The Neuropsychology of Autism

THE NEUROPSYCHOLOGY OF AUTISM

Edited by

Deborah Fein, PhD

Board of Trustees Distinguished Professor
Department of Psychology
Department of Pediatrics
University of Connecticut

OXFORD
UNIVERSITY PRESS

OXFORD
UNIVERSITY PRESS

Oxford University Press, Inc., publishes works that further
Oxford University's objective of excellence
in research, scholarship, and education.

Oxford New York

Auckland   Cape Town   Dar es Salaam   Hong Kong   Karachi
Kuala Lumpur   Madrid   Melbourne   Mexico City   Nairobi
New Delhi   Shanghai   Taipei   Toronto

With offices in

Argentina   Austria   Brazil   Chile   Czech Republic   France   Greece
Guatemala   Hungary   Italy   Japan   Poland   Portugal   Singapore
South Korea   Switzerland   Thailand   Turkey   Ukraine   Vietnam

Copyright © 2011 by Oxford University Press, Inc.

Published by Oxford University Press, Inc.
198 Madison Avenue, New York, New York 10016

www.oup.com

Library of Congress Cataloging-in-Publication Data

The neuropsychology of autism / edited by Deborah Fein.
p. ; cm.
Includes bibliographical references.
ISBN 978-0-19-537831-3   1. Autism–Pathophysiology. 2. Neuropsychology.
I. Fein, Deborah.
[DNLM: 1. Autistic Disorder. 2. Neuropsychology. WM 203.5 N4955 2011]
RC553.A88N535 2011
616.85'88207–dc22
2010022073

9 8 7 6 5 4 3 2 1
Printed in USA
on acid-free paper

To Joe, whose love, knowledge, and wisdom enrich my life every hour
To Elizabeth and Emily, the lights of my life
To Edith, how I wish you were here

Foreword

How can autism, in its variety of manifestations, be explained in terms of what is known about brain function? This is the topic of this comprehensive and exceptional book. This is a question—or more accurately, a program of scientific inquiry—that has challenged many of us in the field of autism research for decades. My own journey of pursuing an understanding of the brain bases of autism started in the late 1970s, when I researched and wrote my doctoral thesis on autism. Over the next three decades, this journey led to my establishing a multidisciplinary research center that brought together scientists from the fields of psychology, psychiatry, genetics, neuroscience, and education, who all worked together to understand the complex set of conditions now referred to as autism spectrum disorders.

Among the people who greatly influenced my scientific journey is Deborah Fein, the editor of this book. Early on in my career, her work had a significant influence on my thinking, beginning with her landmark article, coauthored with Lynn Waterhouse and Charlotte Modahl, on "Neurofunctional Mechanisms in Autism," published in 1996 in *Psychological Review*. From her early multidisciplinary research on identification of neurobiological subtypes, to her work on the role of neuropeptides, to her more recent studies on recovery from autism, Debby has always been a trailblazer in the field. Thus, it is fitting that she has provided leadership in editing this remarkable book, which offers a wide-ranging look at what is known about the brain bases of autism symptoms, including language, memory, attention, and social functioning, among others. The book also provides an in-depth review of the theoretical frameworks that have been proposed to explain how and why the variety of symptoms that make up autism cohere and develop as they do. To accomplish this task, Debby has brought together the best thinkers in the field. Each one offers a unique perspective and up-to-date knowledge on an aspect of autism, or pulls together several lines of knowledge within a theoretical framework.

This book will be helpful and stimulating to a wide range of readers, including scientists studying the molecular basis of autism, applied researchers seeking to understand functional brain circuitry, and clinicians helping individuals with autism spectrum disorders function in their everyday lives. *The Neuropsychology of Autism* provides insight into understanding the behavioral symptoms that define autism. To my knowledge, there is no other single volume that offers a comprehensive and current synopsis of the neuropsychology of autism. I anticipate that, like myself, there will be many others whose thinking and work will be enlightened by Deborah Fein's efforts.

Geraldine Dawson, PhD
Research Professor, The University of North
Carolina at Chapel Hill
Chief Science Officer, Autism Speaks

Acknowledgments

I wish to thank the many people who helped in the creation of this volume. First and foremost I wish to thank the authors, who worked so diligently, and were so responsive to editorial input. They devoted the large amounts of time and creative energy needed to create their high-quality chapters despite multiple other deadlines and pressures, and their work for this volume is very much appreciated indeed. I also wish to thank the extremely supportive, capable, and helpful editors at Oxford who worked on this volume with me, including Joan Bossert, Shelley Reinhardt, and Aaron VanDorn. I owe a great debt of gratitude to my colleagues and graduate students at the University of Connecticut, whose thoughtful and stimulating discussions have been instrumental in my professional development throughout the years, and to the division and department administration, who have created such a warm, collegial, and intellectually rigorous but open environment. I also want to thank the families I have worked with and have come to know over the last 35 years; they have unselfishly shared their considerable wisdom about their children with me, and very often have changed my mind about something I thought I knew. Finally, I want to thank my family, whose patience and endless support have allowed me to devote so much of my time (always more than one expects!) to this book.

Deborah Fein, Ph.D.
Storrs, Connecticut, May, 2010

Contents

Contributors   xv
Introduction   3

Part I.   Fundamental Information about Autism Spectrum Disorders

1. Phenomenology of ASD: Definition, Syndromes, and Major Features   9
   Eva Troyb, Kelley Knoch, and Marianne Barton

2. Genetics: Many Roads to the Autism Spectrum Disorders   35
   Brett S. Abrahams

3. The Neuroanatomy of ASD   47
   Martha R. Herbert

4. The Neurochemistry of ASD   77
   David J. Posey, Zohra Lodin, Craig A. Erickson, Kimberly A. Stigler, and Christopher J. McDougle

5. Major Current Neuropsychological Theories of ASD   97
Agata Rozga, Sharlet A. Anderson, and Diana L. Robins

Part II.   Neuropsychological Functions

6. Language in ASD   123
Elizabeth Kelley

7. Memory in ASD   139
Jill Boucher and Andrew Mayes

8. Attention and Working Memory in ASD   161
Brittany G. Travers, Mark R. Klinger, and Laura Grofer Klinger

9. Executive Functions in ASD   185
Inge-Marie Eigsti

10. Motor Development and its Relation to Social and
Behavioral Manifestations in Children with ASD   205
Ericka L. Wodka and Stewart H. Mostofsky

11. Sensory Functions in ASD   215
Tal Kenet

12. Social Cognition in ASD   225
Mikle South, Robert T. Schultz, and Sally Ozonoff

13. Imitation in ASD   243
Costanza Colombi, Giacomo Vivanti, and Sally J. Rogers

14. Implicit Learning in ASD   267
Inge-Marie Eigsti and Jessica Mayo

15. The Significance of IQ and Differential Cognitive Abilities
for Understanding ASD   281
Robert M. Joseph

16. Clinical Implications for Assessment and Treatment of ASD   295
Julie M. Wolf and Elizabeth Kelley

Part III.   Frontiers of Neuropsychology and Autism

17. Systemizing and Empathizing   317
Sally Wheelwright and Simon Baron-Cohen

18. Entrainment, Mimicry, and Interpersonal Synchrony   339
    Marcel Kinsbourne and Molly Helt

19. Repetitive Movements and Arousal   367
    Marcel Kinsbourne

20. Neural Network Models of Context Utilization   395
    Ananth Narayanan and David Q. Beversdorf

21. Structural and Functional Brain Development in ASD: The Impact of Early
    Brain Overgrowth and Considerations for Treatment   407
    Karen Pierce and Lisa T. Eyler

22. Neuropeptide and Steroid Hormones   451
    Suma Jacob, Maria Demosthenous, and C. Sue Carter

23. Redefining the Concept of Autism as a Unitary Disorder:
    Multiple Causal Deficits of a Single Kind?   469
    Jill Boucher

24. Autism Endophenotypes Are Not Unified by Gene Variants or
    Chromosome Number Variants   483
    Lynn Waterhouse

25. A Whole-Body Systems Approach to ASD   499
    Martha R. Herbert

26. Future Directions in ASD Research   511
    Deborah Fein, Katarzyna Chawarska, and Isabelle Rapin

Index   527

Contributors

BRETT S. ABRAHAMS, PhD
Assistant Professor in Residence
Department of Genetics
Albert Einstein College of Medicine
Bronx, NY

SHARLET A. ANDERSON, MA
Doctoral Candidate
Department of Psychology
Georgia State University
Atlanta, GA

SIMON BARON-COHEN
Professor of Developmental Psychopathology
Director, Autism Research Centre
Cambridge University
Cambridge, UK

MARIANNE BARTON, PhD
Associate Clinical Professor
Director, Psychological Services Clinic
University of Connecticut
Storrs, CT

DAVID Q. BEVERSDORF, MD
Associate Professor
Departments of Radiology, Neurology, and
    Psychology and the Thompson Center
William and Nancy Thompson Endowed Chair in
    Radiology
University of Missouri
Columbia, MO

JILL BOUCHER, PhD
Professor and Honorary Professor
Departments of Psychology
City University and University of Warwick
United Kingdom

C. SUE CARTER, PhD
Professor
Brain Body Center
University of Illinois at Chicago
Chicago, Il

KATARZYNA CHAWARSKA, PhD
Assistant Professor of Psychology
Director of Developmental Disabilities Clinic
    for Infants and Toddlers
Yale University School of Medicine
Child Study Center
New Haven, CT

SIMON BARON-COHEN
Professor of Developmental Psychopathology
Director, Autism Research Centre
Cambridge University
Cambridge, UK

COSTANZA COLOMBI, PhD
Postdoctoral Fellow
Autism and Communication Disorder Center
University of Michigan
Ann Arbor, MI

MARIA DEMOSTHENOUS, MD
Clinical Instructor
Langley Porter Psychiatric Institute
University of California, San Francisco
San Francisco, CA

INGE-MARIE EIGSTI, PhD
Assistant Professor
Department of Psychology
University of Connecticut
Storrs, CT

CRAIG A. ERICKSON, MD
Assistant Professor
Department of Psychiatry
Indiana University School of Medicine
Indianapolis, IN

LISA T. EYLER, PhD
Associate Professor
Department of Psychiatry
University of California, San Diego
San Diego, CA

DEBORAH FEIN, PhD
Board of Trustees Distinguished Professor
Department of Psychology
Department of Pediatrics
University of Connecticut
Storrs, CT

MOLLY HELT, MA
Department of Psychology
University of Connecticut
Storrs, CT

MARTHA R. HERBERT, MD, PhD
Assistant Professor
Department of Neurology
TRANSCEND Research Program
Massachusetts General Hospital
Boston, MA

SUMA JACOB, MD, PhD
Assistant Professor
Institute of Juvenile Research
University of Illinois at Chicago
Chicago, Il

ROBERT M. JOSEPH, PhD
Assistant Professor
Department of Anatomy and Neurobiology
Boston University School of Medicine
Boston, MA

ELIZABETH KELLEY, PhD
Assistant Professor of Psychology
Centre for Neuroscience Studies
Queen's University
Kingston, Ontario

TAL KENET, PhD
Instructor in Neurology
Harvard University School of Medicine
Massachusetts General Hospital
Boston, MA

MARCEL KINSBOURNE, MD
Professor
Department of Psychology
New School for Social Research
New York, NY

LAURA GROFER KLINGER, PhD
Associate Professor
Department of Psychology
The University of Alabama
Tuscaloosa, AL

MARK. R. KLINGER, PhD
Associate Professor
Director of Experimental Training
Department of Psychology
The University of Alabama
Tuscaloosa, AL

KELLEY KNOCH, BA
Graduate Student
Department of Psychology
University of Connecticut
Storrs, CT

ZOHRA LODIN, MD
Child and Adolescent Psychiatry Fellow
Department of Psychiatry
Indiana University School of Medicine
Indianapolis, IN

ANDREW MAYES, D.PHIL.
School of Psychological Sciences
University of Manchester
Manchester, UK

JESSICA MAYO, BA
Department of Psychology
University of Connecticut
Storrs, CT

CHRISTOPHER J. MCDOUGLE, MD
Albert E. Sterne Professor and Chairman
Department of Psychiatry
Indiana University School of Medicine
Indianapolis, IN

STEWART H. MOSTOFSKY, MD
Pediatric Neurologist
Director of the Laboratory for Neurocognitive
    and Imaging Research
Medical Director of the Center for Autism and
    Related Disorders
Associate Professor of Neurology
Johns Hopkins University School of Medicine
Baltimore, MD

ANANTH NARAYANAN
Research Associate
Department of Radiology and Neurology
University of Missouri
Columbia, MO

SALLY OZONOFF, PhD
Endowed Professor and Vice Chair for Research
Department of Psychiatry and Behavioral Sciences
M.I.N.D. Institute
U.C. Davis Medical Center
Sacramento, CA

KAREN PIERCE, PhD
Assistant Professor
Department of Neurosciences, School of Medicine
University of California San Diego
San Diego, CA

DAVID J. POSEY, MD
Associate Professor of Psychiatry
Indiana University School of Medicine
Indianapolis, IN

ISABELLE RAPIN, MD
Saul R. Korey Department of Neurology
Department of Pediatrics
Rose F. Kennedy Center for Research in Mental
    Retardation and Human Development
Albert Einstein College of Medicine
Bronx, NY

DIANA L. ROBINS, PhD
Associate Professor
Department of Psychology
Neuroscience Institute
Georgia State University
Atlanta, GA

SALLY J. ROGERS, PhD
Professor of Psychology and Behavioral Science
UC Davis M.I.N.D. Institute
University of California, Davis
Sacramento, CA

AGATA ROZGA, PhD
Research Faculty
School of Interactive Computing
Georgia Institute of Technology
Atlanta, GA

ROBERT T. SCHULTZ, PhD
Director, Center for Autism Research
Children's Hospital of Philadelphia
R.A.C. Professor of Psychology,
   Department of Pediatrics
University of Pennsylvania
Philadelphia, PA

MIKLE SOUTH, PhD
Assistant Professor of Psychology and Neuroscience
Brigham Young University
Provo, UT

KIMBERLY A. STIGLER, MD
Assistant Professor of Psychiatry
Medical Director, Christian Sarkine Autism
   Treatment Center
Indiana University School of Medicine
Indianapolis, IN

BRITTANY G. TRAVERS, PhD
Department of Psychology
University of Alabama
Tuscaloosa, AL

EVA TROYB
Graduate Student
Department of Psychology
University of Connecticut
Storrs, CT

GIACOMO VIVANTI
Postdoctoral Researcher
UC Davis M.I.N.D. Institute
University of California, Davis
Sacramento, CA

LYNN WATERHOUSE, PhD
Professor, Graduate Global Programs
Director, Child Behavior Study
The College of New Jersey
Trenton, NJ

SALLY WHEELWRIGHT, MA
Autism Research Centre
University of Cambridge
Cambridge, UK

ERICKA L. WODKA, PH.D., ABPP
Instructor, Department of Psychiatry and
   Behavioral Sciences
Johns Hopkins University School of Medicine
Canter for Autism and Related Disorders
Kennedy Krieger Institute
Baltimore, MD

JULIE M. WOLF, PhD
Associate Research Scientist at the
   Child Study Center
Yale School of Medicine
New Haven, CT

The Neuropsychology of Autism

Introduction

Surprisingly, there is no up-to-date, single volume on the neuropsychology of autism currently available. This book aims to bring together, in one place, state-of-the-art reviews of neuropsychological functions in autism as well as presentations of major theoretical viewpoints, all by current leaders in the various fields of autism research.

Section I provides the necessary background information for neuropsychologically oriented readers. These include fundamental topics, so that going forward, readers can share a common ground in understanding the basic phenomena under discussion, and be prepared for the more detailed and theoretical chapters that follow. Chapter 1, by Troyb, Knoch, and Barton, covers definitions and diagnostic criteria for the spectrum disorders, clinical presentation, the clinical picture at different ages, psychiatric comorbidities, and demographic factors. Chapter 2, by Abrahams, presents an overview of what is known about the role of genetics in the autism spectrum disorders;

Chapter 3, by Herbert, does the same for neuroanatomy, while Chapter 4, by Posey, Lodin, Erickson, Stigler, and McDougle, reviews neurochemistry. Finally, Chapter 5, by Rozga, Anderson, and Robins, presents an overview of current neuropsychological theories of autism, presenting a basic introduction to the theories that are covered later in the book in more depth.

In Section II, each chapter reviews an area of neuropsychological function (e.g. language, motor functions). Of course, there is overlap among some of these chapters (e.g., attention and memory, memory and implicit learning), as there is among the topics themselves, since the flow of information through the brain has to be rather arbitrarily divided up to create them to suit our approach. Chapters 6 through 14 cover sensory functioning (Kenet), motor functioning (Wodka and Mostofsky), imitation (Columbi, Vivanti, and Rogers), language (Kelley), implicit learning (Eigsti and Mayo), memory (Boucher), attention and working memory (Travers, Klinger, and Klinger), executive functions (Eigsti), and social cognition (South, Ozonoff, and Schultz). In Chapter 14, Joseph describes the "typical" cognitive profile found in many individuals with autism, and in Chapter 15, Wolf and Kelley draw out some clinical implications for assessment and treatment that follow from the conclusions of the various chapters in this section on specific neuropsychological functions.

Section III contains chapters that present major, overarching, theoretical viewpoints. Some chapters in Section II also take a theoretical viewpoint about their material, but the points of view in Section III entail either a more elaborate theoretical framework or one that attempts to account for multiple aspects of the autistic syndromes. We have attempted to cover most of the current orientations and theories, as well as those that have attracted the most attention by other researchers. In most cases, the theory is represented by one of its leading proponents. In Chapter 17, Wheelwright and Baron-Cohen present evidence for their viewpoint about autistic thinking as representing an extreme of the continuum of systemizing versus empathizing that characterizes normal cognitive processes. In Chapter 18, Kinsbourne and Helt explore deficits in interpersonal entrainment, mimicry, and synchrony and their implications, while in Chapter 19, Kinsbourne reviews the literature on repetitive movements in autism, and their possible relationship to abnormal arousal and to overfocused attention. In Chapter 20, Narayanan and Beversdorf present network models of autism as a deficit in context utilization. Connectivity is considered by some theorists as the leading neuropsychological explanation for many aspects of autism, and in Chapter 21, Pierce and Eyler describe the evidence for this theory. In Chapter 22, Jacob reviews evidence for the involvement of hormones in the development of autistic symptoms.

The next three chapters take a view somewhat different than that of most neuropsychological or neurobiological researchers. In Chapter 23, Boucher considers the view that perhaps we should not be looking for any unitary neuropsychological deficits, with one set of deficits posited to explain the others (but concludes largely in the negative). Waterhouse and Nichols, in Chapter 24, examine a rather similar question but come to somewhat different conclusions; they also examine evidence for possible diagnostic and nondiagnostic autism endophenotypes as a basis for

establishing homogeneous groups for genetic and other neurobiological studies. In Chapter 25, Herbert argues that autism should not be conceptualized as a brain disorder, but rather as a multisystem disorder that affects the brain, and suggests some implications of this view for future biological research. Finally, in Chapter 26, Fein, Rapin, and Chawarska attempt to summarize the major advances of the past 30–40 years, and point to directions that may be most fruitful in the next period of autism research, including classification, epidemiology, genetics and epigenetics, brain structure and function, earliest emergence of symptoms and longitudinal studies, medical comorbidity, assessment, intervention, and outcome.

This book is primarily intended for graduate students, fellows, researchers, and clinicians in neuropsychology, clinical child psychology, pediatrics, neurology, psychiatry, and other fields related to developmental disorders. Professionals with an interest in autism in the fields of school psychology, educational psychology, and special education, as well as members of the lay public with educational backgrounds in any of these areas, will also find much of importance and interest. For neuroscientists, the clinically oriented chapters may present more novel information, while for the clinicians and researchers who are more directly involved with behavior, the neurological information may be particularly new and challenging. In all cases, the authors and I have attempted to provide straightforward definitions and explanations of the most technical concepts and language, but of course, some of the chapters will remain challenging for those with less technical backgrounds.

I also want to point out a hugely important aspect of autism that is not explicitly covered in this volume: the social context of autism. Having a family member with autism changes each family in different and powerful ways. It affects the psychology of each parent, the marriage (in two-parent families), siblings, family dynamics, the extended family, the allocation of emotional, time, and financial resources, and the broader social context (such as jobs and friendships) of each family member. Furthermore, the social context of each child with autism has a dramatic effect on his or her outcome. My clinical impression is that proactive parents who are skilled in bringing out the best in their child and strong advocates for getting the best services can improve the chances of a highly successful outcome (and may even be necessary for it) but sadly, even the actions of such parents do not guarantee it. I hope that a better understanding of the neuropsychology of autism will provide information that will eventually help to ensure that more children with these capable and dedicated parents reach highly successful outcomes. It is hardly possible to overestimate the importance of the social context of the affected child, and the importance of bringing this social context into sharp focus for the child. I regret that this complex, fascinating, and crucial set of relationships cannot be covered in this volume as it deserves to be.

Part I

Fundamental Information about
Autism Spectrum Disorders

Chapter 1

Phenomenology of ASD: Definition, Syndromes, and Major Features

Eva Troyb, Kelley Knoch, and Marianne Barton

Autism Spectrum Disorders (ASDs) are a group of neurodevelopmental disorders that affect up to 1 in 150 individuals (Center for Disease Control [CDC], 2006; Fombonne, Zakarian, Bennett, Meng, & McLean-Heywood, 2006). According to the *Diagnostic and Statistical Manual of Mental Disorders, Fourth Edition, Text Revision* (DSM-IV-TR; American Psychiatric Association [APA], 2000), ASDs are characterized by deficits in communication and socialization, along with repetitive and stereotyped behaviors. A diagnosis of Autistic Disorder (AD) indicates that impairments are present in each of these symptom domains. However, the nature, as well as the severity, of the symptoms of ASDs varies greatly (Hus, Pickles, Cook, Risi, & Lord, 2007). This chapter provides a description of: (a) diagnostic criteria for ASDs; (b) clinical presentation of ASDs throughout childhood, adolescence, and adulthood; (c) recent findings relative to prevalence rates and geographic distribution of ASD; (d) demographic differences in the clinical presentation of ASDs; (e) disorders on the pervasive developmental disorder (PDD)

spectrum; (f) disorders that share symptoms with ASDs, but do not belong to the PDD spectrum; and (g) comorbidity of ASDs with other conditions. Each of these areas has an extensive literature, and therefore, this review will not be comprehensive. Some of the areas are covered in more detail in Section II of this book.

DIAGNOSTIC CRITERIA

A diagnosis of ASD (or a "Pervasive Developmental Disorder," in the nomenclature of the *DSM-IV-TR*) requires that the child display deficits in three areas of development: social relatedness, communication, and restricted interests and repetitive behaviors, with initial onset in one of these areas occurring prior to the age of 3 years. However, the clinical presentation of symptoms within these clusters varies considerably, as does the severity of the behaviors.

To meet criteria for AD, a child must display at least six symptoms described by the *DSM-IV-TR*.

At least two of these six symptoms must come from a subset of four social symptoms, including impaired nonverbal behavior, failure to develop appropriate peer relationships, impaired joint attention, and impaired reciprocity. In addition, the child must display at least one symptom from a cluster pertaining to impaired communication skills, which includes delayed or absent language, impaired ability to converse, repetitive speech, and delayed, repetitive, or absent symbolic play. In addition, one of the six symptoms must be from the cluster that describes restricted interests and repetitive behaviors. That cluster includes unusual preoccupations, rigid rituals, stereotypic movements, and preoccupations with parts of objects (APA, 2000).

Individuals who meet some but not all of the criteria required for a diagnosis of AD may be given the diagnosis of Pervasive Developmental Disorder, Not Otherwise Specified (PDD-NOS). To meet criteria for this diagnostic category, a child must exhibit some degree of social impairment, as well as symptoms from either of the remaining two symptom clusters (communication *or* restricted interests and repetitive behaviors; APA, 2000).

CHARACTERISTICS OF ASDS

Social Impairment

Impaired social relatedness is the defining feature of ASD. This deficit may be manifested in a range of behaviors, including an inability to form relationships, inappropriate social behavior, social isolation, the abnormal use of nonverbal methods of communication (e.g., impaired eye contact or limited use of gestures), lack of awareness of the reactions of others, and failure to share experiences with others (APA, 2000). Individuals with ASD consistently fail to use facial expressions and body posture to regulate social interaction, and often display impaired eye gaze (Charman & Baird, 2002). Children with ASDs struggle with the use of joint attention in dyadic (i.e., child–adult), as well as triadic (i.e., child–adult–object) interactions (Leekam, López, & Moore, 2000; Spence, Sharifi, & Wiznitzer, 2004).

In addition, parents of children with ASDs often describe their child as unaware of others and existing in "his or her own world." Children and adults with ASDs have been found to exhibit a lack of reciprocal conversation and interactive play (Charman & Baird, 2002; Hauck, Fein, Waterhouse, & Feinstein, 1995). Children with ASDs rarely initiate social activities, although they may engage in activities initiated by adults (Hauck et al., 1995; Kasari, Sigman, & Yirmiya, 1993). They infrequently imitate actions performed by others, including gestures (Mostofsky et al., 2006; see also Chapter 13). Play is typically less frequent and less developed than would be expected, given the intellectual ability of the child. Specifically, children with ASDs display restricted imaginative and interactive play and often engage in parallel play instead of cooperative play (Riquet, Taylor, Benaroya, & Klein, 1982; Spence, Sharifi, & Wiznitzer et al., 2004). Impairments in the processing of social information have also been consistently reported in individuals with ASD (see Chapter 12). This deficit is especially evident in the recognition of facially expressed affect, which is impaired even in high functioning individuals with ASDs (Adolphs, Sears, & Piven, 2001).

Communication Impairment

Most children diagnosed with an ASD present some degree of impaired communication; however, the extent of verbal and nonverbal deficits varies considerably. Some children with autism never develop expressive language, while others are fluent (see Chapter 6). Those who go on to develop language often exhibit language delays, and may display immediate and delayed echolalia. Individuals whose language appears fluent usually exhibit communication deficits, most frequently in semantic and pragmatic aspects of language, as well as in abstract or figurative language (Fein et al., 1996; Stevens et al., 2000).

Individuals with ASDs also exhibit deficits in nonverbal communication. Lack of gestures, limited use and interpretation of eye gaze, and atypical speech prosody are common areas of weakness (Baron-Cohen, 1989; Chiang, Soong, Lin, & Rogers, 2008; Mundy, Sigman, & Kasari, 1994; Stone, Ousley, Yoder, Hogan, & Hepburn, 1997).

Restricted Interests and Repetitive Behaviors

Play conducted by children with ASDs may include repetitive behaviors, including preoccupation with parts of toys (e.g., the spinning wheels of a toy car) and other ritualistic behaviors (e.g., lining up toys).

Motor stereotypies (e.g., hand flapping, hand wringing, spinning) are common and are frequently noticed by parents during the child's preschool years. It should be noted that repetitive behaviors are often observed during the first year of life in typically developing children, including kicking, waving, and rocking (Bishop, Luyster, Richler, & Lord, 2008; Thelen, 1979), and hand flapping as a sign of excitement is typical in young children. However, these behaviors diminish as typically developing children age and are seen less frequently after the age of 4 years (Evans et al., 1997). Multiple longitudinal studies of children with ASDs indicate that the prevalence and severity of repetitive behaviors commonly increases during the first 5 years of life (Charman et al., 2005; Moore & Goodson, 2003).

In addition to repetitive behaviors, an individual with an ASD may present with restricted interests or an insistence on sameness. Restricted interests are unusual either in the topic (e.g., metal objects, train schedules) of the preoccupation or the degree of intensity. Insistence on sameness is often manifested in resistance to changes in the routines, daily schedule, or environment of the child, and frequently results in anxiety and tantrums. Similarly to repetitive behaviors, typically developing children also display behaviors that resemble insistence on sameness in routines as well as rigidity in their expectations for tastes, smells, and textures (Bishop et al., 2008). Studies of these behaviors suggest that children with ASDs exhibit more of these behaviors, for longer periods of time and with greater severity, than typically developing children (Richler, Bishop, Kleinke, & Lord, 2007; Thelen, 1979).

Deficits in Attention

Although not considered diagnostic criteria, difficulties with attention and executive functions are very common among children with ASD. Several studies have reported on the presence of attentional abnormalities in individuals diagnosed with ASDs (see Chapter 8). An overly narrow focus of attention to stimuli has been reported and may contribute to the presence of savant skills (isolated exceptional ability in one domain), which are seen in a small portion of individuals with ASDs (Fein, Tinder, & Waterhouse, 1979; Lovaas, Schreibman, Koegel, & Rehm, 1971; Wainwright & Bryson, 1996). In addition, shifting attention from one activity to another appears to be

an area of weakness for individuals with ASDs (Wainwright & Bryson, 1996). However, sustained attention appears to be relatively spared (Pascualvaca, Fantie, Papageorgiou, & Mirsky, 1998; Wainwright & Bryson, 1996). Plaisted, Swettenham, and Rees (1999) examined attentional abilities in individuals with high functioning ASDs and reported that, even in this group, selective attention was not impaired, while divided attention was.

Deficits in Executive Functioning

Numerous studies of executive functioning abilities (e.g., organization, planning, inhibition, working memory) have found these abilities to be impaired in children and adults with ASDs (see Chapter 9). Specifically, studies have indicated that children with ASDs struggle with tasks requiring working memory, inhibition, and set-shifting abilities, when compared with typically developing peers (Hughes, Russell, & Robbins, 1994; Ozonoff & Jensen, 1999; Ozonoff & McEvoy, 1994; Ozonoff, Rogers, & Pennington, 1991; Ozonoff, South, & Provencal, 2005; Rumsey & Hamburger, 1990; Szatmari, Bartolucci, Bremner, & Bond, 1989). Deficits in executive functioning have been presented as a potential explanation for many behavioral features of the disorder.

Recent studies have found that performance on executive functioning tasks appears to vary depending on the age of the group included in the study. Specifically, older children and adults scored worse than peers matched on mental-age, while younger children with ASDs did not exhibit impairments in these skills when compared to peers (Dawson, Meltzoff, Osterling, & Rinaldaldi, 1998; McEvoy, Rogers, & Pennington, 1993; Pennington & Ozonoff, 1996; Yerys, Hepburn, Pennington, & Rogers, 2007). This suggests that executive functioning may not be a primary deficit, but rather a secondary deficit associated with ASDs that becomes manifest as the children develop (Yerys et al., 2007).

DEVELOPMENTAL COURSE AND PROGNOSIS

The presentation of ASD symptomatology varies considerably from early childhood to adolescence and adulthood. As children age and are exposed to intervention, they may gain daily living skills, and the behavioral manifestations of their symptoms may diminish or change (Shea & Mesibov, 2005). In addition, some symptoms of ASDs do not appear consistently in children younger than 3 years of age (e.g., stereotyped and repetitive behaviors; Lord, 1995; Stone et al., 1999). However, when experienced clinicians are given multiple sources of information, ASDs can be reliably diagnosed in children as young as 18 to 24 months (Charman et al., 2005; Eaves & Ho, 2004; Kleinman et al., 2008; Stone et al., 1999). Furthermore, multiple researchers have identified signs of ASDs present in the child's first year of life (Mitchell et al., 2006; Osterling & Dawson, 1994; Zwaigenbaum et al., 2005).

Studies examining early markers of ASDs have relied on videotapes, parental reports, and close monitoring of younger siblings of affected children, who are at elevated risk for developing the disorder (Mitchell et al., 2006; Osterling & Dawson, 1994; Zwaigenbaum et al., 2005). A review of videos recorded during a child's first year of life, before an ASD diagnosis was suspected, suggested that early indicators of ASDs include the presence of inappropriate facial expressions, emotional flatness, low rates of joint attention, limited use of gestures, lack of social smiling, abnormal eye contact, and a preference for being alone (Osterling & Dawson, 1994). Retrospective parental accounts indicated that the earliest symptoms noticed included delayed language, lack of interest in peers, limited use of gestures, and lack of social imitation, sharing, and imaginative play (Stone, 1994). Studies of infant siblings at high risk for ASDs have suggested that early signs of ASDs may be evident in children as young as 6 months of age and include delayed language, failure to respond to name, abnormal visual attention, unusual eye contact, and temperamental aberrations (e.g., lack of responsiveness to caregivers, decreaseed activity level; Mitchell et al., 2006; Zwaigenbaum et al., 2005).

For the majority of children with ASDs, symptoms become more noticeable during the second year of life. Parental reports suggest that during the second year of life, children who have received an ASD diagnosis exhibit a limited range of facial expressions, lack of interest in other children, infrequent imitation of others, low rates of joint attention, and impaired use of gestures (Cox et al., 1999). These findings are confirmed by studies that analyzed videotapes of children diagnosed with an ASD, which had been collected during the second year of life (Wetherby et al., 2004).

An examination of the clinical presentations of children diagnosed with ASDs during the second year of life has produced similar findings. A study of 31 children aged 14–25 months who received an ASD diagnosis indicated that impaired eye contact, failure to respond to name, limited response to joint attention bids, restricted functional and imaginative play, and lack of pointing were commonly present in this age group. Furthermore, frequent symptoms included limited use of nonverbal communication to compensate for delayed speech, fewer directed vocalizations to others, emotional flatness, and the occasional presence of motor stereotypies (Chawarska, Klin, Paul, & Volkmar, 2007).

According to the literature, a portion of children (20–47%) who are diagnosed with ASDs appear to exhibit few of the symptoms until they experience a marked loss of language and/or social interests around 15 to 24 months of age (Bernabei, Cerquiglini, Cortesi, & D'Ardia, 2006; Davidovitch, Glick, Holtzman, Tirosh, & Safir, 2000; Lord, Shulman, & Dilavore, 2004; Werner & Dawson, 2005). Studies reporting higher prevalence rates of regression in children diagnosed with ASDs may have arrived at their estimates from smaller samples, or by using broader definitions for regression (Rogers, 2004; Stefanatos, 2008).

Multiple studies of regression in ASDs have explored the child's development prior to the loss of abilities. Studies examining parent recollection of the child's early development suggest that the majority of children (78.3%) exhibit some level of developmental abnormalities before the onset of regression (Rogers, 2004; Stefanatos, 2008). An analysis of video recordings collected when infants were 12 months of age indicated that children with ASDs who lost skills exhibited similar rates of joint attention as typically developing infants and used complex babble or words more frequently than typically developing children. However, interviews with the parents of these children revealed that a large proportion of the sample exhibited regulatory difficulties (e.g., sleeping problems, oversensitivity to sensory stimulation) prior to the onset of the symptoms of ASDs (Werner & Dawson, 2005). Several studies collected parental reports about potential triggering events that they believe preceded the child's loss of abilities. More than half of the families reported precipitating events that included immunizations, other medical events, and geographical moves, although studies examining a causal relationship between such events and a loss of skills have not supported this claim (Goldberg & Osann, 2003; Shinnar et al., 2001).

Studies examining the prognosis of children with ASDs who experience a regression have yielded mixed results. A number of studies suggest that regression is associated with a poorer long-term outcome, including less developed adaptive abilities and a higher likelihood of IQ scores in the intellectually disabled range. Several studies, however, reported finding no differences in long-term outcome between children with ASDs who lost skills and those who did not. More detailed reviews of the phenomena of regression in ASDs can be found in Rogers (2004), Stefanatos (2008), and Ozonoff (2008).

Manifestations of ASDs change little between the second and third year of life. Studies have indicated that the overall level of language improves over time in many children with ASDs. However, in most cases, as language develops, it begins to include other abnormalities, including echolalia and unusual intonation (Chawarska et al., 2007). Chawarska et al. (2007) reported a marginal increase in use of gestures and a significant increase in the rate of response to bids of joint attention, but not in the rate of initiation of joint attention. Furthermore, the authors reported no change in spontaneous pointing, eye contact, ability to direct facial expressions to others, and responsiveness to name.

Studies examining the clinical presentation of children with ASDs in the fourth and fifth years of life have identified similar symptom manifestations. Cox et al. (1999) examined symptoms of ASDs in children who were 42 months of age and reported that, at this age, these children displayed limited use of conventional gestures, reduced communicative use of pointing, and low rates of sharing enjoyment, offering comfort, and imaginative play. After the age of 4 years, increases in the frequency of restricted interests and repetitive behaviors are commonly observed (Charman et al., 2005; Chawarska et al., 2007).

During middle childhood, deficits in daily living skills may diminish, as children participate in intervention and are better able to acquiesce to the demands placed on them by others. Efforts to accommodate the wishes of others may result in the lessening of public displays of ritualized behaviors and restricted interests. As a result, the child's behavior may appear less consistent with the classic pattern of ASD symptoms, and may appear more similar to the presentation of a hyperactive or intellectually disabled child (Paul, 1987; Shea & Mesibov, 2005).

Less information is available about the manifestation of ASD symptoms during adolescence. Concerns during young adulthood often include a decrease in physical activity, cognitive deteriorations, and the onset of seizures (Eaves & Ho, 2008; Shea & Mesibov, 2005). As many as 25–40% of individuals with autism suffer from seizures, and as many as 50% exhibit abnormal electroencephalography (EEG) results. Studies examining the onset of epileptic activity in individuals with ASDs have indicated that seizures occur most commonly during infancy and adolescence (Gillberg & Steffenberg, 1987; Olsson, Steffenburg, & Gillberg, 1988; Tuchman, Rapin, & Shinnar, 1991; Volkmar & Nelson, 1990). Self-help skills often continue to be impaired in adolescents with ASDs, and these difficulties are compounded by the increasing personal hygiene needs which arise during this period.

Several studies have reported an overall deterioration in behavior during adolescence (Ballaban-Gil, Rapin, Tuchman, & Shinnar, 1996; Koboyashi, Murata, & Yoshinaga, 1992; Nordin & Gillberg, 1998). Multiple studies have reported the presence of difficult behaviors in a substantial proportion of adolescents diagnosed with ASDs, including resistance to change, compulsive behaviors, tantrums, aggression, self-injurious behaviors, and inappropriate sexual behaviors (Ballaban-Gil et al., 1996; Howlin, Goode, Huton, & Rutter, 2004; Rumsey, Rapoport, & Sceery, 1985). Even if behavioral problems decrease in frequency during adolescence, they often become more distressing to families, because as children age, they become taller, heavier, and stronger, and such behaviors can become more dangerous or distressing.

However, in addition to the reports of increased epileptic activity and deteriorating behavior, several studies have reported an improvement in symptoms of ASD during this period (Shea & Mesibov, 2005). For instance, Kobayashi, Murata, and Yoshinaga (1992) surveyed 201 Japanese families and reported than more than a quarter of their sample exhibited improvements between the ages of 10 and 15 years. Similarly, Eaves and Ho (1996) reported behavioral or cognitive improvement in 37% of their sample during adolescence. Byrd (2002) reported improvements in communication, socialization, and behavior in more than 75% of their sample of 100 families. Although the overall level of language continued to improve as the child aged, abnormalities in speech and language persisted throughout adolescence and adulthood for most individuals with ASDs (Ballaban-Gil et al., 1996; Koboyashi et al., 1992).

Improvement in symptoms of ASDs during adolescence has been described as a contributing factor to the willingness of adolescents with average intelligence to participate in therapeutic intervention (Shea & Mesibov, 2005). While these individuals may perform at or above grade level academically, they often struggle with activities of daily living, social expectations, and organizational skills. Many of these individuals become increasingly interested in developing and maintaining close relationships, which they often have difficulty doing. This group may be more eager to partake in intervention that targets social deficits and activities of daily living because of the reduction in symptoms of ASD experienced during adolescence, or perhaps because of their increased social interests, triggered by hormonal changes (Shea & Mesibov, 2005).

Little is known about the clinical presentation of ASDs during adulthood. Early reports of individuals adjusting to adulthood suggested poor outcomes for 60–75% of individuals diagnosed with ASDs. According to these reports, the majority of adults with autism lived in large institutional settings, and few received appropriate services (Kanner, 1971; Lotter, 1978; Rutter, et al., 1967). Recent studies are reporting that most adults with ASD remain highly dependent on others and continue to have difficulty making friends (Billstedt, et al., 2005; Howlin et al., 2004). Ongoing changes in the intervention and treatment of ASDs contribute to changes in adult outcomes.

Studies have suggested that outcomes have improved over the years, with fewer people living in institutions and more working and living independently (Howlin & Goode, 1998). Eaves and Ho (2008) reported on a sample of individuals born during the 1970s and 1980s, and found that 50% of the cases had poor outcomes, in comparison to earlier studies, which reported poor outcomes in 60–75% of adults with ASDs. The majority of the sample examined by Eaves and Ho (2008) lived with their families, and some resided in group homes, but none lived in institutions. Many of these individuals were employed for a few hours each week. Generally, studies have reported that because of the social and communication deficits experienced by adults with ASDs, they suffer from an increased risk of being victims of crime (Shea & Mesibov, 2005). One might expect that as early intervention and school-age services improve, adult outcomes will continue to improve.

Predictors of Long-Term Prognosis

Multiple studies have sought to identify predictors of later outcomes and have consistently pointed to two factors: the presence of communicative language and the child's IQ. A multitude of studies have concluded that children who exhibit functional and communicative speech by the age of 5 have better outcomes than those who do not (Gillberg & Steffenberg, 1987; Rutter, 1970). Lord and Bailey (2002) suggested that children who do not meet this milestone often continue to make improvements in their speech; however, later improvements are associated with greater speech delays and increased dependence on others. In addition, the child's communication at the age of 2 and 3 years, as measured during a systematically collected sample, was found to predict language skills, adaptive functioning, and autism symptom severity for children aged 7 and 9 years (Charman et al., 2005; Luyster, et al., 2007). Nonverbal communication, specifically skills required for joint attention and symbol use (e.g., conventional gestures and symbolic use of gestures) have been proposed as good predictors of outcomes for young children who are not yet speaking (Anderson et al., 2007; Charman et al., 2003; Stone & Yoder, 2001; Wetherby, et al., 2007). Early imitation abilities and imaginative play skills have also been found to predict later language abilities (Charman et al., 2003; Stone & Yoder, 2001; Toth, et al., 2006).

Findings have consistently identified IQ as a predictor of positive outcomes in individuals with ASDs (Stevens et al., 2000). Children with an IQ lower than 55 generally continued to be highly dependent on others through adolescence and adulthood (Eaves & Ho, 2008). Eaves and Ho (2008) also reported that in their longitudinal study of children diagnosed with ASDs, verbal IQ was the best predictor of outcome throughout childhood and adolescence. Similar to previous findings, the authors also reported a correlation between poor outcome and more severe autism symptomatology, as indicated by a higher score on the Children's Autism Rating Scale (CARS; Eaves & Ho, 2008; Gillberg & Steffenberg, 1987; Howlin et al., 2004). To elaborate on these findings, researchers have examined the trajectories of individuals with average IQs who have been diagnosed with an ASD.

Recently, several authors have suggested that a subgroup of high-functioning individuals with ASDs may exist, whose symptoms improve substantially over time (reviewed by Helt et al., 2008).

Furthermore, evidence suggests that a small percentage of individuals diagnosed with ASD in childhood lose their diagnostic label in later years and can function independently in a more or less typical way (Fein et al., 2009; Helt et al., 2008; Sutera et al., 2007; Kelley, Paul, Fein, & Naigles, 2006). These studies indicate that as children move off the autism spectrum, they may show some residual pragmatic language difficulties, especially in the construction of narratives (Kelley et al., 2006); these difficulties tend to resolve as they continue to mature (Fein et al., 2009). Sutera et al. (2007) found that early motor functioning ability was the best single predictor of this "optimal outcome," perhaps because poor motor functioning at age 2 is a proxy for mental retardation. However, ongoing studies at the University of Connecticut (Fein et al., 2009) suggest that these "optimal outcome" children, as they progress through adolescence, retain the same psychiatric vulnerabilities as other children with ASD, particularly anxiety, depression, attention difficulties, and tics. Helt et al. (2008) review this literature and explore possible mechanisms by which early successful intervention might result in the resolution of symptoms and the normalization of development.

EPIDEMIOLOGY

Prevalence

AD was long believed to be a rare disorder, with its prevalence estimated at about 2 to 4 children per 10,000. Beginning in the 1990s, estimates of prevalence increased dramatically; the Centers for Disease Control estimates the prevalence of ASDs in the United States at 6.7 per 1000 children, or 1 in 150 children (CDC, 2006; Fombonne et al., 2006). Wing and Potter (2009) recently reviewed 49 studies of the prevalence of ASDs completed between 1966 and 2006. They described a steady increase in the estimated prevalence of the disorder, with more recent studies revealing higher rates of occurrence. In 1999, Swedish researchers reported a prevalence rate of 120 per 10,000 in Karlstad, Sweden (Kadesjo, Gillberg, & Hagberg, 1999). These authors based their diagnoses

on *International Classification of Diseases, 10th Revision* (ICD-10; World Health Organization, 2007) criteria and reported a prevalence of 60 per 10,000 for AD and 60 per 10,000 for the broader category of ASD. Their estimates remain the highest reported to date in the empirical literature. In another recent study, Baird et al. (2006) reported a prevalence rate of autism of 116 per 10,000 in the South Thames region of London. Their figure is quite similar to that obtained in the Swedish study some 7 years earlier, as well as to the 1 in 91 prevalence figure recently reported by Kogan et al. (2009); however, the Kogan study was based on parent report only.

Most researchers attribute much of the rise in the prevalence of ASDs to methodological and social factors including changes in diagnostic criteria, increased awareness of ASDs, and increased availability of ASD services; they note that increased prevalence cannot be assumed to reflect actual increased occurrence of the disorder (Baird, 2006; Fombonne, 2003, 2005; Wing & Potter, 2009). In a systematic review of 40 studies published between 1980 and 2004, Williams, Higgins, and Brayne (2006) reported that increased prevalence rates for ASDs were associated with the use of more recent diagnostic criteria, evaluation of children at younger ages, and data collection in urban, as opposed to rural, areas. They note that the latter factor is likely associated with social variables such as the availability of evaluation and intervention services, rather than specific environmental factors.

Criteria for the diagnosis of autism changed over time with revisions to the *DSM*. *DSM-III*, published in 1980, introduced the term PDD as a general category of the disorder and described the condition as developmental rather than psychiatric. This model was retained in the 1987 revision, which elaborated the notion of a spectrum of autistic symptoms and added the subgroup PDD-NOS under the general category of PDD. The new sub-category (PDD-NOS) permitted the diagnosis of a PDD in children who do not meet all criteria for a diagnosis of autism. Perhaps for that reason, more children met criteria for an ASD in the *DSM-III-R* than met criteria in the *DSM-III* (Waterhouse et al., 1996). That model was elaborated further in the *DSM-IV*, published in 1994, which added additional subcategories to those listed under the general rubric of PDD. While *ICD-10* and *DSM-IV-TR* criteria are much more specific with regard to the diagnosis of ASDs than the earlier editions of the *DSM*, the later revisions permit the classification of individuals into several other subgroups under the category of PDD. These include Asperger's disorder (AS), which was added to the PDD category in *DSM-IV*.

The inclusion of AS in the *DSM-IV* may have resulted in the identification of more children at the higher functioning end of the spectrum of impairment—that is, children with intact cognitive function and relatively mild impairments. AS was first identified by the Viennese physician Hans Asperger in 1944, at about the same time that Leo Kanner described his American patients with Infantile Autism. Asperger described a milder impairment than did Kanner, which included social immaturity and delayed social reasoning, impaired communication (especially in the area of conversation), and difficulty with empathy and the expression and recognition of emotions (Attwood, 2008). Lorna Wing (1981) drew attention to Asperger's work when she described a similar group of children. Diagnostic criteria for the disorder were proposed by Gillberg (1991a), and were incorporated in modified form into the *DSM-IV* in 1994.

Prevalence rates for AS vary significantly as a function of the diagnostic criteria employed. Studies using the *DSM-IV* or *ICD-10* criteria yield prevalence rates between 0.3 and 8.4 per 10,000 (Baird et al., 2000; Chakrabarti & Fombonne, 2005). Studies which use Gillberg's less restrictive criteria report prevalence rates between 36–48 per 10,000 children (Ehlers & Gillberg, 1993; Kadesjo, Gillberg, & Hagberg, 1999). The introduction of AS into the *DSM-IV* remains a topic of considerable debate, because it can be difficult to distinguish reliably between AS and higher functioning individuals with autism (Klin, McPartland, & Volkmar, 2005). To address this difficulty, the editors of the fifth revision of the DSM have proposed to include a single diagnostic category that does not distinguish between AS and other autism spectrum diagnoses (Lord, 2009). There is little debate, however, that the inclusion of children with relatively milder impairments under the category of PDD has contributed to the increased prevalence of ASDs.

In addition to changes in the diagnostic criteria, procedures for making an ASD diagnosis changed over time. Wing and Potter (2009) and others (Fombonne, 2003, 2005) discussed differences in the methods used to identify and diagnose children with ASDs across studies. Variations in the size of populations studied and methods of case ascertainment

are clearly related to differences in prevalence estimates across studies, with smaller samples and more rigorous case ascertainment associated with higher prevalence estimates (Fombonne, 2003, 2005). The development of reliable diagnostic tools, including the Autism Diagnostic Interview–Revised (Lord, Rutter, & LeCouteur, 1994) and the Autism Diagnostic Observation Schedule (Lord et al., 2000) has permitted more systematic evaluation of children suspected of having an ASD. As these methods have been validated and made available to a wide range of professionals, the range of individuals evaluating children for a potential ASD has increased, as has the frequency with which the diagnosis is made.

Increased advocacy on the part of parent groups has resulted in much greater public awareness of ASDs. In 1991, autism was included for the first time in the educational categories outlined in the Individuals with Disabilities Education Act (IDEA). That change in educational policy has undoubtedly contributed to increased awareness of ASDs and increased identification of children by special education professionals (IDEA, 2004).

The change in educational policy in the United States, and the increased attention to the diagnosis of ASDs, may have contributed to the more accurate diagnosis of children with ASDs who might previously have been identified as intellectually disabled. One group of researchers documented an increase in the diagnosis of ASDs in California and a concomitant decrease in the identification of children with intellectual disability of unknown origin (Croen, Grether, Hoogstrate, & Selvin, 2002). Their study has been criticized on methodological grounds (Blaxill, Baskin, & Sitzer, 2003), but similar findings have been reported elsewhere in the United States (Gurney et al., 2003) and in Sweden (Gillberg, Steffenburg, & Schaumann, 1991). A recent study by Hertz-Picciotto and Delwiche (2009) found that including milder cases, and lowering the age of diagnosis, could not fully account for the rise in prevalence of ASD in California.

Thus, while it seems likely that changes in the diagnostic code and growing awareness of ASDs have been the primary contributors to the increased prevalence of the disorder, it is impossible to rule out a real increase in the incidence of ASDs.

There is strong evidence from a variety of studies that genetic factors are implicated in ASDs, and likely include multiple genes (see Chapter 2).

The concordance rate for monozygotic twins exceeds 90%, as compared to a concordance rate of less than 10% in fraternal twins (Muhle, Trentacoste, & Rapin, 2004). To date, there is no clear evidence that might suggest any increase in the prevalence of these largely unspecified genetic contributors. The concordance rate of less than 100% in monozygotic twins suggests that nongenetic or epigenetic factors may affect the development of the disorder, but thus far there is no evidence in support of specific environmental risk factors (Wing & Potter, 2009). Similarly, while ASDs are associated with a variety of genetic syndromes (see below), there is no consistent evidence that these syndromes may be increasing. One study (Reichenberg et al., 2006) suggested an association between increased paternal age and an increased risk of having a child with an ASD. Such a finding may suggest that social changes that promote deferred child bearing, or the increased use of assistive reproductive technology, may contribute to the increased prevalence of ASDs, but this finding has not yet been replicated.

By far, the most significant controversy regarding potential causes of the increased prevalence of ASDs has surrounded the assertion (Wakefield, 1998) that some forms of ASDs may be associated with the MMR vaccine, or with thimerosal, a preservative used in some vaccines. Multiple epidemiological studies have now investigated a possible link between the MMR vaccine and the regressive form of ASD, and between thimerosal and ASD. All of these studies have yielded negative results (Farrington, Miller, & Taylor, 2001; Fombonne et al, 2006; Honda, Shimizu, & Rutter, 2005; Niehus & Lord, 2006; Stefanatos, 2008; Taylor et al., 2002; Wilson, Mills, Ross, McGowan, & Jadad, 2003). In Japan, health officials initiated a natural experiment when they implemented widespread vaccination in 1989 and then discontinued it in 1993, due to several cases of aseptic meningitis. Japanese officials reported no decrease in the prevalence of ASD after vaccination was suspended; instead, the prevalence of the disorder continued to increase, as it did worldwide (Uchiyama, Kurosawa, & Inaba, 2007).

The best evidence available to date suggests that the increased prevalence of ASDs, while real, is largely (though perhaps not totally) related to improved detection, more comprehensive diagnostic evaluation, and broader definitions of the disorder. While the increased identification of ASDs has undoubtedly raised the costs of providing intervention, it has also made effective services available to many children who would not otherwise have access to them, and may be a significant contributor to the more variable and potentially more positive outcome possible for many of these children.

Geographic Distribution

Epidemiological studies of ASDs have been conducted around the world. Comparable rates of ASDs have been found in the United States (Croen, et al., 2002), Canada (Bryson, Clark, & Smith, 1988), England (Chakrabarti & Fombonne, 2005), France (Fombonne, Du Mazaubrun, Cans, & Grandjean, 1997), Finland (Kielinen, Linna, & Moilanen, 2000), Sweden (Kadesjo et al., 1999), Iceland (Magnússon & Saemundsen, 2001) and Asia (Honda, et al., 2005). These reports suggest that ASDs are widespread and affect individuals across multiple geographic locations.

References to clusters of cases of ASDs within a confined geographic location have been discussed in the popular media. However, only one such case cluster has been published in the literature. Baron-Cohen, Saunders, and Chakrabarti (1999) discussed seven individuals with autism who resided in a single neighborhood in England. The authors concluded that a cluster of that size is likely to occur by chance, but it is important to consider familial relationships and environmental factors that may influence development of the disorder. Given the lack of research on this topic, any conclusions regarding clusters of ASDs are purely speculative.

DEMOGRAPHICS

Gender

ASDs are found disproportionately in males, at a rate of approximately 3–4 males for every female (Bryson, Clark, & Smith, 1988; Fombonne, 1999; Steffenburg & Gillberg, 1986; Volkmar, Szatmari, & Sparrow, 1993). However, the difference in prevalence rates by gender is less pronounced when autism is coupled with intellectual disability. Furthermore, the male to female ratio steadily drops as the severity of intellectual disability rises (Croen, et al., 2002; Fombonne, 2003; Yeargin-Allsopp et al., 2003). A review of epidemiological studies conducted by Fombonne (2003) described the median male to female ratio to be 5.75:1 when comparing individuals within the normal intellectual range. However, this ratio dropped to 1.9:1 when comparing individuals with moderate to severe intellectual disability.

Studies have further shown that females with ASDs display lower verbal and nonverbal intelligence, and more females than males with ASD fall in the severely intellectually disabled range (Banach et al., 2009; Bryson et al., 1988; Konstantareas, Homatidis, & Busch, 1989; Lord, Scopler, & Revicki, 1982; Steffenburg & Gillberg, 1986; Volkmar et al., 1993). Gender differences in intellectual functioning have even been noted in children as young as 28 months. Findings by Carter, et al., (2007) indicate that male and female toddlers with ASDs display different developmental profiles; whereas males perform better on measures of language and motor abilities, females display stronger visual reception skills.

In measuring gender differences on ASD symptomology, studies have yielded conflicting results. Pilowsky, Yirmiya, Shulman, and Dover (1998) found no difference between males and females on the Childhood Autism Rating Scale (Schopler, Reichler, De Vellis, & Daly, 1980) or Autism Diagnostic Interview–Revised (Lord, Storoschuk, Rutter, & Pickles, 1993), when individuals were matched for age and IQ. On the other hand, studies of parental self-report found increased ratings of ASD symptoms for high-functioning (IQ greater than 60) males, compared to high-functioning females (McLennan, Lord, & Schopler, 1993; Posserud, Lundervold, & Gillberg, 2006). Overall, rates of ASDs are disproportionate across gender, as females are less likely to have ASDs, but those that are affected tend to be more severely intellectually disabled.

Socioeconomic Status

The idea of a link between ASDs and socioeconomic status (SES) dates back to Kanner's observation that his 1943 sample consisted mainly of children from well-educated and wealthy families (Kanner, 1943). This observation was initially supported by studies performed in the 1970s and 1980s (Cox, Rutter, Newman, & Bartak, 1975; Finegan & Quarrington, 1979; Hoshino, Kumashiro, Yashima, Tachibana, & Watanabe, 1982; McCarthy, Fitzgerald, & Smith, 1984; Treffert, 1970). However, more recent epidemiological studies have failed to replicate these early findings (Fombonne, 1999, 2003; Larsson et al., 2005;

Powell et al., 2000; Ritvo et al., 1989; Schopler, Andrews, & Strupp, 1979; Steffenburg & Gillberg, 1986; Wing, 1980; Wing & Gould, 1979). Fombonne (2003) reviewed the epidemiological literature and found that only four out of 12 studies supported a link between SES and ASDs, with each of the four supporting studies occurring before 1980. Wing (1980) suggested that earlier reports of an association between SES and ASDs can be explained by referral and diagnostic biases, such that only families with a high SES could afford to have their children examined in specialized clinics. Not surprisingly, the current literature does not support the notion that SES is a factor in the development of ASDs.

In a related body of research, it has also been suggested that rates of ASDs may be higher in immigrant populations (Gillberg, Steffenburg, Borjesson, & Andersson, 1987; Goodman and Richards, 1995; Wing, 1993). The majority of studies examining this phenomenon thus far have not shown a clear correlation, in large part due to the inclusion of relatively small sample sizes, and a lack of information on migration patterns available at the time of the studies. Further investigations in Europe and the United States have found comparable, rather than higher, rates of ASDs across ethnicities (Croen, et al., 2002; Powell et al., 2000; Yeargin-Allsopp et al., 2003). In fact, a California-based study found a lower risk for ASDs in children whose mothers were born in Mexico (Croen, et al., 2002). In all, a clear correlation between immigrant status and ASDs has not been supported by the empirical literature.

DISORDERS INCLUDED IN
THE PERVASIVE DEVELOPMENTAL
DISORDER (PPD) SPECTRUM

In addition to AD, PDD-NOS, and AS, other disorders on the PDD spectrum include Childhood Disintegrative Disorder (CDD), and Rett's Disorder (RD). Children presenting with any disorder on the PDD spectrum exhibit some symptoms of AD, most notably impaired social relatedness. For this reason, at times it may be difficult to accurately assign a diagnostic category that fits best with the child's clinical presentation. To resolve this, researchers have examined each of the disorders on the PDD spectrum in an attempt to identify characteristics that would help clinicians differentiate between ASDs.

Childhood Disintegrative Disorder

CDD was previously known as Heller's disintegrative psychosis and is marked by typical development until the age of two, followed by a period of regression that progresses throughout childhood. During the course of the regression, children experience deterioration of previously acquired social skills and linguistic abilities. Following the regression, children display behavioral features commonly observed in AD; however, the prognosis of CDD is considerably worse (Spence et al., 2004).

Multiple follow-up studies have been conducted to examine the outcomes of children with CDD. These studies have indicated that many children with this disorder never develop language (Evans-Jones & Rosenbloom, 1978; Hill & Rosenbloom, 1986; Volkmar & Cohen, 1989). Volkmar and Cohen (1989) reported on the outcomes of ten cases of individuals diagnosed with CDD. All of the children in their study spoke complete sentences before the onset of the regression. However, in early adulthood, the majority of these individuals were severely intellectually disabled and four were mute. In addition, many exhibited self-injurious behaviors, stereotypies, and aggression.

The development prior to, and the timing of, the regression experienced by children with CDD appear to be helpful in differentiating this disorder from AD and PDD-NOS. The onset of the regression typically seen in AD and PDD-NOS occurs around or before the age of 2 years. Parents of children who are diagnosed with CDD describe a loss of skills that occurs later in childhood, with a mean age of 3.4 years (Volkmar, 1992), and generally occurring between the ages of 2 and 10 years (Spence et al., 2004). Additionally, the regression seen in CDD follows a period of typical development, while the regression experienced by children with AD and PDD-NOS often does not. Studies of children with AD and PDD-NOS who regressed indicate that in a majority of cases parents recall abnormalities that preceded the regression and were most commonly present in the first 12 months of their child's life (Osterling & Dawson, 1994).

Rett's Disorder

RD is diagnosed primarily in females and is relatively rare, affecting 1 in 10,000 to 15,000 children (Hagberg, Goutieres, Hanefeld, Rett, & Wilson, 1985; Hagberg & Hagberg, 1997). This syndrome has been linked to a mutation in the MeCP2 gene at Xq28 in 30–50% of familial cases and 80% of sporadic cases (Amir et al., 1999; Mount, Charman, Hastings, Sheena, & Cass, 2002; Tanguay, 2000). Similarly to CDD, RD is characterized by apparently normal development, which is followed by a period of significant skill loss in the social and psychomotor domains. The syndrome is marked by the deterioration of purposeful use of the hands, which is replaced by complex stereotypic hand mannerisms, most commonly hand-wringing. The regression is also accompanied by progressive cerebral atrophy.

The course of RD progresses through four well-defined stages (Hagberg & Witt-Engestrom, 1986). The first stage lasts for several months and is referred to as early-onset stagnation. Generally, this time is characterized by head growth deceleration, diminished interest in play, unusual hand-waving mannerisms, and diminished communicative abilities and eye contact.

The next stage is referred to as the rapid destructive stage, and can range in length from a few weeks to several months. During this stage, parents report the presence of classic autistic symptoms. Stereotypies common to RD are often observed at this time (e.g., excessive hand wringing, clapping, or washing) and appear to replace purposeful hand movements. The child's gross motor abilities appear to show signs of deterioration, resulting in clumsiness, ataxia and apraxia. In addition, the child may exhibit breathing irregularities, including hyperventilation and breath-holding. Severe dementia is often present at this time, and seizures may develop as well (Hagberg & Witt-Engestrom, 1986).

The psychostationary period is the third stage of RD, and typically lasts several years. During this time, the child's autistic symptoms tend to diminish considerably, and the child makes some cognitive gains. Seizures develop in approximately 70% of cases by this stage, and abnormal EEG results are present in virtually every case. Gross motor abilities often deteriorate further and children often present with gait apraxia, as well as jerky movements of the trunk (Hagberg & Witt-Engestrom, 1986).

The late motor deterioration stage is the final stage of RD. It begins around the age of 5 years and lasts through late adolescence. Epileptic symptoms decrease and emotional interaction with the caregiver improves further during this stage. Motor skills continue to deteriorate and atrophy of muscles progresses, resulting in muscle weakness, severe scoliosis, and trophic foot disturbances. The majority of children suffering from RD become wheelchair-bound during this stage (Hagberg & Witt-Engestrom, 1986).

RD is included on the PDD spectrum because of its phenotypic overlap with autism. The key markers that are helpful in differentiating this syndrome from autism, cerebral palsy, intellectual disability, and encephalopathy are the physical abnormalities typically observed. As noted above, these often include head growth deceleration, loss of purposeful hand movement, the presence of stereotypic hand-wringing, ataxia and other gate abnormalities, scoliosis, hyperventilation, and the holding of the breath (Spence et al., 2004). Furthermore, the regression experienced by children with RD is qualitatively different from the regression seen in AD and PDD-NOS. The regression seen in RD follows a period of typical development, while the regression in AD and PDD-NOS is most commonly predated by abnormalities present in the first year of life (Osterling & Dawson, 1994). In addition, the regression seen in AD and PDD-NOS is not usually accompanied by a loss of motor or adaptive skills, both of which deteriorate in RD (Volkmar & Rutter, 1995).

Asperger's Disorder

AS is a less severe condition than RD and CDD. Similarly to AD, the *DSM-IV-TR* criteria for a diagnosis of AS requires that the child exhibits impaired social relatedness and presents with restricted interests and/or repetitive behaviors. However, unlike AD, criteria for AS specifies that the individual does not experience a delay in language development. Parents often describe their child's behavior as odd, but not peculiar enough to elicit concern until the child reaches school age (Klin & Volkmar, 2000). For this reason, children are frequently not diagnosed with AS until school age, and several studies have suggested that cases that do not present with extreme difficulties in school may go altogether unnoticed (Tantam, 1988a, 1988b).

Parental concerns begin to increase when children with AS begin school and their difficulties become more pronounced. Individuals who meet criteria for AS often flourish in activities based on rote memorization, but struggle with tasks that require more complex conceptualizations or problem-solving skills.

Furthermore, children diagnosed with AS are regularly captivated by one or two topics for many months or years; these interests typically inhibit the development of other interests and knowledge in other areas. The child's commitment to his or her restricted interests begins to interfere with the activities of the structured classroom and may undermine the child's academic performance (Klin & Volkmar, 2000).

Unlike children who are diagnosed with AD, children with AS are interested in interacting with others; however, these interactions are often awkward or odd. They often attempt to tell others about their restricted interests; however, they remain unaware of the responses of others and continue to talk about their interest even when others attempt to switch topics or appear disinterested. Although children with AS do not, by definition, experience language delays, they often display difficulty with pragmatic aspects of language. Specifically, children with AS are frequently overly concrete in their thinking and struggle with sarcasm and humor. In addition, their speech is often pedantic and stilted. The prosody of their speech is also frequently abnormal, as is their use of gestures. Lastly, they engage in imaginative play less frequently than typically developing peers and often have trouble understanding and following rules of games. Combined, these characteristics frequently cause peer rejection and social isolation (Klin & Volkmar, 2000).

As children with AS enter adolescence, they frequently become increasingly interested in developing social relationships and pursuing social contact. Consequently, they are often well aware of the cost of their social difficulties. Adolescents with AS often seek well-defined rules to guide their behaviors when interacting with others. However, their rigidity in following such rules often creates awkward interactions and undermines their efforts. As a result, the inability to form social relationships often results in sexual frustration. In addition, the rigid following of rules to govern behaviors often diminishes the ability of individuals with ASs to meet goals in their employment. Consequently, it is not uncommon for adolescents and adults diagnosed with AS to suffer from depression (Delong & Dwyer, 1988; Gillberg, 1991b; Tantam, 1991).

Several differences have been identified between AS and AD which are helpful in differentiating between these disorders. Unlike AD, the *DSM-IV-TR* criteria for a diagnosis of AS stipulates that there can be no delay in language or adaptive skills, with the exception of social abilities (APA, 2000). In addition, children with AS appear to be less likely to exhibit echolalia, pronominal reversal, and repetition in their speech, than are children with AD or PDD-NOS. However, children with AS are more likely to use idiosyncratic language and to display unusual tones of voice and pedantic speech early in their development than children with AD (Eisenmajer et al., 1996; Kugler, 1998). Furthermore, children with AS generally have a higher verbal than performance IQ, while children with AD are more likely to show the opposite pattern (Kugler, 1998), although there are many individual exceptions.

Other differentiating factors involve an assessment of early communication history, motor development, and the presence of restricted interests and insistence on sameness. Eisenmajer et al. (1996) conducted a structured interview with parents of 48 children diagnosed with high-functioning AD and 69 children diagnosed with AS. The findings indicated that even at a young age, children with AS were more likely to seek out social interactions than children with AD. Additionally, children with AS more commonly exhibited delayed motor milestones and motoric clumsiness than did children with AD or PDD-NOS. Lastly, children with AS were more likely to display restricted interests than children with AD and PDD-NOS, but were less likely to exhibit resistance to change (Kugler, 1998).

Pervasive Developmental Disorder–Not Otherwise Specified

Individuals who meet some, but not all, of the features required for a diagnosis of AD are given the diagnosis of PDD-NOS. To meet criteria for this disorder, individuals must present with some degree of social impairment, along with either a deficit in communication or the presence of restricted interests and/or repetitive behaviors. This diagnostic category is not well defined, and the *DSM-IV-TR* guidelines (APA, 2000) for distinguishing this disorder from other ASDs are based on studies conducted with older children (Chawarska & Volkmar, 2005). For this reason, the diagnostic category may be mistakenly applied to individuals who present with other disorders on the PDD spectrum, as well as other developmental disabilities that are not on the PDD spectrum (Tidmarsh & Volkmar, 2003).

Few studies have compared the clinical presentation of children diagnosed with PDD-NOS to those diagnosed with AD. One such study examined the severity of symptoms exhibited by 135 children who were diagnosed with AD, PDD-NOS, and AS. The findings indicated that the children diagnosed with PDD-NOS exhibited the mildest symptoms of the three groups, displaying the least impaired joint attention skills and fewer deficits across all of the examined domains (Prior et al., 1998). Children with PDD-NOS were also found to have better cognitive, communicative, and social skills than children with AD (Sevin, Matson, Williams, & Kirkpatrick-Sanchez, 1995). Buitelaar, Van der Gaag, Klin, and Volkmar (1999) reported that, when compared to children with AD, children with PDD-NOS displayed fewer restricted interests, engaged in more varied imaginative play, used nonverbal means of communication more frequently, and had a later age of onset. Allen et al. (2001) attempted to make a similar comparison between children with AD and children with PDD-NOS, and found that the groups significantly differed only on restricted stereotyped behaviors, which were less common in the PDD-NOS group. These findings point to a lack of consensus in the literature as to how children with PDD-NOS differ from children with AD, which may be explained by the definition of PDD-NOS.

A lack of a clear definition of PDD-NOS may also contribute to the findings that the diagnosis of PDD-NOS, when made in young children, is less stable than the AD diagnosis (Lord et al., 2006; Stone et al., 1999). Specifically, reliability of the PDD-NOS diagnosis is stronger when it is made in children 4 years of age and older (Klin, Lang, Cicchetti, & Volkmar, 2000). Stone et al. (1999) explained that some of the *DSM-IV-TR* criteria for AD do not apply to very young children, especially those who experience a language delay. These symptoms include failure to develop peer relationships, impaired conversational skills, and stereotyped language. Furthermore, children may not exhibit the required number of symptoms to meet criteria for AD at the age of 2 years, because restricted interests and insistence on sameness often do not emerge until the age of 3 years (Cuccaro et al., 2003; Szatmari et al., 2006).

Multiple studies suggest that the reliability of the diagnosis is considerably stronger when differentiating between ASD and non-ASD, than when differentiating between AD and PDD-NOS (Lord, 1995;

Stone et al., 1999; Volkmar et al., 1994). For this reason, the consolidation of the disorders on the PDD spectrum into a single diagnostic category is being considered for the *DSM-V* (Lord, 2009).

DISORDERS NOT INCLUDED IN THE PERVASIVE DEVELOPMENTAL DISORDER SPECTRUM

Children with ASDs share some symptoms with children diagnosed with other developmental delays and disorders, including global developmental delay, developmental language delay, nonverbal learning disabilities, Obsessive-Compulsive Disorder (OCD), and Tourette's Disorder (TD). As a result of this similarity in symptom presentation, it is often difficult to make an accurate diagnosis. An early and accurate diagnosis of an ASD often allows for earlier commencement of appropriate intervention, which is vital if children with ASDs are to make optimal gains (Eaves & Ho, 2004; Harris & Handleman, 2000). Therefore, it is important to accurately differentiate ASDs from other conditions whose symptoms may resemble disorders on the PDD spectrum.

Developmental Delay

Children with global developmental delays or developmental language delays often exhibit some of the characteristics commonly observed in ASDs. Children with developmental language delays are particularly difficult to differentiate from children with ASDs because language abnormality is one of the core features of ASDs. Young children with developmental disorders often display sensory abnormalities and repetitive behaviors that are frequently observed in children with ASDs (Charman et al., 1998; Lord, 1995; Lord et al., 1993). In addition, children with developmental disabilities often struggle with imaginative play and exhibit communication characteristics that are commonly associated with ASDs. Ventola et al. (2007) compared the clinical presentation of 195 young children with ASDs to 45 similarly aged children with developmental delays in an effort to identify differences the two groups. The results indicated that children with ASDs differentially exhibited impaired socialization skills, specifically joint-attention abilities. Communication skills, sensory sensitivities, and aspects of play also differentiated between the two groups.

Imaginative play is an area of weakness both for toddlers with ASDs and for toddlers with developmental delays (Charman et al., 1998). However, studies examining pretend play in children aged 3.5 to 5 years have reported that these skills are more impaired in children with ASDs than children with other developmental disabilities (Noterdaeme, Sitter, Mildenberger, & Amorosa, 2000; Wainwright and Fein, 1996). Studies suggest that even high-functioning children with ASDs exhibit more impaired imaginative play, when compared to children with developmental language delay (Fein et al., 1996; Wainwright & Fein, 1996).

Studies of communicative abilities in children on the PDD spectrum have also identified specific patterns of deficits in communication that are less likely to be observed in children with developmental delays. Delays in comprehension, appearance of "wh-" questions (i.e., who, what, where, when, and why) and connected sentences, as well as the presence of regression of language skills were found to be the best discriminators between children with ASDs and children with developmental language delay (Fein et al., 1996). In addition, children with ASDs exhibit more echolalia and stereotyped language than children with developmental delays, and are less likely to initiate a verbal exchange or to respond to a verbal communication (Lord, 1995; Loveland, Landry, Hughes, Hall, & McEvoy, 1988; Mildenberger, Sitter, Noterdaeme, & Amorosa, 2001; Noterdaeme et al., 2000; Trillingsgaard, Sorensen, Nemec, & Jorgensen, 2005). Furthermore, children with ASDs display a limited use of conventional gestures and are specifically less likely to nod or shake their head than similarly aged children with developmental delays (Lord et al., 1993, 1994).

A multitude of studies have found a greater degree of impairment in the social abilities of children with ASDs than in children with other developmental disorders (global developmental delay or developmental language delay). Studies comparing the clinical presentation of ASDs and developmental delays in toddlers have found a greater degree of impairment in joint attention, social imitation, pointing to express interest, interest in other children, empathic responding, and displaying a range of facial expressions in toddlers with ASDs (Charman et al., 1998; Landry & Loveland, 1988; Lord, 1995; Rogers, Hepburn, Stackhouse, & Wehner, 2003; Trillingsgaard et al., 2005; Ventola et al., 2007).

Similarly, studies examining social abilities of older children with ASDs have found increased impairment when compared to children of similar ages who suffer from developmental delays. Specifically, these studies have pointed to more pronounced deficits in shared enjoyment, pointing to express interest, offering to share, offering comfort, maintaining eye contact, and the overall quality of social overtures and the level of peer relationships in children with ASDs (Lord et al., 1993; Lord & Pickles, 1996; Noterdaeme et al., 2000).

Although differentiating between children with ASDs and children with developmental delays may be complicated by overlapping deficits, it appears that children with ASDs struggle more significantly in the areas of imaginative play, social interaction, and communication than do children with developmental delays.

Nonverbal Learning Disabilities

Nonverbal Learning Disabilities (NLD) was described by Rourke (1988, 1989) as a syndrome that results from a deficit in the functioning of the right cerebral hemisphere. Rourke's model of NLD describes the presence of a distinct pattern of cognitive strengths and weaknesses that are often combined with impaired social skills, and can resemble the clinical presentation of a child with AS or high-functioning AD. Rourke's model of NLD included deficits in tactile and visual perception, difficulty with assimilation of new materials, and impairments in complex psychomotor abilities, visual attention, and memory. Children with NLD reportedly struggle with visual spatial organization, have difficulty appreciating visual gestalt, and seem to be overwhelmed by visual information. Similarly to individuals with ASD, individuals with NLD tend to perform well on tasks that require rote verbal skills, verbal memory, and auditory attention, but struggle with more complex abilities (e.g., novel problem-solving, concept formation, mathematics). Simple motor abilities, as well as reading and spelling abilities, also appeared to be strong (Rourke, 1988, 1989).

Given the extent of commonality between the diagnostic criteria of ASDs and Rourke's description of NLD, it is likely that these diagnostic categories have been used to describe overlapping groups of children. In attempting to differentiate between ASDs and NLDs, it is helpful to assess the pattern of strengths and weaknesses described by Rourke. It is also useful to examine the degree of social impairment

and presence of restricted interests and repetitive behaviors, which are commonly observed in individuals with ASDs and are typically absent or less severe in individuals with NLD (Green et al., 2003; Rourke, 1988, 1989). However, one should keep in mind that NLD describes a cognitive profile, while ASD describes a set of behaviors, and therefore, there is no reason to think of them as mutually exclusive. Furthermore, NLD is not yet "officially" or universally accepted as a syndrome.

Obsessive-Compulsive Disorder

OCD involves the presence of either intrusive thoughts (obsessions) or repetitive actions (compulsions) that are distressing, time-consuming, or interfere with the individual's daily functioning (APA, 2000). Differentiating obsessions and compulsions observed in individuals with OCD from the behaviors observed in individuals with ASDs is difficult. For instance, it may be difficult to differentiate between an obsession observed in OCD and an unusual interest commonly present in PDDs.

In adults, the distinction between ASDs and OCD is made based on the absence of insight into the senselessness of these behaviors, which by definition is present in adults with OCD. However, children with OCD are not required to have such insight to meet diagnostic criteria (APA, 2000). Because individuals with OCD typically do not display deficits in socialization, social relatedness is a key distinguishing factor between the two disorders in children and adults. Furthermore, a diagnosis of ASD does not preclude a diagnosis of OCD, if the additional diagnosis provides a better description of the child's behavior or intervention needs (see below for more on comorbidity).

Tourette's Disorder

TD is characterized by the presence of multiple motor and vocal tics that persist for at least 1 year. TD typically follows a chronic course, and frequently the tics become increasingly complex over time (APA, 2000). Occasionally, complex tics may be difficult to differentiate from rituals and stereotypies often observed in individuals with ASDs. For instance, complex vocal tics may involve repetition of phrases out of context, which often resembles stereotyped speech. Complex motor tics may involve self-injurious behaviors, such as biting or head-banging, which are also seen in ASDs.

Several characteristics of TD aid clinicians in differentiating it from ASDs. The onset of TD typically occurs later in childhood (the average age of onset is 7 years of age) than does the onset of ASDs. Additionally, social abilities are not typically deficient in individuals suffering from TD unless they present with other comorbid conditions, or unless the TD cause social difficulties. It is worth noting that tics appear to occur more frequently in individuals with ASDs than would be expected, and as such, it is important to consider TD as a comorbid condition in this population (Kerbeshian & Burd, 1986; Marriage, Miles, Strokes, & Davey, 1993). The literature—which is still in its infancy—suggests that tics may sometimes be differentiated from stereotypies on the basis of some distinctive features, such as antecedent conditions, duration, rhythmicity and symmetry, age of onset, and part of body involved (Crosland, Zarcone, Schroeder, Zaronce, & Fowler, 2005; Mahone, Bridges, Prahme, & Singer, 2004).

COMORBID CONDITIONS

A variety of studies have documented a high frequency of intellectual disability in children with ASDs, with some studies suggesting that 70% of children with ASD have IQs below 70 (Fombonne, 2003). More recent studies have found that the incidence of intellectual disability in individuals with ASDs is closer to 50% (CDC, 2006), and suggest that, as the definition of ASDs has broadened, and intervention services have improved, the percentage of children with intellectual functioning within the average range has increased. Seizure disorders are very common among children with ASDs and are estimated to occur in 25–40% of individuals (Tuchman, et al., 1991; Volkmar & Nelson, 1990).

ASDs are known to be comorbid with a variety of genetic syndromes, including Fragile X syndrome, Tuberous Sclerosis (TS), and the partial tetrasomy 15 syndrome. Together these three conditions account for about 15% of all cases of ASDs in which the individual has an IQ below 50. Among individuals with TS, the incidence of ASDs has been estimated at 16–65%; the incidence of TS in the ASD population is 1–4%, although it increases to 8–14% among individuals with an ASD and a seizure disorder (Zafeiriou, Ververi, & Vargiami, 2007).

ASDs are frequently comorbid with Fragile X syndrome, the most common inherited cause of mental retardation. Approximately 25–33% of individuals with Fragile X syndrome have an ASD; among the population of individuals with an ASD, the incidence of Fragile X syndrome is approximately 2%. (Zafeiriou et al., 2007). ASDs may also occur in conjunction with a variety of other genetic conditions, including Moebious syndrome, 22q11 deletion syndrome, Down's syndrome and others, although the prevalence of comorbidity is lower (see Chapter 2 for a more complete discussion of genetic syndromes with autistic features).

Several recent studies have revealed that the comorbidity of ASDs and psychiatric disorders may exceed 70% (Dekker and Koot, 2003; Leyfer et al., 2006). Hyperactivity, inattention, and impulsivity are frequently seen in children with ASDs and are not typically diagnosed as ADHD if a diagnosis of an ASD has been made. Leyfer et al. (2006) reported that 55% of the children with ASDs in their sample had symptoms of ADHD which significantly impaired their functioning, and 31% of their sample met DSM-IV-TR criteria for ADHD. Few children (7%) in their sample met criteria for a diagnosis of Oppositional Defiant Disorder.

As the population of children diagnosed with ASDs has grown, researchers have increasingly reported a significant comorbidity with mood disorders and anxiety disorders. Leyfer et al. (2006) report that 10% of the children in their sample met DSM-IV-TR criteria for depression, and an additional 14% fell just short of meeting criteria for a diagnosis. These data are consistent with earlier reports of a significant incidence of depression among children diagnosed with an ASD, especially among higher functioning adolescent and adult samples (Brereton, Tonge, & Enfield, 2006; Ghaziuddin, Ghaziuddin, & Greden, 2002). The incidence of bipolar disorder, in contrast, appears to be quite low among children with ASDs (Leyfer et al., 2006).

Several studies have revealed that the prevalence of anxiety disorders among individuals with ASDs may be higher than that in the general population. Lecavalier et al. (2006) reported a prevalence of anxiety disorders between 14% and 21% in their large, community-based sample of children with ASD diagnoses. Weisbrot, Gadow, DeVincent, and Pomeroy (2005) reported prevalence rates of 24% and 59%, respectively, for generalized anxiety disorder and specific phobias in their sample of 6- to 12-year-olds with ASDs. They note that anxiety symptoms seemed to increase with age and are both more common and more severe in children with AS and PDD-NOS than in children with AD. Several studies have found that specific phobias are especially common in children and adolescents with ASDs (Leyfer, 2006, Tyson et al., 2009). As noted earlier, the question of comorbidity of ASDs and OCD is more complicated. Many children with autism exhibit ritualistic behaviors which can be confused with the compulsions seen in OCD. In most cases, however, these behaviors are not associated with the extreme anxiety or intrusive thoughts seen in OCD, or it is not possible to assess the presence of these factors. Most authors recommend that the diagnosis of comorbid ASD and OCD should be made very rarely, and only when there is clear evidence of obsessive thinking (Bejerot, 2007; Deprey & Ozonoff, 2009).

SUMMARY

PDDs are a group of neurodevelopmental disorders that are characterized by deficits in social interaction and communication, as well as the presence of repetitive and stereotyped behavior patterns. Individuals with ASDs struggle with forming normal relationships and developing social reciprocity. Many are unable to utilize nonverbal forms of communication, show a lack of awareness of the reactions of others, and fail to share experiences with other people. Individuals with ASDs generally present with some degree of language impairment and frequently exhibit attentional difficulties and deficits in executive functioning (see Part II of this volume for more on cognitive difficulties, and specifically Chapter 15, for a discussion of cognitive profiles).

The developmental course of ASD varies considerably from younger to older ages. In young children, early markers of ASDs include infrequent bids for joint attention, failure to respond to name, emotional flatness, limited social orienting, and poor disengagement of attention. As children with ASDs age and participate in intervention, behavioral abnormalities and deficits in activities of daily living may diminish. Adolescence is often a particularly challenging period for individuals with ASDs. Difficult behaviors often increase in frequency during this period, and the onset of seizures and abnormal EEG results are not uncommon during adolescence. Recent studies of adult outcomes indicate that a substantial proportion of adults with ASDs do not live independently and continue to exhibit social difficulties.

Historically, the prevalence of ASDs was estimated to be about 2–4 per 10,000 children. Recent studies of prevalence rates indicate that in the United States, 1 in 150 children are diagnosed with ASDs. Although there is considerable evidence that the rise in prevalence rates of ASD reflects increased awareness and changes in the diagnostic procedures, a real increase in the incidence of ASDscannot be ruled out.

PDD is a diagnostic category that encompasses a spectrum of disorders, including AD, PDD-NOS, AS, CDD, and RD. Disorders on the PDD spectrum share similar behavioral presentation. In addition, ASDs share symptoms with other developmental delays and disorders. Consequently, it is often difficult to differentiate ASDs from one another, as well as from other conditions. Furthermore, individuals with ASDs frequently present with comorbid conditions, making assessment more difficult still. Further research into the clinical presentation and neurobiology of these disorders should advance our understanding of the nature of ASDs, and allow clinicians to make more accurate diagnoses and more specific recommendations for treatment.

References

Adolphs, R., Sears, L., & Piven, J. (2001). Abnormal processing of social information from faces in autism. *Journal of Cognitive Neuroscience, 13*, 232–240.

Allen, D. A., Steinberg, M., Dunn, M., Fein, D., Feinstein, C., Waterhouse, L., & Rapin, I. (2001). Autistic disorder versus other pervasive developmental disorders in young children: Same or different? *European Child & Adolescent Psychiatry, 10*, 67–78.

American Psychiatric Association. (1994). *Diagnostic and statistical manual of mental disorders* (4th ed.). Washington, DC: American Psychiatric Association.

American Psychiatric Association. (2000). *Diagnostic and statistical manual of mental disorders* (4th ed., text revision). Washington, DC: American Psychiatric Association.

Amir, R. E., Van den Veyver, I. B., Wan, M., Tran, C. Q., Francke, U., Zoghbi, H. Y. (1999). Rett syndrome is caused by mutations in X-linked MECP2, encoding methyl-CpG-binding protein 2. *Nature Genetics, 23*(2), 127–128.

Anderson, D. K., Lord, C., Risi, S., DiLavore, P. S., Shulman, C., Thurm, A. … Pickles, A. (2007). Patterns of growth in verbal abilities among children with autism spectrum disorders. *Journal of Consulting and Clinical Psychology, 75*(4), 594–604.

Attwood, T. (2008). *The complete guide to Asperger's disorder*. London: Kingsley Publishers.

Baird, G., Charman, T., Baron-Cohen, S., Cox, A., Swettenham, J., Wheelwright, S. … Drew, A. (2000). A screening instrument for autism at 18 months of age: A 6 year follow-up study. *Journal of the American Academy of Child and Adolescent psychiatry, 39*, 694–702.

Baird, G., Simonoff, E., Pickles, A., Chandler, S., Loucas, T. Meldrum, D., & Charman, T. (2006). Prevalence of disorders of the autism spectrum in a population cohort of children in South Thames: The Special Needs and Autism Project. *Lancet, 368*, 210–215.

Ballaban-Gil, K., Rapin, I., Tuchman, R., & Shinnar, S. (1996). Longitudinal examination of the behavioral, language and social changes in a population of adolescents and young adults with autistic disorder. *Pediatric Neurology, 15*, 217–223.

Banach, R., Thompson, A., Szatmari, P., Goldberg, J., Tuff, L., & Zwaigenbaum, L. (2009). Brief report: Relationship between non-verbal IQ and gender in autism. *Journal of Autism and Developmental Disorders, 39*(1), 188–193.

Baron-Cohen, S. (1989). Perceptual role taking and protodeclarative pointing in autism. *British Journal of Developmental Psychology, 7*, 113–127.

Baron-Cohen, S., Saunders, K., & Chakrabarti, S. (1999). Does autism cluster geographically? A research note. *Autism, 3*(1), 39–43.

Bejerot, S. (2007). An autistic dimension: A proposed subtype of obsessive-compulsive disorder. *Autism, 11*, 101–110.

Bernabei, P., Cerquiglini, A., Cortesi, F., & D'Ardia, C. (2006). Regression versus no regression in the autistic disorder: Developmental trajectories. *Journal of Autism and Developmental Disorders, 37*(3), 580–588.

Billstedt, E., Gillberg, C., & Gillberg, C. (2005). Autism after adolescence: Population-based 13–22-year follow-up study of 120 individuals with autism diagnosed in childhood. *Journal of Autism and Developmental Disorders, 15*(3), 351–360.

Bishop, S. L., Luyster, R., Richler, J., & Lord, C. (2008). Diagnostic assessment. In K. Chawarska, A. Klin, & F. R. Volkmar (Eds.), *Autism spectrum disorders in infants and toddlers: Diagnosis, assessment, and treatment* (pp. 23–49). New York: Guilford Press.

Blaxill, M., Baskin, D., & Spitzer, W. (2003). Commentary: Blaxill, Baskin & Spitzer on Croen et al. (2002). The changing prevalence of autism in California. *Journal of Autism and Developmental Disorders, 33*, 223–226.

Brereton, A. V., Tonge, B. J. & Einfeld, S. L. (2006). Psychopathology in children and adolescents with autism compared to young people with intellectual disability. *Journal of Autism and Developmental Disorders, 36*(7), 863–870.

Bryson, S. E., Clark, B. S., & Smith, I. M. (1988). First report of a Canadian epidemiological study of autistic syndromes. *Journal of Child Psychology and Psychiatry, 29*(4), 433–445.

Buitelaar, J. K., Van der Gaag, R., Klin, A., & Volkmar, F. (1999). Exploring the boundaries of pervasive developmental disorder not otherwise specified: Analysis of data from the DSM-IV autistic disorder field trial. *Journal of Autism and Developmental Disorders, 29*, 33–43.

Byrd, R. (2002). *Report in the legislature on the principle findings from the epidemiology of autism in California: A comprehensive pilot study*. University of California Davis, MIND Institute. Retrieved August 18, 2010, from http://www.feat.org/LinkClick.aspx?fileticket=RRD%2FsTcWUmc%3D&tabid=78&mid=583

Carter, A., Black, D., Tewani, S., Connolly, C., Kadlec, M., & Tager-Flusberg, H. (2007). Sex differences in toddlers with autism spectrum disorders. *Journal of Autism and Developmental Disorders, 37*(1), 86–97.

Centers for Disease Control (2006). Autism spectrum disorders. Retrieved July 29, 2010, from www.cdc.gov/ncbddd/autism

Chakrabarti, S., & Fombonne, E. (2005). Pervasive developmental disorders in preschool children: Confirmation of high prevalence. *American Journal of Psychiatry, 162*(6), 1133–1141.

Charman, T., & Baird, G. (2002). Practitioner review: Diagnosis of autism spectrum disorder in 2- and 3-year-old children. *Journal of Child Psychology and Psychiatry, 43*, 289–305.

Charman, T., Baron-Cohen, S., Swettenham, J., Baird, G., Drew, A., & Cox, A. (2003). Predicting language outcome in infants with autism and pervasive developmental disorders. *The International Journal of Language and Communication Disorders, 38*, 265–285.

Charman, T., Swettenham, J., Baron-Cohen, S., Cox, A., Baird, G., & Drew, A. (1998). An experimental investigation of social-cognitive abilities in infants with autism: Clinical implications. *Infant Mental Health Journal, 19*(2), 260–275.

Charman, T., Taylor, E., Drew, A., Cockerill, H., Brown, J. A., & Baird, G. (2005). Outcome at 7 years of children diagnosed with autism at age 2: Predictive validity of assessments conducted at 2 and 3 years of age and pattern of symptom change over time. *Journal of Child Psychology and Psychiatry, 46*, 500–513.

Chawarska, K., Klin, A., Paul, R., & Volkmar, F. (2007). Autism spectrum disorder in the second year: Stability and change in syndrome expression. *Journal of Child Psychology and Psychiatry, 48*(2), 128–138.

Chawarska, K., & Volkmar, F. R. (2005). Autism in infancy and early childhood. In F. R. Volkmar,

R. Paul, A. Klin, & D. Cohen (Eds.), *Handbook of autism and pervasive developmental disorders, Vol. 1. Diagnosis, development, neurobiology, and behavior* (3rd ed., pp. 223–246). Hoboken, NJ: Wiley.

Chiang, C., Soong, W., Lin, T., & Rogers, S. J. (2008). Nonverbal communication skills in young children with autism. *Journal of Autism and Developmental Disorders, 38,* 1898–1906.

Cox, A., Klein, K., Charman, T., Baird, G., Baron-Cohen, S., Swettenham, J. ... Wheelwright, S. (1999). Autism spectrum disorders at 20 and 42 months of age: Stability of clinical and ADI-R diagnosis. *Journal of Child Psychology and Psychiatry, 40,* 719–732.

Cox, A., Rutter, M., Newman, S., & Bartak, L. (1975). A comparative study of infantile autism and specific developmental receptive language disorder: II. Parental characteristics. *The British Journal of Psychiatry, 126*(2), 146–159.

Croen, L. A., Grether, J. K., Hoogstrate, J., & Selvin, S. (2002). The changing prevalence of autism in California. *Journal of Autism and Developmental Disorders, 32*(3), 207–215.

Croen, L. A., Grether, J. K., & Selvin, S. (2002). Descriptive epidemiology of autism in a California population: Who is at risk? *Journal of Autism and Developmental Disorders, 32*(3), 217–224.

Crosland, K., Zarcone, J., Schroeder, S., Zaronce, T., and Fowler, S. (2005). Use of an antecedent analysis and a force sensitive platform to compare stereotyped movements and motor tics. *American Journal on Mental Retardation, 110,* 181–192.

Cuccaro, M. L., Shao, Y., Grubber, J., Slifer, M., Wolpert, C. M., Donnelly, S. L. ... Pericak-Vance, M. A. (2003). Factor analysis of restricted and repetitive behaviors in autism using the Autism Diagnostic Interview-R. *Child Psychiatry & Human Development, 34*(1), 3–17.

Davidovitch, M., Glick, L., Holtzman, G., Tirosh, E., & Sarif, M. P. (2000). Developmental regression in autism: Maternal perception. *Journal of Autism and Developmental Disorders, 30*(2), 113–119.

Dawson, G., Meltzoff, A. N., Osterling, J., & Rindaldi, J. (1998). Neuropsychological correlates of early symptoms of autism. *Child Development, 69,* 1276–1285.

Dekker, M., & Koot, H. (2003). DSM-IV disorders in children with borderline to moderate intellectual disability: Prevalence and impact. *Journal of the American Academy of Child and Adolescent Psychiatry, 42,* 915–922.

Delong, G., & Dwyer, J. (1988). Correlation of family history with specific autistic subgroups: Aspereger's syndrome and bipolar affective disease. *Journal of Autism and Developmental Disorders, 18,* 593–600.

Deprey, L., & Ozonoff, S. (2009). Assessment of comorbid psychiatric conditions in autism. In S. Goldstein, J. Naglieri, & S. Ozonoff, (Eds.). *Assessment of Autism Spectrum Disorders* (pp. 290–317). New York: Guilford.

Eaves, L. C., & Ho, H. (1996). Stability and change in cognitive and behavioral characteristics of autism through childhood. *Journal of Autism and Developmental Disorders, 26*(5), 557–569.

Eaves, L. C., & Ho, H. H. (2004). The very early identification of autism: Outcome to age 4 1/2–5. *Journal of Autism and Developmental Disorders, 34,* 367–378.

Eaves, L. C., & Ho, H. H. (2008). Young adult outcome of autism spectrum disorders. *Journal of Autism and Developmental Disorders, 38,* 739–747.

Ehlers, S., & Gillberg, C. (1993). The epidemiology of Asperger syndrome: A total population study. *Journal of Child Psychiatry and Psychology, 34,* 1327–1350.

Eisenmajer, R., Prior, M., Leekam, S., Wing, L., Gould, J., Welham, M., et al. (1996). Comparison of clinical symptoms in autism and Asperger's disorder. *Journal of the American Academy of Child & Adolescent Psychiatry, 35*(11), 1523–1531.

Evans, D. W., Leckman, J. F., Carter, A., Reznick, J. S., Henshaw, D., King, R. A., & Pauls, D.(1997). Ritual, habit, and perfectionism: The prevalence and development of compulsive-like behavior in normal young children. *Child Development, 68,* 58–68.

Evans-Jones, L., & Rosenbloom, L. (1978). Disintegrative psychosis in childhood. *Developmental Medicine and Child Neurology, 20,* 717–724.

Farrington, C. P., Miller, E., & Taylor, B. (2001). MMR and autism: Further evidence against a causal association. *Vaccine, 19*(27), 3632–3635.

Fein, D., Barton, M., Eigsti, I. M., Naigles, L., Rosenthal, M., Tyson, K. ... Helt, M. (2009, May). *Cognitive and Behavioral Profiles of Children Who Recover From Autism.* Paper presented at the International Meeting for Autism Research, Chicago.

Fein, D., Dunn, M., Allen, D. A., Aram, D. M., Hall, N., Morris, R., & Wilson, B. C. (1996). Neuropsychological and language data. In: I. Rapin (Ed.), *Preschool children with inadequate communication: Developmental language disorder, autism, low IQ. Clinics in developmental medicine* (pp. 123–154). London: MacKeith Press.

Fein, D., Tinder, P., & Waterhouse, L. (1979). Stimulus generalization in autistic and normal children. *Journal of Child Psychology and Psychiatry, 20,* 325–335.

Finegan, J. A., & Quarrington, B. (1979). Pre-, peri-, and neonatal factors and infantile autism. *Journal of Child Psychology and Psychiatry, 20*(2), 119–128.

Fombonne, E. (1999). The epidemiology of autism: A review. *Psychological Medicine, 29*(04), 769–786.

Fombonne, E. (2003). Epidemiological surveys of autism and other pervasive developmental disorders: An update. *Journal of Autism and Developmental Disorders, 33*(4), 365–382.

Fombonne, E. (2005). The changing epidemiology of autism. *Journal of Applied Research in Developmental Disabilities*, 18, 281–290.

Fombonne, E., Du Mazaubrun, C., Cans, C., & Grandjean, H. (1997). Autism and associated medical disorders in a French epidemiological survey. *Journal of the American Academy of Child & Adolescent Psychiatry*, 36(11), 1561–1569.

Fombonne, E., Zakarian, R., Bennett, A., Meng, L., & McLean-Heywood, D. (2006). Pervasive developmental disorders in Montreal, Quebec, Canada: Prevalence and links with immunizations. *Pediatrics*, 118(1), e139–150.

Ghaziuddin, M., Ghaziuddin, N., & Greden, J. (2002). Depression in persons with autism: Implications for research and clinical care. *Journal of Autism and Developmental Disorders*, 32(4), 299–306.

Gillberg, C. (1991a). Clinical and neurobiological aspects of Asperger syndrome in six family studies. In U. Frith (Ed.), *Autism and Asperger syndrome* (pp. 122–147). Cambridge: Cambridge University Press.

Gillberg, C. (1991b). Outcome in autism and autistic like conditions. *Journal of the American Academy of Child and Adolescent Psychiatry*, 30, 375–382.

Gillberg, C., & Steffenberg, S. (1987). Outcome and prognostic factors in infantile autism and similar conditions: A population based study of 46 cases followed through puberty. *Journal of Autism and Developmental Disorders*, 17, 273–287.

Gillberg, C., Steffenburg, S., Borjesson, B., & Andersson, L. (1987). Infantile autism in children of immigrant parents. A population-based study from Goteborg, Sweden. *The British Journal of Psychiatry*, 150(6), 856–858.

Gillberg, C., Steffenburg, S., & Schaumann, H. (1991). Is autism more common now than ten years ago? *British Journal of Psychiatry*, 158, 403–409.

Goldberg, W. A., & Osann, K. (2003). Language and other regression: Assessment and timing. *Journal of Autism and Developmental Disorders*, 33, 607–615.

Goodman, R., & Richards, H. (1995). Child and adolescent psychiatric presentations of second-generation Afro-Caribbeans in Britain. *The British Journal of Psychiatry*, 167(3), 362–369.

Green, L., Joy, S., Robins, D., Brooklier, K., Waterhouse, L., & Fein, D. (2003). Autism and pervasive developmental disorders. In R. Schiffer, S. Rao, & B. Fogel (Eds.), *Neuropsychiatry* (2nd ed., pp. 503–551). Baltimore: Williams & Wilkins.

Gurney, J., Fritz, M., Ness, K., Sievers, P., Newschaffer, C. & Shapiro, E. (2003). Analysis of the prevalence trends of autism spectrum disorders in Minnesota. *Archives of Pediatrics and Adolescent Medicine*, 157, 622–627.

Hagberg, B., Goutieres, F., Hanefeld, F., Rett, A., & Wilson, J. (1985). Rett syndrome: Criteria for inclusion and exclusion. *Brain Development*, 7, 372–373.

Hagberg, B., & Hagberg, G. (1997). Rett syndrome: Epidemiology and geographical variability. *European Child and Adolescent Psychiatry*, 6, 55–57.

Hagberg, B., & Witt-Engerstrom, I. (1986). Rett syndrome: A suggested staging system for describing impairment profile with increasing age towards adolescence. *American Journal of Medical Genetics*, 24, 47–59.

Harris, S., & Handleman, J. (2000). Age and IQ at intake as predictors of placement for young children with autism: A four to six-year follow-up. *Journal of Autism and Developmental Disorders*, 30, 137–142.

Hauck, M., Fein, D., Waterhouse, L., & Feinstein, C. (1995). Social initiations by autistic children to adults and other children. *Journal of Autism and Developmental Disorders*, 25(6), 579–595.

Helt, M., Kelley, E., Kinsbourne, M., Pandey, J., Boorstein, H., Herbert, M., & Fein, D.(2008). Can children with autism recover? If so, how? *Neuropsychology Review*, 18(4), 339–366.

Hertz-Picciotto, I., and Delwiche, L. (2009). The rise in autism and the role of age at diagnosis. *Epidemiology*, 20, 84–90.

Hill, A., & Rosenbloom, L. (1986). Disintegrative psychosis of childhood: Teenage follow-up. *Developmental Medicine and Child Neurology*, 28, 34–40.

Honda, H., Shimizu, Y., Imai, M., & Nitto, Y. (2005). Cumulative incidence of childhood autism: A total population study of better accuracy and precision. *Developmental Medicine & Child Neurology*, 47(1), 10–18.

Honda, H., Shimizu, Y., & Rutter, M. (2005). No effect of MMR withdrawal on the incidence of autism: a total population study. *J Child Psychol Psychiatry*, 46(6), 572–579.

Hoshino, Y., Kumashiro, H., Yashima, Y., Tachibana, R., & Watanabe, M. (1982). The epidemiological study of autism in Fukushima-ken. *Psychiatry and Clinical Neurosciences*, 36(2), 115–124.

Howlin, P., & Goode, S. (1998). Outcome in adult life for people with autism and Asperger's disorder. In F. R. Volkmar (Ed.), *Autism and pervasive developmental disorders* (pp. 209–241). Cambridge: Cambridge University Press.

Howlin, P., Goode, S., Hutton, J., & Rutter, M. (2004). Adult outcome for children with autism. *Journal of Child Psychology and Psychiatry*, 45(2), 212.

Hughes, C., Russell, J., & Robbins, T. W. (1994). Evidence for executive dysfunction in autism. *Neuropsychologia*, 32, 477–492.

Hus, V., Pickles, A., Cook, E. H., Risi, S., & Lord, C. (2007). Using the Autism Diagnostic Interview–Revised to increase phenotypic homogeneity in genetic studies of autism. *Journal of Biological Psychiatry*, 61, 438–448.

Individuals with Disabilities Act, (2004). http://frwebgate. access.gpo.gov/cgi-bin/getdoc.cgi?dbname=108_ cong_public_laws&docid=f:publ446.108

Kadesjo, B., Gillberg, C., & Hagberg, B. (1999). Brief report: Autism and Asperger syndrome in seven-year-old children: A total population study. *Journal of Autism and Developmental Disorders*, 29(4), 327–331.

Kanner, L. (1943). Autistic disturbances of affective contact. *Nervous Child*, 2, 217–250.

Kanner, L. (1971). Follow-up study of eleven autistic children originally reported in 1943. *Journal of Autism and Childhood Schizophrenia*, 1, 119–145.

Kasari, C., Sigman, M., & Yirmiya, N. (1993). Focused and social attention of autistic children in interactions with familiar and unfamiliar adults: A comparison of autistic, mentally retarded, and normal children. *Developmental Psychopathology*, 5, 403–414.

Kelley, E., Paul, J. J., Fein, D., & Naigles, L. R. (2006). Residual language deficits in optimal outcome children with a history of autism. *Journal of Autism and Developmental Disorders*, 36, 807–828.

Kerbeshian, J., & Burd, L. (1986). Asperger's disorder and Tourette syndrome: The case of the pinball wizard. *British Journal of Psychiatry: The Journal of Mental Science*, 148, 731–736.

Kielinen, M., Linna, S. L., & Moilanen, I. (2000). Autism in northern Finland. *European Child & Adolescent Psychiatry*, 9(3), 162–167.

Kleinman, J., Ventola, P., Pandey, J., Verbalis, A., Barton, M., Hodgson, S., & Fein, D. (2008). Diagnostic stability in very young children with autism spectrum disorders. *Journal of Autism and Developmental Disorders*, 38, 606–615.

Klin, A., Lang, J., Cicchetti, D. V., & Volkmar, F. R. (2000). Brief report: Interrater reliability of clinical diagnosis and DSM-IV criteria for autistic disorder. Results of the DSM-IV autism field trial. *Journal of Autism and Developmental Disorders*, 30(2), 163–167.

Klin, A., McPartland, J. & Volkmar, F. (2005). Asperger Syndrome. In F. Volkmar, R. Paul, A. Klin & D. Cohen (Eds.). *Handbook of Autism and Pervasive Developmental Disorders*, (3rd ed., pp. 88–125). Hoboken, NJ: Wiley.

Klin, A., & Volkmar, F. R. (Eds.) (2000). *Asperger syndrome*. New York: Guilford Press.

Koboyashi, R., Murata, T., & Yoshinaga, K., (1992). A follow-up study of 201 children with autism in Kyushu and Yamaguchi areas. Japan. *Journal of Autism and Developmental Disorders*, 22, 395–411.

Kogan, M., Blumberg, S., Schieve, L., Boyle, C., Perrin, J., Ghandour, R.,... and van Cyck, P. (2009). Prevalence of parent-reported diagnosis of autism spectrum disorder among children in the US, 2007. *Pediatrics*, 124, 1395–1403.

Konstantareas, M. M., Homatidis, S., & Busch, J. (1989). Cognitive, communication, and social differences between autistic boys and girls. *Journal of Applied Developmental Psychology*, 10, 411–424.

Kugler, B. (1998). The differentiation between autism and Asperger syndrome. *Autism: The International Journal of Research and Practice*, 2, 11–32.

Landry, S. H., & Loveland, K. A. (1988). Communication behaviors in autism and developmental language delay. *Journal of Child Psychology and Psychiatry and Allied Disciplines*, 29(5), 621–634.

Larsson, H. J., Eaton, W. W., Madsen, K. M., Vestergaard, M., Olesen, A. V., Agerbo, E., ... Mortensen, P. B. (2005). Risk factors for autism: Perinatal factors, parental psychiatric history, and socioeconomic status. *American Journal of Epidemiology*, 161(10), 916–925.

Lecavalier, L. (2006). Behavioral and emotional problems in young people with pervasive developmental disorders: Relative prevalence, effects of subject characteristics and empirical classification. *Journal of Autism and Developmental Disorders*, 36(8), 1101–1114.

Leekam, S., López, B., & Moore, C. (2000). Attention and joint attention in preschool children with autism. *Developmental Psychology*, 36, 261–273.

Leyfer, O., Folstein, S., Bacalman, S., Davis, N., Dinh, E. Morgan, J.,... Lainhart, J. (2006). Comorbid psychiatric disorders in children with autism: Interview development and rates of disorder. *Journal of Autism and Developmental Disorders*, 36, 849–861.

Lord, C. (1995). Follow-up of two-year-olds referred for possible autism. *Journal of Child Psychology and Psychiatry*, 36, 1365–1382.

Lord, C. (2009, May). *What would "better" diagnoses of ASDs look like?* Paper presented at the International Meeting for Autism Research, Chicago.

Lord, C., & Bailey, A. (2002). Autism spectrum disorders. In M. Rutter & E. Taylor (Eds.), *Child and adolescent psychiatry* (4th ed., pp. 636–663). Malden, MA: Blackwell Science.

Lord, C., & Pickles, A. (1996). Language level and non-verbal social-communicative behaviors in autistic and language delayed children. *Journal of the American Academy of Child and Adolescent Psychiatry*, 35(11), 1542–1550.

Lord, C., Risi, S., DiLavore, P., Shulman, C., Thurm., & Pickles, A. (2006). Autism from two to nine. *Archives of General Psychiatry*, 63, 694–701.

Lord, C., Risi, S., Lambrecht, L., Cook, E., Levanthal, B., DiLavore, P.,... Rutter, M.(2000). The Autism Diagnostic Observation Schedule–Generic: A standard measure of social and communication deficits associated with the spectrum of autism. *Journal of Autism and Developmental Disorders*, 30, 205–223.

Lord, C., Rutter, M., & Le Couteur, A. (1994). Autism Diagnostic Interview–Revised: A revised version of a diagnostic interview for caregivers of individuals with possible pervasive developmental disorders.

Journal of Autism and Developmental Disorders, 24(5), 659–685.

Lord, C., Schopler, E., & Revicki, D. (1982). Sex differences in autism. *Journal of Autism and Developmental Disorders,* 12(4), 317–330.

Lord, C., Shulman, C., & DiLavore, P. (2004). Regression and word loss in autistic spectrum disorders. *Journal of Child Psychology and Psychiatry,* 45, 936–955.

Lord, C., Storoschuk, S., Rutter, M., & Pickles, A. (1993). Using the ADI-R to diagnose autism in preschool children. *Infant Mental Health Journal,* 14(3), 234–252.

Lotter, V. (1978). Follow-up studies. In M. Rutter & E. Schopler (Eds.), *Autism: A reappraisal of concepts and treatment* (pp. 187–199). New York: Plenum.

Lovaas, O., Schreibman, L., Koegel, R., & Rehm, R. (1971). Selective responding by autistic children to multiple sensory input. *Journal of Abnormal Psychology,* 77(3), 211–222.

Loveland, K. A., Landry, S. H., Hughes, S. O., Hall, S. K., & McEvoy, R. E. (1988). Speech acts and the pragmatic deficits of autism. *Journal of Speech and Hearing Research,* 31(4), 593–604.

Luyster, R., Qui, S., Lopez, K., & Lord, C. (2007). Predicting outcomes of children referred for autism using MacArthur-Bates Communicative Developmental Inventory. *Journal of Speech, Language, and Hearing Research,* 50, 667–681.

Magnússon, P., & Saemundsen, E. (2001). Prevalence of autism in Iceland. *Journal of Autism and Developmental Disorders,* 31(2), 153–163.

Mahone, E.M., Bridges, D., Prahme, C. and Singer, H. (2004). Repetitive arm and hand movements (complex motor stereotypies) in children. *The Journal of Pediatrics,* 145, 391–395.

Marriage, K., Miles, T., Strokes, D., & Davey, M. (1993). Clinical and research implication of the co-occurrence of Asperger's and Tourette syndrome. *Australian and New Zealand Journal of Psychiatry,* 27, 1440–1614.

McCarthy, P., Fitzgerald, M., & Smith, M. A. (1884). Prevalence of childhood autism in Ireland. *Ireland Medical Journal,* 77(5), 129–130.

McEvoy, R., Rogers, S. J., & Pennington, B. F. (1993). Executive function and social communication deficits in young autistic children. *Journal of Child Psychology and Psychiatry,* 34, 563–578.

McLennan, J. D., Lord, C., & Schopler, E. (1993). Sex differences in higher functioning people with autism. *Journal of Autism and Developmental Disorders,* 23(2), 217–227.

Mildenberger, K., Sitter, S., Noterdaeme, M., & Amorosa, H. (2001). The use of the ADI-R as a diagnostic tool in the differential diagnosis of children with infantile autism and children with a receptive language disorder. *European Journal and Child and Adolescent Psychiatry,* 10(5), 248–255.

Mitchell, S., Brian, J., Zwaigenbaum, L., Roberts,W., Szatmari, P., Smith, I., & Bryson, S. (2006). Early language and communication development of infants later diagnosed with autism spectrum disorder. *Journal of Developmental Behavioral Pediatrics,* 27, S69–S78.

Moore, V., & Goodson, S. (2003). How well does early diagnosis of autism stand the test of time? Follow-up study of children assessed for autism at age 2 and development of an early diagnostic service. *Autism,* 7, 47–63.

Mostofsky, S., Dubey, P., Jerath, V., Jansiewicz, E., Goldberg, M., & Denckla, M. (2006). Developmental dyspraxia is not limited to imitation in children with autism spectrum disorders. *Journal of the International Neuropsychological Society,* 12, 314–326.

Mount, R. H., Charman, T., Hastings, R. P., Sheena, R., & Cass, H. (2002). The Rett Syndrome Behaviour Questionnaire (RSBQ): Refining the behavioural phenotype of Rett syndrome. *Journal of Child Psychology and Psychiatry and Allied Disciplines,* 43(8), 1099–1110.

Muhle, R., Trentacoste, S.V., & Rapin, I. (2004). The genetics of autism. *Pediatrics,* 113, e472–e486.

Mundy, P., Sigman, M., & Kasari, C. (1994). Joint attention, developmental level, and symptom presentation in autism. *Development and Psychopathology,* 6, 389–401.

Niehus, R., & Lord, C. (2006). Early medical history of children with autism spectrum disorders. *Developmental and Behavioral Pediatrics,* 27(2), S120–S126.

Nordin, V., & Gillberg, C. (1998). The long-term course of autistic disorders: Update on follow-up studies. *Acta Psychiatrica Scandinavica,* 97, 99–108.

Noterdaeme, M., Sitter, S., Mildenberger, K., & Amorosa, H. (2000). Diagnostic assessment of communicative and interactive behaviours in children with autism and receptive language disorder. *European Child and Adolescent Psychiatry,* 9(4), 295–300.

Olsson, I., Steffenburg, S., & Gillberg, C. (1988). Epilepsy in autism and autisticlike conditions: A population-based study. *Archives of Neurology,* 45, 666–668.

Osterling, J., & Dawson, G. (1994). Early recognition of children with autism: A study of first birthday home videotapes. *Journal of Autism and Developmental Disorders,* 24, 247–257.

Ozonoff, S., & Jensen, J. (1999). Specific executive profiles in three neurodevelopmental disorders. *Journal of Autism and Developmental Disorders,* 29, 171–177.

Ozonoff, S., Heung, K., Byrd, R., Hansen, R., & Hertz-Picciotto, I. (2008). The onset of autism: Patterns of symptom emergence in the first years of life. *Autism Research,* 1, 320–328.

Ozonoff, S., & McEvoy, R. (1994). A longitudinal study of executive function and theory of mind development in autism. *Development and Psychopathology, 6*(3), 415–431.

Ozonoff, S., Rogers, S., & Pennington, B. (1991). Asperger's disorder: Evidence of an empirical distinction from high-functioning autism. *Journal of Child Psychology and Psychiatry, 32,* 1107–1122.

Ozonoff, S., South, M., & Provencal, S. (2005). Executive functions. In F.R. Volkmar, R. Paul, A. Klin, & D. Cohen (Eds.), *Handbook of Autism and Developmental Disorders* (3rd ed., pp. 606–627). New York: John Wiley & Sons.

Pascualvaca, D., Fantie, B., Papageorgiou, M., & Mirsky, A. (1998). Attentional capacities in children with autism: Is there a general deficit in shifting focus? *Journal of Autism and Developmental Disorders, 28,* 467–478.

Paul, R. (1987). Natural history. In D. Cohen, A. Donnellan, R. Paul (Eds.), *Handbook of Autism and Developmental Disorders* (pp. 121–130). New York: John Wiley & Sons.

Pennington, B. F., & Ozonoff, S. (1996). Executive functions and developmental psychopathologies. *Journal of Child Psychology & Psychiatry, 37,* 51–87.

Pilowsky, T., Yirmiya, N., Shulman, C., & Dover, R. (1998). The Autism Diagnostic Interview-Revised and the Childhood Autism Rating Scale: Differences between diagnostic systems and comparison between genders. *Journal of Autism and Developmental Disorders, 28*(2), 143–151.

Plaisted, K., Swettenham, J., & Rees, L. (1999). Children with autism show local precedence in a divided attention task and global precedence in selective attention task. *Journal of Child Psychology and Psychiatry, 40,* 733–742.

Posserud, M. B., Lundervold, A., J., & Gillberg, C. (2006). Autistic features in a total population of 7–9-year-old children assessed by the ASSQ (Autism Spectrum Screening Questionnaire). *Journal of Child Psychology and Psychiatry, 47*(2), 167–175.

Powell, J. E., Edwards, A., Edwards, M., Pandit, B. S., Sungum-Paliwal, S. R., & Whitehouse, W. (2000). Changes in the incidence of childhood autism and other autistic spectrum disorders in preschool children from two areas in the West Midlands, UK. *Developmental Medicine & Child Neurology, 42*(09), 624–628.

Prior, M., Eisenmajer, R., Leekman, S., Wing, L., Gould, J., Ong, B., & Dowe, D. (1998). Are there subgroups within the autistic spectrum? A cluster analysis of a group of children with autistic spectrum disorders. *Journal of Child Psychology and Psychiatry, 39,* 893–902.

Reichenberg, A., Gross, R., Weiser, M., Bresnahan, M., Silverman, J., Harlap, S. ... Lubin, G.(2006). Advancing paternal age and autism. *Archives of Geeral Psychiatry, 63,* 1026–1032.

Richler, J., Bishop, S. L., Kleinke, J., & Lord, C. (2007). Restricted and repetitive behaviors in young children with autism spectrum disorders. *Journal of Autism and Developmental Disorders, 37,* 73–85.

Riquet, C. B., Taylor, N. D., Benaroya, S., & Klein, L. S. (1982). Symbolic play in autistic, Down's, and normal children of equivalent mental age. *Journal of Autism and Developmental Disorders, 11*(4), 439–448.

Ritvo, E. R., Freeman, B. J., Pingree, C., Mason-Brothers, A., Jorde, L., Jenson, W. R.... Ritvo, A. (1989). The UCLA-University of Utah epidemiologic survey of autism: prevalence. *American Journal of Psychiatry, 146*(2), 194–199.

Rogers, S. J. (2004). Developmental regression in autism spectrum disorders. *Mental Retardation and Developmental Disabilities Research Reviews, 10,* 139–143.

Rogers, S. J., Hepburn, S., Stackhouse, T., & Wehner, E. (2003). Parent reports of sensory symptoms in toddlers with autism and those with other developmental disorders. *Journal of Autism and Developmental Disorders, 33*(6), 631–642.

Rourke, B. (1988). The syndrome of nonverbal learning disabilities: Developmental manifestation in neurological disease, disorder, and dysfunction. *The Clinical Neuropsychologist, 2,* 293–330.

Rourke, B. (1989). *Nonverbal learning disabilities: The syndrome and the model.* New York: Guilford.

Rumsey, J., & Hamburger, S. (1990). Neuropsychological findings in high-functioning men with infantile autism, residual state. *Journal of Autism and Developmental Disorders, 20,* 155–168.

Rumsey, J. M., Rapoport, J. L., & Sceery, W. R. (1985). Autistic children as adults: Psychiatric, social, and behavioral outcomes. *Journal of the American Academy of Child Psychiatry, 24,* 465–473.

Rutter, M. (1970). Autistic children: Infancy to adulthood. *Seminars in Psychiatry, 2,* 435–450.

Rutter, M., Greenfield, D., & Lockyer, L. (1967). A five to fifteen year follow-up study of infantile psychosis. II. Social and behavioral outcome. *British Journal of Psychiatry: The Journal of Mental Science, 113,* 1183–1199.

Schopler, E., Andrews, C.E., & Strupp, K. (1979). Do autistic children come from upper-middle-class parents? *Journal of Autism and Developmental Disorders, 9*(2), 139–152.

Schopler, E., Reichler, R. J., De Vellis, R. F., & Daly, K. (1980). Toward objective classification of childhood autism: Childhood Autism Rating Scale (CARS). *Journal of Autism and Developmental Disorders, 10*(1), 91–103.

Sevin, J. A., Matson, J. L., Williams, D., & Kirkpatrick-Sanchez, S. (1995). Reliability of emotional problems with the Diagnostic Assessment for the Severely Handicapped (DASH). *The British Journal of Clinical Psychology, 34,* 93–94.

Shea, V. S. & Mesibov, G. B. (2005). Adolescents and adults with autism. In F. R. Volkmar, R. Paul, A. Klin, and D. J. Cohen (Eds.). *Handbook of autism and pervasive developmental disorders: Vol 1. Diagnosis, development, neurobiology, and behavior* (3rd ed.; pp. 288–311). New York: John Wiley & Sons.

Shinnar, S., Rapin, I., Arnold, S., Tuchman, R. F., Shulman, L., Ballaban-Gil, K. … Volkmar, F. R. (2001). Language regression in childhood. *Pediatric neurology, 24*(3), 183–189.

Spence, S. J., Sharifi, P., & Wiznitzer, M. (2004). Autism spectrum disorder: Screening, diagnosis, and medical evaluation. *Seminars in Pediatric Neurology, 11,* 186–195.

Stefanatos, G. A. (2008). Regression in autistic spectrum disorders. *Neuropsychology Reviews, 18*(4), 305–319.

Steffenburg, S., & Gillberg, C. (1986). Autism and autistic-like conditions in Swedish rural and urban areas: a population study. *The British Journal of Psychiatry, 149*(1), 81–87.

Stevens, M., Fein, D., Dunn, M., Allen, D., Waterhouse, L., Feinstein, C., & Rapin, I. (2000). Subgroups of children with autism by cluster analysis: A longitudinal examination. *Journal of the American Academy of Child & Adolescent Psychiatry, 39,* 346–352.

Stone, W. L., Hoffman, E. L., Lewis, S. L., & Ousley, O. Y. (1994). Early recognition of autism: Parental report vs. clinical observation. *American Journal of Diseases of Children, 148,* 174–179.

Stone, W. L., Ousley, O. Y., Yoder, P. J., Hogan, K. L., & Hepburn, S. L. (1997). Nonverbal communication in two and three-year-old children with autism. *Journal of Autism and Developmental Disorders, 27*(6), 677–696.

Stone, W. L., Lee, E. B., Ashford, L., Brissie, J., Hepburn, S. L., Coonrod, E.E., & Weiss, B. H. (1999). Can autism be diagnosed accurately in children under 3 years? *Journal of Child Psychology and Psychiatry, 40,* 219–226.

Stone, W. L. & Yoder, P. J. (2001). Predicting spoken language level in children with autism spectrum disorders. *Autism, 5,* 341–361.

Sutera, S., Pandey, J., Esser, E., Rosenthal, M., Wilson, L., Barton, M., … Fein, D. (2007). Predictors of optimal outcome in toddlers diagnosed with autism spectrum disorders. *Journal of Autism and Developmental Disorders, 37,* 98–107.

Szatmari, P., Bartolucci, G., Bremner, R., & Bond, S. (1989). A follow-up study of high-functioning autistic children. *Journal of Autism and Developmental Disorders, 19,* 213–225.

Szatmari, P., Georgiades, S., Bryson, S., Zwaigenbaum, L., Roberts, W. Mahoney, W., … Tuff, L. (2006). Investigating the structure of the restricted, repetitive behaviours and interests domain of autism. *Journal of Child Psychology and Psychiatry, 47*(6), 582–590.

Tanguay, P. E. (2000). Pervasive developmental disorders: A 10-year review. *Journal of the American Academy of Child and Adolescent Psychiatry, 39,* 1079–1095.

Tantam, D. (1988a). Lifelong eccentricity and social isolation: I. Psychiatric, social, and forensic aspects. *British Journal of Psychiatry: The Journal of Mental Science, 153,* 777–782.

Tantam, D. (1988b). Lifelong eccentricity and social isolation: II. Asperger's disorder or schizoid personality disorder? *British Journal of Psychiatry: The Journal of Mental Science, 153,* 783–791.

Tantam, D. (1991). Asperger syndrome in adulthood. In U. Frith (Ed.), *Autism and Asperger syndrome* (pp. 147–183). Cambridge: Cambridge University Press.

Taylor, B., Miller, E., Lingam, R., Andrews, N., Simmons, A., & Stowe, J. (2002). Measles, mumps, and rubella vaccination and bowel problems or developmental regression in children with autism: population study. *British Medical Journal, 324*(7334), 393–396.

Thelen, E. (1979). Rhythmical stereotypies in normal human infants. *Animal Behaviour, 27,* 699–715.

Tidmarsh, L., & Volkmar, F. R. (2003). Diagnosis and epidemiology of autism spectrum disorders. *The Canadian Journal of Psychiatry, 48,* 517–525.

Toth, K., Munson, J., Meltzoff, A. N., & Dawson, G. (2006). Early predictors of communication development in young children with autism spectrum disorder: Joint attention, imitation, and toy play. *Journal of Autism and Developmental Disorders, 36,* 993–1005.

Treffert, D. A. (1970). Epidemiology of infantile autism. *Archives of General Psychiatry, 22*(5), 431–438.

Trillingsgaard, A., Sorensen, E. U., Nemec, G., & Jorgensen, M. (2005). What distinguishes autism spectrum disorders from other developmental disorders before the age of four years? *European Journal of Child and Adolescent Psychiatry, 14,* 65–72.

Tuchman, R. F., Rapin, I., & Shinnar, S. (1991). Autistic and dysphasic children. II. Epilepsy. *Pediatrics, 88,* 1219–1225.

Tyson, K., Troyb, E., Rosenthal, M., Helt, M., Eigsti, I. M., Naigles, L., … Fein, D. (2009, May). *Psychiatric Disorders in Optimal Outcome Children with a History of Autism Spectrum Disorders.* Poster presented at the International Meeting for Autism Research, Chicago.

Uchiyama, T., Kurosawa, M., & Inaba, Y. (2007). MMR-vaccine and regression in autism spectrum disorders: negative results presented from Japan. *Journal of Autism and Developmental Disorders, 37*(2), 210–217.

Ventola, P., Kleinman, J., Pandey, P., Wilson, L., Esser, E., Boorstein, et al. (2007). Differentiating between Autism Spectrum Disorders and other developmental disabilities in children who failed a screening instrument for ASD. *Journal of Autism and Developmental Disorders, 37*(3), 425–436.

Volkmar, F. (1992). Childhood disintegrative disorder: Issues for DSM-IV. *Journal of Autism and Developmental Disorders, 22,* 625–642.

Volkmar, F., & Cohen, D. (1989). Disintegrative disorder or "late onset" autism. *Journal of Child Psychology and Psychiatry, 30*, 462–470.

Volkmar, F. R., Klin, A., Siegel, B., Szatmari, P., Lord, C., Campbell, M., ... Kline, W. (1994). Field trial for autistic disorder in DSM-IV. *The American Journal of Psychiatry, 151*(9), 1361–1367.

Volkmar, F., & Nelson, D. (1990). Seizure disorders in autism. *Journal of the American Academy of Child and Adolescent Psychiary, 29*, 127–129.

Volkmar, F. R., & Rutter, M. (1995). Childhood Disintegrative Disorder: Results of the DSM-IV autism field trial. *Journal of the American Academy of Child & Adolescent Psychiatry, 34*(8), 1092–1095.

Volkmar, F. R., Szatmari, P., & Sparrow, S. S. (1993). Sex differences in pervasive developmental disorders. *Journal of Autism and Developmental Disorders, 23*(4), 579–591.

Wainwright, J., & Bryson, S. (1996). Visual-spatial orienting in autism. *Journal of Autism and Developmental Disorders, 26*, 423–438.

Wainwright, L., & Fein, D. (1996). Results of play analyses. In Rapin, I. (Ed.), *Preschool children with inadequate communication: Developmental language disorder, autism, low IQ. Clinics in developmental medicine* (pp. 173–189). London: Mac Keith Press.

Wakefield, A. J., Murch, S. H., Anthony, A., Linnell, J., Casson, D. M., Malik, M., ... Walker-Smith, J. A. (1998). Ileal-lymphoid-nodular hyperplasia, nonspecific colitis, and pervasive developmental disorder in children. *Lancet, 351*(9103), 637–641.

Waterhouse, L., Morris, R., Allen, D., Dunn, M., Fein, D., Feinstein, C., Rapin, I and Wing, L. (1996). Diagnosis and classification in autism. *Journal of Autism and Developmental Disorders, 26*, 59–86.

Weisbrot, D., Gadow, K., DeVincent, C., & Pomeroy, J. (2005). The prsentation of anxiety in pervasive developmental delay. *Journal of Child and Adolescent Psychophrmacology, 15*(3), 477–496.

Werner, E., & Dawson, G. (2005). Validation of the phenomenon of autistic regression using home videotapes. *Archives of General Psychiatry, 62*, 889–895.

Wetherby, A. M., Watt, N., Morgan, L., & Shumway, S. (2007). Social communication profiles of children with autism spectrum disorders late in the second year of life. *Journal of Autism and Developmental Disorders, 37*(5), pp. 960–975.

Wetherby, A., Woods, J., Allen, L., Cleary, J., Dickinson, H., & Lord, C. (2004). Early indicators of autism spectrum disorders in the second year of life.

Journal of Autism and Developmental Disorders, 34(5), 473–493.

Williams, J.G., Higgins, J.P. & Brayne, C.E. (2006). Systematic review of previous studies of autism spectrum disorders. *Archives of Disease in Childhood, 91*(1), 365–382.

Wilson, K., Mills, E., Ross, C., McGowan, J., & Jadad, A. (2003). Association of autistic spectrum disorder and the measles, mumps, and rubella vaccine: a systematic review of current epidemiological evidence. *Archives of Pediatric and Adolescent Medicine, 157*(7), 628–634.

Wing, L. (1980). Childhood autism and social class: a question of selection? *The British Journal of Psychiatry, 137*(5), 410–417.

Wing, L. (1981). Asperger's disorder: A clinical account. *Psychological Medicine, 11*, 115–129.

Wing, L. (1993). The definition and prevalence of autism: A review. *European Child & Adolescent Psychiatry, 2*(1), 61–74.

Wing, L., & Gould, J. (1979). Severe impairments of social interaction and associated abnormalities in children: Epidemiology and classification. *Journal of Autism and Developmental Disorders, 9*(1), 11–29.

Wing, L. & Potter, D. (2009). The epidemiology of autism spectrum disorders: Is the prevalence Rising? In Goldstein, S., Naglieri, J. & Ozonoff, S. (Eds.) *Assessment of Autsim Spectrum Disorders* (pp. 18–54). New York: Guilford Press.

World Health Organization. (2007). *International classification of diseases* (10th revision). Geneva, Switzerland: Author.

Yeargin-Allsopp, M., Rice, C., Karapurkar, T., Doernberg, N., Boyle, C., & Murphy, C. (2003). Prevalence of Autism in a US Metropolitan Area. *JAMA, 289*(1), 49–55.

Yerys, B. E., Hepburn, S. L., Pennington, B. F., & Rogers, S. J. (2007). Executive function in preschoolers with autism: Evidence consistent with a secondary deficit. *Journal of Autism and Developmental Disorders, 37*, 1068–1079.

Zafeiriou, D., Ververi, A., & Vargiami, E. (2007). Childhood autism and associated comorbidities. *Brain and Development, 29*(5), 257–272.

Zwaigenbaum, L., Bryson, S., Rogers, T., Roberts, W., Brian, J., & Szatmari, P. (2005). Behavioral manifestations of autism in the first year of life. *International Journal of Developmental Neuroscience, 23*, 143–152.

Chapter 2

Genetics: Many Roads to the Autism Spectrum Disorders

Brett S. Abrahams

Defined entirely in terms of behavior, the autism spectrum disorders (ASDs) represent a range of conditions involving deficits in language use, social behavior, and range of interests. Technological advances, together with the collection of large, systematically-assessed patient cohorts, have resulted in important new insights regarding the manner by which genetic variation may come to shape risk and presentation. As important as the identification of individual genes and nascent signaling pathways, however, is the recognition of the massive etiological heterogeneity at play. Although an estimated 20% of cases may be attributable to a mutation involving a known risk gene, available evidence suggests that no single region within the genome can account for more than 1–2% of cases. This results in a classic "inverse problem," whereby the outcome (an ASD) is known, but the underlying explanation for any given individual remains obscure. Recent insights into this conundrum are discussed in this chapter, along with thoughts on the direction of future efforts.

The term *autism* was not originally used to describe individuals with the corresponding *DSM-IV* diagnosis in use today, but rather was introduced by the Swiss psychiatrist Eugen Bleuler almost 100 years ago to describe the social withdrawl he observed in people with schizophrenia. Building on work from Leo Kanner and Hans Asperger, the modern clinical concept reflecting a triad of features is much more recent, having been introduced only 30 years ago (Wing & Gould, 1979). This conceptualization has played an enormous role in influencing the direction of genetic research, with the majority of studies employing diagnostic status (affected or unaffected) as the sole endpoint under investigation. As outlined below, such work has identified important loci likely to contribute to core features present within the ASDs. The observation that variation at such loci appears to contribute to a *range* of neurodevelopmental conditions, however, together with the isolation of variants related to intermediate phenotypes, suggests that more refined endpoints—particularly those more directly coupled with neurological development and function—are warranted.

STRONG SUPPORT FOR GENETIC INVOLVEMENT

Multiple convergent lines of evidence support the importance of genetic factors in the modulation of risk. First and foremost, rare events at defined genomic positions (or loci) have been shown to confer as much as a 50-fold increase in relative risk, compared to population prevalence estimates (Kumar et al., 2008; Weiss et al., 2008). Additional strong support for the importance of genetic factors in the ASDs comes from the isolation of common genetic variants that modulate risk and presentation in a more subtle fashion (Wang et al., 2009; Weiss et al., 2009). These findings are consistent with the earlier observation that having a sibling with an ASD diagnosis increases the risk of being on the spectrum 20-fold (Jorde et al., 1991; Lauritsen, Pedersen, & Mortensen, 2005), and with twin studies demonstrating higher concordance rates in monozygotic versus dizygotic twins (Bailey et al., 1995; Steffenburg et al., 1989). As discussed below, however, few if any known genetic variants show a 1:1 relationship with disease, a phenomenon referred to by geneticists as incomplete penetrance, complicating matters greatly. Allelic diversity—the notion that multiple variants with distinct functional effects may exist within genomic regions of interest—adds an additional layer of complexity. That the increased incidence of the ASDs (Fombonne, 2009) appears not to be simply the result of a broadening of diagnostic categories or heightened awareness (Hertz-Picciotto & Delwiche, 2009) is likewise supportive of the importance of environmental contributors. Matters are further obscured by the absence of more knowledge regarding gene–gene and gene–environment interactions—mechanisms most recognize to be important with regard to outcome. The aim of this chapter is to review the current state of affairs in autism genetics, emphasizing both recent progress and limitations in current knowledge.

BASIC GENETIC CONCEPTS

Prior to discussing particular findings relative to the ASDs, a brief review of some basic genetic concepts may prove helpful for some readers. The human genome, comprised of DNA segments distributed across 23 chromosomes, is defined at each of three billion positions by nucleotide identity (A, T, C, or G). Sex chromosomes aside, each position in the genome is present in two copies, which are either identical to one another or distinct from one another. Much of the genome is under strong positive selection, in that variation results in reduced fitness; such regions are largely identical between individuals. This is contrasted with extensive diversity at other genomic positions, where distinct variants (alleles) are tolerated and can be present at high frequencies. These common variants can also contribute to disease, although the individual impact of each is typically more modest. Because common variants do not individually give rise to disease—at least within the ASDs—such alleles are present in both cases and controls, albeit at different frequencies. Ultimate presentation is likely a result of the interaction between such variants, together with contributions from rare alleles of larger effect and environmental risk factors.

At the most basic level, all genetic studies attempt to identify or quantify the relationship between genetic variation and phenotypic outcome. Genetic variation can take on several forms, but of key importance is the distinction between diversity at individual nucleotide positions, and structural variation in which regions comprised of a thousand or more nucleotides are considered as a unit. At the base pair level, variants present at some appreciable population frequency, typically ≥ 5%, are referred to as single nucleotide polymorphisms (SNPs). Base pair variation at intervening positions is also observed, and when both rare and related to some adverse outcome, termed a mutation. Among structural variants, the term *copy number variation* (CNV) is used to refer the phenomenon whereby defined genetic material is not present in the standard two-copy state, but rather absent altogether, present on one chromosome but not the other, or increased in terms of dosage. Not included among CNV are events in which dosage remains unchanged, but relative position within the genome has been altered. Inversions, events in which the standard orientation of genetic material is reversed, and translocations, in which material is present but located in an atypical genomic position, are illustrative here. This distinction is important, as such events have been shown to underlie many rare genetic syndromes, but cannot typically be detected with current array-based methodology.

This said, regardless of the kind of variation under consideration, individuals are genotyped at one or many positions and allele frequencies compared between groups. The study of candidate genes—work which predominated in earlier genetic investigations—employed functional information to prioritize genotyping. For example, in the context of repeated observations of hyperserotonemia in autism (Abramson et al., 1989; Anderson et al., 1987; Piven et al., 1991; Schain & Freedman, 1961), the serotonin transporter emerged as an attractive target for genetic investigation (Cook et al., 1997; Devlin et al., 2005; Kim et al., 2002; Sutcliffe et al. 2005). Although such prioritization was necessary when genotyping was costly and labor intensive, recent technological advances now permit hypothesis-free evaluation of hundreds of thousands of distinct variants within the genome in single experiments. Regardless of scale, all studies have the goal of finding correlations between genetic variation and an endpoint of interest. As discussed below, outcomes can be evaluated either in terms of categorical (e.g. case vs. control) or quantitative (e.g. blood serotonin) differences, with relative merits and distinctions associated with each.

ASD-RELATED SYNDROMES

The earliest clues suggesting a strong genetic basis for the ASDs came from the observation of rare chromosomal aberrations in cases, and evidence for co-occurrence of autistic features with a variety of clinically identified syndromes (see Table 2-1). More than a dozen such entities, in which ASDs are observed at higher than expected frequencies, are well recognized and have recently been discussed elsewhere (Abrahams & Geschwind 2008, 2010; Zafeiriou, Ververi, & Vargiami, 2007). That many such conditions have been determined to be the result of mutations in individual genes (e.g. CACNA1C, CNTNAP2, DHCR7, and MECP2) is important, providing investigators with potential entry points into mechanistic studies. Such entities contribute individually to only a small fraction of total ASD cases, but multiple features appear common to each. Mild to severe deficits in intellectual ability with impaired language appears to be a relatively constant feature. Seizures, impaired motor skills, and hypotonia are also frequently observed.

Complicating matters greatly, however, is the fact that only a subset of individuals diagnosed with such syndromes actually present with an ASD. Fragile X syndrome, typically resulting from the expansion of a repeated three-base-pair motif (CGG) within the non-protein portion of the FMR1 gene, is illustrative here; study of large cohorts suggests that only ~25% of symptomatic carrier males meet criteria for an ASD (Hatton et al., 2006). This point—that defined mutations in individual genes are typically insufficient to give an ASD diagnosis in all carriers—is critical (see also Chapter 24). This incomplete penetrance challenges the notion of single-gene explanations for autism even in rare cases, and places some caveats on the interpretation of results from animal models with regard to the constellation of behavioral abnormalities seen in this diverse set of disorders.

Allelic heterogeneity–the manner by which different kinds of genetic variation at a locus may give rise to distinct phenotypic outcomes–arises here as a second concern. The manner by which distinct FMR1 variants differently impact presentation is illustrative (De Boulle et al., 1993). Similarly, at CNTNAP2 alone, at least 10 distinct alleles, ranging from common contributory variants to fully causal mutations, have been described. The impact of allelic heterogeneity is discussed at length elsewhere (Abrahams & Geschwind, 2010), but typically receives insufficient attention.

Less well explored, but important to this discussion, is the manner by which gender effects, both in autism and related syndromes, may confound attempts to estimate ASD penetrance. Well established is the fact that boys are strongly overrepresented among children with an ASD. Less well reported but similarly clear is that the typical 3- to 4-fold increased incidence in males is skewed further when study is limited to individuals with Asperger syndrome (>6:1; Fombonne, 2005) or without obvious dysmorphism (>7:1; Miles & Hillman, 2000). Because of this sex discrepancy within autism, equal inclusion of males and females for children with a particular syndrome might reasonably be expected to underestimate penetrance. This is precisely what would happen in the case of fragile X, were rates to be evaluated without consideration of child sex. ASD rates in boys and girls with fragile X are 25% and 6%, respectively (Hatton et al., 2006).

Conversely, the absence or reduced numbers of females for various X-linked or Y-linked syndromes

Table 2-1 ASD-related Syndromes a, b

ASD-related syndrome	Associated gene(s)	Proportion with ASD	Proportion ASD with syndrome	References
1q21 Duplication	Many	50%	~1%?	(Szatmari, Paterson et al. 2007; Mefford, Sharp et al. 2008)
3p Deletion/ duplication	CNTN4	<50%	~1%	(Fernandez, Morgan et al. 2004; Glessner, Wang et al. 2009; Roohi, Montagna et al. 2009)
7q11 Duplication	Many	40%	Unknown	(Somerville, Mervis et al. 2005; Van der Aa, Rooms et al. 2009)
15q Duplication (maternal)	Many (including UBE3A, GABRB3, SNRPN, & SNURF)	High	~1%	(Cook, Lindgren et al. 1997)
15q13 Deletion	Many (including CHRNA7)	<50%	Unknown	(Sharp, Mefford et al. 2008; Ben-Shachar, Lanpher et al. 2009)
16p11 Deletion	Many (including SEZ6L2)	High	~1%	(Kumar, KaraMohamed et al. 2008; Marshall, Noor et al. 2008; Weiss, Shen et al. 2008; Kumar, Marshall et al. 2009)
22q11 Deletion (aka VCFS/DiGeorge)	Many (including TBX1 and COMT)	15–50%	<1%	(Fine, Weissman et al. 2005; Vorstman, Morcus et al. 2006; Niklasson, Rasmussen et al. 2009)
22q13 Deletion	SHANK3	High	~1%	(Manning, Cassidy et al. 2004; Durand, Betancur et al. 2007; Moessner, Marshall et al. 2007)
Angelman (15q11-13)	Maternal UBE3A	40–80%	<1%	(Peters, Beaudet et al. 2004; Bonati, Russo et al. 2007)
Beckwith Weidemann (11p15)	IGF2 and CDKN1C	~7%	Unknown	(Kent, Bowdin et al. 2008)
Cortical dysplasia focal epilepsy (7q35-36)	CNTNAP2	70%	Negligible	(Strauss, Puffenberger et al. 2006)
Cowden/Bannayan Riley-Ruvalcaba syndrome (10q23)	PTEN	20%	>10% with macrocephaly	(Orrico, Galli et al. 2009; Varga, Pastore et al. 2009)
Down's syndrome (Trisomy Chr.21)	Many	6–15%	Unknown	(Lowenthal, Paula et al. 2007)
Fragile X (Xq27)	FMR1	25% of Males 6% of Females	1-2%	(Hatton, Sideris et al. 2006)
Potocki-Lupski Duplication (17p11)	Many (including RAI1)	~90%	Unknown	(Potocki, Bi et al. 2007)
Smith-Lemli-Opitz (11q13)	DHCR7	50%	Negligible	(Tierney, Nwokoro et al. 2001)
Prader-Willi (15q11-13)	Paternal deletions	20–25%	Unknown	(Descheemaeker, Govers et al. 2006)
Rett (Xq26)	MECP2	N/A	~0.5%	(Amir, Van den Veyver et al. 1999)
Timothy syndrome (12p13)	CACNA1C	60–80%	Negligible	(Splawski, Timothy et al. 2004)

(continued)

Table 2-1 (continued)

ASD-related syndrome	Associated gene(s)	Proportion with ASD	Proportion ASD with syndrome	References
Tuberous sclerosis (9q34 and 16p13)	TSC1, TSC2	20%	~1%	(Baker, Piven et al. 1998)

[a] The reader should compare values listed above to ASD prevalence in the general public (0.2 - 0.7%) and among individuals with nonsyndromic MR (~ 15%) (Descheemaeker, Govers et al. 2006; CDC 2007). Other etiologically heterogeneous clinical entities that show unexpectedly high overlap with the ASDs include: bipolar disorder, epilepsy, Joubert syndrome, schizophrenia, specific language impairment, and Tourette syndrome.

[b] Gene names are as follows: *CACNA1C* calcium channel voltage-dependent L type alpha 1C subunit, *CDKN1C* cyclin-dependent kinase inhibitor 1C, *CNTN4* contactin 4, *CNTNAP2* contactin-associated protein-like 2, *DHCR7* 7-dehydrocholesterol reductase, *FMR1* fragile X mental retardation 1, *GABRB3* GABA A Receptor, beta 3 subunit, *IGF2* insulin-like growth factor 2, *MECP2* methyl CpG-binding protein 2, *PTEN* phosphotase and tenoin homolog deleted on chromosome 10, *RAI1*, retinoic acid-induced 1, *SEZL6* seizure-related 6 homolog (mouse)-like 2, *SHANK3* SH3 and multiple ankyrin repeat domains 3, *SNURF SNRPN* upstream reading frame, *SNRPN* small nuclear ribonucleoprotein polypeptide N, *TSC1* tuberous sclerosis 1, *TSC2* tuberous sclerosis 2, *UBE3A* ubiquitin protein ligase E3A). CHRNA7 cholinergic receptor, nicotinic, alpha, COMT catechol-O-methyltransferase CDKN1C cyclin-dependent kinase inhibitor 1C, TBX1 T-box 1

would result in higher frequencies among males. Although difficult to assess for rare conditions, ASD incidence within syndromes should be determined independently for each sex. This is increasingly important, as more and more investigators adopt reverse-genetic approaches, where one begins with a collection of individuals with a defined genotype (Mefford et al., 2008; Sharp et al., 2008) and work toward an understanding of function through subsequent phenotypic characterization.

COMMON VARIATION

Rare alleles of major effect can be an important contributor to phenotype, but by definition are absent from most individuals. Common alleles, present in greater than 5% of individuals, can also modulate risk and are likely to account for a substantial proportion of phenotypic variation, when considered in the context of entire populations. Results from candidate gene studies (Abrahams & Geschwind 2008) and recently published genome-wide association studies (GWAS; Wang et al., 2009; Weiss et al., 2009) highlight variants of modest effect, with the inheritance of a risk allele increasing the likelihood of disease between 1.2- to 3-fold.

Although it is reasonable in many other scenarios to employ $p < 0.05$ as a threshold for evaluating statistical significance, modern genetic studies can evaluate hundreds of thousands of independent variants in parallel. Because one might, with a threshold of $p < 0.05$, reasonably expect to obtain a "significant" result by chance alone every 20 trials, correction for multiple comparisons must be made. Following such correction, accepted thresholds of $p < 10^{-7}$ is generally an upper boundary for GWAS. At the same time, because each such experiment is typically evaluated in a diverse number of ways, some have argued recently that still lower thresholds (e.g. $p < 10^{-9}$) may be more appropriate (Ioannidis, Thomas, & Daly, 2009).

Meeting statistical rigor permits assessment of the extent to which an observed effect is likely to occur by chance, but does nothing to address how such variation may impact function either in development or adulthood. In fact, variants highlighted by GWAS are not actually assumed to impact the specific endpoint under investigation, but rather serve as a proxy for nearby alleles which may be contributory. Finding true functional variants that modulate risk will be difficult, given that significantly associated alleles localize predominantly to regions between genes (Wang et al., 2009; Weiss et al., 2009) or in non-coding regions without established functionality (Alarcon et al., 2008; Arking et al., 2008; Vernes et al., 2008).

Finally, and perhaps most important, it should be noted that results from GWAS highlight hundreds of distinct variants for which statistical support is better than that available for variants identified previously by candidate-driven strategies. Although not meeting thresholds discussed above for genome-wide significance, such results raise the important question of what to make of both sets of findings. I would assert that genetic variation at more than a hundred loci is likely to impact risk, making the simple cataloging of such results challenging. If it is true that the number of loci is substantial, and moreover that each may harbor distinct variants with a range of functional consequences, the importance of carefully constructed and widely accessible online databases (see Table 2-2) cannot be overemphasized. As larger cohorts are assembled and phenotypic endpoints refined, clarity regarding how individual genetic variants may be associated with distinct aspects of disease will hopefully emerge. Genetic variants that show a statistically significant association with disease likely shape outcome through action on specific and potentially distinct aspects of brain development, and need not map precisely onto clinical endpoints.

THE COMPLICATED IN-BETWEENS

One method for aligning traditional phenotype to genotype-based approaches is increased use of the

Table 2-2 Resources for the Evaluation of Genetic Findings in Autism and Related Neurodevelopmental Disorders

Database (dB)	Data ^	Scope	Web Address	Reference
1000 genomes	G	Human Variation	http://www.1000genomes.org	(Kuehn 2008)
SFARI Gene	L	ASDs	http://gene.sfari.org/	(Basu, Kollu et al. 2009)
Autism Genetic dB (AGD)	L	ASDs	http://wren.bcf.ku.edu/	(Matuszek and Talebizadeh 2009)
Autism Chromosome Rearrangement dB (ACRD)	G	ASDs	http://projects.tcag.ca/autism/	(Marshall, Noor et al. 2008)
CHOP CNV dB	G	Healthy Controls	http://cnv.chop.edu/	(Shaikh, Gai et al. 2009)
Database of Chromosomal Imbalance and Phenotype in Humans using Ensembl Resources (DeCIPHER)	G vs P	Patients & Syndromes	https://decipher.sanger.ac.uk/application/	(Firth, Richards et al. 2009)
Database of Genotypes and Phenotypes (dbGaP)	G vs P	Various	http://www.ncbi.nlm.nih.gov/gap	(Mailman, Feolo et al. 2007)
Database of Genomic Variants (DGV)	G	Human Variation	http://projects.tcag.ca/variation/	(Iafrate, Feuk et al. 2004)
European Cytogeneticists Association Register of Unbalanced Chromosome Aberrations (ECARUCA)	G vs P	Patients & Syndromes	www.ECARUCA.net	(Feenstra, Fang et al. 2006)
Genetic Association dB (GAD)	L	Phenotypic Variation	http://geneticassociationdb.nih.gov/	(Becker, Barnes et al. 2004)
Human Genome Structural Variation Project (HGSV)	G	Human Variation	http://humanparalogy.gs.washington.edu/structuralvariation/	(Sharp, Cheng et al. 2006)
Human Genome Variation dB of Genotype to Phenotype information (HGVbaseG2P)	L	Phenotypic Variation	http://www.hgvbaseg2p.org/index	(Thorisson, Lancaster et al. 2009)
Online Mendelian Inheritance in Man (OMIM)	L	Syndromes	http://www.ncbi.nlm.nih.gov/omim	

^ L = literature; P = patient phenotypes; G = genotypes

reverse paradigm, in which individuals observed to harbor defined variants are contrasted with non-carriers to find associated phenotypes. A recent example here is identification of individuals harboring characteristic 1.5 Mb deletions at 15q13.3 involving *CHRNA7*, and the subsequent elucidation of a potential relationship to intellectual disability with epileptiform abnormalities (Sharp et al., 2008). Additional multigene loci, including 16p11 and 15q11, which each account for an estimated 1% of ASD cases, were arrived at by similar "genotype-first" methods. Less clear here, however, is whether clinical outcomes are attributable to major effects from individual genes or smaller contributions from multiple adjacent genes. Results of sequence analysis of candidates within the 16p11 locus are most consistent with major independent contributions of multiple genes (Kumar et al., 2009), but little is known and results from one locus are unlikely to generalize to all others. At the same time, the question of what within such disease-related intervals may be contributory is critical for a move toward mechanistic studies.

Evidence for involvement of additional loci has emerged from genome-wide characterization of structural variation in larger cohorts at increased resolution (Bucan et al., 2009; Glessner et al., 2009). Cases were observed to harbor a significant enrichment of rare events at a subset of previously identified ASD-related loci including: 15q11-13, 22q11, Contactin 4 (*CNTN4*), and Neurexin 1 (*NRXN1*). A comparable number of deletions in cases and controls at established loci, however (e.g. 16p11 (5/5) and *SHANK3* (2/2), challenges the specificity and/or penetrance of such rare variants. Importantly, novel ASD-loci were also identified in such studies, using complementary regional and gene-based methods. As with common variants, a major challenge for future work will be to determine how specific variants that may be enriched in cases relative to controls might come to modulate risk and presentation. Given the enormous genomic diversity uncovered by recent work (Conrad et al., 2010), a functional understanding of individual variants that are present in cases represents a massive undertaking.

As discussed above the interpretation of results from all such work is compounded by the fact that multiple distinct variants—likely to differ significantly with regards to effect size and function—can be observed at particular loci of interest. Therefore, while

collapsing across alleles within a region will dilute real effects that may be present, without averaging across events at individual loci, power is limited. This is a key issue in interpretation of CNV data, and in the context of larger datasets is something that should be considered. For example, whereas the deletion at 7q11.23 associated with Williams–Beuren Syndrome gives rise to mental retardation with a relative sparing of expressive language, the reciprocal duplication typically results in consistent speech delay with only mild cognitive impairment (Somerville et al., 2005). Similarly, deletions and duplications at 1q21.1 appear to be associated with differential effects on head size (Brunetti-Pierri et al., 2008): deletion carriers show dramatically increased rates of microcephaly, and a similar, albeit weaker, effect is seen between the corresponding duplication and macrocephaly. Likewise relevant, and adding additional complexity here, is consideration of instances in which variants not only differ with regard to type (deletion or duplication) but do not necessarily overlap. This issue was nicely addressed in recent work which considered CNVs in *NRXN1* and evaluated separately events encompassing regions of clear functional importance (exons) to those outside such regions (Rujescu et al., 2009). We employed a similar exon-focused strategy in separate work and came to similar results (Bucan et al., 2009). Given such phenotypic diversity associated with different alleles at the same locus, caution should be used in inferring specific genotype–phenotype relationships.

One means of resolving some of this complexity is to evaluate involvement of pathways as opposed to individual loci. Results from a Portuguese cohort identified an excess of phosphatidylinositol-related genes within rare CNVs observed in cases but not controls (Cusco et al. 2009). Because each of these CNVs was observed only once, available data is insufficient to answer the separate questions of whether any of these variants might be specific to cases or statistically enriched in cases versus controls. At the same time, overrepresentation of events within pathway members in cases but not controls is intriguing when taken together with the observation that particular syndromic ASDs (e.g. *PTEN*, *NF1*, *TSC1/2*) are the result of mutations at loci that operate within this pathway. Emerging evidence likewise exists for involvement of multiple cell-adhesion molecules (Betancur, Sakurai, & Buxbaum, 2009), although much additional work is needed in this area to understand which subset from this large class of genes may be contributory.

ON GENETIC MODELS

Much progress thus far has come from study of rare families in which ASD-related disorders appear to segregate in a Mendelian manner. Results here are consistent with the interpretation that variation in individual genes can have a major impact on clinical outcome. Such results are likewise consistent with factor analyses carried out on phenotypic data from individuals ascertained for ASD, which suggest that deficits in language, social interaction, and behavioral flexibility can segregate as a unitary entity (Constantino et al., 2004).

This said, identical mutations in well-established ASD-related genes often result in diverse outcomes (Laumonnier et al., 2004), challenging single-gene explanations. Similarly, work evaluating the co-occurrence of triad deficits in each behavioral phenotype found only modest overlap among individuals at the extremes of a community-ascertained cohort (Ronald et al., 2006). The very existence of Asperger syndrome, defined by deficits in social interaction and behavioral flexibility but with language skills intact, suggests that the triad of features can indeed be observed separately. Finally, mounting evidence suggests that variants implicated in the ASDs are relevant to multiple distinct disorders of cognition (Burmeister, McInnis, & Zollner, 2008; Rzhetsky, Wajngurt, Park, & Zheng, 2007; Vernes et al., 2008), raising important questions around how such variation may actually modulate risk, and what phenotypes may prove most informative in the context of genetic investigations.

In attempting to move toward a synthesis of these seemingly contradictory findings, it seems reasonable to suggest that rare and common variations alike act in concert to shape presentation. Individual events can be extremely important, but are typically neither necessary nor sufficient to give rise to disease. As discussed above, the presence of deletions at each of *SHANK3* and 16p11 in typically developing controls without features of neurodevelopmental disease (Bucan et al., 2009; Glessner et al., 2009) makes this point difficult to dispute. These data also argue strongly for distinct etiologies and/or disorders even within sibling pairs, and highlight the importance of combinatorial effects. At the level of individuals, this makes for a classic inverse problem in which the outcome is known (affected child) but multiple possible explanations (genetic and environmental contributors) might account for what is observed. Better appreciation of such complexity will presumably lead to new knowledge.

FUTURE DIRECTIONS

Relative frequencies of the ASDs have been estimated as follows: autism or autistic disorder, ~35%, Asperger syndrome, ~10%), childhood disintegrative disorder (CDD), ~1%, pervasive developmental disorder—not otherwise specified (PDD), ~55%, and Rett syndrome, ~1%. At the same time, available genetic data supports conceptualization in terms of *hundreds* of related disorders with varying degrees of overlap. Leo Kanner, among the first to describe what we recognize today as autism, is quoted as saying "each case merits a detailed consideration of its fascinating peculiarities." Although referring to phenotypic variation he observed in his patients, he might equally have been describing the underlying etiological heterogeneity apparent to us today. Emergence of low-cost genomes will further reinforce the importance of understanding cases as unique entities best understood by parallel analysis of intra- and inter-individual variation.[1]

1. Thanks to Daniel Geschwind, members of the Geschwind lab, and collaborators within the Autism Genome Project for insightful discussion. This work was supported by development funds from the Albert Einstein College of Medicine to the author, as well as an NIMH award to Daniel Geschwind (5R01MH081754-02). The author serves as a consultant for IntegraGen SA and receives financial remuneration for work aimed toward molecular diagnostics in autism.

References

Online Mendelian Inheritance in Man, OMIM. McKusick-Nathans Institute of Genetic Medicine, Johns Hopkins University (Baltimore, MD) and National Center for Biotechnology Information, National Library of Medicine (Bethesda, MD). http://www.ncbi.nlm.nih.gov/omim/

Abrahams, B. S. and D. H. Geschwind (2008). "Advances in autism genetics: on the threshold of a new neurobiology." *Nat Rev Genet* 9(5): 341–355.

Abrahams, B. S. and D. H. Geschwind (2010). Genetics of Autism. *Human Genetics: Problems & Approaches*. M. R. Speicher, S. E. Antonarakis and A. G. Motulsky, Springer–Verlag. 4th Edition.

Abramson, R. K., H. H. Wright, R. Carpenter, W. Brennan, O. Lumpuy, E. Cole and S. R. Young (1989). "Elevated blood serotonin in autistic probands and their first-degree relatives." *J Autism Dev Disord* 19(3): 397–407.

Alarcon, M., B. S. Abrahams, J. L. Stone, J. A. Duvall, J. V. Perederiy, J. M. Bomar, … D. H. Geschwind (2008). "Linkage, Association, and Gene-Expression Analyses Identify CNTNAP2 as an Autism-Susceptibility Gene." *Am J Hum Genet* 82(1): 150–159.

Amir, R. E., I. B. Van den Veyver, M. Wan, C. Q. Tran, U. Francke and H. Y. Zoghbi (1999). "Rett syndrome is caused by mutations in X-linked MECP2, encoding methyl-CpG-binding protein 2." *Nat Genet* 23(2): 185–188.

Anderson, G. M., D. X. Freedman, D. J. Cohen, F. R. Volkmar, E. L. Hoder, P. McPhedran, … J. G. Young (1987). "Whole blood serotonin in autistic and normal subjects." *J Child Psychol Psychiatry* 28(6): 885–900.

Arking, D. E., D. J. Cutler, C. W. Brune, T. M. Teslovich, K. West, M. Ikeda, … A. Chakravarti (2008). "A Common Genetic Variant in the Neurexin Superfamily Member CNTNAP2 Increases Familial Risk of Autism." *Am J Hum Genet* 82(1): 160–164.

Bailey, A., A. Le Couteur, I. Gottesman, P. Bolton, E. Simonoff, E. Yuzda and M. Rutter (1995). "Autism as a strongly genetic disorder: evidence from a British twin study." *Psychol Med* 25(1): 63–77.

Baker, P., J. Piven and Y. Sato (1998). "Autism and tuberous sclerosis complex: prevalence and clinical features." *J Autism Dev Disord* 28(4): 279–285.

Basu, S. N., R. Kollu and S. Banerjee-Basu (2009). "AutDB: a gene reference resource for autism research." *Nucleic Acids Res* 37(Database issue): D832–836.

Becker, K. G., K. C. Barnes, T. J. Bright and S. A. Wang (2004). "The genetic association database." *Nat Genet* 36(5): 431–432.

Ben-Shachar, S., B. Lanpher, J. R. German, M. Qasaymeh, L. Potocki, S. C. Nagamani, … T. Sahoo (2009). "Microdeletion 15q13.3: a locus with incomplete penetrance for autism, mental retardation, and psychiatric disorders." *J Med Genet* 46(6): 382–388.

Betancur, C., T. Sakurai and J. D. Buxbaum (2009). "The emerging role of synaptic cell-adhesion pathways in the pathogenesis of autism spectrum disorders." *Trends Neurosci* 32(7): 402–412.

Bonati, M. T., S. Russo, P. Finelli, M. R. Valsecchi, F. Cogliati, F. Cavalleri, … L. Larizza (2007). "Evaluation of autism traits in Angelman syndrome: a resource to unfold autism genes." *Neurogenetics* 8(3): 169–178.

Brunetti-Pierri, N., J. S. Berg, F. Scaglia, J. Belmont, C. A. Bacino, T. Sahoo, … A. Patel (2008). "Recurrent reciprocal 1q21.1 deletions and duplications associated with microcephaly or macrocephaly and developmental and behavioral abnormalities." *Nat Genet* 40(12): 1466–1471.

Bucan, M., B. S. Abrahams, K. Wang, J. T. Glessner, E. I. Herman, L. I. Sonnenblick, … H. Hakonarson (2009). "Genome-wide analyses of exonic copy number variants in a family-based study point to novel autism susceptibility genes." *PLoS Genet* 5(6): e1000536.

Burmeister, M., M. G. McInnis and S. Zollner (2008). "Psychiatric genetics: progress amid controversy." *Nat Rev Genet* 9(7): 527–540.

CDC (2007). "Prevalence of autism spectrum disorders-Autism and Developmental Disabilities Monitoring Network." *Morbidity and Mortality Weekly Report Surveillance Summaries* 56:1–28.

Conrad, D. F., D. Pinto, R. Redon, L. Feuk, O. Gokcumen, Y. Zhang, … M. E. Hurles (2009). "Origins and functional impact of copy number variation in the human genome." *Nature*.

Constantino, J. N., C. P. Gruber, S. Davis, S. Hayes, N. Passanante and T. Przybeck (2004). "The factor structure of autistic traits." *J Child Psychol Psychiatry* 45(4): 719–726.

Cook, E. H., Jr., R. Courchesne, C. Lord, N. J. Cox, S. Yan, A. Lincoln, … B. L. Leventhal (1997). "Evidence of linkage between the serotonin transporter and autistic disorder." *Mol Psychiatry* 2(3): 247–250.

Cook, E. H., Jr., V. Lindgren, B. L. Leventhal, R. Courchesne, A. Lincoln, C. Shulman, … E. Courchesne (1997). "Autism or atypical autism in maternally but not paternally derived proximal 15q duplication." *Am J Hum Genet* 60(4): 928–934.

Cusco, I., A. Medrano, B. Gener, M. Vilardell, F. Gallastegui, O. Villa, … L. A. Perez-Jurado (2009). "Autism-specific copy number variants further implicate the phosphatidylinositol signaling pathway and the glutamatergic synapse in the etiology of the disorder." *Hum Mol Genet*.

De Boulle, K., A. J. Verkerk, E. Reyniers, L. Vits, J. Hendrickx, E. Van Roy, … P. J. Willems (1993). "A point mutation in the FMR-1 gene associated with fragile X mental retardation." *Nat Genet* 3(1): 31–35.

Descheemaeker, M. J., V. Govers, P. Vermeulen and J. P. Fryns (2006). "Pervasive developmental disorders in Prader-Willi syndrome: the Leuven experience in 59 subjects and controls." *Am J Med Genet A* **140**(11): 1136–1142.

Devlin, B., E. H. Cook, Jr., H. Coon, G. Dawson, E. L. Grigorenko, W. McMahon, ... G. D. Schellenberg (2005). "Autism and the serotonin transporter: the long and short of it." *Mol Psychiatry* **10**(12): 1110–1116.

Durand, C. M., C. Betancur, T. M. Boeckers, J. Bockmann, P. Chaste, F. Fauchereau, ... T. Bourgeron (2007). "Mutations in the gene encoding the synaptic scaffolding protein SHANK3 are associated with autism spectrum disorders." *Nat Genet* **39**(1): 25–27.

Feenstra, I., J. Fang, D. A. Koolen, A. Siezen, C. Evans, R. M. Winter, ... A. Schinzel (2006). "European Cytogeneticists Association Register of Unbalanced Chromosome Aberrations (ECARUCA); an online database for rare chromosome abnormalities." *Eur J Med Genet* **49**(4): 279–291.

Fernandez, T., T. Morgan, N. Davis, A. Klin, A. Morris, A. Farhi, ... M. W. State (2004). "Disruption of contactin 4 (CNTN4) results in developmental delay and other features of 3p deletion syndrome." *Am J Hum Genet* **74**(6): 1286–1293.

Fine, S. E., A. Weissman, M. Gerdes, J. Pinto-Martin, E. H. Zackai, D. M. McDonald-McGinn and B. S. Emanuel (2005). "Autism spectrum disorders and symptoms in children with molecularly confirmed 22q11.2 deletion syndrome." *J Autism Dev Disord* **35**(4): 461–470.

Firth, H. V., S. M. Richards, A. P. Bevan, S. Clayton, M. Corpas, D. Rajan, ... N. P. Carter (2009). "DECIPHER: Database of Chromosomal Imbalance and Phenotype in Humans Using Ensembl Resources." *Am J Hum Genet* **84**(4): 524–533.

Fombonne, E. (2005). Epidemiological Studies of Pervasive Developmental Disorders. *Handbook of Autism and Pervasive Developmental Disorders.* F. R. Volkmar. Hoboken, New Jersey, John Wiley & Sons. 2.

Fombonne, E. (2009). "Epidemiology of pervasive developmental disorders." *Pediatr Res* **65**(6): 591–598.

Glessner, J. T., K. Wang, G. Cai, O. Korvatska, C. E. Kim, S. Wood, ... H. Hakonarson (2009). "Autism genome-wide copy number variation reveals ubiquitin and neuronal genes." *Nature* **459**(7246): 569–573.

Hatton, D. D., J. Sideris, M. Skinner, J. Mankowski, D. B. Bailey, Jr., J. Roberts and P. Mirrett (2006). "Autistic behavior in children with fragile X syndrome: prevalence, stability, and the impact of FMRP." *Am J Med Genet A* **140**(17): 1804–1813.

Hertz-Picciotto, I. and L. Delwiche (2009). "The rise in autism and the role of age at diagnosis." *Epidemiology* **20**(1): 84–90.

Iafrate, A. J., L. Feuk, M. N. Rivera, M. L. Listewnik, P. K. Donahoe, Y. Qi, ... C. Lee (2004). "Detection of large-scale variation in the human genome." *Nat Genet* **36**(9): 949–951.

Ioannidis, J. P., G. Thomas and M. J. Daly (2009). "Validating, augmenting and refining genome-wide association signals." *Nat Rev Genet* **10**(5): 318–329.

Jorde, L. B., S. J. Hasstedt, E. R. Ritvo, A. Mason-Brothers, B. J. Freeman, C. Pingree, ... A. Mo (1991). "Complex segregation analysis of autism." *Am J Hum Genet* **49**(5): 932–938.

Kent, L., S. Bowdin, G. A. Kirby, W. N. Cooper and E. R. Maher (2008). "Beckwith Weidemann syndrome: a behavioral phenotype-genotype study." *Am J Med Genet B Neuropsychiatr Genet* **147B**(7): 1295–1297.

Kim, S. J., N. Cox, R. Courchesne, C. Lord, C. Corsello, N. Akshoomoff,... E. H. Cook, Jr. (2002). "Transmission disequilibrium mapping at the serotonin transporter gene (SLC6A4) region in autistic disorder." *Mol Psychiatry* **7**(3): 278–288.

Kuehn, B. M. (2008). "1000 Genomes Project promises closer look at variation in human genome." *JAMA* **300**(23): 2715.

Kumar, R. A., S. KaraMohamed, J. Sudi, D. F. Conrad, C. Brune, J. A. Badner, ... S. L. Christian (2008). "Recurrent 16p11.2 microdeletions in autism." *Hum Mol Genet* **17**(4): 628–638.

Kumar, R. A., C. R. Marshall, J. A. Badner, T. D. Babatz, Z. Mukamel, K. A. Aldinger, ... S. L. Christian (2009). "Association and mutation analyses of 16p11.2 autism candidate genes." *PLoS ONE* **4**(2): e4582.

Laumonnier, F., F. Bonnet-Brilhault, M. Gomot, R. Blanc, A. David, M. P. Moizard, ... S. Briault (2004). "X-linked mental retardation and autism are associated with a mutation in the NLGN4 gene, a member of the neuroligin family." *Am J Hum Genet* **74**(3): 552–557.

Lauritsen, M. B., C. B. Pedersen and P. B. Mortensen (2005). "Effects of familial risk factors and place of birth on the risk of autism: a nationwide register-based study." *J Child Psychol Psychiatry* **46**(9): 963–971.

Lowenthal, R., C. S. Paula, J. S. Schwartzman, D. Brunoni and M. T. Mercadante (2007). "Prevalence of pervasive developmental disorder in Down's syndrome." *J Autism Dev Disord* **37**(7): 1394–1395.

Mailman, M. D., M. Feolo, Y. Jin, M. Kimura, K. Tryka, R. Bagoutdinov, ... S. T. Sherry (2007). "The NCBI dbGaP database of genotypes and phenotypes." *Nat Genet* **39**(10): 1181–1186.

Manning, M. A., S. B. Cassidy, C. Clericuzio, A. M. Cherry, S. Schwartz, L. Hudgins, ... H. E. Hoyme (2004). "Terminal 22q deletion syndrome: a newly recognized cause of speech and language disability in the autism spectrum." *Pediatrics* **114**(2): 451–457.

Marshall, C. R., A. Noor, J. B. Vincent, A. C. Lionel, L. Feuk, J. Skaug, ... S. W. Scherer (2008).

"Structural variation of chromosomes in autism spectrum disorder." *Am J Hum Genet* 82(2): 477–488.

Matuszek, G. and Z. Talebizadeh (2009). "Autism Genetic Database (AGD): a comprehensive database including autism susceptibility gene-CNVs integrated with known noncoding RNAs and fragile sites." *BMC Med Genet* 10: 102.

Mefford, H. C., A. J. Sharp, C. Baker, A. Itsara, Z. Jiang, K. Buysse, ... E. E. Eichler (2008). "Recurrent rearrangements of chromosome 1q21.1 and variable pediatric phenotypes." *N Engl J Med* 359(16): 1685–1699.

Miles, J. H. and R. E. Hillman (2000). "Value of a clinical morphology examination in autism." *Am J Med Genet* 91(4): 245–253.

Moessner, R., C. R. Marshall, J. S. Sutcliffe, J. Skaug, D. Pinto, J. Vincent, ... S. W. Scherer (2007). "Contribution of SHANK3 mutations to autism spectrum disorder." *Am J Hum Genet* 81(6): 1289–1297.

Niklasson, L., P. Rasmussen, S. Oskarsdottir and C. Gillberg (2009). "Autism, ADHD, mental retardation and behavior problems in 100 individuals with 22q11 deletion syndrome." *Res Dev Disabil* 30(4): 763–773.

Orrico, A., L. Galli, S. Buoni, A. Orsi, G. Vonella and V. Sorrentino (2009). "Novel PTEN mutations in neurodevelopmental disorders and macrocephaly." *Clin Genet* 75(2): 195–198.

Peters, S. U., A. L. Beaudet, N. Madduri and C. A. Bacino (2004). "Autism in Angelman syndrome: implications for autism research." *Clin Genet* 66(6): 530–536.

Piven, J., G. C. Tsai, E. Nehme, J. T. Coyle, G. A. Chase and S. E. Folstein (1991). "Platelet serotonin, a possible marker for familial autism." *J Autism Dev Disord* 21(1): 51–59.

Potocki, L., W. Bi, D. Treadwell-Deering, C. M. Carvalho, A. Eifert, E. M. Friedman, ... J. R. Lupski (2007). "Characterization of Potocki-Lupski syndrome (dup(17)(p11.2p11.2)) and delineation of a dosage-sensitive critical interval that can convey an autism phenotype." *Am J Hum Genet* 80(4): 633–649.

Ronald, A., F. Happe, P. Bolton, L. M. Butcher, T. S. Price, S. Wheelwright, ... R. Plomin (2006). "Genetic heterogeneity between the three components of the autism spectrum: a twin study." *J Am Acad Child Adolesc Psychiatry* 45(6): 691–699.

Roohi, J., C. Montagna, D. H. Tegay, L. E. Palmer, C. DeVincent, J. C. Pomeroy, ... E. Hatchwell (2009). "Disruption of contactin 4 in three subjects with autism spectrum disorder." *J Med Genet* 46(3): 176–182.

Rujescu, D., A. Ingason, S. Cichon, O. P. Pietilainen, M. R. Barnes, T. Toulopoulou, ... D. A. Collier (2009). "Disruption of the neurexin 1 gene is associated with schizophrenia." *Hum Mol Genet* 18(5): 988–996.

Rzhetsky, A., D. Wajngurt, N. Park and T. Zheng (2007). "Probing genetic overlap among complex human phenotypes." *Proc Natl Acad Sci U S A* 104(28): 11694–11699.

Schain, R. J. and D. X. Freedman (1961). "Studies on 5-hydroxyindole metabolism in autistic and other mentally retarded children." *J Pediatr* 58: 315–320.

Shaikh, T. H., X. Gai, J. C. Perin, J. T. Glessner, H. Xie, K. Murphy, ... H. Hakonarson (2009). "High-resolution mapping and analysis of copy number variations in the human genome: A data resource for clinical and research applications." *Genome Res.*

Sharp, A. J., Z. Cheng and E. E. Eichler (2006). "Structural variation of the human genome." *Annu Rev Genomics Hum Genet* 7: 407–442.

Sharp, A. J., H. C. Mefford, K. Li, C. Baker, C. Skinner, R. E. Stevenson, ... E. E. Eichler (2008). "A recurrent 15q13.3 microdeletion syndrome associated with mental retardation and seizures." *Nat Genet* 40(3): 322–328.

Somerville, M. J., C. B. Mervis, E. J. Young, E. J. Seo, M. del Campo, S. Bamforth, ... L. R. Osborne (2005). "Severe expressive-language delay related to duplication of the Williams-Beuren locus." *N Engl J Med* 353(16): 1694–1701.

Splawski, I., K. W. Timothy, L. M. Sharpe, N. Decher, P. Kumar, R. Bloise, ... M. T. Keating (2004). "Ca(V)1.2 calcium channel dysfunction causes a multisystem disorder including arrhythmia and autism." *Cell* 119(1): 19–31.

Steffenburg, S., C. Gillberg, L. Hellgren, L. Andersson, I. C. Gillberg, G. Jakobsson and M. Bohman (1989). "A twin study of autism in Denmark, Finland, Iceland, Norway and Sweden." *J Child Psychol Psychiatry* 30(3): 405–416.

Strauss, K. A., E. G. Puffenberger, M. J. Huentelman, S. Gottlieb, S. E. Dobrin, J. M. Parod, ... D. H. Morton (2006). "Recessive symptomatic focal epilepsy and mutant contactin-associated protein-like 2." *N Engl J Med* 354(13): 1370–1377.

Sutcliffe, J. S., R. J. Delahanty, H. C. Prasad, J. L. McCauley, Q. Han, L. Jiang, ... R. D. Blakely (2005). "Allelic heterogeneity at the serotonin transporter locus (SLC6A4) confers susceptibility to autism and rigid-compulsive behaviors." *Am J Hum Genet* 77(2): 265–279.

Szatmari, P., A. D. Paterson, L. Zwaigenbaum, W. Roberts, J. Brian, X. Q. Liu, ... A. Shih (2007). "Mapping autism risk loci using genetic linkage and chromosomal rearrangements." *Nat Genet* 39(3): 319–328.

Thorisson, G. A., O. Lancaster, R. C. Free, R. K. Hastings, P. Sarmah, D. Dash, ... A. J. Brookes (2009). "HGVbaseG2P: a central genetic association database." *Nucleic Acids Res* 37(Database issue): D797–802.

Tierney, E., N. A. Nwokoro, F. D. Porter, L. S. Freund, J. K. Ghuman and R. I. Kelley (2001). "Behavior phenotype in the RSH/Smith-Lemli-Opitz syndrome." *Am J Med Genet* 98(2): 191–200.

Van der Aa, N., L. Rooms, G. Vandeweyer, J. van den Ende, E. Reyniers, M. Fichera, ... R. F. Kooy (2009).

"Fourteen new cases contribute to the characterization of the 7q11.23 microduplication syndrome." *Eur J Med Genet.*

Varga, E. A., M. Pastore, T. Prior, G. E. Herman and K. L. McBride (2009). "The prevalence of PTEN mutations in a clinical pediatric cohort with autism spectrum disorders, developmental delay, and macrocephaly." *Genet Med* 11(2): 111–117.

Vernes, S. C., D. F. Newbury, B. S. Abrahams, L. Winchester, J. Nicod, M. Groszer, … S. E. Fisher (2008). "A functional genetic link between distinct developmental language disorders." *N Engl J Med* 359(22): 2337–2345.

Vorstman, J. A., M. E. Morcus, S. N. Duijff, P. W. Klaassen, J. A. Heineman-de Boer, F. A. Beemer, … H. van Engeland (2006). "The 22q11.2 deletion in children: high rate of autistic disorders and early onset of psychotic symptoms." *J Am Acad Child Adolesc Psychiatry* 45(9): 1104–1113.

Wang, K., H. Zhang, D. Ma, M. Bucan, J. T. Glessner, B. S. Abrahams, … H. Hakonarson (2009).

"Common genetic variants on 5p14.1 associate with autism spectrum disorders." *Nature* 459(7246): 528–533.

Weiss, L. A., D. E. Arking, H. Gene Discovery Project of Johns, C. the Autism, M. J. Daly and A. Chakravarti (2009). "A genome-wide linkage and association scan reveals novel loci for autism." *Nature* 461(7265): 802–808.

Weiss, L. A., Y. Shen, J. M. Korn, D. E. Arking, D. T. Miller, R. Fossdal, … M. J. Daly (2008). "Association between microdeletion and microduplication at 16p11.2 and autism." *N Engl J Med* 358(7): 667–675.

Wing, L. and J. Gould (1979). "Severe impairments of social interaction and associated abnormalities in children: epidemiology and classification." *J Autism Dev Disord* 9(1): 11–29.

Zafeiriou, D. I., Ververi, A. and E. Vargiami (2007). "Childhood autism and associated comorbidities." *Brain Dev* 29(5): 257–272.

Chapter 3

The Neuroanatomy of ASD

Martha R. Herbert

INTRODUCTION

The neuroanatomy of autism presents us with a diverse array of findings that are hard to encompass within a single explanatory framework. What we know about the neuroanatomy of autism has been derived from descriptive observations of imaging and tissue samples, hypotheses derived from neuropsychological inferences, and measures driven by prior observations, some of which could not have been predicted by any existing knowledge of brain–behavior correlation.

Out of this sprawling array of investigations has come evidence of the involvement of the limbic system, corpus callosum, basal ganglia, thalamus, cerebral cortex, white matter, cerebellum, brainstem, and ventricles — in short, pretty much the entire brain. Moreover, the brain as a whole appears to be affected in ways that cannot simply be reduced to discrete impacts on its individual parts. In order to make sense of these findings, it is important to be sensitive to the range of assumptions in various study designs and interpretations, and the capabilities and limitations of the technologies used to generate the data. This is particularly important in organizing the brain data with the intention of making sense of the behavioral features of autism spectrum disorders (ASD). Consequently, these considerations will be reviewed in order to bring them to bear on the findings.

Observing individuals with ASD, we note a range of features suggesting functions that are some combination of atypical (extraordinary as well as deficient), maladaptive (in relation to social norms or comfortable ranges of biopsychosocial regulation, or both), and dysfunctional (functions that cannot be performed as desired or needed). These features clearly suggest a role for nervous system function in the development of autism spectrum disorders. We also find neuroanatomical features that are different than those found in individuals who are not on the autism spectrum. To understand the anatomy findings and how they may contribute to functional features, we utilize what we know about how the brain controls and modulates the functions we perform. This immediately confronts us with a problem: many of the functions that are so meticulously described at the psychological level as atypical in ASD do not have a clearly understood anatomical basis. Therefore, we cannot simply make an a priori selection of specific brain regions relevant to ASD features, dive into the brain, measure those regions, and come out with the answers. In fact, this "modular" strategy was dominant earlier in autism brain research but it was only mildly fruitful, in that neither initial nor subsequent efforts found any localized region with a clear abnormality that was specific to autism, present in everyone with autism, or present in the same way at different points in development or in different cohorts. Instead, unexpected findings have emerged, such as a tendency toward increased brain size and widespread alterations in functional connectivity, that challenge a modular approach to brain–behavior correlation (Herbert & Anderson, 2008).

The modular approach to brain–behavior correlations and neuroanatomical investigations of autism is further challenged by the question of how to anticipate anatomical findings in a condition with early-life onset. So much of our knowledge of neuroanatomy is based on research on the impact of brain lesions acquired after brain maturation (due to, for example, injuries or disease processes such as tumors). But how do we work back in developmental time from our knowledge of the impact of such lesions on behaviors in adults or older children to valid or useful inferences about the origins of the brain underpinnings of these behaviors? We are far from possessing a detailed picture of the stages of brain–neurofunction relationships through early development—indeed, our very capacity to measure such things is just emerging from its own early infancy. This issue can be framed in the context of the debate between "nativist" and "neuroconstructivist" positions regarding development (Karmiloff-Smith, 2006). A "nativist" position would impute the presence of all of the neurofunctional capabilities exercised in childhood and adulthood as innate, inborn features, almost as if there were a little "neurofunctional homunculus" imprinted on the fetus or the gene. By contrast, a neuroconstructivist position posits a dynamic interaction of genes, brain, cognition, and environment, so that development is a process of constructing emergent features—interactively building both neurofunctional capabilities and the underlying neural systems.

Investigations into the brain basis of autism can be, and have been, designed from both nativist and neuroconstructivist perspectives. A nativist study design might investigate direct correlations between genetic differences and altered neurocognitive functions, with the implicit or explicit assumption that functions emerging in mid-childhood or adulthood have direct correlates in both genes and brain, and that the genes and brain components contain these functions from the start. In a neuroconstructivist framework, the biological and developmental pathways from genes to brain development and neurocognitive function are seen as much more complex and interactive (Morton & Frith, 1995), so that genes are thought to "code for" something prior to neurocognitive function, rather than these functions themselves. This prior "something" (presumably at the level of protein and molecular signaling pathways) needs to interact with other factors in a dynamic and developmental interaction that creates emergent new capabilities in the brain and in neurofunctional capability—and creates these both simultaneously and in relation to each other. Neuroconstructivist investigators would therefore be less likely to infer innate capabilities from anatomy or function described in older individuals, but instead would look for trajectories of differentiation and maturation beyond the fetal and infant stages that could lead to what could be observed later in life. These distinctions are pertinent to the interpretation of neuroanatomical findings in autism.

One can also approach neuroanatomical investigation from a physical point of view: Can the nature or localization of the physical changes give any indication of the timing or characteristics of the agent that could have caused them? This is an approach much used in neuroteratology, the study of developmental brain malformations. But if we apply this approach to findings in autism brain research, we face a challenge. Some neurogenetic and neurotoxic syndromes present us with evidence of striking alterations in brain development where the features of the brain abnormalities are clearly associated with brain developmental processes known to occur in a certain interval of time, generally in utero. The time of action and the molecular targets of the genes, drugs, or toxins that disturb the brain have been inferred in this manner for a variety of agents (Slikker & Chang, 1998). But in ASD, brain changes have a number of features that in the aggregate make it difficult to use this methodology to locate the origin of the changes at one clearly

THE NEUROANATOMY OF ASD 49

delineated point in development. These include: the subtlety of most of the observed findings; the distribution of these findings through many parts of the brain whose developmental timetables may vary; and the involvement of processes at many different biological levels, so that it is not easy to encompass them all in a simple model of causation. It appears unlikely that any single gene, infectious agent, or xenobiotic exposure can uniquely account for the panoply of findings identified to date.

Moreover, most of the anatomical changes identified to date in ASD, particularly as compared to the dramatic abnormalities identified in neurogenetic syndromes of brain malformation, are subtle. Thus some researchers have held that since the autistic brain lacks major dysmorphology, it is unlikely to have suffered significant insult prior to the late gestational or early postnatal period (Ciaranello, VandenBerg, & Anders, 1982; Coleman, Romano, Lapham, & Simon, 1985; Raymond, Bauman, & Kemper, 1996).

The pervasiveness of neuroanatomical findings extends not only across the anatomical landscape, but also across biological levels, with differences from controls having been documented from genes, proteins, and other molecules, to the hierarchy of "levels of integration" ranging from subcellular assemblies to cells, tissues, brain regions, neural systems, and large brain units such as lobes and hemispheres (Salthe, 1985). This pervasiveness suggests the potential presence of a complex range of underlying mechanisms. While a nativist or genetic determinist might assume that all of the higher-order levels of integration derive their characteristics from the underlying genetic blueprint, this is more a belief than a demonstrated fact; physiological science suggests that the situation is much more complex and multidirectional (Noble, 2008). If one elaborates the neuroconstructivist position biologically, it becomes apparent that feedback back and forth across levels becomes a potentially important ongoing modulator of both development and function. In fact, gene expression can be modulated by both environment (including behavior and feedbacks to the organism from that behavior) and endogenous physiology. While the neuroanatomical literature generally contains investigations of one or just a few levels at a time, all are active simultaneously and in fundamental integration with each other. Thus, for example, higher cognitive functions can be traced back to the cellular level, and alterations in each of these levels ought to be related to the other.

Observations are generally made at one or a few levels at a time, but usually then are subjected to interpretation regarding their pertinence to other levels; for example, a neuropathological or microanatomical measurement of alterations in a neurotransmitter receptor is likely to be interpreted as having implications for behaviors associated with that neurotransmitter, even though careful behavioral assessment could not have been performed on subjects contributing postmortem specimens under study. A major challenge not limited to the field of autism research is validating such inferences with careful experimental data.

METHODS AND MEASURES: SENSITIVITIES AND CONSTRAINTS

In addressing this complexity, it is important to be familiar with the means by which information about the brain is acquired—not only the methods and sensitivities of the techniques, but also the constraints on and limitations of what can be detected. Information about neuroanatomy is collected from living subjects and from postmortem tissue samples. Currently, the major methods for investigation of structural neuroanatomy in vivo (in living human beings) include measures of head circumference, ultrasound (USG), computed tomography (CT), and magnetic resonance imaging (MRI). With these techniques, we can take measures of size (area and volume), shape, tissue types (e.g. gray matter, white matter, cerebrospinal fluid, bone, blood), density, and tissue integrity. There are also dynamical measures of anatomy, including perfusion measures (which we will review, since they can be measured at rest and construed as indices of microanatomy); functional imaging techniques measuring surrogates of neural activity (such as functional MRI [fMRI], electroencephalography [EEG], and magnetoencephalography [MEG], as well as PET [positron emission tomography] and SPECT [single photon emission computed tomography]) are for the most part beyond the scope of this chapter.

In neuroanatomical investigations using postmortem tissue specimens, it is possible to report microscopic as well as gross (visible to the eye) measures. Grossly, one can report weight, size, and shape, as well as description of injury, atrophy, disease processes (e.g. bleeding, tumor, or macroscopically visible inflammation), and disproportion or malformation. Microscopic investigation opens the possibility of utilizing stains sensitive to particular cellular characteristics; techniques for tracing the trajectories of fibers are available, and quantitative cell counting techniques (known as stereology) are advancing.

Because so many of the advances in neuroanatomical understanding in autism are both enabled and constrained by the limits of the resolution of the measurement methods employed, the following will review the major methods in a little more detail.

Methods: Macroscopic and In vivo

Volumetric imaging

Volumetric imaging, one of the most broadly used methods, can be performed on any type of scan that yields a physical picture of the brain (USG, CT, MRI), but the acquisition method with the greatest spatial resolution is CT, while that with the best contrast resolution is MRI. The size of a delineated piece of brain tissue reflects the influence of cell types, cell size, cell density, cell composition, intracellular and extracellular fluid characteristics, density of vasculature, and extracellular matrix, among other factors (Caviness, Lange, Makris, Herbert, & Kennedy. 1999). Size can be measured as the area on a single MRI slice by tracing the boundaries of a region—a task which can be accomplished computationally. When CT and MRI are used to image the whole brain or a large part of it, they produce a series of slices through the brain. In MRI, each slice captures a slab of a specific thickness. These slabs can be captured continuously without gaps, or with gaps between the slices. When the slices are continuous it becomes possible to calculate the volume of regions that are included in more than one slice. This is done by deriving the "area" of the region on each slice, turning it into a volume measurement by multiplying by the slice thickness, and adding up the volumes of the region on all of the slices in which that region appears. Limits to resolution are more prominent when the slice is thicker: since the surfaces in the brain are highly curved and convoluted, the boundaries of a region can cross the thickness of a slice at an oblique angle. The boundaries of a region in an MRI slice cannot capture these kinds of angles, but are instead perpendicular to the slice surfaces. This is potentially also true of each voxel (the unit volume of measurement in a scan, whose dimensions are specified by the scanning acquisition protocol parameters). This leads to a phenomenon called "partial voluming," in which a voxel (or region) as defined on a scan can contain elements of more than one tissue type—that is, it can have gray matter, white matter, or even cerebrospinal fluid, yielding a value that averages the signal characteristics of the different components, and is therefore ambiguous and difficult to interpret. As MRI technology has advanced, it has become possible to acquire thinner slices so that there is less partial voluming, and boundaries are clearer.

Several MRI-based morphometric methods have been developed that expand what one can learn about contributors to volume. One set of methods gives information about tissue; the other set of methods goes beyond the limitations of traditional volumetrics with regard to surfaces and shapes.

Tissue information.

1). Tissue parameter mapping exploits the capabilities of certain volumetric imaging acquisitions by extracting further information from signal properties, in order to give indications of tissue composition (lipid, water, or protein) present in each voxel, or unit of imaging acquisition.
2). Quantitative T2 transverse relaxation time is an additional way to identify tissue abnormalities, with an increase in time measured largely reflecting tissue water.
3). Voxel-based morphometry (VBM; Ashburner & Friston, 2000) uses a voxel-based comparison of local tissue concentration—typically grey or white matter—between two groups of subjects, to generate metrics of gray- and white-matter "density." VBM is distinct from classical volumetric or morphometric techniques, which deal with regional or total tissue volume, because it localizes group differences in a brain that has been spatially normalized (aligning images from multiple subjects to increase validity of across-subject comparisons) against a standard template. The method outputs a three-dimensional statistical parametric map (SPM) showing regions where the concentration or the density of the tissue differs significantly between the groups. Density is not the same as volume.
4). Deformation-based morphometry (DBM) is a complementary class of methods that analyzes the deformations used in the normalization process, as opposed to the resulting normalized images. These can be used to study differences in brain shapes at various scales, or to identify differences in relative positions of brain structures (Ashburner et al., 1998).

Surface and shape information. Partial voluming issues in volume-based normalizations illustrate the inability of this method to address adequately the complexity of the shape and folding of the cerebral cortex, which is extremely convoluted and quite variable across individuals, and even between identical twins (Eckert et al. 2002). Two regions can have the same volume and still have different shapes—for example, a longer, thinner region could have the same volume as a shorter, thicker one. Accurate alignment of sulci is difficult to achieve using volume-based techniques. Surface-based measures have been developed to resolve this problem (Anticevic et al. 2008). Surface-based analysis involves reconstruction and display of the cortical surface in multiple representations, including 3-D formats, 2-D slices, smooth surfaces, and ellipsoidal, spherical, and flat maps. These visualizations are often used to display functional data, because they are more sensitive and accurate than volume-based analysis, particularly in detecting neural activation in buried cortical regions, in analyzing geometrical and topological relationships, in assessing structural properties like cortical thickness, and in generating surface-based atlases (Van Essen, Drury, Joshi, & Miller, 1998).

Measures derived from raw brain-size data. There are several possible types of basic calculations that can be made with volumetric, tissue quantification, or shape quantification data. If both the left and right sides of a region are measured, it becomes possible to calculate an asymmetry index, allowing the comparison of size on both the left and right sides and an assessment of statistical significance of differences. If a measure of total brain volume is available, it becomes possible to calculate proportion, and consider such questions as, is a brain region really larger in autism cases than in control cases, or is it just larger because the whole brain is larger?) (O'Brien et al., 2006). If quantifications of several regions are available, it becomes possible to calculate ratios. This allows one to ask, for example, whether thalamus volume change is proportional to cortical volume change, or whether there is a disturbance in proportion that could be reflected in altered thalamocortical functional relationships. Another significant question of this type is whether corpus callosum size has the same ratio to white-matter size across different groups, or whether this relationship is different between groups. Volumetric and other tissue-quantification findings can be important

indicators of issues that need further research, whether using the same or other methods. For example, a deviation in thalamocortical or corpus callosum-white matter proportion may suggest follow-up studies using functional MRI, EEG, or MEG to study the impact on brain function and connectivity, looking at thalamocortical dysrhythmia (Llinas, Urbano, Leznik, Ramirez, & Marle, 2005) or interhemispheric information transfer (Ringo, Doty, Demeter, & Simard, 1994).

Diffusion tensor imaging. Diffusion tensor imaging (DTI) is often thought of as a way to measure white-matter tracts, but it is important to remember that it does not really take a direct measurement of them. This is due to the nature of what it measures, and the limits to resolution in this imaging modality. It may be better described as a measure of "white-matter integrity." DTI measures restrictions to the free movement or diffusion of water in tissue. In a glass of water, the molecules are free to diffuse without restriction. This is called isotropy: "tropy" refers to direction and "iso" refers to the dispersion being the same in all directions. But in brain tissue, the properties of the cells in which the water molecules exist, or which border on water molecules in extracellular tissues, restrict the direction of diffusion; here, the water shows "anisotropy," that is, diffusion that is *not* the same in all directions. In white-matter tracts, the water movement appears to be restricted to the direction along the tract, because water cannot diffuse across the fatty lipids in the myelin that wraps the axons in these tracts. Quantitative data generated by DTI include measures of apparent diffusion coefficient (ADC) and fractional anisotropy (FA). ADC is a measure of diffusivity, or the degree with which water moves freely within the tissue, with high ADC suggesting increase in water or decrease in restriction to water motion. FA, on the other hand, is a measure of directional coherence, or the fraction or extent to which water motion is restricted in a given part of tissue, with a high FA indicating a large amount of restriction of water motion. Higher FA indicates more restriction and higher ADC less restriction.

DTI has a number of limitations. While DTI tractography can generate dramatically stunning multicolor pictures of fibers within the brain, these figures are of qualitative but not quantitative use. In addition, ambiguity arises in DTI imaging in areas where white matter tracts cross each other. This crossing is especially prominent in the white matter right under the cerebral cortex, where fibers are going in many different directions. Standard DTI techniques cannot track a specific fiber through an area of crossing fibers and out the other side. However, recent advances in diffusion imaging allow us to resolve these "crossing" and "kissing" fibers.

DTI images are constructed from magnetic signals that make contact with the brain tissue from a number of directions. The more directions used, the greater is the resolution of the image. But the price for this increased resolution is a longer scan, which makes it hard to acquire the highest quality images on individuals who may have difficulty staying still. Recent formidable technical advances have considerably shortened the time needed for a high-resolution acquisition, but the application to fully awake children with attentional or neurodevelopmental impairment is still limited.

Magnetic resonance spectroscopy. Magnetic resonance spectroscopy (MRS) is a way of using MRI to quantify levels of substances in living individuals. To do this, MRS takes advantage of the way that different substances resonate differently in a uniform magnetic field. The substances measured are related to different tissues and physiological processes in the brain, so that the measured increases or decreases in a substance give an indication of underlying cellular or anatomical differences or disease processes.

However, MRS has a number of technical limitations. Proton magnetic resonance spectroscopy is the variant most commonly used, but other methods exist of potential relevance, particularly phosphorus magnetic resonance spectroscopy, which can offer insights into brain energy metabolism. Since these other methods often involve very lengthy imaging acquisitions, their practical utilization is limited, particularly with children or impaired individuals. Unlike the other MRI techniques discussed above, MRS cannot be performed on the whole brain at once, and a lot of the variability between studies is due to major inconsistencies between studies in choice of brain region scanned, and the approach taken to imaging the region in question (not to speak of cohort age ranges). In the method most commonly used, single voxel spectroscopy (SVS), the size of the one voxel imaged is so large that many different types of tissue, and/or a large area of tissue, are included in one measurement. Even so, this method has yielded intriguing insights into autism anatomy, which will be reviewed later in this chapter. When MRS is performed in more powerful MRI magnetic fields, it is possible to get much greater resolution; however, at the time of this writing, almost all studies have been performed on relatively low-field-strength 1.5 Tesla (1.5T) magnets. More powerful scanners are increasingly available, and this development, along with increased replication of choice of regions and approaches, may further improve the yield of this approach.

Perfusion imaging. Perfusion refers to blood flow in the brain, which has been studied nearly two dozen publications on autism (reviewed later in this chapter). Three major methods of measuring brain perfusion are single photon emission computed tomography (SPECT), positron emission tomography (PET), and arterial spin labeling (ASL). SPECT and PET are both invasive, involving injection of radioactive tracers that are detected directly (SPECT) or indirectly (PET). PET has higher resolution than SPECT due to its selection of photons for simultaneous arrival at the detection device, but SPECT is cheaper and uses longer-lasting and more readily available radioisotopes. Both of these methods, while valuable, are severely limited in clinical and research applicability, particularly in minors, given the need to inject radioactive material. Arterial spin labelling (ASL) is an attractive alternative because it is performed in an MRI scanner without isotopes or contrast. ASL uses endogenous blood water as a contrast agent, by magnetically tagging arterial blood, tracking the decay of the magnetization of the tag as it enters the tissue of interest, and computing perfusion maps by comparing images of tagged versus with untagged blood water (Deibler et al., 2008b). ASL is in widespread clinical use in the imaging of tumors, stroke, and other cerebrovascular disorders (Deibler et al., 2008a). Moreover, because it is MRI-based and noninvasive, this technique is potentially widely available. Yet while ASL is being advocated as a tool in psychiatric diagnosis, because of its capacity to make discriminations in a number of psychiatric disorders such as schizophrenia and depression (Theberge, 2008), its use at present has been limited to a small set of research studies, with no studies to date in autism.

Methods: Postmortem and Microscopic

While this review predominantly focuses on in vivo neuroimaging data, neuropathological findings will be included when relevant. Neuropathological studies clearly have the potential for much finer resolution than microscopic imaging, but they also have a range of limitations. Most prominent among them is the great scarcity of brain tissue. Autism is not a fatal condition; deaths in childhood in individuals with autism are mainly from accidents, drowning, suffocation and seizures (Shavelle, Strauss & Pickett, 2001), and are relatively rare. Autopsies are performed much less commonly today than they were in the years preceding neuroimaging, and this contributes to the third problem, which is the difficulty in educating families about the importance of brain donation, and encouraging families to donate brains when they are dealing with the profound grief and massive stress associated with the death of a child (the Autism Tissue Program is one resource that is addressing this issue).

An additional major limitation is unavoidable variability in the postmortem interval, or length of time between death and processing (fixing or freezing) of the brain tissue, which can have many types of impacts on the state of the tissue. In addition, the processing itself can alter cells and regional volumes in a fashion that is not uniform across the brain (Lodin, Mares, Faltin, & Karasek, 1969).

Overall, it is exceedingly important to remember that interpreting the significance of neuroanatomical findings in a developmental disorder is extremely complicated. Insofar as one is trying to reconstruct the past from present evidence, one needs to be aware that there might be trajectories other than the ones that easily come to mind that could have led to the present state of the tissue. One's interpretations also need to be mindful of the limitations of the study sample, the depth of characterization of the sample, and the resolution and sensitivity of the instrumentation used.

ANATOMICAL IMAGING IN REVIEW

In this next section, autism neuroanatomical imaging will be reviewed within a neuroconstructivist context, and with a sense of the historical development of our understanding as it is influenced by models, by data available at each point in time, and by the growing availability of technologies capable of producing new classes of data. A core theme is the discovery and elucidation of overall brain enlargement in autism. Although the investigations of regional abnormalities in autism predate a concerted attempt to understand

brain enlargement in autism, these will be reviewed following the discussion of brain enlargement, so that the insights gained from the general enlargement can be brought to bear on the features noted in specific brain regions. The review will begin with some of the early neuroanatomical observations in autism. It will then move to observations and measures of differences between autistic and control brains at the largest scales, and will trace the exploration of these measures through a range of dimensions and the techniques used to elucidate these dimensions. The review will then turn to measures of a number of regions that have been explored in more detail, and describe the dimensions and techniques of some additional techniques used to study them. Finally, reflections will be shared regarding the linkages between large-scale and regional measures, and directions important to future progress will be shared, particularly those that hold the clearest relevance to clinical evaluation and intervention.

Clinical Imaging

Clinical neuroradiological imaging involves the acquisition of brain images from individual patients (rather than from individuals chosen to be members of a specifically defined cohort) to look for explanations for diseases and symptom complexes, and to seek targets for treatment interventions., Most of the findings in autism neuroanatomy have been generated using quantitative methods, because these findings are generally too subtle to be detected qualitatively by non-computational clinical radiological assessments which for the most part are qualitative rather than quantitative. On the other hand, the findings discerned quantitatively to date are group findings that substantially overlap with findings in non-autistic individuals, rather than pathognomonic findings that can be used for clinical diagnosis. Presently, therefore, while clinical assessment has not proven useful for identifying diagnostic features, research imaging has thus far not had much influence on clinical practice.

A number of publications have collected and tabulated clinical neuroradiological observations in autism. A 1983 study observed gross abnormalities in 26% of an autism cohort (Gillberg & Svendsen 1983). A 2006 study of imaging findings in children with autism and developmental delay reported that 15 of the 32 children with autism or pervasive developmental disorders (PDD) showed structural abnormalities

(Zeegers et al., 2006). A 2009 study found abnormalities in 48% of a cohort of 77 children with nonsyndromic autism (Boddaert et al., 2009). However, in all of these clinical studies, the abnormalities that were observed, while common in the aggregate, were quite variable in their nature and distribution. These included white-matter lesions in various locations, reduced corpus callosum size, wide or asymmetrical ventricles, arachnoid cysts, Chiari I malformations, cavum septum pellucidum, and dilated Virchow-Robin spaces. These findings are all nonspecific and do not obviously point to any clear avenues of medical intervention. Consequently, brain imaging is not considered to be an essential component of the medical or neurological evaluation of autism, and tends to be ordered only when additional abnormalities are found that suggest that imaging will assist with clinical management.

Early CT findings: Asymmetries and Ventricular Differences

The earliest macroanatomical studies of autism utilized computerized tomography (CT) scans, a method of using x-ray technology to generate a large series of two-dimensional images along a single axis through tissue, such as brain tissue. What distinguishes these studies from the above clinical studies is that consistent anatomical features were measured across all subjects. As these scans have very limited resolution within the gray and white matter, however, observations were confined to the level of overall size, overall asymmetries, and differences in the size of cerebral ventricles, which are easily discerned in this imaging modality (Gillberg & Svendsen, 1983; Hier, LeMay, & Rosenberger, 1979; Hoshino, Manome, Kaneko, Yashima, & Kumashiro, 1984). Some attempt at quantification was made in these images, but due to the level of resolution, these measures and indices were crude. While the findings in these early CT studies suggest differences in the physical status and/or development of the brain, they are not clear enough to offer etiological or functional insight.

Brain size in autism

One of the most replicated findings in autism brain investigations has been the observation of a tendency toward increased brain size, particularly in younger autistic individuals. Although large head size was

observed by Leo Kanner in his initial paper identifying autism as a syndrome (Kanner, 1943), this observation were initially buried in studies performed for other purposes; eventually its relevance was noticed, and the phenomenon investigated deliberately. The earliest measures were of brain weight. There is some source of artifact in brain weight measures because of variability due to the postmortem interval (time from death to removal and fixation of brain), or cause of death (e.g. an illness that involved swelling might change brain size and weight), but even so a trend toward larger brains was noted. In 1985 Bauman and Kemper observed that 8 out of 11 brains in autistic individuals less than 12 years of age showed a significant increase in weight as compared with controls, but 6 out of 8 of those over 18 years of age weighed less than expected (Bauman & Kemper, 1985). Bailey and colleagues (1998) noted that four of six brains in their sample (one four year old, remainder ages 20–27) were greater than the normal range for brain weight for age.

Head circumference

Head circumference (HC) has been an important measure in documenting head-size trends in autism. Davidovitch, Patterson, and Gartside (1996) reported that 18.2% of a group of 148 brain head circumference measures in autistic individuals were at or above the 98th percentile (though, interestingly, while this 1996 paper showed macrocephaly in an American cohort, a 2009 poster by the same author could not replicate this phenomenon in an Israeli autistic sample [Davidovitch, Golan, Vardi, Lev, & Lerman-Sagie, 2009]). Woodhouse and colleagues (1996) noted that 19.7% of a PDD cohort had macrocephaly and 48.7% had head circumference greater than the 90th percentile. Fidler and colleagues noted more macrocephaly in probands with autism and their first-degree relatives (Fidler, Bailey, & Smalley, 2000). Miles and colleagues (2000) reported increased HC in probands in a range of subgroups based on phenotype, onset, seizure status, and IQ, and also found macrocephaly in at least one parent in 45% of cases. Dementieva and colleagues (2005) found macrocephaly in 19% of a cohort of 251 with autism.

MRI

Head circumference measures have made a great contribution to studies of autism, but they have obvious limits, including not only an inability to address anything specific about the brain, but also potential inaccuracy stemming from inconsistent placement of the tape measure on the skull. Head circumference is insensitive to shape differences, such as wide versus long and narrow or taller heads; but shape may be relevant in autism, where a higher preponderance of wide heads has been noted (Deutsch & Joseph, 2003). Starting in the late 1980s and developing into the early 1990s, the advent of brain imaging utilizing structural MRI emerged and allowed a new kind of measure to contribute to our knowledge of brain size in autism. Filipek and colleagues (1992) reported on brain volumes in a cohort of 92 children with high-functioning autism (HFA, IQ > 80), developmental language disorder (DLD, IQ > 80), low-functioning autism (LFA, IQ < 80), and non-autistic low IQ (NALIQ, IQ < 80), as well as controls (CTRL). They found that for total brain volume, HFA > LFA = DLD > CTRL > NALIQ. Large brain size was also reported earlier on by several other research teams (Courchesne et al., 2001; Deutsch & Joseph 2003; Piven, Arndt, Bailey, & Andreasen, 1996; Sparks et al., 2002). By now, structural MRI measures have documented increased total brain volume multiple times; an excellent meta-analysis of these findings has been performed by Stanfield and colleagues (2007).

When does brain size increase occur?

Lainhart and colleagues (2003) generated longitudinal data by performing a retrospective study of head circumference of infants later diagnosed with autism. This brought to light the issue of a postnatal-head-size developmental trajectory. Lainhart found that most of the macrocephalic autistic subjects did not manifest macrocephaly at birth, but developed it during early childhood, as they manifested accelerated increase in head size during this period. This finding has since been replicated multiple times. Courchesne and colleagues (2003) performed a retrospective study of head circumference in children diagnosed with autism as compared with HC norms from the Centers for Disease Control (CDC) and found that, while mean head circumference at birth was at the 30th percentile in this group (as compared with Lainhart's group, where it was in the normal range), it increased 2 standard deviations in the first year and a half of life. Mraz and colleagues (2007) replicated this trajectory, finding a significantly smaller head circumference at

birth to two weeks, and a significantly larger head circumference by 10–14 months of age, although when overall length and weight were controlled for, this difference disappeared. This group also found that children with an early history of autism who subsequently moved off the autism spectrum showed the same head circumference trajectory as did the stable autism group (Mraz, Dixon, Dumont-Mathieu, & Fein, 2009). Lainhart's group subsequently performed a retrospective study of fetal ultrasounds in children who had later been diagnosed with autism, and did not find abnormalities of fetal head circumference in autism (Hobbs et al. 2007). Hazlett and colleagues (2005) found enlargement of head circumference beginning at about 12 months of age. Of the 79 individuals in Dementieva's sample (2005) for which two consecutive HC measures were available (not necessarily starting at birth), 35% had accelerated head growth between the two available measures, while the remainder did not. Of the 37 of these individuals whose consecutive HC measures began at birth, 65% showed abnormal head growth starting at birth.

A number of researchers have been able to use volumetric MRI to document brain volume in small children. Courchesne and colleagues reported increased brain volume in 2–4-year-olds, with 90% above average and 37% meeting criteria for developmental macrocephaly (Courchesne et al., 2001). Hazlett and colleagues (2005) also found significantly increased brain volume in 2-year-olds. A large multi-center prospective at-risk infant MRI imaging study is presently underway at the National Institutes of Health that will greatly enlarge the data available, by documenting changes in total brain and regional volumes during the earliest postnatal development (NIH).

Does accelerated head growth have behavioral correlates?

While Courchesne and colleagues (2003) found that greater head size increase was associated with lower ADI scores, Dementieva (2005) did not replicate this correlation, finding that accelerated head growth, whether or not it started at birth, was associated with increases in several composite scores on the Vineland Adaptive Behavior Scales. Elder and colleagues (2008) found that large brain size at 12 months, followed by a more marked slowing of head growth, predicted the manifestation of autism symptoms. The impact of body weight and length on head circumference has not been consistent across studies (Mraz et al., 2007).

What parts of the brain are driving brain size increase?

To understand brain enlargement in autism, it has become important to understand the neuroanatomy of autism in much more detail. Given that autism is classified as a developmental disorder, theories about a range of developmental disruptions that could lead to this phenomenon have been advanced (Courchesne & Pierce, 2005a, 2005b; McCaffery & Deutsch, 2005). One prominent model is that brain enlargement early in life is due to persistence of the early exuberant proliferation of neurons in the developing brain, presumably because of a failure of pruning, or apoptosis. To understand what is happening with these brains during development, and to assess the merits of various models and hypotheses, it is necessary to measure subcomponents of the brain, in order to assess their respective contributions to this enlargement. Volumetric or morphometric profiling has been a major tool in getting this information, but it has also revealed its own limits; there are questions that can only be answered with other methodologies. To address the brain size question, volumetrics has been applied to quantifying sizes of large regions of the brain, such as the cerebral cortex, white matter, or cerebellum, and to comparing these measures between autistic and control populations. It has also involved measuring the whole brain and comparing proportional volumes between groups.

Gray matter and white matter during development

While the model of "failure of pruning" would predict a larger cerebral cortex, data on cerebral cortex volume are contradictory. One recent paper identified increased cortical thickness (Hardan, Muddasani, Vemulapalli, Keshavan, & Minshew, 2006), whereas Hadjikhani and colleagues (2006) found that cortical thickness of the right inferior frontal cortex was inversely correlated with autism severity. Some of the differences between cohorts seem to map in an age-dependent fashion, suggesting that reconciliation of contradictions may in part come from recognizing a developmental process where volumetric trajectories are non-uniform across brain regions. In early childhood there appears to be an increase in both gray and white matter volumes. Ben Bashat and colleagues (2007), using a form of DTI imaging, measured an accelerated maturation of white matter in 1.8–3.3-year-olds. In middle childhood the data vary. Cerebral cortex has been measured to be absolutely the same, but relatively smaller, than controls in school-aged, high-functioning autistic children (Herbert et al., 2003), but it has also been measured to be larger in the same age group (Palmen et al., 2005).

In a landmark study comparing cross-sectional findings from a large number of subjects ranging in age from 2 through 16 years, growth trajectories were presented for cerebral and cerebellar gray and white matter (Courchesne et al., 2001). Cerebral cortical gray matter was 12% greater in 2–3-year-old autistic subjects than in controls, but by middle childhood (6–9 years of age), distinct trajectories had led to different changes: the control volume had increased 12%, while the autistic group volume had decreased by 2%. Cerebral white matter also appears to have a different growth trajectory in autistic individuals than control subjects. In the autistic subjects, it grew in a linear fashion, starting out 18% larger in the 2–3-year-old autistic group, but having a much flatter slope of volume increase than in controls, and ending up in adolescence being only 10% larger than in early childhood. In controls there was a 12% increase in volume from the 2–3-year-old to the 6–9-year-old age group, and a 59% increase compared to early childhood in the adolescent group. Cerebellar white matter was, dramatically, 39% larger in 2–3-year-old autistic children than in controls; however, in the cross sectional 12–16-year-old adolescent comparison sample, cerebellar white matter was only 7% larger than in the 2–3-year-old autistic subjects, but 50% larger than in early childhood in the comparison control sample.

Distribution of white matter changes

To address the question of whether the white-matter changes were uniform throughout the brain or were non-uniformly distributed in different subregions, our own group utilized a white-matter parcellation technique designed to subdivide the white matter from volumetric images according to the white-matter tract architecture (Makris et al., 1999; Meyer, Makris, Bates, Caviness, & Kennedy, 1999). Although white-matter tracts cannot be discerned or discriminated utilizing the standard MRI acquisition techniques used for volumetric imaging analysis, it is possible to identify their probable locations based on proximal visible gray matter landmarks. Using this technique, a division was made between outer (radiate), sagittal (long tracts such as those going from front to back), and descending tracts. This analysis revealed that high-functioning, autistic, school-aged children (from the same sample as Filipek et al., 1992) had enlargements in radiate white matter in all four lobes as compared to controls, but no enlargements in the deeper white matter in either the sagittal or descending tracts. Interestingly, the developmental language disorder sample showed a similar radiate white-matter involvement, but to a lesser degree, and not involving the parietal lobe. This localization of enlargement is intriguing in light of the neurodevelopmental myelination sequence: the radiate white matter myelinates late in development (late in the first and into the second postnatal year), with the prefrontal white matter myelinating last and for the longest duration. In this analysis, prefrontal white matter, a component of radiate white matter, showed the largest increase, being 36% larger in the autistic sample and 25% larger in the DLD sample than in controls; these marked increases suggest some kind of process affecting late-myelinating white matter, which approximately coincides with the period of postnatal brain enlargement described above.

Corpus callosum

If the overall white matter volume is larger in younger autistic children, and if this enlargement is non-uniform with the deep white matter not being involved, then is this also true for the corpus callosum, the major inter-hemispheric deep white matter structure? The answer is mostly yes. One research group found corpus callosum enlargement in autism, and this only in autistic individuals (as well as non-autistic individuals) with macrocephaly (Kilian et al., 2008). Most other researchers have found the corpus callosum to be reduced in size, and a few reported no differences in size between the two groups (Rice et al., 2005). Within this size reduction there has been some variability between studies in localizing corpus callosum size changes; for example, using mid-sagittal area measures, Egaas and colleagues (1995) found reduction in the mid-sagittal area, while Hardan and colleagues (2000) found anterior reductions. Piven and colleagues (1997) found the body and splenium (posterior) to be smaller.

Additional methods have been utilized, and have yielded generally consistent findings. Using voxel-based morphometry, Waiter and colleagues (2005) found reductions in anterior splenium and isthmus, and using surface-based methods, Freitag and colleagues (2009) discerned reduced posterior thickness. Vidal and colleagues (2006) showed that, while traditional morphometric techniques discerned a reduction in total area and anterior third area, spatial maps discerned significant reduction in both splenium and genus. Recently, additional imaging methods have been applied, adding new dimensions to our understanding of corpus callosum changes in autism. Alexander and colleagues (2007) utilized DTI, and found that higher diffusivity and lower FA were associated with slower processing speeds. Just and colleagues (2007) linked functional and anatomical connectivity measures, and found corpus callosum size reduction that correlated with a lower degree of integration of information. Mason and colleagues (2008) found a correlation between connectivity within the brain regions associated with Theory of Mind and the size of a portion of the anterior corpus callosum.

Asymmetry

Since the corpus callosum is critical to connections between the cerebral hemispheres, this area's alterations in autism might be expected to be associated with brain asymmetries that differ from those in neurotypical individuals. In autism spectrum disorders (ASD), abnormal brain asymmetries have been documented at a variety of levels. At the macroanatomical level, deviations from normal asymmetries have been documented in localized regions (De Fosse et al., 2004; Herbert et al. 2002; Hier, LeMay, & Rosenberger, 1979; Rojas, Camou, Reite, & Rogers, 2005; Rojas, Bawn, Benkers, Reite, & Rogers, 2002), widely distributed, volumetrically measured regions (Herbert et al., 2005), metabolism (Burroni et al. 2008; Chandana et al., 2005; Chiron et al., 1995; Chugani et al., 1997), functional activation (Muller et al., 2004; Takeuchi et al., 2004), neurophysiology (Bruneau et al., 2003; Dawson et al., 1989; Flagg et al., 2005; Khalfa et al., 2001; Lazarev, Pontes, & Deazevedo, 2008; Stroganova et al. 2007), and neurocognitive assessments (Dawson et al., 1986, 1988; Dawson, Warrenburg, & Fuller 1983; Ozonoff & Miller, 1996). Architectonic asymmetries, such as in mini-columns, as has been identified in schizophrenia (Buxhoeveden et al., 2001), have apparently not been investigated in ASD (Chance et al., 2008). Brain asymmetry has been documented in a fairly widespread distribution (Herbert et al., 2005), and may involve a developmental trajectory into adolescence (Flagg et al., 2005). This developmental trajectory may be indirectly supported by the finding by Herbert and colleagues (2005) of greater cortical asymmetry in higher-order associational areas, but not primary sensory and motor areas, since the development of higher-order associational areas is more experience-dependent than that of the primary sensory and motor areas. Although right-hemisphere dysfunction may predominate in autism (McKelvey et al., 1995; Ozonoff & Miller, 1996;), it may not be universal, but rather a marker for specific subtypes distinguished by language impairment (De Fosse et al., 2004; Whitehouse & Bishop, 2008).

Magnetic resonance spectroscopy and neuronal integrity

If it is true that brain enlargement is due to a failure of pruning, it should follow that there would be a greater number of neurons in the cerebral cortex. The metabolite N-Acetyl-aspartate (NAA), detectable by proton magnetic resonance imaging (1H-MRS), is a measure of neuronal integrity or neuronal function, and is sometimes considered a measure of neuronal density. Several 1H-MRS studies have been performed to test this hypothesis, but their findings have contradicted their predictions. Out of 22 magnetic resonance imaging papers in the autism literature, 80 measures of NAA were performed in all studied brain regions combined; 25 found reductions in NAA, 1 found an increase, and 54 showed no change (Shetty et al., 2009). The lack of change in the majority of measures may be in part a reflection of 19 out of 22 of the studies having been performed on a relatively low field-strength 1.5T rather than a 3T magnet; 3T was used in only one study to date (DeVito et al., 2007).

Despite the need for further studies at higher field strength, it is worth noting that when differences were found, the strongly predominant finding was of reduction, rather than increase, of this metabolite. This suggests either reduced neuronal density, a lower level of neuronal functioning, impaired mitochondrial function, or less elaborate neuronal architecture (e.g. dendrites). It is also notable that in the epilepsy-surgery literature, following surgical resection of epileptic foci, there has been documented reversibility of

reduced NAA in secondarily affected brain tissue (Hugg et al., 1996). Moreover, in the overall body of autism spectroscopy literature in children, other metabolites measured are lower rather than higher in autism than controls, suggesting a lower rather than a higher density of cells and metabolic components; this matter is exceedingly well reviewed (Dager, Friedman, Petropoulos, & Shaw, 2008). A problem with drawing inferences from this literature is that a number of spectroscopy studies in autism encompass wide age ranges, some with cohorts ranging in age from early childhood to adulthood; this may potentially reduce the chance of detecting changes in metabolites whose concentrations change during development.

Diffusion tensor imaging, transverse relaxation imaging, and white matter integrity

If the prediction is correct that brain enlargement is due to a failure of pruning, it should also follow that there would be a greater density of axonal processes emanating from the predicted larger number of neurons. There are now a number of DTI papers with findings related to the testing of this model; these are summarized in Table 3-1. Almost all of the studies showed either reduced FA, increased ADC, or both; Ben Bashat and colleagues (2007), who studied the youngest cohort, were also the only ones to utilize a variant "high b value" diffusion tensor imaging study, which is more sensitive than the more standard DTI acquisition to diffusion in areas with high restriction; it is unclear whether the difference between the findings in the younger as compared with the older groups is age- or methodology-related.

The short-range fibers investigated by Sundaram and colleagues (2008) are quite consistent in distribution with the radiate white matter that was reported as enlarged in Herbert and colleagues (2004), as described above. Sundaram and colleagues note that their findings of reduced FA and increased ADC, which suggest reduced rather than increased white matter integrity in this area, are not consistent with the hypothesis that this white-matter volumetric enlargement is composed of a larger number of myelinated axons. Cheung and colleagues (2009) also explicitly ponder how to reconcile lower FA with greater white-matter volume, which they described as counterintuitive. They suggest that white-matter

Table 3-1 Diffusion Tensor Imaging Findings

Study	Subject characteristics	FA	ADC	Regions
Barnea-Goraly et al. (2004)	7 Aut 14.6±3.4 yo 9 TD 13.4±2.8 yo	-		Ventromedial prefrontal cortices, anterior cingulate gyri, temporal parietal sulcus, superior temporal sulci, near the amygdala bilaterally, in occipitemporal tracts and in the corpus callosum
Lee et al. (2007)	43 ASD 7-33 yo 34 TD 8-29 yo	-	+	Superior temporal gyrus, temporal stem
Thakkar et al. (2008)	12 ASD 30±11 yo 14 TD 27±2.8 yo	-		Right anterior cingulate cortex (associated with severity in repetitive behavior ratings)
Sundaram et al. (2008)	50 ASD 57.5 ± 29.2 months 16 TD 82.1 ± 41.4 months	-	+	All frontal fibers ADC: Mean ADC in ASD children was significantly higher FA: No significant differences but there was a trend to lower FA in ASD Long Range Association Fibers ADC:Mean ADC in ASD was higher FA : No changes Short Association fibers ADC: Mean ADC was higher in ASD than in TD FA: Mean FA was significantly lower in ASD Negative correlation between FA and GARS AQ and social isolation subscale . . . but not significant after Bonferroni correction
Cheung et al. (2009)	14 ASD 6-14 yo 14 TD 6-14 yo	-		*Reduced FA:* bilateral prefrontal and temporal regions, especially adjacent to the fusiform gyrus in the right ventral temporal lobe *Increased FA:* right inferior frontal gyrus and left occipital lobe Correlations of lower FA in subsets of these regions with higher ADI-R diagnostic algorithm subscale scores
Ben Bashat et al. (2007)	7 Autism (1.8-3.3 yo) 18 TD (4 months to 23 years)	+		Increased FA and probability and decreased displacement in left sides of all of the following: posterior limb of internal capsule, external capsule and forceps minor, corpus callosum genu, corpus callosum splenium and corticospinal tract

volumetric indices are rather nonspecific, and that given their findings, volume increase might even be due to non-neuronal proliferative processes, such as the activation and cell swelling of microglia and astroglia that have been reported by Vargas and colleagues (2005), which will be discussed shortly. The finding that increased motor cortex white matter predicts motor impairment in autism, not enhanced motor performance (Mostofsky, Burgess, & Gidley Larson, 2007), could conceivably be interpreted as consistent with these reflections on tissue underpinnings. These diffusion tensor imaging findings highlight the limitations of volumetric imaging: it is indeed true that a volumetric measure of increased white matter can by no means be attributed with any certainty to an increase in myelinated axons, since the imaging acquisition used for volumetric analyses simply measures the size of the total white matter compartment,

and does not distinguish between different types of cells and materials that contribute to the volume. It is also important to remember here that increases or decreases in FA or diffusivity can only be considered consistent with, and not proof of changes in, tract or myelinated fiber density.

Neuropathology: Minicolumns; neuroinflammation

Two neuropathology findings of potential relevance to the phenomenon of brain enlargement in autism are altered minicolumns, and evidence of innate immune activation in postmortem tissue from individuals with autism. Minicolumns, a microscopic architectural feature of the brain, were described as being smaller but less compact in their cellular configuration using a number of methods (Casanova, Buxhoeveden,

& Brown, 2002; Casanova, Buxhoeveden, Switala, & Roy, 2002a, 2002b; This phenomenon is pertinent to interneurons that are an important part of the structure of minicolumns, which play a critical inhibitory role in neuronal activity, and that thereby may alter functional connectivity. Casanova has proposed a relationship between minicolumnar alterations and structural connectivity—specifically, increased short-corticortical white matter, suggesting that larger brains require more white matter, and in particular short-range associational fibers, to maintain connectivity (Casanova, 2004). If, as recent DTI studies reviewed just above suggest, there is not in fact increased short-range associational fiber density, it is not obvious what implications this may have for the connectivity impacts of such minicolumns.

While neither MRI scans nor neuropathological investigations have identified focal patches of inflammation in postmortem brain tissue specimens from autistic individuals, neuropathological evidence of innate immune activation has been identified using specific staining techniques (Vargas et al., 2005). This immune activation was identified in the cerebral cortex, white matter, and cerebellum, and consisted of activated astroglial and microglial cells, as well as altered cytokine profiles. More recently, an increase in pro-inflammatory cytokines or glial activation in brain tissue has been identified by other groups (Li et al., 2009; Morgan et al., 2010). A much larger number of studies have identified a range of systemic immune abnormalities (Ashwood & Van de Water, 2004; Ashwood, Wills, & Van de Water, 2006), although the specific details of the immune profiles are not identical between the central nervous system and the organism systemically. Innate immune activation is a prominent feature of a variety of neurodegenerative diseases such as Alzheimer's but it is not detectable by MRI scan or by other in vivo imaging techniques, other than through use of an experimental PET scan ligand, PK11195, which is no longer in use due to side effects. Inflammation can affect the neuroanatomical milieu due to the swelling that accompanies astroglial activation, which may affect volume and may also compress capillary lumen by as much as 50% (Aschner, Allen, Kimelberg, LoPachin, & Streit, 1999), compromising blood perfusion (perfusion will be discussed below). Inflammation may also alter the neurochemical milieu by impairing the reuptake of glutamate and leading to excessive extracellular glutamate (Pardo & Eberhart, 2007), an excitatory neurotransmitter, which may secondarily affect connectivity through increasing the excitation/inhibition ratio which could also have cascading developmental effects (see Chapter 4 for a review of neurochemistry in autism).

The volume enlargement that may be related to swelling of immune-activated glial cells may also conceivably be related to DTI measures of increased water diffusion and reduced FA. Neuroinflammation and biochemical changes also belong to a set of factors that in the broader neuroscience literature have been shown to have some influence on brain asymmetry. A prediction of asymmetry can be made mathematically on the basis of efficiencies of cross-hemispheric communication, where lateralization becomes more efficient with larger brain size (Ringo, 1991; Ringo et al., 1994); however, this does not account for the specifically rightward predominance of this asymmetry. In the broader neuroscience literature, there are papers documenting an influence on brain asymmetry specifically toward rightward asymmetry from various visceral and regulatory factors; these include autonomic (Craig, 2005), neuropeptides (Ramirez, Prieto, Vives, de Gasparo, & Alba, 2004), gonadal steroids (Wisniewski, 1998), and immune (Kang et al. 1991; Shen et al., 2005; Wittling, 1995); but at present, although all these factors have some documented pertinence to autism, their connection to asymmetry in autism has not been pursued.

Perfusion

Cerebral perfusion abnormalities have been identified in at least 18 papers studying autistic cohorts. Cerebral perfusion refers to the quantity of blood flow in the brain. Abnormal regulation of cerebral perfusion is found in a range of severe medical conditions including tumors, vascular disease, and epilepsy. Cerebral hypoperfusion has also been found in a range of psychiatric disorders (Theberge, 2008). Of the 18 papers found in a recent literature search for positron emission tomography (PET) and single photon emission computed tomography (SPECT or SPET) studies of brain perfusion in autism or ASD, 15 were performed using SPECT, two with PET, and one with both SPECT and PET. Neurocognitive hypotheses and conclusions, as well as localization of perfusion changes, were heterogeneous across these papers. Hypoperfusion has been identified in frontal regions (Degirmenci et al., 2008; Galuska et al., 2002; George et al., 1992; Gupta & Ratnam, 2009; Ohnishi et al., 2000; Wilcox et al., 2002), temporal lobes

(Boddaert et al., 2002; Burroni et al., 2008; Degirmenci et al., 2008; Galuska et al., 2002; George et al., 1992; Hashimoto et al., 2000; Ohnishi et al., 2000; Ryu et al., 1999; Starkstein et al., 2000; Zilbovicius et al., 2000), as well as a variety of subcortical regions including basal ganglia (Degirmenci et al., 2008; Ryu et al., 1999; Starkstein et al., 2000), cerebellum (Ryu et al., 1999), limbic structures (Ito et al., 2005; Ohnishi et al., 2000), and thalamus (Ito et al., 2005; Ryu et al., 1999; Starkstein et al., 2000)—i.e., in a widely distributed set of brain regions. It is interesting to note that even with this regional variation in localization, 17 of the 18 publications showed that cerebral perfusion was *reduced*; in the only study reporting some areas of localized hyperfusion, these areas were found in the middle of the frontal pole and temporal lobe, which were more broadly hypoperfused (McKelvey et al., 1995). Only one study showed no difference in perfusion between autistic and control subjects (Herold et al., 1988). It is interesting to note that the variably located small white matter hyperintensities identified in a fair number of clinical scans, as noted earlier, may possibly be attributable to localized areas of hypoperfusion (Brickman et al., 2009). Possibly because virtually all of the autism perfusion studies studies were oriented toward testing neuropsychological rather than pathophysiological hypotheses, there were no probes or tests reported to unearth the tissue-level alterations that might be underlying these reductions in blood flow in these brains.

Regional findings

One of the lessons of the above explorations of the tendency toward large brain size in autism is that bigger is not always better. Large is easily assumed to be constituted by more neurons performing more neural processing in a usefully organized fashion—but this may not be the case. Another way of stating this is that it is not size, so much as function and mechanism, that determine impact. This lesson is pertinent not only in addressing the phenomenon of large brains, but also in making sense of the findings that have emerged in investigating regions of interest in the autistic brain. Region-oriented neuroanatomical studies in autism have been challenged by three major factors: the heterogeneity of findings across subjects and cohorts, the subtlety of the bulk of the findings, and the technical challenges involved in measuring subtle findings (e.g. the greater degree of error in measuring the volume of small-brain regions).

Because of these challenges, more advanced imaging techniques beyond volumetrics have increasingly been applied to extend the resolution and discernment of investigations.

Region-based investigations in autism are based both upon descriptive observations and on localized brain areas suggested by behavioral, communication, sensory, motor epileptic, immune-endocrine, and visceral-system characteristics of autism. An early review by Damasio and Maurer, written before the vast bulk of neuroanatomical investigations in autism, is still cogent for its clinically based predictions of the location of anatomical involvement, as well as its reflections on the reasons for, and potential causes of, this distribution of brain change (Damasio & Maurer, 1978). These authors posited that autism arose from abnormalities in the mesolimbic structures associated with neurotransmitter imbalance that might be a consequence of perinatal viral infection, insult to the periventricular watershed area, or genetically determined neurochemical abnormalities; they also posited basal ganglia circuitry abnormalities based on the presence of gait and movement abnormalities. This set of inferences covers a broad range of possibilities, all of which—and more—are still under investigation today.

Limbic System

An obvious set of brain regions to consider as potentially implicated in autism neuroanatomy is the limbic system, given its role in emotional and social processing—functions that are so prominently atypical in the phenotype. Limbic cortical areas are an evolutionarily ancient set of structures, with a less differentiated cortical layering structure but a much denser set of interconnections than most other parts of the cerebral cortex. The limbic area connections with multiple polymodal and premotor cortex regions as well as with subcortical structure (Barbas, 1995; Tucker, 1992) and the robust connections of orbitofrontal and medial prefrontal areas to the amygdala (Ghashghaei & Barbas, 2002) allows these areas to address representations of experience which are less differentiated than those processed by primary sensory and motor cortex. Such a heavily connected set of regions might be preferentially vulnerable to underlying pathophysiological processes that impact connectivity. Certain infectious processes, such as herpes encephalopathy, also are known to preferentially impact some limbic structures.

Neuropathology

The importance of abnormalities in limbic systems was given early support by neuropathological identification of smaller and more tightly packed cells in the hippocampus, subiculum, entorhinal cortex, amygdala, mamillary body, anterior cingulate cortex, and septum. In the amygdala, the most significant increases in cell-packing density were noted in the medial, cortical, and central nuclei, whereas the lateral nucleus did not manifest this phenomenon (Bauman & Kemper, 1994). A later study by this group identified differences in hippocampal CA4 neurons in two cases of infantile autism, with smaller perikaryon area and less dendritic branching (Raymond et al., 1996). This finding could indicate a cellular basis for impaired information processing. A recent study by members of the same group identified reductions in the limbic system of γ-Aminobutyric acid – i.e. GABAergic systems (Blatt et al., 2001; Guptill et al. 2006), but not of six other receptors studied (Blatt et al., 2001). Since GABA is an inhibitory neurotransmitter, a reduction in GABAergic systems could impact a range of functional domains vulnerable to excessive excitation, including sleep, anxiety, sensory processing, and seizures. A number of other neuropathological studies have not found amygdala or other limbic abnormalities (Bailey et al. 1998; Coleman et al., 1985; Guerin et al., 1996; Rodier et al., 1996; Williams et al. 1980).

Neuroimaging

In neuroimaging, the hippocampus and amygdala have been studied both separately and together. Neuroimaging is particularly challenged here not only due to the previously mentioned greater degree of error in measuring the volume of small brain regions, but also due to the difficulties, particularly in earlier imaging studies performed with older scanners and acquisition protocols, in making a clear delineation between the two structures. The volumetric studies of these regions have not yielded consistent results. Piven and colleagues (1998) showed no difference between 35 autistic and 36 control subjects in hippocampal volume. Saitoh (1995) and colleagues found no difference in the cross-sectional area of the posterior hippocampal formation between autistic and control subjects aged 6 to 42, but in a later study found smaller hippocampal volume by a measure of cross-sectional area of the area dentata, sibiculum,

and CA1-CA3 in subjects 29 months to 42 years of age, with the smallest sizes noted in the youngest age group of 4 years and younger (Saitoh, Karns, & Courchesne, 2001). Alyward and colleagues (1999) found amygdala to be significantly smaller in non-retarded adolescents, with greater significance for absolute volume and lesser, but still significant, difference when volumes were adjusted for the impact of total brain volume. Herbert and colleagues (2003) found a trend toward proportional reduction, while Schumann and colleagues (2004) found hippocampal volume to be increased on the right in low-functioning autistic children and adolescents, and bilaterally in high-functioning autistic children and adolescents. Findings of increased size were reported in several other studies using a variety of methods (Abell et al., 1999; Howard et al., 2000; Sparks et al., 2002), with the last of these studies reporting a subgroup with proportional enlargement and another subgroup with greater than proportional enlargement. On the other hand, no amygdala volume differences were found by Haznedar and colleagues (2000).

A number of studies of amygdala volume have included suggestive correlations with other clinically pertinent variables. Schumann and colleagues (2004) showed an enlargement of the amygdala in children with autism ages 7.5–12.5 years, but not in adolescents as compared with controls; furthermore, whereas the amygdala at the start of the younger age range was already enlarged, in the control group it was smaller in the younger children and larger in the older children within that age group. Nacewicz and colleagues (2006) included psychological correlates in their measures of change with age in their 8- to 25-year-old subjects, showing an earlier and more pronounced increase in amygdala volume in those individuals who had normal eye fixation, but little difference in amygdala volume across the same age range in individuals whose level of eye fixation was low (Nacewicz et al., 2006).

Nacewicz and colleagues (2006) also showed that a smaller amygdala was associated with slowness in distinguishing emotional from neutral expression and reduced fixation of eye regions, as well as greater social impairment in childhood according to ADI-R, a parent report measure. Juranek and colleagues (2006) found that anxious/depressed symptoms were significantly correlated with increased total and right amygdala volume, utilizing the Child Behavior Checklist.

Shape

Shape measurement methodologies have provided another way to show differences between limbic structures in autistic, as compared to control, subjects. Several studies aimed at detecting hippocampal shape and thickness differences not detectable through standard volumetric approaches have recently been published. Dager and colleagues (2007) reported an inward deformation of the subiculum, accentuated in a more severe subgroup and associated with deficits in medial temporal lobe function but not in prefrontal function; this shape deformation had previously been reported in studies of medial temporal lobe epilepsy. Nicolson and colleagues used 3-dimensional surface meshes and discerned localized differences with right medial posterior hippocampus volume reduction, that might be consistent with specific abnormalities of the dentate gyrus or hippocampal CA1, CA3, or CA4 regions (Nicolson et al., 2006).

MRS

Proton magnetic resonance spectroscopy has been used to investigate underlying tissue changes in the amygdala-hippocampal region. There have been a number of findings, but the methodologies are not consistent, which as mentioned above is a function of the restriction of MRS to specific regions rather than whole brain, and the wide range of variability in voxel placement that exacerbates the differences produced by disparities in cohort phenotypes, cohort age, and imaging acquisition methodologies. The most consistent finding was lower n-acetyl-aspartate (NAA) (17 out of 49 measures, with 41 showing no change), and NAA/creatine ratios (4 out or 14 measures, with 10 showing no change) (Shetty et al., 2009). Endo and colleagues (2007) examined this with neuropsychological correlates, and found lower NAA/Cr ratios in the right medial temporal lobe particularly pronounced in the autistic, as compared with PDD-NOS and control, groups, which correlated with their performance on the Childhood Autistic Rating Scale-Tokyo Version. Additional findings include higher glutamine and creatine/phosphocreatine in the amygdala-hippocampus than in the parietal lobe (Page et al., 2006), an increase in myo-inositol/creatine in the amygdala-hippocampus as well as cerebellum, and an increase in choline/creatine in left hippocampus and left cerebellum (Gabis et al., 2008).

Two papers by Kleinhans and colleagues (2007 & 2009) have identified a correlation between metabolic and functional abnormalities utilizing MRS and functional MRI in the same subjects. In the 2007 study, five voxels were placed, including three in regions that were centers of activation in functional MRI in a verbal fluency task in healthy controls. NAA was lower in all regions, particularly the left frontal cortex. Among the behavior-neuronal integrity (i.e., MRS) correlations reported, there was a significant positive correlation between the amount of fMRI signal change in the autistic subjects, but not in the controls. In the 2009 study by Kleinhans and colleagues of high-functioning autistic and Asperger adults, there were no group differences in metabolites, but those autistic or Aspergers individuals with the lowest NAA or Cre (creatine/phosphocreatine) levels were found by ADI to have had the most significant clinical impairment in childhood (Kleinhans et al., 2009).

DTI

Diffusion tensor tracking methodologies have been utilized to study hippocampal-fusiform and amygdala-fusiform pathways (Conturo et al., 2008). In this methodology the measures were subtle, with the macrostructural measures (pathway volume, length, and area) sensitive at the millimeter scale and the microstructural measures (maximum and minimum diffusion coefficients) sensitive at the micron scale; these measures clearly go beyond the sensitivity or resolution of volumetrics. The main finding, noted to be worse in individuals with poorer face recognition or lower IQ scores, was a micron-scale reduction in the diffusion perpendicular to the axis of the white-matter tracts in right hippocampal-fugal pathways. In contrast, there were no detectable macrostructural abnormalities, which led the authors to suggest that the appropriate "machinery" is in place, but its operations are abnormal—in essence inferring that their findings point to underlying mechanisms of autism that are functional rather than structural.

Cerebellum

Studies of the cerebellum have been motivated by a combination of empirical observations of abnormalities and a growing body of literature implicating the cerebellum not only in motor coordination, but in a range of cognitive, affective, and language functions highly pertinent to autism (Schmahmann, 2004; Schmahmann & Caplan 2006; Schmahmann & Pandya, 2008).

Early neuropathological studies indicated abnormalities in the cerebellum. These included a reduction in the number of Purkinje cell alterations in cerebellar nuclei (Bauman & Kemper, 1996). Of the two dozen postmortem cases of autism in the literature, 19 showed decreased density of Purkinje cells (Amaral, Schumann, & Nordahl, 2008). Whether this is due to a loss of cells, or to an alteration of cell functions or properties affecting their binding to histopathological stains, has not been clarified. A recent study suggests that the latter might be contributory. This study used a different staining technique; whereas prior studies had used Nissl staining, here calbindin was chosen because it is a more reliable marker for Purkinje cells. When this method was used, no group differences between autistic and control tissue samples were found in the density of Purkinje cells, with three of the six showing normal density, and the other three showing reduced density, but no correlation of density reduction with severity of autism (Whitney, Kemper, Bauman, Rosene, & Blatt, 2008). The poor uptake of Nissl stain by Purkinje cells in tissue from individuals with autism might nevertheless have some significance, in that it could indicate impaired function of these cells, such as chromatolysis (a depletion of somatic rough endoplasmic reticulum) related to chronically diseased and weakened cells during life.

More recently, the same group has reported a series of microanatomical findings pertinent to the functional features of cerebellar circuitry. A 40% reduction in the level of glutamate decarboxylase 67 isoform (GAD67, which catalyzes GABA synthesis) was identified in Purkinje cells, suggesting that these cells were contributing less inhibitory input to neural circuitry, presumably leading to a net gain in excitation (Yip, Soghomonian, & Blatt, 2007). Interestingly, upstream of Purkinje cells, there appear to be alterations in cerebellar basket and stellate cell interneurons also related to the balance of excitation and inhibition: an upregulation of GAD67 in basket cells was identified, and in the same study a trend toward a small increase was also noted in stellate cells. This seems to suggest an increased feed-forward inhibition to Purkinje cells whose inhibitory GAD67 production is already reduced. This yields a combination of mutually reinforcing alterations: upstream cells are inhibiting the Purkinje cell, lessening its inhibitory functioning, and at the same time the

Purkinje cell itself is also showing reduced intrinsic contribution to inhibitory circuitry. The net result is a loss of inhibition, reducing the denominator in the excitation/inhibition ratio and thereby increasing net excitation. This is consistent with a widely discussed model of an increase in the ratio of excitation to inhibition as underlying autism (Levitt, Eagleson, & Powell, 2004; Rubenstein & Merzenich, 2003). Kern has argued that Purkinje cell loss or dysfunction could result from injury and not necessarily developmental derangement, and presents literature evidence that Purkinje cells are selectively vulnerable to ischemia, hypoxia, excitotoxicity, G protein dysfunction, viral infections (e.g. thiamine), heavy metals, various toxins, and chronic malabsorption syndrome (e.g. celiac disease, inflammatory bowel disease; Kern, 2003).

There have been a variety of other cerebellar neuropathological findings. Abnormalities in the cerebellar cholinergic system have been identified. Lee and colleagues identified a reduction in the high-affinity a4 receptor in the granule cell, as well as the Purkinje and molecular layers, with a possibly compensatory increase in the a7 receptor subunit that was significant in the granule cell layer (Lee et al., 2002). The above-mentioned Vargas study identifying innate immune activation (including microglial and astroglial activation and proinflammatory cytokines) in the brains of individuals with autism found that the cerebellum was a main focus of this neuroinflammation among the regions studied (Vargas et al., 2005). It has also been noted that serum from children with ASD contains autoantibodies to specific cells in the cerebellum (Wills et al., 2009), and that in animal models of mid-gestation respiratory infection, postnatal cerebellar pathology in the offspring resembles that observed in autism (Shi et al., 2009).

Vermis area

The vermal lobules are midline structures in the cerebellum, the areas of which can be measured by tracing their outline on a single mid-sagittal section of a scan. An early report of cerebellar vermal lobules VI-VII hypoplasia (Courchesne et al., 1988) was followed by a substantial number of further papers reporting measurements of this area. These have been reviewed and debated in detail elsewhere (Courchesne, 1999; Courchesne, Townsend, & Saitoh, 1995; Filipek, 1995; Piven & Arndt, 1995; Piven et al., 1999). While some of the papers replicated the findings of hypoplasia, other did not.

Smaller cerebellar vermal lobules VI-VII were found in several studies (Courchesne et al., 1988; Gaffney et al., 1987; Murakami et al., 1989; Saitoh et al., 1995), while some later studies discerned a subgroup with an area increase (Courchesne et al. 1994). However, several other studies found no difference in cerebellar vermal lobules (Elia et al., 2000; Filipek et al., 1992; Garber & Ritvo, 1992; Holttum et al., 1992; Kleiman, Neff, & Rosman, 1992;Nowell et al., 1990; Piven et al. 1992, 1997; Rumsey & Hamburger, 1988). It was also argued that vermal hypoplasia was found in a number of other neurodevelopmental disorders, and therefore was not specific to autism (Ciesielski & Knight, 1994; Schaefer et al., 1996).

Volume

Cerebellar volume is a less frequently performed measure because it requires assessment of slices throughout the entire structure (which in the earlier days of MRI scans was visualized with poor resolution); when performed it has generally yielded increased volume in autism, although to different degrees. Two studies (Piven et al., 1997; Sparks et al., 2002) showed cerebellar increase proportional to increased total brain volume. Herbert and colleagues (2003) similarly found that total cerebellar volume was greater in autism than in controls, but not different after adjustment for total brain volume; this finding was in the same set of brains where earlier analysis had found no difference in midline vermal lobule VI-VI areas (Filipek et al., 1992). However, Hardan and colleagues (2001) found cerebellar volumes to be both relatively and absolutely larger. Using voxel-based morphometry, the metrics of which (as discussed in the earlier methodology section) are not directly comparable to those used in the above studies, Abell and colleagues (1999) also found increased gray matter volume bilaterally in the cerebellum. Cerebellar volume increase was not found in a comparison of autistic subjects with and without macrocephaly to normocephalic and macrocephalic typically developing individuals (Cleavinger et al., 2008).

Cerebellar white matter

Improvements in posterior fossa resolution have more recently allowed the segmentation of cerebellar gray and white matter; this measure has led to findings suggesting that overall cerebellar volume increase may be due to an increase in cerebellar white matter. The above-mentioned neuroinflammation in the cerebellum (Vargas et al., 2005) was prominent in the cerebellar white matter. In the only study in which this was measured, cerebellar white matter was as much as 39% larger in autism than in controls aged 2 to 4 years (Courchesne et al., 2001). Boddaert's group found a mean decrease in the voxel-based morphometry measure discussed above of cerebellar "white matter concentration" in 21 school-age children with autism (Boddaert et al., 2004), though this measure cannot be mapped onto volume measurements, as it is a metric of different physical properties, and a metric of reduced density cannot distinguish between increased water and reduced size.

Thalamus

The thalamus is a critical relay station in brain information processing and is of great potential interest in autism research, due to its central role in connectivity, coordination, and sensory modulation. Abnormalities in the thalamus have been found by various measures. Volumetric findings are not entirely consistent. One study showed reduced thalamic volume relative to total brain volume (Tsatsanis et al., 2003), while another showed proportional increase in thalamic volume that lost significance when adjusted for overall brain size (Herbert et al., 2003); a third study showed a lack of linear relationship between the volumes of thalamus and brain (Hardan et al., 2006). Decreased "gray matter concentration" was found in the thalamus using voxel-based morphometry (Waiter et al., 2005). Perfusion abnormalities have been found by SPECT (Ito et al., 2005; Ryu et al., 1999; Starkstein et al., 2000) and by PET (Haznedar et al., 2006; Horwitz et al. 1988). MRS has shown reduced NAA in thalamus (Friedman et al., 2003). Hardan and colleagues investigated the possibility of a relationship between metabolic and functional abnormalities in the thalamus; their findings included lower levels of N-acetylaspartate (NAA), phosphocreatine and creatine, and choline-containing metabolites in the left thalamus autism group, compared with controls even in the absence of volumetric differences, and some limited relationships between questionnaire measures of sensory abnormalities and proton MRS metabolites (Hardan et al., 2008). Nicotinic abnormalities in the cholinergic system in the thalamus have been identified in autism (Ray et al., 2005). Brain-specific antibodies to proteins in the thalamus and hypothalamus have been identified in plasma from a subset of children with autism (Cabanlit et al., 2007).

Basal Ganglia

The basal ganglia are of potential interest in autism because of their contributions to movement and movement abnormalities such as tics and stereotypies, as well as for to the role they play in motivation, repetitive behaviors, and obsessiveness. These regions have been investigated using volumetrics, spectroscopy, perfusion measures, immune measures, and animal models, with findings summarized in Table 3-2. MacFabe and colleagues (2007) identified histopathological abnormalities and electrophysiological spiking in the caudate associated with tics in an animal model of environmentally induced autistic-like behaviors (MacFabe et al., 2007). A relationship has been identified of larger caudate volume at times of episodes of symptoms of PANDAS (an acronym for Pediatric Autoimmune Neuropsychiatric Disorders Associated with Streptotoccus)(Giedd et al., 2000), but there is no direct evidence of an analogous immune-infectious syndrome with brain volume in the case of autism.

Table 3-2 Basal Ganglia Findings

Study	Subject characteristics	Measure	Regions
Hardan et al., 2003	40 Aut Non-MR, 41 TD 8-45 yo	Volume Motor	Weaker motor functioniong in autistic group not accompanied by basal ganglia volumetric differences
Hollander et al., 2005	18 ASD, 17TD 17-57 yo	Volume ADI	Larger right caudate volume Correlation of total caudate and putamen volumes with repetitive behaviors on the ADI-C subscale
Haznedar et al., 2006	17 ASD, 17 TD 17-56 yo	Volume ADI Glucose metabolism	Greater right caudate volume with reduced glucose metabolism in the ventral caudate
Rojas et al., 2006	24 Aut, 23 TD 7-44 yo	VBM	Enlarged caudate nucleus
Langen et al., 2007	Sample 1: 21 HFA, 21 TD, 10-14 yo Sample 2 21 HFA, 21 TD, 15-24yo	Volume	Increased caudate volume associated with repetitive behaviors Caudate changes localize to head of caudate Caudate grew bigger over time in autism but decreased in volume over time in controls
Degirmenci et al., 2008	10 Aut, 6.7±1.7 yo; 5 TD, 6.4±1.4 yo Relatives: (8 mothers, 39± 4 yo; 8 fathers 36 ± 5 yo; 7 siblings, 13 ± 5 yo Controls for Relatives: Parents: 5M, 5F, 37±3 yo 22 controls for siblings, 5.4-15.7yo	SPECT	Reduced right caudate perfusion Other findings reviewed in section on perfusion
Levitt et al., 2003	22 Aut + ASD 5.4-15.7 yo 20 TD 6.8-16.3 yo	MRS	Creatine/Phosphocreatine ratio higher in head of right caudate but lower in body of left caudate
Singh and Rivas, 2004	68 Aut, 4-12 yo 30 TD, 5-12 yo	Immuno-blotting	Serum antibodies to caudate nucleus in 49% of subjects studied
MacFabe et al., 2007	74 adult male Long–Evans	Animal model	Animal model of environmentally induced autistic features using proprionic acid Histopathological abnormalities and caudate spiking associated with tics

Cerebral lobes

While a growing body of functional imaging evidence suggests that the connectivity between frontal lobes and other parts of the brain is particularly affected in autism, this literature is beyond the scope of the present neuroanatomical review (see Chapter 21). What insights into lobar anatomy have emerged from anatomical investigations? The substantial impact upon frontal lobe volumes of overall brain enlargement has already been reviewed above (Carper et al., 2002; Herbert et al. 2004). Frontal lobe volume has been measured as inversely correlated with cerebellar volume (Carper & Courchesne, 2000), and localized enlargement of the frontal lobes early in autism development has been noted (Carper & Courchesne, 2005). Orbitofrontal cortical (OFC) gray matter volume was measured as reduced in the right lateral OFC, and correlations between social deficits and white matter OFC structures were observed.

Temporal lobe involvement has also been noted. Superior temporal lobe abnormalities have been noted in a number of studies (Boddaert et al., 2004; Herbert et al., 2002). While Lainhart's group did not observe overall differences in temporal lobe volume (Bigler et al., 2003), they measured abnormalities in the left fusiform gyrus, the right temporal stem, and the right inferior temporal gyrus gray matter, with similarities noted between subjects with autism and subjects with reading difficulties (Neeley et al., 2007). White matter microstructure was also noted to be abnormal in these subregions of the temporal lobe (Lee et al., 2007). Reduced left planum temporale volume (Rojas et al., 2002) and lack of normal planum temporale asymmetry (Rojas et al., 2005) have been measured.

Parietal lobe involvement has been variable, with reductions noted in a subgroup (Courchesne, Press, & Yeung-Courchesne, 1993) and in parietal white matter (Ke et al., 2008), enlargement noted by others (Carper et al., 2002; Herbert et al., 2004; Piven et al., 1996), and lack of difference by yet others (Hazlett et al., 2006). Occipital lobe changes have not been strongly observed, perhaps because of an apparent anterior-to-posterior gradient in the degree of hyperplasia (Carper et al., 2002).

SUMMARY AND CONCLUSION

Overall, we clearly have a massive amount of evidence that there are differences in anatomy between autistic and non-autistic individuals. However, these differences are not always consistent, and while there are many potential contributors and explanations, it is not always clear specifically how to account for the inconsistencies. Developmental trajectory undoubtedly plays a role in total brain volume and in the volumes of regions such as the caudate and the amygdala. Technical issues may complicate measures, such as the greater risk of error involved in quantifying volumes of small regions. Imaging analysis methods may yield somewhat different boundaries between laboratories, and regional naming conventions may be idiosyncratic and inconsistent across sites. A study may have hypothesis-driven reasons for focusing on a subset of regions, and may give the impression that the findings they report are localized, when in fact a more broadly focused study of the same sample might identify similar findings in other regions as well. For example, Herbert and colleagues (2002) reported altered brain asymmetry in language-associated regions; however, using the same set of brains but performing a whole-brain analysis, they reported a much more widespread set of asymmetry alterations (Herbert et al., 2005). There is also the issue of heterogeneity in autism. It is by now clear that it is possible to meet the behaviourally defined criteria of "autism spectrum disorders" through a wide range of underlying biological challenges to brain function. It is likely, for example, that brain connectivity may be challenged by a variety of different underlying mechanisms (e.g., various gene variants affecting synapses, various environmental challenges reducing mitochondrial efficiency at synapses, astroglial activation that compromises the quality of tripartite synapse function, and much more). Overall, this combination of inconsistent findings, poorly understood impact of development, methodological differences between labs and underlying heterogeneity undoubtedly contributes to the challenge of putting together a coherent picture of autism neuroanatomy.

An additional potential contributor to the heterogeneity of anatomical (and other) findings in autism is the nature of the impact of environmental or physiological factors, such as immune alterations, infectious exposures, and toxic exposures, upon the brain. These factors may alter cellular functioning in a fashion that is either weakly or not at all targeted to specific regions, and whose localization may thus be somewhat accidental rather than necessarily revealing of regional alterations intrinsic to autism. This (along with the region-restricted focus of some of the studies) may contribute to explaining the greatly distributed localization of perfusion abnormalities in autism, even while almost every study reported that perfusion is reduced. Reduced perfusion is what would be expected in the setting of immune alterations or infectious or toxic exposures, given their impact on glial cells, membrane and transport function, and various other physiological factors. Such changes could further alter synaptic, oscillatory, and connectivity dynamics in a way that would change neural systems function. This set of considerations raises the possibility that localizations of anatomical and neural systems dysfunctions may be downstream of pathophysiological impacts, rather than direct outcomes of regionally targeted causal factors.

Despite all of these potential contributors to heterogeneity and inter-study inconsistencies, there are a number of anatomical findings that are consistent across at least a preponderance of studies. Brain size (head circumference, brain volume, brain weight) is on average larger in younger subjects, with an intriguing developmental trajectory, while the corpus callosum is not enlarged proportional to overall enlargement and is mostly measured as smaller. There is involvement in the cerebellum, limbic system, basal ganglia, thalamus, and white matter, though the specific character of this involvement varies markedly across studies and age groups. Perfusion is lower, though the distribution of this perfusion has varied in measures to date. Metabolic and diffusion tensor imaging measures mostly suggest some kind of reduction in density of metabolites and in fiber integrity. Seen together, this picture, even with all its remaining loose ends, still represents a substantial advance over what was known a decade ago, and a stronger pace of progress in the next decade can be reasonably expected.

The comprehensiveness of this discussion is limited by its restriction to physical anatomy. A fuller picture would come from integrating the structural and functional advances being made in the field, but for now that will need to be done by the reader in relation to other chapters in this volume. The fact that we are seeing growing number of studies integrating measures of volume, metabolism, or perfusion with measures of functional activation suggests that we are getting more systematic in probing for the pathophysiological mediators of neuropsychological dysfunction. Pathophysiology is a critical and active intermediary. As DTI, MRS, and perfusion imaging are more widely utilized, as neuropathology advances, and as more

multimodal studies are performed, a more integrated set of empirically grounded linkages across the levels of autism will begin to emerge.

References

Abell, F., Krams, M., Ashburner, J., Passingham, R., Friston, K., Frackowiak, R., Happe, F. Frith, C., & Frith, U. (1999.) The neuroanatomy of autism: A voxel-based whole brain analysis of structural scans. Neuroreport, 10(8), 1647–1651.

Alexander, A. L., Lee, J. E., Lazar, M., Boudos, R., Dubray, M. B., Oakes, T. R., Miller, J. N., Lu, J., Jeong, E. K., McMahon, W. M., Bigler, E. D. & Lainhart, J. E. (2007). Diffusion tensor imaging of the corpus callosum in autism. Neuroimage, 34(1), 61–73.

Amaral, D. G., Schumann, C. M., and Nordahl, C. W. (2008.) Neuroanatomy of autism. Trends Neurosci, 31(3), 137–145.

Anticevic, A., Dierker, D. L., Gillespie, S. K., Repovs, G.,Csernansky, J. G., Van Essen, D. C., & Barch, D. M. (2008). Comparing surface-based and volume-based analyses of functional neuroimaging data in patients with schizophrenia. Neuroimage, 41(3), 835–848.

Aschner, M., Allen, J. W., Kimelberg, H. K., LoPachin, R. M. & Streit, W. J. (1999). Glial cells in neurotoxicity development. Annu Rev Pharmacol Toxicol, 39, 151–173.

Ashburner, J., & Friston, K. J. (2000). Voxel-based morphometry—the methods. Neuroimage, 11(6 Pt 1), 805–821.

Ashburner, J., Hutton, C., Frackowiak, R., Johnsrude, I., Price, C., & Friston, K. (1998). Identifying global anatomical differences: Deformation-based morphometry. Hum Brain Mapp, 6(5-6), 348–357.

Ashwood, P., & Van de Water, J. (2004). A review of autism and the immune response. Clin Dev Immunol, 11(2), 165–174.

Ashwood, P., Wills, S. & Van de Water, J. (2006). The immune response in autism: A new frontier for autism research. J Leukoc Biol, 80(1), 1–15.

Aylward, E. H., Minshew, N. J., Goldstein, G., Honeycutt, N. A., Augustine, A. M., Yates, K. O., Barta, P. E., & Pearlson, G. D. (1999). MRI volumes of amygdala and hippocampus in non-mentally retarded autistic adolescents and adults. Neurology, 53(9), 2145–2150.

Bailey, A., Luthert, P., Dean, A., Harding, B., Janota, I., Montgomery, M., Rutter, M., & Lantos, P. (1998). A clinicopathological study of autism. Brain, 121 (Pt 5), 889–905.

Barbas, H. (1995). Anatomic basis of cognitive-emotional interactions in the primate prefrontal cortex. Neurosci Biobehav Rev, 19(3), 499–510.

Bauman, M. L., & Kemper, T. L. (1985). Histoanatomic observations of the brain in early infantile autism. Neurology, 35, 866–874.

Bauman, M. L., & Kemper, T. L. (1996). Observations on the Purkinje cells in the cerebellar vermis in autism. *J Neuropathol Exp Neurol*, 55, 613.

Bauman, M. L., & Kemper, T. L. (1994). Neuroanatomic observations of the brain in autism. In M. L. Bauman, T. L. Kemper (Eds.), *The Neurobiology of Autism* (pp. 119–145). Baltimore: The Johns Hopkins University Press.

Ben Bashat, D., Kronfeld-Duenias, V., Zachor, D. A., Ekstein, P. M., Hendler, T. Tarrasch, R., Even, A., Levy, Y., & Ben Sira, L. (2007). Accelerated maturation of white matter in young children with autism: A high b value DWI study. *Neuroimage*, 37(1), 40–47.

Bigler, E. D., Tate, D. F., Neeley, E. S., Wolfson, L. J., Miller, M. J., Rice, S. A., Cleavinger, H., Anderson, C., Coon, H.,Ozonoff, S., Johnson, M., Dinh, E., Lu, J., Mc Mahon, W., & Lainhart, J. E. (2003). Temporal lobe, autism, and macrocephaly. *AJNR Am J Neuroradiol*, 24(10), 2066–2076.

Blatt, G. J., Fitzgerald, C. M., Guptill, J. T., Booker, A. B., Kemper, T. L., &Bauman, M. L.(2001). Density and distribution of hippocampal neurotransmitter receptors in autism: An autoradiographic study. *J Autism Dev Disord*, 31(6), 537–543.

Boddaert, N., Chabane, N. Barthelemy, C., Bourgeois, M., Poline, J. B., Brunelle, F., Samson, Y., & Zilbovicius, M.(2002). Bitemporal lobe dysfunction in infantile autism: Positron emission tomography study. *J Radiol*, 83(12 Pt 1), 1829–1833.

Boddaert, N., Chabane, N., Gervais, H., Good, C. D., Bourgeois, M., Plumet, M. H., Barthelemy, C., Mouren, M. C., Artiges, E., Samson, Y., Brunelle, F., Frackowiak, R. S., & Zilbovicius, M. (2004). Superior temporal sulcus anatomical abnormalities in childhood autism: A voxel-based morphometry MRI study. *Neuroimage*, 23(1), 364–369.

Boddaert, N., Zilbovicius, M., Philipe, A., Robel, L., Bourgeois, M., Barthelemy, C., Seidenwurm, D., Meresse, I., Laurier, L., Desguerre, I., Bahi-Buisson, N., Brunelle, F., Munnich, A., Samson, Y., Mouren, M. C., & Chabane, N. (2009). MRI findings in 77 children with non-syndromic autistic disorder. *PLoS One*, 4(2), e4415.

Brickman, A. M., Zahra, A., Muraskin, J., Steffener, J., Holland, C. M., Habeck, C., Borogovac, A., Ramos, M. A., Brown, T. R., Asllani, I., & Stern, Y. (2009). Reduction in cerebral blood flow in areas appearing as white matter hyperintensities on magnetic resonance imaging. *Psychiatry Res*, 172(2), 117–120.

Bruneau, N., Bonnet-Brilhault, F., Gomot, M., Adrien, J. L., & Barthelemy, C. (2003). Cortical auditory processing and communication in children with autism: Electrophysiological/behavioral relations. *Int J Psychophysiol*, 51(1), 17–25.

Burroni, L., Orsi, A., Monti, L., Hayek, Y., Rocchi, R., & Vattimo, A. G . (2008). Regional cerebral blood flow in childhood autism: A SPET study with SPM evaluation. *Nucl Med Commun*, 29(2), 150–156.

Buxhoeveden, D. P., Switala, A. E., Litaker, M., Roy, E., & Casanova, M. F. (2001). Lateralization of minicolumns in human planum temporale is absent in nonhuman primate cortex. *Brain Behav Evol*, 57(6), 349–358.

Cabanlit, M., Wills, S., Goines, P., Ashwood, P., & Van de Water, J. (2007). Brain-specific autoantibodies in the plasma of subjects with autistic spectrum disorder. *Ann N Y Acad Sci*, 1107, 92–103.

Carper, R. A., & Courchesne, E. (2000). Inverse correlation between frontal lobe and cerebellum sizes in children with autism. *Brain*, 123(Pt 4), 836–844.

Carper, R. A., & Courchesne, E. (2005). Localized enlargement of the frontal cortex in early autism. *Biol Psychiatry*, 57(2), 126–133.

Carper, R. A., Moses, P., Tigue, Z. D., & Courchesne, E. (2002). Cerebral lobes in autism: Early hyperplasia and abnormal age effects. *Neuroimage*, 16(4), 1038–1051.

Casanova, M. F. (2004). White matter volume increase and minicolumns in autism. *Ann Neurol*, 56(3), 453; author reply 454.

Casanova, M. F., Buxhoeveden, D. P., & Brown, C. (2002). Clinical and macroscopic correlates of minicolumnar pathology in autism. *J Child Neurol*, 17(9), 692–695.

Casanova, M. F., Buxhoeveden, D. P., Switala, A. E., & Roy, E. (2002a). Minicolumnar pathology in autism. *Neurology*, 58(3), 428–432.

Casanova, M. F., Buxhoeveden, D. P., Switala, A. E., & Roy, E. (2002b). Neuronal density and architecture (Gray Level Index) in the brains of autistic patients. *J Child Neurol*, 17(7), 515–521.

Caviness, V. S. Jr, Lange, N. T., Makris, N., Herbert, M. R., & Kennedy, D. N. (1999). MRI-based brain volumetrics: Emergence of a developmental brain science. *Brain Dev*, 21(5), 289–295.

Chance, S. A., Casanova, M. F., Switala, A. E.,& Crow, T. J. (2008). Auditory cortex asymmetry, altered minicolumn spacing and absence of ageing effects in schizophrenia. *Brain*, 131(Pt 12), 3178–3192.

Chandana, S. R., Behen, M. E., Juhasz, C., Muzik, O., Rothermel, R. D., Mangner, T. J., Chakraborty, P. K., Chugani, H. T., & Chugani, D. C. (2005). Significance of abnormalities in developmental trajectory and asymmetry of cortical serotonin synthesis in autism. *Int J Dev Neurosci*, 23(2–3), 171–182.

Chiron, C., Leboyer, M., Leon, F., Jambaque, I., Nuttin, C., & Syrota, A. (1995). SPECT of the brain in childhood autism: Evidence for a lack of normal hemispheric asymmetry. *Dev Med Child Neurol*, 37(10), 849–860.

Chugani, D. C., Muzik, O., Rothermel, R., Behen, M., Chakraborty, P., Mangner, T., da Silva, E. A., & Chugani, H. T. (1997). Altered serotonin synthesis in the dentatothalamocortical pathway in autistic boys. *Ann Neurol*, 42(4), 666–669.

Ciaranello, R. D., VandenBerg, S. R., & T. F. Anders. (1982). Intrinsic and extrinsic determinants of neuronal development: relation to infantile autism. *J Autism Dev Disord*, 12(2), 115–145.

Ciesielski, K. T., & Knight, J. E. (1994). Cerebellar abnormality in autism: A nonspecific effect of early brain damage? *Acta Neurobiol Exp (Warsz)* 54(2), 151–154.

Coleman, P. D., Romano, J., Lapham, L., & Simon, W. (1985). Cell counts in cerebral cortex of an autistic patient. *Journal of Autism and Developmental Disorders*, 15, 245–255.

Conturo, T. E., Williams, D. L., Smith, C. D., Gultepe, E. Akbudak, E., & Minshew, N. J. (2008). Neuronal fiber pathway abnormalities in autism: An initial MRI diffusion tensor tracking study of hippocampo-fusiform and amygdalo-fusiform pathways. *J Int Neuropsychol Soc*, 14(6), 933–946.

Courchesne, E. (1999). An MRI study of autism: the cerebellum revisited. *Neurology*, 52(5), 1106.

Courchesne, E., Carper, R., & Akshoomoff, N. (2003). Evidence of brain overgrowth in the first year of life in autism. *JAMA* 290(3), 337–344.

Courchesne, E., Karns, C. M., Davis, H. R., Ziccardi, R., Carper, R. A., Tigue, Z. D., Chisum, H. J., Moses, P., Pierce, K., Lord, C., Lincoln, A. J., Pizzo, S., Schreibman, L., Haas, R. H., Akshoomoff, N. A., & Courchesne, R. Y. (2001). Unusual brain growth patterns in early life in patients with autistic disorder: An MRI study. *Neurology*, 57(2), 245–254.

Courchesne, E., & Pierce, K. (2005a). Why the frontal cortex in autism might be talking only to itself: local over-connectivity but long-distance disconnection. *Curr Opin Neurobiol*, 15(2), 225–230.

Courchesne, E., & Pierce, K. (2005b.) Brain overgrowth in autism during a critical time in development: Implications for frontal pyramidal neuron and interneuron development and connectivity. *Int J Dev Neurosci*, 23(2–3), 153–170.

Courchesne, E., Press, G. A., & Yeung-Courchesne, R. (1993). Parietal lobe abnormalities detected with MR in patients with infantile autism [see comments]. *Am J Roentgenol*, 160(2), 387–393.

Courchesne, E., Saitoh, O., Yeung-Courchesne, R., Press, G. A., Lincoln, A. J., Haas, R. H., & Schreibman, L. (1994). Abnormality of cerebellar vermian lobules VI and VII in patients with infantile autism: Identification of hypoplastic and hyperplastic subgroups with MR imaging. *Am J Roentgenol*, 162(1), 123–130.

Courchesne, E., Yeung-Courchesne, R., Pres, G. A., Hesselink, J. R., & Jernigan, T. L. (1988). Hypoplasia of cerebellar vermal lobules VI and VII in autism. *New England Journal of Medicine*, 318(21), 1349–1354.

Courchesne, E., Townsend, J., & Saitoh, O. (1995). Reply from the authors to Piven & Arndt. *Neurology*, 45, 399–402.

Craig, A. D. (2005). Forebrain emotional asymmetry: A neuroanatomical basis? *Trends Cogn Sci*, 9(12), 566–571.

Dager, S. R., Friedman, S. D., Petropoulos, H., & Shaw, D. W. W. (2008). Imaging evidence for pathological brain development in Autism Spectrum Disorders. In A. Zimmerman (Ed.), *Autism: Current theories and evidence* (361–379). Totowa, NJ: Humana Press.

Dager, S. R., Wang, L., Friedman, S. D., Shaw, D. W., Constantino, J. N., Artru, A. A., Dawson, G., & Csernansky, J. G. (2007). Shape mapping of the hippocampus in young children with autism spectrum disorder. *AJNR Am J Neuroradiol*, 28(4), 672–677.

Damasio, A. R., & Maurer, R. G. (1978). A neurological model for childhood autism. *Archives of Neurology*, 35, 777–786.

Davidovitch, M., Golan, D., Vardi, O., Lev, D., & Lerman-Sagie, T. (2009). Head circumference of Israeli children with autism spectrum disorder. International Meeting for Autism, Chicago, Poster.

Davidovitch, M., Patterson, B., & Gartside, P. (1996). Head circumference measurements in children with autism. *J Child Neurol*, 11, 389–393.

Dawson, G., Finley, C., Phillips, S., & Galpert, L. (1986). Hemispheric specialization and the language abilities of autistic children. *Child Dev*, 57(6), 1440–1453.

Dawson, G., Finley, C., Phillips, S., Galpert, L., & Lewy, A. (1988). Reduced P3 amplitude of the event-related brain potential: Its relationship to language ability in autism. *J Autism Dev Disord*, 18(4), 493–504.

Dawson, G., Finley, C., Phillips, S., & Lewy, A. (1989). A comparison of hemispheric asymmetries in speech-related brain potentials of autistic and dysphasic children. *Brain Lang*, 37(1), 26–41.

Dawson, G., Warrenburg, S., & Fuller, P. (1983). Hemisphere functioning and motor imitation in autistic persons. *Brain Cogn*, 2(4), 346–354.

De Fosse, L., Hodge, S. M., Makris, N., Kennedy, D. N., Caviness, V. S., Mcgrath, L., Steele, S., Ziegler, D. A., Herbert, M. R., Frazier, J. A., Tager-Flusberg, H., & Harris, G. J. (2004). Language-association cortex asymmetry in autism and specific language impairment. *Annals of Neurology*, 56(6), 757–766.

Degirmenci, B., Miral, S., Kaya, G. C., Iyilikci, L., Arslan, G., Baykara, A., Evren, I., & Durak, H. (2008). Technetium-99m HMPAO brain SPECT in autistic children and their families. *Psychiatry Res*, 162(3), 236–243.

Deibler, A. R., Pollock, J. M., Kraft, R. A., Tan, H., Burdette, J. H., & Maldjian, J. A. (2008a). Arterial spin-labeling in routine clinical practice, part 2: Hypoperfusion patterns. *AJNR Am J Neuroradiol*, 29(7), 1235–1241.

Deibler, A. R., Pollock, J. M., Kraft, R. A., Tan, H., Burdette, J. H., & Maldjian, J. A. (2008b). Arterial spin-labeling in routine clinical practice, part 1: Technique and artifacts. *AJNR Am J Neuroradiol*, 29(7), 1228–1234.

Dementieva, Y. A., Vance, D. D., Donnelly, S. L., Elston, L. A., Wolpert, C. M., Ravan, S. A., DeLong, G. R., Abramson, R. K., Wright, H. H., &. Cuccaro, M. L. (2005). Accelerated head growth in early development of individuals with autism. *Pediatr Neurol*, 32(2), 102–108.

Deutsch, C. K., &. Joseph, R. M. . (2003). Brief report: Cognitive correlates of enlarged head circumference in children with autism. *J Autism Dev Disord*, 33(2), 209–215.

DeVito, T. J., Drost, D. J., Neufeld, R. W., Rajakumar, N., Pavlosky, W., Williamson, P., & Nicolson, R. (2007). Evidence for cortical dysfunction in autism: A proton magnetic resonance spectroscopic imaging study. *Biol Psychiatry*, 61(4), 465–473.

Eckert, M. A., Leonard, C. M., Molloy, E. A., Blumenthal, J., Zijdenbos, A., & Giedd, J. N. (2002). The epigenesis of planum temporale asymmetry in twins. *Cerebral Cortex*, 12(7), 749–755.

Egaas, B., Courchesne, E., & Saitoh, O. (1995). Reduced size of corpus callosum in autism. *Arch Neurol*, 52(8), 794–801.

Elder, L. M., Dawson, G., Toth, K., Fein, D., & Munson, J. (2008). Head circumference as an early predictor of autism symptoms in younger siblings of children with autism spectrum disorder. *J Autism Dev Disord*, 38(6), 1104–1111.

Elia, M., Ferri, R., Musumeci, S. A., Panerai, S., Bottitta, M., & Scuderi, C. (2000). Clinical correlates of brain morphometric features of subjects with low- functioning autistic disorder. *J Child Neurol*, 15(8), 504–508.

Endo, T., Shioiri, T., Kitamura, H., Kimura, T., Endo, S., Masuzawa, N., & Someya, T. (2007). Altered chemical metabolites in the amygdala-hippocampus region contribute to autistic symptoms of autism spectrum disorders. *Biol Psychiatry*, 62(9), 1030–1037.

Fidler, D. J., Bailey, J. N., & Smalley, S. L. (2000). Macrocephaly in autism and other pervasive developmental disorders. *Dev Med Child Neurol*, 42, 11: 737–740.

Filipek, P. A., Richelme, C., Kennedy, D. N., Rademacher, J., Pitcher, D. A., Zidel S., &Caviness, V. S. (1992). Morphometric analysis of the brain in developmental language disorders and autism (abstract). *Ann Neurol*, 32, 475.

Filipek, P. A. (1995). Quantitative magnetic resonance imaging in autism: The cerebellar vermis. *Current Opinion in Neurology*, 8(2), 134–138.

Flagg, E. J., Cardy, J. E., Roberts, W., & Roberts, T. P. (2005). Language lateralization development in children with autism: insights from the late field magnetoencephalogram. *Neurosci Lett*, 386(2), 82–87.

Freitag, C. M., Luders, E., Hulst, H. E., Narr, K. L., Thompson, P. M., Toga, A. W., Krick, C., & Konrad, C. (2009). Total brain volume and corpus callosum size in medication-naive adolescents and young adults with autism spectrum disorder. *Biol Psychiatry*, 66(4), 316–319.

Friedman, S. D., Shaw, D. W., Artru, A. A., Richards, T. L., Gardner, J., Dawson, G., Posse, S., & Dager. S. R. (2003). Regional brain chemical alterations in young children with autism spectrum disorder. *Neurology*, 60(1), 100–107.

Gabis, L., Huang, W., Azizian, A., DeVincent, C., Tudorica, A., Kesner-Baruch, Y., Roche, P., & Pomeroy, J. (2008). 1H-magnetic resonance spectroscopy markers of cognitive and language ability in clinical subtypes of autism spectrum disorders. *J Child Neurol*, 23(7), 766–774.

Gaffney, G. R., Tsai, L. Y., Kuperman, S., & Minchin, S. (1987). Cerebellar structure in autism. *Am J Dis Child*, 141(12), 1330–1332.

Galuska, L., Szakall Jr., S., Emri, M., Olah, R., Varga, J., Garai, I., Kollar, J., Pataki, I., & Tron, L. (2002). PET and SPECT scans in autistic children. *Orv Hetil*, 143(21 Suppl 3), 1302–1304.

Garber, H. I., & Ritvo, E. R. (1992). Magnetic resonance imaging of the posterior fossa in autistic adults. *American Journal of Psychiatry*, 149, 245–247.

George, M. S., Costa, D. C., Kouris, K., Ring, H. A., & Ell, P. J. (1992). Cerebral blood flow abnormalities in adults with infantile autism. *J Nerv Ment Dis*, 180(7), 413–417.

Ghashghaei, H. T., & Barbas, H. (2002). Pathways for emotion: Interactions of prefrontal and anterior temporal pathways in the amygdala of the rhesus monkey. *Neuroscience*, 115(4), 1261–1279.

Giedd, J. N., Rapoport, J. L., Garvey, M. A., Perlmutter, S., & Swedo, S. E. (2000). MRI assessment of children with obsessive-compulsive disorder or tics associated with streptococcal infection. *Am J Psychiatry*, 157(2), 281–283.

Gillberg, C., & Svendsen, P. (1983). Childhood psychosis and computed tomographic brain scan findings. *J Autism Dev Disord*, 13(1), 19–32.

Guerin, P., Lyon, G., Barthelemy, C., Sostak, E., Chevrollier, V., Garreau, B., & Lelord, G. (1996). Neuropathological study of a case of autistic syndrome with severe mental retardation. *Dev Med Child Neurol*, 38(3), 203–211.

Gupta, S. K., & Ratnam, B. V. (2009). Cerebral perfusion abnormalities in children with autism and mental retardation: A segmental quantitative SPECT study. *Indian Pediatr.*, 46(2), 161–164.

Guptill, J. T., Booker, A. B, Bauman, M. L., Kemper, T. L., & Blatt, G. J. (2006). 3Hflunitrazepam-labeled benzodiazepine binding sites in the hippocampal formation in autism: A multiple concentration autoradiographic study. *Journal of Autism and Developmental Disorder*, 37(5), 911–920.

Hadjikhani, N., Joseph, R. M., Snyder, J., & Tager-Flusberg, H. (2006). Anatomical differences in the mirror neuron system and social cognition network in autism. *Cereb Cortex*, 16(9), 1276–1282.

Hardan, A. Y., Minshew, N. J., Harenski, K., & Keshavan, M. S. (2001). Posterior fossa magnetic resonance imaging in autism. *J Am Acad Child Adolesc Psychiatry*, 40(6), 666–672.

Hardan, A. Y., Minshew, N. J., & Keshavan, M. S. (2000). Corpus callosum size in autism. *Neurology*, 55(7), 1033–1036.

Hardan, A. Y., Minshew, N. J., Melhem, N. M., Srihari, S., Jo, B., Bansal, R., Keshavan, M. S., & Stanley, J. A. (2008). An MRI and proton spectroscopy study of the thalamus in children with autism. *Psychiatry Res*, 163(2), 97–105.

Hardan, A. Y., Muddasani, S., Vemulapalli, M., Keshavan, M. S., & Minshew, N. J. (2006). An MRI study of increased cortical thickness in autism. *Am J Psychiatry*, 163(7), 1290–1292.

Hashimoto, T., Sasaki, M., Fukumizu, M., Hanaoka, S., Sugai, K., & Matsuda, H. (2000). Single-photon emission computed tomography of the brain in autism: effect of the developmental level. *Pediatr Neurol*, 23(5), 416–420.

Hazlett, H. C., Poe, M., Gerig, G., Smith, R. G., Provenzale, J., Ross, A., Gilmore, J., & Piven, J. (2005). Magnetic resonance imaging and head circumference study of brain size in autism: Birth through age 2 years. *Arch Gen Psychiatry*, 62(12), 1366–1376.

Hazlett, H. C., Poe, M., Gerig, G., Smith, R. G., & Piven, J. (2006). Cortical gray and white brain tissue volume in adolescents and adults with autism. *Biol Psychiatry*, 59(1), 1–6.

Haznedar, M. M., Buchsbaum, M. S., Hazlett, E. A., LiCalzi, E. M., Cartwright, C., & Hollander, E. (2006). Volumetric analysis and three-dimensional glucose metabolic mapping of the striatum and thalamus in patients with autism spectrum disorders. *Am J Psychiatry*, 163(7), 1252–1263.

Haznedar, M. M., Buchsbaum, M. S., Wei, T. C., Hof, P. R., Cartwright, C., Bienstock, C. A., & Hollander, E. (2000). Limbic circuitry in patients with autism spectrum disorders studied with positron emission tomography and magnetic resonance imaging. *Am J Psychiatry*, 157(12), 1994–2001.

Herbert, M. R., & Anderson, M. P. (2008). An expanding spectrum of autism models: From fixed developmental defects to reversible functional impairments. In A. Zimmerman (Ed.), *Autism: Current Theories and Evidence* (pp. 429–463). New York: Humana Press.

Herbert, M. R., Harris, G. J., Adrien, K. T., Ziegler, D. A., Makris, N., Kennedy, D. N., Lange, N. T., Chabris, C. F., Bakardjiev, A., Hodgson, J., Takeoka, M., Tager-Flusberg, H., & Caviness Jr., V. S. (2002). Abnormal asymmetry in language association cortex in autism. *Ann Neurol*, 52(5), 588–596.

Herbert, M. R., Ziegler, D. A., Deutsch, C. K., O'brien, L. M., Kennedy, D. N., Filipek, P. A., Bakardjiev, A. I., Hodgson, J., Takeoka, M., Makris, N., & Caviness Jr., V. S. (2005). Brain asymmetries in autism and developmental language disorder: A nested whole-brain analysis. *Brain*, 128(Pt 1), 213–226.

Herbert, M. R., Ziegler, D. A., Deutsch, C. K., O'brien, Lange, N., Bakardjiev, A., Hodgson, J., Adrien, K. T., Steele, S., Makris, N., Kennedy, D., Harris, G. J., & Caviness, V. S. (2003). Dissociations of cerebral cortex, subcortical and cerebral white matter volumes in autistic boys. *Brain*, 126(Pt 5), 1182–1192.

Herbert, M. R., Ziegler, D. A., Makris, N., Filipek, P. A., Kemper, T. L., Normandin, J. J., Sanders, H. A., Kennedy, D. N., & Caviness Jr., V. S. (2004). Localization of white matter volume increase in autism and developmental language disorder. *Ann Neurol*, 55(4), 530–540.

Herold, S., Frackowiak, R. S., Le Couteur, A., Rutter, M., & Howlin, P. (1988). Cerebral blood flow and metabolism of oxygen and glucose in young autistic adults. *Psychol Med*, 18(4), 823–831.

Hier, D. B., LeMay, M., & Rosenberger, P. B. (1979). Autism and unfavorable left-right asymmetries of the brain. *J Autism Dev Disord*, 9(2), 153–159.

Hobbs, K., Kennedy, A., Dubray, M., Bigler, E. D., Petersen, P. B., McMahon, W., & Lainhart, J. E. (2007). A retrospective fetal ultrasound study of brain size in autism. *Biol Psychiatry*, 62(9), 1048–1055.

Holttum, J. R., Minshew, N. J., Sanders, R. S., & Phillips, N. E. (1992). Magnetic resonance imaging of the posterior fossa in autism. *Biol Psychiatry*, 32(12), 1091–1101.

Horwitz, B., Rumsey, J. M., Grady, C. L., & Rapoport, S. I. (1988). The cerebral metabolic landscape in autism. Intercorrelations of regional glucose utilization. *Arch Neurol*, 45(7), 749–755.

Hoshino, Y., Manome, T., Kaneko, M., Yashima, Y., & Kumashiro, H. (1984). Computed tomography of the brain in children with early infantile autism. *Folia Psychiatr Neurol Jpn*, 38(1), 33–43.

Howard, M. A., Cowell, P. E., Boucher, J., Broks, P., Mayes, A., Farrant, A., & Roberts, N. (2000). Convergent neuroanatomical and behavioural evidence of an amygdala hypothesis of autism. *Neuroreport*, 11(13), 2931–2935.

Hugg, J. W., Kuzniecky, R. I., Gilliam, F. G., Morawetz, R. B., Fraught, R. E., & Hetherington, H. P. (1996). Normalization of contralateral metabolic function following temporal lobectomy demonstrated by 1H magnetic resonance spectroscopic imaging. *Ann Neurol*, 40(2), 236–239.

Ito, H., Mori, K., Hashimoto, T., Miyazaki, M., Hori, A., Kagami, S., & Kuroda, Y. (2005). Findings of brain 99mTc-ECD SPECT in high-functioning autism—3-dimensional stereotactic ROI template analysis of brain SPECT. *J Med Invest*, 52(1–2), 49–56.

Juranek, J., Filipek, P. A., Berenji, G. R., Modahl, C., Osann, K., & Spence, M. A. (2006). Association between amygdala volume and anxiety level:

Magnetic resonance imaging (MRI) study in autistic children. *J Child Neurol*, 21(12), 1051–1058.

Just, M. A., Cherkassky, V. L., Keller, T. A., Kana, R. K., & Minshew, N. J. (2007). Functional and anatomical cortical underconnectivity in autism: Evidence from an FMRI study of an executive function task and corpus callosum morphometry. *Cereb Cortex*, 17(4), 951–961.

Kang, D. H., Davidson, R. J., Coe, C. L., Wheeler, R. E., Tomarken, A. J., & Ershler, W. B. (1991). Frontal brain asymmetry and immune function. *Behav Neurosci*, 105(6), 860–869.

Kanner, L. (1943). Autistic disturbances of affective contact. *Nervous Child*, 10, 217–250.

Karmiloff-Smith, A. (2006). The tortuous route from genes to behavior: A neuroconstructivist approach. *Cogn Affect Behav Neurosci*, 6(1), 9–17.

Ke, X., Hong, S., Tang, T., Zou, B., Li, H., Hang, Y., Zhou, Z., Ruan, Z., Lu, Z., Tao, G., & Liu, Y. (2008). Voxel-based morphometry study on brain structure in children with high-functioning autism. *Neuroreport*, 19(9), 921–925.

Kern, J. K. (2003). Purkinje cell vulnerability and autism: A possible etiological connection. *Brain Dev*, 25(6), 377–382.

Khalfa, S., Bruneau, N., Roge, B., Georgieff, N., Veuillet, E., Adrien, J. L., Barthelemy, C., & Collet, L. (2001). Peripheral auditory asymmetry in infantile autism. *Eur J Neurosci*, 13(3), 628–632.

Kilian, S., Brown, W. S., Hallam, B. J., McMahon, W., Lu, J., Johnson, M., Bigler, E. D., & Lainhart, J. (2008). Regional callosal morphology in autism and macrocephaly. *Dev Neuropsychol*, 33(1), 74–99.

Kleiman, M. D., Neff, S., & Rosman, N. P. (1992). The brain in infantile autism: Are posterior fossa structures abnormal? *Neurology*, 42, 753–760.

Kleinhans, N. M., Richards, T., Weaver, K. E., Liang, O., Dawson, G., & Aylward, E. (2009). Brief Report: Biochemical correlates of clinical impairment in high functioning autism and Asperger's disorder. *J Autism Dev Disord*, 39(7), 1079–1086.

Kleinhans, N. M., Schweinsburg, B. C., Cohen, D. N., Muller, R. A., & Courchesne, E. (2007). N-acetyl aspartate in autism spectrum disorders: regional effects and relationship to fMRI activation. *Brain Res.*, 1162, 85–97.

Lainhart, J. E. (2003). Increased rate of head growth during infancy in autism. *JAMA*, 290(3), 393–394.

Lazarev, V. V., Pontes, A., & Deazevedo, L. C. (2008). EEG photic driving: Right-hemisphere reactivity deficit in childhood autism. A pilot study. *Int J Psychophysiol*, 71(2), 177–183.

Lee, J. E., Bigler, E. D., Alexander, A. L., Lazar, M., DuBray, M. B., Chung, M. K., Johnson, M., Morgan, J., Miller, J. N., McMahon, W. M., Lu, J., Jeong, E. K., & Lainhart, J. E. (2007). Diffusion tensor imaging of white matter in the superior temporal gyrus and temporal stem in autism. *Neurosci Lett*, 424(2), 127–132.

Lee, M., Martin-Ruiz, C., Graham, A., Court, J., Jaros, E., Perry, R., Iversen, P., Bauman, M., & Perry, E. (2002). Nicotinic receptor abnormalities in the cerebellar cortex in autism. *Brain*, 125(Pt 7), 1483–1495.

Levitt, P., Eagleson, K. L., & Powell, E. M. (2004). Regulation of neocortical interneuron development and the implications for neurodevelopmental disorders. *Trends Neurosci*, 27(7), 400–406.

Li, X., Chauhan, A., Sheikh, A. M., Patil, S., Chauhan, V., Li, X. M., Ji, L., Brown, T., & Malik, M. (2009). Elevated immune response in the brain of autistic patients. *J Neuroimmunol*, 207(1-2), 111–6.

Llinas, R., Urbano, F. J., Leznik, E., Ramirez, R. R., & van Marle, H. J. (2005). Rhythmic and dysrhythmic thalamocortical dynamics: GABA systems and the edge effect. *Trends Neurosci*, 28(6), 325–333.

Lodin, Z., Mares, V., Faltin, J., & Karasek, J. (1969). Studies on the effect of fixation on nervous tissue. IV. Volumetric changes of cerebellar structures due to preparation of the tissue for electron microscopy. *Acta Histochem*, 34(1), 1–9.

MacFabe, D. F., Cain, D. P., Rodriguez-Capote, K., Franklin, A. E., Hoffman, J. E., Boon, F., Taylor, A. R., Kavaliers, M., & Ossenkopp, K. P. (2007). Neurobiological effects of intraventricular propionic acid in rats: Possible role of short chain fatty acids on the pathogenesis and characteristics of autism spectrum disorders. *Behav Brain Res*, 176(1), 149–169.

Makris, N., Meyer, J. W., Bates, J. F., Yeterian, E. H., Kennedy, D. N., & Caviness, V. S. (1999). MRI-Based topographic parcellation of human cerebral white matter and nuclei II. Rationale and applications with systematics of cerebral connectivity. *Neuroimage*, 9(1), 18–45.

Mason, R. A., Williams, D. L., Kana, R. K., Minshew, N., & Just, M. A. (2008). Theory of mind disruption and recruitment of the right hemisphere during narrative comprehension in autism. *Neuropsychologia*, 46(1), 269–280.

McCaffery, P., & Deutsch, C. K. (2005). Macrocephaly and the control of brain growth in autistic disorders. *Prog Neurobiol*, 77(1–2), 38–56.

McKelvey, J. R., Lambert, R., Mottron, L., & Shevell, M. I. (1995). Right-hemisphere dysfunction in Asperger's syndrome. *J Child Neurol*, 10(4), 310–314.

Meyer, J. W., Makris, N., Bates, J. F., Caviness, V. S., & Kennedy, D. N. (1999). MRI-Based topographic parcellation of human cerebral white matter I: Technical foundations. *Neuroimage*, 9(1), 1–17.

Miles, J. H., Hadden, L. L., Takahashi, T. N., & Hillman, R. E. (2000). Head circumference is an independent clinical finding associated with autism. *Am J Med Genet*, 95(4), 339–350.

Morgan, J. T., G. Chana, C. A. Pardo, C. Achim, K. Semendeferi, J. Buckwalter, E. Courchesne, and I. P. Everall. (2010). Microglial activation and increased microglial density observed in the dorsolateral prefrontal cortex in autism. *Biol Psychiatry 68*(4), 368–76.

Morton, J., & Frith, U. (1995). Causal modelling: A structural approach to developmental psychopathology. In D. Cicchetti and D. J. Cohen (Eds.), *Manual of developmental psychopathology* (pp. 357–390). New York: John Wiley.

Mostofsky, S. H., Burgess, M. P., & Gidley Larson, J. C. (2007). Increased motor cortex white matter volume predicts motor impairment in autism. *Brain, 130* (Pt 8), 2117–2122.

Mraz, K. D., Dixon, J., Dumont-Mathieu, T., & Fein, D. (2009). Accelerated head and body growth in infants later diagnosed with autism spectrum disorders: A comparative study of optimal outcome children. *J Child Neurol, 24*(7), 833–845.

Mraz, K. D., Green, J., Dumont-Mathieu, T., Makin, S., & Fein, D. (2007). Correlates of head circumference growth in infants later diagnosed with autism spectrum disorders. *J Child Neurol, 22*(6), 700–713.

Muller, R. A., Cauich, C., Rubio, M. A., Mizuno, A., & Courchesne, E. (2004). Abnormal activity patterns in premotor cortex during sequence learning in autistic patients. *Biol Psychiatry, 56*(5), 323–332.

Murakami, J. W., Courchesne, E., Press, G. A., Yeung-Courchesne, R., & Hesselink, J. R. (1989). Reduced cerebellar hemisphere size and its relationship to vermal hypoplasia in autism. *Arch Neurol, 46*(6), 689–694.

Nacewicz, B. M.,Dalton, K. M., Johnstone, T., Long, M. T., McAuliff, E. M., Oakes, T. R., Alexander, A. L., & Davidson, R. J. (2006). Amygdala volume and nonverbal social impairment in adolescent and adult males with autism. *Arch Gen Psychiatry, 63*(12), 1417–1428.

Neeley, E. S., Bigler, E. D., Krasny, L., Ozonoff, S., McMahon, W., & Lainhart, J. E. (2007). Quantitative temporal lobe differences: Autism distinguished from controls using classification and regression tree analysis. *Brain Dev, 29*(7), 389–399.

Nicolson, R., DeVito, T. J., Vidal, C. N., Sui, Y., Hayashi, K. M., Drost, D. J., Williamson, P. C., Rajakumar, N., Toga, A. W., & Thompson, P. M. (2006). Detection and mapping of hippocampal abnormalities in autism. *Psychiatry Res, 148*(1), 11–21.

National Institutes of Health. A longitudinal MRI study of infants at risk for autism. *Brain Development in Autism: Infant Siblings*. Retrieved August 3, 2010, from http://www.ibis-network.org/default.html.

Noble, D. (2008). *The music of life*. New York: Oxford University Press.

Nowell, M. A., Hackney, D. B., Muraki, A. S., & Coleman, M. (1990). Varied MR appearance of autism: Fifty-three pediatric patients having the full autistic syndrome. *Magn Reson Imaging, 8*(6), 811–816.

O'brien, L. M., Ziegler, D. A., Deutsch, C. K., Kennedy, D. N., Goldstein, J. M., Seidman,L. J., Hodge, S, Makris, N., Caviness, V., Frazier, J. A., & Herbert, M. R. (2006). Adjustment for whole brain and cranial size in volumetric brain studies: A review of common adjustment factors and statistical methods. *Harv Rev Psychiatry, 14*(3), 141–151.

Ohnishi, T., Matsuda, H., Hashimoto, T., Kunihiro, T., Nishikawa, M., Uema, T., & Sasaki, M. (2000). Abnormal regional cerebral blood flow in childhood autism. *Brain, 123*(Pt 9), 1838–1844.

Ozonoff, S., & Miller, J. N. (1996). An exploration of right-hemisphere contributions to the pragmatic impairments of autism. *Brain Lang, 52*(3), 411–434.

Page, L. A., Daly, E., Schmitz, N. A. Simmons, Toal, F., Deeley, Q., Ambery, F., McAlonan, G. M., Murphy, K. C., & Murphy, D. G. (2006). In vivo 1H-magnetic resonance spectroscopy study of amygdala-hippocampal and parietal regions in autism. *Am J Psychiatry, 163*(12), 2189–2192.

Palmen, S. J., Hulshoff Pol, H. E., Kemner, C., Schnack, H. G., Durston, S., Lahuis, B. E., Kahn, R. S., & Van Engeland, H. (2005). Increased gray-matter volume in medication-naive high-functioning children with autism spectrum disorder. *Psychol Med, 35*(4), 561–570.

Pardo C. A., & Eberhart, C. G. (2007). The neurobiology of autism. *Brain Patho., 17*(4), 434–47.

Piven, J., Bailey, J., Ranson, B. J., & Arndt, S. (1998). No difference in hippocampus volume detected on magnetic resonance imaging in autistic individuals. *J Autism Dev Disord, 28*(2), 105–110.

Piven, J., Nehme, E., Simon, J., Barta, P., Pearlson, G., and Folstein, S. E. (1992). Magnetic resonance imaging in autism: Measurement of the cerebellum, pons, and fourth ventricle. *Biological Psychiatry, 31*(5), 491–504.

Piven, J., Saliba, K., Bailey, J., & Arndt, S. (1997). An MRI study of autism: The cerebellum revisited. *Neurology, 49*, 546–551.

Piven, J., Saliba, K., Bailey, J., & Arndt, S. (1999). An MRI study of autism: The cerebellum revisited — reply. *Neurology, 52*(5), 1106–1107.

Piven, J., & Arndt, S. (1995). The cerebellum and autism. *Neurology, 45*, 398–399.

Piven, J., Arndt, S., Bailey, J., & Andreasen, N. (1996). Regional brain enlargement in autism: A magnetic resonance imaging study. *Journal of the American Academy of Child and Adolescent Psychiatry, 35*(4), 530–536.

Piven, J., Bailey, J., Ranson, B. J. & Arndt, S.(1997). An MRI study of the corpus callosum in autism. *Am J Psychiatry, 154*(8), 1051–1056.

Ramirez, M., Prieto, I., Vives, F., de Gasparo, M., & Alba, F. (2004). Neuropeptides, neuropeptidases and brain asymmetry. *Curr Protein Pept Sci, 5*(6), 497–506.

Ray, M. A., Graham, A. J., Lee, M., Perry, R. H., Court, J. A., & Perry, E. K. (2005). Neuronal nicotinic acetylcholine receptor subunits in autism: An immunohistochemical investigation in the thalamus. *Neurobiol Dis*, 19(3), 366–377.

Raymond, G. V., Bauman, M. L., & Kemper, T. L. (1996). Hippocampus in autism: A Golgi analysis. *Acta Neuropathol (Berl,)* 91(1), 117–119.

Rice, S. A., Bigler, E. D., Cleavinger, H. B., Tate, D. F., Sayer, J., McMahon, W., Ozonoff, S., Lu, J., & Lainhart, J. E. (2005). Macrocephaly, corpus callosum morphology, and autism. *J Child Neurol*, 20(1), 34–41.

Ringo, J. L. (1991). Neuronal interconnection as a function of brain size. *Brain Behav Evol*, 38(1), 1–6.

Ringo, J. L., Doty, R. W., Demeter, S., & Simard, P. Y. (1994). Time is of the essence: A conjecture that hemispheric specialization arises from interhemispheric conduction delay. *Cereb Cortex*, 4(4), 331–343.

Rodier, P. M., Ingram, J. L., Tisdale, B., Nelson, S., & Roma, J. (1996). Embryological origins for autism: Developmental anomalies of the cranial nerve motor nuclei. *Journal of Comparative Neurology*, 370, 247–261.

Rojas, D. C., Bawn, S. D., Benkers, T. L., Reite, M. L., & Rogers, S. J. (2002). Smaller left hemisphere planum temporale in adults with autistic disorder. *Neurosci Lett*, 328(3), 237–240.

Rojas, D. C., Camou, S. L., Reite, M. L., & Rogers, S. J. (2005). Planum temporale volume in children and adolescents with autism. *J Autism Dev Disord*, 35(4), 479–486.

Rubenstein, J. L., and M. M. Merzenich. 2003. Model of autism: increased ratio of excitation/inhibition in key neural systems. *Genes Brain Behav* 2, 5: 255–267.

Rumsey, J. M., & Hamburger, S. D. (1988). Neuropsychological findings in high-functioning men with infantile autism residual state. *Journal of Clinical and Experimental Neuropsychology*, 10, 201–221.

Ryu, Y. H., Lee, J. D., Yoon, P. H., Kim, D. I., Lee, H. B., & Shin, Y. J. (1999). Perfusion impairments in infantile autism on technetium-99m ethyl cysteinate dimer brain single-photon emission tomography: Comparison with findings on magnetic resonance imaging. *Eur J Nucl Med*, 26(3), 253–259.

Saitoh, O., Courchesne, E., Egaas, B., Lincoln, A. J., & Schreibman, L. (1995). Cross-sectional area of the posterior hippocampus in autistic patients with cerebellar and corpus callosum abnormalities. *Neurology*, 45(2), 317–324.

Saitoh, O., Karns, C. M., & Courchesne, E. (2001). Development of the hippocampal formation from 2 to 42 years: MRI evidence of smaller area dentata in autism. *Brain*, 124(Pt 7), 1317–1324.

Salthe, S. (1985). *Evolving hierarchical systems*. New York: Columbia University Press.

Schaefer, G. B., Thompson, J. N., Bodensteiner, J. B., McConnell, J. M., Kimberling, W. J., Gay, C. T.,

Dutton, W. D., Hutchings, D. C., & Gray, S. B. (1996). Hypoplasia of the cerebellar vermis in neurogenetic syndromes. *Ann Neurol*, 39(3), 382–385.

Schmahmann, J. D. (2004). Disorders of the cerebellum: Ataxia, dysmetria of thought, and the cerebellar cognitive affective syndrome. *J Neuropsychiatry Clin Neurosci*, 16(3), 367–378.

Schmahmann, J. D., & Caplan, D. (2006). Cognition, emotion and the cerebellum. *Brain*, 129(Pt 2), 290–292.

Schmahmann, J. D., & Pandya, D. N. (2008). Disconnection syndromes of basal ganglia, thalamus, and cerebrocerebellar systems. *Cortex*, 44(8), 1037–1066.

Schumann, C. M., Hamstra, J., Goodlin-Jones, B. L., Lotspeich, L. J., Kwon, H., Buonocore, M. H., Lammers, C. R., Reiss, A. L., & Amaral, D. G. (2004). The amygdala is enlarged in children but not adolescents with autism; the hippocampus is enlarged at all ages. *J Neurosci*, 24(28), 6392–6401.

Shavelle, R. M., Strauss, D. J., Pickett, J. Causes of death in autism. *Journal of Autism and Developmental Disorders*, 31(6), 569–576.

Shen, Y. Q., Hebert, G., Moze, E., Li, K. S., & Neveu, P. J. (2005). Asymmetrical distribution of brain interleukin-6 depends on lateralization in mice. *Neuroimmunomodulation*, 12(3), 189–194.

Shetty, N., Ratai, E., Ringer, A., & Herbert, M. (2009). Magnetic resonance studies in ASD: Review of regions investigated, findings, potential influence of methodology, and directions for future research. *International Meeting for Autism Research*, Poster 4188.

Shi, L., Smith, S. E., Malkova, N., Tse, D., Su, Y., & Patterson, P. H. (2009). Activation of the maternal immune system alters cerebellar development in the offspring. *Brain Behav Immun*, 23(1), 116–123.

Slikker, W., & Chang, L. W. (1998). *Handbook of developmental neurotoxicology*. San Diego, CA: Academic Press.

Sparks, B. F., Friedman, S. D., Shaw, D. W., Aylward, E. H., Echelard, D., Artru, A. A., Maravilla, K. R., Giedd, J. N., Munson, J., Dawson, G., & Dager, S. R. (2002). Brain structural abnormalities in young children with autism spectrum disorder. *Neurology*, 59(2), 184–192.

Stanfield, A. C., McIntosh, A. M., Spencer, M. D., Philip, R., Gaur, S., & Lawrie, S. M. (2007). Towards a neuroanatomy of autism: A systematic review and meta-analysis of structural magnetic resonance imaging studies. *Eur Psychiatry*, 23(4), 289–299.

Starkstein, S. E., Vazquez, S., Vrancic, D., Nanclares, V., Manes, F., Piven, J., & Plebst, C. (2000). SPECT findings in mentally retarded autistic individuals. *J Neuropsychiatry Clin Neurosci*, 12(3), 370–375.

Stroganova, T. A., Nygren, G., Tsetlin, M. M., Posikera, I. N., Gillberg, C., Elam, M., & Orekhova, E. V.

(2007). Abnormal EEG lateralization in boys with autism. *Clin Neurophysiol, 118*(8), 1842–1854.

Sundaram, S.K., Kumar, A.J., Makki, M.I., Behen, M.E., Chugani, H.T. & Chugani, D.C.(2008). Diffusion tensor imaging of frontal lobe in autism spectrum disorder. *Cerebral Cortex, 18*(11), 2659–65.

Takeuchi, M., Harada, M., Matsuzaki, K., Nishitani, H., & Mori, K. (2004). Difference of signal change by a language task on autistic patients using functional MRI. *J Med Invest, 51*(1–2), 59–62.

Theberge, J. (2008). Perfusion magnetic resonance imaging in psychiatry. *Top Magn Reson Imaging, 19*(2), 111–130.

Tsatsanis, K. D., Rourke, B. P., Klin, A., Volkmar, F. R., Cicchetti, D., & Schultz, R. T. (2003). Reduced thalamic volume in high-functioning individuals with autism. *Biol Psychiatry, 53*(2), 121–129.

Tucker, D. M. 1992. Developing emotions and cortical networks. In M. R. Gunnar & C. A. Nelson (Eds.), *Developmental behavioral neuroscience, vol. 24* (pp. 75–128). Hillsdale, NJ: Lawrence Erlbaum Associates.

Van Essen, D. C., Drury, H. A., Joshi, S., & Miller, M. I. (1998). Functional and structural mapping of human cerebral cortex: Solutions are in the surfaces. *Proc Natl Acad Sci U S A, 95*(3), 788–795.

Vargas, D. L., Nascimbene, C. Krishnan, C., Zimmerman, A. W., & Pardo, C. A. (2005). Neuroglial activation and neuroinflammation in the brain of patients with autism. *Ann Neurol, 57*(1), 67–81.

Vidal, C. N., Nicolson, R., DeVito, T. J., Hayashi, K. M., Geaga, J. A., Drost, D. J., Williamson, P. C., Rajakumar, N., Sui, Y., Dutton, R. A., Toga, A. W., & Thompson, P. M. (2006). Mapping corpus callosum deficits in autism: an index of aberrant cortical connectivity. *Biol Psychiatry, 60*(3), 218–225.

Waiter, G. D., Williams, J. H., Murray, A. D., Gilchrist, A., Perrett, D. I., & Whiten, A. (2005). Structural white matter deficits in high-functioning individuals with autistic spectrum disorder: a voxel-based investigation. *Neuroimage, 24*(2), 455–461.

Whitehouse, A. J., & Bishop, D. V.(2008). Cerebral dominance for language function in adults with specific language impairment or autism. *Brain, 131*(Pt 12), 3193–3200.

Whitney, E. R., Kemper, T. L., Bauman, M. L., Rosene, D. L., & Blatt, G. J. (2008). Cerebellar Purkinje cells are reduced in a subpopulation of autistic brains: A stereological experiment using Calbindin-D28k. *Cerebellum, 7*(3), 406–16.

Wilcox, J., Tsuang, M. T., Ledger, E., Algeo, J., & Schnurr, T.(2002). Brain perfusion in autism varies with age. *Neuropsychobiology, 46*(1), 13–16.

Williams, R. S., Hauser, S. L., Purpura, D. P., DeLong, G. R., & Swisher, C. N. (1980). Autism and mental retardation: Neuropathologic studies performed in four retarded persons with autistic behavior. *Arch Neurol, 37*(12), 749–753.

Wills, S., Cabanlit, M., Bennett, J., Ashwood, P., Amaral, D. G., & Van de Water, J. (2009). Detection of autoantibodies to neural cells of the cerebellum in the plasma of subjects with autism spectrum disorders. *Brain Behav Immun, 23*(1), 64–74.

Wisniewski, A. B.(1998). Sexually-dimorphic patterns of cortical asymmetry, and the role for sex steroid hormones in determining cortical patterns of lateralization. *Psychoneuroendocrinology, 23*(5), 519–547.

Wittling, W. (1995). Brain asymmetry in the control of autonomic-physiologic activity. In R. J. Davidson & K. Hugdahl (Eds.), *Brain asymmetry* (pp. 305–357). Cambridge, MA: MIT Press.

Woodhouse, W., Bailey, A., Rutter, M., Bolton, P., Baird, G., & Le Couteur, A. (1996). Head circumference in autism and other pervasive developmental disorders. *J Child Psychol Psychiatry, 37*(6), 665–671.

Yip, J., Soghomonian, J. J., & Blatt, G. J. (2007). Decreased GAD67 mRNA levels in cerebellar Purkinje cells in autism: pathophysiological implications. *Acta Neuropathol, 113*(5), 559–568.

Zeegers, M., Van Der Grond, J., Durston, S., Nievelstein, R. J., Witkamp, T., Van Daalen, E., Buitelaar, J., & Engeland, H. V. (2006). Radiological findings in autistic and developmentally delayed children. *Brain Dev, 28*(8), 495–499.

Zilbovicius, M., Boddaert, N., Belin, P., Poline, J. B., Remy, P., Mangin, J. F., Thivard, L., Barthelemy, C., & Samson, Y. (2000). Temporal lobe dysfunction in childhood autism: A PET study. Positron emission tomography. *Am J Psychiatry, 157*(12), 1988–1993.

Chapter 4

The Neurochemistry of ASD

David J. Posey, Zohra Lodin, Craig A. Erickson, Kimberly A. Stigler, and Christopher J. McDougle

Investigations into the neurochemistry of autistic disorder (autism) began with early studies that measured the concentration of various neurotransmitters and metabolites in blood, urine, and cerebrospinal fluid (CSF). This was followed by both drug treatment studies, as well as drug challenge studies, which aimed to determine how both acute and chronic pharmacological manipulation of neurochemistry affects biomarkers and symptoms. Postmortem studies have revealed additional neurochemical findings. Genetic and neuroimaging studies are greatly expanding the pace of discovery and further informing our understanding of the neurochemistry of autism.

Significant progress has been made in the search for the underlying pathophysiology of autism over the past 50 years. In this span of time, the concept of autism has gone from that of a poorly understood psychiatric disorder with dubious psychosocial causes to that of a neurodevelopmental syndrome highly determined by genetics. Like many neuropsychiatric disorders affecting complex brain functions, its exact causes

are unknown. The heritability of autism, based on twin studies, is high. It is currently thought that genetic polymorphisms acting together, and possibly influenced by environmental contributions, are related to etiology. More is known about the underlying pathophysiology of autism, but limitations remain, given many of the challenges of conducting clinical investigations in this population. These challenges include the heterogeneity in clinical presentation, presence of significant comorbidities (e.g., mental retardation, seizures), and the fact that many patients are very young, nonverbal, or treated with psychotropic medications.

This chapter reviews the neurochemistry of autism with a focus on three broad categories: (1) monoamines [serotonin (5-hydroxytryptamine, 5-HT), dopamine (DA), and norepinephrine (NE)]; (2) glutamate (Glu)/γ-aminobutyric acid (GABA) systems, and; (3) neuropeptides. Studies measuring these compounds and metabolites in both peripheral (e.g., blood) and central (e.g., CSF) fluids will be reviewed. Genetic, neuroimaging, and postmortem findings are also summarized.

MONOAMINES

Serotonin neurons are widely distributed throughout the mammalian brain. This neuronal system is one of the earliest to develop, and the turnover rate of 5-HT is higher in the immature mammalian brain than at any other time in life. Serotonin plays a critical role as a growth factor in the immature brain, directing both proliferation and maturation (Whitaker-Azmitia, 1993). Serotonergic dysfunction dysfunction has been implicated in several areas relevant to autism including obsessive-compulsive disorder, mood disorders, and aggression. Studies assessing the 5-HT neurotransmitter system in autism are summarized in Table 4-1. The role of other monoamines in autism is less clear.

Serotonin and Metabolites

Early neurochemical studies of autism focused on the 5-HT system. Schain and Freedman (1961) were the first to study whole blood serotonin (WBS) in autism. Their sample included three pediatric groups: autism plus severe mental retardation, mild mental retardation alone, and severe mental retardation alone. WBS was highest in children with autism, but was also elevated in children with severe mental retardation, compared to those children with mild mental retardation. The clinical presentation of the six autistic children with the highest WBS levels was no different from those who had normal levels. The finding of hyperserotonemia in a substantial minority of children is one of the more consistent findings in autism (Ritvo et al., 1970). More recent studies have found that elevated WBS is mainly present in prepubertal children with autism and that race may also affect 5-HT levels (McBride et al., 1998).

Leboyer and colleagues (1999) measured WBS levels in 62 subjects with autism aged 3–23 years, 91 healthy controls aged 2–16 years, and 118 healthy subjects over 16 years of age. Twenty-nine (48%) of the 60 autistic subjects, for whom there was available blood, met criteria for hyperserotonemia. WBS levels diminished with age in controls, but not in subjects with autism. In this same study, non-affected, first-degree relatives of subjects with autism also exhibited hyperserotonemia (51% of mothers, 45% of fathers, and 87% of siblings) suggesting that the finding may relate to underlying genetics, and not necessarily to the presence or absence of autism.

Recently, platelet 5-HT was investigated in 53 adults with autism spectrum disorders (ASDs) and 45 healthy controls (Hranilovic et al., 2007). Ninety-nine percent of WBS is found in platelets. Adults treated with selective serotonin reuptake inhibitors (SSRIs) had platelet 5-HT levels four times lower than subjects treated without SSRIs. These subjects were excluded from subsequent analyses. There were no effects of gender or degree of mental retardation on 5-HT levels. Subjects with better speech had lower 5-HT levels; the degree of mental retardation and overall autism severity had no effect. Platelet 5-HT levels in subjects with ASDs were significantly higher compared to controls. Fifteen of 47 (32%) subjects with ASDs met criteria for hyperserotonemia (> 2 standard deviations above the mean level for control subjects).

In another study of 17 pediatric subjects with autism, their first-degree relatives, and eight mothers of typically developing children, platelet-poor plasma 5-HT levels were found to be low in mothers of autistic children compared to control mothers (Connors et al., 2006). Plasma 5-HT levels of subjects with autism correlated with the levels of their mothers and were significantly lower than those of their fathers (p = .028), but not those of their siblings (p = .063). The authors hypothesized that low serotonin levels may affect fetal brain development and increase the risk of autism, although the methodology used in obtaining and measuring 5-HT in platelet-poor plasma has been questioned (Anderson, 2007).

Urinary levels of 5-hydroxyindoleacetic acid (5-HIAA), the primary metabolite of 5-HT, are not significantly different between subjects with autism and controls (Minderaa, Anderson, Volkmar, Akkerhuis, & Cohen, 1987). CSF 5-HIAA, which may better reflect central 5-HT function, is also not significantly different in children with autism (Gillberg & Svennerholm, 1987; Gillberg, Svennerholm, & Hamilton-Hellberg, 1983; Narayan, Srinath, Anderson, & Meundi, 1993). Two studies that utilized probenecid to block the transport of 5-HIAA out of the CSF found similar (Cohen, Shaywitz, Johnson, & Bowers, 1974), or slightly lower (Cohen, Caparulo, Shaywitz, & Bowers, 1977), levels in children with autism, compared to controls with psychosis.

Serotonin Challenge Studies

Behavioral and neuroendocrine challenge studies involving 5-HT have also been conducted in autistic subjects.

Table 4-1 Selected Studies of the 5-HT Neurotransmitter System in Autism Spectrum Disorders

Type of Study	Author	Year	Sample	Findings
Blood	Minderaa et al.	1987	autism unmedicated (n=16), autism medicated (n=20), controls (n=27)	WBS in unmedicated autistics > controls. No significant differences in 5-HIAA excretion.
	Leboyer et al.	1999	autism (n=62); controls (n=118), first-degree relatives (n=122)	Elevated WBS in autism as well as 51% of mothers, 45% of fathers and 87% of siblings.
	Hranilovic et al.	2007	adults with autism (n=53), controls (n=45)	PSL in autism > controls.
	Connors et al.	2006	Mothers of children with autism (n=17), Mothers of TD children (n=8)	Plasma 5-HT levels in autism mothers < TD mothers.
Urine	Gillberg & Svennerholm	1987	autism (n=25), psychosis (n=12), historical controls	CSF 5-HIAA autism = controls.
CSF	McBride et al.	1989	autism (n=7), controls (N=7)	Blunted prolactin release in response to 60-mg oral dose of fenfluramine in autism compared to controls.
	Narayan et al.	1993	autism (n=17), neurologically impaired controls (n=15)	CSF 5-HIAA autism = neurologically impaired.
Challenge Study	McDougle et al.	1996	autism (n=17)	Worsening of anxiety and stereotypies in 11 (65%) subjects with tryptophan depletion compared to 0 subjects with sham depletion in this randomized placebo-controlled crossover study.
	Novotny et al.	2000	ASD (n=11), controls (n=9)	GH response to sumatriptan in autism > controls in this placebo-controlled challenge study.
	Hollander et al.	2000	ASD (n=11)	Sumatriptan elicited GH response correlated with severity of repetitive behaviors.
	Novotny et al.	2004	ASD (n=11), controls (n=8)	m-CPP induced increase in repetitive behavior and prolactin in ASD > controls in this randomized double-blind study.
Genetic	Cook et al.	1997	autism trios (n=86)	Preferential transmission of short allele variant of polymorphism in the promoter region of the 5-HTT (HTTLPR) gene (SLC6A4) in autism.
	Klauck et al.	1997	ASD trios (n=65)	Preferential transmission of the long allele variant of the 5-HTTLPR gene in ASD.
	Lassig et al.	1999	autism trios (n=53)	No evidence of unequal transmission of 5-HTR7 haplotypes.
	Veenstra-VanderWeele et al.	2002	ASD trios (n=115)	No evidence of unequal transmission of 5-HTR2A haplotypes.
	Yirmiya et al.	2002	ASD families (n=49), controls (n=108)	MAOA not associated with ASD.
	Cohen et al.	2003	ASD (n=41)	Low-activity MAOA allele associated with lower IQ and autism severity.

(continued)

Table 4-1 (continued)

Type of Study	Author	Year	Sample	Findings
	Brune et al.	2006	autism (n=73)	Short variant of 5-HTTLPR associated with ADI-R "failure to use nonverbal communication to regulate social interaction." Long variant of 5-HTTLPR associated with ADI-R "stereotyped and repetitive motor mannerisms," aggression, and ADOS "directed facial expressions" and "unusual sensory interests."
	Guhathakurta et al.	2006	autism (n=79), parents (n=136), controls (n=143)	SLC6A4 not associated with autism (Indian population).
	Koishi et al.	2006	autism trios (n=140)	5-HTTLPR not associated with autism (Japanese population).
	Ramoz et al.,	2006	ASD families (n=352)	TPH1 and TPH2 not associated with autism.
	Cho et al.	2007	ASD trios (n=126)	Preferential transmission of the long allele variant of 5-HTTLPR in ASD.
	Huang et al.	2008	Meta-analysis of 16 studies	SLC6A4 not associated with autism.
	Davis et al.	2008	autism (n=29), controls (n=39)	Low-activity MAOA allele associated with larger cortical brain volumes in autism.
	Orabona et al.	2009	ASD males (n=252), controls	Undertransmission of 5-HTR1B haplotypes in ASD. No association of 5-HTR2C and ASD (case-control study; Brazilian population of European ancestry).
Neuroimaging	Chugani et al.	1997	autism (n=8), siblings (n=5)	Using PET, gross asymmetries found in 5-HT synthesis in frontal cortex, thalamus, and cerebellum in males with autism.
	Chugani et al.	1999	autism (n=30), siblings (n=8), epilepsy (n=16)	Using PET, disrupted serotonin synthesis capacity in autism.
	Friedman et al.	2006	ASD (n=45), DD (n=12), TD (n=10)	Using H1-MRS, Gray matter CHO, creatine plus phosphocreatine, N-acetylaspartate, and MI in ASD < TD. Gray matter Cho and MI in ASD < DD. White matter differences in ASD = DD.
	Murphy et al.	2006	Asperger's (n=8); controls (n=10)	Using SPECT, reduced 5-HTR2A receptor binding in the anterior and posterior cingulate, frontal and superior temporal lobes, and left parietal lobe in Asperger's.
	Makkonen	2008	autistic (n=15); control (n=10)	Using SPECT, reduced 5-HTT binding capacity in the medial frontal cortex.

Controls are healthy controls unless specified.

Abbreviations used: 5-HIAA=5-hydroxyindoleacetic acid, 5-HT=serotonin, 5-HTR= serotonin receptor, 5-HTT=serotonin transporter, ADI-R=Autism Diagnostic Interview-Revised, ADOS=Autism Diagnostic Observation Schedule, ASD=autism spectrum disorder, CHO=choline-containing compounds, DAT=dopamine transporter, DD=developmentally delayed, GH=growth hormone, H1-MRS=proton magnetic resonance spectroscopy, MAOA=monoamine oxidase A, m-CPP=m-chlorophenylpiperazine, MI=myo-inositol, MR/CI= mental retardation or otherwise cognitively impaired, PET=positron emission tomography, PSL=Platelet serotonin level, SERT=serotonin transporter, SPECT= single photon emission computed tomography, TDT=transmission/disequilibrium test, TD=typical development, TPH-tyryptophan hydroxy-lase, uVNTR=upstream variable-number tandem repeat region, WBS=whole blood serotonin.

The immediate precursor of 5-HT, 5-hydroxytrypto-phan (5-HTP), was administered to children with autism and adult normal control subjects (Hoshino et al., 1983, 1984). Prolactin response to 5-HTP was reduced in the children with autism, suggesting dimin-ished central 5-HT responsiveness. Blunted prolactin release was also found in response to fenfluramine (an indirect 5-HT agonist) 60 mg given orally, in an inves-tigation of seven male young adults with autism and matched healthy controls (McBride et al., 1989).

Acute tryptophan depletion was conducted with 17 drug-free adults with autism (McDougle et al., 1996). Tryptophan depletion led to significant reduc-tions in plasma free and total tryptophan, whereas administration of sham depletion (containing trypto-phan) led to a significant increase in these plasma measures. Eleven of the 17 subjects showed a worsen-ing of symptoms, including a significant increase in whirling, flapping, pacing, banging, self-hitting, rock-ing, and toe walking, with tryptophan depletion com-pared to sham depletion.

Another set of challenge studies used the 5-HT_{1D} receptor agonist sumatriptan, which increases growth hormone release. Eleven adults with autism or Asperger's disorder and nine controls were given sub-cutaneous sumatriptan and placebo, separated by 1 week (Novotny et al., 2000). The subjects had a sig-nificantly greater growth hormone response than con-trols, suggesting hypersensitivity of the 5-HT_{1D} receptor. The severity of repetitive behavior at base-line in these subjects was positively correlated with the growth hormone response to sumatriptan (Hollander et al., 2000). The same investigators also found that the oral administration of m-chlorophe-nylpiperazine (m-CPP), a 5-HT agonist, resulted in a significant increase in repetitive behaviors and prolac-tin in adults with autism or Asperger's disorder, in comparison with controls (Novotny et al., 2004).

Serotonin Genetics

A number of investigations of genes involved in the 5-HT system have been conducted in autism. The 5-HT transporter (5-HTT), the site of action of sero-tonin reuptake inhibitors, has long been considered a candidate gene for autism. Cook et al. (1997) were the first to report an association between the short variant of a functional insertion-deletion polymorphism in the promoter region of 5-HTT (HTTLPR) gene (SLC6A4) and autism. In contrast, Klauck et al.

(1997) identified preferential transmission of the long variant of HTTLPR in their sample of autistic sub-jects. In another study, 126 Korean trios of ASD patients (both parents plus affected child), the long allelic variant was preferentially transmitted in the ASD subjects (Cho, Yoo, Park, Lee, & Kim, 2007).

Other studies have not found an association between SLC6A4 and autism. The transmission of the short or long variant of the 5-HTTLPR locus in affected individuals was determined in a large cohort of 352 families (Ramoz et al., 2006). The study did not find an association between autism and the 5-HT-TLPR locus, or any of the nine single nucleotide poly-morphisms (SNPs) covering the SLC6A4 gene, or any of their haplotypes. No association was found between these variants and autism in another study involving a smaller sample from India (Guhathakurta et al., 2006). In a study of 104 trios, all ethnically Japanese, an analysis using the transmission/disequilibrium test (TDT) between the 5-HTT gene promoter polymor-phism and autism, showed no significant linkage dis-equilibrium (Koishi et al., 2006).

Huang and Santangelo (2008) conducted a sys-tematic review and meta-analysis of all published family-based and population based studies (n=16) and failed to find an overall association between 5-HTT gene polymorphisms and autism. In ethnically hetero-geneous family-based studies of United States mixed population samples, however, significant preferential transmission of the short variant of 5-HTTLPR was found. There were no differences between short and long variant transmission among family-based studies of European and Asian samples.

Other investigators have explored different pheno-typic presentations of 5-HTTLPR polymorphisms in autism. Brune et al. (2006) found that subjects who were heterozygous or homozygous for the short variant of 5-HTTLPR were rated as more severe on the Autism Diagnostic Interview-Revised (ADI-R) subdomain of "failure to use nonverbal communication to regulate social interaction." Subjects homozygous for the long variant were rated as more severe on the "stereotyped and repetitive motor mannerisms" domain and on aggression. On the Autism Diagnostic Observation Schedule (ADOS), subjects having the long variant were more impaired on directed facial expressions and unusual sensory interests. Variants of the SLC6A4 gene have also been shown to be related to the finding of hyperserotonemia in ASD (Coutinho et al., 2004).

Genes encoding 5-HT receptors have also been studied. Orabona et al. (2009) reported undertransmission of the gene encoding the 5-HT_{1B} receptor in 252 Brazilian males with ASDs of European descent. Results from studies involving other 5-HT receptor genes, including genes encoding the 5-HT_{2A} (Veenstra-VanderWeele et al., 2002), 5-HT_{2C} (Orabona et al., 2009), and 5-HT_7 (Lassig et al., 1999) receptors, have not identified a significant association with autism.

Tryptophan 2,3 dioxygenase (TDO2) is the rate-limiting enzyme in the catabolism of tryptophan, the precursor of 5-HT. Nabi, Serajee, Chugani, Zhong & Huq (2004) demonstrated a significant difference in the transmission of TDO2 haplotypes to autistic subjects, suggesting the presence of a susceptibility mutation in the TDO2 or a nearby gene. Monoamine oxidase A (MAOA) metabolizes 5-HT and other monoamines. A variable number tandem repeat (VNTR) polymorphism exists within the promoter region of the MAOA gene that influences MAOA expression levels so that the "low activity'" allele (MAOA-L) is associated with increased neurotransmitter levels in the brain. MAOA-L has been associated with lower IQ (Yirmiya et al., 2002), greater symptom severity (Cohen et al., 2003), and larger cortical brain volumes (Davis et al., 2008) in autism. The tryptophan hydroxylase genes, TPH1 and TPH2, encode the rate-limiting enzymes that control 5-HT biosynthesis. In a family-based association test in 352 families with autism and in clinically defined subsets of these families with either severe obsessive-compulsive behaviors or self-stimulatory behaviors, no evidence for association between autism and single SNPs or haplotypes of TPH1 or TPH2 were found (Ramoz et al., 2006).

Serotonin Neuroimaging

Neuroimaging studies of the 5-HT system have also been completed in autism. The first investigation utilized positron emission tomography (PET) to assess the tracer alpha-[^{11}C]methyl-L-tryptophan (AMT) as an indicator of 5-HT synthesis in eight autistic children and five of their siblings (Chugani et al., 1997). Gross asymmetries of 5-HT synthesis in the frontal cortex, thalamus, and cerebellum were found in all seven of the autistic boys studied, but not in the only female autistic subject. The investigators concluded that the focal abnormalities in [^{11}C]AMT accumulation may represent either aberrant innervation by 5-HT terminals or altered function in anatomically normal pathways. A subsequent study by the same investigators (Chugani et al., 1999), again using PET and [^{11}C]AMT, found that for non-autistic children, 5-HT synthesis capacity was more than 200% of adult values until the age of 5 years and then declined toward adult values. In autistic children, 5-HT synthesis capacity increased gradually between the ages of 2 years and 15 years to values 1.5 times higher than adult normal values. It was concluded that humans undergo a period of high-brain 5-HT synthesis capacity during childhood, and that this developmental process is disrupted in autistic children.

In a study utilizing single photon emission computed tomography (SPECT), children with autism showed reduced 5-HT transporter binding capacity in the medial frontal cortex (Makkonen 2008). DA transporter binding was no different between subjects (n=15) and controls (n=10). Cortical 5-HT_{2A} receptor binding and density as measured by SPECT was significantly reduced in eight adults with Asperger's disorder, in comparison to 10 controls with SPECT (Murphy et al. 2006). Proton magnetic resonance spectroscopy (H1-MRS) was used in a study of 45 preschool-aged children with ASDs, 12 age-matched children with developmental delay (DD), and 10 typically developing children (Friedman et al., 2006). Decreased gray matter concentrations of choline-containing compounds (Cho), creatine plus phosphocreatine, N-acetylaspartate, and myo-inositol (mI) were found compared with typically developing children. Compared to children with developmental delays, children with ASDs demonstrated decreased levels of Cho and mI in gray matter. White matter differences were similar in the ASD and DD groups.

Dopamine and Metabolites

The monoamine DA is integral to motor functioning, cognition, and hormone release (Moore and Bloom, 1979). A role for DA in autism has been postulated, based upon the beneficial effects observed with the use of DA D_2 receptor antagonists, such as haloperidol and risperidone. This class of drugs has been shown to effectively target symptoms commonly exhibited by individuals with autism, such as aggression, self-injurious behavior, and hyperactivity (Posey, Stigler, Erickson, & McDougle, 2008), but is not clearly effective for the core symptoms of social and communication impairment.

To a large extent, neurochemical research in this area has centered on the measurement of the major

DA metabolite, homovanillic acid (HVA), in urine and plasma, as well as CSF. When considering this research, it is important to bear in mind that only approximately 25% of urine and plasma HVA appears to result from central DA turnover, and that peripheral measures are primarily able to identify only substantial alterations in central DA metabolism (Maas, Hattox, Greene, & Landis, 1980).

Conflicting results have been found in studies examining DA and its metabolites in plasma and urine. In a study of catecholamine metabolism in 22 youth with autism aged 5–16 years and controls matched for age and sex, no significant difference in urinary DA was found between groups (Launay et al., 1987). In 17 unmedicated subjects with autism, no difference was found in levels of DA and HVA in urine and plasma HVA and prolactin, the release of which is inhibited by DA (Minderaa, Anderson, Volkmar, Akkerhuis, & Cohen, 1989). Autistic subjects treated with antipsychotics (n=23) had significant elevations in plasma prolactin, and both plasma and urinary HVA, but not DA. However, Martineau et al. (1992) did find abnormalities in a larger sample (n=156) measuring urine levels of DA and its derivatives, including HVA, 3-methoxytyramine (3MT), and NE + epinephrine (EPI), compared with age-matched intellectually disabled and normal controls. The levels were found to decrease significantly with age in all three groups. Interestingly, decreased levels of DA and HVA were found in medicated versus unmedicated autistic youth in contrast to the findings of Minderaa et al. (1989).

Several studies that measured CSF HVA levels have been published. Gillberg & Svennerholm (1987) reported a 50% elevation in CSF HVA in children with autism, compared to an age- and sex-matched control group with other neurological disorders. However, other investigators have not replicated this elevation (Cohen et al., 1974; Cohen et al., 1977; Narayan et al., 1993; Ross et al., 1985).

Dopamine Genetics

In a case-control study, the A1 allele of the DA D_2 receptor gene was found to be more prevalent in autism (55%) and other neuropsychiatric disorders, including attention-deficit/hyperactivity disorder (ADHD), Tourette's disorder, and alcohol dependence, compared to controls (25%; Comings et al., 1991). The DA D_1 receptor (DRD1) gene was examined in 112 male-only affected sibling-pair families to determine whether there

was any association between ASDs and the mothers' or sons' DRD1 genotypes. A risk haplotype in the DRD1 gene was identified which was over-transmitted from mothers to sons with ASDs. This haplotype was associated with more severe impairments in measures of social interaction, communication, and stereotypies (Hettinger, Liu, Schwartz, Michaelis, & Holden, 2008).

Robinson, Schutz, Macciardi, White, & Holden (2001) examined the DA-ß-hydroxylase (DßH) gene as a candidate locus in 37 families with two or more children with ASDs, using the affected sibling-pair method. DßH catalyzes DA to NE. There was no increased concordance for DßH alleles in affected siblings, but the mothers had a higher frequency of alleles containing a 19-base pair deletion. The authors hypothesized that lowered maternal serum DßH activity might produce a suboptimal uterine environment, which in combination with a genetic susceptibility, could result in ASD.

A variable number tandem repeat (VNTR) functional polymorphism located in the 3'–untranslated region of the dopamine transporter (DAT1) gene was examined in 67 children with ASD to look for an association with various associated symptoms (Gadow, Roohi, DeVincent, & Hatchwell, 2008). According to parent ratings, children with the 10–10 repeat allele exhibited less severe symptoms of hyperactivity and impulsivity, as well as less severe language deficits. However, teacher ratings indicated that social anxiety and tic symptoms were more severe for children with the 10–10 genotype.

Dopamine Neuroimaging

PET has been used to examine DA function in autism. Using [^{18}F]fluorodopa (FDOPA), Ernst and colleagues (1997) studied 14 children and adolescents with autism and 10 controls. In the autistic group, regional FDOPA accumulation in the anteriomedial prefrontal cortex was reduced by 39%.

In another PET study, 6 children (ages 3–5 years) with autism were treated with 6R-L-erythro-5,6,7, 8,-tetrahydrobiopterin (R-BH$_4$), a cofactor for tyrosine hydroxylase in the biosynthetic pathway of catecholamines (Fernell et al., 1997). Subjects were included only if they demonstrated a relatively low level of R-BH$_4$ in the CSF. Prior to treatment, PET revealed increased DA D_2 receptor binding in the caudate and putamen as a whole. Treatment led to increases in CSF R-BH$_4$ and a 10% decrease in DA D_2 receptor binding.

Norepinephrine and Metabolites

The neurotransmitter NE is associated with arousal, memory, anxiety, and autonomic activity (Moore & Bloom, 1979). Produced from DA, NE is metabolized to vanillylmandelic acid (VMA) in the periphery, and to 3-methoxy-4-hydroxyphenylglycol (MHPG) in the central nervous system (CNS). Plasma and urine levels of NE and its metabolites have been considered to be generally well correlated with central functioning (Roy, Pickar, De Jong, Karoum, & Linnoila, 1988). However, research has also shown that estimates of the proportion of MHPG in blood and urine originating in the CNS, relative to that from the periphery, have been uncertain, ranging from 10%–60% (Blombery et al., 1980).

An early study found higher levels of blood NE and lower levels of DßH in autism compared to age-matched controls (Lake, Zeigler, & Murphy, 1977). Minderaa et al. (1994) also found no significant difference in plasma MHPG between subjects with autism and age-matched controls regardless of medication status. Urinary levels of MHPG, NE, and EPI were recorded between subjects with autism and normal controls. The authors concluded that notable abnormalities in basal NE measures did not appear to be present in autism. CSF MHPG levels also do not appear to be significantly different from normal in autism (Young et al., 1981; Gillberg & Svennerholm, 1987).

GLUTAMATE/GABA

Glutamate, the primary excitatory amino acid neurotransmitter, is found in high concentrations throughout the brain. It is thought to play a crucial role in both neuronal plasticity and higher cognitive functioning (Cotman Kahle, Miller, Ulas, & Bridges, 1995). Glutamate receptors are divided into metabotropic and ionotropic types. The ionotropic receptors are further classified into the following three families: N-methyl-D-aspartate (NMDA), alpha-amino-3-hydroxy-5-methyl-4-isoxazole propionic acid (AMPA), and kainate. Several researchers have postulated that glutamate dysfunction may play a role in autism (Carlsson, 1998; McDougle, 2002).

GABA, another amino acid neurotransmitter, is the primary inhibitory neurotransmitter in the brain. It is synthesized from glutamate by glutamic acid decarboxylase (GAD). Investigators have also hypothesized that GABA may play an important role in the

pathophysiology of autism (Dhossche et al., 2002). Rubenstein and Merzenich (2003) have emphasized the importance of excitation/inhibition balance, and theorized that mechanisms leading to either increased excitation or decreased inhibition during neurodevelopment could manifest as autism. Selected studies assessing the glutamate and GABA neurotransmitter are summarized in Table 4-2.

Glutamate/GABA Measurements

Several reports have suggested that peripheral levels of glutamate are elevated in the plasma of subjects with autism and other ASDs. Aldred, Moore, Fitzgerald, & Waring (2003) collected blood from 23 subjects, ages 4–29 years, with autism or Asperger's disorder, and 55 of their family members (32 parents, 23 siblings), and measured amino acid concentrations. They found that concentrations of glutamate, phenylalanine, lysine, and asparagine were significantly higher in both subjects and family members, compared to age-matched controls. Glutamine levels were significantly lower. Moreno-Fuenmayor, Borjas, Arrieta, Valera, & Socorro-Candanoza (1996) also measured amino acid levels in 14 children with autism (all under 10 years of age) and age- and sex-matched controls. They found that aspartate was higher and glutamine and asparagine were lower in subjects than in controls. Increased levels of serum glutamate were also found n a study of 18 Japanese male adults with autism compared to 19 age-matched controls; levels of glutamine, glycine, d-serine, and l-serine did not differ between groups (Shinohe et al., 2007).

In contrast to the majority of studies showing elevated glutamate, Rolf, Haarmann, Grotemeyer, & Kehrer (1993) found that aspartate and glutamate were decreased in 18 drug-free children aged 8–14 years with autism compared, to 14 age-matched healthy controls. GABA and glutamine levels were also significantly lower. However, Dhossche et al. (2002) reported elevated plasma GABA levels (measured by gas chromatography/mass spectrometry) in a small, heterogeneous sample of nine subjects with autism aged 5–15 years, compared to nine control subjects with ADHD. Most of the autistic subjects were taking prescribed psychotropic or anticonvulsant drugs, and all of the ADHD controls were taking psychostimulants.

Neuroimaging is beginning to be used to better understand the glutamate system. Using H1-MRS, high-functioning adults (n=25) with ASDs showed higher concentration of glutamate/glutamine and

Table 4-2 Selected Studies of the Glutamate and GABA Neurotransmitter Systems in Autism Spectrum Disorders

Type of Study	Author	Year	Sample	Findings
Blood	Rolf et al.	1993	autism unmedicated (n=18), controls (n=14)	Glutamate and GABA decreased in autism.
	Moreno-Fuenmayor et al.	1996	autism (n=14), historical controls	Glutamate increased in autism.
	Dhossche et al.	2002	autism medicated (n=9), ADHD medicated (n=9)	GABA increased in autism.
	Aldred et al.	2003	ASD (n=23), first-degree relatives (n=55), historical controls	Glutamate increased in ASD and first-degree relatives.
	Shinohe et al.	2007	autism (n=18), controls (n=19)	Glutamate increased in autism.
Genetic	Cook et al.	1998	autism trios (n=140)	GABRB3 marker 155CA-2 associated with autism.
	Salmon et al.	1999	multiplex autism families (n=139)	GABRB3 marker 155CA-2 not associated with autism.
	Martin et al.	2000	autism trios (n=54)	GABRB3 marker 155CA-2 not associated with autism. Suggestive linkage for another marker GABRB3.
	Nurmi et al.,	2001	multiplex autism families (n=94)	GABRB3 markers (including 155CA-2 and GABRB3) not associated with autism.
	Buxbaum et al.	2002	autism families (n=80)	GABRB3 marker (155CA-2) associated with autism.
	Menold et al.	2001	Autistic patients and parents (n=226)	Two GABRG3 markers associated with autism.
	Jamain et al.	2002	autism families (n=59), autism trios (n=107)	GRIK2 associated with autism.
	Shuang et al.	2004	autism trios (n=174)	GRIK2 associated with autism (Chinese population).
	McCauley et al.	2004	multiplex autism families (n=123)	Six GABRB3 and GABRA5 markers nominally associated with autism.
	Rabionet et al.	2004	multiplex autism families (n=110)	GAD1 not associated with autism.
	Ma et al.	2005	Caucasian autism families (n=470)	GABRA4 and GABRB1 interaction associated with autism.
	Seguarado et al.	2005	autism trios (n=158)	SLC25A12 associated with autism.
	Blasi et al.	2006	autism multiplex families (n=261);	SLC25A12 not associated with autism.
	Correia et al.	2006	autism trios (n=241)	SLC25A12 not associated with autism.
	Rabionet et al.	2006	Autism families (n=327)	SLC25A12 not associated autism.
	Collins et al.	2006	Caucasian autism families (n=557), African-American autism families (n=54)	GABRA4 and GABRB1 genes associated with autism in both Caucasian and African-American families. GABRA4-GABRB1 interaction in Caucasian families.
	Dutta et al	2007	ASD (n=101), parents (n=180), controls (n=152)	GRIK2 not associated with autism (Indian population).
	Kim et al.	2007	ASD trios (n=126)	GRIK2 associated with autism (Korean population).

(continued)

Table 4-2 (continued)

Type of Study	Author	Year	Sample	Findings
	Li et al.	2008	ASD (n=213), controls (n=160)	GRM8 not associated with autism.
	Buttenschøn et al.	2009	autism (n=444), controls (n=444)	No association with common GAD1 markers and autism. However, a rare nine-marker haplotype in this gene region was associated with autism.
Neuroimaging	Page et al.	2006	ASD (n=25), controls (n=21)	Using H1-MRS, elevated glutamate/glutamine and creatine/phosphocreatine in amygdala-hippocampal region but not parietal region.
Postmortem	Blatt et al.	2001	autism (n=4); controls (n=3)	Using autoradiography, decreased GABA receptor binding in hippocampus. No differences in 5-HT, cholinergic, or glutamatergic receptor density.
	Purcell et al.	2001	autism (n=10), controls (n=23)	Up-regulation of GluR1 (AMPA 1) and increase in GluR1 receptor. Decreased AMPA receptor density in cerebellum.
	Fatemi et al.	2002	autism (n=8), controls (n=5)	GAD 65 reduced in parietal cortex. GAD 67 reduced in cerebellum.
	Guptill et al.	2007	autism (n=4), controls (n=3)	Decreased number of GABA receptors in hippocampus.
	Yip et al.	2007	autism (n=8), controls (n=8)	GAD67 mRNA level was reduced by 40% in the autistic group compared to controls.
	Lepagnol-Bestel et al.	2008	autism (n=9), controls (n=8)	SLC25A12 expression increased in prefrontal cortex, but not in cerebellum.
	Palmieri et al.	2008	autism (n=6) matched controls (n=6)	Increase in GRIA1 and aspartate/glutamate exchange (calcium-dependent) in temporocortical gray matter.
	Fatemi et al.	2009a	autism (n=9), controls (n=12)	Reduced GABA (A) receptor subunit expression in parietal cortex, superior frontal cortex, and cerebellum.
	Fatemi et al.	2009b	autism (n=9), controls (n=12)	Reduced GABA (B) receptor subunit expression in parietal cortex, superior frontal cortex, and cerebellum.

Controls are healthy controls unless specified.

Abbreviations used: ADHD=attention-deficit/hyperactivity disorder, AMPA=alpha-amino-3-hydroxy-5-methyl-4-isoxazole propionic acid, ASD=autism spectrum disorder, GABA= γ-aminobutyric acid, GABR=GABA A receptor, GAD=glutamate acid decarboxylase, GRIA1=glutamate receptor ionotropic AMPA 1, GRIK2=glutamate receptor ionotropic kainate 2, GRM8=glutamate receptor metabotropic 8, H1-MRS=proton magnetic resonance spectroscopy.

creatine/phosphocreatine in the amygdala-hippocampal region, but not in the parietal region (Page et al 2006).

Glutamate Receptors

A number of genetic studies of the glutamate and GABA systems have been conducted in autism. Jamain et al. (2002) showed that the glutamate receptor ionotropic kainate 2 gene (GRIK2), also known as the glutamate receptor 6 (GluR6) gene, is in disequilibrium with autism, and that an excess of maternal transmission of the GRIK2 haplotype exists. This finding has been replicated in persons from China (Shuang et al., 2004) and Korea (Kim, Kim, Park, Cho, & Yoo, 2007), but not India (Dutta et al., 2007). Individuals homozygous for a mutation in the GluR6 gene were found to have moderate to severe mental retardation in an extended Iranian family, suggesting that GluR6 function is crucial to higher cognitive function (Motazacker et al., 2007).

Serajee, Zhong, Nabi, & Huq (2003) found suggestive evidence for linkage disequilibrium between autism and the metabotropic glutamate receptor 8 (GRM8) gene, which occurs on chromosom 7q, a region implicated in genome-wide scans. Li et al. (2008), however, did not find significant linkage with polymorphisms of GRM8 in 213 children with ASDs and 160 controls.

Postmortem studies have occasionally found glutamate receptor abnormalities. Purcell, Jeon, Zimmerman, Blue, & Pevsner (2001) examined the cerebellum and hippocampi of 10 persons with autism and 23 matched controls using cDNA microarray technology, additional measurements of mRNA and protein levels, as well as receptor autoradiography, and found upregulation of the glutamate receptor AMPA 1 (GluR1) gene. Higher levels of the corresponding protein were also found. Finally, AMPA receptor density was decreased in both the granule cell layer and molecular cell layer of the cerebellum.

GABA Receptors

Several lines of evidence implicate the 15q11-q13 chromosome region as potentially harboring autism-susceptibility genes. This includes numerous reports suggesting that duplications and other abnormalities in this region may occur in as many as 3% of autistic individuals (Sutcliffe et al., 2003). Abnormalities in this genetic region are also responsible for disorders with significant overlap with autism, including Prader-Willi and Angelman syndromes.

Cook et al. (1998) tested several loci in this region for linkage disequilibrium and were the first to report an association between a marker (155CA-2) within the GABA receptor subunit ß-3 gene (GABRB3) and autism in a sample of 140 trios. Linkage disequilibrium for 155CA-2 has been found in one other sample (Buxbaum et al., 2002), but not others (Maestrini et al., 1999; Martin et al., 2000; Nurmi et al., 2001; Salmon et al., 1999). However, Martin et al. (2000) did report linkage disequilibrium with another nearby marker (GABRB3) in this same region.

Menold et al. (2001) found linkage disequilibrium for two SNPs located within the GABRG3 gene. McCauley et al. (2004) performed linkage disequilibrium mapping across a region containing a cluster of GABA receptor subunit genes on chromosome 15q12. Six markers individually, across GABRB3 and GABRA5,

and several haplotypes inclusive of those markers, demonstrated nominally significant association.

Ma et al. (2005) found that GABRA4 is involved in autism through an interaction with GABRB1. A follow-up study also showed GABRA4 and GABRB1 associations with autism in both Caucasian and African American samples (Collins et al., 2006). A subset of families with seizures in at least one family member with autism did not show an association with GABRA4, but did with three SNPS within GABRB1.

In an autoradiographic study, Blatt et al. (2001) reported decreased density of GABA receptors in the hippocampal sections of brain in cases with autism (n = 4) compared to controls (n = 3). This appears to be due to a decreased number of GABA receptors, rather than reduced affinity (Guptill et al., 2007). Reduced GABA A (Fatemi et al., 2009a) and GABA B (Fatemi et al., 2009b) subunit expression has also been demonstrated in the cerebellum, as well as in the superior frontal cortex (BA9), and parietal cortex (BA40).

Glutamic Acid Decarboxylase

Glutamic Acid Decarboxylase (GAD) is an enzyme important in the conversion of Glu to GABA. Two GAD isoforms, GAD67 and GAD65, are encoded by GAD1 and GAD2, respectively. As decarboxylases, they require Vitamin B_6 as a cofactor, which some believe may have efficacy in autism (Pfeiffer, Norton, Nelson, & Shott, 1995). However, candidate-gene studies have not found consistent association between GAD1 and autism (Buttenschøn et al., 2009; Rabionet et al., 2004). However, Buttenschøn and colleagues (2009) did report a rare nine-marker haplotype in this gene region as being associated with autism.

Both GAD65 and GAD67 levels were measured in postmortem cerebellar (n = 5) and parietal cortices (n = 5) of persons with autism compared to controls (Fatemi et al., 2002). In this study, GAD65 was significantly lower in cerebellar cortices and GAD67 was significantly reduced in parietal cortices. Using in situ hybridization, cerebellar GAD 67 mRNA levels have also been shown to be reduced by approximately 40% in autism (n=8) compared to controls (n=8) (Yip et al., 2007).

Mitochondrial Aspartate/Glutamate Carrier

The mitochondrial aspartate/glutamate carrier is encoded by the SLC25A12 gene on chromosome 2q, another region implicated in genome-wide scans.

SLC25A12 polymorphisms have been linked to autism in some (Ramoz et al., 2004; Seguarado et al., 2005; Turunen et al., 2008), but not all (Blasi et al., 2006; Correia et al., 2006), Rabionet et al., 2006) candidate gene studies. Postmortem studies have found overexpression of SLC25A12 in Brodmann's Area (BA) 46 prefrontal cortex but not in the cerebellum (Lepagnol-Bestel et al., 2008). Palmieri et al. (2008) reported increased aspartate/glutamate exchange rates that were dependent on significantly higher calcium concentrations in postmortem neocortical tissue of six autistic patients compared to controls, although no specific SLC25A12 polymorphisms were linked to this excess activity.

NEUROPEPTIDES

This section will review studies examining the role of opioids, melatonin, and other neuropeptides and neurotrophins in autism. Oxytocin and other hormones are the focus of Chapter 22.

Opioids

Several observations of autistic children led to the early evaluation of opioid dysregulaton as a possible etiologic explanation of ASDs. These have included elevated pain threshold, little interest in social interactions, and episodes of motor hyperactivity (Sher et al., 1997). These findings appeared to match those seen in infant animals administered opiates (Panskepp et al., 1985).

Evaluations of ß-endorphin (and ß-endorphin metabolites in some cases) levels in the serum, CSF, and urine of patients with ASDs, compared to controls, have yielded conflicting results (Tordjman et al., 1997). Ten studies enrolling a total of 142 patients with ASDs have evaluated serum ß-endorphin levels, and the results represent a relatively equal mix of increased, decreased, or similar ß-endorphin levels found in the patients compared to control subjects. In two investigations of CSF ß-endorphin levels in patients with ASDs, one reported increased and one reported decreased levels in affected patients.

Investigation of urinary opioid peptides has attempted to look at whether inadequate processing of exogenous opioids by the gastrointestinal (GI) tract may result in over-absorption, and finally urinary excretion, of the peptides. Such an evaluation analyzed the urine of 10 children with autism, compared to 11 adult controls, and found no difference between groups

(Hunter et al., 2003). This study also specifically evaluated dipeptidyl peptidase in the serum of patients and found no difference compared with controls. This enzyme is present at the intestinal brush border, and is expected to be involved in the cleaving of exogenous dietary opioids. Cass et al. (2008) also were unable to demonstrate opioid peptiduria in another case-control study of 65 boys with autism and 158 controls.

The use of naltrexone, an opioid receptor antagonist, has been evaluated in several open-label and placebo-controlled trials in patients with ASDs having unknown, elevated, or normal levels of serum ß-endorphin (Erickson et al., 2007). Again, as in the studies looking at serum and CSF ß-endorphin levels, conflicting results on the efficacy of naltrexone exist, but most controlled studies suggest that the core symptoms of autism and associated maladaptive behavior are not significantly affected by naltrexone.

Melatonin

Melatonin is important in sleep and other circadian rhythms. It is synthesized in the pineal gland by the conversion of 5-HT to N-acetylserotonin via arylalkylamine N-acetyltransferase). N-acetylserotonin is then converted to melatonin via acetylserotonin methyltransferase (ASMT).

Decreased melatonin secretion during the dark phase of a 24-hour collection period was demonstrated in 14 children with autism, compared to 20 controls (Kulman et al., 2000). Tordjman et al. (2005) found decreased urinary excretion of 6-sulphatoxymelatonin in youth with autism (n=49), compared to matched controls (n=88).

Melke et al. (2008) found two polymorphisms of ASMT to be more frequent in autism (n=250), compared to controls (n=255). Biochemical analyses in the same subjects revealed decreased ASMT activity and low melatonin levels in subjects with autism.

Other Neuropeptides and Neurotrophins

A novel analysis of neuropeptides and neurotrophins from frozen blood samples of neonates subsequently diagnosed with an ASDs (n=69), mental retardation (MR) without autism (n=54), or cerebral palsy (n=63), as well as normal control patients (n=54), found significantly elevated levels of several measured substances in the ASD and MR groups (Nelson et al., 2001). Concentrations of neonatal vasoactive intestinal peptide (VIP), calcitonin gene-related peptide (CGRP), brain-derived neurotrophic factor (BDNF), and neurotrophin 4/5 were significantly higher in both the ASD and MR groups. No significant differences between the ASD and MR groups were noted. Concentrations of substance P, pituitary adenylate cyclase-activating polypeptide (PACAP), nerve growth factor (NGF), and neurotrophin 3 were all similar among all groups tested. In another study, CSF levels of the neurotrophic factor insulin-like growth factor-I were found to be similar in an analysis of 11 autistic patients and 11 age-matched "disabled" controls (Vanhalia et al., 2001).

More recently, Croen et al. (2008) measured BDNF levels during pregnancy and at the time of birth from archived samples in three groups: autism (n=84), developmental delay/mental retardation (n=49), and typical development (n=159). In contrast to the earlier positive finding, no significant differences were found in BDNF levels between the three groups.

BDNF has previously been found to be elevated in postmortem studies of adults with autism (Perry et al., 2001). BDNF and BDNF autoantibodies were measured in groups of children with autism, childhood disintegrative disorder (CDD), Pprvasive developmental disorder not otherwise specified (PDD-NOS), as well as healthy controls and children with other neurological and non-neurological illness (Connolly et al., 2006). Elevated BDNF levels were found in children with autism and CDD compared to healthy controls. BDNF autoantibodies were also elevated in children with autism, CDD, and epilepsy, compared to controls.

SUMMARY

This chapter has explored the available literature on neurochemical contributions to the pathophysiology of autism, with a focus on monoamines (5-HT, DA, NE), glutamate/GABA systems, and neuropeptides. With respect to monoamines, the majority of studies that have focused on basal measures of plasma, urine, and CSF have been negative. The one exception is that of elevated WBS or "hyperserotonemia," which has been replicated in multiple investigations. Its underlying mechanism, however, remains unclear. Pharmacological manipulation of the 5-HT system via the acute administration of various drugs under controlled laboratory conditions has been shown to affect behavior in adults with autism. These challenge studies have not yet been replicated, and have not been integrated with neuroimaging to allow better assessment of changes in neurochemistry. Preliminary PET studies involving 5-HT and DA systems have identified abnormalities in 5-HT synthesis capacity. Postmortem assessment of monoaminergic involvement needs to be completed. The roles of DA and NE are less clear, but may be involved in areas that are commonly impaired in autism including mood, arousal, and attention.

Encouraging results from preliminary genetic studies of the glutamate and GABA systems are emerging. This includes a number of postmortem studies showing decreased GABA function in the brains of persons with autism. Multiple genetic studies are finding abnormalities in glutamate and GABA receptors, although these results have not been replicated in all samples. Initial MRS studies are also suggesting glutamatergic abnormalities.

The role of neuropeptides and neurotrophins in the pathophysiology of autism is less clear. Findings from recent studies of opioid abnormalities are not supportive of this hypothesis. Melatonin abnormalities have recently been found by Tordjman et al. (2005) and other groups. Interesting initial results suggesting elevated neonatal BDNF as a biomarker of autism and intellectual disability have failed to be replicated. However, BDNF levels have been shown to be elevated in older children and adults with autism as well as other neurological illness.

Future high-quality studies should continue to include controls groups in order to assess the impact of race, age, sex, concomitant drugs, comorbid medical illness (e.g., epilepsy), and IQ on the obtained results. New methodologies such as MRS may greatly expand our knowledge of the in vivo neurochemistry of autism. Studies that simultaneously capture data from multiple modalities including peripheral blood, neuroimaging, and genetics may also be important in advancing our understanding of the underlying pathophysiology of autism.[1]

1. Supported in part by NIMH grants R01 MH077600 (Dr. Posey), R01 MH072964 (Dr. McDougle), and K23 MH082119 (Dr. Stigler), as well as a National Institute of Health grant K12 UL1 RR025761, Indiana University Clinical and Translational Sciences Institute Career Development Award (Dr. Erickson), the Daniel X. and Mary Freedman Fellowship in Academic Psychiatry (Dr. Stigler), and the Division of Disability & Rehabilitative Services, Indiana Family and Social Services Administration (Drs. Erickson and McDougle).

References

Aldred, S., Moore, K. M., Fitzgerald M., & Waring R. H. (2003). Plasma amino acid levels in children with autism and their families. *Journal of Autism Development Disorder, 33,* 93–97.

Anderson, G. M. (2007). Measurement of plasma serotonin in autism. *Pediatric Neurology, 36,* 138.

Blasi, F., Bacchelli, E., Carone, S., Toma, C., Monaco, A. P., Bailey, A. J., Maestrini, E., International Molecular Genetic Study of Autism Consortium (IMGSAC) (2006). SLC25A12 and CMYA3 gene variants are not associated with autism in the IMGSAC multiplex family sample. *The European Journal of Human Genetics, 14,* 123–126.

Blatt G. J., Fitzgerald C. M., Guptill J. T., Brooker, A. B., Kemper, T. L., Bauman, M. L. (2001). Density and distribution of hippocampal neurotransmitter receptors in autism: an autoradiographic study. *Journal of Autism and Developmental Disorders, 31,* 537–543.

Blombery, P. A., Kopin, I. J., Gordon, E. K., Markey, S. P., Ebert, M. H. (1980). Conversion of MHPG to vanillylmandelic acid. Implications for the importance of urinary MHPG. *Archives of General Psychiatry, 37,* 195–198.

Brune, C. W., Kim, S. J., Salt, J., Leventhal, B. L., Lord, C., Cook, E. H. (2006). 5-HTTLPR genotype-specific phenotype in children and adolescents with autism. *The American Journal of Psychiatry, 163,* 2148–2156.

Buttenschøn, H. N., Lauritsen, M. B., Daoud, A., Hollegaard, M., Jorgensen, M., Tvedegaard, K., . . . NAME, INITIAL(2009). A population-based association study of glutamate decarboxylase 1 as a candidate gene for autism. *Journal of Neural Transmission, 116,* 381–388.

Buxbaum, J. D., Silverman, J. M., Smith, C. J., Greenberg, D. A., Kilifarski, M., Reichert, J., . . . NAME, INITIAL. (2002). Association between GABRB3 polymorphism and autism. *Molecular Psychiatry, 7,* 311–316.

Carlsson, M. L. (1998). Hypothesis: Is infantile autism a hypoglutamatergic disorder? Relevance of glutamate-serotonin interactions for pharmacotherapy. *Journal of Neural Transmission, 105,* 525–535.

Cass, H., Gringras, P., March, J., McKendrick, I., O'Hare, A. E., Owen, L., . . . NAME, INITIAL. (2008). Absence of urinary opioid in children with autism. *Archives of Disease in Childhood, 93,* 745–750.

Cho, I., Yoo, H., Park, M., Lee, Y. S., & Kim, S. A. (2007). Family-based association study of 5-HTTLPR and the 5-HT2A receptor gene polymorphisms with autism spectrum disorder in Korean trios. *Brain Research, 1139,* 34–41.

Chugani, D. C., Muzik, O., Rothermel, R., Behen, M., Chakraborty, P., Mangner, T., . . . Chugani, H. T. (1997). Altered serotonin synthesis in the dentatothalamocortical pathway in autistic boys. *Annals of Neurology, 42,* 666–669.

Chugani, D. C., Muzik, O., Behen, M., Rothermal, R., Janisse, J. J., Lee, J.,Chugani, H. T. (1999). Developmental changes in brain serotonin synthesis capacity in autistic and nonautistic children. *Annals of Neurology, 45,* 287–295.

Cohen, D. J., Shaywitz, B. A., Johnson, W. T., & Bowers, M. (1974). Biogenic amines in autistic and atypical children: cerebrospinal fluid measures of homovanillic acid and 5-hydroxyindoleacetic acid. *Archives of Gen Psychiatry, 31,* 845–853.

Cohen, D. J., Caparulo, B. K., Shaywitz, B. A., & Bowers, M. B. (1977). Dopamine and serotonin metabolism in neuropsychiatrically disturbed children: CSF homovanillic acid and 5-hydroxyindoleacetic acid. *Archives of General Psychiatry, 34,* 545–550.

Cohen, I. L., Liu, X., Schutz, C., White, B. N., Jenkins, E. C., Brown, W. T., Holden, J. J. (2003). Association of autism severity with a monoamine oxidase A functional polymorphism. *Clinical Genetics, 64,* 190–197.

Collins, A., Ma, D., Whitehead, P., Martin, E., Wright, H., Abramson, R., . . . Pericak-Vance, M. A. (2006). Investigation of autism and GABA receptor subunit genes in multiple ethnic groups. *Neurogenetics, 7,* 167–174.

Comings, D. E., Comings, B. G., Muhleman, D., Dietz, G., Shahbahrami, B., Tast, D., . . . Flanagan, S. D. (1991). The dopamine D2 receptor locus as a modifying gene in neuropsychiatric disorders. *JAMA, 266,* 1793–1800.

Connolly, A. M., Chez, M., Streif, E. M., Keeling, R. M., Golumbek, P. T., Kwon, J. M., . . . Deuel, R. M. (2006). Brain-derived neurotrophic factor and autoantibodies to neural antigens in sera of children with autistic spectrum disorders, Landau-Kleffner syndrome, and epilepsy. *Biological Psychiatry, 59,* 354–363.

Connors, S. L., Matteson, K. J., Sega, G. A., Lozzio, C. B., Carroll, R. C., & Zimmerman, A.W. (2006). Plasma Serotonin in Autism. *Pediatric Neurology, 35,* 182–186.

Cook, E. H., Courchesne, R., Lord, C., Cox, N. J., Yan, S., Lincoln, A., . . . NAME, INITIAL (1997). Evidence of linkage between the serotonin transporter and autistic disorder. *Molecular Psychiatry, 2,* 247–250.

Cook, E. H., Courchesne, R.Y., Cox, N. J., Lord, C., Gonen, D., Guter, S. J., . . . Courchesne, E. (1998). Linkage disequilibrium mapping of autistic disorder, with 15q11-13 markers. *American Journal of Human Genetics, 62,* 1077–1083.

Correia, C., Coutinho, A. M., Diogo, L., Grazina, M., Marques, C., Miguel, T., . . . Vicente, A. M. (2006). Brief report: High frequency of biochemical markers for mitochondrial dysfunction in autism: No association with the mitochondrial aspartate/glutamate carrier SLC25A12 gene. *Journal of Autism and Developmental Disorders, 36,* 1137–1140.

Cotman, C. W., Kahle, J. S., Miller, S. E., Ulas, J., & Bridges, R. J. (1995). Excitatory amino acid neurotransmission. In F. E. Bloom & D. J. Kupfer (Eds.), *Psychopharmacology: The Fourth Generation of Progress* (pp. 75–85). *New York: Raven Press.*

Croen, L. A., Goines, P., Braunschweig, D., Yolken, R., Grether, J. K., Fireman, B., et al. (2008). Brain-derived neurotrophic factor and autism: maternal and infant peripheral blood levels in the Early Markers for Autism (EMA) Study. *Autism Research, 1*, 130–137.

Coutinho, A. M., Oliveira, G., Morgadinho, T., Fesel, C., Macedo, T. R., Bento, C., . . . Vicente, A. M. (2004). Variants of the serotonin transporter gene (SLC6A4) significantly contribute to hyperserotonemia in autism. *Molecular Psychiatry, 9*, 264–271.

Davis, L., Hazlett, H., Librant, A., Nopoulos, P., Sheffield, V., Piven, J., Wassink, T.H. (2008). Cortical Enlargement in Autism is Associated With a Functional VNTR in the Monoamine Oxidase A Gene. *Neuropsychiatric Genetics, 147B*, 1145–1151.

Dhossche, D., Applegate, H., Abraham, A., Maertens, P., Bland, L., Bencsath, A., Martinez, J. (2002). Elevated plasma gamma-aminobutyric acid (GABA) levels in autistic youngsters: stimulus for a GABA hypothesis of autism. *Medical Science Monitor, 8*, 1–6.

Dutta, S., Das, S., Guhathakurta, S., Sen, B., Sinha, S., Chatterjee, A., . . . Usha, R. (2007). Glutamate receptor 6 gene (GluR6 or GRIK2) polymorphisms in the Indian population: a genetic association study on autism spectrum disorder. *Cellular and Molecular Neurobiology, 27*, 1035–1047.

Ernst, M., Zametkin, A. J., Matochik, J. A., Pascualvaca, D., & Cohen, R. M. (1997). Low medial prefrontal dopaminergic activity in autistic children. *Lancet, 350*, 638.

Erickson, C. A., Stigler, K. A., Posey, D. J., & McDougle, C. J. (2007). Psychopharmacology. In F. R. Volkmar (Ed.), *Autism and Pervasive Developmental Disorders, 2nd ed.* (pp. 221–253). Cambridge, U.K.: Cambridge University Press.

Fatemi, S. H., Halt, A. R., Stary, J. M., Kanodia, R., Schulz, S. C., & Realmuto, G. R. (2002). Glutamic acid decarboxylase 65 and 67 kDa proteins are reduced in the autistic parietal and cerebellar cortices. *Biological Psychiatry, 52*, 805–810.

Fatemi, S.H., Reutiman, T.J., Folsom, T.D., & Thuras, P.D. (2009). GABAA Receptor Downregulation in Brains of Subjects with Autism. *Journal of Autism and Developmental Disorders, 39*, 223–230.

Fatemi, S. H., Folsom, T. D., Reutiman, T. J., & Thuras, P. D. (2009). Expression of GABA(B) receptors is altered in brains of subjects with autism. *Cerebellum, 8*, 64–69.

Fernell, E., Watanabe, Y., Adolfsson, I., Tani, Y., Bergstrom, M., Hartvig, P., Lilja, A., von Knorring, A. L., Gillberg, C. (1997). Possible effects of tetrahydrobiopterin treatment in six children with autism—clinical and positron emission tomography data: a pilot study. *Dev Med Child Neurol, 39*, 313–318.

Friedman, S., Shaw, D., Artu, A., Dawson, G., Petropoulos, H., & Dager, S. R. (2006). Gray and White Matter Brain Chemistry in Young Children With Autism. *Archives of General Psychiatry, 63*, 786–794.

Gadow, K. D, Roohi, C. J., DeVincent, C., & Hatchwell, E. (2008). Association of ADHD, tics, and anxiety with dopamine transporter (DAT1) genotype in autism spectrum disorder. *Journal of Child Psychology and Psychiatry, 49*, 1331–1338.

Gillberg, C., Svennerholm, L., & Hamilton-Hellberg, C. (1983). Childhood psychosis and monoamine metabolites in spinal fluid. *Journal of Autism and Developmental Disorders, 13*, 383–396.

Gillberg, C., & Svennerholm, L. (1987). CSF monoamines in autistic syndromes and other pervasive developmental disorders of early childhood. *British Journal of Psychiatry, 151*, 89–94.

Guhathakurta, S., Ghosh, S., Sinha, S., Chatterjee, A., Ahmed, S., Chowdhury, S.R., . . . Usha, R. NAME, INITIAL. (2006). Serotonin transporter promoter variants: Analysis in Indian autistic and control population. *Brain Research, 1092*, 28–35.

Guptill, J. T., Brooker, A. B., Gibbs, T. T., Kemper, T. L., Bauman, M. L., & Blatt, G. J. (2007). [3H]-flunitrazepam-labeled benzodiazepine binding sites in the hippocampal formation in autism: A multiple concentration autoradiographic study. *Journal of Autism and Developmental Disorders, 37*, 911–920.

Hettinger, J., Liu, X., Schwartz, C., Michaelis, R., & Holden, J. (2008). A DRD1 haplotype is associated with risk for autism spectrum disorders in male-only affected sib-pair families. *American Journal of Medical Genetics Part B (Neuropsychiatric Genetics) 147B*, 628–636.

Hollander, E., Novotny, S., Allen, A., Aronowitz, B., Cartwright, C., & DeCaria, C. (2000). The relationship between repetitive behaviors and growth hormone response to sumatriptan challenge in autistic disorder. *Neuropsychopharmacoly, 22*, 163–167.

Hoshino, Y., Watanabe, M., Tachibana, R., Murata, S., Kaneko, M., Yashimo, Y., Kumashiro, H., . . . NAME, INITIAL.(1983). A study of the hypothalamus-pituitary function in autistic children by the loading test of 5HTP, TRH, and LH-RH. *Japanese Journal of Brain Research, 9*, 94–95.

Hoshino, Y., Tachibana, J. R., Watanabe, M., Murata, S., Yokoyama, F., Kaneko, M., . . . Kumashiro, H. NAME, INITIAL.(1984). Serotonin metabolism and hypothalamic-pituitary function in children with infantile autism and minimal brain dysfunction. *Japanese Journal of Psychiatry and Neurology, 26*, 937–945.

Hranilovic, D., Bujas-Petkovic, Z., Vragovic, R., Vuk, T., Hock, K., & Jernej, B. (2007). Hyperserotonemia in adults with autistic disorder. *Journal of Autism and Developmental Disorders, 37*, 1934–1940.

Huang, C., & Santangelol, S. (2008). Autism and serotonin transporter gene polymorphisms: A systematic review and meta-analysis. *American Journal of Medical Genetics Part B (Neuropsychiatric Genetics)* 147B, 903–913.

Hunter, L. C., O'Hare, A., Herron, W. J., Fisher, L. A., & Jones, G. E. (2003). Opioid peptides and dipeptidyl peptidase in autism. *Developmental Medicine and Child Neurology, 45,* 121–128.

Jamain, S., Betancur, C., Quach, H., Philippe, A., Fellous, M., Giros, B., . . . Bourgeron, T.; Paris Autism Research International Sibpair (PARIS) Study NAME, INITIAL.(2002). Linkage and association of the glutamate receptor 6 gene with autism. *Molecular Psychiatry, 7,* 302–310.

Kim, S. A., Kim, J. H., Park, M., Cho, I. H., & Yoo, H. J. (2007). Family-based association study between GRIK2 polymorphisms and autism spectrum disorders in the Korean trios. *Neuroscience Research, 58,* 332–335.

Klauck, S. M., Poustka, F., Benner, A., Lesch, K. P., & Poustka, A. (1997). Serotonin transporter (5-HTT) gene variants associated with autism? *Human Molecular Genetics, 6,* 2233–2238.

Koishi, S., Yamamoto, K., Matsumoto, H., Koishi, S., Enseki, Y., Ova, A., . . . Yamazaki, K. NAME, INITIAL.(2006). Serotonin transporter gene promoter polymorphism and autism: A family-based genetic association study in Japanese population. *Brain & Development, 28,* 257–260.

Kulman, G., Lissoni, P., Rovelli, F., Roselli, M. G., Brivio, F., & Sequeri, P. (2000). Evidence of pineal endocrine hypofunction in autistic children. *Neuro Endocrinology Letters, 21,* 31–34.

Lake, R., Zeigler, M. G., Murphy, D. L. (1977). Increased norepinephrine levels and decreased DBH activity in primary autism. *Archives of General Psychiatry, 35,* 553–556.

Lassig, J. P., Vachirasomtoon, K., Hartzell, K., Leventhal, M., Courchesne, E., Courchesne, R., . . . Cook, E.H. NAME, INITIAL.(1999). Physical mapping of the serotonin 5-HT7 receptor gene (HTR7) to chromosome 10 and pseudogene (HTR7P) to chromosome 12, and testing of linkage disequilibrium between HTR7 and autistic disorder. *American Journal of Medical Genetics, 88,* 472–475.

Launay, J. M., Ferrari, P., Haimart, M., Bursztejn, C., Tabuteau, F., Braconnier, A., . . . Fermanian, J. NAME, INITIAL. (1987). Catecholamine metabolism in infantile autism: A controlled study of 22 autistic children. *Journal of Autism and Developmental Disorders, 17,* 333–347.

Leboyer, M., Philippe, A., Bouvard, M., Guilloud-Bataille, M., Bondoux, D., Tabuteau, F., . . . Launay, J. M. NAME, INITIAL.(1999). Whole blood serotonin and plasma beta-endorphin in autistic probands and their first-degree relatives. *Biological Psychiatry, 45,* 158–163.

Lepagnol-Bestel, A. M., Maussion, G., Boda, B., Cardona, A., Iwayama, Y., Delezoide, A.L., . . . Simonneau, M. NAME, INITIAL.(2008). SLC25A12 expression is associated with neurite outgrowth and is upregulated in the prefrontal cortex of autistic subjects *Molecular Psychiatry, 13,* 385–397.

Li, H., Li, Y., Shao, J., Li, R., Qin, Y., Xie, C., Zhao, Z. NAME, INITIAL.(2008). The Association Analysis of RELN and GRM8 Genes With Autistic Spectrum Disorder in Chinese Han Population. *American Journal of Medical Genetics Part B (Neuropsychiatric Genetics) 147B,* 194–200.

McBride, P. A., Anderson, G. M., Hertzig, M. E., Sweeney, J. A., Kream, J., Cohen, D. J., Mann, J. J. NAME, INITIAL.(1989). Serotonergic responsivity in male young adults with autistic disorder: results of a pilot study. *Archives of General Psychiatry, 46,* 213–221.

McBride, P. A., Anderson, G. M., Hertzig, M. E., Snow, M. E., Thompson, S. M., Khait, V. D., . . . Cohen, D. J. NAME, INITIAL.(1998). Effects of diagnosis, race, and puberty on platelet serotonin levels in autism and mental retardation. *The Journal of American Academy of Child and Adolescent Psychiatry, 37,* 767–776.

McCauley, J. L., Olsen, L. M., Delahanty, R., Amin, T., Nurmi, E. L., Organ, E. L., . . . Sutcliffe, J. S. NAME, INITIAL.(2004). A linkage disequilibrium map of the 1-Mb 15q12 GABA$_A$ receptor subunit cluster and association to autism. *American Journal of Medical Genetics, 131B,* 51–59.

McDougle C. J., Naylor S. T., Cohen D. J., Aghajanian, G. K., Herninger, G. R., & Price, L. H. (1996). Effects of tryptophan depletion in drug-free adults with autistic disorder. *Archives of General Psychiatry, 53,* 993–1000.

McDougle, C. J. (2002). Current and emerging therapeutics of autistic disorder and related pervasive developmental disorders. In K. L. Davis, D. Charney, J. T. Coyle, C. Nemeroff (Eds.), *Psychopharmacology: The Fifth Generation of Progress* (pp. 565–576). . Philadelphia: Lippincott Williams & Wilkins.

Ma, D., Whitehead, P., Menold, M., Martin, E., Ashley-Koch, A., Mei, H., . . . Pericak-Vance, M. A. NAME, INITIAL.(2005). Identification of significant association and gene-gene interaction of GABA receptor subunit genes in autism. *American Journal of Human Genetics, 77,* 377–388.

Maestrini, E., Lai, C., Marlow, A., Matthews, N., Wallace, S., Bailey, A., . . . Monaco, A. P. NAME, INITIAL. (1999). Serotonin transporter (5-HTT) and gamma-aminobutyric acid receptor subunit beta 3 (GABRB3) gene polymorphisms are not associated with autism in the IMGSA families. *American Journal of Medical Genetics, 88,* 492–496.

Martin, E. R., Menold, M. M., Wolpert, C. M., Bass, M. P., Donnelly, S. L., Ravan, S. A., . . . Pericak-Vance, M. A. NAME, INITIAL.(2000). Analysis of linkage disequilibrium in gamma-aminobutyric acid receptor subunit genes in autistic disorder. *American Journal of Medical Genetics, 96,* 43–48.

Martineau, J., Barthelemy, C., Jouve, J., Muh, J. P., & Lelord, G. (1992). Monoamines (serotonin and catecholamines) and their derivatives in infantile autism: Age-related changes and drug effects. *Developmental Medicine and Child Neurology, 34,* 593–603.

Maas, J. W., Hattox, S. E., Greene, N. M., & Landis, D. H. (1980). Estimates of dopamine and serotonin synthesis by the awake human brain. *Journal of Neurochemistry, 34,* 1547–1549.

Makkonen, I., Riikonen, R., Kokki, H., Airaksinen, M. M., & Kuikka, J. T. (2008). Serotonin and dopamine transporter binding in children with autism determined by SPECT. *Developmental Medicine and Child Neurology, 50,* 593–597.

Melke, J., Botros, G., Chaste, P., Betancur, C., Nygren, G., Anckarsater, H., . . . Bourgeron, T. NAME, INITIAL. (2008). Abnormal melatonin synthesis in autism spectrum disorders. *Molecular Psychiatry, 13,* 90–98.

Menold, M. M., Shao, Y., Wolpert, C. M., Donnelly, S. L., Raiford, K. L., Martin, E. R., . . . Gilbert, J. R. NAME, INITIAL.(2001). Association analysis of chromosome 15 $GABA_A$ receptor subunit genes in autistic disorder. *Journal of Neurogenetics, 15,* 245–259.

Minderaa, R. B., Anderson, G. M., Volkmar, F. R., Akkerhuis, G. W., & Cohen, D. J. (1987). Urinary 5-hydroxyindoleacetic acid and whole blood serotonin and tryptophan in autistic and normal subjects. *Biological Psychiatry, 22,* 933–940.

Minderaa, R. B., Anderson, G. M., Volkmar, F. R., Akkerhuis, G. W., & Cohen, D. J. (1989). Neurochemical study of dopamine functioning in autistic and normal subjects. *Journal of American Academy of Child and Adolescent Psychiatry, 28,* 200–206.

Minderaa, R. B., Anderson, G. M., Volkmar, F. R., Akkerhuis, G. W., & Cohen, D. J. (1994). Noradrenergic and adrenergic functioning in autism. *Biological Psychiatry, 36,* 237–241.

Moore R.Y., & Bloom F. E. (1979). Central catecholamine neuron systems: anatomy and physiology of the norepinephrine and epinephrine systems. *Annual Review of Neuroscience, 2,* 113–168.

Moreno-Fuenmayor, H., Borjas, L., Arrieta, A., Valera, V., & Socorro-Candanoza, L. (1996). Plasma excitatory amino acids in autism. *The Journal of Clinical Investigation, 37,* 113–128.

Motazacker, M. M., Rost, B. R., Hucho, T., Garshasbi, M., Kahrizi, K., Ullmann, R., . . . Kuss, A. W. NAME, INITIAL.(2007). A defect in the ionotropic glutamate receptor 6 gene (GRIK2) is associated with autosomal recessive mental retardation. *American Journal of Human Genetics, 81,* 792–798.

Murphy, D., Daly, E., Schmitz, N., Toal, F., Murphy, K., Curran, S., . . . Travis, M. NAME, INITIAL (2006). Cortical serotonin 5-HT2A receptor binding and social communication in adults with Asperger's disorder: An in vivo SPECT study. *American Journal of Psychiatry, 163,* 934–936.

Nabi, R., Serajee, F. J., Chugani, D. C., Zhong, H., & Huq, A., H. (2004). Association of tryptophan 2,3 dioxygenase gene polymorphism with autism. *American Journal of Medical Genetics, 125B,* 63–68.

Narayan, M., Srinath, S., Anderson, G. M., & Meundi, D. B. (1993). Cerebrospinal fluid levels of homovanillic acid and 5-hydroxyindoleacetic acid in autism. *Biological Psychiatry, 33,* 630–635.

Nelson, K. B., Grether, J. K., Croen, L. A., Dambrosia, J. M., Dickens, B. F., Jelliffe, L. L., . . . Phillips, T. M. NAME, INITIAL.(2001). Neuropeptides and neurotrophins in neonatal blood of children with autism or mental retardation. *Annals of Neurology, 49,* 597–606.

Novotny, S., Hollander, E., Allen, A., Mosovich, S., Aronowitz, B., Cartwright, C., . . . Dolgoff-Kaspar, R. NAME, INITIAL.(2000). Increased growth hormone response to sumatriptan challenge in adult autistic disorders. *Psychiatry Research, 94,* 173–177.

Novotny, S., Hollander, E., Phillips, A., Allen, A., Wasserman, S., & Iyengar, R. (2004). Increased repetitive behaviours and prolactin responsivity to oral m-chlorophenylpiperazine in adults with autism spectrum disorders. *The International Journal of Neuropsychopharmacology, 7,* 249–254.

Nurmi, E. L., Bradford, Y., Chen, Y., Hall, J., Arnone, B., Gardiner, M. B., . . . Sutcliffe, J. S. NAME, INITIAL. (2001). Linkage disequilibrium at the Angelman syndrome gene UBE3A in autism families. *Genomics, 77,* 105–113.

Orabona, G., Griesi-Oliveira, K., Vadasz, E., Bulcao, V. L., Takahashi, V. N., Moreira, E. S., . . . Passos-Bueno, M. R. NAME, INITIAL.(2009). HTR1B and HTR2C in autism spectrum disorders in Brazilian families. *Brain Research 1250,* 14–19.

Page, L., Daly, E., Schmitz, N., Simmons, A., Toal, F., Deeley, Q., . . . Murphy, D. G. NAME, INITIAL. (2006). In vivo 1H-magnetic resonance spectroscopy study of amygdala-hippocampal and parietal regions in autism. *American Journal Psychiatry, 163,* 2189–2192.

Palmieri, L., Papaleo, V., Porcelli, V., Scarcia, P., Gaita, L., Sacco, R., . . . Persico, A. M. NAME, INITIAL. (2008). Altered calcium homeostasis in autism-spectrum disorders: evidence from biochemical and genetic studies of the mitochondrial aspartate/glutamate carrier AGC1. *Molecular Psychiatry,* 1–15.

Panskepp, J., Siviy, S. M., & Normansell, L. A. (1985). Brain opioids and social emotions. In M. Reite, T. Field (Eds.), *The psychobiology of attachment and emotion* (pp. 3–49). New York: Academic Press.

Perry, E. K., Lee, M. L., Martin-Ruiz, C. M., Court, J. A., Volsen, S. G., Merrit, J., . . . Wenk, G. L. NAME, INITIAL.(2001). Cholinergic activity in autism: abnormalities in the cerebral cortex and basal forebrain. *American Journal of Psychiatry, 158,* 1058–1066.

Pfeiffer, S. L., Norton, J., Nelson, L., & Shott, S. (1995). Efficacy of vitamin B6 and magnesium in the treatment of autism: a methodology review and summary of outcomes. *Journal of Autism and Developmental Disorders, 25,* 481–493.

Posey, D. J., Stigler, K. A., Erickson, C. A., & McDougle, C. J. (2008). Antipsychotics in the treatment of autism. *The Journal of Clinical Investigation, 118,* 6–14.

Purcell, A.E., Jeon, O.H., Zimmerman, A.W., Blue M. E., & Pevsner, J. (2001). Postmortem brain abnormalities of the glutamate neurotransmitter system in autism. *Neurology, 57,* 1618–1628.

Rabionet, R., Jaworski, J. M., Ashley-Koch, A. E., Martin, E. R., Sutcliffe, J. S., Haines, J. L., . . . Pericak-Vance, M. A. NAME, INITIAL.(2004). Analysis of the autism chromosome 2 linkage region: GAD1 and other candidate genes. *Neuroscience Letters, 372,* 209–214.

Rabionet, R., McCauley, J. L., Jaworski J. M., Ashley-Koch A. E., Martin, E. R., Sutcliffe, J. S., . . . Pericak-Vance, M. A. NAME, INITIAL.(2006). Lack of association between autism and SLC25A12. *American Journal of Psychiatry, 163,* 929–931.

Ramoz, N., Reichert J. G., Smith, C. J., Silverman, J. M., Vespalova, I. N., Davis, K. L., Buxbaum, J.D. (2004). Linkage and association of the mitochondrial aspartate/glutamate carrier SLC25A12 gene with autism. *Am J Psychiatry, 161,* 662–669.

Ramoz, N., Reichert, J., Corwin, T., Smith, C., Silverman, J., Hollander, E., Buxbaum, J. D. NAME, INITIAL. (2006). Lack of evidence for association of the serotonin transporter gene SLC6A4 with autism. *Biological Psychiatry, 60,* 186–191.

Ritvo, E. R., Yuwiler, A., Geller, E., Ornitz, E. M., Saeger, K., & Plotkin, S. (1970). Increased blood serotonin and platelets in early infantile autism. *Archives of General Psychiatry, 23,* 566–572.

Robinson, P. D., Schutz, C. K., Macciardi, F, White, B. N., & Holden, J. J. (2001). Genetically determined low maternal serum dopamine β-Hydroxylase levels and the etiology of autism spectrum disorders. *American Journal of Medical Genetics, 100,* 30–36.

Rolf, L. H., Haarmann, F.Y., Grotemeyer, K.H., & Kehrer, H. (1993). Serotonin and amino acid content in platelets of autistic children. *Acta Psychiatrica Scandinavica, 87,* 312–316.

Ross, D. L., Klykylo, W. M., Anderson, G.M. (1985). Cerebrospinal fluid indoleamine and monoamine effects in fenfluramine treatment of autism. *Annals of Neurology, 18,* 394.

Roy, A., Pickar, D., De Jong, J., Karoum, F., Linnoila, M. (1988). Norepinephrine and its metabolits in cerebrospinal fluid, plasma, and urine. Relationship to hypothalamic-pituitary-adrenal axis function in depression. *Arch Gen Psychiatry, 45,* 849–857.

Rubenstein, J. L. R., Merzenich, M. M. (2003). Model of autism: increased ratio of excitation/inhibition in key neural systems. *Genes Brain Behav, 2,* 255–267.

Salmon, B., Hallmayer, J., Rogers, T., Kalaydjieva, L., Petersen, P. B., Nicholas, P., . . . Risch, N. NAME, INITIAL.(1999). Absence of linkage and linkage disequilibrium to chromosome 15q11-q13 markers in 139 multiplex families with autism. *American Journal of Medical Genetics, 88,* 551–556.

Segurado, R., Conroy, J., Meally, E., Fitzgerald, M., Gill, M., & Gallagher, L. (2005). Confirmation of association between autism and the mitochondrial aspartate/glutamate carrier SLC25A12 gene on chromosome 2q31. *American Journal of Psychiatry, 162,* 2182–2184.

Serajee, F. J., Zhong, H., Nabi, R., & Huq, A. H. (2003). The metabotropic glutamate receptor 8 gene at 7q31: partial duplication and possible association with autism. *Journal of Medical Genetics, 40,* e42.

Schain, R. J., & Freedman, D. X. (1961). Studies on 5-hydroxyindole metabolism in autistic and other mentally retarded children. *Journal of Pediatrics, 58,* 315–320.

Sher, L. (1997). Autistic disorder and the endogenous opioid system. *Medical Hypotheses, 48,* 413–414.

Shinohe, A., Hashimoto, K., Nakamura, K., Tsujii, M., Iwata, Y., Tsuchiya, K. J., . . . Mori, N. NAME, INITIAL.(2007). Increased serum levels of glutamate in adult patients with autism. *Progress in Neuropsychopharmacology and Biological Psychiatry, 31,* 590.

Shuang, M., Liu, J., Jia, M. X., Yang, J. Z., Wu, S. P., Gong, X. H., . . . Zhang, D. NAME, INITIAL. (2004). Family-based association study between autism and glutamate receptor 6 gene in Chinese Han trios. *American Journal of Medical Genetics, 131B,* 48–50.

Sutcliffe, J.S., Nurmi, E.L., & Lombroso, P. J. (2003). Genetics of childhood disorders: XLVII. Autism, part 6: duplication and inherited susceptibility of chromosome 15q11-q13 genes in autism. *Developmental Neurobiology, 42,* 253–256.

Tordjman, S., Anderson, G. M., McBride, P.A., Hertzig, M. E., Snow, M. E., Hall, L. M., . . . Cohen, D. J. NAME, INITIAL.(1997). Plasma beta-endorphin, adrenocorticotropin hormone, and cortisol in autism. *Journal of Child Psychology and Psychiatry, 38,* 705–715.

Tordjman, S., Anderson, G. M., Pichard, N., Charbuy, H., & Touitou, Y. (2005). Nocturnal excretion of 6-sulphatoxymelatonin in children and adolescents with autistic disorder. *Biological Psychiatry, 57,* 134–138.

Turunen, J. A., Rehnstrom, K., Kilpinen, H., Kuokkanen, M., Kempas, E., & Ylisaukko-Oja, T. (2008). Mitochondrial aspartate/glutamate carrier SLC25A12 gene is associated with autism. *Autism Research, 1,* 189–192.

Vanhalia, R., Turpeinen, U., & Riikonen, R. (2001). Low levels of insulin-like growth factor-I in cerebrospinal fluid in children with autism. *Developmental and Medical Child Neurology, 43,* 614–616.

Veenstra-VanderWeele, J., Kim, S.J., Lord, C., Courchesne, R., Akshoomoff, N., Leventhal, B. L., . . . Cook, E. H. NAME, INITIAL. (2002). Transmission disequilibrium studies of the serotonin 5-HT2A receptor gene (HTR2A) in autism. *American Journal of Medical Genetics, 114*, 277–283.

Whitaker-Azmitia, P.M. (1993). The role of serotonin and serotonin receptors in development of the mammalian nervous system. In I. S. Zagon, P. J. McLaughlin (Eds.), *Receptors in the developing nervous system, vol 2. Neurotransmitters* (pp. 43–53). London: Chapman & Hall.

Yip, J., Soghomonian, J., & Blatt, G. (2007). Decreased GAD67 mRNA levels in cerebellar Purkinje cells in autism: Pathophysiological implications. *Acta Neuropathologica, 113*, 559–568.

Yirmiya, N., Pilowsky, T., Tidhar, S., Nemanov, L., Altmark, L., & Ebstein, R. P. (2002). Family-based and population study of a functional promoter-region monoamine oxidase A polymorphism in autism: Possible association with IQ. *American Journal of Medical Genetics, 114*, 284–287.

Young, J.G., Cohen, D.J., Kavanaugh, M.E., Landis, H. D., Shaywitz, B. A., & Maas, J. W. (1981). Cerebrospinal fluid, plasma, and urinary MHPG in children. *Life Science, 28*, 2837–2845.

Chapter 5

Major Current Neuropsychological Theories of ASD

Agata Rozga, Sharlet A. Anderson, and Diana L. Robins

Since 1943, when Leo Kanner first described autism, numerous neuropsychological theories have attempted to explain the triad of deficits in social relatedness, communication, and restricted, repetitive, and stereotyped behaviors and interests that characterize autism spectrum disorders (ASD). A strong neuropsychological theory explicitly connects observable behavior to brain function and/or structure, elucidating the brain–behavior relationships. However, a strong neuropsychological theory of autism also should address all three domains of symptoms seen in autism. The hypotheses regarding autism's etiology have varied in their ability to explain all three areas of deficit. In fact, rather than a broad approach that ties together the three symptom domains, many theories instead take the approach of identifying the "core deficit" from which the other symptoms develop as a cascade.

This chapter reviews the major neuropsychological theories of ASD that have emerged in the last several decades, which we have sorted into the following categories: executive functioning, information pro-

cessing, social motivation, and social cognition. We close with a section on emerging topics, and relatively recent theories and models for which researchers are building empirical support, such as mirror neurons and their relevance to mimicry and imitation, animal models, and neural networks. Some of the theories discussed here are dealt with in more detail in other chapters in this volume.

EXECUTIVE FUNCTIONING

Although many psychological theories of autism focus on the social and communicative impairments considered to be the hallmark features of the disorder, the executive function (EF) theory hypothesizes the key impairment to be located within a set of higher-level cognitive skills that underlie independent, goal-oriented behavior (Lezak, Howieson, Loring, Hannay, & Fischer, 2004), mediated by the prefrontal cortex (see Chapter 9 for a more detailed review of executive functioning in autism). Deficits in a range of such skills, including working memory, planning, inhibition, cognitive flexibility, and self-monitoring (Minshew, Webb, Williams, & Dawson, 2006), are thought to underlie the problems that individuals with ASD exhibit in everyday contexts, including difficulties in adaptive functioning and academic performance. Importantly, many of the restricted, repetitive, and stereotyped behaviors and interests seen in autism appear to be related to executive functioning deficits, including rigidity, difficulty with change, and lack of planning (Ozonoff, Pennington, & Rogers, 1991).

Early studies that set the stage for executive functioning deficits as a theory of autism identified problems in cognitive flexibility, including perseveration and set-shifting difficulties, using classic tests of executive functioning such as the Wisconsin Card Sorting Test, in which the individual must attend to changing cues regarding rules for sorting a set of pictures across multiple trials, and the Tower of London and Tower of Hanoi tasks, in which the individual must come up with a strategy for completing a puzzle that requires planning and inhibition of short-term solutions (Hughes, Russell, & Robbins, 1994; Pennington & Ozonoff, 1996). However, these early studies utilized measures that were imprecise, insofar as they tapped multiple executive functions within a single task. Consequently, more recent studies have sought to examine which specific EF component skills, such as inhibitory control, cognitive flexibility, and working memory, may be intact or deficient in autism. In a recent review, Ozonoff, South, and Provencal (2005) presented findings in support of intact inhibitory functions coupled with deficits in attentional disengagement and cognitive flexibility in individuals with autism. The researchers attempted to resolve early conflicting findings regarding the presence of verbal working memory deficits in autism (Bennetto, Pennington, & Rogers, 1996; Russell, Jarrold, & Henry, 1996) by highlighting the imprecise measurements of the early tests of executive functioning due to confounding component processes, and proposed that an information-processing approach to the analysis of individual components of executive functions may be more appropriate than an attempt to assess executive functioning as a whole.

One criticism of the EF account of autism has been that executive function deficits can be observed in a variety of neurodevelopmental conditions, leading researchers to evaluate the extent to which autism

may be characterized by a unique profile of EF impairments distinct from that observed in ADHD, learning disorders, and other conditions. This profile appears to be characterized by intact cognitive and motor inhibition (Ozonoff et al., 2005; Ozonoff & Jensen, 1999; Ozonoff & Strayer, 1997) along with deficits in cognitive flexibility, including attentional set-shifting and planning (Courchesne et al., 1994; Hughes et al., 1994; Ozonoff et al., 2005; Ozonoff & Jensen, 1999). Using discriminant function analysis, Barnard and colleagues (2008) examined five domains of executive functioning (planning, set-shifting, inhibition, working memory, and fluency) and found that a composite score of working memory and planning successfully classified 75% of their sample of adults with autism and learning disability and 65% of their control group, which consisted of adults with learning disability alone. These results support the claim made by Ozonoff and colleagues (2005) that more finely grained assessment strategies to differentiate executive functioning deficiency profiles are necessary.

Functional and anatomical differences underlying executive functioning deficits in autism involve a number of specific brain regions. Courchesne and colleagues (1994) cite MRI and autopsy evidence of both cerebellar hypo- and hyperplasia in autism. They postulate a hypothesis that the inability to shift attention quickly underlies many of the social difficulties in autism, and discuss the cerebellum's role in preparing for rapid shifts in attention by priming selective attention and arousal, so as to be able to detect subtle signals from noise in complex situations. However, Minshew, Luna, and Sweeney (1999) explored Courchesne and colleagues' (1994) findings using an eye-tracking paradigm with a visually guided saccade task, an oculomotor delayed-response task, and an anti-saccade task, and found evidence for neocortical dysfunction in spatial working memory, with intact functioning in cerebellar regions. Two recent fMRI studies report reduced activity in dorsolateral prefrontal regions during working memory tasks in high-functioning individuals with ASD (Koshino et al., 2008; Luna et al., 2002). Schmitz and colleagues (2006) found increased activation of the left inferior and orbitofrontal cortex during a motor response inhibition task, the left insula during a cognitive interference inhibition task, and left inferior and right mesial parietal cortex during a set-shifting task, as well as corresponding increased inferior frontal cortex gray matter density. Dawson, Meltzoff, Osterling, and

Rinaldi (1998) investigated executive functioning tasks mediated by either medial temporal/limbic structures (delayed non-matching to sample) or dorsolateral prefrontal cortex (delayed response), and their respective relationships to severity of core autism symptom domains (social orienting, immediate and delayed imitation, shared attention, response to distress, and symbolic play). Children with autism were matched on verbal ability to a clinical sample of children with Down Syndrome and a typically developing control sample. Results showed that all domains of social functioning were associated with performance on the medial temporal tasks, whereas only immediate imitation was associated with the dorsolateral prefrontal cortex task.

Methods to examine the issue of primacy and universality of executive function deficits in autism include looking for attenuated forms of the deficit in unaffected relatives, and determining how early in development these deficits appear (see Chapter 9). Several papers have identified executive functioning deficits that may represent behavioral markers for the broader autism phenotype among undiagnosed first-degree relatives of individuals with autism (Hughes, Plumet, & Leboyer, 1999; Ozonoff, Rogers, Farnham, & Pennington, 1993; Piven & Palmer, 1997). Early development of executive functions in ASD is equivocal, and appears to depend on the age of the sample, the task used, and the comparison group (Dawson et al., 2002; Griffith, Pennington, Wehner, & Rogers, 1999; McEvoy, Rogers, & Pennington, 1993).

A key question for any theory is the extent to which it can account for all three symptom domains of autism. Several researchers have proposed that verbal working memory deficits impact social functioning, given the need for individuals to cope with rapidly changing verbal (and nonverbal) stimuli that occur in natural social discourse, to select an appropriate response to these cues, and to maintain social norms and unspoken rules of engagement throughout the subtle and fluid stream of changing stimuli (Bennetto et al., 1996; Gilotty, Kenworthy, Sirian, Black, & Wagner, 2002). Executive functioning deficits may also significantly impact children's ability to maintain goals and inhibit impulsive behaviors in social interactions. Indeed, significant correlations have been reported between EF and social interaction measures, including perseverative errors and joint attention behaviors in young children with autism (Griffith et al., 1999; McEvoy et al., 1993). Finally, relations

between performance on EF tests and Theory of Mind (this concept will be discussed in more detail later in this chapter) tasks have been reported among children with autism (e.g., Ozonoff et al., 1991), though at present it is not clear whether this association is a developmental one (i.e., EF is a pre-requisite for ToM), or whether both impairments stem from another shared causal factor.

In sum, refinements to the EF theory of autism over the last three decades have made great strides toward characterizing a specific profile of EF impairments that are unique to autism and the neural underpinnings of this profile, and toward linking specific aspects of EF dysfunction with social and adaptive functioning in ASD. However, due to the inherent componential approach both in terms of function and structure, the EF theory has not yet been able to fully account for the particular constellation of symptoms that define autism phenotype as we currently know it. Moreover, a relative lack of longitudinal studies prevents clear conclusions regarding the developmental primacy of EF impairments in autism. Chapter 9 in this volume emphasizes the importance of studying the role of EF in autistic symptomatology, whether or not it is a core deficit. Given that EF is foundational in the ability to manage the demands of everyday life, it will be important to continue to examine the role of EF in autism, with particular attention to the development of EF in early life, and with more refined assessment tools that tease apart the different aspects of EF.

INFORMATION PROCESSING

Although the EF theory accounts well for the difficulties individuals with autism exhibit in cognitive flexibility and higher-order planning, it does not address areas of relative strength often found in autistic individuals, particularly in visuospatial skills. Frith (1989) was the first to propose that these strengths and weaknesses may have the same origin, attributing them to weak "central coherence," or a poor ability to integrate pieces of information from the environment into a gestalt, or a meaningful whole, in context (Frith, 1989; Frith & Hill, 2003). The weak central coherence (WCC) account proposes that autism is characterized by a bias toward processing featural and local elements of stimuli at the expense of global meaning. Thus, a key prediction of this theory is that individuals with autism may be expected to perform well on tasks that favor attention to detail, and poorly on tasks requiring attention to the global context. In line with this proposal, a large number of studies have demonstrated intact, and even superior, performance among individuals with autism, relative to matched controls, on tasks that favor local processing (Bölte, Holtmann, Poustka, Scheurich, & Schmidt, 2007; Jolliffe & Baron-Cohen, 1997; Shah & Frith, 1993) and impaired performance on tasks requiring global processing (Brosnan, Scott, Fox, & Pye, 2004; Pellicano, Gibson, Maybery, Durkin, & Badcock, 2005), though the findings are not unequivocal (Mottron, Burack, Iarocci, Belleville, & Enns, 2003).

Studies of patients with acquired right hemisphere damage, as well as imaging and ERP studies, implicate the right hemisphere in global, integrative processing (Gallace, Imbornone, & Vallar, 2008; Robertson & Lamb, 1991; Stiles et al., 2008), suggesting that right hemisphere abnormalities may underlie some of the global deficits and local biases that have been found in autism. In addition, Fein and colleagues (1984) analyzed patterns of strength and impairment within language and concluded that strongly lateralized left hemisphere dysfunction was not supported, in contrast to the prevailing notions of the day. Neural mechanisms that may underlie the local processing bias in autism include abnormalities in the ventral occipito-temporal region, and dorsolateral prefrontal and parietal regions (Ring et al., 1999). Reduced connectivity in the autistic brain may provide an additional neural mechanism explaining weak central coherence (see review by Happé & Frith, 2006).

Although weak central coherence was first postulated to account for both social (e.g., Theory of Mind) impairments and nonsocial asset/deficit profiles in autism (Frith, 1989), studies analyzing the relationship between central coherence and Theory of Mind in autism have yielded mixed results. Several studies failed to find a relationship between weak central coherence and Theory of Mind abilities in children and adults with autism (Happé, 1997; Morgan, Maybery, & Durkin, 2003). However, other studies have shown a positive relationship between performance on central coherence and Theory of Mind tasks among children with autism (Jarrold, Butler, Cottington, & Jimenez, 2000). The mixed results regarding the link between Theory of Mind and central coherence may be due to methodological issues, such as differing factors that were controlled for across

studies. Ultimately, any potential causal relationship between weak central coherence and Theory of Mind deficits in autism needs to be studied using longitudinal designs.

Evidence of weak central coherence has also been found in first-degree relatives of children diagnosed with autism. An early study by Baron-Cohen and Hammer (1997) found Theory of Mind deficits and local processing bias in parents of children with ASDs (Baron-Cohen & Hammer, 1997; Bölte & Poustka, 2006; Happé, Briskman, and Frith, 2001). Thus, evidence suggests that a cognitive style favoring detail-oriented processing may capture features of the broader autism phenotype among first-degree relatives of individuals with autism. However, as Happé and Booth (2008) note in a recent review, local and global processing may be confounded in many studies, and new evidence indicating that individuals with autism are capable of global processing if explicitly instructed to do so suggests that weak central coherence may be more appropriately thought of as a *cognitive style* that includes distinct information processing biases, rather than as *deficits* in global processing (Happé & Frith, 2006; Happé & Booth, 2008). The researchers further suggest that weak coherence may best be characterized as two independent dimensions, including a reduced tendency to integrate information and an increased tendency to process features, and thus that potential experimental tasks should assess these dimensions independently of one another. Moreover, empirical evidence also suggests that weak central coherence does not appear to be a characteristic of all individuals with autism, and its presence in other clinical populations such as those with Williams syndrome, schizophrenia, depression, and right hemisphere damage (Happé & Frith, 2006), indicates it is neither universal nor specific.

Another information-processing theory has developed from work done by Minshew and colleagues (Minshew & Goldstein, 1998; Minshew, Johnson, & Luna, 2001; Williams, Goldstein, & Minshew, 2006), who have proposed a model of autism as a disorder of complex information processing or higher-order integrative functioning which, similar to the weak central coherence account, aims to account for the profile of deficits and intact abilities previously documented in neuropsychological investigations of individuals with autism. In a seminal study comparing the performance of high-functioning adolescents and adults with autism to that of age, sex, and IQ-matched typically developing controls on a comprehensive battery of neuropsychological tasks, Minshew and Goldstein (1998) found that individuals with autism demonstrated intact or even superior performance on tasks with low information-processing demands (e.g., simple memory and language, rule learning, attention, sensory perception, visuospatial), whereas their performance was quite impaired on tasks that required complex information processing (e.g., concept formation, problem solving, skilled motor abilities, complex memory, and language). This cognitive profile of the selective impact on higher-order cognitive abilities across multiple domains and intact simpler abilities within those same domains led to a conceptualization of autism as a disorder of complex information processing (Minshew & Goldstein, 1998), which may be characteristic of autism across development, rather than representing the outcome of an earlier-occurring primary deficit (Williams et al., 2006).

The neural basis underlying the profile of intact lower-order information-processing, coupled with impaired higher-order complex information in autism, may involve underdevelopment of functional connections within and between neural systems, with preserved or overdeveloped local circuitry (Minshew et al., 2006; Minshew, Sweeney, & Luna, 2002; Minshew & Williams, 2007). In line with this prediction, a number of neuroimaging studies have provided evidence of functional under-connectivity underlying the performance of individuals with autism on a range of tasks involving higher-order processing, including executive functions, language comprehension, Theory of Mind, and face processing (Just, Cherkassky, Keller, Kana, & Minshew, 2007; Just, Cherkassky, Keller, & Minshew, 2004; Kana, Keller, Cherkassky, Minshew, & Just, 2006; Koshino et al., 2008; Luna, et al., 2002; Mason, Williams, Kana, Minshew, & Just, 2008; see Chapter 21 for more detail).

Both the weak central coherence and complex information-processing theories can potentially account for the patterns of strengths and weaknesses observed in ASD, the former by positing differential abilities in processing information that differs in kind (global/featural), and the latter by highlighting differences in processing information that differs in level of complexity. A further strength of these accounts is that they do not rely on a single mechanism or a specific neural substrate, but locate atypicality at the level of whole-brain processing. A synthesis of these two theories has the potential to create a more comprehensive

account of information processing biases that may underlie the behavioral manifestations of autism.

SOCIAL MOTIVATION AND SOCIAL COGNITION

Whereas in previous sections we focused on neuropsychological theories that emphasize cognitive disturbance as a precipitating factor in the emergence of autistic symptomatology, we now turn our attention to theories that emphasize early social deficits in autism, and the resulting developmental cascade that disrupts subsequent social and communicative development.

Social Motivation Theories

The first set of theories, which we will refer to as social motivation theories, views autistic impairments in the context of transactional processes that underlie the emergence of neural systems that support social information processing. A central tenet of these theories is that a biologically based attenuation of the motivation to orient to social stimuli in autism, particularly a decreased tendency to spontaneously orient to human faces, voices, and gestures (Adrien et al., 1991; Baranek, 1999; Fein, Pennington, Markowitz, Braverman, & Waterhouse, 1986; Klin, 1991, 1992; Lord, 1995; Osterling & Dawson, 1994; Osterling, Dawson, & Munson, 2002; Swettenham et al., 1998; Werner, Dawson, Osterling, & Dinno, 2000), derails normal developmental pathways for the emergence of social and communication skills (Dawson et al., 2002; Klin, Jones, Schultz, & Volkmar, 2003; Mundy & Neal, 2001; Schultz, et al., 2003). Although the models vary to some extent in the hypothesized mechanism underlying impairment, the early-emerging lack of motivation for social engagement in autism is presumed to limit the child's social experiences, which in turn negatively impacts the development of neural systems which critically depend on social input (Dawson, Webb, & McPartland, 2005; Mundy & Neal, 2001). Thus, critical to these models is the notion that autistic deficits stem from a disruption of normative experience-expectant neurodevelopmental processes, and the subsequent disorganization and impairment of more complex brain systems that subserve social-emotional and social-cognitive skill development. Waterhouse, Fein, and Modahl (1996) specifically suggest two neurofunctional mechanisms relevant to social motivation that might underlie autistic symptomatology: (a) impaired assignment of the affective significance of stimuli, in which abnormal amygdala system function disrupts association of social stimuli with emotional salience, and (b) asociality, in which impaired oxytocin system function flattens social bonding and affiliativeness.

Dawson and colleagues' social motivation model places autistic impairments within the context of the normal emergence of social brain circuitry in infancy, with particular emphasis on the role of the reward system in the development of this circuitry (Dawson & Faja, 2008; Dawson, Webb, Wijsman, et al., 2005). Infants' early preference for social stimuli is largely shaped by the fact that they anticipate that pleasure will be associated with such stimuli. This early preference may be driven by activation of the dopamine reward circuit, which itself is modulated by oxytocin and vasopressin, with dopaminergic projections to the prefrontal cortex and the amygdala involved in the formation of representations of the reward value of social stimuli (Carver & Dawson, 2002; Dawson, Webb, & McPartland, 2005). The resulting propensity for directing attention to faces and voices assures that cortical specialization for processing these stimuli occurs, with more complex social brain networks emerging as the brain regions specialized for processing these social stimuli, including the fusiform gyrus (FG) and superior temporal sulcus (STS), become integrated with those involved in reward, particularly the amygdala and those that guide attention and action (e.g., prefrontal cortex; Dawson & Faja, 2008; Dawson, Webb, Wijsman, et al., 2005)

As applied to autism, this model posits that due to an early disruption in the reward circuit, infants with autism find social stimuli inherently less rewarding, and thus spend less time attending to faces and voices (Bernier, Webb, & Dawson, 2006). This, in turn, translates to a failure to develop expertise for processing social stimuli; consequently, decreased cortical specialization and abnormal brain circuitry for social information processing occurs (Bernier et al., 2006; Dawson & Faja, 2008; Dawson, Webb, & McPartland, 2005; Minshew et al., 2006). Evidence of oxytocin and vasopressin disruption in autism (Green et al., 2001; Kim et al., 2002; Modahl et al., 1998; see also Chapter 22), and previous research indicating these neuropeptides modulate the dopamine reward circuit (Insel & Fernald, 2004; Insel, O'Brien, & Leckman, 1999; Young & Wang, 2004), points to one possible

mechanism underlying the social motivation deficit that is the starting point for this developmental cascade.

Dawson and colleagues (2005) focus on face-processing impairments as one of the earliest systems derailed by social motivation impairments, noting that many of the earliest social behaviors disrupted in autism—including eye contact, joint attention, responsiveness to emotional displays, face recognition, and emotion perception—rely on information that can be gathered from the face. Face processing is also posited to play a critical role in the development of social relationships and Theory of Mind, two core impairments among older individuals with autism (Baron-Cohen, 1995). In line with the hypothesized decreased cortical specialization and abnormal brain circuitry for face processing in autism, Dawson and colleagues (2002) have documented that by three years of age, children with autism fail to show a differential ERP response to familiar versus unfamiliar faces, and fail to demonstrate increased amplitude to fear faces at both an early and late component of the ERP wave (Dawson, Webb, Carver, Panagiotides, & McPartland, 2004). Importantly, in the 2004 study, longer ERP latency to fear was associated with less attention to an experimenter expressing distress, fewer joint attention episodes, and fewer instances of social orienting, further underscoring the developmental consequences of early face processing impairments for subsequent social and communicative functioning in autism. Studies with older individuals suggest that by middle childhood, individuals with ASD fail to preferentially activate the fusiform gyrus during face processing tasks, and may instead recruit areas that are typically involved in object processing, such as the inferior temporal gyrus (Pierce, Müller, Ambrose, Allen, & Courchesne, 2001; Schultz, Gauthier, et al., 2000), although there is some evidence indicating that this hypoactivation may be driven by a failure to pay attention to the eyes (Dalton et al., 2005, Dalton, Holsen, Abbeduto, & Davidson, 2008).

In further support of this social motivation hypothesis, Sung and colleagues (2005) have recently demonstrated that a social motivation trait, measured by a subset of items on the Broader Phenotype of Autism Symptom Scale that reflect how much an individual enjoys spending time with others, is heritable in multiplex families. Moreover, similar to findings with children and adults with autism, parents of children with autism demonstrate a decrement in face recognition ability on standardized neurocognitive tasks, and show slower than expected neural processing of faces and abnormal cortical specialization for faces (Dawson, Webb, Wijsman, et al., 2005). Thus, two central aspects of the model—namely, a lack of social motivation and the subsequent impact on face processing—appear to also capture features of the broader autism phenotype among parents of individuals with autism.

The model proposed by Schultz and colleagues similarly focuses on lack of face-processing expertise as the precipitating factor in subsequent social impairment in autism, and traces the origins of these deficits to a social-orienting impairment driven by early abnormality in the amygdala (Klin et al., 1999; Schultz, Gauthier, et al., 2000; Schultz, Romanski, & Tsatsanis, 2000; see Chapter 12 also). Specifically, Schultz and colleagues argue that individuals with autism fail to attend to faces because they do not find them emotionally salient (Grelotti, Gauthier, & Schultz, 2002; Klin, 2000; Klin et al., 2003; Schultz, Romanski, et al., 2000). Consistent with this model, neuroimaging studies show hypoactivation of the amygdala (e.g., Castelli, Frith, Happé, & Frith, 2002; Critchley et al., 2000) and the fusiform face area (FFA; e.g., Critchley et al., 2000; Schultz et al., 2000) in reaction to a variety of social stimuli. Recent experimental work by Klin and colleagues has documented the earliest manifestations of face-processing impairments in autism—specifically, altered visual scanning of faces in toddlers with ASD that is characterized by reduced fixation on the eye region and increased gaze to the mouth (Jones, Carr, & Klin, 2008; Klin & Jones, 2008). Evidence that the viewing patterns of toddlers with ASD also indicate a particular sensitivity to physical contingencies, such as those present in audiovisual synchrony (Klin & Jones, 2008; Klin, Lin, Gorrido, Ramsey, & Jones, 2009), has led to the proposal that the increased fixations on the mouth region may be the result of the ongoing synchrony between lip movements and speech sounds (Klin et al., 2009).

The social motivation model presented by Mundy also grounds autistic impairments in a biologically-based attenuation of sensitivity to the reward value of social interaction, which contributes to a decrement in the tendency to spontaneously orient to social stimuli. Impoverished social information processing during infancy leads to subsequent disruptions of neurobehavioral development via a negative feedback loop, as lack of social information input disrupts

normative, experience-driven developmental processes (Mundy, 1995; Mundy & Acra, 2006; Mundy & Neal, 2001). Two key aspects of the model bear highlighting. First, the model shifts focus from the neural systems underlying social-perceptual processes (e.g., face processing) to systems that mediate the spontaneous *generation* of social attention and behavior, especially initiation of joint attention (Mundy & Thorp, 2007). Second, it emphasizes the self-organizing nature of early neurobehavioral development, focusing on the extent to which the child's tendency to initiate social attention coordination with others assures social information input and social experience presumed crucial to promoting normative behavioral and neural development (Mundy & Crowson, 1997; Mundy & Neal, 2001; Mundy, Sigman, & Kasari, 1994; Mundy & Thorp, 2007). Notably, these tenets are central to the *Enactive Mind* model recently proposed by Klin and colleagues (Klin et al., 2003; Klin, Jones, Schultz, & Volkmar, 2005), who similarly focus on motivational predispositions toward social action, and the extent to which social cognition may result from the child's repeated experiences in acting upon their social world (see Chapters 12 and 18).

Within the model presented by Mundy and colleagues, early-emerging deficits in joint attention in autism are viewed as part of a basic social approach impairment hypothesized to reflect disturbance in a frontal motivational executive system that typically prioritizes social information input and processing via social orienting (Mundy, 1995; Mundy, Card, & Fox, 2000). Similar to the proposals of Dawson, Waterhouse, and Schultz presented above, the hypothesized mechanisms underlying the failure to prioritize social orienting in autism involve neuropeptide systems that mediate sensitivity to the reward of engaging in social approach behaviors, and midbrain systems that signal the affective significance of these behaviors and link them with positive affective states (Mundy, 1995). The notion that a disturbance in frontal and midbrain functions that support reward sensitivity may reduce the motivation for social approach behaviors, such as joint attention, in autism derives empirical support from two lines of research. The first includes studies with typically developing toddlers linking the development of initiating joint attention with activity of the dorsomedial prefrontal cortex and medial orbitofrontal cortex (Caplan et al., 1993; Dawson et al., 2002; Henderson, Yoder, Yale, & McDuffie, 2002;

Mundy et al., 2000). Second, Dawson and colleagues (2002) have demonstrated that the severity of joint attention impairments in three-year-old children with autism correlates with neurocognitive abilities previously linked with functioning of the medial temporal lobe-orbitofrontal circuit (involved in reward perception), but not with tasks that reflect activity of the dorsolateral prefrontal cortex. Finally, Mundy and colleagues have demonstrated that typically developing infants are much more likely to convey positive affect to their interactive partners in the context of joint attention bids than during requesting (Kasari, Sigman, Mundy, & Yirmiya, 1990; Mundy, Kasari, & Sigman, 1992; Venezia, Messinger, Thorp, & Mundy, 2004), whereas positive affect rarely accompanies the joint attention bids of children with autism (Kasari et al., 1990; Kasari, Sigman, Yirmiya, & Mundy, 1993). Thus, the joint attention behaviors of children with autism reflect a failure of normative, potentially intrinsic, motivation for sharing positive affective experiences with others (Mundy & Acra, 2006; Mundy & Thorp, 2007).

Turning to the consequences of joint attention impairment in autism for subsequent development, Mundy focuses on the self-organizing function of joint attention in language development. A child's initiation of joint attention, for example by shifting gaze or pointing to an object of interest, provides the caregiver with an opportunity to use the shared attentional focus and label the object (e.g., Tomasello, 1995). In addition, the child's ability to follow the caregiver's line of regard, pointing, and gestures during verbally mediated social interactions may be critical to acquiring new words, because it reduces the likelihood of referential mapping errors (e.g., Baldwin, 1995). In autism, evidence that impairment in initiating and responding to joint attention bids of others may emerge by the second year of life (Charman et al., 1997; Landa, Holman, & Garrett-Mayer, 2007; Sullivan et al., 2007; Yirmiya et al., 2006) suggests that from the outset, children with autism may be poorly equipped to take advantage of incidental social learning opportunities. A number of longitudinal studies have now documented predictive links between joint attention impairments in autism and language development, even after children's initial language skills and IQ are covaried (Charman et al., 2003; Mundy, Sigman, & Kasari, 1990; Sigman & Ruskin, 1999; Toth, Munson, Meltzoff, & Dawson, 2006).

To the extent that the emergence of joint attention skill reflects infants' developing understanding of others as intentional agents (Tomasello, 1995), and may thus be a precursor of more advanced social cognitive skills such as Theory of Mind (Baron-Cohen, 1995; Charman, 2000), impairment in joint attention skills could have tremendous implications for social cognitive development in autism (Baron-Cohen, 1991a, 1995; Mundy et al., 1994). Indeed, imaging evidence indicates that patterns of activation during theory of mind tasks, which include the dorsal medial cortex and adjacent subcortical areas of the anterior cingulate (Frith & Frith, 2003) overlap considerably with areas that have been implicated in initiating joint attention. Joint attention also has been shown to predict Theory of Mind task performance (Charman, 2000) and prosocial behavior and play with peers (Sigman & Ruskin, 1999; Travis, Sigman, & Ruskin, 2001) among high-functioning children with autism.

Finally, the potential key role of joint attention in the pathology of autism is also underscored by a growing number of studies of very young non-affected siblings of children with autism, which indicate that delays in the use of attention sharing and requesting gestures, and deficits in the ability to follow the gaze and point gestures of others across the 14–24 month period, may represent early features of the broader autism phenotype in this group (Goldberg et al., 2005; Landa & Garrett-Mayer, 2006; Sullivan et al., 2007; Toth, Dawson, Meltzoff, Greenson, & Fein, 2007; Yirmiya et al., 2006; Zwaigenbaum et al., 2005).

The theories summarized above share a common focus on a biologically based, early-emerging lack of motivation for social engagement in autism, which derails experience-expectant neurodevelopmental processes that underlie the emergence of a wide range of social communicative behaviors known to be impaired in autism. As these theories are deeply grounded in normative developmental processes, they provide a cohesive account of not only the presence but, more importantly, the emergence of the behavioral and neural manifestations of autism, as well as their interdependence. However, whereas the hypothesized neural mechanisms underlying the lack of salience of social stimuli in autism—including disrupted functioning of neuropeptide systems and the amygdala—have been documented among older children and adults with autism, empirical evidence linking these mechanisms to the earliest behavioral manifestations of autism in infancy remain speculative. Moreover, although these theories account well for the social-communicative impairments observed in autism, as currently presented, they do not adequately address key aspects of the autism phenotype, including repetitive behaviors and restricted interests, as well as cognitive profiles.

Social Cognitive Theories

Social cognitive theories of autism focus on impairments in the capacity to represent and reason about the thoughts, beliefs, and feelings of others, which is key to navigating everyday social interactions. This phenomenon, called *Theory of Mind*, was first thought to be mediated by a dedicated cognitive mechanism subserved by specific neural subsystems (Baron-Cohen, Tager-Flusberg, & Cohen, 1994; Leslie, 1987), though more recent proposals suggest that impairments in social perception and behavior in autism reflect disturbance in ventral "social brain" systems that support social cognition (Baron-Cohen et al., 1999; Critchley et al., 2000).

In its original formulation, the Theory of Mind (ToM) or Mindblindness theory of autism posited that a disturbance in the capacity to cognitively represent the mental states of others gives rise to the social communication deficits observed autism (Baron-Cohen, 1995; Baron-Cohen, Leslie, & Frith, 1985; Frith, 1989). Since the ToM account of autism was first proposed, a range of mentalizing impairments have been documented, including impaired performance on tests of reasoning about "false beliefs" and "beliefs about beliefs" (Baron-Cohen, 1989a; Baron-Cohen et al., 1985), making mental-physical and appearance-reality distinctions (Baron-Cohen, 1989b), understanding that "seeing leads to knowing" (Leslie & Frith, 1988), and understanding subtle and figurative aspects of speech such as irony, metaphor, and sarcasm (Happé, 1993, 1995; for a review, see Baron-Cohen, 2000). Importantly, although some older and cognitively advanced individuals with autism demonstrate intact ToM ability on experimental tasks that tap false-belief understanding, they nonetheless continue to show impairments on more open-ended and interaction-based assessments, including a decreased tendency to use mental-state terms in narrative and discourse (Capps, Losh, & Thurber, 2000; Tager-Flusberg, 1992), or engage in pretend play (Baron-Cohen, 1987; Jarrold, 2003), and pragmatic difficulties, such as a lack of appreciation for social conventions regarding topic maintenance, and judging the informational needs of conversational partners (Baltaxe, 1977; Capps, Kehres, & Sigman, 1998).

From a developmental perspective, behaviors presumed to reflect the earliest signs of a child's emerging sensitivity to the mental states of others, including coordination of shared attention via gaze-following and referential looking, imitation of others' intentional actions, and pretense, have all been shown to be delayed within the first two years of life in autism (Charman et al., 1997, 1998; Landa et al., 2007; Sullivan et al., 2007). Moreover, a lack of attentional preference for the human face and voice among infants with autism, described previously, suggests that the emergence of ToM may already be compromised early on in autism by a lack of social input presumed to be an important trigger for the emergence of the mentalizing mechanism (Frith, 2001). Developmental repercussions of an early impairment in ToM in autism are predicted to be most clearly evident in social and communication domains. A number of studies have directly linked ToM abilities, as assessed using experimental tasks, to the degree to which real-life social skills and pragmatic skill deficits are displayed among individuals with autism (Frith, Happé, & Siddons, 1994; Happé, 1993; Tager-Flusberg, 2003). Impaired emotional processing in autism, including well-documented deficits in the ability to interpret and reason about complex social emotions (Adolphs, Sears, & Piven, 2001; Baron-Cohen, 1991b; Capps, Yirmiya, & Sigman, 1992), may similarly represent a secondary deficit to impaired ToM.

As the behavioral evidence for ToM impairments in autism has mounted, researchers have begun to examine the possible neural substrates for mentalizing, and the extent of the dysfunction of this system in autism. Although a review of this large body of work is beyond the scope of this chapter, the converging evidence suggests a network of brain regions that appear to be consistently activated during both verbal and nonverbal tasks that tap mentalizing skills, including the medial prefrontal cortex/anterior cingulate cortex, the temporal poles adjacent to the amygdala, and the temporo-parietal junction at the top of the superior temporal sulcus (Brunet, Sarfati, Hardy-Bayle, & Decety, 2000; Castelli et al., 2002; Fletcher et al., 1995; Frith & Frith, 2003; Gallagher et al., 2000; Goel, Grafman, Sadato, & Hallett, 1995; Schultz et al., 2000). Preliminary findings suggest that the brain abnormality in autism involves reduced activation in these regions on a variety of social-cognitive tasks, including reading stories and answering questions about complex mental states (Happé et al., 1996), inferring mental and emotional states from the eye region (Baron-Cohen et al., 1999), interpreting potentially ironic statements (Wang, Lee, Sigman, & Dapretto, 2007), and passive viewing of silent animations of moving geometric shapes that have previously been shown to elicit attributions involving goal-directed actions (Castelli et al., 2002; Kana, Keller, Cherkassky, Minshew, & Just, 2008).

Notably, Kana and colleagues (2008) have recently demonstrated that impaired ToM processing in autism may be the result of disruption at the level of inter-region connectivity of the social brain network. Utilizing a task in which participants were asked to attribute mental states to moving geometric figures, the researchers found that relative to control participants, high-functioning adults with autism showed reduced functional connectivity between frontal ToM regions (including the medial frontal gyrus, anterior paracingulate, and orbital frontal gyrus) and posterior ToM regions (right middle and superior temporal gyrus). This decreased synchronization among frontal and posterior cortical ToM areas during mental-state attribution in autism provides one possible neural mechanism by which ToM impairments in autism may arise.

Based on a growing body of evidence that, in addition to deficits in attributing mental states to others, children with autism have similar difficulty in reasoning about complex emotions (Baron-Cohen, 1991b; Capps et al., 1992) and showing concern for other's distress (Yirmiya, Sigman, Kasari, & Mundy, 1992), the ToM theory has been extended to include the ability to attribute emotional states to others, and consequently, to have an appropriate emotional reaction in relation to that inferred state (Baron-Cohen, Wheelwright, Lawson, Griffin, & Hill, 2002). In its most recent formulation, the Empathizing-Systemizing theory of autism (Baron-Cohen et al., 2005) posits that alongside difficulties in reasoning about, and appropriately responding to, the cognitive and emotional states of others (i.e., empathizing), which presumably underlie the social and communication deficits, there is intact, even enhanced, capacity for reasoning about and predicting the behavior of systems and non-agentive events (systemizing), which may account for repetitive behaviors and narrow obsessional interests (see Chapter 17). Baron-Cohen and colleagues (2005) propose that one avenue for looking into the underlying brain abnormalities in autism may be to examine areas that have demonstrated sex differences, given that systematizing is a more male trait, whereas empathizing is a more female trait. For example, there is some

evidence indirectly suggesting a pattern of increased local connectivity and decreased long-range connectivity in the male brain, with a similar imbalance between local and long-range connectivity recently reported in autism (Courchesne & Pierce, 2005; Just et al., 2004).

Family studies of autism indicate that a similar imbalance in empathizing and systemizing may be found among parents of children with autism. Parents of children with autism spectrum disorders show mild but significant deficits and atypical brain activation on empathizing tasks (Baron-Cohen & Hammer, 1997; Baron-Cohen et al., 2006), but are faster than sex-matched controls on the embedded figures test, and may be overrepresented in occupations that rely on systemizing skills, such as engineering (Baron-Cohen & Hammer, 1997; Baron-Cohen, Wheelwright, Stott, Bolton, & Goodyer, 1997; see Chapter 17).

Ever since the Theory of Mind hypothesis of autism was first proposed nearly 25 years ago, there has been much disagreement about how universal such mentalizing deficits are, and how well they can account for other aspects of the disorder. Nonetheless, the difficulties individuals with ASD exhibit in relying on an understanding of another person's beliefs, goals, motivations, and feelings in order to navigate social interactions are undisputable. The key question is not whether ToM impairments are a characteristic of individuals with autism, but rather, whether they represent an early-emerging, core deficit that precipitates the subsequent emergence of the profile of symptoms observed in ASD. Although conceptualizing the earliest manifestations of ToM in infancy remains a challenge, the field needs longitudinal studies that can disentangle the relative contribution of ToM impairments to the emergence of autism in the first years of life. The Systemizing-Empathizing extension of the ToM hypothesis is provocative and appears to fit well with a growing appreciation of autism as potentially representing the extreme of a continuum of traits observed in the general population. However, replication of key aspects of the theory by independent research groups is a goal for future research.

EMERGING TOPICS
IN NEUROPSYCHOLOGICAL
ACCOUNTS OF AUTISM

This section introduces a number of newer neuropsychological theories of autism, as well as some that have received less empirical testing. Many of these theories are covered in more depth in subsequent chapters, and others are quite recently published and the field has not yet tested them empirically. However, the novel approaches incorporated into these theories may lead us to a better understanding of the neuropsychological basis of autism.

Mirror Neuron Theory, Mimicry, and Imitation

Discovery of a set of *mirror neurons* in the inferior frontal and parietal regions of the macaque monkey brain that is active both upon performing a goal-directed action and watching the same action performed by another (Gallese, Fadiga, Fogassi, & Rizzolatti, 1996; Rizzolatti et al., 1996), and subsequent elaboration of an analogous network in humans involving the pars opercularis of the inferior frontal gyrus and rostral posterior parietal cortex (Iacoboni et al., 1999; Parsons et al., 1995; Rizzolatti & Craighero, 2004), has led to the proposal that a dysfunctional mirror neuron system (MNS) in autism may underlie the widely documented deficits in imitation (Rogers, Bennetto, McEvoy, & Pennington, 1996; Rogers, Hepburn, Stackhouse, & Wehner, 2003; Stone, Ousley, & Littleford, 1997), and subsequent impairments in social cognition (Williams, Whiten, Suddendorf, & Perrett, 2001) that are regularly observed in individuals with autism (see Chapters 12, 13, and 18, for extended discussion of this idea).

Recent imaging work suggests, that in addition to supporting action imitation, the MNS may also support action understanding, particularly inferences regarding the goals behind the actions (Fogassi et al., 2005; Hamilton & Grafton, 2006; Iacoboni et al., 2005; Koski et al., 2002; Rizzolatti & Craighero, 2004). The ability to understand actions and goals via the MNS may provide the basis for more advanced Theory of Mind and related social cognitive skills (Gallese & Goldman, 1998; Gallese, Keysers, & Rizzolatti, 2004; Oberman & Ramachandran, 2007); a deficient MNS may underlie impaired performance on tasks involving imitation and goal inference, playing a causal role in social cognitive disturbance in autism. Moreover, MNS modulation of limbic activity via the insula to give observed or imitated actions emotional significance (Carr, Iacoboni, Dubeau, Mazziotta, & Lenzi, 2003) may explain impaired emotion processing and empathy in autism. A related

theory notes that the MNS may enable intersubjectivity through so-called "embodied simulation," or internal representations of others' body states and associated actions and emotions, which provides experiential understanding of others (Gallese, 2006), and which may be disrupted in autism.

A few imaging studies have reported altered activation of putative mirror neuron regions in the brains of adults and adolescents during action imitation (Dapretto et al., 2006; Nishitani, Avikainen, & Hari, 2004; Williams & Waiter, 2006) and observation (Dapretto et al., 2006; Oberman et al., 2005; Theoret et al., 2005). A related argument articulated by Winkielman and colleagues (Winkielman, McIntosh, & Oberman, 2009; Winkielman, Niedenthal, & Oberman, 2008) focuses on the role of embodied simulation, specifically in emotion perception. The authors base their theory partly upon a large body of research utilizing facial electromyography (EMG), which demonstrates that presentation of emotional stimuli evokes patterns of activation in facial movements in the observer that differentially represent the valance of the perceived emotion. Such "facial mimicry" allows for somatic feedback that represents one source of information during emotion recognition. The role of facial mimicry in emotional recognition is highlighted by evidence that these responses can initiate and modulate emotional experience, and that blocking mimicry (e.g., asking participants to bite down on a pen) selectively impairs recognition of specific emotions (Niedenthal, Brauer, Halberstadt, & Innes-Ker, 2001; Oberman, Winkielman, & Ramachandran, 2007).

Although activation of the aforementioned mirror neuron system represents one potential mechanism underlying embodied simulation (e.g., Carr et al., 2003; Dapretto et al., 2006), a number of other mirror-like phenomena—whereby an area of the brain is involved both in perception and action—have been documented, suggesting other potential mechanisms. As summarized by Winkielman and colleagues (2009), these include evidence of activation of somatosensory and ventromedial cortices during explicit judgments of emotion from faces, compared to an indirect task of judging the gender of the individuals posing the emotion (Winston, O'Doherty, & Dolan, 2003), recruitment of the insula and anterior cingulate during observation of another's emotional state (Jackson, Meltzoff, & Decety, 2005; Singer et al., 2004), impaired performance on a range of emotion recognition tasks among patients with lesions in soma-tosensory cortices (Adolphs, 2006; Adolphs, Damasio, Tranel, Cooper, & Damasio, 2000), and a drop in per-formance on a facial discrimination task upon a tem-porary block of brain activity in the right somatosensory cortex via targeted transcranial magnetic stimulation (Pitcher, Garrido, Walsh, & Duchaine, 2008).

With respect to ASD, there is a small but growing empirical base supporting atypical EMG responses during implicit emotion recognition, tasks such as passive viewing of static and dynamic emotionally expressive faces (Beall, Moody, McIntosh, Hepburn, & Reed, 2008; McIntosh, Reichmann-Decker, Winkielman, & Wilbarger, 2006; Rozga, Mumaw, King, & Robins, 2009), though one study utilizing an explicit task where participants were asked to classify the emotionally expressive faces reported a delayed EMG response (Oberman, Winkielman, & Ramachandran, 2009). Moreover, at least one study reported EMG responses in individuals with ASD that were of comparable amplitude to those observed in typically developing controls during a task involving perception of emotional faces paired with emotionally congruent or incongruent auditory cues (Magnée, de Gelder, van Engeland, & Kemner, 2007), though Winkielman and colleagues have argued that the pairing of emotionally expressive voices with faces may have cued participants with ASD to attend to the emotional dimension of the stimuli (Winkielman et al., 2009).

Connectivity

Neuroimaging is a powerful tool to examine brain-behavior relationships. Initial studies using neuroim-aging focused on specific brain regions demonstrating altered structure or function; however, more sophisti-cated methods have been developed to examine sys-tems as a whole, which may map onto behavior more completely than does examination of discrete units or brain regions. Connectivity analyses examine relation-ships between specific brain regions, using a number of approaches. Diffusion tensor imaging (DTI) has been used to examine the organization and struc-tural integrity of white matter tracts in ASD, using fractional anisotropy (FA) and DTI-based tractogra-phy. A number of studies of autism have demonstrated white matter abnormalities in corresponding brain regions that have also been implicated in emotion perception studies, including anterior cingulate,

ventromedial prefrontal, temporal, and frontal regions (Barnea-Goraly et al., 2004; Ke et al., 2009; Lee et al., 2007; Sundaram et al., 2008; Thakkar et al., 2008). Particularly relevant to evidence of emotion process-ing deficits in autism is a study by Conturo and col-leagues (2008) which reported that, although there were no gross anatomical aberrations in hippocampo-fusiform (HF) and amygdalo-fusiform (AF) pathways in ASD detected by traditional structural MRI, white matter as measured by DTI showed evidence of poor fiber diffusivity in the right HF pathway in ASD com-pared with controls, consistent with decreases in fiber diameters and slower neural transmission. Results indicating white matter abnormalities in pathways interconnecting medial-temporal and fusiform struc-tures converge nicely with the large body of fMRI research suggesting atypical amygdala and fusiform activity during emotion processing in autism, as well as abnormal long-range connectivity in the socioemo-tional network in autism. Additional approaches to connectivity analyses include functional and effective connectivity, which correlate regional brain activations with one another during rest and task-specific periods, respectively. For example, there is evidence of reduced effective connectivity among regions of the limbic system during emotion perception tasks (Welchew et al., 2005; Wicker et al., 2008). It has been hypoth-esized that connectivity in autism is disrupted by reduced pruning, also known as brain overgrowth, which leads to inefficient communication across brain regions (see Chapters 3 and 21 for more in-depth review of this point).

Animal Models

The neuropsychological models discussed thus far aim to account for the wide range of social, communi-cative, and cognitive impairments observed in autism; in contrast, the use of animal models to investigate neurobiological mechanisms underlying specific fea-tures of the autistic phenotype has the potential to provide critical insight into the neuropathology of this disorder. One such area involves the stereotyped and repetitive behaviors and restricted interests that, despite being quite common among individuals with ASD, are often not adequately addressed by cognitive and social neuropsychological models (see Chapter 19). Models of the pathogenesis of stereotyped, repeti-tive, and injurious behaviors often focus both on their genetic and neurological underpinnings, as well as environmental and psychological factors that modulate their expression (Bodfish, 2007). Animal models relevant to these behaviors include those repetitive and stereotyped behaviors associated with targeted insults to the central nervous system (e.g., genetic mutation, viral exposure, lesions), those induced by psychopharmacological means, and those produced by restricted environments and experience (Lewis, Tanimura, Lee, & Bodfish, 2007). One major issue concerns the degree to which such animal models can not only account for lower–order repetitive behaviors observed in autism—including stereotyped movements, repetitive object manipulation, and self-injury (Moy et al., 2004; Moy et al., 2007)—but for the cognitive or higher-order behaviors, such as compulsions, rituals, and circumscribed interests (Moy et al., 2007). Animal models addressing the latter draw on evidence linking rates of restricted and repetitive behavior in autism to executive function tasks tapping cognitive flexibility (Colacicco, Welzl, Lipp, & Wurbel, 2002; Garner & Mason, 2002; Garner, Meehan, & Mench, 2003).

Given the complexity of social-interactive and social-cognitive impairments in autism, animal models of this aspect of the autism phenotype that can be readily generalized are inherently quite challenging to develop. One animal model focusing on social symptomatology is based on research with prairie voles and transgenic and knockout[1] mice implicating the neuropeptides oxytocin and vasopressin in the regulation of affiliation, social attachments, and social recognition (Choleris et al., 2003; Ferguson, Aldag, Insel, & Young, 2001; Hammock & Young, 2002; Insel, 1997; Pitkow et al., 2001; Young, Lim, Gingrich, & Insel, 2001). Given the core deficits in social engagement in autism, a number of researchers have suggested that oxytocin might be implicated in the etiology of the disorder (Green et al., 2001; Insel et al., 1999; Lim, Bielsky, & Young, 2005; Modahl et al., 1998; Panksepp, 1993; Waterhouse et al., 1996). Studies suggesting the oxytocin system may be dysfunctional in autism report evidence of lower levels of plasma oxytocin and concomitant association with the degree of social impairments in severely

affected children with autism (Modahl et al., 1998), decreases in repetitive behaviors and facilitation of social information processing in adults with ASDs following intravenous oxytocin infusion (Hollander et al., 2007; Hollander et al., 2003), and linkage studies of the oxytocin receptor gene in autism (Jacob et al., 2007; Kim et al., 2002; Wassink et al., 2004; see Chapter 22).

Neural Network Models

The growing field of computational neuroscience has provided researchers with a new avenue for examining the possible neural underpinnings of specific cognitive impairments in autism. Artificial neural networks mathematically model neurons and nervous systems, and thus the neural and cognitive functioning subserved by these systems, by running computer simulations of groups of neurons, synaptic connections, and changes in synaptic strength due to learning (Rumelhart & McClelland, 1986). One advantage of these models is that they can generate testable hypotheses with implications for the pathogenesis in autism. Indeed, such models have been used to explore the extent to which an overabundance versus deficiency in neuronal connections may explain the selective attention and generalization deficits observed in autism (Cohen, 1994), to explore the extent to which attentional impairments in autism may be caused by impaired attention shifting, versus a strong familiarity preference or negative response to novelty (Gustafsson & Paplinski, 2004), to propose accounts for hyperspecificity of memory and difficulty with generalization in autism (McClelland, 2000), and to examine the extent to which impaired feature detection may explain memory function and the lack of drive for central coherence in autism (Gustafsson, 1997).

Beversdorf and colleagues (2007; also see Chapter 20) have developed a neural network model to examine the extent to which restricted semantic and associative networks in autism could result in an impaired ability to utilize context for information processing, as suggested in the weak central coherence account (Frith & Happé, 1994). The focus on restricted semantic and associative networks stemmed from a behavioral study which indicated that individuals with ASD were less susceptible than typically developing controls to (incorrectly) reporting they recognized an index word from a list of semantically and associatively related words. This failure to experience a normative

---

1. A transgenic mouse is a mouse that has had DNA or genes introduced into its cells artificially. A knockout mouse is a mouse that has had the function of one or more of its genes deleted or made non-functional.

"false memory" effect was accompanied by decreased performance relative to typical controls on free recall of the words (Beversdorf et al., 2000). The authors found that applying decreased efficiency in search strategies in the neural network model (less widespread node activation) was sufficient to result in decreased performance on free recall in the same network that yielded superior recognition performance in ASD (Beversdorf et al., 2007). Evidence of a restricted semantic network in autism was placed within the context of previous behavioral findings of local bias and difficulty utilizing meaning in context, as well as recent fMRI evidence indicating decreased functional cortical connectivity in autism (Cherkassky, Kana, Keller, & Just, 2006; Just et al., 2004; Kana et al., 2006). Restricted semantic and associative network in autism, possibly underpinned by a lower degree of coordination among activated brain areas, could potentially address some of the problems with generalizing observed among individuals with autism, including the rigidity evident in many of the restricted/repetitive symptoms, the literal mindedness, and poor generalization of learning.

Arousal

The idea that chronic states of overarousal or unstable arousal may underlie some of the behaviors in autism goes back to the work of the Hutts (Hutt, Hutt, Lee, & Ounsted, 1965), and is reflected in subsequent theories by Kinsbourne (1987) and Dawson and Lewy (1989), and a recent, elaborated "polyvagal" theory by Porges (2004). These are reviewed in Chapter 19. In addition to direct evidence of arousal abnormalities in autism, animal studies support the expression of repetitive motor behaviors as indicative of high arousal. Estimates of comorbid anxiety disorders in children with ASDs are high (e.g., Kim, Szatmari, Bryson, Streiner, & Wilson, 2000; Leyfer et al., 2006; Muris, Steeneman, Merckelbach, Holdrinet, & Meesters, 1998), and family studies indicate a predisposition to Obsessive-Compulsive Disorder (OCD) and other anxiety disorders in autism families (Bolton, Pickles, Murphy, & Rutter, 1998; Piven, Chase, Landa, & Wzorek, 1991). Although anxiety and overarousal per se may not account for all of the characteristics of autism, they are clearly common, and may contribute strongly to repetitive behaviors and social avoidance, especially in high-functioning children.

Contingency Preferences

Gergely and Watson (1999) outlined a contingency detection mechanism, operational from early infancy, in which stimuli can be judged along several dimensions as perfectly, highly, or less contingent on each other. In earliest infancy, detection of perfect contingency between, for example, motor effort and sensory feedback, is critical in the infant's development of the self. Gergely (2001) argues that around three months of age, the infant's preferences switch from focusing on perfect contingencies to input with high, but imperfect, contingencies, and that this switch enables the infant to learn about social interaction contingencies. He further argues that the switch fails to occur, or occurs incompletely, in infants with autism, thus focusing the infant's attention on situations involving perfect contingency. This, in effect, focuses the infants on the physical rather than the social world. He demonstrates experimentally that older typical children prefer to look at a stimulus with imperfect predictability to their own movements, while children with autism prefer to look at the perfectly contingent feedback. This seems consistent with the phenomenon reported by Klin and colleagues (2009), that is, that toddlers with ASD are particularly attuned to physical (and presumably perfect) contingencies within biological motion point-light displays. It also seems consistent with the notion of "systematizing" discussed in Chapter 17. Thus, although recent and relatively untested, this theoretical notion seems consistent with some extant theories and data, and pushes the possible deviation from normal development into the first half of the first year.

CONCLUSIONS

A number of the theories presented in this chapter have a growing body of empirical support. We anticipate that as the field continues to develop, the brain-behavior relationships evident in typical development, but disrupted, altered, or absent in autism, will become clearer. In addition, the integration of methodological expertise from several different areas, including neuroimaging, psychophysiology, genetics, animal models, and computational neuroscience, has the potential to lead to sophisticated theories that may develop by combining aspects of the theories presented here. Furthermore, compelling evidence in support of these theories may come from applying these varied methods in concert using a developmental approach, to better understand the cascade of deficits that arise from a very early disruption to the brain in autism.

References

Adolphs, R. (2006). How do we know the minds of others? Domain specificity, simulation, and inactive social cognition. *Brain Research, 1079,* 25–35.

Adolphs, R., Damasio, H., Tranel, D., Cooper, G., & Damasio, A. (2000). A role for somatosensory cortices in the visual recognition of emotion as revealed by three-dimensional lesion mapping. *Journal of Neuroscience, 20,* 2683–2690.

Adolphs, R., Sears, L., & Piven, J. (2001). Abnormal processing of social information from faces in autism. *Journal of Cognitive Neuroscience, 13*(2), 232–240.

Adrien, J. L., Perrot, A., Hameury, L., Martineau, J., Roux, S., & Sauvage, D. (1991). Family home movies: Identification of early autistic signs in infants later diagnosed as autistics. *Brain Dysfunction, 4*(6), 355–362.

Baldwin, D. A. (1995). Understanding the link between joint attention and language. In C. Moore & P. J. Dunham (Eds.), *Joint attention: Its origins and role in development* (pp. 131–158). Hillsdale, NJ: Lawrence Erlbaum.

Baltaxe, C. A. (1977). Pragmatic deficits in the language of autistic adolescents. *Journal of Pediatric Psychology, 2*(4), 176–180.

Baranek, G. T. (1999). Autism during infancy: A retrospective video analysis of sensory-motor and social behaviors at 9-12 months of age. *Journal of Autism and Developmental Disorders, 29*(3), 213–224.

Barnard, L., Muldoon, K., Hasan, R., O'Brien, G., & Stewart, M. (2008). Profiling executive dysfunction in adults with autism and comorbid learning disability. *Autism, 12*(2), 125–141.

Barnea-Goraly, N., Kwon, H., Menon, V., Eliez, S., Lotspeich, L., & Reiss, A. L. (2004). White matter structure in autism: Preliminary evidence from diffusion tensor imaging. *Biological Psychiatry, 55*(3), 323–326.

Baron-Cohen, S. (1987). Autism and symbolic play. *British Journal of Developmental Psychology, 5*(2), 139–148.

Baron-Cohen, S. (1989a). The autistic child's theory of mind: A case of specific developmental delay. *Journal of Child Psychology and Psychiatry, 30*(2), 285–297.

Baron-Cohen, S. (1989b). Are autistic children "behaviorists"? An examination of their mental-physical and appearance-reality distinctions. *Journal of Autism and Developmental Disorders, 19*(4), 579–600.

Baron-Cohen, S. (1991a). Precursors to a theory of mind: Understanding attention in others. In A. Whiten (Ed.), *Natural theories of mind: Evolution, development and simulation of everyday mindreading* (pp. 233–251). Cambridge, MA: Basil Blackwell.

Baron-Cohen, S. (1991b). Do people with autism understand what causes emotion? *Child Development, 62*(2), 385–395.

Baron-Cohen, S. (1995). *Mindblindness: An essay on autism and theory of mind.* Cambridge, MA: MIT Press.

Baron-Cohen, S. (2000). Theory of mind and autism: A fifteen year review. In S. Baron-Cohen, H. Tager-Flusberg, & D. J. Cohen (Eds.), *Understanding other minds: Perspectives from Developmental Cognitive Neuroscience* (pp. 3–20). New York: Oxford University Press.

Baron-Cohen, S. & Hammer, J. (1997). Parents of children with Asperger syndrome: What is the cognitive phenotype? *Journal of Cognitive Neuroscience, 9*(4), 548–554.

Baron-Cohen, S., Leslie, A. M., & Frith, U. (1985). Does the autistic child have a "theory of mind"? *Cognition, 21*(1), 37–46.

Baron-Cohen, S., Ring, H., Chitnis, X., Wheelwright, S., Gregory, L., Williams, S., ... Bullmore, E. (2006). fMRI of parents of children with Asperger Syndrome: A pilot study. *Brain and Cognition, 61*(1), 122–130.

Baron-Cohen, S., Ring, H., Wheelwright, S., Bullmore, E. T., Brammer, M., Simmons, A., & Williams, S.C.R. (1999). Social intelligence in the normal and autistic brain: An fMRI study. *European Journal of Neuroscience, 11*(6), 1891–1898.

Baron-Cohen, S., Tager-Flusberg, H., & Cohen, D. J. (1994). *Understanding other minds: Perspectives from autism.* New York: Oxford University Press.

Baron-Cohen, S., Wheelwright, S., Lawson, J., Griffin, R., Ashwin, C., Billington, J., & Chakrabarti, B. (2005). Empathizing and systemizing in autism spectrum conditions. In F. R. Volkmar, R. Paul, A. Klin, & D. J. Cohen (Eds.), *Handbook of autism and pervasive developmental disorders, Vol. 1* (pp. 628–663). Hoboken, NJ: John Wiley & Sons Inc.

Baron-Cohen, S., Wheelwright, S., Lawson, J., Griffin, R., & Hill, J. (2002). The exact mind: Empathizing and systemizing in autism spectrum conditions. In U. Goswami (Ed.), *Blackwell handbook of childhood cognitive development* (pp. 491–508). Malden, MA: Blackwell Publishing.

Baron-Cohen, S., Wheelwright, S., Stott, C., Bolton, P., & Goodyer, I. (1997). Is there a link between engineering and autism? *Autism, 1*(1), 101–109.

Beall, P. M., Moody, E. J., McIntosh, D. N., Hepburn, S. L., & Reed, C. L. (2008). Rapid facial reactions to emotional facial expressions in typically developing children and children with autism spectrum disorder. *Journal of Experimental Child Psychology, 101*(3), 206–223.

Bennetto, L., Pennington, B. F., & Rogers, S. J. (1996). Intact and impaired memory functions in autism. *Child Development*, 67(4), 1816–1835.

Bernier, R., Webb, S. J., & Dawson, G. (2006). Understanding impairments in social engagement in autism. In P. J. Marshall & N. A. Fox (Eds.), *The development of social engagement: Neurobiological perspectives*. (pp. 304–330). New York: Oxford University Press.

Beversdorf, D. Q., Narayanan, A., Hillier, A., & Hughes, J. D. (2007). Network model of decreased context utilization in autism spectrum disorder. *Journal of Autism and Developmental Disorders*, 37(6), 1040–1048.

Beversdorf, D. Q., Smith, B. W., Crucian, G. P., Anderson, J. M., Keillor, J., Barrett, A. M., ... Heilmanlet, K. M. (2000). Increased discrimination of "false memories" in autism spectrum disorder. *Proceedings of the National Academy of Sciences*, 97, 8734–8737.

Bodfish, J. W. (2007). Stereotypy, self-injury, and related abnormal repetitive behaviors. In J. W. Jacobson, J. A. Mulick, & J. Rojahn (Eds.), *Handbook of Intellectual and Developmental Disabilities* (pp. 481–505). New York: Springer Publishing Co.

Bölte, S., Holtmann, M., Poustka, F., Scheurich, A., & Schmidt, L. (2007). Gestalt perception and local-global processing in high-functioning autism. *Journal of Autism and Developmental Disorders*, 37(8), 1493–1504.

Bölte, S., & Poustka, F. (2006). The broader cognitive phenotype of autism in parents: How specific is the tendency for local processing and executive dysfunction? *Journal of Child Psychology and Psychiatry*, 47(6), 639–645.

Bolton, P.F., Pickles, A., Murphy, M., & Rutter, M. (1998). Autism, affective and other psychiatric disorders: patterns of familial aggregation. *Psychological Medicine*, 28(2), 385–395.

Brosnan, M. J., Scott, F. J., Fox, S., & Pye, J. (2004). Gestalt processing in autism: Failure to process perceptual relationships and the implications for contextual understanding. *Journal of Child Psychology and Psychiatry*, 45(3), 459–469.

Brunet, E., Sarfati, Y., Hardy-Bayle, M., & Decety, J. (2000). A PET Investigation of the Attribution of Intentions with a Nonverbal Task. *Neuroimage*, 11(2), 157–166.

Caplan, R., Chugani, H., Messa, C., Guthrie, D., Sigman, M., de Traversay, J., Mundy, P. (1993). Hemispherectomy for intractable seizures: Presurgical cerebral glucose metabolism and post-surgical non-verbal communication. *Developmental Medicine & Child Neurology*, 35(7), 582–592.

Capps, L., Kehres, J., & Sigman, M. (1998). Conversational abilities among children with autism and children with developmental delays. *Autism*, 2(4), 325–344.

Capps, L., Losh, M., & Thurber, C. (2000). "The frog ate the bug and made his mouth sad": Narrative competence in children with autism. *Journal of Abnormal Child Psychology*, 28(2), 193–204.

Capps, L., Yirmiya, N., & Sigman, M. (1992). Understanding of simple and complex emotions in non-retarded children with autism. *Journal of Child Psychology and Psychiatry*, 33(7), 1169–1182.

Carr, L., Iacoboni, M., Dubeau, M. C., Mazziotta, J. C., & Lenzi, G. L. (2003). Neural mechanisms of empathy in humans: A relay from neural systems for imitation to limbic areas. *Proceedings of the National Academy of Sciences*, 100, 5497–5502.

Carver, L. J., & Dawson, G. (2002). Development and neural bases of face recognition in autism. *Molecular Psychiatry*, 7(Suppl 2), S18–S20.

Castelli, F., Frith, C., Happé, F., & Frith, U. (2002). Autism, Asperger syndrome and brain mechanisms for the attribution of mental states to animated shapes. *Brain: A Journal of Neurology*, 125(8), 1839–1849.

Charman, T. (2000). Theory of mind and the early diagnosis of autism. In S. Baron-Cohen, H. Tager-Flusberg, and D. J. Cohen (Eds.), *Understanding Other Minds: Perspectives from Developmental Cognitive Neuroscience* (pp. 422–441). New York: Oxford University Press.

Charman, T., Baron-Cohen, S., Swettenham, J., Baird, G., Drew, A., & Cox, A. (2003). Predicting language outcome in infants with autism and pervasive developmental disorder. *International Journal of Language & Communication Disorders*, 38(3), 265–285.

Charman, T., Swettenham, J., Baron-Cohen, S., Cox, A., Baird, G., & Drew, A. (1997). Infants with autism: An investigation of empathy, pretend play, joint attention, and imitation. *Developmental Psychology*, 33(5), 781–789.

Charman, T., Swettenham, J., Baron-Cohen, S., Cox, A., Baird, G., & Drew, A. (1998). An experimental investigation of social-cognitive abilities in infants with autism: Clinical implications. *Infant Mental Health Journal*, 19(2), 260–275.

Cherkassky, V. L., Kana, R. K., Keller, T. A., & Just, M. A. (2006). Functional connectivity in a baseline resting-state network in autism. *Neuroreport*, 17(16), 1687–1690.

Choleris, E., Gustafsson, J. A., Korach, K. S., Muglia, L. J., Pfaff, D. W., & Ogawa, S. (2003). An estrogen-dependent four-gene micronet regulating social recognition: A study with oxytocin and estrogen receptor-α and -β knockout mice. *Proceedings of the National Academy of Sciences*, 100(10), 6192–6197.

Cohen, I. L. (1994). An artificial neural network analogue of learning in autism. *Biological Psychiatry*, 36(1), 5–20.

Colacicco, G., Welzl, H., Lipp, H.-P., & Wurbel, H. (2002). Attentional set-shifting in mice: Modification of a rat paradigm, and evidence for strain-dependent variation. *Behavioural Brain Research*, 132(1), 95–102.

Conturo, T. E., Williams, D. L., Smith, C. D., Gultepe, E., Akbudak, E., & Minshew, N. J. (2008). Neuronal fiber pathway abnormalities in autism: An initial MRI diffusion tensor tracking study of hippocampo-fusiform and amygdalo-fusiform pathways. *Journal of the International Neuropsychological Society*, 14(6), 933–946.

Courchesne, E., & Pierce, K. (2005). Why the frontal cortex in autism might be talking only to itself: Local over-connectivity but long-distance discon-nection. *Current Opinion in Neurobiology*, 15(2), 225–230.

Courchesne, E., Townsend, J., Akshoomoff, N. A., Saitoh, O., Yeung-Courchesne, R., Lincoln, A. J., ... Lau, L. (1994). Impairment in shifting attention in autistic and cerebellar patients. *Behavioral Neuroscience*, 108(5), 848–865.

Critchley, H. D., Daly, E. M., Bullmore, E. T., Williams, S. C. R., Van Amelsvoort, T., Robertson, D. M., ... Murphy, D. G. M. (2000). The functional neuroanatomy of social behaviour: Changes in cerebral blood flow when people with autistic disorder process facial expressions. *Brain: A Journal of Neurology*, 123(11), 2203–2212.

Dalton, K. M., Holsen, L., Abbeduto, L., & Davidson, R. J. (2008). Brain function and gaze fixation during facial-emotion processing in fragile x and autism. *Autism Research*, 1(4), 231–239.

Dalton, K. M., Nacewicz, B. M., Johnstone, T., Schaefer, H. S., Gernsbacher, M. A., Goldsmith, H. H., ... Davidson, R. J. (2005). Gaze fixation and the neural circuitry of face processing in autism. *Nature Neuroscience*, 8(4), 519–526.

Dapretto, M., Davies, M. S., Pfeifer, J. H., Scott, A. A., Sigman, M., Bookheimer, S. Y., Iacoboni. M. (2006). Understanding emotions in others: Mirror neuron dysfunction in children with autism spectrum disorders. *Nature Neuroscience*, 9(1), 28–30.

Dawson, G., Carver, L., Meltzoff, A. N., Panagiotides, H., McPartland, J., & Webb, S. J. (2002). Neural corre-lates of face and object recognition in young children with autism spectrum disorder, develop-mental delay and typical development. *Child Development*, 73(3), 700–717.

Dawson, G., & Faja, S. (2008). Autism spectrum disorders: A developmental perspective. In T. P. Beauchaine and S. Hinshaw (Eds.), *Child and Adolescent Psychopathology* (pp. 575–613). Hoboken, NJ: John Wiley & Sons Inc.

Dawson, G., & Lewy, A. (1989). Arousal, attention, and the socioemotional impairments of individuals with autism. In G. Dawson (Ed.), *Autism: Nature, diagnosis, and treatment* (pp. 49–74). New York, NY: Guilford Press.

Dawson, G., Meltzoff, A. N., Osterling, J., & Rinaldi, J. (1998). Neuropsychological correlates of early symptoms of autism. *Child Development*, 69(5), 1276–1285.

Dawson, G., Munson, J., Estes, A., Osterling, J., McPartland, J., Toth, K., ... Abbott, R. (2002b). Neurocognitive function and joint attention ability in young children with autism spectrum disorder versus developmental delay. *Child Development*, 73(2), 345–358.

Dawson, G., Webb, S. J., Carver, L., Panagiotides, H., & McPartland, J. (2004). Young children with autism show atypical brain responses to fearful versus neutral facial expressions of emotion. *Developmental Science*, 7(3), 340–359.

Dawson, G., Webb, S. J., & McPartland, J. (2005). Understanding the nature of face processing impairment in autism: Insights from behavioral and electrophysiological studies. *Developmental Neuropsychology*, 27(3), 403–424.

Dawson, G., Webb, S. J., Wijsman, E., Schellenberg, G., Estes, A., Munson, J., Faja, S. (2005). Neurocognitive and electrophysiological evidence of altered face processing in parents of children with autism: Implications for a model of abnormal development of social brain circuitry in autism. *Development and Psychopathology*, 17(3), 679–697.

Fein, D., Humes, M., Kaplan, E., Lucci, D. & Waterhouse, L. (1984). The question of left hemi-sphere dysfunction in autistic children. *Psychological Bulletin*, 95, 258–281.

Fein, D., Pennington, B., Markowitz, P., Braverman, M. & Waterhouse, L. (1986). Towards a neuropsycho-logical model of infantile autism: Are the social deficits primary? *Journal of the American Academy of Child Psychiatry*, 25, 198–212.

Ferguson, J. N., Aldag, J. M., Insel, T. R., & Young, L. J. (2001). Oxytocin in the medial amygdala is essential for social recognition in the mouse. *Journal of Neuroscience*, 21(20), 8278–8285.

Fletcher, P. C., Happé, F., Frith, U., Baker, S. C., Dolan, R. J., Frackowiak, R. S. J., & Frith, C. D. (1995). Other minds in the brain: A functional imaging study of "theory of mind" in story compre-hension. *Cognition*, 57(2), 109–128.

Fogassi, L., Ferrari, P. F., Gesierich, B., Rozzi, S., Chersi, F., & Rizzolatti, G. (2005). Parietal lobe: From action organization to intention understanding. *Science*, 308(5722), 662–667.

Frith, U. (1989). Autism and "theory of mind." In C. Gillberg (Ed.), *Diagnosis and treatment of autism* (pp. 33–52). New York: Plenum Press.

Frith, U. (2001). Mind blindness and the brain in autism. *Neuron*, 32(6), 969–979.

Frith, U., & Frith, C. (2003). Development and neuro-physiology of mentalizing. *Philosophical Transactions of the Royal Society of London*, 358(1431), 459–473.

Frith, U., & Happé, F. (1994). Autism: Beyond "theory of mind." *Cognition*, 50, 115–132.

Frith, U., & Hill, E. (2003). *Autism: Mind and brain.* New York: Oxford University Press.

Gallace, A., Imbornone, E., & Vallar, G. (2008). When the whole is more than the sum of the parts: Evidence from visuospatial neglect. *Journal of Neuropsychology*, 2(2), 387–413.

Gallagher, H. L., Happé, F., Brunswick, N., Fletcher, P. C., Frith, U., & Frith, C. D. (2000). Reading the mind in cartoons and stories: An fMRI study of "theory of the mind" in verbal and nonverbal tasks. *Neuropsychologia*, 38(1), 11–21.

Gallese, V. (2006). Intentional attunement: A neurophysiological perspective on social cognition and its disruption in autism. *Brain Research*, 1079(1), 15–24.

Gallese, V., Fadiga, L., Fogassi, L., & Rizzolatti, G. (1996). Action recognition in the premotor cortex. *Brain*, 119, 593–609.

Gallese, V., & Goldman, A. (1998). Mirror neurons and the simulation theory of mind-reading. *Trends in Cognitive Sciences*, 2(12), 493–501.

Gallese, V., Keysers, C., & Rizzolatti, G. (2004). A unifying view of the basis of social cognition. *Trends in Cognitive Sciences*, 8(9), 396–403.

Garner, J. P., & Mason, G. J. (2002). Evidence for a relationship between cage stereotypies and behavioural disinhibition in laboratory rodents. *Behavioural Brain Research*, 136(1), 83–92.

Garner, J. P., Meehan, C. L., & Mench, J. A. (2003). Stereotypies in caged parrots, schizophrenia and autism: Evidence for a common mechanism. *Behavioural Brain Research*, 145(1–2), 125–134.

Gergely, G. (2001). The obscure object of desire: "Nearly, but clearly not, like me": Contingency preference in normal children versus children with autism. *Bulletin of the Menninger Clinic*, 65, 411–426.

Gergely, G., & Watson, J. S. (1999). Early socio–emotional development: Contingency perception and the social-biofeedback model. In P. Rochat (Ed.), *Early social cognition: Understanding others in the first months of life* (pp. 101–136). Mahwah, NJ: Lawrence Erlbaum Associates Publishers.

Gilotty, L., Kenworthy, L., Sirian, L., Black, D. O., & Wagner, A. E. (2002). Adaptive skills and executive function in autism spectrum disorders. *Child Neuropsychology*, 8(4), 241–248.

Goel, V., Grafman, J., Sadato, N., & Hallett, M. (1995). Modeling other minds. *Neuroreport*, 6(13), 1741–1746.

Goldberg, W. A., Jarvis, K. L., Osann, K., Laulhere, T. M., Straub, C., Thomas, E., … Spence, M. A. (2005). Brief report: Early social communication behaviors in the younger siblings of children with autism. *Journal of Autism and Developmental Disorders*, 35(5), 657–664.

Green, L., Fein, D., Modahl, C., Feinstein, C., Waterhouse, L., & Morris, M. (2001). Oxytocin and autistic disorder: Alterations in peptide forms. *Biological Psychiatry*, 50(8), 609–613.

Grelotti, D. J., Gauthier, I., & Schultz, R. T. (2002). Social interest and the development of cortical face specialization: What autism teaches us about face processing. *Developmental Psychobiology*, 40(3), 213–225.

Griffith, E. M., Pennington, B. F., Wehner, E. A., & Rogers, S. J. (1999). Executive functions in young children with autism. *Child Development*, 70(4), 817–832.

Gustafsson, L. (1997). Inadequate cortical feature maps: A neural circuit theory of autism. *Biological Psychiatry*, 42(12), 1138–1147.

Gustafsson, L., & Paplinski, A. P. (2004). Self-organization of an artificial neural network subjected to attention shift impairments and familiarity preference, characteristics studied in autism. *Journal of Autism and Developmental Disorders*, 34(2), 189–198.

Hamilton, A. F., & Grafton, S. T. (2006). Goal representation in human anterior intraparietal sulcus. *Journal of Neuroscience*, 26(4), 1133–1137.

Hammock, E. A. D., & Young, L. J. (2002). Variation in the vasopressin V1a receptor promoter and expression: Implications for inter- and intraspecific variation in social behaviour. *European Journal of Neuroscience*, 16(3), 399–402.

Happé, F. (1993). Communicative competence and theory of mind in autism: A test of relevance theory. *Cognition*, 48(2), 101–119.

Happé, F. (1995). Understanding minds and metaphors: Insights from the study of figurative language in autism. *Metaphor and Symbol*, 10(4), 275–295.

Happé, F. (1997). Central coherence and theory of mind in autism: Reading homographs in context. *British Journal of Developmental Psychology*, 15, 1–12.

Happé, F., & Booth, R. D. L. (2008). The power of the positive: Revisiting weak coherence in autism spectrum disorders. *The Quarterly Journal of Experimental Psychology*, 61(1), 50–63.

Happé, F., Briskman, J., & Frith, U. (2001). Exploring the cognitive phenotype of autism: Weak "central coherence" in parents and siblings of children with autism: I. experimental tests. *Journal of Child Psychology and Psychiatry*, 42(3), 299–307.

Happé, F., Ehlers, S., Fletcher, P., Frith, U., Johansson, M., Gillberg, C., … Frith, C. (1996). "Theory of mind" in the brain. Evidence from a PET scan study of Asperger syndrome. *Neuroreport*, 8(1), 197–201.

Happé, F., & Frith, U. (2006). The weak coherence account: Detail-focused cognitive style in autism spectrum disorders. *Journal of Autism and Developmental Disorders*, 36(1), 5–25.

Henderson, L. M., Yoder, P. J., Yale, M. E., & McDuffie, A. (2002). Getting the point: Electrophysiological correlates of protodeclarative pointing. *International Journal of Developmental Neuroscience*, 20(3–5), 449–458.

Hollander, E., Bartz, J., Chaplin, W., Phillips, A., Sumner, J., Soorya, L., … Wasserman, S. (2007). Oxytocin increases retention of social cognition in autism. *Biological Psychiatry*, 61(4), 498–503.

Hollander, E., Novotny, S., Hanratty, M., Yaffe, R., DeCaria, C. M., Aronowitz, B. R., & Mosovich, S. (2003). Oxytocin infusion reduces repetitive behaviors in adults with autistic and Asperger's disorders. *Neuropsychopharmacology*, 28(1), 193–198.

Hughes, C., Plumet, M., & Leboyer, M. (1999). Towards a cognitive phenotype for autism: Increased prevalence of executive dysfunction and superior spatial span amongst siblings of children with autism. *Journal of Child Psychology and Psychiatry*, 40(5), 705–718.

Hughes, C., Russell, J., & Robbins, T. W. (1994). Evidence for executive dysfunction in autism. *Neuropsychologia*, 32(4), 477–492.

Hutt, S. J., Hutt, C., Lee, D., & Ounsted, C. (1965). A behavioural and electroencephalographic study of autistic children. *Journal of Psychiatric Research*, 3(3), 181–197.

Iacoboni, M., Molnar-Szakacs, I., Gallese, V., Buccino, G., Mazziotta, J. C., & Rizzolatti, G. (2005). Grasping the intentions of others with one's own mirror neuron system. *PLoS Biology*, 3, 529–535.

Iacoboni, M., Woods, R. P., Brass, M., Bekkering, H., Mazziotta, J. C., & Rizzolatti, G. (1999). Cortical mechanisms of human imitation. *Science*, 286(5449), 2526–2528.

Insel, T. R. (1997). A neurobiological basis of social attachment. *American Journal of Psychiatry*, 154(6), 726–735.

Insel, T. R., & Fernald, R. D. (2004). How the brain processes social information: Searching for the social brain. *Annual Review of Neuroscience*, 27, 697–722.

Insel, T. R., O'Brien, D. J., & Leckman, J. F. (1999). Oxytocin, vasopressin, and autism: Is there a connection? *Biological Psychiatry*, 45(2), 145–157.

Jackson, P. L., Meltzoff, A., & Decety, J. (2005). How do we perceive the pain of others? A window into the neural processes involved in empathy. *Neuroimage*, 24(3), 771–779.

Jacob, S., Brune, C. W., Carter, C. S., Leventhal, B. L., Lord, C., & Cook, E. H. (2007). Association of the oxytocin receptor gene (OXTR) in Caucasian children and adolescents with autism. *Neuroscience Letters*, 417(1), 6–9.

Jarrold, C. (2003). A review of research into pretend play in autism. *Autism*, 7(4), 379–390.

Jarrold, C., Butler, D. W., Cottington, E. M., & Jimenez, F. (2000). Linking theory of mind and central coherence bias in autism and in the general population. *Developmental Psychology*, 36(1), 126–138.

Jolliffe, T., & Baron-Cohen, S. (1997). Are people with autism and Asperger syndrome faster than normal on the Embedded Figures Test? *Journal of Child Psychology and Psychiatry*, 38(5), 527–534.

Jones, W., Carr, K. & Klin, A. (2008). Absence of preferential looking to the eyes of approaching adults predicts level of social disability in 2-year-olds with autism spectrum disorder. *Archives of General Psychiatry*, 65, 946–954.

Just, M. A., Cherkassky, V. L., Keller, T. A., Kana, R. K., & Minshew, N. J. (2007). Functional and anatomical cortical underconnectivity in autism: Evidence from an fMRI study of an executive function task and corpus callosum morphometry. *Cerebral Cortex*, 17(4), 951–961.

Just, M. A., Cherkassky, V. L., Keller, T. A., & Minshew, N. J. (2004). Cortical activation and synchronization during sentence comprehension in high-functioning autism: Evidence of underconnectivity. *Brain: A Journal of Neurology*, 127(8), 1811–1821.

Kana, R. K., Keller, T. A., Cherkassky, V. L., Minshew, N. J., & Just, M. A. (2006). Sentence comprehension in autism: Thinking in pictures with decreased functional connectivity. *Brain: A Journal of Neurology*, 129(9), 2484–2493.

Kana, R. K., Keller, T. A., Cherkassky, V. L., Minshew, N. J., & Just, M. A. (2008). Atypical frontal-posterior synchronization of Theory of Mind regions in autism during mental state attribution. *Social Neuroscience*, 4(2), 135.

Kasari, C., Sigman, M., Mundy, P., & Yirmiya, N. (1990). Affective sharing in the context of joint attention interactions of normal, autistic, and mentally retarded children. *Journal of Autism and Developmental Disorders*, 20(1), 87–100.

Kasari, C., Sigman, M., Yirmiya, N., & Mundy, P. (1993). Affective development and communication in young children with autism. In A. P. Kaiser & D. B. Gray (Eds.), *Enhancing children's communication: Research foundations for intervention. Communication and language intervention series*, Vol. 2. (pp. 201–222). Baltimore, MD: Paul H. Brookes Publishing.

Ke, X., Tang, T., Hong, S., Hang, Y., Zou, B., Li, H., ... Liu, Y. (2009). White matter impairments in autism, evidence from voxel-based morphometry and diffusion tensor imaging. *Brain Research*, 1265, 171–177.

Kim, J. A., Szatmari, P., Bryson, S. E., Streiner, D. L., Wilson, F. J. (2000). The prevalence of anxiety and mood problems among children with autism and Asperger syndrome. *Autism*, 4, 117–132.

Kim, S. J., Young, L. J., Gonen, D., Veenstra-VanderWeele, J., Courchesne, R., Courchesne, E., ... Insel, T. R. (2002). Transmission disequilibrium testing of arginine vasopressin receptor 1A (AVPR1A) polymorphisms in autism. *Molecular Psychiatry*, 7(5), 503–507.

Kinsbourne, M. (1987). Cerebral-brainstem relations in infantile autism. In E. Schopler, & G. B. Mesibov (Eds.), *Neurobiological issues in autism* (pp. 107–125). New York, NY: Plenum Press.

Klin, A. (1991). Young autistic children's listening preferences in regard to speech: a possible characterization of the symptom of social withdrawal. *Journal of Autism and Developmental Disorders*, 21, 29–42.

Klin, A. (1992). Listening preferences in regard to speech in four children with developmental disabilities. *Journal of Child Psychology and Psychiatry*, 33, 763–769.

Klin, A. (2000). Attributing social meaning to ambiguous visual stimuli in higher-functioning autism and

Asperger syndrome: The Social Attribution Task. *Journal of Child Psychology and Psychiatry*, 41(7), 831–846.

Klin, A., & Jones, W. (2008). Altered face scanning and impaired recognition of biological motion in a 15-month-old infant with autism. *Developmental Science*, 11, 40–46.

Klin, A., Jones, W., Schultz, R., & Volkmar, F. (2003). The enactive mind, or from actions to cognition: Lessons from autism. *Philosophical Transactions of the Royal Society of London*, 358(1430): 345–360.

Klin, A., Jones, W., Schultz, R. T., & Volkmar, F. R. (2005). The enactive mind-from actions to cognition: Lessons from autism. In F. R. Volkmar, R. Paul, A. Klin, & D. J. Cohen (Eds.), *Handbook of autism and pervasive developmental disorders*, Vol. 1 (pp. 682–703). Hoboken, NJ: John Wiley & Sons.

Klin, A., Lin, D. J., Gorrindo, P., Ramsay, G., Jones, W. (2009). Two-year-olds with autism orient to non-social contingencies rather than biological motion. *Nature*, 459, 257–261.

Klin, A., Sparrow, S. S., de Bildt, A., Cicchetti, D. V., Cohen, D. J., & Volkmar, F. R. (1999). A normed study of face recognition in autism and related disorders. *Journal of Autism and Developmental Disorders*, 29(6), 499–508.

Koshino, H., Kana, R. K., Keller, T. A., Cherkassky, V. L., Minshew, N. J., & Just, M. A. (2008). fMRI investigation of working memory for faces in autism: Visual coding and underconnectivity with frontal areas. *Cerebral Cortex*, 18(2), 289–300.

Koski, L., Wohlschlager, A., Bekkering, H., Woods, R. P., Dubeau, M.-C., Mazziotta, J. C., & Iacoboni, M. (2002). Modulation of motor and premotor activity during imitation of target-directed actions. *Cerebral Cortex*, 12(8), 847–855.

Landa, R., & Garrett-Mayer, E. (2006). Development in infants with autism spectrum disorders: A prospective study. *Journal of Child Psychology and Psychiatry*, 47(6), 629–638.

Landa, R., Holman, K. C., & Garrett-Mayer, E. (2007). Social and communication development in toddlers with early and later diagnosis of Autism Spectrum Disorders. *Archives of General Psychiatry*, 64, 853–864.

Lee, J. E., Bigler, E. D., Alexander, A. L., Lazar, M., DuBray, M. B., Chung, M. K., ... Lainhart, J. E. (2007). Diffusion tensor imaging of white matter in the superior temporal gyrus and temporal stem in autism. *Neuroscience Letters*, 424(2), 127–132.

Leslie, A. M. (1987). Pretense and representation: The origins of "theory of mind." *Psychological Review*, 94(4), 412–426.

Leslie, A. M., & Frith, U. (1988). Autistic children's understanding of seeing, knowing and believing. *British Journal of Developmental Psychology*, 6(4), 315–324.

Lewis, M. H., Tanimura, Y., Lee, L. W., & Bodfish, J. W. (2007). Animal models of restricted repetitive behavior in autism. *Behavioural Brain Research*, 176(1), 66–74.

Leyfer, O. T., Folstein, S. E., Bacalman, S., Davis, N. O., Dinh, E., Morgan, J., ... Lainhart, J. E. (2006). Comorbid psychiatric disorders in children with autism: Interview development and rates of disorders. *Journal of Autism and Developmental Disorders*, 36(7), 849–861.

Lezak, M. D., Howieson, D. B., Loring, D. W., Hannay, H. J., & Fischer, J. S. (2004). *Neuropsychological assessment (4th ed.)*. New York: Oxford University Press.

Lim, M. M., Bielsky, I. F., & Young, L. J. (2005). Neuropeptides and the social brain: Potential rodent models of autism. *International Journal of Developmental Neuroscience*, 23(2–3), 235–243.

Lord, C. (1995). Follow-up of two-year-olds referred for possible autism. *Journal of Child Psychology and Psychiatry*, 36(8), 1365–1382.

Luna, B., Minshew, N. J., Garver, K. E., Lazar, N. A., Thulborn, K. R., Eddy, W. F., & Sweeney, J. A. (2002). Neocortical system abnormalities in autism: An fMRI study of spatial working memory. *Neurology*, 59(6), 834–840.

Magnée, M. J. C. M., de Gelder, B., van Engeland, H., & Kemner, C. (2007). Facial electromyographic responses to emotional information from faces and voices in individuals with pervasive developmental disorder. *Journal of Child Psychology and Psychiatry*, 48(11), 1122–1130.

Mason, R. A., Williams, D. L., Kana, R. K., Minshew, N., & Just, M. A. (2008). Theory of mind disruption and recruitment of the right hemisphere during narrative comprehension in autism. *Neuropsychologia*, 46(1), 269–280.

McClelland, J. (2000). The basis of hyperspecificity in autism: A preliminary suggestion based on properties of neural nets. *Journal of Autism and Developmental Disorders*, 30(5), 497–502.

McEvoy, R. E., Rogers, S. J., & Pennington, B. F. (1993). Executive function and social communication deficits in young autistic children. *Journal of Child Psychology and Psychiatry*, 34(4), 563–578.

McIntosh, D. N., Reichmann-Decker, A., Winkielman, P., & Wilbarger, J. L. (2006). When the social mirror breaks: deficits in automatic, but not voluntary, mimicry of emotional facial expressions in autism. *Developmental Science*, 9(3), 295–302.

Minshew, N. J., & Goldstein, G. (1998). Autism as a disorder of complex information processing. *Mental Retardation and Developmental Disabilities Research Reviews*, 4(2), 129–136.

Minshew, N. J., Johnson, C., & Luna, B. (2001). The cognitive and neural basis of autism: A disorder of complex information processing and dysfunction of neocortical systems. In L. M. Glidden (Ed.), *International Review of Research in Mental Retardation* (pp. 111–138). New York: Academic Press.

Minshew, N. J., Luna, B., & Sweeney, J. A. (1999). Oculomotor evidence for neocortical systems but not cerebellar dysfunction in autism. *Neurology*, 52(5), 917–922.

Minshew, N. J., Sweeney, J., & Luna, B. (2002). Autism as a selective disorder of complex information processing and underdevelopment of neocortical systems. *Molecular Psychiatry*, 7(2), S14–s15.

Minshew, N. J., Webb, S. J., Williams, D. L., & Dawson, G. (2006). Neuropsychology and neurophysiology of autism spectrum disorders. In S.O. Moldin & J. L. R. Rubenstein (Eds.), *Understanding autism: From basic neuroscience to treatment* (pp. 379–415). Boca Raton, FL: CRC Press.

Minshew, N. J., & Williams, D. L. (2007). The new neurobiology of autism: Cortex, connectivity, and neuronal organization. *Archives of Neurology*, 64(7), 945–950.

Modahl, C., Green, L., Fein, D., Morris, M., Waterhouse, L., Feinstein, C., Levin, H. (1998). Plasma oxytocin levels in autistic children. *Biological Psychiatry*, 43(4), 270–277.

Morgan, B., Maybery, M., & Durkin, K. (2003). Weak central coherence, poor joint attention, and low verbal ability: Independent deficits in early autism. *Developmental Psychology*, 39(4), 646–656.

Mottron, L., Burack, J. A., Iarocci, G., Belleville, S., & Enns, J. T. (2003). Locally oriented perception with intact global processing among adolescents with high-functioning autism: Evidence from multiple paradigms. *Journal of Child Psychology and Psychiatry*, 44(6), 904–913.

Moy, S. S., Nadler, J. J., Perez, A., Barbaro, R. P., Johns, J. M., Magnuson, T. R., ... Crawley, J. N. (2004). Sociability and preference for social novelty in five inbred strains: An approach to assess autistic-like behavior in mice. *Genes, Brain & Behavior*, 3(5), 287–302.

Moy, S. S., Nadler, J. J., Young, N. B., Perez, A., Holloway, L. P., Barbaro, R. P., ... Crawley, J. N. (2007). Mouse behavioral tasks relevant to autism: Phenotypes of 10 inbred strains. *Behavioural Brain Research*, 176(1), 4–20.

Mundy, P. (1995). Joint attention and social-emotional approach behavior in children with autism. *Development and Psychopathology*, 7(1), 63–82.

Mundy, P., & Acra, C. F. (2006). Joint Attention, Social Engagement, and the Development of Social Competence. In P. J. Marshall & N. A. Fox (Eds.), *The development of social engagement: Neurobiological perspectives* (pp. 81–117). New York, NY: Oxford University Press.

Mundy, P., Card, J., & Fox, N. (2000). EEG correlates of the development of infant joint attention skills. *Developmental Psychobiology*, 36(4), 325–338.

Mundy, P., & Crowson, M. (1997). Joint attention and early social communication: Implications for research on intervention with autism. *Journal of Autism and Developmental Disorders*, 27(6), 653–676.

Mundy, P., Kasari, C., & Sigman, M. (1992). Nonverbal communication, affective sharing, and inter-subjectivity. *Infant Behavior & Development*, 15(3), 377–381.

Mundy, P., & Neal, A. R. (2001). Neural plasticity, joint attention, and a transactional social-orienting model of autism. In L. M. Glidden (Ed.), *International review of research in mental retardation: Autism, Vol. 23*. (pp. 139–168). San Diego: Academic Press.

Mundy, P., Sigman, M., & Kasari, C. (1990). A longitudinal study of joint attention and language development in autistic children. *Journal of Autism and Developmental Disorders*, 20(1), 115–128.

Mundy, P., Sigman, M., & Kasari, C. (1994). The theory of mind and joint-attention deficits in autism. In S. Baron-Cohen, H. Tager-Flusberg, & D. J. Cohen (Eds.), *Understanding other minds: Perspectives from autism* (pp. 181–203). New York: Oxford University Press.

Mundy, P., & Thorp, D. (2007). Joint attention and autism: Theory, assessment and neurodevelopment. In T. Charman & W. Stone (Eds.), *Social and communication development in autism spectrum disorders: Early identification, diagnosis and intervention* (pp. 104–138). London, England: Jessica Kingsley Publishers.

Muris, P., Steerneman, P., Merckelbach, H., Holdrinet, I., & Meesters, C. (1998). Comorbid anxiety symptoms in children with pervasive developmental disorders. *Journal of Anxiety Disorders*, 12(4), 387–393.

Niedenthal, P., Brauer, M., Halberstadt, J. B., & Innes-Ker, A. (2001). When did her smile drop? Facial mimicry and the influences of emotional state on the detection of change in emotional expression. *Cognition & Emotion*, 15, 853–864.

Nishitani, N., Avikainen, S., & Hari, R. (2004). Abnormal imitation-related cortical activation sequences in Asperger's disorder. *Annals of Neurology*, 55(4), 558–562.

Oberman, L. M., Hubbard, E. M., McCleery, J. P., Altschuler, E. L., Ramachandran, V., & Pineda, J. A. (2005). EEG evidence for mirror neuron dysfunction in autism spectrum disorders. *Cognitive Brain Research*, 24(2), 190–198.

Oberman, L. M., & Ramachandran, V. S. (2007). The simulating social mind: The role of the mirror neuron system and simulation in the social and communicative deficits of autism spectrum disorders. *Psychological Bulletin*, 133(2), 310–327.

Oberman, L. M., Winkielman, P., & Ramachandran, V. (2007). Face to face: Blocking expression-specific muscles can selectively impair recognition of emotional faces. *Social Neuroscience*, 2, 167–178.

Oberman, L. M., Winkielman, P., & Ramachandran, V. S. (2009). Slow echo: Facial EMG evidence for the delay of spontaneous, but not voluntary, emotional mimicry in children with autism spectrum disorders. *Developmental Science*, 12(4), 510–520.

Osterling, J., & Dawson, G. (1994). Early recognition of children with autism: A study of first birthday home videotapes. *Journal of Autism and Developmental Disorders*, 24(3), 247–257.

Osterling, J., Dawson, G., & Munson, J. A. (2002). Early recognition of 1-year-old infants with autism spectrum disorder versus mental retardation. *Development and Psychopathology*, 14(2), 239–251.

Ozonoff, S., & Jensen, J. (1999). Specific executive function profiles in three neurodevelopmental disorders. *Journal of Autism and Developmental Disorders*, 29(2), 171–177.

Ozonoff, S., Pennington, B. F., & Rogers, S. J. (1991). Executive function deficits in high-functioning autistic individuals: Relationship to theory of mind. *Journal of Child Psychology and Psychiatry*, 32(7), 1081–1105.

Ozonoff, S., Rogers, S. J., Farnham, J. M., & Pennington, B. F. (1993). Can standard measures identify subclinical markers of autism. *Journal of Autism and Developmental Disorders*, 23(3), 429–441.

Ozonoff, S., South, M., & Provencal, S. (2005). Executive functions. In F. R. Volkmar, R. Paul, A. Klin, & D. J. Cohen (Eds.), *Handbook of autism and pervasive developmental disorders*, Vol. 1 (pp. 606–627). Hoboken, NJ: John Wiley & Sons.

Ozonoff, S., & Strayer, D. L. (1997). Inhibitory function in nonretarded children with autism. *Journal of Autism and Developmental Disorders*, 27(1), 59–77.

Panksepp, J. (1993). Commentary on the possible role of oxytocin in autism. *Journal of Autism and Developmental Disorders*, 23(3), 567–569.

Parsons, L. M., Fox, P. T., Downs, J. H., Glass, T., Hirsch, T. B., Martin, C. M., ... Lancaster, J. L. (1995). Use of implicit motor imagery for visual shape discrimination as revealed by PET. *Nature*, 375(6526), 54–58.

Pellicano, E., Gibson, L., Maybery, M., Durkin, K., & Badcock, D. R. (2005). Abnormal global processing along the dorsal visual pathway in autism: A possible mechanism for weak visuospatial coherence? *Neuropsychologia*, 43(7), 1044–1053.

Pennington, B. F., & Ozonoff, S. (1996). Executive functions and developmental psychopathology. *Journal of Child Psychology and Psychiatry*, 37(1), 51–87.

Pierce, K., Müller, R. A., Ambrose, J., Allen, G., & Courchesne, E. (2001). Face processing occurs outside the fusiform "face area" in autism: Evidence from functional MRI. *Brain: A Journal of Neurology*, 124(10), 2059–2073.

Pitcher, D., Garrido, L., Walsh, V., & Duchaine, B. (2008). TMS disrupts the perception and embodiment of facial expressions. *Journal of Neuroscience*, 28, 8929–8933.

Pitkow, L. J., Sharer, C. A., Ren, X., Insel, T. R., Terwilliger, E. F., & Young, L. J. (2001). Facilitation of affiliation and pair-bond formation by vasopressin receptor gene transfer into the ventral forebrain of a monogamous vole. *Journal of Neuroscience*, 21(18), 7392–7396.

Piven, J., Chase, G., Landa, R., & Wzorek, M. (1991). Psychiatric disorders in the parents of autistic individuals. *Journal of the American Academy of Child & Adolescent Psychiatry*, 30(3), 471–478.

Piven, J., & Palmer, P. (1997). Cognitive deficits in parents from multiple-incidence autism families. *Journal of Child Psychology and Psychiatry*, 38(8), 1011–1021.

Porges, S. W. (2004). The Vagus: A mediator of behavioral and physiologic features associated with autism. In M. L. Bauman & T. L. Kemper (Eds.), *The Neurobiology of Autism* (pp. 65–78). Baltimore: Johns Hopkins University Press.

Ring, H. A., Baron-Cohen, S., Wheelwright, S., Williams, S. C. R., Brammer, M., Andrew, C., & Bullmore, E. T. (1999). Cerebral correlates of preserved cognitive skills in autism: A functional MRI study of embedded figures task performance. *Brain: A Journal of Neurology*, 122(7), 1305–1315.

Rizzolatti, G., & Craighero, L. (2004). The mirror-neuron system. *Annual Review of Neuroscience*, 27, 169–192.

Rizzolatti, G., Fadiga, L., Matelli, M., Bettinardi, V., Paulesu, E., Perani, D., & Fazio, F. (1996). Localization of grasp representations in humans by PET: 1. Observation versus execution. *Experimental Brain Research*, 111(2), 1432–1106.

Robertson, L. C., & Lamb, M. R. (1991). Neuropsychological contributions to theories of part/whole organization. *Cognitive Psychology*, 23(2), 299–330.

Rogers, S. J., Bennetto, L., McEvoy, R., & Pennington, B. F. (1996). Imitation and pantomime in high-functioning adolescents with autism spectrum disorders. *Child Development*, 67(5), 2060–2073.

Rogers, S. J., Hepburn, S. L., Stackhouse, T., & Wehner, E. (2003). Imitation performance in toddlers with autism and those with other developmental disorders. *Journal of Child Psychology and Psychiatry*, 44(5), 763–781.

Rozga, A., Mumaw, M., King, T. Z., & Robins, D. L. (2009). Lack of emotion-specific facial mimicry responses among high-functioning individuals with an autism spectrum disorder. Poster presented at the International Meeting for Autism Research, Chicago, IL.

Rumelhart, J. L., & McClelland, D. E. (1986). *Parallel distributed processing: Exploitations in the microstructure of cognition. Vol. 1*. Foundations. Cambridge, MA: MIT University Press.

Russell, J., Jarrold, C., & Henry, L. (1996). Working memory in children with autism and with moderate learning difficulties. *Journal of Child Psychology and Psychiatry*, 37(6), 673–686.

Schmitz, N., Rubia, K., Daly, E., Smith, A., Williams, S., & Murphy, D. G. M. (2006). Neural correlates of executive function in autistic spectrum disorders. *Biological Psychiatry*, 59(1), 7–16.

Schultz, R. T., Gauthier, I., Klin, A., Fulbright, R. K., Anderson, A. W., Volkmar, F., … Gore, J. C. (2000). Abnormal ventral temporal cortical activity during face discrimination among individuals with autism and Asperger syndrome. *Archives of General Psychiatry*, 57(4), 331–340.

Schultz, R. T., Grelotti, D. J., Klin, A., Kleinman, J., Van der Gaag, C., Marois, R., & Skudlarski, P. (2003). The role of the fusiform face area in social cognition: Implications for the pathobiology of autism. *Philosophical Transactions of the Royal Society of London*, 358(1430), 415–427.

Schultz, R. T., Romanski, L. M., & Tsatsanis, K. D. (2000). Neurofunctional models of autistic disorder and Asperger syndrome: Clues from neuroimaging. In A. Klin, F. R. Volkmar, & S. Sparrow (Eds.), *Asperger syndrome* (pp. 172–209). New York: Guilford Press.

Shah, A., & Frith, U. (1993). Why do autistic individuals show superior performance on the block design task? *Journal of Child Psychology and Psychiatry and Allied Disciplines*, 34(8), 1351–1364.

Sigman, M., & Ruskin, E. (1999). Continuity and change in the social competence of children with autism, Down syndrome, and developmental delays. *Monographs of the Society for Research in Child Development*, 64(1), v–114.

Singer, T., Seymour, B., O'Doherty, J., Kaube, H., Dolan, R., & Frith, C. D. (2004). Empathy for pain involves the affective but not somatosensory components of pain. *Science*, 303, 1157–1162.

Stiles, J., Stern, C., Appelbaum, M., Nass, R., Trauner, D., & Hesselink, J. (2008). Effects of early focal brain injury on memory for visuospatial patterns: Selective deficits of global-local processing. *Neuropsychology*, 22(1), 61–73.

Stone, W. L., Ousley, O. Y., & Littleford, C. D. (1997). Motor imitation in young children with autism: What's the object? *Journal of Abnormal Child Psychology*, 25, 475–485.

Sullivan, M., Finelli, J., Marvin, A., Garrett-Mayer, E., Bauman, M., & Landa, R. (2007). Response to joint attention in toddlers at risk for autism spectrum disorder: A prospective study. *Journal of Autism and Developmental Disorders*, 37(1), 37–48.

Sundaram, S. K., Kumar, A., Makki, M. I., Behen, M. E., Chugani, H. T., & Chugani, D. C. (2008). Diffusion tensor imaging of frontal lobe in autism spectrum disorder. *Cerebral Cortex*, 18(11), 2659–2665.

Sung, Y., Dawson, G., Munson, J. A., Estes, A., Schellenberg, G., & Wijsman, E. (2005). Genetic investigation of quantitative traits related to autism: Use of multivariate polygenic models with ascertainment adjustment. *The American Journal of Human Genetics*, 76(1), 68–81.

Swettenham, J., Baron-Cohen, S., Charman, T., Cox, A, Baird, G., Drew, A., … Wheelwright, S. (1998). The frequency and distribution of spontaneous attention shifts between social and nonsocial stimuli in autistic, typically developing, and nonautistic developmentally delayed infants. *Journal of Child Psychology and Psychiatry*, 39(5), 747–753.

Tager-Flusberg, H. (1992). Autistic children's talk about psychological states: Deficits in the early acquisition of a theory of mind *Child Development*, 63(1), 161–172.

Tager-Flusberg, H. (2003). Exploring the relationship between theory of mind and social-communicative functioning in children with autism. In B. Repacholi & V. Slaughter (Eds.), *Individual differences in theory of mind: Implications for typical and atypical development* (pp. 197–212). New York: Psychology Press.

Thakkar, K. N., Polli, F. E., Joseph, R. M., Tuch, D. S., Hadjikhani, N., Barton, J. J. S., & Manoach, D. S. (2008). Response monitoring, repetitive behaviour and anterior cingulate abnormalities in autism spectrum disorders (ASD). *Brain: A Journal of Neurology*, 131(9), 2464–2478.

Theoret, H., Halligan, E., Kobayashi, M., Fregni, F., Tager-Flusberg, H., & Pascual-Leone, A. (2005). Impaired motor facilitation during action observation in individuals with autism spectrum disorder. *Current Biology*, 15, R84–R85.

Tomasello, M. (1995). Joint attention as social cognition. In C. Moore & P. J. Dunham (Eds.), *Joint attention: Its origins and role in development* (pp. 103–130). Hillsdale, NJ: Lawrence Erlbaum Associates.

Toth, K., Dawson, G., Meltzoff, A. N., Greenson, J., & Fein, D. (2007). Early social, imitation, play, and language abilities of young non-autistic siblings of children with autism. *Journal of Autism and Developmental Disorders*, 37(1), 145–157.

Toth, K., Munson, J., Meltzoff, A. N., & Dawson, G. (2006). Early predictors of communication development in young children with autism spectrum disorder: Joint attention, imitation, and toy play. *Journal of Autism and Developmental Disorders*, 36(8), 993–1005.

Travis, L., Sigman, M., & Ruskin, E. (2001). Links between social understanding and social behavior in verbally able children with autism. *Journal of Autism and Developmental Disorders*, 31(2), 119–130.

Venezia, M., Messinger, D. S., Thorp, D., & Mundy, P. (2004). The development of anticipatory smiling. *Infancy*, 6(3), 397–406.

Wang, A. T., Lee, S. S., Sigman, M., & Dapretto, M. (2007). Reading affect in the face and voice: Neural correlates of interpreting communicative intent in children and adolescents with autism spectrum disorders. *Archives of General Psychiatry*, 64(6), 698–708.

Wassink, T. H., Piven, J., Vieland, V. J., Pietila, J., Goedken, R. J., Folstein, S. E., & Sheffield, V. C. (2004). Examination of AVPR1a as an autism susceptibility gene. *Molecular Psychiatry*, 9, 968–972.

Waterhouse, L., Fein, D., & Modahl, C. (1996). Neurofunctional mechanisms in autism. *Psychological Review*, 103(3), 457–489.

Welchew, D. E., Ashwin, C., Berkouk, K., Salvador, R., Suckling, J., Baron-Cohen, S., & Bulmore, E. (2005). Functional disconnectivity of the medial temporal lobe in Asperger's disorder. *Biological Psychiatry*, 57(9), 991–998.

Werner, E., Dawson, G., Osterling, J., & Dinno, N. (2000). Brief report: Recognition of autism spectrum disorder before one year of age: A retrospective study based on home videotapes. *Journal of Autism and Developmental Disorders*, 30(2), 157–162.

Wicker, B., Fonlupt, P., Hubert, B., Tardif, C., Gepner, B., & Deruelle, C. (2008). Abnormal cerebral effective connectivity during explicit emotional processing in adults with autism spectrum disorder. *Social Cognitive and Affective Neuroscience*, 3(2), 135–143.

Williams, D. L., Goldstein, G., & Minshew, N. J. (2006). Neuropsychologic functioning in children with autism: Further evidence for disordered complex information-processing. *Child Neuropsychology*, 12(4), 279–298.

Williams, J. H. G., & Waiter, G. D. (2006). Neuroimaging self-other mapping in autism. In S. J. Rogers & J. H. G. Willams (Eds.), *Imitation and the social mind: Autism and typical development* (pp. 352–376). New York: Guilford Press.

Williams, J. H. G., Whiten, A., Suddendorf, T., & Perrett, D. I. (2001). Imitation, mirror neurons and autism. *Neuroscience & Biobehavioral Reviews*, 25(4), 287–295.

Winkielman, P., McIntosh, D. N., & Oberman, L. M. (2009). Embodied and disembodied emotion processing: Learning from and about typical and autistic individuals. *Emotion Review*, 1(2), 178–190.

Winkielman, P., Niedenthal, P., & Oberman, L. M. (2008). The embodied emotional mind. In G. R. Semin & E. R. Smith (Eds.), *Embodied grounding: Social, cognitive, affective, and neuroscientific approaches* (pp. 263–288). New York: Cambridge University Press.

Winston, J. S., O'Doherty, J., & Dolan, R. (2003). Common and distinct neural responses during direct and incidental processing of multiple facial expressions. *Neuroimage*, 20, 84–97.

Yirmiya, N., Gamliel, I., Pilowsky, T., Feldman, R., Baron-Cohen, S., & Sigman, M. (2006). The development of siblings of children with autism at 4 and 14 months: Social engagement, communication, and cognition. *Journal of Child Psychology and Psychiatry*, 47(5), 511–523.

Yirmiya, N., Sigman, M. D., Kasari, C., & Mundy, P. (1992). Empathy and cognition in high-functioning children with autism. *Child Development*, 63(1), 150–160.

Young, L. J., Lim, M. M., Gingrich, B., & Insel, T. R. (2001). Cellular mechanisms of social attachment. *Hormones and Behavior*, 40(2), 133–138.

Young, L. J., & Wang, Z. (2004). The neurobiology of pair bonding. *Nature Neuroscience*, 7(1327), 1048–1054.

Zwaigenbaum, L., Bryson, S., Rogers, T., Roberts, W., Brian, J., & Szatmari, P. (2005). Behavioral manifestations of autism in the first year of life. *International Journal of Developmental Neuroscience*, 23(2–3), 143–152.

Part II

Neuropsychological Functions

Chapter 6

Language in ASD

Elizabeth Kelley

Language and communication difficulties are one of the three main categories of impairments experienced by individuals with autism spectrum disorders (ASDs), the so-called "triad" of impairment (Wing, 1981). Research in the field of language in autism has been relatively extensive, yet several questions remain unanswered. In this chapter, I will first discuss the patterns of difficulties and strengths that individuals with ASD experience in each of four distinct aspects of language functioning: phonology and prosody, grammar, semantics, and pragmatics. I will then discuss some of the more commonly held theories to account for these patterns of difficulties. Finally, I will conclude with a discussion of clinical implications of language difficulties in ASD for the assessment, treatment, and prognosis of these individuals.

HISTORY AND OVERVIEW OF LANGUAGE IN AUTISM

Shortly after Kanner (1943) first proposed the diagnosis of autism, the psychology community began to speculate that autism was caused by poor parenting. The Freudian zeitgeist influenced this causal explanation; while Kanner originally stated that autism was probably due to some sort of organic brain dysfunction, he very shortly thereafter proposed that the cause could be environmental. Bettelheim (1967) coined the term "refrigerator mother" to refer to mothers who were so emotionally cold that they left their children no choice but to withdraw into themselves for self-protection. While this psychoanalytic perspective held sway, there was little research conducted on the language abilities of individuals with autism—indeed, there was little research conducted at all with these individuals. What little research was conducted was designed to support the poor-parenting theory.

By the late 1960s and early 1970s, the tide was beginning to turn against the psychoanalytic theories of autism, and other possible causes and key symptoms of the disorder began to be investigated. Around this time, a number of, prominent theorists in the field stated that language problems in individuals with autism were key symptoms in understanding the disorder (Churchill, 1972; Creak, 1972; Rutter, 1968). These theorists proposed that a dense language disorder was the key to understanding the social and cognitive difficulties that individuals with autism experience. Upon further study, however, it was soon discovered that autism, and the triad of symptoms that individuals with autism experience, stem from a far more complex disorder than simple language difficulties would produce. Indeed, there are many individuals with ASDs whose basic language abilities are relatively intact, yet they continue to exhibit a clear autistic profile of social withdrawal, difficulties in communication with others, and restricted and repetitive behaviors and interests. Moreover, children with Specific Language Impairment (SLI) have extreme difficulties in the linguistic realm, yet do not show the social withdrawal and repetitive behaviors that children with ASD exhibit (Rapin, 1996).

In fact, language functioning may appear at first blush to be unrelated to a diagnosis on the autism spectrum. Individuals with ASDs vary greatly in their language abilities; they range from being completely mute, to having limited functional language, to being verbally quite fluent. Even the most verbal of individuals on the autism spectrum, however, experience clear difficulties with the social and communicative aspects of language, or using language in an appropriate social manner (Tager-Flusberg, 2001). Although for a long time it was estimated that approximately 50% of individuals on the autism spectrum had no functional speech (Lord & Paul, 1997), more recently it has been suggested that this estimate is too high, and that fewer individuals with an ASD are completely nonverbal than was previously estimated (Eigsti, de Marchena, Schuh, & Kelley, in press). This increase in the percentage of verbal children with ASD is likely due to two factors: Not only is the prognosis generally improving for individuals with ASDs, but more high-functioning individuals are also being diagnosed, because of greater awareness of Asperger's disorder

and high-functioning autism. Thus, both a greater number of individuals are attaining functional speech through early intervention programs, and more high-functioning children with relatively intact language abilities are being diagnosed with an ASD than in the past.

Language profiles vary not only among individuals, but also within individuals across the course of development. Young children who go on to obtain a diagnosis on the autism spectrum often speak quite late. Indeed, one study found that language delay is the most common presenting concern when parents of these children first contact a doctor or other professional (DeGiacomo & Fombonne, 1998). Children are often thought to have a simple language delay or are tested for deafness before a diagnosis on the autism spectrum is given (DeGiacomo & Fombonne, 1998). Howlin (2003) found in a retrospective study that parents reported that the average age at which a group of children with ASDs said their first words was 38 months, compared to an overall range of 8–14 months for typically developing children. Even if young children with ASD do have some words, these children still generally experience difficulties with language comprehension (Fein et al., 1996; Lord & Paul, 1997). Young children on the autism spectrum do not orient to their own names and are often unable to follow simple instructions.

Early in development, the language profile of the child with ASD may look similar to those of children with SLI. Unlike children with SLI, however, children with an ASD show a lack of interest in engaging in communication with others, and make no attempt to communicate through nonverbal gestures or facial expressions (Rapin, 1996). As children with an ASD approach middle childhood, they may perform well on standardized tests of vocabulary, but continue to have difficulty using words in the appropriate contexts and formulating sentences and paragraphs in a coherent stream of speech (Fein et al., 1996). Pragmatics, or the understanding of appropriate language use for social purposes, remains a difficulty for all individuals with ASD throughout the life span (Dunn & Rapin, 1997).

Phonology and Prosody

Phonemes are the smallest units of sound in a language. An individual's phonological ability is their facility with producing and comprehending the phonemes of their native language. Difficulties with phoneme production (i.e., articulation) are often found in lower-functioning children with ASD, and also generally early in these children's language development (Lord & Paul, 1997). However, phonological ability in individuals with ASD has generally been thought to be commensurate with their overall developmental and language levels (Kjelgaard & Tager-Flusberg, 2001).

More recently, however, some researchers have proposed that at least some children with ASD may have particular difficulties in the phonological realm. Rogers and Bennetto (2000), for example, have proposed that some children with ASD may have particular problems with articulation due to an oro-motor dyspraxia (an inability to gain fine motor control over the muscles in one's mouth and tongue). One recent study found that the overall motor fluency of children with ASDs predicted their speech fluency (Gernsbacher, Sauer, Geye, Schweigert, & Goldsmith, 2008). It should be noted, however, that developmental level was not controlled for in this study, and thus might have been the variable that was driving both motor and speech fluency. Other researchers have proposed that receptive phonology may be particularly problematic for individuals with ASD (Dunn & Rapin, 1997). An inability to comprehend the particular phonemes of their native language could explain why young children with ASD have such difficulty understanding speech early in development. A number of recent studies have found that individuals with ASD do process auditory and linguistic information atypically at the cortical level, suggesting possible difficulties (or at least different neurological processes) in processing linguistic information (Bigler et al., 2007; Boddaert et al., 2003; Bruneau, Bonnet-Brillhaut, Gomot, Adrien, & Barthelemy, 2003; Dunn, Vaughan, Kreuzer and Kurtzberg (1999); Gage, Siegel, & Roberts, 2003; Müller et al., 1999).

In summary, productive phonology (i.e., articulation) appears to be strongly tied to overall language level in most children with ASD, such that it is problematic primarily for younger and lower-functioning children. Although some children with ASD may have some difficulty with oro-motor functioning, this is likely the exception rather than the rule. While individuals with ASD may have difficulties processing phonemic input, or process it in an unusual manner in the auditory cortex, it is unclear as of yet what impact this has on overall language functioning in these individuals. More studies are needed to determine what effects differences in auditory processing in the brain have on the linguistic behavior of individuals with ASD.

Prosody is commonly grouped with phonology in the study of language because both are aspects of the acoustic signal of speech. The study of prosody has to do with the production and comprehension of the melodic contour of language, the stress placed on important words or new information, and specific aspects of speech, such as the rising intonation at the end of a question to indicate a lack of certainty. Individuals with ASD are often reported by clinicians to have unusual prosody, speaking either in a monotone voice or an exaggerated, singsong prosody (Fay & Schuler, 1980). Despite strong agreement among clinicians of unusual prosodic production in individuals with ASD, relatively little research has been conducted in this area.

In one of the first research studies conducted in this area, researchers found that adults with ASD generally used less appropriate prosodic phrasing, placing stress in the wrong place in a sentence or using unusual melodic contour (Shriberg, Paul, McSweeney, Klin, & Cohen, 2001). In addition to unusual use of prosody, individuals with ASD also seem to have difficulties in understanding the use of prosody in language. A recent study found that adolescents with ASD were unable to use prosody to resolve syntactic ambiguity in embedded sentences (Diehl, Bennetto, Watson, Gunlogson, & McDunough, 2008). In sum, it appears that both the production and comprehension of prosody are affected in individuals with ASD, though more research is needed to pinpoint the nature and cause of their difficulties.

Grammar

Syntactic ability is the ability of individuals to use the ordering of words in a sentence to convey and comprehend meaning. Morphemes are the smallest units of meaning in a language, and are used to convey aspects of grammar that are not covered by syntax. Both syntax and morphology are subsumed under the individual's comprehension and production of grammar. In the 1980s and 1990s, a number of studies were conducted that led to the conclusion that grammar in individuals with ASD was generally appropriate for their mental age and overall language level. These studies found that grammatical development in children with ASD was similar to that of typically developing children, but merely delayed (Jordan, 1993; Landa, 2000; Lord & Paul, 1997; Minshew, Goldstein, & Siegel, 1995). For example, Tager-Flusberg (1981) found that children with ASD were able to use word order to act out sentences. Children with ASD seemed to show a normal (if delayed) pattern of grammatical development over time in both longitudinal (Tager-Flusberg et al., 1990) and cross-sectional (Waterhouse & Fein, 1982) studies.

More recently, however, some researchers have begun to question whether syntax and morphology really do really develop in a typical, but delayed, manner in children with ASD. Researchers have found that children with ASD do not use a wide range of syntactic forms in spontaneous speech (Dunn & Rapin, 1997; Pierce & Bartolucci, 1977; Scarborough, Rescorla, Tager-Flusberg, Fowler, & Sudhalter, 1991). One study found that individuals with ASD were less likely to use complex syntax, such as embedded sentences and relative clauses, in their spontaneous speech (Eigsti, Bennetto, & Dadlani, 2007). Interestingly, unlike syntactic forms in typically developing children, the syntactic forms of children with ASD have been found to be less complex than would be expected from their mean length of utterance (Scarborough et al., 1991); that is, although children with ASD were speaking in relatively long sentences, they were less likely to use a wide range of syntactic structures, such as asking questions and using embedded sentences (where one clause is embedded in a larger sentence structure). Thus, individuals with ASD may use simpler and more repetitive syntactic structures than would be expected, given their overall language level or verbal mental age.

On closer examination, it appears that there also are some difficulties experienced by individuals with ASD in the morphological realm. Children with autism frequently have difficulty with pronoun reversal, that is, saying "I" when they mean "you" and vice versa (Fay & Schuler, 1980). Pronoun reversal has been hypothesized to be due to echolalia (Fay & Schuler, 1980), as individuals with autism may only repeat back what they themselves hear to convey meaning, for example, saying, "Do you want a cookie?" when they themselves want a cookie, because that is what they had heard directed at themselves on previous occasions. Some researchers have also hypothesized that pronoun reversal is caused by difficulties with deixis (i.e., the ability to switch perspectives or

take context into account in understanding an utterance; Lord & Paul, 1997). Indeed, an early study found that while morphological development in children with ASD for the most part proceeded according to the children's developmental level, these children seemed to experience particular problems with person and time deixis (Bartolucci, Pierce, & Streiner, 1980); that is, they frequently engaged in personal pronoun reversal and were unable to use verb tenses appropriately to talk about the present versus the past.

More recently, some authors have proposed that there is a subgroup of individuals with ASD whose language profile is similar to that of individuals with SLI (Kjelgaard & Tager-Flusberg, 2001). These authors found a subgroup of verbal children with ASD whose language skills were quite poor in comparison to their overall mental age, and whose linguistic difficulties were found in several areas of language including syntax, semantics, and pragmatics (although their phonological development was mental-age appropriate). In a study of these same children's spontaneous speech, Roberts and her colleagues (2004) found that they displayed high rates of omission of obligatory tense markers, for example, saying "I walk to the store yesterday." This is a pattern of error that is commonly seen in English speakers with SLI. It should be noted that these types of tense markers were very similar to the difficulties found in the Bartolucci et al (1980) study, and could be a reflection of perspective-taking problems in the realm of past and future thought, rather than a strict grammatical competence issue.

One of the most common difficulties that individuals with ASD seem to experience in the linguistic realm is that of formulating output, or putting together a coherent narrative with well-formed sentences that carry a consistent train of thought (Cantwell, Baker, & Rutter, 1978; Fein et al., 1996; Lord & Paul, 1997; Minshew et al., 1995). It is possible that these formulation deficits may disallow children with ASD from using syntactic structures that they nonetheless have in their repertoire. That is, children with ASD may use very simple sentence structures (even though they know more complex structures) because they are principally having difficulty formulating their thoughts and expressing themselves clearly. Another issue that has been discussed extensively in the literature is the so-called "form-function distinction." This distinction refers to the idea that because individuals with ASD do not necessarily use language for the same functions as typically developing individuals do (i.e., to engage in shared communication, rather than to simply make their needs known), they may be displaying a limited number of syntactic forms due to the limited number of functions of their speech (Lord & Paul, 1997; Tager-Flusberg, 1994; Wilkinson, 1998). In other words, they may have a range of syntactic structures, but have no use for them when they are only using communication to make their needs known.

In sum, although individuals with ASD appear to generally have grammatical competence in line with their overall mental age, there may be specific aspects of grammar (such as person and time deixis and complex syntax) with which these individuals have particular difficulty. More research is needed to explore whether these difficulties are due to perspective-taking issues (deixis), or the limited communicative functions that individuals with ASD engage in. Moreover, it is critical to explore whether there is indeed a subgroup of individuals with ASD who are comorbid for SLI, as this could have important implications for the treatment of these individuals.

Semantics

The semantic aspect of language refers to the understanding of the meanings of words (and, to a lesser degree, the deep meaning of sentences). Here too, the accepted theory for much of the 1980s and 1990s (perhaps in a pendulum-swing against the focus on language deficits in the 1970s) was that semantic language was commensurate with the overall developmental and language level of the individual with ASD. There are a number of findings which would suggest that semantics, as a rule, develop typically (although in a delayed manner) in children with ASD. Standardized vocabulary tests tend to be a relative strength for individuals with ASD (Fein et al., 1996; Kelley, Paul, Fein, & Naigles, 2006; Kjelgaard & Tager-Flusberg, 2001; Mottron, 2004; Waterhouse & Fein, 1982). As Mottron (2004) has stressed, this is an important factor to keep in mind when conducting and also interpreting research, as individuals with ASD are often matched only on receptive vocabulary (e.g. the Peabody Picture Vocabulary Test) and not other, more complex, aspects of language. Estimating the language level of these children based only on receptive vocabulary may severely overestimate their true language ability.

One commonly occurring symptom found in individuals with ASD is the use of neologisms, or words that are made up and have no shared meaning with others (except perhaps those who know the individual well). The fact that individuals with autism use neologisms suggests that they do not understand the importance of shared meaning to the communicative process (Dunn & Rapin, 1997; Wilkinson, 1998). In a study of the use of neologisms by children with ASD and a control group of children with developmental delay, Volden and Lord (1991) found that the use of neologisms in the ASD group was not related to the social or cognitive ability of these children. Interestingly, the use of neologisms in the ASD group increased with increased language comprehension, whereas the developmentally delayed (non-autistic) children with higher language comprehension used fewer neologisms.

The ability to categorize words is a key component of semantic understanding. In an early study of categorization ability, Tager-Flusberg (1981) found that children with ASD were just as able as their mental-age-matched peers to sort line drawings into familiar categories, such as "animals" or "furniture." Dunn and her colleagues (1996) asked children to name as many animals as they could in one minute, and found that children with ASD were able to name just as many animals as their mental-age-matched peers, an ability known as *lexical fluency*. Interestingly, though, they found that the children with ASD named significantly more atypical animals; that is, they gave examples like "aardvark" and "ostrich" where the typical children named animals like "dog" and "horse." Another study which measured a greater number of lexical fluency types (e.g. different categories and words that start with different letters) found that children with ASD had reduced lexical fluency in comparison to the control group (Turner, 1999).

Other studies suggest that semantic categories may be differently organized in the brains of individuals with ASD. Dunn and her colleagues (1999) found that individuals with ASD displayed more errors classifying whether target words belonged to the category of animal or not, though this difference was not significant with their small sample size (N=8). Perhaps more interestingly, however, they found that, unlike typically developing individuals, the individuals with ASD showed no difference in N4 brainwaves for targets versus non-targets. Because 50% of the words belonged to the target category of animals, the typically developing individuals appeared to build up a "selective expectancy" (p.79) (an expectancy that the words presented would be animal words) of the category of animal, and showed a clear N4 waveform when the words presented were not animal words (the N4 generally indicates a violation of expectancy). The individuals with ASD did not demonstrate a clear N4 waveform, however, which the researchers interpreted as a lack of concrete category expectations.

There is also some evidence that semantic categories are not constructed in the same manner in individuals with ASD as they are in typically developing individuals. For example, Klinger and Dawson (2001) found that children with ASD, unlike their typically developing counterparts, were able to categorize nonsense animals if they were given rules about them, but they were unable to extract the rules in order to form prototypes of these nonsense animals. Furthermore, early research found that children with autism had particular difficulties learning category names (Menyuk & Quill, 1985).

Other researchers have found evidence to indicate that the semantic aspect of language may be problematic for individuals with ASD. While Tager-Flusberg (1981) found that children with ASD were able to use word order to act out sentences, unlike typical children they were not affected by the semantic probability of the sentence. That is, they were just as likely to act out *The car kissed the baby* as they were to act out *The mother kissed the baby*; typically developing children were much more likely to act out the latter than the former. Kamio and her colleagues (Kamio, Kelley, Robins, Swainson, & Fein, 2007; Kamio & Toichi, 2000) have found that individuals with ASD are less likely than typical individuals to be primed by semantically related words in a lexical decision task, even if those individuals with ASD had no reported history of language delay and had verbal intelligence within the average range.

One area of semantics that has consistently been found to be problematic for individuals with ASD is the comprehension and production of mental-state verbs (Baron-Cohen et al., 1994; Kazak, Collis, & Lewis, 1997; Kelley et al., 2006; Ziatas, Durkin, & Pratt, 1998). Lord (1996) hypothesized that children with ASD use mental-state verbs less in their spontaneous speech because they simply think about, and therefore talk about, other people's mental states to a lesser degree than typically developing individuals. Not only do individuals with ASD use fewer mental-state verbs in their spontaneous speech, however, they are also less able than mental-age-matched peers to understand the meaning of these verbs, such as the certainty difference between *guess* and *know*. Indeed, my colleagues and I found that even optimal-outcome children with a history of autism who no longer met the criteria for a diagnosis of ASD were less able than their typically developing peers to understand the certainty differences between *know* and either *think* or *guess* (Kelley et al., 2006).

Some authors have hypothesized that semantics are always a problem to some degree in individuals with ASD (Dunn & Rapin, 1997). Whether or not individuals form semantic categories and organize those categories in the same manner as typically developing individuals is currently unclear and more research is needed in this area. Furthermore, there have been no systematic studies of the process of lexical development over the course of development in individuals with ASD (Tager-Flusberg, 2001).

Pragmatics

Unlike other aspects of language, it is widely recognized that individuals with ASD consistently have difficulty with the pragmatic aspect of language. Pragmatic language involves the use of language within a social context for communication. Many abilities are covered under the umbrella of pragmatics, including taking the perspective of the listener; maintaining the topic of interest; giving enough (but not too much) information to the listener; using humor, sarcasm, metaphor, and idiom; and using nonverbal communication (e.g. facial expressions and gesture).

Individuals with ASD generally have problems, to at least some degree, with initiating conversation, maintaining the topic of the conversation, and considering the perspective of the listener (Dunn & Rapin, 1997). Higher-functioning children and adolescents with ASD quite commonly have a pedantic speaking style, using vocabulary far beyond their years and a more formal manner of speech than their peers (Rutter, Mawhood, & Howlin, 1992). Even individuals with no language delay demonstrate deep pragmatic problems (Lewis, Murdoch, & Woodyatt, 2007). Children who have improved to such an extent that they no longer meet the criteria for a diagnosis on the autism spectrum continue to demonstrate pragmatic difficulties (Kelley et al, 2006), although they may grow out of all but the most subtle difficulties in this area (Kelley, Naigles, & Fein, 2010). Indeed, studies have even found higher pragmatic problems in the parents of children with an ASD, suggesting there may be a genetic predisposition to pragmatic difficulties (Whitehouse, Barry, & Bishop, 2007).

Individuals with ASDs seem to have particular difficulty engaging in conversations. A recent study found that high-functioning adolescents with ASD had difficulty staying on topic, providing the right amount of information, and engaging in reciprocity in conversations (Paul, Orlovski, Marcinko, & Volkmar, 2009). Several studies have been conducted to examine whether children with an ASD were able to rephrase their statements if they were misunderstood (i.e., if were they able to repair a conversational breakdown). One study found that high-functioning children with ASD were just as able as mental-age-matched peers to engage in conversational repair, although they gave more irrelevant answers (Volden, 2004). However, another study found that younger children with ASD were completely unable to repair conversational breakdowns and simply repeated what they had already said, perhaps in a louder voice (Geller, 1998). Several studies have found that individuals with ASD do not respond appropriately to questions (Capps, Kehres, & Sigman, 1998); even adults have difficulty giving relevant answers that provide enough information to the listener (Eales, 1993).

Several studies have demonstrated that individuals with ASD do not understand figurative language and idioms, at least as they are measured by standardized tests (Dennis, Lazenby, & Lockyer, 2001; MacKay & Shaw, 2004; Ozonoff & Miller, 1996. Individuals with ASD also have a great deal of difficulty understanding inferences (Dennis et al., 2001; Norbury & Bishop, 2002; Ozonoff & Miller 1996). In these tasks, participants are given the beginning and the end of a scenario and have to figure out what could have happened in the middle; children and adults with ASD perform far below their verbal mental age on this task.

Another way to measure pragmatic language ability is to have children with ASD tell a story. Generally in these studies the children are given a wordless picture book, and they are asked to retell the story in their own words. Several studies in this area have found that the children's narratives lacked causal structure, that is, unlike their typically developing counterparts, they did not spontaneously discuss how the events of the story were related to one another and the overall goals of the characters (Capps, Losh, & Thurber, 2000; Diehl, Bennetto, & Young, 2006; Kelley et al., 2006). Capps and her colleagues found that the children with ASD used fewer narrative devices—such as repeating words for emphasis, or calling attention to the action through dramatic language—than their typically developing counterparts (Capps et al., 2000; Losh & Capps, 2003). In a study conducted with optimal-outcome children with a history of autism (i.e., those who no longer met diagnostic criteria), it was found that these children were still less likely than their typically developing peers to talk about causal structure, and were more likely than their typically developing counterparts to misinterpret what was occurring in the story (Kelley et al., 2006).

Pragmatic difficulties are thought of as one of the most stigmatizing features of having an ASD (Landa, 2000). Although older and higher-functioning individuals with ASD often do wish to communicate with others, they find it very difficult to understand other people's communication, as it is generally rife with inferences, metaphors, idioms, and subtle nonverbal cues. Volden and her colleagues (2009) recently found that, while language ability and nonverbal intelligence did contribute to pragmatic language ability, a significant proportion of variance was not accounted for by these variables. Perhaps unsurprisingly, pragmatic language difficulties were strongly related to level of autism symptoms.

Given that the research indicates a universal deficit in pragmatic language for individuals with ASD, perhaps the most fruitful area in which to focus research in the future is the effectiveness of various interventions designed to improve pragmatic language and social skills. Numerous books and treatment programs for parents and clinicians exist that focus on increasing the pragmatic language and social skills of children with ASDs (Gray, 2000; McAfee & Attwood, 2001), yet very little research has been dedicated to examining their effectiveness.

THEORIES OF LANGUAGE DIFFICULTIES IN INDIVIDUALS WITH ASD

The three main theories that are currently used to explain the language (and cognitive) difficulties exhibited by individuals with ASD are the central-coherence theory (Shah & Frith, 1983, 1993;

Happé, 1999), the executive-dysfunction theory (Hughes & Russell, 1993; Ruble & Scott, 2002), and the Theory of Mind (ToM; Baron-Cohen, Leslie, & Frith, 1985; Baron-Cohen, 1988). These theories for the most part do not propose etiological mechanisms or processes; rather, they are generally used as a theoretical framework to guide research. There is evidence in support of all three theories, and research pitting these theories against one another has generally yielded mixed findings. It has become increasingly clear in recent years that all three theories have their merit, and individuals with ASD do indeed experience difficulties in all three areas which lead to their pervasive difficulties in development. However, all three also have shortcomings when viewed as theories of the prime cause of the entire syndrome.

The Central-Coherence Theory

The Central-Coherence theory of autism states that the primary difficulty that individuals with ASD experience is their inability to organize information into a coherent whole; in other words, an inability to see the forest for the trees. This theory was put forth in response to research that found that individuals with ASD showed particular strengths in tasks such as the Embedded Figures task, which requires the individual to find a particular small shape in a larger, more complex pattern (Shah & Frith, 1983). This theory was given support by the finding that individuals with ASD also are not helped in the same way as typically developing individuals by overlaying the larger pattern onto the blocks when completing the block design task of the Wechsler intelligence tests (Shah & Frith, 1993). Although little research has been conducted to examine the relationship between central coherence and language development, Noens and van Berckelaar-Onnes (2005) have hypothesized that this theory would explain why individuals with ASD are relatively adept at handling the more mechanical aspects of language, such as grammar, and relatively poor at dealing with the more formal and symbolic aspects of language, such as reasoning, concept formation, and inference. It is also possible that central coherence would be related to the difficulty that individuals with autism experience with interpreting language in context. More research is needed to clarify the effects of central coherence on the development of language and communication in individuals with ASD.

The Executive-Dysfunction Theory

The Executive-Dysfunction theory of autism proposes that the primary deficit in these individuals lies in the executive-functioning realm. Individuals with ASD are proposed to have the most severe deficits in cognitive inhibition and flexibility. Researchers in this area have generally focused more on cognitive and social functioning and less on language development. However, some have hypothesized that a lack of cognitive flexibility might have a profound effect on ToM skills, which in turn would affect language development (Rogers & Bennetto, 2000). If the individual with ASD is unable to flexibly switch attention and perspective between speakers, it would indeed make language learning quite difficult. However, little research has investigated direct links between executive dysfunction and language development in this population.

The Theory of Mind (ToM)

The theory that has been studied the most in relationship to language deficits in autism is probably the Theory of Mind (ToM). Theory of Mind is the ability of an individual to understand that others have desires, beliefs, and thoughts that are different from one's own, and that they will act on those different desires, beliefs, and thoughts. Individuals with ASD are known to have deficits in this area (Baron-Cohen, Leslie, & Frith, 1985; Brent, Rios, Happé, & Charman, 2004; Happe, 1994; Kleinman, Marciano, & Ault, 2001). Baron-Cohen (1988) proposed that a lack of ToM abilities is the key to understanding cognitive and language difficulties in individuals with ASD.

Jordan (1993) has suggested that in typical development, the earliest aspects of communication (gesture, babbling, joint attention, and so forth) are learned before language, but this is often not true of the child with ASD. There is some support for this idea; for example, Carpenter, Pennington, and Rogers (2002) found that children with ASD learned some language before they learned to engage in joint attention (that is, sharing a gaze with another in regards to an object), or before they began to gesture. Another study found that children with ASD were unable to use the speaker's direction of gaze to learn the name of a new object, and unlike the control group, instead paired the word that was uttered with the object that they themselves were focused on at the time of the utterance (Baron-Cohen, Baldwin, & Crowson, 1997).

As mentioned above, all three of these theories have found some support in the literature and it is likely that central coherence, executive-functioning difficulties, and problems in ToM are all related to the difficulties that individuals with ASD experience in the realm of language and communication. More research is needed to investigate the relationship between these various difficulties and language development in order to better understand the implications for treating children with ASD and supporting their optimal language development. Although there may be correlations between central coherence, executive functioning, and ToM with language ability, this nonetheless does not imply that these factors are directly responsible for the difficulties that individuals with ASD experience with language and communication.

CLINICAL IMPLICATIONS

Assessment

There are a number of issues that the clinician should keep in mind when assessing the language of the individual with ASD. Perhaps one of the most obvious is the issue of diagnostic subtype; that is, are there differences in the linguistic profiles of individuals with autistic disorder, Asperger's syndrome, or pervasive developmental disorder—not otherwise specified? Although a lack of language delay is a defining characteristic of a diagnosis of Asperger's, there in nonetheless a great deal of overlap in the profiles of individuals with Asperger's and those with high-functioning autism, particularly as the children get older (Gilchrist et al., 2001; Szatmari, Tuff, Finlayson, & Bartolucci, 1990; Witwer & Lecavalier, 2008). In general, children with Asperger's tend to have higher verbal than nonverbal intelligence, with the opposite being true of children with high-functioning autism. This discrepant pattern becomes less clear over the course of development, however (Joseph, Tager-Flusberg, & Lord, 2002). Some researchers have hypothesized that the best way to separate individuals on the autism spectrum is by intelligence levels, not by subtypes, as intelligence levels are far more predictive of outcome than diagnostic categories (Fein et al., 1999; Witwer & Lecavalier, 2008).

Another important issue for clinicians is the question of which are the best tests to use to assess

individuals with ASD. The tests used to assess these individuals are important, as results can vary widely between tests (Magiati & Howlin, 2001. As mentioned earlier, individuals with ASD may be particularly good at rote naming, and so simply using a test of their receptive or expressive vocabulary will not assess their key difficulties. The Clinical Evaluation of Language Fundamentals, Version 4 (CELF-4: Semel, Wiig, & Secord, 2003) and the Test for Reception of Grammar, Second Edition (TROG-2; Bishop, 2003) are two widely used standardized tests that assess a number of different aspects of the individual's language ability (for a comprehensive discussion of language assessment in children, see Kelley, Jones, & Fein, 2003).

It is also important to assess the individual's ability to communicate, not just their "verbal behavior" (Wetherby, Prizant & Schuler, 2000). One of the easiest ways to do this is to collect a spontaneous speech sample (Tager-Flusberg, 2000). One does not need to have an extensive background in linguistics to determine whether the individual is able to clearly communicate intent, stay on topic, provide enough information for the context, and understand other pragmatic factors, such as humor and irony. There are also a number of standardized tests that assess pragmatic understanding, such as the Test of Pragmatic Language, Second Edition (TOPL2; Phelps-Teraski & Phelps-Gunn, 2007) and the Test of Language Competence, Expanded Edition (Wiig & Secord, 1989). The Comprehensive Assessment of Spoken Language (Carrow-Woolfolk, 1999) includes both more traditional language tests and pragmatic subtests, which are suitable for testing multiple aspects of language in the same individual.

Also very important to keep in mind when administering tests to individuals with ASD is their level of motivation and attention (Tager-Flusberg, 2000). Because individuals with ASD do not have the same level of social motivation as typically developing individuals, they do not respond as well to social feedback, nor do they demonstrate the desire to please their tester that typically developing individuals generally demonstrate. Individuals with ASD commonly have comorbid attention difficulties, and so keeping them on task may be challenging. It is important for the clinician to remember these factors and provide frequent breaks, and tangible reinforcement where appropriate. When computerized testing is available it is recommended, as individuals with ASD often find interacting with a computer less stressful than interacting with another person (Tager-Flusberg, 2000).

Treatment

Language is an essential treatment focus in children with ASD. The inability to communicate with their children causes a great deal of stress for families (Wetherby, et al., 2000). It is also quite likely that the child's frustration with his or her inability to communicate is related to self-injurious behaviors; improving the child's communication skills often alleviates self-injurious and tantrum-throwing behaviors (Koegel, 2000; Wetherby et al., 2000). It has also been found that social, cognitive, and language abilities are more interdependent in children with ASD, in comparison to their typically developing peers (Dyck, Pick, Hay, Smith, & Hallmayer, 2006); thus, improving language should improve social and cognitive abilities as well.

What type of treatment the child receives often varies greatly by geographic region; while most children in North America receive treatment based at least in part on behavioral principles (the so-called Lovaas method, also known as Applied Behavior Analysis or discrete trial training), there are an increasing number of treatment programs that focus on teaching the child in a more naturalistic setting. Unfortunately, very little good research exists in the field of autism treatment. There are virtually no double-blind randomized controlled trials, every study uses different outcome measures, it is very difficult to measure the amount and fidelity of treatment, and most studies suffer from small sample sizes (Charman & Howlin, 2003). Assessing the treatment literature is beyond the scope of this chapter; however, there are a number of treatment issues relevant to the development of language and communication that the clinician should keep in mind.

Autism spectrum disorders are heterogeneous in their presentation, and it is possible that different children may need different treatments (Wetherby et al., 2000); however, little research to date has assessed which children respond to which treatments. Often, the type of treatment determines the type of progress the child will make (Yoder & Stone, 2006). That is, children who are taught using strict, discrete, trial methods with little focus on generalization may have an expansive vocabulary, yet little generalization to different contexts (Koegel, Dell, & Koegel, 1987).

Therefore, it is crucial to ensure that behavioral programming includes work on generalizing language to different contexts, is taught for different pragmatic functions, and includes maintenance practice as well.

Some research also suggests that treatment that focuses on some of the precursors to a Theory of Mind might be beneficial to young children with ASD. Researchers have suggested that a focus on fostering joint-attention and imitation skills leads to better overall outcomes, including better language development (Mundy & Crowson, 1997; Sigman, 1998). One study found that children who had better joint attention in the early years had better grammar approximately two years later (Rosenthal-Rollins & Snow, 1998). Joint attention and imitation are known to be precursors to Theory of Mind in typically developing children; therefore, increasing these abilities may simply increase social understanding, which leads in turn to more desire to communicate.

Treatments based on behavioral principles have been the only treatments which have demonstrated children improving to such a great extent that they lose their diagnosis (Kelley et al., 2006; McEachin, Smith, & Lovaas, 1993). The best treatments likely use behavioral principles, and also provide the child with some treatment in the social realm. It is extremely important for the treatment to be started as early as possible, and for the child to receive as many hours of treatment per week as is feasible. Indeed, Mundy and Crowson (1997) have stated that it may be less important what type of intervention the child receives, than whether they receive it in an intensive manner early in development.

There are some children with ASD who will remain mute no matter how much intervention they receive. These children should be taught to communicate with others through the use of some sort of nonverbal communication system, be it sign language or other methods, in order to make their needs known and reduce their own and their families' frustration. One method of communication for nonverbal children which has shown some promise in the research field is the Picture Exchange Communication System (PECS; Bondy & Frost, 2001). Children are taught to use pictures in a social context to communicate their needs. When working with children with ASD, it is always a good idea for the clinician to consult with a registered speech and language pathologist (SLP); this is perhaps particularly important in the case of the nonverbal child.

Prognosis

The range of prognosis for individuals with ASD is quite large; while many individuals with these disorders have a relatively poor prognosis (i.e., an inability to live independently, hold a job for a significant length of time, or have meaningful peer relationships), others function relatively well. It is important to remember that autism is both affected by and affects development (Lord & Risi, 2000); that is, although young children with ASD may have a particular symptom profile, that does not mean that symptom profile will remain fixed over the course of their development. The young child with ASD who is quite socially withdrawn and nonverbal may become an adolescent who has language skills in the typical range on standardized tests, although he or she is likely to experience continuing difficulties with pragmatics. Early language skills are a strong predictor of later outcome (Lord, 1996; Stone & Yoder, 2001), and thus it is crucial to try to develop language skills as early as possible. Prognosis can be quite good for some children with early intensive intervention and, as mentioned earlier, it may matter less what the intervention is than whether it is early and intense—i.e., at least 20 hours per week and preferably closer to 40 (Mundy & Crowson, 1997).

Children may even improve to such an extent that they no longer meet criteria for a diagnosis on the autism spectrum, yet these children may (but not in all cases) retain subtle social, emotional, and pragmatic language difficulties (Kelley et al., 2006; Kelley et al, 2010; McEachin et al., 1993).

Language is a highly valued skill in our society, and those who cannot communicate effectively may not be fully integrated into it. All efforts should be made to provide enough intervention with children with ASD so that they can reach their full potential. For this to occur, the focus of language interventions should not just be on learning vocabulary and grammar, but on teaching the child to communicate effectively with others. Language is about more than simply words and sentences; language is about sharing one's feelings, perspectives, and beliefs.

References

Baron-Cohen, S. (1988). Social and pragmatic deficits in autism: Cognitive or affective? *Journal of Autism and Developmental Disorders, 18*, 379–402.

Baron-Cohen, S., Baldwin, D. A., & Crowson, M. (1997). Do children with autism use the speaker's direction of gaze strategy to crack the code of language? *Child Development, 68*, 48–57.

Baron-Cohen, S., Leslie, A. M., & Frith, U. (1985). Does the autistic child have a theory of mind? *Cognition, 21*, 37–46.

Baron-Cohen, S., Ring, H., Moriarity, J., Schmitz, B., Costa, D., & Ell, P. (1994). Recognition of mental state terms: Clinical findings in children with autism and a functional neuroimaging study of adults. *British Journal of Psychiatry, 165*, 640–649.

Bartolucci, G., Pierce, S. J., & Streiner, D. (1980). Cross-sectional studies of grammatical morphemes in autistic and mentally retarded children. *Journal of Autism and Developmental Disorders, 10*, 39–50.

Bettelheim, B. (1967). *The empty fortress: Infantile autism and the birth of the self.* New York: Free Press.

Bigler, E. D., Mortensen, S., Neeley, E. S., Ozonoff, S., Krasny, L., Johnson, M., … Lainhart, J. E. (2007). Superior temporal gyrus, language function, and autism. *Developmental Neuropsychology, 31*, 217–238.

Bishop, D. V. M. (2003). *Test for reception of grammar, second edition.* San Antonio, TX: The Psychological Corporation.

Boddaert, N., Belin, P., Chabane, N., Poline, J., Barthelemey, C., Mouren-Simeoni, M., … Zilbovicius, M. (2003). Perception of complex sounds: Abnormal pattern of cortical activation in autism. *American Journal of Psychiatry, 160*, 2057–2060.

Bondy, A., & Frost, L. (2001). The picture exchange communication system. *Behavior Modification, 25*, 725–744.

Brent, E., Rios, P., Happe, F., & Charman, T. (2004). Performance of children with autism spectrum disorders on advanced theory of mind tasks. *Autism, 8*, 283–299.

Bruneau, N., Bonnet-Brilhault, F., Gomot, M., Adrien, J. L., & Barthelemy, C. (2003). Cortical auditory processing and communication in children with autism: Electrophysiological and behavioral relations. *International Journal of Psychophysiology, 51*, 17–25.

Cantwell, D., Baker, L., & Rutter, M. (1978). A comparative study of infantile autism and specific developmental receptive language disorder IV. Analysis of syntax and language function. *Journal of Child Psychology and Psychiatry, 19*, 351–362.

Capps, L., Kehres, J., & Sigman, M. (1998). Conversational abilities among children with autism and children with developmental delays. *Autism, 2*, 325–344.

Capps, L., Losh, M., & Thurber, C. (2000). "The frog ate the bug and made his mouth sad": Narrative competence in children with autism. *Journal of Abnormal Child Psychology, 28*, 193–204.

Carpenter, M., Pennington, B. F., & Rogers, S. J. (2002). Interrelations among social-cognitive skills in young children with autism. *Journal of Autism and Developmental Disorders, 32*, 91–106.

Carrow-Woolfolk, E. (1999). *Comprehensive assessment of spoken language*. Bloomington, MN: Pearson Corp.

Charman, T., & Howlin, P. (2003). Research into early intervention for children with autism and related disorders: Methodological and design issues. *Autism, 7*, 217–225.

Churchill, D. W. (1972). The relation of infantile autism and early childhood schizophrenia to developmental language disorders of childhood. *Journal of Autism and Childhood Schizophrenia, 2*, 182–197.

Creak, M. (1972). Reflections on communication and autistic children. *Journal of Autism and Childhood Schizophrenia, 2*, 1–8.

DeGiacomo, A., & Fombonne, E. (1998). Parental recognition of developmental abnormalities in autism. *European Child and Adolescent Psychiatry, 7*, 131–136.

Dennis, M., Lazenby, A. L., & Lockyer, L. (2001). Inferential language in high-function children with autism. *Journal of Autism and Developmental Disorders, 31*, 47–54.

Diehl, J. J., Bennetto, L., Watson, D., Gunlogson, C. & McDunough, J. (2008). Resolving ambiguity: A psycholinguistic approach to understanding prosody processing in high-functioning autism. *Brain and Language, 106*, 144–152.

Diehl, J. J., Bennetto, L., & Young, E. C. (2006). Story recall and narrative coherence in high-functioning autism spectrum disorders. *Journal of Abnormal Child Psychology, 34*(1), 87–102.

Dunn, M., Gomes, H., & Sebastian, M. (1996). Prototypicality of responses in autistic, language-disordered, and normal children in a word fluency task. *Child Neuropsychology, 2*, 99–108.

Dunn, M., & Rapin, I. (1997). Communication in autistic children. In P.J. Accardo, B.K. Shapiro, & A.J. Capute (Eds.) *Behavior Belongs in the Brain* (pp. 97–111). Baltimore: York Press.

Dunn, M. Vaughan, H., Kreuzer, J., & Kurtzberg, D. (1999). Electrophysiologic correlates of semantic classification in autistic and normal children. *Developmental Neuropsychology, 16*, 79–99.

Dyck, M. J., Pick, J. P., Hay, D., Smith, L., & Hallmayer, J. (2006). Are abilities abnormally interdependent in children with autism? *Journal of Clinical Child and Adolescent Psychology, 35*, 20–33.

Eales, M. J. (1993). Pragmatic impairments in adults with childhood diagnosis of autism or developmental receptive language disorder. *Journal of Autism and Developmental Disorders, 23*, 593–617.

Eigsti, I-M., Bennetto, L., & Dadlani, M. B. (2007). Beyond pragmatics: Morpho-syntactic development in autism. *Journal of Autism and Developmental Disorders, 37*, 1007–1023.

Eigsti, I. M., de Marchena, A., Schuh, J. & Kelley, E. (in press). Language acquisition in autism spectrum disorders: A developmental review. *Research in Autism Spectrum Disorders*.

Fay, W. H., & Schuler, A. L. (1980). *Emerging language in autistic children*. Baltimore: University Park Press.

Fein, D., Dunn, M., Allen, D. A., Aram, D. M., Hall, N., Morris, R., & Wilson, B. C. (1996). Language and neuropsychological findings. In I. Rapin (Ed.), *Preschool children with inadequate communication* (pp. 123–154). London: MacKeith Press.

Fein, D., Stevens, M., Dunn, M., Waterhouse, L., Allen, D., Rapin, I., & Feinstein, C. (1999). Subtypes of pervasive developmental disorder: Clinical characteristics. *Child Neuropsychology, 5*, 1–23.

Gage, N. M., Siegel, B., & Roberts, T. P. L. (2003). Cortical auditory system maturational abnormalities in children with autism disorder: An MEG investigation. *Developmental Brain Research, 144*, 201–209.

Geller, E. (1998). An investigation of communication breakdowns and repairs in verbal autistic children. *The British Journal of Developmental Disabilities, 44*, 71–85.

Gernsbacher, M. A., Sauer, E. A., Geye, H. M., Schwiegert, E. K., & Goldsmith, H. H. (2008). Infant and toddler oral- and manual-motor skills predict later speech fluency in autism. *Journal of Child Psychology and Psychiatry, 49*, 43–50.

Gilchrist, A., Green, J., Cox, A., Burton, D., Rutter, M., & LeCouteur, A. (2001). Development and current functioning in adolescents with Asperger syndrome: A comparative study. *Journal of Child Psychology and Psychiatry, 42*, 227–239.

Gray, C. (2000). *The new social story book: Illustrated edition*. Arlington, TX: Future Horizons.

Happé, F. (1999). Autism: Cognitive deficit or cognitive style? *Trends in Cognitive Sciences, 3*, 216–222.

Howlin, P. (2003). Outcome in high-functioning adults with autism with and without early language delays: Implications for the difference between autism and Asperger syndrome. *Journal of Autism and Developmental Disorders, 33*, 3–13.

Hughes, C., & Russell, J. (1993). Autistic children's difficulty with mental disengagement from an object: Its implications for theories of autism. *Developmental Psychology, 29*, 498–510.

Jordan, R. (1993). The nature of the linguistic and communication difficulties of children with autism. In D.J. Messer & G.T. Turner (Eds.), *Critical influences on child language acquisition and development* (pp. 229–249). New York: St. Martin's Press.

Joseph, R. M., Tager-Flusberg, H., & Lord, C. (2002). Cognitive profiles and social-communicative functioning in children with autism spectrum disorder. *Journal of Child Psychology and Psychiatry, 43*, 807–821.

Kamio, Y., Kelley, E., Robins, D., Swainson, B., & Fein, D (2007). Atypical lexical/semantic processing in high-functioning pervasive developmental disorders without early language delay. *Journal of Autism and Developmental Disorders, 37*, 1116–1122.

Kamio, Y., & Toichi, M. (2000). Dual access to semantics in autism: Is pictorial access superior to verbal access? *Journal of Child Psychology and Psychiatry, 31*, 859–867.

Kanner, L. (1943). Autistic disturbances of affective contact. *Nervous Child, 2*, 217–250.

Kazak, S., Collis, G. M., & Lewis, V. (1997). Can young people with autism refer to knowledge states? Evidence from their understanding of "know" and "guess." *Journal of Child Psychology and Psychiatry, 38*, 1001–1009.

Kelley, E., Jones, G., & Fein, D. (2003). Language assessment in children. In M. Hersen, G. Goldstein, & S. R. Beers (Eds.), *The comprehensive handbook of psychological assessment, Volume 1: Intellectual and neuropsychological assessment* (pp. 191–215). New York: Wiley and Sons.

Kelley, E., Naigles, L., & Fein, D. (2010). An in-depth examination of optimal outcome children with a history of autism spectrum disorders. *Research in Autism Spectrum Disorders, 4*, 526–538.

Kelley, E., Paul, J., Fein, D., & Naigles, L. R. (2006). Residual language deficits in optimal outcome children with a history of autism. *Journal of Autism and Developmental Disorders, 36*, 807–828.

Kjelgaard, M. M., & Tager-Flusberg, H. (2001). An investigation of language impairment in autism: Implications for genetic subgroups. *Language and Cognitive Processes, 16*, 287–308.

Kleinman, J., Marciano, P. L., & Ault, R. L. (2001). Advanced theory of mind in high-functioning adults with autism. *Journal of Autism and Developmental Disorders, 31*, 29–36.

Klinger, L. G., & Dawson, G. (2001). Prototype formation in autism. *Development and Psychopathology, 13*, 111–124.

Koegel, L. K. (2000). Interventions to facilitate communication in autism. *Journal of Autism and Developmental Disorders, 30*, 383–390.

Koegel, R. L., O'Dell, M. C., & Koegel, L. K. (1987). A natural language teaching paradigm for nonverbal autistic children. *Journal of Autism and Developmental Disorders, 17*, 187–199.

Landa, R. (2000). Social language use in Asperger syndrome and high-functioning autism. In A. Klin, F. R. Volkmar, & S. S. Sparrow (Eds.), *Asperger syndrome* (pp. 125–155). New York: Guilford Press.

Lewis, F. M., Murdoch, B. E., & Woodyatt, G. C. (2007). Communicative competence and metalinguistic ability: Performance by children and adults with autism spectrum disorder. *Journal of Autism and Developmental Disorders, 37*, 1525–1538.

Lord, C. (1996). Language in high-functioning adolescents with autism: Questions about deviance and delay. In D. Cicchetti & S.L. Toth (Eds.), *Rochester symposium on developmental psychopathology: Volume 7: Adolescence: Opportunities and challenges* (pp. 149–165). Rochester, NY: Rochester University Press.

Lord, C., & Paul, R. (1997). Language and communication in autism. In D. J. Cohen & F. R. Volkmar (Eds.), *Handbook of autism and pervasive developmental disorders* (pp. 195–225). New York: Wiley Press.

Lord, C., & Risi, S. (2000). Diagnosis of autism spectrum disorders in young children In A. M. Wetherby & B. M. Prizant (Eds.), *Autism spectrum disorders: A transactional developmental perspective* (pp. 11–30). Baltimore: Brookes Publishing.

Losh, M., & Capps, L. (2003). Narrative ability in high-functioning children with autism or Asperger's disorder. *Journal of Autism and Developmental Disorders, 33*, 239–251.

MacKay, G., & Shaw, A. (2004). A comparative study of figurative language in children with autism spectrum disorders. *Child Language Teaching and Therapy, 20*, 13–32.

Magiati, J., & Howlin, P. (2001). Monitoring the progress of preschool children with autism enrolled in early intervention programs. *Autism, 5*, 399–406.

McAfee, J., & Atwood, T. (2001). *Navigating the social world: A curriculum for individuals with Asperger's disorder, high functioning autism and related disorders*. Arlington, TX: Future Horizons.

McEachin, J. J., Smith, T., & Lovaas, I.O. (1993). Long-term outcome for children with autism who received early intensive behavioral treatment. *American Journal on Mental Retardation, 97*, 359–372.

Mcnyuk, P., & Quill, K. (1985). Semantic problems in autistic children. In E. Schopler & G. B. Mesibov (Eds.), *Communication problems in autism* (pp. 127–146). New York: Plennum Press.

Minshew, N. J., Goldstein, G., & Siegel, D. J. (1995). Speech and language in high-functioning autistic individuals. *Neuropsychology, 9*, 255–261.

Mottron, L. (2004). Matching strategies in cognitive research in individuals with high-functioning autism: Current practices, instrument biases, and recommendations. *Journal of Autism and Developmental Disabilities, 34*, 19–27.

Müller, R. A., Behen, M. E., Rothermel, R. D., Chugani, D. C., Muzik, O., Mangner, T. J., & Chugani, H. T. (1999). Brain-mapping of language and auditory perception in high-functioning autistic adults: A PET study. *Journal of Autism and Developmental Disorders, 29*, 19–31.

Mundy, P., & Crowson, M. (1997). Joint attention and early social communication: Implications for research on intervention with autism. *Journal of Autism and Developmental Disorders, 27*, 653–676.

Noens, I. L. J., & van Berckelaer-Onnes, I. A. (2005). Captured by details: Sense-making, language, and communication in autism. *Journal of Communication Disorders, 38*, 123–141.

Norbury, C. F., & Bishop, D. V. M. (2002). Inferential processing and story recall in children with communication problems: A comparison of specific language impairment, pragmatic language impairment, and high-functioning autism. *International Journal of Language and Communication Disorders, 37,* 227–251.

Ozonoff, S., & Miller, J. N. (1996). An exploration of right-hemisphere contributions to the pragmatic impairments of autism. *Brain and Language, 52,* 411–434.

Paul, R., Orlovski, C. M., Marcinko, H. C., & Volkmar, F. (2009). Conversational behaviors in youth with high-functioning ASD and Asperger syndrome. *Journal of Autism and Developmental Disorders, 39,* 115–125.

Phelps-Teraski, D., & Phelps-Gunn, T. (2007). *Test of pragmatic language, Second edition.* Bloomington, MN: Pearson Corp.

Pierce, S., & Bartolucci, G. (1977). A syntactic investigation of verbal autistic, mentally-retarded, and normal children. *Journal of Autism and Childhood Schizophrenia, 7,* 121–134.

Rapin, I. (1996). *Preschool children with inadequate communication.* London, UK: MacKeith Press.

Roberts, J. A., Rice, M. L., & Tager-Flusberg, H. (2004). Tense marking in children with autism. *Applied Psycholinguistics, 25,* 429–448.

Rogers, S. J. & Bennetto, L. (2000). Intersubjectivity in autism: The roles of imitation and Executive Function. In A.M. Wetherby & B.M. Prizant (Eds.), *Autism spectrum disorders: A transactional developmental perspective* (pp. 79–107). Baltimore: Brookes Publishing.

Rosenthal-Rollins, P., & Snow, C. E. (1998). Shared attention and grammatical development in typical children and children with autism. *Journal of Child Language, 25,* 653–673.

Ruble, L. A., & Scott, M. M. (2002). Executive functions and the natural habitat behaviors of children with autism. *Autism, 6,* 365–381.

Rutter, M. (1968). Concepts of autism: A review of research. *Journal of Child Psychology and Psychiatry, 9,* 1–25.

Rutter, M., Mawhood, L., & Howlin, P. (1992). Language delay and social development. In P. Fletcher & D. Hall (Eds.), *Specific speech and language disorders in children: Correlates, characteristics, and outcomes* (pp. 63–78). London: Whurr.

Scarborough, H. S., Rescorla, L., Tager-Flusberg, H., Fowler, A. E., & Sudhalter, V. (1991). The relation of utterance length to grammatical complexity in normal and language-delayed groups. *Psycholinguistics, 12,* 23–45.

Semel, E., Wiig, E. H., & Secord, W. A. (2003). *Clinical Evaluation of Language Fundamentals, Fourth edition.* San Antonio, TX: The Psychological Corporation.

Shah, A., & Frith, U. (1983). An islet of ability in autistic children: A research note. *Journal of Child Psychology and Psychiatry, 24,* 613–620.

Shah, A., & Frith, U. (1993). Why do autistic individuals show superior performance on the block design task? *Journal of Child Psychology and Psychiatry, 34,* 1351–1364.

Shriberg, L. D., Paul, R., McSweeney, J. L., Klin, A., & Cohen, D. J. (2001). Speech and prosody characteristics of adolescents and adults with high-functioning autism and Asperger syndrome. *Journal of Speech, Language, and Hearing Research, 44,* 1097–1115.

Sigman, M. (1998). Change and continuity in the development of children with autism. *Journal of Child Psychology and Psychiatry, 39,* 817–827.

Stone, W. L. & Yoder, P.J. (2001). Predicting spoken language level in children with autism spectrum disorders. *Autism, 5,* 341–361.

Szatmari, P., Tuff, L., Finlayson, M. A. J., & Bartolucci, G. (1990). Asperger's disorder and autism: Neurocognitive aspects. *Journal of the American Academy of Child and Adolescent Psychiatry, 29,* 130–136.

Tager-Flusberg, H. (1981). Sentence comprehension in autistic children. *Applied Psycholinguistics, 2,* 5–24.

Tager-Flusberg, H. (1994). Dissociations in form and function in the acquisition of language by autistic children. In H. Tager-Flusberg (Ed.), *Constraints on language acquisition: Studies of atypical childre.* (pp. 175–194). Hillsdale, NJ: Erlbaum Publishers.

Tager-Flusberg, H. (2000). The challenge of studying language development in children with autism. In L. Menn & N. B. Ratner (Eds.), *Methods for studying language production.* (pp. 313–332). Mahwah, NJ: Erlbaum.

Tager-Flusberg, H. (2001). Understanding the language and communicative impairments in autism. *International Review of Research in Mental Retardation, 23,* 185–205.

Tager-Flusberg, H., Calkins, S., Nolin, T., Baumberger, T., Anderson, M., & Chadwick-Dias, A. (1990). A longitudinal study of language acquisition in autistic and Down syndrome children. *Journal of Autism and Developmental Disorders, 20,* 1–21.

Turner, M. A. (1999). Generating novel ideas: Fluency performance in high-functioning and learning disabled individuals with autism. *Journal of Child Psychology and Psychiatry, 40,* 189–201.

Volden, J. (2004). Conversational repair in speakers with autism spectrum disorder. *International Journal of Language and Communication Disorders, 39,* 171–189.

Volden, J., Coolican, J., Garon, N., White, J., & Bryson, S. (2009). Brief report: Pragmatic language in autism spectrum disorders: Relationships to measures of ability and disability. *Journal of Autism and Developmental Disorders, 39,* 388–393.

Volden, J., & Lord, C. (1991). Neologisms and idiosyncratic language in autistic speakers. *Journal of Autism and Developmental Disorders, 21,* 109–129.

Waterhouse, L., & Fein, D. (1982). Language skills in developmentally disabled children. *Brain and Language, 15,* 307–333.

Wetherby, A. M., Prizant, B. M., & Schuler, A. L. (2000). Understanding the nature of communication and language impairments. In A. M. Wetherby & B. M. Prizant (Eds.), *Autism spectrum disorders: A transactional developmental perspective* (pp. 109–142). Baltimore: Brookes Publishing.

Whitehouse, A. J. O., Barry, J. G., & Bishop, D. V. M. (2007). The broader language phenotype of autism: A comparison with specific language impairment. *Journal of Child Psychology and Psychiatry, 48,* 822–830.

Wiig, E., & Secord, W. (1989) *Test of language competence—Expanded edition.* San Antonio, TX: The Psychological Corporation.

Wilkinson, K. M. (1998). Profiles of language and communication skills in autism. *Mental Retardation and Developmental Disabilities Research, 4,* 73–79.

Wing, L. (1981). Language, social, and cognitive impairment in autism and severe mental retardation. *Journal of Autism and Developmental Disorders, 11,* 31–44.

Witwer, A. N., & Lecavalier, L. (2008). Examining the validity of autism spectrum disorder subtypes. *Journal of Autism and Developmental Disorders, 38,* 1611–1624.

Yoder, P., & Stone, W. (2006). Randomized control comparison of two communication interventions for preschoolers with autism spectrum disorders. *Journal of Consulting and Clinical Psychology, 74,* 426–435.

Ziatas, K., Durkin, K., & Pratt, C. (1998). Belief term development in children with autism, Asperger syndrome, Specific Language Impairment, and normal development: Links to Theory of Mind development. *Journal of Child Psychology and Psychiatry, 39,* 755–761.

Chapter 7

Memory in ASD

Jill Boucher and Andrew Mayes

INTRODUCTION

Why is the study of memory important for understanding autism spectrum disorders (ASDs)? The answer is that memory and learning are inseparable, so any memory atypicalities will affect how and what people with ASDs learn, and this will be evident in the course and outcomes of behavioral and brain development, and in the ways in which individuals with ASDs experience and respond to the external world. But do people with ASDs have memory impairments? The aims of this chapter are, first, to confirm that they do; second, to argue that impairments in lower-functioning people with ASDs are related to, but more extensive than, those in high-functioning individuals; and third, to suggest that the different patterns of spared and impaired abilities across the spectrum have greater explanatory significance than is generally recognized.

The chapter opens with a section providing some historical context for research into memory in ASDs, and introducing the theoretical framework and

terminology to be used. Clinical and research findings on memory in individuals with Asperger's disorder (AS) or high-functioning autism (HFA), defined here in terms of the triad of ASD-related impairments plus currently normal language and cognitive function following early language delay or abnormality, are then reviewed, and interpretations of the findings are discussed. Clinical and research findings on memory in people with low-functioning autism (LFA), defined in terms of the triad of ASD-related impairments plus clinically significant intellectual disability and structural language impairment, are then presented and discussed.

BACKGROUND

History

The history of research into memory in ASDs shows an uneven pattern of interest. When psychogenic explanations were largely abandoned in the 1960s, attention turned to cognitive and linguistic impairments as possible causes of ASDs, and several early researchers included tests of memory among their experiments. Some of these researchers, including Boucher and Warrington (1976), Hauser et al. (1975), and Rimland (1964), speculated that autism might derive at least in part from a form of developmental amnesia associated with hippocampal and/or diencephalic brain abnormalities. It is important to note that a diagnostic criterion for autism as understood at that time included clinically significant structural language impairment in addition to impaired use of language in interpersonal communication (Ritvo & Freeman, 1971; Rutter, 1968). Structural language impairment was not, in fact, omitted as a necessary diagnostic feature until the *Diagnostic and Statistical Manual of Mental Disorders—III* (*DSM-III*) was published by the American Psychiatric Association in 1987. The developmental amnesia hypothesis was therefore based on the study of individuals with LFA, not those with AS or HFA, as currently understood.[1]

From the late 1980s, however, it was increasingly recognized that the triad of ASD-related impairments could occur in people with normal intellectual and language abilities, and attention shifted to investigating high-functioning individuals in place of those with LFA. Tests of the theory of mind, central coherence and executive function theories dominated over the next two decades, and research into memory declined. Moreover, such studies of memory in high-functioning individuals as were carried out demonstrated predominantly normal abilities, indicating that a developmental amnesia hypothesis cannot explain "pure" autism, or autism *per se* (Bennetto et al., 1996; Bowler et al., 1997; Minshew & Goldstein, 1993; Renner et al., 2000; Rumsey & Hamburger, 1988).

However, these studies all demonstrated selective anomalies and impairments of memory, and further probing of memory abilities in high-functioning individuals has confirmed and extended the list of differences in the ways in which people with AS or HFA remember and learn, as compared to neurotypical individuals. At the same time, developments in the understanding of normal and abnormal memory

provide a much richer theoretical framework than was available 30 years ago within which to study memory in both higher- and lower-functioning individuals with ASDs. This is, therefore, an appropriate time to re-evaluate the role of memory anomalies and impairments within explanations of atypical behaviors across the spectrum (see Boucher & Bowler, 2008, for more detailed coverage).

Theoretical Framework and Terminology

The psychology of memory is complex, and there is no agreed-upon theoretical framework within which to study it. Two complementary approaches can be identified, however: one focusing on analysis of the psychological processes contributing to memory; and another that is more concerned with identifying systems involved in memory for different kinds of information, mediated by different brain regions (Gardiner, 2008). Theories concerning memory processes revolve round distinctions such as those between encoding, storage, and retrieval; short- and long-term memory; deep and shallow levels of encoding; item-specific and relational encoding; rapid, single-trial learning and slow, repetition-based learning; and effortful and automatic retrieval. All these distinctions have some relevance for characterizing and understanding memory in ASDs, and will be referred to in the reviews and discussions below. A further distinction can be made between declarative (or explicit) and nondeclarative (or implicit) forms of memory and learning. This distinction is based in part on a continuum of levels of conscious awareness at retrieval, ranging from no conscious awareness (in the case of, for example, the effects of perceptual priming, or driving on autopilot), through borderline cases where, for example, one might say of a memory "I don't *think* I imagined it", to a fully conscious awareness that what is remembered is a "true" memory rather than fantasy or déjà vu.

Within the systems approach to the psychology of memory, Tulving's (1984) taxonomy is best known. According to Tulving's taxonomy, *procedural memory* processes information needed for the acquisition and use of sensorimotor and cognitive skills and habits, and for simple conditioning; *perceptual memory* processes discrete single items, whether simple or complex; *semantic memory* processes factual, decontextualized information, including word meanings; and *episodic memory* processes information about unique events

---

1. The term "relatively able" that was sometimes used to describe participants in these experiments implied only that the participants had some useful language; it did not imply that they had normal language, as in AS or HFA.

experienced by the individual. These four memory systems all acquire and hold information in the long term. The fifth system, *working memory*, is defined in terms of what the system does, with emphasis on the short-term maintenance, manipulation, and use of visuospatial, linguistic, and (Baddeley, 2002) episodic information in thinking and reasoning.

Tulving's systems approach has proved useful heuristically and remains the dominant model underlying research into memory in ASDs (see, for example, the review by BenShalom, 2003). However, the approach is unsatisfactory in ways that are important for the analysis of memory in ASDs to be presented here, following the literature review on memory in HFA. Rather, a three-systems model comprising declarative memory (subsuming Tulving's semantic and episodic systems), nondeclarative memory (subsuming Tulving's implicit perceptual and procedural systems), and short-term and working memory is more suitable. In subsequent sections, clinical and research findings on memory in people with ASDs are presented and discussed under these three headings.

MEMORY IN HIGH-FUNCTIONING INDIVIDUALS

Review of Findings

Some of the studies cited in this section have assessed only individuals with AS, and some others have assessed only individuals with HFA, as defined earlier. Other studies report findings on mixed groups of individuals with AS or HFA, sometimes specifying the numbers in each subgroup but sometimes using the term "HFA" to refer to any currently high-functioning individual with an ASD, regardless of whether or not there is a history of language delay. There is not a sufficiently extensive literature to justify considering memory in AS and in HFA separately. Nor is there currently any robust evidence of persistent behavioral differences between high-functioning individuals with ASDs with or without a history of language delay (Frith, 2004; Macintosh & Dissanayake, 2004; Volkmar & Klin, 2000). For these reasons, studies of memory in "AS/HFA" generally are reviewed, with only occasional reference to participants' diagnoses.

Ability-criteria for HFA vary, with some studies describing participants with verbal IQs as low as 60 as "high-functioning." Here, a cut-off point of minimum verbal and full-scale IQs of 70 for all participants will be adhered to where ability ranges are available. However, an exception is made in the case of studies that include participants with a very wide range of ability (e.g. VQs between 60 and 125) but where mean verbal and full-scale IQs for the group are comfortably within the high-functioning range, i.e., 75 or above.

Nondeclarative memory

Research findings suggest that most but not all forms of nondeclarative memory are unimpaired in people with AS/HFA. Both perceptual and conceptual priming have been shown to be normal in groups with AS/HFA (Gardiner et al., 2003; Hala et al., 2007; Renner et al., 2000; Toichi, 2008). Implicit category formation was unimpaired in studies by Molesworth et al. (2005) and by Bott et al. (2006). Implicit learning of spatial context and of a hierarchical temporal sequence was shown in a study by Barnes et al. (2008). Finally, classical conditioning was found to be normal in a study by Sears et al. (1994).

Evidence indicative of impairments of nondeclarative memory comes from a study of fear conditioning by Gaigg and Bowler (2007), and a study of sequence learning by Mostofsky et al. (2000). Impaired fear conditioning, contrasting with the finding by Sears et al. (1994) of normal classical conditioning, is consistent with the fact that emotion-based and motoric classical conditioning are dependent on different brain systems, as noted below. However, Mostofsky and colleagues' (2000) finding of impaired sequence learning has been criticized by Barnes et al. (2008), also by Gordon & Stark (2007), and may be unreliable.

Apart from experimental studies of nondeclarative forms of learning and memory, it has been argued that impaired motor skills are consistent with impaired procedural memory (Walenski et al., 2006). Motor skills are undoubtedly impaired across the spectrum, not excluding people with AS (Jansiewicz et al., 2006). However, patterns of impaired and spared motor skills are heterogeneous, and it is certain that multiple factors are involved in shaping the different profiles that occur. Some of these do not implicate procedural learning. For example, abnormal muscle tone (Rapin, 1996), impaired proprioception (Weimer et al., 2001), or comorbid dyspraxia (Mostofsky et al., 2006) may contribute to impaired motor skills. Other causes would, therefore, have to be ruled out before concluding that procedural memory impairments contribute to motor impairments.

Such evidence as there is concerning the integrity of brain structures and circuits subserving nondeclarative memory supports the general conclusion that procedural learning is predominantly, but not completely, intact in high-functioning groups. Thus, there is no evidence to suggest that regions of sensory neocortex involved in perceptual priming are structurally or functionally abnormal. Equally, the widely accepted view that abnormalities of the amygdala and associated circuitry underlie socio-emotional impairments in ASDs is consistent with impaired fear conditioning—and with impaired memory for emotionally significant material more generally (Gaigg & Bowler, 2008). The possibility that procedural memory deficits contribute to motor abnormalities is supported by evidence of functional anomalies within the basal-ganglia frontostriatal pathways that subserve gait and locomotion (McAlonan et al., 2008; Rinehart et al., 2006). Less consistency between behavioral and neurobiological evidence might be inferred from the fact that motoric classical conditioning, which is dependent on cerebellar function, is intact in people with AS/HFA, although cerebellar abnormalities are almost certainly implicated in brain dysgenesis in ASDs (Belmonte et al., 2004; Courchesne, 2004). However, the cerebellum is a complex structure contributing to many different facets of learning and behavior, some others of which have been shown to be intact in individuals with ASDs (Mostofsky et al., 2004, 2006), indicating that cerebellar anomalies are not pervasive.

Immediate memory span and working memory

There is ample evidence of intact short-term memory capacity for unstructured verbal inputs in people with AS/HFA. For example, digit span is in the average or above-average range on standardized IQ tests (Fein et al., 1996; Manjiviona & Prior, 1999; Minshew et al., 2005) and is unimpaired in studies using matched comparison groups (e.g., Bennetto et al., 1996). Unelaborated verbal rehearsal utilizing the phonological loop also appears to be intact (Joseph et al., 2005; Smith & Gardiner, 2008) and may be exploited by high-functioning individuals to compensate for selective memory difficulties (BenShalom et al., in press). Only one study has reported a negative finding on

an immediate serial recall task using verbal material. This study showed a small but consistent overall impairment associated with weak recall of item order with intact item recall (Martin et al., 2006; see also Bennetto et al., 1996 for other evidence of impaired memory for temporal order). Evidence on immediate memory for visuospatial stimuli is sparse. However, Verté et al. (2006) and Zinke et al. (2010) reported normal performance on the Corsi blocks task.

Findings concerning the executive component of working memory are more varied. Verbal working memory appears to be predominantly intact (Ozonoff & Strayer, 2001; Pennington et al., 1997; Williams et al., 2005a; but see Joseph et al., 2005, also Manjiviona & Prior, 1999 for contrary evidence). Visuospatial working memory is less secure, impairments having been shown in most relevant studies (Minshew et al., 1999; Morris et al., 1999; Steele et al., 2007; Williams et al., 2005a).

Evidence relating to brain correlates of short-term and working memory in people with AS/HFA is limited, but generally consistent with the behavioral findings. Thus, there is no evidence to suggest that either the posterior parietal region that holds representations of verbal inputs in unmodified form, nor the parieto-occipital and inferior frontal regions associated with the visuospatial sketchpad, are structurally or functionally abnormal in people with AS/HFA. Conversely, there is evidence of abnormalities of prefrontal regions associated with central executive functions generally. In particular, subregions of dorsolateral prefrontal cortex contributing to the neural circuit subserving visuospatial working memory have been shown to function abnormally in some studies of AS/HFA (Koshino et al., 2005; Luna et al., 2002).

Long-term declarative memory

Numerous studies show that *recognition* using a variety of meaningful verbal and visual stimuli is unimpaired in groups with AS/HFA (Ambery et al., 2006; Barth et al., 1995; Bennetto et al.; 1996; Boucher et al., 2005; Bowler et al., 2000a, 2007; Hala et al., 2005; Joseph et al., 2005; Minshew et al., 1992; O'Shea et al., 2005; Renner et al., 2000). Moreover, superior, as opposed to intact, recognition of pictures of static objects, such as buildings, was shown by Blair et al. (2002). Similarly, superior recognition of geometric shapes and symbols was shown by Hillier et al. (2007), with fewer false-positive responses than in neurotypical controls. Fewer false positives were also shown on a test of the ability to recognize semantically related words (Beversdorf et al., 2000; Kamio & Toichi, 2007), although the studies by Hillier et al. (2007) and Bowler et al. (2000a) showed a more typical rate of false positive responses in this particular type of test. Superior word recognition was reported by Toichi (2008; see also Toichi & Kamio, 2002) when attention was drawn to the written forms of words or to their phonological characteristics during presentation. When attention was drawn to the semantic characteristics of stimuli during presentation, performance was enhanced relative to performance in the other two presentation conditions, as it was in the comparison group. However, performance in the semantic-processing condition was similar to, rather than superior to, performance in the comparison group. These findings suggest that word recognition is usually achieved atypically by people with AS/HFA, with superior memory for the physical, as opposed to the semantic, characteristics of verbal stimuli. Only one study of individuals with AS/HFA has shown impaired word recognition in high-functioning individuals, and the impairment in this study was slight, although statistically significant (Bowler et al., 2004).

By contrast, impaired recognition of previously unfamiliar faces has been shown in numerous studies, including some in which intact recognition of non-social stimuli has been shown in the same participants (Blair et al., 2002; Boucher et al., 2005; Davies et al., 1994; Ellis, Ellis, Fraser, & Deb, 1994; Williams, Goldstein, & Minshew, 2005b). There have also been occasional reports of impaired recognition of non-meaningful shapes (Ameli et al., 1988; Davies et al., 1994).

Free recall is considered next. However, before reviewing the relevant evidence, it is important to point out that the term "free recall" is inaccurate, because all recall is cued in some way or other, although the kinds of cue, and the usefulness of different kinds of cue, vary. Thus, some cue types, including those utilized in "cued recall" as commonly understood, usually lead directly to a target stimulus, typically using informative associations (e.g., "an animal") or parts of target items (e.g., "a word beginning with /sh/") as cues to individual items. Other cue types, including those used in free recall (as commonly understood) do not lead directly to individual target items. Thus, tests of "free recall" typically identify a set of items to be recalled by providing information about the study context, such as "the words you heard just now" or "the pictures I showed

you yesterday". This kind of cue often requires the participant to generate their own further cues before individual target items can be retrieved. These contrasting kinds of (cued) recall may depend on psychological and neural processes that do not completely overlap with each other. It is therefore useful to mark the different types of recall by using the terms "cued recall" and "free recall", despite the inaccuracy of the latter term, and despite the fact that there is a continuum rather than a dichotomy of cue types utilized in recall (better captured by the term "task support" as used by Bowler et al., 1997, 2004).

Evidence from experimental or clinical tests of free recall by individuals with AS/HFA is mixed, sometimes showing intact, sometimes impaired, performance overall, and sometimes indicating that good performance has been achieved in atypical ways. Least impaired is the recall of supraspan lists of unrelated items, such as single words or pictures of everyday objects. Unimpaired performance for this type of material has been shown in tests of delayed recall (e.g., Minshew & Goldstein, 2001; Mottron et al., 2001; Renner et al., 2000; Williams et al., 2006), as well as in tests of immediate recall (e.g., Bennetto et al., 1996; Bowler et al., 1997; Buitelaar et al., 1999; Minshew & Goldstein, 1993; Smith & Gardiner, 2008). However, Toichi and Kamio (2003) reported impaired immediate recall of concrete words, with unimpaired recall of abstract words in an HFA group. There may also be a lack of the usual primacy effect in single-trial recall (Renner et al., 2000; Toichi & Kamio, 2003; but see Bowler et al., 2000 for contrary evidence). The ability to learn long lists of unrelated words over repeated trials is unimpaired (Bennetto et al., 1996; Bowler et al., 2008a; Bowler et al., 2009; Minshew et al., 1992; Minshew & Goldstein, 1993). However, the study by Bowler et al. (2008a) showed that whereas neurotypical individuals developed broadly similar word groupings to each other over repeated trials, the groupings developed by the AS participants were idiosyncratic— that is, particular to each individual. In addition, Bowler et al. (2009) observed that the primacy effect does not increase over repeated trials, as it does in neurotypical individuals.

Free recall of semantically or syntactically structured verbal material is less secure than free recall of unrelated or uniformly related items. So, for example, immediate recall of lists of words from two different categories was shown to be impaired in two studies, associated with failure to use a semantic-clustering strategy (Bowler et al., 1997; Minshew & Goldstein, 1993). However, these findings were only partially replicated in another study (Lopez & Leekam, 2003). Free recall of sentences has been shown to be impaired in some studies (Botting & Conti-Ramsden, 2003; Kelley, Paul, Fein, & Naigles, 2006; Minshew & Goldstein, 2001; Williams et al., 2006) but not in others (Fein et al., 1996; Kjelgaard & Tager-Flusberg, 2001; Whitehouse et al., 2008). A study comparing the performances of preschool-aged children with either AS or HFA showed impaired recall of sentences in the latter but not the former group (Iwanaga et al., 2000). Free recall of stories has also been found to be impaired in some studies (Minshew & Goldstein, 2001; O'Shea et al., 2005; Rumsey & Hamburger, 1988; Williams et al., 2006), but not in others (Ambery et al., 2006; Boucher et al., 2005; Jolliffe & Baron-Cohen, 2000; Williams et al., 2005b).

Findings on the free recall of complex, non-meaningful visual material (e.g., drawing from memory a copy of a recently seen figure, or retracing a maze from memory) are also mixed. Performance has been shown to be impaired in some studies (Minshew & Goldstein, 2001; Rumsey & Hamburger, 1988; Verté et al., 2006; Williams et al., 2006) but not in others (Boucher et al., 2005; Buitelaar et al., 1999; Gunter et al., 2002; Minshew et al., 1997). Free verbal recall of the content of pictures showing social scenes has been found to be impaired in one group study (Williams et al., 2005b), and was also reported in a single-case study of an exceptionally high-functioning individual (BenShalom et al., in press). Free verbal recall of passively observed naturalistic events is also impaired (McCrory et al., 2007).

Two studies of autobiographical memory have shown impaired recall of autobiographical episodes in combination with unimpaired recall of autobiographical facts (Crane & Goddard, 2008; Klein et al., 1999). Good average scores on the Information subtest of the Wechsler scales (Wechsler, 1997a,b) also indicate unimpaired free recall of overlearnt factual information (Manjiviona & Prior, 1999; Minshew et al., 2005; Ozonoff et al., 2000). In addition, high-functioning individuals have a well-known tendency to amass factual knowledge on topics of special interest. Taken together, these observations might suggest that free recall of factual information acquired naturalistically, typically over many "trials," is intact or superior. However, retrieval of individual items in these instances may be cued either by the questions asked, or by habitual self-cueing strategies.

In sum, free recall is somewhat fragile in people with AS/HFA, in contrast to the robust findings of unimpaired or superior performance on recognition tests, with a number of different factors determining whether performance is intact (even if atypical) or impaired.

Cued recall is intact in people with AS/HFA when a cue such as a category name or an initial letter is provided for the recall of individual items (e.g., Bennetto et al., 1996; Mottron et al., 2001). In the study by McCrory et al. (2007) in which free recall of passively observed naturalistic events was impaired, recall cued by leading questions was unimpaired. Paired-associate learning, in which the first word of an arbitrarily associated pair is provided as a cue to the second word, is unimpaired regardless of whether testing is immediate or delayed (Minshew & Goldstein, 2001; Williams et al., 2005b; Ambery et al., 2006). Sound-symbol paired-associate learning was unimpaired in a study by Williams et al. (2006), as was face-name associative learning in the studies by Ambery et al. (2006) and Salmond et al. (2005).

In *source memory* tests, items that have been correctly identified in a standard recognition task are used as cues for the recognition or recall of information associated with that item when it was presented. So, for example, a participant who has correctly recognized a word might be asked "Which of these colors was it printed in?" (a recognition test); or "What color was it printed in?" (a recall test). In some source memory recall tests the request for contextual information is more open-ended than in the above example. In particular, in the "remember-know" paradigm, participants who have correctly recognized an item are asked to say whether they recall anything unique to the occasion when the item was presented (e.g. that it reminded them of x; that it came after item y; or that a clock struck just as the item was presented).

Intact source recognition in people with AS/HFA has been reported in three studies (Bowler et al., 2004; Gaigg et al., 2008; Williams et al., 2005b). O'Shea et al. (2005) reported intact recognition of impersonal contextual information, but impaired recognition of social contextual information. A striking dissociation between intact source recognition and impaired source recall was shown in the studies by Bowler et al. and by Gaigg et al. Impaired recall of contextual information by high-functioning individuals was also shown in a study by Bowler et al. (2000b) using the remember-know paradigm, and in a study by Bigham et al. (2010) using a non-verbal analog of the remember-know test.

In what are sometimes referred to as source-monitoring tasks (Johnson et al., 1993), interest focuses on the external and internal source of a recognized stimulus, where internal refers to the participant themselves and external refers to some other person or persons. So, for example, a participant who has correctly recognized a previously heard word might be asked "Was it spoken by a man or a woman?" (two external sources); or "Did I say it, or did you?" (one external one internal source–sometimes referred to as reality monitoring); or "Did you say it, or did you just think it?" (two internal sources). The capacity to recall internal (i.e., self-performed) actions is of particular interest in relation to memory in people with ASDs, because recall of personally experienced episodes necessarily involves a re-experiencing of one's own presence and role within the episode (Lind & Bowler, 2008; Wheeler et al., 1998). Hala and colleagues (2005) showed impairment on all three types of source monitoring in a group of children with HFA. The pattern of performance across the three types was, however, the same in the experimental and comparison groups, with reality monitoring ("Did you say it, or did I?") superior to both the external-external and the internal-internal conditions. Thus, there was no clear evidence of better memory for self-performed, as opposed to other-performed, tasks in either group. By contrast, in their test of source recognition and source recall cited above, Bowler et al. (2004) found that active participant involvement during stimulus presentation improved source memory in an adult AS group without, however, overcoming a significant impairment of source recall.

In sum, performance by people with AS/HFA is unimpaired in source-memory tasks where contextual information is available within the immediate environment and can be recognized, but impaired in tasks where contextual information must be recalled. Performance on source-monitoring tasks is generally poor, in keeping with other findings on memory for information with social connotations, whether involving self or others (see Webb, 2008, and Lind, in press for reviews).

Discussion of Findings

The two research groups that have studied memory in AS/HFA most intensively—namely the groups headed by Minshew and by Bowler—have offered different interpretations of the data, concentrating in particular on their own findings. These interpretations are outlined first. Our interpretation of the findings reviewed follows, and similarities and differences between the three interpretations are discussed.

Minshew and her colleagues describe their findings on memory in HFA as an impairment of complex information processing leaving the processing of simple information unimpaired (e.g., Minshew et al., 1997; Williams et al., 2006). Other behavioral findings by this group on language processing, abstract reasoning, and motor skills are also explained in this way. "Complex information processing" is variously identified with the detection or use of organizational strategies, high processing load, or a requirement for the integration of information; whereas "simple information processing" is identified with basic association processes or a low information-processing load.

Problems of complex information processing have been ascribed by this group to impaired brain connectivity (Minshew & Williams, 2007), the pattern of spared and impaired abilities being explained in terms of "a generalized dysfunction of the association cortex, with sparing of primary sensory and motor cortex." In aligning themselves with the model of ASDs as a disconnection syndrome (Belmonte et al., 2004; Courchesne, 2004; Geschwind & Levitt, 2007), Minshew and Williams (2007) explicitly distance themselves from explanations in terms of regional brain dysfunctions including "the disproved amnesia hypothesis." However, they note certain structural anomalies including increased numbers of minicolumns in prefrontal and temporal cortices (Casanova et al., 2006) and lack of normal frontal development in adolescence (Courchesne, 2004; Courchesne & Pierce, 2005).

Bowler and his colleagues bring a more cautious, but more analytic, approach to their interpretation of findings on declarative memory in high-functioning individuals, especially adults with AS (see Bowler et al., 2010 for a summary of this group's current views). Utilizing Tulving's division of declarative memory into memory for personally experienced episodes and memory for factual information, they note a "subtle but persistent" impairment of episodic memory, combined with anomalies in the processing of certain kinds of semantic information on certain tasks, especially those providing little support at retrieval, such as standard free recall tasks. Bowler et al.'s (2010) explanation of these observations is that there is an imbalance between complex relational encoding and single-item or associative item-item encoding in people with AS/HFA, in favor of the latter. They argue that an impairment or under-usage of complex relational encoding is consistent with impaired memory for personally experienced events in which multi-modal information including spatio-temporal information and autonoetic awareness must be encoded, stored, and retrieved. They also argue that their hypothesis is consistent with evidence of intact use of item-item associations in learning and memory, combined with multiple instances of difficulty in progressing to the level of encoding and utilizing 3-way hierarchic relations across a wide range of behaviors.

Bowler et al. (2010) note that their impaired relational encoding hypothesis is consistent with Minshew and her colleagues' observations of pervasive difficulties in tasks involving complex information processing. Bowler et al.'s identification of impaired relational encoding with problems of neural binding is also consistent with disconnection models of ASDs. Moreover, like Minshew and Williams (2007), Bowler and colleagues note that regions of the frontal and medial temporal lobes are likely sites of cellular and functional abnormalities in people with ASDs. However, they go beyond Minshew and Williams in suggesting that hippocampal dysfunction is implicated as a cause of impaired relational encoding (Gaigg et al., 2008), explicitly excluding likely involvement of perirhinal or entorhinal cortex (Bowler et al., 2010).

The interpretation of data on declarative memory in AS/HFA (and in lower-functioning autism) proposed in Boucher et al. (2008b; see also Boucher, 2009) pivots on the assumption that two distinct, but interactive and mutually supportive processes contribute to declarative memory, namely recollection (probably with other kinds of recall), and familiarity (Aggleton & Brown, 2006; Jacoby, 1991; Yonelinas, 2002). Recollection is a kind of recall in which a recognized stimulus cues recall of diverse kinds of contextual information from a personally experienced episode in which the stimulus was encountered. Recollection is a central feature of relational and episodic memory, and some hold that it may be essential for them (e.g., Eichenbaum et al., 2007). It contributes to rapid, single-trial learning, and is almost certainly dependent on intact hippocampal function and connectivity, and possibly also on intact function and connectivity of subregions of dorsolateral prefrontal cortex and other regions of the prefrontal corex (Aggleton & Brown, 2006; Kirwan et al., 2008).

Familiarity is defined as a feeling that one has experienced a stimulus before without necessarily recalling any other information about it, including any episodic contextual detail. Familiarity relates to single percepts or items (including complex items such as scenes or faces), although it may also contribute to recognition of certain kinds of association between items, such as those between similar kinds of item (Mayes et al., 2007; Yonelinas, 2002). Familiarity increases with stimulus repetition, possibly building on initially implicit perceptual representations. It is important for slow, incremental learning, and is probably (though not certainly) dependent at least in part on intact function and connectivity of perirhinal and entorhinal medial temporal lobe cortex (Aggleton & Brown, 2006; Montaldi et al., 2006).

The processes of recollection and familiarity do not map precisely onto Tulving's content-based distinction between episodic and semantic memory. Specifically, recollection is usually and possibly always involved in memory for personally experienced episodes, as noted above. Equally, the retrieval of factual (semantic) information involves a form of cued recall very similar to that involved in recollection, and thus semantic and episodic memory are likely to depend on some of the same brain mechanisms.

Nor is there a precise correspondence between recollection and familiarity on the one hand, and tests of free recall or recognition on the other. Although recollection and other kinds of cued recall generally contribute to "free" recall test performance, recall may sometimes be achieved by randomly generating possible target memories and then deciding whether these feel familiar. Equally, performance on most clinical or research recognition tests partially depends on recollection of contextual information encoded during presentation of a stimulus.

According to our interpretation, the data on declarative memory in individuals with AS/HFA are consistent with a relatively mild impairment of recollection leaving familiarity intact (as well as most facets of implicit perceptual and procedural learning, immediate short-term memory, and verbal – but possibly not visual - working memory). This combination of selectively impaired and predominantly spared memory abilities is consistent with the fact that memory in people with AS/HFA is in most ways efficient and in some ways superior. For example, individuals with AS/HFA often have encyclopedic factual knowledge of topics of special interest to them, as noted above.

This may be explained partly in terms of restricted interests and obsessive tendencies. However, exploitation of intact memory for decontextualized information and intact capacities for verbatim rehearsal in the absence of relational memory may also contribute (see Ullman, 2001 for the suggestion of compensatory overuse of intact memory abilities). Similarly, exploitation of intact procedural learning is consistent with a preference for routines and other habitual patterns of behavior in everyday life.

At the same time, impaired recollection is consistent with the "subtle but persistent" impairment of personally experienced episodes noted by Bowler et al. (2010; see also BenShalom, 2003). Related to this, impaired recollection would adversely affect performance on any clinical or laboratory memory test in which material to be remembered is presented in a single-trial learning episode. The adverse effects would be greatest in delayed recall tests using novel (trial-unique) material such as stories, sentences, or meaningless visual stimuli. Although intact perceptual memory would contribute to immediate recognition or recall of these kinds of materials, the contribution of explicit familiarity after a single exposure would be relatively low, increasing dependence on recollection and other kinds of cued recall. The adverse effects of selectively impaired recollection would also be greatest in recall tests where the retrieval cue provided identifies study context rather than providing target-specific information. Impaired recollection would also diminish associative networks supporting factual knowledge including word meanings, with consequences for performance on tests in which semantic organization and associative networks play a critical role (Holdstock et al., 2002). Finally, a habitual reliance on perceptual and immediate short-term memory would predispose people with AS/HFA towards shallow (phonological, graphical) levels of encoding of stimuli in preference to deeper (semantic) encoding. Habitual reliance on immediate short-term memory would also interfere with the reorganization of material at recall (e.g., semantic clustering) which improves performance on some memory tests in neurotypical individuals.

An impaired recollection/spared familiarity hypothesis is broadly compatible with Bowler and colleagues' impaired relational/spared single-item memory hypothesis, and with Minshew and colleagues' impaired complex/spared simple information processing hypothesis. An impaired recollection hypothesis is also compatible with evidence cited by Minshew and Williams (2007),

Gaigg et al. (2010) and others (e.g. Loveland et al., 2008; Salmond et al., 2005) concerning dysfunction within hippocampal-prefrontal circuitry. Positive evidence includes some of our own in which reduced hippocampal and parahippocampal volumes were demonstrated in a mixed-ability, predominantly high-functioning group of adults with ASDs (Boucher et al., 2005). Most interestingly from the point of view of the hypothesis (to be discussed in detail later in this chapter) concerning the consequences of memory impairments in lower-functioning individuals with ASDs, was the fact that hippocampal volume correlated negatively with scores on a clinical measure of communication. However, hippocampal lesions have not been consistently reported, and such abnormalities as have been reported have often differed in kind (see Cody et al., 2002; Rojas et al., 2004 for reviews); but see also (Nicolson et al., 2006; Dell'Acqua et al., 2009; Gaigg et al., 2010; and Nicolson et al., 2006 for recent positive evidence).

The above explanation of declarative memory problems in people with AS/HFA is, like the hypothesis proposed by Bowler and colleagues, a form of "developmental amnesia" hypothesis, without entailing a claim that memory impairment is the main cause of the most characteristic features of ASD-related behavior. This raises the question of the relationship between AS/HFA and cases of developmental amnesia without autism, as described in the broader literature. Best known of these cases is a group of individuals studied by Vargha-Khadem and her colleagues (Baddeley et al., 2001; De Haan et al., 2006; Vargha-Khadem et al., 1997). These individuals have selective but marked episodic/recollective memory impairments associated with congenital or early acquired bilateral and extensive hippocampal lesions. They have none of the socio-emotional impairments diagnostic of ASDs, no doubt because their brain lesions do not include the amygdalae and associated circuitry. However, at least one well-studied individual has a particular interest in the kinds of overlearnt factual knowledge such as is often a peak ability in people with AS/HFA (he enjoys setting questions for quizzes). Vargha-Khadem (personal communication) also notes a "reduced drive to generate new plans and ideas" in people with developmental amnesia, which she attributes to "a memory impairment, in that for an idea to be pursued and actively developed, one has to keep the goal in mind and work towards its accomplishment." It may be the case, therefore, as we have argued elsewhere (Boucher, 2009; Boucher et al., 2008b) that the combination of spared and impaired memory abilities can help to explain the generativity and planning impairments associated with ASDs.

Recollection and episodic memory are not, however, as severely impaired in people with AS/HFA as in Vargha-Khadem et al.'s cases of developmental amnesia, resembling more closely the mild impairments observed in individuals born pre-term (Isaacs et al., 2000; Salmond et al., 2008). Hippocampal lesions in pre-term individuals are less extensive than those in people with the severe form of developmental amnesia, and have sometimes proved difficult to demonstrate—which may bear on the fact that evidence of hippocampal lesions in individuals with ASDs is not robust. People with AS/HFA also differ from those with developmental amnesia (also individuals born pre-term) in having additional impairments of memory for stimuli with social or emotional significance. These person-related impairments spread across nondeclarative as well as declarative forms of learning, and are no doubt associated with pathology additional to that underlying developmental amnesia.

People with AS/HFA also have one strikingly spared memory ability which may not be shared by individuals with either the severe or mild forms of developmental amnesia, or by adults with acquired hippocampal-related amnesia, although this has not been adequately tested. This is a capacity for recall when cues identify specific target items (e.g., "an animal", "something blue"; see the discussion of different types of recall cue, above). A spared capacity for this kind of cued recall extends to testable individuals with lower-functioning autism, and constitutes a major challenge to the analogy between memory impairments in ASDs and those associated with hippocampal lesions. This discrepancy could indicate that impaired recollection and episodic memory in people with AS/HFA, and in verbal individuals with lower-functioning autism, result from disruptions of anatomical or functional connectivity within hippocampal-prefrontal circuitry, rather than from hippocampal lesions. Bowler et al. (1994, 2008b; Gaigg & Bowler, 2008) have commented on the similarities between patterns of memory strengths and weaknesses in people with AS and those of older people, considered by some to derive from loss of frontal tissue and associated executive impairments. This suggestion

is consistent with Minshew and Williams' (2007) interpretation of findings on AS/HFA and, as they point out, is attractive in view of evidence that top-down control of processing is impaired across a range of behaviors, not just declarative memory (Frith, 2003; Happé & Frith, 2006). The explanation is also consistent with evidence of a relative lack of growth of frontal efferents during adolescence (Courchesne, 2004). It may also be the case that a variety of different lesions or functional disturbances underlie the impairments of recollection and episodic memory in AS/HFA, helping to explain some of the inconsistencies in the findings on memory reviewed above.

MEMORY IN PEOPLE WITH LOWER-FUNCTIONING AUTISM

Review of Findings

We assume that there is a continuum of memory impairments across the autism spectrum, from highly selective impairments and anomalies in individuals with AS/HFA, through increases in the severity and pervasiveness of memory impairments in middle- and lower-functioning individuals with some language (referred to here as the verbal, or "V-LFA," group), to a total loss of most forms of memory in individuals with nonverbal LFA[2]. Because there are almost no studies of memory in individuals with nonverbal LFA, the large majority of studies reviewed below relate to individuals in the V-LFA group. If the assumption of a continuum of memory abilities is correct, then mild to moderate, rather than severe or profound, memory impairments would be predicted in this intermediate group. There is, moreover, some overlap between individual participants in studies reported in the section on memory in AS/HFA (where mean VQ for the group is 75 or above) and participants in studies to be reported in this section (where mean VQ is below 75). Ideally, the comparison of memory in higher- and lower-functioning individuals with ASDs would be made between participants with non-overlapping verbal abilities. However, this would severely limit the material that could be covered in this review.

---

2. It is an open question as to whether some individuals with partial or atypical forms of ASD may have entirely normal memory.

The predominance of research into high-functioning forms of ASD over recent decades has resulted in there being less empirical data on memory in V-LFA than on memory in AS/HFA. Moreover, early studies of declarative memory in lower-functioning individuals often used participant groups that are small by today's standards, reducing statistical power and biasing towards negative findings. In addition, participants were selected using less rigorous diagnostic ascertainment methods than are available today, as well as using diagnostic criteria that included structural language impairment. Participants in early studies were always children, because few diagnosed cases had reached adulthood. These limitations and differences must be kept in mind when evaluating findings published before the 1990s. However, it is not true to suggest, as is sometimes done, that matching procedures were inadequate in early studies. Although a few very early studies equated experimental and comparison groups only for digit span (which biases toward findings of impairment), most studies used the same or similar tests of vocabulary comprehension and nonverbal intelligence as are used today.

Nondeclarative memory

There is too little robust behavioral evidence to form any firm conclusions concerning spared or impaired nondeclarative memory abilities in individuals with V-LFA. However, Gordon and Stark (2007) demonstrated that children with LFA, including some who were nonverbal, were able to learn a visual sequence, though at a slower rate than children without autism. This suggests that at least one kind of procedural learning is relatively intact. Priming has not been assessed in V-LFA groups, to the best of our knowledge. Impaired prototype formation was reported by Klinger and Dawson (2001), but the methodology used was strongly criticized by Molesworth et al. (2005) and also by Bott et al. (2006). Classical conditioning, whether emotion-related or motoric, has not been experimentally investigated in people with V-LFA, to the best of our knowledge. Impaired motor skills might be indicative of impaired procedural learning, as suggested in the section on memory in AS/HFA. However, other causes would have to be ruled out before reaching this conclusion, as argued above.

Diagnostic description and day-to-day observation do, however, suggest that most kinds of nondeclarative learning are intact in people with V-LFA, and may in fact be relied on to an unusual extent. Most conspicuously, spontaneous behavior in this group is dominated by habits and routines such as are acquired via various forms of nondeclarative memory. Similarly, from the fact that behavioral training is used successfully in educational programs and is the intervention of choice for low-ability individuals with challenging behavior, it can be inferred that instrumental—if not classical—conditioning is intact in low-functioning individuals. Some of the research evidence on declarative memory reviewed below may also be interpreted as suggesting that individuals with V-LFA rely to an unusual extent on perceptual and procedural learning in formal memory tests. So, for example, Russell and Jarrold (1999) reported that children with V-LFA, unlike children without autism, performed better in an incidental than an intentional learning condition, consistent with implicit, as opposed to explicit, learning. Farrant et al. (1998), Hauck et al. (1998), and Hill & Russell (2002) also showed unimpaired learning on unexpected recognition tasks. Analyses of savant abilities also suggest that low-functioning individuals can achieve exceptional feats in calculation, memory, foreign language acquisition, drawing, or music, using implicitly acquired procedures (Miller, 1999; Pring, 2008).

Immediate short-term and working memory

Wechsler subtest profiles show that the immediate serial order recall of digits is relatively spared in individuals with V-LFA (Lincoln et al., 1995; Siegel et al., 1996), where "relatively" is used to indicate that scores on this subtest are higher than on other verbal subtests for that individual or group, even if below standardized norms. Unimpaired or superior digit span relative to ability-matched comparison groups has been confirmed in studies by Frith (1970), Boucher and Warrington (1976), and Russell et al. (1996). Similarly, serial recall of short random word strings was reported by Hermelin and O'Connor (1967) to be superior to that of a comparison group. Russell et al. (1996) reported that children in a V-LFA group were as likely to use verbal rehearsal as an ability-matched comparison group, indicating relatively intact use of the phonological loop (see also Farrant et al., 1999). However, V-LFA participants in Hermelin and O'Connor's (1967) study did not perform significantly better on strings of high- as opposed to low-frequency words (cf. Toichi and Kamio, 2003, on recall of concrete and abstract words by high-functioning individuals). Nor did participants in Hermelin and O'Connor's study perform better on the recall of syntactically structured as opposed to random word strings, unlike low-ability children without ASDs.

Immediate serial recall of visual material was assessed in a picture-sequencing task by O'Connor and Hermelin (1967) and reported to be unimpaired relative to performance by young, typically developing children. In addition, the children with V-LFA resembled the typically developing children in performing better on the reconstruction of meaningful as opposed to non-meaningful sequences. Farrant et al. (1999) also showed unimpaired serial memory span for pictures of common objects. O'Connor and Hermelin's demonstration that the meaningfulness of picture sequences enhances performance in children with V-LFA to the same extent as in comparison groups might appear to conflict with reports of impaired use of meaning in verbal recall tasks. However, the visual task used by O'Connor and Hermelin supplied items and required only memory for order, reducing the episodic memory load. In addition, their visual task did not lend itself to a strategy utilizing non-meaningful perceptual information, whereas words may be encoded phonologically (if heard) or graphically (if read). In an unpublished study replicating and extending O'Connor and Hermelin's study, Boucher observed that when non-meaningful shape cues were added to the pictures, most children with V-LFA used the shape cues to order a sequence, whereas children without autism used meaning cues. This strengthens the suggestion that failure to utilize structure and meaning in verbal tests is associated with an atypical hierarchy of encoding strategies, in which non-meaningful features preempt attention over the processing of meaning when both types of cue are available.

Russell et al. (1996) reported relatively intact central-executive capacity on verbal working memory tasks, whereas Reed (2004) reported impaired performance on a visual working-memory task. These observations parallel the fuller set of findings on working memory in AS/HFA, although more evidence is clearly needed.

Declarative memory

Recognition

Summers and Craik (1994) reported impairment on a test of immediate recognition of spoken words.

Recognition was impaired regardless of whether stimulus words had only been spoken by the experimenter during presentation, or whether the child had also been instructed to do something with named objects during presentation (e.g. "Put the glasses on"). Recognition of the names of objects the child had handled was better than recognition of words only spoken by the experimenter, but the improvement was less than that occurring in children without autism. Delayed word recognition was unimpaired in a study by Farrant et al. (1998) using an unexpected memory test.

Three studies assessing immediate recognition of meaningful non-social visual stimuli reported unimpaired performance in children with V-LFA, relative to comparison groups (Boucher & Lewis, 1992; Brian & Bryson, 1996; Hauck et al., 1998). However, in the study by Brian and Bryson (1996), immediate recognition of meaningless designs or fragmented pictures was at chance levels in the experimental group. Impaired performance by children with V-LFA on a delayed picture-recognition task was reported by Boucher and Warrington (1976). Similarly, two studies testing delayed recognition of non-meaningful visual stimuli in both low- and high-functioning groups reported impairment in a V-LFA, but not an HFA, group (Barth et al., 1995; Boucher et al., 2008a). A study by Prior and Chen (1976) showed that children with V-LFA learned a sequence of 2-choice discriminations between junk objects in the same number of trials as participants without autism. However, the pattern of performance differed in the two groups, with the experimental group doing less well than controls on Trial 1 and improving more rapidly than controls in later trials.

The studies by Boucher and Lewis (1992) and Hauck et al. (1998) that showed intact recognition of non-social visual stimuli (buildings and common objects, respectively) both demonstrated impaired recognition of previously unfamiliar faces in the same participants. Boucher et al. (1998) showed that impaired recognition of unfamiliar faces extends to impaired recognition of familiar faces and voices in individuals with V-LFA.

In sum, although too few studies have been reported for any firm conclusions to be drawn, it may be provisionally concluded that recognition is fragile in individuals with V-LFA, contrasting with consistently intact recognition in AS/HFA (apart from the fact that recognition of social stimuli is impaired across the spectrum).

Free recall

Immediate free recall of supraspan random word lists was reported to be unimpaired in most of the early studies (Boucher, 1981a; Fyffe & Prior, 1978; Hermelin & O'Connor, 1967; O'Connor & Hermelin, 1967; Ramondo & Milech, 1984; Tager-Flusberg, 1991; but see Boucher, 1978, for a contrary finding). All of these studies showed unimpaired or enhanced recency effects relative to comparison groups, in combination with reduced primacy effects. In the study by Summers and Craik (1994) in which recognition was impaired regardless of whether or not the children had handled the objects the names of which had to be remembered, recall of items not handled was impaired. However, recall of items handled by the participant was unimpaired.

Frith (1970) assessed immediate serial recall of minimally structured supraspan word strings (e.g. "pig pig horse horse pig horse pig horse"). A high-digit-span subgroup of children with V-LFA was unimpaired on this task, whereas a low-digit-span subgroup was impaired. Neither subgroup showed evidence of pattern detection, and impaired recall in the low-span group was associated with reliance on recall of the most recently occurring items, disrupting serial-order recall. The studies by Hermelin & O'Connor (1967), O'Connor and Hermelin (1967), Fyffe and Prior (1978), and Ramondo and Milech (1984) showing unimpaired recall of supraspan random word lists also demonstrated that increases in semantic meaningfulness or syntactic structure does not improve recall by children with V-LFA as much as in comparison groups. Thus, in one experiment Hermelin and O'Connor (1967) gave children words from two categories in jumbled order, and found that the children with V-LFA, unlike ability matched children without autism, did not use a clustering strategy in recall. This finding was replicated by Tager-Flusberg (1991). Tests of the immediate recall of supraspan sets of visual material by individuals with V-LFA have not, to our knowledge, been reported.

We turn now to tests of delayed recall. Boucher and Warrington (1976) reported impairments in the delayed recall of named pictures of everyday objects and of supraspan random word lists. Prior and Hoffman (1990) showed impaired delayed recall of visual material using the Rey Osterreith figure recall test. Boucher and Lewis (1989) showed impaired ability to carry out spoken or demonstrated instructions

with or without an intervening delay (with intact ability to carry out written instructions). Boucher and Lewis also showed that participants with V-LFA asked more repeat questions than non-autistic participants in a simplified "20 questions" game, suggesting impaired memory for their own recent utterances. Boucher (1981b), Boucher and Lewis (1989) and Millward et al. (2000) showed impaired delayed recall of personally experienced events. Finally, poor performance on the Information, Similarities, and Vocabulary subtests of the Wechsler scales relative to performance on digit span and nonverbal subtests (Lord & Paul, 1997; Seigel et al., 1996) indicates impaired recall of factual information from semantic memory, even when the prescribed questions supply relatively informative cues.

In sum, immediate free recall of unrelated words is unimpaired and associated with strong recency effects, suggesting reliance on the short-term immediate memory component of working memory. By contrast, immediate recall of verbal material with semantic or syntactic structure is impaired, as is delayed recall for all types of material assessed to date. The pattern of spared and impaired abilities on single-trial clinical or experimental tests resembles that reported for AS/HFA groups in some respects. However, such evidence as is available suggests that delayed recall on single-trial tests is more impaired in lower-functioning than in high-functioning groups.

Cued recall is superior or intact in individuals with V-LFA, relative to appropriate comparison groups, as tested on the same kinds of task that show unimpaired cued recall in people with AS/HFA. Thus, unimpaired cued recall of words using either phonological or semantic prompts was shown in studies by Boucher and Warrington (1976) and by Tager-Flusberg (1991), and unimpaired category-cued recall of named pictures of common objects was shown by Farrant et al. (1999). It is worth noting that unimpaired cued recall in the Boucher and Warrington and Tager-Flusberg studies occurred in the same children in whom impaired free recall was demonstrated. Similarly, all three studies cited above as showing impaired free recall of personally experienced events in response to open questions showed unimpaired cued recall in response to leading—i.e., more informative— questions (Boucher, 1981b; Boucher & Lewis, 1989; Millward, Powell, Messer, & Jordan, 2000). In a study of low-functioning adults, Hare, Mellor, and Azmi (2007) reported that cueing significantly improved recall of actions that had been carried out either by the participant or by the experimenter (however, the kinds of cues given are not specified in the report). In contrast to Millward et al.'s (2000) observation of better recall of other-performed over self-performed acts, Hare et al. showed significantly better cued recall of self-performed over other-performed acts.

Most strikingly, verbal paired associate learning was shown by Boucher and Warrington (1976) to be at age-appropriate level and superior to that of ability-matched controls. Similarly, Morton-Evans and Hensley (1978) reported unimpaired ability to learn visual-visual (i.e., same domain) paired stimuli. However, the children in this study were markedly impaired in their ability to learn a set of auditory-visual (i.e., between domain) associations. This potentially interesting observation must be viewed with caution, however, as only 5 participants with V-LFA were tested.

Source memory

Only three studies of source memory in lower-functioning individuals with ASDs have been reported. In the first of these studies, Farrant et al. (1998) found unimpaired reality-monitoring ("Did you say this word, or did I?") in a 2-choice source recognition task using supplementary non-social cues (the child and the experimenter each held a different colored block). In the second study, Russell and Jarrold (1999) reported a similar finding in a 4-choice color recognition task ("Did the picture come from the green/red/blue/yellow box?"). However, in the same study Russell and Jarrold found impaired performance in a complex 4-choice reality-monitoring task requiring participants to remember whether picture cards on a board had been placed by themselves, by themselves on behalf of a doll, by the experimenter, or by the experimenter on behalf of a doll. Unlike children in the two comparison groups, children with V-LFA did not show better memory for cards they had placed themselves as opposed to those placed by the experimenter (a finding that differs from those reported by Summers and Craik, 1994, and by Hare et al., 2007). Moreover, performance by the children with V-LFA did not improve when the experiment was run in an intentional as opposed to an incidental memory condition, whereas it did improve in the comparison group. In the third source-memory study, Bigham et al. (2010) found impaired recall of temporal

information ("Did you see that before or after you saw the banana?").

There are too few findings on source memory in people with LFA to reach any conclusions concerning the extent to which source memory may or may not be impaired. In addition, neither of the tests of color recognition was highly sensitive, and the complexity of Russell and Jarrold's test of memory for self- v. other-performed actions makes their finding here somewhat questionable.

Discussion of Findings

The major interpreter of findings on memory in lower-functioning autism over many years is DeLong (e.g., 1978, 1992, 2003, 2008), who has consistently argued that pathology affecting the hippocampus and associated medial temporal lobe cortex is causally implicated in the language and learning impairments associated with LFA. As noted in the Introduction, Boucher & Warrington (1976) were amongst others writing at the time who, like DeLong, hypothesised that memory impairments might be causally implicated in 'early infantile autism'. Since that time, understanding of normal memory, of different forms of acquired amnesia, and of developmental amnesia has enormously increased. Utilizing this increased understanding, we have hypothesised (Boucher et al. 2008a, 2008b; Boucher, 2009) that individuals with LFA may have a combined impairment of recollection and familiarity, hence impaired declarative memory for both episodic and semantic information. In the case of individuals with V-LFA, the declarative memory impairment is hypothesised to be mild or moderate, leaving procedural memory and immediate short-term working memory processes intact. We have further suggested that an impairment of semantic memory additional to the episodic memory impairment common to all individuals with ASDs could help to explain anomalous language development and the close links between linguistic and intellectual impairments in low-functioning autism[3]. The arguments linking a certain pattern of memory strengths

---

3. Some individuals with ASDs are not intellectually impaired but do have structural language impairment. It is not argued that language impairment in these cases derives from declarative memory deficits. Nor is it argued that impaired declarative memory is the sole cause of language impairments in LFA: other factors such as

and weaknesses to anomalous language development and intellectual disability in LFA are presented in the papers cited above and are not repeated here. In what follows, predictions from the hypothesis concerning memory strengths and weaknesses in individuals with V-LFA are summarized, and evidence relating to each prediction is considered.

Our hypothesis predicts that individuals with V-LFA will have: (1) predominantly intact procedural memory processes; (2) intact short-term immediate memory and working memory slave systems, allowing for rehearsal of unmodified inputs and hence rote learning; (3) impaired recall of personally experienced events; (4) impoverished factual knowledge, including general knowledge and knowledge of word meanings; and (5) impaired performance on all clinical and research tests of long-term declarative memory, where intact abilities cannot be effectively used to compensate. Summary conclusions regarding the strength of the evidence relating to each prediction follow, drawing on the results of studies reviewed in the previous subsection.

1. There is almost no experimental evidence relating to the prediction of predominantly intact procedural memory (automatic, implicit learning), but clinical and observational evidence suggests that most kinds of procedural memory are relatively intact. However, it may be inferred from studies of individuals with AS/HFA that emotion-related conditioning is impaired across the spectrum.
2. There is strong experimental support for the prediction of intact, short-term, immediate memory and working memory slave systems, as reviewed above.
3. Three studies of event memory support the prediction of impaired free recall of personally experienced events.
4. Poor performance on the Information subtest of the Wechsler scales relative to performance on nonverbal subtests contrasts sharply with performance on this subtest in people with AS/HFA, and supports the prediction of impaired fact memory. Moreover, there is no evidence to suggest that lower-functioning individuals with ASDs amass factual information in the way typical of people with AS/HFA.

5. Regarding the prediction of impaired performance on clinical and research tests of declarative memory where intact abilities cannot be effectively used, it was concluded above that recognition in people with LFA is fragile and easily disrupted by the introduction of a delay between presentation and test, or by increased novelty of the material to be recognized. Free recall is, as predicted, impaired except when methodology maximizes opportunities for compensating using perceptual memory and working memory slave systems, i.e., in tests of the immediate recall of unstructured material.

Such evidence as is available on memory in individuals with V-LFA is, therefore, largely supportive of our predictions. The behavioral evidence is also mainly consistent with suggestions of hippocampal dysfunction extending into ento-rhinal and perirhinal regions of medial temporal lobe cortex. However in one notable respect the behavioral evidence on memory in V-LFA is inconsistent with suggestions of hippocampal plus medial temporal lobe cortex pathology, in that cued recall (as commonly understood) and within-domain, paired-associate learning are unimpaired in individuals with V-LFA, which is not the case in individuals with hippocampal-related forms of either acquired or developmental amnesia. This discrepancy has already been noted and discussed in relation to findings on memory in people with AS/HFA, where it was suggested that if cued recall and paired-associate learning were confirmed as impaired in hippocampal-related developmental and acquired amnesia but unimpaired in people with ASDs, then it would be necessary to look for the neurological origins of memory impairments in ASDs elsewhere in the brain, possibly in prefrontal regions. The discrepancy between free and cued forms of recall are more striking in V-LFA than in AS/HFA, underlining the need for further research assessing cued recall and paired associate learning (within and across domains) using sensitive tests and including individuals with known hippocampal lesions, in addition to individuals with ASDs.

There is an equally clear need for studies of brain structure and function in groups of lower-functioning individuals with ASDs. Early postmortem studies of the brains of lower-functioning individuals with autism showed hippocampal and hippocampal-region

---

hearing loss, comorbid SLI, and deprivation may also contribute.

structural abnormalities consistent with a dual impairment of recollection and familiarity (see Bauman & Kemper, 2005 for a review). A structural brain imaging study of low-functioning adults by Rojas et al. (2004) also showed clear evidence of hippocampal abnormality. In addition, case studies reported by DeLong and Heinz (1997) of individuals with autism and profound language and intellectual impairment associated with widespread bilateral-medial-temporal lobe lesions are consistent with our hypothesis. However, other postmortem studies of brains of individuals with LFA (notably that by Bailey et al., 1998) have not reported hippocampal region abnormalities.

In sum, such data as are available on memory in lower-functioning individuals indicate more than a "subtle but persistent impairment of episodic memory" (Bowler et al., 2010), such as has been observed in people with Asperger's syndrome or high-functioning autism. These data also suggest that memory impairments in lower-functioning individuals extend beyond difficulties in remembering complex material as suggested by Minshew and her colleagues, in as far as delayed recognition of pictures of everyday objects and of single unfamiliar shapes has been shown to be impaired, as has delayed recall of single words and the names of pictured objects in some studies. In view of this evidence it is, we argue, not helpful to consider findings on memory in ASDs without making distinctions between individuals with normal language and intellectual ability and those in whom language and intelligence are significantly impaired. It is also unhelpful (not least to less able individuals and their families, in addition to theoreticians) to continue to research only the memory abilities of the most able people with ASDs. The overriding message of this chapter is, therefore, that researchers interested in memory in autism should turn at least some of their attention to the problems of the less able.

References

Aggleton, J., & Brown, M. (2006). Interleaving brain systems for episodic and recognition memory. *Trends in Cognitive Sciences, 10*, 455–463.

Ambery, F., Russell, A., Perry, K., Morris, R., & Murphy, D. (2006). Neuropsychological functioning in adults with Asperger syndrome. *Autism, 10*, 551–564.

Ameli, R., Courchesne, E., Lincoln, A., Kaufman, A., & Grillon, C. (1988). Visual memory processes in high functioning individuals with autism. *Journal of Autism and Developmental Disorders, 18*, 601–615.

American Psychiatric Association (1987). *Diagnostic and statistical manual of mental disorders*, 3rd edition revised (DSM III-R). Washington D.C.: Author.

Baddeley, A. (2002). Is working memory still working? *European Psychologist, 7*, 85–97.

Baddeley, A., Vargha-Khadem, F., & Mishkin, M. (2001). Preserved recognition in a case of developmental amnesia: Implications for the development of semantic memory? *Journal of Cognitive Neuroscience, 13*, 357–369.

Bailey, A., Luther, P., Dean, A., Harding, B., Janota, I., Montgomery, M., Rutter, M., & Lantos, P. (1998). A clinicopathological study of autism. *Brain, 121*, 889–905.

Barnes, K., Howard, J., Howard, D., Kenworthy, L., Vaidya, C., Gaillard, W., et al. (2008). Intact implicit learning of spatial context and temporal sequences in childhood autism spectrum disorder. *Neuropsychology, 22*, 563–570.

Barth, C., Fein, D., & Waterhouse, L. (1995). Delayed match-to-sample performance in autistic children. *Developmental Neuropsychology, 11*, 53–69.

Bauman, M. L., & Kemper, T. L. (2005). Neuroanatomic observations of the brain in autism: A review and future directions. *International Journal of Developmental Neuroscience, 23*, 183–187.

Belmonte, M., Cook, E., Anderson, G., Rubenstein, R., Greenough, W., Beckel-Mitchener, A., Tierney, E. (2004). Autism as a disorder of neural information processing: Directions for research and targets for therapy. *Molecular Psychiatry, 9*, 646–663.

Bennetto, L., Pennington, B., & Rogers, S. (1996). Intact and impaired memory functions in autism. *Child Development, 67*, 1816–1835.

BenShalom, D. (2003). Memory in autism: Review and synthesis. *Cortex, 39*, 1129–1138.

BenShalom, D., Faran, Y., & Boucher, J. (in press). A quantitive measure of JS's memory. *Autism.*

Beversdorf, D., Smith, B. W., Crucian, G., Anderson, J., Keillor, J., Barrett, A., Heilman, K. (2000). Increased discrimination of "false memories" in autism spectrum disorder. *Proceedings of the National Academy of Sciences, USA 97*, 8734–8737.

Bigham, S., Boucher, J., Mayes, A., & Anns, S. (2010) Assessing recollection and familiarity in autistic spectrum disorders: Methods and findings. *Journal of Autism and Developmental Disorders, 40*, 878–889.

Blair, R., Frith, U., Smith, N., Abell, F., & Cipolotti, L. (2002). Fractionation of visual memory: Agency detection and its impairment in autism. *Neuropsychologia, 40*, 108–118.

Bott, L., Brock, J., Brockdorff, N., Boucher, J. & Lamberts, K. (2006). Perceptual similarity in autism. *Quarterly Journal of Experimental Psychology, 59*, 1237–1254.

Botting, N., & Conti-Ramsden, G. (2003). Autism, primary pragmatic difficulties, and specific language impairment: Can we distinguish them using psycholinguistic markers? *Developmental Medicine and Child Neurology, 45*, 515–524.

Boucher, J. (1978). Echoic memory capacity in autistic children. *Journal of Child Psychology and Psychiatry, 19*, 161–166.

Boucher, J. (1981a). Immediate free recall in early childhood autism: Another point of behavioural similarity with the amnesic syndrome. *British Journal of Psychology, 72*, 211–215.

Boucher, J. (1981b). Memory for recent events in autistic children. *Journal of Autism and Developmental Disorders, 11*, 293–302.

Boucher, J. (2009. *The autistic spectrum: Characteristics, causes, and practical issues*. London: Sage.

Boucher, J., Bigham, S., Mayes, A., & Muskett, T. (2008a). Recognition and language in low-functioning autism. *Journal of Autism and Developmental Disorders, 38*, 1259–1269.

Boucher, J. & Bowler, D. (2008). *Memory in autism: Theories and evidence*. Cambridge: Cambridge University Press.

Boucher, J., Cowell, P., Howard, M., Broks, P., Mayes, A., & Roberts, N. (2005). A combined clinical neuropsychological and neuroanatomical study of adults with high-functioning autism. *Cognitive Neuropsychiatry, 10*, 165–214.

Boucher, J., & Lewis, V. (1989). Memory impairments and communication in relatively able autistic children. *Journal of Child Psychology and Psychiatry, 30*, 99–122.

Boucher, J., & Lewis, V. (1992). Unfamiliar face recognition in relatively able autistic children. *Journal of Child Psychology and Psychiatry, 33*, 843–860.

Boucher, J., Lewis, V., & Collis, G. (1998). Familiar face and voice matching and recognition in children with autism. *Journal of Child Psychology and Psychiatry, 39*, 171–181.

Boucher, J., Mayes, A., & Bigham, S. (2008b). Memory, language, and intellectual ability in low functioning autism. In J. Boucher & D. M. Bowler (Eds.), *Memory in Autism: Theories and Evidence* (pp. 268–290). Cambridge: Cambridge University Press.

Boucher, J., & Warrington, E. (1976). Memory deficits in early infantile autism: Some similarities to the amnesic syndrome. *British Journal of Psychology, 67*, 73–87.

Bowler, D. M., Gaigg, S. B. & Gardiner, J. M. (2008a). Subjective organisation in the free recall of adults with 'Asperger's syndrome. *Journal of Autism and Developmental Disorders, 38*, 104–113.

Bowler, D. M., Gaigg, S. B. & Gardiner, J. M. (2008b). Effects of related and unrelated context on recall and recognition by adults with high-functioning autism spectrum disorder. *Neuropsychologia, 46*, 993–999.

Bowler, D. M., Gaigg, S. B. & Gardiner, J. M. (2009). Free recall learning of hierarchically organized lists by adults with Asperger's syndrome: Additional evidence for diminished relational processing. *Journal of Autism and Developmental Disorders, 39*, 589–595.

Bowler, D. M., Gaigg, S., & Lind, S. (2010). Memory in autism: Binding, self and brain. In I. Roth & P. Rezaie (Eds.), *Researching the autistic spectrum: Contemporary perspectives* (pp. 316–347). Cambridge: Cambridge University Press.

Bowler, D. M., Gardiner, J., & Berthollier, N. (2004). Source memory in adolescents and adults with Asperger syndrome. *Journal of Autism and Developmental Disorders, 34*, 533–542.

Bowler, D. M., Gardiner, J., & Gaigg, S. (2007). Factors affecting conscious awareness in the recollective experience of adults with Asperger's syndrome. *Consciousness and Cognition, 16*, 124–143.

Bowler, D. M., Gardiner, J. M., Grice, S., & Saavalainen, P. (2000a). Memory illusions: False recall and recognition in high functioning adults with autism. *Journal of Abnormal Psychology, 109*, 663–672.

Bowler, D. M, Gardiner, J., & Grice, S. (2000b). Episodic memory and remembering in adults with Asperger syndrome. *Journal of Autism and Developmental Disorders, 30*, 295–304.

Bowler, D. M., Limoges, E., & Mottron, L. (2009b). Different verbal learning strategies in high-functioning autism: evidence from the Rey Auditory Verbal Learning Test. *Journal of Autism and Developmental Disorders, 39*, 910–915.

Bowler, D. M., Matthews, N. J., & Gardiner, J. M. (1997). Asperger's syndrome and memory: Similarity to autism but not amnesia. *Neuropsychologia, 35*, 65–70.

Brian, J., & Bryson, S. (1996). Disembedding performance and recognition memory in autism/PDD. *Journal of Child Psychology and Psychiatry, 37*, 865–872.

Buitelaar, J., van der Wees, M., Swaab-Barneveld, H., & van der Gaag, R. (1999). Verbal memory and performance IQ predict theory of mind and emotion recognition ability in children with autistic spectrum disorders and in psychiatric control children. *Journal of Child Psychology and Psychiatry, 40*, 869–882.

Casanova, M., van Kooten, I., Switala, A., van Engeland, H., Heinsen, H., Schmitz, C. (2006). Minicolumnar abnormalities in autism. *Acta Neuropathologica, 112*, 287–303.

Cody, H., Pelphrey, K., & Piven, J. (2002). Structural and functional magnetic resonance imaging of autism. *International Journal of Developmental Neuroscience, 20*, 421–438.

Courchesne, E. (2004). Brain development in autism: Early overgrowth followed by premature arrest of growth. *Mental Retardation and Developmental Disabilities Research Reviews, 10*, 106–111.

Crane, L., & Goddard, L. (2008). Episodic and semantic autobiographical memory in adults with autism spectrum disorder. *Journal of Autism and Developmental Disorders, 38*, 498–506.

Davies, S., Bishop, D., Manstead, A., & Tantam, D. (1994). Face perception in autistic children. *Journal of Child Psychology and Psychiatry, 35*, 1033–1058.

Dell'Acqua, F., Thiebaut de Schotten, M., Murphy, C., Robertson, D., Deeley, Q., Daly, E., & Murphy, D. (2009). The anatomy of extended limbic pathways in Asperger syndrome: A preliminary diffusion tensor imaging tractography study. *Neuroimage, 47*, 427–434.

DeLong, G. R. (1978). A neuropsychological interpretation of infantile autism. In M. Rutter & E. Schopler (Eds.), *Autism* (pp. 207–218). New York: Plenum Press.

DeLong, G. R. (1992). Autism, amnesia, hippocampus, and learning. *Neuroscience and Biobehavioural Reviews, 16*, 63–72.

DeLong, G. R. (2003). Disorders of memory in childhood with a focus on temporal lobe disease and autism. In S. Segalowitz & I. Rapin (Eds.), *Handbook of Neuropsychology (2nd edition), Vol 8, Part II: Child Neuropsychology, Part II* (pp. 731–751). Amsterdam: Elsevier.

DeLong, G.R. (2008). Dysfunction and hyperfunction of the hippocampus in autism? In J. Boucher & D. M. Bowler (Eds.), *Memory in Autism: Theories and Evidence* (pp. 103–121). Cambridge: CUP.

DeLong, G. R., & Heinz, E. (1997). The clinical syndrome of early-life bilateral hippocampal sclerosis. *Annals of Neurology, 43*, 687.

Eichenbaum, H., Yonelinas, A. P., & Ranganath, C. (2007) The medial temporal lobe and recognition memory. *Annual Review of Neuroscience, 30*, 123–152.

Ellis, H. D., Ellis, D. M., Fraser, W., & Deb, S. (1994). A preliminary study of right hemisphere cognitive deficits and impaired social judgments among young people with Asperger syndrome. *European Child and Adolescent Psychiatry, 3*, 255–266.

Farrant, A., Blades, M., & Boucher, J. (1998). Source monitoring in children with autism. *Journal of Autism and Developmental Disorders, 28*, 43–50.

Farrant, A., Boucher, J., & Blades, M. (1999). Metamemory in children with autism. *Child Development, 70*, 107–131.

Fein, D., Dunn M., Allen, D. A., Aram, D. M., Hall, N. Morris, R., & Wilson, B. C. (1996). Neuropsychological and language data. In Rapin, I. (Ed.), *Preschool children with inadequate communication: Developmental language disorder, autism, low IQ* (pp. 123–154). London: Mac Keith Press.

Frith, C. (2003). What do imaging studies tell us about the neural basis of autism? In G. Bock and Jamie Goode (Eds.), *Autism: Neural basis and treatment possibilities* (pp. 149–176). Chichester, UK: John Wiley & Sons for the Novartis Foundation.

Frith, U. (1970). Studies in pattern detection in normal and autistic children. *Journal of Abnormal Psychology, 76*, 413–420.

Frith, U. (2004). Confusions and controversies about Asperger syndrome. *Journal of Child Psychology and Psychiatry, 42*, 672–686.

Fyffe, C., & Prior, M. (1978). Evidence for language recoding in autistic, retarded and normal children: A re-examination. *British Journal of Psychology, 69*, 393–402.

Gaigg, S.B., & Bowler, D.M. (2007). Differential fear conditioning in Asperger's syndrome. Implications for an amygdala theory of autism. *Neuropsychologia, 45*, 2125–2134.

Gaigg, S. B., & Bowler, D. M. (2008). Free recall and forgetting of emotionally arousing words in autism spectrum disorder. *Neuropsychologia, 46*, 2336–2343.

Gaigg, S., Bowler, D.M., Ecker, C., Calvo-Merino, B., & Murphy, D.G. (2010). fMRI correlates of relational memory difficulties in Autism Spectrum Disorders. Poster presented at International Meeting for Autism Research, Philadelphia.

Gaigg, S. B., Gardiner, J. M., & Bowler, D.M. (2008). Free recall in autism spectrum disorder: The role of relational and item-specific encoding. *Neuropsychologia, 46*, 986–992.

Gardiner, J. M. (2008). Concepts and theories of memory. In J. Boucher & D. M. Bowler (Eds.), *Memory in autism: Theory and evidence* (pp. 3–20). Cambridge: Cambridge University Press.

Gardiner, J. M., Bowler, D. M., & Grice, S. (2003). Perceptual and conceptual priming in autism: An extension and replication. *Journal of Autism and Developmental Disorders, 33*, 259–269.

Gordon, B., & Stark, S. (2007). Procedural learning of a visual sequence in individuals with autism. *Focus on Autism and Other Developmental Disabilities, 22*, 14–22.

Gunter, H., Ghaziuddin, M., & Ellis, H.D. (2002). Asperger syndrome: Tests of right hemisphere functioning and interhemispheric communication. *Journal of Autism and Developmental Disorders, 32*, 263–282.

De Haan, M., Mishkin, M., Baldeweg, T., & Vargha-Khadem, F. (2006). Human memory development and its dysfunction after early hippocampal injury. *Trends in Neurosciences, 29*, 374–381.

Hala, S., Paxman, P., & Glenwright, M. (2007). Priming the meaning of homographs in typically developing children and children with autism. *Journal of Autism and Developmental Disorders, 37*, 329–340.

Hala, S., Rasmussen, C., & Henderson, A. (2005). Three types of source monitoring in children with and without autism: The role of executive function. *Journal of Autism and Developmental Disorders, 35*, 75–89.

Happé, F., & Frith, U. (2006). The weak coherence account: Detail-focused cognitive e style in autistic spectrum disorders. *Journal of Autism and Developmental Disorders, 36*, 5–23.

Hare, D. J., Mellor, C., & Azmi, S. (2007). Episodic memory in adults with autistic spectrum disorders: Recall for self- versus other-experienced events. *Research in Developmental Disabilities, 28,* 317–329.

Hauser, S., DeLong, G. R., & Rosman, N. (1975). Pneumographic findings in the infantile autism syndrome. *Brain, 98,* 667–688.

Hauck, M., Fein, D., Maltby, N., Waterhouse, L., & Feinstein, C. (1998). Memory for faces in children with autism. *Child Neuropsychology, 4,* 187–198.

Hermelin, B., & O'Connor, N. (1967). Remembering of words by psychotic and normal children. *British Journal of Psychology, 68,* 213–218.

Hill, E., & Russell, J. (2002). Action memory and self-monitoring. *Infant and Child Development, 11,* 159–170.

Hillier, A., Campbell, H., Kiellor, J., Phillips, N., & Beversdorf, D. Q. (2007). Decreased false memory for visually presented shapes and symbols among adults on the autism spectrum. *Journal of Clinical and Experimental Neuropsychology, 29,* 610–616.

Holdstock, J., Mayes, A., Isaac, C., Gong, Q., & Roberts, N. (2002). Differential involvement of the hippocampus and temporal lob cortices in rapid and slow learning of new semantic information. *Neuropsychologia, 40,* 748–768.

Isaacs, E., Lucas, A., Chong, W., Wood, S., Johnson, C., Marshall, C., … Gadian, D. (2000). Hippocampal volume and everyday memory in children of very low birth-weight. *Pediatric Research, 47,* 713–720.

Iwanaga, R., Kawasaki, C., & Tsuchida, R. (2000). Comparison of sensory-motor and cognitive function between autism and Asperger syndrome in preschool children. *Journal of Autism and Developmental Disorders, 30,* 169–174.

Jacoby, L. L. (1991). A process dissociation framework: Separating automatic from intentional uses of memory. *Journal of Memory and Language, 30,* 513–541.

Jansiewicz, E., Goldberg, M., Newschaffer, C., Denckla, M., Landa, R., & Mostofsky, S. (2006). Motor signs distinguish children with high functioning autism and Asperger's syndrome from controls. *Journal of Autism and Developmental Disorders, 36,* 613–621.

Johnson, M., Hashtroudi, S., & Lindsay, D. (1993). Reality monitoring. *Psychological Bulletin, 114,* 3–28.

Jolliffe, T., & Baron-Cohen, S. (2000). Linguistic processing in high-functioning adults with autism or Asperger syndrome. *Psychological Medicine, 30,* 1169–1187.

Joseph, R., Steele, S., Meyer, E., & Tager-Flusberg, H. (2005). Self-ordered pointing in children with autism: Failure to use verbal mediation in the service of working memory? *Neuropsychologia, 43,* 1400–1411.

Kamio, Y., & Toichi, M. (2007). Memory illusion in high-functioning autism and Asperger's disorder. *Journal of Autism and Developmental Disorders, 37,* 867–876.

Kelley, E., Paul, J., Fein, D., & Naigles, L. (2006). Residual language deficits in optimal outcome children with a history of autism. *Journal of Autism and Developmental Disorders, 36,* 807–828.

Kirwan, C. B., Wixted, J. T., & Squire, L. R. (2008) Activity in the medial temporal lobe predicts memory strength, whereas activity in the prefrontal cortex predicts recollection. *Journal of Neuroscience, 28,* 10541–10548.

Kjelgaard, M., & Tager-Flusberg, H. (2001). An investigation of language profiles in autism: Implications for genetic subgroups. *Language and Cognitive Processes, 16,* 287–308.

Klein, S., Chan, R., & Loftus, J. (1999). Independence of episodic and semantic self-knowledge: The case from autism. *Social Cognition, 17,* 413–437.

Klinger, L., & Dawson, G. (2001). Prototype formation in autism. *Development and Psychopathology, 13,* 111–124.

Koshino, H., Carpenter, P., Minshew, N., Cherkassky, V., Keller, T., & Just, M.A. (2005). Functional connectivity in an fMRI working memory task in high-functioning autism. *Neuroimage, 24,* 810–824.

Leekam, S., & Lopez, B. (2003). Do children with autism fail to process information in context? *Journal of Child Psychology and Psychiatry, 44,* 285–300.

Lincoln, A. J., Allen, M., & Killman, A. (1995). The assessment and interpretation of intellectual abilities in people with autism. In E. Schopler & G. Mesibov (Eds.), *Learning and cognition in autism* (pp. 89–118). New York: Plenum Press.

Lind, S. (in press). Memory and the self in autism spectrum disorder: A review and theoretical framework. *Autism.*

Lind, S., & Bowler, D. M. (2008). Episodic memory and autonoetic consciousnes in autism spectrum disorders. In J. Boucher & D. M. Bowler (Eds.), *Memory in autism: theories and evidence* (pp. 166–187). Cambridge UK: Cambridge University Press.

Lord, C., & Paul, R. (1997). Language and communication in autism. In D. Cohen & F. Volkmar (Eds.), *Handbook of pervasive developmental disorders, 2nd ed.* (pp. 195–225). New York: John Wiley.

Loveland, K. A., Bachevalier, J., Pearson, D., & Lane, D. (2008). Fronto-limbic functioning in children and adults with and without autism. *Neuropsychologia, 46,* 49–62.

Luna, B., Minshew, N., Garver, K., Lazar, N., Thulborn, J., Eddy, W., & Sweeney, J. (2002). Neocortical system abnormalities in autism: An fMRI study of spatial working memory. *Neurology, 59,* 834–840.

Macintosh, K., & Dissanayake, C. (2004). The similarities and differences between autistic disorder and Asperger's disorder: A review of the empirical evidence. *Journal of Child Psychology and Psychiatry, 45,* 421–434.

Manjiviona, J., & Prior, M. (1999). Neuropsychological profiles of children with Asperger syndrome and autism. *Autism, 3,* 327–356.

Martin, J., Poirier, M., Bowler. D., & Gaigg. S. (2006). Short-term serial recall in individuals with Asperger's syndrome. Poster presented at the International Meeting for Autism Research, Montreal.

Mayes, A., Montaldi, D., & Migo, E. (2007). Associative memory and the medial temporal lobes. *Trends in Cognitive Sciences, 11,* 126–135.

McAlonan, G., Suckling, J., Wong, N., Cheung, V., Lienenkaemper, N., Cheung, C., & Chua, S. (2008). Distinct patterns of gray matter abnormality in high-functioning autism and Asperger syndrome. *Journal of Child Psychology and Psychiatry, 49,* 1287–1285.

McCrory, E., Henry, L., & Happé, F. (2007). Eye-witness memory and suggestibility in children with Asperger syndrome. *Journal of Child Psychology and Psychiatry, 48,* 482–489.

Miller, L.K. (1999). The savant syndrome: Intellectual impairment and exceptional skill. *Psychological Bulletin, 125,* 31–46.

Millward, C., Powell, S., Messer, D., & Jordan, R. (2000). Recall for self and other in autism: Children's memory for events experienced by themselves and their peers. *Journal of Autism and Developmental Disorders, 30,* 15–28.

Minshew, N., & Goldstein, G. (1993). Is autism an amnesic disorder? Evidence from the California Verbal Learning Test. *Neuropsychology, 7,* 209–216.

Minshew, N., & Goldstein, G. (2001). The pattern of intact and impaired memory functions in autism. *Journal of Child Psychology and Psychiatry, 42,* 1095–1101.

Minshew, N., Goldstein, G., Muenz, L. R., & Payton, J. (1992). Neuropsychological functioning in non-mentally retarded autistic individuals. *Journal of Clinical and Experimental Neuropsychology, 14,* 749–761.

Minshew, N., Goldstein, G., & Siegel, D. (1997). Neuropsychologic functioning in autism: Profile of a complex information processing disorder. *Journal of the International Neuropsychological Society, 3,* 303–317.

Minshew, N., Luna, B., & Sweeney, J. (1999). Oculomotor evidenc for neocortical systems but not cerebellar dysfunction in autism. *Neurology, 52,* 917–922.

Minshew, N., Turner, C., & Goldstein, G. (2005). The application of short forms of the Wechsler Intelligence Scales in adults and children with high functioning autism. *Journal of Autism and Developmental Disorders, 35,* 45–52.

Minshew, N., & Williams, D. (2007). The new neurobiology of autism. *Archives of Neurology, 64,* 945–950.

Molesworth, C., Bowler, D., & Hampton, J. (2005). The prototype effect in recognition memory: Intact in autism? *Journal of Child Psychology and Psychiatry, 46,* 661–672.

Montaldi, D., Spencer, T. J., Roberts, N., & Mayes, A. R. (2006). The neural system that mediates familiarity memory. *Hippocampus, 16,* 504–520.

Morris, R., Rowe, A., Fox, N., Feigenbaum, J., Miotto, E., & Howlin, P. (1999). Spatial working memory in Asperger's syndrome and in patients with focal frontal and temporal lob lesions. *Brain and Cognition, 41,* 9–26.

Morton-Evans, A., & Hensley, R. (1978). Paired associate learning in early infantile autism and receptive developmental aphasia. *Journal of Autism and Childhood Schizophrenia, 8,* 61–69.

Mostofsky, S., Bunoski, R., Morton, S., Goldberg, M., & Bastian, A. (2004). Children with autism adapt normally during a catching task requiring the cerebellum. *Neurocase, 10,* 60–64.

Mostofsky, S., Dubey, P., Jerath, V., Jansiewicz, E., Goldberg, M., & Denkla, M. (2006). Developmental dyspraxia is not limited to imitation in children with autistic spectrum disorders. *Journal of the International Neuropsychological Society, 12,* 314–326.

Mostofsky, S., Goldberg, M., Landa, R., & Denkla, M. (2000). Evidence for a deficit in procedural learning in children and adolescents with autism: Implications for cerebellar contribution. *Journal of the International Neuropsychological Society, 6,* 752–759.

Mottron, L., Morasse, K., & Belleville, S. (2001). A study of memory functioning in individuals with autism. *Journal of Child Psychology and Psychiatry, 42,* 253–260.

Nicolson, R., DeVito, T., Vidal, C., Sui, Y., Hayashi, K., Drost, D., Williamson, P., Rajakumar, N., Toga, A., & Thompson, P.C. (2006). Detection and mapping of hippocampal abnormalities in autism. *Psychiatry Research: Neuroimaging, 148,* 11–21.

O'Connor, N., & Hermelin, B. (1967). Auditory and visual memory in autistic and normal children. *Journal of Mental Deficiency Research, 11,* 126–131.

O'Shea, A., Fein, D., Cillessen, D., Klin, A., & Schultz, R. (2005). Source memory in children with autism spectrum disorders. *Developmental Neuropsychology, 27,* 337–360.

Ozonoff, S., South, M., & Miller, J. (2000). DSM-IV-defined Asperger syndrome: Cognitive, behavioural, and early history differentiation from autism. *Autism, 4,* 29–46.

Ozonoff, S., & Strayer, D. (2001). Further evidence of intact working memory in autism. *Journal of Autism and Developmental Disorders, 31,* 257–263.

Pennington, B., Rogers, S., Bennetto, L., McMahon Griffith, E., Reed, D. T., & Shyu, V. (1997). Validity tests of the impairments of executive function hypothesis of autism. In J. Russell (Ed.), *Autism as an executive disorder* (pp. 143–178). Oxford: Oxford University Press.

Pring, L. (2008). Memory characteristics in individuals with savant skills. In J. Boucher & D.M. Bowler (Eds.), *Memory in autism: Theories and evidence* (pp. 210–230). Cambridge: Cambridge University Press.

Prior, M., & Chen, C. (1976). Short-term and serial memory in autistic, retarded, and normal children.

Journal of Autism and Childhood Schizophrenia, 6, 121–131.

Prior, M., & Hoffman, W. (1990). Neuropsychological testing of autistic children through an exploration with frontal lobe tests. *Journal of Autism and Developmental Disorders, 20,* 581–590.

Ramondo, N., & Milech, D. (1984). The nature and specificity of language coding deficit in autistic children. *British Journal of Psychology, 75,* 95–103.

Rapin, I. (1996). Neurological issues. In I. Rapin (Ed.), *Preschool children with inadequate communication* (pp. 98–112). Cambridge: Mac Keith Press.

Reed, T. (2004). Visual perspective taking as a measure of working memory in participants with autism. *Journal of Developmental and Physical Disabilities, 14,* 63–76.

Renner, P., Klinger, L., & Klinger, M. (2000). Implicit and explicit memory in autism: Is autism an amnesic disorder? *Journal of Child Psychology and Psychiatry, 30,* 3–14.

Rimland, B. (1964). *Infantile autism.* New York: Appleton-Century-Crofts.

Rinehart, N., Tonge, B., Iansek, R., McGinley, J., Brereton, A., Enticott, P., & Bradshaw, J. (2006). Gait function in newly diagnosed children with autism: Cerebellar and basal ganglia related motor disorder. *Developmental Medicine and Child Neurology, 48,* 819–824.

Ritvo, E., & Freeman, B. (1971). National Society for Autistic Children definition of autism. *Journal of Pediatric Psychology, 2,* 146–148.

Rojas, D., Allegra-Smith, E., Benkers, T., Camou, S., Reite, M., & Rogers, S. (2004). Hippocampus and amygdala volumes in parents of children with autistic disorder. *American Journal of Psychiatry, 161,* 2038–2044.

Rumsey, J., & Hamburger, S. (1988). Neuropsychological findings in high-functioning men with infantile autism, residual state. *Journal of Clinical and Experimental Psychology, 10,* 201–221.

Russell, J., Jarrold, C., & Henry, L. (1996). Working memory in children with autism and with moderate learning difficulties. *Journal of Child Psychology and Psychiatry, 37,* 673–687.

Russell, J., & Jarrold, C. (1999). Memory for actions in children with autism: Self versus other. *Cognitive Neuropsychiatry, 4,* 303–331.

Rutter, M. (1968). Concepts of autism: A review of research. *Journal of Child Psychology and Psychiatry, 24,* 513–531.

Salmond, C., Ashburner, J., Connelly, A., Friston, K., Gadian, D., & Vargha-Khadem, F. (2005). The role of the medial temporal lobe in autistic spectrum disorders. *European Journal of Neuroscience, 22,* 764–772.

Salmond, C., Adlam, A., Gadian, D., & Vargha-Khadem, F. (2008). A comparison of memory profiles in relation to neuropathology in autism, developmental amnesia, and children born prematurely. In J. Boucher & D.M. Bowler (Eds.), *Memory in*

autism: Theory and evidence (pp. 63–85). Cambridge: Cambridge University Press.

Sears, L. L., Finn, P., & Steinmetz, J. (1994). Abnormal classical eye-blink conditioning in autism. *Journal of Autism and Developmental Disorders, 24,* 737–751.

Siegel, D., Minshew, N., & Goldstein, G. (1996). Wechsler IQ profiles in diagnosis of high functioning autism. *Journal of Autism and Developmental Disorders, 26,* 389–407.

Smith, B., & Gardiner, J. (2008). Rehearsal and directed forgetting in Asperger syndrome. In J. Boucher & D. M. Bowler (Eds.), *Memory in autism: Theory and evidence* (pp. 249–267). Cambridge: Cambridge University Press.

Steele, S., Minshew, N., Luna, B., & Sweeney, J. (2007). Spatial working memory deficits in autism. *Journal of Autism and Developmental Disorders, 37,* 605–612.

Summers, J., & Craik, F. (1994). The effect of subject-performed tasks on the memory performance of verbal autistic children. *Journal of Autism and Developmental Disorders, 24,* 773–783.

Tager-Flusberg, H. (1991). Semantic processing in the free recall of autistic children: Further evidence of a cognitive deficit. In G. Dawson (Ed.), *Autism: Nature, diagnosis, and treatment* (pp. 92–109). New York: Guilford Press.

Toichi, M., & Kamio, Y. (2003). Long term memory in high functioning autism: Controversy on episodic memory reconsidered. *Journal of Autism and Developmental Disorders, 33,* 151–161.

Toichi, M. (2008). Episodic memory, semantic memory and self-awareness in high-functioning autism. In J. Boucher & D. Bowler (Eds.), *Memory in autism: Theory and evidence* (pp. 143–165). Cambridge: Cambridge University Press.

Tulving, E. (1984). How many memory systems are there? *American Psychologist, 40,* 385–398.

Ullman, M. (2001). Contributions of brain memory circuits to language: The declarative/procedural model. *Cognition, 92,* 231–270.

Vargha-Khadem, F., Gadian, D., Watkins, K., Connelly, A., van Paesschen, W., & Mishkin, M. (1997). Differential effects of early hippocampal pathology on episodic and semantic memory. *Science, 277,* 376–380.

Verté, S., Geurts, H., Roeyers, H., Oosterlaan, J., & Sergeant, J. (2006). Executive functioning in children with an autism spectrum disorder: Can we differentiate within the spectrum? *Journal of Autism and Developmental Disorders, 36,* 351–362.

Volkmar, F. R., & Klin, A. (2000). Diagnostic issues in Asperger syndrome. In A. Klin, F.R. Volkmar, & S. Sparrow (Eds.), *Asperger syndrome* (pp. 25–71). Guilford: New York.

Walenski, M., Tager-Flusberg, H., & Ullman, M. (2006). Chapter title. Language in autism. In S. Moldin & J. Rubenstein (Eds.), *Understanding autism: From* basic neuroscience to treatment (pp. 175–203). New York: Taylor and Francis.

Webb, S. (2008). Impairments in social memory in autism. Evidence from behavior and neuroimaging. In J. Boucher & D. M. Bowler (Eds.), *Memory in autism: Theories and evidence* (pp. 188–209). Cambridge: Cambridge University Press.

Wechsler, D. (1997a). *Wechsler Adult Intelligence Scale—Third edition*. San Antonio, TX: The Psychological Corporation.

Wechsler, D. (1997b). *Wechsler Intelligence Scale for Children—Third edition*. San Antonio, TX: The Psychological Corporation.

Weimer, A., Schatz, A., Lincoln, A., Ballantyne, A., & Trauner, D. (2001). "Motor" impairment in Asperger syndrome: Evidence for a deficit in proprioception. *Journal of Developmental and Behavioral Pediatrics, 22*, 92–101.

Wheeler, M., Stuss, D., & Tulving, E. (1998). Toward a theory of episodic memory: The frontal lobes and autonoetic consciousness. *Psychological Bulletin, 121*, 331–354.

Williams, D. L., Goldstein, G., Carpenter, P., & Minshew, N. (2005a). Verbal and spatial working memory in autism. *Journal of Autism and Developmental Disorders, 35*, 747–756.

Williams, D. L., Goldstein, G., & Minshew, N. J. (2005b). Impaired memory for faces and social scenes in autism: Clinical implications of memory dysfunction. *Archives of Clinical Neuropsychology, 20*, 1–15.

Williams, D. L., Goldstein, G., Minshew, & N. J. (2006). Neuropsychologic functioning in children with autism: Further evidence for disordered complex information-processing. *Child Neuropsychology, 12*, 279–298.

Whitehouse, A. J. O., Barry, J. G., & Bishop, D. V. M. (2008). Further defining the language impairment of autism: Is there a specific language impairment subtype? *Journal of Communication Disorders, 41*, 319–336.

Yonelinas, A. (2002). The nature of recollection and familiarity: A review of 30 years research. *Journal of Memory and Language, 46*, 441–517.

Zinke, K., Fries, E., Altgassen, M., Kirschbaum, C., Dettenborn, L., & Kliegal, M. (2010). Visuospatial short-term memory explains deficits in tower task planning in high-functioning children with autism spectrum disorder. *Child Neuropsychology, 16*, 229–241.

Chapter 8

Attention and Working Memory in ASD

Brittany G. Travers, Mark. R. Klinger, and Laura Grofer Klinger

She didn't seem to be aware of her surroundings… If she was focusing on anything, it was on minute particles of dust or hair that she now picked up from the rug to study with intense concentration. (Maurice, 1993, pp. 32–33)

In this description of her 2-year-old daughter, Catherine Maurice captures the often confusing nature of attention in individuals with autism spectrum disorder (ASD). At times, individuals with ASD seem to have poor attention skills and a tendency to attend to irrelevant details, while missing more relevant information in the environment. However, at other times, the same person has the ability to intensely focus their attention on the matter at hand. This seeming contrast between poor and excellent attention skills has intrigued clinicians and researchers alike. In this chapter, we explore the nature of attention in individuals with ASD, with a particular emphasis on explaining this seeming contradictory evidence for whether attention is impaired or enhanced in individuals on the autism spectrum.

Attention is certainly one of the most important, pervasive, complex, and, in many ways, ill-defined topics in cognitive neuroscience. While some of our thinking processes occur seemingly automatically with minimal attention, clearly many of our thoughts and behaviors require attentional control. Attention plays an important role in both our automatic and intentional thoughts and actions. As you intentionally direct attention to the words on this page, you can both read the words and dwell upon their underlying meaning. However, you may experience an automatic shift away from this book, and your thoughts about it, when a noise occurs outside your window. Then, you may find yourself shifting attention again to thinking about your plans for tomorrow. Even in this brief "window" of your day, attention is with you at every moment of your thoughts. Thus, the term *attention* encompasses a wide variety of thinking processes from the relatively simple process of alertness to one's surroundings, to the very complex thinking processes of careful balancing of our own goals and the goals of others in social negotiation and problem-solving. Individuals with autism spectrum disorders (ASD) have been hypothesized to struggle with many of the different aspects of attention.

In this chapter, we will organize our discussion of this complex construct by discussing three kinds of attention. First, we will discuss the ability to orient and direct one's attention to some parts of the environment while ignoring other aspects of the environment. This kind of attention has been referred to as *input* (or *spatial*) *attention*, because it influences which information from the world is examined and "passed on" for further processing, and which information is ignored.

A second kind of attentional process refers to thinking that is consciously controlled, manipulated with effort, and often aimed at accomplishing goal-directed behavior. This kind of attention has been referred to as *controlled* (or *selective*) *attention*. This can include selecting which aspects of the world to focus on, and which aspects to deliberately suppress or ignore. Clearly, some thought processes require a great deal of attentional control to perform, while others seemingly occur automatically. In Catherine Maurice's description of her daughter's attention, it is unclear whether her input attention is impaired such that she is focusing on the wrong information, or whether this is a more "controlled" choice to look at dust and hair rather than other information in the environment.

Finally, a concept that is closely linked to attention will be discussed. This related construct is *working memory*, which refers to the structures and processes used for temporarily storing and manipulating information. As such, working memory is involved in maintaining information in our current thoughts, directing attention to relevant information, and coordinating cognitive processes when more than one task must be done at the same time. We begin each section with a review of the typical development of these attentional processes and then review the current literature on these processes in individuals with ASD. Finally, we link each review to clinical implications with regards to the assessment and treatment of ASD.

INPUT ATTENTION

Input (or spatial) attention determines the scope of information that is attended in the world. It is the gateway from the outer world to the inner world of thoughts and perceptions. Information that is attended at input is passed along for further processing, whereas information that is not attended may be registered in sensory cortex but is not passed along for further processing, and quickly fades from brain activation. Input attention is relatively automatic and often occurs without conscious intention. Two aspects of input attention have been studied extensively: the ability to orient and shift one's attentional focus, and the ability to widen or narrow one's attentional focus or spotlight.

Measuring Input Attention

Traditionally, each aspect of input attention (orienting/shifting and the spotlight of attention) has been studied using separate paradigms. Posner, Walker, Friedrich, and Rafal (1984) proposed that the ability to orient and shift attention occurs in three steps: disengagement, shift, and engagement. Disengagement refers to breaking attention away from the current focus. The shift is simply the movement from the previous stimulus to the next stimulus. Engagement is the focus of attention onto the new stimulus. These three elements of orienting and shifting attention are commonly measured using the Posner et al. (1984) target-detection task. In this task, the goal of the participant is to remain focused on a central point while detecting peripheral stimuli to the left and right of the central focal point. The task includes valid and invalid cues to the target location and variable cue-to-target delays, manipulating the amount of time one has to use the cue. Within the traditional paradigm, peripheral cues (e.g., a flash or square at one of the target locations) measure automatic or exogenous (externally pulled) orienting of attention (see Figure 8-1). Central cues (e.g., an arrow at the central focus point that shows the participant where to shift attention) measure more controlled or endogenous (internally directed) attention. In this task, with either type of cue, attention is measured by the cue-validity effect, which is the difference in accuracy or response speed to trials in which the cue validly predicts the target location, versus trials in which the cue invalidly predicts the wrong target location.

The ability to widen or narrow one's attention focus or "spotlight" has traditionally been measured through the use of the Navon letter task (Navon, 1977) or one of many similar variations. In this task, the goal of the participant is to look for a particular target item

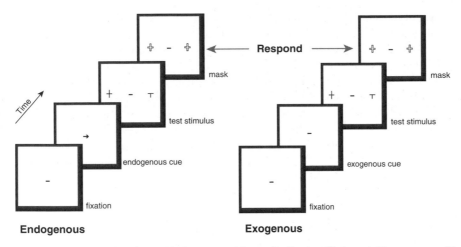

Figure 8-1 Input Attention Paradigm: Endogenous (Central) Cueing Task and Exogeneous (Peripheral) Cueing Task.

(e.g., an H). Stimuli presented to participants are large letters (the global level) composed of many small letters (the local level). Attention to either the global level or the local level is measured by looking at reaction-time differences in detecting the target at either the global level (a large H made up of small S's) or the local level (a large S made up of small H's). Within this task a researcher can investigate an individual's preference for looking at either the local or global level, but other issues can also be investigated, like the ease of shifting from looking at local level to the global level or vice versa.

Neural Basis of Input Attention

Posner and Petersen (1990) theorized that specific regions of the brain were responsible for each part of this spatial attention system. The parietal lobe is theorized to be responsible for disengaging attention from the current stimulus. For example, Posner et al. (1984) reported that patients with parietal lobe lesions showed decreased disengagement of attention in the opposite visual field. In contrast, this disengagement of attention was not affected by temporal-lobe lesions. The midbrain is thought to be responsible for shifting attention to the new location. Specifically, patients with injury to the superior colliculus demonstrated significant slowing in the shifting of attention, regardless of whether or not attention was previously engaged. While individuals without injury to this area, as well as patients with other cortical lesions including

the parietal lobe, are less likely to return attention to a previously attended spatial location, patients with deterioration of the superior colliculus return attention to previously attended locales as much as they do to new spatial locations (Sapir, Soroker, Berger, & Henik, 1999). Finally, there is evidence for the involvement of the thalamus and pulvinar in the engagement part of attention (Petersen, Robinson, & Morris, 1987; Posner, 1988). Patients with thalamic lesions were shown to be slower to respond to targets even when delay times were very long (giving patients enough time to orient).

The ability to widen or narrow the spotlight of attention has been found to rely on many of the same brain regions as orienting and shifting of attention (Weissman & Woldorff, 2005). Lesion studies have shown that the parieto-temporal area is important to the size of attentional focus. Recent neuroimaging studies show findings that are generally consistent with the suggestion that attention to the global level is more tied to the temporal cortex and the inferior parietal lobe/superior temporal gyrus, and that attention to the local level is more tied to the superior parietal cortex and the intraparietal sulcus (Han, Jiang, & Gu, 2004; Weissman & Woldorff, 2005). In addition, the size of the attentional spotlight is lateralized such that damage to the left parietal and temporal areas leads to poor analysis of local information, but damage to the right parietal and temporal areas leads to poor analysis of global information (Lamb & Robertson, 1990; Lamb, Robertson, & Knight, 1989; Robertson, Lamb, & Knight, 1988).

Typical Development of Input Attention

The ability to orient toward a visual stimulus (e.g., follow a toy that moves across the field of vision) is typically present at birth (see Ruff & Rothbart, 1996, for a review of the development of attention). By 3 to 4 months of age, infants are able to disengage their attention and shift it toward another stimulus (e.g., shift from looking at one toy to another toy; Atkinson, Hood, Wattam-Bell, & Braddick, 1992; Johnson, Posner, & Rothbart, 1994). During the first few months of life, attention is thought to be controlled by exogenous (i.e., automatic) processes (Atkinson et al., 1992), such that attention is automatically drawn toward events occurring in the environment (e.g., a flash of color). Exogenous attention is stimulus-driven and occurs with minimal mental effort or conscious awareness. Between 3 and 6 months of age, infants begin to develop more endogenous (i.e., controlled) attention processes (Hood, 1995; Johnson et al., 1994). Endogenous orienting is intentional, is goal driven, and requires mental effort and conscious awareness that directs attention toward a specific location. Enns and Brodeur (1989) demonstrated that, while 6-year-old children and adults showed similar levels of exogenous orienting, endogenous orienting continued to develop throughout childhood.

The ability to adjust attentional focus or spotlight has not yet been studied in infants and young children. However, there have been several studies examining whether there is a preference to use a narrow or a wider spotlight of attention (Cassia, Simion, Milani, & Umiltà, 2002; Poirel, Mellet, Houdé, & Pineau, 2008; Scherf, Behrmann, Kimchi, & Luna, 2009). Specifically, within a few hours after birth, infants show evidence that they attend to more global than local information (Cassia et al., 2002). This preference appears to wane in the preschool years, where a more local, narrow attentional focus has been reported (Poirel et al., 2008). By nine years of age, a more adult-like global preference has been reported across several studies, and this global preference appears to increase across development (Poirel et al., 2008; Scherf et al., 2009).

Input Attention in Individuals with ASD

Visual Orienting

Several studies have specifically examined exogenous orienting in persons with ASD using Posner-style cuing paradigms. Studies using a peripheral cue have shown fairly consistent evidence that exogenous orienting is impaired in high-functioning children, adolescents, and adults with ASD (Greenaway & Plaisted, 2005; Renner, Klinger, & Klinger, 2006; Townsend et al., 1999; Townsend, Courchesne, & Egaas, 1996; Townsend, Harris, & Courchesne, 1996). Specifically, each of these studies has shown that individuals with ASD show decreased cue validity effects when a peripheral cue is followed quickly by a target. In each study, participants were given a brief time (i.e., cue-to-target delays ranged from 100 milliseconds [ms] to 250 ms) to orient to the cue and shift their attention to the possible target location. These effects have been found using reaction time and accuracy measures to compute cue-validity effects. However, one study (Iarocci & Burack, 2004) did not find impaired exogenous cuing in children with ASD and comorbid intellectual disability. In this study, the fixation stimulus was removed before cue presentation. This could be a crucial methodological difference, because when the fixation stimulus remains on the screen, participants are obliged to disengage their attention from the fixation stimulus before they are able to shift their attention. That is, they must stop attending to the current location before they can shift and engage their attention at the cued location. Indeed, several investigators (Courchesne et al., 1994; Landry & Bryson, 2004) have found that disengaging attention from a current location may be particularly difficult for persons with ASD.

The literature examining endogenous orienting is more mixed. Typically, studies have used a central cue (e.g., an arrow) to direct the participant's attention toward a target stimulus location. In participants with ASD, this type of orienting seems to be impaired when there is a shorter latency between the onset of the arrow and the onset of the target (i.e., cue-to-target delays ranging from 100–200 ms; Landry, Mitchell, & Burack, 2009; Wainwright-Sharp & Bryson, 1993). However, when there were longer latencies, individuals with ASD performed similarly to individuals with typical development (i.e., cue-to-target delays ranging from 400–800 ms; Landry et al., 2009; Wainright-Sharp & Bryson, 1993). To date, there has been one study (Senju, Tojo, Dairoku, & Hasegawa, 2004) that found intact endogenous cuing at short cue-to-target delay intervals.

Taken together, the literature on attention orienting suggests that individuals with ASD have difficulty shifting and refocusing their attention across the life span. This is particularly true when there is an abrupt distraction in the periphery that automatically "pulls" attention toward the interruption. Townsend and colleagues (Townsend et al., 1999; Townsend, Courchesne et al., 1996; Townsend, Harris et al., 1996) proposed that persons with ASD are indeed capable of attention orienting, but they require more time to do so than individuals with typical development (the slowing hypothesis). Renner et al. (2006) hypothesized that this slow attention orienting suggests that attention orienting in ASD is more effortful or controlled and may simply take longer than the automatic orienting of attention that is typically used to process abrupt onset environmental information. Whether this difficulty is due to a problem in disengaging attention or whether it is due to a problem in shifting attention remains to be determined. However, either way, individuals with ASD are likely to "miss" quickly occurring environmental information that requires rapid shifts of attention.

Spotlight of Attention

In terms of the widening or narrowing of input attention, research has found evidence of both an overly narrow and an overly broad spotlight of attention in persons with ASD. Evidence for an overly narrow spotlight of attention comes from early studies demonstrating "stimulus overselectivity" in ASD (Lovaas & Schreibman, 1971; Rincover & Ducharme, 1987), and from more recent studies examining "weak central coherence" (Frith, 1989; Frith & Happé, 1994; Happé & Frith, 2006) and "enhanced perceptual functioning" (Mottron, Dawson, Soulières, Hubert, & Burack, 2006) theories of ASD. Central coherence theory proposes that individuals with ASD have a tendency to focus on details and have difficulty integrating "local" or specific features into a whole (i.e., have a weak central coherence). Enhanced perceptual functioning theory suggests that persons with ASD have a tendency to process visual information at a narrow or "local" level. The primary difference between these two theories is that weak central coherence suggests a global processing deficit, whereas enhanced perceptual functioning suggests intact global processing, but enhanced attention to local processing. In spite of this difference, these two theories both suggest that persons with ASD will have better local processing (i.e., a narrower spotlight of attention). This narrower focus of attention can lead to superior performance on tasks requiring attention to details (e.g., embedded figures or block design tasks) and poor performance on tasks that require the ability to integrate global information (e.g., a homophone reading task in which the sentence context determines the correct pronunciation of a word). There is a large body of literature supporting this type of superior attention to details (Shah & Frith, 1983, 1993) and impaired attention to global features (Happé, 1997; Jolliffe & Baron-Cohen, 1999) in persons with ASD. For example, across multiple conditions, persons with ASD tend to focus on the individual letters rather than the overall picture in a Navon letter task (e.g., they focus on the smaller letter A's that compose a single large letter H; Wang, Mottron, Peng, Berthiaume, & Dawson, 2007). Thus, there is quite a bit of support for the notion that individuals with ASD have a narrow spotlight of attention.

However, there is also a body of literature that provides evidence for an overly broad spotlight of attention in persons with ASD. Some of this information comes from reports of sensitivities to sensory information (e.g., touch, taste, smell), and evidence suggesting that these sensitivities may be due to difficulty filtering out perceptual information (Wiggins, Robins, Bakeman, & Adamson, 2009). These sensory sensitivities may be due to an overly broad spotlight of attention that does not filter out peripheral sensory information. Empirical evidence for an overly broad spotlight of attention comes from Burack (1994), who asked participants with ASD to identify a particular shape in the presence of distracters, while the search area was small or large. He found that participants with ASD had the most difficulty when distracters were present, suggesting that they were using a broader spotlight of attention that was not filtering out the distracters. When the search area was made smaller (thus externally imposing a narrower spotlight of attention on the participant), participants with ASD were able to identify the target more quickly, once again suggesting an overly broad spotlight of attention. Similarly, Smith and Milne (2009) found that adolescents with ASD were more observant of irrelevant changes in a movie (e.g., pants changing colors from one scene to the next) than adolescents with typical development. They interpreted this result as being caused by an abnormally broad spotlight of attention in persons with ASD. In contrast, individuals with typical development typically show "change blind-ness" in which these types of changes are not noticed. However, three other studies of change blindness in ASD did not find differences between the perfor-mance of participants with ASD and participants with typical development (Burack et al., 2009; Fletcher-Watson, Leekam, Findlay, & Stanton, 2008; Fletcher-Watson, Leekam, Turner, & Moxon, 2006).

In sum, there is evidence for both an overly narrow and an overly broad spotlight of attention in ASD. One possibility that could explain the inconsistency of the literature is that persons with ASD exhibit anomalies in flexibly switching between narrow and broad spotlights of attention. Indeed, in individuals with typical development, the spotlight of attention may narrow and widen many times over the course of seconds, depending on the task at hand or the varying perceptual load. Remington, Swettenham, Campbell, & Coleman (2009) found that participants with ASD had to have more distracters (a higher perceptual load) before they narrowed their spotlight of attention compared to individuals with typical development. This result suggests that individuals with ASD may have difficulty switching from a broader spotlight of attention to a narrow spotlight. There is also evi-dence that persons with ASD may also have difficulty switching from a narrow spotlight of attention to a broader spotlight of attention. For example, using a design with differently sized crosshairs, Mann and Walker (2003) found that individuals with ASD took significantly longer to attend to stimuli when the crosshairs directed attention to move from a small focus to a larger focus of attention. Like the visual-orienting literature, these findings suggest that indi-viduals with autism likely "miss" important information in their environment when their attentional focus is overly narrow or overly broad.

Neuroimaging of Input Attention in ASD

Several neuroimaging studies have investigated the neural mechanisms underlying input (automatic) atten-tion in persons with ASD. Haist, Adamo, Westerfield, Courchesne, & Townsend (2005) reported that individu-als with ASD exhibited less activation in the bilateral inferior parietal lobule, a key attention area, compared to individuals with typical development in a short cue-to-target delay condition (i.e., 100 ms). Furthermore, across both short and long cue-to-target delay conditions, persons with ASD recruited the posterior

cerebellar vermis less than persons with typical devel-opment. The authors interpreted these findings as evidence for abnormalities of the cerebellar-frontal attentional system in ASD. An additional study examined the neural underpinnings of covert shifts of attention between two lateral spatial locations (Belmonte & Yurgelun-Todd, 2003). It found that individuals with ASD tended to activate the ventral occipital regions instead of the regions typically associated with attentional shifts (e.g., the superior parietal cortex, middle temporal cortex, dorsolateral prefrontal cortex, premotor cortex, and medial frontal cortex). Combined, these results suggest that there is decreased activation in typical attentional circuits in persons with ASD compared to typically developing participants.

Using the embedded figures task (EFT), studies have examined the brain mechanisms of the attention spotlight in children (Lee et al., 2007), adolescents (Manjaly et al., 2007), and adults (Manjaly et al., 2003; Ring et al., 1999) with ASD. These studies have consistently found less activation of the prefron-tal regions (including the premotor cortex and dorsolateral prefrontal cortex) in persons with ASD. Furthermore, similar to the neuroimaging results of Belmonte and Yurgelun-Todd (2003), all but one of these studies (Lee et al., 2007) has found increased activation in the occipito-temporal areas in the ASD group. Taken with the behavioral results of persons with ASD excelling in local-component processing, these neuroimaging results suggest that local process-ing may be less effortful for persons with ASD. Because additional behavioral results suggest difficulties in the transition between a narrow and broader spotlight of attention, future neuroimaging research should examine the neural mechanisms in persons with ASD that underlie the transition between local and global processing.

Summary

Across both types of input attention discussed— orienting to cues and changing or adjusting the size of the spotlight of attention—there is evidence that individuals with ASD across the life span have impairments in the relatively automatic allocation of attention that occurs without conscious thought. In both types of attention research, there is evidence for a type of "sticky" attention in which individuals with ASD do not flexibly adjust their focus of attention to attend to relevant information. This can be seen in their difficulty reorienting their attention to cues in the environment, especially to sudden movement or the appearance of objects in the periphery, and in their difficulty changing the size of their spotlight of attention, that is, going from a narrow to wide focus or a wide to narrow focus. These difficulties seem to be especially present when attention must be allocated swiftly, without time for more controlled decision-making. Both types of input attention involve a complex network of brain regions, with the temporo-parietal junction being seen as especially important for both attentional orienting and changing the spotlight of attention. Studies with attentional cuing in ASD have confirmed that functioning in the parietal attention system seems to be impaired in ASD. While some studies have examined the neural underpinnings of the spotlight of attention in ASD, no study has yet directly examined the brain functioning of shifts of the spotlight of attention (e.g., from local to global focus).

CONTROLLED ATTENTION

Controlled (or selective) attention governs the control and flow of the processing of our thoughts and perceptions. The ability to focus attention on one issue or goal while ignoring and inhibiting others, the ability to sustain attention on a task even when it becomes tiresome, and the ability to divide attention and do two things simultaneously or by quick alternation, all imply control over a limited attentional resource that is essential to goal-directed action. Models of controlled attention generally suggest that there are attentional processes that both enhance performance of selected goals and inhibit or suppress performance of nonselected goals. There are presumably large individual differences in this resource; some persons have strong attentional resources and others do not. Also, there are presumably large intra-individual differences in this resource; any given individual has times where they have more attentional resources and other times where their attention is more limited. From this description, it should come as no surprise that this form of attention is highly similar to those processes described as executive functioning in the neuropsychology literature and to the central executive process within working memory discussed later in this chapter. While there is a great deal of overlap between

these topic areas, in the sections that follow, we will discuss those studies that have described themselves as controlled or selective attention studies, or used experimental tasks that were originally designed to measure aspects of controlled attention (see Chapter 9 for a review of executive functioning in ASD).

Measuring Controlled Attention

Much of the work on controlled attention has focused on the ability to control responses by a process of inhibition. This has included research using the Stroop task, the Go/No-Go task, and the Stop Signal task. In all of these tasks a participant has a dominant, perhaps relatively automatic response that must be stopped by forcibly inhibiting this dominant response so that the nondominant response may be enacted. Perhaps the most common task in the field of attention is the Stroop task (Stroop, 1935). In this task, participants are told to name the color of the ink in which a color word is printed (e.g., to say "red" for the word "green" printed in red ink); in order to do this accurately, the potent automatic word-reading response has to be inhibited. Another task designed to measure inhibition of responses is the Go/No-Go task. While there are many versions of this task, most involve responding quickly to objects that appear on a screen but withholding responses to certain stimuli (e.g., a blue square). The Stop Signal Task measures the ability to switch between enacting and inhibiting a prepotent response (Logan & Cowan, 1984). In this task, participants are instructed to respond to a target (e.g., an X) except when a stop-signal (e.g., a tone) immediately precedes the target (see Figure 8-2). This task is similar to the Go/No-Go task in many ways, with the chief difference being that the cue to discontinue responding occurs before the target in the Stop-Signal task, but is part of the target presentation in the Go/No-Go task.

Neural Basis of Controlled Attention

Research on the neural basis for controlled attention has implicated many different areas of the brain. However, across studies there is some consistency suggesting that the fronto-striatal network may underlie much of controlled attention. Casey (2001) argued that the basal ganglia are involved in the inhibition of inappropriate behaviors (Mink, 1996), whereas the prefrontal cortex (PFC) is involved in protecting

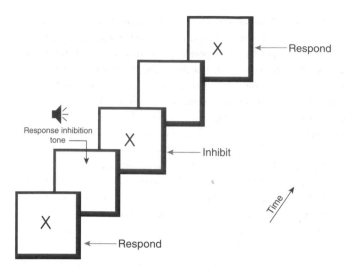

Figure 8-2 Controlled Attention Paradigm: Stop Signal Task.

representations of relevant information from interference due to competing information (Miller & Cohen, 2001). These regions interact and share information across many pathways, creating a fronto-striatal network that plays an important role in motor planning, initiation, and timing (Deiber, Honda, Ibañez, Sadato, & Hallett, 1999). The PFC in this model is theorized to exert control over both input (sensory) and output (motor) neurons within this system, and to be influenced by both input and output neurons. Several studies have used the Go/No-Go task to examine the neural correlates of inhibitory control. Generally, these studies have shown activation in prefrontal, basal ganglia, and supplementary motor regions (Kawashima et al., 1996; Liddle, Kiehl, & Smith, 2001; Rubia et al., 2000). Studies using the Go/No-Go task have suggested that the anterior cingulate is also activated during the Go/No-Go task, but is not involved directly in response inhibition, being instead involved in monitoring performance (Braver, Barch, Gray, Molfese, & Snyder, 2001; Liddle et al., 2001).

Typical Development of Controlled Attention

Relatively large developmental differences in accuracy and reaction time have been reported in many controlled attention tasks. For instance, children improve dramatically in the Go/No-Go task from the preschool years (Levy, 1980), through school age and into adulthood (Becker, Isaac, & Hynd, 1987). Similarly, studies using stop-signal tasks have also shown that the speed

of suppressing a response becomes faster throughout childhood (Williams, Ponesse, Schachar, Logan, & Tannock, 1999). Many have interpreted the late development of inhibitory processes as a reflection of the slow maturation of the prefrontal cortex (Bjorklund & Harnishfeger, 1990; Dempster, 1992). Booth et al. (2003) compared the neural activation patterns for adults and children aged 9 to 11 years to examine how controlled attention and inhibition develop, using fMRI. They found that there were large developmental differences, with children showing greater activation than adults in the fronto-striatal regions, including the middle cingulate, the medial frontal gyrus, medial aspects of the bilateral superior frontal gyrus, and the left caudate nucleus. In this case, greater activation reflects the fact that more resources were needed to perform the task in children than adults.

Controlled Attention in Individuals with ASD

A variety of measures, including the Stroop, Go/No-Go, and Stop Signal tasks, have been used to examine controlled attention in individuals with ASD. Results have varied across tasks and participant characteristics. Thus, we will review the data for each task separately.

Stroop Tasks

Two studies have used a traditional Stroop task with children and adolescents across a wide age range

(6–19 years) and reported no differences in inhibition in participants with ASD, compared to participants with typical development matched on reading ability (Eskes, Bryson, & McCormick, 1990; Ozonoff & Jensen, 1999). That is, both groups were affected to a similar degree by the word meaning, suggesting that persons with ASD have capabilities for inhibiting responses similar to those of persons with typical development. This intact inhibitory control has also been found in children with ASD who have comorbid intellectual disability. Specifically, Russell, Jarrold, and Hood (1999) used the day/night version of the Stroop task (Gerstadt, Hong, & Diamond, 1994), designed for younger children and with no reading prerequisite, in a sample of 10- to 18-year-old children with ASD who had verbal mental ages of 5 to 8 years old. Compared to a control group with mild intellectual impairments, participants with ASD showed no differences in Stroop task performance. Across studies, persons with ASD seem to show no reliable differences in inhibiting responses in Stroop tasks.

Stop-Signal Tasks

Ozonoff and Strayer (1997) compared 9- to 17-year-old high-functioning children with ASD to children and adolescents with typical development on a Stop-Signal task that involved categorizing words except when the stop-signal (a tone) occurred just prior to the presentation of a word. They found that participants with ASD responded similarly to the control participants on all aspects of this task.

Go/No-Go Tasks

In contrast to results with the Stroop Task and Stop-Signal Task, results with the Go/No-Go paradigm have been mixed, with some studies showing intact inhibition (Happé, Booth, Charlton, & Hughes, 2006; Raymaekers, Antrop, van der Meere, Wiersema, & Roeyers, 2007), and other studies showing impaired inhibition (Raymaekers, van der Meere, & Roeyers, 2004). For example, Happé and colleagues (2006) compared participants with ASD (mean age = 10.9 years), participants with ADHD, and participants with typical development on a Go/No-Go task in which pictures of airplanes and bombs were presented on the screen. Participants were instructed to press a key whenever an airplane was presented (70% of presented objects) but to not respond to images of a bomb

(30% of objects). They found that both younger and older participants with ASD were equally adept at selectively responding to airplanes and inhibiting responding to bombs as the participants with typical development. Furthermore, participants with ASD outperformed participants with ADHD.

In a similar study, Raymaekers et al. (2004) found that adults with high-functioning ASD showed intact inhibition skills when the presentation rate was relatively slow or moderate (one stimulus every 6 seconds or every 2 seconds). However, when the stimulus rate was increased to a stimulus every second, participants with ASD made nearly three times as many errors as participants with typical development. Interestingly, this result was not replicated in a study of 7- to 13-year-old children by Raymaekers et al. (2007). They found no differences between children with ASD children with typical development, even when stimuli appeared once every second or more frequently. Raymaekers et al. (2007) suggested that the differing pattern across studies may be due to differences in the development of these abilities between childhood and adulthood. In typically developing children, these inhibition abilities continue to develop and improve from childhood to adulthood. However, it was suggested that these abilities may not continue to develop from childhood to adulthood in persons with ASD. Certainly, longitudinal studies are needed to directly test this hypothesis.

Preparing to Overcome Prepotency (POP) Task

Solomon, Ozonoff, Cumming, and Carter (2008) asked 8- to 18-year-old participants with ASD to respond to the direction indicated by a target (an arrow). The target was preceded by a cue (a green or red square) that indicated whether to respond using the common, dominant response (indicate the direction in which the arrow is pointed) or a reverse mapping (indicate the opposite direction from which the arrow is pointed). Younger children with ASD (less than 12 years old) performed similarly to control participants. However, those participants older than 12 years of age performed worse than older control participants. This result replicates the pattern across studies observed by Raymaekers and colleagues (2004, 2007) of younger individuals with ASD showing more similar inhibition skills to age- and IQ-matched typically developing participants, but older individuals with ASD not showing as much continued improve-ment as typically developing older participants. These results suggest that the development of inhibition skills may stall in ASD such that less improvement is seen from childhood to adulthood than is seen in typical development. Future longitudinal studies are vital here to clarify this pattern.

Continuous Performance Test (CPT)

In addition to the tasks described above that empha-size inhibitory control, it is also important to examine attentional control as the ability to sustain attention on a task that otherwise may not be considered particularly interesting, or may become repetitive or boring. The primary task to measure sustained attention in this way is the Continuous Performance Test (CPT; Rosvold, Mirsky, Saranson, Branscome, & Beck, 1956). While there are many variations of this task, in a typical ver-sion, participants are simply asked to watch (or listen) for a rare event (e.g., an X appearing on a screen) and to press a button when that rare event occurs. Because the task can be somewhat long and the critical event is somewhat rare, participants must use attentional control to force themselves to continue to sustain their attention to the stream of incoming information. Several studies have used the CPT to examine sus-tained attention in persons with ASD. Pascualvaca, Fantie, Papageorgiou, and Mirsky (1998) compared 6- to 12-year-olds with ASD to mental-age-matched controls on three CPTs. Across all three measures, the ASD group showed similar performance to the control groups, suggesting that sustained attention is relatively intact in persons with ASD. Similar results have been seen in other studies with children with ASD (Casey, Gordon, Mannheim, & Rumsey, 1993; Garretson, Fein, & Waterhouse, 1990). Only two studies have found any significant differences in sustained attention in persons with ASD. One study manipulated the motivational conditions used to encourage participants to work hard on their CPT performance (Garretson et al., 1990). They used one condition in which a tan-gible motivator (either a pretzel or a penny) was given after every fifth target hit. The other condition used a social motivator (being told "Good work") after every fifth hit. Garretson and colleagues only found evi-dence for impaired sustained attention in the social motivation condition, suggesting that the ability to sustain attention itself is not impaired in ASD, but that social motivators are less effective in ASD.

All of these studies used child participants, and like the other studies of attentional control, found no impairments in controlled attention in children with ASD. It is important to examine whether adults with ASD show intact sustained-attention abilities in order to test whether all controlled attention abilities show some impairment in adults, or whether only those tasks that involve inhibition show such impairment. Only one study has examined the sustained-attention performance of adults with ASD. Goldstein, Johnson, and Minshew (2001) compared a large group of children and adults with ASD on a version of the CPT. Like others, they found no group-level differ-ences between ASD and control participants. Additionally, there was not a significant interaction between diagnostic group and age, indicating that the two groups were similar at all age groups. This result indicates that adults with ASD do not seem to show the same developmental plateau for sustained atten-tion as they show for aspects of controlled attention that involve inhibition. Future studies examining the differences between inhibitory attention and sustained attention in adults with ASD will be important in order to help us better understand where attentional development in adults with ASD may go awry.

Neuroimaging of Controlled Attention in ASD

Two published studies have examined patterns of neural activation during controlled attention tasks in adults with high-functioning ASD. Schmitz and colleagues (2006) found similar behavioral inhibition across participants with ASD and participants with typical development on three executive functioning tasks, including a Go/No-Go task and a spatial Stroop task. Despite identical behavioral responses, partici-pants with ASD showed *greater* neural activation in key areas associated with inhibitory control, including increased activation in the left middle/inferior frontal gyrus and the left orbitofrontal gyrus for the Go/No-Go task, and in the insula for the spatial Stroop task. They interpret these findings as likely indicative of the use of different inhibitory processes in persons with ASD. In particular, persons with ASD may use different cognitive strategies to inhibit responses than persons with typical development. Persons with ASD may rely more upon verbal, effortful strategies, which may cause more activation in the left frontal lobe than is seen in persons with typical development.

However, this result must be approached tentatively, because the one other fMRI study examining controlled inhibition found quite different results. Kana, Keller, Minshew, and Just (2007) compared performance on a simple Go/No-Go task and a 1-Back version of the Go/No-Go task. In the 1-Back task participants must remember the prior item and respond when the new item is different from the prior item (a "go" trial) but not respond to the new item if it repeats the prior item (a "no-go" trial). Kana and colleagues (2007) found *less* activation in a large number of areas, including the cingulate cortex, the calcarine, the right inferior frontal gyrus, and the insula (all areas typically involved in inhibition), in the participants with ASD, compared to participants with typical development. Kana and colleagues also found less connectivity between the anterior cingulate cortex (ACC) and the frontal-parietal circuitry in the group with ASD. It is difficult to know what to make of these conflicting results. One study showed a consistent pattern across several tasks of hyperactivation in the brain during inhibitory control tasks (Schmitz et al., 2006); the other study showed a pattern of hypoactivation during reasonably similar inhibitory control tasks (Kana et al., 2007). The only commonality is that both studies found similar behavioral inhibition in ASD and typical groups. It is a somewhat unsatisfying conclusion that persons with ASD may achieve similar controlled attentional abilities by using different brain regions, but we do not really know which different brain areas underlie these differences. Certainly future studies need to seek to replicate and clarify these results.

Summary

A wide variety of tasks have been used to examine whether deficits in controlled attention are commonly seen in ASD. Studies have tested participants, who ranged in age from 6 years to adulthood and had a wide range of intellectual abilities. Overall, there does not seem to be a global impairment in controlled attention. The vast majority of studies have found that most persons with ASD have similar controlled attention capabilities as their age- and IQ-matched typically developing peers. However, when impairments are seen, they are most likely to be found in high-functioning adults with ASD, particularly for tasks involving inhibitory control. This is a somewhat paradoxical result. When ASD is discussed as a

development disorder, it is often suggested that early impairments lead to later difficulties. In this particular case, the developmental trajectory of controlled-attention abilities seems relatively normal through early adolescence, at which point persons with ASD may "fall off" the typical developmental trajectory. Further research is certainly needed to confirm this developmental pattern and to more fully investigate the neural underpinnings of this difficulty.

WORKING MEMORY

It has long been acknowledged that the ability to attend to information is closely related to the ability to hold that information in one's most immediate thoughts. Thus, one cannot accurately examine attention without also examining its working memory counterpart. Working memory is the system that underlies our ability to actively maintain and manipulate information on a moment-to-moment basis. According to Baddeley's (2003) model, working memory is composed of four subsystems: the phonological loop for auditory or verbally-rehearsed information, the visuospatial sketchpad for visual information, the episodic buffer to integrate information and allow access to conscious awareness, and the central executive for the direction of attention and the manipulation of information provided by the other three subsystems.

Measuring Working Memory

Many tasks have been employed in the measurement of working memory. These tasks can broadly be classified as tasks that require *maintenance* of information in working memory and tasks that require the *manipulation* of information in working memory. Maintenance tasks typically require memory for strings of information and include forward verbal digit span tasks (e.g., present in the Wechsler Intelligence Scales for Children; WISC-IV: Wechsler, 2003), forward spatial span tasks (e.g., present in the Cambridge Neuropsychological Testing Automated Battery; CANTAB), n-back tests in which participants are asked to respond if a target appeared previously (see Figure 8-3), the spatial working memory test (present in the CANTAB), and the Oculomotor Delayed Response (ODR) task. Manipulation tasks are more complex and require changing information while it is

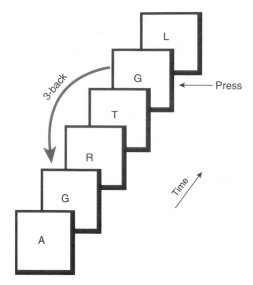

Figure 8-3 Working Memory Paradigm: N-Back Task.

stored in memory (e.g., listening to a string of letters, rearranging them, and then repeating them in reverse order). Common manipulation tasks include letter-number sequencing (e.g., WISC-IV), backward verbal digit span (e.g., WISC-IV), backward spatial span, and spatial mental rotation.

The distinction between maintenance versus manipulation tasks can broadly separate working memory tasks in terms of complexity. However, even within these groups, it is difficult to determine the relative complexity of one task compared to another. Additionally, it is unclear if poorer performance on more complex working memory tasks indicates lower working memory capacity, or greater difficulty recruiting and utilizing additional cognitive processes above and beyond working memory. Indeed, working memory has been found to be highly correlated with other cognitive processes, such as processing speed (Schmiedek, Oberauer, Wilhelm, Süß, & Wittmann, 2007), attentional control (Fukuda & Vogel, 2009; Kane & Engle, 2003), and reasoning ability (Krumm et al., 2009). Thus, what may appear to be an impairment in working memory on a particular task may actually be due to an impairment in a related cognitive domain. For persons with ASD, there may be additional confounding cognitive processes at work. For example, persons with ASD often demonstrate language production difficulty, verbal imitation difficulty, and motor difficulty. Most phonological working-memory tasks require verbalization, and even

a degree of verbal imitation, by the participant. Similarly, most spatial working-memory tasks require motor responses. Because of language production and motor difficulties, persons with ASD may appear to have poor verbal and spatial working-memory ability, when in fact they are limited not in working memory, but in their ability to express their knowledge on tests of working memory.

Neural Correlates of Working Memory

Consistent with Baddeley's (2003) model, neuroimaging studies have found distinct neural activation patterns with phonological and spatial information in working memory tasks. Specifically, phonological information in working memory typically activates Broca's area, the left supplementary motor area, and the pre-motor cortex (Smith & Jonides, 1999), whereas spatial information in working memory typically activates the right pre-motor cortex (Smith & Jonides, 1999), the inferior parietal cortex, the supplementary motor area, and the frontal eye fields (Sweeney et al.,1996). Thus, phonological working memory appears to heavily rely on speech perception and speech production regions of the brain, and spatial working memory appears to heavily rely on spatial-analysis and motor regions of the brain. These results suggest that the neural correlates of working memory heavily depend on what type of information is being held in memory. Furthermore, these results indicate substantial overlap between working memory, the perception of stimuli, and the reaction to stimuli (i.e., verbal or motor responses), suggesting that working memory performance likely depends on the degree to which information is attended to and perceived by the individual.

In addition to the type of information being processed, the neural correlates of working memory also appear to depend on how the information is preserved in working memory. For example, information that requires maintenance (e.g., trying to remember a phone number in working memory) appears to have neural correlates that are distinct from information that requires manipulation (e.g., doing math problems without a pen or pencil). Specifically, in maintenance working-memory tasks, activation is typically seen in the ventral prefrontal cortex (VPFC), whereas in manipulation working-memory tasks, activation is typically seen in the mid-dorsolateral prefrontal cortex (m-DLPFC; Owen, 1997, 2000). Thus, the neural organization of working memory appears to be dictated by both the type of information, and how this information is processed (that is, whether it is passively stored or actively manipulated).

Typical Development of Working Memory

Because working memory appears to require the integration of many diverse regions of the brain, understanding the development of these diverse regions, and the development of the connections between these regions, is extremely important. Working memory appears to have a prolonged period of development, with the greatest leaps in working-memory performance occurring in mid-to-late adolescence (Hale, Bronik, & Fry, 1997; Luciana, Conklin, Hooper, & Yarger, 2005; Luciana & Nelson, 2002; Luna, Garver, Urban, Lazar, & Sweeney, 2004). The timing of this relatively late developmental trajectory also appears to depend on whether the information is merely maintained or manipulated. For example, Conklin, Luciana, Hooper, and Yarger (2007) found that verbal and spatial backward-span tasks that require both manipulation and maintenance continued to develop and improve later into adolescence (16 to17 years of age) than the forward span counterpart that required only maintenance (13 to 15 years of age for phonological items; 11 to 12 years of age for spatial items). This result suggests that the ability to passively maintain information in working memory develops earlier than the ability to actively manipulate information. In line with this prediction, adults have demonstrated increased proficiency in complex, manipulation-based working memory tasks compared to children (Luciana et al., 2005). The development of working memory mirrors the development of the frontal lobes, which have been suggested to be one of the last parts of the brain to be fully myelinated (Sowell et al., 2003).

Working Memory in Individuals with ASD

Because the developmental trajectory of working memory extends into mid-adolescence, it is extremely challenging to compare the results of studies that have used different age groups. Furthermore, whether a study matches the ASD and typically developing groups on chronological age or mental age might determine the outcome of the study (Russo et al., 2007).

Therefore, we believe it is best to view the literature through a developmental lens while also taking into account task complexity (maintenance or manipulation tasks) and type of stimuli (phonological or spatial).

Maintenance Working-Memory Tasks

In preschool-age children with ASD, studies have primarily used maintenance working-memory tasks, asking participants to immediately recall digits, words, or stories. Studies using phonological maintenance tasks typically have found evidence of a working-memory impairment in preschoolers with ASD, such that when the to-be-retained information increases in complexity, the immediate recall for the information appears more impaired (Fein et al., 1996; Gabig, 2008). In contrast, Russell, Jarrold, and Henry (1996) found no phonological working-memory performance impairment in school-age children with ASD, compared to children with developmental delays and children with typical development. However, in adolescents evidence for a phonological working-memory impairment reemerges. Bennetto, Pennington, and Rogers (1996) found impaired phonological working memory on a maintenance counting and sentence-span task in persons with ASD. Subsequently, there is no clear developmental trend when we examine phonological maintenance working-memory in isolation. The discrepancy between findings across studies may be due to differences in task complexity, or due to developmental maturation. These studies reaffirm the importance of taking task complexity into account when examining working memory.

Spatial maintenance working-memory tasks have been administered to persons with ASD across the life span. In preschoolers, Griffith, Pennington, Wehner, and Rogers (1999) found no difference between preschoolers with ASD and developmentally delayed children on a battery of spatial working memory tasks. Similarly, in school-age children no spatial working memory differences emerged in one-back, two-back, spatial memory, or box search tasks (Ozonoff & Strayer, 2001) or in a Morris water maze or CANTAB spatial working memory task (Edgin & Pennington, 2005). Consequently, there does not appear to be a spatial maintenance working- memory impairment in children with ASD. However, there is a growing body of literature suggesting that spatial maintenance working memory impairments seem to emerge during adolescence and adulthood. For example, poorer spatial working memory performance in this age group have been found on the CANTAB spatial working memory task (Steele, Minshew, Luna, & Sweeney, 2007) and on Occulomotor Delayed Response (ODR) tasks (Goldberg et al., 2002; Luna, Doll, Hegedus, Minshew, & Sweeney, 2007; Luna et al., 2002; Minshew, Luna, & Sweeney, 1999; Takarae, Minshew, Luna, & Sweeney, 2004).

To directly address whether individuals with ASD are more likely to exhibit spatial working memory impairments with age, Luna and colleagues (2007) used a cross-sectional design to examine spatial working memory in the ODR task. Differing developmental trends in ODR performance between the diagnostic groups were found. Specifically, during late adolescence and adulthood, participants with typical development continued to show improvements in spatial working memory, whereas participants with ASD did not show this continued improvement. These results suggest that a spatial working memory impairment in persons with ASD may become more pronounced during adolescence and adulthood.

In addition to age, the complexity of the spatial task may influence whether a spatial working memory impairment is detected or not. In a battery of verbal and spatial working memory tasks, Minshew and Goldstein (2001) found that on most basic tests of working memory, adolescents and adults with ASD performed similarly to participants with typical development. However, when task difficulty and memory load increased, participants with ASD performed more poorly. These results suggest that in both phonological and spatial maintenance tasks, the complexity of the to-be-remembered information may have an especially large influence on the working memory capabilities of persons with ASD.

Manipulation Working Memory Tasks

Manipulation working memory tasks are frequently incorporated into standardized intellectual assessments (e.g., the Digits Backwards task on the WISC-IV). Oftentimes, these tasks measure both maintenance and manipulation working memory. For example, the WISC-IV digit span subtest includes both forward digit span and backward digit span items. Nevertheless, standardized tests such as the WISC-IV have relatively more manipulation working memory items than maintenance items suggesting that manipulation

working memory may contribute to overall working memory index scores on these subtests. School-age children with ASD have typically shown poorer working memory on these standardized tests. For example, children with ASD had lower working memory index scores (and processing speed index scores) on the WISC-IV, compared to their scores on the other indices (Mayes & Calhoun, 2008). Similarly, children with ASD with higher IQs had working memory scores below their full-scale IQ scores in digit span and arithmetic subtests of the WISC-III and in the memory for sentences subtest of the Stanford-Binet IV (Mayes & Calhoun, 2003). Thus, there is some evidence for phonological manipulation working memory impairments in preschoolers and school-age children with ASD.

Direct Comparison of Maintenance and Manipulation Working Memory

Empirical tests using both maintenance and manipulation working memory tasks have generally found preserved working memory performance in the maintenance tasks, but impaired working memory performance in at least some of the manipulation tasks. For example, Joseph, McGrath, and Tager-Flusberg (2005) found no difference in performance between children with ASD and age- and IQ-matched peers with typical development on maintenance working memory tasks, including word span forward and block span forward tasks. However, on manipulation working memory tasks, Joseph and colleagues found equivalent performance in the word span backward task but not in the block span backward task, in which the children with ASD performed more poorly than children with typical development. This pattern of results suggests maintenance working memory may be intact in this group, but manipulation working memory may be somewhat impaired. Similarly, Williams, Goldstein, and Minshew (2006) assessed phonological and spatial working memory in high-functioning children with ASD (average age 11.36) and age-matched controls, and they did not find significantly different performances in maintenance working memory tasks, such as a three-word short term memory task, or a maze task. However, they did find poorer performance in the ASD group in more complex working memory tasks that required the integration of information (suggestive of a manipulation task). Taken together, these results suggest that there is evidence of intact maintenance working memory in school-age children with ASD. However, with the increased need for manipulation of information in working memory, school-age children with ASD may be more likely to perform poorly. This result is consistent with maintenance working memory developing earlier than manipulation working memory (Luciana et al., 2005).

Neuroimaging of Working Memory in ASD

Four studies have examined working memory in adults with ASD using fMRI technology (Koshino et al., 2005, 2008; Luna et al., 2002; Silk et al., 2006). All four studies have found similar behavioral performance across individuals with ASD and comparison individuals. However, all of these studies have found group differences in the neurological patterns of activation.

In terms of the neuroimaging of phonological maintenance working memory, two studies using different versions of n-back tasks have been conducted. Koshino et al. (2005) reported that participants with ASD showed less activation in the left dorsolateral prefrontal cortex (DLPFC), inferior frontal gyrus, and posterior precentral sulcus, suggesting that participants with ASD might be rehearsing the stimuli using the visuospatial sketchpad instead of the phonological loop. Additionally, the participants with ASD exhibited more activation in the right inferior parietal region compared to the left. As mentioned previously, the inferior parietal regions are thought to mediate the orienting of attention to allow for the verbal rehearsal of the information (Jonides et al., 1998; Owen, McMillan, Laird, & Bullmore, 2005). Thus, this result suggests possible differences in input attention during the working memory task. In the second n-back study, Koshino et al. (2008) used an n-back task with facial stimuli. Similar to their previous n-back findings, they found less activation in the left inferior frontal gyrus in the group with ASD and less synchronization between activated brain regions suggesting less reliance on verbal rehearsal in the phonological loop in the participants with ASD.

To examine the neural correlates of spatial manipulation working memory, Silk and colleagues (2006) used a mental rotation task. They found less activation in the DLPFC, ACC, and caudate nucleus in the participants with ASD, compared to participants with typical development. Similarly, on a spatial memory task, Luna et al. (2002) found that the participants with ASD had less activation than controls in the posterior ACC and DLPFC.

In sum, despite the different types of working memory tasks, there appears to be converging evidence that there are differing patterns of activation in the DLPFC and ACC in persons with ASD during working memory tasks. In some of the studies there was more activation in the DLPFC, whereas in others, there was less, compared to participants with typical development. Additionally, Koshino et al. (2005) found the opposite pattern of hemispheric DLPFC activation in participants with ASD, compared to participants with typical development. Typically, the DLPFC is one of the last brain regions to develop, and synaptic pruning in this area continues into late adolescence (15–20 years of age; Sowell et al., 2003). Therefore, differences in the DLPFC might underlie the age-related behavioral findings in persons with ASD. Furthermore, the DLPFC is implicated in controlled attention and top-down attention orienting (Rees, Frackowiak, & Frith, 1997). This suggests that the controlled attention may also have a distinct developmental trajectory in this population.

These results suggest that persons with ASD may use different working memory strategies that behaviorally lead to similar performance (O'Hearn, Asato, Ordaz, & Luna, 2008). Another suggestion is that the working memory tasks used in these neuroimaging studies were slightly less complex than previous working memory tasks used (i.e., the ODR), which possibly could have led to the similar behavioral results but different patterns of neural activation.

Summary

In examining working memory in ASD via a developmental lens, the evidence for a global working memory impairment is still inconsistent. Nevertheless, some interesting patterns of working memory ability do emerge. In general, persons with ASD appear to have more difficulty with working memory when the stimuli are complex, when the task requires manipulation instead of maintenance, and when the individual is an adolescent or adult. Furthermore, the literature suggests that the developmental trajectory for working memory performance in people with ASD is different in that it does not continue at the same rate into adulthood (Luna et al., 2007). Neuroimaging studies suggest that this developmental difference may stem from neuroanatomical differences in regions such as the DLPFC and ACC that have shown differing patterns of activation during working memory tasks in persons with ASD. Future studies that examine working memory should take a longitudinal approach in examining working memory development in persons with ASD across the life span. This approach would benefit from structural brain imaging that could speak to the white matter growth and pruning in areas such as the ACC and DLPFC across the life span of persons with ASD.

CONCLUSIONS AND CLINICAL IMPLICATIONS

This review provides converging evidence that individuals with ASD across the life span have impairments in the relatively automatic allocation of attention that occurs without conscious thought. This can be seen in their difficulty reorienting their attention to cues in the environment, especially to sudden movement or the appearance of objects in the periphery, and in their difficulty with changing the size of their spotlight of attention, whether from a narrow-to-wide or wide-to-narrow focus. These difficulties seem to be especially present when attention must be allocated swiftly, without time for more controlled decision making. This type of automatic attention allocation involves a complex network of brain regions, with the temporo-parietal junction being seen as especially important for both attentional orienting and changing the spotlight of attention.

Generally, there are fewer impairments in controlled attention, including inhibition and sustained attention. However, where there are differences, the differences are typically larger in adults than children with ASD. This finding has led researchers to suggest that development of these abilities may become stalled or plateau in individuals with ASD. This is not a regression, but rather a lack of continued development into adolescence and adulthood. This pattern has also been observed in the research in working memory. Research in both controlled attention and working memory implicates similar brain areas as functioning differently in persons with ASD including the PFC, the ACC, and the basal ganglia. The PFC is considered especially important for decision-making and problem-solving. If there is a plateau or delay in development of the PFC in persons with ASD,

difficulties with decision-making and problem-solving ought to also be more noticeable in adults with ASD, especially when the problems and the decisions that need to be made concerning them are complex (see Minshew and Goldstein, 1998 and Minshew, Goldstein, and Siegel, 1997).

The pattern of strengths and weaknesses in attention that have been described throughout this chapter have significant implications for our understanding and treatment of ASD. Input- attention difficulties most likely develop very early. Indeed, within the first few months of life, infants are typically able to quickly and flexibly disengage and shift their attention, and show a preference for using a wide spotlight of attention. Impairments in these early developing attentional mechanisms are likely to have a cascading effect on individuals with ASD such that they fail to learn about important information in the environment. Impaired input attention suggests that individuals with ASD are less likely to detect changes in their environment and are less likely to shift their attention or adjust the size of the attention spotlight when a change is detected. If they do not detect a change, or simply cannot shift their attention when change is detected, a great deal of information is simply "missed." This is particularly true in settings that involve quickly presented, peripheral information. Certainly, social gatherings require this type of attention allocation, and are likely to be particularly difficult for individuals with ASD. Other nonsocial activities such as driving also require this skill, as being able to simultaneously focus on the road ahead and detect abrupt changes in the environment, including the periphery are required. Indeed, many individuals with ASD with average or above average intelligence seem to realize that this kind of situation is difficult for them and often avoid social gatherings or learning to drive, expressing fear and self-doubt about their ability to manage all of the unexpected events that occur in these situations.

Symptomatology

Given the early developing input-attention impairments in ASD, it is possible that some of the "core" symptoms of ASD may be a result of inefficient attention allocation. Indeed, the ability to orient one's attention by disengaging and shifting it has been linked to the Theory of Mind (i.e., the ability to understand that others have a different perspective from one's own) and joint attention impairments that are present in ASD (e.g., Dawson et al., 2004; Leekam & Moore, 2001). Dawson et al. (2004) proposed that there is a specific impairment in social orienting. They reported that 3- to 4-year-old children with ASD demonstrated less social orienting (e.g., response to name being called, response to the experimenter snapping his or her fingers, or response to the experimenter humming) compared to mental-age-matched children with developmental delay and children with typical development. It is unclear whether this impairment in social orienting is specific to social stimuli, or linked to overall impairments in input attention that have been discussed in this chapter. Dawson and colleagues (Dawson et al., 2004; Dawson, Meltzoff, Osterling, Rinaldi, & Brown, 1998) found that the orienting of attention to nonsocial stimuli was also impaired in young children with ASD. Thus, it may be that individuals with ASD have a general impairment in their ability to orient attention to both social and nonsocial stimuli. However, there is also evidence that social orienting is even more impaired than nonsocial orienting. For example, Goldberg and colleagues (2008) reported that 8- to 13-year-old children were impaired on an endogenous cueing task when eyes instead of an arrow were used as a central cue. While the majority of research using long (e.g., 700 ms) endogenous cues shows intact orienting, this social cue was difficult for children with ASD to process. Taken together, this review suggests that social orienting may be linked to overall input attention impairments, although there is something "special" about social information that makes it even more difficult to process than nonsocial information. Perhaps the dynamic nature of social information is particularly impacted by the "sticky" attention in ASD that makes it difficult to quickly adjust one's attentional focus.

Intervention

Clinically, this body of research supports interventions geared toward focusing attention on the most relevant (e.g., pivotal) information in the environment. This is particularly true for very young children with ASD, whose atypical attentional focus is thought to produce an ever-expanding impairment in social understanding. For example, Klin and colleagues (Klin, Jones, Schultz, Volkmar, & Cohen, 2002) have found that young children with ASD prefer to attend to another person's mouth instead of their eyes, which likely

leads to later difficulty understanding emotions that are typically "read" in the eyes. Thus, interventions such as Pivotal Response Therapy (Koegel, Koegel, & McNerney, 2001), Discrete Trial Instruction (Eikeseth, Smith, Jahr, & Eldevik, 2007; Lovaas, 2003), Early Start Denver Model (Dawson et al., 2009), and TEACCH (Mesibov, Shea, & Schopler, 2004), that focus attention on the most important aspects of the environment while minimizing distractions, are likely to be the most effective at treating input attention impairments.

Findings of relatively intact controlled attention coupled with impaired input attention offer some intriguing ideas for developing interventions. For older individuals with ASD, a compensation approach, in which more controlled "effortful" attention mechanisms are taught in order to compensate for impaired automatic attention, may be successful. Indeed, many of the most commonly used social skills interventions, including social stories (Gray, 2000) and social scripts, are designed to teach specific rules for managing social situations, including how to recognize the important aspects of the situation that need to be attended (see Klinger & Williams, 2009 for a review). In our clinical work with adults, we often use controlled attention techniques to explicitly teach individuals with ASD how to both narrow and widen their attentional spotlight. For example, when teaching a college student with ASD how to read a textbook, we typically instruct the student to identify both specific facts from the chapter and also big-picture information that is in the chapter (see Table 8-1). However, this compensation approach cannot teach quick, flexible attention allocation. Thus, this type of compensation often takes a greater amount of time (e.g., college students with ASD will likely need to study many more hours than other students who are able to adjust their attentional spotlight more automatically), and does not guarantee success in situations that do not allow for extra time to allocate attention (e.g., driving or timed test-taking).

The research suggesting that controlled attention, specifically complex inhibition, becomes progressively more impaired in adults with ASD has significant implications. The data do not suggest a worsening, but rather a plateau in inhibition skills, where they do not improve as much from adolescence to adulthood as individuals with typical development. This plateau is certainly seen in the poor decision-making skills that clinicians and family members often report in

Table 8-1 Tips for Narrowing and Broadening the Attention Spotlight During Reading Two Different Ways to Read the Same Text

Narrow *Learning the Details*	Big *Learning how the Details Fit Together (The BIG Picture)*
Read the title and highlight title words in each chapter.	Write a big picture question that fits the title.
Read and highlight key terms in the chapter.	Read the discussion questions before reading the chapter.
Type a list of key terms and their definitions. For each term, write two narrow facts.	Go back to your key terms. For each term, write two big picture facts.
Create some flash cards	Write a summary note at the end of each chapter.

adults with ASD. Oftentimes, these poor decisions are due to a failure to inhibit inappropriate or disadvantageous behaviors, particularly in situations that require quite a bit of effortful control (e.g., some repetitive behaviors or spending one's paycheck on special interests, such as video games or magazines, rather than on necessities, such as food and rent). Similarly, adults with ASD often demonstrate impaired working memory skills that are important for daily living (e.g., remembering phone numbers, or completing mathematical calculations, including making change). There is a paucity of intervention research directed toward identifying effective approaches to teaching independent living, academic, and employment skills to adults with ASD. The most successful approaches are likely to take into account the literature on controlled attention in ASD.

Assessment

The attention literature may partially explain the profile of strengths and weaknesses that individuals with ASD display on standardized intellectual assessments (see Klinger, O'Kelley, & Mussey, 2009 for a review). Indeed, children and adolescents with ASD often show their strongest performance on tasks requiring a narrow spotlight of attention, including the WISC-IV Block Design (Lincoln, Hanzel, & Quirmbach, 2007). In contrast, even high-functioning individuals with ASD tend to struggle on subtests examining processing speed and manipulation working memory (Wechsler, 2003). Attention and working memory clearly influence many different aspects of standardized assessment. Thus, an overall IQ score may be an average of widely discrepant scores, and may not meaningfully describe a child's true ability. Klin, Saulnier, Tsatsanis, and Volkmar (2005) noted

that it is critical for the evaluator to have knowledge of the cognitive profiles that occur in ASD, in order to avoid erroneous conclusions by focusing on islets of strengths when interpreting testing results.

FINAL NOTE

Attention and working memory serve as the gateway between our external environment and our internal selves, determining what information is processed and what information is not. From this review, it appears that there are atypicalities in input attention (orienting and spotlight), controlled attention (inhibition and sustained), and working memory in persons with ASD. These atypicalities sometimes lead to enhanced performance in locating and identifying local elements, and at other times they lead to difficulties in social processing, learning, and traditional academic study. At the beginning of this chapter, we quoted Catherine Maurice's description of her young daughter, who was tuned into the most delicate of dust and carpet particles, but seemingly unaware of the surrounding environment. Hopefully, future research examining attention in persons with ASD will be able to find ways for people like Maurice's daughter to utilize their attentional strengths to their benefit, and to minimize their attentional weaknesses.

References

Atkinson, J., Hood, B., Wattam-Bell, J., & Braddick, O. (1992). Changes in infants' ability to switch visual attention in the first three months of life. *Perception*, 21(5), 643–653.

Baddeley, A. (2003). Working memory: Looking back and looking forward. *Nature Reviews Neuroscience*, 4(10), 829–839.

Becker, M., Isaac, W., & Hynd, G. (1987). Neuropsychological development of nonverbal behaviors attributed to "frontal lobe" functioning. *Developmental Neuropsychology*, 3(3-4), 275–298.

Belmonte, M., & Yurgelun-Todd, D. (2003). Functional anatomy of impaired selective attention and compensatory processing in autism. *Cognitive Brain Research*, 17(3), 651–664.

Bennetto, L., Pennington, B. F., & Rogers, S. J. (1996). Intact and impaired memory functions in autism. *Child Development*, 67(4), 1816–1835.

Bjorklund, D., & Harnishfeger, K. (1990). The resources construct in cognitive development: Diverse sources of evidence and a theory of inefficient inhibition. *Developmental Review*, 10(1), 48–71.

Booth, J. R., Burman, D. D., Meyer, J. R., Lei, Z., Trommer, B. L., Davenport, N. D., ... Mesulam, M. M. (2003). Neural development of selective attention and response inhibition. *Neuroimage*, 20, 737–751.

Braver, T., Barch, D., Gray, J., Molfese, D., & Snyder, A. (2001). Anterior cingulate cortex and response conflict: Effects of frequency, inhibition and errors. *Cerebral Cortex*, 11(9), 825–836.

Burack, J. (1994). Selective attention deficits in persons with autism: Preliminary evidence of an inefficient attentional lens. *Journal of Abnormal Psychology*, 103(3), 535–543.

Burack, J., Joseph, S., Russo, N., Shore, D., Porporino, M., & Enns, J. (2009). Change detection in naturalistic pictures among children with autism. *Journal of Autism and Developmental Disorders*, 39(3), 471–479.

Casey, B. (2001). Disruption of inhibitory control in developmental disorders: A mechanistic model of implicated frontostriatal circuitry. In J. L. McClelland (Ed.), *Mechanisms of cognitive development: Behavioral and neural perspectives* (pp. 327–349). Mahwah, NJ: Lawrence Erlbaum Associates Publishers.

Casey, B. J., Gordon, C. T., Mannheim, G. B., & Rumsey, J. M. (1993). Dysfunctional attention in autistic savants. *Journal of Clinical and Experimental Neuropsychology*, 15, 933–946.

Cassia, V., Simion, F., Milani, I., & Umiltà, C. (2002). Dominance of global visual properties at birth. *Journal of Experimental Psychology: General*, 131(3), 398–411.

Conklin, H. M., Luciana, M., Hooper, C. J., & Yarger, R. S. (2007). Working memory performance in typically developing children and adolescents: Behavioral evidence of protracted frontal lobe development. *Developmental Neuropsychology*, 31(1), 103–128.

Courchesne, R., Townsend, J., Akshoomoff, N. A., Yeung-Courchesne, R., Press, G., Murakami, J., ... Lau, L. (1994). A new finding: Impairment in shifting attention in autistic and cerebellar patients. In S. H. Browman & J. Graffman (Eds.), *Atypical cognitive deficits in developmental disorders: Implications for brain function* (pp. 101–137). Hillsdale, NJ: Erlbaum.

Dawson, G., Meltzoff, A. N., Osterling, J., Rinaldi, J., & Brown, E. (1998). Children with autism fail to orient to naturally occurring social stimuli. *Journal of Autism and Developmental Disorders*, 28, 479–485.

Dawson, G., Rogers, S., Munson, J., Smith, M., Winter, J., Greenson, J., ... Varley, J. (2009). Randomized, controlled trial of an intervention for toddlers with autism: The Early Start Denver Model. *Pediatrics*, 125, 17–23.

Dawson, G., Toth, K., Abbott, R., Osterling, J., Munson, J., Estes, A., & Liaw, J. (2004). Early social attention impairments in autism: Social orienting, joint attention, and attention to distress. *Developmental Psychology*, 40, 271–283.

Deiber, M., Honda, M., Ibañez, V., Sadato, N., & Hallett, M. (1999). Mesial motor areas in self-initiated versus externally triggered movements examined with fMRI: Effect of movement type and rate. *Journal of Neurophysiology*, 81(6), 3065–3077.

Dempster, F. (1992). The rise and fall of the inhibitory mechanism: Toward a unified theory of cognitive development and aging. *Developmental Review*, 12(1), 45–75.

Edgin, J. O., & Pennington, B. F. (2005). Spatial cognition in autism spectrum disorders: Superior, impaired, or just intact? *Journal of Autism and Developmental Disorders*, 35(6), 729–745.

Eikeseth, S., Smith, T., Jahr, E., & Eldevik, S. (2007). Outcome for children with autism who began intensive behavioral treatment between ages 4 and 7: A comparison controlled study. *Behavior Modification*, 31, 264–278.

Enns, J., & Brodeur, D. (1989). A developmental study of covert orienting to peripheral visual cues. *Journal of Experimental Child Psychology*, 48(2), 171–189.

Eskes, G. A., Bryson, S. E., & McCormick, T. (1990). Comprehension of concrete and abstract words in autistic children. *Journal of Autism and Developmental Disorders*, 20, 61–73.

Fein, D., Dunn, M. A., Allen, D. M., Aram, R., Hall, N., Morris, R., & Wilson, B. C. (1996). Neuropsychological and language findings. In I. Rapin (Ed.), *Preschool children with inadequate communication: Developmental language disorder, autism, low IQ* (pp. 123–154). London: MacKeith Press.

Fletcher-Watson, S., Leekam, S., Findlay, J., & Stanton, E. (2008). Brief report: Young adults with autism spectrum disorder show normal attention to eye-gaze information—Evidence from a new change blindness paradigm. *Journal of Autism and Developmental Disorders*, 38(9), 1785–1790.

Fletcher-Watson, S., Leekam, S. R., Turner, M. A., & Moxon, L. (2006). Do people with autistic spectrum disorder show normal selection for attention?

Evidence from change blindness. *British Journal of Psychology*, 97, 537–554.

Frith, U., (1989). *Autism: Explaining the Enigma*. Oxford: Blackwell.

Frith, U., & Happe´, F. (1994). Autism: Beyond "'theory of mind.'" *Cognition*, 50, 115–132.

Fukuda, K., & Vogel, E. (2009). Human variation in overriding attentional capture. *The Journal of Neuroscience*, 29(27), 8726–8733.

Gabig, C. S. (2008). Verbal working memory and story retelling in school-age children with autism. *Language, Speech, and Hearing Services in Schools*, 39, 498–511.

Garretson, H. B., Fein, D., & Waterhouse, L. (1990). Sustained attention in children with autism. *Journal of Autism and Developmental Disorders*, 20, 101–114.

Gerstadt, C., Hong, Y., & Diamond, A. (1994). The relationship between cognition and action: Performance of children 3 1/2-7 years old on a Stroop-like day-night test. *Cognition*, 53(2), 129–153.

Goldberg, M. C., Lasker, A. G., Zee, D. S., Garth, E., Tien, A., & Landa, R. J. (2002). Deficits in the initiation of eye movements in the absence of a visual target in adolescents with high functioning autism. *Neuropsychologia*, 40, 2039–2049.

Goldberg, M., Mostow, A., Vecera, S., Larson, J., Mostofsky, S., Mahone, E., & Denckla, M. B. (2008). Evidence for impairments in using static line drawings of eye gaze cues to orient visual-spatial attention in children with high functioning autism. *Journal of Autism and Developmental Disorders*, 38, 1405–1413.

Goldstein, G., Johnson, C. R., & Minshew, N. J. (2001). Attentional processes in autism. *Journal of Autism and Developmental Disorders*, 31, 433–440.

Gray, C. (2000). *The new social stories book*. Texas: Future Horizons.

Greenaway, R., & Plaisted, K. (2005). Top-down attentional modulation in autistic spectrum disorders is stimulus-specific. *Psychological Science*, 16(12), 987–993.

Griffith, E., Pennington, B., Wehner, E., & Rogers, S. (1999). Executive functions in young children with autism. *Child Development*, 70(4), 817–832.

Haist, F., Adamo, M., Westerfield, M., Courchesne, E., & Townsend, J. (2005). The functional neuroanatomy of spatial attention in autism spectrum disorder. *Developmental Neuropsychology*, 27(3), 425–458.

Han, S., Jiang, Y., & Gu, H. (2004). Neural substrates differentiating global/local processing of bilateral visual inputs. *Human Brain Mapping*, 22(4), 321–328.

Hale, S., Bronik, M. D., & Fry, A. F. (1997). Verbal and spatial working memory in school-age children: Developmental differences in susceptibility to interference. *Developmental Psychology*, 33, 364–371.

Happé, F. (1997). Central coherence and theory of mind in autism: Reading homographs in context.

British Journal of Developmental Psychology, 15 (Pt 1), 1–12.

Happé, F., Booth, R., Charlton, R., & Hughes, C. (2006). Executive function deficits in autism spectrum disorders and attention-deficit/hyperactivity disorder: Examining profiles across domains and ages. *Brain and Cognition*, 61(1), 25–39.

Happé, F., & Frith, U. (2006). The weak coherence account: Detail-focused cognitive style in autism spectrum disorders. *Journal of Autism and Developmental Disorders*, 36(1), 5–25.

Hood, B. (1995). Shifts of visual attention in the human infant: A neuroscientific approach. In C. Rover-Collier & L. Lipsett (Eds.), *Advances in infancy research* (pp. 63–216). Norwood, NJ: Ablex.

Iarocci, G., & Burack, J. A. (2004). Intact covert orienting to peripheral cues among children with autism. *Journal of Autism and Developmental Disorders*, 34, 257–264.

Johnson, M., Posner, M., & Rothbart, M. (1994). Facilitation of saccades toward a covertly attended location in early infancy. *Psychological Science*, 5(2), 90–93.

Jolliffe, T., & Baron-Cohen, S. (1999). A test of central coherence theory: Linguistic processing in high-functioning adults with autism or Asperger syndrome: Is local coherence impaired? *Cognition*, 71(2), 149–185.

Jonides, J., Schumacher, E. H., Smith, E. E., Koeppe, R. A., Awh, E., Reuter-Lorenz, P. A., ... Willis, C. R. (1998). The role of parietal cortex in verbal working memory. *Journal of Neuroscience*, 18(13), 5026–5034.

Joseph, R. M., McGrath, L. M., & Tager-Flusberg, H. (2005). Executive dysfunction and its relation to language ability in verbal school-age children with autism. *Developmental Neuropsychology*, 27, 361–378.

Kana, R., Keller, T., Minshew, N., & Just, M. (2007). Inhibitory control in high-functioning autism: Decreased activation and underconnectivity in inhibition networks. *Biological Psychiatry*, 62(3), 198–206.

Kane, M., & Engle, R. (2003). Working-memory capacity and the control of attention: The contributions of goal neglect, response competition, and task set to Stroop interference. *Journal of Experimental Psychology: General*, 132(1), 47–70.

Kawashima, R., Satoh, K., Itoh, H., Ono, S., Furumoto, S., Gotoh, R., ... Fukuda, H. (1996). Functional anatomy of GO/NO-GO discrimination and response selection—a PET study in man. *Brain Research*, 728(1), 79–89.

Klin, A., Jones, W., Schultz, R., Volkmar, F., & Cohen, D. (2002). Visual fixation patterns during viewing of naturalistic social situations as predictors of social competence in individuals with autism. *Archives of General Psychiatry*, 59(9), 809–816.

Klin, A., Saulnier, C., Tsatsanis, K., & Volkmar, F. (2005). Clinical evaluation in autism spectrum disorders: psychological assessment within a transdisciplinary framework. In F.R. Volkmar, R. Paul, A. Klin, & D. J. Cohen (Eds.), *Handbook of autism and pervasive developmental disorders, Vol. 2: Assessment, interventions, and policy* (3rd ed.) (pp. 772–798). Hoboken, NJ: John Wiley & Sons Inc.

Klinger, L. G., O'Kelley, S. E., & Mussey, J. L. (2009). Assessment of intellectual functioning in Autism Spectrum Disorders. In S. Goldstein, J.A. Naglieri, & S. Ozonoff (Eds.), *Assessment of autism spectrum disorders* (pp. 209–252). New York: Guilford.

Klinger, L. G., & Williams, A. (2009). Cognitive-behavioral interventions for students with Autism Spectrum Disorders. In M.J. Mayer, R. Van Acker, J.E. Lochman, & F.M. Gresham (Eds.), *Cognitive-behavioral interventions for emotional and behavioral disorders: School-based practice* (pp. 328–362). New York: Guilford.

Koegel, R. L., Koegel, L. K., & McNerney, E. K. (2001). Pivotal areas in intervention for autism. *Journal of Clinical Child Psychology, 30,* 19–32.

Koshino, H., Carpenter, P. A., Minshew, N. J., Cherkassky, V. L., Keller, T. A., & Just, M. A. (2005). Functional connectivity in an fMRI working memory task in high-functioning autism. *NeuroImage, 24,* 810–821.

Koshino, H., Kana, R. K., Keller, T. A., Cherkassky, V. L., Minshew, N. J., & Just, M. A. (2008). fMRI investigation of working memory for faces in autism: Visual coding and underconnectivity with frontal areas. *Cerebral Cortex, 18,* 289–300.

Krumm, S., Schmidt-Atzert, L., Buehner, M., Ziegler, M., Michalczyk, K., & Arrow, K. (2009). Storage and non-storage components of working memory predicting reasoning: A simultaneous examination of a wide range of ability factors. *Intelligence, 37(4),* 347–364.

Lamb, M., & Robertson, L. (1990). The effect of visual angle on global and local reaction times depends on the set of visual angles presented. *Perception & Psychophysics, 47(5),* 489–496.

Lamb, M., Robertson, L., & Knight, R. (1989). Attention and interference in the processing of global and local information: Effects of unilateral temporal-parietal junction lesions. *Neuropsychologia, 27(4),* 471–483.

Landry, R., & Bryson, S. E. (2004). Impaired disengagement of attention in young children with autism. *Journal of Child Psychology and Psychiatry, 45,* 1115–1122.

Landry, O., Mitchell, P., & Burack, J. (2009). Orienting of visual attention among persons with autism spectrum disorders: Reading versus responding to symbolic cues. *Journal of Child Psychology and Psychiatry, 50(7),* 862–870.

Lee, P. S., Foss-Feig, J., Henderson, J. G., Kenworthy, L. E., Gilotty, L., Gaillard, W. D., & Vaidya, C. J.(2007). Atypical neural substrates of embedded figures task performance in children with autism spectrum disorders. *Neuroimage, 38(1),* 184–193.

Leekam, S., & Moore, C. (2001). The development of attention and joint attention in children with autism. In J. A. Burack, T. Charman, N. Yirmiya, & P. R. Zelazo (Eds.), *The development of autism: Perspectives from theory and research* (pp. 105–129). Mahwah, NJ: Lawrence Erlbaum.

Levy, F. (1980). The development of sustained attention (vigilance) in children: Some normative data. *Journal of Child Psychology and Psychiatry, 21(1),* 77–84.

Liddle, P., Kiehl, K., & Smith, A. (2001). Event-related fMRI study of response inhibition. *Human Brain Mapping, 12(2),* 100–109.

Lincoln, A., Hanzel, E., & Quirmbach, L. (2007). Assessing intellectual abilities of children and adolescents with autism and related disorders. In S. R. Smith & L. Handler (Eds.), *The clinical assessment of children and adolescents: A practitioner's handbook* (pp. 527–544). Mahwah, NJ: Lawrence Erlbaum Associates Publishers.

Logan G. D., & Cowan W. B. (1984). On the ability to inhibit thought and action: A theory of an act of control. *Psychological Review, 91,* 295–327.

Lovaas, O. I. (2003). *Teaching individuals with developmental delays: Basic intervention techniques.* Austin, TX: Pro-Ed.

Lovaas, O., & Schreibman, L. (1971). Stimulus overselectivity of autistic children in a two stimulus situation. *Behaviour Research and Therapy, 9(4),* 305–310.

Luciana, M., Conklin, H. M., Hooper, C. J., & Yarger, R. S. (2005). The development of nonverbal working memory and executive control processes in adolescents. *Child Development, 76,* 697–712.

Luciana, M., & Nelson, C. A. (2002). Assessment of neuropsychological function through use of the Cambridge Neuropsychological Testing Automated Battery: Performance in 4- to 12-year-old children. *Developmental Neuropsychology, 22,* 595–624.

Luna, B., Doll, S. K., Hegedus, S. J., Minshew, N. J., & Sweeney, J. A. (2007). Maturation of executive function in autism. *Biological Psychiatry, 61(4),* 474–481.

Luna, B., Garver, K. E., Urban, T. A., Lazar, N. A., & Sweeney, J. A. (2004). Maturation of cognitive processes from late childhood. *Child Development, 75,* 1357–1372.

Luna, B., Minshew, N. J., Garver, K. E., Lazar, N. A., Thulborn, K. R., Eddy, W. F., & Sweeney, J. A. (2002). Neocortical system abnormalities in autism: An fMRI study of spatial working memory. *Neurology, 59(6),* 834–840.

Manjaly, Z. M., Bruning, N., Neufang, S., Stephan, K. E., Brieber, S., Marshall, J. C., … Fink, J. R. (2007). Neurophysiological correlates of relatively enhanced local visual search in autistic adolescents. *Neuroimage, 35(1),* 283–291.

Manjaly, Z. M., Marshall, J. C., Stephan, K. E., Gurd, J. M., Zilles, K., & Fink, G. R. (2003). In search of the hidden: An fMRI study with implications for the study of patients with autism and with acquired brain injury. *Neuroimage. 19*(3), 674–683.

Mann, T., & Walker, P. (2003). Autism and a deficit in broadening the spread of visual attention. *Journal of Child Psychology and Psychiatry, 44*(2), 272–284.

Maurice, C. (1993). *Let me hear your voice: A family's triumph over autism.* New York: Fawcett Columbine.

Mayes, S. D., & Calhoun, S. L. (2003). Analysis of WISC-III, Stanford-Binet IV, and academic achievement test scores in children with autism. *Journal of Autism and Developmental Disorders, 33*, 329–341.

Mayes, S. D., & Calhoun, S. L. (2008). WISC-IV and WIAT-II profiles in children with high-functioning autism. *Journal of Autism and Developmental Disorders, 38*, 428–439.

Mesibov, G., Shea, V., & Schopler, E. (2004). *The TEACCH approach to autism spectrum disorders.* New York: Springer.

Miller, E., & Cohen, J. (2001). An integrative theory of prefrontal cortex function. *Annual Review of Neuroscience, 24*, 167–202.

Mink, J. W. (1996). The basal ganglia: Focused selection and inhibition of competing motor programs. *Progress in Neurobiology, 50*, 381–425.

Minshew, N. J., & Goldstein, G. (1998). Autism as a complex disorder of information-processing. *Mental Retardation and Developmental Disabilities Research Reviews, 4*, 129–136.

Minshew, N. J., & Goldstein, G. (2001). The pattern of intact and impaired memory function in autism. *Journal of Child Psychology and Psychiatry, 42*, 1095–1101.

Minshew, N. J., Goldstein, G., & Siegel, D. J. (1997). Neuropsychologic functioning in autism: Profile of a complex information-processing disorder. *Journal of the International Neuropsychological Society, 3*, 303–316.

Minshew, N. J., Luna, B., & Sweeney, J. A. (1999). Oculomotor evidence for neocortical systems but not cerebellar dysfunction in autism. *Neurology, 52*, 917–922.

Mottron, L., Dawson, M., Soulières, I., Hubert, B., & Burack, J. (2006). Enhanced perceptual functioning in autism: An update, and eight principles of autistic perception. *Journal of Autism and Developmental Disorders, 36*(1), 27–43.

Navon, D. (1977). Forest before trees: The precedence of global features in visual perception. *Cognitive Psychology, 9*(3), 353–383.

O'Hearn, K., Asato, M., Ordaz, S., & Luna, B. (2008). Neurodevelopment and executive function in autism. *Development and Psychopathology, 20*, 1103–1132.

Owen, A. M. (1997). The functional organization of working memory processes within human lateral frontal cortex: The contribution of functional neuroimaging. *European Journal of Neuroscience, 9*, 1329–1339.

Owen, A. M. (2000). The role of the lateral frontal cortex in mnemonic processing: The contribution of functional neuroimaging. *Experimental Brain Research, 133*, 33–43.

Owen, A. M., McMillan, K. M., Laird, A. R., & Bullmore, E. (2005). N-Back working memory paradigm: A meta-analysis of normative functional neuroimaging studies. *Human Brain Mapping, 25*(1), 46–59.

Ozonoff, S., & Jensen, J. (1999). Brief report: Specific executive function profiles in three neurodevelopmental disorders. *Journal of Autism and Developmental Disorders, 29*(2), 171–177.

Ozonoff, S., & Strayer, D. (1997). Inhibitory function in nonretarded children with autism. *Journal of Autism and Developmental Disorders, 27*(1), 59–77.

Ozonoff, S., & Strayer, D. L. (2001). Further evidence of intact working memory in autism. *Journal of Autism and Developmental Disorders, 31*(3), 257–263.

Pascualvaca, D. M., Fantie, B. D., Papageorgiou, M., & Mirsky, A. F. (1998). Attentional capacities in children with autism: Is there a general deficit in shifting focus. *Journal of Autism and Developmental Disabilities, 28*, 467–478.

Petersen, S., Robinson, D., & Morris, J. (1987). Contributions of the pulvinar to visual spatial attention. *Neuropsychologia, 25*(1-A), 97–105.

Poirel, N., Mellet, E., Houdé, O., & Pineau, A. (2008). First came the trees, then the forest: Developmental changes during childhood in the processing of visual local-global patterns according to the meaningfulness of the stimuli. *Developmental Psychology, 44*(1), 245–253.

Posner, M. I. (1988). Structures and functions of selective attention. In T. Boll & B. Bryant (Eds.), *Master lectures in clinical neuropsychology and brain function: Research, measurement, and practice* (pp. 171–202). Washington, DC: American Psychological Association.

Posner, M., & Petersen, S. (1990). The attention system of the human brain. *Annual Review of Neuroscience, 13*, 25–42.

Posner, M. I., Walker, J. A., Friedrich, F. J., & Rafal, R. D. (1984). Effects of parietal lobe injury on covert orienting of visual attention. *Journal of Neuroscience, 4*(7), 1863–1874.

Raymaekers, R., Antrop, I., van der Meere, J., Wiersema, J., & Roeyers, H. (2007). HFA and ADHD: A direct comparison on state regulation and response inhibition. *Journal of Clinical and Experimental Neuropsychology, 29*(4), 418–427.

Raymaekers, R., van der Meere, J., & Roeyers, H. (2004). Event-rate manipulation and its effect on arousal modulation and response inhibition in adults with high functioning autism. *Journal of Clinical and Experimental Neuropsychology, 26*(1), 74–82.

Remington, A., Swettenham, J., Campbell, R., & Coleman, M. (2009). Selective attention and perceptual load in autism spectrum disorder. *Psychological Science, 20*(11), 1388–1393.

Rees, G., Frackowiak, R., & Frith, C. (1997). Two modulatory effects of attention that mediate object categorization in human cortex. *Science, 275*, 835–838.

Renner, P., Klinger, L., & Klinger, M. (2006). Exogenous and endogenous attention orienting in autism spectrum disorders. *Child Neuropsychology, 12*(4-5), 361–382.

Rincover, A., & Ducharme, J. (1987). Variables influencing stimulus overselectivity and "tunnel vision" in developmentally delayed children. *American Journal of Mental Deficiency, 91*(4), 422–430.

Ring, H. A., Baron-Cohen, S., Wheelwright, S., Williams, S. C., Brammer, M., Andrew, C., & Bullmore, E. T. (1999). Cerebral correlates of preserved cognitive skills in autism: A functional MRI study of embedded figures task performance. *Brain, 122*(7), 1305–1315.

Robertson, L. C., Lamb, M. R., & Knight, R. T. (1988). Effect of lesions on temporal-parietal junction on perceptual and attentional processing in humans. *The Journal of Neuroscience, 8*, 3757–3769.

Rosvold, H., Mirsky, A. F., Saranson, I., Bransome, E. D., & Beck, L. H. (1956). A continuous performance test of brain damage. *Journal of Consulting Psychology, 20*, 343–350.

Rubia, K., Overmeyer, S., Taylor, E., Brammer, M., Williams, S., Simmons, A., ... Bullmore, E. T. (2000). Functional frontalisation with age: Mapping neurodevelopmental trajectories with fMRI. *Neuroscience & Biobehavioral Reviews, 24*(1), 13–19.

Ruff, H., & Rothbart, M. (1996). *Attention in early development: Themes and variations.* New York: Oxford University Press.

Russell, J., Jarrold, C., & Henry, L. (1996). Working memory in children with autism and with moderate learning difficulties. *Journal of Child Psychology and Psychiatry, 37*(6), 673–686.

Russell, J., Jarrold, C., & Hood, B. (1999). Two intact executive capacities in children with autism: Implications for the core executive dysfunctions in the disorder. *Journal of Autism and Developmental Disorders, 29*(2), 103–112.

Russo, N., Flanagan, T., Iarocci, G., Berringer, D., Zelazo, P. D., & Burack, J. A. (2007). Deconstructing executive deficits among persons with autism: implications for cognitive neuroscience. *Brain and Cognition, 65*, 77–86.

Sapir, A., Soroker, N., Berger, A., & Henik, A. (1999). Inhibition of return in spatial attention: Direct evidence for collicular generation. *Nature Neuroscience, 2*(12), 1053–1054.

Scherf, K., Behrmann, M., Kimchi, R., & Luna, B. (2009). Emergence of global shape processing continues through adolescence. *Child Development, 80*(1), 162–177.

Schmiedek, F., Oberauer, K., Wilhelm, O., Süß, H., & Wittmann, W. (2007). Individual differences in components of reaction time distributions and their relations to working memory and intelligence. *Journal of Experimental Psychology: General, 136*(3), 414–429.

Schmitz, N., Rubia, K., Daly, E., Smith, A., Williams, S., & Murphy, D. (2006). Neural correlates of executive function in autistic spectrum disorders. *Biological Psychiatry, 59*(1), 7–16.

Senju, A., Tojo, Y., Dairoku, H., & Hasegawa, T. (2004). Reflexive orienting in response to eye gaze and an arrow in children with and without autism. *Journal of Child Psychology and Psychiatry, 45*, 445–458.

Shah, A., & Frith, U. (1983). An islet of ability in autistic children: A research note. *Journal of Child Psychology and Psychiatry, 24*(4), 613–620.

Shah, A., & Frith, U. (1993). Why do autistic individuals show superior performance on the block design task? *Journal of Child Psychology and Psychiatry, 34*(8), 1351–1364.

Silk, T. J., Rinehart, N., Bradshaw, J. L., Tonge, B., Egan, G., O'Boyle, M., & Cunnington, R. (2006). Visuospatial processing and the function of prefrontal-parietal networks in autism spectrum disorders: A functional MRI study. *American Journal of Psychiatry, 163*(8), 1440–1443.

Smith, E. E., & Jonides, J. (1999). Storage and executive processes in the frontal lobes. *Science, 283*(5408), 1657–1661.

Smith, H., & Milne, E. (2009). Reduced change blindness suggests enhanced attention to detail in individuals with autism. *Journal of Child Psychology and Psychiatry, 50*(3), 300–306.

Solomon, M., Ozonoff, S., Cummings, N., & Carter, C. (2008). Cognitive control in autism spectrum disorders. *International Journal of Developmental Neuroscience, 26*(2), 239–247.

Sowell, E. R., Peterson, B. S., Thompson, P. M., Welcome, S. E., Hekenius, A.L., & Toga, A. W. (2003). Mapping cortical change across the human life span. *Nature Neuroscience, 6*, 309–315.

Steele, S. D., Minshew, N. J., Luna, B., & Sweeney, J. A. (2007). Spatial working memory deficits in autism. *Journal of Autism and Developmental Disorders, 37*(4), 605–612.

Stroop, J. (1935). Studies of interference in serial verbal reactions. *Journal of Experimental Psychology, 18*(6), 643–662.

Sweeney, J. A., Mintun, M. A., Kwee, S., Wiseman, M. B., Brown, D. L., Rosenberg, D. R., ... Carl, J. R. (1996). Positron emission tomography study of voluntary saccadic eye movements and spatial working memory. *Journal of Neurophysiology, 75*, 454–468.

Takarae, Y., Minshew, N. J., Luna, B., & Sweeney, J. A. (2004). Oculomotor abnormalities parallel cerebellar histopathology in autism. *Journal of Neurology, Neurosurgery and Psychiatry, 75*, 1359–1361.

Townsend, J., Courchesne, E., Covington, J., Westerfield, M., Harris, N. S., Lyden, P., ... Press, G. A. (1999). Spatial attention deficits in patients with acquired or developmental cerebellar abnormality. *The Journal of Neuroscience, 19,* 5632–5643.

Townsend, J., Courchesne, E., & Egaas, B. (1996). Slowed orienting of covert visual-spatial attention in autism: Specific deficits associated with cerebellar and parietal abnormality. *Development and Psychopathology, 8,* 563–584.

Townsend, J., Harris, N. S., & Courchesne, E. (1996). Visual attention abnormalities in autism:Delayed orienting to location. *Journal of International Neuropsychological Society, 2,* 541–550.

Wainwright-Sharp, J. A., & Bryson, S. E. (1993). Visual orienting deficits in high functioning People with autism. *Journal of Autism and Developmental Disorders, 23,* 1–13.

Wang, L., Mottron, L., Peng, D., Berthiaume, C., & Dawson, M. (2007). Local bias and local-to-global interference without global deficit: A robust finding in autism under various conditions of attention, exposure time, and visual angle. *Cognitive Neuropsychology, 24*(5), 550–574.

Wechsler, D. (2003). *Wechsler intelligence scale for children, fourth edition. administration and scoring manual.* San Antonio, TX: Harcourt Assessment, Inc.

Weissman, D., & Woldorff, M. (2005). Hemispheric asymmetries for different components of global/local attention occur in distinct temporo-parietal loci. *Cerebral Cortex, 15*(6), 870–876.

Wiggins, L., Robins, D., Bakeman, R., & Adamson, L. (2009). Brief report: Sensory abnormalities as distinguishing symptoms of autism spectrum disorders in young children. *Journal of Autism and Developmental Disorders, 39*(7), 1087–1091.

Williams, D. L., Goldstein, G., & Minshew, N. J. (2006). Neuropsychologic functioning in children with autism: Further evidence for disordered complex information-processing. *Child Neuropsychology, 12,* 279–298.

Williams, B., Ponesse, J., Schachar, R., Logan, G., & Tannock, R. (1999). Development of inhibitory control across the life span. *Developmental Psychology, 35*(1), 205–213.

Chapter 9

Executive Functions in ASD

Inge-Marie Eigsti

In 1985, Judith Rumsey described findings from a sample of 10 adult men with autism who showed significant impairments in their performance of a task assessing the integrity of the frontal lobes of the brain (Rumsey, 1985). Frontal-lobe pathology has long been associated with difficulty in organizing and planning; these supervisory, or regulatory, processes are known as the "executive functions." The link between executive functions and the frontal lobes is supported both by many lesion studies and by functional brain imaging studies, where performance of executive function tasks is associated with increased brain activity in frontal regions (e.g., Baker et al., 1996). Since Rumsey's influential study, researchers have speculated that the executive functions (EF) are a possible "core deficit" of autism.

In addition to EF, two other prominent theories have postulated candidate core deficits in autism. These include the weak central coherence (Frith & Happé, 1994), and related connectivity (Baron-Cohen, Leslie, & Frith, 1985) arguments, as discussed

in Chapters 5, 17, and 21, and Theory of Mind, as discussed in Chapter 12. Three criteria are relevant in evaluating a "core deficit" for a developmental disorder (Sigman, Dijamco, Gratier, & Rozga, 2004). First, the deficit should be *universal* in affected individuals; that is, every person with that disorder should display the impairment at some developmental period, regardless of symptom severity. Second, performance should be *specific*; affected individuals should show a profile with strengths in some areas, as well as weaknesses in the core deficit. Thirdly, the deficit should be *unique*; that is, individuals with the disorder should show a unique profile or pattern on that function, compared with individuals with other disorders. These criteria have all been brought to bear in studies of EF in ASD.

Some researchers argue that the search for a single unifying theory of autism is fruitless, because the three domains of autism (that is, social reciprocity, language and communication, and repetitive and stereotyped behaviors) appear to derive from distinct genes and to separate in factor analyses (Happé, Ronald, & Plomin, 2006), and because attempts to develop a single explanation have not been uniformly successful (see Chapters 23 and 24).

We agree that it is possible that EF may not explain "all" of autism. However, the search for cognitive underpinnings of at least some of the characteristic symptoms of the spectrum may be fruitful for several reasons. Whether or not deficits in EF are at the "core" of the autism spectrum, understanding these deficits in an affected individual will help clinicians and researchers to better predict and interpret that individual's developmental course, as well as specific challenges and areas of strength. For example, longitudinal studies indicate that EF is a central contributor to the development of Theory of Mind skills in typically developing children ages 2 to 4 years (Hughes & Ensor, 2007), and in children with autism specifically (Pellicano, 2007). Given the importance of Theory of Mind in the study of autism, it behooves us to better understand its possible building blocks. Conversely, fulfilling the promise of the field of developmental psychopathology (Cicchetti & Rogosch, 1996), the study of EF in autism may further inform our understanding of EF as a whole (how different subcomponents may interact, which impair the development of others, what are the neural substrates of EF, and so on). Studying EF in autism as a class of processes will promote the development of improved assessment and intervention strategies that are relevant for a variety of disorders. Finally, the current evidence suggests that a significant, clinically meaningful proportion of individuals with autism spectrum disorders struggle with difficulties that reflect executive dysfunction. This conclusion is buttressed by exciting intervention data indicating that gains in EF can translate into decreased impairment in other domains (as in, e.g, Fisher & Happé, 2005). Thus, whether or not EF is a core deficit in ASD, it merits empirical attention.

DEFINING THE EXECUTIVE FUNCTIONS

While there has been vigorous debate on exactly what processes or functions are involved in EF, research suggests that they primarily involve attentional shifting or mental flexibility, inhibition, working memory, planning, and fluency (Engle, Kane, & Tuholski, 1999; Hill, 2004). EF has been construed in two primary ways, according to Garon, Bryson, and Smith (2008).

First, EF could be described as a single "system" built up from a number of components (e.g., Baddeley, 1992), driven by a central attentional (Posner & Rothbart, 2007) or inhibitory (Dempster, 1992) system. In another formulation, EF might comprise a variety of functions, each having a unique prefrontal functional basis and a unique developmental trajectory (Casey, Durston, & Fossella, 2001).

There is strong support for both approaches when assessing typically developing children. On the one hand, data have been marshalled to suggest process-specific trajectories. For example, there are measurable improvements on inhibitory control from ages 1 to 6 years (Diamond & Taylor, 1996), in response speed and verbal fluency from ages 3 to 5 years (Espy, 1997), in processing speed and fluency improvements through middle childhood (Welsh, Pennington, & Groisser, 1991) and again between 9 and 12 years of age (Kail, 1986), with a flattening after age 16 (Kail, 1986); cognitive flexibility increases during early and middle childhood (Welsh, et al., 1991), and attention-shifting task performance improves dramatically between ages 7 and 9 (Anderson, 2002). Planning and organizational task performance improves dramatically from age 7 to 10, and then more gradually into adolescence (Anderson, 2002). These findings seem to suggest that each EF has an individual neural substrate and developmental trajectory. On the other hand, there is significant across-the-board improvement in EF abilities during the first six years of life, with some additional leaps occurring in early adolescence. Generally, there appear to be two primary stages of EF development: a first phase, from birth to 3 years, when basic skills for component EFs develop; then a second stage, from 3–5 years, when basic EF skills are coordinated. It is possible that these differing periods of change in apparently "component" EF processes could actually reflect a developmental cascade, in which one process precedes the fine-tuning of a subsequent process because the latter invokes or depends upon the former. The study of atypical populations who struggle with EF deficits may allow for a particularly sensitive window into the nature and organization of EF in development.

The earliest investigations of EF presumed a developmentally late emergence of these functions. This was based in part on findings that the frontal lobes are the last brain structures to develop (Huttenlocher, 1979, 1990). As such, EF was thought to play a relatively minor role in behavioral functioning (and behavioral impairments) in the early years of childhood. The field of autism research has been instrumental in pushing EF researchers to more carefully investigate the development of EF in childhood. A second shift in perspective hinged on our understanding of the brain networks involved in EF. Because of the early focus on lesions to frontal cortex and their resultant EF impairments, the first conceptualizations of EF focused on frontal brain areas. However, researchers now agree that EF deficits likely reflect disruptions not just to frontal lobes, but to multiple bidirectional pathways between frontal areas and posterior and subcortical regions, especially the basal ganglia (Casey, et al., 2001; Stuss & Benson, 1984).

This chapter provides an overview of specific EF abilities in individuals with autism spectrum disorders (ASD), and the tasks assessing these processes. The executive processes are thought to comprise three primary functions: *set-shifting*, *inhibition*, and *working memory* (which includes updating, monitoring), as well as two potentially more peripheral processes of *planning* and *fluency*, and a newer construct, *cognitive control*. Unless otherwise noted, "ASD" samples include individuals with Autistic disorder, Asperger's disorder, and pervasive developmental disorder, not otherwise specified (PDD-NOS). In some cases, good tasks exist to tap executive processes that have not been tried with autistic populations; these are mentioned in order to identify gaps in the research.

SET-SHIFTING

Set-shifting is an executive process characterized primarily by the concept of flexibility, and in particular by the ability to update, or "shift," one's cognitive strategy or "response set" in reaction to changes in the environment. Findings consistently indicate difficulties in patients with frontal lobe damage, particularly dorsolateral frontal cortex, with set-shifting; their responses are characterized by perseveration (sticking with a maladaptive or incorrect response).

The Wisconsin Card Sort Test (WCST; Berg, 1948), one of the most well-studied set-shifting tasks, has been deemed the "gold standard" of EF (Ozonoff, et al., 2004). This task assesses set-shifting, but also strategic planning, holding in mind a future goal, moderating previously reinforced responses, attention, working memory, and visual processing. Although WCST performance reflects multiple

cognitive functions, it is thought to tap primarily into frontal (and thus executive) functions.

The WCST consists of a set of cards which vary by 1) the shape pictured, 2) the number of shapes pictured, and 3) the color of those shapes. The participant attempts to match her card to one of those properties by laying it on any of several piles, and then receives the examiner's verbal feedback of "correct" or "incorrect;" response accuracy for the first trial is at chance. Once the participant has correctly matched to a given property for a specified number of consecutive trials, the examiner switches to a new category (giving appropriate feedback) without reporting the category shift. Response variables for the WCST typically include Categories Achieved (that is, number of properties on which the participant was able to match), Perseverative Errors (number of times that a participant continues to match to a property which the experimenter has designated as incorrect), and Loss of Set Errors (matching to a new property after "correct" feedback to a different property on the previous trial). Additional variables include Total Errors, Total Correct Trials, and Number of Trials to First Category. Children's performance increases steadily with age, reaching a plateau at about 10 years of age (Chelune & Baer, 1986). A computerized version of the WCST has been found to enhance performance in children with autism (Pascualvaca, Fantie, Papageorgiou, & Mirsky, 1998; Tien et al. 1996 cited in Shu, Lung, Tien, & Chen, 2001), though computer and examiner administrations are not necessarily comparable for typically developing children either (Feldstein, et al., 1999).

Despite the WCST's popularity as a measure of executive function, there is growing data that it is insufficiently *specific*; patients with non-frontal and frontal damage can perform similarly (Anderson, Damasio, Jones, & Tranel, 1991). Furthermore, the WCST may be insufficiently *sensitive*; that is, patients with frontal damage who exhibit executive dysfunction in daily living may perform in the normal range (Damasio, Tranel, & Damasio, 1991; Shallice & Burgess, 1991).

WCST findings in autism

A wide variety of studies have demonstrated impairments (especially, perseverative responding) in autism across a variety of ages (Ozonoff & Jensen, 1999; Ozonoff, Pennington, & Rogers, 1991; Rumsey, 1985).

Individuals with high-functioning autism (HFA) show more perseverative responding and fewer categories completed relative to typically developing controls and individuals with attention-deficit/hyperactivity disorder (Szatmari, Tuff, Finlayson, & Bartolucci, 1990) and dyslexia (Rumsey & Hamburger, 1990). Adults with both HFA and Asperger's disorder exhibit impairments on the WCST relative to matched controls (Ozonoff, Rogers, & Pennington, 1991), though several studies have failed to find impairments (Barnard, Muldoon, Hasan, O'Brien, & Stewart, 2008; Minshew, Goldstein, Muenz, & Payton, 1992; Turner, 1999). It should be noted that in the Minshew et al. 1992 study, participants did make many perseverative errors relative to task norms.

Perseverative performance on the WCST has also been demonstrated in children and adolescents with ASD. One study of 13 adolescents with Asperger's or high-functioning autism (HFA), compared to typically developing controls, indicated poorer performance on a computerized version of the WCST, with the greatest differences in loss of set errors (Kaland, Smith, & Mortensen, 2008); similar results were found for adolescents with ASD using the standard WCST (Bennetto, Pennington, & Rogers, 1996). Shu and colleagues (2001) assessed 26 children with autism ages 6–12 years (described as "average" in intellectual ability; IQ data were available for only 15 participants), and compared their performance on a computerized version of the WCST to 52 control children, matched on age. The autism group completed fewer categories, had fewer "conceptual level" responses, and had more perseverative and loss-of-set errors. Finally, a large study of 34 children with language delay, compared with 21 children with HFA, indicated that the HFA group made more perseverative errors, and that error rates were significantly correlated with severity of autism symptoms (Liss et al., 2001). Interestingly, group differences in perseveration on the WCST, as well as correlations with perseveration in everyday life, no longer held when covarying verbal IQ.

In summary, studies utilizing the WCST to compare the performance of individuals with ASD to controls generally find that the ASD group is more perseverative and completes fewer different sets. There is a version of the WCST, the Dimensional Change Card Sort (Zelazo, et al., 2003), that is appropriate for younger children (ages 3 and older) and has been found to correlate with Theory of Mind skills; unfortunately, there are no published data for children with ASD.

Additional set-shifting tasks: Intradimensional/Extradimensional (ID/ED) Shift

As noted above, the WCST may not be appropriately sensitive or specific. At the least, it draws on multiple EF processes. The computerized CANTAB battery (described in full below) provides an alternative, potentially more specific task, the Intradimensional/ Extradimensional (ID/ED) Shift, which assesses the ability to respond to specific attributes of complex stimuli (shapes with superimposed white lines) and to shift attention between attributes (shapes versus white lines). An influential multisite study, including data from 79 individuals with autism across a wide range of ages (6–47 years) and intellectual level (full-scale IQs ranging from 50–150), indicated that the autism group was impaired in extra-dimensional shifting relative to 70 age-, gender-, and IQ-matched typically developing controls (Ozonoff, et al., 2004). This suggests a difficulty in shifting attention to the new aspect of the stimulus, rather than inhibiting the previously reinforced response on the same dimension. Performance was also correlated with adaptive behavior skills (though not with severity of autism symptomatology). Similarly, 35 children and adolescents with autism (ages 7–18) had deficits on the ID/ED shift task relative to typically developing and mildly learning-delayed comparison groups (Hughes, Russell, & Robbins, 1994). Finally, preliminary data from a functional MRI version of the ID/ED shift task suggest that adolescents with ASD show the typical prefrontal (dorsolateral prefrontal cortical) activation seen in controls, but not the associated parietal activity (Mak-Fan, Morris, Roberts, & Taylor, 2008). In contrast, one study failed to find differences in set-shifting errors on the ID/ED task in school-aged children with autism (Landa & Goldberg, 2005).

The Brixton Test

The Brixton Test (Burgess & Shallice, 1997) is a visuospatial sequencing task that assesses rule-shifting abilities. A child must predict which of 10 numbered turtles on a card will be colored. Accurate prediction requires the child to determine a rule, as in the WSCT. However, the rules are more abstract, and switch at set intervals (rather than being contingent on the participant reaching some criterion). Data from a study of 10 high-functioning adults with autism, compared with chronological age- and IQ-matched controls, found no differences in performance on this task (Boucher, et al., 2005). However, there is to date very little available data.

Altogether, set-shifting in ASD is vulnerable to disruption, particularly in older and more impaired individuals; data from younger children are less consistent.

INHIBITION

Inhibition is an executive process that describes the ability to selectively attend to relevant information, while inhibiting attention or responses to irrelevant (but often salient and interfering) stimuli. In adults, inhibition has often been assessed with the Stroop task, in which an individual is presented with a highly familiar stimulus class, printed words that spell out the names of colors. In the inhibitory condition of the task, the participant must overlook or ignore the word that is spelled out, and instead name the ink color in which the word is printed. The contrast between simple color-naming (typically, of X's printed in three ink colors), and inhibitory color naming (of the ink color of printed color names), provides an elegant assessment of a person's ability to inhibit attention to salient but task-irrelevant information (as well as to maintain a representation of a rule). Although some of the earliest Stroop studies with adults with ASD suggested poor inhibitory functioning (Rumsey, 1985; Rumsey & Hamburger, 1988), most studies find no group differences (Barnard et al., 2008; Eskes, Bryson, & McCormick, 1990; Ozonoff & Jensen, 1999). Younger individuals have also been found to have intact inhibitory skills on the Stroop (Ozonoff & Strayer, 1997).

The traditional Stroop can only assess inhibitory impairments in fluent readers. In the Go/Nogo task, participants are asked to give a button-press response to frequently presented target stimuli (such as pictures of various Pokemon cartoon characters), but to inhibit this simple response to a similar distractor stimulus (e.g., Eigsti, et al., 2006). While Go/Nogo studies of ASD are few in number, they are consistent in demonstrating intact performance for individuals on the spectrum (Ozonoff, Strayer, McMahon, & Filloux, 1994).

A second inhibitory task for adults is the Hayling test (Burgess & Shallice, 1997), a measure of response

initiation and suppression. First, participants are asked to complete 15 sentences by generating a semantically sensible or congruent word. In a second condition, participants must generate 15 illogical or incongruent sentence endings. Somewhat surprisingly, one small study of 10 high-functioning adults indicated that the ASD group made significantly more errors (14 vs. 3) on this task (Hill & Bird, 2006), indicating significant difficulty in following the rule or in inhibiting a salient response. James Russell has argued that inhibition deficits in ASD are observed when rules are arbitrary *and* must be verbally encoded; because Stroop performance does not include both these criteria, individuals with ASD are likely to show intact performance. In contrast, the Hayling test meets both these conditions.

While the Stroop and the Hayling are best suited for older individuals, researchers have developed tasks suitable for children that tap into the same inhibitory processes. These tasks can be divided into simple and complex inhibitory tasks (following Garon et al., 2008), a division that reflects the demand to engage in several tasks simultaneously.

Simple response inhibition

Object retrieval and the *delay of gratification task* are both simple measures of response inhibition that are appropriate for young children. There are no data on performance in ASD. In the *anti-saccade task*, the child views a screen on which target stimuli are displayed to one side. The child must move her gaze to the opposite side. Initially developed in the field of cognitive neuroscience to tap cognitive control (discussed below), this task can be administered with nonverbal individuals, infants, and others. One study reported impairments (more directional errors) in 11 adolescents with high-functioning autism, relative to typically developing controls (Goldberg et al., 2002).

Complex response inhibition

The *Kiddie Stroop* tasks (e.g., Day/Night Stroop) require children to generate a word that mismatches a presented picture (e.g., the word "day" when shown a picture of a moon, and the word "night" when shown a picture of a sun). As is the case with the traditional Stroop, the required response conflicts with a more automatic or prepotent response. The Kiddie Stroop can be administered with children ages 2 and older (Russell, Jarrold, & Hood, 1999). In the *Detour-reaching* task, for ages three and older, children are asked to retrieve a reward that is inside a box. There is a transparent window on the box, through which the reward is visible; the box has a bulb that can illuminate as yellow or green, and the color determines whether the child should turn a knob (prepotent action) or press a switch (detour action) to access the reward. In a study of 40 children with autism ages 6–19 years, matched on verbal mental age to developmentally delayed controls, Hughes and Russell (1993) found that the autism group performed poorly. Other complex response inhibition tasks that can be administered with children of mental ages 3 and older include the *Bear and Dragon task*, versions of the children's game "*Simon Says*," the *Knock and Tap task*, and in the *Spatial Conflict task*.

While data are largely unavailable from these inhibition tasks in samples of individuals with ASD, findings indicate that a) there are some aspects of response inhibition which are strikingly impaired in individuals with autism (specifically, the anti-saccade, detour-reaching, and Hayling tasks), and b) that the simpler inhibition tasks are highly promising for studies of high-risk infant siblings of individuals with autism or other young, potentially affected individuals, because tasks are sensitive to processes that may be impaired at a very early developmental stage.

WORKING MEMORY

Working memory (WM) has been construed in several ways over the past three decades. The foundational model, proposed by Baddeley and Hitch (1974), involved a central executive or supervisory system which controlled information flow among two subsystems: a phonological loop (which maintains active representations of auditory information); and a visuospatial "scratchpad" (which maintains active representations of visual information). In this model, the central-executive regulates attentional and cognitive control processes to permit the simultaneous storage and processing of information while performing cognitive tasks. The notion that storage and processing are discrete is implemented in many studies as a distinction between "short-term" and "working" memory processes (e.g., Case, Kurland, & Goldberg, 1982).

Many researchers have argued that simple span tasks measure the storage aspects that are central to short-term memory (STM), whereas complex span tasks measure the processing aspects that are central

to WM (Daneman & Carpenter, 1980); complex span tasks are found to correlate more strongly with measures of higher-order cognition (Ackerman, Beier, & Boyle, 2005). In contrast, some have argued that both simple and complex tasks assess the same construct, but with differential relative involvement of subcomponent processes such as phonological rehearsal, maintenance, updating, and controlled search (Unsworth & Engle, 2007). While this is an active area of debate, findings suggest that simple span tasks may be *relatively less* sensitive to subtle individual variability in performance. Thus, the current discussion is split into simple span and complex WM tasks; we argue that working memory deficits in ASD are most apparent in the latter case. This distinction accounts for the lack of WM findings in some studies of younger children with autism (average age, 36 months), which has led some researchers to conclude that deficits are a later-occurring outcome in ASD, secondary to living with the symptoms of autism over development, or reflecting the operation of an unmeasured cognitive risk factor (Yerys, Hepburn, Pennington, & Rogers, 2007); see Chapter 7 for additional discussion of working memory and autism.)

Simple span/STM

Working memory researchers have drawn on some tasks initially developed for non-human primates to assess the efficiency of working memory in young preverbal human children. These tasks are appropriate for very young children because they require only a simple manual response, and because rewards are integral to task administration, making participation inherently reinforcing (Espy, Kaufmann, McDiarmid, & Glisky, 1999).

The tasks reviewed here involve both WM and inhibition. Clearly, these processes are closely intertwined; action selection typically implies non-selection of some competing action, and stronger competition from these alternatives requires greater and more consistent WM to avoid incorrect response. We have grouped these tasks under the WM heading because an individual must maintain information about the preceding trial in order to guide responding on the subsequent trial.

In the *Delayed Response* task (Goldman-Rakic, 1987), administered to children as young as 5 months, an object is hidden in one of two wells; after a brief delay, the child retrieves (and consumes) the rewarding object. A study of children with ASD with a mean age of 5 years indicated significant impairments on Delayed Response compared to control groups with Down's syndrome and typical development (Dawson, Meltzoff, Osterling, & Rinaldi, 1998). In contrast, an ASD group aged 3 to 6 showed no impairments on this task, compared to similar control groups (McEvoy, Rogers, & Pennington, 1993). *Delayed Alternation* (Elder & Nissen, 1933) requires the child to alternate in searching between left and right wells on alternate trials; McEvoy and colleagues (1993) again found no difference in their ASD group. The *Delayed Non-Match-to-Sample* task requires the child to choose a novel object (rather than the more familiar object presented on the prior trial) in order to receive the reward. In a 1998 study, children with autism were impaired on this task, and their performance was correlated with social impairments (Dawson, et al., 1998), but, surprisingly, in a study of a younger group (33–57 months) with autism, there were no group differences (Dawson et al., 2002). *Object Discrimination* requires the child to remember which of two objects is associated with a reward. After five correct trials, the contingency is reversed. Children with autism ages 33–57 months did not differ on this task (Dawson et al., 2002).

In *Spatial Reversal* (and the related *Object Reversal*), as in many of the primate EF tasks, there are wells (sometimes, inverted opaque plastic cups). Two wells are stationed at opposite sides of the child's midline, and one is "baited" with a reward. After the child retrieves the reward at one side, the same side is baited for several successive trials, after which the side of hiding is switched. This task can be administered to children ages 2 and older. Participants must determine the rewarded response, remember this response, and then shift to a new response when the original response is no longer rewarded. A small study ($n = 7$ each in three groups of autism, typically developing chronological age-matched, and typically developing verbal age-matched groups, ages 4–7 years), found that the group with autism was more likely to perseverate on spatial reversal (Coldren & Halloran, 2003). Perseveration was also found for an ASD group ages 3–6 years (McEvoy, et al., 1993). In contrast, three studies found no group differences in Spatial Reversal when comparing preschoolers with autism to age-matched controls at ages 3–5 (Dawson, et al., 2002; Griffith, Pennington, Wehner, & Rogers, 1999) and 2–3 years (Yerys, et al., 2007).

The *A Not B task* dates back to Piaget's explorations of object permanence (Piaget, 1954), and can be administered to children as young as 6 months old. A child watches while a reward is hidden beneath a cup at the midline, which is then moved to one side. After a 5-second delay, the child can retrieve the reward. After a successful series of retrievals on the first side, the reward is hidden on the opposite side. In *A Not B with Invisible Displacement*, a slightly more difficult task, the reward is concealed inside a box. Three studies found no impairments in a sample of children with autism on this task (Dawson et al., 2002; Griffith et al., 1999; Yerys et al., 2007). In the *Windows task*, a child sees two boxes with transparent windows that reveal the contents; one box contains an attractive object. The child must select the empty box to receive a reward. Children with autism, ages 2–3, years performed similarly to controls on this task (Yerys et al., 2007).

To summarize briefly the findings so far: in simple tasks that assess WM (but with a significant inhibitory component), data from 11 tasks, for children with autism ages 2 to 6 years, found no differences from controls; data from 6 tasks, for children ages 3–14 years, found differences between autism and control groups. Why have findings been so inconsistent, and why are studies with younger children less likely to find differences? One possibility is, of course, that children with ASD do not differ in WM capacity; the many studies documenting significant differences, as reviewed above, however, argue against this. Another possibility is that these WM deficits are "secondary" to ASD and emerge as a consequence of living with the disorder. A third possibility is that these tasks are relatively insensitive to WM deficits, in part because the WM capacity they measure may not be fully developed until later, perhaps in the early school-age period. In this case, "everyone" tends to perform relatively poorly at these WM tasks at young ages, making it difficult to establish group differences. In addition, these simpler WM tasks all rely on memory for visual location, with a variety of rule manipulations, and it is possible that this is a relative strength for individuals with ASD (Yerys, et al., 2007).

Children ages 3 and older are able to complete span tasks such as *Digit Span*, which requires a child to listen to and repeat back a series of digits of increasing length, and its visuospatial counterpart, *Block Span*, which requires a child to watch and then imitate the examiner as she taps several blocks in a series.

One study of 37 children with autism ages 5–11 indicated deficits in Block Span relative to typically developing controls matched on age and IQ; no verbal span task was administered (Joseph, McGrath, & Tager-Flusberg, 2005). A related task, *non-word repetition*, is thought to assess simple phonological WM. Kjelgaard and Tager-Flusberg (2001) reported impairments in a language-impaired subset of high-functioning children with autism ages 4–14, relative to controls, on non-word repetition.

Two studies have found deficits in simple span tasks for adults with ASD. Twenty adults with autism were impaired on the forward spatial span task from the Wechsler Memory Scales (Barnard, et al., 2008). Twenty-six adults with HFA had deficits on a very simple visuospatial delayed-response task, in which participants saw a single target presented in the visual periphery while fixating on a central target; after a delay, they were cued to shift fixation to the target (Minshew, Luna, & Sweeney, 1999). These tasks appear to be more the exception than the rule; in general, adults with autism are not impaired on simple visual span tasks. In contrast, impairments are often observed when the information to be encoded is more complex, or when organizational processes to aid recall are required.

Complex tasks/WM

While the simple span tasks are thought to assess primarily "storage" or active maintenance processes, the hallmark of complex WM tasks is the involvement of both the storage and updating of information. In *Digit Span Backward*, the participant hears a series of digits, and must repeat them in reverse order. Similarly, in *Block Span Backward*, the child must tap, in reverse order, the same blocks that were tapped by the examiner. These tasks can be completed by typical children with a mental age of 3 years and older (Carlson, Moses, & Claxton, 2004), though unpublished data from our laboratory suggest that children with autism younger than 6 years (mental age) are unable to comprehend task instructions. A group of 37 children with autism, ages 5–11, matched on IQ with controls (but differing on vocabulary) scored lower on block-span-backward; word-span-backward results did not reach significance but were in the same direction (Joseph, et al., 2005). As the autism group was relatively strong on forward span, it would be useful to know whether group differences might emerge if one held simple span constant in this comparison. More data on these tasks, ideally in a single sample, are needed to better establish whether deficits are limited to visuospatial backward span tasks.

Self-ordered pointing (also known as *Box and Cup Scramble*; Petrides & Milner, 1982) requires children to compare a potential response to responses already made and updated in WM; this task can be given to children ages 3 and older. A child must search for rewards hidden under cups; after each search trial, a delay is imposed and the cups are scrambled. The child must remember which cups have already been searched and inhibit a response to the previously searched location. Griffith and colleagues (1999) found no impairments in children with autism ages 3–5 years. In a more complex variant of the task, children hear a series of items named, and then must point to those items on a page. Children with autism ages 5–14 were impaired relative to controls, in a verbal (but not a nonverbal) condition of such a self-ordered pointing task, even when controlling for simple span (Joseph, Steele, Meyer, & Tager-Flusberg, 2005). Similar deficits were found for a slightly older group, ages 6–18 (Russo et al., 2005). Using the computerized CANTAB version of this task in 29 individuals with HFA, ages 8–29, Steele and colleagues found clear WM impairments in ASD, with the greatest impairments when the number of items to be recalled was large (Steele, Minshew, Luna, & Sweeney, 2007). Findings from a study of individuals with Asperger's disorder using a spatial WM task with a high load also indicated ASD-specific deficits (Morris et al., 1999). Thus, a number of studies find deficits for complex and visual WM tasks.

In contrast, one study asked children to point, in the correct order, to 12 visually presented cards, over six trials. Eleven boys with HFA, ages 6–12 years, had *no* impairments in this task (Bebko & Ricciuti, 2000). In another visuospatial memory task, a sample of individuals with autism, ages 8–17, had no impairments on an N-back task (which required continuous updating in WM; Ozonoff & Strayer, 2001).

The California Verbal Learning Test (CVLT) has often served as a WM measure. In this task, the participant hears a "shopping list" of 15 objects (fruits, clothing, furniture), and is asked to repeat back the list. The process is repeated five times, and an interference list of similar items is presented. The original list must then be recalled. There is a 20-minute delayed recall trial as well as a recognition memory trial.

Studies have explored the number of items recalled, and whether participants strategically group items into semantically organized categories. An influential early study gave the CVLT to adolescents with autism and to learning-disabled controls and found deficits for the autism group, even when controlling for digit span; performance correlated with autistic symptomatology[1] (Bennetto et al., 1996). More recently, a study of individuals ages 11–40 on a CVLT-like task found poorer recall using semantic cues for the autism group, but no differences for phonological cues (Mottron, Mottron, Morasse, & Belleville, 2001). Again, performance was correlated with severity of scores on the ADI-R. A somewhat different pattern of results emerged in another study of high-functioning individuals with autism ages 15–40, who had no differences on the CVLT list memory trials (unlike Bennetto et al.), but were impaired relative to controls on cued delayed recall (Minshew et al., 1992).

The CVLT taps into accumulated memory for relatively simple items. Memory for context and order, however, is a distinct component of memory. Two independent groups have documented deficits in children with autism on tasks assessing this aspect of memory (Boucher, 1981; O'Shea, Fein, Cillessen, Klin, & Shultz, 2005), with the finding that individuals with ASD fail to encode socially salient information—in particular, when attending to events.

One influential well-controlled study failed to document WM deficits in autism using complex "dual tasks." Russell, Jarrold, and Henry (1996) found similar WM spans in the autism, typically developing, and developmentally delayed participants who completed the study; there were 33 children per group with a mean age of 12 years. The complex WM tasks included a counting task (track the number of black dots seen on a card over several trials, then tally the numbers across trials); an odd-man-out task (identify the position of a black dot in three positions, then locate a dot whose pattern had differed in an intervening presentation); and a sums task (recall the answers to a series of simple addition questions). There were both simple and complex conditions for each of these tasks, and findings showed that the autism group was superior to the developmentally delayed control group

in the simple span tasks, and did not differ from this group for complex tasks. Both clinical groups were impaired relative to the typically developing control participants. Russell and colleagues interpreted these findings as indicating that when information must be held in working memory while other information is processed, children with autism perform similarly to mental-age-matched controls. Given that the autism group had superior simple spans, but were unable to "harness" this superiority in the complex tasks, we suggest that this conclusion may be too strongly formulated, and that more evidence is needed before determining that there are *no* complex verbal WM deficits in ASD.

Working memory in ASD

If working memory is a process that interacts with declarative and procedural knowledge in long-term memory over the course of task performance, one would predict that tasks that demand significant input or contribution from stored knowledge might be more challenging that those that involve simple short-term storage only. Many findings in studies of autism are consistent with this conceptualization, in that the complexity of material that is encoded in working memory appears to influence whether individuals with autism show deficits or not. Studies of preschoolers (Fein et al., 1996), children ages 5–8 (Gabig, 2008), and children ages 8–16 (Williams, Goldstein, & Minshew, 2006) document a specific profile for working memory tasks for the ASD groups, with non-word repetition less impaired than digit span, which in turn is less impaired than on sentence imitation tasks. In each of these studies, the autism group was impaired relative to controls, and controls showed a flat profile across tasks. This complexity-sensitive pattern is to be expected when task performance demands simultaneous processing from multiple input sources, including phonology, semantics, and syntax (Gabig, 2008). Alternatively, the flat profile observed in controls may reflect the test norming process, which is designed to give mean scores at group averages for typically developing children.

The literature on WM in ASD is a complex and inconsistent one, with many findings of ASD-specific differences, but many null findings as well. As reviewed above, there are some notable gaps in the literature to date, with very limited data on digit-backward tasks and complex span tasks of the type studied by Russell

---

1. Results were not significantly different after stringent correction for the number of comparisons, an adjustment that many statisticians have indicated may lead to Type II error.

and colleagues. In addition, most studies simply administer a task and measure group differences between samples; few studies use a within-subject experimental manipulation of processing demands (e.g., Ozonoff & Strayer, 2001, or Russell, Jarrold & Henry, 1996); such parametric manipulations have been highly informative in cognitive neuroscience. A variety of findings from the developmental WM literature suggests that increasing WM by extending delays or introducing secondary tasks increases the probability of prepotent errors (Roberts & Pennington, 1996). When findings vary so dramatically across tasks, modalities, and ages, within-subjects manipulations of WM demands may provide insight into whether deficits are present.

We briefly raise one consideration here about current conceptualizations of WM. Research in the connectionist and modeling domain has questioned the utility of an isolated construct of verbal WM, suggesting that any so-called WM task is assessing language processing (MacDonald & Christiansen, 2002). In this view, deficits in WM tasks may be attributed to language processing constraints, such as variability in the strength and accuracy of phonological, semantic, and syntactic representations. This is highly relevant to the notion (discussed in Dennis et al., 2009, and in Footnote 2 below) that covarying language ability when analyzing WM tasks is likely to remove the very source of variance that is of central interest, and we encourage future studies to reconsider this practice or to approach it with great care.

In addition to the three primary EF constructs reviewed in detail (set-shifting, inhibition, and working memory), factor analyses in typically developing populations and other work have identified two EF constructs, planning and fluency, that may contribute to additional non-overlapping variance in individual performance and development.

PLANNING

Planning involves the identification and organization of steps towards a goal. One task commonly used to assess planning is the *Tower of London task,* or the related *Tower of Hanoi task.* These have been frequently used in research as markers of damage to prefrontal cortex (Shallice, 1982). In the *Tower of London task,* the participant arranges colored balls on three posts (or into three sockets) laid out in a horizontal line, and must obey several rules about ball movement. The examiner provides an illustration of a configuration of balls, which the participant must match. Scores include Time to First Move, Number of Correct Trials, and Time to Complete Each Trial. A sample scoring procedure is described by Anderson (1996). The similar *Tower of Hanoi task* has disks or rings of increasing size. Participants are asked to move the "tower" of disks along a row of three pegs, while following rules governing disk movement.

Findings from the Tower tasks with individuals with ASD are fairly consistent in documenting deficits in ASD. A study of 35 individuals with autism, ages 7 to 18, exhibited planning deficits on the Tower relative to IQ-matched controls with learning disabilities or typical development (Hughes, et al., 1994); similar deficits were demonstrated in 19 adolescents with HFA compared to learning disabled controls (Bennetto et al., 1996); in children with HFA ages 8–14 (O'Shea et al., 2005); in 37 children with autism ages 5–11 (Joseph et al., 2005); and in a computerized version of the Tower for adults (Just, Cherkassky, Keller, Kana, & Minshew, 2007) and children with autism (Ozonoff et al., 1991).

The lone null result to our knowledge, comes from a study of 30 adults with autism with IQs ranging from 50–85, relative to IQ-matched developmentally delayed controls (mean age of 30 years). Though the autism group *seemed* less able to pass the Tower task (30% vs. 59% accuracy), results (relative to an arbitrarily-set threshold) did not reach significance (Barnard et al., 2008). In general, studies of planning suggest deficits in ASD.

FLUENCY

Fluency involves the ability to generate multiple specific responses. It can be seen as an index of creativity and flexibility, and is assessed in a variety of modalities, typically by asking participants to generate as many items as possible within a limited amount of time (often, 60 seconds). Tasks include generating words beginning with a given letter (typically, F, A, and S; this is often called "Controlled Oral Word Association"), visuospatial designs, items in a given category (e.g., zoo animals), and ideas (e.g., identify uses for a hat).

Data from studies of ASD are inconsistent, but generally suggest fluency impairments. One study of adults with ASD found decreased fluency, relative to controls, for generating novel words and novel ideas; the ASD group's visual designs were also more repetitive (Turner, 1999). In addition, these fluency results were significantly associated with repetitive behaviors. Similarly, Craig and Baron-Cohen (1999) found impaired fluency in children with Asperger's and autism with an average age of 12 years. Finally, Bishop and Norbury (2005) found a relationship between verbal fluency and other aspects of communicative deficits in a sample of 14 children with high-functioning autism; with pragmatic language delays (but not autism; $n = 25$); with specific language impairment (but no pragmatic deficits; $n = 17$); and with typical development ($n = 18$). Both the autism and pragmatic delay groups generated more incorrect responses; and for the three clinical groups, fluency was associated with communication impairments. In contrast, a study of 20 lower-functioning (mean FSIQ of 67) adults with autism compared to IQ-matched adults, found that the autism group performed similarly to controls on word (FAS) fluency and design fluency (Barnard, et al., 2008). However, it should be noted that in this study, results were calculated in an atypical fashion: a pass/fail threshold was set at the level of the mean performance for the entire sample. As such, group means are by necessity raised or lowered according to the performance level of the autism group. In general, data seems fairly consistent in demonstrating that, across a variety of ages, ASD is associated with decreased fluency of responding.

COGNITIVE CONTROL

Cognitive control refers to the ability to flexibly allocate mental resources to guide thoughts and actions in light of internal goals. Theoreticians have suggested that cognitive control is a more "useful" construct than EF, because it may be more clearly specified and identified with neural structures (specifically, dorsolateral prefrontal cortex, medial frontal cortex [including anterior cingulate], and parietal cortex). Although individuals with ASD exhibit prominent symptoms of behavioral inflexibility, researchers have been unable to identify the cognitive correlates of this inflexibility. Given the pattern of strengths and weaknesses in inhibitory tasks, we propose that cognitive control may provide a more parsimonious way to interpret inhibitory task findings from ASD. One particular strength

of the cognitive-control approach is that tasks in this literature are typically highly molar, that is, they isolate specific processes, as described below.

To date, only few studies have directly assessed cognitive control in ASD. Results, however, are provocative. A study of 31 children and adolescents with ASD, ages 8–17 years, and age- and IQ-matched controls suggested deficits in a cognitive control "POP" task, in which participants were asked to respond with a simple button press following a green cue (pressing the button on the side that a central arrow points to) and to respond with an incompatible response following a red cue (pressing the button on the opposite side that is indicated by the central arrow). Because incompatible "red" trials occurred less frequently (30%), they were less salient or prepotent. Participants with autism made significantly more errors on these incompatible trials, particularly in older (> 12 years) participants, and error rates were correlated with autistic symptomatology (Solomon, Ozonoff, Cummings, & Carter, 2008). A second study assessed 18 individuals with ASD, compared to age- and IQ-matched controls, as they performed two cognitive control tasks (Mosconi, et al., 2009). In the *saccadic control task*, participants must visually fixate on a central cue, and then disengage from that cue to look at a target; in the *anti-saccade task*, the same stimuli were given, but the participant was asked to look the opposite direction from the cue. Results indicated a greater difficulty in the ASD group in the anti-saccade task, and error rates were correlated with ritualistic and compulsive behaviors as assessed on the ADI-R. Preliminary data from a functional brain imaging (fMRI) study using a similar visual cognitive control task, conducted in our laboratory, suggests a differentially activated network in response to invalid cues, and higher error rates in adults with autism, relative to controls.

Finally, fMRI studies of cognitive control in ASD have assessed changes in cognitive control as a function of the social salience of cues. The first study found hypoactivation (relatively decreased activity) in an ASD group in response to a "gaze" stimulus, relative to an arrow cue, which these researchers took as suggesting that processing of social stimuli can interfere with cognitive control (Dichter & Belger, 2007). A second study by the same group demonstrated that participants showed less activation than controls in performing a cognitive control task in conditions of heightened arousal (after seeing highly unpleasant or pleasant pictures), suggesting a differential response to socially salient images (Dichter & Belger, 2008).

CONSTRUCT VALIDITY

As is true for most standardized assessment measures, EF tasks are administered in a calm, quiet, distraction-free environment, in a time-limited period; furthermore, these tasks include explicit task instructions and lots of structure. In contrast, in the real world, EF demands are presented with conflicting stimuli, multiple implicit task demands, unclear goals, and sometimes ill-defined task onset and completion times. Thus, structured EF assessments may not reveal the deficits that become apparent in a multidimensional, real-world situation. Researchers have designed several caregiver questionnaires to address this issue of "construct validity"—that is, whether an assessment is measuring what it purports to measure. This is a particularly meaningful issue in the study of EF in individuals with ASD, because caregivers and teachers generally report such strong impressions of cognitive inflexibility, WM challenges, and planning deficits, in the everyday lives of affected individuals.

The Behavioral Rating Inventory of Executive Functioning (BRIEF) is one such parent questionnaire. In one study, parents of 54 high-functioning children with ASD completed the BRIEF (Gioia, Isquith, Kenworthy, & Barton, 2002). Compared to typically-developing (n = 208), reading disordered (n = 34), ADHD (n = 53), and traumatic brain injury (n = 67) groups, matched on age, gender, ethnicity and SES, the ASD group scored higher (and in the clinically-significant range, with the percentage in that range as noted) on most subscales: Shift (69%), Working Memory (57%), Monitor (65%), and Plan (70%).

Cannon and colleagues developed another construct-valid EF task in which participants are provided with "problem scenarios" (e.g., an apartment-dweller has upstairs neighbors with noisy dogs) and are asked to generate multiple possible solutions, to rate those solutions for how well they solved the problem, and also to rate given solutions for how well they solved the problem (Channon, Charman, Heap, Crawford, & Rios, 2001). Compared to typically developing control participants, 15 adolescents with Asperger's disorder generated fewer solutions and were less able to distinguish between good and poor solutions. This may reflect both impaired social judgment and impaired EF processes.

In addition to concerns about construct validity, many of the EF assessments reviewed here assess multiple putative EF processes, in a small group of individuals. Responding to these concerns, researchers have designed "omnibus" tasks, normed on a single sample, which aim at assessing multiple EFs within a single battery. We review here four batteries: the Cambridge Neuropsychological Test Automated Battery, the Delis Kaplan Executive Function System (D-KEFS; Delis, Kaplan, & Kramer, 2001), the NEPSY (Kemp, Kirk, & Korkman, 1998), and the Behavioral Assessment of Dysexecutive Syndrome (BADS; Wilson, Alderman, Burgess, Emslie, & Evans, 1996).

CANTAB

The Cambridge Neuropsychological Test Automated Battery (CANTAB; Sahakian & Owen, 1992) is a computer-administered nonverbal set of nine tasks which the participant completes via touchscreen. The EF tasks include 1) the *Intradimensional/ Extradimensional (ID/ED) Set-Shift*, described in detail above; 2) *Match-to-Sample Visual Search*, in which the participant is presented with an abstract pattern as well as similar pattern options and must match them; 3) *Paired Associates Learning*, in which the individual must remember patterns associated with different locations on the screen; 4) *Big/Little Circle*, in which the participant must alternate in pointing to one size circle for 20 trials and then the other size circle; 5) *Delayed-Match-to-Sample*, in which the participant must match one of four patterns to a complex visual pattern; 6) *Rapid Visual Information Processing*, a test of sustained attention with an additional working memory component, in which the individual must monitor a series of presented numbers for a given number sequence; 7) *Pattern and Spatial Recognition Memory*, in which the individual is presented with a series of visual patterns and must distinguish presented and novel patterns—in a second component, the individual watches a square move to specific locations and must later recall those locations; 8) *Spatial Working Memory*, in which the participant must keep track of which of an increasingly-long series of boxes has already been opened; and 9) *Stockings of Cambridge*, a computerized analog to the Tower of London task, in which balls are placed in "socks" rather than onto pegs. One notable gap is the lack of a verbal working memory assessment.

This well-studied measure has been helpful in EF studies of a variety of populations, including patients with bipolar disorder, schizophrenia, and fetal alcohol exposure, as well as aging populations. A major consideration is whether the computer-based approach renders the CANTAB less sensitive to deficits that would be present in ASD groups if assessed in a face-to-face, human interaction (Feldstein et al., 1999; Ozonoff, 1995; Tien et al., 1996). Despite this concern, one major study of a large sample of participants with ASD, across a wide age and IQ range, was successful in demonstrating significant deficits in set-shifting abilities (Ozonoff et al., 2004).

D-KEFS

The Delis-Kaplan Executive Function System (Delis et al., 2001) was designed to assess inhibition, planning, impulsivity, concept formation, abstract thinking, fluency (or creativity), and flexibility in individuals ages 8 to 89 years. It appears to have clinical utility and to be a helpful tool in EF research (Homack, Lee, & Riccio, 2005). As with the CANTAB, there are nine tasks: 1) *Twenty Questions*, based on the common game of the same name, which assesses the ability to identify categories and subcategories; 2) *California Card Sorting Test*, a variant of the WCST, which assesses problem-solving behavior; 3) *California Stroop Test*, a variant of the traditional Stroop, with an ID/ED shift condition; 4) *California Trails*, a variant of the Trail-Making Test; 5) *Verbal Fluency*, in which a participant must generate as many items as possible in a specific timeframe, within a specific category; 6) *Design Fluency*, which assesses visuospatial fluency as well as response inhibition, and cognitive flexibility; 7) *California Proverb Test*, which assesses pragmatic knowledge; 8) *California Word Context Test*, which assesses semantic knowledge and creativity; and 9) *Tower of California*, an analog of the Tower of Hanoi, with five disks and a board with three pegs.

A recent study found significant deficits in planning on the D-KEFS Tower task (Lopez, Lincoln, Ozonoff, & Lai, 2005), though group differences did not hold when controlling for verbal IQ[2]. In addition,

scores for flexibility (WCST and Trails), working memory (tasks taken from the Wechsler Adult Intelligence Scale), and response inhibition (California Stroop) tasks were strongly associated with restrictive and repetitive behaviors in ASD. Similarly, another study of 12 males with ASD (ages 14–42) included the DKEFS. Results showed lower overall EF scores, relative to the normative database, with notable impairments in complex verbal tasks requiring efficient cognitive search strategies and problem-solving techniques; there were no impairments in design fluency (Kleinhans, Akshoomoff, & Delis, 2005). However, interpretation is limited by the lack of data from a comparison group.

NEPSY

The NEPSY (Kemp et al., 1998) is based on many of the EF tasks initially designed for use with adults. As such, it is somewhat limited in specificity, but has an excellent normative base, extended in a recent revision (2007) to cover children ages 3 years–16 years, 11 months. The NEPSY-II is not designed to be administered as a whole. Rather, any of eight subtest groupings might be administered, depending on the assessment question. The test consists of 32 subtests, tapping into six domains: Attention and Executive Functioning, Language, Memory and Learning, Social Perception, Sensorimotor, and Visuospatial Processing. The Attention/EF domain comprises assessments of inhibition, self-regulation, monitoring, vigilance, selective and sustained attention, maintenance of response set, planning, flexibility in thinking and figural fluency. These tasks are similar to the tests described throughout the chapter. While data from children with ASD is scarce, one study documented impairments in 23 children with HFA, relative to typically developing controls matched on age, race, gender, and SES (Hooper, Poon, Marcus, & Fine, 2006). The HFA group scored lower on Tower, Phonological Processing, Auditory Attention

---

group-specific deficits, researchers have begun to voice powerful arguments against this practice, as it may involve removing significant variance that is actually syndrome-specific; that is, "it is false that any measure on which groups differ and which its not itself the comparison of interest must be controlled because it is related to the assignment (to groups) mechanism" (Dennis et al., 2009, p. 8).

and Response Set, Speeded Naming, Imitation of Hand Positions, Visuomotor Precision, Arrows, Comprehension of Instructions and Narrative Memory.

A final "omnibus" assessment of EF is the Behavioral Assessment of Dysexecutive Syndrome (BADS, Wilson, et al., 1996), which consists of six tasks: 1) *Temporal Judgment*; 2) *Rule Shift* (a modified WCST); 3) *Practical Problem-solving*, in which the participant must determine how to extract a cork from a tube; 4) *Strategy Formation*, in which the participant must generate multiple strategies to find a lost item; 5) *Planning*, in which the participant must devise an optimal route on a map; and 6) a task which combines planning, performance monitoring, and task ordering, in which the participant must at least attempt each of six tasks in 10 minutes, in any order, with the single constraint being that he must not multi-task.

Using the BADS (among other tasks), Hill and Bird examined EF skills in a sample of 22 adults with Asperger's, compared with 22 typically developing control adults matched on FSIQ and chronological age (Hill & Bird, 2006). Their findings demonstrated significant impairments in the Asperger's group in the planning and multitasking "combination" tasks from the BADS, as well as the Hayling sentence completion task (which assesses fluency and inhibition; see description above). Interestingly, 21 of the 22 participants with Asperger's scored below the 5th percentile (relative to the control group) on at least one task; in addition, scores were correlated with autistic symptomatology (scores on a questionnaire about pragmatic and communicative competence, and scores on the Autism Spectrum Quotient; Baron-Cohen, Wheelwright, Skinner, Martin, & Clubley, 2001). Hill and Bird suggest that modular EF tasks are helpful for assessing EF skills in ASD, and that impairments reflect a difficulty with engaging and disengaging from responses or activities while maintaining a goal representation.

EF IN THE BROADER AUTISM PHENOTYPE

There has been generally strong support for findings of EF deficits in family members of affected individuals, compared to family members of developmentally delayed individuals or other control groups. For example, Hughes and colleagues found deficits in

set-shifting, visuospatial planning, and working memory, but not in spatial memory, in 40 parents of children with autism relative to 40 parents of LD and 36 adults from unaffected families (Hughes, Leboyer, & Bouvard, 1997). A follow-up study reported poor set-shifting, planning, and fluency performance, but intact spatial span, in siblings of affected children relative to children with typically developing or globally developmentally delayed siblings (Hughes, Plumet, & Leboyer, 1999). A study of unaffected parents and siblings of individuals with autism (n = 58) and obsessive-compulsive disorder (n = 64), as well healthy controls (n = 47), indicated impairments in planning and working memory (Tower of London), but no differences in four other EF tasks (verbal fluency, design fluency, trail making, and association fluency), and no differences between family members in the ASD and obsessive groups (Delorme, et al., 2007). However, some studies fail to find differences in EF for relatives of individuals with ASD; for example, a study of parents of individuals with ASD (n = 62), compared to early onset schizophrenia (n = 36) and mental retardation (n = 30), found no group differences in WCST, Tower of Hanoi, or the Trail-making Test (Bölte & Poustka, 2006).

Generally, data suggest difficulties in family members with planning, set-shifting, and working memory, though findings are only as consistent as most others in the behavioral genetics of autism; that is, no firm conclusions can be drawn. However, the approach of studying family members of affected individuals is likely to prove fruitful, particularly in an era when large, well-characterized samples with associated genotype data are increasingly available (see Chapter 2).

SUMMARY AND FUTURE DIRECTIONS

This chapter has reviewed executive processes in autism spectrum disorder, focusing primarily on set-shifting, inhibition, and working memory, as well as planning, fluency, and cognitive control. Both clinicians and basic scientists agree that the executive functions are central to everyday functioning, and particularly in classroom and vocational settings. For example, EF abilities are critical for understanding how to initiate an open-ended task, to set realistic goals, to organize new information for subsequent recall, to generate multiple potential solutions for problems, to inhibit impulses, and to consider the consequences of one's actions. EF deficits have been used to understand difficulties in symbolic play (McDonough, Stahmer, Schreibman, & Thompson, 1997), pragmatic language skills (Schuh, Mirman, Gustafson, & Eigsti, May, 2009), syntactic development (Eigsti, 2001), Theory of Mind abilities (Pellicano, 2007), and even the response to intervention (Fisher & Happé, 2005).

While there are many conflicting findings about EF skills in ASD, the data generally suggest deficits in set-shifting and complex aspects of WM (e.g., conditions of high load). Most studies find evidence of deficits in planning and fluency, as well. While data from "typical" response inhibition tasks suggest that this EF is generally unimpaired, the few studies that have examined inhibition of responses in service of simple goals (e.g., cognitive control) suggest that cognitive control deficits may play a role in ASD.

A better understanding of regulatory capacities characterized by EF in large samples of affected and unaffected individuals—ideally, followed longitudinally—will be critical to our understanding of the development and "use" of EF in autism. As Garon and colleagues (2008) point out, while the extended developmental trajectory of EF means that this set of capacities is highly vulnerable to insult, it also means that EF may be amenable to intervention for an extended period. The use of "omnibus" tasks, which permit the assessment of different EF constructs in a single sample, of highly construct-valid questionnaires, and of modern tasks drawn from cognitive neuroscience to examine parametrically-varied, molar aspects of EF, are all likely to be fruitful avenues for understanding this construct.

Language appears particularly entwined with EF. Dating from early proposals that language is required to help regulate behavior (e.g., Luria, 1959), theoreticians have pondered the role of language skills in our ability to control, plan, and regulate our behavior. Given the salient and primary difficulties with language that are central to the autism spectrum disorders, it seems likely that the relationship between EF processes and language development will continue to reveal important new facets of the disorder, whether or not EF is a core deficit. More broadly, EF is likely to be central to our understanding of many symptoms of autism, including repetitive activities and circumscribed interests, where individuals perseverate on a given non-functional behavior or a highly specific (and again, typically non-functional) topic or idea. Certainly, the exciting arena of EF holds great promise for those who hope to better understand the underpinnings of the many strengths and weaknesses that characterize the autism spectrum disorders, and to intervene to allow affected individuals to reach their potential.

References

Ackerman, P. L., Beier, M. E., & Boyle, M. O. (2005). Working memory and intelligence: The same or different constructs? *Psychological Bulletin, 131*(1), 30–60.

Anderson, P. (2002). Assessment and development of executive function (EF) during childhood. *Child Neuropsychology, 8*(2), 71–82.

Anderson, P., Anderson, V., & Lajoie, G. (1996). The Tower of London Test: Validation and standardization for pediatric populations. *The Clinical Neuropsychologist, 10*, 54–65.

Anderson, S. W., Damasio, H., Jones, R. D., & Tranel, D. (1991). Wisconsin Card Sorting Test performance as a measure of frontal lobe damage. *Journal of Clinical and Experimental Neuropsychology, 13*(6), 909–922.

Baddeley, A. (1992). Working memory. *Science, 255*(5044), 556–559.

Baddeley, A., & Hitch, G. (1974). Working memory. In G. A. Bower (Ed.), *The Psychology of Learning and Motivation* (pp. 47–89). New York: Academic Press.

Baker, S. C., Rogers, R. D., Owen, A. M., Frith, C. D., Dolan, R. J., Frackowiak, R. S.,& Robbins, T.W.(1996). Neural systems engaged by planning: a PET study of the Tower of London task. *Neuropsychologia, 34*(6), 515–526.

Barnard, L., Muldoon, K., Hasan, R., O'Brien, G., & Stewart, M. (2008). Profiling executive dysfunction in adults with autism and comorbid learning disability. *Autism, 12*(2), 125–141.

Baron-Cohen, S., Leslie, A., & Frith, U. (1985). Does the autistic child have a "theory of mind"? *Cognition, 21*, 37–36.

Baron-Cohen, S., Wheelwright, S., Skinner, R., Martin, J., & Clubley, E. (2001). The autism spectrum quotient (AQ): Evidence from Asperger syndrome, high-functioning autism, males and females, scientists and mathematicians. *Journal of Autism and Developmental Disorders, 31*(1), 5–17.

Bebko, J., & Ricciuti, C. (2000). Executive functioning and memory strategy use in children with autism: The influence of task constraints on spontaneous rehearsal. *Autism, 4*(3), 299–320.

Bennetto, L., Pennington, B. F., & Rogers, S. J. (1996). Intact and impaired memory functions in autism. *Child Development, 67*, 1816–1835.

Berg, E. A. (1948). A simple objective technique for measuring flexibility in thinking. *Journal of General Psychology, 39*, 15–22.

Bishop, D. V., & Norbury, C. F. (2005). Executive functions in children with communication impairments, in relation to autistic symptomatology. 1: Generativity. *Autism*, 9(1), 7–27.

Bölte, S., & Poustka, F. (2006). The broader cognitive phenotype of autism in parents: How specific is the tendency for local processing and executive dysfunction? *Journal of Child Psychology and Psychiatry*, 47(6), 639–645.

Boucher, J. (1981). Memory for recent events in autism. *Journal of Autism and Developmental Disorders, 11*, 293–301.

Boucher, J., Cowell, P., Howard, M., Broks, P., Farrant, A., Roberts, N., & Mayes, A. (2005). A combined clinical, neuropsychological, and neuroanatomical study of adults with high functioning autism. *Cognitive Neuropsychiatry*, 10(3), 165–213.

Burgess, P. W., & Shallice, T. (1997). *The Hayling and Brixton tests*. Bury, St. Edmonds: Thames Valley Test Company.

Carlson, S. M., Moses, L. J., & Claxton, L. J. (2004). Individual differences in executive functioning and theory of mind: An investigation of inhibitory control and planning ability. *Journal of Experimental Child Psychology*, 87(4), 299–319.

Case, R., Kurland, M. D., & Goldberg, J. (1982). Operational efficiency and the growth of short-term memory span. *Journal of Experimental Child Psychology, 33*, 386–404.

Casey, B. J., Durston, S., & Fossella, J. A. (2001). Evidence for a mechanistic model of cognitive control. *Clinical Neuroscience Research, 1*, 267–282.

Channon, S., Charman, T., Heap, J., Crawford, S., & Rios, P. (2001). Real-life-type problem-solving in Asperger's syndrome. *Journal of Autism and Developmental Disorders*, 31(5), 461–469.

Chelune, G. J., & Baer, R. A. (1986). Developmental norms for the Wisconsin Card Sorting test. *Journal of Clinical and Experimental Neuropsychology*, 8(3), 219–228.

Cicchetti, D., & Rogosch, F. (1996). Equifinality and multifinality in developmental psychopathology. *Development and Psychopathology*, 8(4), 597–600.

Coldren, J. T., & Halloran, C. (2003). Spatial reversal as a measure of executive functioning in children with autism. *Journal of Genetic Psychology*, 164(1), 29–41.

Craig, J., & Baron-Cohen, S. (1999). Creativity and imagination in autism and Asperger syndrome. *Journal of Autism and Developmental Disorders*, 29(4), 319–326.

Damasio, A. R., Tranel, D., & Damasio, H. C. (1991). Somatic markers and the guidance of behavior: Theory and preliminary testing. In H. S. Levin, H. M. Eisenberg, & A. L. Benton (Eds.), *Frontal Lobe Function and Dysfunction* (pp. 217–229). New York: Oxford.

Daneman, M., & Carpenter, P. A. (1980). Individual differences in working memory and reading. *Journal of Verbal Learning and Verbal Behavior, 19*, 450–466.

Dawson, G., Meltzoff, A. N., Osterling, J., & Rinaldi, J. (1998). Neuropsychological correlates of early symptoms of autism. *Child Development, 69*(5), 1276–1285.

Dawson, G., Munson, J., Estes, A., Osterling, J., McPartland, J., Toth, K., …, Abbott, R. (2002). Neurocognitive function and joint attention ability in young children with autism spectrum disorder versus developmental delay. *Child Development*, 73(2), 345–358.

Delis, D. C., Kaplan, E., & Kramer, J. (2001). *Delis Kaplan executive function system*. San Antonio, TX: Psychological Corporation.

Delorme, R., Gousse, V., Roy, I., Trandafir, A., Mathieu, F., Mouren-Simeoni, M. C., …, Leboyer, M. (2007). Shared executive dysfunctions in unaffected relatives of patients with autism and obsessive-compulsive disorder. *European Psychiatry*, 22(1), 32–38.

Dempster, F. N. (1992). The rise and fall of the inhibitory mechanism: Toward a unified theory of cognitive development and aging. *Developmental Review, 12*(1), 45–75.

Dennis, M., Francis, D. J., Cirino, P. T., Schachar, R., Barnes, M. A., & Fletcher, J. M. (2009). Why IQ is not a covariate in cognitive studies of neurodevelopmental disorders. *Journal of the International Neuropsychological Society, 15*, 1–13.

Diamond, A., & Taylor, C. (1996). Development of an aspect of executive control: development of the abilities to remember what I said and to "do as I say, not as I do." *Developmental Psychobiology*, 29(4), 315–334.

Dichter, G. S., & Belger, A. (2007). Social stimuli interfere with cognitive control in autism. *Neuroimage*, 35(3), 1219–1230.

Dichter, G. S., & Belger, A. (2008). Atypical modulation of cognitive control by arousal in autism. *Psychiatry Research*, 164(3), 185–197.

Eigsti, I. M. (2001). *Word learning and memory functions in young children with autism*. (Unpublished doctoral dissertation). University of Rochester, Rochester, NY.

Eigsti, I. M., Zayas, V., Mischel, W., Shoda, Y., Ayduk, O., Dadlani, M. B., …, Casey, B.J. (2006). Predicting cognitive control from preschool to late adolescence and young adulthood. *Psychological Science*, 17(6), 478–484.

Elder, J. H., & Nissen, H. W. (1933). Delayed alternation in raccoons. *Journal of Comparative Psychology, 16*, 117–135.

Engle, R. W., Kane, M. J., & Tuholski, S. W. (1999). Working memory and controlled attention. In A. Miyake & P. Shah (Eds.), *Models of working memory: Mechanisms of active maintenance and executive control* (pp. 102–134). New York, NY: Cambridge University Press.

Eskes, G. A., Bryson, S. E., & McCormick, T. A. (1990). Comprehension of concrete and abstract words in autistic children. *Journal of Autism and Developmental Disorders, 20*(1), 61–73.

Espy, K. A. (1997). The shape school: Assessing executive function in preschool children. *Developmental Neuropsychology, 13,* 495–499.

Espy, K. A., Kaufmann, P. M., McDiarmid, M. D., & Glisky, M. L. (1999). Executive functioning in preschool children: performance on A-not-B and other delayed response format tasks. *Brain and Cognition, 41*(2), 178–199.

Fein, D., Dunn, M. A., Allen, D. M., Aram, R., Hall, N., Morris, R., et al. (1996). Neuropsychological and language findings. In I. Rapin (Ed.), *Preschool children with inadequate communication: Developmental language disorder, autism, low IQ* (pp. 123–154). London: MacKeith Press.

Feldstein, S. N., Keller, F. R., Portman, R. E., Durham, R. L., Klebe, K. J., & Davis, H. P. (1999). A comparison of computerized and standard versions of the Wisconsin Card Sorting Test. *Clin Neuropsychol, 13*(3), 303–313.

Fisher, N., & Happé, F. (2005). A training study of theory of mind and executive function in children with autistic spectrum disorders. *Journal of Autism and Developmental Disorders, 35*(6), 757–771.

Frith, U., & Happé, F. (1994). Autism: Beyond "theory of mind." *Cognition, 50,* 115–132.

Gabig, C. S. (2008). Verbal working memory and story retelling in school-age children with autism. *Language, Speech and Hearing Services in Schools, 39*(4), 498–511.

Garon, N., Bryson, S. E., & Smith, I. M. (2008). Executive function in preschoolers: A review using an integrative framework. *Psychological Bulletin, 134*(1), 31–60.

Gioia, G. A., Isquith, P. K., Kenworthy, L., & Barton, R. M. (2002). Profiles of everyday executive function in acquired and developmental disorders. *Child Neuropsychology, 8*(2), 121–137.

Goldberg, M. C., Lasker, A. G., Zee, D. S., Garth, E., Tien, A., & Landa, R. J. (2002). Deficits in the initiation of eye movements in the absence of a visual target in adolescents with high functioning autism. *Neuropsychologia, 40*(12), 2039–2049.

Goldman-Rakic, P. S. (1987). Development of cortical circuitry and cognitive function. *Child Development, 58,* 601–622.

Griffith, E. M., Pennington, B. F., Wehner, E. A., & Rogers, S. J. (1999). Executive functions in young children with autism. *Child Development, 70*(4), 817–832.

Happé, F., Ronald, A., & Plomin, R. (2006). Time to give up on a single explanation for autism. *Nature Neuroscience, 9*(10), 1218–1220.

Hill, E. L. (2004). Executive dysfunction in autism. *Trends in Cognitive Sciences, 8*(1), 26–32.

Hill, E. L., & Bird, C. M. (2006). Executive processes in Asperger syndrome: Patterns of performance in a multiple case series. *Neuropsychologia, 44*(14), 2822–2835.

Homack, S., Lee, D., & Riccio, C. A. (2005). Test review: Delis-Kaplan executive function system. *Journal of Clinical and Experimental Neuropsychology, 27*(5), 599–609.

Hooper, S. R., Poon, K. K., Marcus, L., & Fine, C. (2006). Neuropsychological characteristics of school-age children with high-functioning autism: performance on the NEPSY. *Child Neuropsychology, 12*(4-5), 299–305.

Hughes, C., & Ensor, R. (2007). Executive function and theory of mind: Predictive relations from ages 2 to 4. *Developmental Psychology, 43*(6), 1447–1459.

Hughes, C., Leboyer, M., & Bouvard, M. (1997). Executive function in parents of children with autism. *Psychological Medicine, 27,* 209–220.

Hughes, C., Plumet, M.-H., & Leboyer, M. (1999). Towards a cognitive phenotype for autism: Increased prevalence of executive dysfunction and superior spatial span amongst siblings of children with autism. *Journal of Child Psychology and Psychiatry, 40*(5), 705–718.

Hughes, C., & Russell, J. (1993). Autistic children's difficulty with mental disengagement from an object: Its implications for theories of autism. *Developmental Psychology, 29*(3), 498–510.

Hughes, C., Russell, J., & Robbins, T. W. (1994). Evidence for executive dysfunction in autism. *Neuropsychologia, 32*(4), 477–492.

Huttenlocher, P. R. (1979). Synaptic density in human frontal cortex - developmental changes and effects of aging. *Brain Research, 163,* 195–205.

Huttenlocher, P. R. (1990). Morphometric study of human cerebral cortex development. *Neuropsychologia, 28*(6), 517–527.

Joseph, R., Steele, S., Meyer, E., & Tager-Flusberg, H. (2005). Self-ordered pointing in children with autism: failure to use verbal mediation in the service of working memory? *Neuropsychologia, 43*(10), 1400–1411.

Joseph, R. M., McGrath, L. M., & Tager-Flusberg, H. (2005). Executive dysfunction and its relation to language ability in verbal school-age children with autism. *Developmental Neuropsychology, 27*(3), 361–378.

Just, M. A., Cherkassky, V. L., Keller, T. A., Kana, R. K., & Minshew, N. J. (2007). Functional and anatomical cortical underconnectivity in autism: evidence from an FMRI study of an executive function task and corpus callosum morphometry. *Cerebral Cortex, 17*(4), 951–961.

Kail, R. (1986). Sources of age differences in speed of processing. *Child Development, 57*(4), 969–987.

Kaland, N., Smith, L., & Mortensen, E. (2008). Brief report: Cognitive flexibility and focused attention in children and adolescents with Asperger syndrome or high-functioning autism as measured on the computerized version of the Wisconsin Card Sorting Test. *Journal of Autism and Developmental Disorders, 38*(6), 1161–1165.

Kemp, S., Kirk, U., & Korkman, M. (1998). *Essentials of NEPSY assessment*. New York: Wiley.

Kjelgaard, M.M., & Tager-Flusberg, H. (2001). An investigation of language impairment in autism: Implications for genetic subgroups. *Language and Cognitive Processes, 16*, 287–308.

Kleinhans, N., Akshoomoff, N., & Delis, D. C. (2005). Executive functions in autism and Asperger's disorder: Flexibility, fluency, and inhibition. *Developmental Neuropsychology, 27*(3), 379–401.

Landa, R. J., & Goldberg, M. (2005). Language, social, and executive functions in high functioning autism: a continuum of performance. *Journal of Autism and Developmental Disorders, 35*(5), 557–573.

Liss, M., Fein, D., Allen, D., Dunn, M., Feinstein, C., Morris, R., … Rapin, I. (2001). Executive functioning in high-functioning children with autism. *Journal of Child Psychology and Psychiatry and Allied Disciplines, 42*(2), 261–270.

Lopez, B., Lincoln, A., Ozonoff, S., & Lai, Z. (2005). Examining the relationship between executive functions and restricted, repetitive symptoms of Autistic Disorder. *Journal of Autism and Developmental Disorders, 35*(4), 445–460.

Luria, Z. (1959). A semantic analysis of a normal and a neurotic therapy group. *Journal of Abnormal Psychology, 58*(2), 216–220.

MacDonald, M. C., & Christiansen, M. H. (2002). Reassessing working memory: Comment on Just and Carpenter (1992) and Waters and Caplan (1996). *Psychological Review, 109*, 35–54.

Mak-Fan, K., Morris, D., Roberts, W., & Taylor, M. (2008). *Functional neuroimaging of set shifting in children with autism spectrum disorder*. Paper presented at the International Meeting for Autism Research (IMFAR), London, England.

McDonough, L., Stahmer, A., Schreibman, L., & Thompson, S. J. (1997). Deficits, delays, and distractions: An evaluation of symbolic play and memory in children with autism. *Development and Psychopathology, 9*, 17–41.

McEvoy, R. E., Rogers, S. J., & Pennington, B. F. (1993). Executive function and social communication deficits in young autistic children. *Journal of Child Psychology and Psychiatry, and Allied Disciplines, 34*(4), 563–578.

Minshew, N. J., Goldstein, G., Muenz, L. R., & Payton, J. B. (1992). Neuropsychological functioning in nonmentally retarded autistic individuals. *Journal of Clinical and Experimental Neuropsychology, 14*, 749–761.

Minshew, N. J., Luna, B., & Sweeney, J. A. (1999). Oculomotor evidence for neocortical systems but not cerebellar dysfunction in autism. *Neurology, 52*(5), 917–922.

Morris, R. G., Rowe, A., Fox, N., Feigenbaum, J. D., Miotto, E. C., & Howlin, P. (1999). Spatial working memory in Asperger's syndrome and in patients with focal frontal and temporal lobe lesions. *Brain and Cognition, 41*, 9–26.

Mosconi, M. W., Kay, M., D'Cruz, A. M., Seidenfeld, A., Guter, S., Stanford, L. D., & Sweeney, J.A. (2009). Impaired inhibitory control is associated with higher-order repetitive behaviors in autism spectrum disorders. *Psychological Medicine, 39*, 1–8.

Mottron, L., Mottron, L., Morasse, K., & Belleville, S. (2001). A study of memory functioning in individuals with autism. *Journal of Child Psychology and Psychiatry, 42*(2), 253.

O'Shea, A. G., Fein, D. A., Cillessen, A. H. N., Klin, A., & Shultz, R. T. (2005). Source memory in children with autism spectrum disorders. *Developmental Neuropsychology, 27*(3), 337–360.

Ozonoff, S. (1995). Reliability and validity of the Wisconsin Card Sorting Test in autism. *Neuropsychology, 4*, 491–500.

Ozonoff, S., Cook, I., Coon, H., Dawson, G., Joseph, R. M., Klin, A., … & Wrathall, D. (2004). Performance on Cambridge Neuropsychological Test Automated Battery subtests sensitive to frontal lobe function in people with autistic disorder: Evidence from the Collaborative Programs of Excellence in Autism network. *Journal of Autism and Developmental Disorders, 34*(2), 139–150.

Ozonoff, S., & Jensen, J. (1999). Brief report: Specific executive function profiles in three neurodevelopmental disorders. *Journal of Autism and Developmental Disorders, 29*(2), 171–177.

Ozonoff, S., Pennington, B. F., & Rogers, S. J. (1991). Executive function deficits in high-functioning autistic individuals: Relationship to theory of mind. *Journal of Child Psychology and Psychiatry & Allied Disciplines, 32*, 1081–1105.

Ozonoff, S., Rogers, S. J., & Pennington, B. F. (1991). Asperger's syndrome: Evidence of an empirical distinction from high-functioning autism. *Journal of Child Psychology and Psychiatry, and Allied Disciplines, 32*(7), 1107–1122.

Ozonoff, S., & Strayer, D. L. (1997). Inhibitory function in nonretarded children with autism. *Journal of Autism and Developmental Disorders, 27*(1), 59–77.

Ozonoff, S., & Strayer, D. L. (2001). Further evidence of intact working memory in autism. *Journal of Autism & Developmental Disorders, 31*(3), 257–263.

Ozonoff, S., Strayer, D. L., McMahon, W. M., & Filloux, F. (1994). Executive function abilities in autism and Tourette syndrome: an information processing approach. *Journal of Child Psychology and Psychiatry, and Allied Disciplines, 35*(6), 1015–1032.

Pascualvaca, D. M., Fantie, B. D., Papageorgiou, M., & Mirsky, A. F. (1998). Attentional capacities in children with autism: is there a general deficit in shifting focus? *Journal of Autism and Developmental Disorders, 28*(6), 467–478.

Pellicano, E. (2007). Links between theory of mind and executive function in young children with autism: Clues to developmental primacy. *Developmental Psychology, 43*(4), 974–990.

Petrides, M., & Milner, B. (1982). Deficits on subject-ordered tasks after frontal- and temporal-lobe lesions in man. *Neuropsychologia, 20*(3), 249–262.

Piaget, J. (1954). *The construction of reality in the child.* New York: Basic Books.

Posner, M. I., & Rothbart, M. K. (2007). Research on attention networks as a model for the integration of psychological science. *Annual Review of Psychology, 58,* 1–23.

Roberts, R. J. J., & Pennington, B. F. (1996). An interactive framework for examining prefrontal cognitive processes. *Developmental Neuropsychology, 12*(1), 105–126.

Rumsey, J. M. (1985). Conceptual problem-solving in highly verbal, nonretarded autistic men. *Journal of Autism and Developmental Disorders, 15*(1), 23–36.

Rumsey, J. M., & Hamburger, S. D. (1988). Neuropsychological findings in high-functioning men with infantile autism, residual state. *Journal of Clinical and Experimental Neuropsychology, 10*(2), 201–221.

Rumsey, J. M., & Hamburger, S. D. (1990). Neuropsychological divergence of high-level autism and severe dyslexia. *Journal of Autism and Developmental Disorders, 20*(2), 155–168.

Russell, J., Jarrold, C., & Henry, L. (1996). Working memory in children with autism and moderate learning difficulties. *Journal of Child Psychology and Psychiatry, and Allied Disciplines, 37*(6), 673–686.

Russell, J., Jarrold, C., & Hood, B. (1999). Two intact executive capacities in children with autism: implications for the core executive dysfunctions in the disorder. *Journal of Autism and Developmental Disorders, 29*(2), 103–112.

Russo, N., Landry, O., Hongwanishkul, D., Lee, W., Burack, J. A., & Zelazo, P. D. (2005, May). *Working memory and executive function in autism.* Paper presented at the International Meeting for Autism Research (IMFAR), Boston, MA.

Sahakian, B. J., & Owen, A. M. (1992). Computerized assessment in neuropsychiatry using CANTAB: Discussion paper. *Journal of the Royal Society of Medicine, 85*(7), 399–402.

Schuh, J. M., Mirman, D., Gustafson, T., & Eigsti, I. M. (May, 2009). *Do you see what I see? The influence of working memory on shared knowledge in children with autism and typical development.* Paper presented at the International Meeting for Autism Research (IMFAR-09), Philadelphia, PA.

Shallice, T. (1982). Specific impairments in planning. *Philosophical Transactions of the Royal Society of London, 298,* 199–209.

Shallice, T., & Burgess, P. W. (1991). Higher-order cognitive impairments and frontal lobe lesions in man. In H. S. Levin, H. M. Eisenberg & A. L. Benton (Eds.), *Frontal lobe function and dysfunction* (pp. 125–138). New York: Oxford.

Shu, B. C., Lung, F. W., Tien, A. Y., & Chen, B. C. (2001). Executive function deficits in non-retarded autistic children. *Autism, 5*(2), 165–174.

Sigman, M., Dijamco, A., Gratier, M., & Rozga, A. (2004). Early detection of core deficits in autism. *Mental Retardation and Developmental Disabilities Research Reviews, 10*(4), 221–233.

Solomon, M., Ozonoff, S. J., Cummings, N., & Carter, C. S. (2008). Cognitive control in autism spectrum disorders. *International Journal of Developmental Neuroscience, 26*(2), 239–247.

Steele, S., Minshew, N. J., Luna, B., & Sweeney, J. (2007). Spatial working memory deficits in autism. *Journal of Autism and Developmental Disorders, 37*(4), 605–612.

Stuss, D., & Benson, D. (1984). Neuropsychological studies of the frontal lobes. *Psychological Bulletin, 95,* 3–28.

Szatmari, P., Tuff, L., Finlayson, A., & Bartolucci, G. (1990). Asperger's syndrome and autism: Neurocognitive aspects. *Journal of the American Academy of Child and Adolescent Psychiatry, 29,* 130–136.

Tien, A. Y., Spevack, T. V., Jones, D. W., Pearlson, G. D., Schlaepfer, T. E., & Strauss, M. E. (1996). Computerized Wisconsin Card Sorting Test: Comparison with manual administration. *Kaohsiung Journal of Medical Science, 12*(8), 479–485.

Turner, M. A. (1999). Generating novel ideas: Fluency performance in high-functioning and learning disabled individuals with autism. *Journal of Child Psychology and Psychiatry, 40,* 189–201.

Unsworth, N., & Engle, R. W. (2007). On the division of short-term and working memory: An examination of simple and complex span and their relation to higher order abilities. *Psychological Bulletin, 133*(6), 1038–1066.

Welsh, M. C., Pennington, B. F., & Groisser, D. (1991). A normative-developmental study of executive function: A window on prefrontal function in children. *Developmental Neuropsychology, 7,* 131–149.

Williams, D., Goldstein, G., & Minshew, N. J. (2006). The profile of memory function in children with autism. *Neuropsychology, 20*(1), 21–29.

Wilson, B. A., Alderman, N., Burgess, P. W., Emslie, H., & Evans, J. J. (1996). *Behavioural assessment of the dysexecutive syndrome: Manual.* Bury St. Edmunds, England: Thames Valley Test Company.

Yerys, B. E., Hepburn, S. L., Pennington, B. F., & Rogers, S. J. (2007). Executive function in preschoolers with autism: evidence consistent with a secondary deficit. *Journal of Autism and Developmental Disorders, 37*(6), 1068–1079.

Zelazo, P. D., Muller, U., Frye, D., Marcovitch, S., Argitis, G., Boseovski, J., Chiang, J. K., Hongwanishkul, D., Schuster, B. V. & Sutherland, A. (2003). The development of executive function in early childhood. *Monographs of the Society for Research in Child Development, 68,* vii–137.

Chapter 10

Motor Development and its Relation to Social and Behavioral Manifestations in Children with ASD

Ericka L. Wodka and Stewart H. Mostofsky

INTRODUCTION

The clinical conceptualization of autism is characterized by impairments in three core areas of functioning: communication, socialization, and repetitive/stereotyped patterns of behavior. Other areas of difficulty are also described, but not considered diagnostic of autism spectrum disorders (ASD). Developmental motor impairments exemplify a deficit often seen in children with ASD, but are not considered diagnostic either. In fact, in Kanner's first description of 11 cases of "infantile autism" (1943), stereotyped behaviors and clumsiness in both gait and gross motor performance were noted. Similarly, in an early study examining basic motor functioning in autism, Ornitz, Guthrie, and Farley (1977) found that disturbances in motility (hand flaps, finger flicks, body posture, incorrect gesturing, toe walking, and darting/lunging movements) were present in about 70% of their ASD sample. Since then, there has been accumulating evidence documenting motor impairments as a prominent feature of ASD, with findings suggesting these impairments are seen in children across the spectrum of autism diagnosis, including both high- and low-functioning individuals (Freitag, Kleser, Schneider, & von Gontard, 2007; Gidley Larson & Mostofsky, 2006; Green et al., 2002; Haas et al., 1996; Hallett et al., 1993; Jansiewicz et al., 2006; Jones & Prior, 1985, Manjiviona & Prior, 1995; Mostofsky et al., 2006; Noterdaemem Mildenberger, Minow, & Amorosa, 2002; Rapin, 1991; Rogers, Bennetto, McEvoy, & Pennington, 1996, Smith & Bryson, 1994; Teitelbaum, Teitelbaum, Nye, Fryman, & Maurer, 1998; Vilensky, Damasio, & Maurer, 1981). Observed motor deficits include abnormalities in basic aspects of motor control, such as gait, posture, coordination, and tone, as well as difficulties in performing higher-order skills, including imitation and pantomime of complex gestures.

In addition to being an observable area of developmental weakness for children with ASD, there are multiple characteristics of motor functioning that are amenable to examination, providing a basis for understanding the neurologic basis of autism: 1) motor signs are highly quantifiable and reproducible and are more overtly observable than measures of more complex social and behavioral systems; 2) motor function can be examined in a manner that minimizes potential confounds of attention and socioemotional relatedness; and 3) the neuroanatomic and physiologic basis of motor control is better understood in contrast to that for complex social behavior, such that one knows where to look in the brain when examining for anatomic correlates of functional impairment. As such, the motor system provides a model for understanding deficits in parallel systems, such as those necessary for development of social and communicative behaviors. Consistent with this notion, in children with ASD, motor deficits appear to be associated with core impairments in socialization and communication (Iacoboni, 2005; Rizzolatti, Fogassi, & Gallese, 2001; Rizzolatti, Fogassi, & Gallese, 2001; Williams, & Whiten, & Singh, 2004).

The purpose of this chapter is to describe the motor impairments that have been documented in children with ASD, as well as their relationship to the social and behavioral manifestations of the disorder. Particular emphasis will be placed on recently described abnormalities in the acquisition of internal models for motor control in ASD, suggesting that children with ASD build stronger than normal associations between motor commands and proprioceptive feedback, and weaker than normal associations between the same commands and visual feedback. Additionally, the neurological underpinnings of motor abnormalities in ASD will be reviewed, highlighting newly described abnormalities in cortical and subcortical connectivity, and concluding with a discussion of the clinical relevance of these associations, particularly regarding the development of social and communicative behaviors.

MEASURES OF MOTOR DYSFUNCTION IN ASD

While motor skills develop simultaneously with other skills (e.g., early communication), observable gains in motor skills are evident before other domains of functioning. Difficulties in the development of motor function can occur at multiple levels, ranging from gross ability (e.g., walking, running) to fine

motor (e.g., buttoning up a shirt, writing), and basic ability (e.g., posture), to complex tasks involving motor planning, execution, and persistence (e.g., riding a bicycle). Basic motor impairments, including low muscle tone, imbalance, clumsy gait, and poor manual dexterity and coordination, have been observed in children with ASD across a range of functional ability, and offer a high level of discrimination in distinguishing children with ASD from typically developing (TD) children (Jansiewicz et al., 2006).

Retrospective studies, including video analysis, have identified abnormalities as early as infancy in sensory-motor behaviors (i.e., anticipatory posturing) and motor development (e.g., lying down, sitting, and standing) (Baranek, 1999; Teitelbaum et al., 1998, 2004). Throughout childhood and into adolescence and adulthood, motor deficits continue to be observed in ASD. Using retrospective clinical record reviews, Ming, Brimacombe, and Wagner (2007) reported on the prevalence of motor difficulties in 154 children with ASD. In this cohort, hypotonia was most frequently described (51% of the sample), followed by motor apraxia (34%), intermittent toe walking (19%), and gross motor delay (9%). Notably, hypotonia and motor apraxia appeared to improve with age, as prevalence rates were significantly higher in younger than older children. In addition, multiple studies (Damasio & Maurer, 1978; Maurer & Damasio, 1982; Vilensky et al., 1981) have documented unusual gait (i.e., slower pace, decreased step length, increased knee flexion), coordination, and posturing (i.e., asymmetrical postures while standing and walking) in children with ASD. More recently, Rinehart and colleagues (2006) reported increased difficulty in walking a straight line with the coexistence of variable stride length/duration for children with autism. These findings were comparable to that from patients with cerebellar ataxia. Perhaps of greatest importance, Sutera and colleagues (2007) reported that delayed motor skills at age 2 years emerged as the clearest distinguishing factor in identifying children who continued to meet criteria for an ASD diagnosis at age 4 years.

Ozonoff and colleagues (2008) have criticized the positive motor findings described in ASD, stating that many conclusions are limited by the lack of use of a clinical control group. Additionally, Ozonoff pointed out that, when clinical groups are used for comparison (i.e., groups other than typically developing controls), differences between children with ASD and children with mental retardation have not been shown on measures of running, jumping, throwing, catching, and balance (Morin & Reid, 1985); differences between children with ASD and general developmental delay have not been shown on measures of reflex, balance, locomotion, grasping, object manipulation, or visuomotor integration (Provost, Lopez, & Heimerl, 2006); and differences between children with ASD and language disability have not been shown on measures of fine and gross motor skill, coordination, and balance (Noterdaeme et al., 2002). As such, it appears that difficulties with basic motor skill development are often present in, but not specific to, ASD.

In contrast, higher-level motor learning tasks may offer some level of specificity in ASD. Children with ASD often show impairments in performance of skilled motor tasks and gestures, often referred to as "developmental dyspraxia" (Dewey, 1991; Minshew, Goldstein, & Siegel, 1997; Mostofsky et al., 2006; Rogers et al., 1996). While the term *apraxia* is traditionally used in the adult literature to refer to an acquired impairment in the ability to carry out skilled movements in the absence of fundamental sensorimotor, language, or general cognitive impairment sufficient to preclude it, *developmental dyspraxia* is more encompassing, as unlike acquired adult-onset apraxia, coexisting sensory and basic motor problems may also be present. More specifically, developmental dyspraxia could be considered a neurologic sign, where impaired execution of skilled movements or gestures is out of proportion to, and not wholly explained by, basic motor impairment or perceptuomotor impairment. This is exemplified in ASD. For instance, Dziuk and colleagues (2007) reported that, while performance on measures of praxis were strongly predicted by basic motor skill (i.e., times to complete repetitive limb movements on standardized motor exam), children with ASD continued to demonstrate poorer performance on praxis exam as compared to TD children, even after accounting for basic motor skill. As evidence for specificity of dyspraxia in autism, Dewey, Cantell, and Crawford (2007) recently reported that while children with ASD, attention deficit/hyperactivity disorder (ADHD), and developmental coordination disorder (DCD) plus ADHD all showed impairments in basic motor development, only children with ASD showed deficits in gestural performance (of note, given the neuropsychological

context of this paper, *gesture* was a term used to refer to a previously learned skilled motor action, not simply a communicative movement).

A thorough examination of praxis involves careful assessment of the types of errors made by the individual (transitive versus intransitive) and the means used to elicit these errors (Heilman & Gonzalez Rothi, 2003). Transitive actions, the predominant category for praxis assessment, refer to pantomimed tool use to command (e.g. brushing hair), while intransitive actions are symbolic (e.g. waving goodbye, saluting). Imitative transitive (e.g. touching your nose) and intransitive (e.g. wiggling your fingers) gestures are also assessed under the umbrella of praxis. Given the hypothesized link of imitation to theory of mind (the ability to understand that another's perspective is separate from one's own)—a skill often identified as impaired in ASD—praxis tasks utilizing imitation have been emphasized in ASD, documenting fairly consistent deficits (Rogers and Pennington, 1991). Additionally, however, there have been several studies from our laboratory and others suggesting a more pervasive deficit in praxis (not just limited to imitation), with documented impairments in performance of gestures to *command and with actual tool use* comparable to those of imitation (Dowell, Mahone, & Mostofsky, 2009; Dziuk et al., 2007, Mostofsky et al., 2006). Specifically, in two fairly distinct samples of subjects, these pervasive praxis deficits were shown to be associated with the core behavioral features of ASD, including social and communicative impairments as measured by the ADOS (Dowell et al., 2009; Dzuik et al., 2007). Additionally, these core behavioral features of ASD (as measured by the ADOS) were predicted not only by imitation, but also gesture to command and tool use. As such, it appears that multiple areas of praxis abnormalities are associated with some of the defining features of ASD.

To further explore this concept, impairments in postural knowledge (i.e., the representational knowledge of skilled movements), as well as autism-associated impairments in basic motor skills, have been examined and shown as correlated with praxis (Dowell et al.,2009). Postural knowledge was assessed using a test adapted for children from Mozaz et al. (2002). Children are presented with pictures of a person with a missing hand performing either transitive or intransitive gestures (one involving the use of a tool—hammering or painting—or not involving a tool—waving goodbye or clapping); they are then asked to choose (from three options) the hand that best depicts how the tool should be held or how the gesture should be performed. Alternatively, the child is presented with three pictures of hands holding a tool and asked to identify which of the three pictures best depicts how the tool should be held (e.g., a hammer held by the handle or the head).

Common to all three aspects of praxis examination is the ability to access parietal representations of skilled movement necessary to guide proper movement selection/sequencing mediated by the premotor cortex (Heilman & Gonzalez Rothi, 2003). We have found that children with ASD are impaired in both their ability to accurately identify representations of skilled movements (by assessing one's identification of appropriate movements and use of tools through pictures; Dowell et al.,2009), and in their ability to execute sequenced motor commands (Dzuik et al., 2007; Jansiewicz et al., 2006; Mostofsky et al., 2006), suggesting that both parietal and motor/premotor dysfunction may be contributing to impaired performance of skilled gestures. Yet, the fact that these impairments cannot entirely account for impaired praxis in ASD suggests that additional deficits in transformation of perceptual representations into motor sequences—perhaps related to abnormalities in connectivity between parietal and premotor regions—may be an important factor contributing to impaired development of skilled gestures in ASD. These abnormalities in connectivity may be tied to anomalous acquisition of internal models of movements necessary for skill development, as discussed in the next section.

MOTOR LEARNING IN ASD

Given the developmental context of autism, it is critical to evaluate not only performance of motor skills, but also the ability to learn motor patterns and carry out more complex motor tasks, as difficulty with gestural performance could reflect a fundamental problem with acquiring motor skills, i.e., motor skill learning. In fact, in a review of "Imitation and Action in Autism," Smith and Bryson (1994) cited Wing (1969), noting that "clumsy children with autism reportedly have particular difficulty with *learning* organized patterns of movements (e.g., skipping and dancing)" (p. 267).

Over the last decade, one important new concept developed in the field of neuroscience has been that of *internal models* (Shadmehr & Mussa-Ivaldi, 1994), whereby the brain learns to perform movements by building internal models that associate one's own motor commands with sensory feedback. Specifically, associations between motor learning, praxis, and the formation of internal models have been suggested, with attempts made to tease apart specific aspects of motor learning most contributory to the deficits observed in ASD.

Examination of motor learning has revealed fundamental differences in the way that children with ASD learn motor patterns and form internal models. In particular, anomalous visuomotor sequence learning has been documented in ASD in comparison to TD controls (Gidley Larson & Mostofsky, 2008; Mostofsky, Goldberg, Cutting, & Denckla, 2001; Mostofsky, Goldberg, Landa, & Denckla, 2000).

Initial examination of motor adaptation, using a range of tasks that required a change in the motor output in response to a change in the environment, revealed that regardless of task demand, children with ASD were able to adapt their motor output by forming a predictive internal model, with rates of acquisition and decay that were not different from those of TD children (Gidley Larson et al., 2008; Mostofsky, Bunoski, Morton, Goldberg, & Bastian 2004). In interpreting these findings, we considered that adaptation of movement is a basic function central to successful performance of simple tasks necessary for survival. Humans are constantly adjusting their internal models to account for the effects of the external environment (i.e., moving while holding an object, the weight of the object, etc.), as well as internal changes (i.e., fatigue, growth, etc.). For instance, in order to reach out, grab a piece of food, and bring it to one's mouth to eat, the internal model must constantly be adjusting for the distance of the food from the body, the type of grip required to grasp the food, the weight of the food, the movement trajectory of the arm from the table to the mouth, the width of the mouth, etc.

Given that motor adaptation is likely critical for survival, we considered that adaptation may be preserved at the expense of other functions in children with ASD, and that closer examination of motor adaptation may better describe the deficiencies in motor learning in children with ASD. In a recent follow-up study of motor adaptation (Haswell, Izawa, Mostofsky, & Shadmehr, 2009), children used a novel tool (a robotic arm) and learned to compensate for force perturbations produced by the robotic device. Analysis of the patterns of generalization revealed that in learning an internal model of the novel tool, children with ASD relied upon the association between self-generated motor commands and proprioception, to a much greater extent than did TD children, with less reliance on the association between the same motor commands and visual feedback. That is, the sense of proprioception and its association with motor commands, which is mediated by connections between primary motor and somatosensory cortices, appeared to be abnormally upregulated in children with ASD. In contrast, the association between visual input and motor commands, which is mediated by longer-range connections between premotor and posterior parietal cortices, appears to be abnormally downregulated. The results are consistent with those from a study of prism adaptation revealing that, in contrast to children with mental retardation and TD controls, children with autism appeared to rely on proprioceptive rather than visual feedback to adapt arm movement (Masterson & Biederman, 1983). Similarly, unpublished findings from our laboratory have shown that while blindfolded, children with ASD perform better than TD children on a maze-tracing task (relying on proprioceptive feedback for success).

These findings help to explain consistently reported observations of dyspraxia in children with autism, as the acquisition and performance of skilled gestures is dependent on connections between posterior parietal and premotor cortices. It also helps to explain observations from studies of motor sequence learning: under certain conditions, children with ASD show impaired acquisition of novel visuomotor sequences (Dowell & Mostofsky, 2009; Gidley Larson et al., 2008; Mostofsky et al., 2000), whereas children with ASD show superior ability during a blindfolded maze-tracing task, where visual input is removed and sequence learning instead relies on somatosensory feedback (Dowell et al., 2009).

THE ASSOCIATION OF MOTOR LEARNING AND SENSORY/SOCIAL FUNCTIONING

For children with ASD, observed motor skill difficulties appear to parallel social skill deficits. For instance, in 1953, Ritvo and Provence reported deficient imitative learning in a 21-month-old boy with autism. Specifically, this child's mother reported that her son could not play pat-a-cake simply by watching her, and instead, she had to move his hands through the appropriate actions of the game for him to learn the pattern of movements.

Parallels between social/communicative and motor development may in large part be attributable to overlap in neural mechanisms underlying acquisition of motor and social skills, a concept particularly relevant for a developmental disorder such as autism. As described above, it appears that the development of effective non-verbal social and communicative gestures (i.e., waving, blowing a kiss) is reliant on creating internal models of movement necessary to learning complex movement sequences.

Formation of these internal models may also contribute to development of perceptual constructs of social interaction. Specifically, it has been hypothesized that the same internal models that are the basis of learning skilled movements are also the basis for how our brain understands the actions of others (Iacoboni, 2005; Rizzolatti, Fogassi, & Gallese, 2001; Williams, Ehiten, & Singh, 2004). Theory suggests that, in learning to perform a movement, the brain builds an association between self-generated motor commands and sensory feedback (Shadmehr & Krakauer, 2008), forming an internal model that allows it to predict the sensory consequences of self-generated motor commands. While this ability is crucial for performing skillful movements, it may also play a fundamental role in the ability of our brain to imitate the actions of others (Miall, 2003; Rizzolatti et al., 2001). Indeed, one can view the problem of imitation as one of observing visual consequences of other people's actions, and then producing motor commands that mimic them (Mattar & Gribble, 2005). From a theoretical perspective, successful imitation is possible only if the brain already has access to an internal model that has built an association between motor commands and visual consequences. If imitation is impaired, then there is probably a deficit in the association between self-generated motor commands and sensory consequences. Specifically, as imitation and not the formation of internal models is impaired in ASD, a deficit in the visuomotor circuit is implicated.

The idea of this imitation-dependent "mirror neuron system" is related to internal models of motor control, as it suggests that when we look at others performing movements, we imagine the motor commands that they may be producing and predict the sensory consequences of those motor commands, as if they were our own. In this way, we can interpret the purpose and consequences of the actions that we see.

Consistent with these observations, several investigators have found autism to be associated with impaired imitation (Rogers, Hepburn, Stackhouse, & Wehner, 2003; Smith & Bryson 1994), and have hypothesized that "impaired formation of self-other representation" leads to abnormal development of empathy and a sense of others' minds (Rogers & Pennington, 1991; Williams et al., 2004). Asperger (1961) in fact stated that children on the autism spectrum have movement problems because *they do not learn by watching other people in daily life* (cited in Miyahara et al., 1997). Further, in recent findings from our laboratory, we found children with ASD to be particularly impaired on imitation-dependent visuomotor sequence learning (Dowell & Mostofsky, 2009).

As discussed above, the preferential association between motor commands and proprioceptive, as opposed to visual, feedback in children with ASD therefore offers a rationale for observed impairments in the ability of children with ASD to acquire models of action through visually based imitation, subsequently impacting their ability to understand and interpret the meaning of social and communicative behavior of others. Put another way, the consequence of a weaker than normal association between motor commands and visual feedback, which is mediated by connections between posterior parietal and premotor cortices, is that children with ASD may develop a "dyspraxia" for social (as well as motor) skills. Findings reported by Haswell and colleagues (2009) support this idea, revealing that reliance on proprioceptive feedback is significantly correlated with measures of both motor *and social* impairment. Emerging knowledge identifying potential mechanisms that contribute to difficulty with engaging the external world can lead to greater understanding of the neural underpinnings of autism and, most importantly, provide a basis for effective treatment.

NEUROANATOMICAL MOTOR CORRELATES IN ASD AND ASSOCIATED BEHAVIORAL IMPLICATIONS

ASD has been linked to abnormalities in multiple brain regions and systems, many of which are associated with motor function. Increased brain volume is the most consistent neuroimaging finding in children with ASD, with several studies revealing prominent differences during early childhood that are no longer seen by adolescence (Carper, Moses, Tigue, & Courchesne, 2002; Courchesne et al., 2001; Hazlett et al., 2005; Redcay & Courchesne, 2005;). In particular, anatomic MRI (aMRI) studies have revealed enlarged cerebral white matter volume that is localized to outer "radiate" areas, comprising short-range connections between neighboring brain regions (Herbert et al., 2004; Minshew & Williams, 2007).

Consistent with these findings, investigators have proposed that the pattern of impairments associated with autism, as well as some relative strengths in "local" perceptual processing, are secondary to differences in structural and functional connectivity (Happé & Frith, 2006; Herbert et al., 2004; Minshew et al., 1997). Specifically, overgrowth of localized cortical connections and undergrowth of more distant connections (Happé & Frith, 2006; Herbert et al., 2004) have been hypothesized to result in impaired complex information processing (Minshew et al., 1997) and "weak central coherence" (Happé & Frith, 2006).

Acquisition of motor skills is also dependent on coordinated activity across a network of cortical (motor, premotor, parietal) and subcortical (basal ganglia and cerebellum) regions (Doyon et al., 2002). For children with ASD, a striking dissociation was recently described (Mostofsky, Burgess, & Gidley Larson, 2007), whereby increased local white-matter volume in the primary motor cortex was a robust predictor of motor impairment. In contrast, for TD children and children with ADHD, the opposite pattern was observed—that is, increased primary motor white-matter volume predicted better (rather than worse) motor-skill performance. These findings suggest that impaired motor development in autism is associated with overgrowth of localized connections within the primary motor cortex; furthermore, this association appears specific to autism. Additionally, findings from postmortem studies of individuals diagnosed with ASD suggest that this overgrowth of localized white-mater connections may be a consequence of disorganized development of cortical minicolumns (Casanova, Buxhoeveden, & Brown, 2002). It follows that for children with ASD, localized white-matter connections may not only be larger in volume, they may also be more disorganized, and that this disorganization may be an important biomarker for behavioral dysfunction characterizing autism. As such, altered patterns of motor learning in autism may have their basis in differences in the wiring of connections between cortical and subcortical regions, with resulting impaired development of motor skills, including complex gestures necessary for social and communicative behavior (Gidley Larson & Mostofsky, 2006; Mostofsky et al., 2007). Coupled with our findings showing that children with ASD have a bias toward proprioceptive feedback, these reports provide useful insights into the way in which children with ASD learn social and communicative behaviors, which will be further described below.

Observations of white-matter abnormalities in autism have led to investigations into functional connectivity, or how distant brain regions are "connected" based on similarities in their profiles of functional activity during fMRI (so-called functional connectivity MRI, or fcMRI). Decreased functional connectivity has been observed in autism during performance of a range of cognitive tasks (Just et al., 2007; Just, Cherkassky, Keller, & Minshew, 2004; Kana et al., 2006; Kana, Keller, Minshew, & Just, 2007) and, as recently published, we found that compared with TD children, children with high-functioning autism (HFA) showed significantly decreased functional connectivity between distant brain regions during performance of a simple finger-sequencing task (Mostofsky et al., 2009. Furthermore, we found the TD group showed greater activation in the ipsilateral anterior cerebellum, while the HFA group showed greater activation in the supplementary motor area (SMA). Taken together, the findings suggest that decreased functional connectivity between distant brain regions may contribute to an inability to shift motor execution from cortical regions associated with effortful control to regions associated with habitual execution, a process critical to motor learning.

The relevance of this combination of neuroanatomical, connectivity, functionality, and behavioral findings is quite substantial. In the motor-adaptation task that we considered in the section above, learning to move a robotic arm with force perturbations produces changes in the activity fields of cells in both the primary motor cortex (Li, Padoa-Schioppa, & Bizzi, 2001) and the premotor cortex (Xiao, Padoa-Schioppa, & Bizzi 2006). These two areas have fundamentally different anatomical and physiological characteristics. The primary motor cortex is strongly connected to the neighboring somatosensory cortex

and has activity fields that, during reaching, depend on the configuration of the arm in proprioceptive coordinates (Scott & Kalaska, 1997). In contrast, the premotor cortex is strongly connected to the more distant posterior-parietal cortex and has activity fields that during reaching depend on displacement of the hand in extrinsic or visual coordinates (Scott, Serigo, & Kalaska, 1997). Our findings in children with ASD of a stronger than normal association between proprioception and motor commands, and a weaker than normal association between vision and motor commands, thereby appear to be consistent with imaging and postmortem studies (Casanova et al., 2006; Herbert et al., 2004), revealing an overexpression of short-range axons, including those connecting primary motor and somatosensory cortices. These "primary sensorimotor" connections are established very early in life, which is coincident with the timing of brain overgrowth in autism; and, recent magnetoencepholgraphy (MEG) findings indeed reveal that the somatosensory field is expanded in autism (Coskun et al., 2009). Accordingly, if plasticity in the autistic brain is upregulated in the primary sensorimotor cortex due to increased localized connectivity, then it may explain the excessive reliance on proprioception during motor learning observed in ASD.

These findings may have important implications for intervention aimed at helping children with ASD to better rely on external cues, improving their ability to acquire skills important for social, communicative, and motor functions. For instance, it may be possible that targeted excitation and inhibition of areas and networks of undergrowth and overgrowth may be achieved though behavioral, biofeedback, or cortical stimulation methods that reinforce reliance on visual feedback during motor learning. Specifically, upregulating the association between motor commands and visual feedback in children with ASD, by enhancing the excitability of visuomotor association areas in the posterior parietal cortex or decreasing the excitability of somatosensory cortex, could result in an improvement in both the ability to control movements and the ability to interpret the actions of others.

CONCLUSIONS

While not diagnostic, ASD is associated with impairments in basic motor coordination, as well as in the performance of skilled motor gestures (dyspraxia) and motor learning activities, all of which interact and correlate with the core social and communicative deficiencies of ASD. In addition, neural correlates of these motor-based deficits have been identified, and may serve as parallel models for understanding the social difficulties experienced by children with ASD. Using an example from our laboratory, recent research has shown that while children with ASD can adapt their movements in response to both visual and somatosensory perturbations, they show anomalous patterns of motor learning, suggesting a bias toward excessive reliance on proprioceptive, rather than visual, feedback. Consistent with this, assessment of motor-sequence learning in ASD revealed a striking dissociation, whereby children with ASD show impaired acquisition of visuomotor sequences, but superior performance when learning instead depends on proprioceptive feedback. Additionally, neuroimaging suggests a dissociative pattern of association between motor skill and connectivity, showing an autism-specific association between impaired motor development in autism and overgrowth of localized connections within the primary motor cortex. These observations provide an emerging rationale explaining why children with autism are impaired in their ability to acquire models of action through visually based imitation, including those necessary to understand and interpret the meaning of others' social and communicative behaviors. However, questions remain regarding the clinical relevance and neural basis of the stronger than normal association between motor commands and proprioceptive feedback in autism, and whether a change in this bias can be achieved, providing an effective method of treating impaired skill acquisition, potentially impacting social interest and reciprocity.[1]

---

1. This work was supported by grants from the National Alliance for Autism Research/Autism Speaks and from NIH: K02 NS 044850 (SHM), RO1NS048527, M01 RR00052 (Johns Hopkins General Clinical Research Center). We would also like to thank the children and families for participating in our research project.

References

Baranek, G. (1999). Autism during infancy: A retrospective video analysis of sensory-motor and social behaviors at 9–12 months of age. *J Autism Dev Disord*, 29, 213–224.

Carper, R. A., Moses, P., Tigue, Z. D., & Courchesne, E. (2002). Cerebral lobes in autism: Early hyperplasia and abnormal age effects. *Neuroimage*, 16, 1038–1051.

Casanova, M. F., Buxhoeveden, D. P., & Brown, C. (2002). Clinical and macroscopic correlates of minicolumnar pathology in autism. *J Child Neurol*, 17(9), 692–695.

Casanova, M. F., van Kooten, I. A., Switala, A. E., van Engeland, H., Heinsen, H., Steinbusch, H.W. ... Schmitz, C. (2006). Minicolumnar abnormalities in autism. *Acta Neuropathol (Berl)*, 112, 287–303.

Coskun, M. A., Varghese, L., Reddoch, S., Castillo, E.M., Pearson, D.A., Loveland, K.A. ... Sheth, B.R. (2009). How somatic cortical maps differ in autistic and typical brains. *Neuroreport*, 20, 175–179.

Courchesne, E., Karns, C. M., Davis, H. R., Ziccardi, R., Carper, R.A., Tigue, Z.D. ... Courchesne, R.Y. (2001). Unusual brain growth patterns in early life in patients with autistic disorder: An MRI study. *Neurology*, 57, 245–254.

Damasio, A. R., & Maurer, R.G. (1978). A neurological model for childhood autism. *Arch Neurol*, 35, 777–786.

Dewey, D. (1991). Praxis and sequencing skills in children with sensorimotor dysfunction. *Dev Neuropsychol*, 7(2), 197–206.

Dewey, D., Cantell, M., & Crawford, S. G. (2007). Motor and gestural performance in children with autism spectrum disorders, developmental coordination disorder, and/or attention deficit hyperactivity disorder. *Journal of the International Neuropsychological Society*, 13, 246–256.

Dowell L. R., Mahone E. M., & Mostofsky, S. H. (2009). Associations of postural knowledge and basic motor skill with dyspraxia in autism: Implication for abnormalities in distributed connectivity and motor learning. *Neuropsychology*. 23, 563–570.

Dowell, L. R., & Mostofsky, S. H. (2009) *Imitation-dependent visuomotor sequence learning in ASD*. Accepted for presentation at the 8th International Meeting for Autism Research, Chicago, Illinois.

Doyon, J., Song, A.W., Karni, A. et al. (2002). Experience-dependent changes in cerebellar contributions to motor sequence learning. *Proc Natl Acad Sci*, 99, 1017–1022.

Dziuk, M., Gidley Larson, J., Apostu, A., Mahone, E., Denckla, M., & Mostofsky, S. (2007). Dyspraxia in autism: Association with motor, social, and communicative deficits. *Dev Med Child Neurol*, 49(10), 734–739.

Freitag, C., Kleser, C., Schneider, M., & von Gontard, A. (2007). Quantitative assessment of neuromotor function in adolescents with high functioning autism and Asperger syndrome. *J Autism Dev Disord*, 37, 948–959.

Gidley Larson, J. C., Bastian, A. J., Donchin, O., Shadmehr, R., & Mostofsky, S. H. (2008). Acquisition of internal models of motor tasks in children with autism. *Brain*, 131, 2894–2903.

Gidley Larson J. C. & Mostofsky, S. H. (2008). Evidence that the pattern of visuomotor sequence learning is altered in children with autism. *Autism Research*, 1, 341–353.

Green, D., Baird, G., Barnett, A. L., Henderson, L., Huber, J., & Henderson, S. E. (2002). The severity and nature of motor impairment in Asperger's disorder: A comparison with specific developmental disorder of motor function. *J Child Psychol Psychiatry*, 43, 655–668.

Haas, R. H., Townsend, J., Courchesne, E., Lincoln, A.J., Schriebman, L., & Yeung-Courchesne, R. (1996). Neurologic abnormalities in infantile autism. *Journal of Child Neurology*, 11, 84–92.

Hallett, M., Lebiedowska, M. K., Thomas, S.L., Stanhope, S. J., Denckla, M.B., & Rumsey, J. (1993). Locomotion of autistic adults. *Archives of Neurology*, 50, 1304–1308.

Happé, F., & Frith, U. (2006). The weak coherence account: Detail-focused cognitive style in autism spectrum disorders. *J Autism Dev Disord*, 36, 5–25.

Haswell, C. C., Izawa, J., Mostofsky, S. H., & Shadmehr, R. (2009). *Children with autism show excessive reliance on proprioception in building internal models of action*. Accepted for presentation at the 8th International Meeting for Autism Research, Chicago, Illinois.

Hazlett, H. C., Poe, M., Gerig, G., Gimpel Smith, R., Provenzale, J., Ross, A. ... Piven, J. (2005). Magnetic resonance imaging and head circumference study of brain size in autism: Birth through age 2 years. *Arch Gen Psychiatry*, 62, 1366–1376.

Heilman, K. M., & Gonzalez Rothi, L. J. (2003). *Apraxia (4th ed.)*. New York: Oxford University Press.

Herbert, M. R., Ziegler, D. A., Makris, N., Filipek, P. A., Kemper, T. L., Normandin, J. J. ... Caviness, V.S. (2004). Localization of white matter volume increase in autism and developmental language disorder. *Ann Neurol*, 55(4), 530–540.

Iacoboni, M. (2005). Neural mechanisms of imitation. *Curr Opin Neurobiol*, 15, 632–637.

Jansiewicz, E. M., Goldberg, M. C., Newschaffer, C. J., Denckla, M., Landa, R. J., & Mostofsky, S. (2006). Motor signs distinguish children with high functioning autism and Asperger's disorder from controls. *J Autism Dev Disord*, 36(5), 613–621.

Jones, V., & Prior, M. (1985). Motor imitation abilities and neurological signs in autistic children. *J Autism Dev Disord*, 15, 37–46.

Just, M. A., Cherkassky, V. L., Keller, T. A., Kana, R.K., & Minshew, N.J. (2007). Functional and anatomical cortical underconnectivity in autism: Evidence

from an FMRI study of an executive function task and corpus callosum morphometry. *Cereb Cortex*, 17, 951–961.

Just, M. A., Cherkassky, V. L., Keller, T. A., & Minshew, N. J. (2004). Cortical activation and synchronization during sentence comprehension in high-functioning autism: Evidence of underconnectivity. *Brain*, 127, 1811–1821.

Kana, R. K., Keller, T. A., Cherkassky, V. L., Minshew, N.J., & Just, M.A. (2006). Sentence comprehension in autism: thinking in pictures with decreased functional connectivity. *Brain*, 129, 2484–2493.

Kana, R. K., Keller, T. A., Minshew, N. J., & Just, M. A. (2007). Inhibitory control in high-functioning autism: decreased activation and underconnectivity in inhibition networks. *Biol Psychiatry*, 62, 198–206.

Kanner, L. (1943). Autistic disturbances of affective contact. *Nervous Child*, 2, 217–250.

Li, C. S., Padoa-Schioppa, C., & Bizzi, E. (2001). Neuronal correlates of motor performance and motor learning in the primary motor cortex of monkeys adapting to an external force field. *Neuron*, 30, 593–607.

Manjiviona, J., & Prior, M. (1995). Comparison of Asperger syndrome and high-functioning autistic children on a test of motor impairment. *J Autism Dev Disord*, 25(1), 23–39.

Masterton, B., & Biederman, G. (1983). Proprioceptive versus visual control in autistic children. *J Autism Dev Disord*, 13(2), 141–152.

Mattar, A. A., & Gribble, P. L. (2005). Motor learning by observing. *Neuron*, 46, 153–160.

Maurer, R. G., & Damasio, A. R., (1982). Childhood autism from the point of view of behavioral neurology. *J Autism Dev Disord*, 12, 195–205.

Miall, R. C. (2003). Connecting mirror neurons and forward models. *Neuroreport*, 14, 2135–2137.

Ming, X., Brimacombe, M., & Wagner, G. C. (2007). Prevalence of motor impairment in autism spectrum disorders. *Brain Dev*, 29, 565–570.

Minshew, N. J., Goldstein, G., & Siegel, D. J. (1997). Neuropsychologic functioning in autism: Profile of a complex information processing disorder. *J Int Neuropsychol Soc*, 3(4), 303–316.

Minshew, N. J., & Williams, D. L. (2007). The new neurobiology of autism: Cortex, connectivity, and neuronal organization. *Arch Neurol*, 64, 945–950.

Miyahara, M. Tsujii, M., Hori, M., Nakanishi, K., Kageyama, H. & Sugiyama, T. (1997). Brief report: motor incoordination in children with Asperger syndrome and learning disabilities. *Journal of Autism and Developmental Disorders*, 27, 595–603.

Morin, B., & Reid, G. (1985). A quantitative and qualitative assessment of autistic individuals on selected motor tasks. *Adapted Physical Activity Quarterly*, 2, 43–55.

Mostofsky, S. H., Bunoski, R., Morton, S. M., Goldberg, M., & Bastian, A. J. (2004). Children with autism adapt normally during a catching task requiring the cerebellum. *Neurocase, 10*, 60–64.

Mostofsky, S., Burgess, M., & Gidley Larson, J. (2007). Increased motor cortex white matter volume predicts motor impairment in autism. *Brain, 32*(1), 543–562.

Mostofsky, S., Dubey, P., Jerath, V. K., Jansiewicz, E. M., Goldberg, M. C., & Denckla, M. B. (2006). Developmental dyspraxia is not limited to imitation in children with autism spectrum disorders. *J Int Neuropsychol Soc, 12*(3), 314–326.

Mostofsky, S., Goldberg, M. C., Cutting, L., & Denckla, M. (2001). *Impaired procedural learning of rotary pursuit in children with autism.* Paper presented at the International Meeting for Autism Research, San Diego, CA.

Mostofsky, S., Goldberg, M. C., Landa, R. J., & Denckla, M. B. (2000). Evidence for a deficit in procedural learning in children and adolescents with autism: Implications for cerebellar contribution. *J Int Neuropsychol Soc, 6*, 752–759.

Mostofsky, S. H., Powell, S. K., Simmonds, D. J., Goldberg, M.C., Caffo, B., & Pekar, J. (2009). Decreased connectivity and cerebellar activity in autism during motor task performance. *Brain, 132*, 2413–2425.

Mozaz, M., Rothi, L.J.G., Anderson, J.M., Crucuan, G.P. & Heilman, K.M. (2002). Postural knowledge of transitive pantomimes and intransitive gestures. *Journal of the International Neuropsychological Society, 8*, 958–962.

Noterdaeme, M., Mildenberger, K., Minow, F., & Amorosa, H. (2002). Evaluation of neuromotor deficits in children with autism and children with specific speech and language disorder. *Eur Child Adolesc Psyhciatry, 11*, 219–225.

Ornitz, E. M., Guthrie, D., & Farley, A. H. (1977). The early development of autistic children. *Journal of Autism and Child Schizophrenia, 7*, 207–229.

Ozonoff, S., Young, G. S., Goldring, S., Greiss-Hess, L., Herrera, A. M., Steele, J. ... Rogers, S.J. (2008). Gross motor development, movement abnormalities, and early identification of autism. *J Autism Dev Disord, 38*(4), 644–656.

Provost, B., Lopez, B. R., & Heimerl, S. (2006). A comparison of motor delays in young children: Autism spectrum disorder, developmental delay, and developmental concerns. *J of Autism Dev Disord, 37*, 321–328.

Rapin, I. (1991). Autistic children: Diagnosis and clinical features. *Pediatrics, 87*, 751–760.

Redcay, E., & Courchesne, E. (2005). When is the brain enlarged in autism? A meta-analysis of all brain size reports. *Biol Psychiatry, 58*, 1–9.

Rinehart, N. J., Tonge, B. J., Iansek, R., McGinley, J., Brereton, A. V., Enticott, P., & Bradshaw, J.L. (2006). Gait function in newly diagnosed children with autism: Cerebellar and basal ganglia related motor disorder. *Dev Med Child Neurol, 48*(10), 819–824.

Rizzolatti, G., Fogassi, L., & Gallese, V. (2001). Neurophysiological mechanisms underlying the understanding and imitation of action. *Nat Rev Neurosci, 2*, 661–670.

Rogers, S., Bennetto, L., McEvoy, R., & Pennington, B. (1996). Imitation and pantomime in high-functioning adolescents with autism spectrum disorders. *Child Dev, 67*, 2060–2073.

Rogers, S. J., Hepburn, S. L., Stackhouse, T., & Wehner, E. (2003). Imitation performance in toddlers with autism and those with other developmental disorders. *J Child Psychol Psychiatry, 44*, 763–781.

Rogers, S. J., & Pennington, B. F. (1991). A theoretical approach to the deficits in infantile autism. *Dev Psychopathol, 3*, 137–162.

Scott, S., & Kalaska, J. F. (1997). Reaching movements with similar hand paths but different arm orientations. I. Activity of individual cells in motor cortex. *J Neurophysiol, 77*, 826–852.

Scott, S. H., Sergio, L. E., & Kalaska, J. F. (1997). Reaching movements with similar hand paths but different arm orientations. II. Activity of individual cells in dorsal premotor cortex and parietal area 5. *J Neurophysiol, 78*, 2413–2426.

Shadmehr, R., & Krakauer, J. W. (2008). A computational neuroanatomy for motor control. *Exp Brain Res, 185*, 359–381.

Shadmehr, R., & Mussa-Ivaldi, F. A. (1994). Adaptive representation of dynamics during learning of a motor task. *J Neurosci. 14*, 3208–3224.

Smith, I. M., & Bryson, S. E. (1994). Imitation and action in autism: A critical review. *Psychol Bull, 116*(2), 259–273.

Sutera, S., Pandey, J., Esser, E. L., Rosenthal, M. A., Wilson, L. B., Barton, M. ... Fein, D. (2007). Predictors of optimal outcome in toddlers diagnosed with autism spectrum disorders. *J Autism Dev Disord, 37*, 98–107.

Teitelbaum, O., Benton, T., Shah, P. K., Prince, A., Kelly, J. L., & Teitelbaum, P. (2004). Eshkol-Wachman movement notation in diagnosis: The early detection of Asperger's disorder. *PNAS, 101*(32), 11909–11914.

Teitelbaum, P., Teitelbaum, O., Nye, J., Fryman, J., & Maurer, R. G. (1998). Movement analysis in infancy may be useful for early diagnosis of autism. *Proc Natl Acad Sci, 95*, 13982–13987.

Vilensky, J. A., Damasio, A. R., & Maurer, R. G. (1981). Gait disturbances in patients with autistic behavior: A preliminary study. *Arch Neurol, 38*, 646–649.

Williams, J. H., Whiten, A., & Singh, T. (2004). A systematic review of action imitation in autistic spectrum disorder. *J Autism Dev Disord, 34*, 285–299.

Wing, L. (1969). The handicaps of autistic children- A comparative study. *Journal of Child Psychology and Psychiatry, 10*, 1–40.

Xiao, J., Padoa-Schioppa, C., & Bizzi, E. (2006). Neuronal correlates of movement dynamics in the dorsal and ventral premotor area in the monkey. *Exp Brain Res, 168*, 106–119.

Chapter 11

Sensory Functions in ASD

Tal Kenet

INTRODUCTION

Sensory abnormalities do not define autism, and are not required in order to meet diagnostic criteria for autism. However, each and every parent, guardian, or clinician dealing with individuals with autism spectrum disorders (ASD) will readily testify that sensory-processing abnormalities are a core feature of the challenges associated with the disorder. These challenges are manifested in all sensory modalities, spanning olfactory functions as well as the three topographically mapped sensory modalities: visual, auditory, and tactile. This review will focus on primary (early cortical) abnormalities in these three modalities, as abnormalities in these modalities have been studied to a greater extent. As ubiquitous and diverse as sensory abnormalities in ASD are, to date, the correlation between sensory function and the behavioral phenotype or severity of autism remains unknown. From a neurophysiological point of view, the degree to which repetitive behaviors and the social and communication deficits associated with autism could be downstream consequences of sensory perception abnormalities is still an open question.

A fundamental reason to focus attention on sensory processing is that the interaction between individuals and the world around them is mediated entirely through the sensory domains. Abnormal perception and processing of sensory input at the earliest cortical levels propagates throughout the cortical hierarchy through feedforward as well as feedback connections, resulting in multiple levels of abnormal cortical activation and aberrant signal to noise ratios. The normal cortical response to a sensory stimulus is a highly coordinated and well-orchestrated process, in which neuronal assemblies dedicated to respond to particular aspects of the external inputs fire in patterns that have functionally significant and precise spatial and temporal structures.

Such orchestrated responses are highly dependent, first and foremost, on three factors: (i) the exact nature and structure of connections among the neurons that make up the assemblies, and between a cortical area and the areas that feedback/forward to it; (ii) the relative timing of action potentials; and (iii) the ratio between excitatory and inhibitory processes, which essentially dominates the level of activity of the network. These factors are, naturally, not independent, and disruption in any one of them will affect the others, and thus will necessarily affect the signal-to-noise ratio of the internal representation of the sensory stimulus. Consequently, the response of neuronal assemblies to incoming inputs will no longer be optimized for sensory representation, leading to the inevitable outcome of disruption in the salience—i.e., differentiability and stability—of the cortical representations of signals. Such a decrease in cortical salience will inexorably be manifested behaviorally in a myriad of ways, including hypersensitivities, distortions, and altered pathways for responding to sensory stimuli, all of which are characteristic of autism.

Additionally, synchronization both between and within neuronal assemblies is disrupted, thus reinforcing abnormal patterns of connectivity, which in turn affects the propagation of the signal from lower areas in the cortical hierarchy to higher ones. Thus, abnormal signal to noise ratio representing sensory stimulation in early sensory processing areas will inevitably also have downstream consequences on higher cognitive functions. It is worth noting that such a scenario also allows for hyper-performance, as well as hypo-performance, as local signals are affected to a lesser degree by adjacent neuronal assemblies, thus potentially facilitating the processing of local features.

Many of the neurophysiological abnormalities already documented in ASD might lead to altered sensory perception. Reduced inhibition and/or increased excitation can lead to altered signal representation in the cortex (Rubenstein & Merzenich, 2003). An altered ratio of excitation to inhibition can be a consequence of multiple mechanisms, including GABA (inhibitory neurotransmitter) abnormalities (Buxbaum et al., 2002; Casanova et al., 2003; Hussman, 2001; Ma et al., 2005) or increases in glutamate (excitatory neurotransmitter; Buxbaum et al., 2002; Hussman, 2001; Menold et al., 2001). Neuroinflammation, documented in inferior frontal, cingulate and cerebellar tissue from postmortem brain samples from autistic individuals age 5–44 (Vargas et al., 2005), is also likely to alter neuronal properties related to both cortical excitability and connectivity. Finally, abnormal neuromodulator levels and receptor abnormalities would surely affect sensory processing, and several key neuromodulators have been implicated in autism. Those include BDNF (Miyazaki et al., 2004; Nelson et al., 2001), which participates in regulation of critical period closure; serotonin and dopamine (Cook et al., 1997; Ernst et al., 1997), both of which affect sensory regulations and reward systems; nicotinic receptors (Lee et al., 2002; Martin-Ruiz et al., 2004; Perry et al., 2001; Ray et al., 2005), and the acetylcholine (Perry et al., 2001) system, which play an important role in learning; and upregulated/abnormal glutamate receptor activity (Jamain et al., 2002; Purcell et al., 2001; Ramoz et al., 2004; Serajee et al., 2003), which would affect the inhibition to excitation ratio (Lam et al., 2005; See Chapter 4).

Given that this is only a partial list of neurophysiological abnormalities documented in ASD, it is not surprising that sensory-processing abnormalities are as prevalent as they are. It is difficult to assess, given the breadth and vagueness of some of the findings, how such physiological abnormalities might affect sensory processing; on the other hand, it is possible that a better understanding of sensory perception abnormalities, their scope, and their manifestations across different domains might help to inform us about the neural substrates that underlie those abnormalities, thus providing us with a better insight into the causes of ASD. Understanding sensory-processing abnormalities in ASD might also provide us with neural or behavioral markers that could be used for early diagnosis and risk assessment in infants, as well as with potential treatment venues for older individuals who meet diagnostic criteria. In order to achieve these goals, we need to first gain a better understanding of the nature of sensory processing abnormalities in autism, at both the behavioral and neurophysiological levels. This review examines some of the recent findings in the field, in the three cortically and topographically mapped sensory domains: visual, auditory, and somatosensory.

VISUAL PROCESSING IN AUTISM SPECTRUM DISORDERS

Many groups have studied visual perception in autism, both neurophysiologically and behaviorally, documenting instances of both superior and inferior visual processing. In spite of a multitude of studies, to date no single underlying theory has emerged which could account for all of the observed abnormalities in the visual system evident in ASD. In fact, one fMRI study of the early visual cortex in high-functioning adults with ASD found a perfectly normal V1 (Hadjikhani et al., 2004). In this review, the focus will be on two subtypes of abnormalities documented in the visual cortex of individuals with ASD: first, processing of visual motion that has no social or biological component (this class of stimuli triggers V5 primarily); and second, processing of figures that have no biological or social significance, and are composed primarily of small lines or gratings—stimuli that are known to activate early visual cortex (V1 and V2 primarily) extremely well. Both of these classes of visual stimuli trigger cortical processes that are relatively well understood from animal models, but do not tend to heavily engage higher cognitive skills, and thus allow us to focus on cortical areas that are lowest in the processing hierarchy.

Visual Processing of Non-Biological Motion

A common paradigm used to study the perception of motion uses randomly placed moving dots with varying levels of coherence, known as a random dots kinematogram (RDK). The percentage of dots moving in the same direction is defined as coherence; i.e., if 40% of the dots are moving to the right, and another 60% are moving randomly, the stimulus has 40% coherence. The goal is to determine the threshold, or the minimal coherence level, for detection of the direction of motion of the coherent dots. This measure is defined as the motion coherence threshold (MCT). The paradigm is highly effective in activating MT/V5 (Newsome & Pare, 1988), is well correlated with behavioral reports (Salzman & Newsome, 1994), and has been explored extensively in dyslexia and in ASD. There is a general agreement between groups that individuals with dyslexia are impaired on this task and, on average, have higher MCT indicating a deficit in this paradigm (Hansen et al., 2001; Ridder et al., 2001; Schulte-Korne et al., 2004; Talcott et al., 2000). In autism, the RDK paradigm has been explored behaviorally by several groups, with variable interpretations (de Jonge et al., 2007; Del Viva et al., 2006; Milne et al., 2002; Pellicano et al., 2005; Spencer et al., 2000), all of whom, with the exception of one (Del Viva et al., 2006) found that individuals with autism have significantly higher MCT than controls,

with one (de Jonge et al., 2007) finding such an effect in the younger (7_12 year old) PDD group, but not in the older PDD group. Some groups interpret the higher MCT in autism as evidence for a "dorsal stream deficit" that has been hypothesized also in dyslexia (Milne et al., 2002; Pellicano et al., 2005; Spencer et al., 2000). In support of this claim, Spencer et al. (2000) tested performance on a parallel non-dorsal-stream task using static lines oriented concentrically, instead of dots. On this task, children with autism performed very similarly to controls, and hence the group concluded that the deficits are confined to the dorsal stream. In a parallel exploration, Pellicano et al. (2005) compared the performance of the autism group on the RDK task to their performance on a flicker contrast task. Their hypothesis was that the former targets *later* dorsal stream functions, while the latter targets *earlier* levels of the cortical dorsal stream. They found that children with autism were impaired on the RDK task, but normal on the flicker task; thus, they ruled out attentional and other confounding effects, and concluded that it is the later levels of the dorsal stream (V5), which must be affected, while earlier levels of the dorsal stream (V1/V2) remain intact. Pellicano et al. (2005) also raised the possibility that it is the integration across the moving dots that is impaired in autism (see also Dakin & Frith, 2005). Indeed, Talcott et al. (2000) used the RDK stimulus described above to examine motion perception in dyslexia. They found that as more dots were added to the RDK, children with dyslexia improved, and at a high dot density, become indistinguishable from controls. They suggest this positive effect of increasing the motion energy could imply that individuals with dyslexia have inherently lower signal-to-noise ratios, without speculating on the origins. In parallel, it is interesting to note that at least one study found normal MCT in individuals with ASD (Del Viva et al., 2006). In that paradigm, however, the moving dots were larger and in two colors, thus effectively increasing the local signal-to-noise ratio.

In light of these findings, several groups proceeded to test motion coherence thresholds in autism using different paradigms, to further investigate the dorsal processing stream deficit hypothesis of ASD. Tsermentseli et al. (2008) used a slightly modified version of the RDK task, where dot coherence formed a circular shape at some random area on the screen, rather than giving the impression of directional motion. Their results are intriguing, showing normal performance for three of their groups (controls, dyslexia, Asperger's syndrome), and impaired performance only in the high-functioning autism group, with a far greater variability in that group; a similar difference between the Asperger's group and the autism group was also noted in at least one other study (Spencer & O'Brien, 2006). Such studies underscore the importance of correct diagnosis and group assignment when choosing a study population. While both studies did find a motion perception impairment in the autism group, an identical deficit was also found for a stationary but similar stimulus defined by form only, undermining the motion perception deficit hypothesis, and thus the dorsal stream hypothesis as well. In their study of the perception of visual motion in autism, Bertone et al. (2003) used a different approach from the one presented above. The group differentiated between luminance-defined (first order) motion, and texture-defined (second order) motion. They found that individuals with autism have thresholds of detection that are similar to controls for first-order motion stimuli, but are impaired on detecting second-order motion stimuli. The authors interpret their results as a deficit in the perception of complex stimuli, rather than a deficit along the magnocellular stream. Another group (2008b) used plaid pattern motion to assess thresholds, and found no performance differences between controls and the ASD group. Finally, a recent study (Sanchez-Marin & Padilla-Medina, 2008) found that detection of motion of a vertical line embedded in noise is impaired in ASD individuals relative to controls, but the same degree of impairment was also found for the same stimulus when stationary, meaning the observed impairment is not generated by the motion, but by the nature of the stimulus itself. This last study in particular supports the hypothesis that lower motion detection thresholds in ASD might be a function of internal signal-to-noise ratios, rather than a dorsal stream deficit. Indeed, it is possible that it is the lower signal-to-noise ratio of stimuli defined as complex by Bertone et al (2003, 2005) that was driving the impairment observed in second-order motion, but not first-order motion, in that study. An alternative hypothesis (Vandenbroucke et al., 2008a) relates to the spatial frequency nature of the stimulus; all the studies finding a deficit in motion perception in ASD used stimuli (such as the RDK) that had inherently high spatial frequency, while those finding no deficits used low-spatial frequency stimuli.

Visual Processing of Stationary "Low-Level" Visual Stimuli

Several of the studies mentioned in the previous section tested motion paradigms alongside similar stationary paradigms as control conditions. While at least one study showed normal performance in their ASD group on the stationary task but elevated thresholds for form-based tasks (de Jonge et al., 2007; Spencer et al., 2000), other studies show elevated thresholds in the autism group for both the motion condition and the corresponding stationary condition (Sanchez-Marin & Padilla-Medina, 2008; Spencer & O'Brien, 2006; Tsermentseli et al., 2008). The stationary conditions for which deficits were observed in the autism group vary, from stimuli defining a form using dense, tiny, oriented lines (a high-spatial-frequency stimulus with varying signal to noise ratio;Spencer et al., 2000; Tsermentseli et al., 2008), through a simple line embedded in Gaussian noise (Sanchez-Marin & Padilla-Medina, 2008), to flickering stimuli tapping into contrast sensitivity with low spatial and high temporal frequencies, which taps into the magnocellular stream (Pellicano et al., 2005; Pellicano & Gibson, 2008), and have variable signal-to-noise ratios. In combination, no single theme emerges as a unifying explanation for all of the above observations.

The picture grows even more complex when additional findings are considered. A recent study (Ashwin et al., 2008) showed that individuals with ASD (both autism and Asperger's) have superior visual acuity. The authors speculate the phenomenon is retinal in origin, and how it might affect some of the other observed deficits, if at all, remains unknown. Finally, two studies looked at EEG-evoked potential activity in response to simple visual stimuli. In one study (Vandenbroucke et al., 2008b), the stimulus consists of figure and ground made up of small, oriented lines, where orientation defines boundaries. This is a naturally high spatial frequency and low signal-to-noise stimulus. The authors saw diminished differentiation between stimulus types in the ASD group, as early as 120ms after stimulus onset, which would imply a deficit at the level of early visual cortex (V1/V2). Another study used simple Gabor patches (black and white gratings with a superimposed Gaussian) to measure how the EEG signal changes with spatial frequency. They found that the ASD group did not modulate latency or amplitude with varying spatial frequency, while the control group exhibited delayed response onset and increased response amplitude with increasing spatial frequency. This latter finding hints that spatial frequency is indeed likely to play an important role in the visual abnormalities observed in autism. That said, other studies discussed above suggest that the signal-to-noise ratio of the stimulus is also likely to contribute to the observed phenomenon. Furthermore, whether or not the magnocellular processing stream in autism is more impacted than the parvocellular stream, still remains to be firmly established. Finally, many of the studies discussed here show great variability within the autism group, as well as differences across the autism phenotype (in particular high functioning autism versus Asperger's). These studies underscore the importance of developing a better understanding of subtypes within ASD, where visual perception might be one avenue to accomplish just such a task.

AUDITORY PROCESSING IN AUTISM SPECTRUM DISORDERS

Like visual processing, auditory processing in autism has been studied both behaviorally and neurophysiologically by multiple groups. And as in the visual domain, impairments and superior performance have both been documented. There is ample evidence that children with autism process the sounds of speech (Flagg et al., 2005; Kasai et al., 2005; Kuhl et al., 2005; Lepisto et al., 2005b; Oram Cardy et al., 2005) and voices (Gervais et al., 2004; Kujala et al., 2005) differently from typically developing children. It is easy to imagine how abnormal processing of sound early in the cortical hierarchy of auditory processing might affect the processing of more complex auditory information, such as language, higher up in the cortical hierarchy, . However, there is also evidence of normal, or even superior, performance in ASD for pitch discrimination and musical abilities (Bonnel et al., 2003; Jarvinen-Pasley and Heaton, 2007; Kellerman et al., 2005; Lepisto et al., 2005a; Mottron et al., 2000). Music, like language, is also a specialized function, and like language, also depends on the processing of sounds earlier in the auditory hierarchy. The two sets of findings—impairments for the processing of language and voices, but superior or normal performance for music—are hard to reconcile. It is possible that abnormal processing of sound early in the cortical hierarchy would result in deficits for auditory processing of language sounds, and normal or superior performance for auditory processing of music. Note that there is a large body of literature on subcortical or peripheral auditory processing showing both abnormalities and normal responses in ASD (Galbraith, 2008; Klin, 1993; Khalfa et al., 2001; King et al., 2002; Kwon et al., 2007; Russo et al., 2008; Tas et al., 2007), but here we will focus only on behavioral measures, as well as cortical processing as measured using EEG or MEG.

The Auditory Mismatch Paradigm

The highly reliable auditory mismtach paradigm (Kujala et al., 2001; Naatanen, 1995; Naatanen & Alho, 1995a, 1995b, 1995c;Novitski et al., 2004; Pekkonen et al., 1995; Tervaniemi et al., 2005) consists of playing one sound (the "standard") repeatedly with relatively constant intervals for 80–90% of the trials, and randomly playing a "deviant" sound in 10–20% of the trials. Ideally, the two sounds are identical in all but one parameter (e.g., frequency). The cortical response to the deviant sound is generally larger than the response to the standard sound, and is followed by a mismatch specific response. Most importantly, the magnitude of the neurophysiological mismatch response measured using EEG (termed MisMatch Negativity, or MMN) or MEG (termed MisMatch Field, or MMF) correlates reliably with behavioral discrimination data. The value of this paradigm lies in its being preattentive, that is, generating reliable responses even when the subject is otherwise engaged (e.g. watching a movie with the sound off). This paradigm is therefore excellent for investigating auditory processing in children with autism and other disorders, for whom maintaining attention on an otherwise relatively boring task is difficult; there is no need to control for attentional effects in this design, making it relatively popular.

Multiple groups have used this paradigm to study frequency discrimination using simple tones in ASD, with results ranging from shortening of the latency of the MMN response in autism (Gomot et al., 2002), to longer MMN latencies in Asperger's disorder children (Jansson-Verkasalo et al., 2003), to no latency shifts but amplitude differences in children with comorbid mental retardation (Ferri et al., 2003), or no difference at all from controls (Ceponiene et al., 2002). One group used a 28-channel MEG system to record MMN paradigm in a mixed group of individuals with autism, aged 8–32, and found no MMN response in the autistic group, as opposed to controls (Tecchio et al., 2003). Potential confounding factors include the different locations of the EEG electrodes in the EEG studies, slight variations in specific stimulus properties, and perhaps most importantly, the probable large heterogeneity of the ASD group within and across studies.

In addition to frequency discrimination, the mismatch paradigm has also been used to study tone duration discrimination in ASD. Here too, results differ across studies; while one study found no significant differences between the ASD group and the control group for tone-duration discrimination (Kasai et al., 2005), other studies (one of autism and one of Asperger's, by the same group) did find diminished MMNs in the ASD groups for tone-duration discrimination (Lepisto et al., 2005a, 2006). Here too, it is likely that the differences in results could be accounted for by the large probable variability of the ASD groups across studies.

Other findings of auditory processing in ASD

Auditory processing abnormalities in autism are not limited to frequency or duration discrimination. Perhaps the most commonly reported auditory processing abnormality in ASD is sensitivity to loud noises. While the neural basis of this phenomenon remains unexplored, it was shown behaviorally that children with ASD do have increased perception of loudness, indicating hyperacusis, and have a smaller auditory dynamic range (Khalfa et al., 2004). Two related EEG studies of loudness perception in autism (Bruneau et al., 1999, 2003) find that children with autism ages 4 to 8 have markedly smaller amplitudes of response to all presented intensities (50–80 dB), with bilateral temporal delayed onset latency of the N100. They also find that the growth of magnitude function—the increase in response amplitude as a function of increasing stimulus intensity—is apparent in both hemispheres in the control group, but flat in the autism group in the left hemisphere. Finally, multiple groups documented differences in the early components of the auditory response in ASD, N1b and N1c in EEG (Bomba and Pang, 2004; Bruneau et al., 1999; 2003), and its magnetic equivalent in the MEG, the M100, with M100 abnormalities (increased latencies) occurring primarily for frequencies below 1000 Hz (Gage et al., 2003).

It is evident that there is a plethora of findings showing abnormal auditory processing in autism. Some of the above studies found correlations between the processing of simple tones and language skills, while others did not. There is clearly a range of findings that sometimes have conflicting results, and to date no coherent theory has been put forth that might unite this broad range of observations of auditory processing abnormalities into a single hypothesis about the neural substrates that may underlie these processes.

SOMATOSENSORY PROCESSING IN AUTISM SPECTRUM DISORDERS

Of all the three topographically mapped sensory modalities, this is the one least studied in autism. This is surprising, given the ample anecdotal evidence that somatosensory perception is abnormal in autism (Edelson et al., 1999; Grandin, 1983; Ratey et al., 1992). Two recent studies examine sensory adaptation and synchronization in autism, and find abnormalities in both. In one study, it was shown that adults with autism spectrum disorders have superior cutaneous localization relative to typical adults following a short adaptation period, and a longer adaptation period did not alter spatial localization capacity in the autism group, whereas it enhanced spatial localization in the control group (Tommerdahl et al., 2007). Furthermore, somatosensory temporal order judgments thresholds (at two adjacent fingertips) are drastically reduced in the presence of simultaneous vibrotactile stimuli (25 Hz), but no such reduction was observed in the ASD group (Tommerdahl et al., 2008). In fact, the ASD group had similar temporal order judgment thresholds, regardless of background stimulation. Such rapid vibrotactile stimulation excites and synchronizes adjacent cortical neuronal assemblies representing adjacent fingers; the fact that the ASD group was not affected by the background vibrations means that those vibrations failed to synchronize adjacent neuronal assemblies (that govern the adjacent finger), thus indicating local functional under-connectivity between adjacent cortical columns/neuronal assemblies in primary somatosensory cortex. The authors attribute the findings to the deficient cerebral cortical GABAergic inhibitory neurotransmission. Finally, in another recent study of tactile perception in ASD (Cascio et al., 2008), the authors showed that individuals with ASD were more sensitive than controls to vibrations on their forearm, and to thermal pain on both the forearm and the palm. In contract, there were no differences between groups in detection of light touch or innocuous thermal stimuli.

In combination, these findings are a clear indication that somatosensory inputs are processed differently in ASD individuals, even at the earliest cortical levels—areas far lower in the cortical hierarchy than regions that subserve social function, language, or communications. Such findings underscore the importance of investigating the link between sensory-processing abnormalities early in the cortical hierarchy, classic ASD behavioral traits, and abnormal cortical processing of social- and communication-based stimuli.

POSSIBLE NEURAL SUBSTRATES OF ABNORMAL SENSORY PROCESSING IN ASD

It is obvious, from the breadth of studies described above, which are only a small fraction of published studies on the topic, that sensory-processing abnormalities in ASD are distributed rather than localized; sensory abnormalities in ASD obviously span multiple dimensions of latency, adaptation, magnitude, and behavior abnormalities, with both enhanced and impaired behavior associated with aberrant cortical responses. Given this diversity in findings, the heterogeneity of ASD, and the broad variability seen over and over again in the ASD groups almost irrespective of the study, it is hard to imagine that one single theory could account for all of these observations. It is also worth bearing in mind that autism is a developmental disorder, and that each of these three sensory modalities matures on a different trajectory and timescale; thus, one abnormality (for example, reduced excitation-to-inhibition ratio), might affect each of these modalities differently during development, further contributing to the confusion. Some of the more prominent recent theories of autism (not necessarily specific to sensory processing) include local over-connectivity (Belmonte et al., 2004), a deficit in processing more complex stimuli (the "complexity" hypothesis; (Bertone et al., 2003, 2005), and a reduced signal-to-noise ratio (Rubenstein & Merzenich, 2003; Sanchez-Marin & Padilla-Medina, 2008). While all of these have highly promising aspects, they all also fall short of explaining the full gamut of observed phenomena. Local overconnectivity, which would favor local over global sensory processing, cannot account for deficits in auditory loudness processing or lack of somatosensory adaptation for instance. The complexity theory is compelling, but it too cannot account for the above observations, nor is it possible to reliably differentiate a complex stimulus from one which simply has a reduced signal-to-noise ratio; furthermore, the concept of "complex" cannot easily be correlated with specific neural substrates. The theory that the cortex in ASD represents stimuli with reduced-signal to-noise ratio cannot fully account for some of the superior sensory abilities observed in ASD, nor can it explain spatial-frequency effects in the visual domain, or delayed M100 only for low frequencies in the auditory domain, for example. It is therefore probable that several mechanisms and neuronal abnormalities, most likely at multiple levels (from single neurons through to inter-area connections), all contribute to varying degrees to the abnormal sensory processing observed in ASD. It is also likely that no single mechanism is unique to one sensory modality, which is why we see such a widely distributed range of abnormalities across modalities. To date, the nature of the specific neural substrates underlying these observations, and how they combine in the population as a whole to result in the observed abnormalities, and in individuals to result in the observed heterogeneity, remain open questions.

References

Ashwin, E., Ashwin, C., Rhydderch, D., Howells, J., & Baron-Cohen, S. (2008). Eagle-eyed visual acuity: An experimental investigation of enhanced perception in autism. *Biol Psychiatry*, X, XX–XX.

Belmonte, M. K, Allen, G., Beckel-Mitchener, A., Boulanger, L. M., Carper, R. A., & Webb S. J. (2004). Autism and abnormal development of brain connectivity. *J Neurosci*, 24, 9228–9231.

Bertone, A., Mottron, L., Jelenic, P., & Faubert, J. (2003). Motion perception in autism: A "complex" issue. *J Cogn Neurosci*, 15, 218–225.

Bertone, A., Mottron, L., Jelenic, P., & Faubert, J. (2005). Enhanced and diminished visuo-spatial information processing in autism depends on stimulus complexity. *Brain*, 128, 2430–2441.

Bomba, M. D., & Pang, E. W. (2004). Cortical auditory evoked potentials in autism: A review. *Int J Psychophysiol*, 53, 161–169.

Bonnel, A., Mottron, L., Peretz, I,. Trudel, M., Gallun, E., & Bonnel, A. M. (2003). Enhanced pitch sensitivity in individuals with autism: A signal detection analysis. *J Cogn Neurosci*, 15, 226–235.

Bruneau, N., Roux, S., Adrien, J. L., & Barthelemy, C. (1999). Auditory associative cortex dysfunction in children with autism: Evidence from late auditory evoked potentials (N1 wave-T complex). *Clin Neurophysiol*, 110, 1927–1934.

Bruneau, N., Bonnet-Brilhault, F., Gomot, M., Adrien, J. L., & Barthelemy, C. (2003). Cortical auditory processing and communication in children with autism: Electrophysiological/behavioral relations. *Int J Psychophysiol*, 51, 17–25.

Buxbaum, J. D., Silverman, J. M., Smith, C. J., Greenberg, D. A., Kilifarski, M., Reichert, J., Cook, E. H., Jr., Fang, Y., Song, C. Y., & Vitale, R. (2002). Association between a GABRB3 polymorphism and autism. *Mol Psychiatry*, 7, 311–316.

Casanova, M. F., Buxhoeveden, D., & Gomez, J. (2003). Disruption in the inhibitory architecture of the cell minicolumn: Implications for autisim. *Neuroscientist*, 9, 496–507.

Cascio, C., McGlone, F., Folger, S., Tannan, V., Baranek, G., Pelphrey, K. A., & Essick, G. (2008). Tactile perception in adults with autism: A multidimensional psychophysical study. *J Autism Dev Disord*, 38, 127–137.

Cook, E. H., Jr., Courchesne, R., Lord, C., Cox, N. J., Yan, S., Lincoln, A., Haas, R., Courchesne, E., & Leventhal, B. L. (1997). Evidence of linkage between the serotonin transporter and autistic disorder. *Mol Psychiatry*, 2, 247–250.

Dakin, S., & Frith, U. (2005). Vagaries of visual perception in autism. *Neuron*, 48, 497–507.

de Jonge, M. V., Kemner, C., de Haan, E. H., Coppens, J. E., van den Berg, T. J., & van Engeland, H. (2007). Visual information processing in high-functioning individuals with autism spectrum disorders and their parents. *Neuropsychology*, 21, 65–73.

Del Viva, M. M., Igliozzi, R., Tancredi, R., & Brizzolara, D. (2006). Spatial and motion integration in children with autism. *Vision Res*, 46, 1242–1252.

Edelson, S. M., Edelson, M. G., Kerr, D. C., & Grandin, T. (1999). Behavioral and physiological effects of deep pressure on children with autism: A pilot study evaluating the efficacy of Grandin's Hug Machine. *Am J Occup Ther*, 53, 145–152.

Ernst, M., Zametkin, A. J., Matochik, J. A., Pascualvaca, D., & Cohen, R. M. (1997). Low medial prefrontal dopaminergic activity in autistic children. *Lancet*, 350, 638.

Flagg, E. J., Cardy, J. E. O., Roberts, W., & Roberts, T. P. L. (2005). Language lateralization development in children with autism: Insights from the late field magnetoencephalogram. *Neuroscience Letters*, 386, 82–87.

Gage, N. M., Siegel, B., Callen, M., & Roberts, T. P. (2003). Cortical sound processing in children with autism disorder: An MEG investigation. *Neuroreport*, 14, 2047–2051.

Galbraith, G. C. (2008). Deficient brainstem encoding in autism. *Clin Neurophysiol*, 119, 1697–1700.

Gervais, H., Belin, P., Boddaert, N., Leboyer, M., Coez, A., Sfaello, I., Barthelemy, C., Brunelle, F., Samson, Y., & Zilbovicius, M. (2004). Abnormal cortical voice processing in autism. *Nat Neurosci*, 7, 801–802.

Grandin, T. (1983). Coping strategies. *J Autism Dev Disord*, 13, 217–222.

Hadjikhani, N., Chabris, C. F., Joseph, R. M., Clark, J., McGrath, L., Aharon, I., Feczko, E., Tager-Flusberg, H., & Harris, G. J. (2004). Early visual cortex organization in autism: An fMRI study. *Neuroreport*, 15, 267–270.

Hansen, P. C., Stein, J. F., Orde, S. R., Winter, J. L., & Talcott, J. B. (2001). Are dyslexics' visual deficits limited to measures of dorsal stream function? *Neuroreport*, 12, 1527–1530.

Hussman, J. P. (2001). Suppressed GABAergic inhibition as a common factor in suspected etiologies of autism. *J Autism Dev Disord*, 31, 247–248.

Jamain, S., Betancur, C., Quach, H., Philippe, A., Fellous, M., Giros, B., Gillberg, C., Leboyer, M., & Bourgeron, T. (2002). Linkage and association of the glutamate receptor 6 gene with autism. *Mol Psychiatry*, 7, 302–310.

Jarvinen-Pasley, A., & Heaton, P. (2007). Evidence for reduced domain-specificity in auditory processing in autism. *Dev Sci*, 10, 786–793.

Kasai, K., Hashimoto, O., Kawakubo, Y., Yumoto, M., Kamio, S., Itoh, K., Koshida, I., Iwanami, A., Nakagome, K., & Fukuda, M. (2005). Delayed automatic detection of change in speech sounds in adults with autism: A magnetoencephalographic study. *Clinical Neurophysiology*, 116, 1655–1664.

Kellerman, G. R., Fan, J., & Gorman, J. M. (2005). Auditory abnormalities in autism: Toward functional distinctions among findings. *CNS Spectr*, 10, 748–756.

Khalfa, S., Bruneau, N., Roge, B., Georgieff, N., Veuillet, E., Adrien, J. L., Barthelemy, C., & Collet, L. (2001). Peripheral auditory asymmetry in infantile autism. *Eur J Neurosci*, 13, 628–632.

Khalfa, S., Bruneau, N., Roge, B., Georgieff, N., Veuillet, E., Adrien, J. L., Barthelemy, C., & Collet, L. (2004). Increased perception of loudness in autism. *Hear Res*, 198, 87–92.

King, C., Warrier, C. M., Hayes, E., & Kraus, N. (2002). Deficits in auditory brainstem pathway encoding of speech sounds in children with learning problems. *Neuroscience Letters*, 319, 111–115.

Klin, A. (1993). Auditory brainstem responses in autism: Brainstem dysfunction or peripheral hearing loss? *J Autism Dev Disord*, 23, 15–35.

Kuhl, P. K., Coffey-Corina, S., Padden, D., & Dawson, G. (2005). Links between social and linguistic processing of speech in preschool children with autism: Behavioral and electrophysiological measures. *Dev Sci*, 8, F1–F12.

Kujala T, Kallio J, Tervaniemi M, Naatanen R (2001). The mismatch negativity as an index of temporal processing in audition. Clin Neurophysiol 112:1712–1719.

Kujala, T., Lepisto, T., Nieminen-von Wendt, T., Naatanen, P., & Naatanen, R. (2005). Neurophysiological evidence for cortical discrimination impairment of prosody in Asperger syndrome. Neuroscience Letters, 383, 260–265.

Kwon, S., Kim, J., Choe, B. H., Ko, C., & Park, S. (2007). Electrophysiologic assessment of central auditory processing by auditory brainstem responses in children with autism spectrum disorders. J Korean Med Sci, 22, 656–659.

Lam, K. S., Aman, M. G., & Arnold, L. E. (2005). Neurochemical correlates of autistic disorder: A review of the literature. Res Dev Disabil, X, XX–XX.

Lee, M., Martin-Ruiz, C., Graham, A., Court, J., Jaros, E., Perry, R., Iversen, P., Bauman, M., & Perry, E. (2002). Nicotinic receptor abnormalities in the cerebellar cortex in autism. Brain, 125, 1483–1495.

Lepisto, T., Kujala, T., Vanhala, R., Alku, P., Huotilainen, M., & Naatanen, R. (2005a). The discrimination of and orienting to speech and non-speech sounds in children with autism. Brain Res, 1066, 147–157.

Lepisto, T., Kujala, T., Vanhala, R., Alku, P., Huotilainen, M., & Naatanen, R. (2005b). The discrimination of and orienting to speech and non-speech sounds in children with autism. Brain Research, 1066, 147–157.

Lepisto, T., Silokallio, S., Nieminen-von Wendt, T., Alku, P., Naatanen, R., Kujala, T. (2006). Auditory perception and attention as reflected by the brain event-related potentials in children with Asperger syndrome. Clin Neurophysiol, 117, 2161–2171.

Ma, D. Q., Whitehead, P. L., Menold, M. M., Martin, E. R., Ashley-Koch, A. E., Mei, H., Ritchie, M. D., Delong, G. R., Abramson, R. K., Wright, H. H., Cuccaro, M. L., Hussman, J. P., Gilbert, J. R., & Pericak-Vance, M. A. (2005). Identification of significant association and gene-gene interaction of GABA receptor subunit genes in autism. Am J Hum Genet, 77, 377–388.

Martin-Ruiz, C. M., Lee, M., Perry, R. H., Baumann, M., Court, J. A., & Perry, E. K. (2004). Molecular analysis of nicotinic receptor expression in autism. Brain Res Mol Brain Res, 123, 81–90.

Menold, M. M., Shao, Y., Wolpert, C. M., Donnelly, S. L., Raiford, K. L., Martin, E. R., Ravan, S. A., Abramson, R. K., Wright, H. H., Delong, G. R., Cuccaro, M. L., Pericak-Vance, M. A., & Gilbert, J. R. (2001). Association analysis of chromosome 15 gabaa receptor subunit genes in autistic disorder. J Neurogenet, 15, 245–259.

Milne, E., Swettenham, J., Hansen, P., Campbell, R., Jeffries, H., & Plaisted, K. (2002). High motion coherence thresholds in children with autism. J Child Psychol Psychiatry, 43, 255–263.

Miyazaki, K., Narita, N., Sakuta, R., Miyahara, T., Naruse, H., Okado, N., & Narita, M. (2004). Serum neurotrophin concentrations in autism and mental retardation: A pilot study. Brain Dev, 26, 292–295.

Mottron, L., Peretz, I., & Menard, E. (2000). Local and global processing of music in high-functioning persons with autism: beyond central coherence? J Child Psychol Psychiatry, 41, 1057–1065.

Naatanen, R. (1995). The mismatch negativity: A powerful tool for cognitive neuroscience. Ear Hear, 16, 6–18.

Naatanen, R., & Alho, K. (1995a). Mismatch negativity to change in complex spectrotemporal sound pattern: A new way to study neural learning in the human brain. Electroencephalogr Clin Neurophysiol Suppl, 44, 179–184.

Naatanen, R., & Alho, K. (1995b). Mismatch negativity — a unique measure of sensory processing in audition. Int J Neurosci, 80, 317–337.

Naatanen, R., & Alho, K. (1995c). Generators of electrical and magnetic mismatch responses in humans. Brain Topogr, 7, 315–320.

Nelson, K. B., Grether, J. K., Croen, L. A., Dambrosia, J. M., Dickens, B. F., Jelliffe, L. L., Hansen, R. L., & Phillips, T. M. (2001). Neuropeptides and neurotrophins in neonatal blood of children with autism or mental retardation. Ann Neurol, 49, 597–606.

Newsome, W. T., & Pare, E. B. (1988). A selective impairment of motion perception following lesions of the middle temporal visual area (MT). J Neurosci, 8, 2201–2211.

Novitski, N., Tervaniemi, M., Huotilainen, M., & Naatanen, R. (2004). Frequency discrimination at different frequency levels as indexed by electrophysiological and behavioral measures. Brain Res Cogn Brain Res, 20, 26–36.

Oram Cardy, J. E., Flagg, E. J., Roberts, W., & Roberts, T. P. (2005). Delayed mismatch field for speech and non-speech sounds in children with autism. Neuroreport, 16, 521–525.

Pekkonen, E., Rinne, T., & Naatanen, R. (1995). Variability and replicability of the mismatch negativity. Electroencephalogr Clin Neurophysiol, 96, 546–554.

Pellicano, E., & Gibson, L. Y. (2008). Investigating the functional integrity of the dorsal visual pathway in autism and dyslexia. Neuropsychologia, 46, 2593–2596.

Pellicano, E., Gibson, L., Maybery, M., Durkin, K., & Badcock, D. R. (2005). Abnormal global processing along the dorsal visual pathway in autism: a possible mechanism for weak visuospatial coherence? Neuropsychologia, 43, 1044–1053.

Perry, E. K., Lee, M. L., Martin-Ruiz, C. M., Court, J. A., Volsen, S. G., Merrit, J., Folly, E., Iversen, P. E., Bauman, M. L., Perry, R. H., & Wenk, G. L. (2001). Cholinergic activity in autism: Abnormalities in the cerebral cortex and basal forebrain. Am J Psychiatry, 158, 1058–1066.

Purcell, A. E., Jeon, O. H., Zimmerman, A. W., Blue, M. E., & Pevsner, J. (2001). Postmortem brain abnormalities of the glutamate neurotransmitter system in autism. *Neurology, 57,* 1618–1628.

Ramoz, N., Reichert, J. G., Smith, C. J., Silverman, J. M., Bespalova, I. N., Davis, K. L., & Buxbaum, J. D. (2004). Linkage and association of the mitochondrial aspartate/glutamate carrier SLC25A12 gene with autism. *Am J Psychiatry, 161,* 662–669.

Ratey, J. J., Grandin, T., & Miller, A. (1992). Defense behavior and coping in an autistic savant: The story of Temple Grandin, PhD. *Psychiatry, 55,* 382–391.

Ray, M. A., Graham, A. J., Lee, M., Perry, R. H., Court, J. A., & Perry, E. K. (2005). Neuronal nicotinic acetylcholine receptor subunits in autism: An immunohistochemical investigation in the thalamus. *Neurobiol Dis, 19,* 366–377.

Ridder, W. H., 3rd, Borsting, E., & Banton, T. (2001). All developmental dyslexic subtypes display an elevated motion coherence threshold. *Optom Vis Sci, 78,* 510–517.

Rubenstein, J. L., & Merzenich, M. M. (2003). Model of autism: Increased ratio of excitation/inhibition in key neural systems. *Genes Brain Behav, 2,* 255–267.

Russo, N. M., Skoe, E., Trommer, B., Nicol, T., Zecker, S., Bradlow, A., & Kraus, N. (2008). Deficient brainstem encoding of pitch in children with autism spectrum disorders. *Clin Neurophysiol, 119,* 1720–1731.

Salzman, C. D., & Newsome, W. T. (1994). Neural mechanisms for forming a perceptual decision. *Science, 264,* 231–237.

Sanchez-Marin, F. J., & Padilla-Medina, J. A. (2008). A psychophysical test of the visual pathway of children with autism. *J Autism Dev Disord, 38,* 1270–1277.

Schulte-Korne, G., Bartling, J., Deimel, W., & Remschmidt, H. (2004). Visual evoked potentials elicited by coherently moving dots in dyslexic children. *Neuroscience Letters, 357,* 207–210.

Serajee, F. J., Zhong, H., Nabi, R., & Huq, A. H. (2003). The metabotropic glutamate receptor 8 gene at 7q31: Partial duplication and possible association with autism. *J Med Genet, 40,* e42.

Spencer, J., O'Brien, J., Riggs, K., Braddick, O., Atkinson, J., & Wattam-Bell, J. (2000). Motion processing in autism: Evidence for a dorsal stream deficiency. *Neuroreport, 11,* 2765–2767.

Spencer, J. V., & O'Brien, J. M. (2006). Visual form-processing deficits in autism. *Perception, 35,* 1047–1055.

Talcott, J. B., Hansen, P. C., Assoku, E. L., & Stein, J. F. (2000). Visual motion sensitivity in dyslexia: Evidence for temporal and energy integration deficits. *Neuropsychologia, 38,* 935–943.

Tas, A., Yagiz, R., Tas, M., Esme, M., Uzun, C., & Karasalihoglu, A. R. (2007). Evaluation of hearing in children with autism by using TEOAE and ABR. *Autism, 11,* 73–79.

Tervaniemi, M., Sinkkonen, J., Virtanen, J., Kallio, J., Ilmoniemi, R. J., Salonen, O., & Naatanen, R. (2005). Test-retest stability of the magnetic mismatch response (MMNm). *Clin Neurophysiol, 116,* 1897–1905.

Tommerdahl, M., Tannan, V., Holden, J. K., & Baranek, G. T. (2008). Absence of stimulus-driven synchronization effects on sensory perception in autism: Evidence for local underconnectivity? *Behav Brain Funct, 4,* 19.

Tommerdahl, M., Tannan, V., Cascio, C. J., Baranek, G. T., & Whitsel, B. L. (2007). Vibrotactile adaptation fails to enhance spatial localization in adults with autism. *Brain Res, 1154,* 116–123.

Tsermentseli, S., O'Brien, J. M., & Spencer, J. V. (2008). Comparison of form and motion coherence processing in autistic spectrum disorders and dyslexia. *J Autism Dev Disord, 38,* 1201–1210.

Vandenbroucke, M. W., Scholte, H. S., van Engeland, H., Lamme, V. A., & Kemner, C. (2008a). Coherent versus component motion perception in autism spectrum disorder. *J Autism Dev Disord, 38,* 941–949.

Vandenbroucke, M. W., Scholte, H. S., van Engeland, H., Lamme, V. A., & Kemner, C. (2008b). A neural substrate for atypical low-level visual processing in autism spectrum disorder. *Brain, 131,* 1013–1024.

Vargas, D. L., Nascimbene, C., Krishnan, C., Zimmerman, A. W., & Pardo, C. A. (2005). Neuroglial activation and neuroinflammation in the brain of patients with autism. *Ann Neurol, 57,* 67–81.

Chapter 12

Social Cognition in ASD

Mikle South, Robert T. Schultz, and Sally Ozonoff

Leo Kanner described children with autism as "[unable] to relate themselves in an ordinary way to people … from the beginning of life" (1943, p. 242). Kanner's summary succinctly frames the main theme for this chapter: How do individuals diagnosed with autism spectrum disorders (ASD) perceive and think about their social interactions? We begin the chapter by reviewing the primacy of social deficits in autism from the earliest ages. We then consider evidence for impairments in both social perception and motivation, including research aimed at discovering fundamental biomarkers in these areas; we also briefly consider how underconnectivity in key brain regions may affect social cognition in autism. We finish with a discussion of how research into social cognition can support effective clinical intervention. Traditional neuropsychological research is now supplemented by rapid advances in technology and methodology across a number of areas, including eye tracking studies, neuroimaging, psychophysiology, and the development of targeted animal models. Throughout the

chapter, we strive to apply the information that is available from many different approaches to the study of ASD.

PRIMACY OF SOCIAL DEFICITS IN ASD

Early Markers of Atypical Social Development

Parents of children with ASD often begin to be concerned when language fails to develop as expected. However, several symptoms of atypical social interaction seem to predate the language abnormalities that parents report at the time of recognition. By the middle of their second year, children later diagnosed with ASD show less interest in looking at faces, decreased orienting to name, decreased pointing, limited imitation, and lack of sharing enjoyment and interests with others (see Ozonoff et al., 2008; Zwaigenbaum et al., 2005). It has been proposed that these early skill differences may lead to subsequent delays or detours in the development of more complex social abilities, such as building a "Theory of Mind" about others' intentions (Sodian & Thoermer, 2008). (Theory of Mind is defined as the realization that others have thoughts different than one's own; this concept will be discussed more fully later in the chapter). Differential development of fundamental social skills may predict developmental course, including possible "regression," in which previous skills diminish, or developmental plateau, in which they slow or stop progressing in their maturation; firm conclusions in this area are limited, however, by the current small number of prospective studies, and by significant measurement limitations in retrospective studies (Ozonoff et al., 2008).

Social Ability Separate from General Cognitive Ability

Because the triad of symptoms that define autism is rather broad in nature, it has been presumed that the syndrome disrupts a widely distributed set of neural systems (Robins, Hunyadi, & Schultz, 2005). However, there are also areas of spared function in autism, including basic perceptual skills and certain cognitive functions; thus, significant social disability in autism may be accompanied by average or above-average general intelligence. This implies that social intelligence and cognitive ability (at least as measured by traditional IQ and memory tests) arise from largely distinct neural systems. Although social skills do develop with age in individuals with ASD, the definition of autism requires that social development is both delayed and deviant.

Heterogeneity of Social Cognition in ASD

It is now widely accepted that there are multiple forms of autism (Bill & Geschwind, 2009; Happé, Ronald, & Plomin, 2006); it is also likely that these various forms arise from multiple genotypes, subject to multiple gene-gene and/or gene-environment influences (Anderson, 2008; Happe & Ronald, 2008). For instance, although one frequent symptom of autism is impaired use of nonverbal behaviors such as eye-to-eye gaze, there may be multiple underlying reasons for the limited use of eye contact that should be considered separately: one child may be less motivated than usual to interact with other people, perhaps because of *under-*

activity in the motivational systems including the amygdala (Schultz, 2005); a different child may actively avoid eye contact because of social anxiety that arises due to *overactivity* of the amygdala (Dalton et al., 2005). The similar outward behavior of these two children—defined symptomatically as markedly impaired eye gaze—is based on different genetic makeups that might respond differently to the same interventions, and might require distinct forms of treatment.

Social cognition in ASD vis-à-vis other conditions

In general, social deficits appear to be more unique to autism, and less shared with other neuropsychiatric disabilities, than the other core autism deficits (Schultz, 2005). Nonetheless, a number of reported exceptions highlight the need for research regarding specific markers of social cognition within the autism spectrum, and in relation to other psychiatric and cognitive factors. For example, Chawarska and Volkmar (2007) studied three groups of 2-year-olds: one group of children diagnosed with autism, one group of children diagnosed with developmental delay (DD) but not autism, matched on nonverbal mental age; and a younger typical comparison group matched on nonverbal mental age. On a discrimination task for monkey and human faces, the autism and DD groups were both impaired relative to the typical group; a second study of older children (3- and 4-year-olds) found that face recognition ability was positively correlated with nonverbal cognitive ability and age, but not with social interaction skills. An fMRI study comparing autism with subtypes of schizophrenia found similar patterns of reduced activation in paranoid schizophrenia and autism, in key areas of the social brain (i.e., amygdala, fusiform face area, and ventrolateral prefrontal cortex), in response to judging the trustworthiness of faces (Pinkham, Hopfinger, Pelphrey, Piven, & Penn, 2008). Finally, a behavioral study comparing face processing between children diagnosed with Williams syndrome and children diagnosed with autism found that emotional face processing was more impaired in the Williams group than the autism group (Lacroix, Guidetti, Rogé, & Reilly, 2009). These "exceptions" underscore the difficulties of doing research in samples marked by tremendous heterogeneity of symptom expression.

Dimensional definitions and social endophenotypes

Categorical diagnostic systems, such as the *DSM-IV*, do not readily account for overlap of symptoms across diagnostic boundaries within ASDs; with other neuro-psychiatric conditions; nor for the variation that can occur within the same child, depending on the situation or the day (Klin, Pauls, Schultz, & Volkmar, 2005; South, Wolf, & Herlihy, 2009; see also Chapters 23, 24, and 25). As an alternative to categorical definitions, proponents of a dimensional-systems approach view both typical and atypical behavior as variations in degree along one or more continuous dimensions of behavior or personality (Cuthbert, 2005), such as the example of variation in eye gaze discussed above.

Another fruitful approach to understanding the variety of behavioral symptoms in autism is to look for possible intermediate endophenotypes, defined as measurable characteristics that lie on the pathway between genes and observed symptom expression (Gottesman & Gould, 2003). Such endophenotypes may serve to create more genetically homogenous subgroups, and to indicate shared traits in relatives with subclinical symptom expression, as indicators of susceptibility genes (Coon, 2006). These subclinical behavioral and biomarkers may include a wide variety of features; in the case of autism, for example, there are observable variations in head growth, serotonin levels, eye gaze behavior, and language development. Because atypical social development appears to be uniquely important to autism, research regarding potential endophenotypes, such as deficits in social motivation, social perception, and social cognition, are explored further below.

SOCIAL PERCEPTION IN ASD

Ever since Langdell's (1978) seminal studies of atypical face processing in ASD (see also Hobson, Ouston, & Lee, 1988a; 1988b), research has generally shown that individuals with ASD do not utilize typical strategies for organizing and integrating social cues from faces (reviewed in Sasson, 2006) and voices (see Gervais et al., 2004). One vein of research has focused directly on deficits in sensory or perceptual processing of social information (see Schultz & Robbins, 2005); another fruitful avenue has explored the foundations of social motivation in autism, which may in turn

directly affect perceptual processes (reviewed in Schultz, 2005). Most recently, studies of neural under-connectivity in ASD have focused on how information is processed over long distances in the brain, suggesting that it may be the complexity of social information processing, and the integration of various strands of information across the brain, that contributes to the unique social deficits seen in ASD (see Koshino et al, 2008; also see Chapter 21 for more on connectivity).

Facial Identity Processing

In typical development, "face expertise" usually develops naturally, rapidly, and vigorously in young children (Johnson, 2005). Evidence for a rudimentary face-specific N170 response is seen in event-related potential (ERP) studies of infants as young as 3 months old (Johnson, 2006). Localization of specialized face-processing functions at the fusiform face area (FFA; a small region in the lateral edge of the middle portion of the temporal lobe fusiform gyrus) appears to be complete before adolescence (Gathers, Bhatt, Corbly, Farley, & Joseph, 2004). Yet many individuals with ASD struggle with recognizing facial identity through-out their life. This difficulty occurs despite intact vision both generally and for other complex visual objects (reviewed in Grelotti, Gauthier, & Schultz, 2002; Wolf et al., 2008).

Ongoing work suggests that the magnitude of the deficit in recognizing facial identity in ASD is as large as, or larger than, that in any other neuropsychological domain. This deficit is marked by an overemphasis on individual features and an underemphasis on the holistic gestalt configuration of the face. For example, ASD individuals show less performance degradation with inverted faces than do comparison groups (e.g., Teunisse& de Gelder, 2003). Whereas typically developing individuals demonstrate facili-tated face recognition for "low-spatial-frequency" information (i.e., the position of features in space), children with ASD do better on behavioral tasks that emphasize high-spatial-frequency information (i.e., sharp changes in brightness around the edges; Deruelle, Rondan, Gepner, & Tardiff, 2004). Dawson et al. (2005) have found face recognition difficulties in behavioral and ERP studies of parents of children with autism, strongly suggesting that face processing is a functional trait marker (i.e., a valid endophenotype) for autism.

Autism and the FFA

In typical development, the FFA shows selectivity (i.e., enhanced activation) for faces compared to other complex objects (Kanwisher, McDermott, & Chun, 1997). Schultz et al. (2000) published the first functional neuroimaging study of face perception among individuals with ASD, reporting that the FFA was hypoactive in a group of 14 persons with autism or Asperger syndrome, compared to two independent samples of 14 control participants (see Figure 12-1 for an example illustration). Findings of hypoactivity of the FFA in autism have been replicated by at least nine other labs (e.g., Pierce et al., 2001; Wang et al., 2004), making this the first reliable functional MRI marker of ASD in the literature. Preliminary data show that individual differences in autism symptom severity strongly predict individual differences in degree of FFA activation, such that less FFA activation is associated with greater social disability. Preliminary data from one of us (R.T. Schultz) also indicates that accuracy on face identity perception tests also correlates with degree of FFA activation.

Despite the consistency of FFA findings across so many studies in autism, recent research has demonstrated that hypoactivation of the FFA may be, at least to some degree, task specific. Speer, Cook, McMahon, and Clark (2007) report that children and adolescents with autism show atypical eye-gaze patterns only for stimuli that are both social and dynamic, and not to non-social or social-but-static conditions. An fMRI study by Hadjikhani, Joseph, Snyder, and Tager-Flusberg (2007) found no differences in FFA activation between ASD and controls, although their sample size was very small, and the specific tasks used have been shown elsewhere to be weak modulators of FFA activity and relatively insensitive to fusiform activation abnormalities in ASD (Schultz et al., 2008). An fMRI study by Pierce and Redcay (2008) found that children diagnosed with autism (ages 6–12) showed hypoactivation in the FFA while viewing faces of adult strangers, but showed no difference in activation to familiar faces (i.e., their mothers and friends) or faces of other children. Better understanding about the specificity of the FFA for face-identity processing is therefore a critical topic for further research.

There also remains considerable controversy surrounding the question of whether face-processing deficits in ASD are indeed specific to faces, or whether this reflects a more general problem in visual processing.

As noted above, children with autism show an atypical benefit when viewing high-frequency versus low-frequency spatial information. More support of a fundamental visual-processing deficit comes from a study of perceptual discrimination that compared faces with novel, complex, homogenous objects (Greebles) and novel, heterogenous objects, where the ASD group was equally impaired for discriminating faces and Greebles (Scherf, Berhmann, Minshew, & Luna, 2008). A small EEG study found that ASD participants had difficulty with detecting the boundaries of non-face objects, suggesting a low-level visual processing impairment (Vandenbroucke, Scholte, van Engeland, Lamme, & Kemner, 2008).

In contrast, in the largest sample studied to date, with exquisite matching on age and IQ, Wolf et al. (2008) found specific deficits for faces versus objects across a battery of tests of basic perceptual processing strategies. Effect sizes for group differences averaged around 1 standard deviation, indicating that the real face processing deficit in ASD is likely large. Another behavioral study (Wallace, Coleman, & Bailey, 2008) found intact object processing but impaired face processing especially when stimuli were presented for just a short time (as short as 40 milliseconds [ms]), as expected by theories of a holistic processing deficit in ASD that particularly disrupts processing of faces. A recent fMRI study of face processing in ASD (Bookheimer, Wang, Scott, Sigman, & Dapretto, 2008) found that FFA activity was greater in response to inverted versus upright faces in both ASD and comparison groups, but that amygdala and prefrontal cortex were hypoactive in the ASD group; the authors conclude that attention to social significance, not deficits in visual information processing, is what drives face-processing deficits in autism.

The nature and extent of face-processing differences in autism thus continues to be an area of active research to define more precisely the nature, extent and biological underpinnings of these social perceptual abnormalities in ASD. Theories of neural underconnectivity in autism (e.g., Minshew & Williams, 2007; Renner, Klinger, & Klinger, 2006) may provide a somewhat parsimonious consolidation of these divergent viewpoints. Just and colleagues (e.g., Just, Cherkassky, Kana, Keller, & Minshew, 1997; Kana, Keller, Cherkassky, Minshew, & Just, 2009) report data from a number of fMRI studies that demonstrate limitations in connectivity between posterior and anterior brain regions. They suggest that posterior

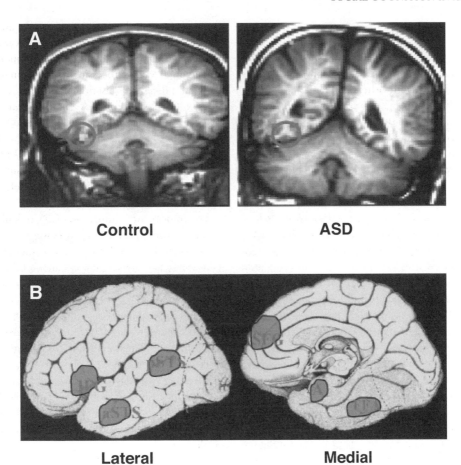

Figure 12-1 Functional MRI abnormalities observed in autism spectrum disorders (ASD). A, these coronal MRI images show the cerebral hemispheres above, the cerebellum below, and a circle over the fusiform gyrus of the temporal lobe. The examples illustrate the frequent finding of hypoactivation of the fusiform gyrus to faces in an adolescent male with ASD (right) compared with an age- and IQ-matched healthy control male (left). The red/yellow signal shows brain areas that are significantly more active during perception of faces; signals in blue show areas more active during perception of nonface objects. Note the lack of face activation in the boy with ASD but average levels of nonface object activation. B, Schematic diagrams of the brain from lateral and medial orientations illustrating the broader array of brain areas found to be hypoactive in ASD during a variety of cognitive and perceptual tasks that are explicitly social in nature. Some evidence suggests that these areas are linked to form a "social brain" network. IFG, Inferior frontal gyrus (hypoactive during facial expression imitation); pSTS, posterior superior temporal sulcus (hypoactive during perception of facial expression and eye gaze tasks); SFG, superior frontal gyrus (hypoactive during theory of mind tasks, i.e., when taking another person's perspective); A, amygdala (hypoactive during a variety of social tasks); FFA, fusiform face area (hypoactive during perception of personal identity). (From DiCocco-Bloom et al., 2006). (See color Figure 12-1.)

areas are unable to be guided by top down regulatory goals. An alternative model (see Bölte et al., 2008; Haist et al., 2005; Takarae et al., 2007) develops the idea that there are increased short-range connections in autism that arise from early brain overgrowth in ASD (Bigler et al. 2003; Carper & Courchesne 2005). This leads to hyperconnectivity, increased neural noise, and reduced efficiency of information processing, creating an information "bottleneck"; that is, too few numbers of long-range connections prevent sharing and synthesis of information across distributed brain networks. As a consequence, higher-level cortical areas (e.g., the frontal lobes) are required to assist in processing lower-level information, leaving these areas less available for more complex cognitive tasks, such as executive functions and Theory of Mind tasks.

Facial Expression Processing

There are also many studies of facial expression processing. It appears that children and adults with ASD demonstrate deficits in perceiving, labeling, and understanding facial expressions that may underlie more complex difficulties in empathy and social reciprocity (see Fein, Lucci, Braverman, & Waterhouse, 1992; Hobson, Ouston, & Lee, 1988a, 1988b; Yirmiya et al., 1992). While recognition of facial identity is largely under the purview of the fusiform region, the superior temporal sulcus and neighboring gyrus are critically involved in decoding nonverbal communications through facial expressions (Robins, Hunyadi, & Schultz, 2009). Pelphrey and colleagues (Pelphrey et al., 2007; Pelphrey, Morris, & McCarthy, 2005) report that perception of dynamic facial expressions in ASD is associated with not only with hypoactivity in the FFA, but also in the amygdala and in the posterior superior temporal sulcus (pSTS), a region associated with perception of biological motion and inferences about intentionality (see also Humphreys, Hasson, Avidan, Minshew, & Berhmann, 2008). A study of typical development by Wyc, Hudac, Carter, Sobel, and Pelphrey (2009) has recently shown differential activation of the posterior STS depending on the type of body movement: perception of mouth movements elicited activity along the mid-posterior STS, while eye movements elicited activity that was somewhat more posterior. Consistent with these functional deficits, there are now also at least two reports of the morphology of the STS being altered in adolescents and young adults with autism (Boddaert et al., 2004; Waiter et al., 2005).

Eye-tracking studies

Infrared eye tracking has been used to measure eye movements, another form of nonverbal behavior that communicates a person's internal affective state and interest. Klin et al. (2002) measured visual scan paths in adults with autism as they tried to make sense of interpersonal social interactions. They found that individuals with autism focused much more than typical viewers on the mouth, while focusing much less on the rest of the face, particularly the eye region. The distribution of percent viewing time on the eye region for

each group did not overlap at all, showing that this one behavioral variable could classify participants with 100% sensitivity and specificity in this sample. Although other studies have not always seen quite the same degree of separation between autism and comparison groups, there is ample evidence for eye tracking abnormalities in autism (e.g., Hernandez et al., 2009; Pelphrey et al., 2002; Sterling et al., 2008). This is consistent with behavioral results showing that persons with ASD are less skilled overall on tasks involving fine-grained perceptual discriminations of the eye region, as opposed to the mouth region (Wolf et al., 2008).

Studies of younger siblings of children with autism have found that infants who are diagnosed with autism at later ages show impaired visual tracking during infancy (Zwaigenbaum et al., 2005). Some 6-month-old siblings at familial risk for autism also demonstrate decreased eye contact and increased gaze at the mouth during eye tracking studies of a "still face" paradigm (Merin, Young, Ozonoff, & Rogers, 2007), although none of these infants went on to develop autism (Young, Merin, Rogers, & Ozonoff, 2009). Klin and colleagues have shown visual scanning abnormalities in two-year-olds diagnosed with autism, both in response to human adults who are approaching the infant (Jones, Carr, & Klin, 2008) and in orienting to point-light displays of biological motion (Klin et al., 2009). The ability to quantify primary social functions such as eye gaze, in a variety of naturalistic and experimental settings and across a range of ages and developmental levels, promises to provide valuable insight into the neural mechanisms underlying autism. Evidence for these early-appearing face-processing differences are also important in clarifying that the accuracy deficits on person identification and facial expression discrimination in later childhood and adulthood are not merely "end states" of a life long lack of motivation to interact with others, i.e., less time on task, but rather are part of a constellation of early-appearing markers, and hallmarks of ASD.

SOCIAL MOTIVATION AND THE AMYGDALA

Functional Connectivity for Face Processing

Given the multiple findings of individual areas of abnormal activation during social perception in ASD, there are now a number of ongoing research projects examining the functional connectivity between these regions. Specifically, it is hypothesized that reduced long-range connectivity affects the integration of information across an extended social network in the brain (Kleinhans et al., 2008; see Chapter 21). There is strong preliminary evidence showing altered functional connectivity between the amygdala, FFA, and frontal lobes in autism (Bookheimer et al., 2008; Kleinhans et al., 2008; Koshino et al., 2008; Schultz et al, 2005). Although face processing is known to be critically dependent on aspects of the fusiform gyrus (e.g., prosopagnosia only results from lesions to the fusiform gyrus, not other brain regions), other areas communicate and possibly modulate FFA activity, and become important in the context of a broader set of social functioning.

The amygdala, motivation, and attention

What might precede or underlie the deficits in social perception that we have just described? It has been hypothesized that limited levels of social motivation, when deficient from birth, may derail a whole host of normal developmental processes (reviewed in Baron-Cohen et al., 2000; Schultz, Romanski, & Tsatsanis, 2000). One example of the developmental consequences of congenitally low levels of social motivation would be a failure to develop normal perceptual expertise for faces (Grelotti et al., 2002; Schultz, 2005). More broadly, insufficient motivation for social engagement would be expected to lead to less social experience, which would impact social perceptual and social cognitive skill development. From the perspective of this model, congenital deficits in social motivation are a lynchpin of the development of autism, affecting early patterns of gaze as well as later social perceptual and social cognitive abilities (Schultz, 2005; see Figure 12-2).

This model further postulates that the connections between various nodes in a larger social network are responsible for mediating these behavioral deficits. As reviewed above, both the STS and the FFA support critical social-perceptual functions that are abnormal in autism. However, neither the STS nor the fusiform gyrus (FG) function are encapsulated modules that can perform functions in an autonomous manner; rather, they operate as part of larger neural systems, and information processing subserving social perception likely reflects the interactions between multiple nodes within these systems. The precise interactions between nodes have not yet been well specified, but it

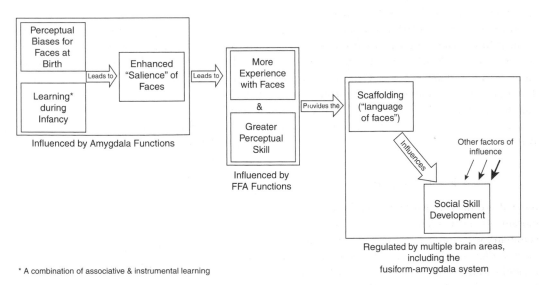

Figure 12-2 A heuristic model of the relationship between the development of face perceptual skills and social skills as mediated by a system involving the amygdala and select cortical regions such as the fusiform gyrus and the superior temporal sulcus. The amygdala is hypothesized to have a critical role early in development, while the cortical areas are believed to have a protracted development across childhood so as to allow the advanced computations characteristic of adult levels of face and facial expression recognition. (From Schultz, 2005).

appears that the FFA has a special relationship with the amygdala to form the core of one functional neural network (Schultz, 2005).

Damage to the amygdala appears to cause reduced levels of FFA activity to faces (Vuilleumier et al., 2004), suggesting that there are direct and active inputs from the amygdala to the FFA that support or "prime" its computational activities. The FFA also appears to be involved in other select aspects of social cognition beyond social perception. Studies employing visual theory of mind type tasks have now shown the FFA to be active during social judgments, even in the absence of any presentation of a face or a face-like object (e.g., Schultz et al., 2003). One interpretation of the FFA's activity during social cognitive tasks is that it also integrates perceptual information with conceptual knowledge. South, Grupe, & Schultz (2008) report a study where typical young adults who were trained to associate novel, abstract visual stimuli ("Blobs") with word triads of descriptive traits. During an fMRI task that required only visual discrimination of the Blobs with no reference to the semantic traits, there was significant activation in the FFA for viewing the Blobs when the associated traits were social personality traits ("friendly," "jealous"), but not when the associated traits were non-social physical descriptors ("heavy," "moist,"). They suggest that what one knows about a person (e.g., personality traits) has a marked influence on how the person is view perceptually. Thus, in typical development, "what you know" has an important influence on "what you see" (Barsalou, 2008). In this context, the FFA's low activity level during face perception in individuals with ASD might reflect a failure to connect social concepts together, as well as deficits in face perception.

Amygdala-frontal connections

Beyond its role as modulator and interpreter of the emotional significance of data processed in perceptual regions, the amygdala has dense reciprocal connections to orbital and medial prefrontal cortices (PFC; Carmichael & Price, 1995; Mufson et al., 1981; Price et al., 1996). The amygdala is known to be necessary for learning to associate sensory perceptions with emotional reinforcers; contemporary models of its functions suggest that it adds an emotional tag to incoming sensory stimuli, which is important for triaging information in terms of motivational salience (Aggleton, 2003).

The amygdala forms an integral part of a loop with PFC to link sensory information with prior knowledge and experience, in order to formulate decisions and initiate subsequent actions. In autism samples, orbital and medial PFC areas have shown reduced fMRI activity during Theory of Mind tasks (Castelli, Frith, Happé, & Frith, 2002), as well as reduced dopaminergic activity using positron emission topography (Ernst et al., 1997). Behaviorally, damage to the amygdala causes impairment in recognizing facial expressions, detecting social faux pas, judging trustworthiness, and interpreting social intentions (see Adolphs et al., 2005).

Questions about the Amgydala's Role in Autism

A different perspective regarding the amygdala's role in social cognition highlights its importance in mediating physiological arousal and related reward-based processes (see Davis & Whalen, 2001). In this scenario, the magnitude of amygdala activation depends on stimulus intensity. Thus, hypoactivation of the amygdala in autism may reflect nonspecific factors such as generally low arousal, rather than a specific deficit in social cognition. From this perspective, amygdala hypoarousal may be a principal source of low social motivation in autism, which in turn leads to a broad array of social perceptual and social deficits across the course of development.

Although this model is likely an oversimplification, it does provide a structure for future studies, which are clearly needed for testing the precise role of these and other neural substrates of social motivation deficits in autism. One fruitful area of study will be to define the specificity of amygdala dysfunction with regard to social-information processing. For example, a recent behavioral study of adolescents and adults with autism found that emotional stimuli facilitated learning and memory to the same degree as in the comparison group, as long as the tasks did not include overtly social elements (South et al., 2008). South et al. (2008) suggested that amygdala function is disrupted in autism only for social information, perhaps as a result of atypical feedback from social perception areas such as the FFA. Animal models, reviewed below, also do not support a direct role for the amygdala in social impairment in autism (see especially, Amaral & Corbett, 2003).

It will likewise be important to characterize the specificity of the "amygdala phenotype" for autism vis-à-vis other developmental psychopathologies: very similar models of pathophysiology have been suggested for anxiety, depression, psychopathy, bipolar disorder, substance abuse, schizophrenia, and post-traumatic stress disorder (see, e.g., Davidson & Slagter, 2000; Morris, Weickert, & Loughland, 2009; Shin & Liberzon, 2010 2009). Identification of focused contributions to behavior by specific amygdala regions and pathways in autism may benefit from the use of multiple techniques, including neuroimaging, as well as from techniques used to study other disorders (such as startle paradigms used in PTSD and psychopathy). This in turn may be compatible with research to identify endophenotypes and associated genetic markers that correspond directly to subnuclei of the amygdala (Zirlinger & Anderson, 2003).

ADDITIONAL THEMES IN
SOCIAL COGNITION

Thus far, this review has primarily focused on face processing research, which has contributed to the bulk of social cognitive research in ASD to date. Nonetheless, there are a number of additional research areas that are important to consider with regard to how individuals diagnosed with ASD view their social interactions. These include links to empathy and Theory of Mind; to other perceptual modalities, such as voice; to other symptoms of autism, specifically restricted and repetitive behaviors; and to the potential for animal models to inform understanding of the neuropsychology of autism.

Mirror Neurons

Impaired social-communicative behaviors are the earliest observable symptoms of autism in young children (Toth, Munson, Meltzoff, & Dawson, 2006). These include impairments in joint attention (sharing attention to objects or events with another person; see Chapter 1); the use of communicative gestures (pointing to objects, reaching for objects to request them); and imitation (immediate and deferred imitation of actions on objects; imitation of facial and body movements; see Chapters 13 and 18). These behaviors appear to form essential building blocks to later communicative and social development—in particular, the development of language and a Theory of Mind.

Neuroimaging studies of potential early-onset markers recently have been energized by paradigms used to investigate motor mirror neurons, named for highly specific neural firing in the monkey ventral premotor cortex (area F5) not just while executing an action with an object (e.g. reaching for a glass), but also while viewing somebody else do the same ("mirror") action. It has been suggested that this system is critical for understanding others' intentions, perhaps by internally simulating the actions of others so as to derive an understanding of what is seen on a more personal ground. Mirror neurons thus may be an essential building block for developing a theory of mind (reviewed in Williams et al., 2006). Williams et al. (2006) found decreased fMRI BOLD activation in right parietal areas for adolescents with ASD compared to controls during motor mirroring activities; they also report atypical activation for the ASD group in the right temporo-parietal junction thought to subserve Theory of Mind, as well as decreased left amygdala activity. Iacoboni and colleagues (Dapretto et al., 2006) reported reduced fMRI activity for children with high-functioning autism, relative to controls, in the inferior frontal gyrus during a task comparison of observing vs. imitating facial expressions. One challenge to mirror neuron hypotheses of autism is that most of the studies referenced above studies do not find any deficits on intentionality tasks, when one is trying to guess what is the actors purpose for making the movement. Future iterations of the mirror neuron account will need to describe neural models that effectively link motor system function with the affective dysfunction that is a hallmark of autism.

Neuroscience approaches to theory of mind

Research regarding Theory of Mind, (ToM) which, as noted earlier, is defined as the realization that others have thoughts different than one's own, has long been a prominent topic in autism studies. Nonetheless, very few relevant neuroimaging studies have been reported. Williams et al. (2006) utilized an imitation paradigm during fMRI, where participants raised one of their fingers in response to different kinds of cues, including an imitation cue (an animated finger), a symbolic execution cue (a cross showed which finger to raise) or a spatial cue (a cross on either side of the screen), in adolescents diagnosed with ASD. Relative to the comparison group, the ASD group showed hypoactivation at the right temporoparietal junction that has been previously linked with theory of mind, and in the left amygdala, perhaps indicating reduced emotional reactivity as reviewed above. Mason et al. (2008) found that the ASD group recruited this ToM region at the right temporoparietal junction when making judgments of both physical and social (intentional) causality, whereas the comparison group recruited this region only for socially relevant judgments. The ASD group also demonstrated reduced functional connectivity between the right temporoparietal junction and another key region in the ToM network in the left medial frontal gyrus.

The ability to differentiate between one's own thoughts and intentions and those of others is crucial for effective social interaction. Happé (2003) has theorized that reflecting on one's own thoughts utilizes the same neural mechanisms as thinking about the thoughts of others. Vanderwal and colleagues (2008) showed in a typical control sample with fMRI how the distributed system engaged when one reflects about oneself is essentially identical to the neural system used when one reflects about the minds of others. Other recent fMRI evidence in ASD samples lends support to this hypothesis. Chiu et al. (2008) report that, despite intact cognitive understanding of an economic task played with a partner, their ASD group did not activate a region of medial cingulate cortex associated with a sense of self-identity or self-intention that was clearly evident in two comparison groups. Moreover, this measure was positively correlated with autism symptom severity. Kennedy et al. (2006) found no difference in activation of midline "default mode" structures between task and resting conditions for an ASD sample. The authors suggest that ASD individuals may not develop a typical pattern of self-referential thought; rather, they may have more externally directed thoughts, e.g. toward obsessive interests or environmental distractions. In sum, existing evidence consistently indicates impaired functionality in self- and other-referential networks in ASD; there is tremendous potential for expanded work in this area to define the next frontier of research on social cognition along the autism spectrum.

Voice Perception

Although most previous research on social perception in autism has dealt with visual stimuli (e.g, faces),

the human voice also contributes rich social and emotional information. It is known that autism is associated with a number of deficits in auditory and voice processing such as prosody comprehension, auditory filtering, and verbal content comprehension (reviewed in Tager-Flusberg, Paul, & Lord, 2005). Samson et al. (2006) review a number of studies by their group showing deficits in auditory processing in response to non-voice stimuli (e.g. tones, environmental sounds) across multiple behavioral and psychophysiological methods. A consistent theme of their work is that dysfunction in autism corresponds to the level of stimulus and/or task complexity, in line with the complex-information-processing model (Minshew, Goldstein, & Siegel, 1997; however, see Mongillo et al., 2008, for evidence that social information per se, not the complex of information, is the core problem). Gervais et al. (2004) report a study where adults diagnosed with ASD did not activate the STS in response to vocal, compared to non-vocal sounds. However, Boucher, Lewis, & Collis (2000) did not find impairments in autism for familiar or unfamiliar voice recognition, compared to typical or selective language impairment groups.

An important theme that is now receiving considerable attention is how visual and auditory stimuli are integrated together (Loveland, Steinberg, Pearson, Mansour, & Reddoch, 2008). There are now several reports of atypical multi-sensory integration in autism, using behavioral (Mongillo et al., 2008), fMRI (Loveland et al., 2008) and EEG (Magnee, Oranje, van Engeland, Kahn, & Kemner, 2009) techniques.

Animal Models of Social Cognition

There are several important obstacles to developing valid animal models of social cognition in autism. Patterns of social interaction and communication are typically more complex in humans than those seen in various animal species. Although laboratory-rearing conditions allow for careful control of environmental influences on development, such studies may lack ecological validity regarding the influence of environment on social context and brain-behavior relationships (Insel & Fernald, 2004). Scientists who are approaching the problem of autism need to understand the complexity and heterogeneity of the autism spectrum and carefully consider the adequacy of symptom matching between animals and humans (Crawley, 2004).

Despite these challenges, animal models can be useful for identifying and subtyping specific neurochemical, neuroanatomic, and neurobehavioral pathways in autism. Crawley (2004) postulates that using a variety of inbred strains and mutant mouse lines, scientists will soon identify genes that are linked to phenotypic extremes of behavior that are common in autism. In parallel to this approach, there is a substantial body of ongoing research using mice with knockout genes, mutated genes, or altered neurotransmitter expression that provide intriguing models of autism-like behaviors. Although mice do not demonstrate complex human behaviors such as language or theory of mind, they have a clear repertoire of social behavior that is relevant to human social interactions. For example, proximity-seeking behavior (for parent-child relationships as well as for potential mating relationships) is reduced in the BALB/c strain of mice that also show other characteristics of autism including large brain size, underdevelopment of the corpus callosum, and high levels of anxiety (Brodkin, 2007). An intriguing recent mouse study by Tabuchi et al. (2007) explored the effects of a specific knockout of the Neuroligin 3 gene–a mutation seen in a small percentage of individuals diagnosed with ASD. In addition to poor social function, the animals surprisingly showed an increase in *inhibitory* synaptic transmission with no effect on excitatory transmission. Theoretically, such increased inhibition of neural impulses in the developing brain could lead to underdevelopment of neural connectivity.

Insel and Fernald (2004) have described a framework in which the evolutionary significance of affiliative and reproductive behaviors means that their neural and hormonal correlates are likely to be highly conserved within species. Insel and Fernald suggest that social learning and social motivation are hardwired, rapid, and strong due to their evolutionary importance, and that selective neuropeptides in the mesolimbic dopamine system, especially vasopressin and oxytocin, form the essential link between perception and evaluation of the reward value of a stimulus in species-specific behaviors (see Chapter 22). Oxytocin knockout mice show profound deficits in social recognition, while pair bonding in prairie voles is affected by manipulations of the vasopressin or oxytocin systems (Lim, Bielsky, & Young, 2005). One published study has shown a possible association between autism and markers of the vasopressin V1a receptor (Kim et al., 2002).

In addition to generating new hypotheses, animal models are also important for putting existing theories of social cognition to the test. Amaral and colleagues (e.g., Amaral & Corbett, 2003) have designed experiments based on the theory that atypical amygdala function may lie at the foundation of social difficulties in autism. They report that early amygdala lesions in rhesus monkeys do not impair social behaviors, nor the monkeys' ability to recognize species-specific social cues. Amaral suggests that amygdala dysfunction may be an important contributor to the development and maintenance of the anxiety that so often accompanies autism, but that the amygdala is not essential for reciprocal social interaction. However, it is important to note that there is no parallel between ablation studies of the amygdala in nonhuman primates and models of amygdala dysfunction in humans with ASD. The former destroys the entire amygdala and asks what happens to social behavior development. The latter suggests that the amygdala's functions are poorly regulated for optimal social functioning. It may be that an atypically connected and a suboptimally functioning amygdala is more problematic for the development of social reciprocity skills than having no amygdala at all (see also work by Bachevalier, summarized in Bachevalier and Loveland, 2006).

Social Cognition and Repetitive Behavior

It remains unclear whether repetitive behaviors and impaired reciprocal social interaction share an underlying genetic basis, or whether these are orthogonal genetic factors. With current data, the answer to this question hinges on whether one studies an autism population or the general population. In a study of children with an autism spectrum disorder, Constantino et al. (2004) presented cluster analyses from maternal-report instruments that suggest a "singular underlying factor of major effect" for autism symptoms (p. 724). In contrast, Ronald, Happé, and Plomin (2006), using parent and teacher data from a very large community sample of twin pairs not selected for autistic symptomatology, report only modest associations between deficits in social behavior and levels of stereotyped, repetitive behavior; Ronald et al. (2006) suggest that both classes of behavior are highly heritable, but they share limited genetic overlap in the general population, and therefore should be studied separately. A related view comes from the recent factor analysis of the Autism Diagnostic Observation Schedules (Gotham et al. 2008), which suggests that social and communication skills are grouped together, but repetitive behaviors stand alone.

Moy et al. (2008) report at least 11 knockout mouse strains that show both repetitive behaviors and social deficits. It is possible that genetic mechanisms which normally moderate the development of social behavior and repetitive behaviors are distinct and separate, but that the genes which cause autism also create linkages between these phenotypic elements (see Anderson, 2008, for a discussion of such emergent phenomena). It is also possible that one behavioral deficit leads to another, so that the space left by a lack of social interaction becomes filled with stereotyped behaviors; or that a tendency toward repetitive behavior interferes with social interaction. This latter suggestion is supported by recent findings from Sasson et al. (2008), where the viewing patterns of both social and non-social stimuli in children diagnosed with ASD were more circumscribed, perseverative, and detail-oriented.

IMPLICATIONS FOR TREATMENT

Knowledge regarding atypical neural connectivity in the social brain in autism helps to explain how existing treatments work, and emphatically underscores the need for intervention as early as possible. Hebb's Law (1949) is over-simplistically summarized as "neurons that fire together, wire together." Following this maxim, the requirements for therapeutic intervention in autism are to artificially build, through targeted and repeated practice, those neural networks for social cognition that have not developed naturally. Because subsequent brain development greatly depends on what has come before, the creation of better functional networks earlier in life should lead to healthier later development. Therefore, concerns about the risk for ASD (either due to family history or early observations of the child), should lead to intervention as soon as possible, focused on building both the motivation to attend to social information, and on the explicit skills that are required to successfully interact with others.

In line with a social-motivation theory of autism, several recent models of social skill development have moved away from the traditional focus on explicit behavioral teaching, in favor of a more social experiential approach. These interventions seek to increase the motivation that underlies social behavior, rather than to simply teach explicit skills with no attention to the underlying motivation, including models such as Relationship Development Intervention (RDI; see Gutstein, Burgess, & Montfort, 2007). More research is needed to determine the effectiveness of RDI and other experiential models (see review by Rogers & Vismara, 2008).

There are now several programs that seek to combine the benefits of both explicit and experiential models by teaching necessary skills while also addressing participants' motivation toward social stimuli. "Let's Face It!" (LFI; Tanaka, Lincoln, & Hegg, 2003; Wolf et al., 2008) is a computer-based intervention designed to provide ASD children with intensive training in face- processing skills. The software includes a number of arcade-like games that target skills including face-matching, emotion identification, facial identity recognition, face salience, immediate memory for faces, and eye gaze interpretation. Thus, specific face-processing skills are taught while the computer-game medium creates a motivating and fun platform for skill development. Significant improvement in face recognition skills have been demonstrated for LFI in a recently completed randomized clinical trial with 42 children in active treatment, as compared to 37 children with ASD in a waitlist control group (Tanaka et al., 2010). Other studies have also shown the effectiveness of computer-based platforms used to teach face-processing skills to individuals with ASD (e.g., Faja, Aylward, Bernier, & Dawson, 2008). Gray's (1998) "social stories" and "comic strip conversations" also help children to learn social information through a medium that may be more fun and motivating than traditional instructional techniques.

CONCLUSIONS

Neuropsychological research regarding social cognition in autism has consistently focused on themes of atypical social perception, especially for faces. The availability of new techniques—especially for in vivo neuroimaging as well as for the refinement of effective eye-tracking systems—now allows for more sophisticated experimental paradigms and application to a wide range of severity and age, including at-risk infants. The recognition that the behavioral symptoms of autism emerge through numerous genotypic pathways has advanced the field from a focus on categorical definitions to a search for observable endophenotypes that link behaviors with underlying biological mechanisms. For most current research in social cognition, there is truly a case of "the more we know, the more there is to learn." Even the most consistent findings—for example, a decreased face inversion effect in autism, and hypoactivation of the fusiform gyrus in face perception studies—appear to be influenced by task-specific and age-specific factors, as well as individual differences in areas such as language, intelligence, and motivation.

We suggest that future research on cross-modal integration of social information is a crucial next step. Experimental studies of autism have long suffered from poor external validity, because the complexity of everyday life, beyond a simple task or two done in the lab, is so overwhelming for individuals and families affected by autism. For example, Ozonoff's (1995) study of cognitive flexibility using the Wisconsin Card Sorting Test demonstrated that non-cognitive factors (i.e., whether the test was administered by computer or by a human) have a substantial influence on performance. Theories of neuronal underconnectivity perhaps hold more promise for explaining how incoming information is so difficult for individuals diagnosed with ASD to process; whether and how these processing difficulties are specific to social information is not yet firmly established.

Conceptually, it is essential to consider how any number of etiological pathways may converge in neurodevelopment to comprise the behaviorally defined autism spectrum disorders. What are the neural organizing principles and shared pathways that lead to a group of behaviors that can be defined by the common term of autism? The development of dimensional approaches to autism symptoms should lead to more rapid progress in understanding how people affected by autism understand everyday social interaction.[1]

---

1. We thank Julie Wolf, Lauren Herlihy, and Joshua Diehl for their contributions to portions of this chapter. Thanks also to Sarah White for her invaluable assistance in preparing the manuscript.

References

Adolphs, R., Gosselin, F., Buchanan, T. W., Tranel, D., Schyns, P., & Damasio, A. R. (2005). A mechanism for impaired fear recognition after amygdala damage. *Nature, 433*, 68–72.

Aggleton, J. P. (2003). The contribution of the amygdala to normal and abnormal emotional states. *Trends in Neruoscience, 16*, 328–333.

Amaral, D. G., & Corbett, B. A. (2003). The amygdala, autism and anxiety. *Novartis Foundation Symposium, 251*, 177.

Anderson, G. M. (2008). The potential role for emergence in autism. *Autism Research, 1*, 18–30.

Bachevalier, J., & Loveland, K.A. (2006). The orbitofrontal-amygdala circuit and self-regulation of social-emotional behavior in autism. *Neuroscience and Biobehavioral Reviews, 30*, 97–117.

Baron-Cohen, S., Ring, H. A., Bullmore, E. T., Wheelwright, S., Ashwin, C., & Williams, S. C. (2000). The amygdala theory of autism. *Neuroscience And Biobehavioral Reviews, 24*, 355–364.

Barsalou, L. (2008). Grounded cognition. *Annual Review of Psychology, 59*, 617–645.

Bigler, E. D., Tate, D. F., Neeley, E. S., Wolfson, L. J., Miller, M. J., Rice, S. A. ... Lainhart, J.E. (2003). Temporal lobe, autism, and macrocephaly. *American Journal Of Neuroradiology, 24*, 2066–2076.

Bill, B. R., & Geschwind, D. H. (2009). Genetic advances in autism: Heterogeneity and convergence on shared pathways. *Current Opinion In Genetics & Development, 19*, 271–278.

Boddaert, N., Chabane, N., Gervais, H., Good, C. D., Bourgeois, M., Plumet, M. H. ... Zilbovicius, M. (2004). Superior temporal sulcus anatomical abnormalities in childhood autism: A voxel-based morphometry MRI study. *Neuroimage, 23*, 364–369.

Bölte, S., Hubl, D., Dierks, T., Holtmann, M., & Poustka, F. (2008). An fMRI-study of locally oriented perception in autism: Altered early visual processing of the block design test. *Journal Of Neural Transmission, 115*, 545–552.

Bookheimer, S. Y., Wang, A. T., Scott, A., Sigman, M., & Dapretto, M. (2008). Frontal contributions to face processing differences in autism: Evidence from fMRI of inverted face processing. *Journal Of The International Neuropsychological Society, 14*, 922–932.

Boucher, J., Lewis, V., & Collis, G. M. (2000). Voice processing abilities in children with autism, children with specific language impairments, and young typically developing children. *Journal Of Child Psychology And Psychiatry, 41*, 847–857.

Brodkin, E. S. (2007). BALB/c mice: Low sociability and other phenotypes that may be relevant to autism. *Behavioural Brain Research, 176*, 53–65.

Carmichael, S.T., & Price, J. L. (1995). Limbic connections of the orbital and medial prefrontal cortex in macaque monkeys. *Journal of Comparative Neurology, 363*, 615–641.

Carper, R. A., & Courchesne, E. (2005). Localized enlargement of the frontal cortex in early autism. *Biological Psychiatry, 57*, 126–133.

Castelli, F., Frith, C., Happé, F., & Frith, U. (2002). Autism, Asperger syndrome and brain mechanisms for the attribution of mental states to animated shapes. *Brain, 125*, 1839–1849.

Chawarska, K., & Volkmar, F. (2007). Impairments in monkey and human face recognition in 2-year-old toddlers with autism spectrum disorder and developmental delay. *Developmental Science, 10*, 266–279.

Chiu, P. H., Kayali, M. A., Kishida, K. T., Tomlin, D., Klinger, L. G., Klinger, M. R. … Montague, P.R. (2008). Self responses along cingulate cortex reveal quantitative neural phenotype for high-functioning autism. *Neuron, 57*, 463–473.

Constantino, J. N., Gruber, C. P., Davis, S., Hayes, S., Passanante, N., & Przybeck, T. (2004). The factor structure of autistic traits. *Journal Of Child Psychology And Psychiatry, 45*, 719–726.

Coon, H. (2006). Current perspectives on the genetic analysis of autism. *American Journal Of Medical Genetics, 142C*, 24–32.

Crawley, J. N. (2004). Designing mouse behavioral tasks relevant to autistic-like behaviors. *Mental Retardation And Developmental Disabilities Research Reviews, 10*, 248–258.

Cuthbert, B. N. (2005). Dimensional models of psychopathology: Research agenda and clinical utility. *Journal Of Abnormal Psychology, 114*, 565–569.

Dalton, K. M., Nacewicz, B. M., Johnstone, T., Schaefer, H. S., Gernsbacher, M. A., Goldsmith, H. H. … XXX. (2005). Gaze fixation and the neural circuitry of face processing in autism. *Nature Neuroscience, 8*, 519–526.

Dapretto, M., Davies, M. S., Pfeifer, J. H., Scott, A. A., Sigman, M., Bookheimer, S. Y. … Davidson, R.J. (2006). Understanding emotions in others: Mirror neuron dysfunction in children with autism spectrum disorders. *Nature Neuroscience, 9*, 28–30.

Davidson, R. J., & Slagter, H. A. (2000). Probing emotion in the developing brain: Functional neuroimaging in the assessment of the neural substrates of emotion in normal and disordered children and adolescents. *Mental Retardation and Developmental Disabilities Research Reviews, 6*, 166–170.

Davis, M., & Whalen, P. (2001). The amygdala: Vigilance and emotion. *Molecular Psychiatry, 6*, 13–34.

Dawson, G., Webb, S. J., & McPartland, J. (2005). Understanding the nature of face processing impairment in autism: Insights from behavioral and electrophysiological studies. *Developmental Neuropsychology, 27*, 403–424.

Deruelle, C., Rondan, C., Gepner, B., & Tardif, C. (2004). Spatial frequency and face processing in children with autism and Asperger syndrome. *Journal of Autism and Developmental Disorders, 34*, 199–210.

Ernst, M., Zametkin, A. J., Matochik, J. A., Pascualvaca, D., & Cohen, R. M. (1997). Low medial prefrontal dopaminergic activity in autistic children. *Lancet, 350*, 638.

Faja, S., Aylward, E., Bernier, R., & Dawson, G. (2008). Becoming a face expert: A computerized face-training program for high-functioning individuals with autism spectrum disorders. *Developmental Neuropsychology, 33*, 1–24.

Fein, D., Lucci, D., Braverman, M., & Waterhouse, L. (1992). Comprehension of affect in context in children with pervasive developmental disorders. *Journal of Child Psychology and Psychiatry, 33*, 1157–1167.

Gathers, A. D., Bhatt, R., Corbly, C. R., Farley, A. B., & Joseph, J. E. (2004). Developmental shifts in cortical loci for face and object recognition. *Neuroreport, 15*, 1549–1553.

Gervais, H., Belin, P., Boddaert, N., Leboyer, M., Coez, A., Sfaello, I. … Zilboviscius, M. (2004). Abnormal cortical voice processing in autism. *Nature Neuroscience, 7*, 801–802.

Gotham, K., Risi, S., Dawson, G., Tager-Flusberg, H., Joseph, R., Carter, A., Hepburn, S. … Lord, C. (2008).A replication of the Autism Diagnostic Observation Schedule (ADOS) revised algorithms. *Journal of the American Academy of Child and Adolescent Psychiatry, 47*, 642–651.

Gottesman, I. I., & Gould, T. D. (2003). The endophenotype concept in psychiatry: Etymology and strategic intentions. *The American Journal Of Psychiatry, 160*, 636–645.

Gray, C. A. (1998). Social stories and comic strip conversations with students with Asperger Syndrome and high-functioning autism. In E. Schopler, G. B. Mesibov, & L. J. Kunce (Eds.), *Asperger syndrome or high-functioning autism?* (pp. 167–198). New York: Plenum Press.

Grelotti, D. J., Gauthier, I., & Schultz, R. T. (2002). Social interest and the development of cortical face specialization: What autism teaches us about face processing. *Developmental Psychobiology, 40*, 213–225.

Gutstein, S. E., Burgess, A. F., & Montfort, K. (2007). Evaluation of the relationship development intervention program. *Autism, 11*, 397–411.

Hadjikhani, N., Joseph, R. M., Snyder, J., & Tager-Flusberg, H. (2007). Abnormal activation of the social brain during face perception in autism. *Human Brain Mapping, 28*, 441–449.

Haist, F., Adamo, M., Westerfield, M., Courchesne, E., & Townsend, J. (2005). The functional neuroanatomy of spatial attention in autism spectrum disorder. *Developmental Neuropsychology, 27*, 425–458.

Happé, F. (2003). Theory of mind and the self. *Annals Of The New York Academy Of Sciences, 1001*, 134–144.

Happé, F., & Ronald, A. (2008). The "fractionable autism triad": A review of evidence from behavioural, genetic, cognitive and neural research. *Neuropsychology Review, 18*, 287–304.

Happé, F., Ronald, A., & Plomin, R. (2006). Time to give up on a single explanation for autism. *Nature Neuroscience, 9*, 1218–1220.

Hebb, D. O. (1949), *The organization of behavior.* New York: Wiley.

Hernandez, N., Metzger, A., Magné, R., Bonnet-Brilhault, F., Roux, S., Barthelemy, C., & Martineau, J. (2009). Exploration of core features of a human face by healthy and autistic adults analyzed by visual scanning. *Neuropsychologia, 47*, 1004–1012.

Hobson, R. P., Ouston, J., & Lee, A. (1988a). Emotion recognition in autism: Coordinating faces and voices. *Psychological Medicine, 18*, 911–923.

Hobson, R. P., Ouston, J., & Lee, A. (1988b). What's in a face? The case of autism. *British Journal Of Psychology, 79*, 441–453.

Humphreys, K., Hasson, U., Avidan, G., Minshew, N., & Behrmann, M. (2008). Cortical patterns of category-selective activation for faces, places and objects in adults with autism. *Autism Research, 1*, 52–63.

Insel, T. R., & Fernald, R. D. (2004). How the brain processes social information: Searching for the social brain. *Annual Review Of Neuroscience, 27*, 697–722.

Johnson, M. H. (2005). Subcortical face processing. *Nature Reviews Neuroscience, 6*, 766–774.

Jones, W., Carr, K., & Klin, A. (2008). Absence of preferential looking to the eyes of approaching adults predicts level of social disability in 2-year-old toddlers with autism spectrum disorder. *Archives Of General Psychiatry, 65*, 946–954.

Kana, R. K., Keller, T. A., Cherkassky, V. L., Minshew, N. J., & Just, M.A. (2009). Atypical frontal-posterior synchronization of theory of mind regions in autism during mental state attribution. *Social Neuroscience, 4*, 135–152.

Kanner, L. (1943). Autistic disturbances of affective contact. *Nervous Child, 2*, 217–253.

Kanwisher, N., McDermott, J., & Chun, M. M. (1997). The fusiform face area: A module in human extrastriate cortex specialized for face perception. *The Journal Of Neuroscience, 17*, 4302–4311.

Kennedy, D. P., Redcay, E., & Courchesne, E. (2006). Failing to deactivate: Resting functional abnormalities in autism. *Proceedings Of The National Academy Of Sciences, 103*, 8275–8280.

Kim, S. J., Young, L. J., Gonen, D., Veenstra-VanderWeele, J., Courchesne, R., Courchesne, E. ... Insel, T.R. (2002). Transmission disequilibrium testing of arginine vasopressin receptor 1A (AVPR1A) polymorphisms in autism. *Molecular Psychiatry, 7*, 503–507.

Kleinhans, N. M., Richards, T., Sterling, L., Stegbauer, K. C., Mahurin, R., Johnson, L. C. ... Aylward, E. (2008). Abnormal functional connectivity in autism spectrum disorders during face processing. *Brain, 131*, 1000–1012.

Klin, A., Jones, W., Schultz, R., Volkmar, F., & Cohen, D. (2002). Visual fixation patterns during viewing of naturalistic social situations as predictors of social competence in individuals with autism. *Archives Of General Psychiatry, 59*, 809–816.

Klin, A., Lin, D. J., Gorrindo, P., Ramsay, G., & Jones, W. (2009). Two-year-olds with autism orient to non-social contingencies rather than biological motion. *Nature, 459*, 257–261.

Klin, A., Pauls, D., Schultz, R., & Volkmar, F. (2005). Three diagnostic approaches to Asperger syndrome: Implications for research. *Journal of Autism and Developmental Disorders, 35*, 221–234.

Koshino, H., Kana, R. K., Keller, T. A., Cherkassky, V. L., Minshew, N. J., & Just, M. A. (2008). fMRI investigation of working memory for faces in autism: Visual coding and underconnectivity with frontal areas. *Cerebral Cortex, 18*, 289–300.

Lacroix, A., Guidetti, M., RogÃ©, B., & Reilly, J. (2009). Recognition of emotional and nonemotional facial expressions: a comparison between Williams syndrome and autism. *Research In Developmental Disabilities, 30*, 976–985.

Langdell, T. (1978). Recognition of faces: An approach to the study of autism. *Journal of Child Psychology and Psychiatry, 19*, 255–268.

Lim, M. M., Bielsky, I. F., & Young, L. J. (2005). Neuropeptides and the social brain: Potential rodent models of autism. *International Journal Of Developmental Neuroscience, 23*, 235–243.

Loveland, K. A., Steinberg, J. L., Pearson, D. A., Mansour, R., & Reddoch, S. (2008). Judgments of auditory-visual affective congruence in adolescents with and without autism: a pilot study of a new task using fMRI. *Perceptual And Motor Skills, 107*, 557–575.

Magnee, M. J., Oranje, B., van Engeland, H., Kahn, R. S., & Kemner, C. (2009). Cross-sensory gating in schizophrenia and autism spectrum disorder: EEG evidence for impaired brain connectivity? *Neuropsychologia, 47*, 1728–1732.

Mason, R. A., Williams, D. L., Kana, R. K., Minshew, N., & Just, M. A. (2008). Theory of mind disruption and recruitment of the right hemisphere during narrative comprehension in autism. *Neuropsychologia, 46*, 269–280.

Merin, N., Young, G. S., Ozonoff, S., & Rogers, S. J. (2007). Visual fixation patterns during reciprocal social interaction distinguish a subgroup of 6-month-old infants at-risk for autism from comparison infants. *Journal of Autism and Developmental Disorders, 37*, 108–121.

Minshew, N. J., Goldstein, G., & Siegel, D. J. (1997). Neuropsychologic functioning in autism: Profile of a complex information processing disorder. *Journal Of The International Neuropsychological Society, 3*, 303–316.

Minshew, N. J., & Williams, D. L. (2007). The new neurobiology of autism: Cortex, connectivity, and neuronal organization. *Archives Of Neurology*, *64*, 945–950.

Mongillo, E. A., Irwin, J. R., Whalen, D. H., Klaiman, C., Carter, A. S., & Schultz, R. T. (2008). Audiovisual processing in children with and without autism spectrum disorders. *Journal of Autism and Developmental Disorders*, *38*, 1349–1358.

Morris, R. W., Weickert, C. S., & Loughland, C. M. (2009). Emotional face processing in schizophrenia. *Current Opinions in Psychiatry*, *47*, 642–651.

Moy, S. S., Nadler, J. J., Young, N. B., Nonneman, R. J., Segall, S.K., Andrade, G.M. ... Magnuson, T.R. (2009). Emotional face processing in schizophrenia. *Current Opinions in Psychiatry*, *47*, 642–651.

Mufson, E. J., Mesulam, M. M., & Pandya, D. N. (1981). Insular interconnections with the amygdala in the rhesus monkey. *Neuroscience*, *6*, 1231–1248.

Ozonoff, S. (1995). Reliability and validity of the Wisconsin Card Sorting Test in studies of autism. *Neuropsychology*, *9*, 491–500.

Ozonoff, S., Heung, K., Byrd, R., Hansen, R., & Hertz-Picciotto, I. (2008). The onset of autism: Patterns of symptom emergence in the first years of life. *Autism Research*, *1*, 320–328.

Pelphrey, K. A., Morris, J. P., & McCarthy, G. (2005). Neural basis of eye gaze processing deficits in autism. *Brain*, *128*, 1038–1048.

Pelphrey, K. A., Morris, J. P., McCarthy, G., & Labar, K. S. (2007). Perception of dynamic changes in facial affect and identity in autism. *Social Cognitive And Affective Neuroscience*, *2*, 140–149.

Pelphrey, K. A., Sasson, N. J., Reznick, J. S., Paul, G., Goldman, B. D., & Piven, J. (2002). Visual scanning of faces in autism. *Journal of Autism and Developmental Disorders*, *32*, 249–261.

Pierce, K., Müller, R. A., Ambrose, J., Allen, G., & Courchesne, E. (2001). Face processing occurs outside the fusiform "face area" in autism: evidence from functional MRI. *Brain*, *124*, 2059–2073.

Pierce, K., & Redcay, E. (2008). Fusiform function in children with an autism spectrum disorder is a matter of "who." *Biological Psychiatry*, *64*, 552–560.

Pinkham, A. E., Hopfinger, J. B., Pelphrey, K. A., Piven, J., & Penn, D. L. (2008). Neural bases for impaired social cognition in schizophrenia and autism spectrum disorders. *Schizophrenia Research*, *99*, 164–175.

Price, J. L., Carmichael, S. T., & Drevets, W. C. (1996). Networks related to the orbital and medial prefrontal cortex; a substrate for emotional behavior? *Progress in Brain Research*, *107*, 523–536.

Renner, P., Grofer Klinger, L., & Klinger, M. R. (2006). Exogenous and endogenous attention orienting in autism spectrum disorders. *Child Neuropsychology*, *12*, 361–382.

Robins, D. L., Hunyadi, E. T., & Schultz, R. T. (2005, May). *Perception of emotion through facial expression and tone of voice in autism spectrum disorders: An fMRI study*. Paper presented at the International Meeting for Autism Research, Boston, MA.

Robins, D. L., Hunyadi, E. & Schultz, R. T. (2009) Superior temporal activation in response to dynamic audio-visual emotional cues. *Brain and Cognition*, *69*, 269–278.

Rogers, S. J. & Vismara, L. A. (2008). Evidence-based comprehensive treatments for early autism. *Journal of Clinical Child and Adolescent Psychology*, *37*, 8–38.

Ronald, A., Happé, F., Bolton, P., Butcher, L. M., Price, T. S., Wheelwright, S. ... Plomin, R. (2006). Genetic heterogeneity between the three components of the autism spectrum: A twin study. *Journal of the American Academy of Child and Adolescent Psychiatry*, *45*, 691–699.

Samson, F., Mottron, L., Jemel, B., Belin, P., & Ciocca, V. (2006). Can spectro-temporal complexity explain the autistic pattern of performance on auditory tasks? *Journal of Autism and Developmental Disorders*, *36*, 65–76.

Sasson, N. J. (2006). The development of face processing in autism. *Journal of Autism and Developmental Disorders*, *36*, 381–394.

Sasson, N. J., Turner-Brown, L. M., Holtzclaw, T. N., Lam, K. S., & Bodfish, J. W. (2008). Children with autism demonstrate circumscribed attention during passive viewing of complex social and nonsocial picture arrays. *Autism Research*, *1*, 31–42.

Scherf, K. S., Behrmann, M., Minshew, N., & Luna, B. (2008). Atypical development of face and greeble recognition in autism. *Journal Of Child Psychology And Psychiatry*, *49*, 838–847.

Schultz, R. T. (2005). Developmental deficits in social perception in autism: The role of the amygdala and fusiform face area. *International Journal Of Developmental Neuroscience*, *23*, 125–141.

Schultz, R. T., Gauthier, I., Klin, A., Fulbright, R. K., Anderson, A. W., Volkmar, F. ... XXX. (2000). Abnormal ventral temporal cortical activity during face discrimination among individuals with autism and Asperger syndrome. *Archives Of General Psychiatry*, *57*, 331–340.

Schultz, R. T., Grelotti, D. J., Klin, A., Kleinman, J., Van der Gaag, C., Marois, R. ... XXX. (2003). The role of the fusiform face area in social cognition: Implications for the pathobiology of autism. *Philosophical Transactions Of The Royal Society Of London. Series B, Biological Sciences*, *358*, 415–427.

Schultz, R. T., Grupe, D. W., Hunyadi, E., Jones, W., Wolf, J., Hoyt, E. G., Lin, D., & Herlihy, L.E. (2008, May). *The effect of task differences on FFA activity in autism spectrum disorders*. Paper presented at the International Meeting for Autism Research, London, England.

Schultz, R. T., Romanski, L. M., & Tsatsanis, K. D. (2000). Neurofunctional models of autistic disorder and Asperger syndrome: Clues from neuroimaging. In A. Klin, F. R. Volkmar, & S. S. Sparrow (Eds.), *Asperger syndrome* (pp. 172–209). New York: Guilford.

Shin, L. M., & Liberzon, I. (2010).The neurocircuitry of fear, stress, and anxiety disorders. *Neuropsychopharmacology*, 35, 169–191.

Sodian, B., & Thoermer, C. (2006). Precursors to a theory of mind in infancy: Perspectives for research on autism. *Quarterly Journal Of Experimental Psychology*, 61, 27–39.

South, M., Grupe, D. G., & Schultz, R. T. (2008, May). *Activation of the fusiform face area in response to implicit social semantic attributions.* Poster presented at the 7th Annual Meeting for Autism Research, London, England.

South, M., Wolf, J., & Herlihy, L. (2009). New directions: translating clinical child neuroscience to practice. In M.C. Roberts & R.G. Steele (Eds.), *Handbook of Pediatric Psychology* (4th Edition, pp. 737–754). New York: Guilford.

South, M., Ozonoff, S., Suchy, Y., Kesner, R. P., McMahon, W. M., & Lainhart, J. E. (2008). Intact emotion facilitation for nonsocial stimuli in autism: Is amygdala impairment in autism specific for social information? *Journal of the International Neuropsychological Society*, 14, 42–54.

Speer, L. L., Cook, A. E., McMahon, W. M., & Clark, E. (2007). Face processing in children with autism: effects of stimulus contents and type. *Autism*, 11, 265–277.

Sterling, L., Dawson, G., Webb, S., Murias, M., Munson, J., Panagiotides, H. ... Aylward, E. (2008). The role of face familiarity in eye tracking of faces by individuals with autism spectrum disorders. *Journal of Autism and Developmental Disorders*, 38, 1666–1675.

Tabuchi, K., Blundell, J., Etherton, M. R., Hammer, R. E., Liu, X., Powell, C. M. & Südhoff, T. (2007). A neuroligin-3 mutation implicated in autism increases inhibitory synaptic transmission in mice. *Science*, 318, 71–76.

Tager-Flusberg, H., Paul, R., & Lord, C. (2005). Language and communication. In F. R. Volkmar, A. Klin, R. Paul, & D. Cohen (Eds.), *Handbook of Autism and Developmental Disorders* (3rd Edition) (pp. 335–363). New York: Wiley.

Takarae, Y., Minshew, N. J., Luna, B., & Sweeney, J. A. (2007). Atypical involvement of frontostriatal systems during sensorimotor control in autism. *Psychiatry Research*, 156, 117–127.

Tanaka, J., Lincoln, S., & Hegg, L. (2003). A framework for the study and treatment of face processing deficits in autism. In H. Leder & G. Swartzer (Eds.), *The Development of Face Processing* (pp. 101–119). Berlin: Hogrefe Publishers.

Tanaka, J. W., Wolf, J. M., Klaiman, C., Koenig, K., Cockburn, J., Herlihy, L., Brown, C., Stahl, S., Kaiser, M. D., & Schultz, R.T. (2010). Using computerized games to teach face recognition skills to children with autism spectrum disorder: The Let's Face It! program. *Journal of Child Psychology and Psychiatry*, 51, 944–952.

Teunisse, J. P., & de Gelder, B. (2003). Face processing in adolescents with autistic disorder: The inversion and composite effects. *Brain And Cognition*, 52, 285–294.

Toth, K., Munson, J., Meltzoff, A. N., & Dawson, G. (2006). Early predictors of communication development in young children with autism spectrum disorder: Joint attention, imitation, and toy play. *Journal of Autism and Developmental Disorders*, 36, 993–1005.

Vandenbroucke, M. W., Scholte, H. S., van Engeland, H., Lamme, V. A., & Kemner, C. (2008). A neural substrate for atypical low-level visual processing in autism spectrum disorder. *Brain*, 131, 1013–1024.

Vanderwal, T., Hunyadi, E., Grupe, D.W., Connors, C.M., Schultz, R.T. (2008). Self, mother and abstract other: an fMRI study of reflective social processing. *Neuroimage*, 41, 1437–1446.

Vuilleumier, P., Richardson, M. P., Armony, J. L., Driver, J., & Dolan, R. J. (2004). Distant influences of amygdala lesion on visual cortical activation during emotional face processing. *Nature Neuroscience*, 7, 1271–1278.

Waiter, G. D., Williams, J. H., Murray, A. D., Gilchrist, A., Perrett, D. I., & Whiten, A. (2005). Structural white matter deficits in high-functioning individuals with autistic spectrum disorder: A voxel-based investigation. *Neuroimage*, 24, 455–461.

Wallace, S., Coleman, M., & Bailey, A. (2008). Face and object processing in autism spectrum disorders. *Autism Research*, 1, 43–51.

Wang, A. T., Dapretto, M., Hariri, A. R., Sigman, M., & Bookheimer, S. Y. (2004). Neural correlates of facial affect processing in children and adolescents with autism spectrum disorder. *Journal of the American Academy of Child and Adolescent Psychiatry*, 43, 481–490.

Williams, J. H., Waiter, G. D., Gilchrist, A., Perrett, D. I., Murray, A. D., & Whiten, A. (2006). Neural mechanisms of imitation and "mirror neuron" functioning in autistic spectrum disorder. *Neuropsychologia*, 44, 610–621.

Wolf, J. M., Tanaka, J. W., Klaiman, C., Cockburn, J., Herlihy, L., Brown, C. ... Schultz, R.T. (2008). Specific impairment of face-processing abilities in children with autism spectrum disorder using the Let's Face It! skills battery. *Autism Research*, 1, 329–340.

Wyc, B. C., Hudac, C. M., Carter, E. J., Sobel, D. M., & Pelphrey, K. A. (2009). Action understanding in the superior temporal sulcus region. *Psychological Science*, 20, 771–777.

Yirmiya, N. Sigman, M. D., Kasari, C., & Mundy, P. (1992). Empathy and cognition in high-functioning children with autism. *Child Development*, 63, 150–160.

Young, G.S., Merin, N., Rogers, S.J., & Ozonoff, S. (2009). Gaze behavior and affect at 6 months: predicting clinical outcomes and language development in typically developing infants and infants at risk for autism. *Developmental Science, 12,* 798–814.

Zirlinger, M., & Anderson, D. (2003). Molecular dissection of the amygdala and its relevance to autism. *Genes, Brain, And Behavior, 2,* 282–294.

Zwaigenbaum, L., Bryson, S., Rogers, T., Roberts, W., Brian, J., & Szatmari, P. (2005). Behavioral manifestations of autism in the first year of life. *International Journal Of Developmental Neuroscience, 23,* 143–152.

Chapter 13

Imitation in ASD

Costanza Colombi, Giacomo Vivanti, and Sally J. Rogers

INTRODUCTION

In the child development field, the importance of imitation for social development is widely recognized. Imitation is considered a central ability for cultural transmission, serving a learning or *apprenticeship function*, which allows children to learn goal-directed patterns of behaviors from others (Baldwin, 1906; Bruner, 1972; Piaget, 1962; Rogers, Cook, & Meryl, 2005; Rogoff, Mistry, Goncu, & Mosier, 1993; Tomasello, Kruger, & Ratner, 1993; Uzgiris, 1999). A second function of imitation entails *social interpersonal communication*. Imitation of facial expressions and body movements is embedded in social-emotional exchanges, serving as a mechanism for communication between social partners (Gopnik, & Meltzoff, 1994; Hatfield, Cacioppo, & Rapson, 1994; Uzgiris, 1981). These two functions may operate fairly independently of each other, at both the behavior level (see Rogers, Young, Cook, Giolzetti, & Ozonoff, [2010]), and at the neurocognitive level (see Iacoboni, 2005).

The centrality of imitation as a general learning mechanism in early childhood (Meltzoff, 1985; Tomasello, 1999; Uzgiris, 1981) is supported by evidence that, in typically developing young children, a variety of key developmental accomplishments demonstrate strong relationships with imitation skills, including general cognitive abilities (Strid, Tjus, Smith, Meltzoff, & Heimann, 2006), language development (Bates, Thal, Whitesell, Fenson, & Oakes, 1989; Masur & Eichorst, 2002), sharing of affect (Uzgiris, 1999), cooperation (Colombi et al., 2009), and social responsiveness (Heimann, 1998, 2002), although the nature of these relationships is not fully understood. A model of early childhood learning built on imitation as a key learning tool predicts that children with impaired imitation skills would demonstrate a variety of developmental sequelae; such a model was offered almost 20 years ago by Rogers and Pennington (1991). Their model focused on children with autism spectrum disorder (ASD), for whom imitation is often found to be impaired.

In fact, imitation of others represents a well-demonstrated deficit in autism (see Williams, Whiten, & Singh, 2004 for a recent systematic review). Because of the relationship between imitation and several other developmental domains, it is plausible that an early imitation deficit in autism may contribute to impairments in cognition, social communication, and adaptive skills (DeMyer, Hintgen, & Jackson, 1981; Hepburn & Stone, 2006; Rogers & Pennington, 1991). Given the presumed fundamental role of imitation in the development of more mature socioemotional skills (e.g., Meltzoff, 1990; Rogers & Pennington, 1991), imitative skills are now being studied intensively, with the aim to understand their role in autism (see Williams et al., 2004).

Imitative difficulties in children with autism were first identified and studied almost 40 years ago by DeMyer and colleagues (1972). During the 20 years following that study, only seven studies testing imitation deficits in autism were published (Bartak, Rutter, & Cox, 1977; Hammes & Langdell, 1981; Hertzig, Snow, & Sherman, 1989; Jones,& Prior, 1985; Morgan, Cutrer, Coplin, & Rodrigue, 1989; Ohta, 1987; Sigman & Ungerer, 1984).

In 1991, Rogers and Pennington reviewed these seven studies, confirming the presence of an autism-specific deficit in imitation, and suggesting a developmental model of autism based on Stern's (1985) theory of interpersonal development. They conceptualized the imitation problem in autism as a difficulty coordinating representations of self and other, and they hypothesized that the primary deficit in imitation would lead to impairments in joint attention, language, symbolic play, and Theory of Mind. After the publication of Rogers and Pennington's model in 1991, the number of studies investigating imitation in autism increased exponentially over the following two and half decades. The imitation deficit in autism has been confirmed by many methodologically rigorous studies using comparison groups of developmentally matched children with typical development, as well as matched groups involving children or adults with other developmental disorders, and several systematic reviews, including a meta-analysis (e.g., Charman et al.,1997; Rogers, 1999; Rogers et al., 2003; Rogers & Pennington, 1991; Sigman & Ungerer, 1984; Smith & Bryson, 1994; Stone et al., 1997; Williams, Whiten, & Singh, 2004).

Interestingly, not all aspects of imitation seem to be equally impaired in ASD. While both frequency of imitation and precision of imitation appear to be affected, people with autism show relatively poorer performance in spontaneous and automatic imitation (mimicry) than in structured imitation. Additionally, across different types of structured imitation tasks, people with ASD are relatively less deficient in imitating goal-directed actions on objects than gestural and facial movements. Let us briefly review the main components of areas of impairment and relative strength in autism.

Automatic imitation

Mimicry is a rapid, automatic, and unintentional matching response to others' emotional expressions and actions (Hatfield et al., 1994). Seeing someone smiling provokes us to move our muscles to prepare for a smile, and seeing someone moving activates our body to perform a similar movement. These rapid reactions are very likely to be minimally influenced by learning, motivation, and inferential understanding of others' behavior. Individuals with ASD appear to lack this response when observing emotional expression (Beall et al., 2008; McIntosh et al., 2006; Scambler et al., 2007) but not when observing actions (Bird et al., 2007; see Chapter 18 in this volume).

Imitation of non-meaningful body gestures and oral-facial movements

Early studies on imitation in autism reported a significantly impaired ability to imitate gestures, that is, body movements that do not involve objects (DeMyer et al., 1972; Ohta, 1987). This finding has since been replicated by many studies using different stimuli, coding systems, amd comparison groups (including different clinical populations), and across a wide range of IQ and language levels, and chronological ages (Aldridge et al., 2000; Bennetto, 1999; Bernabei et al., 2003; Dawson et al., 1998; Rogers et al., 1996; Rogers et al., 2003; Smith, & Bryson, 1998). Similarly, the ability to imitate facial movements is consistently reported to be severely affected in ASD across different ages, language levels, and IQ levels (Dawson et al., 1998; Rogers et al., 1996; Rogers et al., 2003). However, facial movement imitation has received less attention than imitation of movement with other body parts (Rogers et al., 2005).

Imitation of actions involving objects

The imitation of goal-directed actions on objects seems to be less impaired than gestural and facial imitation in autism. Rogers et al. (2005), after reviewing the literature involving imitation of actions on objects, concluded that studies in this area provide the most mixed findings and stronger developmental relations, in comparison to gestural and facial imitation. Autism-specific deficits in object imitation have been found in several studies involving preschoolers (Dawson et al., 1998; Rogers et al., 2003; Rogers et al., 2010); however, McDonough et al. (1997), using a similar population, did not find such a deficit. Moreover, other studies involving older subjects did not find group differences (Hammes & Langdell, 1981; Hobson & Lee, 1999). An autism-specific deficit in social imitation may explain difficulties with gestural imitation, mimicry, and embodiment, combined with areas of relative strength in imitating actions on objects. These findings may represent evidence that the apprenticeship function of imitation, and the neural networks underlying this ability, may be less affected by autism than the neural networks underlying social communicative functions.

Spontaneous versus elicited imitation

The lack of spontaneous imitation in ASD was identified in early studies of imitation by Ungerer and Sigman (1987), who found more frequent imitative performance in ASD under elicited conditions than in spontaneous situations. This finding has been replicated by many others (e.g., Brown & Whiten, 2000).

Imitation of incomplete acts

In three independent studies modeled on Meltzoff's (1995) unfulfilled intentions paradigm (where an actor begins, but does not complete, actions on objects), children with ASD were found to perform the intended actions on objects. While this task is not typically thought of as an imitation task, in fact the adult models an action in which the final act of completion is aborted. Given the paradigm, it appears reasonable to assume that imitation plays *some* role in performing this task, and the performance of children with ASD in this paradigm has been interpreted as demonstrating both that the ability to imitate actions on objects is preserved in ASD, and also

that the imitation problem is one of performance, not competence (Aldridge et al., 2000; Carpenter, Pennington, & Rogers, 2001; Colombi, Rogers, & Young, 2005).

As illustrated by the studies discussed above, the imitation deficit in autism is a well-established finding. The current questions now driving studies of imitation in autism concern the underlying mechanisms that might be disrupting imitation performance in persons with autism. Studies have begun to test a number of candidate mechanisms: Do children with autism have difficulties *paying attention* to the demonstration? Are they motivated to imitate the model? Do they have difficulties *understanding* the actions they observe? Are they able to *map the visual input onto their body schema*? Are they able to *create a motor representation* of the perceived action? And, finally, do they have difficulties *executing* the action?

NEUROPSYCHOLOGICAL MODELS OF IMITATION: TYPICAL DEVELOPMENT AND AUTISM

Researchers who examine the specific cognitive operations and subcomponents that underlie imitation difficulties in autism work from complex models of the cognitive processes involved in accurate imitation performance. Neuropsychological models of imitation have been provided by Rothi, Ochipa, & Heilman (1991) and Tessari, Canessa, Ukmar, & Rumiati (2007) and include three main phases:

1. *Encoding phase.* This step involves the formation of a representation of the action based on the imitator's visual attention to relevant properties of the demonstrator's action.
2. *Cross-modal or transformation/matching phase:* In this process, the imitator's previous knowledge of the meaning and motor aspects of the action is recruited, allowing for an efficient transfer from a perceptual code to a semantic and motor code. When the observed action is novel and cannot be mapped onto the imitator's motor vocabulary, the action, rather than being processed as a unit, is decomposed in a series of chunks that are each maintained "online" in working memory. In this case, imitation relies on a direct mapping from the perceptual to the motor features of the action, without a "semantic" mediation.

3. *Execution phase:* During this phase, the action is executed and the perceptual analysis of the performed action is compared to the representation of the action to provide online feedback and corrections on the motor plan.

While there are current controversies about such a neuropsychological model, which will be reviewed in the upcoming sections, this type of model has provided a productive framework for experimental explorations concerning the nature of the imitative deficit in autism. In the following sections of the chapter, we will use this model to organize a review of both neurocognitive and behavioral studies, beginning with studies that examine the encoding phase, then covering those that examine the cross-modal transfer from visual to motor representation, and ending with the motor execution phase. It is important to remember that, while these aspects of imitation are often conceptualized and studied as if they were separate mechanisms, there are both theoretical and empirical reasons suggesting that common processes underlie the perception and the execution of actions (Gallagher, 2007; Giorello & Sinigaglia, 2007; Hurley & Noe, 2003; Merleau-Ponty, 1945). We will address this crucial issue later, when discussing how to interpret the behavioral findings and neuroimaging correlates of imitation in autism and typical development.

Current brain-based models of imitation processing

Recent neurocognitive research suggests that the following process might be at work during the encoding of to-be-imitated actions. The process begins with an observation of an action. The occipital cortex maps the observed action, and projects to the superior temporal sulcus (STS) region. The STS is a high-level visual-processing area that is selectively activated by the perception of biological movements (Allison et al., 2000; Decety & Grezes, 1999; Pelphrey, Adolphs, & Morris, 2004). Recent findings suggest that the STS is specialized in interpreting dynamic social signs, such as gaze and head directions, and in processing social information conveyed by biological motion. Moreover, this region provides a somatotopic representation of the observed actions (Pelphrey, Morris, & McCarthy, 2005). Therefore, one role of STS is to distinguish social/biological motion, to translate

perceived information into body knowledge, and possibly to detect intentionality in the perceived movement (Castelli et al., 2000, 2002; Pelphrey et al., 2003; Schultz, Chawarska, & Volkmar, 2006). The STS then projects to the inferior parietal lobule (IPL).

The inferior parietal lobule has "mirror properties:" neurons in this area are activated by both observing an action and executing it (Gallese et al., 1996). This mirroring capacity is believed to mediate an "automatic" understanding of the action, based on the direct matching of the visual information onto the imitator's motor repertoire (Fogassi & Luppino, 2005). The inferior parietal lobule projects to the inferior frontal gyrus (Broca's area).

The inferior frontal gyrus (IFG; Brodmann area 44), plus the adjacent portion of the premotor area, also contains a significant number of mirror neurons, namely, those motor neurons that are activated both when observing and performing a specific action. Crucially, some neurons in this area are also activated by observing and performing nonidentical actions that are related to the same goal. This process allows the attribution of the semantic value of the observed action. In other words, the activation of this region during the observation of the action mediates the mapping of the visuomotor pattern into the imitator's semantic vocabulary of purposeful action,s and the goals that are accomplished with them (Iacoboni & Dapretto, 2006; Kohler et al., 2002; Koski et al., 2002; Rumiati et al., 2005). The final step in the neural pathways involves sending efferent copies of motor plans from the IFG back to the STS, so that the visual description of the observed action is compared to the predicted sensory consequences of the planned imitative action (Carr et al., 2003; Iacoboni, 2005; Iacoboni et al., 2001), an evaluative step in the process that allows one to determine if the goal was reached.

Two aspects of this model stand out: 1) both the visual and the motor system are involved in the action understanding process. Rather than relying on low-level visuospatial properties of the action to derive a motor representation, we exploit our motor system to represent, or map, what we see via our action repertoire (Grezes & Decety, 2001; Iacoboni, 2008; Rumiati et al., 2005); and 2) seeing an action elicits the motor program for implementing the same *goal*—that is, the specific conditions of the setting and the observer then determine how the action is imitated (e.g., whether or not the observer has the same effectors available to perform the action, or whether or not the same goal can be achieved with a more familiar or efficient motor program).

This ability to encode goals, in addition to the kinematics of the demonstrator's action, is what makes imitation flexible and selective in typical development. Such a "semantic" coding, as opposed to a "visuospatial" coding, results in a decreased demand on information processing resources, and more efficient imitative performance (Gattis, Bekkering, & Wohlschlager, 2002; Tessari & Rumiati, 2004).

However, when the demonstration's action does not have a goal or a predefined meaning, the imitator cannot "translate" the action into a motor schema using his "semantic vocabulary." The action, rather than being encoded on the basis of its goal, has to be processed in terms of its visuomotor properties via a non-semantic, "sub-lexical" route. Tessari and Rumiati (2004; see also Rumiati et al., 2005; Tessari et al., 2007) documented that the neurocognitive basis of processing "meaningless" actions, which must be mapped via the visual-spatial and kinematic pathways, overlaps only in part with neural network implementing the encoding of goal-directed actions. In particular, during the encoding of meaningless actions, less activation of the inferior frontal gyrus and more activation of the right occipital-parietal junction is observed (Rumiati et al., 2005). These neuroimaging data indicate that when we cannot exploit the semantics of the action (a process mediated by the inferior frontal gyrus), we need to rely on a more pictorial description of the action. In this case the action, rather than being encoded as a unit, has to be broken down into a series of chunks that are each maintained "online" in working memory. Crucially, nothing in the kinematics of the action indicates when the action starts and when it ends. The imitator needs to rely on the demonstrator's ostensive cues to "isolate" the action to be imitated in the stream of the demonstrator's behavior.

These different routes are activated by the properties of the action stimulus. When an action is recognized as familiar and meaningful, the semantic coding is automatically activated; when the action is meaningless and it has no correspondence in the imitator's semantic vocabulary, the "sub-lexical" (more pictorial) route is selected (Press, Bird, Walsh, & Heyes, 2008). For the semantic coding process to take place, the imitator needs to have expertise with the action observed; the action observed needs to be present in his semantic vocabulary. This has important implications for autism, as children with autism, by definition, have a more limited range of activities in their repertoire (American Psychiatric Association, 2000) and less social expertise (Klin et al., 2003) than age-mates.

Now we will proceed to describe the research base for examining autism-specific difficulties in each main phase of producing an imitation: encoding, transfer, and output.

THE ENCODING PROCESS IN TYPICAL DEVELOPMENT: GOING BEYOND THE MOTOR INFORMATION

Research on imitation in autism has mainly focused on motor execution of imitation, or, what kinds of difficulties might impact children's ability to reproduce others' actions. However, the first stage that enables imitation (i.e., the encoding of the action to be imitated) has been much less investigated. Investigating the encoding phase of imitation involves understanding how the imitator forms, retains, and operates on that specific representation (Whiten, 2002). We cannot read the mind of the imitator to see how he or she represents an action; however, we can access this process by 1) observing how the imitator will imitate the same action under different conditions (does the imitator process an action differently if we manipulate variables such as the demonstrator's gaze direction, length of exposure, or the context of the action?), 2) analyzing the imitator's visual attention pattern during the demonstration (what elements of the demonstration is the imitator considering?), and 3) determining what parts of the brain are active during the demonstration (what functional circuitries are implementing the encoding process?). Using these techniques, scientists are starting to uncover information on how actions are encoded in the imitation process by typically developing individuals. The most relevant of these notions, in relation to autism, is that when we encode an action, we encode more than the action itself.

For an efficient imitative learning process to take place, the imitator, given all the potential information available in the demonstrator's behavior, needs to take in some stimuli and ignore other stimuli (Behne, Carpenter, & Tomasello, 2005; Bekkering, Wohlschlager, & Gattis, 2000; Brass, Schmitt, Spengler, & Gergely, 2007; Carpenter, & Call, 2007; Carpenter, Tomasello, & Savage-Rumbaugh, 1995; Tomasello, & Carpenter, 2005). The demonstrator's goal, and the context in which the action takes place, appear to be particularly relevant in the imitator's representation of the demonstrator's action (Bekkering, Wohlschlager, & Gattis, 2000; Gergely et al., 2002; Iacoboni, 2005). Consider the following example: The demonstrator is sitting at a table with a bottle (close to him) and a teacup (on the other side of the table). He moves his arm toward the teacup and grasps it. In doing so, he touches the bottle with his elbow, causing the bottle to move. If, while doing this action, the demonstrator looks at the bottle, the imitator might conclude that his goal was to deliberately move the bottle and then grasp the cup; if, instead, the demonstrator is looking at the teacup the whole time, the imitator might conclude that he is reaching for the teacup and, while doing so, accidentally touched the bottle. If asked to observe and then imitate the model, the imitator will, in the first situation, imitate both actions, and in the second situation, imitate only the action of grasping the teacup (Carpenter, & Call, 2007; Southgate, Johnson, & Csibra, 2008). Therefore, the demonstrator's behaviors toward the object that he or she is acting upon crucially influences the way the action is encoded, and, ultimately, reproduced.

The imitator's encoding and reproduction of the action is also influenced by contextual aspects, such as objects and physical constraints in the environment. If the demonstrator is moving aside the bottle with his elbow while holding a large box in his hands, the imitator is very likely to move the bottle aside using his hand rather than the elbow (Gergely et al., 2002). However, if the demonstrator's hands are empty, the imitator is more likely to move the bottle with his elbow. This pattern has been found in very young children as well as adults (Carpenter, Akhtar, & Tomasello, 1998; Kiraly, 2009; Southgate, Johnson, & Csibra, 2008). The interpretation of this imitative behavior is that the imitator evaluates the actions of the demonstrator in terms of goals, and means and assumes that another person will generally use the most efficient action available to accomplish a goal. In the example above, the observer assumes that the only reason the person holding the box is using his elbow is because his hands are otherwise occupied, and not because it is important to the task, and so the imitator uses the most rational and common action in order to achieve the same goal. However, if his hands are free, then the observer assumes there is a specific reason to use the elbow, and thus uses it as well.

This tendency of children to interpret an action as goal-directed appears to be a general bias of humans and develops very early. Behavioral data show that encoding an action as goal-directed represents the "default" output of the action understanding process from infancy on (Csibra, 2008; Csibra & Gergely, 2007). However, there are some motor acts that appear to be non-goal-directed. What happens when an observer sees an individual performing actions that are not directed toward any recognizable goal? Behavioral data indicate that children consider the demonstration's actions as goal-directed even when the action itself does not lead to an end-state. When the demonstrator is doing an apparently meaningless action or gesture and *he is providing some kind of ostensive cue*, then the imitator encodes the action as a deliberate action to be attended to and imitated (in this case, observer interprets the ostensive cue to signal the demonstrator's goal to have the imitator attend and imitate his actions).

Indeed, imitation typically occurs in the framework of a social exchange in which the demonstrator provides communicative cues that help the imitator to understand *what* and *how* to imitate (Frith, 2008; Kiraly, 2009). In this framework, the demonstrator adopts a pedagogical stance by deliberately guiding the imitator through gesture, facial expressions, gaze, posture, and or vocalizations; the imitator, in turn, is socially motivated and cognitively able to participate in the exchange, and the imitation process takes place in a sort of mutually reinforcing choreography (Fonagy, Gergely, & Target, 2007; Gergely, Egyed, & Kiraly, 2007; Stern, 1985). These kinds of exchanges are mediated by shared communicative meanings. The ostensive direct gaze is a particularly important communicative signal that precedes actions to which the demonstrator wants the imitator to pay attention (Sperber & Wilson, 1995). Children show special sensitivity to the direct gaze of another person, and appear to ascribe more salience to the actions that follow such a gaze, shown in their increased attention and exact imitation (Kiraly, 2009; Senju & Csibra, 2008). Therefore, the demonstrator's behavior toward the imitator crucially influences the way the action is encoded.

In these examples, the imitator observes the same exact motor action (touching a bottle with his elbow); however, he "sees" and imitates four different actions under specific circumstances. The same input is encoded so as to lead to four different outputs. The reverse phenomenon is also observed in human imitation: different inputs lead to the same output, apparently for the same reason: the underlying interpretation of the goal-directedness of the action. Noy, Rumiati, and Flash (2008) documented that variations in features such as the orientation of the action do not change the way the action is imitated. In summary, children go beyond the "literal" information (Bruner, 1957). They do not "echo" an action via imitation, but rather frame the actions they see in a broader context that assumes a logical relation among the demonstrator's action, his intentions, and his communication.

However, another step is necessary for determining how actions will be processed: the properties of the action stimulus, rather than being a *datum*, depend on the imitator's selective attention to the relevant properties of the action. Encoding of a critical aspect of the demonstrator's action (i.e., where is he looking, what is he doing?) occurs only when attention is directed toward that feature (Klin, 2008). Children are exposed to a myriad of movements in daily life situations—how do they know what are the relevant aspects to be attended and imitated? Empirical data suggest that from infancy, children show very powerful preferential looking behaviors; they are strongly biased to selectively attend to specific features, namely faces, eyes (Morton & Johnson, 1991; Turati, Macchi Cassia, Simion, & Leo, 2006), and hands (particularly when hands are manipulating objects; Amano, Kezuka, & Yamamoto, 2004). These features are those that are crucially involved in determining how the input is encoded and imitated (see above). This suggests that the mechanism gating perceptual input to the mirror-system-mediated action-understanding process is based on the imitator's preferential orientation toward specific features of the action. In other words, children are "programmed to learn" (Del Giudice, Manera, & Keysers, 2009), and possess a topology of salience (see Klin et al., 2003; Rogers et al.,) that biases them to select those features of the demonstration that lead to the semantic encoding of the action. This encoding process allows the child to combine information from past experiences (the semantic store) with information contained in the current experience, allowing the child to "go beyond the information given" to understand the current situation, flexibly learning within a social/pedagogical framework. Do children with autism also go "beyond the information given" when observing and imitating?

The encoding process in children with autism: Looking at the demonstration versus looking at the demonstrator

The process of analysis and interpretation of the demonstrator's action described above, in which information in addition to the action itself is recruited, is mediated by a series of specific abilities, including efficient gaze processing, integration of different sources of information (Vivanti et al., 2008), joint attention (Carpenter, Tomasello, & Savage-Rumbaugh, 1995; Hobson & Hobson, 2007), and understanding of emotion, intentions, and communicative cues conveyed by the demonstrator's face and body (Carpenter & Call, 2007; Southgate, Csibra, Kaufman, & Johnson, 2008). All of these abilities, which appear to be crucially involved in encoding and understanding, and ultimately imitating, others' actions, appear to be deficient in individuals with autism (Dawson,& Bernier, 2007; Mundy & Burnette, 2005; Mundy & Neal, 2001; Pennington, 2009; Schultz, Chawarska, & Volkmar, 2006). Therefore, there are reasons to hypothesize that abnormalities in the way children with autism encode and understand the demonstrator's action might crucially contribute to their imitation deficit.

First of all, do children with autism pay attention to the demonstration? It is very common to hear parents of children with autism saying, "I try to teach him how to do that, but he doesn't pay attention to me!" Is that what really happens? Do they fail to imitate because they do not look at the demonstration? A basic grasp of the demonstrator's actions by individuals with autism is supported by studies using recognition tests (Bennetto, 1999; Smith & Bryson, 1998). In these studies, participants with autism, like comparison participants, were able to recognize the actions they had imitated from an array of actions represented in pictures. Although participants' observations of the demonstrator's action was adequate to permit later recognition, these studies leave open the question of differences in the focus and relative amount of visual attention during the demonstration.

Recently, Vivanti, Nadig, Ozonoff, & Rogers (2008) empirically tested this hypothesis. They employed eye-tracking technology to examine what children with autism and typically developing children look at when actions to be imitated are being demonstrated to them. Their findings indicated that well-matched groups of children with autism and typically developing children look at to-be-imitated actions for similar durations; however, typically developing children, as a group, looked to the demonstrator's neutral face twice as long as the group of children with autism did. In the experiment, children were observing two different types of to-be-imitated actions: meaningful and non-meaningful actions. In the first case, the actions themselves (e.g., drawing a line, striking a xylophone) provided all of the elements necessary for the imitator's interpretation: the actions were "self-explaining," that is, no additional information was needed for the imitator to make sense of them. In the second case, the actions (e.g., flexing the arm at the elbow, moving the arm across the forehead) were ambiguous and did not have an obvious end-state or goal. When observing these latter actions, the group of typically developing children greatly increased their attention to the face of the demonstrator, as if searching for additional information to explain the action.

Interestingly, the group with autism also demonstrated increased looks to the face when the action to be imitated was not goal-directed. What strongly differentiated the two groups was the decreased quantity of visual attention to the demonstrator's face in the group with autism in both conditions.

These eye-tracking data indicate that children with autism, as a group, are actually looking at the *demonstration*, but they fail to look at the *demonstrator* as much as typically developing children do. Similar findings in an imitation task were obtained by Hobson and Hobson (2007) using a behavioral paradigm. They found that children with autism, compared to children with other developmental disabilities, were less inclined to look at the demonstrator during both the observation and the execution of an imitative task. Moreover, they found visual attention to the demonstrator's face to be related to better imitative performance. The tendency to look at the demonstrator's face has been documented in infancy as well as childhood in both typically developing children and those with intellectual deficits (Carpenter, Tomasello, & Savage-Rumbaugh, 1995; Hobson & Hobson, 2007). These data are consistent with the abundant research literature demonstrating that children with autism have reduced attention to social stimuli (Dalton et al., 2005; Dawson et al., 2002; Grelotti, Gauthier, & Schultz, 2002; Pelphrey et al., 2002), difficulties in face processing (Ashwin, Baron-Cohen, Wheelwright, O'Riordan, & Bullmore, 2007; Scherf et al., 2008), and abnormal visual scanning patterns (Anderson, Colombo, & Shaddy, 2006; Klin et al., 2003; Speer et al., 2007). Converging evidence is provided by a study by Castiello (2003), which demonstrated that the observation of a person performing a goal-directed movement facilitated imitation only if the observer could see the actor's gaze, though children with autism have not shown this same type of facilitation (Pierno et al., 2008). Thus, the current data suggest

that, when a child with autism and a typically developing child are observing someone's action, they are both observing the action, but they are not encoding the same breadth of social information (see also Rogers et al., 2010). Differences in how children with autism imitate others appear to begin in the very first step of the process, with selective attention guiding the perceptual input to the rest of the system.

Imitation in autism might rely mainly on the encoding and reproduction of the motor information (i.e., the action itself), while typically developing children select and integrate extra-motor information to support a semantic coding of the action. Failure to detect cues provided by the demonstrator's face might result in difficulties in processing more complex goal-directed actions, in which information provided by the demonstrator's face is necessary to interpret the goal of the action. Imitation of simple goal-directed actions, in which the action itself is "self-explaining" and no extra-motor information is necessary to understand the demonstrator's goal, might not be affected by this difference in visual attention, thus resulting in the often-replicated finding that children with autism show less deficit in imitating simple actions on objects than other types of imitations.

This interpretation is supported by findings from a recent study (Vivanti et al., under review) that tested the ability of children with autism to predict the outcome of an action in two conditions: (1) when the end-state of the action could be inferred on the basis of the objects involved in the action; and (2) when the demonstrator's gaze direction was crucial for determining the course of the action. The group with autism performed as well as the group with typical development in the first condition, but were significantly impaired in the second condition. Gaze-pattern analyses revealed that children with autism showed significantly reduced attention to the direction of the demonstrator's gaze compared to the contrast group, suggesting that failure to interpret this ostensive cue to the demonstrator's goal led to their poor performance.

It is tempting to speculate that failure to capture this type of social information results in persons with autism processing the action to be modeled via the "sublexical" route (see above) more frequently than others, and using the "semantic" route less frequently. This interpretation seems to be supported by studies documenting that, in contrast to typically developing children, children with ASD tend to imitate "accidental" actions performed by the demonstrator, thus reproducing the exact motor pattern observed, without appreciating the difference between "intentional" and "accidental" acts of the demonstrator (D'Entremont & Yazbek, 2007), though see contradictory evidence from Rogers et al., 2010; see also Chapter 18). Moreover, children with autism, unlike those with other developmental disabilities, are more likely to imitate the action itself (the motor pattern) but not the affective style of the demonstrator (e.g., knocking on a door gently versus harshly; Hobson, 1986, 1995; Hobson, & Lee, 1999).

However, we also found that children with autism are able to predict the outcome of an action on the basis of the actor's emotions (Vivanti et al., under review). This dissociation between the ability to understand the goals of an action on the basis of emotional expressions and gaze direction suggests that children with autism, rather than having a general inability to select and appreciate information conveyed from the face, are less sensitive to some specific social cues, in particular referential cues (e.g., gaze direction) that are particularly relevant to understand an action's goals.

The atypical visual pattern observed in autism might also affect the imitation of meaningless actions and the frequency of imitative acts, as the demonstrator's communicative cues conveyed by the face, such as the ostensive direct gaze, are crucial to tell the child when to imitate and to "isolate" the to-be-imitated action in the stream of the demonstrator's behavior. Children show special sensitivity to the ostensive direct gaze from infancy, and appear to ascribe more relevancy to the actions that follow it, attending to and imitating them (Gergely & Csibra, 2006; Senju & Csibra, 2008).

In a recent study, we asked participants with and without autism to imitate a series of actions on objects that were associated with either a direct or averted demonstrator's gaze. While the direct gaze helped typically developing children pay attention to the action, this was not the case for children with autism. In fact, they imitated the actions in the Averted Gaze condition as accurately as typically developing children; however, in the Direct Gaze condition, their performance was significantly worse than that of the control group. This finding suggests that children with autism might not appreciate the communicative signals conveyed by the face for guiding imitation.

Following Hobson's thinking (see Hobson, & Lee, 1999), it is tempting to suggest that children with autism copy *an action* (as they encode motor information—the action itself) while typically developing children copy *a person* who is performing an action (as they encode the action itself in the framework of the demonstrator's goals and communicative signals). More empirical research is needed in this area; however, these preliminary data suggest that abnormalities in the way the action is encoded are present in autism, and they cannot be fully explained by basic social or low-level visual impairments.

Encoding actions without intending to: The case of mimicry

Within a second of seeing an emotional facial expression, typically developing individuals automatically and unintentionally match that expression in a phenomenon known as *mimicry* or *emotional contagion* (Cacioppo et al., 1986; Hatfield et al., 1994) These rapid "mirroring" reactions, along with other forms of "unconscious" interpersonal matching behaviors, typically involve facilitation of previously existing movements, rather than learning new actions (Orgs et al., 2008). However, it has been proposed that the mirror neuron system facilitates imitative learning, intersubjective engagement, and social understanding (Decety & Chaminade, 2003; Rogers & Williams, 2006). The interpersonal significance of mimicry is evidenced through studies demonstrating positive affiliative effects on social partners when being mimicked (Chartrand & Bargh, 1999), and those demonstrating that mimicked facial expressions are associated with changes in one's emotional experience in the direction of the mirrored partner's emotions (McIntosh, 1996). Thus, a deficit in interpersonal mirroring could have considerable significance on interpersonal relations. It has been suggested that the mechanism underlying these rapid and automatic reactions is the perceptual-motor direct matching implemented by the mirror neuron system (Buccino, Binkofski, & Riggio, 2004; Niedenthal et al., 2005); however, alternative mechanisms have also been proposed (Beall et al., 2008).

Four recent studies have found reduced automatic matching responses during the observation of different facial expressions in ASD (Beall et al., 2008; McIntosh et al., 2006; Scambler et al., 2007; Senju, & Csibra, 2008; see Chapter 18); note however, that one study, (Bird et al., 2007), reports intact automatic imitation tendency in persons with autism in a paradigm involving hand gestures). These findings taken together suggest that a deficit in automatic imitation in ASD might be specific for facial expressions, and might be related to an emotion-specific deficit in ASD, rather than a deficit in automatic action-perception coupling (Beall et al., 2008). Moreover, some authors argue that echolalia and echopraxia, two phenomena observed in autism, should be incompatible with an automatic imitation deficit (Griffin, 2002; Southgate, Csibra, Kaufman, & Johnson, 2008; although see Rogers & Pennington, 1991, who suggest that different neural systems underlie motor imitation and verbal echolalia). Sorting out this dichotomy involving reduced imitation of all types, on the one hand, and the presence of echopraxia and echolalia in some persons with autism, on the other (and also persons without autism but with other types of brain dysfunction), will take detailed study.

One possible reason for reduced mimicry involves the possibility that participants with autism do not attend to the "critical" parts of the stimuli (Klin, 2008; Senju, & Csibra et al., 2008)—a problem of encoding, and a possibility that requires eye-tracking technology to address. However, there is also evidence suggesting that a disruption of output processes implemented by the mirror system might be present in persons with autism, and this might contribute to their difficulties in imitation. In the following section, we review the literature in this area.

THE TRANSFORMATION PHASE: FROM THE INPUT TO THE OUTPUT, THE ACTION-PERCEPTION MECHANISM

Scholars seem to agree that in order to imitate, it is necessary to have an action-perception correspondence mechanism between the model and the observer. Among the different mechanisms involved in imitation, the process of mapping observed actions onto motor representations has received the most attention in the last decade, with research on imitation in typical development. Infants imitate a small number of facial movements from very early in life (Meltzoff & Moore, 1977). How do they translate perceptual knowledge into motor knowledge? This crucial issue, known as the correspondence problem (Hurley, 2008; Hurley & Chater, 2005; Nehaniv &

Dautenhahn, 2002), cannot be addressed by associative learning mechanisms (Meltzoff, 2005) when one is studying newborns. The way most scientists address the correspondence problem is to invoke a common code for visual and motor representation, so that the observed actions are encoded in a perceptual/motor format, enabling the individual to map the visual information directly onto motor representation.

Mirror neurons, discovered in the 1990s by a University of Parma group directed by Giacomo Rizzolatti, may represent the neurocognitive substrate of such an action-perception equivalence mechanism. Mirror neurons are visual motor neurons that, in the macaque monkey, activate both during the observation and the performance of a goal-directed action, as demonstrated through intracortical recording. In humans, the existence of mirror neurons can only be inferred indirectly, as intracortical electrophysiology is only possible in rare circumstances. Thus, in the human literature, researchers usually refer to mirror neuron system (MNS) or mirror areas studied through indirect techniques. In humans, the presence of an MNS has been inferred by a series of studies via electroencephalography (EEG; e.g., Lepage & Theoret; 2006; Oberman, Ramachandran, & Pineda, 2008), magnetoencephalography (MEG; e.g., Hari, Forss, Avikainen, Kirveskari, Salenius, & Rizzolatti 1998), transcranial magnetic stimulation (TMS; e.g., Fadiga, Fogassi, Pavesi, & Rizzolatti., 1995; Strafella & Paus, 2000), and functional brain imaging such as positron emission tomography (PET; e.g., Decety et al., 1997; Grafton, Arbib, Fadiga, & Rizzolatti, 1996; Grezes, Costes, & Decety, 1998; Rizzolatti, Fadiga, Gallese, & Fogassi, 1995), and functional MRI (fMRI; e.g., Buccino et al., 2004; Grezes, Armony, Rowe, & Passingham, 2003).

One main functional difference between monkey and human MNS involves the nature of actions that stimulate the MNS. While monkeys' MNS becomes activated only during observation of transitive actions (goal-directed actions on objects), in humans, even the observation of intransitive actions (limb movements that do not involve objects and are not goal-directed) may produce activation of the motor cortex (Rizzolatti & Craighero, 2004). This difference is crucial, as it could constitute the most recently evolved part of the MNS that allows humans to flexibly and promptly imitate other individuals and send and receive communicative signals (Arbib, 2005).

Fadiga et al. (1995), using TMS, conducted the first study investigating the presence of MNS activity in humans. Fadiga et al. (1995) recorded motor evoked potentials (MEPs), elicited by stimulation of the left motor cortex, from the right hand and arm muscles of volunteers asked to observe an experimenter grasping an object (transitive hand actions) or performing meaningless arm gestures (intransitive arm movements). The presentation of lights and 3-D objects was used as a control condition. Fadiga et al. (1995) assumed that if seeing a movement activates the premotor cortex in humans, this activation should be accompanied by an increase of MEPs triggered by the magnetic stimulation of the motor cortex. The observation of both transitive and intransitive actions was accompanied by an increase of the recorded MEPs, in comparison to the control conditions. These findings led Fadiga et al. (1995) to conclude that an MNS is also present in humans.

After Fadiga et al.'s (1995) study, several experimental and theoretical accounts related mirror neurons to various functions involving action understanding (Rizzolatti, Fogassi, & Gallese, 2002), imitation (e.g., Iacoboni, 2005; Iacoboni et al.,1999), intention understanding (e.g., Fogassi et al., 2005; Iacoboni et al., 2005), empathy (Gallese, Keysers, & Rizzolatti, 2004), and communication (Rizzolatti & Arbib, 1998; Rizzolatti & Craighero, 2004). In 2005, Rizzolatti suggested that the question of which is the function of the MNS is incorrectly formulated, given the current theoretical accounts and empirical evidence regarding the MNS in both humans and monkeys. According to the author, based on current empirical evidence on mirror neurons, we can only confidently infer that: (1) the primate brain possesses an observation-execution matching mechanism mapping the visual description of actions onto their motor counterpart; and (2) this mechanism may underlie several functions depending on what aspect of the action is coded and the interactions of the MNS with other systems. Rizzolatti (2005) also suggested that given that mirror neurons do not possess a single functional role, and that several areas of the human brain are characterized by this observation/execution property, rather than talking about a mirror system or mirror functions, it may be more appropriate to talk about a *mirror mechanism*. For these reasons, the coexistence of typical and abnormal mirror areas of function may be a reasonable hypothesis.

Given that the MNS activates in neurotypical humans during imitation and other social cognitive tasks in which people with autism show impairment,

and given Williams et al.'s (2001) hypothesis that MNS activation is abnormal in autism, the field has moved quickly to examine MNS functioning as a possible neurobiological substrate of autism social impairment. So far, ten published studies have tested the hypothesis of a deficient functioning of the MNS in autism with a variety of methodologies.

Nishitani et al. (2004) assessed MNS in adults with Asperger syndrome and typical adults, through magnetoencephalography (MEG), during imitation of still pictures of lip forms. In both groups, they found similar activation in the occipital cortex, occipital temporal sulcus, inferior parietal lobe, and primary motor cortex of both hemispheres. However, in the AS group, the activation of the inferior frontal lobe was delayed and activations in the frontal lobe and in the primary motor cortex were weaker than in control subjects. The main abnormality was observed in Broca's area on the left, and its counterpart in the right hemisphere. The authors suggest that this abnormal activation could partially account for imitation and social impairment in AS.

Williams et al. (2005) employed Iacoboni et al.'s (2005) fMRI protocol involving imitation of finger movements to study MNS activation in adolescents with ASD, compared to typically developing adolescents. In the ASD group, they found attenuated activation in areas of the right parietal lobe associated with the MNS, in Broca's area, and in an area at the right temporo-parietal junction associated with a Theory of Mind (ToM) function. Moreover, the ASD group did not present modulation of left amygdala activity during imitation compared to the control group. According to the authors, in the ASD group the differential MNS activation during imitation is part of a more complex deficit in the neural substrate of imitation.

Dapretto et al. (2006) examined MNS activity in high-functioning children with autism and matched controls through fMRI while imitating and observing emotional expressions. The ASD group showed MNS activity in the inferior frontal gyrus (pars opercularis), while both groups performed the tasks similarly. As activity in the inferior frontal gyrus was related to ADOS scores, the authors concluded that a malfunctioning related to the MNS may underlie the social deficits in autism.

Oberman et al. (2005) measured mu wave suppression, an index thought to reflect MNS activity, in high-functioning individuals with ASD and age- and gender-matched control subjects. The ASD group showed mu suppression to self-performed hand movements but not to observed hand movements. The authors suggest that these findings support the hypothesis of a dysfunctional MNS in high functioning individuals with autism.

Additionally, Bernier, Dawson, Murias, & Webb (2007) investigated mu rhythm attenuation during the observation, execution, and imitation of movements in 14 high-functioning adults with ASD and 15 IQ- and age-matched typical adults. Both groups demonstrated significant attenuation of the mu rhythm when executing an action. However, when observing movement, the individuals with ASD showed significantly reduced attenuation of the mu wave. Behaviorally assessed imitation skills were correlated with degree of mu wave attenuation during observation of movement. The authors concluded that there is an execution/observation matching system dysfunction in individuals with autism and that this matching system is related to degree of impairment in imitation abilities.

Moreover, Martineau, Cochin, Magne, and Barthelemy (2008) compared EEG activity in typically developing children and children with autism while they observed videos depicting human actions or still scenes. Desynchronization of the EEG in the motor cortex and frontal and temporal locations to the observation of human actions was found in the typically developing children but not in the children with autism. The authors consider these findings as supportive of an MNS deficit in autism.

Hadijikani et al. (2006) reported that adults with ASD showed reduced cortical thickness in areas ascribed to the MNS, the bilateral pars opercularis of the inferior frontal gyrus. These are the same areas that failed to activate during imitation and observation of facial expressions in Dapretto et al. (2006). Furthermore, Hadijikani et al. (2006) found that cortical thinning in these areas was correlated with severity of ASD symptoms.

Cattaneo et al. (2007) observed, in children with autism as compared to typically developing children, diminished electromyography (EMG) activity of the mouth-opening mylohyoid (MH) muscle to the observation and execution of action involving intentions' understanding. According to these authors, their findings support the involvement of MNS in intentions understanding and its consequent involvement in autism.

Despite these accounts supporting impairments in the MNS of individuals with autism, at least three studies identified preserved areas of functioning in this population. Oberman, Ramachandran, and Pineda (2008), via EEG recording, reported in children with autism mu suppression similar to that identified in a control group comprising typically developing children, to the observation of a grasp performed by the hand of a familiar actor such as a parent. As reported by these authors, their findings suggest that the MNS of children with autism activates similarly to that of typical individuals when some familiar characteristics can be identified in the observed stimuli.

Gowen, Stanley, and Miall (2008) used a movement interference paradigm to study MNS in a group of children with autism and children with typical development. Movement interference occurs with the observation and execution of incongruent actions, and it is supposed to be related to the activation of mirror neurons. The authors found equivalent interference effects for both ASD and control participants. While they suggest that their findings are inconsistent with a global mirror neuron dysfunction in the autism group, they proposed three explanations for their results: (1) MNS is unrelated to the interference effect; (2) the MNS of the participants with autism was not affected; and (3) certain components of the MNS are not impaired.

Recently, we further tested the hypothesis of preserved MNS activation in autism (Colombi, 2009). We examined mu wave suppression through EEG recording (power in the 8–13Hz band recorded over motor cortex), as an index of MNS activation, in a group of high functioning 9- to 16- year-old children with autism and a carefully matched typical control group, when they were presented with (1) actions on objects (transitive actions) and (2) body movements (intransitive actions). Children with autism showed mu suppression similar to the control group to the presentation of both transitive and intransitive actions. Both groups showed larger mu suppression in the central area when presented with transitive actions in comparison to intransitive actions. These findings suggest that the MNS of children with autism responds to the observation of actions on objects as well as to body movements.

While the majority of the studies (8 out of 11), describe a malfunctioning in the MNS of children with autism, three recent studies (Colombi, 2009; Gowen et al., 2008; Oberman et al., 2008) suggested preserved areas of functioning in the MNS of children with autism. Further research is certainly necessary to better characterize preserved and affected areas of functioning in the MNS of children with autism.

These three studies suggest that the action-perception mechanism may be preserved in autism. Abnormalities in autism have been documented in areas and processes that extend beyond the mirror system. Therefore, multiple mechanisms can contribute to the inefficiency of the imitative process in this population. Besides abnormalities detected at the structural or functional level, recent works investigated connectivity of these different regions in ASD. The study by Hari, and Nishitani (2004) compared latencies in the activation of the neural regions underlying imitation in subjects with Asperger syndrome (AS) and typically developing controls (TD). They showed that the flow of information from occipital areas to STS and from STS to IPL in Asperger's subjects was associated with a normal time latency—however, activation intervals from IPL to IFG were significantly longer, suggesting a problem in connectivity between the two mirror areas underlying imitation. Moreover, reduced functional connectivity between visual cortex and IFG has been documented by Villalobos et al. (2005) in a non-imitative task. An area of research that needs further investigation is the relationship between these impairments and the MNS, and how this translates into the imitation deficit in autism.

Though some empirical evidence suggests the possibility of an MNS impairment in autism (e.g., Dapretto et al., 2006; Oberman et al., 2005), we propose that the neural-cognitive action-perception mechanism may be preserved, at least partially, in autism. As previously reviewed, behavioral studies suggest dissociation in imitative abilities of people with autism between learning or *apprenticeship* function and *social interpersonal communication* function (e.g., Rogers et al.,2010). Interestingly, Iacoboni (2005) suggested a model of the neural mechanisms involving the presence of a core circuitry of imitation comprising the superior temporal sulcus (STS) and the MNS. According to Iacoboni, this core circuitry interacts with other neural systems in ways that depend on the type of imitation to be performed. In the model, two subsystems of imitation are identified. Imitative learning is supported by a neural system comprising the core circuitry of imitation interacting with the dorsolateral prefrontal cortex and motor preparation areas. On the other hand, imitation as a form of social interaction is supported by a neural system comprising the core circuitry of imitation interacting with the limbic system. Additionally, the ventral premotor mirror neurons were mainly associated with the imitation of goal directed or transitive actions, while the activation of superior and inferior parietal lobules was associated to a greater extent with nonmeaningful or intransitive actions (Decety et al., 1997; Grezes, Costes, & Decety, 1998; Koski et al., 2002). The existence of these two neural pathways of imitation may explain the dissociation between imitation for instrumental learning and social communication found in autism. If the imitation for learning function and its corresponding neural substrate are intact, then it can be argued that the action-perception mechanism and its neural substrate are not necessarily impaired in autism. The impairment may reside in the brain areas (such as the limbic system) that interact with the MNS.

EXECUTION PHASE: THE OUTPUT

Several accounts suggest that motor difficulties are common in autism (see Chapter 10). Manjiviona and Prior (1995) evaluated motor impairments in Asperger syndrome and high-functioning autistic children using the Test of Motor Impairment-Henderson Revision. They found motor impairment in 50% of a group of children with a diagnosis of Asperger syndrome and 67% of a group with Autistic disorder. Dewey, Cantell, and Crawford (2007) identified significant impairment in motor coordination skills in 49 children with autism, in comparison to a control group of typical children using the Bruininks-Oseretsky Test of Motor Proficiency-Short Form. Ghaziuddin, and Butler (1998) assessed evaluated motor coordination using the Bruininks Oseretsky test in a group of children with Asperger syndrome, a group with autistic disorder, and a group with pervasive developmental disorder not otherwise specified (PDD-NOS). Motor coordination deficits were found in all three groups, with the autistic group more severely impaired compared to the other two groups.

Green et al. (2002) evaluated motor impairment in children with Asperger syndrome using the Movement Assessment Battery for Children (Henderson & Sugden, 1992). In this study, all the children with Asperger syndrome met diagnostic criteria of motor impairment. Green et al. (2009) identified definite movement impairments in 79% of children with autistic spectrum disorders evaluated with the Movement

Assessment Battery for Children. They also found that children with an IQ of less than 70 were more impaired than those with an IQ more than 70.

The neural correlates of motor functioning in autism have been investigated in several neuroimaging studies. Several accounts describe evidence of pathology in the cerebellum, an area considered critical for motor functioning, in autism (Bailey et al., 1998; Courchesne, 1991, 1997; Gaffney, Tsai, Kuperman, & Minchin, 1987; Guerin et al., 1996). Moreover, Carper and Courchesne (2000) found that in some individuals with autism, the degree of abnormality of the cerebellum was related to increased volume of the frontal lobe.

While motor abnormalities are well-documented in at least a substantial portion of individuals with ASD, the extent to which motor difficulties explain the variability in imitation performance is not yet known (Bennetto, 1999; Green et al., 2002; Rogers et al., 2003; Smith & Bryson, 1998). Smith and Bryson (1998) reported that difficulties in motor skills accounted for 37% of the variance in gesture imitation scores in their sample. More recently, McDuffie et al. (2005) found a strong correlation between imitation and motor skills, while Rogers et al. (2003) found no significant association between the two measures in a group of preschoolers with autism. Vanvuchelen, Roeyers, & de Weerdt (2007) reported that motor abilities accounted for 80% of the imitative performance in a group of low-functioning children with autism. Among the various imitative skills tested in research, oral-facial imitation appears to be the most influenced by motor difficulties (e.g., oral dyspraxia; Rogers et al., 2005). One major issue in interpreting the relation between motor and imitation abilities in experimental studies is that different studies assess motor abilities using different motor tests, which, in turn have different imitation demands inherent in their instructions.

DO WE IMITATE OTHERS BECAUSE WE UNDERSTAND THEM, OR DO WE UNDERSTAND OTHERS BECAUSE WE IMITATE THEM? THE DEBATE ON THE NATURE OF IMITATION AND ITS IMPLICATIONS FOR AUTISM

The debate on the nature of the imitation deficit in autism is embedded in broader debates in cognitive science, such as those comparing the "Theory-Theory"

to the "Simulation Theory," or those comparing "embodied cognition" models to computational models for action understanding, perception, and social cognition (Barsalou, 2008; Dennett, 1991; Fodor, 1992; Gallese, 2003). The heuristic value of these models is limited in some cases because, rather than providing predictions of specific patterns of strengths and weaknesses in imitative behavior in autism, proponents of different models "use" the imitation deficit in autism as an argument for the goodness of their theory. As we reviewed in the first part of the chapter, the imitation deficit in autism cannot be characterized as a unitary phenomenon. Moreover, both "autism" and "imitation" are somewhat elusive concepts for science. Autism researchers recognize that autism exists in a wide range of distinct conditions. Researchers in the last decade became increasingly skeptical about the usefulness of models providing a single explanation for autism (Happè, Ronald, & Plomin, 2006; see Chapters 23 and 24). Furthermore, as we have been describing, a wide range of behaviors falls under the umbrella of "imitation." Scholars from different disciplines—including philosophy of mind, developmental psychology, and ethology—are still debating the nature, definition, and conceptualization of the different kinds of imitative behaviors (see, for example, Hurley, 2008).

These debates concerning the relationship between autism and imitation, in our opinion, are very unlikely to generate further heuristics in autism, unless they include the idea that different imitative behaviors and different aspects of the imitative process are based on different neurocognitive processes, and are likely impaired for different reasons in different individuals and different diagnostic groups. We build this concept from two elements: the complementarity of inferential and non-inferential processes in imitation, and the perspective of system inefficiency and vulnerability in autism and other neurological and neurodevelopmental disorders. Inferential and non-inferential processes may both be involved in different types of imitative behaviors and in the same imitative act. It might be the case that simpler forms of mirroring-based imitation occur earlier in development than simpler forms of inferential understanding. Simpler forms of inferential understanding likely precede more complex forms of imitative learning (Hurley, 2008). At the process level, an earlier mirror-based response to the demonstrator's action might be re-scripted in more flexible formats as greater awareness of the attentional and intentional stance of the demonstrator develops, to permit more flexible and selective imitation. In other words, a top-down re-description of the demonstrator's action might be built upon a base grounded in bottom-up perception-action encoding. The nature of the stimulus, the nature of the context, and the learning history of the observer all will influence the nature of the information processes that are involved in any particular imitative act. This perspective suggests that there is not convincing evidence for either a "bottom-up" or "top-down" account of the imitation deficit in autism; furthermore, framing the problem in such terms may not be the most productive, given our growing understanding of the imitation problem.

The second point we wish to highlight is that imitation competence involves a complex system of neurocognitive processes, including visual attention, social motivation, understanding of communicative cues, integration of multiple sources of information, working memory, transfer of visual input into the body schema (for novel movements and actions) as well as linked observation-action responses for familiar movements and actions, motor planning, executive processes, and inhibitory processes. All will be influenced by development and previous experiences. Imitation, even at the level of mimicry, must involve much more than the mirror neuron system. Complex information processing systems can be disrupted in many ways, and imitation research in autism has identified many differences in the performance of persons with ASD compared to others. It might be the case that this heterogeneous vulnerability in the components of the system causes the system to be inefficient, thus affecting many, but not all, imitative behaviors, in many, but not all, individuals with autism. The research into neurocognitive componential aspects of imitation in autism is steadily yielding more detailed information about imitative behavior and underlying brain activity. However, there is another question underlying the theories: To what extent does the imitation problem affect symptom expression and development in persons with autism? This question requires a different research approach, particularly from two study designs: longitudinal studies of infants who develop ASD, and treatment studies that allow imitation to be experimentally manipulated. Both types of studies are currently being conducted.

The longitudinal studies of infant siblings of children with autism have the potential to reveal much about the interaction of imitative abilities, developmental trajectories, and symptoms of autism. Zwaigenbaum et al. (2005) have demonstrated that imitation impairments are present by the age of 12 months in children who will later develop autism, though Young et al. (in review) did not find specific imitation deficits until 18 months in a similar sample. However, few longitudinal studies have thus far examined the relation between imitation abilities in the preschool period and social development or autism symptomatology at the level of individual differences, and this type of study is necessary for testing the theory that the imitation problems in autism contribute to the developing autism phenotype. Such studies are badly needed and should begin to emerge from the infant-sibling studies.

The second type of study needed involves treatment. Can one affect outcomes in ASD by teaching imitation early? Does teaching imitation confer a specific benefit that is not conferred by teaching speech, joint attention, or pretend play? There is only indirect evidence for this at present. The interventions that have demonstrated the most powerful effects of intensive early intervention in ASD focus very heavily on imitation training at the start of the intervention, though it is taught in different ways (; Lovaas, 1987; Rogers, & Dawson, 2010; Smith et al., 2000). Additionally, Ingersoll and Schreibman (2006) have described secondary advances in joint attention and other core skill areas resulting from imitation training. However, this question needs a design like that provided by Kasari et al. (2008), in which two different interventions are delivered to randomized groups with long-term follow-up to examine relative effects.

Both study designs—the longitudinal follow-along and the longitudinal comparative treatment interventions—are expensive and complex to carry out, but these designs are necessary to determine the specific role that imitation skills play in outcomes of young children with ASD. Determining the essential ingredients of early intervention programs is necessary if we are to eventually develop more targeted, individualized, and powerful intervention approaches for specific children, but given both the economic challenges of early intervention for autism and the poor outcomes that still result for so many, we must continue to isolate and examine the nature and the role of the imitation deficit in ASD.[1]

1. This chapter was partially supported by grants from the National Institutes of Mental Health T32 MH073124-6 (Rogers and Vivanti), 1R01 MH081757-3, funded by NIMH and the National Institute of Child Development (Rogers and Colombi) and the MIND Institute, UCDavis. We wish to acknowledge Diane Larzelere's support for manuscript preparation.

References

Aldridge, M.A., Stone, K.R., Sweeney, M.H., & Bower, T.G.R. (2000). Preverbal children with autism understand the intentions of others. *Developmental Science, 3,* 294–301.

Allison, T., Puce, A., & McCarthy, G. (2000). Social perception from visual cues: Role of the STS region. *Trends in Cognitive Sciences, 4,* 267–278.

Amano, S., Kezuka, E., & Yamamoto, A. (2004). Infant shifting attention from an adult's face to an adult's hand: A precursor of joint attention. *Infant Behavior and Development, 27*(1), 64–80.

American Psychiatric Association. (2000). *Diagnostic and statistical manual of mental disorders, 4th Edition, text revision (DSM-IV-TR).* Washington, D.C.: American Psychiatric Association.

Anderson, C.J., Colombo, J., & Shaddy D.J. (2006). Visual scanning and papillary responses in young children with autism spectrum disorder. *Journal of Clinical and Experimental Neuropsychology, 28,* 1238–1256.

Arbib, M.A. (2005). From monkey-like action recognition to human language: An evolutionary framework for neurolinguistics. *Behavioral and Brain Ssciences, 28,* 105–124.

Ashwin, C., Baron-Cohen, S., Wheelwright, S., O'Riordan, M., & Bullmore, E.T. (2007). Differential activation of the amygdala and the "social brain" during fearful face-processing in Asperger Syndrome. *Neuropsychologia, 45*(1), 2–14.

Bailey, A., Luthert, P., Dean, A., Harding, B., Janota, I., Montgomery, M., Rutter, M., & Lantos, P. (1998). A clinicopathological study of autism. *Brain, 121*(5), 889–905.

Baldwin, J.M. (1906). *Social and ethical interpretations in mental development.* New York: Macmillan.

Barsalou, L.W. (2008). Cognitive and neural contributions to understanding the conceptual system. *Current Directions in Psychological Science, 17*(2), 91–95.

Bartak, L., Rutter, M., & Cox, A. (1977). A comparative study of infantile autism and specific developmental receptive language disorders III. Discriminant function analysis. *Journal of Autism and Developmental Disorders, 7*(4), 383–396.

Bates, E., Thal, D., Whitesell, K., Fenson, L., & Oakes, L. (1989). Integrating language and gesture in infancy. *Developmental Psychology, 25*(6), 1004–1019.

Beall, P.M., Moody, E.J., McIntosh, D.N., Hepburn, S.L., & Reed, C.L. (2008). Rapid facial reactions to emotional facial expressions in typically developing children and children with autism spectrum disorder. *Journal of Experimental Child Psychology, 101*(3), 206–223.

Behne, T., Carpenter, M., & Tomasello, M. (2005). One-year-olds comprehend the communicative intentions behind gestures in a hiding game. *Developmental Science, 8*(6), 492–499.

Bekkering, H., Wohlschalger, A., & Gattis, M. (2000). Imitation of gestures in children is goal-directed. *The Quarterly Journal of Experimental Psychology: A Human Experimental Psychology, 53A*(1), 153–164.

Bennetto, L. (1999). A componential approach to imitation and movement deficits in autism. *Dissertation Abstracts International, 60,* 8–19.

Bernabei, P., Fenton, G., Fabrizi, A., Camioni, L., & Perucchini, P. (2003). Profiles of sensorimotor development in children with autism and with developmental delay. *Perceptual Motor Skills, 96* (3 Pt 2), 1107–1116.

Bernier, R., Dawson, G., Murias, M., & Webb, S. (2007). EEG mu rhythm and imitation impairments in individuals with autism spectrum disorder. *Brain and Cognition, 64*(3), 228–237.

Bird, B., Leighton, J., Press, C., & Heyes, C. (2007). Intact automatic imitation of human and robot actions in autism spectrum disorders. *Proceedings of the Royal Society Biological Sciences, 274*(1628), 3027–3031.

Brass, M., Schmitt, R., Spengler, S., & Gergely, G. (2007). Investigating action understanding: Inferential processes versus action simulation. *Current Biology, 17*(24), 2117–2121.

Brown, J., & Whiten, A. (2000). Imitation, theory of mind and related activities in autism: An observational study of spontaneous behaviour in everyday contacts. *Autism, 4*(2), 185–204.

Bruner, J. (1957). From joint attention to the meeting of minds: An introduction. In C. Moore & P.J. Dunham (Eds.), *Joint attention: Its origins and role in development* (pp. 1–14). Hillsdale, NJ: Lawrence Erlbaum Associates, Inc.

Bruner, J. (1972). Nature and uses of immaturity. *American Psychologist, 27,* 687–708.

Buccino, G., Binkofski, F., & Riggio, L. (2004). The mirror neuron system and action recognition. *Brain and Language, 89*(2), 370–376.

Cacioppo, J.T., Petty, R.E., Kao, C.F., & Rodriguez, R. (1986). Central and peripheral routes to persuasion: An individual difference perspective. *Journal of Personality and Social Psychology, 51*(5), 1032–1043.

Carpenter, M., Akhtar, N., & Tomasello, M. (1998). Fourteen- through 18-month-old infants differentially imitate intentional and accidental actions. *Infant Behavior and Development, 21*(2), 315–330.

Carpenter, M., & Call, J. (2007). The question of "what to imitate": Inferring goals and intentions from demonstrations. In K. Dautenhahn & C. Nehaniv (Eds.), *Imitation and social learning in robots, humans and animals: Behavioural, social and communicative dimensions* (pp. 135–151). Cambridge: Cambridge University Press.

Carpenter, M., Pennington, B.F., & Rogers, S.J. (2001). Understanding of others' intentions in children with autism. *Journal of Autism and Developmental Disorders, 31*(6), 589–600.

Carpenter, M., Tomasello, M., & Savage-Rumbaugh, S. (1995). Joint attention and imitative learning in children, chimpanzees, and enculturated chimpanzees. *Social Development, 4*, 217–237.

Carper, R.A., & Courchesne, E. (2000). Inverse correlation between frontal lobe and cerebellum sizes in children with autism. *Brain, 123*(4), 836–844.

Carr, L., Iacoboni, M., Dubeau, M.C., Mazziotta, J.C., & Lenzi, G.L. (2003). Neural mechanisms of empathy in humans: A relay from neural systems for imitation to limbic areas. *Proceedings of the National Academy of Sciences, 100*(9), 5497–5502.

Castelli, F., Frith, C., Happé, F., & Frith, U. (2002). Autism, Asperger syndrome and brain mechanisms for the attribution of mental states to animated shapes. *Brain, 125*, 1839–1849.

Castelli, F., Happé, F., Frith, U., & Frith, C. (2000). Movement and mind: A functional imaging study of perception and interpretation of complex intentional movement patterns. *Neuroimage, 12*, 314–325.

Castiello, U. (2003). Understanding other people's actions: Intention and attention. *Journal of Experimental Psychology: Human Perception and Performance, 29*, 416–430.

Cattaneo, L., Fabbri-Destro, M., Boria, S., Pieraccini, C., Monti, A., Cossu, G., & Rizzolatti, G. (2007). Impairment of actions chains in autism and its possible role in intention understanding. *Proceedings of the National Academy of Sciences of the United States of America, 104*(45), 17825–17830.

Charman, T., Swettenham, J., Baron-Cohen, S., Cox, A., Baird, G., & Drew, A. (1997). Infants with autism: An investigation of empathy, pretend play, joint attention, and imitation. *Developmental Psychology, 33*, 781–789.

Chartrand, T.L., & Bargh, J.A. (1999). The chameleon effect: The perception-behavior link and social interaction. *Journal of Personality and Social Psychology, 76*, 893–910.

Colombi, C. (2009). Mirror neuron system activation in autism in response to transitive and intransitive actions. *Dissertation Abstracts International, 70*, 1500.

Colombi, C., Liebal, K., Tomasello, M., Young, G., Warneken, F., & Rogers, S. (2009). Examining correlates of cooperation in autism: Imitation, joint attention, and understanding intentions. *Autism, 13*(2), 143–163.

Colombi, C., Rogers, S., & Young, G. (2005, MONTHMay). *Understanding intentions on objects, imitation, and social engagement in children with autism.* Paper presented at the International Meeting for Autism Research (IMFAR), Boston, MA.

Courchesne, E. (1991). Neuroanatomic imaging in autism. *Pediatrics, 87*(5 Pt 2), 781–790.

Courchesne, E. (1997). Brainstem, cerebellar and limbic neuronatomical abnormalities in autism. *Current Opinion in Neurobiology, 7*(2), 269–278.

Csibra, G. (2008). Goal attribution to inanimate agents by 6.5-month-old infants. *Cognition, 107*(2), 705–717.

Csibra, G., & Gergely, G. (2007). Obsessed with goals: Functions and mechanisms of teleological interpretation of actions in humans. *Acta Psychologica, 124*, 60–78.

Dalton, K.M, Nacewicz, B.M., Johnstone, T., Schaefer, H.S., Gernsbacher, M.A., Goldsmith, H.H., Alexander, A.L., & Davidson, R.J. (2005). Gaze fixation and the neural circuitry of face processing in autism. *Nature Neuroscience, 8*(4), 519–526.

Dapretto, M., Davies, M., Pfeifer, J.H., Scott, A., Sigman, M., Bookheimer, S., & Iacoboni, M. (2006). Understanding emotions in others: Mirror neuron dysfunction in children with autism spectrum disorders. *Nature Neuroscience, 9*, 28–30.

Dawson, G., & Bernier, R. (2007). Development of social brain circuitry in autism. In D. Coch, K.W. Fischer & G. Dawson (Eds.), *Human behavior, learning, and the developing brain* (pp. 28–55). New York: Guilford Press.

Dawson, G., Meltzoff, A.N., Osterling, J., & Rinaldi, J. (1998). Neuropsychological correlates of early symptoms of autism. *Child Development, 69*(5), 1276–1285.

Dawson, G., Munson, J., Estes, A., Osterling, J., McPartland, J., Toth, K., Carver, L., & Abbott, R. (2002). Neurocognitive function and joint attention ability in young children with autism spectrum disorder versus developmental delay. *Child Development, 73*(2), 345–358.

Dawson, G., Rogers, S., Munson, J., Smith, M., Jamie, W., Greenson, J., et al. (2009). Randomized controlled trial of the Early Start Denver Model: A developmental behavioral intervention for toddlers with autism: Effects on IQ, adaptive behavior, and autism diagnosis. *Pediatrics*, doi/10.1542/peds.2009-0958.

Dawson, G., Rogers, S., Munson, J., Smith, M., Jamie, W., Greenson, J. . . . LAST AUTHOR. (2009). Randomized controlled trial of the Early Start Denver Model: A developmental behavioral intervention for toddlers with autism: Effects on IQ, adaptive behavior, and autism diagnosis. *Pediatrics*, X, XX–XX. doi: 10.1542/peds.2009-0958.

Decety, J., & Chaminade, T. (2003). When the self represents the other: A new cognitive neuroscience view on psychological identification. *Consciousness and Cognition, 12*, 577–596.

Decety, J., & Grèzes, J. (1999). Neural mechanisms subserving the perception of human actions. *Trends in Cognitive Science 3*, 172–178.

Decety, J., Grezes, J., Costes, N., Perani, D., Jeannerod, M., Procyk, E., Grassi, F., & Fazio, F. (1997). Brain activity during observation of actions. *Influence of action content and subject's strategy. Brain, 120*(10), 1763–1777.

Del Giudice, M., Manera, V., & Keysers, C. (2009). Programmed to learn? The ontogeny of mirror neurons. *Developmental Science, 12*(2), 350–363.

DeMyer, M.K., Alpern, G.D., Barton, S., DeMyer, W.E., Churchill, D.W., Hingtgen, J.N. (1972). Imitation in autistic, early schizophrenic, and nonpsychotic subnormal children. *Journal of Autism and Childhood Schizophrenia, 2,* 264–287.

DeMyer, M.K., Hingtgen, J.N., & Jackson, R.K. (1981). Infantile autism reviewed: A decade of research. *Schizophrenia Bulletin, 7*(3), 388–451.

Dennett, D. (1991). *Consciousness explained.* Boston, MA: Little, Brown & Company.

D'Etremont, B., & Yazbek, A. (2007). Imitation of intentional and accidental actions for children with autism. *Journal of Autism and Developmental Disorders, 37*(9), 1665–1678.

Dewey, D., Cantell, M., & Crawford, S.G. (2007). Motor and gestural performance in children with autism spectrum disorders, developmental coordination disorder, and/or attention deficit hyperactivity disorder. *Journal of the International Neuropsychological Society, 13,* 246–256.

Fadiga, L., Fogassi, L., Pavesi, G., & Rizzolatti, G. (1995). Motor facilitation during action observation: A magnetic stimulation study. *Journal of Neurophysiology, 73,* 2608–2611.

Fodor, J.A. (1992). A theory of the child's theory of mind. *Cognition, 44*(3), 283–296.

Fogassi, L., Ferrari, P.F., Gesierich, B., Rozzi, S., Chersi, F., & Rizzolatti, G. (2005). Parietal lobe: From action organization to intention understanding. *Science, 308*(5722), 662–667.

Fogassi, L., & Luppino, G. (2005). Motor functions of the parietal lobe. *Current Opinion in Neurobiology, 15*(6), 626–631.

Fonagy, P., Gergely, G., & Target, M. (2007). The parent-infant dyad and the construction of the subjective self. *Journal of Child Psychology and Psychiatry, 48*(3-4), 288–328.

Frith, C.D. (2008). Social cognition. *Philosophical Transactions of the Royal Society B, 363*(1499), 2033–2039.

Gaffney, G.R., Tasi, L.Y., Kuperman, S., & Minchin, S. (1987). Cerebellar structure in autism. *American Journal of Diseases of Childhood, 141,* 1330–1333.

Gallagher, S. (2007). Moral agency, self-consciousness, and practical wisdom. *Journal of Consciousness Studies, 14*(5-6), 199–223.

Gallese, V. (2003) The roots of empathy: The shared manifold hypothesis and the neural basis of inter-subjectivity. *Psychopathology, 36*(4), 171–180.

Gallese, V., Fadiga, L., Fogassi, L., & Rizzolatti, G. (1996). Action recognition in the premotor cortex. *Brain, 119,* 593–609.

Gallese, V., Keysers, C., & Rizzolatti, G. (2004). A unifying view of the basis of social cognition. *Trends in Cognitive Sciences, 8*(9), 396–403.

Gattis, M., Bekkering, H., & Wohlschlager, A. (2002). Goal-directed imitation. In A. Meltzoff & W. Prinz (Eds.), *The Imitative Mind* (pp. 183–205XX–XX). New York: Cambridge University Press.

Gergely, G., Bekkering, H., & Kiraly, I. (2002). Rational imitation in preverbal infants. *Nature, 415,* 755.

Gergely, G., & Csibra, G. (2006). Sylvia's recipe: The role of imitation and pedagogy in the transmission of cultural knowledge. In N.J. Enfield & S.C. Levinson (Eds.), *Roots of Human Sociality: Culture, Cognition and Interaction* (pp. 229–258). Oxford: Oxford International Publishers, Ltd.

Gergely, G., Egyed, K., & Kiraly, I. (2007). On pedagogy. *Developmental Science, 10*(1), 139–146.

Ghaziuddin, M., & Butler, E. (1998). Clumsiness in autism and Asperger syndrome: A further report. *Journal of Intellectual Disability Research, 42*(1), 43–48.

Giorello, G., & Sinigaglia, C. (2007). Perception in action. *Acta Bio Medica, 78*(S1), 49–57.

Gopnik, A., & Meltzoff, A.N. (1994). Minds, bodies, and persons: Young children's understanding of the self and others as reflected in imitation and theory of mind research. In S.T. Parker, R.W. Mitchell, & M.L. Bochia (Eds.), *Self-awareness in animals and humans* (pp. 166–186). New York: Cambridge University Press.

Gowen, E., Stanley, J., & Miall, R.C. (2008). Movement interference in autism-spectrum disorder Title of article. *Neuropsychologia, 46*(4), 1060–1068.

Grafton, S.T., Arbib, M.A., Fadiga, L., & Rizzolatti, G. (1996). Localization of grasp representation in human by PET 2. *Observation versus imagination. Experimental Brain Research, 112*(3), 103–111.

Green, D., Baird, G., Barnett, A.L., Henderson, L., Huber, J., & Henderson, S.E. (2002). The severity and nature of motor impairment in Asperger's disorder: A comparison with specific developmental disorder of motor function. *Journal of Child Psychology and Psychiatry, 43*(5), 655–668.

Green, D., Charman, T., Pickles, A., Chandler, S., Loucas, T., Simonoff, E., & Baird, G. (2009). Impairment in movement skills of children with autistic spectrum disorder. *Developmental Medicine and Child Neurology, 51*(4), 311–316.

Grelotti, D.J., Gauthier, I., & Schultz, R.T. (2002). Social interest and the development of cortical face specialization: What autism teaches us about face processing. *Developmental Psychobiology, 40*(3), 213–225.

Grezes, J., Armony, J.L., Rowe, J., & Passingham, R.E. (2003). Activations related to "mirror" and "canonical" neurons in the human brain: An fMRI study. *NeuroImage, 18*(4), 928–937.

Grezes, J., Costes, N., & Decety, J. (1998). Top-down effect of strategy on the perception of human biological motion: A PET investigation. *Cognitive Neuropsychology, 15*(6/7/8), 553–582.

Grezes, J., & Decety, J. (2001). Functional anatomy of execution, mental simulation, observation, and verb generation of actions: A meta-analysis. *Human Brain Mapping, 12,* 1–19.

Griffin, R. (2002). Social learning in the nonsocial: Imitation, intentions, and autism. *Developmental Science, 5*(1), 30–32.

Guerinii, P., Lyon, G., Barthelemy, C., Sostak, E., Chevrollier, V., Garreauit, & Lelord, G. B. . . . NAME. (1996). Neuropathological study of a case of autistic syndrome with severe mental retardation. *Developmental Medicine & Child Neurology*, 38(3), 203–211.

Hadjikhani, N., Joseph, R.M., Snyder, J., & Tager-Flusberg, H. (2006). Anatomical differences in the mirror neuron system and social cognition network in autism. *Cerebral Cortex*, 16(9), 1276–1282.

Hammes, J.G.W., & Langdell, T. (1981). Precursors of symbol formation and childhood autism. *Journal of Autism and Developmental Disorders*, 11(3), 331–346.

Happé, F., Ronald, A., & Plomin, R. (2006). Time to give up on a single explanation for autism. *Nature Neuroscience*, 9(10), 1218–1220.

Hari, R., Forss, N., Avikainen, S., Kirveskari, E., Salenius, S., & Rizzolatti, G. (1998) Activation of human primary motor cortex during action observation: A neuromagnetic study. *Proceedings of the National Academy of Sciences USA*, 95, 15061–15065.

Hari, R., & Nishitani, N. (2004). From viewing of movement to imitation and understanding of other persons' acts: MEG studies of the human mirror-neuron system. In N. Kanwisher & J. Duncan (Eds.), *Functional neuroimaging of visual cognition. Attention and performance XX* (pp. 463–479). Oxford: Oxford University Press.

Hatfield, E., Cacioppo, J. T., & Rapson, R. L. (1994). *Emotional contagion*. New York: Cambridge University Press.

Heimann, M. (1998). Imitation in neonates, in older infants and in children with autism: Feedback to theory. In S. Braten (Ed.), *Intersubjective communication and emotion in early ontogeny* (pp. 89–104). Cambridge: Cambridge University Press.

Heimann, M. (2002). Notes on individual differences and the assumed elusiveness of neonatal imitation. In A.N. Meltzoff & W. Prinz (Eds.), *The imitative mind: Development, evolution, and brain bases* (pp. 74–84). Cambridge: Cambridge University Press.Add Helt Chapter 8 from this book????.

Henderson, S.E., & Sugden, D. (1992). *The movement assessment battery for children*. London: The Psychological Corporation.

Hepburn, S.L., & Stone, W.L. (2006). Longitudinal research on motor imitation in autism. In S.J. Rogers & J.H.G. Williams (Eds.), *Imitation and the social mind: Autism and typical development* (pp. XX–XX310–329). New York: Guilford.

Hertzig, M.E., Snow, M.E., & Sherman, M. (1989). Affect and cognition in autism. *Child and Adolescent Psychiatry*, 28(2), 195–199.

Hobson, J.A., & Hobson, R.P. (2007). Identification: The missing link between joint attention and imitation? *Development and Psychopathology*, 19, 411–431.

Hobson, R.P. (1986). The autistic child's appraisal of expressions of emotion. *Journal of Child Psychology and Psychiatry*, 27, 321–342.

Hobson, R.P. (1995). Apprehending attitudes and actions: Separable abilities in early development? *Development and Psychopathology*, 7, 171–182.

Hobson, R.P., & Lee, A. (1999). Imitation and identification in autism. *Journal of Child Psychology and Psychiatry*, 40, 649–660.

Hurley, S. (2008). The shared circuits model (SCM): How control, mirroring, and simulation can enable imitation, deliberation, and mindreading. *Behavioral and Brain Sciences*, 31, 1–22.

Hurley, S., & Chater, N. (2005). *Perspectives on imitation: From neuroscience to social science*. Cambridge, MA: MIT Press.

Hurley, S.L., & Noe, A. (2003). Neural plasticity and consciousness. *Biological Philosophy*, 18, 131–168.

Iacoboni, M. (2005). Understanding others: Imitation, language, empathy. In S. Hurley & N. Chater (Eds.), *Perspectives on imitation: From neuroscience to social science* (pp. XX–XX77–100). Cambridge, MA: MIT Press.

Iacoboni, M. (2008). The role of premotor cortex in speech perception: Evidence from fMRI and rTMS. *Journal of Physiology-Paris*, 102(1-3), 31–34.

Iacoboni, M., & Dapretto, M. (2006) The mirror neuron system and the consequences of its dysfunction. *Nature Reviews Neuroscience*, 7, 942–951.

Iacoboni, M., Koski, L., Brass, M., Bekkering, H., Woods, R.P., Dubeau, M.-C., Mazziotta, J.C., & Rizzolatti, G. (2001). Re-afferent copies of imitated actions in the right superior temporal cortex. *Proceedings of the National Academy of Science USA*, 98, 13995–13999.

Iacoboni, M., Woods, R.P., Brass, M., Bekkering, H., Mazziotta, J.C., & Rizzolatti, G. (1999). Cortical mechanisms of human imitation. *Science*, 286, 2526–2528.

Ingersoll, B., & Schreibman, L. (2006). Teaching reciprocal imitation skills to young children with autism using a naturalistic behavioral approach: Effects on language, pretend play, and joint attention. *Journal of Autism and Developmental Disorders*, 36, 487–505.

Jones, V., & Prior, M. (1985). Motor imitation abilities and neurological signs in autistic children. *Journal of Autism and Developmental Disorders*, 15(1), 37–46.

Kasari, C., Paparella, T., Freeman, S., & Jahromi, L.B. (2008). Language outcome in autism: Randomized comparison of joint attention and play interventions. *Journal of Consulting and Clinical Psychology*, 76(1), 125–137.

Kiraly, I. (2009). The effect of the model's presence and of negative evidence on infants' selective imitation. *Journal of Experimental Child Psychology*, 102, 14–25.

Klin, A. (2008). Three things to remember if you are a functional magnetic resonance imaging researcher of face processing in autism spectrum disorders. *Biological Psychiatry, 64*(7), 549–551.

Klin, A., Jones, W., Schultz, R., & Volkmar, F. (2003). The enactive mind, or from actions to cognition: Lessons from autism. *Philosophical Transactions Royal Society of London B Biological Sciences, 358*(1430), 345–360.

Kohler, E., Keysers, C., Umiltà, M.A., Fogassi, L., Gallese, V., & Rizzolatti, G. (2002). Hearing sounds, understanding actions: Action representation in mirror neurons. *Science, 297,* 846–848.

Koski, L., Wohschlager, A., Bekkering, H., Woods, R.P., Dubeau, M.C., Mazziotta, J.C., & Iacoboni, M. (2002). Modulation of motor and premotor activity during imitation of target-directed actions. *Cerebral Cortex, 12*(8), 847–855.

Lepage, J.F., & Theoret, H. (2006). EEG evidence for the presence of an action observation-execution matching system in children. *European Journal of Neuroscience, 23*(9), 2505–2510.

Lovaas, O.I. (1987). Behavioral treatment and normal educational and intellectual functioning in young autistic children. *Journal of Consulting and Clinical Psychology, 55*(1), 3–9.

Manjiviona, J., & Prior, M. (1995). Comparison of Asperger syndrome and high-functioning autistic children on a test of motor impairment. *Journal of Autism and Developmental Disorders, 25*(1), 23–39.

Martineau, J., Cochin, S., Magne, R., & Barthelemy, C. (2008). Impaired cortical activity in autistic children: Is the mirror neuron system involved? *International Journal of Psychophysiology, 68*(1), 35–40.

Masur, E.F., & Eichorst, D.L. (2002). Infants' spontaneous imitation of novel versus familiar words: Relations to observational and maternal report measures of their lexicons. *Merrill-Palmer Quarterly, 48.*4(202), 405–426.

McDonough, L., Stahmer, A., Schreibman, L., & Thompson, S.J. (1997). Deficits, delays, and distractions: An evaluation of symbolic play and memory in children with autism. *Development and Psychopathology, 9*(1), 17–41.

McDuffie, A., Yoder, P., & Stone, W. (2005). Prelinguistic predictors of vocabulary in young children with autism spectrum disorders. *Journal of Speech, Language, and Hearing Research, 48,* 1080–1097.

McIntosh, D.N. (1996). Facial feedback hypothesis: Evidence, implications, and directions. *Motivation and Emotion, 20,* 121–147.

McIntosh, D.N., Reichmann-Decker, A., Winkielman, P., & Wilbarger, J.L. (2006). Title of articleWhen the social mirror breaks: Deficits in automatic, but not voluntary, mimicry of emotional facial expressions in autism. *Developmental Science, 9*(3), 295–302.

Meltzoff, A. (1985). The roots of social and cognitive development: Models of man's original nature. In T. M. Field & N. Fox (Eds.), *Social perception in infants* (pp. 1–30). New Jersey: Able.

Meltzoff, A. (2005). Imitation and other minds: The "like me" hypothesis. In S. Hurley & N. Chater (Eds.), *Perspectives on imitation: From neuroscience to social science,* vol. 2 (pp. XX–XX55–78). Cambridge, MA: MIT Press.

Meltzoff, A., & Moore, M. (1977). Imitation of facial and manual gestures by human neonates. *Science, 198,* 75–78.

Meltzoff, A.N. (1990). Foundations for developing a concept of self: The role of imitation in relating self to other and the value of social mirroring, social modeling, and self practice in infancy. The self in transition: Infancy to childhood. In D. Cicchetti & M. Beeghly (Eds.), *The self in transition: Infancy to childhood. The John D. and Catherine T. MacArthur foundation series on mental health and development* (pp. 139–164). Chicago: University of Chicago Press.

Meltzoff, A.N. (1995). What infant memory tells us about infantile amnesia: Long-term recall and deferred imitation. *Journal of Experimental Child Psychology, 59*(3), 497–515.

Merleau-Ponty, M. (1945). *The phenomenology of perception (C. Smith, Trans.).* London: Routledge & Kegan Paul.

Morgan, S.B., Cutrer, P.S., Coplin, J.W., & Rodrigue, J.R. (1989). Do autistic children differ from retarded and normal children in Piagetian sensorimotor functioning? *Journal of Child Psychology and Psychiatry, 30*(6), 857–864.

Morton, J., & Johnson, M.H. (1991). CONSPEC and CONLERN: A two-process theory of infant face recognition. *Psychological Review, 98*(2), 164–181.

Mundy, P., & Burnette, C. (2005). Joint attention and neurodevelopment. In F. Volkmar, A. Klin, & R. Paul (Eds.), *Handbook of autism and pervasive developmental disorders,* Vol. 3 (pp. 650–681). Hoboken, NJ: John Wiley.

Mundy, P., & Neal, R.A. (2001). Neural plasticity, joint attention, and a transactional social-orienting model of autism. In L.M. Glidden (Ed.), *International review of research in mental retardation* (pp. 139–168). San Diego, CA: Academic Press.

Nehaniv, C., & Dautenhahn, K. (2002). The correspondence problem. In K. Dautenhahn & C. Nehaniv (Eds.), *Imitation in animals and artifacts* (pp. 41–62). Cambridge, MA: MIT Press.

Niedenthal, P.M., Barsalou, L.W., Winkielman, P., Krauth-Gruber, S., & Ric, F. (2005). Embodiment in attitudes, social perception, and emotion. *Personality and Social Psychology Review, 9*(3), 184–211.

Nishitani, N., Avikaienen, S., & Hari, R. (2004). Abnormal imitation-related cortical activation sequences in Asperger's disorder. *Annals of Neurology, 55*(4), 558–562.

Noy, L., Rumiati, R.I., & Flash, T. (2008). Simple movement imitation: Are kinematic features sufficient to map perceptions into actions? *Brain and Cognition, 69*(2), 360–368.

Oberman, L.M., Hubbard, E.M., McCleery, J.P., Altschuler, E.L., Ramachandran, V.S., & Pineda, J.A. (2005). EEG evidence for mirror neuron dysfunction in autism spectrum disorders. *Cognitive Brain Research, 24*(2), 190–198.

Oberman, L.M., Ramachandran, V.S., & Pineda, J.A. (2008). Modulation of mu suppression in children with autism spectrum disorders in response to familiar or unfamiliar stimuli: The mirror neuron hypothesis. *Neuropsychologia, 46*(5), 1558–1565.

Ohta, M. (1987). Cognitive disorders of infantile autism: A study employing the WISC, spatial relationships, conceptualization, and gestural imitation. *Journal of Autism and Developmental Disorders, 17*, 45–62.

Orgs, G., Dombrowski, J.H., Heil, M., & Jansen-Osmann, P. (2008). Expertise in dance modulates alpha/beta event-related desynchronization during action observation. *European Journal of Neuroscience, 27*(12), 3380–3384.

Pelphrey, K.A., Adolphs, R., & Morris, J.P. (2004). Neuroanatomical substrates of social cognition dysfunction in autism. *Mental Retardation and Developmental Disabilities Research Reviews, 10*, 259–271.

Pelphrey, K.A., Morris, J.P., & McCarthy, G. (2005). Neural basis of eye gaze processing deficits in autism. *Brain, 128*, 1038–1048.

Pelphrey, K.A., Sasson, N.J., Reznick, S., Paul, G., Goldman, B.D., & Piven, J. (2002). Visual scanning of faces in autism. *Journal of Autism and Developmental Disorders, 32*(4), 249–261.

Pelphrey, K., Singerman, J.D., Allison, T., & McCarthy, G. (2003). Brain activation evoked by perception of gaze shifts: The influence of context. *Neuropsychologia, 41*(2), 156–170.

Piaget, O. J. (1962). *Play, dreams, and imitation in childhood*. New York: Norton.

Pennington, B.F.J. (2009). How neuropsychology informs our understanding of developmental disorders. *Journal of Child Psychology and Psychiatry, 50*(1-2), 72–78.

Piaget, O.J. (1962). *Play, dreams, and imitation in childhood*. New York: Norton.

Pierno, A.C., Becchio, C., Turella, L., Tubaldi, F., & Castiello, U. (2008). Observing social interactions: The effect of gaze. *Society for Neuroscience, 3*(1), 51–59.

Press, C., Bird, G., Walsh, E., & Heyes, C. (2008). Automatic imitation of intransitive actions. *Brain and Cognition, 67*, 44–50.

Rizzolatti, G. (2005). The mirror neuron system and imitation. In S. Hurley & N. Chater (Eds.), *Perspectives on imitation: From neuroscience to social science*, vol. 1 (pp. 55–76). Cambridge, MA: MIT Press.

Rizzolatti, G., & Arbib, M. (1998) Language within our grasp. *Trends in Neurosciences, 21*, 188–194.

Rizzolatti, G., & Craighero, L. (2004). The mirror-neuron system. *Annual Review of Neuroscience, 27*, 169–192.

Rizzolatti, G., Fadiga, L., Gallese, V., & Fogassi, L. (1995). Premotor cortex and the recognition of motor actions. *Cognitive Brain Research, 3*, 131–141.

Rizzolatti, G., Fogassi, L., & Gallese, V. (2002). Motor and cognitive functions of the ventral premotor cortex. *Current Opinion in Neurobiology, 12*(2), 149–154.

Rogers, S.J. (1999). Intervention for young children with autism: From research to practice. *Infants and Young Children, 12*(2), 1–16.

Rogers, S.J., Bennetto, L., McEvoy, R., & Pennington, B.F. (1996). Imitation and pantomime in high functioning adolescents with autism spectrum disorders. *Child Development, 67*, 2060–2073.

Rogers, S.J., Cook, I., & Meryl, A. (2005). Imitation and play in autism. In F. Volkmar, R. Paul, A. Klin, & D. Cohen (Eds.), *Handbook of autism and pervasive developmental disorders*, 3rd edition (pp. 382–405). New York: Wiley.

Rogers, S.J., & Dawson, G. (2010). *Early Start Denver Model for young children with autism: Promoting language, learning and engagement. Play and engagement in early autism: The Early Start Denver Model*. New York: Guilford.

Rogers, S.J., & Pennington, B.F. (1991). A theoretical approach to the deficits in infantile autism. *Development and Psychopathology, 3*, 137–162.

Rogers, S.J., Stackhouse, T., Hepburn, S.L., & Wehner, E.A. (2003). Imitation performance in toddlers with autism and those with other developmental disorders. *Journal of Child Psychology and Psychiatry, 44*(5), 763–781.

Rogers, S.J., & Williams, J.H.G. (2006). Imitation in autism. In S.J. Rogers & J.H.G. Williams (Eds.), *Imitation and the social mind: Autism and typical development*. New York: Guilford Press.

Rogers, S.J., Young, G.S., Cook, I., Giolzetti, A., & Ozonoff, S. (2010). Imitating actions on objects in early-onset and regressive autism: Effects and implications of task characteristics on performance. *Development and Psychopathology, 22*, 71–85.

Rogoff, B., Mistry, J., Goncu, A., & Mosier, C. (1993). Guided participation in cultural activity by toddlers and caregivers. *Monographs of the SRCD, 58*(1), 1–161.

Rothi, L.J.G., Ochipa, C., & Heilman, K.M. (1991). A cognitive neuropsychological model of limb praxis. *Cognitive Neuropsychology, 8*, 443–458.

Rumiati, R.I., Weiss, P.H., Tessari, A., Assmus, A., Zilles, K., Herzog, H., & Fink, G.R. (2005). Common and differential neural mechanisms supporting imitation of meaningful and meaningless actions. *Journal of Cognitive Neuroscience, 17*, 1420–1431.

Scambler, D.J., Hepburn, S., Rutherford, M.D., Wehner, E.A., & Rogers, S.J. (2007). Emotional responsivity in children with autism, children with other developmental disabilities, and children with typical development. *Journal of Autism and Developmental Disorders, 37*(3), 553–563.

Scherf, K.S., Behrmann, M., Minshew, N., & Luna, B. (2008). Atypical development of face and greeble recognition in autism. *Journal of Child Psychology and Psychiatry, 49*(8), 838–847.

Schulz, R., Chawarska, K., & Volkmar, F. (2006). The social brain in autism: Perspectives from neuropsychology and neuroimaging. In S.O. Moldin & J.L.R. Rubinstein (Eds.), *Understanding autism: From basic neuroscience to treatment* (pp. XX–XX323–348). Boca Raton, FL: CRC Press.

Senju, A., & Csibra, G. (2008). Gaze following in human infants depends on communicative signals. *Current Biology, 18*(9), 668–671.

Sigman, M., & Ungerer, J. (1984). Cognitive and language skills in autistic, mentally retarded, and normal children. *Developmental Psychology, 20,* 293–302.

Smith, I.M., & Bryson, S.E. (1994). Imitation and action in autism: A critical review. *Psychological Bulletin, 116*(2), 259–273.

Smith, I.M., & Bryson, S.E. (1998). Gesture imitation in autism I: Nonsymbolic postures and sequences. *Cognitive Neuropsychology, 15,* 747–770.

Smith, T., Groen, A.D., & Wynn, J.W. (2000). Randomized trial of intensive early intervention for children with pervasive developmental disorder. *American Journal on Mental Retardation, 105*(4), 269–285.

Southgate, V., Csibra, G., Kaufman, J., & Johnson, M. H. (2008). Distinct processing of objects and faces in the infant brain. *Journal of Cognitive Neuroscience, 20*(4), 741–749.

Southgate, V., Johnson, M.H., & Csibra, G. (2008). Infants attribute goals even to biomechanically impossible actions. *Cognition, 107*(3), 1059–1069.

Speer, L.L., Cook, A.E., McMahon, W.M., & Clark, E. (2007). Face processing in children with autism. *Autism, 11*(3), 265–277.

Sperber, D., & Wilson, D. (1995). *Relevance: Communication and cognition.* Oxford: Blackwell.

Stern, D. (1985). *The interpersonal world of the infant.* New York: Basic Books.

Stone, W.L., Ousley, O.Y., & Littleford, C.D. (1997). Motor imitation in young children with autism: What's the object? *Journal of Abnormal Child Psychology, 25,* 475–485.

Strafella, A.P., & Paus, T. (2000). Modulation of cortical excitability during action observation: A transcranial magnetic stimulation study. *NeuroReport, 11*(10), 2289–2292.

Strid, K., Tjus, T., Smith, L., Meltzoff, A.N., & Heimann, M. (2006). Infant recall memory and communication predicts later cognitive development. *Infant Behavior and Development, 29*(4), 545–553.

Tessari, A., Canessa, N., Ukmar, M., & Rumiati, R.I. (2007). Neuropsychological evidence for a strategic control of multiple routes in imitation. *Brain, X,* XX–XX 139(4), 1111–1126. doi:10.1093/brain/awm003.

Tessari, A., & Rumiati, R. I. (2004). The strategic control of multiple routes in imitation of actions. *Journal of Experimental Psychology: Human Perception and Performance, 30*(6), 1107–1116.

Tomasello, M. (1999). *The cultural origins of human cognition.* Cambridge, MA: Harvard University Press.

Tomasello, M., & Carpenter, M. (2005). The emergence of social cognition in three young chimpanzees. *Monographs of the Society for Research in Child Development, 70*(1), 1–136.

Tomasello, M., Kruger, A.C., & Ratner, H.H. (1993). Cultural learning. *Behavioral and Brain Sciences, 16,* 495–552.

Turati, C., Macchi Cassia, V., Simion, F., & Leo, I. (2006). Newborns' face recognition: Role of inner and outer facial features. *Child Development, 77*(2), 297–311.

Ungerer, J.A., & Sigman, M. (1987). Categorization skills and receptive language development in autistic children. *Journal of Autism and Developmental Disorders, 17*(1), 3–16.

Uzgiris, I. (1981). Two functions of imitation during infancy. *International Journal of Behavioral Development, 4,* 1–17.

Uzgiris, I. (1999). Imitation as activity: Its developmental aspects. In J. Nadel & G. Butterworth (Eds.), *Imitation in infancy* (pp. 186–206). Cambridge: Cambridge University Press.

Vanvuchelen, M., Roeyers, H., & DeWeerdt, W. (2007). Nature of motor imitation problems in school-aged males with autism: How congruent are the error types? *Developmental Medicine & Child Neurology, 49,* 6–12.

Villalobos, M.E., Mizuno, A., Dahl, B.C., Kemmotsu, N., & Muller, R.A. (2005). Reduced functional connectivity between V1 and inferior frontal cortex associated with visuomotor performance in autism. *Neuroimage, 25,* 916–925.

Vivanti, G., Nadig, A., Ozonoff, S., & Rogers, S.J. (2008). What do children with autism attend to during imitation tasks? *Journal of Experimental Child Psychology, 101*(3), 186–205.

Vivanti, G., McCormick, C., Young, G., Abucayan, F., Hatt, N., Nadig, A., Ozonoff, S., & Rogers, S.J. (under review) Mechanisms of action understanding in autism.

Whiten, A. (2002). Imitation of sequential and hierarchical structure in action: Experimental studies with children and chimpanzees. In K. Dautenham & C. Nehaniv (Eds.), *Imitation in animals and artifacts* (pp. 191–209). Cambridge, MA: MIT Press.

Williams, J.H.G., Waiter, G.D., Perra, O., Perrett, D.L., & Whiten, A. (2005). An fMRI study of joint attention experience. *NeuroImage, 25*(1), 133–140.

Williams, J.H.G., Whiten, A., & Singh, T. (2004). A systematic review of action imitation in autistic spectrum disorder. *Journal of Autism and Developmental Disorders, 34*(3), 285–299.

Williams, J.H.G., Whiten, A., Suddendorf, T., & Perrett, D.I. (2001). Imitation, mirror neurons and autism. *Neuroscience and Biobehavioral Reviews*, *25*, 287–295.

Young, G.S., Rogers, S. J., Hutman, T., Ozonoff, S., Rozga, A., & Sigman, M. (in review). Imitation in autism from 12 to 24 months: A longitudinal study using a random coefficient multilevel Rasch measurement model.

Zwaigenbaum, L., Bryson, S., Rogers, T., Roberts, W., Brian, J., & Szatmari, P. (2005). Behavioral manifestations of autism in the first year of life. *International Journal of Developmental Neuroscience*, *23*, 143–152.

Chapter 14

Implicit Learning in ASD

Inge-Marie Eigsti and Jessica Mayo

Kanner's (1943) earliest descriptions of what came to be known as "autistic disorder" were characterized by a puzzling contradiction: the individuals he described were often exceptionally good at acquiring certain classes of information—such as stretches of dialogue from favorite cartoons, or multiple individuals' birthdays—but they had difficulty in learning other kinds of information, such as some complex motor sequences (e.g., tying one's shoes) or understanding implications that are not explicitly spelled out. More generally, individuals with autism often have the ability to master material that they find interesting and that has a flat "profile"—that is, facts that are organized with only a limited hierarchical structure (e.g., license plate numbers for a series of cars). On the other hand, these same individuals often struggle to extract hierarchical patterned information from a series of situations; that is, they often have difficulty generalizing from multiple instances of a given situation (Hwang & Hughes, 2000; Lovaas, Koegel, Simmons, & Long, 1973; Lovaas & Smith, 1989;

Ozonoff & Miller, 1995) These distinct kinds of learning have been described as forming the basis of explicit learning (for a series of facts or separate pieces of information), and implicit learning (for the extraction of underlying regularities or patterns), respectively.

The ability to learn and respond to systematicity or regularity in one's environment, or to implicitly learn, is thought to relate to a variety of high-level skills, including language and motor skills (Perruchet & Pacton, 2006) and social interaction (Lieberman, 2000). Given that these domains are so importantly involved in the presentation of autism spectrum disorders (ASD), a variety of researchers have explored the possibility that implicit learning impairments might play a central role in the symptoms of this disorder.

The focus of this chapter is to review implicit learning abilities in ASD, with a focus on the apparent contradiction between the *clinical impressions of impaired implicit learning* abilities, and *research findings suggesting largely intact implicit learning*. Of note, *learning* and *memory* processes are closely intertwined.

The former is defined as a process that modifies a subsequent behavior, whereas the latter refers to the retrieval of past experiences. Memory could be thought of as secondary to learning, because it is, in essence, the stored representation of a learning process. As such, this chapter will review primarily research on implicit learning, rather than implicit memory. In addition, the terms "implicit" and "explicit" map closely onto "procedural" and "declarative" (Cohen & Squire, 1980) in the research literature; we hew to the former set for the sake of clarity.

NEURAL FOUNDATIONS OF
IMPLICIT LEARNING

A history of early studies described two distinct systems in the human brain (Claparede, 1951; Korsakoff, 1889; as reviewed in Renner et al., 2000). These data were based on animal models, developmental studies, and lesion studies, especially findings of spared implicit learning in cases of dense amnesia (Gabrieli et al., 1994). These early suggestions have been supported by more recent studies of patients with Parkinson's disease (Kim et al., 2004), Tourette's syndrome (Marsh et al., 2004), and brain imaging studies (Forkstam & Petersson, 2005).

Implicit learning appears to involve two general sets of brain areas (Conway & Pisoni, 2008), based on findings from functional brain imaging (fMRI) studies of various implicit learning tasks. First, learning appears to activate modality-specific regions involved in stimulus recognition and task performance. For example, the auditory cortex mediates the learning of tone sequences (Gottselig, Brandeis, Hofer-Tinguely, Borbely, & Achermann, 2004), whereas occipital (visual) cortex mediates the learning of visual sequences (Lieberman, Chang, Chiao, Bookheimer, & Knowlton, 2004). Second, implicit learning appears to involve a set of somewhat modality-independent regions; across a wide variety of distinct tasks and modalities, learning recruits frontal cortical areas (prefrontal cortex, premotor cortex, supplementary motor areas) areas, often including Broca's area (Forkstam, Hagoort, Fernandez, Ingvar, & Petersson, 2006), as well as subcortical areas (basal ganglia, particularly the striatum, which is comprised of the caudate and putamen; see review in Bapi, Pammi, Miyapuram, & Ahmed, 2005). The basal ganglia connect to multiple cortical sites including motor cortex, premotor cortex, and prefrontal cortex. Thus, sequence learning relies heavily on a complex dynamic interplay of multiple corticostriatal loops (Seger, 2006), with specific interactions being dependent in part on task demands. Finally, other brain regions, including the parietal cortex (Menghini, Hagberg, Caltagirone, Petrosini, & Vicari, 2006) and the cerebellum (Desmond & Fiez, 1998), are also implicated in implicit learning.

Some regions relevant to implicit learning also exhibit anatomical differences in ASD. Research using PET has found reduced F-fluorodopa activity in the anterior medial prefrontal cortex, compared with the occipital cortex, in ASD (Ernst, Zametkin, Matochik, Pascualvaca, & Cohen, 1997). This finding of decreased dopaminergic function in the prefrontal cortex could also be related to implicit learning abilities, as the dopamine system is critical throughout a large network of brain areas, including the frontal lobes and related structures of the basal ganglia, medial-temporal lobs, and thalamic nuclei. Some of these regions (the basal ganglia in particular) are centrally involved in implicit learning processes, as reviewed above.

Furthermore, many forms of implicit learning involve the acquisition of motor skills (see Chapter 10). One brain structure that is central to the production and planning of motor movements is the cerebellum. In turn, one of the most consistent neuroanatomical findings in ASD involves changes in the size of structures within the cerebellum, and specifically, the posterior fossa area (the cerebellum, pons, and fourth ventricle). Some reports suggest decreased cerebellar volume as well as a smaller ratio of cerebellum to posterior fossa and cerebellum to total brain (Gaffney, Kuperman, Tsai, Minchin, & Hassanein, 1987); smaller area of pons (Gaffney, Kuperman, Tsai, & Minchin, 1988); smaller ratio of cerebellar lobules VI-VII to I-V (Courchesne, Yeung-Courchesne, Press, Hesselink, & Jernigan, 1988); and a smaller volume of cerebellar hemispheres (Murakami, Courchesne, Press, Yeung-Courchesne, & Hesselink, 1989). We should note that these findings of decreased cerebellar volume have not always been replicated (Garber & Ritvo, 1992; Holttum, Minshew, Sanders, & Phillips, 1992), and some data suggest that cerebellar differences may be secondary to IQ differences, rather than specific to autism (Piven, Saliba, Bailey, & Arndt, 1997). Neuropathology studies have shown a paucity of cerebellar Purkinje cells (Bailey et al., 1998).

Although sample sizes are small and based on post-mortem samples, data indicate that the neurons of the deep cerebellar nuclei and the inferior olive are atypical in autism. Thus, a number of approaches suggest that cerebellar anomalies play a role in the disorder, and could potentially be relevant to implicit motor learning abilities.

Given these neurobiological differences, one would expect differences in behavioral performance of tasks that centrally involve the cerebellum. Lesion studies of animals and humans have demonstrated that the cerebellum is involved in motor learning tasks (Daum et al., 1993). One such task is a simple test of classical conditioning of the eyeblink response, in which a participant hears a short tone just before a puff of air is delivered to the eye. The puff elicits a reflexive automatic eye blink. Learning has occurred when the tone also elicits the eyeblink (signifying a learned association between the tone and then the puff). This form of learning has been shown to occur during sleep for newborn infants, who appear to actively process and remember relationships between events during sleep (Fifer et al., 2010). Eyeblink conditioning was examined in 11 children with ASD 6–17 years old, with IQ in the average range, compared to 17 typically developing (TD) children matched on age, gender and performance IQ (Sears, Finn, & Steinmetz, 1994). Results showed that, while the TD group learned effectively, the ASD group had significant differences in timing of the blink. While they did learn the association between the puff and the tone, such that they blinked when the tone was presented, the blink occurred at a highly maladaptive point, such that their eyes were maximally open when the puff occurred. Differences in learning within such a simple conditioning paradigm might in turn lead to impaired implicit learning abilities for more complex procedures.

A more recent study argues against the suggestion that children with ASD show generalized implicit learning deficits for cerebellum-mediated processes. Mostofsky and colleagues had a small group of children with high-functioning autism[1] (HFA; $n = 8$) and TD controls ($n = 8$) perform an adaptive catching task, in which the weight of a ball changed across trials of catching (Mostofsky, Bunoski, Morton, Goldberg, & Bastian, 2004). Participants adapted to the changing weight of the ball, and implicit learning of weight change was measured by the displacement of participants' catching arm. Findings indicated no group differences. This might suggest that other implicit tasks (e.g., eyeblink conditioning) tap a different region of the cerebellum than that recruited for this motor adaptation task, or that implicit-learning deficits are present only for tasks with a significant demand for visually guided learning. Wodka and Mostofsky, in Chapter 10, argued that performance on this catching task reflects motor *adaptation* as opposed to learning of a *sequence* (a central component of implicit learning, discussed in detail below).

Another factor that may resolve this inconsistency is the presence of timing abnormalities in ASD that recruit non-cerebellar systems. One study demonstrated specific deficits in the timing of responses in ASD (D'Cruz et al., 2009). Participants with HFA ($n = 52$) and TD controls ($n = 54$), ages 8–52 years, matched on gender and age, performed a predictive saccade task known to draw on a frontostriatal brain system. Subjects tracked visual targets that alternated between two locations at a fixed time interval; anticipatory (faster) RT for the next target was the measure of learning. Results demonstrated no differences in *overall* reduction in response latencies for the ASD group; however, members of the ASD group were faster with *rightward* predictive and anticipatory responses. These data suggested that there may be an acceleration of temporal coding in a left hemisphere frontostriatal system involved in the timing of internally generated motor response sequences. These data are consistent with neuroanatomical findings of left hemisphere abnormalities in ASD (Rinehart, Bradshaw, Brereton, & Tonge, 2002), as well as of atypical lateralization of many cognitive processes in autism (Knaus et al., 2010).

STUDIES OF IMPLICIT VISUO-MOTOR LEARNING

One of the most well-studied forms of implicit learning involves the acquisition of novel motor skills. Also termed *procedural learning*, this kind of motor learning involves fronto-striatal and cerebellar circuits. Individuals with impairments in these brain regions typically have difficulty in learning new patterned

---

1. High functioning autism (HFA) is defined by individuals with an ASD diagnosis and a measured IQ score in the average range (above 80), unless otherwise noted.

movements, such as riding a bicycle or dancing. For example, motor learning is impaired in people with prefrontal lesions (Gomez Beldarrain, Grafman, Pascual-Leone, & Garcia-Monco, 1999) and those with Parkinson's disease (Sommer, Grafman, Clark, & Hallett, 1999).

The serial reaction time (SRT) test has been used extensively as a measure of implicit motor learning (Thomas & Nelson, 2001). In a typical version of this task, participants sit in front of a computer screen which has displaying a horizontal row of four squares. The squares serve as possible locations for a target stimulus (e.g., picture of a dog). The target appears at intervals in each of the locations; the specific location is predicted by a sequence, often 10 items in length (e.g., the target appears at the leftmost or first square, then the third, then the fourth, then the second, etc.). The participant is asked to either tap the target on a touch screen, or to press a numbered button associated with that target. With a sequence of 10 items, it is difficult for participants to become consciously aware that a sequence is reliably predicting where the target will appear. However, reaction times become reliably faster for participants who learn the sequence. It is possible to demonstrate that the change in RT is due to learning, rather than simple motor rehearsal of the response action, because when the sequence is disrupted and the target appears in randomly selected locations, RTs are slowed.

Several researchers have used the SRT paradigm to explore implicit learning skills in ASD. Findings across studies have suggested varying degrees of implicit learning deficits among individuals with ASD. The first such study explored performance on a standard 10-item SRT task in a group of 11 children with HFA, ages 8–16, compared to a group of 17 TD participants matched for age (Mostofsky, Goldberg, Landa, & Denckla, 2000). While IQs for both groups were in the same range, they were not explicitly matched on IQ. Results showed that HFA group showed significantly less change in RT than the TD control group, suggesting a lack of implicit learning on this SRT task, and the authors took this finding as an indication that implicit learning impairments could contribute to the core symptom presentation in ASD.

The researchers followed up on this result using a different visuomotor sequence learning task to demonstrate ASD-specific differences that were less likely to reflect simple motor impairments (Gidley Larson

& Mostofsky, 2008). Participants with ASD ($n = 52$), ADHD ($n = 39$) and TD ($n = 62$), matched on age, all of whom had Full Scale IQs over 70, performed two rotary pursuit tasks in which they were asked to use a "wand" to track a target on a spinning disk (an apparatus that resembles an old-school LP record player). The ASD group accrued significantly less time on target than other groups in one version of the task, and showed less change in performance (improvement) over time than the comparison groups, suggesting that they had poorer implicit learning for this motor task. Additionally, when presented with a novel (i.e., interference) pattern, the ASD group showed a decreased interference effect as compared to the other two groups. Findings were taken to suggest that the ASD group may have been using an atypical strategy to approach the task. Unlike the other two groups, the ASD group might have been relying more heavily on *explicit learning of the task*—that is, explicit memorization of the movement pattern—rather than *implicit learning*; this would lead to a decreased interference effect as seen for the ASD group. Reliance on explicit memorization of the movement pattern rather than implicit learning of the task may explain the difficulty the ASD group exhibited.

Another group has attempted to replicate the initial findings of impaired implicit motor learning (Mostofsky et al., 2000), addressing the possibility that the challenging 10-item sequence may have been the sole source of group differences (Gordon & Stark, 2007). A group of seven low-functioning children with ASD (IQs ranging from <50 – 108) was compared with a group of nine TD children, matched on age. Of note, the ASD group included two children aged six years, while the youngest TD participant was aged nine years. In their first study, ASD participants completed an 8-item SRT task during six testing sessions (usually one session/week for six weeks). The task comprised 48 trials (eight-item sequence, repeated six times) delivered across 12 blocks. TD participants completed the same 48-trial task in a single testing session. Although the TD group demonstrated significant sequence learning after a single session, the ASD group showed only marginal evidence of learning, even after the six training sessions, and learning was observed only at the group (and not an individual) level. In a second SRT experiment, involving many of the same children (nine in total), a shorter, 4-item sequence was tested. Again, ASD participants completed the SRT task for six sessions; TD participants completed only a single testing session. As in the first study, TD children learned after a single session. The ASD group did show evidence of learning when the six sessions were averaged together. While the authors concluded that sensitivity to sequence detection is possible for children with ASD given sufficient exposure, the data also suggest significant ASD-specific impairments on sequence learning tasks. This study is one of only two in total, to our knowledge, including lower-functioning individuals.

Several subsequent studies found intact implicit learning in groups of children with ASD. Barnes and colleagues (2008) found equivalent performance on two tests of implicit learning in 14 participants with HFA and Asperger's disorder, ages 8 to 14, compared to 14 TD participants who were matched for gender, age and IQ. First, participants completed a modified SRT task, in which participants saw a row of three target locations (here denoted A, B, and C), and were exposed to a 6-item sequence; the sequence consisted of A-r-C-r-B-r, where "r" denotes a random location interposed between the fixed locations. In a second study of implicit learning, participants were asked to locate a cue in a complex visual pattern. Both studies found no group differences, suggesting intact implicit learning of temporal sequences and of spatial context. Finally, a case study of an adult with autism and savant skills (calendrical calculation, drawing) found no impairments in learning in an SRT task compared to seven adult TD control participants (Wallace, Happé & Giedd, 2009).

Functional imaging studies have demonstrated subtle abnormalities in neural activation during implicit learning tasks in individuals with ASD. In a study of individuals with ASD and TD ($n = 8$ per group) matched on gender, both groups demonstrated similar rates of implicit learning on a 6-item SRT visuomotor sequence task based on their behavioral data (Muller et al., 2003). Interestingly, neural activation differed between groups despite their similar behavioral performance. Although both groups had activation of the bilateral premotor cortex, superior parietal cortex, and occipital cortex, the ASD group had *less* activation of superior parietal cortex and *more* activation of prefrontal cortex and posterior parietal areas. Further, the ASD group had significantly more scattered activation in these areas. These data suggest that the neural regions typically involved in higher-order functioning are recruited for lower-order tasks (simple motor control and visual perception) in

individuals with ASD, making complex, higher-order tasks more difficult.

A follow-up fMRI study showed differences in neural activation in an ASD group ($n = 8$) as compared to a TD group ($n = 8$) matched on age, gender, and handedness (Muller, Cauich, Rubio, Mizuno, & Courchesne, 2004). As in Muller and colleagues (2003), the ASD and TD groups showed similar intact implicit learning of an 8-item visuomotor sequence learning task, but distinct patterns of neural activation. During the early stages of learning, the TD group had activation in the premotor and primary motor cortices. As learning continued, activation in these motor areas decreased, and there was an increase in prefrontal activation. In contrast, the ASD group continued to activate premotor and primary motor cortices throughout the test, and did *not* show increased prefrontal activation during the later stages of learning. The authors suggested that individuals with ASD recruit brain regions that do not optimally support implicit learning.

LANGUAGE AND COMMUNICATION

Implicit Verbal Learning

Implicit learning goes beyond movement sequences, to also involve the nonconscious acquisition and use of verbal information. While the empirical literature on verbal aspects of implicit learning in ASD is limited, it is characterized by the use of several well-designed tasks. One of the earliest studies made use of a semantic priming paradigm to assess automatic aspects of lexical access, likely related to implicit knowledge of semantic information, in a group of adolescents with HFA, compared to a group of age, IQ, and gender-matched TD individuals (Toichi & Kamio, 2001). Participants completed a word completion task in which the word fragment was semantically related, or unrelated, to a preceding word prime. All participants benefited from the semantically related prime, indicating that they may have stored and accessed similar semantic information. One distinction between groups was that priming performance was related to nonverbal IQ, but only for the HFA group. The same researchers followed up with a subsequent study involving a semantic decision task in a group of 11 individuals with Asperger's disorder or HFA, compared to a group of age, IQ, and gender-matched TD individuals (Kamio, Robins,

Kelley, Swainson, & Fein, 2007). Participants made decisions about words after hearing a semantically related word. Results indicated a lack of semantic priming effects in the ASD group, which suggested a deficit in lexical-semantic processing in ASD.

Researchers have investigated another form of priming involving the reading of ambiguous homograph words (e.g., "bank" as in a financial institution versus "bank" as in the side of a river). A study of 16 adolescents with ASD required participants to read aloud sentences containing homographs, where the meaning of the sentence was consistent with only one pronunciation (Happé, 1997). The ASD group performed more poorly than a comparison sample. A more recent study used a similar homographs paradigm, this time investigating whether children with ASD make use of priming information from homographs, semantically related, and unrelated targets (Hala, Pexman, & Glenwright, 2007). The ASD group used primes to correctly pronounce homographs, indicating intact semantic priming, though they continued to use the same pronunciation upon later presentation of homographs, indicating deficits in inhibition.

While not drawing on an experimental paradigm, another study reported intact implicit learning in a small sample of children with ASD (Ledford, Gast, Luscre, & Ayres, 2008). During small group instruction time, three dyads of children were repeatedly shown 12 spelling words or important phrases that were printed on small index cards. Each of the spelling words or phrases was paired with a small symbol (e.g., a picture of a caution sign was paired with the word "caution"). Though never instructed to attend to the symbol, the children were generally able to show which symbol matched each spelling word, up to several days following the training.

There is a related literature involving categorization and prototype formation. These processes are relevant to implicit learning, though not precisely examples of such learning; we briefly review the most important findings here. First, one of the earliest studies of prototype formation, or the ability to extract similar features from a set of superficially different stimuli, explored category learning in children with ASD, Down's syndrome, and typical development (Klinger & Dawson, 2001). In two complementary tasks, children across groups were able to identify the correct solution in a rule-based paradigm, but neither clinical group was able to develop prototype features in a category-learning paradigm. Results suggested

difficulty in category-formation for children with ASD and Down's syndrome. Similar deficits in extracting prototype information was exhibited by children and adults with ASD in a face processing task (Gastgeb, Rump, Best, Minshew, & Strauss, 2009). Finally, a visuospatial categorization study revealed significantly slower performance by adults with HFA in learning category structure (Bott, Brock, Brockdorff, Boucher, & Lamberts, 2006). Across studies, findings suggest significant difficulty in extracting or forming categories and prototypes in ASD, a difficulty that might be related to implicit learning skills.

Implicit learning of verbal transitional probabilities

Implicit aspects of learning language have been less well studied than motor learning. Research using an artificial language paradigm has shown that typically developing adults, and even infants, are sensitive to transitional probabilities—that is, the probability that one syllable in a language will be followed by another syllable (Saffran, Aslin, & Newport, 1996). Using transitional probabilities to determine word boundaries is critical for learning language; extracting words from a continuous speech stream, in order to learn their meanings, hinges upon this ability. In contrast to typically developing children, children with Specific Language Impairment (SLI) show an insensitivity to transitional probabilities and have difficulty extracting words from a continuous speech stream (Evans, Saffran, & Robe-Torres, 2009).

To examine the ability to detect transitional probabilities of words in children with autism, we used the same artificial language learning paradigm (Mayo & Eigsti, 2010). Seventeen children with autism and 24 children with typical development (TD), ages 7 to 17, matched on gender, age, full-scale IQ, and receptive vocabulary, listened to a 21-minute speech stream containing 12 syllables. Six combinations of syllables formed trisyllabic "words" with high internal transitional probabilities (32–100%); transitional probabilities of syllables not forming "words" were lower (10–20%). As they listened, children drew pictures. Immediately following presentation of the speech stream, children completed a 36-trial, two-alternative forced-choice (2AFC) test, choosing the trisyllabic "word" that sounded more like the speech sounds that they heard while drawing.

On the 2AFC test, both groups performed better than chance (ASD, $p = .01$; TD, $p <.001$) and did not perform differently from one another. Similar group performance suggests children with ASD implicitly learned statistical cues within the language as well as their TD peers. However, a closer examination of group performance suggests subtle group differences. After the 21-minute exposure to the syllable stream, children were presented with the 2AFC test that contained both a target word in the artificial language as well as a foil non-word. An ideal learner might be sensitive to the presence of the foil words and update her representation of the language's statistics to take additional exemplars into account. This is particularly likely, given the high salience of these words, presented in isolation, relative to words presented in the speech stream. In other words, exposure to the foils during the test makes them sound more familiar.

Results in this task suggested a group difference in response to the 2AFC test. The TD group performed better on the first half of the test than on the second half of the 2AFC test, and performance (% correct) on the second portion of the 2AFC test was negatively correlated with performance on language measures including receptive vocabulary (PPVT-3 score, $r(22) = -0.46$, $p = .24$, and phonological processing, $r(22) = -0.42$, $p = .04$, and with nonverbal IQ, $r(22) = -0.41$, $p < .05$. Children with the highest scores for language and IQ were more sensitive to interference from the foils and performed poorly on the second portion of the test (evidence of updated learning). In contrast, the group of children with ASD performed consistently throughout the forced-choice test; their performance on the second half of the test was only associated with scores on an experimental measure of joint attention, a social ability (Bean & Eigsti, 2010), $r(15) = -0.57$, $p - .02$.

These results may suggest that, although both the ASD and TD groups were able to implicitly learn information regarding transitional probabilities when exposed to a lengthy language stream (21 minutes), the ASD group failed to show evidence of continually updated learning as they were exposed to items on the forced-choice test. These group differences on performance throughout the test may suggest subtle differences in implicit language learning abilities that disadvantage children with ASD.

Implicit Learning of Social Cues

One important correlate of implicit learning is the ability to acquire knowledge of language conventions through exposure, rather than through explicit explanation or teaching. While empirical studies of this phenomenon in ASD are not available, there is a large literature documenting pragmatic language difficulties in ASD that appear associated with this process. For example, unlike TD children, individuals with ASD exhibit significant difficulty in learning the meaning of common metaphors such as "That's the way the cookie crumbles" (Lord, 1996; Tager-Flusberg, Paul, & Lord, 2005). A child with an ASD who hears an adult say, "What a good trick! What else have you got up your sleeve?" might actually peer into his sleeve. Similarly, children with ASD appear to require explicit instruction about social conventions such as how to address peers versus adults; they may be able to produce appropriate variation in register in structured, directive situations (Volden & Sorenson, 2009), but show difficulty in more spontaneous interactions. Some related work has explored the role of social "priming" in ASD. Specifically, two children with ASD were able to increase their rates of spontaneous social initiations when "primed" to do so via a high-reinforcement session providing multiple practice opportunities (Zanolli, Daggett, & Adams, 1996).

The Iowa Gambling Task has been described as measuring implicit learning that is highly relevant to social and emotional aspects of learning (Bechara, Damasio, Tranel, & Damasio, 2005). In this task, participants see 4 virtual decks of cards; on each trial, they must choose a card from one deck; with each choice they may win or lose money. Their goal is to win as much money as possible. The four decks each have a built-in probability structure, such that some decks are characterized by occasional large wins but more frequent losses, and others by smaller wins but fewer losses. Healthy participants sample cards from each deck, and settle on consistent selections from the most profitable decks, after 40–50 trials. In contrast, individuals with orbitofrontal cortex lesions perseveratively choose the bad decks, despite losing money, and show no physiological reactivity (e.g., galvanic skin response; GSR) to their losses, which is seen as evidence that these patients are not benefiting from reinforcement learning via physiological affective states (Damasio, 1994). Two studies have examined the performance of individuals with ASD on such tasks. In one, 14 participants with Asperger's disorder were shown to be as likely as 14 TD participants to select cards from "good decks" (Johnson, Yechiam, Murphy, Queller, & Stout, 2006). However, they shifted between decks more often, and showed reduced GSR.

In a second study, half of the sample of adolescents with ASD showed atypical reinforcement learning; they appeared more motivated to explore novel possibilities (Yechiam, Arshavsky, Shamay-Tsoory, Yaniv, & Aharon, 2009). While these data are limited to studies with high-functioning individuals, they seem to suggest an atypical link between the emotional underpinnings of reward-related decision-making and learning.

Implicit Learning and Savant Skills

Differences in implicit learning are associated with both the social and communicative domains of impairment in ASD. Research has also probed the degree to which implicit learning deficits might contribute to the presence of repetitive behaviors and stereotyped interests, and moreover, to the presence of splinter or savant skills. For example, Happé and Vital (2009) have proposed that reduced awareness of one's own mental states (i.e., less "Theory of Mind") could decrease the degree to which conscious attempts to understand explicit rules interfere with implicit rule learning; it is known that conscious consideration of a rule can impair implicit acquisition of that rule (Reber, 1993). Cardoso-Martins and da Silva (2008) attempted to explore the relationship between implicit learning and the presentation of hyperlexia, or highly-skilled word decoding (reading) in the context of limited word comprehension. They studied eight children with ASD and hyperlexia, compared to children with ASD but without hyperlexia as well as to TD children. The hyperlexia group performed similarly to the TD group on nonword reading, but worse on reading comprehension, consistent with the hyperlexia presentation; surprisingly, the hyperlexia group performed worse on a letter-sound spelling task and on a phoneme awareness task as well. These data were taken to suggest that the hyperlexic group had learned letter-sound relations implicitly, on the basis of statistical learning, with a suggestion that a lack of interest in language implied reduced interference from language *meaning* on word reading (i.e., less explicit top-down influence on this more automatic implicit process).

Summary

On the surface, the difficulties that individuals with ASD exhibit in generalizing from one social situation to another, in understanding metaphors from context, in interpreting subtle but frequent social cues, and so on, strongly suggest the presence of difficulties with implicit learning. Findings that individuals perform much better given explicit prompts provide additional support for this hypothesis (Bartak, Rutter, & Cox, 1975; Oberman, Winkielman, & Ramachandran, 2009). Additional support for an impaired implicit learning hypothesis comes from studies that demonstrate neuroanatomical differences between ASD and TD groups in areas that have been demonstrated to be critical to implicit learning. Given the seemingly obvious behavioral difficulties and the anatomical differences between ASD and TD groups, one would expect experimental testing of implicit learning to provide clear and convincing evidence of such an impairment. However, as this review indicates, the empirical data are mixed, with several studies demonstrating intact skills, others pointing to subtle differences between ASD and TD groups, and still others showing significant deficits. These results are summarized in Table 14-1.

It should be noted that a number of implicit learning tasks have been reported in the cognitive science literature, with no reported data from individuals with ASD. As shown in Table 14-1, there are a number of implicit learning tasks for which there are no reported data in ASD, which may help to address the inconsistencies in the literature to date. These measures are as follows: (1) fragmented pictures as primes (Snodgrass & Corwin, 1988; Snodgrass & Feenan, 1990; Weldon & Jackson-Barrett, 1993); (2) word generation with implicit reinforcement, in which the participant is asked to generate as many words as possible—if the experimenter responds with "mm-hmm" to only plurals (for example), participants are likely to increase their rate of plural production (Greenspoon, 1955); and (3) studies relying on "liking" judgments, in which participants are presented with a long series of very rapidly-presented geometrical figures (e.g. for 40 milliseconds)—at subsequent testing, participants make judgments about which picture they have previously seen, given a pair of old and new pictures (Kunst-Wilson & Zajonc, 1980), and while typically performing at chance when asked to make recognition memory judgments, participants nevertheless show a sensitivity to familiarity when making a liking judgment; and (4) paradigms in which participants are presented with a set of auditory clicks and must press a response key to match the number of clicks, and receive feedback when they respond correctly

Table 14-1 Implicit Learning in ASD: Tasks and Findings

Task	Findings	Population	Reference
Eyeblink conditioning:	Maladaptive response timing	n =11, ages 7–22, HFA	Sears et al., 1994
Motor adaption–catching	ASD = TD	n = 8, ages 8–13, HFA	Mostofsky et al., 2004
Visuo-motor learning: SRT tasks			
4-item sequence	Intact learning, but dramatically slowed	n = 9, ages 6–14, LFA	Gordon & Stark, 2007
6-item sequence	Intact learning, atypical pattern of brain activity	n = 8, adults, HFA	Muller et al., 2003
Modified 6-item sequence	ASD = TD	n = 14, ages 8–14, HFA	Barnes et al., 2008
8-item sequence	Intact learning, atypical pattern of brain activity	n = 8, adults, HFA	Muller et al., 2004
8-item sequence	Intact learning, but dramatically slowed	n = 9, ages 6–14, LFA	Gordon & Stark, 2007
10-item sequence	No learning	n = 11, ages 8–16, HFA	Mostofsky et al., 2000
10-item sequence	ASD = TD	Case study of savant skills	Wallace et al., 2009
Rotary/pursuit task	Atypical pattern of learning	n = 38, ages 8–13, HFA	Gidley Larson et al., 2008
Implicit Verbal Learning			
Semantic priming	ASD = TD	n = 25, ages 14–28, HFA	Toichi & Kamio, 2001
Semantic decision	No priming	n = 11, ages 9–21, HFA	Kamio et al., 2007
Priming of word homographs by sentence context	No priming	n = 16, HFA	Happe, 1997
Prototype/categorization: Words	Decreased prototype use	n = 12, ages 5–21, LFA	Klinger & Dawson, 2001
Transitional probabilities in novel syllable stream	Subtle deficits	n = 17, ages 7–17, HFA	Mayo & Eigsti, May, 2010
Implicit Visual Learning			
Prototype/categorization: Faces	Decreased prototype use	ages 8-13 & 17–53, HFA	Gastgeb et al., 2009
Visuospatial categorization study	Slower to learn category structure	n = 12, ages 20–62, HFA	Bott et al., 2006
Reinforcement Learning			
Iowa Gambling Task	More shifting and less physiological response	n = 15, mean age 16, HFA	Johnson et al., 2006
Iowa Gambling Task	More exploration, failure to settle on best-paying decks	n = 15, mean age 15, HFA	Yechiam et al., 2009
Unstudied Implicit Learning Tasks			
Priming of pictures using visual fragments			Snodgrass & Feenan, 1990
Implicit reinforcement during word generation			Greenspoon, 1955
Familiarity versus "liking" judgment for briefly-presented stimuli			Kunst-Wilson & Zajonc, 1980
Implicit reinforcement of speed of responding			Svartdal, 1989

Note: All results refer to performance by the ASD group. Rows that are shaded indicate intact performance by the ASD group.

(Svartdal, 1989). When feedback is contingent on speed of responding (slower or faster), participants implicitly change their speed of responding in that direction. Studies with ASD participants using these tasks may illuminate the role of implicit learning deficits in autism.

We now attempt to provide an interpretation of the somewhat inconsistent results from studies of implicit learning in ASD. First, task complexity appears to play an important role. In more simple implicit paradigms, individuals with ASD show fewer impairments (for example, in a shorter SRT sequence of 6 rather than 10 items, Gordon & Stark, 2007). Second, subtle differences in performance may be detected only when a detailed examination of task approach and performance is considered. Measuring implicit learning by the end states of a learning task may be too gross to detect differences between ASD and TD groups. Examination of learning curves, error types, and differences in functional activation during imaging studies may help capture the subtle differences between ASD and TD groups. A third consideration is that very few studies have investigated performance of implicit learning by individuals with lower intellectual functioning. That said, if implicit deficits are playing an important role in the symptoms and presentation of ASD, one would expect those deficits to be equally prominent in low- and high-functioning individuals.

A fourth important limitation of existing studies is that many of them fail to report or take handedness into account. The saccade task reviewed above (D'Cruz et al., 2009) suggested dramatic differences in left- versus right-mediated performance, with impairments seen only for left-hemisphere processing. Future studies should be sure to at least consider the role of hemispheric lateralization and the atypical pattern that appears to characterize individuals with ASD. Fifth, individuals with ASD, both high- and low-functioning, exhibit increased clumsiness, more motor slowing, and more impairment on complex motor tasks (see Chapter 10). Many implicit learning tasks critically hinge on changes in RT (e.g., via button presses) as a measure of learning, and given that motor slowing is already present, it is critical to control for baseline differences in RT. Differences in the timing and coordination of motor movements seem to be an important feature of communicative and language skills in ASD (e.g., de Marchena & Eigsti, in press), and also appear to play an important role in differences in implicit learning (D'Cruz et al., 2009; Sears

& Steinmetz, 2000). Finally, future studies should consider the role of attentional demands, or dual-tasking, in implicit learning. Specifically, data suggest that implicit learning is negatively affected by the performance of simultaneous unrelated tasks (Shanks & Johnstone, 1999). While the suggestion is speculative, it is possible that in tasks involving cues or stimuli that require greater processing (such as, e.g., faces or language), individuals with ASD may be devoting greater attentional resources to the surface-level aspects of stimulus processing, leaving fewer resources available for deeper processing of sequences or cross-stimulus relationships. It is only after we take these factors into account that we may begin to understand why, despite the common intuition that implicit deficits could be present in ASD and lead to the symptoms, we see so many null findings.

Implicit learning appears to underlie multiple aspects of healthy functioning, including social interactions, language acquisition, discourse processes, participation in physical activities (e.g., sports), and many other activities. As such, the presence or absence of implicit learning deficits or differences has significant potential to inform intervention for individuals with ASD. More broadly, such a central cognitive process may provide clues to the core mechanisms underlying the symptom presentation in ASD.

References

Bailey, A., Luthert, P., Dean, A., Harding, B., Janota, I., Montgomery, M. ... Lantos, P. (1998). A clinico-pathological study of autism. *Brain, 121*, 889–905.

Bapi, R., Pammi, V., Miyapuram, K., & Ahmed, S. (2005). Investigation of sequence processing: A cognitive and computational neuroscience perspective. *Current Science, 89*, 1690–1698.

Barnes, K. A., Howard, J. H., Jr., Howard, D. V., Gilotty, L., Kenworthy, L., Gaillard, W. D. ... Vaidya, C. (2008). Intact implicit learning of spatial context and temporal sequences in childhood autism spectrum disorder. *Neuropsychology, 22*, 563–570.

Bartak, L., Rutter, M., & Cox, A. (1975). A comparative study of infantile autism and specific developmental language disorder: I. The Children. *British Journal of Psychiatry 126*, 127–145.

Bean, J., & Eigsti, I. M. (2010, May). *A novel measure of joint attention for use with older children and adolescents: evidence for clinical utility and external validity.* Paper presented at the International Meeting for Autism Research (IMFAR-10), Philadelphia, PA.

Bechara, A., Damasio, H., Tranel, D., & Damasio, A. R. (2005). The Iowa Gambling Task and the somatic marker hypothesis: Some questions and answers.

Trends in Cognitive Sciences, 9, 159–62; discussion 62–64.

Bott, L., Brock, J., Brockdorff, N., Boucher, J., & Lamberts, K. (2006). Perceptual similarity in autism. Quarterly Journal of Experimental Psychology, 59, 1237–1254.

Cardoso-Martins, C., & da Silva, J. R. (2008). Cognitive and language correlates of hyperlexia: Evidence from children with autism spectrum disorders. Reading and Writing, 23, 1–17.

Claparede, E. (1951). Recognition and "me-ness. In D. Rapaport (Ed.), Organization and pathology of thought (pp. 58–75). New York: Columbia University Press; Reprinted from Archives de Psychologies, (1911), 11, 79–90.

Cohen, N. J., & Squire, L. R. (1980). Preserved learning and retention of pattern-analyzing skill in amnesia: dissociation of knowing how and knowing that. Science, 210, 207–210.

Conway, C. M., & Pisoni, D. B. (2008). Neurocognitive basis of implicit learning of sequential structure and its relation to language processing. Annals of the New York Academy of Sciences, 1145, 113–131.

Courchesne, E., Yeung-Courchesne, R., Press, A. G., Hesselink, J. R., & Jernigan, T. L. (1988). Hypoplasia of cerebellar lobules VI and VII in infantile autism. New England Journal of Medicine, 318, 1349–1354.

D'Cruz, A. M., Mosconi, M. W., Steele, S., Rubin, L. H., Luna, B., Minshew, N., & Sweeney, J. A. (2009). Lateralized response timing deficits in autism. Biological Psychiatry, 66, 393–397.

Damasio, A. R. (1994). Descartes' error: Emotion, reason, and the human brain. New York: Grosset/Putnam.

Daum, I., Schugens, M. M., Ackermann, H., Lutzenberger, W., Dichgans, J., & Birbaumer, N. (1993). Classical conditioning after cerebellar lesions in humans. Behavioral Neuroscience, 107, 748–756.

de Marchena, A., & Eigsti, I. M. (in press). Conversational gestures in autism spectrum disorders: Asynchrony but not decreased frequency. Autism Research.

Desmond, J., & Fiez, J. (1998). Neuroimaging studies of the cerebellum: Language, learning, and memory. Trends in Cognitive Sciences, 2, 355–361.

Ernst, M., Zametkin, A., Matochik, J., Pascualvaca, D., & Cohen, R. (1997). Low medial prefrontal dopaminergic activity in autistic children. Lancet, 350, 638.

Evans, J. L., Saffran, J. R., & Robe-Torres, K. (2009). Statistical learning in children with specific language impairment. Journal of Speech, Language, and Hearing Research, 52, 321–335.

Fifer, W. P., Byrd, D. L., Kaku, M., Eigsti, I. M., Isler, J. R., Grose-Fifer, J., Tarullo, A. R., Balsam, P.D. (2010). Newborn infants learn during sleep. Proceedings of the National Academy of Sciences of the United States of America, 107, 10320-10323.

Forkstam, C., Hagoort, P., Fernandez, G., Ingvar, M., & Petersson, K. M. (2006). Neural correlates of artificial syntactic structure classification. Neuroimage, 32, 956–967.

Forkstam, C., & Petersson, K. M. (2005). Towards an explicit account of implicit learning. Current Opinions in Neurology, 18, 435–441.

Gabrieli, J. D., Keane, M. M., Stanger, B. Z., Kjelgaard, M. M., Corkin, S., & Growdon, J. H. (1994). Dissociations among structural-perceptual, lexical-semantic, and event-fact memory systems in Alzheimer, amnesic, and normal subjects. Cortex, 30, 75–103.

Gaffney, G. R., Kuperman, S., Tsai, L. Y., & Minchin, S. (1988). Morphological evidence for brainstem involvement in infantile autism. Biological Psychiatry, 24, 578–586.

Gaffney, G. R., Kuperman, S., Tsai, L. Y., Minchin, S., & Hassanein, K. M. (1987). Midsagittal magnetic resonance imaging of autism. British Journal of Psychiatry 151, 831–833.

Garber, H. J., & Ritvo, E. R. (1992). Magnetic resonance imaging of the posterior fossa in autistic adults. American Journal of Psychiatry, 149, 245–247.

Gastgeb, H. Z., Rump, K. M., Best, C. A., Minshew, N. J., & Strauss, M. S. (2009). Prototype formation in autism: Can individuals with autism abstract facial prototypes? Autism Research, 2, 279–284.

Gidley Larson, J. C., & Mostofsky, S. H. (2008). Evidence that the pattern of visuomotor sequence learning is altered in children with autism. Autism Research, 1, 341–353.

Gomez Beldarrain, M., Grafman, J., Pascual-Leone, A., & Garcia-Monco, J. C. (1999). Procedural learning is impaired in patients with prefrontal lesions. Neurology, 52, 1853–1860.

Gordon, B., & Stark, S. (2007). Procedural learning of a visual sequence in individuals with autism. Focus on Autism and Other Developmental Disabilities, 22, 14–22.

Gottselig, J. M., Brandeis, D., Hofer-Tinguely, G., Borbely, A. A., & Achermann, P. (2004). Human central auditory plasticity associated with tone sequence learning. Learning and Memory, 11, 162–171.

Greenspoon, J. (1955). The reinforcing effect of two spoken sounds on the frequency of two responses. American Journal of Psychiatry, 68, 409–416.

Hala, S., Pexman, P. M., & Glenwright, M. (2007). Priming the meaning of homographs in typically developing children and children with autism. Journal of Autism and Developmental Disorders, 37, 329–340.

Happé, F. (1997). Central coherence and theory of mind in autism: Reading homographs in context. British Journal of Developmental Psychology, 15, 1–12.

Happé, F., & Vital, P. (2009). What aspects of autism predispose to talent? Philosophical Transactions of the Royal Society B: Biological Sciences, 364, 1369–1375.

Holttum, J. R., Minshew, N. J., Sanders, R. S., & Phillips, N. E. (1992). Magnetic resonance imaging of the posterior fossa in autism. *Biological Psychiatry*, 32, 1091–1101.

Hwang, B., & Hughes, C. (2000). The effects of social interactive training on early social communicative skills of children with autism. *Journal of Autism and Developmental Disorders*, 30, 331–343.

Johnson, S. A., Yechiam, E., Murphy, R. R., Queller, S., & Stout, J. C. (2006). Motivational processes and autonomic responsivity in Asperger's disorder: Evidence from the Iowa Gambling Task. *Journal of the International Neuropsychological Society*, 12, 668–676.

Kamio, Y., Robins, D., Kelley, E., Swainson, B., & Fein, D. (2007). Atypical lexical/semantic processing in high-functioning autism spectrum disorders without early language delay. *Journal of Autism and Developmental Disorders*, 37, 1116–1122.

Kanner, L. (1943). Autistic disturbances of affective contact. *Nervous Child*, 2, 217–250.

Kim, J. S., Reading, S. A., Brashers-Krug, T., Calhoun, V. D., Ross, C. A., & Pearlson, G. D. (2004). Functional MRI study of a serial reaction time task in Huntington's disease. *Psychiatry Research*, 131, 23–30.

Klinger, L. G., & Dawson, G. (2001). Prototype formation in autism. *Development and Psychopathology*, 13, 111–124.

Knaus, T. A., Silver, A. M., Kennedy, M., Lindgren, K. A., Dominick, K. C., Siegel, J., & Tager-Flusberg, H. (2010). Language laterality in autism spectrum disorder and typical controls: A functional, volumetric, and diffusion tensor MRI study. *Brain and Language*, 112, 113–120.

Korsakoff, S. S. (1889). Etude medico-psychologique sur une formes des maladies de la memoire [Medical-psychological study of diseases of memory]. *Revue Philosophique*, 28, 501–530.

Kunst-Wilson, W. R., & Zajonc, R. B. (1980). Affective discrimination of stimuli that cannot be recognized. *Science*, 207, 557–558.

Ledford, J. R., Gast, D. L., Luscre, D., & Ayres, K. M. (2008). Observational and incidental learning by children with autism during small group instruction. *Journal of Autism and Developmental Disorders*, 38, 86–103.

Lieberman, M. D. (2000). Intuition: A social cognitive neuroscience approach. *Psychological Bulletin*, 126, 109–137.

Lieberman, M. D., Chang, G. Y., Chiao, J., Bookheimer, S. Y., & Knowlton, B. J. (2004). An event-related fMRI study of artificial grammar learning in a balanced chunk strength design. *Journal of Cognitive Neuroscience*, 16, 427–438.

Lord, C. (1996). Language in high-functioning adolescents with autism: Questions about deviance and delay. In D. Cicchetti & S. L. Toth (Eds.), *Rochester symposium on developmental psychopathology: Adolescence: Opportunities and challenges, Vol. 7* (pp. 149–165). Rochester: University of Rochester Press.

Lovaas, O. I., Koegel, R., Simmons, J. Q., & Long, J. S. (1973). Some generalization and follow-up measures on autistic children in behavior therapy. *Journal of Applied Behavior Analysis*, 6, 131–165.

Lovaas, O. I., & Smith, T. (1989). A comprehensive behavioral theory of autistic children: paradigm for research and treatment. *Journal of Behavior Therapy and Experimental Psychiatry*, 20, 17–29.

Marsh, R., Alexander, G. M., Packard, M. G., Zhu, H., Wingard, J. C., Quackenbush, G., & Peterson, B. S. (2004). Habit learning in Tourette syndrome: A translational neuroscience approach to a developmental psychopathology. *Archives of General Psychiatry*, 61, 1259–1268.

Mayo, J., & Eigsti, I. M. (2010, May). *Statistical word learning in children with ASD*. Paper presented at the International Meeting for Autism Research (IMFAR-10), Philadelphia, PA.

Menghini, D., Hagberg, G. E., Caltagirone, C., Petrosini, L., & Vicari, S. (2006). Implicit learning deficits in dyslexic adults: An fMRI study. *Neuroimage*, 33, 1218–1226.

Mostofsky, S. H., Bunoski, R., Morton, S. M., Goldberg, M. C., & Bastian, A. J. (2004). Children with autism adapt normally during a catching task requiring the cerebellum. *Neurocase*, 10, 60–64.

Mostofsky, S. H., Goldberg, M. C., Landa, R. J., & Denckla, M. B. (2000). Evidence for a deficit in procedural learning in children and adolescents with autism: Implications for cerebellar contribution. *International Neuropsychological Society*, 6, 752–759.

Muller, R., Cauich, C., Rubio, M., Mizuno, A., & Courchesne, E. (2004). Abnormal activity patterns in premotor cortex during sequence learning in autistic patients. *Biological Psychiatry*, 56, 323–332.

Muller, R. A., Kleinhans, N., Kemmotsu, N., Pierce, K., & Courchesne, E. (2003). Abnormal variability and distribution of functional maps in autism: An FMRI study of visuomotor learning. *American Journal of Psychiatry*, 160, 1847–1862.

Murakami, J. W., Courchesne, E., Press, G. A., Yeung-Courchesne, R., & Hesselink, J. R. (1989). Reduced cerebellar hemisphere size and its relationship to vermal hypoplasia in autism. *Archives of Neurology*, 46, 689–694.

Oberman, L. M., Winkielman, P., & Ramachandran, V. S. (2009). Slow echo: Facial EMG evidence for the delay of spontaneous, but not voluntary, emotional mimicry in children with autism spectrum disorders. *Developmental Science*, 12, 510–520.

Ozonoff, S., & Miller, J. (1995). Teaching theory of mind: A new approach to social skills training for individuals with autism. *Journal of Autism and Developmental Disorders*, 25, 415–33.

Perruchet, P., & Pacton, S. (2006). Implicit learning and statistical learning: One phenomenon, two approaches. *Trends in Cognitive Sciences*, 10, 233–238.

Piven, J., Saliba, K., Bailey, J., & Arndt, S. (1997). An MRI study of autism: The cerebellum revisited. *Neurology, 49*, 546–551.

Reber, A. S. (1993). *Implicit learning and tacit knowledge: An essay on the cognitive unconscious.* New York: Oxford University Press.

Renner, P., Grofer Klinger, L., & Klinger, M. R. (2000). Implicit and explicit memory in autism: Is autism an amnestic disorder? *Journal of Autism and Developmental Disorders, 30*, 3–14.

Rinehart, N. J., Bradshaw, J. L., Brereton, A. V., & Tonge, B. J. (2002). Lateralization in individuals with high-functioning autism and Asperger's disorder: A frontostriatal model. *Journal of Autism and Developmental Disorders, 32*, 321–331.

Saffran, J. R., Aslin, R. N., & Newport, E. L. (1996). Statistical learning by 8-month-old infants. *Science, 274*, 1926–1928.

Sears, L. L., Finn, P. R., & Steinmetz, J. E. (1994). Abnormal classical eye-blink conditioning in autism. *Journal of Autism and Developmental Disorders, 24*, 737–751.

Sears, L. L., & Steinmetz, J. E. (2000). Classical eyeblink conditioning in normal and autistic children. In D. Woodruff-Pak & J. E. Steinmetz (Eds.), *Eyeblink classical conditioning Volume 1: Applications in humans* (pp. 143–162). Boston: Kluwer Academic Publishers.

Seger, C. A. (2006). The basal ganglia in human learning. *Neuroscientist, 12*, 285–290.

Shanks, D. R., & Johnstone, T. (1999). Evaluating the relationship between explicit and implicit knowledge in a sequential reaction time task. *Journal of Experimental Psychology: Learning, Memory and Cognition, 25*, 1435–1451.

Snodgrass, J. G., & Corwin, J. (1988). Perceptual identification thresholds for 150 fragmented pictures from the Snodgrass and Vanderwart picture set. *Perceptual and Motor Skills, 67*, 3–36.

Snodgrass, J. G., & Feenan, K. (1990). Priming effects in picture fragment completion: support for the perceptual closure hypothesis. *Journal of Experimental Psychology: General, 119*, 276–296.

Sommer, M., Grafman, J., Clark, K., & Hallett, M. (1999). Learning in Parkinson's disease: Eyeblink conditioning, declarative learning, and procedural learning. *Journal of Neurology, Neurosurgery, and Psychiatry, 67*, 27–34.

Svartdal, F. (1989). Shaping of rule-governed behaviour. *Scandinavian Journal of Psychology, 30*, 304–314.

Tager-Flusberg, H., Paul, R., & Lord, C. (2005). Language and communication in autism. In F. R. Volkmar, R. Paul, A. Klin, & D. Cohen (Eds.), *Handbook of autism and pervasive developmental disorders* (3rd ed.). 335–364. New York: Wiley.

Thomas, K. M., & Nelson, C. A. (2001). Serial reaction time learning in preschool- and school-age children. *Journal of Experimental Child Psychology, 79*, 364–387.

Toichi, M., & Kamio, Y. (2001). Verbal association for simple common words in high-functioning autism. *Journal of Autism and Developmental Disorders, 31*, 483–490.

Volden, J., & Sorenson, A. (2009). Bossy and nice requests: Varying language register in speakers with autism spectrum disorder (ASD). *Journal of Communication Disorders, 42*, 58–73.

Wallace, G. L., Happé, F., & Giedd, J.N. (2009). A case study of a multiply talented savant with an autism spectrum disorder: Neuropsychological functioning and brain morphometry. *Philosophical Transactions of the Royal Society B: Biological Sciences, 364*, 1425–1432.

Weldon, M. S., & Jackson-Barrett, J. L. (1993). Why do pictures produce priming on the word-fragment completion test? A study of encoding and retrieval factors. *Memory and Cognition, 21*, 519–528.

Yechiam, E., Arshavsky, O., Shamay-Tsoory, S. C., Yaniv, S., & Aharon, J. (2009). Adapted to explore: reinforcement learning in Autistic Spectrum Conditions. *Brain and Cognition, 72*, 317–324.

Zanolli, K., Daggett, J., & Adams, T. (1996). Teaching preschool age autistic children to make spontaneous initiations to peers using priming. *Journal of Autism and Developmental Disorders, 26*, 407–422.

Chapter 15

The Significance of IQ and Differential Cognitive Abilities for Understanding ASD

Robert M. Joseph

INTRODUCTION

Individuals with autism spectrum disorder (ASD) are remarkably varied in their intellectual abilities. Current estimates suggest that, whereas approximately half of all individuals with ASD are mildly to profoundly cognitively impaired, half have cognitive abilities within the normal range of intelligence, and a substantial minority have intelligent quotients well above normal. In addition, individuals with autism frequently present with an unusual degree of unevenness in their cognitive abilities, and often with strengths that significantly exceed not only their own general-level ability, but general population norms as well. The occurrence of autism in association with such a wide range of IQ easily leads to the mistaken impression that intellectual ability, whether impaired or not, is a coincidental feature of this complex disorder, and of limited significance with regard to its causes or course. But this is far from the truth. This chapter considers the significance of IQ and IQ profiles in

understanding ASD from clinical and research perspectives. It addresses the limitations as well as the value of IQ measures, both with regard to current practices and possible future uses. Particular attention is devoted to the proven and potential contributions that IQ and measures of differential cognitive abilities can make to the understanding of genetic and neurobiological heterogeneity in ASD.

THE DISTRIBUTION OF IQ IN ASD

Until recently, it was commonly estimated that approximately three-quarters of individuals with autism were intellectually impaired (IQ < 70; Bailey, Phillips, & Rutter, 1996; Rutter, 1979). In a review of 32 epidemiological surveys of autism published from 1966 to 2001, Fombonne (2003) reported that 30% of cases were within the normal range of cognitive ability, 30% were mildly to moderately impaired, and 40% were severely to profoundly impaired. Yet, over

281

the past decade, as the estimated prevalence of ASD has increased, the IQ distribution of individuals identified with ASD has also changed. For example, in two large-scale, records-based surveillance studies conducted by the Centers for Disease Control and Prevention in 2000 and 2002 (CDCP, 2007a, 2007b), intellectual disability was found to occur in only about 50% of children classified as having ASD—significantly lower than prior estimates of 75%. In studies using active screening to identify all ASD cases, rates of cognitive impairment have been estimated to be even lower, from 40% (Baird et al., 2000) to as low as 24% (Chakrabarti & Fombonne, 2001) and 30% (Chakrabarti & Fombonne, 2003). However, it is important to recognize that recent increases in the estimated prevalence of ASD, and the shift in distribution of IQ, are in large part attributable to a broadening of case definition and improved recognition (Fombonne, 1999, 2003), developments which have resulted in the inclusion of more mildly affected individuals with higher levels of adaptive functioning. Thus, it is still not clear whether earlier estimates that three-quarters of individuals with autistic disorder are cognitively impaired are wholly inaccurate. In fact, two studies that have reported IQ distributions for children with narrowly defined autism separately from those meeting criteria for any ASD have reported that 69% (Chakrabarti & Fombonne, 2001) and 67% (Chakrabarti & Fombonne, 2003) of the former tested as cognitively impaired.

SEX DIFFERENCES IN IQ IN ASD

It has been well-established by epidemiological research that ASD occurs predominantly in males, by a ratio of about 4 to 1 (Fombonne, 1999; 2003; Yeargin-Allsopp et al., 2003). It has also been well-established that females with ASD have generally lower IQs than males, and are much more likely to have IQs in the impaired range (Bryson, Clark, & Smith, 1988; Lord & Schopler, 1985; Lord, Schopler, & Revicki, 1982; Volkmar, Szatmari, & Sparrow, 1993). A corollary finding is that the male-female sex ratio in autism decreases with lower IQ. For example, in an epidemiological sample of 965 children identified with ASD at ages 3 to 10 years, Yeargin-Allsopp et al. (2003) reported a male-female sex ratio of 7:3 among children with no cognitive impairment, 4:4 among children with mild impairment, 3:5 among

children with moderate impairment, 2:1 among children with severe impairment, and 1:3 among children with profound impairment. Sex differences in IQ in ASD are not well understood. For many years it has been theorized that females have a higher threshold, and thus require a greater genetic load for the expression of autism (Tsai & Beisler, 1983), resulting in more severe cognitive impairment. However, recent evidence suggests that girls are most likely to acquire autism via non-familial genetic mutations that are more strongly associated with low IQ in both females and males than are familial modes of transmission (Banach et al., 2009).

PREDICTABILITY AND STABILITY OF IQ IN ASD

The reliability of measures of IQ in children with ASD has been a topic of long-standing research interest, particularly because of the potentially confounding effects of children's social-communicative disability and related behavioral issues on a valid assessment of IQ. These include language delay or impairment, pragmatic difficulties with the imitation and turn-taking routines that are often used in testing, susceptibility to preoccupations and special interests, low threshold for distractibility, and motivational differences. Nonetheless, research findings indicate fairly good predictability and stability of nonverbal IQ scores in children with ASD, comparable to that found for non-autistic children with language impairment or other developmental delays (Freeman, Ritvo, Needleman, Yokota, 1985; Lord & Schopler, 1989a, 1989b; Sigman & Ruskin, 1999). Yet, this conclusion requires two important qualifications.

First, research evidence indicates that the predictability and stability of IQ in ASD increases as a function of age of first assessment, at least until the end of the preschool years. In a study of children whose IQ was assessed two times five years apart, Lord and Schopler (1989a) found cross-time correlations of .68 for children first tested at ages 2–3 years, as compared to .81 and .83 for children first tested at ages 4–5 and 6–7 years, respectively. Charman et al. (2005) reported that IQ scores at age 7 were not predicted by scores from the same measure at age 2 years ($r = .00$), but were at age 3 years ($r = .52$). Sigman and Ruskin (1999) found that the correlation between IQ measures taken during preschool (mean age = 3;11) and middle school age (mean age = 12;11) was .44, which was comparable to the medium-sized correlations found for 3-year-olds in the studies by Lord & Schopler and Charman et al. In contrast, in a subsequent follow-up of the same group, middle-school-age IQ scores were strongly predictive of IQ scores in young adulthood (mean age = 19;0) with a cross-time correlation of .95 (Sigman & McGovern, 2005).

The second qualification regards the degree of stability in individuals' absolute scores over time. Lord and Schopler (1989a) observed that, despite the substantial predictability of preschool IQ measures over a 5-year interval, children with autism, like typically developing children, frequently showed sizeable changes in absolute scores, but that these were generally within 10 to 12 points (see also Charman et al., 2005). They also reported that when children exhibited categorical shifts (e.g., unimpaired, mildly impaired, severely impaired) in IQ, these shifts tended to be between contiguous categories. Children who initially scored in the unimpaired range of IQ were as a group the most stable, with 75% remaining in the unimpaired range 5 years later (see also Howlin et al., 2004). Children who initially scored in the mildly impaired range were almost as likely to move into the unimpaired range (35%; see also Sigman & Ruskin, 1999) as they were to remain in the mildly impaired range (39%). Although 38% of children who initially scored in the severely impaired range of IQ moved into the mildly impaired range at follow-up, only 11% were found to be functioning in the unimpaired range. Thus, even among young preschool children with autism, nonverbal IQ measured below a score of 50 appears to be a reliable indicator of long-term cognitive impairment (rather than cognitive delay), and is thus likely to be clinically meaningful with regard to a child's prognosis.

As with predictability, there is a clear increase in the stability of IQ scores by the school-age years. For example, in a longitudinal study of 48 children diagnosed with autism at 3 to 5 years of age, Sigman and Ruskin (1999) found that 11 of 39 children (33%) who had scored in the cognitively impaired range in preschool scored in the unimpaired range in middle childhood. In contrast, when this same group of children was re-tested in later adolescence, none who had scored in the impaired range in middle childhood advanced into the unimpaired range by later adolescence (Sigman & McGovern, 2005).

The development of improved measures for the assessment of cognitive abilities in children with ASD and other developmental disabilities will be important both for clinical and research purposes. IQ tests serve a critical role in identifying cognitive strengths and weakness relevant to educational planning, in helping to determine appropriate therapeutic interventions, and in establishing eligibility for government-mandated services based on IQ (Ozonoff, Goodlin-Jones, & Solomon, 2005). In research, reliable and stable measures of IQ and differential cognitive abilities are necessary for understanding the course of development and the best predictors of outcome, and for potentially helping to resolve the remarkable heterogeneity in the causes and expression of ASD.

Several measures now commonly used in IQ testing of children with autism, but less known outside of ASD-related clinical practice and research, represent progress toward these ends. For example, the Differential Ability Scales (Elliot, 1990, 2007) can be administered across a wide range of chronological age, from 2.5 through 17 years, as well as mental age, yielding standard scores as low as 25. In addition, only 6 subtests are necessary to generate verbal and nonverbal IQ estimates, making administration time relatively brief. In addition, it has been argued (Joseph, Tager-Flusberg, & Lord, 2002) that its subscales provide more conceptually homogenous and coherent measures of differential cognitive abilities in individuals with autism than do the more widely administered Wechsler intelligence scales (1991, 1997). The Mullen Scales of Early Learning (1995) have been widely adopted for the assessment of cognitive abilities in younger children with autism. The Mullen can be administered to children from one to 68 months of age and yields five separate subtests scores, as well as verbal and nonverbal composite scores. For this reason, it has been cited as preferable to the also widely used Bayley Scales of Infant Development (Bayley, 1993), which yield only a single, global developmental score based on abilities assessed in several different cognitive domains (Akshoomoff, 2006; Ozonoff et al., 2005), although the recently revised Bayley III also provides separate scaled scores for cognitive, motor, and language functioning. Recently published longitudinal studies following children with ASD from age 2 through preschool and school age have shown that age-2 Mullen scores are robustly predictive of later cognitive functioning as measured with the Differential Ability Scales (Anderson et al., 2007; Thurm, Lord, Lee, &

Newschaffer, 2007), underscoring the usefulness of these measures. Nonetheless, further research and development of cognitive assessment tools that can generate predictive and comparable estimates of differential cognitive abilities from toddlerhood through adolescence will be of great value to both clinical assessment and research.

THE RELATIONSHIP OF IQ TO AUTISM SYMPTOM SEVERITY, ADAPTIVE FUNCTIONING, AND LONG-TERM OUTCOME

Autism symptoms, and the associated impairments in adaptive social, communication, and daily living skills, can occur with equal severity in a person who is cognitively impaired and a person with above-average IQ. This would seem to suggest that there is no relationship between IQ and the severity of autism, and that IQ is of little value in understanding the causes of autism or the remarkable variability in its severity. Yet, along with early childhood language development, IQ has long been recognized as one of the strongest predictors of adaptive functioning and adult outcome in ASD (Gillberg & Steffenburg, 1987; Kobayashi, Murata, & Yashinaga, 1992; Lockyer & Rutter, 1969; Lotter, 1974; Venter, Lord, & Schopler, 1992; Volkmar, Cicchetti, Cohen, & Bregman, 1992). Research published in the past decade continues to support the predictive value of IQ for later outcomes in autism. For example, in a cluster analysis of 132 children divided into better and poorer outcome subgroups according to symptom severity and adaptive functioning scores, Stevens et al. (2000) found that preschool-age nonverbal IQ was the strongest predictor of group membership at school age. In contrast, preschool ratings of adaptive behavior and symptom severity were not strongly predictive of school-age outcome. In one of the largest and most methodologically rigorous follow-up studies of adults with autism, Howlin, Goode, Hutton, and Rutter (2004) investigated the relationship between childhood cognitive ability and quality of adult outcome in 68 individuals aged 21 to 48 years. Outcomes were rated primarily in terms of level of independence achieved in daily living and employment. These authors found that individuals with a childhood nonverbal IQ of at least 70 had significantly better outcomes than those with IQs

below 70. It is notable, however, that both Stevens et al. (2000) and Howlin et al. (2004) found significantly more variability in the outcomes of individuals with normal or near-normal IQ in childhood. In other words, in both studies, low IQ was more reliably associated with poorer outcomes than higher IQ was associated with better outcomes.

Evidence that normal or near-normal IQ is necessary but not sufficient for better outcomes is consistent with the well-established finding that level of adaptive functioning is typically significantly lower than would be expected based on cognitive ability in ASD (Bolte & Poutska, 2002; Carter et al., 1998; Freeman et al., 1999), and that this discrepancy is especially prominent among higher-ability individuals (e.g., Liss et al., 2000). The most widely used measure of adaptive functioning in autism research has been the Vineland Adaptive Behavior Scales (Sparrow, Balla, & Cicchetti, 1984). The Vineland is a standardized, semi-structured parent interview that assesses an individual's "real-life" behaviors and provides ratings of adaptive skills in communication (e.g., listening when another person is speaking, telling another person what happened), socialization (e.g., initiating interpersonal interactions, taking turns in conversation, maintaining friendships), and daily living (e.g., taking care of personal hygiene, using money). Research with the Vineland has revealed a profile of adaptive behavior skills in ASD characterized by marked impairment in socialization skills, moderately impairment in communications skills, and generally adequate daily living skills relative to overall cognitive ability (Bolte & Poutska, 2002; Carter et al., 1998).

Two recent studies investigated whether IQ differentially predicts social and behavioral adaptive-behavior skills and symptom severity in higher-ability children with ASD. In a longitudinal investigation of 68 children with ASD, Szatmari et al. (2003) examined the explanatory power of nonverbal IQ and language level measured at ages 4–6 years on outcomes at 6–8 years and 10–13 years. They found that the predictive ability of language and nonverbal IQ was stable over the two time points, and that the variance explained in outcomes that was overlapping for the language and nonverbal IQ predictors far outweighed variance that was uniquely associated with either factor. On average, the amount of variance in adaptive behaviors explained by these predictors was 60% for Vineland communication scores,

40% for Vineland socialization scores, and 20% for autism symptom ratings, as measured with the Autism Behavior Checklist (Krug, Arik, & Almond, 1980). In a cross-sectional study of 187 male children and adolescents with ASD, Klin et al. (2007) similarly found that verbal and nonverbal IQ were moderately and positively correlated with Vineland communication scores, but unrelated to Vineland socialization scores, and had relatively small, inverse relationships with autism symptom scores, as measured with the Autism Diagnostic Observation Schedule (ADOS; Lord, Rutter, DiLavore, & Risi, 1999). Another recent study conducted by Hus et al. (2007) investigated the relationship between IQ and ADOS symptom severity in 983 individuals and found generally medium-sized, inverse correlations between both verbal and nonverbal IQ and ADOS scores (see also Joseph, Tager-Flusberg, & Lord, 2002, discussed below). The much wider range of IQ investigated in the Hus et al. study might account for the larger correlations found, as IQ was restricted to scores of 70 and above in the Klin et al. and Szatmari et al. studies.

Several implications follow from the above findings. First, even though IQ scores are predictive of adaptive functioning, they typically exceed Vineland scores in absolute terms and often do not serve as a valid indicator of adaptive living skills, particularly in higher-ability individuals who have IQ scores that are within the normal range. Thus, measures of adaptive functioning, in addition to IQ, are of critical importance in assessment and therapeutic, educational, and vocational planning for individuals with ASD. Second, general intelligence appears to have a larger moderating influence on communication than on socialization skills in ASD. This may be explained in part by the fact that communications skills, especially as measured on the Vineland, are largely dependent on language level, which in turn is strongly related to IQ. In addition, this finding suggests that there is less overlap in the cognitive processes involved in the learning and application of the skills measured in IQ tests (e.g., inductive reasoning) and those involved in the learning and application of social skills (e.g., social and affective reciprocity). This is consistent with prior empirical findings (Joseph & Tager-Flusberg, 2004; Klin et al., 2003) and may help to explain the typical failure of social skills to generalize beyond the context in which they are explicitly taught (Bellini & Peters, 2008).

THE ROLE OF IQ IN THE SEARCH FOR THE GENETIC CAUSES OF ASD

Although autism is known to be strongly heritable, the past decade of genetic research has revealed that it is as heterogeneous in its genetic causes as it is in its behavioral manifestations (Geschwind, 2008; also see Chapters 2 and 24). Since large-scale behavioral genetic studies of autism were first initiated over a decade ago, IQ has been an important factor in attempts to reduce genetic heterogeneity, and potentially reveal differential modes of transmission of ASD. For example, MacLean et al. (1999) investigated whether the risk of autism-like traits in non-affected families (referred to as the broader autism phenotype or lesser variant) varied as a function of the nonverbal IQ of the affected family member (or proband). They found that relatives of probands with IQ > 60 had a higher risk of the lesser variant than relatives of probands with IQ < 60, leading them to conclude that IQ may provide a marker of genetic heterogeneity and differential mechanisms of familial transmission of ASD. In a similar vein, in a genome-wide linkage analyses of 976 multiplex families, Liu et al. (2008) grouped families according to various quantitative or categorical traits (e.g., symptom severity, language onset, nonverbal IQ) in an effort to reduce genetic heterogeneity. In doing so, they obtained their strongest linkage signal when they divided their sample based on nonverbal IQ. This signal was found for a subset of 313 families with IQ > 70 on chromosome 15q13.3-q14 (logarithm of odds score of 4.01), and was particularly interesting because of its proximity to 15q11-q13, the locus of three GABA receptor subunit genes identified as significant in several prior association studies of autism (e.g., Ashley-Koch, 2006).

Despite evidence that IQ, at least categorically defined, may mark differences in the genetic transmission of ASD, whether the genes controlling IQ in ASD contribute directly to autism susceptibility, or rather simply alter the severity of its expression, remains a question. Skuse (2007) has strongly endorsed the latter point of view, arguing that the strong association between autism and cognitive impairment results from reduced capacity for cognitive compensation for independently inherited autistic traits. From this point of view, autism risk genes are much more prevalent in the general population than currently thought, but the brain is better able to compensate for that risk in individuals with intact cognitive abilities. Skuse also suggests that the association of autism phenotypes with an increasing number of genetic and chromosomal disorders, such as Smith-Lemli-Opitz syndrome, Williams syndrome, Timothy syndrome, and Duchenne muscular dystrophy, is not because these disorders have a genetic relation to autism, but because they are associated with cognitive disability, and thus have a lower threshold for expressing autism susceptibility genes that are independently inherited. Although Skuse's argument is provocative, it is not clear how it would accommodate findings from association studies linking mutations of genes involved in neuronal migration, synaptogenesis, and axonal path-finding to both non-autistic mental retardation and autism without mental retardation (Geschwind & Levitt, 2007). Regardless, whether in favor of or against the idea that IQ marks genetic heterogeneity in ASD, both points of view lead to the conclusion that IQ is a key variable to consider in genetic studies of autism.

DIFFERENTIAL COGNITIVE ABILITIES AND THEIR ETIOLOGICAL SIGNIFICANCE IN ASD

Autism spectrum disorder is not only characterized by a remarkably wide range of general intelligence between individuals, but also by frequently uneven development of cognitive abilities within individuals. The Wechsler child and adult intelligence scales (1991, 1997) have been the most widely used instruments for the assessment of IQ profiles in individuals with ASD. A Wechsler IQ profile with Verbal IQ (VIQ) lower than Performance IQ (PIQ) has often been associated with autism (Happé, 1994; Lincoln, Allen, & Kilman, 1995; Lincoln, Courchesne, Allen, Hanson, & Ene, 1998), and has even been viewed as a useful criterion in the differential diagnosis of autism (Lincoln, Courshesne, Kilman, Elmasian, & Allen, 1988). However, although group means from Wechsler IQ testing often appear to support a prototypical VIQ<PIQ profile, closer scrutiny has shown that a VIQ<PIQ is far from universal among individuals with autism. For example, in a review of 16 studies, Siegel, Minshew, and Goldstein (1996) found that mean VIQ scores were significantly lower than mean PIQ scores in only 9 studies. An obvious limitation of inferring a prototypical IQ profile from group means is the possibility of "averaging out" significant

individual discrepancies that may occur in both directions in any given sample. Siegel et al. (1996) addressed this problem by examining the actual frequency of Wechsler VIQ-PIQ discrepancies in either direction in relatively large samples of high-ability children and adults with autism. They found a significant discrepancy favoring PIQ in 20% of children and 11% of adults, and a significant discrepancy favoring VIQ in 16% of children and 28% of adults. These frequencies were not markedly different from, and if anything were lower than, general population norms. The authors concluded that there is no prototypical Wechsler VIQ-PIQ profile in autism, at least among higher-ability individuals (see also Williams et al., 2008), but with the qualification that IQ discrepancies, particularly those favoring PIQ over VIQ, may be more frequent at lower levels of cognitive ability (Rumsey, 1992). On the basis of these findings, the authors cautioned against the use of IQ profiles for diagnostic purposes, given their limited sensitivity and specificity, arguing that their use should be reserved for educational and vocational planning (see also Mesibov, 1996). Similar findings have also led to the conclusion that a VIQ-PIQ discrepancy, in this case one favoring verbal over nonverbal abilities, is not a valid criterion for differentiating Asperger from autistic disorder (Manjiova & Prior, 1999; Ozonoff, South, & Miller, 2000)

Although IQ profiles appear to be of little value in the differential diagnosis of autism, at least as currently defined (APA, 1994), it is possible that differences in cognitive profiles may index etiologically meaningful variation in symptom severity and developmental course within ASD. As such, cognitive profiles, particularly those marking uneven development of cognitive abilities, could help to identify important variants in genetic and brain architecture which account for the highly heterogeneous expression of ASD. To address these possibilities, Joseph and colleagues (Deutsch & Joseph, 2003; Joseph, Tager-Flusberg, & Lord, 2002; Tager-Flusberg & Joseph, 2003) conducted a series of three studies relating patterns of uneven development between verbal and nonverbal IQ in ASD to differences in symptom severity, head circumference, and brain volume.

In our initial study (Joseph et al., 2002), our first goal was to examine whether significant discrepancies between VIQ and NVIQ occur at a higher frequency than normal in preschool and school-age children with ASD and, further, to determine if any such discrepancies occur as a function of overall ability, as suggested by Siegel et al. (1996). To assess IQ profiles, we used the Differential Ability Scales (DAS; Elliott, 1990). The DAS includes a preschool and a school-age version, each consisting of 6 core subtests that yield a verbal and nonverbal IQ score. In the school-age version, nonverbal ability is further differentiated into nonverbal reasoning and spatial components, so as to distinguish between nonverbal inductive reasoning ability and more purely visual-perceptual processing skills. In addition to the advantages of its relative brevity, our rationale for using the DAS was the arguably increased coherence of its subscale measures, especially relative to the Wechsler verbal and performance subscales, which are known for a high degree of subtest scatter (Happé, 1994), and which do not necessarily conform to the same factor structure in autism as in the general population (Lincoln et al., 1988).

Participants included 73 children (mean age = 5;5, SD = 0;10) who were administered the preschool DAS and 47 children (mean age = 8;11, SD = 2;0) who were administered the school-age DAS. The sample as a whole was selected for having sufficiently high overall ability (full-scale IQ > 55) to minimize the possibility that floor effects would prevent detection of discrepancies between verbal (V) and nonverbal (NV) abilities. Analysis of children's DAS scores revealed a high frequency of significant V-NV discrepancies in the preschool (56%) and school-age (62%) groups, which in both cases occurred at a much higher

rate than in the DAS normative sample (~30%). As shown in Figure 15-1, V-NV discrepancies in the preschool group were strongly in favor of nonverbal ability. The three preschool V-NV discrepancy groups did not differ in age, but full-scale IQ was significantly lower in the V=NV group than in the two discrepancy groups. Although verbal score was significantly lower than nonverbal score for the preschool sample as a whole, these two measures were significantly correlated (r = .42, p < .001), as they were in the DAS normative sample (r = .51). Unlike in the preschool group, mean verbal and nonverbal did not differ for the school-age group as a whole, and V-NV discrepancies occurred nearly equally in both directions. The school-age V-NV groups did not differ in age, but full-scale IQ was marginally higher in the V<NV group than in the V=NV group. As can be seen in Figure 15-2, verbal and nonverbal scores in the two discrepancy groups were approximately the converse of each other, indicating that the V-NV discrepancies reflected a true strength in one domain or the other rather than different levels of verbal ability between two groups that shared the same level of nonverbal ability. The dissociation of verbal and nonverbal abilities in the V<NV discrepancy group was most marked in the comparison of verbal and spatial ability scores. This dissociation was also reflected in the weak correlation between verbal and spatial scores for the entire school-age sample, r = .28, n.s., compared to r = .50 in the DAS normative sample. In contrast, strong correlations were found between verbal and

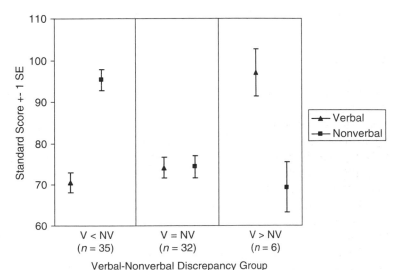

Figure 15-1 Preschool DAS Subscale Scores by Verbal-Nonverbal Discrepancy Groups.

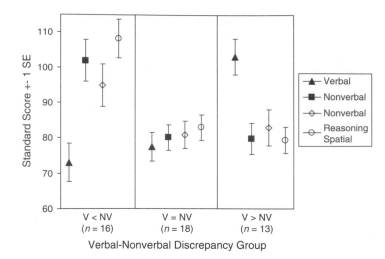

Figure 15-2 School-Age DAS Subscale Scores by Verbal-Nonverbal Discrepancy Groups.

nonverbal reasoning scores, $r = .61$, $p < .001$, and between nonverbal reasoning and spatial scores, $r = .68$, $p < .001$, similar to those found in the DAS normative sample ($r = .59$ and $r = .61$, respectively).

To summarize, we found a high level of unevenness in the cognitive abilities of children with ASD, and no evidence of a prototypical cognitive profile. Further, both preschool and school-age children with V<NV profiles tended to have higher full-scale IQs, contradicting the proposal that V<NV discrepancies are associated with overall lower ability in ASD (Rumsey et al, 1992; Siegel et al., 1996). Our main developmental finding was that significant V<NV discrepancies occurred more frequently in younger children (48%) than in older children (34%). Additional analyses revealed that children with V<NV profiles in the preschool group were significantly more delayed in independently measured language milestones (first words, phrase speech) than the other two preschool V-NV groups. There were no differences in language milestones between the school-age V-NV groups. This led us to conclude that the greater rate of V<NV discrepancies in the preschool group may have been attributable, at least in part, to the effects of developmental language delay, and that a portion of these discrepancies might resolve over time. This interpretation is consistent with the fact that the preschool DAS verbal subtests measure expressive vocabulary and listening comprehension and are thus more strictly language-based in nature. In contrast, the DAS school-age verbal subtests measure, in addition to general language-level, higher-level verbal reasoning and concept formation (similar to the Wechsler Vocabulary

and Similarities subtests). Our findings also suggested that the preschool DAS may not be the optimal measure to chart the development of the dissociation of verbal and nonverbal abilities we found in our school-age V<NV discrepancy group. Of particular interest in this regard is a recent study conducted by Kuschner, Bennetto, and Yost (2007), who used the Brief IQ (BIQ) Screening Assessment from the Leiter-R (Roid & Miller, 1997) to assess patterns of strength and weakness in nonverbal cognitive functioning in preschool children with ASD. Using deviance scores to identify discrepancies from each participants' mean performance, Kuschner et al. (2007) found that 88% of children with ASD exhibited positive deviance scores on visual-perceptual measures and 63% exhibited negative deviance on nonverbal reasoning measures. Typically developing and non-ASD developmentally delayed comparison participants were much less likely to show significant deviations from their mean scores. These findings suggest that a nonverbal measure, such as the Leiter-R BIQ Screening Assessment, that is not confounded by language level might provide a more sensitive measure of the V<NV discrepancy we found in older children with the School-Age DAS, particularly given that these discrepancies appeared to be driven by strengths in visual-perceptual processing.

Our finding that severity of impairment in reciprocal social interaction was associated with strengths particularly in the domain of visual-spatial cognition, although based on a routinely administered IQ test, is consistent with a long line of experimental inquiry demonstrating enhanced visual-perceptual processing abilities in individuals with ASD, which have been conceptualized in terms of weak central coherence (Happé, 1999) and, more recently, enhanced perceptual functioning (Mottron, Dawson, Soulieres, Hubert, & Burack, 2006). Individuals with ASD have been shown to excel, for example, on the Wechsler Block Design task (Caron, Mottron, Berthiaume, & Dawson, 2006; Shah & Frith, 1983, 1993), the Embedded Figures Task (Joliffe & Baron-Cohen, 1997; Shah & Frith, 1983), and in visual search (O'Riordan, Plaisted, Driver, & Baron-Cohen, 2001; Plaisted, O'Riordan, & Baron-Cohen,1998). Although this research has generally sought to establish a local bias in visual perception or attention as a component of the autism neurocognitive phenotype, without consideration of individual differences within ASD (but see Jarrold and Russell, 1997), Happé and Frith (2006) recently acknowledged that weak central coherence and associated strengths in visual-perceptual processing are likely characteristic of only a subset of individuals with ASD, given the heterogeneous nature of the disorder.

Our second goal was to determine whether differential development of verbal and nonverbal abilities might be associated with etiologically relevant differences in core autistic symptomatology. To assess symptom severity, we used the Autism Diagnostic Observation Schedule (ADOS; Lord et al., 1999), a semi-structured, interactive observation scale that provides quantitative ratings of communicative and social behaviors corresponding to DSM-IV (APA, 1994) criteria for autism. To assess the associations between differential verbal-nonverbal abilities and symptom severity, a V-NV difference score was calculated by subtracting the nonverbal from the verbal score for each participant, such that negative scores indicated relatively superior nonverbal skills. In both the preschool and school-age groups, communication symptom severity was significantly and inversely related to verbal IQ scores, but not to nonverbal IQ scores, indicating that better communicative functioning was specifically associated with higher verbal ability across age groups. However, the pattern of correlations between IQ scores and social symptoms differed across the age groups. In the preschool group, social symptom severity was significantly and inversely related to both verbal and nonverbal score, indicating that better functioning in the social domain was associated with overall cognitive ability. In contrast, in the school-age group, social symptom severity was unrelated to

nonverbal scores, but was inversely related to verbal score and, to an even greater degree, to the V-N difference score, $r = -.45, p < .01$. Thus, the higher a child's nonverbal score was relative to his or her verbal score, the more impaired he or she was in social functioning. This association remained significant, $r = -.35, p < .02$, when the variance explained by verbal ability was partialled from the correlation. In addition, a MANCOVA, covarying for verbal ability, showed significantly higher social symptom scores in the school-age V<NV relative to the V>NV and V=NV groups, but no group differences in communication symptoms. In the preschool group, there was no relation between V-NV difference score and social or communicative symptom scores, and no differences between V-NV discrepancy groups in symptom severity.

In summary, school-age children with discrepantly superior visual-spatial skills evidenced greater social impairment than other children with ASD, and this impairment was independent of their generally lower verbal skills (see also Joseph, Keehn, Connolly, Wolfe, & Horowitz, 2009, for complementary findings from a visual search task). Whether school-age children had discrepantly superior verbal skills, or presented with no discrepancy, had no bearing on social symptom severity. These findings suggested that, even if a V<NV IQ profile is not prototypical of ASD, it is nonetheless special. Accordingly, we hypothesized that the imbalance in cognitive functioning represented by the V<NV profile, and its specific association with increased impairment in reciprocal social interaction, may reflect a particularly severe disturbance in brain organization and, as such, might provide a categorical or dimensional marker for an etiologically significant subtype of autism.

To test this hypothesis further, we assessed whether V<NV discrepancies might be specifically related to enlarged head circumference and increased brain volume. Although not found in all individuals, group trends toward increased head size and increased brain size are thus far the most replicated neurobiological findings on ASD (Lainhart et al., 2006; Redcay & Courchesne, 2005). Deutsch and Joseph (2003) examined the relationship of head circumference to DAS V-NV differences in a sample of 63 children with a mean age of 7.3 years and a mean full-scale IQ of 76. We found that macrocephaly (> 97th percentile) occurred at a rate of 14%, and large head size (> 90th percentile) occurred at a rate of 33%, which in both cases was significantly higher than expected based on norms ($p < .001$) and consistent with previous findings. As in Joseph et al. (2002), we examined the effects of V-NV discrepancies categorically and dimensionally. The three V-NV discrepancy groups did not differ in age or in full-scale IQ, although the V<NV group trended toward higher full-scale IQ than the other two groups. Head circumference was significantly larger in the V<NV group than the other two discrepancy groups. Correlational analyses for the entire sample showed V-NV discrepancy scores were not correlated with full-scale, verbal or nonverbal IQ scores, but were significantly and inversely correlated with head circumference, $r = .38$, $p < .01$, and this correlation remained significant when verbal score was partialled, $r = .35$, $p < .02$. Our finding that discrepantly higher nonverbal abilities were associated with increased head circumference in children with ASD was replicated in a much larger sample of 208 individuals (Lainhart et al., 2006). However, although the correlation was significant ($p < .007$), it was rather small ($r = -.21$), perhaps owing to the use of multiple different IQ test and the much broader range of age and full-scale IQ in this multi-site sample. We followed up our head circumference study by assessing the relationship of V-NV discrepancies to differences in brain volume (Tager-Flusberg & Joseph, 2003). In this study, we compared 8 children who had significant V<NV discrepancies on the DAS and 8 children without a V-NV discrepancy. The groups did not differ in age ($M = 9.9$ years) or in full-scale IQ ($M = 88$). We found that the V<NV group had significantly increased cerebral gray matter volume relative to the V=NV group, and that the increase was generally consistent across frontal, parietal, temporal, occipital, and paralimbic cortex.

Our findings linking discrepantly superior visual-perceptual abilities to increased head and brain size in children with ASD converge with recent proposals that brain overgrowth in ASD reflects a fundamental disturbance in early neural development and organization that disrupts structural and functional cortical connectivity (Geschwind & Levitt, 2007; Lewis & Elman, 2008). The exact nature of this neurodevelopmental disturbance is unknown, but could involve any of a number of prenatal and postnatal processes, including neural genesis and migration, axon guidance, formation of synapses and dendrites, programmed cell death, axonal and syntactic pruning, and myelination. From this perspective, disturbances in longer-range cortical connectivity, particularly between higher-level association cortex and the sensory cortices, results in diminished top-down modulation or integration of lower-level visual-perceptual inputs (Courchesne & Pierce, 2005; Just, Cherkassky, Keller, Kana, & Minshew, 2007). Alternatively, local anomalies at the site of early visual processing, such as malformation of cortical minicolumn microcircuitry (Casanova, Buxhoeveden, & Gomez, 2003), or an imbalance in neurotransmitters regulating the ratio of excitation to inhibition in cortical cell assemblies (Rubenstein & Merzenich, 2003), might result in an over-amplification of lower-level visual information (e.g., Bertone, Mottron, Jelenic, & Faubert, 2005; Plaisted, Saksida, Alcantara, & Weisblatt, 2003; see Chapter 11). As reviewed by Geschwind and Levitt (2007), mutations of a number of genes regulating early neurodevelopment, including neural connectivity, have already been identified in ASD, but show only weak-to-moderate associations, likely owing to complex multigenic interactions and significant genetic heterogeneity. Given evidence linking unevenly developed visual-perceptual skills, increased brain size, and developmental perturbations in cortical connectivity, V-NV IQ discrepancies could plausibly provide a highly efficient neurocognitive subtyping tool for reducing the heterogeneity impeding the search for genes involved in cerebral overgrowth and disconnection in ASD.

CONCLUSIONS

IQ tests have proven to be informative and useful measures in both the clinical care of individuals with ASD, and in scientific inquiry aimed at understanding the complex etiology of ASD. Research has shown that IQ can be reliably and validly measured even in young children with ASD, but at the same time suggests that improvements can be made, particularly in the assessment of toddlers and younger preschool-age children. Moreover, research has shown IQ to be one of the most robust predictors of outcome for individuals with ASD, but with important qualifications. One is that low IQ is more reliably predictive of a poorer outcome than high IQ is of a better outcome. Another is that IQ, especially among higher-ability individuals, often significantly exceeds "real-life" adaptive skills, particularly in the domain of social functioning. From a clinical-care perspective, normal-range IQ scores can be extremely misleading regarding the continued need for therapeutic intervention and special accommodations for social disability, particularly in educational and vocational settings. From a research perspective, further inquiry is needed to better understand the relatively limited moderating effects of IQ on adaptive social functioning, and to develop treatments based on the learning processes through which social skills are actually acquired.

IQ testing, and identification of cognitive strengths and weaknesses, is useful in educational planning for children with ASD, as it is for all children, but cognitive profiles derived from IQ tests do not appear to be useful in the differential diagnosis of autism, or in differentiating between ASD diagnoses, at least as they are currently defined according to *DSM-IV* criteria. However, global IQ measures, as has long been recognized, and measures of differential cognitive abilities, as has been argued in this chapter, do appear to have value in parsing some of the immense variability that characterizes ASD at the level of neurobiological cause as well as the level of behavioral expression. Standardized cognitive assessment instruments are particularly valuable in this regard, for the very reason that they are standardized and can be reliably administered across very large multisite research samples, which are necessary for resolving etiological heterogeneity. Such tests will be most useful and informative when they are designed to yield homogenous, robust measures of differential cognitive abilities across the widest range of age and development possible.

References

Akshoomof, N. (2006). Use of the Mullen Scales of Early Learning for the assessment of young children with autism spectrum disorders. *Child Neuropsychology*, 12, 269–277.

American Psychiatric Association (1994). *Diagnostic and Statistical Manual of Mental Disorders (DSM-IV)*. 4th Edition. Washington, D.C: APA.

Anderson, D. K., Lord, C., Risi, S., DiLavore, P. S., Shulman, C., Thurm, A., Welch, K., & Pickles, A. (2007). Patterns of growth in verbal abilities among children with autism spectrum disorder. *Journal of Consulting and Clinical Psychology*, 75, 594–604.

Ashley-Koch, A. E., Mei, H., Jaworski, J., Ma, D. Q., Ritchie, M. D., Menold, M. M. . . . Pericak-Vance, M. A. (2006). An analysis paradigm for investigating multi-locus effects in complex disease: Examination of three GABA receptor subunit genes on 15q11-q13 as risk factors for autistic disorder. *Annals of Human Genetics*, 70, 281–292.

Baird, G., Charman, T., Baron-Cohen, S., Cox, A., Swettenham, J., Wheelwright, S., & Drew, A. (2000). A screening instrument for autism at 18 months of age: A 6-year follow-up study. *Journal of the American Academy of Child and Adolescent Psychiatry*, 39, 694–702.

Banach, R., Szatmari, P., Goldberg, J., Tuff, L. P., Zwaigenbaum, L., Mahoney, W. J., & Thompson, A. (2009). Brief report: Relationship between nonverbal IQ and gender in Autism. *Journal of Autism and Developmental Disorders*, 39, 188–193.

Bellini, S., & Peters, J. K. (2008). Social skills training for youth with autism spectrum disorders. *Child and Adolescent Psychiatric Clinics of North America*, 17, 857–873.

Bertone, A., Mottron, L., Jelenic, P., & Faubert, J. (2005). Enhanced and diminished visuo-spatial information processing in autism depends on stimulus complexity. *Brain*, 128, 2430–2441.

Boltë, S., & Poustka, F. (2002). The relation between general cognitive level and adaptive behavior domains in individuals with autism with and without co-morbid mental retardation. *Child Psychiatric and Human Development*, 33, 165–172.

Bryson, S. E., Clark, B. S., & Smith, I. (1988). First report of a Canadian epidemiological study of autistic syndromes. *Journal of Child Psychology and Psychiatry and Allied Disciplines*, 29, 433–446.

Caron, M. J., Mottron, L., Berthiaume, C., & Dawson, M. (2006). Cognitive mechanisms, specificity and neural underpinnings of visuospatial peaks in autism. *Brain*, 129, 1789–1802.

Carter, A. S., Volkmar, F. R., Sparrow, S. S., Wang, J. J., Lord, C., Dawson, G., . . . & Schopler, E. (1998). The Vineland Adaptive Behavior Scales: Supplementary norms for individuals with autism. *Journal of Autism and Developmental Disorders*, 28, 287–302.

Casanova, M. F., Buxhoeveden, D. P., & Gomez, J. (2003). Disruption in the inhibitory architecture of the cell minicolumn: Implications for autism. *Neuroscientist*, 9, 496–507.

Courchesne, E., & Pierce, K. (2005). Why the frontal cortex in autism might be talking only to itself: Local over-connectivity but long-distance disconnection. *Current Opinion in Neurobiology*, 15, 225–230.

Centers for Disease Control and Prevention (2007a). Prevalence of autism spectrum disorders—autism and developmental disabilities monitoring network, 6 sites, United States, 2000. *Surveillance Summaries, Feb. 9, 2007. MMWR*, 56, 1–11.

Centers for Disease Control and Prevention (2007b). Prevalence of autism spectrum disorders—autism and developmental disabilities monitoring network, 14 sites, United States, 2002. *Surveillance Summaries, Feb. 9, 2007. MMWR*, 56, 12–28.

Chakrabarti, S., & Fombonne, E. (2001). Pervasive developmental disorders in preschool children.

Journal of the American Medical Association, 285, 3093–3099.

Chakrabarti, S., & Fombonne, E. (2003). Pervasive developmental disorders in preschool children: Confirmation of high prevalence. *American Journal of Psychiatry, 162,* 1133–1141.

Charman, T., Taylor, E., Drew, A., Cockerill, H., Brown, J., & Baird, G. (2005). Outcome at 7 years of children diagnosed with autism at age 2. *Journal of Child Psychology and Psychiatry, 46,* 500–513.

Deutsch, C., & Joseph, R. M. (2003). Brief report: Cognitive correlates of enlarged head circumference in children with autism. *Journal of Autism and Developmental Disorders, 33,* 209–215.

Elliott, C. D. (1990). *Differential ability scales.* New York: The Psychological Corporation.

Elliott, C. D. (2007). *Differential ability scales* (2nd ed.). New York: The Psychological Corporation.

Fombonne, E. (1999). The epidemiology of autism: A review. *Psychological Medicine, 29,* 769–786.

Fombonne, E. (2003). Epidemiological surveys of autism and other pervasive developmental disorders: An update. *Journal of Autism and Developmental Disorders, 33,* 365–382.

Freeman, B. J., Del'Homme, M., Guthrie, D., & Zhang, F. (1999). Vineland adaptive behavior scale scores as a function of age and initial IQ in 210 autistic children. *Journal of Autism and Developmental Disorders, 5,* 379–384.

Geschwind, D. H. (2008). Autism: Many genes, common pathways? *Cell, 135,* 391–395.

Geschwind, D. H., & Levitt, P. (2007). Autism spectrum disorders: Developmental disconnection syndromes. *Current Opinion in Neurobiology, 17,* 103–111.

Gillberg, C., & Steffenburg, S. (1987). Outcome and prognostic factors in infantile autism and similar conditions: A population-based study of 46 cases followed through puberty. *Journal of Autism and Developmental Disorders, 17,* 273–287.

Happé, F. G. E. (1994). Wechsler IQ profile and theory of mind in autism: A research note. *Journal of Child Psychology and Psychiatry, 35,* 1461–1471.

Happé, F. (1999). Autism: Cognitive deficit or cognitive style? *Trends in Cognitive Sciences, 3,* 216–222.

Happé, F., & Frith, U. (2006). The weak coherence account: Detail-focused cognitive style in autism spectrum disorders. *Journal of Autism and Developmental Disorders, 36,* 5–25.

Howlin, P., Goode, S., Hutton, J., & Rutter, M. (2004). Adult outcome for children with autism. *Journal of Child Psychology and Psychiatry, 45,* 212–229.

Hus, V., Pickles, A., Cook, E. H., Risi, S., & Lord, C. (2007). Using the autism diagnostic interview — Revised to increase the phenotypic homogeneity in genetic studies of autism. *Biological Psychiatry, 61,* 438–448.

Jarrold, C., & Russell, J. (1997). Counting abilities in autism: Possible implications for central coherence theory. *Journal of Autism and Developmental Disorders, 27,* 25–37.

Jolliffe, T., & Baron-Cohen, S. (1997). Are people with autism and Asperger syndrome faster than normal on the Embedded Figures Test? *Journal of Child Psychology and Psychiatry, 38,* 527–534.

Joseph, R. M., Keehn, B., Connolly, C. E., Wolfe, J. M., & Horowitz, T. S. (2009). Why is visual search superior in autism spectrum disorder? *Developmental Science, 12,* 1083–1096.

Joseph, R. M., & Tager-Flusberg, H. (2004). The relationship of theory of mind and executive functions to symptom type and severity in children with autism. *Development and Psychopathology, 16,* 137–155.

Joseph, R. M., Tager-Flusberg, H., & Lord, C. (2002). Cognitive profiles and social-communicative functioning in children with autism. *Journal of Child Psychology and Psychiatry, 6,* 807–821.

Just, M. A., Cherkassky, V.L., Keller, T. A., Kana, R. K., & Minshew, N. J. (2007). Functional and anatomical cortical underconnectivity in autism: Evidence from an fMRI study of an executive function task and corpus callosum morphometry. *Cerebral Cortex, 17,* 951–961.

Klin, A., Jones, W., Schultz, R., & Volkmar, F. (2003). The enactive mind, or from actions to cognition: Lessons from autism. *Philosophical Transactions: Biological Sciences, 358*(1430), 345–360.

Klin, A., Saulnier, C. A., Sparrow, S. S., Cicchetti, D. V., Volkmar, F. R., & Lord, C. (2007). Social and communication abilities and disabilities in higher-functioning individuals with autism spectrum disorders: The Vineland and ADOS. *Journal of Autism and Developmental Disorders, 37,* 748–759.

Kobayashi, R., Murata, T., & Yoshinaga, K. (1992). A follow-up study of 201 children with autism in Kyushu and Yamaguchi areas, Japan. *Journal of Autism and Developmental Disorders, 22,* 395–411.

Krug, D. A., Arik, J. L., & Almond, P. (1980). Behavior checklist for identifying severely handicappe6d individuals with high levels of autistic behaviour. *Journal of Child Psychology and Psychiatry, 21,* 221–229.

Kuschner, E. S., Bennetto, L., & Yost, K. (2007). Patterns of nonverbal cognitive functioning in young children with autism spectrum disorders. *Journal of Autism and Developmental Disorders, 37,* 795–807.

Lainhart, J. E., Bigler, E. D., Bocian, M., Coon, H., Dinh, E., Dawson, G., . . . Volkmar, F. (2006). Head circumference and height in autism: A study by the Collaborative Program of Excellence in Autism. *American Journal of Medical Genetics Part A, 140,* 2257–2274.

Lewis, J. D., & Elman, J. L. (2008). Growth-related neural reorganization and the autism phenotype: A test of the hypothesis that altered brain growth leads to altered connectivity. *Developmental Science, 11,* 135–155.

Lincoln, A. J., Allen, M., & Kilman, A. (1995). The assessment and interpretation of intellectual abilities in people with autism. In E. Schopler & G. Mesibov (Eds.), *Learning and cognition in autism* (pp. 89–117). New York: Plenum.

Lincoln, A., Courchesne, E., Allen, M., Hanson, E., & Ene, M. (1998). Neurobiology of Asperger syndrome: Seven case studies and quantitative magnetic resonance imaging findings. In E. Schopler, G. Mesibov, & L. J. Kunce (Eds.), *Asperger syndrome or high-functioning autism?* (pp. 145–166). New York: Plenum.

Lincoln, A. J., Courchesne, E., Kilman, B. A., Elmasian, R., & Allen, M. (1988). A study of intellectual abilities in high-functioning people with autism. *Journal of Autism and Developmental Disorders, 18,* 505–523.

Liu, X. Q., Paterson, A. D., Szatmari, P., & The Autism Genome Project Consortium. (2008). Genome-wide linkage analyses of quantitative and categorical autism subphenotypes. *Biological Psychiatry, 64,* 561–570.

Lockyer, L., & Rutter, M. (1969). A five- to fifteen-year follow-up study of infantile psychosis: III. Psychological aspects. *British Journal of Psychiatry, 115,* 865–882.

Lord, C., Rutter, M., DiLavore, P. C., & Risi, S. (1999). *Autism diagnostic observation schedule—WPS (ADOS-WPS).* Los Angeles, CA: Western Psychological Services.

Lord, C., & Schopler, E. (1985). Differences in sex ratios in autism as a function of measured intelligence. *Journal of Autism and Developmental Disorders, 15,* 185–193.

Lord, C., & Schopler, E. (1989a). The role of age at assessment, developmental level, and test in the stability of intelligence scores in young autistic children. *Journal of Autism and Developmental Disorders, 19,* 483–499.

Lord, C., & Schopler, E. (1989b). Stability of assessment results of autistic and nonautistic language-impaired children from preschool years to early school age. *Journal of Child Psychology and Psychiatry, 30,* 575–590.

Lord, C., Schopler, E., & Revicki, D. (1982). Sex differences in autism. *Journal of Autism and Developmental Disorders, 12*(4), 317–330.

Lotter, V. (1974). Factors related to outcome in autistic children. *Journal of Autism and Developmental Disorders, 4,* 263–277.

MacLean, J. E., Szatmari, P., Jones, M.B., Bryson, S .E., Mahoney, W. J., Bartolucci G., & Tuff, L. (1999). Familial factors influence level of functioning in pervasive developmental disorder. *Journal of the American Academy of Child and Adolescent Psychiatry, 38,* 746–753.

Manjiviona, J., & Prior, M. (1999). Neuropsychological profiles of children with Asperger syndrome and autism. *Autism, 3,* 327–356.

Mesibov, G. (1996). Commentary on Siegel, Minshew, and Goldstein. *Journal of Autism and Developmental Disorders, 26,* 387–388.

Mottron, L., Dawson, M. Soulieres, I., Hubert, B., & Burack, J. (2006). Enhanced perceptual functioning in autism: An update, and eight principles of autistic perception. *Journal of Autism and Developmental Disorders, 36,* 27–43.

Mullen, E. M. (1995). *Mullen scales of early learning* (AGS ed.). Circle Pines, MN: American Guidance Service Inc.

O'Riordan, M. A., Plaisted, K. C., Driver, J., & Baron-Cohen, S. (2001). Superior visual search in autism. *Journal of Experimental Psychology: Human Perception and Performance, 27,* 719–730.

Ozonoff, S., Goodlin-Jones, B. L., Solomon, M. (2005). Evidence-based assessment of autism spectrum disorders in children and adolescents. *Journal of Clinical Child and Adolescent Psychology, 34,* 523–540.

Ozonoff, S., South, M., & Miller, J. (2000). DSM-IV-defined Asperger disorder: Cognitive, behavioral, and early history differentiation from high-functioning autism. *Autism, 4,* 29–46.

Plaisted, K., O'Riordan, M., & Baron-Cohen, S. (1998). Enhanced visual search for a conjunctive target in autism: A research note. *Journal of Child Psychology and Psychiatry, 39,* 777–783.

Plaisted, K., Saksida, L., Alcantara, J., & Weisblatt, E. (2003). Towards an understanding of the mechanisms of weak central coherence effects: Experiments in visual configural learning and auditory perception. *Philosophical Transactions of the Royal Society: B (Biological Sciences), 358* (1430), 375–386.

Redcay, E., & Courchesne, E. (2005). When is the brain enlarged in autism? A meta-analysis of all brain size reports. *Biological Psychiatry, 58,* 1–9.

Roid, G. H., & Miller, L. J. (1997). *Leiter International Performance Scale-Revised.* Wood Dale, IL: Stoelting.

Rubenstein, J. L. R., & Merzenich, M. M. (2003). Model of autism: increased ratio of excitation/inhibition in key neural systems. *Genes, Brain and Behavior, 2,* 255–267.

Rumsey, J. M. (1992). Neuropsychological studies of high-level autism. In E. Schopler & G. B. Mesibov (Eds.), *High-functioning individuals with autism* (pp. 41–64). New York: Plenum Press.

Shah, A., & Frith, U. (1983). An islet of ability in autistic children: A research note. *Journal of Child Psychology and Psychiatry, 24,* 613–620.

Shah, A., & Frith, U. (1993). Why do autistic individuals show superior performance on the block design task? *Journal of Child Psychology and Psychiatry, 34,* 1351–1364.

Siegel, D. J., Minshew, N. J., & Goldstein, G. (1996). Wechsler IQ profiles in diagnosis of high-functioning autism. *Journal of Autism and Developmental Disorders, 26,* 389–406.

Sigman, M., & McGovern, C. W. (2005). Improvement in cognitive and language skills from preschool to adolescence in autism. *Journal of Autism and Developmental Disorders, 35*, 15–23.

Sigman, M., & Ruskin, E. (1999). Change and continuity in the social competence of children with Autism, Down syndrome, and developmental delays. *Monograph of the Society for Research in Child Development.* London, England: Blackwell.

Skuse, D.H. (2007). Rethinking the nature of genetic vulnerability to autistic spectrum disorders. *Trends in Genetics, 23*, 387–395.

Sparrow, S., Balla, D., & Cicchetti, D. V. (1984). *Vineland adaptive behavior scales.* Circle Pines, MN: American Guidance Service.

Stevens, M. C., Fein, D. A., Dunn, M., Allen, D., Waterhouse, L. H., Feinstein, C., & Rapin I. (2000). Subgroups of children with autism by cluster analysis: A longitudinal examination. *Journal of the American Academy of Child and Adolescent Psychiatry, 39*, 346–352.

Szatmari, P., Bryson, S. E., Boyle, M. H., Streiner, D. L., & Duku, E. (2003). Predictors of outcome among high functioning children with autism and Asperger syndrome. *Journal of Child Psychology and Psychiatry, 44*(4), 520–528.

Thurm, A. E., Lord, C., Lee, L.-C., Newschaffer, C. J. (2007). Predictors of language acquisition in preschool children with autism spectrum disorders. *Journal of Autism and Developmental Disorders, 37*, 1721–1734.

Tsai, L. Y., & Beisler, J. M. (1983). The development of sex differences in infantile autism. *The British Journal of Psychiatry, 142*, 373–378.

Venter, A., Lord, C., & Schopler, E. (1992). A follow-up study of high functioning autistic children. *Journal of Child Psychology and Psychiatry, 33*, 489–507.

Volkmar, F. R., Cicchetti, D. V., Cohen, D. J., & Bregman, J. (1992). Brief report: Developmental aspects of DSM-III-R criteria for autism. *Journal of Autism and Developmental Disorders, 22*, 657–662.

Volkmar, F. R., Szatmari, P., & Sparrow, S. S. (1993). Sex differences in pervasive developmental disorders. *Journal of Autism and Developmental Disorders, 23*(4), 579–591.

Wechsler, D. (1997). *Wechsler adult intelligence scale* (3rd ed.). San Antonio, TX: The Psychological Corporation.

Wechsler, D. (1991). *Wechsler intelligence scale for children* (3rd ed.). San Antonio, TX: Psychological Corporation.

Williams, D. L., Goldstein, G., Kojkowski, N., & Minshew, N. J. (2008). Do individuals with high functioning autism have the IQ profile associated with nonverbal learning disability? *Research in Autism Spectrum Disorders, 2*, 353–361.

Yeargin-Allsopp, M., Rice, C., Karapurkar, T., Doernberg, N., Boyle, C., & Murphy, C. (2003). Prevalence of autism in a US metropolitan area. *Journal of the American Medical Association, 289*(1), 49–55.

Chapter 16

Clinical Implications for Assessment and Treatment of ASD

Julie M. Wolf and Elizabeth Kelley

While the signs of autism are generally not visible until the second year of life (Landa & Garrett-Mayer, 2006; Zwaigenbaum et al., 2005), the effectiveness of early intervention has led to an increase in research aiming to identify even earlier markers of autism spectrum disorders (ASD). Many research centers are now conducting prospective studies of infants at risk for developing ASD, in an attempt to identify such early markers. Meanwhile, multiple theorists have posited possible early origins of the impairments characteristic of ASD. Theorists often suggest a single deficit (e.g., in social motivation, imitation, Theory of Mind) that in turn impacts other areas of development, thus resulting in the complex presentation of ASD in childhood. What is noted throughout this section, and elaborated in this chapter, is the complex interplay between these various functions even in early development, suggesting that the pattern of impairments is likely a complex one from very early in development.

As noted in Chapter 12 of this volume, some have hypothesized that the social impairments observed in individuals with ASD arise from a motivational impairment, which in turn leads to a decreased attention to social stimuli during a critical period in early development (Dawson, 2008; Grelotti, Gauthier, & Schultz, 2002). This in turn impacts the subsequent development of social skills that are dependent upon this initial learning. For example, in chapter 13, Colombi et al. discussed how the failure to attend to the demonstrator (as opposed to the demonstration) while viewing an imitable action limits the child's ability to determine the goal directedness or intentions of the demonstrator. Thus, from very early on, the posited impairment in social motivation directs children's attention away from socially meaningful stimuli, and they in turn fail to learn to infer social intent or meaning. This missed opportunity for learning in early childhood reverberates throughout development, leading to the impairments in joint attention, language, symbolic play,

Theory of Mind, and interpretation of social nuance observed in individuals with ASD.

The early social and imitation impairment has close ties to motor development, in that it is necessary to create internal models of movement in order to learn to perform complex movements, and this learning happens socially. As Wodka and Mostofsky note in Chapter 10, the internal models used for learning movements may be the same ones by which the brain understands the actions of others (Iacoboni, 2005; Rizzolatti, Fogassi, & Gallese, 2001; Williams, Whiten, & Singh, 2004). Thus, some movement impairments in individuals with ASD may be secondary to social impairments, consistent with Dowell & Mostofsky's (2009) finding that individuals with ASD are particularly impaired on visuomotor sequence learning that is depending on imitation. However, it should be noted that many individuals with ASD also have primary motor deficits (e.g. low muscle tone) that likely cannot be attributed to social impairments.

As Eigsti discussed in Chapter 9, deficits in executive functions may also underlie some of the social impairments experienced by individuals with ASD. Links between executive functioning and Theory of Mind have been found in children as young as preschool age (see Pellicano, 2007 for a review). In young adults, degree of social skill has been found to be related to the ability to engage in cognitive shifting (Berger et al., 2003). It is further plausible that deficits in response inhibition (Hughes & Russell, 1993) could contribute to a failure to inhibit inappropriate social behaviors. Executive functioning impairments may also be related to restricted and repetitive behaviors exhibited by children with ASD. Although Eigsti notes that children with ASD do not have impairments in cognitive control, impairments in set-shifting may account for some perseverative behaviors, as well as the tendency to become fixated on topics or objects of interest (and hence, to fail to shift attention to other topics or objects).

Regardless of the specific etiology of ASD, or whether one area represents a "core" deficit that is the antecedent to all other impairments, what is clear is that the various neuropsychological functions impact and interact with one another throughout development. As a result of this complex interplay of functions, it is critical that assessment and treatment be comprehensive, and explore the child's needs in each of these domains. The remainder of this chapter is devoted to a discussion of assessment and treatment considerations both generally and with regard to the specific domains of neuropsychological functioning discussed throughout this section.

CONSIDERATIONS IN DIAGNOSTIC AND NEUROPSYCHOLOGICAL ASSESSMENT OF ASD

General Considerations in Assessment

Diagnostic assessment

Diagnostic assessment of ASDs should include both direct observation of the child, as well as a parent interview to obtain information about early development. The current "gold standard" diagnostic measures are the Autism Diagnostic Observation Schedule (ADOS; Lord, Rutter, DiLavore, & Risi, 2002) and the Autism Diagnostic Interview (ADI; Rutter, LeCouteur, & Lord, 2003), although a number of other measures are available as well, including the Diagnostic Interview of Social and Communication Disorders (DISCO; Wing, Leekam, Libby, Gould, & Larcombe, 2002), the Childhood Autism Rating Scale (CARS; Schopler, Reichler, & Renner, 1986), and the Autism Observational Scale for Infants (AOSI; Bryson, McDermott, Rombough, & Zwaigenbaum, 2008).

In conducting a diagnostic evaluation, the child's presentation should be considered within the context of a number of demographic factors. Ethnicity and Socioeconomic Status (SES) are among the considerations, as Klaver, Heurta, Guter, and Cook (2009) found that minority subjects may not be as likely to receive an ASD diagnosis as their first diagnosis, despite this being the best diagnosis for the child. Age is also a consideration, in that symptoms may change dramatically across the life span (Klinger & Renner, 2000). While the young child with autism may have very little language and no interest in other people, the adolescent with autism may have much more functional language (though still be impaired with regard to pragmatic language) and have interest in others, yet have continuing social difficulties. Likewise, repetitive behaviors that are common in young children (such as unusual sensory interests, lining up objects, and characteristic finger and hand mannerisms) may be replaced by ritualized behavior and a restricted pattern of interests in adolescence (Bishop, Richler, & Lord, 2006).

A child's presentation should also be considered in the context of his or her language and cognitive abilities. For example, which ADOS module is administered can have important effects on how the child scores on the diagnostic algorithm (Klein-Tasman, Risi, & Lord, 2007). Administering an ADOS module that is too easy linguistically or developmentally for the child will likely underestimate the degree of autism symptoms. Conversely, administering an ADOS module beyond the child's linguistic level may overestimate the degree of autism symptoms. If in doubt, elements of more than one module can be combined.

Similarly, when a child has a profound intellectual disability, it can be difficult to ascertain whether an autism spectrum disorder is also present (Lord, Rutter, & LeCouteur, 1994). This is because individuals with intellectual disabilities may exhibit a number of traits associated with ASD, such as language impairments and repetitive behaviors. However, they tend to be more socially motivated than individuals with autism, and this becomes an important differentiating factor. It may be particularly difficult to differentiate between autism and intellectual disability before a mental age of 18 months and a chronological age of 3 years (Lord & Risi, 2000), and therefore in young children it may be necessary to provide a provisional diagnosis that can be clarified over time.

In addition to child-specific factors impacting diagnosis, clinicians differ from one another with regard to which specific diagnosis (Autistic disorder, Asperger's disorder, Pervasive Developmental Disorder Not Otherwise Specified [PDD-NOS]) they choose to give. It is often the case that a child receives one diagnosis from one clinician and a different diagnosis when they seek a second opinion. This may be attributable to the fact that children's presentations do not always neatly fit within the diagnostic criteria set forth by the DSM-IV. Prior et al. (1998) note that differences in presentation within a diagnostic category are no greater than differences between diagnostic groups. Furthermore, in a systematic review of the literature, Witwer & Lecavalier (2008) found more differences between low- and high-IQ groups than between diagnostic subtypes with regard to clinical characteristics, neuropsychological profiles, comorbidity, and prognosis.

Reliability and validity considerations

In interpreting test results, it is important to take into account that almost no standardized measures include norms for individuals with ASD, with the Vineland Adaptive Behavior Scales, 2nd Edition (Sparrow et al., 2005) being one exception. In addition, there are few instruments designed to measure the stability of autistic traits over time. The AQ child (Auyeung, Baron-Cohen, Wheelwright, & Allison, 2008) and PDD-BI (Cohen, Schmidt-Lackner, S., Romanczyk, & Sudhalter, 2003), are exceptions; however, these two measures are not yet very widely used.

Furthermore, different tests may assess developmental level very differently, particularly in early childhood. For example, the Bayley Scales of Infant Development often underestimate the developmental level of young children with autism because there is a very strong social component to this test (Lord & Schopler, 1989).

Another reliability concern is the agreement between raters. Parents and teachers may give very different behavioral ratings, reflecting the fact that many measures assess state, rather than trait characteristics (Kanne, Abbachi, & Constantino, 2009). In particular, low levels of agreement have been found between parents and teachers on the Behavior Assessment System for Children, Child Behavior Checklist, Behavior Rating Inventory of Executive Function (Kanne, Abbachi, & Constantino, 2009), Abberant Behavior Checklist, and Vineland (Szatmari, Archer, Fisman, & Streiner, 1994).

Characteristics of individuals with ASD that may impact test performance

In evaluating an individual with an autism spectrum disorder, the examiner must consider aspects of the individual's diagnosis that may influence their presentation during the testing session, and therefore may impact test performance. Due to their pragmatic language impairments, individuals with ASD may not understand the nature of the testing situation. They may have more difficulty than typically developing individuals staying on task, paying attention to the examiner, and answering questions in a relevant manner (Kelley, Jones, & Fein, 2003). The examiner should make a concerted effort to ascertain the extent to which performance weaknesses may be due a failure to comprehend task expectations.

Attentional difficulties may also hinder performance in the testing situation (see Chapter 8). Individuals with ASD have great difficulty in disengaging their attention (Landry & Bryson, 2004), and may perseverate on topics or tasks of interest. The examiner must be certain that the individual being assessed is indeed focused on the task at hand, and is not still thinking about the last task given or one of their obsessive interests. Individuals with ASD may also have difficulty perceiving speech in noise (Alcantara, Weisblatt, Moore, & Bolton, 2004), and therefore testing rooms should be as quiet and free of distractions as possible, to ensure that the individual with ASD can fully attend to the task at hand and process instructions.

Speed of information processing is also a factor to consider when administering any assessment measure. Individuals with ASD may have particular difficulty with stimuli presented at a fast rate, leading to hyperarousal and performance deficits (Raymaekers, van der Meere, & Roeyers, 2004). Thus, it is important when testing to allow ample time, whenever possible, for the individual to provide his or her response.

Social factors also affect test performance for individuals with ASD. Some individuals experience social anxiety, and this may affect how they respond to the examiner (Kuusiko et al., 2008). Other individuals may lack a motivation to please the examiner, and therefore not put forth their best effort. For example, Pascualvaca and colleagues (1998) showed that deficits in examiner-administered Wisconsin Card Sorting Test performance were not present when a computer-administered analogue of the task was presented instead. Examiners should note these observations, and consider them when interpreting test results.

Older, higher-functioning individuals on the autism spectrum will often have the skills to comment on their own experiences and perceptions of their difficulties. It is important to include an interview with these individuals as part of the assessment process. However, examiners should also take into consideration that even high-functioning individuals on the autism spectrum may not have the same degree of insight and ability to reflect on their own experiences as neurotypical individuals (Bishop, Gotham, Seltzer, & Lord, 2009).

Domain-Specific Considerations in Assessment

Cognitive Ability and Adaptive Skills

Cognitive testing is a critical component of the evaluation of individuals with ASD, as it is necessary to obtain a complete picture of the individual's cognitive strengths and weaknesses, rather than a simple focus on autistic symptoms. Common cognitive measures

utilized in the ASD population include the Wechsler intelligence scales (Wechsler, 1999, 2003), the Differential Ability Scales, 2nd Edition (DAS-II; Elliott, 2007), and the Leiter International Performance Scale, Revised (Roid & Miller, 1997; this is a nonverbal measure of intelligence useful in evaluating individuals with little or no spoken language).

As Joseph discussed in Chapter 15, individuals with ASD tend to exhibit cognitive profiles with a high degree of variability between domains and subtests, and yet there is no prototypical profile. A profile involving strengths in the nonverbal domain, as compared to the verbal domain, has often been associated with Autistic disorder, while the opposite pattern has been associated with Asperger's syndrome. However, not all children show these patterns, and as such, IQ profiles should not inform diagnostic decisions. Knowledge of an individual's cognitive profile is very helpful in treatment planning, however, in that the clinician can make recommendations that utilize a child's strengths and provide intervention and accommodations for areas of weakness.

Cognitive testing is also useful in documenting changes in the child's profile over the course of development, or progress over time. Outcomes vary tremendously, with many children making great gains in cognitive, language, and social development, while other children show less progress. As Joseph notes, preschool children with cognitive test scores in the severely impaired range are likely to remain in the intellectually impaired range throughout their lives. While this does not suggest that clinicians and educators should "give up" on these children, or assume that they will not make progress, it does suggest consideration of a greater focus on functional "life skills" and skills that will foster vocational success, rather than a focus on strict academics.

In this regard, an evaluation of adaptive behavior is also a critical component of an autism evaluation. The Vineland Adaptive Behavior Scales (Sparrow et al., 2005) are the most commonly used measure of adaptive functioning in the assessment of autism spectrum disorders, and assess functioning in the areas of communication, daily living, socialization, and motor skills. Individuals with autism typically display a highly variable profile on the Vineland, with the most pronounced deficits in socialization (Carter et al., 1998). Results from the Vineland are very useful in planning interventions targeting development of functional, adaptive life skills.

Language

As was discussed in Chapter 6 of this volume, there are a number of different components to language, and these may be differentially affected across children with ASD, and even may be differentially affected across development of the individual child with ASD. Most children on the autism spectrum have very low levels of language in toddlerhood and preschool, yet these very same children may become quite verbal with time and treatment.

As discussed in Chapter 6, verbal individuals with ASD show relative strengths in phonology and articulation, basic grammar, and single-word receptive vocabulary, although there may be a subgroup of children who have grammatical difficulties similar to those children with Specific Language Impairment, so grammar is an important area to assess. Individuals with ASD experience the most severe difficulties with semantics, output and comprehension of formulated speech, and pragmatic language.

A comprehensive speech/language evaluation is an important component in evaluating a child on the autism spectrum. Comprehensive language batteries such as the Clinical Evaluation of Language Fundamentals–Fourth Edition (CELF-IV; Semel, Wiig, & Secord, 2003) and Comprehensive Assessment of Spoken Language (CASL; Carrow-Woolfolk, 1999) are useful measures in this regard. For less verbal children, measures of single-word vocabulary, such as the Peabody Picture Vocabulary Test-Fourth Edition (PPVT-IV; Dunn & Dunn, 2007) can provide a basic estimate of receptive single-word knowledge. There are also measures of specific aspects of language; measures of pragmatic language, such as the Test of Pragmatic Language (TOPL; Phelps-Terasaki & Phelps-Gunn, 1992) and the Pragmatic Checklist on the CELF-IV can be particularly helpful in planning social skills interventions for children with ASD. However, it should be kept in mind that many children with autism have been taught what to say in certain social situations, and can answer questions about such situations correctly, but are unable to apply what they know in naturalistic social situations.

Imitation

As discussed in Chapter 13, individuals with ASD are impaired in imitation involving facial expressions and gestures, but are less impaired at imitating actions involving objects. Thus, it appears to be the social-communication function of imitation that is impaired, at least in part. The authors suggest that there may be different neurocircuitries underlying different types of imitation, with limbic system involvement in imitation that serves a social purpose, which may contribute to the social imitative impairments in ASD. This suggests that neuropsychological assessment should include a variety of tasks that can help to isolate the individual's deficit. In the case of imitation, this may mean including social imitative tasks as well as simple motor imitation tasks. If the individual is indeed impaired at the former, but not the latter, this would suggest limbic involvement, and a different approach to intervention than for a child whose imitation difficulties were more global (e.g. related to motor functioning).

Attention to social information may also play a role in imitation skill. As Columbi and colleagues discussed in Chapter 13, humans are biased to interpret others' actions as goal-directed, and from infancy, selectively attend to socially relevant aspects of others (faces, eyes, and hands). This tendency focuses their attention toward those aspects of the action that allow for semantic encoding. Children with ASD show reduced social attention from very young ages, and in turn, tend to look at the demonstration rather than the demonstrator when imitating an action. Columbi and colleagues suggest that they use a sublexical route rather than a semantic route for encoding actions to be imitated; as such, their method of encoding is not facilitated by a reading of the actor's intentions. Interestingly, Columbi et al. also cite recent data suggesting that individuals with ASD are able to predict the outcome of an action based on the actor's emotional state. This suggests that individuals with ASD may not have an inability to attend to social information, but rather fail to do so (a similar conclusion is reached by Kinsbourne and Helt in Chapter 18). As Columbi et al. note, there are multiple explanations that may account for this; it may be that individuals with ASD are not motivated to attend to social information; they may fail to pick up on subtle cues that would direct their attention toward social information; they may find attending to social information anxiety-arousing and therefore aversive; or they may have a low-level visual-processing impairment that prevents them from attending to socially relevant information. These various possibilities highlight the importance of a comprehensive neuropsychological evaluation to determine what may underlie the social attention/imitation impairment in a given individual.

For example, measures of visual attention, observation of social motivation, and a psychiatric evaluation of anxiety, as well as evaluation of motor disability or overall intellectual disability, may all help to shed light on the factors contributing to an individual's social presentation, and in turn inform treatment approaches.

Social Behavior and Social Cognition

Social impairments are often considered the "core" deficit in ASDs, and yet there are few measures to effectively assess a child's social functioning. Such assessment is largely made through observational measures (e.g., the ADOS), and subsequent coding of the quality of the child's social interactions, and through interviews of knowledgeable informants such as parents and teachers. Measures of pragmatic language also provide information about a child's social functioning. However, as noted above, pragmatic language tests assess whether the children know what they are *supposed* to say in a given situation, which may not reflect what the child actually does in naturalistic settings. A number of rating scales are available, such as the Social Skills Improvement System (SSRS; Gresham & Elliot, 2009), which can be completed by both parent and teacher, and can nicely supplement direct observation measures by providing input into a child's functioning in naturalistic environments, such as the home and school.

In addition to general measures of social functioning, neuropsychological assessment may include measures of specific aspects of social cognition. For example, as South and colleagues discuss in Chapter 12, extensive research has identified face-processing deficits in individuals with ASD, which suggests that individuals with ASD utilize a feature-based, rather than holistic, approach to processing faces. The Let's Face It! Assessment battery (Wolf et al., 2008) has been developed as a comprehensive measure of face-processing skills, and includes measures of both holistic and part-based processing, allowing for an assessment of the types of strategies the individual may use. Other published, standardized measures of face recognition and memory are also available, such as the Benton Test of Facial Recognition (Benton et al., 1983), as well as face memory subtests of the Children's Memory Scales (Cohen, 1997) and NEPSY-II Affect Recognition and Theory of Mind subtests (Korkman, Kirk, & Kirk, 2007)). While these measures of face processing are not diagnostic, they can provide useful information in planning social interventions.

Sensory Function

Although not specific to ASD, children on the autism spectrum often have sensory impairments (both over- and under-sensitivity; Iarocci & MacDonald, 2006; Liss, Saulnier, Fein, & Kinsbourne, 2006; see also Chapter 11). An evaluation by an occupational therapist, and parent- and teacher-report measures such as the Sensory Profile (Dunn, 1999), are useful components for determining the sensory sensitivities of the child, and in planning appropriate therapy and accommodations to address these needs, such as desensitization or environmental accommodations.

As was discussed by Kenet in Chapter 11, sensory processing problems are not diagnostic of ASD, but they are very commonly found in the ASD population. Moreover, these sensory-processing problems have important downstream effects on cognition and behavior, as individuals who are overwhelmed by sensory stimuli may engage in a very limited range of behaviors and environments in order to protect themselves from overstimulation (see Chapter 19 for a discussion of the relationship between repetitive behaviors and overarousal). Kenet eloquently discusses the issue of signal-to-noise ratios in sensory processing, and how many individuals with ASD do not seem able to pick the relevant stimuli out of the incoming sensory stream. This may lead to either hypersensitivity or hyposensitivity in sensory processing in any of the sensory domains.

These sensory difficulties have important implications for the assessment of individuals with ASD. Testing should take place in a quiet environment, with little sensory distraction so that the individual being tested is able to focus on the relevant sensory information. However, it can also be revealing to observe the child's ability to attend under distracting conditions, since the environment he will encounter in school, for example, may contain multiple distractions.

Repetitive Behavior

The most common method used to assess repetitive behaviors in individuals with ASD is the Repetitive Behavior Scales–Revised (Bodfish et al., 2000; Lewis & Bodfish, 1998). This is a parent-administered checklist which assesses numerous restricted, repetitive, stereotypical, and ritualistic behaviors that individuals with ASD display. This checklist also assesses the extent to which these behaviors interfere with an individual's functioning.

Children with ASD, particularly younger and lower-functioning children, may demonstrate a great deal of repetitive behavior in the clinical setting, given the unfamiliarity of the setting and the demands being placed upon them (Horner, Carr, Strain, Todd, & Reed, 2002; Turner, 1999). Often the child will demonstrate such behaviors when she or he is frustrated and trying to escape the testing situation. The clinician must be very careful not to reinforce these behaviors by allowing the child to stop testing; —that is, reinforcing these behaviors by providing an escape from frustration (Joosten, Bundy, & Einfield, 2009; Lewis & Bodfish, 1998). Repetitive behaviors may also be seen when the individual with ASD is over-aroused (Chapter 19),and thus the testing room should be kept as quiet and calm as possible, in order to not overwhelm the patient.

Motor Function

Wodka and Mostofsky (Chapter 10) discuss the many motor difficulties that individuals with ASD may experience, including impairments in fine motor skills, gross motor skills, basic motor skills, and more complex motor skills involving planning and execution. These motor difficulties may affect gait, posture, coordination, and muscle tone. Although the motor difficulties of individuals with ASD have not been researched to the same extent that social and communicative difficulties have been, recent research indicates that motor impairments seem to be the norm rather than the exception in individuals with ASD.

Because of their difficulties with social interaction in the testing situation, as well as their known difficulties with imitation, it is important to assess motor skills without requiring the examinee to imitate actions performed by the clinician. Pegboard tests can be useful in this regard, as can graphomotor tests such as mazes, and tests that require the individual to act out a number of everyday actions, such as brushing one's teeth or combing one's hair. If motor difficulties are suspected, assessment by a neurologist, a physical therapist, or an occupational therapist is suggested.

Attention

As noted by Travers, Klinger and Klinger in Chapter 8, the attentional abilities of individuals with ASD are highly variable. Individuals with ASD may show impairments in many aspects of attention, including the automatic allocation of attention, controlled attention (particularly in higher-functioning individuals), and working memory. At the same time, individuals with ASD may have heightened attention to stimuli that are salient to them. This is consistent with the findings of Garretson, Fein, and Waterhouse (1990) suggesting that sustained attention in individuals with ASD improves when strong incentives are used.

Travers et al. (Chapter 8) review a number of measures for assessing attentional capacities. These include the Navon letter task (for assessing local vs. global attention), Stroop, Go/No-Go, and the Continuous Performance Test (CPT). In addition, measures of working memory (such as the Working Memory Index of the Wechsler scales) are impacted by attentional skills. A comprehensive battery of measures such as these can be an important component of a neuropsychological battery for individuals with ASD when attentional difficulties are suspected.

Attentional difficulties may impact an individual's performance during neuropsychological testing. As such, the clinician must keep in mind that distractions need to be kept to a minimum in order for the individual with ASD to perform to the best of their abilities. However, the clinician may also wish to test how resistant the individual is to distraction, as it is very difficult to avoid distracting environments in daily life. It is also often revealing to observe attentional difficulties evident during different types of tasks. It is not unusual to observe children with ASD who are highly inattentive and resistant to language tasks, but become much more able to attend and self-monitor during nonverbal tasks, which should suggest specific difficulties with language rather than basic attentional capacity.

Executive Function

Executive functioning deficits are frequently found in individuals with ASD, as was discussed by Eigsti (Chapter 9), although there are mixed findings in the literature with regard to this issue. Standard tests of executive functioning, such as the Wisconsin Card Sort Test and the Stroop, often do not find significant differences between individuals with ASD and well-matched control groups. Shifting attention and cognitive flexibility appear to be more impaired; however, there are some mixed findings in this literature as well.

As Eigsti mentions, problems with planning, shifting attention, monitoring performance, and cognitive flexibility are almost universally reported as difficulties that individuals with ASD experience in their day-to-day lives.

A number of comprehensive batteries exist for assessing executive functioning skills, such as the Delis-Kaplan Executive Function System (D-KEFS; Delis, Kaplan, & Kramer, 2001)] which includes planning, organization, fluency, attention, mental flexibility, set shifting, and concept formation. It should be noted, however, that executive functioning deficits may be subtle and therefore difficult to detect in older, higher-functioning children (Goldberg et al., 2005). Furthermore, children may perform well on measures of executive functioning in the structured testing environment, and yet show impairments in their ability to implement these skills in naturalistic settings (Geurts, Corbett, & Solomon, 2009; see also Chapter 9). As such, parent and teacher report measures, such as the Behavior Rating Inventory of Executive Function (BRIEF; Gioia, Isquith, Guy, & Kenworthy, 2000), can be informative as a supplement to test data.

Memory

The findings with regard to memory skills of individuals with autism are mixed. Some studies suggest impairments in verbal memory (Toichi & Kamio, 1998) and source memory (O'Shea et al., 2005). Deficits in episodic memory are also reported (Millward et al., 2000), although there are many clinical accounts of individuals with ASD who have exceptional episodic memory, as well as exceptional memory in general for topics that interest them.

In Chapter 7, Boucher and Mayes provided a comprehensive summary of memory functioning in individuals with ASD. In high-functioning individuals, classical conditioning and most forms of nondeclarative memory are unimpaired, although subtle procedural memory impairments may underlie some aspects of motor impairments in certain individuals. Memory for social and emotional information tends to be particularly impaired. Findings with regard to working memory are somewhat inconsistent, but Boucher notes in Chapter 23 that while verbal working memory is often intact in high-functioning individuals, visuospatial working memory tends to be impaired. With regard to long-term memory, recognition memory

is generally unimpaired (with the exception of some types of social information, such as recognition of unfamiliar faces). Findings with regard to free recall are mixed. Recall of autobiographical information tends to be impaired, while recall of factual information tends to be intact.

In lower-functioning individuals, findings are generally similar, although they show impairments in both recall and recognition memory. In addition, lower-functioning individuals may particularly rely upon procedural forms of learning. Boucher and Mayes argue that in individuals with high functioning autism, familiarity is intact while recollection is impaired, whereas in individuals with low functioning autism, both familiarity and recollection are impaired.

Thus, an important implication for neuropsychological assessment is that a cursory evaluation of memory functioning may fail to uncover important information about the individual. An evaluation of memory needs to include measures of free recall, cued recall, and recognition, as findings may be quite different from one individual to another. Furthermore, a comprehensive evaluation of memory, including comparisons of memory for social and nonsocial information (e.g. faces vs. objects), as well as measures of procedural learning (see Chapter 14), declarative memory, and working memory, will allow for the most comprehensive understanding of an individual's learning style, and guide intervention accordingly. Subtests of the NEPSY, the D-KEFS, and the California Verbal Learning Test assess many of these aspects of memory. For very low-functioning children, an observation that procedural or rote learning is more intact than episodic or semantic memory may be helpful for those teaching the child basic skills.

CONSIDERATIONS IN TREATMENT OF ASD

General Considerations in Intervention

Models of intervention

While many treatments are available for ASD, very few have extensive empirical support. Unfortunately, many treatments lacking empirical support are promoted and marketed in order to profit from parents who are eager to do whatever they can to help their child, or advocated sincerely by proponents who are not aware of or deterred by lack of evidence. In worst-case scenarios, such treatments may even be harmful (Woznicki, 2005). Thus, parents should be cautioned to be skeptical of treatments making bold claims of offering a "cure," and responsible clinicians should guide parents toward appropriate, scientifically validated interventions. Intensive early intervention is critical for long-term positive outcomes, although the specific manner of intervention may be less important than the fact that it is early, intensive, and involves individual instruction (Mundy, 2003).

The treatment approach that has garnered the most empirical support is based upon the principles of applied behavioral analysis (ABA), which involves intensive discrete trial instruction in a one-on-one context, with emphasis on generalizing learned skills to other settings. Discrete trials involve providing the child with an instruction (e.g. "touch cup"), awaiting the child's response, providing a prompt if needed (e.g. guiding the child's hand toward the cup), and feedback (e.g. reinforcement for a correct response). Behavioral interventions are most effective when begun early (prior to age 4), when treatment is intensive (up to 40 hours per week) and long term, and when generalization to the natural environment is emphasized (Lovaas, 2003). Support for the effectiveness of ABA comes from Lovaas' (2003) work suggesting significant long-term improvement in children who had received the intervention, as well as from numerous follow-up studies (e.g. Kelley, Paul, Fein, & Naigles, 2006). Despite its extensive empirical support, ABA has been criticized for producing "robotic" behaviors, and because it is expensive and time-intensive, making it infeasible for many families. Recent modifications to ABA focus on the use of intrinsic reinforcers when possible, a focus on generalization and maintenance, the gaining of fluency and communicative use, emphasis on development of positive affect, and a focus on specific "pivotal" skills that may underlie the learning of other skills. For a recent review of the efficacy of various forms of ABA and other interventions, see Rogers and Vismara (2008).

Other intervention models focus on providing environmental supports to foster learning. For example, the Treatment and Education of Autism and Related Communication-Handicapped Children (TEACCH) model (Mesibov, Shea, & Schopler, 2004) is a structured teaching program which places emphasis on providing visual and other supports to foster independence. Although the TEACCH method has not undergone extensive empirical investigation, there are some studies supporting its effectiveness (Panerai, Ferrante, & Zingale, 2002; Van Bourgondien, Reichle, & Schopler, 2003).

Educational setting

The appropriate educational setting should be based upon the individual needs of the child. Some children with autism spectrum disorders require a self-contained setting with intensive one-on-one instruction for optimal learning. Other children gain most from a mainstream placement and the maximal exposure to typically developing peers that it affords. Some children require a one-on-one aide who can adapt the curriculum to meet the needs of the child, while others need less support and may have resource room time devoted to work on particular areas of weakness. In general, it is important that educational goals be tailored to the individual child.

It is also important that educational plans include an emphasis on generalization. Children with autism may master a skill in one setting, and be unable to apply the same skill in another setting or with another individual. Once a skill is mastered in one setting, generalization can be encouraged by teaching or testing that skill in other settings or by other teachers. In the same vein, consistency across settings with regard to specific goals and structure of the environment will aid in learning and in generalization of skills across settings. Therefore, frequent communication between home and school, and among intervention providers, is essential for ensuring that similar goals and strategies are being emphasized in various settings.

Pharmacotherapy

Although no medications are available to treat the core symptoms of ASD, pharmacotherapy can be beneficial in alleviating some of the symptoms that are associated with ASD. Selective serotonin reuptake inhibitors (SSRIs), mood stabilizers, psychostimulants, and atypical antipsychotics may be effective in treating disruptive behaviors, self-injury, mood, and anxiety (Aman, 2004). For a summary of pharmacotherapeutic approaches to address emotional and behavioral regulation concerns in ASD, see Owley (2007).

Domain-Specific Considerations in Intervention

Cognitive Ability and Adaptive Skills

Individuals with ASD have difficulties with top-down processing or "central coherence" (or perhaps have heightened low-level or bottom-up processing; see Minshew, Johnson, & Luna, 2001 for further discussion of this issue). This contributes to a difficulty among many individuals with ASD in seeing the "big picture." Without this big-picture view, individuals with ASD may lack an organizational framework upon which to map their experiences and information they learn, which may contribute to their difficulties with implicit learning. Thus, treatment approaches need to incorporate explicit task instructions and expectations. Skills that typically developing individuals acquire implicitly need to be explicitly taught. The success of ABA-based treatment speaks to the effectiveness of explicit teaching methods for individuals with ASD.

IQ is one of the best predictors of adult outcomes in individuals with ASD (Billstedt, Gillberg, & Gillberg, 2005), although as Joseph noted in Chapter 15, low IQ is predictive of a poor outcome more than high IQ is predictive of a positive outcome. In high-functioning individuals, IQ often exceeds adaptive functioning, and therefore measures of adaptive functioning are critical in guiding intervention. In young children, basic self-help skills should be targeted, including toileting, feeding, and dressing. As children age, the focus should shift to more advanced skills, including cooking, cleaning, and managing money. In adolescence and adulthood, careful consideration should be given to educational or vocational placement and career planning. The provision of a job coach can be critical in ensuring the initial success of the individual in the workplace, and increase the likelihood of successful long-term employment (Keel, Mesibov, & Woods, 1997).

Language

Early language skills are a strong predictor of outcome (Billstedt, Gillberg, & Gillberg, 2007), and therefore, early language intervention is a critical component of a child's educational plan. Continued speech and language therapy throughout childhood is integral in the educational plan of a child on the autism spectrum. Treatment should not only focus on word acquisition,

but should place an emphasis on functional communication as well. Communication goals should be targeted throughout the day, in multiple settings, including opportunities to practice communicative skills in vivo. Specific target goals that may be appropriate include: making requests and communicating desires; narrating play; language comprehension; responding to questions; asking questions (using who, what, where, when, why, how many); increasing semantic knowledge; increasing complexity of utterances; using prepositions, quantitative terms, and qualitative adjectives; understanding spatial and temporal relationships; describing events; asking for clarification or help; verbal problem solving; and reciprocal conversation. Training in the area of conversational skills should involve initiating and maintaining a conversational topic, turn-taking, expanding and elaborating upon the topic at hand, taking the perspective of the conversational partner, and appropriately closing a conversation. Other common pragmatic language difficulties include: speaking a lot but not listening, inappropriately changing the topic to one of interest to the child, perseverating on topics of interest to the child/adolescent despite the listener's lack of interest, inappropriate use of eye contact and personal space, difficulties with idioms and figures of speech, difficulty with multiple conversational partners, use of inappropriately formal vocabulary, not saying everything you think, and many more. Specific programs and suggestions for helping the child with some of these issues can be found in Dunn (2005), Fein and Dunn (2007), and Goldstein and McGinnis (1997).

Children with ASD with limited language may also benefit from a number of assistive devices and technologies to aid in communication. These include the Picture Exchange Communication System (PECS; Bondy & Frost, 2001), sign language, and keyboards. Some evidence suggests that these communicative aids may help to increase the use of spoken language, including an increase in number of words used and in complexity of utterances (Ganz & Simpson, 2004).

Imitation

As Columbi et al. discussed in Chapter 13, the imitation impairments observed in individuals with ASD may be related to social inattention. Children with ASD tend to attend to the demonstration rather than the demonstrator when viewing an action to be imitated.

Furthermore, semantic coding of the action to be imitated is activated by actions that are familiar and meaningful, and thus this activation may not occur in children who lack social expertise. From an intervention standpoint, the question becomes whether it is possible to improve imitation skills by directing attention to social information from early in development. A further question is whether such early intervention would then have automatic sequellae in improving social attention and motivation in later development, or whether continued intervention would be necessary to help individuals with ASD to continue to prioritize social information throughout development. As Colombi et al. noted, longitudinal studies are needed in order to understand the connection between early social attention and imitation skills and later social functioning. Furthermore, they noted that it is unknown whether specific interventions are needed to teach social imitation skills in early development, or whether existing early interventions may be sufficient toward this end.

Whatever the underlying factors behind failure to develop imitation, it is clear that deficient imitation will preclude an extremely important route to learning, one on which typically developing children rely from the first year of life. Consequently, most ABA programs focus early on the development of imitation skills, starting with simple vocal and motor imitation, and progressing to more complex and more social skills, and consider the development of imitation to be a foundational skill for most later learning.

Social Cognition

A number of interventions targeting social skills development have been developed with some empirical support. Many of these models involve explicit teaching, given the impairments individuals with ASD have in implicit learning. These models have demonstrated effectiveness in improving social skills such as greeting and play skills (Barry et al., 2003); social initiation, eye contact, experience sharing, interest in peers, problem-solving skills, and emotional knowledge (Bauminger, 2002); conversational skills, topic selection, and self-perception (Mesibov, 1984); and increased social interaction time with peers (Morrison et al., 2001). Involvement of typically developing peers as models has also been shown to be effective (Chan et al., 2009).

Social skills interventions should be adapted to the needs of the individual child. In younger and lower-functioning individuals, social skill interventions typically target basic skills such as eye contact, social imitation, social communication, or simple reciprocal interactions (e.g. peek-a-boo). As Colombi et al. noted in Chapter 13, children with ASD may exhibit impairments in their ability to imitate social behaviors (such as facial expressions), while their basic imitation skills are intact. Thus, targeting imitation of social behaviors in early development may set the stage for the development of more complex understanding of social intentions. In middle childhood, intervention may focus on skills such as interactive play, awareness of self and others, reciprocal conversation, initiation of social interaction, and appropriate social responses. Once these skills are mastered, the focus of social skills intervention turns to fostering understanding of the complexities of social interactions, including abstract and subtle social cues, the emotions of self and others, appreciation of humor and sarcasm, and perspective taking.

As South et al. noted in Chapter 12, social skills impairments may have different etiologies from one child to the next, and treatment should be tailored accordingly. For example, social anxiety is very common in higher-functioning individuals with ASD (Kuusiko et al., 2008). These individuals are often quite interested in social interaction, yet are unable to engage with others due to their anxiety and their difficulties understanding the social world. Interventions for these individuals might therefore target relieving their anxiety through therapy and medication, in addition to traditional social skills interventions.

Intervention may also target specific aspects of social cognition. For example, the Let's Face It! intervention (Wolf et al., 2008) targets face-processing abilities (with regard to both facial identity and expression) via a computer game platform that is fun and motivating for children. Faja et al. (2008) also report on a computer-based intervention that was successful in remediating face-processing deficits in adults with ASD. A question is whether such interventions might have increased effectiveness if implemented during a sensitive period in early development in which typically developing children naturally acquire expertise with faces. An additional question is the extent to which gains can be generalized from a computer-based platform to real-world environments. As such, it may be beneficial to supplement computer-based interventions with additional strategies to aid the child in developing these skills (e.g. explicit teaching of emotion labels; modeling labeling of one's own affective experiences), and to foster generalization (e.g. practice in recognizing classroom peers).

In Chapter 12, South et al. reviewed a number of recent intervention approaches that aim to increase motivation associated with social interaction. These include the Relationship Development Intervention (RDI; Gutstein, 2000), which aims to teach children the inherent rewards associated with social interaction, and the Let's Face It! computer game intervention for teaching the face-processing skills mentioned above (Wolf et al., 2008). Carol Gray's (1998) "social stories" and "comic strip conversations" may serve this purpose as well, by presenting social skills lessons in an engaging story or cartoon format. Social stories and comic strip conversations have shown some effectiveness, but with limited generalization and maintenance of improvements (Delano & Snell, 2006; Greenway, 2000; Thiemann & Goldstein, 2001).

Sensory and Motor Function

As with other domains of functioning, children with ASD are quite heterogeneous with regard to their sensorimotor functioning. Sensory impairments, if present, range from sensory-seeking and self-stimulatory behaviors, to extreme aversion to certain sensory inputs. Thus, treatment should be tailored to the child's individual needs. Sensorimotor function is related to physical safety (e.g. children with gross motor impairments are susceptible to falling or other injury; children with sensory avoidance may unsafely bolt away from aversive stimuli; and self-injury may reflect an extreme form of sensory-seeking behavior). Thus, addressing a child's sensorimotor needs is a critical component of intervention.

Sensorimotor impairments in ASD are typically addressed through occupational therapy, although behavior therapy can be useful in desensitizing the children to aversive stimuli by teaching them relaxation procedures. Auditory processing may also be a focus of treatment (Lincoln, Dickstein, Courchesne, Elmasan, & Tallal, 1992). Sensory Integration Therapy is commonly included in the treatment of individuals with autism, including techniques such as swinging, deep pressure, weighted vests, and tactile stimulation. Despite the frequent inclusion of such treatments in the educational plans of children with autism, very little empirical research has been conducted investigating their effectiveness (Dawson & Watling, 2000);

it is possible that such techniques may benefit some children because they provide reinforcing activities, opportunities for a social relationship and a gross motor activity as a break from academics.

In addition to occupational therapy, environmental accommodations can be made to address a child's sensory needs. For a child with sensory sensitivities, quiet work areas, removal of distracting stimuli, and frequent sensory breaks may provide relief and increase on-task behavior. As children age, graphomotor demands of academic tasks increase (i.e., writing, drawing), and children with graphomotor weaknesses may require additional supports. For example, developing a child's keyboarding skills so that written tasks can be completed on the computer is a useful support for a child with a graphomotor weakness.

Repetitive Behaviors

As was mentioned in Chapter 19, many researchers have hypothesized that repetitive behaviors stem from chronic under- or over-arousal, although there is little direct evidence for this hypothesis, due at least in part to the relative lack of research assessing repetitive behaviors in this population. Others have hypothesized that repetitive behaviors are maintained through their reinforcing sensory qualities (Cunningham & Schreibman, 2008; Lewis & Bodfish, 1998; Lovaas, Newsom & Hickman, 1987); are an attempt to control the sensory input (Gabriels et al, 2008; Turner, 1999); or serve as a way of escaping aversive stimuli or frustrating situations (Horner et al, 2002; Lewis & Bodfish, 1998). Indeed, it is possible that all of these mechanisms are involved in the maintenance of repetitive behaviors in individuals with ASD, and thus it is strongly advised to conduct a functional assessment of these behaviors (Horner et al, 2002). A functional assessment involves carefully observing the situations in which the behavior occurs and allows the clinician to begin to understand the reasons for the behavior and thus be better able to respond to the underlying cause of the behavior itself.

There are many reasons why it is important to try to reduce the restricted and repetitive behaviors that are so frequently seen in ASD. As Kinsbourne noted in Chapter 19, these behaviors focus the individual's attention inwards and thus prohibit the individual from attending to their surroundings. Repetitive behaviors can be very socially stigmatizing (Cunningham & Schreibman, 2008), and their disruptive nature may preclude the child from being mainstreamed into a regular classroom (Horner et al., 2002).

Behavioral treatments have generally been the method of choice in treating repetitive behaviors in individuals with ASD, although drugs which stabilize the serotenergic, dominergic, and opiate systems may have some positive effects (see Chapter 19). It should be noted that while many of the most commonly seen repetitive behaviors may arise in typically developing infants (hand-flapping, spinning, rocking, lining up objects), these behaviors do not disappear in individuals with ASD. Thus, the mechanisms which lead to these behaviors may not be the same mechanisms that serve to maintain them; unlike in typical development, these behaviors are not outgrown (Horner et al, 2002).

The form of these behaviors may be irrelevant (with the exception of self-injurious behavior, which for obvious reasons is important to extinguish by whatever means necessary), and clinicians' focus should be on the function of these behaviors. Is the child engaging in these behaviors because they are overanxious, or understimulated, or trying to get out of something that they do not want to do? By assessing the reasons for the behavior, it will be easier to find a replacement behavior, or a way of ameliorating the anxiety, that is more socially and functionally acceptable. If the child is engaging in these behaviors purely for sensory stimulation, the sensory feedback can be removed, or the behavior can be replaced with a more appropriate one.

It should be noted that many repetitive behaviors are highly resistant to extinction. It is important to continually be vigilant in assessing the cause of the behaviors, enlist the caregiver's help in ensuring that these behaviors are never reinforced, try to widen the child's behavioral repertoire as much as possible, and attempt to eliminate the behavior as early as possible in its presentation (Horner et al, 2002; Lovaas et al, 1987; Turner, 1999).

Attention

While there are very few interventions that aim to directly improve attention (other than psychopharmacological intervention, e.g. with psychostimulants), a number of environmental supports and accommodations may be provided in order to help individuals with ASD to focus on the most relevant or salient information, and sustain their attention in order to complete tasks. These strategies include classroom modifications, such as removing distracters or seating the child near the teacher, simplifying complex tasks, and providing the child with frequent breaks.

Motivation appears to play a key role in sustained attention among individuals with ASD, as is anecdotally evident from their heightened attention to objects and topics of interest. Garretson et al. (1990) found that deficits in sustained attention in individuals with ASD were remediated by providing strong reinforcers. Similarly, Pascualvaca et al. (1998) found that individuals with ASD performed better on a computer-administered version of the Wisconsin Card Sorting Test than on a human-administered version, which they note may be attributable to the increased motivation associated with the computer-based task. Thus, an intervention strategy is to ensure that tasks are sufficiently motivating to individuals with ASD, either through utilizing strong reinforcers or through incorporating a child's interests into academic material (Jennett, Harris, & Mesibov, 2003).

Executive Function

Impairments in executive functions can be addressed via supports and environmental accommodations to aide in the child's planning and organizational skills (Rogers & Bennetto, 2000). Children with fluency or processing-speed impairments may be provided extended time for completing assignments and exams. Those with difficulty shifting set may benefit from tasks that have a clear beginning and end, and from being given warnings ("5 minutes left," "1 minute left") in order to cue the child that it is time to move on to the next activity, and to prevent the child from perseverating on any one activity. Planning and organizational skills can be taught and supported with visual aids. These include visual schedules (in words or pictures) of the day's activities; timers that help to monitor work pace and signify the end of an activity; "to-do" lists utilizing words and pictures to represent the tasks that must be completed; and visual sequence strips demonstrating the steps required to complete a task, as well as space organizers for notebooks and desks. Individuals with ASD may have particular difficulty with novel tasks with poorly defined rules (Ciesielski & Harris, 1997; Rogers & Bennetto, 2000), and as Eigsti noted in Chapter 9, often have difficulty with complex working-memory tasks. Both of these findings argue for breaking down complex or novel tasks into their component parts, so that the child can focus on the individual components without becoming overwhelmed by the complexity of the entire task. Eigsti suggested that the impairments in working-memory abilities, relative to typically developing peers, may not emerge until the child reaches school age. Notably, the onset of these impairments often coincides with late elementary school or the beginning of middle school, a time when academic task complexity and working-memory demands tend to increase (Gioia, Isquith, & Guy, 2001). Thus, accommodating the child's executive functioning deficits becomes critically important.

Memory

While few interventions have been developed to directly address memory impairments in individuals with ASD, the findings with regard to memory may point to some possible treatment directions. As Boucher and Mayes discussed in Chapter 7, cued recall appears to be intact in individuals with ASD. This supports the use of prompting as a teaching method (as is employed in discrete trial methods) and as a testing method, and other external supports and cues to facilitate learning and recall. For low-functioning children in particular, interventions that utilize their generally intact procedural learning may also be beneficial. With regard to the meaningfulness of information to be learned, Boucher reports finding that when both meaningful and non-meaningful cues are present, the attention of children with ASD may be drawn to the non-meaningful information. This suggests intervening to eliminate distracters and to isolate the child's attention on the task at hand in order to facilitate learning. This may also tie into findings related to source memory, in which recognition of non-social contextual information is intact, while recognition of social contextual information is impaired (O'Shea et al., 2005). This may be an example of non-meaningful (non-social) information pulling their attention away from more meaningful social information. This suggests that individuals with ASD may benefit from interventions aimed at guiding their attention toward social information. Finally, Minshew argues that individuals with ASD may have impairments in complex information processing, while simple information processing remains intact. This argues for accommodations and supports to help reduce the complexity of information to be remembered, such as simplifying instructions and breaking

down tasks and information into components, rather than presenting the full complexity of the information in its entirety.

CONCLUSIONS AND FUTURE DIRECTIONS

Autism is a complex neurobiological disorder, the etiology of which is largely unknown, but that involves contributions from the various neuropsychological functions discussed in this section. An important future direction for research is to further elucidate the genetic and neurobiological mechanisms that contribute to the development of autistic symptoms.

With regard to diagnosis of ASDs, an important direction concerns the diagnostic classification system. Despite the *DSM-IV's* categorical system for diagnosing autism spectrum disorders, individuals on the spectrum do not always demonstrate characteristics that fall neatly into any one of the diagnostic categories, and the differences between subtypes may reflect degree of impairment, rather than qualitative differences. As such, the upcoming *DSM-V* will include a single classification of "Autism Spectrum Disorder," with emphasis on dimensional classification and specifiers to denote degree of impairment (Lord, 2009). Research will be necessary to substantiate the validity of this new diagnostic system.

Given the benefit of early intervention, an important area of continued research is the development of methods for improving the early detection of children with autism. While screening methods have been developed to identify autism as early as possible (Robins, Fein, Barton, & Green, 2001), continued work is needed to ensure that these screeners are being implemented effectively. For example, Croen, Grether, and Selvin (2002) found that children from ethnic minority backgrounds are not identified as early as children from the majority culture. A challenge for researchers, clinicians, and policy makers is to ensure that all children across demographic groups are identified as early as possible, and to ensure that early intervention services are available to all children.

Continued development of assessment tools is also an area of high priority. Psychological and neuropsychological assessment tools often do not map onto cognitive functions that more recent and more basic science indicates are the natural categories of function. Assessment tools driven by cognitive neuroscience will ultimately shed more light on basic areas of spared and impaired functioning for each individual.

Finally, continued research is needed to provide empirical support for interventions used in the treatment of autism, and to develop new empirically validated interventions. Despite the numerous interventions available to individuals with ASD, only behavioral interventions have received extensive empirical support. In particular, while social skills are a primary target area for intervention among children with autism spectrum disorders, studies evaluating the effectiveness of social skills interventions tend to be inconclusive. This may be due to the nature of the social impairments themselves. Koenig et al. (2009) argue that traditional clinical trial methods may be inappropriate for evaluating social skills group interventions in that: a) social impairments in ASD are complex and multidimensional and, as such, improvements cannot be determined on the basis of uni-dimensional, "single indicator" outcome measures; and b) unlike psychiatric symptoms (i.e., depression) that have a clear onset and the ability to be fully alleviated, developmental symptoms do not lend themselves to conclusive, unambiguous determination of remediation. Thus, empirical support utilizing novel or observational means of evaluation may be necessary to substantiate the effectiveness of social skills interventions. Finally, research is needed to determine methods of tailoring intervention to a child's individual needs, to identify the components of various interventions that are most effective, and to develop new treatments that combine the most effective components of existing interventions.

References

Alcantara, J. I., Weisblatt, E. J. L., Moore, B. C. J., & Bolton, P. F. (2004). Speech-in-noise perception in high-functioning individuals with autism or Asperger's disorder. *Journal of Child Psychology and Psychiatry*, 45, 1107–1114.

Aman, M. G. (2004). Management of hyperactivity and other acting-out problems in patients with autism spectrum disorder. *Seminars in Pediatric Neurology*, 11(3), 225–228.

Auyeung, B., Baron-Cohen, S., Wheelwright, S., & Allison, C. (2008). The autism spectrum quotient: Children's version (AQ-Child). *Journal of Autism and Developmental Disorders*, 38, 1230–1240.

Barry, T. D., Klinger, L. G., Lee, J. M., Palardy, N., Gilmore, T., & Bodin, S. D. (2003). Examining the effectiveness of an outpatient clinic-based social skills group for high-functioning children with autism. *Journal of Autism and Developmental Disorders*, 33(6), 685–701.

Bauminger, N. (2002). The facilitation of social-emotional understanding and social interaction in high-functioning children with autism: Intervention outcomes. *Journal of Autism and Developmental Disorders*, 32(4), 283–298.

Benton, A. L., Hamsher, K. D. S., Varney, N. R., & Spreen, O. (1983). *Contributions to neuropsychological assessment*. New York: Oxford University Press.

Berger, H. J. C., Aerts, F. H. T. M., van Spaendonck, K. P. M., Cools, A. R., & Tuenisse, J. P. (2003). Central coherence and cognitive shifting in relation to social improvement in high-functioning adults with autism. *Journal of Clinical and Experimental Neuropsychology*, 25, 502–511.

Billstedt, E., Gillberg, C. & Gillberg, C. (2005). Autism after adolescence: Population-based 13- to 22-year follow-up study of 120 individuals diagnosed with autism in childhood. *Journal of Autism and Developmental Disorders*, 35, 351–360.

Billstedt, E, Gillberg, I. C., & Gillberg, C. (2007). Autism in adults: Symptom patterns and early childhood predictors. Use of the DISCO in a community sample followed from childhood. *Journal of Child Psychology and Psychiatry*, 48, 1102–1110.

Bishop, S. L., Gotham, K., Seltzer, M. M., & Lord, C. (2009, May). *Self-report in adolescents and adults with ASD: Implications for diagnostic assessment and for evaluation of the broader autism phenotype*. Paper presented at the Eighth Annual Meeting for Autism Research, Chicago, IL.

Bishop, S. L., Richler, J., & Lord, C. (2006). Association between restricted and repetitive behaviors and nonverbal IQ n children with autism spectrum disorders. *Child Neuropsychology*, 12, 247–267.

Bodfish, J. W., Symons, F. J., Parker, D. E., & Lewis, M. H. (2000). Varieties of repetitive behavior in autism: Comparisons to mental retardation. *Journal of Autism and Developmental Disorders*, 20(3), 237–243.

Bondy, A., & Frost, L. (2001). The picture exchange communication system. *Behavior Modification*, 25(5), 725–744.

Bryson, S. E., McDermott, C., Rombough, V., & Zwaigenbaum, L. (2008). The autism observational scale for infants: Scale development and assessment of reliability. *Journal of Autism and Developmental Disabilities*, 38 (4), 731–738.

Carrow-Woolfolk, E. (1999). *Comprehensive assessment of spoken language*. Circle Pines, MN: American Guidance Service.

Carter, A. S., Volkmar, F. R., Sparrow, S. S., Wang, J. J., Lord, C., Dawson, G., . . . Schopler, E. (1998). The Vineland adaptive behavior scales: Supplementary norms for individuals with autism. *Journal of Autism and Developmental Disorders*, 28(4), 287–302.

Chan, J.M., Lang, R., Rispoli, M., O'Reilly, M., Sigafoos, J., & Cole, H. (2009). Use of peer-mediated interventions in the treatment of autism spectrum disorders: A systematic review. *Research in Autism Spectrum Disorders, 3*(4), 876–889.

Ciesielski, K. T. & Harris, R. J. (1997). Factors related to performance failure on executive tasks in autism. *Child Neuropsychology, 3*, 1–12.

Cohen, M. J. (1997). *Children's memory scale.* San Antonio, TX: The Psychological Corporation, Harcourt Brace & Company.

Cohen, I. L., Schmidt-Lackner, S., Romanczyk, R., & Sudhalter, V. (2003). The PDD Behavior Inventory: A rating scale for assessing response to intervention in children with Pervasive Developmental Disorder. *Journal of Autism and Developmental Disorders, 33*, 31–45.

Croen, L. A., Grether, J. K., & Selvin, S. (2002). Descriptive epidemiology of autism in a California population: Who is at risk? *Journal of Autism and Developmental Disorders, 32*(3), 217–224.

Cunningham, A. B., & Schreibman, L. (2008). Stereotypy in autism: The importance of function. *Research in Autism Spectrum Disorders, 2*, 469–479.

Dawson, G. (2008). Early behavioral intervention, brain plasticity, and the prevention of autism spectrum disorder. *Development and Psychopathology, 20*, 775–803.

Dawson, G., & Watling, R. (2000). Interventions to facilitate auditory, visual, and motor integration in autism: A review of the evidence. *Journal of Autism and Developmental Disorders, 30*, 415–421.

Delano, M. & Snell, M. E. (2006). The effects of social stories on the social engagement of children with autism. *Journal of Positive Behavior Interventions, 8*(1), 29–42.

Dellis, D. C., Kaplan, E., & Kramer, J. H. (2001). *Delis-Kaplan executive functioning system.* Bloomington, MN: Pearson Assessments.

Dowell, L. R. & Mostofsky, S. H. (2009) Imitation-dependent visuomotor sequence learning in ASD. Accepted for presentation at the 8th International Meeting for Autism Research, Chicago, Illinois.

Dunn, L. M., & Dunn, D. M. (2007). *The Peabody picture vocabulary test* (4th ed.). Bloomington, MN: Pearson Assessments.

Dunn, M (2005). S.O.S.: Social skills in our schools: A social skills program for children with pervasive developmental disorders. Shawnee Mission, KS: Autism Asperger Publishing Company.

Dunn, W. (1999). *Sensory profile.* San Antonio, TX: Pearson Assessments.

Elliott, C. D. (2007). *Differential abilities scales-II.* Bloomington, MN: Pearson Assessments.

Faja, S., Aylward, E., Bernier, R., & Dawson, G. (2008). Becoming a face expert: A computerized face-training program for high-functioning individuals with autism spectrum disorders. *Developmental Neuropsychology, 33*(1), 1–24.

Fein, D., and Dunn, M. (2007) *Autism in your classroom: A general educator's guide to students with autism spectrum disorders.* NY: Woodbine House.

Gabriels, R. L., Agnew, J. A., Miller, L. J., Gralla, J., Pan, Z., Goldson, . . . Hooks, E. (2008). Is there a relationship between restricted, repetitive, stereotyped behaviors and interests and abnormal sensory response in children with autism spectrum disorders? *Research in Autism Spectrum Disorders, 2*, 660–670.

Ganz, J. B., & Simpson, R. L. (2004). Effects on communicative requesting and speech development of the Picture Exchange Communication System in children with characteristics of autism. *Journal of Autism & Developmental Disorders, 34*, 395–409.

Garretson, H. B., Fein, D., & Waterhouse, L. (1990). Sustained attention in children with autism. *Journal of Autism and Developmental Disorders, 20*, 101–114.

Guerts, H. M., Corbett, B., & Solomon, M. (2009). The paradox of cognitive flexibility in autism. *Trends in Cognitive Sciences, 13*, 74–82.

Gioia, G. A., Isquith, P. K., & Guy, S. C. (2001). Assessment of Executive Function in Children with Neurological Impairments. In R. Simeonsson & S. Rosenthal (Eds.), *Psychological and Developmental Assessment* (pp. 317–356). New York: The Guilford Press.

Gioia, G. A., Isquith, P. K., Guy, S. C., & Kenworthy, L. (2000). *Behavior rating inventory of executive function.* Odessa, FL: Psychological Assessment Resources, Inc.

Goldberg, M. C., Mostofsky, S. H., Cutting, L. E., Mahone, E. M., Astor, B. K., Denckla, M. B., & Landa, R. J. (2005). Subtle executive impairments in children with autism and children with ADHD. *Journal of Autism and Developmental Disorders, 35*, 279–293.

Goldstein, A., & McGinnis, E. (1997) *Skillstreaming the adolescent: New strategies and perspectives for teaching prosocial skills.* Champaign, IL: Research Press.

Gray, C. A. (1998). Social stories and comic strip conversations with students with Asperger Syndrome and high-functioning autism. In E. Schopler, G. B. Mesibov, & L. J. Kunce (Eds.), *Asperger syndrome or high-functioning autism?* (pp. 167–198). New York: Plenum Press.

Greenway, C. (2000). Autism and Asperger Syndrome: Strategies to promote prosocial behaviours. *Educational Psychology in Practice, 16*(4), 469–486.

Grelotti, D. J., Gauthier, I., & Schultz, R. T. (2002). Social interest and the development of cortical face specialization: What autism teaches us about face processing. *Developmental Psychobiology, 40*, 213–225.

Gresham, F. M., & Elliot, S.N. (2009). *Social skills improvement system.* Circle Pines, MN: American Guidance Service.

Gutstein, S. E. (2000). *Solving the relationship puzzle: A new developmental program that opens the door to lifelong social and emotional growth.* Texas: Future Horizons.

Horner, R. H., Carr, E. G., Strain, P. S., Todd, A. W., & Reed, H. K. (2002). Problem behavior interventions for young children with autism: A research synthesis. *Journal of Autism and Developmental Disabilities*, 32, 423–446.

Hughes, C., & Russell, J. (1993). Autistic children's difficulty with mental disengagement from an object: Its implications for theories of autism. *Developmental Psychology*, 29, 498–510.

Iacoboni, M. (2005). Neural mechanisms of imitation. *Current Opinions in Neurobioogy*, 15, 632–637.

Iarocci, G., & McDonald, J. (2006). Sensory integration and the perceptual experiencesof persons with autism. *Journal of Autism and Developmental Disorders*, 36, 77–90.

Jennett, H. K., Harris, S. L., & Mesibov, G. B. (2003). Commitment to philosophy, teacher efficacy, and burnout among teachers of children with autism. *Journal of Autism and Developmental Disorders*, 33, 583–593.

Joosten, A. V., Bundy, A. C., & Einfeld, S. L. (2009). Intrinsic and extrinsic motivation for stereotypic and repetitive behavior. *Journal of Autism and Developmental Disorders*, 39, 521–531.

Kanne, S. M., Abbachi, A. M., & Constantino, J. N. (2009). Multi-informant ratings of psychiatric symptom severity in children with autism spectrum disorders: The importance of environmental context. *Journal of Autism and Developmental Disorders*, 39, 856–864.

Keel, J. H., Mesibov, G. B., & Woods, A. V. (1997). TEACCH-supported employment program. *Journal of Autism and Developmental Disorders*, 27(1), 3–9.

Kelley, E., Jones, G., & Fein, D. (2003). Language assessment in children. In M. Hersen, G. Goldstein, & S. R. Beers (Eds.), *The comprehensive handbook of psychological assessment, Volume 1: Intellectual and neuropsychological assessment* (pp. 191–215). New York: Wiley and Sons.

Kelley, E., Paul, J., Fein, D., & Naigles, L. R. (2006). Residual language deficits in optimal outcome children with a history of autism. *Journal of Autism and Developmental Disorders*, 36, 807–828.

Klaver, J. M., Heurta, M., Guter, S. J., & Cook, E. H. (2009, May). *Demographics and diagnosis: Early findings from the Autism Center of Excellence and Simons Simplex Collection studies at UIC*. Poster presented at the Eighth Annual Meeting for Autism Research, Chicago, IL.

Klein-Tasman, B. P., Risi, S., & Lord, C. E. (2007). Effect of language and task demands on the diagnostic effectiveness of the Autism Diagnostic Observation Schedule: The impact of module choice. *Journal of Autism and Developmental Disorders*, 37, 1224–1234.

Klinger, L. G. & Renner, P. (2000). Performance-based measures in autism: Implications for diagnosis, early detection, and identification of cognitive profiles. *Journal of Clinical Child Psychology*, 29, 479–492.

Koenig, K., De Los Reyes, A., Cicchetti, D., Scahill, L., & Klin, A. (2009). Group intervention to promote social skills in school-age children with pervasive developmental disorders: Reconsidering efficacy. *Journal of Autism and Developmental Disorders*, 39(8), 1163–1172.

Korkman, M., Kirk, S., & Kirk, U. (2007). *NEPSY-II*. San Antonio: Pearson.

Kuusiko, S., Pollock-Wurman, R., Jussila, K., Carter, A. S., Mattila, M-L., Ebeling, H., . . . Moilanen, I. (2008). Social anxiety in high-functioning children and adolescents with autism and Asperger syndrome. *Journal of Autism and Developmental Disorders*, 38, 1697–1709.

Landa, R., & Garrett-Mayer, E. (2006). Development in infants with autism spectrum disorder: A prospective study. *Journal of Child Psychology and Psychiatry*, 47, 629–638.

Landry, R., & Bryson, S. E. (2004). Impaired disengagement of attention in young children with autism. *Journal of Child Psychology and Psychiatry*, 45, 1115–1122.

Lewis, M. H., & Bodfish, J. W. (1998). Repetitive behaviors disorders in autism. *Mental Retardation and Developmental Disabilities Research Reviews*, 4, 80–89.

Lincoln, A. J., Dickstein, P., Courchesne, E., Elmasian, R., & Tallal, P. (1992). Auditory processing abilities in non-retarded adolescents and young adults with developmental receptive language disorder and autism. *Brain and Language*, 43, 613–622.

Liss, M., Sauliner, C. & Fein, D. & Kinsbourne, M. (2006). Sensory and attention abnormalities in autistic spectrum disorders. *Autism*, 10(2), 155–172.

Lord, C. (2009, May). *What would "better" diagnosis of ASDs look like?* Paper presented at the Eighth Annual International Meeting for Autism Research, Chicago, IL.

Lord, C. & Risi, S. (2000). Diagnosis of autism spectrum disorders in young children. In A.M. Wetherby & B.M. Prizant (Eds.),*Autism spectrum disorders: A transactional developmental perspective* (pp. 11–30). Baltimore, MD: Brookes.

Lord, C., Rutter, M., DiLavore, P. C., & Risi, S. (2002). *Autism diagnostic observation schedule*. Los Angeles, CA: Western Psychological Services.

Lord, C., Rutter, M., & LeCouteur, A. (1994). Autism diagnostic interview–revised: A revised version of a diagnostic instrument for caregivers of individuals with possible Pervasive Developmental Disorders. *Journal of Autism and Developmental Disorders*, 24, 659–685.

Lord, C., & Schopler, E. (1989). The role of age at assessment, developmental level, and test in the stability of intelligence scores in young autistic children. *Journal of Autism and Developmental Disorders*, 19, 483–499.

Lovaas, O. I. (2003). *Teaching individuals with developmental delays: Basic intervention techniques*. Austin, TX: Pro-Ed.

Lovaas, I., Newsom, C., & Hickman, C. (1987). Self-stimulatory behavior and perceptual reinforcement. *Journal of Applied Behavior Analysis, 20*, 45–68.

Mesibov, G. B. (1984). Social skills training with verbal autistic adolescents and adults: A program model. *Journal of Autism and Developmental Disorders, 14*(4), 395–404.

Mesibov, G. B., Shea, V., & Schopler, E. (2004). *The TEACCH approach to autism spectrum disorders.* New York: Springer.

Millward, C., Powell, S., Messer, D., & Jordan, R. (2000). Recall for self and other in autism: Children's memory for events experienced by themselves and their peers. *Journal of Autism and Developmental Disorders, 30*(1), 15–28.

Minshew, N. J., Johnson, C., & Luna, B. (2001). The cognitive and neural basis of autism: A disorder of complex information processing and dysfunction of neocortical systems. *International Review of Research in Mental Retardation, 23*, 111–138.

Morrison, L., Kamps, D., Garcia, J., & Parker, D. (2001). Peer mediation and monitoring strategies to improve initiations and social skills for students with autism. *Journal of Positive Behavior Interventions, 3*(4), 237–250.

Mundy, P. (2003). Annotation: The neural basis of social impairments in autism: The role of the dorsal medial frontal cortex and anterior cingulate system. *Journal of Child Psychology and Psychiatry, 44*, 793–809.

O'Shea, A. G., Fein, D. A., Cillessen, A. H., Klin, A., & Schultz, R. T. (2005). Source memory in children with autism spectrum disorders. *Developmental Neuropsychology, 27*(3), 337–360.

Owley, T. (2007). Pharmacological interventions for neurodevelopmental disorders. In S. J. Hunter & J. Donders (Eds.), *Pediatric neuropsychological intervention: A critical review of science and practice* (pp. 369–391). Boston, MA: Cambridge University Press.

Panerai, S., Ferrante, L., & Zingale, M. (2002). Benefits of the treatment and education of autistic and communication handicapped children (TEACCH) programme as compared with a non-specific approach. *Journal of Intellectual Disability Research, 46*(4), 318–327.

Pascualvaca, D., Fantie, B., Papageorgiou, M., & Mirsky, A. (1998) Attentional capacities in children with autism: Is there a general deficit in shifting focus? *Journal of Autism and Developmental Disorder, 28*, 467–478.

Pellicano, E. (2007). Links between theory of mind and executive function in young children with autism: clues to developmental primacy. *Developmental Psychology, 43*(4), 974–990.

Phelps-Terasaki, D., & Phelps-Gunn, T. (1992). *Test of pragmatic language.* San Antonio, TX: Harcourt Assessment.

Prior, M., Eisenmajor, R., Leekam, S., Wing, L., Gould, J., Ong, B., & Dowe, D. (1998). Are there subgroups within the autism spectrum? A cluster analysis of a group of children with autism spectrum disorders. *Journal of Child Psychology and Psychiatry, 39*, 893–902.

Raymaekers, R., van der Meere, J., & Roeyers, H. (2004). Event-rate manipulation and its effect on arousal modulation and response inhibition in adults with high functioning autism. *Journal of Clinical and Experimental Neuropsychology, 26*, 74–82.

Rizzolatti, G., Fogassi, L., & Gallese, V. (2001). Neurophysiological mechanisms underlying the understanding and imitation of action. *Nature Reviews Neuroscience, 2*, 661–670.

Robins, D. L., Fein, D., Barton, M. L., & Green, J. A. (2001). The modified checklist for autism in toddlers: An initial study investigating the early detection of autism and pervasive developmental disorders. *Journal of Autism and Developmental Disorders, 31*(2), 131–144.

Rogers, S. J., & Bennetto, L. (2000). Intersubjectivity in autism: The roles of imitation and executive function. In A. M. Wetherby & B. M. Prizant (Eds.), *Autism spectrum disorders: A transactional developmental perspective* (pp. 79–107). Baltimore, MD: Brookes.

Rogers, S., & Vismara, L. (2008) Evidence-based comprehensive treatments for early autism. *Journal of Clinical Child & Adolescent Psychology, 37*(1), 8–38.

Roid, G., & Miller, L. (1997). *Leiter international performance scale–revised.* Wood Dale, IL: Stoelting.

Rutter, M., LeCouteur, A., & Lord, C. (2003). *The autism diagnostic interview–revised.* Los Angeles, CA: Western Psychological Services.

Schopler, E., Reichler, R. J., & Renner, B. R. (1986). *Childhood autism rating scale.* Circle Pines, MN: AGS Publishing.

Semel, E., Wiig, E.H., & Secord, W.A. (2003). *Clinical evaluation of language fundamentals* (4th ed.). San Antonio, TX: The Psychological Corporation.

Sparrow, S. S., Cicchetti, D., & Balla, D. A. (2005). *Vineland adaptive behavior scales* (2nd ed.). Circle Pines, MN: AGS Publishing.

Szatmari, P., Archer, L., Fisman, S., & Streiner, D. L. (1994). Parent and teacher agreement in the assessment of pervasive developmental disorders. *Journal of Autism and Developmental Disorders, 24*, 703–717.

Thiemann, K. S., & Goldstein, H. (2001). Social stories, written text cues, and video feedback: Effects on social communication of children with autism. *Journal of Applied Behavior Analysis, 34*(4), 425–446.

Toichi, M., & Kamio, Y. (1998). Verbal memory in autistic adolescents. *Japanese Journal of Child and Adolescent Psychiatry, 39*, 364–373.

Turner, M. (1999). Annotation: Repetitive behavior in autism: A review of psychological research. *Journal of Child Psychology and Psychiatry, 40*, 839–849.

Van Bourgondien, M. E., Reichle, N. C., & Schopler, E. (2003). Effects of a model treatment approach on adults with autism. *Journal of Autism and Developmental Disorders*, 33(2), 131–140.

Wechsler, D. (1999). *Wechsler abbreviated scale of intelligence*. San Antonio, TX: Harcourt Assessment, Inc.

Wechsler, D. (2003). *Wechsler intelligence scale for children* (4th ed.). San Antonio, TX: The Psychological Corporation.

Williams, J. H., Whiten, A., & Singh, T. (2004). A systematic review of action imitation in autistic spectrum disorder. *Journal of Autism and Developmental Disorders*, 34, 285–299.

Wing, L., Leekam, S. R., Libby, S. J., Gould, J., & Larcombe, M. (2002). the diagnostic interview for social and communication disorders: Background, inter-rater reliability and clinical use. *Journal of Child Psychology and Psychiatry and Allied Disciplines*, 43, 307–325.

Witwer, A. N., & Lecavalier, L. (2008). Examining the validity of autism spectrum disorder subtypes. *Journal of Autism and Developmental Disorders*, 38, 1611–1624.

Wolf, J. M., Tanaka, J. W., Klaiman, C., Koenig, K., Cockburn, J., Herlihy, L., . . . Schultz, R.T. (2008). *Let's Face It! A computer-based intervention for strengthening face processing skills in individuals with autism spectrum disorders*. Presented at the 7th International Meeting for Autism Research, London, England.

Woznicki, K. (2005). British boy dies after chelation therapy for autism. Retrieved from http://www.medpagetoday.com/Neurology/Autism/1616.

Zwaigenbaum, L., Bryson, S., Rogers, T., Roberts, W., Brian, J., & Szatmari, P. (2005). Behavioral manifestations of autism in the first year of life. *International Journal of Developmental Neuroscience*, 23, 143–152.

Part III

Frontiers of Neuropsychology and Autism

Chapter 17

Systemizing and Empathizing

Sally Wheelwright and Simon Baron-Cohen

According to Professor Stephen Hawking in *A Brief History of Time*, "A theory is a good theory if it satisfies two requirements: It must accurately describe a large class of observations on the basis of a model that contains only a few arbitrary elements, and it must make definite predictions about the results of future observations." (Hawking, 1988, p. 10). Using these principles, a useful psychological theory of autism has to account for a large proportion of behaviors seen in individuals across the whole autism spectrum. It needs to account for the triad of impairments which currently form the diagnostic criteria for autism, i.e., social and communicative impairments in the presence of restricted and repetitive activities and interests. In addition to providing a framework for understanding the clinical picture presented by individuals with autism, a good psychological theory also needs to make predictions about performance on relevant cognitive tests. Finally, it should help inform research at other levels of explanation and make predictions beyond the realm

of cognition, for example in the realm of genetics or neurobiology, or even treatment.

Whether one cognitive account can accomplish all this is discussed in Chapters 23 and 24. In the present chapter, we present the systemizing and empathizing account of autism. In a nutshell, this theory states that people with autism have intact or even superior systemizing skills but are impaired at empathizing. Systemizing refers to the drive to create or impose systems on the world and to analyze these systems. Empathizing comprises two parts: a cognitive component which is linked with the ability to identify and predict the behavior of others, and an affective component which is the ability to have an appropriate emotional response to others.

In this chapter, we discuss the definition of empathizing and systemizing more fully, and present the evidence for the empathizing-systemizing (E-S) theory of autism. We describe the relationship between empathizing and systemizing in people with and without autism, and how the E-S theory relates to a second theory, the extreme male brain theory of autism. We discuss how the E-S theory accounts for clinical presentation for both the diagnostic features and associated characteristics and how the E-S theory can be used as a theoretical basis for interventions. We include a section on the neural underpinnings of empathizing. Finally, we consider the opposite cognitive profile: individuals who are hyperempathizers and hyposystemizers.

NOTE ON TERMINOLOGY

In the rest of this chapter, we use the term autism spectrum conditions (ASC) as an umbrella term for all conditions on the autism spectrum. We choose to use this term because it is a neutral description of all the relevant conditions, including Asperger syndrome, autism, autism spectrum disorder, and pervasive developmental disorder.

DEFINING SYSTEMIZING

The fundamental concept of a system is that it is predictable: if you know the input, then you can predict the output. The essential structure of a system can therefore be considered as input → operation → output (Baron-Cohen, 2002). Systemizing involves working out what the operation does so that for any given input, you can predict the output. The operation may be somewhat of a "black box," in that you do not have to have a full understanding of the operation in order to be able to use the system. For example, when you hit the "Return" key on the computer keyboard, you do not need to understand how a computer works to predict that the cursor will move to the next line. However, if you do understand the "black box" more fully, you will be able to make better use of the system.

In some systems, the systemizer has to abstract the system themselves, e.g., weather patterns. In others, there is already a system in place, e.g., train timetables. A calendar is an example of a system which falls into both camps—the average calendar user will simply use it to find that, say March 7 in 2008 was a Friday. Some systemizers, however, will take calendar use to another level and work out how to predict what day March 7 falls in any given year, past or present.

In the world, some things can only be understood as systems, while some things can be approached in a systematic manner, but it is not essential to do so. And for yet other things, using a systematic approach will never be the best strategy. An example of a "pure" system is arithmetic: performing the same calculation will always produce the same answer, and if you know what the input is, and what operation is being performed on the input, you can predict with 100% certainty what the output is. There is no other way to approach arithmetic, other than in a purely systematic way.

An example of an activity which can be approached with differing degrees of systemizing is cooking. The systemizing cook will follow the recipe exactly: he will fry exactly 1 cup of onions for precisely 7 minutes before adding 1 clove of crushed garlic, and two minutes later, a 5-ounce tin of tomatoes, one quarter-teaspoon of salt, five dashes of pepper, and after another 30 minutes of gentle simmering, 3 tablespoons of chopped fresh basil. The non-systemizing cook will randomly change their basic recipe, adding more seasoning without measuring the quantities exactly, changing the cooking time in a rough and ready way, or cutting corners in different ways. Whereas the systemizing cook will produce very similar dishes every time, those produced by the less systemizing cook will be more variable.

The best example of something which cannot be systemized successfully is probably the social world. Using a systemizing approach here will only ever work at a very basic level. Systemizing is not adaptable enough to be the best strategy for social interaction—there are simply too many variables to take into consideration, and it is not always possible to identify which inputs are relevant and important in a straightforward manner. There is an infinite range of possible directions in which any social interaction might go, and the simple input → operation → output systemizing approach is not equipped to deal with this. In the same way that the systematic cook will be thrown off if he does not have an ingredient he needs (whilst the non-systemizing cook will find a substitute), the social world systemizer will not have the strategies to adapt when someone does not behave in the usual way. People are not always predictable, and not only that, in social interactions you may have to process input from several people at the same time. Systemizing is just not an efficient strategy to use in the social world. We suggest that the key skill needed in the social world is, in fact, empathizing, a process described in the next section.

Another way of describing this idea that some things can be systemized more easily than others is by considering how lawful systems are (Baron-Cohen, 2008a). Some systems, e.g. light switches, are 100% lawful: they have zero variance, or only one degree of freedom, and can therefore be predicted, and controlled, 100% of the time. Other systems, e.g., planetary orbits, may be 90% lawful—there is slightly more variance and a few more degrees of freedom. The lawfulness of social interactions will vary depending on the situation, but in general it will be quite low, with high variance and many degrees of freedom. Hence, systemizing the social world is of little predictive value.

There is evidence that typical adults use social-specific strategies to solve logic problems, if the logic problems are set in the social world, and that these strategies make solving the task much easier. A good example of this is the Wason Selection Task. In the original version of this task, participants are given four cards which, face-up, show A, D, 4, and 7. Participants are told that each card has one number on one side and one letter on the other side. Participants have to select the minimum number of card(s) to turn over to check the rule, "If a card has a vowel on one side, then it has an even number on the other side." The correct answer is that you need to turn over A and 7 but very few people get this answer, typically less than 10% (Manktelow & Evans, 1979). However, if the logically equivalent problem is presented in a more social context, performance dramatically improves. For example, the four cards might show "drank beer," "drank lemonade," "is 21 years old," and "is 16 years old" and the participant must choose which cards to turn over to check the rule that if you drink alcohol, you have to be over 21 years of age. Typically about 75% of people get the correct answer, that you have to turn "drank beer" and "is 16 years old" over (Griggs & Cox, 1982).

Having described how some things must be analyzed in terms of systems, and noting it is possible to do this with other things, we now turn our attention to the actual process of systemizing. Understanding a system can be either a passive or active process. If it is a passive process, the systemizer is purely an observer, watching the input and output of the system and formulating rules based on these observations. If the systemizer takes a more active role, she may deliberately manipulate the input to see what effect this has on the output.

Systemizing is not a unitary process: it can be broken down into different steps. These steps will also be affected by whether the systemizer is active or passive.

The passive systemizer may simply take pleasure from observing systems and recognizing patterns within the system. For the active systemizer, step one is identifying exactly what is going to be systemized, e.g., predicting whether it's going to rain in the next 24 hours, how to add a phone number to the address book in a cell phone, or how to grow tomatoes successfully. Step two involves identifying the relevant information or data and looking for patterns within this information. In the growing tomatoes example, soil type, temperature, moisture, and light levels may all be important, whereas whether or not you sing to your plants is irrelevant. In step three, a model is formulated and tested against the known data, e.g., what conditions produce the most tomatoes. This step is repeated until the model passes this stage. In the final stage, the model is used to make predictions and tested against new data, e.g., comparing tomatoes grown in and outside. If the model fails at this stage, step three is repeated. When the model passes the final stage, the systemizer has a successful model which can be used repeatedly. Good systemizers will effectively continue with the final stage *ad infinitum*, always ready to adapt the model if it no longer fits the evidence or fails to make useful predictions (Baron-Cohen, 2006).

Note that in this analysis of systemizing, there are many parallels to be drawn with scientific methodology. This observation leads to one potential criticism of the E-S theory: namely, that systemizing is only applicable to individuals with a high IQ. There are two points to make in response to this criticism. First, it is important to recognize that, although there may be a desire and drive to systemize, the individual may not always be successful in his endeavors. The clinical implication of this could be frustration and anxiety in the individual. A second response to the IQ issue is that in fact, many behaviors associated with lower-functioning individuals can be viewed in a systemizing context (see Table 17-1).

DEFINING EMPATHIZING

Systemizing is a very recent concept and may not be very familiar to some readers. Empathizing, on the other hand, is a much more common concept and most people will have a better understanding of it. Despite this, the word "empathy" has only been around for about 100 years. It was invented by Titchener as a translation of the German word "Einfuhlung," itself

Table 17-1 Examples of Systemising in Low Functioning and High Functioning Individuals

Type of systemising	Examples of behaviour in low functioning individuals	Examples of behaviour in high functioning individuals
Sensory	Tapping surfaces, letting sand run through fingers	Insisting on the same foods each day
Motoric	Spinning round and round, rocking back and forth	Learning knitting patterns or a tennis technique
Collectible	Collecting leaves or baseball cards	Making lists and catalogues
Numerical	Obsessions with calendars or train timetables	Solving math problems
Motion	Watching washing machines spin round and round	Analyzing exactly when a specific event occurs in a repeating cycle
Spatial	Obsessions with routes	Developing drawing techniques
Environmental	Insisting on bricks being lined up in an invariant order	Insisting that nothing is moved from its usual position
Social	Saying the first half of a phrase and waiting for the other person to complete it	Insisting on playing the same game whenever a child comes to play
Natural world	Asking over and over again what the weather will be today	Learning the Latin names of every plant
Mechanical	Learning to operate the DVD player	Fixing bicycles or taking apart gadgets and reassembling them
Vocal/auditory/ verbal	Echoing sounds	Collecting words and word meanings
Action sequences	Watching the same DVD over and over again	Analyzing dance techniques
Music	Playing the same tune over and over again	Analyzing the musical structure of a song

a term from aesthetics meaning "to project yourself into what you observe" (Titchener, 1909). In relation to ASC, the idea of empathizing in part arose from the Mindblindness theory of autism (Baron-Cohen, 1995), and in part from the affective theory (Hobson, 1986). Research in the 1980s explored the idea that children with ASC were delayed in developing a Theory of Mind (ToM). ToM refers to the ability to attribute mental states to others, and the understanding that other people have thoughts and feelings, and that these may not be the same as your own thoughts and feelings. If you have a ToM, you can understand other people and even predict what they are going to do.

The classic false belief test is used as a marker for the presence of ToM (Premack & Woodruff, 1978). To pass the false belief test, you have to understand that a protagonist will look for an object where they *think* it is, rather than in the location that you, the participant, *know* it is. Typically, children with ASC are delayed at passing the false belief test, so they are thought to be delayed in developing a ToM (Baron-Cohen, 1995). The consequence of this is mindblindness (albeit to different degrees). In other words, people with ASC find it difficult to understand that other people have thoughts and feelings, which they act on, and that these thoughts

and feelings can be different from one's own. It is not surprising then that other people's behavior may be confusing, unpredictable, and sometimes even disturbing.

The concept of mindblindness seemed to offer a good explanation for the social and communication difficulties seen in people with ASC, and indeed the idea of degrees of mindblindness has been retained in the E-S theory. However, we now conceptualize ToM to be one of the components of empathy. Empathy consists of a cognitive component, which largely overlaps with ToM, and in addition, an affective component (Baron-Cohen & Wheelwright, 2004). The affective component refers to having an appropriate emotional response to someone else. The term appropriate is not synonymous with "same." For example, if you saw someone else falling over in the street you may not have the feelings of embarrassment and discomfort that that person has, but you would probably feel sorry for them—and this would be an appropriate response.

Putting the cognitive and affective components of empathy together, it is clear that empathizing allows us to make sense of the behavior of others, predict what they might do next, understand how they feel, and on top of this, feel connected to that other person, and respond appropriately to them.

TYPICAL EMPATHY DEVELOPMENT AND DEFICITS IN PEOPLE WITH ASC

Having described systemizing and empathizing in some detail, we now look at the typical pattern of development of these traits, and we present evidence relevant to the E-S theory–specifically, deficits in empathizing and preserved or superior systemizing in people with ASC. We start with empathy.

From the earliest days of life in the typically developing child, there is evidence for skills, such as emotion sharing, which are the precursors for empathizing (Rochat, 2002). For example, babies who are just one day old will selectively cry in response to the vocal characteristics of another infant's cry (Hoffman, 1975). Infants exposed to cries of other newborns cry significantly more than those exposed to an intensity-matched synthetic cry or silence (Sagi & Hoffman, 1976), and interestingly, neonates do not respond to the sound of their own cries (Martin & Clark, 1982). These findings demonstrate that a neonate's perception of another's distressed affective state elicits a behavior-matching response in the self. This emotion sharing, sometimes referred to as *emotional contagion* or *emotional resonance*, is one of the building blocks of empathy (Decety & Meyer, 2008). Reduced emotional resonance has been demonstrated experimentally in young children with autism compared with children with other developmental conditions (Corona, Dissanayake, et al., 1998; Scambler, Hepburn, et al., 2007; Sigman, Kasari, et al. 1992).

Emotional contagion is not generally considered to be true empathy, since the infant is imitating the emotional distress of another without the cognitive skills required to understand why the other person is distressed (Ungerer et al., 1990). As the typical child develops, more of the skills that are required for true empathy emerge. The typical infant can judge whether something is an agent or not and for agents, what their goal or basic intention is (Premack, 1990). They can judge whether an agent is looking at them or not (Baron-Cohen, 1994), if an agent is expressing a basic emotion, and if so, what type (Ekman, 1992). For example, by 10 weeks of age, infants can discriminate their mother's presentation of happy, sad, and angry expressions, and in some conditions, match these expressions (Haviland & Lelwica, 1987). This automatic and spontaneous mimicry of facial expressions is absent in adults and adolescents with ASC, despite voluntary mimicry not being impaired (McIntosh, Reichmann-Decker, Winkielman, & Wilbarger, 2006).

Emotion recognition is a fundamental component of empathy, and in the study reported above, 10-week-old infants were shown to be capable of discrimination of some of the basic emotions. However, there remains some debate about when typical children are capable of emotion recognition: some researchers assert that young babies both recognize and respond to facially and vocally expressed emotions (Izard, 1994; Walker-Andrews & Lennon 1991), whereas other researchers claim that recognition of facial expressions continues to develop into the school years (Camras & Allison, 1985; Widen & Russell, 2008). Some of these differences are likely to be due to differences in study methodology, and also conflation of emotion recognition and emotion labelling (Vicari, Reilly, Pasqualetti, Vizzotto, & Caltagirone, 2000).

Similarly, different study methodologies could account for the debate about whether there is a measurable impairment in emotion recognition for basic and complex emotions, in both high-functioning and low-functioning individuals with ASC (Adolphs, Sears, & Piven, 2001; Hobson, 1991). Whether or not there is a measurable impairment, most researchers agree that emotion-recognition strategies are different in people with and without ASC (Wallace, Coleman, & Bailey, 2008). The evidence suggests that individuals with ASC focus on individual features and use a rule-based strategy, rather than the template strategy typically used by people without ASC (Joseph & Tanaka, 2003; Rutherford & McIntosh, 2007). This means that when tasks use stimuli that are presented for a relatively long time, people with ASC may not differ from controls in terms of scores, because they can successfully use their cognitive skills to make emotion judgements. However, when stimuli are presented more briefly, for durations in the range of microexpressions, people with ASC are selectively impaired at making judgements about emotion (Clark, Winkielman, et al. 2008). The identification of microexpressions is important (Bartlett, Movellan, et al. 2005) for a variety of empathizing skills, including the detection of subtle social cues (Ekman, 1984), the rapid mimicry of emotional expression (Dimberg, Thunberg, et al. 2000), and the perception of rapidly changing emotional states (Ickes, 2003).

As well as (possibly) recognizing basic emotions, very young infants engage in "proto-conversations" with their mothers (Bateson, 1975): they look and listen to each other, and respond appropriately to one another. Again, these behaviors are important precursors to empathy. As infants develop, they engage in shared attention—for example, by following gaze or a point (Mundy & Crowson, 1997; Scaife & Bruner, 1975). By 14 months of age, children are highly sensitive to where another person is looking, and will strive to establish joint attention (Butterworth, 1991; Hood, Willen et al. 1997). Joint attention behaviors include pointing and following another's gaze. In joint attention, the infant not only looks at the face and eyes of the other person, but also pays attention to what the other person is interested in. Children with ASC aged 20 months show reduced frequency of joint attention in toddlerhood (Swettenham et al., 1998).

The first experimental examples of, arguably, true empathy occur at around 18 months, when children begin to show concern at the distress of others (Yirmiya, Sigman, et al. 1992), and instrumental acts of helping may be observed (Thompson, 1987). Experimental studies indicate a lack of empathic concern in children with ASC when a parent or experimenter feigned pain, illness, or fear (Charman, Swettenham, et al. 1997; Sigman, Kasari, et al. 1992).

Although empathic acts may be recordable from the age of 18 months, development of empathy and related skills continues throughout childhood. Children begin to attribute a wider range of mental states to themselves and to others (Leslie, 1987), and they will recognize and respond appropriately to more complex emotions (Harris, Johnson, Hutton, Andrews, & Cooke, 1989). By the age of 3 years, children can understand the relationships between mental states, such as seeing leads to knowing (Pratt & Bryant, 1990), and at 4 years, they know that people can have false beliefs (Wimmer & Perner, 1983). At 5 to 6 years of age, children understand that people can hold beliefs about beliefs (Perner & Wimmer, 1985). People with ASC are impaired or delayed in all these skills (Baron-Cohen, 1989; Baron-Cohen & Goodhart, 1994; Baron-Cohen, Leslie, & Frith, 1985; Leslie & Frith, 1988). By the age of 7, the typical child has learned to recognize faux pas, i.e., she understands that words can sometimes be unintentionally hurtful (Baron-Cohen, O'Riordan, Stone, Jones, & Plaisted, 1999), whereas children with ASC find this task difficult.

In very high-functioning adults with ASC, more ecologically valid tests may provide a measure of empathy deficits in those who have developed strategies to succeed on simple empathizing tasks. For example, in the empathic accuracy test, participants

have to infer the thoughts and feelings of two people who are engaged in a naturally occurring conversation. People with ASC who score in the control range on both Happé's Stories task (Happe, 1994), and a version of the Reading the Mind in the Eyes task (Baron-Cohen, Wheelwright, Hill, Raste, & Plumb, 2001), are still significantly impaired at the empathic accuracy task (Ponnet, Roeyers, Buysse, De Clerq, & Van Der Heyden, 2004).

Recently, it has been suggested that, while people with ASC are impaired in the cognitive component of empathy, the affective or emotional component is preserved (Dziobek, Rogers, et al. 2008; Rogers, Dziobek, Hassenstab, Wolf, & Convit, 2007). It is certainly logical that, if you cannot correctly infer the mental state of another, you will not have an appropriate emotional response to that state. However, there is evidence that adults with ASC do not show sensorimotor resonance when observing painful stimuli directed at another individual (Minio-Paluello, Baron-Cohen, Avenanti, Walsh, & Aglioti, 2009). In this study, participants viewed videos of painful stimuli (a hand being deeply penetrated by a needle) or control stimuli (a needle penetrating a tomato) while motor-evoked potentials were induced in their own hand with single-pulse transcranial magnetic stimulation (TMS). Cortico-spinal inhibition, as indexed by the motor potential, is expected when the subject himself experiences a painful stimulus, and, for empathic individuals, when the subject views another undergoing painful stimulation. Unlike the typical controls, the participants with ASC did not show cortico-spinal inhibition while viewing the painful stimuli delivered to a model's hand. Sensorimotor resonance is a rudimentary form of affective empathy, and this TMS study suggests that changes at very basic levels of neural processing are linked with impaired affective empathy. Consistent with this finding are previous studies indicating a lack of empathic concern in children when a parent or experimenter feigned pain, illness, or fear, as noted earlier (Charman, Swettenham, et al. 1997; Sigman, Kasari, et al. 1992).

PRESERVED SYSTEMIZING IN PEOPLE WITH ASC

As will hopefully have become clear, there is not a single moment when a child suddenly becomes empathic. Rather there are a series of developmental steps which the typical child takes, and empathy skills continue to develop into and throughout adulthood. A similar pattern of development is also seen for skills related to systemizing. Since systemizing is a relatively recent concept, there is not a rich literature on its development in children. Relevant areas may include the development of categorization skills, causal reasoning, deductive reasoning, scientific thinking, and understanding of the physical world, but for the time being, the development of systemizing is certainly an area ripe for research. The following section focuses on studies that have demonstrated the preserved or even superior systemizing skills demonstrated by people with autism.

Systemizing refers to the *drive* to systemize, not just the *ability* to systemize. The E-S theory suggests that people with ASC are *attracted* to systems, whether or not they are measurably successful at systemizing. One of the diagnostic criteria for ASC is narrow interests: people with ASC tend to develop obsessional interests in particular topics or objects. Anecdotally, and from clinical descriptions, these obsessions tend to cluster round systems (Baron-Cohen, 2008b; Hart, 1989; Williams, 1996), e.g., washing machines, trains, calendars, and prime numbers, and this observation is backed up by a survey of the content of obsessions in children with ASC (Baron-Cohen & Wheelwright, 1999).

Not only are people with ASC drawn to systems, but some studies have shown that they are at least as, if not more, competent at systemizing than people without ASC. Children with ASC outperformed mental-age-matched controls when sequencing physical-causal stories, but were significantly worse at sequencing picture stories that required an understanding of intentions (Baron-Cohen, Leslie, et al., 1986). In a study of academic achievement, participants with ASC performed similarly to IQ-matched controls on a mechanical reasoning test, despite scoring significantly lower on a comprehension test (Minshew, Goldstein, Taylor, & Siegel, 1993). Similarly, a mixed group of male and female adults with ASC outperformed control females and matched the performance of male controls on the Physical Prediction Questionnaire (PPQ), in which participants have to predict how levers and bobs will behave by studying mechanical diagrams (Lawson, Baron-Cohen, et al. 2004). In a study with adolescent children, the ASC group outperformed both male and female controls on a folk (intuitive) physics test (Baron-Cohen, Wheelwright, Spong, Scahill, & Lawson, 2001). This test comprises multiple choice

questions covering a wide variety of topics including the best way to pull a boat along, how easy it is to push over solid objects, in which shaped container water will cool the quickest and how to put tent pegs in the ground to provide the best hold.

TESTING SYSTEMIZING AND EMPATHIZING IN THE SAME PARTICIPANTS

Although there are plenty of studies that show that people with ASC are impaired at empathizing, and there is a small, but consistent, body of evidence showing that people with ASC have preserved or superior systemizing skills, ideally we need to test these abilities in the same participants, at the same time. This is because the E-S theory states that people with ASC have preserved or superior systemizing *relative* to their empathizing. In one study, participants were given the PPQ, as described above, along with the Social Stories Questionnaire (SSQ), a test of subtle faux pas detection (Lawson, Baron-Cohen, et al. 2004). The sample sizes for this study were relatively small (18 males with ASC and 89 controls), but the pattern of results was similar to that seen in the study described next, which had a much larger sample size (125 people with ASC and about 2000 controls) and used self-report questionnaires.

We developed the Empathy Quotient (EQ; Baron-Cohen & Wheelwright, 2004) and Systemizing Quotient (SQ; Baron-Cohen, Richler, et al. 2003; Wheelwright et al., 2006) as quick, quantitative measures of empathizing and systemizing skills. The EQ and SQ items are shown in Table 17-2. Each questionnaire consists of a series of statements, and the respondent has to indicate to what extent they agree or disagree with each statement. The higher your score on the EQ, the more empathic you are, and the higher your score on the SQ, the greater is your drive to systemize.

The E-S theory predicts that people with ASC will have lower EQ scores than control adults, but that their SQ scores will be as high, if not higher. To test this prediction, we gave both the EQ and SQ to adults with and without an ASC diagnosis (Wheelwright et al., 2006). As predicted, adults with ASC scored significantly higher than control adults on the SQ, but scored significantly lower on the EQ. The E-S theory also predicts that if you look at the difference

Table 17-2 Items from the Empathy Quotient and Systemising Quotient

Items from the Empathy Quotient

Asterisked items are reverse scored

1.   I can easily tell if someone else wants to enter a conversation.
*2.   I find it difficult to explain to others things that I understand easily, when they don't understand it first time.
3.   I really enjoy caring for other people.
*4.   I find it hard to know what to do in a social situation.
*5.   People often tell me that I went too far in driving my point home in a discussion.
*6.   It doesn't bother me too much if I am late meeting a friend.
*7.   Friendships and relationships are just too difficult, so I tend not to bother with them.
*8.   I often find it difficult to judge if something is rude or polite.
*9.   In a conversation, I tend to focus on my own thoughts rather than on what my listener might be thinking.
*10.   When I was a child, I enjoyed cutting up worms to see what would happen.
11.   I can pick up quickly if someone says one thing but means another.
*12.   It is hard for me to see why some things upset people so much.
13.   I find it easy to put myself in somebody else's shoes.
14.   I am good at predicting how someone will feel.
15.   I am quick to spot when someone in a group is feeling awkward or uncomfortable.
*16.   If I say something that someone else is offended by, I think that that's their problem, not mine.
*17.   If anyone asked me if I like their haricut, I would reply truthfully, even if I didn't like it.
*18.   I can't always see why someone should have felt offended by a remark.
*19.   Seeing people cry doesn't really upset me.
*20.   I am very blunt, which some people take to be rudeness, even though this is unintentional.
21.   I don't tend to find social situations confusing
22.   Other people tell me I am good at understanding how they are feeling and what they are thinking.
23.   When I talk to people, I tend to talk about their experiences rather than my own.
24.   It upsets me to see animals in pain.
*25.   I am able to make decisions without being influenced by people's feelings.
26.   I can easily tell if someone else is interested or bored with what I am saying.
27.   I get upset if I see people suffering on news programs.
28.   Friends usually talk to me about their problems as they say I am very understanding.
29.   I can sense if I am intruding, even if the other person doesn't tell me.
*30.   People sometimes tell me that I have gone too far with teasing.
*31.   Other people often say that I am insensitive, though I don't always see why.
*32.   If I see a stranger in a group, I think that it is up to them to make an effort to join in.
*33.   I usually stay emotionally detached when watching a film.
34.   I can tune into how someone else feels rapidly and intuitively.
35.   I can easily work out what another person might want to talk about.
36.   I can tell if someone is masking their true emotion.
37.   I don't consciously work out the rules of social situations.
38.   I am good at predicting what someone will do.
39.   I tend to get emotionally involved with a friend's problems.
40.   I can usually appreciate the other person's viewpoint, even if I don't agree with it.

Items from the Systemising Quotient

Asterisked items are reverse scored

(continued)

Table 17-2 (continued)

1. I find it very easy to use train timetables, even if this involves several connections.
2. I like music or book shops because they are clearly organized.
*3. I would not enjoy organizing events, e.g. fundraising evenings, fetes, conferences.
4. When I read something, I always notice whether it is grammatically correct.
5. I find myself categorising people into types (in my own mind).
*6. I find it difficult to read and understand maps.
7. When I look at a mountain, I think about how precisely it was formed.
*8. I am not interested in the details of exchange rates, interest rates, stocks and shares.
9. If I were buying a car, I would want to obtain specific information about its engine capacity.
*10. I find it difficult to learn how to programme video recorders.
11. When I like something I like to collect a lot of different examples of that type of object, so I can see how they differ from each other.
12. When I learn a language, I become intrigued by its grammatical rules.
13. I like to know how committees are structured in terms of who the different committee members represent or what their functions are.
14. If I had a collection (e.g. CDs, coins, stamps), it would be highly organized.
*15. I find it difficult to understand instruction manuals for putting appliances together.
16. When I look at a building, I am curious about the precise way it was constructed.
*17. I am not interested in understanding how wireless communication works (e.g. cell phones).
18. When travelling by train, I often wonder exactly how the rail networks are coordinated.
19. I enjoy looking through catalogues of products to see the details of each product and how it compares to others.
20. Whenever I run out of something at home, I always add it to a shopping list.
21. I know, with reasonable accuracy, how much money has come in and gone out of my bank account this month.
*22. When I was young I did not enjoy collecting sets of things e.g. stickers, football cards etc.
23. I am interested in my family tree and in understanding how everyone is related to each other in the family.
*24. When I learn about historical events, I do not focus on exact dates.
25. I find it easy to grasp exactly how odds work in betting.
*26. I do not enjoy games that involve a high degree of strategy (e.g. chess, Risk, Games Workshop).
27. When I learn about a new category I like to go into detail to understand the small differences between different members of that category.
*28. I do not find it distressing if people who live with me upset my routines.
29. When I look at an animal, I like to know the precise species it belongs to.
30. I can remember large amounts of information about a topic that interests me e.g. flags of the world, airline logos.
*31. At home, I do not carefully file all important documents e.g. guarantees, insurance policies
32. I am fascinated by how machines work.
*33. When I look at a piece of furniture, I do not notice the details of how it was constructed.
*34. I know very little about the different stages of the legislation process in my country.
*35. I do not tend to watch science documentaries on television or read articles about science and nature.
36. If someone stops to ask me the way, I'd be able to give directions to any part of my home town.
*37. When I look at a painting, I do not usually think about the technique involved in making it.
38. I prefer social interactions that are structured around a clear activity, e.g. a hobby.
*39. I do not always check off receipts etc. against my bank statement.
*40. I am not interested in how the government is organized into different ministries and departments.
41. I am interested in knowing the path a river takes from its source to the sea.

(continued)

Table 17-2 (continued)

42. I have a large collection e.g. of books, CDs, videos etc.

43. If there was a problem with the electrical wiring in my home, I'd be able to fix it myself.

*44. My clothes are not carefully organised into different types in my wardrobe.

*45. I rarely read articles or webpages about new technology.

46. I can easily visualise how the motorways in my region link up.

*47. When an election is being held, I am not interested in the results for each constituency.

*48. I do not particularly enjoy learning about facts and figures in history.

*49. I do not tend to remember people's birthdays (in terms of which day and month this falls).

50. When I am walking in the country, I am curious about how the various kinds of trees differ.

*51. I find it difficult to understand information the bank sends me on different investment and saving systems.

*52. If I were buying a camera, I would not look carefully into the quality of the lens.

53. If I were buying a computer, I would want to know exact details about its hard drive capacity and processor speed.

*54. I do not read legal documents very carefully.

55. When I get to the checkout at a supermarket I pack different categories of goods into separate bags.

*56. I do not follow any particular system when I'm cleaning at home.

*57. I do not enjoy in-depth political discussions.

*58. I am not very meticulous when I carry out D.I.Y or home improvements.

*59. I would not enjoy planning a business from scratch to completion.

60. If I were buying a stereo, I would want to know about its precise technical features.

61. I tend to keep things that other people might throw away, in case they might be useful for something in the future.

62. I avoid situations which I can not control.

*63. I do not care to know the names of the plants I see.

*64. When I hear the weather forecast, I am not very interested in the meteorological patterns.

*65. It does not bother me if things in the house are not in their proper place.

66. In maths, I am intrigued by the rules and patterns governing numbers.

*67. I find it difficult to learn my way around a new city.

68. I could list my favourite 10 books, recalling titles and authors' names from memory.

69. When I read the newspaper, I am drawn to tables of information, such as football league scores or stock market indices.

*70. When I'm in a plane, I do not think about the aerodynamics.

*71. I do not keep careful records of my household bills.

72. When I have a lot of shopping to do, I like to plan which shops I am going to visit and in what order.

*73. When I cook, I do not think about exactly how different methods and ingredients contribute to the final product.

74. When I listen to a piece of music, I always notice the way it's structured.

75. I could generate a list of my favourite 10 songs from memory, including the title and the artist's name who performed each song.

between the EQ and SQ scores in individuals with ASC, most individuals will score higher on the SQ than the EQ.

To test this, we defined five brain types, based on the difference between standardised EQ and SQ scores. The five types are: Type B (balanced brain), Type E (E>S), Extreme Type E (E>>S), Type S (S>E) and Extreme Type S (S>>E). Table 17-3 shows the percent of individuals with each brain type. As predicted, most adults with ASC have Extreme Type S brains: 62% compared with just 3% in the general population, supporting the idea that systemizing is much better developed than empathizing in people with ASC. The data from this study are also shown in Figure 17-1. This graph plots each individual, with SQ score on the x-axis and EQ score on the y-axis, and the boundaries for each brain type are shown.

Starting in the top left-hand corner (low SQ, high EQ), and moving to the bottom right-hand corner (high SQ, low EQ), the brain types pass from Extreme Type E, Type E, Type B, Type S to Extreme Type S. Following this same axis, you can see that the highest concentration of individuals changes from control females, to control males, and finally to people with ASC. Nearly all individuals with ASC have either a Type S or Extreme Type S brain. Although there is a handful in the balanced brain category, there are none with a Type E or Extreme Type E brain. Looking at the controls, you can see that there are similar proportions of males and females with a Type B brain, but more males with a Type S brain and more females with a Type E brain.

So far, we have described these results in terms of categorical clinical diagnosis: People either do or do not have an ASC diagnosis. Another strategy is to consider these data using a more dimensional approach — and if we are serious about considering autism as a spectrum, this is arguably the better tactic to use. The

Autism Spectrum Quotient (AQ) is a questionnaire in the same format as the EQ and SQ. It provides a measure of the number of autistic traits an individual has: the higher your AQ score, the more traits you have (Baron-Cohen, Wheelwright, et al. 2001). The AQ has been used extensively in both clinical and non-clinical samples (Austin, 2005; Hoekstra, Bartels, Cath, & Boomsma, 2008; Hurst, Mitchell, et al. 2007; Stewart, Watson, et al. 2009; Wakabayashi, Baron-Cohen, et al. 2004; Woodbury-Smith, Robinson, Wheelwright, & Baron-Cohen, 2005), and is approximately normally distributed. Dimensionalizing The E-S theory leads to the prediction that there will be a correlation between the difference score (SQ minus EQ) and the AQ. This is exactly the pattern of results we found for both the sample as a whole, and also in both the control group and the ASC group separately. The correlations were all large, around $r = 0.6$, and highly significant (Wheelwright et al., 2006). In other words, if you score higher on the SQ than the EQ, the greater the discrepancy between your scores, the more autistic traits you have. If you score higher on the EQ than the SQ, the greater the discrepancy between your scores, the fewer autistic traits you have.

WHAT IS THE RELATIONSHIP BETWEEN SYSTEMIZING AND EMPATHIZING?

In the previous section, we described how most people with ASC have a Type S or Extreme Type S brain: they are better at systemizing than empathizing. This suggests that within the ASC group there will be a negative correlation between EQ and SQ scores. This is indeed the case: There is a modest ($r = -0.29$), but significant correlation between the EQ and SQ. Considering the results from the control group, it is not quite as easy to predict whether there is a significant

Table 17-3 Percent of Individuals with Each Brain Type

Brain Type	Definition (E = empathising, S = systemising)	ASC group	Typical males	Typical females
Extreme Type E	E >> S	0	0	4
Type E	E > S	0	15	45
Type B	E = S	6	30	29
Type S	S > E	32	50	21
Extreme Type S	S >> E	62	5	1

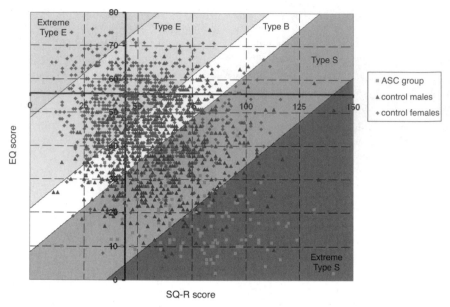

Figure 17-1 SQ and EQ Scores for All Participants with the Boundaries for Each Brain Type. (See color Figure 17-1.)

relationship between systemizing and empathizing. In control males, a large proportion of individuals have Type S or Extreme Type S brains, but many have a balanced brain and about 1 in 7 have a Type E brain. In control females, the mirror image pattern of results is seen: a large proportion have Type E or Extreme Type E brains but again, many have balanced brains and about 1 in 5 have Type S brains. The correlation between the EQ and SQ in the control group is in fact very small, r = -0.09, but because of the large sample size, statistically significant. The difference in the magnitude of the correlations between the ASC and the control group is highly significant i.e., the negative correlation between EQ and SQ in people with ASC is statistically bigger than that in the control group.

THE E-S THEORY AND THE EXTREME MALE BRAIN THEORY OF AUTISM

The E-S theory was originally proposed to explain typical sex differences. Specifically, the E-S theory predicted that more males than females have Type S brain and more females than males have Type E brains. These predictions were confirmed in the study described above using the EQ and SQ. The extreme male brain theory of autism (EMB) predicts that the cognitive profile seen in typical males will be seen to the extreme in people with ASC (Baron-Cohen, 2002; Baron-Cohen & Hammer, 1997). This view was first suggested by Hans Asperger himself (Asperger, 1944). The EQ and SQ study supports this prediction: Most people with ASC have an extreme Type S brain.

Evidence for the EMB theory is also found in observational studies and cognitive tests in areas related to ASC. Starting with the empathizing-related studies, at 12 months of age, girls make more eye contact than boys (Lutchmaya, Baron-Cohen, et al. 2002), and children with ASC make less eye contact than typical boys (Swettenham et al., 1998). Girls tend to pass false belief tests at an earlier age than boys (Charman, Ruffman, et al. 2002; Happé 1995), and children with ASC typically pass at a later age (Baron-Cohen, Leslie, et al. 1985). On the faux pas test, the participant has to recognize that one character in a vignette has said something that could be hurtful to another character. Children with ASC find this test difficult, and there is also a difference in the development of typical boys and girls on this task: girls pass the faux pas test at an earlier age (Baron-Cohen, O'Riordan, et al. 1999). In adults, typical females score higher on the Social Stories Questionnaire described above than typical males, who in turn score higher than adults with AS (Lawson, Baron-Cohen, et al. 2004). On the Reading the Mind in the Eyes

Test, in which participants have to judge what someone is thinking or feeling just by looking at a photograph of their eyes, there is a small female advantage, and again, people with ASC show an impairment on this task (Baron-Cohen, Wheelwright, et al. 2001).

The studies described above are examples where typical females outperform typical males, and people with ASC have below-average performance. The prediction is that in the systemizing-related tests, males will tend to outperform females, and people with ASC will score highest of all. In fact, results have not always been quite as clear-cut as this. Sometimes the prediction has been confirmed but sometimes, although typical males outperform typical females, people with ASC do not have superior scores; rather, they perform at a similar level to typical males. This is exactly the result which has been found on the Physical Prediction Questionnaire, in which participants have to predict how levers and bobs will behave by studying mechanical diagrams (Lawson, Baron-Cohen, et al. 2004). Typical males and males with ASC performed equally well on this task, and both these groups performed better than control females. In the Mental Rotation Test, participants have to judge whether two abstract 3-dimensional shapes in different orientations are the same or different. This is a task on which males generally outperform females (Masters & Sanders, 1993), and people with ASC have been shown to outperform typical controls (Falter, Plaisted, et al. 2008). In a series of experiments with a human-size labyrinth, people with ASC matched the performance of people without ASC on all the tasks, and were faster at a map-learning task, and more accurate in a task involving graphic cued recall of a path (Caron, Mottron, et al. 2004). Other studies have found that typical males tend to outperform typical females on tasks involving learning routes (Galea & Kimura, 1993), navigating computer-generated mazes (Moffat, Hampson, et al. 1998), and way-finding (Silverman, Choi, et al. 2000).

HOW THE E-S THEORY ACCOUNTS FOR CLINICAL PRESENTATION

One of the strengths of the E-S theory is that it is a two-factor theory—that is, it can explain both the social and non-social symptoms of ASC. Deficits in empathizing account well for the qualitative disabilities in social and communication skills. In the definition of empathizing given above, we described how empathizing allows us to make sense of the behavior of others, predict what they might do next, how they feel, and on top of this, feel connected others, and respond appropriately to them. If empathizing is impaired in an individual, it follows that he will struggle with peer relationships, will not want to share experiences and interests with others, will lack social and emotional reciprocity, will have impairments in nonverbal behaviors, will find it difficult to use appropriate language, and will find initiating and sustaining conversations difficult. These are all symptoms for autistic disorder, based on the *DSM-IV* criteria.

Systemizing explains the third axis in the diagnostic criteria: the narrow interests, repetitive behavior, and resistance to change. Narrow interests are sometimes described as obsessions. An obsession involves completely immersing yourself in a particular topic or interest, finding out all the information about it, and understanding everything there is to know—in other words, cracking the system. Repetitive behaviors can be understood in terms of an individual using a system she has developed, or testing out a system repeatedly. Similarly, resistance to change can be thought of as an individual sticking with a nice, safe, predictable system. The E-S theory accounts well for the core symptoms described above, but can it explain the other characteristics which are commonly associated with ASC?

LANGUAGE DELAY

Many people with ASC have language delay, or even a complete absence of expressive language. The E-S theory has one way of explaining why language delay might occur in ASC. This is because the neurotypical route into language is to use empathy, or more specifically, to use joint attention (to establish a topic) and intention-detection (to guess at a speaker's intended meaning; Baldwin, 1995; Tomasello, 1988). If a toddler with ASC has empathy deficits, this route into language may be less accessible to her. Instead, she has to fall back on a systemizing approach to language acquisition. While this is possible, it is much harder, simply because the pragmatics of language are far less rule-based (Baron-Cohen, Baldwin, & Crowson, 1997). But over and above the E-S account of language delay, it may well be that there are specific genetic contributions to this comorbid phenotype (Tager-Flusberg, Rice, et al. 2004).

SENSORY HYPERSENSITIVITY

Sensory hypersensitivity formed part of the diagnostic criteria in *DSM-III*, but was dropped in *DSM-IV*. There are now calls for hypersensitivity to be reintroduced in *DSM-V*. This proposal is supported by questionnaire-based studies, which suggest that over 90% of children with ASC have sensory abnormalities (Kern, Trivedi, et al. 2006, 2007; Leekam, Nieto, et al. 2007; Tomchek & Dunn, 2007; see also Chapter 11). The "enhanced perceptual functioning" (EPF) model was proposed to account for the superior low-level perceptual processing in people with ASC (Mottron & Burack, 2001). There is evidence supporting this model across different modalities. For example, individuals with ASC have enhanced visual acuity (Ashwin, Ashwin, Rhydderch, Howells, & Baron-Cohen, 2009), enhanced pitch discrimination (O'Riordan & Passetti, 2006), and hypersensitivity to vibrotactile stimulation and thermal pain (Blakemore et al., 2006; Cascio, McGlone, et al. 2008). In these studies, and others, the superior processing is all at low levels. Enhanced perceptual functioning is not found at higher levels. This difference in perceptual processing is related to stimulus complexity. For example, individuals with ASC are more accurate at detecting the orientation of simple visual stimuli (luminance-defined gratings), but less accurate at identifying complex visual stimuli (texture-defined gratings; Bertone, Mottron, et al. 2005).

The E-S theory is a cognitive theory, and is concerned with behavior and cognitive functioning at a higher level than the basic perceptual processing which is related to sensory hypersensitivity. The E-S theory cannot, therefore, account for sensory hypersensitivity, but the two are not incompatible. A central tenet for the E-S theory is that a propensity to systemize is associated with having excellent attention to detail. Taking this to the extreme, it is not surprising that people with ASC are hypersensitive, and certainly hypersensitivity is not inconsistent with the E-S theory.

PRACTICAL APPLICATION OF THE E-S THEORY

According to the E-S theory, the typical individual with ASC is impaired at empathizing, but has preserved or even superior systemizing skills. Can this strength in systemizing be used to improve an area of weakness (empathizing)? Can empathy skills be taught using systemizing? In the description of systemizing above, we discussed why using a systemizing strategy is not effective in social situations, but perhaps it could be used as a teaching method for improving empathizing. The *Mind Reading* DVD (Baron-Cohen, Golan, et al. 2004) is an interactive guide to emotions and mental states. It provides users with a *system* of emotions, in the hope that they can harness their systemizing skills to improve their emotion recognition skills (a precursor to empathizing). *Mind Reading* presents 412 emotions and mental states in a taxonomic system based on 24 emotion groups, and 6 developmental levels, for ages 4 years to adulthood. There is a dictionary definition for each emotion and in addition, each emotion is demonstrated with six examples in three modes: facial expression movies, voice recordings and written context examples. The resulting 7416 (412 x 3 x 6) emotional "assets" are organized in a highly systematic manner. The database of emotions can be accessed directly using the Emotion Library application, or users can utilize the Learning Center, which includes lessons and quizzes.

The effectiveness of the *Mind Reading* DVD has been assessed in small groups with high-functioning ASC (Golan & Baron-Cohen, 2006). The general pattern of results is that *Mind Reading* does enhance emotion recognition skills for both faces and voices when these skills are evaluated using stimuli that are similar to the *Mind Reading* assets. Improvements are found after just a few weeks. However, these skills do not generalize to non-*Mind Reading*-like stimuli, and it is clear that additional methods are needed to enhance generalization. This result is not really surprising, given the discussion above relating to why systemizing is ineffective in the social world. The social world is an open system (Lawson, 2003). It is essential to take context into consideration, there is endless variation in inputs, and real-time performance is required for successful functioning in this world.

Using computers for teaching emotion recognition (or other skills relating to empathizing) to people with ASC is attractive; the computer environment is a highly predictable system, free from social demands, users can work at their own speed, material can be tailored to individual's level of understanding, and lessons can be repeated over and over again. But the very reason that the computer environment is attractive means that generalization from the learned material to new tasks or situations is difficult (Bernard-Opitz, Sriram, & Nakhoda-Sapuan, 2001; Bolte, Feineis-Matthews, et al. 2002; Silver & Oakes, 2001; Swettenham, 1996). Future efforts in this direction will need to concentrate on this generalization issue.

NEURAL UNDERPINNINGS OF EMPATHIZING AND SYSTEMIZING

The characterization of the underlying neural circuits for empathizing and systemizing is a rapidly moving target in the fields of social and cognitive neuroscience. Currently, much more is known about the neural systems that implement specific kinds of empathizing "computations" relative to the literature on the neural systems implementing systemizing "computations." In the following section, we highlight the current solid findings with regard to empathizing.

The neural systems underlying specific types of empathic computations are co-opted by relatively spatially distinct neural circuitry. For instance, affective empathy recruits regions such as the anterior insula (AI), caudal anterior/middle cingulate cortex (cACC/MCC), and somatosensory cortex. In one study, individuals experienced a pain stimulus (Self-Pain) or watched their partner receive a similar type of painful stimulus (Other-Pain). Both the experience of Self-Pain and the observation of Other-Pain recruited AI and cACC/MCC (Singer, Seymour, et al. 2004). Similar manipulations, such as simply imagining oneself or others in pain, results in a similar co-opting of AI and cACC/MCC for both self and other (Jackson, Brunet ,et al. 2006; Lamm, Batson, & Decety, 2007). Studies on the self-experience or observation of emotion in others also indicates that AI and cACC/MCC are crucially involved (Wicker and al., 2003). Other areas which are consistently activated during both self-emotion and other-emotion evaluation are the amygdala and dorsomedial prefrontal cortex (dMPFC) (Lee & Siegle, in press). Despite the shared nature of such evaluative emotion representations (i.e., consistently active for self and other), the AI and dMPFC are more biased for responding to the experience of emotion in oneself rather than the perception of emotion in others, while the amygdala is biased in the reverse fashion (e.g., responding more to perception of emotion in others versus self-experience of emotion; Wager, Barrett et al. in press).

Sensorimotor resonance, which we characterize as a rudimentary form of affective empathy, is coded for by the somatosensory and motor cortex, in the same way that these regions code for the sensorimotor quality of one's own experience. The evidence for this comes from studies which expand across a variety of methodologies, from somatosensory or motor evoked potentials via transcranial magnetic stimulation (Avenanti, Bueti, Galati, & Aglioti, 2005; Bufalari, Aprile, et al. 2007; Minio-Paluello et al., 2009) or magnetoencephalography (MEG; Cheng, Yang, et al. 2008), to fMRI (Blakemore, Bristow, et al. 2005; Keysers, Wicker, et al. 2004; Lamm, Nusbaum, Meltzoff, & Decety, 2007), or the study of special patients with mirror-touch synaesthesia (Banissy & Ward, 2007; Blakemore, Bristow, et al. 2005). However, some of the most striking evidence for sensorimotor resonance comes from the literature on mirror neurons. In the monkey brain, mirror neurons have been found to reside in the frontal operculum/ ventral premotor cortex (i.e., pars opercularis or Brodmann Area 44) and inferior parietal lobule (Iacoboni & Dapretto, 2006; Rizzolatti & Craighero, 2004). Neurons in these areas fire during both the self-execution of actions (e.g., reaching), and the observation of others executing goal-directed actions. In humans, fMRI has delineated a more extended neural circuit for shared representation of self-executed action and observation of such actions in others. This circuit incorporates the ventral premotor and inferior parietal regions as well as the primary motor and somatosensory cortex (Gazzola & Keysers, 2009). Individual differences in self-reported empathy also correlate with the activity in these regions during empathic processing (Chakrabarti, Bullmore, et al. 2006) and across development (Pfeifer, Iacoboni, et al. 2008), lending further evidence for the crucial role such circuitry plays in empathic processing. The Chakrabarti study, which included participants with and without ASC, correlated EQ scores with the brain activation evoked by videos of actors portraying different emotions. Independent of emotion type, the inferior frontal gyrus activity was higher for people with higher EQ.

The neural systems underlying cognitive empathy have been very well characterized. The dorsal and ventral medial prefrontal cortex (dMPFC, vMPFC), posterior cingulate/precuneus (PCC), and the temporo-parietal junction (TPJ) are all involved in mentalizing, Theory of Mind, and perspective taking (Amodio & Frith, 2006; Saxe, 2006). The TPJ appears to be especially sensitive to unambiguous or certain cognitive processing of mental states (e.g., beliefs), while dMPFC and vMPFC are more sensitive to mental-state processing that is more ambiguous or uncertain (e.g., preferences; Jenkins & Mitchell in press). Each of these regions however, is recruited during mentalizing both about oneself and others. Furthermore, each of these areas are functionally connected to the same neural circuits during mentalizing about the self or others. This functionally connected neural circuit comprises many of the previously mentioned areas involved in affective and embodied aspects of empathy (e.g., the ventral premotor cortex, somatosensory cortex, AI, cACC/MCC), suggesting that computations implemented at lower-level empathic processing are being integrated with higher-level cognitive empathic processing circuitry (Lombardo, Chakrabarti et al. in press). Similar to this suggestion, it has also been recently found that the degree of empathic accuracy correlates with activity across cognitive empathy, affective empathy, and embodied circuits (Zaki, Bolger et al. in press). Therefore, rather than viewing empathy as fractionated into separate distinct neural systems, it is more likely that empathizing requires distributed neural processing across the circuits that individually may indeed specialize in specific aspects of empathizing. Whereas in the laboratory setting, the specific nature of the tasks used may constrain this distributed neural processing, in the real world it is likely that each of these neural circuits are coordinating their processing, in order to effectively and accurately empathize.

In contrast to the increasing amount of evidence relating to the neural basis of empathizing, evidence relating to the neural systems for processes underlying systemizing has not yet been acquired. The crucial questions—to what extent empathizing and systemizing neural circuits overlap, and whether this overlap is the same in people with and without ASC—currently remain unanswered.

HYPEREMPATHIZERS AND HYPOSYSTEMIZERS

This chapter has described how people with ASC can be characterized as having an Extreme Type S brain: they are hypersystemizers and hypoempathizers. This raises the question, what would a person with the opposite cognitive profile look like? People with the opposite profile cognitive profile will have an Extreme

Type E brain: they are hyposystemizers and hyperempathizers. One, perhaps flippant, way of thinking about these people is that, although they would struggle with systems, e.g., computers and other machines, it would not really matter, as they could use their superior people skills to get someone else to do the job for them. A recent, highly speculative, theory suggests that, while autism is associated with hypo-developed social cognition, hyper-developed social cognition can lead to psychosis (Crespi & Badcock, 2008). This theory does not make sense in the E-S conceptualization of the brain—if you are a hyperempathizer you are unusually accurate at detecting other people's mental states, and you are unusually sensitive to other people. People who have paranoia or some other psychiatric diagnosis, which means they are overwhelmed by their own or other's emotions, do not fit in with this profile of the hyperempathizer. Similarly, the personality disorders are characterized by profound self-centeredness and, if anything, empathy deficits are more likely to be associated with these conditions (Fonagy, 1989).

In the past, it has been suggested that Williams' syndrome (WS) has the opposite phenotype to autism (Peterson & Panksepp, 2004). Children with WS, it has been claimed, have poor spatial cognition, but are hypersocial and have good face processing-skills. This description fits in with the idea that people with WS might have the Extreme Type E profile. However, a recent review concluded that, while individuals with WS do have visuospatial deficits, they also have pragmatic language impairments and peer difficulties (Martens, Wilson, & Reutens, 2008). This suggests that people with WS are not good candidates for the Extreme Type E profile.

Of course, people with an Extreme Type E brain may not have or require any clinical diagnosis. People with this type of brain would, by definition, be able to function very well in the social world. Although they may struggle at school with subjects requiring a high degree of systemizing ability, such as math and science, they would not necessarily be impaired at other subjects which are not so dependent on systemizing, and so would not necessarily come to the attention of teachers. Investigation of the Extreme Type E brain is an area requiring further research.

CONCLUSIONS

In the introduction to this chapter, we outlined the requirements of a useful psychological theory of ASC.

First, it must be consistent with the clinical presentation of ASC. The E-S theory achieves this because the empathizing deficit accounts for the difficulties in social communication, and the systemizing bias explains the narrow interests, repetitive behavior, and resistance to change criteria. Second, the theory must make clear predictions for performance on relevant cognitive tests, which indeed the E-S theory does. Finally, the theory should help inform research at different levels of research. Although it is beyond the scope of this chapter to go into details, the E-S theory has been informing genetic studies (Chakrabarti, Dudridge et al. submitted), hormonal studies (Auyeung et al., 2006, Chapman, Baron Cohen et al. 2006), and brain imaging studies (Chakrabarti & Baron-Cohen, 2006), suggesting that the E-S theory is not just a description at the psychological level, but a useful tool in the hunt for the biological substrate of ASC (Baron-Cohen, Knickmeyer, & Belmonte, 2005).

References

Adolphs, R., Sears, L., & Piven, J. (2001). Abnormal processing of social information from faces in autism. *Journal of Cognitive Neuroscience, 13*, 232–240.

Amodio, D. M., & Frith, C. D. (2006). Meeting of minds: The medial frontal cortex and social cognition. *Nat Rev Neurosci, 7*(4), 268–277.

Ashwin, E., Ashwin, C., Rhydderch, D., Howells, J., Baron-Cohen, S. (2009). Eagle-eyed visual acuity: An experimental investigation of enhanced perception in autism. *Biol Psychiatry, 65*(1), 17–21.

Asperger, H. (1944). Die Autistischen Psychopathen im Kindesalter. *Archiv fur Psychiatrie und Nervenkrankheiten, 117*, 76–136.

Austin, E. J. (2005). Personality correlates of the broader autism phenotype as assessed by the Autism Spectrum Quotient (AQ). *Personality and Individual Differences, 38*(2), 451–460.

Auyeung, B., Baron-Cohen, S., Chapman, E., Knickmeyer, R., Taylor, K., & Hackett, G. (2006). Foetal testosterone and the Child Systemizing Quotient (SQ-C). *European Journal of Endrocrinology, 155*, 123–130.

Avenanti, A., Bueti, D., Galati, G., &Aglioti, S. M. (2005). Transcranial magnetic stimulatioin highlights the sensorimotor side of empathy for pain. *Nature Neuroscience, 8*, 955–960.

Baldwin, D. (1995). Understanding the link between joint attention and language acquisition. In C. Moore & P. Dunham (Eds.), *Joint attention: Its origins and role in development* (pp. 131–158). Hillsdale, NJ: Lawrence Erlbaum Associates.

Banissy, M. J., & Ward, J. (2007). Mirror-touch synesthesia is linked with empathy. *Nat Neurosci, 10*(7), 815–816.

Baron-Cohen, S. (1989). The autistic child's theory of mind: A case of specific developmental delay. *Journal of Child Psychology and Psychiatry, 30*, 285–298.

Baron-Cohen, S. (1994). The Mindreading System: New directions for research. *Current Psychology of Cognition, 13*, 724–750.

Baron-Cohen, S. (2002). The extreme male brain theory of autism. *Trends in Cognitive Science, 6*, 248–254.

Baron-Cohen, S. (2006). Two new theories of autism: Hyper-systemizing and assortative mating. *Archives of Diseases in Childhood, 91*, 2–5.

Baron-Cohen, S. (2008a). Autism, hypersystemizing, and truth. *Q J Exp Psychol (Colchester), 61*(1), 64–75.

Baron-Cohen, S. (2008b). *Autism and Asperger syndrome: The facts.* Oxford: Oxford University Press.

Baron-Cohen, S., Baldwin, D., Crowson, M. (1997). Do children with autism use the Speaker's Direction of Gaze (SDG) strategy to crack the code of language? *Child Development, 68*, 48–57.

Baron-Cohen, S., Golan, O., et al. (2004). *Mind Reading: The interactive guide to emotions.* London: Jessica Kingsley Limited.

Baron-Cohen, S., & Goodhart, F. (1994). The seeing leads to knowing deficit in autism: The Pratt and Bryant probe. *British Journal of Developmental Psychology, 12*, 397–402.

Baron-Cohen, S., & Hammer, J. (1997). Is autism an extreme form of the male brain? *Advances in Infancy Research, 11*, 193–217.

Baron-Cohen, S., Knickmeyer, R., & Belmonte, M. K. (2005). Sex differences in the brain: Implications for explaining autism. *Science, 310*, 819–823.

Baron-Cohen, S., Leslie, A. M., & Frith, U. (1985). Does the autistic child have a theory of mind? *Cognition, 21*, 37–46.

Baron-Cohen, S., Leslie, A. M., & Frith, U. (1986). Mechanical, behavioral and Intentional understanding of picture stories in autistic children. *British Journal of Developmental Psychology, 4*, 113–125.

Baron-Cohen, S., O'Riordan, M., Stone, V., Jones, R., & Plaisted, K.(1999). A new test of social sensitivity: Detection of faux pas in normal children and children with Asperger syndrome. *Journal of Autism and Developmental Disorders, 29*, 407–418.

Baron-Cohen, S., Richler, J., Bisarya, D., Gurunathan, N., & Wheelwright, S (2003). The systemizing quotient: An investigation of adults with Asperger syndrome or high-functioning autism, and normal sex differences. *Philosophical Transactions of the Royal Society of London Series B-Biological Sciences, 358*(1430), 361–374.

Baron-Cohen, S., & Wheelwright, S.(1999). "Obsessions" in children with autism or Asperger syndrome — Content analysis in terms of core domains of cognition. *British Journal of Psychiatry, 175*, 484–490.

Baron-Cohen, S., & Wheelwright, S(2004). The empathy quotient: An investigation of adults with Asperger syndrome or high functioning autism, and normal sex differences. *Journal of Autism and Developmental Disorders* 34(2): 163–175.

Baron-Cohen, S., Wheelwright , S., Hill, J., Raste, Y., & Plumb, I.(2001). The Reading the Mind in the Eyes test revised version: A study with normal adults, and adults with Asperger Syndrome or high-functioning autism. *Journal of Child Psychology and Psychiatry*, 42, 241–252.

Baron-Cohen, S., Wheelwright, S., Spong, A., Scahill, V., & Lawson, J. (2001). Are intuitive physics and intuitive psychology independent? *Journal of Developmental and Learning Disorders*, 5, 47–78.

Baron-Cohen, S., Wheelwright, S., Skinner, R., Martin, J., & Clubley, E. (2001). The Autism-Spectrum Quotient (AQ): Evidence from Asperger syndrome/high-functioning autism, males and females, scientists and mathematicians. *Journal of Autism and Developmental Disorders*, 31(1), 5–17.

Bartlett, M., Movellan, J., Littlewort, G., Braathen, B., Frank, M., & Sejnowski, T. (2005). Towards automatic recognition of spontaneous facial actions. In P. Ekman (Ed.), *What the face reveals* (pp. 393–426). Oxford: Oxford University Press.

Bateson, M. C. (1975). Mother-infant exchanges: The epigenesis of conversational interaction. *Ann N Y Acad Sci*, 263, 101–113.

Bernard-Opitz, V., Sriram, N., & Nakhoda-Sapuan, S. (2001). Enhancing social problem solving with children with autism and normal children through computer-assisted instruction. *Journal of Autism and Developmental Disorders*, 31, 377–398.

Bertone, A., Mottron, L., Jelenic, P., & Faubert, J. (2005). Enhanced and diminished visuo-spatial information processing in autism depends on stimulus complexity. *Brain*, 128, 2430–2441.

Blakemore, S. J., Bristow, D., Bird, G., Frith, C., & Ward, J. (2005). Somatosensory activations during the observation of touch and a case of vision-touch synaesthesia. *Brain*, 128(Pt 7), 1571–1583.

Blakemore, S. J., Tavassoli, T., Calò, S., Thomas, R. M., Catmur, C., Frith, U., & Haggard, P. (2006). Tactile sensitivity in Asperger syndrome. *Brain Cogn*, 61(1), 5–13.

Bolte, S., Feineis-Matthews, S., Leber, S., Dierks, T., Hubl, D., & Poustka, F. (2002). The development and evaluation of a computer-based program to test and to teach the recognition of facial affect. *International Journal of Circumpolar Health*, 61, 61–68.

Bufalari, I., Aprile, T., Avenanti, A., Di Russo, F., & Aglioti, S. M. (2007). Empathy for pain and touch in the human somatosensory cortex. *Cereb Cortex*, 17(11), 2553–2561.

Butterworth, G. (1991). The ontogeny and phylogeny of joint visual attention. In A. Whiten. (Ed.), *Natural theories of mind* (pp. 223–232). Oxford, Blackwell.

Camras, L. A., & Allison, K. (1985). Children's understanding of emotional facial expressions and verbal labels. *Journal of Nonverbal Behavior*, 9(2), 84–94.

Caron, M. J., Mottron, L., Rainville, C., & Chouinard, S. (2004). Do high functioning persons with autism present superior spatial abilities. *Neuropsychologia*, 42, 467–481.

Cascio, C., McGlone, F., Folger, S., Tannan, V., Baranek, G., Pelphrey, K. A., & Essick, G. (2008). Tactile perception in adults with autism: A multidimensional psychophysical study. *J Autism Dev Disord*, 38(1), 127–137.

Chakrabarti, B., & Baron-Cohen, S. (2006). Empathizing: Neurocognitive developmental mechanisms and individual differences. In S. Anders, G. Ende, M. Junghofer, J. Kissler, & D. Wildgruber (Eds.), *Understanding emotions; Progress in brain research* (pp. 403–418). New York: Elsevier.

Chakrabarti, B., Bullmore, E. T., & Baron-Cohen, S. (2006). Empathizing with basic emotions: Common and discrete neural substrates. *Social Neuroscience*, 1, 364–384.

Chakrabarti, B., Dudbridge, F., Kent, L., Wheelwright, S., Hill-Cawthorne, G., Allison, C., ... Baron-Cohen, S. (2009). Genes related to sex steroids, neural growth and socio-emotional behavior are associated with autistic traits, empathy and Asperger syndrome. *Autism Research*, 2, 157–177.

Chapman, E., Baron-Cohen, S., Auyeung, B., Knickmeyer, R., Taylor, K., & Hackett, G. (2006). Foetal testosterone and empathy: Evidence from the Empathy Quotient (EQ) and the Reading the Mind in the Eyes Test. *Social Neuroscience*, 1, 135–148.

Charman, T., Ruffman, T., & Clements, W. (2002). Is there a gender difference in false belief development. *Social Development*, 11, 1–10.

Charman, T., Swettenham, J., Baron-Cohen, S., Cox, A., & Baird, G (1997). Infants with autism: An investigation of empathy, joint attention, pretend play, and imitation. *Developmental Psychology*, 33, 781–789.

Cheng, Y., Yang, C. Y., Lin, C. P., Lee, P. L., & Decety, J. (2008). The perception of pain in others suppresses somatosensory oscillations: A magnetoencephalography study. *Neuroimage*, 40(4), 1833–1840.

Clark, T. F., Winkielman, P., & McIntosh, D. N. (2008). Autism and the extraction of emotion from briefly presented facial expressions: Stumbling at the first step of empathy. *Emotion*, 8(6), 803–809.

Corona, R., Dissanayake, C., Arbelle, S., Wellington, P., & Sigman, M. (1998). Is affect aversive to young children with autism? Behavioral and cardiac responses to experimenter distress. *Child Dev*, 69(6), 1494–1502.

Crespi, B., & Badcock, C. (2008). Psychosis and autism as diametrical disorders of the social brain. *Behavioral and Brain Sciences*, 31(3): 284–320.

Decety, J., & Meyer, M. (2008). From emotion resonance to empathic understanding: A social developmental neuroscience account. *Dev Psychopathol*, 20(4), 1053–1080.

Dimberg, U., Thunberg, M., & Elmehed, K. (2000). Unconscious facial reactions to emotional facial expressions. *Psychol Sci*, 11(1), 86–89.

Dziobek, I., Rogers, K., Fleck, S., Bahnemann, M., Heekeren, H. R., Wolf, O. T., & Convit, A. (2008). Dissociation of cognitive and emotional empathy in adults with asperger syndrome using the multifaceted empathy test (MET). *Journal of Autism and Developmental Disorders*, 38(3), 464–473.

Ekman, P. (1984). Expression and the nature of emotion. In K. Scherer & P. Ekman (Eds.), *Approaches to autism* (pp. 319–343). Hillsdale, NJ: Erlbaum.

Ekman, P. (1992). Facial expressions of emotion: An old controversy and new findings. *Philos Trans R Soc Lond B Biol Sci*, 335, 63–69.

Falter, C. M., Plaisted, K. C., & Davis, G. (2008). Visuospatial processing in autism-testing the predictions of extreme male brain theory. *Journal of Autism and Developmental Disorders*, 38(3), 507–515.

Fonagy, P. (1989). On tolerating mental states: Theory of mind in borderline personality. *Bulletin of the Anna Freud Center*, 12, 91–115.

Galea, L. A. M., & Kimura, D. (1993). Sex differences in route learning. *Personality & Individual Differences*, 14, 53–65.

Gazzola, V., & Keysers, C. (2009). The observation and execution of actions share motor and somatosensory voxels in all tested subjects: Single-subject analyzes of unsmoothed fMRI data. *Cereb Cortex*, 19(6), 1239–1255.

Golan, O., & Baron-Cohen, S. (2006). Systemizing empathy: Teaching adults with Asperger syndrome or high-functioning autism to recognize complex emotions using interactive multimedia. *Dev Psychopathol*, 18(2), 591–617.

Griggs, R. A., & Cox, J. R. (1982). The elusive thematic-materials effect in Wason's selection task. *British Journal of Psychology*, 73(3), 407.

Happé, F. (1994). An advanced test of theory of mind: Understanding of story characters' thoughts and feelings by able autistic, mentally handicapped, and normal children and adults. *Journal of Autism and Development Disorders*, 24, 129–154.

Happé, F. G. E. (1995). The role of age and verbal-ability in the theory of mind task-performance of subjects with autism. *Child Development*, 66(3), 843–855.

Harris, P., Johnson, C. N., Hutton, D., Andrews, G., & Cooke, T. (1989). Young children's theory of mind and emotion. *Cognition and Emotion*, 3, 379–400.

Hart, C. (1989). *Without reason*. New York: Harper & Row, Inc.

Haviland, J. M., & Lelwica, M. (1987). The induced affect response—10-week-old infants responses to 3 emotion expressions. *Developmental Psychology*, 23(1), 97–104.

Hawking, S. (1988). *A Brief History of Time*. New York: Bantam Press.

Hobson, R. P. (1986). The autistic child's appraisal of expressions of emotion. *Journal of Child Psychology and Psychiatry*, 27, 321–342.

Hobson, R. P. (1991). Methodological issues for experiments on autistic individuals' perception and understanding of emotion. *J Child Psychol Psychiatry*, 32(7), 1135–1158.

Hoekstra, R. A., Bartels, M., Cath, D. C., & Boomsma, D. I. (2008). Factor structure, reliability and criterion validity of the Autism-Spectrum Quotient (AQ): A study in Dutch population and patient groups. *J Autism Dev Disord*, 38(8), 1555–1566.

Hoffman, M. L. (1975). Developmental synthesis of affect and cognition and its implications for altruistic motivation. *Developmental Psychology*, 11(5), 607–622.

Hood, B., Willen, J., & Driver, J. (1997). An eye-direction detector triggers shifts of visual attention in human infants. Unpublished ms.: Harvard University.

Hurst, R. MMitchell, ., J. T., Kimbrel, N. A., Kwapil, T. K., & Nelson-Gray, R. O. (2007). Examination of the reliability and factor structure of the Autism Spectrum Quotient (AQ) in a non-clinical sample. *Personality and Individual Differences*, 43(7), 1938–1949.

Iacoboni, M., & Dapretto, M. (2006). The mirror neuron system and the consequences of its dysfunction. *Nat Rev Neurosci*, 7(12), 942–951.

Ickes, W. (2003). *Everyday mind reading: Understanding what other people think and feel*. Amherst, NY: Prometheus Books.

Izard, C. E. (1994). Innate and universal facial expressions: Evidence from developmental and cross-cultural research. *Psychol Bull*, 115(2), 288–299.

Jackson, P. L., Brunet, E., Meltzoff, A. N., & Decety, J. (2006). Empathy examined through the neural mechanisms involved in imagining how I feel versus how you feel pain. *Neuropsychologia*, 44(5), 752–761.

Jenkins, A., & Mitchell, J. (2010). Mentalizing under uncertainty: Dissociating neural responses to ambiguous and unambiguous mental state inferences. *Cereb Cortex*, 20 (2) 404–410.

Joseph, R. M., & Tanaka, J (2003). Holistic and part-based face recognition in children with autism. *Journal of Child Psychology and Psychiatry*, 44, 529–542.

Kern, J. K., Trivedi, M. H., Garver, C. R., Grannemann, B. D., Andrews, A. A., Savla, J. S., ... Schroeder, J. L. (2006). The pattern of sensory processing abnormalities in autism. *Autism*, 10, 480–494.

Kern, J. K., Trivedi, M. H., Grannemann, B. D., Garver, C. R., Johnson, D. G., Andrews, A. A., ... Schroeder, J. L. (2007). Sensory correlations in autism. *Autism*, 11(2), 123–134.

Keysers, C., Wicker, B., Gazzola, V., Anton, J. L., Fogassi, L., & Gallese, V. (2004). A touching sight: SII/PV activation during the observation and experience of touch. *Neuron*, 42(2), 335–346.

Lamm, C., Batson, C. D., & Decety, J. (2007). The neural substrate of human empathy: Effects of perspective-taking and cognitive appraisal. *J Cogn Neurosci*, 19(1), 42–58.

Lamm, C., Nusbaum, H. C., Meltzoff, A. N., & Decety, J. (2007). What are you feeling? Using functional magnetic resonance imaging to assess the modulation of sensory and affective responses during empathy for pain. *PLoS ONE, 2*(12), e1292.

Lawson, J. (2003). Depth accessibility difficulties: An alternative conceptualisation of autism spectrum conditions. *Journal for the Theory of Social Behavior, 33*, 189–202.

Lawson, J., Baron-Cohen, S., & Wheelwright, S. (2004). Empathizing and systemizing in adults with and without Asperger Syndrome. *J. Autism Dev. Disord, 34*, 301–310.

Lee, K., & Siegle, G. (in press). Common and distinct brain networks underlying explicit emotional evaluation: A meta-analytic study. *Social Cognitive and Affective Neuroscience.*

Leekam, S. R., Nieto, C., Libby, S. J., Wing, L., & Gould, J. (2007). Describing the sensory abnormalities of children and adults with autism. *Journal of Autism and Developmental Disorders, 37*(5), 894–910.

Leslie, A. M. (1987). Pretence and representation: The origins of theory of mind. *Psychological Review, 94*, 412–426.

Leslie, A. M., & Frith, U. (1988). Autistic children's understanding of seeing, knowing, and believing. *British Journal of Developmental Psychology, 6*, 315–324.

Lombardo, M., Chakrabarti, B., Bullmore, E., Wheelwright, S., Sadek, S., Suckling, J., ... Baron-Cohen, S. (2010). Shared neural circuits for mentalizing about the self and others. *Journal of Cognitive Neuroscience. 22*(7), 1623–1635.

Lutchmaya, S., Baron-Cohen, S., & Raggatt, P. (2002). Foetal testosterone and eye contact in 12 month old infants. *Infant Behav. Dev, 25*, 327–335.

Manktelow, K. I., & Evans, J. (1979). Facilitation of reasoning by realism—effect or non-effect. *British Journal of Psychology, 70*(NOV), 477–488.

Martens, M. A., Wilson, S. J., & Reutens, D. J. (2008). Research review: Williams syndrome: A critical review of the cognitive, behavioral, and neuroanatomical phenotype. *Journal of Child Psychology and Psychiatry, 49*(6), 576–608.

Martin, G. B., & Clark, R. D. (1982). Distress crying in neonates—Species and peer specificity. *Developmental Psychology, 18*(1), 3–9.

Masters, M. S., & Sanders, B. (1993). Is the gender difference in mental rotation disappearing? *Behavior Genetics, 23*, 337–341.

McIntosh, D. N., Reichmann-Decker, A., Winkielman, P., & Wilbarger, J. L. (2006). When the social mirror breaks: Deficits in automatic, but not voluntary, mimicry of emotional facial expressions in autism. *Developmental Science, 9*(3), 295–302.

Minio-Paluello, I., Baron-Cohen, S., Avenanti, A., Walsh, V., & Aglioti, S. M. (2009). Absence of embodied empathy during pain observation in Asperger syndrome. *Biological Psychiatry, 65*(1), 55–62.

Minshew, N., Goldstein, G., Taylor, H. G., & Siegel, D. J. (1993). Academic achievement in high functioning autistic individuals. *Journal of Clinical and Experimental Neuropsychology, 16*, 261–270.

Moffat, S. D., Hampson, E., & Hatzipantelis, M (1998). Navigation in a virtual maze: Sex differences and correlation with psychometric measures of spatial ability in humans. *Evolution and Human Behavior, 19*(2), 73–87.

Mottron, L., & Burack, J. A. (2001). Enhanced perceptual functioning in the development of autism. In . J. A. Burack, T. Charman, N. Yirmiya, P. Zelazo (Eds.), *The development of autism: Perspectives from theory and research* (pp. 131–148). New York: Routledge.

Mundy, P., & Crowson, M. (1997). Joint attention and early social communication. *Journal of Autism and Developmental Disorders, 27*, 653–676.

O'Riordan, M., & Passetti, F. (2006). Discrimination in autism within different sensory modalities. *J Autism Dev Disord, 36*(5), 665–675.

Perner, J., & Wimmer, H. (1985). John thinks that Mary thinks that ... Attribution of second-order beliefs by 5-10 year old children. *Journal of Experimental Child Psychology, 39*, 437–471.

Peterson, B., & Panksepp, J. (2004). Biological basis of childhood neuropsychiatric disoders. In J. Panksepp (Ed.), *Textbook of biological psychiatry* (pp. 393–436). New York: Wiley-Liss.

Pfeifer, J. H., Iacoboni, M. Mazziotta, J. C., & Dapretto, M. (2008). Mirroring others' emotions relates to empathy and interpersonal competence in children. *Neuroimage, 39*(4), 2076–2085.

Ponnet, K. S., Roeyers, H., Buysse, A., De Clerq, A., & Van Der Heyden, E. (2004). Advanced mind-reading in adults with Asperger syndrome. *Autism, 8*(3), 249–266.

Pratt, C., & Bryant, P. (1990). Young children understand that looking leads to knowing (so long as they are looking into a single barrel). *Child Development, 61*; 973–983.

Premack, D. (1990). The infant's theory of self-propelled objects. *Cognition, 36*, 1–16.

Premack, D., & Woodruff, G. (1978). Does the chimpanzee have a theory of mind? *Behavioral and Brain Sciences, 1*(4), 515–526.

Rizzolatti, G., & Craighero, L. (2004). The mirror-neuron system. *Annu Rev Neurosci, 27*, 169–192.

Rochat, P. (2002). *The infant's world.* Cambridge, MA: Harvard University Press.

Rogers, K., Dziobek, I., Hassenstab, J., Wolf, O. T., & Convit, A. (2007). Who cares? Revisiting empathy in Asperger syndrome. *Journal of Autism and Developmental Disorders, 37*(4), 709–715.

Rutherford, M. D., & McIntosh, D. N. (2007). Rules versus prototype matching: Strategies of perception of emotional facial expressions in the autism spectrum. *Journal of Autism and Developmental Disorders, 37*(2), 187–196.

Sagi, A., & Hoffman, M. L. (1976). Empathic distress in Newborns. *Developmental Psychology, 12*(2), 175–176.

Saxe, R. (2006). Uniquely human social cognition. *Curr Opin Neurobiol, 16*(2), 235–239.

Scaife, M., & Bruner, J. (1975). The capacity for joint visual attention in the infant. *Nature*, 253, 265–266.

Scambler, D. J., Hepburn, S., Rutherford, M. D., Wehner, E. A., & Rogers, S. J. (2007). Emotional responsivity in children with autism, children with other developmental disabilities, and children with typical development. *Journal of Autism and Developmental Disorders*, 37(3), 553–563.

Sigman, M. D., Kasari, C., Kwon, J. H., & Yirmiya, N. (1992). Responses to the negative emotions of others by autistic, mentally-retarded, and normal-children. *Child Development*, 63(4), 796–807.

Silver, M., & Oakes, P. (2001). Evaluation of a new computer intervention to teach people with autism or Asperger syndrome to recognize and predict emotions in others. *Autism*, 5, 299–316.

Silverman, I. I., Choi, J., Mackewn, A., Fisher, M., Moro, J., & Olshansky, E. (2000). Evolved mechanisms underlying wayfinding. Further studies on the hunter-gatherer theory of spatial sex differences. *Evol Hum Behav*, 21(3), 201–213.

Singer, T., Seymour, B., O'Doherty, J., Kaube, H., Dolan, R. J., & Frith, C. D. (2004). Empathy for pain involves t he affective but not sensory components of pain. *Science*, 303, 1157–1167.

Stewart, M. E., Watson, J., Allcock, A. J., & Yaqoob, T. (2009). Autistic traits predict performance on the block design. *Autism*, 13(2), 133–142.

Swettenham, J. (1996). Can children with autism be taught to understand false belief using computers? *Journal of Child Psychology and Psychiatry*, 37, 157–165.

Swettenham, J., Baron-Cohen, S., Charman, T., Cox, A., Baird, G., Drew, A ... . Wheelwright, S. (1998). The frequency and distribution of spontaneous attention shifts between social and non-social stimuli in autistic, typically developing, and non-autistic developmentally delayed infants. *Journal of Child Psychology and Psychiatry*, 9, 747–753.

Tager-Flusberg, H., Rice, M. L., & Warren, S. F. (2004). Do autism and specific language impairment represent overlapping language disorders? In M.L. Rice & S.F. Warren (Eds.), *Developmental language disorders: From phenotypes to etiologies* (pp. 31–52). Mahwah, NJ: Lawrence Erlbaum Associates Publishers.

Thompson, R. (1987). Empathy and emotional understanding: The early development of empathy. In N. Eisenberg & J. Strayer (Eds.), *Empathy and its development* (pp. 119–145). Cambridge: Cambridge University Press.

Titchener, E. (1909). Lectures on the elementary psychology of the thought processes. New York: Macmillan.

Tomasello, M. (1988). The role of joint-attentional processes in early language acquisition. *Language Sciences*, 10, 69–88.

Tomchek, S. D., & Dunn, W. (2007). Sensory processing in children with and without autism: A comparative study using the short sensory profile. *American Journal of Occupational Therapy*, 61(2), 190–200.

Ungerer, J. A., Dolby, R., Waters, B., Barnett, B., Kelk, N., & Lewin, V. (1990). The early development of empathy—Self-regulation and individual-differences in the 1st year. *Motivation and Emotion*, 14(2), 93–106.

Vicari, S., Reilly, J. S., Pasqualetti, P., Vizzotto, A., & Caltagirone, C. (2000). Recognition of facial expressions of emotions in school-age children: the intersection of perceptual and semantic categories. *Acta Paediatr*, 89(7), 836–845.

Wager, T., Barrett, L., Bliss-Moreau, E., Lindquist, K., Duncan, S., Kober, H., ...Mize, J. (2008). The neuroimaging of emotion. In M. Lewis (Ed.), *Handbook of Emotion*. (pp. 249–271). New York: The Guilford Press.

Wakabayashi, A., Baron-Cohen, S., & Wheelwright, S. (2004). The Autism Spectrum Quotient (AQ) Japanese version : Evidence from high-functioning clinical group and normal adults. *Japanese Journal of Psychology*, 75, 78–84.

Walker-Andrews, A. S. , & Lennon, E. (1991). Infants' discrimination of vocal expressions: Contributions of auditory and visual information. *Infant Behavior & Development*, 14(2), 131–142.

Wallace, S., Coleman, M., & Bailey, A. (2008). An investigation of basic facial expression recognition in autism spectrum disorders. *Cognition & Emotion*, 22(7), 1353–1380.

Wheelwright, S., Baron-Cohen, S., Goldenfeld, N., Delaney, J., Fine, D., Smith, R., ... Wakabayashi, A. (2006). Predicting autism spectrum quotient (AQ) from the Systemizing Quotient—Revised (SQ-R) and Empathy Quotient (EQ). *Brain Research*, 1079, 47–56.

Wicker, B., Keysers, C., Plailly, J., Royet, J. P., Gallese, V., & Rizzolatti. G.(2003). Both of us disgusted in *My* insula: The common neural basis of seeing and feeling disgust. *Neuron*, 40, 655–664.

Widen, S. C., & Russell, J. A. (2008). Children acquire emotion categories gradually. *Cognitive Development*, 23(2), 291–312.

Williams, D. (1996). *Autism: An inside-out approach*. London: Jessica Kingsley.

Wimmer, H., & Perner, J. (1983). Beliefs about beliefs: Representation and constraining function of wrong beliefs in young children's understanding of deception. *Cognition*, 13, 103–128.

Woodbury-Smith, M., Robinson, J., Wheelwright, S., & Baron-Cohen, S. (2005). Screening adults for Asperger Syndrome using the AQ: Diagnostic validity in clinical practice. *Journal of Autism and Developmental Disorders*, 35, 331–335.

Yirmiya, N., Sigman, M., Kasari, C., & Mundy, P. (1992). Empathy and cognition in high functioning children with autism. *Child Development*, 63, 150–160.

Zaki, J., Bolger, N., Weber, J., & Ochsner, K. (2009). The neural bases of empathic accuracy. *Proceedings of the National Academy of Sciences*, 106(27), 11382–11387.

Chapter 18

Entrainment, Mimicry, and Interpersonal Synchrony

Marcel Kinsbourne and Molly Helt

INTRODUCTION: SOCIAL SYMPTOMS IN AUTISM

In his pioneering description of autism, Kanner (1943) pinpointed "autistic disturbances of affective contact" as the central features of the disorder, disturbances that reflect "innate inability to form the usual biologically provided contact with people." Children with autistic spectrum disorder (ASD) are unsociable, reticent, and even aloof, especially with strangers. They find the pragmatics of dyadic interactions difficult, avoid full face-to-face confrontation and eye contact, and do not grasp the conventions of turn taking in conversation. Concurrent with, or antecedent to, these anomalies of dyadic interaction, is an apparent lack of interest in, and even awareness of, others' states of mind, as well as a preference for engaging inanimate objects (e.g. Swettenham et al., 1998), or for internalizing attention altogether (Kinsbourne, 1979). In this discussion we first outline systematic and experimental studies of the phenomenology,

development, and neurofunctional correlates of interpersonal coordination. We then examine the ways in which the atypically limited interpersonal coordination of people with autism diverges from the norm, and consider what an adequate preliminary model of the underlying neuropathology might be. Finally, we consider whether autistic impediments to social interaction are primary, or secondary to antecedent deviations in development that are not specifically social in nature.

Apes understand actions, but only humans have the unique social motivation to interact and establish shared intentionality (Tomasello, Carpenter, Call, Behne, & Moll, 2005). Only humans engage in face-to-face, entrained, dyadic interactions that are synchronized with respect to timing and emotional content. Indeed, throughout human evolution (and up to the invention of the telephone) this was the only practical way for people to converse in real time. We might learn what is lost (or gained) from conversing in modes other than face-to-face from high-functioning people with autism, who are averse to interacting face-to-face with others and making eye contact.

For dyadic entrainment to occur, even when there is no important information to transmit, the parties must find it intrinsically rewarding to engage face-to-face with sustained eye contact, and without inducement by extrinsic reinforcers. Should some impediment preclude face-to-face positioning, the opportunity for dyadic entrainment would vanish. Children with autism appear to be averse to the uncertainty that is inherent in other people's facial expressions, although that degree of uncertainty can easily be borne by typically developing individuals. Eye contact carries a cognitive load, and holding direct eye contact with another person leads to physiological arousal, with increased heart rate and skin conductance, and may result in gaze aversion (Doherty-Sneddon, Bonner, Bruce, Longbotham & Doyle 2002). This gaze aversion might be magnified if the individual is in a chronic state of overarousal or unstable arousal, and Kinsbourne explores this possibility in Chapter 19. Such an aversion to uncertainty might cause even an infant to defensively avoid eye contact, and thereby override the basic propensity of the human infant to relate face-to-face with adults.

As Darwin famously recognized, the human face is the most flexible conveyer of social signals (Ohman, 2002). A host of social impediments might flow from the inability to take advantage of facial expressions for receiving socially transmitted information, as well as for acquiring social skills. Alternatively, children with autism might be drawn away from eye contact by a strong preference for turning their attention inward to their own bodily states, as implied by the term autism, derived from the Greek words "self" and "state", which both Kanner (1943) and Asperger (1944) independently chose to name the previously unrecognized syndrome. This inwardly directed attention might also be driven by a disorder of arousal, or by some other unknown subjective force. The idea of inwardly directed attention has received recent support from studies of the "default system" (Buckner, Andrews-Hanna, & Schacter, 2008), a topographic pattern of brain activation when people introspect, and which normally switches off when attention returns to events in the world (Greene & Haidt, 2002). Kennedy & Courchesne (2008) have observed that in people with autism, "default" activations frequently persist even when they undertake tasks that mandate interaction with the environment. Engaging in introspection too often and too long may detract from social learning and social behavior.

Although our emphasis is on the emergence of social symptoms in children with autism, we begin by considering the nonverbal characteristics of interpersonal coordination—the degree to which social interactions are entrained, or synchronous, and patterned after the other, encompassing the phenomena of mimicry and interactional synchrony—between normally functioning adults. The discussion that follows highlights the foundational nature of interpersonal coordination, and the benefits to affiliation and social learning that accrue.

INTERPERSONAL COORDINATION IN TYPICAL INDIVIDUALS

When couples converse, they also entrain into an "embodied" dyad. Typically, they face each other. Each partner's gaze direction and posture resonates with that of the other, and when turn taking becomes due, embodies the anticipated response (Jordan, 2009; Kinsbourne & Jordan, 2009). Each participant mimics the other's postures and expressions, and reflects the other's speech patterns in his own bodily rhythms. Condon and Sander (1974) discovered this reciprocal cycling coordination in infants and mothers and named it "interactional synchrony." It turns out to be a potent effect. As an extreme example, Zajonc, Adelman, Murphy, and Niedenthal (1987) find that long-married couples look more alike than they did at their wedding, apparently because years of mimicking one another in silent empathy shapes facial similarities and wrinkle patterns; indeed, the more they resemble each other at a silver anniversary, the greater marital accord they report. This mutual entrainment is presumably the hallmark of a successful long-term dyadic interaction.

"Face time" is intrinsically rewarding for both parties, regardless of the verbal content that is transmitted. The origins of this motivated entrainment, for purposes even of uninformative ("phatic") interactions, can be seen as early as the reciprocal interactions of newborn babies and their caretakers (Kinsbourne, 2002). To engage with a peer, toddlers imitate the other child's nonverbal behavior. "Imitating another's nonverbal actions is a core behavioral strategy for achieving social coordination during the developmental period, preceding reliance on verbal communication in peer interaction" (Eckerman, Davis, & Dedoc, 1989, p. 60). Even capuchin monkeys move closer to, and cooperate more, with humans who imitate them (Faulkner, Suomi, Visalberghi, & Ferraril, 2009).

Mimicry of Actions and Emotions

Mimicry and imitation differ in a key respect, in that mimicry is automatic, whereas imitation is volitional (see Chapter 13). Tomasello (1996) defined mimicry as "nonvolitional automatic matching responses." In contrast, imitating someone else's actions is intentional, and sometimes even effortful. As human beings interact, we unconsciously mimic (often at a level undetectable to the naked eye) each other's posture, facial expressions, vocal prosody, speech patterns, gestures, and emotional expressions (e.g., Niedenthal, Barsalou, Ric, & Krauth-Gruber, 2005).

A conventional account of the relationship between mimicry and emotional convergence with those around us is the classic James-Lange hypothesis. The observer perceives the other's posture and expressions, her musculature mimics that of the other, and the brain interprets feedback from its own musculature as signaling the emotion in question (e.g., James, 1890). This "empathic coupling" would be an instance of "embodied communication" (e.g., Kinsbourne & Jordan, 2009). Initially thought to be specifically facial (hence named the "facial feedback hypothesis" [Capella, 1993]), embodied communication extends also to gesture, posture, and prosody of speech (McIntosh, 1996; Macrae, Duffy, Miles & Lawrence, 2008). In short, movements that are associated with the expression of an emotion not only signal it to others, but can also cause the observer to feel that emotion, at least to some extent.

However, after repeatedly witnessing and internalizing an emotion, one would presumably learn to experience cognitive empathy on sight, without needing to route the feeling through the body's periphery in order to enable emotional empathy. If autistic individuals do not focus on the face, they might neither learn to recognize emotional expressions, not simulate them internally, and therefore would not later readily identify the emotional expressions of others. Or, they would learn only deliberately to memorize and identify emotional expressions, without the presumed benefit of having that emotional understanding informed by bodily feedback.

In an alternative form, or perhaps at the next level of cognitive and emotional development, the observer may represent and recognize the emotion that he infers from the other's actions; the experience of that emotion may overflow its neuronal representation and become embodied in the observer's musculature, causing overt or covert mimicry. The embodiment may subsequently feed back centrally to generate or increase an emotion that corresponds to the emotion inferred in the other (even if it's inferred incorrectly; see Moody, McIntosh, Mann & Weisser, 2007). Felt emotion may be necessary in infancy for learning to recognize and experience the emotions of others, but once these connections are repeatedly activated, and cognitive factors become more important in assessing the states of others, one may not need to feel the emotion to enable him to recognize how someone else feels.

Our automatic tendency to mimic emotional information represented in the musculature of others, coupled with the effects of this mimicking on our emotional states, may explain emotional contagion (Hatfield, Caccioppo, & Rapson, 1994). Because we unconsciously mimic their emotional movements, we inadvertently feel the emotions of those with whom we interact. Theorists of embodied social cognition argue that vicariously experiencing the emotions of others in our own bodies (albeit in an attenuated form) provides an emotional link between self and other that generates social connection and empathy.

The term empathy is commonly used to refer to multilevel constructs ranging from primitive emotional contagion, which is purely stimulus-driven (that is, emotional contagion due to motor mimicry and feedback without cognitive mediation; Hatfield, et al., 1994), to perspective-taking, that is, representing the mental state of another through top-down inferential, rather than perceptual, processes, which take into account what one knows and what one remembers about the other person. Mimicry could be a rudimentary precursor or building block of empathy. The infant may be born with the capacity for primitive emotional contagion, which in itself offers no basis for the observer to distinguish between himself and someone else as the source of the emotion. True empathic processes emerge as the infant becomes aware that the source of his represented emotion is outside of himself, and is cognitively able to place the emotion into interpersonal context, having the self awareness to realize that what he feels is a reflection of what the other person appears to be feeling. In its most complex use, the term "empathy" requires the individual to use this emotional information to act in a sympathetic manner (Decety & Moriguchi, 2007). Where conscious reflection is called for, midline brain circuitry, notably the medial prefrontal cortex, becomes involved. In short, although the mimicry that is involved in the suggested mechanism for empathy may perhaps be necessary, it is certainly not sufficient for the full range of behavior suggested by the term "empathy." However, if mimicry is the first step to building empathy, and is compromised in individuals with autism, they will have difficulty reaching these later stages or more sophisticated forms of empathy.

The social impact of facial mimicry is bidirectional. The more people like one another, the more they mimic one another, and the more they are induced to mimic one another, the better they report liking each other (Chartrand & Bargh, 1999). The same applies to emotional contagion (Bavelas, Black, Lemery, & Mullett, 1987). The higher a person rates on scales measuring empathy, the more she engages in mimicry, and the more susceptible she herself is to emotional contagion (Chartrand & Bargh, 1999; Sonnby-Borgstrom, 2002). By way of emotional contagion, mimicry increases empathy for the person being mimicked, and this increases prosocial behavior (Stel, van den Heuvel, & Smeets, 2008). Participants who are mimicked (van Baaren, Holland, Kawakami, & van Knippenberg, 2004) and those who mimic another person (Stel, et al., 2008) both donate more money to a charity than controls. Being mimicked appears to increase trust and generosity. Meanwhile, mimicking another person may lead one to move closer to that person (Ashton-James, Van Baaren, Chartrand, Decety, & Karremans, 2007). Mimicry increases feelings of similarity toward the mimicry partner (Lakin, Jefferis, Cheng, & Chartrand, 2003), and in turn increases the mimicry displayed toward the partner (Guéguen & Martin, 2009). According to Lakin et al. (2003), mimicry is "social glue"; it evolved on account of the selective advantage for humans of affiliating and communicating as a group.

Facial mimicry may be mediated by eye gaze. Contagious yawning, a form of mimicry, can be triggered by looking at pictures of the disembodied eyes of people while they yawn, but not their disembodied mouths, indicating that the yawning is triggered by direct gaze (Provine, 1989). When a caregiver mimics her infant during a dyadic interaction, the infant looks at her face more. Striano, Henning, and Stahl (2005) asked mothers to interact with their 3-month-old babies as on a previous occasion, or to interact with them as they normally did, or to imitate all of their infants' facial expressions. Although infants smiled most during the normal interaction condition, infants looked most at their mothers' faces in the imitation condition.

Mimicry and Development

Human infants appear to be born with the potential for mimicry and emotional contagion. As soon as three hours after birth, infants make movements within their motor repertoire, that they see modeled by an adult (Meltzoff & Moore, 1977)–most reliably in the case of tongue protrusion (for a review, see Rogers, 2006). As for emotional contagion, newborn infants cry when they hear other babies crying in the nursery, but not when they hear computer-generated sounds matched to infant crying for acoustic properties (Simner, 1971). Newborn "matching" behaviors have been cited as early examples of the strong link between the perception of actions and emotions in others, and one's own experience of these actions and emotions. They set the stage for imitative abilities that emerge later and underlie critical aspects of social and emotional development. Emotional contagion of crying does not imply that the affected infant cried on account of her deep sympathy with the initially crying child. To credit the newborn infant with the ability to mentalize is unrealistic. Emotional contagion is relevant precisely because it is automatic and does not imply any recognition of the source of the "contagious" mood. Presumably, it allows the infant to develop in a context in which she enacts the feelings of others, a critical first step in the developmental cascade of interpersonal coordination and interaction.

Kinsbourne (2002) proposed that emotional contagion is an instance of enactive perception (Varela, Thompson, & Rosch (1992). When observers perceive actions, or when objects "afford" highly routine actions, they automatically activate their own corresponding motor programs. Infants' mimicry often appears as a full-blown replication of the target's action or expressed emotion, in contrast to the attenuated replications that characterize adult mimicry. Infants lack sufficient frontal lobe development to inhibit the motor overflow from their enactive social perception, and, as stated previously, such inhibition may only be recruited once the infant recognizes the source of the emotion as coming from outside of his own body. When an infant observes an action, the as-yet-immature infant brain cannot inhibit the overt manifestation of the motor planning that accompanies the enactive perception, "The execution of the action makes the infant's perception of the action publicly available, and allows others to 'see' what the infant has seen, 'on the fly'" (Kinsbourne, 2002, p. 316). The infant engages over and over in repetitive reciprocal imitation with the caretaker, both mirroring and anticipating the other's actions. This mutual multiscale entrainment (Kinsbourne and Jordan, 2009) provides the infant with a "scaffold" for joint action and further anticipated entrainment. The infant's conspicuous predilection for entrainment does not derive from material reinforcements, and it would be fanciful to suppose that the infant deliberately engages in these activities in order to practice or learn anything. "This is presumably because the resulting entrainment has evolved to be innately and intrinsically motivating for the infant. The entrainment then becomes secondarily motivating also because it facilitates bonding with a caretaker" (Kinsbourne & Jordan, 2009, p. 109).

Early mimetic behaviors and contagious crying gradually become less frequent. Imitative tongue protrusion disappears by 2–3 months of age (Abravanel & Sigafoos, 1984). Eighty-four percent of newborns, but only 24 percent of 3- to 12-month-old infants, exhibit contagious crying (Bühler & Hetzer, 1928). The mimicry and contagion may have become covert. They are subsequently reinstated in a modified form. At 10–14 months, infants are much more likely to mimic the distressed facial expressions of other crying children, without crying themselves (Zahn-Waxler, Radke-Yarrow, & King, 1979). Thus mimicry and emotional contagion reappear during the second half of the first year, and then continue to expand thereafter. By 9 months of age, babies take on the basic moods and facial expressions of their caregivers, such as joy and sadness (Termine & Izzard, 1988). Jones (1996, 2007) found in longitudinal studies that mimicry of specific actions appeared at distinct periods in development between 6–18 months of age. A special case of mimicry may be the phenomenon of gaze following, a precursor of joint attention, first observed in 6-month-old infants. The infants begin to shift their gaze in the direction of a gaze shift by an adult with whom they are making eye contact

(Johnson, et al., 2005), perhaps enactively, because the represented motor plan is not blocked by inhibition. Thus, automatic mimicry would directly facilitate joint attention.

Some forms of mimicry, such as contagious yawning, remain overt throughout the life span. Contagious yawning is reliably demonstrated by 4 years of age in typically developing children (Helt, Eigsti, Snyder, & Fein, in press), and has been linked to emotional empathy. Arnott, Singhal, and Goodale (2009) studied individual differences in the tendency to yawn when listening to the sound of yawning, whereas Platek, Critton, Myers, and Gallup (2003) investigated individual differences in the tendency to yawn while viewing someone else yawn. In both studies, those participants who were most apt to yawn also scored highest on ratings of empathy.

Among adults, mimicry is usually covert, as adequate frontal lobe development has occurred to inhibit overt mimicry of the targets of our attention, and as we are easily able to recognize the source of the emotion as "other." The most extensive mimicry research has been conducted on facial expressions using electromyography (EMG), which measures minute changes in facial musculature that cannot be observed by the naked eye. Viewing slides of faces that express diverse emotions elicits facial EMG responses that correspond to the perceived expressions (Bush, Barr, McHugo, & Lanzetta, 1989; Dimberg, 1982; Dimberg, Thunberg, & Grunedal, 2002; Vaughan & Lanzetta, 1980). These responses are thought to be automatic because of their speed, and because they are obtained even when the faces are presented subliminally (Dimberg, Thunberg, & Elmehed, 2000). Similar studies have demonstrated mimetic effects for prosody (Neumann & Strack, 2000), gaze direction, speech patterns, gestures, mannerisms, and bodily posture (e.g., McHugo, Lanzetta, Sullivan, Masters, & Englis, 1985).

Mimicry and Synchrony of Rhythm

Mimicry may be a specific instance of a more powerful tool for entrainment: the joint undertaking of rhythmic activity. Marsh, Richardson, and Schmidt (2009) discuss how synchronizing with others enhances mutual feelings of connectedness and facilitates emerging social units. Discussing cultural mechanisms for stimulating the feeling of belonging, Brothers (1997) draws attention to synchronized group behaviors in the public arena. Anthropologists and others have repeatedly remarked that synchronous group movements, such as marching, singing and chanting, improve group cohesion. Wiltermuth and Heath (2009) provide experimental evidence for this concept. Kinsbourne (2002) linked the developmental origin of the powerful affiliative effect of entraining with others to the clearly reinforcing value for infants of engaging in reciprocally alternating activities with caretakers (Beebe, Jaffe, Feldstein, Mays, & Alson, 1985).

Interactional synchrony in infancy involves high-intensity, face-to-face interactions between parent and child, which involve matching of affect, behaviors (e.g., vocalizations), and biological rhythms. From the first day or two after birth, infants move their bodies in synchrony with their mother's speech patterns (Condon & Sander, 1974). Mothers, in turn, may model their early face-to-face play on the burst-pause rhythms that are familiar to infants from crying and sucking (Tronick, Als, & Brazelton, 1977), and synchronous dyads develop entrained heart rhythms (Feldman, 2006; Watanabe, Okubo, & Kuroda, 1996). These highly aroused moments of interpersonal exchange, distinct from the stream of daily life, provide infants with their first mimetic experiences. The temporal aspect of these interactions is their defining feature. Synchrony may be a form of mimicry (or vice versa), wherein the aspect of the other's behavior that is mimicked is its temporal properties (Kinsbourne, 2005). Dowd and Tronick (1986) found that when infants respond to their mothers' speech, they do not so much adopt the mother's underlying speech rhythm, as track and adapt themselves to the parent's varying tempo. Temporally patterned events presumably teach infants contingency, and bind discrete sensory processes into unified organized mental representations.

Several biological factors in both mother and infant predict mother-infant synchrony at 3 months, creating a link between early biological and social rhythms (Feldman, 2006). Specifically, the mother's oxytocin level (Feldman, Levine, Zagoory-Sharon, & Weller, 2007), and her ability to screen out redundant stimuli, as well as the infant's parasympathetic control over his heart rhythm, sleep/wake cycles, newborn orientation, and arousal modulation at term, are each uniquely predictive of more parent-child synchrony at 3 months (Feldman, 2007a). The degree of synchrony between parents and infants at 3 months in turn predicts children's later development of symbol use (Feldman & Greenbaum, 1997), self-regulation (Feldman, Greenbaum, & Yirmiya, 1999), Theory of Mind performance, and capacity for empathy, as it increases into adolescence (Feldman, 2007b). According to Dissanayaka (2000 p. xi) both sexual and generally affiliative love "is originally manifested – expressed and exchanged – by means of emotionally meaningful rhythms and modes" that are jointly created and sustained by mothers and their infants in ritualized evolved interactions".

Neurochemical and Anatomical Underpinnings of Mimicry

The neurochemical underpinnings of mimicry are somewhat clearer than the anatomical mechanisms, although both require further research. The neuro-peptides oxytocin and vasopressin might be involved (Heinrichs & Domes, 2008). In experimental animals, oxytocin reduces the activation of the amygdala, and uncouples the amygdala from brain stem regions that subserve the behavioral and autonomic manifestations of fear (Kirsch et al., 2005). Fear causes sympathetic arousal. Correspondingly, mouse "knock-outs" for oxytocin showed a profound social deficit despite having retained normal olfactory and spatial learning abilities. The social deficit could be fully reversed by injecting oxytocin into the medial amygdala (Ferguson, Aldag, Insel, & Young, 2001). There is evidence from humans to correspond with the animal work. Oxytocin reduces anxiety that might preclude social activity, and, similar to mimicry, intranasal administration of oxytocin has been reported to increase feelings of trust (Kosfeld, Heinrichs, Zak, Fischbacher, & Fare, 2005). Feldman et al. (2007) reported that the mother's oxytocin levels predicted the degree of mother-infant coordination. Andari et al. (2010) reported that high-functioning people with autism engaged in a simulated ball game exhibited more cooperative behavior and more eye contact after oxytocin was administered. (For further discussion of oxytocin and its interaction with the autonomic nervous system, see Chapter 19).

Vasopressin has more complex effects. In males it fosters pair bonding, but also anxiety with respect to unknown persons. In females it facilitates affiliative behavior (Heinrichs & Domes, 2008). Allman, Watson, Tetreault, and Hakeem (2005) suggested that vasopressin function is deficient in ASD. They pointed to a specific type of neuron, spindle-shaped, which they named the Von Economo neuron, after the neuroanatomist who first described them. The Von Economo neurons have receptor sites for vasopressin. Allman et al. (2005) offer evidence that these neurons play a role in social-cognition networks, and discovered that they were disorganized in two autopsied individuals with ASD. Kennedy, Semendeferi, and Courchesne (2007) counted von Economo spindle cells in the frontoinsular cortex in brains of autistic individuals, and found their numbers to be within normal limits (See also Chapter 22).

Common Coding of Perception and Action

William James (1890) first suggested a link between perception and action: "Every representation of a movement awakens to some degree the actual movement which is its object." This early statement of ideomotor theory has taken on new life with the advent of the mirror neuron phenomenon. Prinz (1990) had proposed that perception and action are coded in common, two years before a putative neural substrate for the hypothesized link, the mirror neurons, were discovered in macaque monkeys (di Pelligrino, Fadiga, Fogassi, Gallese, & Rizzolatti, 1992; Gallese, Fadiga, Fogassi, & Rizzolatti, 1996). Although it is the behavior, not the neural activity that may underlie it, that is of primary interest in social evolution and its pathologies, the discovery fueled an ongoing surge in experiments on action/observation congruence, and of theoretical treatments of this phenomenon, with well over 900 articles on mirror neurons on record in PubMed as of this writing.

The common coding theory assumes that actions are coded in terms of the distal events they are intended to bring about; that is, their goals. Perceived actions are also coded in terms of action representations (Prinz, 1990). Electrophysiological recordings in rhesus and macaque monkeys provide direct evidence for perception/action coupling (di Pelligrino et al., 1992; Gallese et al., 1996). Neurons in the ventral premotor and posterior parietal cortices increase their firing rate both while the monkey is engaged in actions, and while the monkey observes the same actions being performed. Correspondingly, functional neuroimaging in humans demonstrates overlap between the areas of brain that are activated during action execution, and when actions are observed. The pattern of brain activation during action observation is quite similar when demonstrated electrophysiologically, by desynchronization of the mu rhythm in the EEG, and by functional imaging (Perry & Bentin, 2009). The mu rhythm occupies much the same bandwidth as the alpha rhythm, but is accessed over the motor, rather than the visual, cortex. It becomes desynchronized when the relevant areas of brain become active, and has therefore been claimed as a proxy marker for mirror neuron activity in humans, the neurons themselves remaining inaccessible to direct observation and verification. The common coding, in overlapping areas of "mirror circuitry," involves premotor cortex, supplementary motor area, parietal lobule and cerebellum (see Chapter 13). In fact, common coding may be a general feature of representational systems. Tkach, Reimer, and Hatsopoulos (2007) offered evidence that congruence between observation and action is a general feature of motor systems, even outside of "canonical" mirror areas. Pineda (2008) argues for an "extended" mirror neuron system that includes the sensorimotor cortex. However, for present purposes, it is common coding that is significant, rather than whether it is instantiated by a particular neural network.

Since mimicry automatically occurs when a person observes or engages with another person, neuroimaging studies in which participants are asked passively to observe the actions or the emotions of others presumably capture the neural correlates of mimicry. Buccino et al. (2004) asked participants to watch videos of humans and animals performing various actions (biting, barking, etc.) Whereas actions that were in the observer's repertoire (e.g., biting) activated "mirror" activity in the observer's motor cortex, actions that were not in the observer's repertoire (e.g., barking) seem to be recognized by the visual system without motor/simulatory involvement. Calvo-Merino, Glaser, Grezes, Passingham and Haggard (2005) asked expert dancers and novices to watch a series of dance movements in two different styles. While viewing, those who were expert in the particular dance style had enhanced motor activity. It seems that when we view actions informed by our personal, embodied experience, it is as-if we were enacting them, too (Damasio, Tranel, & Damasio, 1991).

Common coding between first- and third-person experiences of emotion has been reported for disgust (Wicker et al., 2003), pain (Singer et al., 2004), touch (Keysers et al., 2004), emotional body language (de Gelder & Hadjikhani, 2006), and emotional expressions (Carr, Iacoboni, Dubeau, Mazziotta, & Lenzi, 2003) in the insula and anterior cingulate, similar to the common coding for actions in the inferior frontal cortices and sensorimotor cortices. The insula has been suggested to mediate the transformation of a perceived action into an emotional experience by relaying information about action representation from the superior temporal and inferior frontal cortices (sometimes referred to as "the mirror neuron system") to the limbic system (Carr et al., 2003). This relay is thought to allow information about the actions of others (e.g., a facial expression) to provoke an emotional experience (e.g., empathy).

Neuroimaging research substantiates the link between mimicry and empathy. Two fMRI studies on adults found a positive correlation between empathy scores and activity in premotor areas during action observation, and while listening to action sounds (Gazzola, Aziz-Zadeh, & Keysers, 2006; Kaplan & Iacoboni, 2006), indicating a relationship between the measured degree of covert mimicry and of empathy. Similarly, Pfeifer, Iacoboni, Mazziotta, and Dapretto (2008) reported that activation within the network of inferior frontal "mirror" areas, the insula, and the amygdala of children aged 9–10 years, while they observed and imitated emotional expressions, was positively correlated with ratings of empathy.

SUMMARY

In overview, the amount of automatic mimicry, observed via behavioral coding, measured in movements of the facial muscles via EMG, or inferred from the distribution of brain activation on fMRI activation during passive viewing of actions and emotional expressions, correlates positively with an individual's level of empathy.

The extent to which an infant mimics the caregiver's facial expressions and bodily rhythms predicts later social competencies, not only with respect to empathy, but also communication. Mimicry may serve social development both by increasing a child's motivation to entrain with her caregiver, thereby garnering additional social experience, and by providing the infant with a way to share the emotions of those around him. Mimicry may lay the foundations for the development of communication and empathy later in childhood.

The common coding of percepts and intentions to act no doubt facilitates both rapid response to urgent events and social relatedness. It integrates into the very fabric of the brain the cumulative experience of the perceived actions and inferred motivations of others, fostering a shared point of view and conformity in action within the group. The viewpoints and the conformity in action are shared without the benefit of critical scrutiny. The individuals in the group may not even be aware that this is happening.

INTERPERSONAL COORDINATION IN PEOPLE WITH AUTISM

A Caveat about Interpretation

When typical and autistic participants perform differently on the same task, the explanation may not be straightforward. Whereas typical subjects usually do what they are asked to do, autistic individuals may or may not perform as they are instructed, may perform with less mental effort, or may perform in alternative ways, in each case offering no explanation. This problem is particularly severe when functional neuroimaging is the experimental methodology, as it is in a rapidly growing experimental literature. Attenuated activation of a specialized brain area may indeed derive from a neurological impairment. But alternatively, the participant might not have chosen to act (or been able to act), and therefore to activate, in the manner requested by the investigator. Correspondingly, in many comparisons of typical and ASD children, the ASD group does not so much exhibit the target behavior in attenuated form, as exhibit it less frequently. Such a finding does not indicate a neurological problem, but rather that the child chose to do something else, or to attend to something else. Nonetheless, functional imaging offers unusual advantages beyond the obvious remarkable insights that it offers into functional brain organization. It may assist the interpretations at the behavioral level. For instance, individuals with autism often fail to disclose what they are doing, and what they are feeling. Absent such information, functional imaging may reveal a pattern of brain activation that permits inferences about otherwise covert mental states.

Mimicry of Actions and Emotions

Behavioral Measures of Emotional Contagion

Reports that emotional contagion is diminished in individuals with autism suggest that mimicry is deficient, perhaps even from infancy on. Analysis of home videos reveals that infants who subsequently develop autism are less likely to smile in response to their caregiver's smiles by the end of their first year (Dawson, Meltzoff, Osterling, Rinaldi, & Brown, 1998), although no difference can be detected in affect-sharing between infants who will be diagnosed as autistic and infants whose development will proceed along typical lines (Ozonoff et al., 2010). Preschool-age children with ASD are less susceptible than typical preschool-age children to emotional contagion through prompts that typically elicit emotions that match those of the model: for example, an experimenter opens a box in a child's presence and looks delighted or looks afraid (Scambler, Hepburn, Rutherford, Wehner, & Rogers, 2006), or an experimenter injures herself (Bacon, Fein, Morris, Waterhouse, and Allen, 1998). Participants with ASD are also less susceptible than age-matched, typically developing peers to contagious yawning when they are shown video recordings (Senju, et al., 2007), or during live interactions (Helt, Eigsti, Snyder, & Fein, in press) with other people yawning. Interestingly, in one study, children with autism did not respond with less intensity to such presses for emotional contagion, they simply responded less frequently. The proportion of emotional contagion responses they emitted varied inversely with the severity of their symptoms, as measured by ADOS - Autism Diagnostic Observation Schedule) communication and socialization scores (Scambler et al., 2006). This finding may indicate that children with autism display emotional contagion less frequently not because they lack that capability, but because of reduced social attention, and it is the extent to which their social attention is reduced that relates to their symptom severity.

EMG

Electromyographic studies reveal that autistic individuals display diminished mimicry for actions and emotions under naturalistic conditions, but typical levels of mimicry when the instructional set calls explicit attention to the emotional aspects of the stimuli. The first EMG study of adults with autism spectrum disorders (ASD), by McIntosh et al. (2006), found that they imitated as well as the control group when explicitly asked to copy the expressions they viewed, but, unlike the control group, displayed little automatic mimicry when they viewed emotional expressions passively; that is, when they were told simply, "watch the pictures as they appear on the screen." Beall et al. (2008) replicated these effects with 8- to 13-year-old children with ASD (although the older children did display some mimicry). Stel, van den Heuvel, and Smeets (2008) asked participants to watch a 5-minute video in which a young man expressed happiness while he talked about his adventures in an amusement park. The experimenters coded the facial expressions and gestures of participants as they watched the video. ASD participants showed less spontaneous mimicry than controls, even though they did not differ in how long they spent looking toward the screen. In contrast, when they were asked to imitate the young man, the ASD participants did not differ in how long they engaged in deliberate imitation.

In contrast to the relative dearth of mimicry under passive viewing conditions, EMG paradigms that encourage individuals with ASD to pay explicit attention to the emotional aspects of the facial stimuli have not found them to be lacking in mimicry. Magnee, deGelder, van Engeland, and Kemner (2007) showed high-functioning adults with ASD happy and fearful faces and asked them to judge the sex of the faces, as opposed to passively watching. Meanwhile, congruent- or incongruently valenced voices were paired with the faces, providing additional emotional cueing. The additional cuing resulting in enhanced mimicry by people with ASD, as compared with controls. Wilbarger, McIntosh, and Winkielman, (2009) showed high-functioning adults with ASD emotional expressions embedded in other positively or negatively valenced imagery (e.g., spiders, snakes, car crashes, nature scenes, food, etc.), and monitored their facial responses by EMG. No group differences were found, either between the ASD group and the control group or between the reactions to affective scenes versus faces. Oberman, Winkelman, and Ramachandran (2009) asked 8- to 12-year-old high-functioning children with ASD to watch faces with varied emotional expressions and classify them as happy, sad, angry, fearful, disgusted, or neutral. While the magnitude of mimicry as indicated by EMG in response to facial expressions in individuals with ASD was similar to that of typical controls, the responses were delayed by approximately 160 milliseconds across all emotions.

According to Klin, Jones, Schultz, Volkmar, & Cohen, (2002) the most powerful predictor of diagnostic status in adults with autism is the extent of spontaneous attention to other people's eye rather than their mouth area, or even a focus that altogether bypasses the face (Hermans, van Wingen, Bos, Putnam, and van Honk (2008) separately scored spontaneous mimicry in the muscles surrounding the eyes and the muscles surrounding the mouth in volunteers from the general population who scored at the two extremes on an inventory of autistic traits. The groups did not differ on mimicry of movements of the mouth, but the high-scoring women showed less mimicry around the eyes. These findings further highlight the importance of focus of attention for the presence or absence of mimicry. The issue for individuals with ASD appears not to be a deficiency in the cerebral substrate of mimicry, but in where they are attending. The eye movement studies show that when people with autism look at other people, they preferentially and selectively attend to the mouth (e.g. Neumann. Spezio, Piven & Adolphs, 2006). Indeed, when faces are best recognized by their eyes, children with autisms are apt to fail, but when recognition depends on the mouth, they perform as well as neurotypical control children (de Gelder, Vroomen and van der Heide, 1991, Joseph and Tanaka, 2003). When the faces are familiar, however, children with autism can recogize then as well as control children. (Pierce, Haist, Sedaghat and Courchesne (2004). The investigators concluded that "dysfunction in the FFA (fusiform face area) found in other studies of autism may reflect defects in systems that modulate the FFA, rather than the FFA itself" (p. 2703.) Children with autism differ from the norm not only in whether they mimic, but also in what they mimic, if they mimic at all. Therefore we propose that the neurological determinants of autism severity are not mirror neuron circuits, but circuits for spatial or social attention, which in autism are biased away from the human face, and especially from the eyes.

Mimicry of Rhythm

Parent-child synchrony in dyads in which the child is autistic appears to have the same predictive features as in low-risk dyads. Siller and Sigman (2002) studied 25 parent-child dyads in which the child was 3–6 years of age and had an ASD diagnosis. The extent to which the caregivers synchronized with their child's focus of attention was positively related to the child's language development, one year, 10 years, and even 16 years later. Notably, the parents of autistic children were no less synchronous with their children than were the parents of developmentally delayed and typically developing children (matched for language-age). The parents of autistic children might have become experienced in maintaining their child's focus of attention. The authors suggest that the autistic children might have benefited from unusually high levels of parental synchrony. Alternatively, caregivers may more easily synchronize with children who are less symptomatic. However, on follow-up, the findings could not be explained by differences in initial IQ, or language. The degree to which the individual responds to bids for joint attention also predicted later language development, but independently from parental behavior. The autistic child's level of synchrony with the parent, which is more likely to be compromised, was not measured.

Yirmiya et al. (2006) studied parent-infant synchrony among the infant siblings of children with autism—a group at higher risk for developing the full-blown disorder, or, if not, the broader or extended autism phenotype (Verte, Roeyers, & Buysee, 2003)—prospectively from when they were 4 months of age. The dyads that involved infant siblings of autistic children were less synchronous at 4 months than the dyads involving infant siblings of typically developing children, but only for infant-led interactions. Moreover, synchrony was weaker in those infants who went on to develop language delays by 14 months. Trevarthen and Daniel (2005) reported on the absence of synchrony between a father and his 11-month-old daughter who went on to develop autism, in contrast to his synchronous interactions with her typically developing twin.

Also pointing to the temporal or rhythmic aspect of interpersonal coordination as being particularly problematic in ASD, Feldstein, Konstantareas, Oxman, and Webster (1982) found that adolescents with autism were unable to synchronize the timing of their speech with that of both a familiar and of a novel conversational partner. Goodman, Isenhower, Marsh, Schmidt, and Richardson (2005) discovered that people who sit side-by-side in rocking chairs lapse into unintentional phase entrainment. Sebanz, Bekkering, and Knoeblich (2005) reviewed the tendency of people who are engaged in the same task to coordinate their movements, without being asked to do so. Isenhower, Marsh, Silva, Richardson, & Schmidt (2007) reported autistic children's difficulty in synchronizing rhythmically with their mothers.

When seated next to their mothers in side-by-side rocking chairs, 4- to 8-year-old children with ASD were less likely than controls spontaneously to synchronize their rocking movements with those of their mothers. This finding is likely to be significant with respect to the social problems in ASD, since several studies have reported that synchronizing one's movements induces affiliation between the protagonists (e.g. Marsh, Richardson and Schmidt 2009, Hove and Risen, 2009)

Mimicry and Common Perceptual and Motor Coding

Individuals with ASD have reduced "mirror-like" neural activation when they view other people's actions (e.g., Oberman, McCleery, Altschuler, Ramachandran, & Pineda, 2005) and emotional expressions (Dapretto, Davies, Pfeifer, & Scott, 2006). Furthermore, the amount of "mirror activity" that individuals with autism display while they observe emotional expressions is inversely correlated with their symptom severity (Dapretto et al., 2006).

That at least some of the autistic deficit in spontaneous mimicry is due to reduced social attention is consistent with other reported findings. Wang, Lee, Sigman, & Dapretto (2007) found that, when autistic participants were asked to listen to ironic or neutral sentences without instruction, they showed less activation in regions involved in voice processing (the MPFC) compared with controls. However, when they were instructed to pay attention to the voice and facial expressions of the stimuli, their activation patterns normalized. These instructions, predictably, had no effect on the control group, consistent with the notion that typical individuals naturally attend to social emotional cues, whereas autistic individuals may only do so under special circumstances. Indeed, although children with autism show reduced activation in the fusiform face area when they view the faces of adult strangers, indicating reduced face processing (Schultz et al., 2000), these differences disappear when their attention is directed to the eye region of the faces (Hadjikhani, Joseph, Snyder, & Tager-Flusberg 2006), or when they are shown faces of children (Pierce & Redcay, 2008) or their parents (Pierce, Haist, Sedaghat, & Courchesne, 2004; Pierce & Redcay, 2008).

The design of the studies that did not find mimicry deficits may have inadvertently triggered more careful scrutiny on the part of their autistic participants of the emotional aspects of the faces. People with autism are capable of mimicry when they are explicitly guided to attend to emotional stimuli (Magnee et al., 2007; Oberman et al., 2007, 2009; Wilbarger, McIntosh, & Winkielman, 2009). Conversely, mimicry can prime social attention. Nadel, Prepin, and Okanda (2005) reported that, unlike their typically developing peers, children with autism do not show distress at a "frozen" adult unless the adult first spends some time imitating them. The children needed to be primed with mimicry in order to react in a typical social manner.

In contrast to study designs that employ explicit emotional cueing or social stimuli that are particularly salient to autistic children, study designs that capture individuals with autism gathering social information in a normal, perhaps casual, manner find less mimicry (Beall et al., 2008; Dapretto et al., 2006; McIntosh et al., 2006; Oberman et al. 2005; Stel et al., 2008). The severity of autistic symptoms (Dapretto et al., 2006), diagnostic status (Helt et al. in press), and the degree of subsequent language delay (Yirmiya et al., 2006) are all inversely correlated with the autistic children's amount of mimicry. The severity of autism may be measured by how much mimicry individuals with autism typically engage in, rather than how much they are capable of engaging in, that is, by a performance rather than a competence limitation. Columbi and colleagues draw a similar conclusion in Chapter 13, in relation to imitation. The underproduction of mimicry could be secondary to limitations in attention to emotional cues, gaze, and history with the social partner. These, in turn, might be secondary to an egocentric, inward turning of attention.

Even when children with autism successfully process all relevant emotional information, the timing of their response may still be delayed (Oberman et al., 2009). The difficulty in matching a parent's interactional rhythms may be due to a diminished capacity for perceiving the temporal aspects of interactions necessary for interactional synchrony (Bebko, Weiss, Demark, & Gomez, 2006).

MECHANISMS OF MIMICRY

In order to understand what a mimicry deficit would mean for theories about autism, one would need to understand its mechanism. As mentioned above, Kinsbourne (2002) argued that infant mimicry is the result of enactive perception. Perceiving an attended object (thing or person) is not passive. It is enactive, in that the percept's encodings include the response possibilities that the perceived object "affords" (Gibson, 2003). To an extent, the perceptual encoding activates the motor programs that the agent would use, were he actually to carry out the afforded action. In a sense, one's perception anticipates one's own prospective actions. The infant perceives an action that is within his response repertoire, and, in the course of perception, automatically readies the motor system to respond likewise. This motor planning is not confined to motor imagery, corresponding to an intention but not a commitment to the act, as it would be in an older person, who had developed the needed inhibitory functions. As nothing is holding back the realization of the infant's motor programs; rather, they are openly expressed and become publicly available. The infant's body betrays the infant's thoughts. Objects are encoded in terms of their "affordances," and when an action rather than an object is encoded, the affordance may be to match the salient aspects of that action. Perceiving the action primes the same action in the brain of the observer. This is an effect on motor readiness, a motor contagion, as Blair et al. (2008) and Blakemore and Frith (2004) put it.

Infants appear to be driven to enact the actions, emotional expressions, and rhythms of conspecifics: for example, infants will mimic the eye gaze target of a stuffed animal that either has a face or that interacts with them contingently (Nadel et al., 2005), and will imitate a human being (but not a robot) who is performing the same action (Meltzoff, 1995). Thus, infants may mimic that to which they attend with great interest; other beings, real or simulated. At some time during infancy an autistic child may lose the impulse to engage with others reciprocally (rather than only instrumentally). The lack of mimicry in individuals with autism may reflect the failure to perceive the social aspects of an interaction as the most salient features of the interaction, or an active avoidance of eye contact with just these salient features. This account of mimicry is consistent with diminished mimicry being the result of diminished social perception.

The lack of certain key experiences on account of the avoidance of social interaction, and the preference for objects over people and for repetitive forms of play, has adverse effects on social development. Actions determine percepts. A novel act, or an act in a novel environment, may reveal novel percepts, whereas repetitive actions only offer the repetition of the same or similar percepts. Thus, an autistic child engaged in repetitive play will fail to expand his perceptual repertoire. This theory of deficit in environmental-expectant development is most readily applicable to the majority of children with autism who develop it in the first year of life. However, identifying the deprivation of key social experiences as the major cause of the expansion of autism in the second and third years of life does not account for the quarter of cases of ASD in which regression into autism starts well into the second year of life, from a baseline of normal or near-normal pace of development (Stefanatos, 2008); or at any rate fewer but still clearly regressive cases that have been identified by prospective studies on the at-risk infant siblings of children with autism (Rogers, 2009). Nor will environmental deprivation during development explain full-blown cases of ASD that develop after more than three years of apparently normal development, in childhood disintegrative disorder and in Landau Kleffner syndrome (Stefanatos, Kinsbourne, & Wasserstein 2002). Even less can it explain the sudden onset of autism in cases of herpes encephalitis, in later childhood (DeLong, Bean, & Brown 1981), and even in adolescence (Gillberg, 1986). Evidently, normal prior experience does not mitigate the severity of autism when there is overt acute brain damage (typically of bilateral temporal lobes). The concept of a developmental cascade in which early deficits in mimicry subsequently lead to the elaboration of social deficits applies more readily to the large number of early onset cases. Lack of key experiences during development is not essential for the genesis of autism; nonetheless, it may be operative in many cases. The nature of the key experiences of which the autistic infant is deprived remains unclear. Some suggestions follow.

One of us (MH) has clinically observed stereotypies that involve enacting moving objects (such as the scroll at a bank, or words flying onto the screen during film credits, or marbles dropping down a slide). One child with autism repetitively imitates the motion of hands coming toward him to tickle him, with the orientation of his hands reversed, indicating that he may be focusing on the perceptual features of that engaging activity, rather than the social intentions behind it. If children enact whatever is interesting to them, then autistic children may enact objects at the expense of social stimuli (Klin, Jones, Schultz, &

Volkmar, 2003). This may deprive pre-autistic infants of the experiences that build social cognition. If so, then early deficits in mimicry and in synchrony may both reflect minor deviations in a pre-autistic infant's attention to emotional cues. This deviation of attention away from social stimuli, in this case biological motion, towards physical contingencies was recently demonstrated in an autistic infant (Klin, Lin, Gorrindo, Ramsay, & Jones, 2009). Lack of attention to emotional cues would deprive the growing child of the sufficient social experience necessary for developing an empathic, embodied, mind (Klin et al., 2003).

If lack of social attention were the cause of the diminished use of mimicry in individuals with autism, this would explain reduced activation of mirror circuitry, without the need to hypothesize an unexplained primary failure of the mirror networks to develop. However, the relative disuse of perceptuo-motor (mirror) activity may secondarily limit the connections that normally are made through experience. Mirroring could be the result of the principle that neurons that fire together wire together (Hebb, 1949; Heyes, Bird, Johnson, & Haggard, 2005; Keysers & Perrett, 2004; Kinsbourne, 2005), in the following way.

Mothers automatically and unconsciously mimic their babies throughout infancy. When a baby feels sick and looks at his mother's face, which is mimicking his own pained expression, a connection is formed between the pained facial expression of another and his subjective feeling of pain. As an infant's social experience broadens, repeated temporal associations will cause neural connections to form between the facial expressions and bodily postures of others and the internal feelings in his body, as well as between the actions of others and his own actions. Later in life, when he sees the face of someone in pain (i.e., when one part of his pain network becomes activated), it will activate the rest of the network, calling up for him a semblance of the internal feeling of being in pain (Damasio, et al., 1991). As already discussed, this embodied experience could serve as a basis for empathy.

Another example comes from yawning, which may be contagious because perceived actions prime the enactment of the same actions due to shared coding. But children with autism may not have engaged in enough mimicry and synchrony to engender elaborate networks of common coding. The connections between the facial expressions of others and one's own internal feelings may never be made, may be made

only for salient individuals like parents, or may be made only much later in life. Even though the child might learn, through explicit teaching, that a crinkled brow and downturned lips signal pain, he will have a cognitive, not a visceral reaction (i.e., embodied emotional experience) to such an expression. These embodied links to conceptual knowledge may, through feedback, help direct our attention to what is salient in our environment. They would allow the developing child to become fluent at attending to socio-emotional stimuli, favoring increased affective attunement with others as children age. Children with autism might not have the benefit of this interaction with the environment.

Small deviations in mimicry and synchrony early in life may build on themselves with increasingly severe consequences as the first year draws to a close. Mimicry engenders feelings of closeness and connection between individuals, which in turn increases the amount of mimicry individuals will display toward one another, in a continuously escalating cycle between mother and child. Out of this increasingly synchronous bond could develop abilities (and the motivation to develop abilities) such as imitation, joint attention, and speech. Joint attention—the sharing of one's experience of observing an object or event by following gaze or pointing—which is the first developmental milestone that is reliably observed to be absent among young children with autism spectrum disorders, could develop as the result of emotion contagion between parent and child. When a child looks and sees her mother looking toward a stimulus, her tendency to mimic her mother's expressions may be strong enough by the age of 9–12 months immediately to cause a corresponding orientation toward the stimulus—that is, joint attention (Bacon et al., 1998; Campos & Sternberg, 1981). When Condon and Sander (1974) demonstrated that even 1- to 2-day-old newborns synchronize their movements to their mother's speech patterns, they argued that this rhythmic imprinting scaffolds speech development. If infants with autism do not fully engage, then synchronization and mimicry with their mother and other members of the social group, as well as feelings of psychological connection and opportunities for social learning, would not evolve as expected in the course of development.

An early gap in experience may expand as the child grows older, should the child's odd expressions, postures, and prosody fail to trigger the parent's unconscious mimicry of the child. Buccino et al. (2004) and Calvo-Merino et al. (2005) demonstrated that the brain areas that implement perceptuomotor resonance respond most strongly to actions that are in the observer's own repertoire. Thus, the more idiosyncratic a child's emotional expressions and behaviors are, the less they are likely to trigger mimicry in those around him. Consistent with the idea that contagion depends partially on the child's ability to produce the typical array of affective signals, Fraiberg (1974) reported that when observers watched typically developing infants on screen, there was "resonance of mood," on the viewer's face (viewers smile when babies smile, etc.). The faces of viewers remain solemn when they watch blind babies. She attributed this lack of emotional contagion to the diminished expressiveness of blind babies. Taken further, the diminished mimicry of older children with ASD would not only prevent increasing feelings of psychological connectedness in the child, but also in others toward the child. Interacting with children with ASD and not experiencing the usual emotional contagion during interactions may leave one puzzled as to what the child is feeling, and therefore feeling at a psychological distance.

It has been suggested that children with ASD sometimes engage in too much mimicry, in the form of echolalia. We suggest that echolalia is not a form of mimicry at all. Rather, the inability to read the direction of the caregiver's intentions (beginning with gaze) could result in verbal mislabeling. When parents refer to novel objects and events, the infant may have to choose the referent from an array of stimuli. The infant is subject to "referential mapping errors" (Baldwin, 1995). In a language-learning paradigm, an experimenter speaks a label while gazing into a bucket at a toy. The 18-month-old infant follows the direction of the experimenter's gaze to label the correct toy. In contrast, infants with autism will mistakenly apply the label to the toy with which they are playing when the experimenter speaks (Baron-Cohen, Baldwin, & Crowson, 1997). Thus, the child's labeling mechanism may be intact, in that when his caregiver utters a word and his affective system is engaged, he will learn the word or phrase. However, in contrast to the typically developing child, who assumes that the word represents the target of the caregiver's attention, the egocentric autistic child, unaware of the target of his caregiver's attention, encodes the word as signifying whatever happens to be the focus of his own attention

at the moment. The child who is told "you miss Grandma" may then use the words "you miss Grandma" to label his sad feelings whenever they occur, regardless of the context. Notably, joint attention abilities in toddlers with autism are the strongest predictors of later language development, and the effects of early interventions for ASD may be mediated by the extent to which they succeed in establishing shared attention with the child (Charman, 2003).

Mimicry and Reduced Social Perception

The extant data on mimicry fit with the notion that interpersonal coordination deficits are the result of reduced automatic attention to socioemotional cues. Children with autism fail on tests of social competence and exhibit diminished brain activation while executing corresponding tasks because they are simply not looking at social stimuli with full attention. Indeed, they may actively avoid doing so. This simplifying suggestion makes it unnecessary to invoke anomalous brain development or structural neuronal deficits. It does, however, call for an explanation as to why autistic children ignore, or even actively avoid engaging with, social stimuli.

Children with autism do not refrain from face-to-face interactions because they find them to be meaningless. At least with their mothers, groups of children with ASD have repeatedly been shown to be capable of attachment (Capps, Sigman, & Mundy, 1994, Dissanayake & Crossley 1997, Shapiro, Sherman, Calamari, & Loch, 1987; Sigman & Ungerer, 1984), no less than children in comparison groups. Although they are attached, there is some impediment to their relating to their caretaker in the typical, reciprocal, face-to-face way.

CANDIDATE NEUROBIOLOGICAL MECHANISMS FOR DISRUPTING MIMICRY

Although deficient use of mimicry and synchrony is pervasive in children with autism, children with autism also differ from typical peers in their nonsocial behaviors, such as their lack of representational play, predilection for repetitive movements, and anomalous sensitivities to sensory stimuli. It follows that candidate neurobiological mechanisms for disrupting mimicry may either be specific to social development, or they may encompass both the social and the nonsocial characteristics of the autistic spectrum.

Since children with autism do mimic when their attention is explicitly directed, what ultimately causes their reduced interpersonal coordination? Why do these young children not spontaneously deploy social attention, but only when they are prompted to do so? How might currently topical theories of autism address the issues of impaired synchrony? We favor models that postulate network dysfunctions that implicate multiple brain areas, such as the four outlined below.

1. Mirror Neuron Theory

Mimicry and "Mirror Neurons"

Although the concept of common coding or perceptuomotor resonance is by no means new, it has recently become the subject of an intense investigative effort, spurred by the introduction of a theory as to its brain basis. Weisberg et al. (2008) have studied how psychological theories gain in prominence when they acquire a neuroscience element, however tangential that element might be to the validity and implications of the theory. The concept of mirror neurons is a case in point. Mirror neurons as integrators of self-other actions, and even feelings, have immediate appeal as a simplifying explanatory principle in the burgeoning fields of social cognitive psychology and social psychopathology (e.g. Iacoboni, 2009). The clutter of "widely distributed neural networks" that is revealed by typical functional neuroimaging studies is allegedly reduced to a set of highly specific neurons custom-made for the prototypically intense social interaction among humans. The concept perhaps reached its apotheosis in 2000, when Ramachandran (2000) hailed it "as the driving force behind the great leap forward in human evolution". He anticipated that mirror neurons would explain a host of mental abilities that have hitherto remained mysterious. Indeed, the onrush of studies that attempt just that continues unabated. However, a countercurrent of reservation and skepticism is also becoming more prominent (e.g. Dinstein, Thomas, Behrmann, & Heeger 2008, Hickok, 2009,).

Mirror neurons may not even have the custom-made, special-purpose, integrative function between self and other with which they are widely credited. They may fire both when the action is observed and when it is intended, because they cannot "tell the difference." "Perceptual representations are called

upon (1) when the act is observed (2) when the observer forms the intention to perform the act (3) when the act is accompanied by an efference copy (4) when the act is monitored on completion. In each case the same movement is represented, and in each case mirror neurons may fire, indifferent to which one of these processes is occurring" (Kinsbourne, 2005, p. 165). If this pattern of neuronal firing impacts behavior, then that impact has dubious consequences. It would seem to constrain the observer to emulate the actions of another, whether that is adaptively desirable or not. Whereas perception-action coupling may be very important for social behavior, an additional mechanism would have to evolve to hold in check any responses arising from "mirroring" that are undesirable. However, the impact of mirror neurons as such may be less momentous. Chong, Cunnington, Williams, Kanwisher, and Mattingly (2008) reported that the same territory (right inferior parietal lobe) exhibited fMRI adaptation when subjects pantomimed specific actions and when they observed these actions. They take this to be evidence for the presence of mirror neurons in humans. Two alternative interpretations should also be considered: Neurons that are engaged in action observation and in action execution both inhabit this same enormous neural territory, and overall they are much in the minority. Functional imaging cannot differentiate between individual neurons and interconnected neurons firing during perception and action. Or, the inferior parietal lobe may house representations of these actions, whereas other parts of the brain label them self or other. Areas other than those that house mirror circuitry, such as inferior parietal lobe, are differentially activated by self- versus other-action-related activity (Decety & Chaminade, 2005). Areas other than those that house mirror neurons were activated when deaf signers observed video-clips of pantomime performers (Emmorey, XU, Gannon, Goldin-Meadow & Braun 2009). Left inferior parietal activity is associated with action-related activities of the self, and right inferior parietal activity with action-related activities of the other (Decety, Chaminade, Grezes, & Meltzoff, 2002). The concept of a "mirror neuron deficit" in autism sounds straightforward, but is not.

Williams, Whiten, Suddendorf, and Perrett (2001) first proposed that autism is a deficit of mirror neuron activity. Mirror neuron dysfunction could be "the single primary deficit that explains the behavioral picture that characterizes autism in all its presentations"

(Williams, 2008, p. XX). This vivid if simplistic suggestion has found some support in subsequent studies (Dapretto et al., 2006, Oberman et al., 2005). If mirror circuit activity mediates the development of empathy and other social skills, then deficient mirror activity could account for deficiencies in these skills in people with autism.

However, as reviewed above, individuals with autism do show mimicry and mirror activity under some conditions—for instance when they are viewing their parents, as opposed to strangers (Oberman & Ramachandran, 2007). So the circuitry for "mirroring" must be in place in individuals with autism. The abnormality appears to reside in the frequency with which these circuits are activated; that is, how and when they are used. Mimicry depends on focused attention. People with autism might simply not be looking at the critical displays with as focused attention as the typical individual, and that may be why the "mirror circuitry" is less often activated when they view others' actions. Nor is the impairment in imitation disproportionate to the impairment in comparable non-imitative tasks (Leighton, Bird, Chaiman, & Heyes, 2008), as mirror neuron theory would predict. Indeed, Bird, Leighton, Press, and Hayes (2007) contend that if one excludes "nonspecific defective mechanisms", automatic imitation is intact in individuals with ASD (p. 3030).

Williams (2008) arrived at a more nuanced theoretical formulation than the one he and his colleagues offered in 2001. He points out, "impairments in self-other matching and mirror neuron functioning are not necessarily inextricably linked" (p. 73). Different groups of mirror neurons may code different features of actions, and may serve different social functions. Hamilton (2008) suggested that a network that subserves mimicry is defective in autism, whereas a network that subserves goal emulation and planning is not. These distinctions could prove to be fruitful. However, they diffuse the dramatic simplifying thrust of the mirror neuron theory of autism. Williams (2008) conceded, "the ways that mirror neurons contribute to these (autistic) brain-behavior links are likely to be complex" (p. 73). Finally, when overt brain damage causes autism, as in herpes encephalitis, the brunt of the injury is bitemporal (implicating hippocampus and amygdala), and not in mirror neuron territory.

Dinstein, Thomas, Behrmann and Heeger (2008) address not only the alleged functions of mirror neurons in general, but also their application to the explanation of social impairments in autism. According to Dinstein and colleagues, "there is surprisingly little evidence to support the claim that a dysfunction in mirror neurons is the neural mechanism underlying autism" (p. 15). They point to the obvious facts that there are multiple components of the syndrome of autism that are quite unrelated to the presumed function of mirror circuits, and extensive evidence for malfunction in brain areas of people with autism that are not thought or likely to house mirror neurons. The mirror neuron concept of autism addresses, at best, only one of the multiple components of this syndrome. As Dinstein and colleagues remark, it is insufficient to gather observations that are consistent with the predictions of a theory. "Showing a positive correlation with the predictions of one theory and negative correlations with the predictions of alternative hypotheses provides much stronger support" (p 17).

In a recent survey, Rizzolatti and Sinigaglia (2010) addressed a series of studies interpreted as critical of mirror circuit theory. They came to terms with the fact that the participation of mirror neurons in understanding the behavior of others does not seem to be essential. However, they insisted on the special role of mirror circuits in relationships that humans form. They argued that "the parieto-frontal mechanism is the only one that allows an individual to understand the actions of others 'from the inside' and gives the observer a first-person grasp of the motor goals and intentions of other individuals" (p. 264). This is, of course, an argument along the lines of simulation theory for emotional appreciation, which is quite controversial. The difference between understanding another's actions and understanding them from the inside is not entirely clear, and the implied distinction between mirror and non-mirror neural mechanisms does not appear to have been tested experimentally. This is relevant to our concern with autism, because Rizzolatti and Sinigaglia concluded their essay with the following statement: "Preliminary evidence suggests that the impairment of this natural link may be one of the causes of the striking inability of people with autism to relate to each other" (p. 273).

This claim is significant for mirror neuron theory as well as for autism. In humans the neuroscientific evidence derives from neuroimaging and electrophysiology. These techniques are invaluable for uncovering neural correlates of known behavior. But when they reveal novel neural properties such as "mirror activity," they are at a loss when it comes to proving which, if any, particular behavior not only correlates with, but actually depends on, the circuitry in question. For that level of proof, one must move to human neuropsychology, for the demonstration that without the aid of the circuit in question, a particular behavior is handicapped or abolished. Given that mirror neurons are rather widely distributed, it is unlikely that human lesion studies will abolish mirror neurons without also inactivating much else, so as to accomplish such a proof. Absent the availability of proof from lesion studies, the validity of autism as a case in point for the failure of mirror mechanism is crucial. However, that evidence is not at hand. In fact, most recently a well controlled study has found that mu suppression, considered an electrophysiological surrogate for mirror neuron activity, is to be found and children with autism as it is in neurotypical children (Fan, Decety, Yang, Liu and Cheng 2010). Another study that predicted less interference between simultaneously observed and executed incompatible action based on mirror neuron theory failed to confirm this prediction (Gowen and Miall, 2008).

Even if the mirror neuron theory of autism as such falls short, impairment or disuse of common coding might obscure the correspondence between self and other (self-other mapping). This in turn could prevent mimicry and imitation, and subsequently the development of empathy through embodiment. It could be the recognition that other humans are "like me" (Meltzoff, 2002) that draws an infant's attention preferentially to other humans. This dearth of perceptuomotor resonance in autistic children is probably secondary to their systematically deviant attention.

2. Timing Deficit Theory

The organization of early biological rhythms may lead to better infant regulation of microshifts in arousal and attention (Feldman, 2006) and better information-processing skills (Feldman & Mayes, 1999), resulting in more interpersonal synchrony (Warner, 1992). Jaffe, Beebe, Feldstein, Crown, & Jasnow (2001) have shown that dyadic timing in infancy guides the trajectory of relatedness. Autistic children may have a diminished ability to perceive temporal changes, and so be unable to manage rapid shifts in attention, as is required by joint attention (Courchesne, Townsend, Akshoomoff and Saitoh, 1994). Children's ability to perceive contingencies would be compromised if they

are unable to connect cause to event because of difficulties in shifting visual attention, or perceiving rapid temporal change, both controlled by the cerebellum. Increased latency to disengage visual attention is among the first signs of autism (Zwaigenbaum et al., 2005). Temporal anomalies in autism include disturbed neural synchrony (e.g., Welsh, Ahn, &, Placantonakis, 2005), a disruption in "clock genes" involved in the perception of time (Nicholas, et al., 2007), and disturbances in circadian sleep cycles (Elia, et al., 2000; Limoges, Mottron, Bolduc, Berthiaume, & Godbout, 2005). Histological studies in autism consistently find alterations in the cerebellum, and particularly the Purkinje cells (Kemper & Bauman, 2002). Recent fMRI and EEG/MEG evidence of dysfunctional temporal coordination of neural responses in ASD has been reviewed by Ulhaas, et al. (2009). How far these limitations go toward accounting for autistic symptomatology remains uncertain.

3. Role of the Amygdala

Often implicated in social pathology (e.g. Baron-Cohen et al., 2000), the amygdala generates affective states, directs attention to emotionally salient stimuli (including the eyes), and elicits motivated behavior. Innate lack of preference for faces may be due to amygdala dysfunction (Waterhouse, Fein, & Modahl, 1996). Support for this idea comes from similarities between adults with amygdala lesions and individuals with autism. They include difficulty in: 1) orienting to social stimuli (e.g., Spezio, Huang, Castelli, & Adolphs, 2007; Wang et al., 2007), 2) detecting the gaze direction of others (e.g., Adolphs, 2006; Baron-Cohen et al., 1992); and 3) understanding emotions (Braverman, Fein, Lucci, & Waterhouse 1989; Fein, Lucci, Braverman, & Waterhouse 1992). Sprengelmeyer et al. (1999) reported NM, a patient with bilateral amygdala injury, who had lost the sense of fear. The case of SM, a patient with bilateral amygdala damage, is particularly striking: SM no longer employs any eye contact during conversation, as measured by eye tracking, and instead directs her gaze nearly exclusively to the mouth region of others' faces, or photographs of diverse emotional expressions (Spezio et al., 2007). Of the various emotional expressions, fear is the one that most specifically is signaled by the upper face, eyes, eyelids, brow and forehead (Boucher and Ekman, 1975). SM does not recognize fear. However, when SM is explicitly instructed to attend to the eyes, she can do so, and her recognition of fear normalizes (Adolphs, Baron-Cohen, & Tranel, 2002). The interpretation of these findings may be more complicated, though. Jack, Blais, Scheepers, Schyns, & Caldara, (2009) reported that fear can indeed be inferred from inspection of the lower face, and can even be better differentiated from disgust and anger in this way than by inspection of the eyes.

Critchley et al. (2000) observed hypoactivation of the amygdala when adults with autism labeled the gender of emotional faces (an implicit condition), but comparable activity to controls when they labeled the emotion in the same faces (an explicit condition). Howard et al. (2000) reported smaller than normal amygdala volume in people with high-functioning autism, and suggested incomplete pruning during development as an explanation.

The volume of the amygdala is reportedly correlated with the ability to distinguish between emotional and neutral expressions, and with the amount of social impairment displayed by individuals with autism (Nacewicz et al., 2006). The investigators suggest that, in autism, the amygdala is initially hyperactive, and is involved in an ongoing excitotoxic process, such that its volume initially increases, but subsequently shrinks, especially in the most severe cases. The authors point to comparable findings of initial hypertrophy and ultimate shrinkage of the amygdala in early followed by recurrent depression. The difficulty in evaluating the specificity and significance of volumetric findings is dramatized by the fact that children with Williams syndrome, frequently portrayed as counterpoints to children with ASD on account of their excessive and indiscriminate sociability, also have enlarged amygdalas (Reiss et al. 2004).

Whereas most theoretical formulations of the amygdala in ASD are couched in terms of hypofunction, the evidence suggests that it is hyperfunction that is associated with anxiety and social avoidance (see overarousal theory, below).

4. Overarousal Theory

Hutt, Hutt, Lee, and Ounsted (1964) were the first to proposed that overarousal of the forebrain is a causal mechanism for autism, basing themselves on abnormalities in electrophysiological recordings. Individuals with autism are more easily aroused by sensory stimuli, and overreact to them, treating as aversive stimuli that are not experienced as such by the general population.

This may be the result of an increased ratio of excitation to inhibition in the brain, perhaps due to a preponderance of excitatory neurotransmitters (Rubenstein & Merzenich, 2003). Kleinhans et al. (2009) reported reduced habituation in the amygdala in ASD, indicating the sustained arousal that they believe contributes to the social deficits observed in autism spectrum disorder. The enhanced arousal that attends uncertainty (Critchley et al., 2001) may be exaggerated in ASD, causing the individual to avoid interaction with unpredictable sources of stimulation, such as people they do not know, and to overreact to surprises that they cannot avoid. The preference for the non-human goes beyond the realistic potential for surprise, however. When children with autism were presented with robots with identical potential for action, one clothed to appear humanoid whereas the other was plain in appearance, the autistic children clearly preferred the plain robot (Robins, Dautenhahn, & Dubowski 2006). In addition, toddlers with autism prefer computer-generated noise to "motherese" (Kuhl, Coffey-Corina, Padden, & Dawson, 2005).

Overarousal could also disrupt early parent-child synchrony, if the diminished amount of mutual engagement reflects an infant's neurophysiological intolerance for sensory stimulation, or for the lack of predictability that is involved in social interactions (Penman, Meares, Baker, & Milgrom-Friedman, 2003), resulting in an autistic preference for perfect contingencies (such as occur with self-movement and objects), rather than merely high contingencies (such as occur when interacting with others; Gergely, 2001).

Kinsbourne (1979, 1987) showed that overarousal could account for the anomalies in social behavior that are observed in people with autism. Their low threshold for arousal may drive them to avoid gaze, interaction with strangers, and other socially loaded stimuli as a compensatory mechanism to contain this overarousal, thus depriving them of regularly perceiving cues that would trigger social processes like mimicry. Dawson (1989) summarized "the behavioral and physiological evidence (that) suggests that autism is associated with aversive responses to novelty and with chronic high levels of automatic arousal (e.g., high heart rate)" (p. 163). Casanova, Buxhoeveder, Suitala, and Roy (2002) demonstrated abnormal organization of cortical columns in autopsied brains of individuals with autism, which they determined would cause abnormal chronic arousal, with abnormal behaviors to diminish it. Belmonte and Yurgelun-Todd (2003, p. 651) interpreted findings on functional imaging likewise as indicative of overconnected neural systems, prone to noise and crosstalk resulting in hyperarousal and over selectivity. The central nucleus of the amygdala controls autonomic activation, and its overarousal abolished social behavior in rats, as discussed above. The overarousal theory may be compatible with the potential involvement of the amygdala that was discussed earlier in the chapter. Dalton et al. (2005) showed diminished gaze fixation in individuals with autism. "Variation in fixation within autistic individuals was strongly and positively associated with amygdala activation . . . suggesting a heightened emotional response associated with gaze fixation in autism" (p. 519).

According to "polyvagal theory" (Porges, 2003), the autonomic nervous system plays a role in the clinical picture of ASD, interacting with amygdala overarousal. The vagus nerve, primary mediator of parasympathetic activity in the body, is integrated with the brain in a "social engagement system". This system has autonomic and somatomotor components, and it serves to maintain a state of calm self-regulation and to communicate via facial expression, and gaze- and head orienting, respectively. According to Moore and Calkins (2004), infants who engaged in more synchronous interactions with their parents showed greater vagal brake activity during the still-face procedure (an experimental task in which the mother is asked to "freeze" her face, rather than interact naturally and contingently with her infant). The vagal brake reflects an infant's ability to slow down his heart rate in response to environmental challenges, and so to selectively engage with and disengage from the environment. Porges (2003) presented the mammalian polyvagal system as allowing for quick changes in metabolic feedback from the heart, which engenders adaptation to rapidly changing inputs. This adaptation favors social behavior because it allows for the monitoring of micro-shifts in the emotional signals of others while maintaining the calm state required for social bonding—the abilities that underlie synchrony.

A deficient polyvagal system could explain why infants with autism have difficulty with visual disengagement, and it predicts that young children with autism should actively prefer nonsocial stimuli to social stimuli. As such, it is consistent with: (1) the finding that toddlers with autism prefer computer-generated noise to "motherese" (Kuhl, et al., 2005),

and plain-looking robots to humanoid robots (Robins et al., 2006); (2) the attention to physical contingencies shown by Klin et al. (2009) in an autistic infant; and (3) that the tendency for infants who will develop autism to follow gaze diminishes between 6 and 12 months of age (Zwaigenbaum, et al., 2005). Overactivation could arise from the neuroinflammation that has been documented among individuals with autism (Pardo, Vargas, & Zimmerman, 2005; Vargas, Nascimbene, Krishnan, Zimmerman, & Pardo, 2005). The inflammation results in a hyperglutamatergic state (Evers & Hollander, 2008). This tilts the excitation-inhibition balance in the direction of hyper-excitability of the neuronal network. A corresponding mouse model of ASD has been presented (Gogolla, Le Blanc, Quast, Sudhof, Faglioni & Hensch 2009). Noting the high prevalence of seizures and epileptiform EEGs in ASD, Polleux and Lauder (2004) find "that the cortex of autistic individuals is characterized by an imbalance between excitation-inhibition in the cortex is attractive because it is based on functional evidence characterizing the autistic brain" (p. 314). Overactivation of the amygdala and a tilt toward dominance of the sympathetic limb of the autonomic nervous system may contribute to the overarousal. Also, overarousal theory is consistent with the high risk for anxiety disorders in individuals with autism, and even those who no longer meet criteria for ASD (Helt et al., 2008). The neurobiology of overarousal and the autonomic nervous system, as they concern non-social aspects of autism, are further discussed in Chapter 19.

CONCLUSION

In our overview of the evidence from typical development, we concluded that entrainment, and the opportunity for mimicry that it affords, is foundational for much of social development and communication, development that is compromised in children with ASD.

1. So is a lack of mimicry at the core of the social impairment in ASD?

Any unitary explanation for the autistic syndrome and its wide range of phenotypic expression is likely to be unitary at the neurobiological and mechanistic, rather than the behavioral, level. Nonetheless, much autistic symptomatology reflects difficulty with social interactions, and the individual's attempts to compensate for that difficulty. Mimicry appears early in life as the result of enactive perception of social stimuli. Enactive perception requires focal attention. One of the earliest signs of autism is reduced attention to social stimuli, and consequently reduced frequency of spontaneous mimicry. As mimicry serves to increase affiliation and motivation to engage socially, as well as to form building blocks for the development of empathy, the reduction in mimicry may have serious consequences for social development and perhaps for experience-dependent neural maturation. Importantly, when an individual with autism is offered instructions that encourage explicit processing of emotional cues, even indirectly, mimicry and the corresponding patterns of neural activation tend to normalize. As reviewed, when people with autism are successfully induced to do deliberately, something that they fail to do automatically, they often can do it. This type of observation steers research interest away from theories that propose static ("modular") deficits or the absence of a specific type of neuron, toward accounts that invoke differences in behavioral predispositions that reflect anomalies of attention and motivation.

Although the lack of mimicry may not be a primary deficit in autism, the social handicaps that result begin early in life. Therefore lack of mimicry may contribute to the expansion of autistic symptoms over the first few years. As such, mimicry could be a promising target for intervention.

2. What causes the reduced attention to social stimuli that characterizes autism and drives the characteristic social developmental deficits?

Substantial static neurological deficits, comparable to the discrete areas of inactivated brain that form the basis of classical lesion-based neuropsychology, are unlikely to be the ultimate solution, at least for high-functioning autistic people. Most things that high-functioning autistic people cannot do they actually sometimes can, and indeed do. Correspondingly, a functional imbalance between opponent neural systems and dysregulated interaction between neurotransmitter influences are more likely than static deficits to determine the often narrow boundary conditions within which key functions can still be implemented. Deficient structure, whether of specific regions in the brain, or deficiency in a particular type of neuron, are less likely explanations.

3. Primarily social?

We set out to determine whether the social manifestations of autism are due to a primary deficiency in the brain mechanisms underlying nonverbal interpersonal coordination or synchrony. We arrive at the conclusion that this is not the case. Rather, the brain mechanism of interpersonal engagement is intact, but underused. This is because individuals with autism frequently fail in the preliminaries to social engagement, namely face-to-face confrontation and eye contact.

4. Why do they fail in interpersonal engagement?

There is as yet no convincing answer to this question. Is there a failure to develop, or a gradual deterioration in, a neural system that is requisite for social engagement? This would be a deficit theory. Or have people with autism not developed, or developed but then lost, the human species-specific feeling that engaging in reciprocal interaction with others is its own reward? This is a difference theory. Or is the social neural network in place, the motivation to use it latent, but the consequences of engaging with others so deeply disturbing, that withdrawing attention from the world of people is the only tenable option? This is a compensation theory. Are people with autism socially inept, socially indifferent, or socially averse? Or, within this strikingly distinctive yet heterogeneous population, are instances of each of these pathological states to be found?

References

Abravanel, E., & Sigafoos, A. D. (1984). Exploring the presence of intention during early infancy. *Child Development, 55,* 381–392.

Adolphs, R., Baron-Cohen, S., & Tranel, D. (2002). Impaired recognition of social emotions following amygdala damage. *Journal of Cognitive Neuroscience, 14,* 1264–1274.

Adolphs, R. (2006). How do we know the minds of others? Domain specificity, simulation, and enactive social conjunction. *Brain Research, 1079,* 25–35.

Allman, J. M., Watson, K. K., Tetreault, N. A., & Hakeem, A. Y. (2005). Intuition and autism: A possible role for Von Economo neurons. *Trends in Cognitive Science, 9,* 367–373.

Andari, E., Duhamel, J-R., Zalla, T., Herbrecht, E., Leboyer, M., & Sirigu, A. (2010). Promoting social behavior with oxytocin in high-functioning autism spectrum disorders. *Proceedings of the New York Academy of Sciences, 107,* 4389–4394.

Arnott, S. R., Singhal, A., & Goodale, M. A. (2009). An investigation of auditory contagious yawning. *Cognitive, Affective and Behavioral Neuroscience 9,* 335–342.

Ashton-James, C., Van Baaren, R. B., Chartrand, T. L., Decety, J., & Karremans, J. (2007). Mimicry and me: The impact of mimicry on self-construal. *Social Cognition, 25*, 518–535.

Asperger, H. (1944). Die "Autistischen Psychopathen" im Kindesalter. *European Archives of Clinical Neuroscience, 117*, 76–136.

Bacon, A. L., Fein, D., Morris, R., & Waterhouse, L. (1998). The responses of autistic children to the distress of others. *Journal of Autism and Developmental Disorders, 28*, 129–142.

Baldwin, D. A. (1995). Understanding the link between joint attention and language. In C. Moore & P. J. Dunham (Eds.), *Joint attention: Its origin and role in development* (pp. 131–158). Hillsdale NJ: Erlbaum.

Baron-Cohen, S., Baldwin, D. A., & Crowson, M. (1997). Do children with autism use the speaker's direction of gaze strategy to crack the code of language? *Child Development, 68*, 48–57.

Baron-Cohen S., Ring H. A., Bullmore E. T., Wheelwright S., Ashwin, C., & Williams, S.C.R. (2000). The amygdala theory of autism. *Neuroscience and Biobehavioral Reviews, 24*, 355–364.

Bavelas, J. B., Black, A., Lemery, C. R., & Mullett, J. (1987). Motor mimicry as primitive empathy. In N. Eisenberg & J. Strayer (Eds.), *Empathy and its development* (pp. 317–333). New York: Cambridge University Press.

Beall, P. M., Moody, E. J., McIntosh, D. N., Hepburn, S. L., & Reed, C. L. (2008). Rapid facial reactions to emotional facial expressions in typically developing children and children with autism spectrum disorder. *Journal of Experimental Child Psychology, 101*, 206–223.

Bebko, J. M., Weiss, J. A., Demark, J. L., & Gomez, P. (2006). Discrimination of temporal synchrony in intermodal events by children with autism and children with developmental disabilities without autism. *Journal of Child Psychology and Psychiatry, 47*, 88–98.

Beebe, B., Jaffe, J., Feldstein, S., Mays, A., & Alson, D. (1985). Interpersonal timing: The application of an adult dialog model to infant-mother vocal and kinesic interactions. In T. Fields & N. Fox (Eds.), *Social perception in infants* (pp. 217–246). Norwood, NJ: Ablex.

Belmonte, M. K., & Yurgelun-Todd, D. A. (2003). Functional anatomy of impaired selective attention and compensatory processing in autism. *Cognitive Brain Research, 17*, 651–664.

Bird, G., Leighton, J., Press, C., & Heyes, C. (2007). Intact automatic imitation of human and robot actions in autism spectrum disorders. *Proceedings of the Royal Society B, 274*, 3027–3031.

Blair, R. J. R. (2008). Fine cuts of empathy and the amygdala: Dissociated deficits in psychopathy and autism. *Quarterly Journal of Experimental Psychology, 61*, 157–170.

Blakemore, S.-J., & Frith, C. (2004). The role of motor contagion in the prediction of action. *Neuropsychologia, 43*, 260–267.

Boucher, J. D., & Ekman, P. (1975). Facial areas and emotional information. *Journal of Communication, 25*, 21–29.

Braverman, M., Fein, D., Lucci, D., & Waterhouse, L. (1989). Affect comprehension in children with pervasive developmental disorders. *Journal of Autism and Developmental Disorders, 19*, 301–316.

Brothers, L. (1997). *Friday's footprint: How society shapes the human mind*. Oxford: Oxford University Press.

Buccino, G., Lui, F., Canessa, N., Pastteri, I., Lagravinese, G., Benuzzi, F. . . . Rizzolatti, G. (2004). Neural circuits involved in the recognition of actions performed by nonconspecifics: An fMRI study. *Journal of Cognitive Neuroscience, 16*, 114–126.

Buckner, R. L., Andrews-Hanna, J. R., & Schacter, D. L. (2008). The brain's default network: Anatomy, function, and relevance to disease. *Annals of New York Academy of Sciences, 1124*, 1–38.

Bühler, C. & Hetzer, H. (1928). Das erste Verstandniss fur Ausdruck im ersten Lebensjahr. *(The earliest understanding of expression in the first year of life.) Zeitschrift for Psychologie, 107*, 50–61.

Bush, K., Barr, L. L., McHugo, J., & Lanzetta, T. (1989). The effects of facial control and facial mimicry on subjective reactions to comedy routines. *Motivation and Emotion, 13*, 31–52.

Calvo-Merino, B., Glaser, D. E., Grèzes, J., Passingham, R. E., & Haggard, P. (2005). Action observation and acquired motor skills: An fMRI study with expert dancers. *Cerebral Cortex, 15*, 1243–1249.

Campos, J. J., & Sternberg, C.R. (1981). Perception, appraisal, and emotion: The onset of social referencing. In: M. Lamb & L. Sherrod (Eds.), *Infant social cognition* (pp. 273–314). Hillsdale, NJ: Erlbaum.

Capella, J. N. (1993). The facial feedback hypothesis in human interaction. *Journal of Language and Social Psychology, 12*, 13–29.

Capps, L., Sigman, M., & Mundy, P. (1994). Attachment security in children with autism. *Development and Psychopathology, 6*, 249–261.

Carr, L., Iacoboni, M., Dubeau, M. C., Mazziotta, J. C., & Lenzi, G. L. (2003). Neural mechanisms of empathy in humans: A relay from neural systems for imitation to limbic areas. *Proceedings of the National Academy of Sciences, U S A, 100*, 5497–5502.

Casanova, M. F., Buxhoeveder, D. P., Suitala, A. E., & Roy, E. (2002). Minicolumnar pathology in autism. *Neurology, 58*, 428–432.

Charman, T. C. (2003). Why is join attention a pivotal skill in autism? *Philosophical Transactions of the Royal Society: Biological Sciences, 358*, 345.

Chartrand, T. L., & Bargh, J A. (1999). The chameleon effect: The perception-behavior link and social interaction. *Journal of Personality and Social Psychology, 76*, 893–910.

Chong, T., Cunnington, R., Williams, M., Kanwisher, N., & Mattingly, J. (2008). fMRI adaptation reveals mirror neurons in human inferior parietal cortex. *Current Biology*, 18, 1576–1580.

Condon, W. S., & Sander, L. W. (1974). Neonate movement is synchronized with adult speech: Interactional participation and language acquisition. *Science*, 183, 99–101.

Courchesne, E., Townsend, J., Akshoomoff, N.A., & Saitoh, O. (1994). Impairment in shifting attention in autistic and cerebellar patients. *Behavioral Neuroscience*, 108, 848–865.

Critchley, H. D., Elliot, R., Mattias, C. J., & Dolan, R. J. (2001). Neural activity relating to reward anticipation in the human brain. *Neuron*, 29, 537–545.

Critchley, H. D., Daly, E. M., Bullmore, E. T., Williams, S. C. R., Van Amelsvoort, T., Robertson, D. M. . . . Murphy, D. G. M. (2000). The functional neuroanatomy of social behaviour: Changes in cerebral blood flow when people with autistic disorder process facial expressions. *Brain*, 123, 2203–2212.

Dalton, K. M., Nacewicz, B. M., Johnstone, T., Schaefer, H. S., Gernsbacher, M. A., Goldsmith, H. H. . . . Davidson, R.J. (2005). Gaze fixation and the neural circuitry of face processing in autism. *Nature Neuroscience*, 8, 519–526.

Damasio, A. R., Tranel, D., & Damasio, H. C. (1991). Somatic markers and the guidance of Behavior: Theory and preliminary testing. In H. S. Levin, H. M. Eisenberg, & A. L. Benton (Eds.), *Frontal lobe function and dysfunction* (pp. 217–229). New York: Oxford University Press.

Dapretto, M., Davies, M. S., Pfeifer, J. H., Scott, A. A., Sigman, M., Bookheimer, S. Y., Iacoboni M. (2006). Understanding emotions in others: Mirror neuron dysfunction in children with autism spectrum disorders. *Nature Neuroscience*, 9, 28–30.

Dawson, G. (1989). *Autism: Nature, diagnosis, and treatment*. New York: Guilford Press.

Dawson, G., Meltzoff, A., Osterling, J., Rinaldi, E., & Brown, B. (1998). Children with autism fail to orient to naturally occurring social stimuli. *Journal of Autism and Developmental Disorders*, 28, 479–485.

Decety, J., & Chaminade, T. (2005). The neurophysiology of imitation and intersubjectivity. In S. Hurley & N. Cater (Eds.), *Perspectives on imitation: From neuroscience to social science* (pp. 119–140). Cambridge: MA: MIT Press.

Decety, J., Chaminade, T., Grezes, J., & Meltzoff, A. N. (2002). A PET exploration of the neural mechanisms involved in reciprocal imitation. *Neuroimage*, 15, 265–272.

Decety, J., & Moriguchi, Y. (2007). The empathic brain and its dysfunction in psychiatric populations: implications for intervention across different clinical conditions. *BioPsychoSocial Medicine*, 1, 22–65.

de Gelder, B., & Hadjikhani, N. (2006). Non-conscious recognition of emotional body language. *Neuroreport*, 17, 583–586.

De Gelder B, Vroomen J & van der Heide L (1991) Face recognition and lip reading in autism. *European Journal of Cognitive Psychology* 3, 69–86.

DeLong, G., Bean, S. C., & Brown, F. R. (1981). Acquired reversible autistic syndrome in acute encephalopathic illness in children. *Archives of Neurology*, 38, 191–194.

di Pelligrino, G., Fadiga, L., Fogassi, L., Gallese, V., & Rizzolatti, G. (1992). Understanding motor events: A neurophysiological study. *Experimental Brain Research*, 91, 176–180.

Dimberg, U. (1982). Facial reactions to facial expressions. *Psychophysiology*, 19, 643–647.

Dimberg, U., Thunberg M., & Elmehed K. (2000). Unconscious facial reactions to emotional facial expressions. *Psychological Science*, 11, 86–89.

Dimberg, U., Thunberg, M., & Grunedal, S. (2002). Facial reactions to emotional stimuli: Automatically controlled emotional responses. *Cognition & Emotion*, 16, 449–472.

Dinstein, I., Thomas, C., Behrmann, M., & Heeger, D. J. (2008). A mirror up to nature. *Current Biology*, 18, R13–R18.

Dissanayake E. (2000). *Art and Intimacy: How the Arts began*. University of Washington Press.

Dissanayake, C., & Crossley, S. A. (1997). Proximity and social behaviors in autism: Evidence for attachment. *Journal of Child Psychology and Psychiatry*, 37, 149–156.

Doherty-Sneddon, G., Bruce, V., Bonner, L., Longbotham S., Doyle, C. 2002). Development of gaze aversion as disengagement from visual information. *Developmental Psychology*, 38, 438–445.

Dowd, J. M., & Tronick, E. Z. (1986). Temporal coordination of arm movements in early infancy: Do infants move in synchrony with adult speech? *Child Development*, 57, 762–776.

Eckerman, C. O., Davis, C. C., & Dedoc, S. M. (1989). Toddlers' emerging ways of achieving social coordination with a peer. *Child Development*, 60, 440–453.

Elia, M., Ferri, R., Musumeci, S.A., Del Gracco, S., Bottitta, M., Scuderi, C., . . . Grubar, J-C., (2000). Sleep in subjects with autistic disorder: A neurophysiological and psychological study. *Brain Development*, 22, 88–92.

Emmorey K., Xu, J., Gannon, P., Goldin-Meadow S., Braun, A. (2010). CNS activation and regional connectivity during pantomime observation: No engagement of the mirror neuron system for deaf signers. *Neuroimage* 49, 994–1005.

Evers, M., & Hollander, E. (2008) Excitotoxicity in autism: The role of glutamate in pathogenesis and treatment. In A. W. Zimmerman (Ed.), *Autism: Current theories and evidence* (pp. 133–146). Totswa, NJ: Humana Press.

Faulkner, A., Suomi, S. J., Visalberghi, E., & Ferraril, P. F. (2009). Capuchin monkeys display affiliation to humans who imitate them. *Science, 325,* 880–883.

Fein, D., Lucci, D., Braverman, M., & Waterhouse, L. (1992). Comprehension of affect in context in children with pervasive developmental disorders. *Journal of Child Psychology and Psychiatry, 33,* 1157–1167.

Feldman, R. (2006). From biological rhythms to social rhythms: Physiological precursors of mother–infant synchrony. *Developmental Psychology, 42,* 175–188.

Feldman, R. (2007a). Maternal versus child's risk and the development of parent–infant and family relationships in five high-risk populations. *Development and Psychopathology, 19,* 293–312.

Feldman, R. (2007b). Parent infant synchrony. *Biological foundations and developmental outcomes. Current Directions in Psychological Science, 16,* 340–345.

Feldman, R., & Greenbaum, C. W. (1997). Affect regulation and synchrony in mother–infant play as precursors to the development of symbolic competence. *Infant Mental Health Journal, 18,* 4–23.

Feldman, R., Greenbaum, C. W., & Yirmiya, N. (1999). Mother–infant affect synchrony as an antecedent to the emergence of self-control. *Developmental Psychology, 35,* 223–231.

Feldman, R., Levine, A., Zagoory-Sharon, O., & Weller, A. (2007). Evidence for a neuroendocrinological foundation of human affiliation: Plasma oxytocin levels across pregnancy and the postpartum predict maternal–infant bonding. *Psychological Science, 18,* 965–970.

Feldman, R. & Mayes, L. C. (1999). The cyclic organization of attention during habituation is related to infants' information processing. *Infant Behavior and Development, 22,* 37–49.

Feldstein, S., Konstantareas, M. M., Oxman, J., & Webster, C. D. (1982). The chronography of interactions with autistic speakers: An initial report. *Journal of Communication Disorders, 15,* 451–460.

Ferguson, J. N., Aldag, J. M., Insel, T. R., & Young, L.J. (2001). Oxytocin in the medial amygdala is essential for social recognition in the mouse. *Journal of Neuroscience, 21,* 8278–8285.

Fraiberg, S. (1974). The effect of the infant on its caregiver. In S. Fraiberg, M. Lewis, & L. A. Rosenblum (Eds.), *Blind infants and their mothers: An examination of their sign system* (pp. 149–169). New York: Wiley.

Gallese, V., Fadiga, L., Fogassi, L., & Rizzolatti, G. (1996). Action recognition in the premotor cortex. *Brain, 119,* 593–609.

Gazzola, V., Aziz-Zadeh, L., & Keysers, C. (2006). Empathy and the somatotopic auditory mirror system. *Current Biology, 16,* 1824–1829.

Gergely, G. (2001). The obscure object of desire: "Nearly, but clearly not, like me": Contingency preference in normal children versus children with autism. *Bulletin of the Menninger Clinic, 65,* 411.

Gibson, J. J. (2003). The ecological approach to visual perception. In M. P. Munger (Ed.), *The history of psychology: Fundamental questions* (pp. 468–477). New York: Oxford University Press.

Gillberg, C (1986). Brief report: Onset at age 14 of a typical autistic syndrome. A case report of a girl with herpes simplex encephalitis. *Journal of Autism and Developmental Disorders, 16,* 369–375.

Gogolla, N., LeBlanc, C., Quast, K.B., Sudhof, T. E., Faglioni, M., Hensch, T. K. (2009). Common circuit defect of excitatory-inhibitory balance in mouse models of autism. *Journal of Neurodevelopmental Disorders, 1,* 172–181.

Goodman, J. R. L., Isenhower, R.W., Marsh, K. L., Schmidt, R. C., & Richardson, M. J. (2005). In H. Heft & L. Marsh (Eds.), *The interpersonal phase entrainment of rocking chair movements. Studies in Perception and Action XIII* (pp. XX–XX). New Jersey: Erlbaum.

Gowen, J. S., and Miall R. C. (2007) Movement interference in autism-spectrum disorder. *Neuropsychologia 46,* 1060–1068.

Greene, J., & Haidt, J. (2002). How (and where) does moral judgment work? *Trends in Cognitive Sciences, 6,* 517–523.

Guéguen, N., & Martin, A. (2009). Incidental similarity facilitates behavioral mimicry. *Social Psychology, 40,* 88–92.

Hadjikhani, N., Joseph., R., Snyder, J., & Tager-Flusberg, H. (2006). Anatomical differences in the mirror neuron system and social cognition network in autism. *Cerebral Cortex, 16,* 1276–1282.

Hamilton, A. C. (2008). Emulation and mimicry for social interaction: A theoretical approach to imitation in autism. *Quarterly Journal of Experimental Psychology, 6,* 101–115.

Hatfield, E., Caccioppo, J., & Rapson, R. (1994). *Emotional contagion.* New York: Cambridge University Press.

Hebb, D. (1949). *The organization of behavior: A neurophysiological theory.* New York: Wiley.

Heinrichs, M., & Domes, G. (2008). Neuropeptides and social behavior effects of oxytocin and vasopressin in humans. *Progress in Brain Research, 170,* 337–350.

Helt, M., Eigsti, I-M., Snyder, P. J., & Fein, D. A. (in press). Contagious yawning in autistic and typical development. *Child Development.*

Helt, M., Kelley, E., Kinsbourne, M., Pandey, J., Boorstein, H., Herbert, M., & Fein, D. (2008). Can children with autism recover? If so, how? *Neuropsychology Reviews, 18,* 339–366.

Hermans, E. J., van Wingen, G., Bos, P. A., Putnam, P., & van Honk, J. (2008). Reduced spontaneous facial mimicry in women with autistic traits. *Biological Psychology, 80,* 348–353.

Heyes, C., Bird, G., Johnson, H., & Haggard, P. (2005). Experience modulates automatic attention. *Cognitive Brain Research, 22,* 233–240.

Hove M. J. and Risen J. L. (2009) It's all in the timing: Interpersonal synchrony increases affiliation. *Social Cognition 27*, 949–960.

Howard, M. A., Cowell P. E., Boucher, J., Broks, P., Farrant, A. & Roberts, N. (2000). Convergent neuroanatomical and behavioural evidence of an amygdala hypothesis of autism. *Neuroreport, 11*, 2931–2935.

Hutt, C., Hutt, S. J., Lee, D., & Ounsted, C. (1964). Arousal and childhood autism. *Nature, 204*, 908–909.

Iacoboni, M. (2009). Imitation, empathy, and mirror neurons. *Annual Review of Psychology, 60*, 653–670.

Isenhower, R. W., Marsh, K. L., Silva, P., Richardson, M. J., & Schmidt, R. C., (2007, July). *Interpersonal coordination in autistic and typically-developing children*. Paper presented at the 14th International Conference on Perception and Action, Yokahama, Japan.

Jack, R. E., Blais, C., Scheepers, C., Schyne, P. G., & Caldara, R. (2009). Cultural confusions show facial expressions are not universal. *Current Biology, 19*, 1–6.

Jaffe, J., Beebe, B., Feldstein, S., Crown, C. L., & Jasnow, M. D. (2001). Rhythms of dialogue in infancy: Coordinated timing in development. *Monographs of the Society for Research in Child Development, 66* (2, Serial No. 265).

James, W. (1890). *The principles of psychology*. New York: Holt.

Johnson, M. H., Griffin, R., Csibra, G., & Halit, H. (2005). The emergence of the social brain network: Evidence from typical and atypical development. *Development and Psychopathology, 17*, 599–619.

Jones, S. S. (1996). Imitation or exploration? Young infants' matching of adults' oral gestures. *Child Development, 67*, 1952–1969.

Jones, S. (2007). Imitation in infancy: The development of mimicry. *Psychological Science, 18*, 593–599.

Jordan, J. S. (2009). Forward-looking aspects of perception-action coupling as a basis for embodied communication. *Discourse Processes, 46*, 127–144.

Joseph R.M., and Tanaka J. (2003) Holistic and part-based face recognition in children with autism. *Journal of Child Psychology and Psychiatry 44*, 529–542.

Kanner, L. (1943). Autistic disturbances of affective contact. *Nervous Child, 2*, 217–250.

Kaplan, J. T., & Iacoboni, M. (2006). Multimodal action representation in human left ventral premotor cortex. *Cognitive Processing, 8*, 103–113.

Kemper, T. L., & Bauman, M. L. (2002). Neuropathology of infantile autism. *Molecular Psychiatry, 7*, 512–513.

Kennedy, D. P., & Courchesne, E. (2008). The intrinsic functional organization of the brain is altered in autism. *Neuroimage, 39*, 1877–1885.

Kennedy D. P., Semendeferi, K., & Courchesne, E. (2007). No reduction of spindle neuron number in frontoinsular cortex in autism. *Brain and Cognition, 64*, 124–129.

Keysers, C., & Perrett, D. (2004). Demystifying social cognition: A Hebbian perspective. *Trends in Cognitive Sciences, 8*, 501–507.

Keysers, C., Wicker, B, Gazzola, V., Anton, J., Fogassi, L., & Gallese, V. (2004). A touching sight: SII/PV activation during the observation and experience of touch. *Neuron, 42*, 335–346.

Kinsbourne, M. (1979). The neuropsychology of infantile autism. In L. A. Lockman, K. F. Swaiman, J. S. Drage, K. B. Nelson & K. M. Marsden (Eds.), *Workshop on the Neurobiological Basis of Autism. NINCDS Monograph N 23* (pp. XX–XX). Bethesda, MD: Department of HEW.

Kinsbourne, M. (1987). Cerebral-brainstem interactions in infantile autism. In E. Schopler & G. Mesibov (Eds.), *Neurobiological Theories of Arousal and Autism*. New York, Plenum.

Kinsbourne, M. (2002). The role of imitation in body ownership and mental growth. In Meltzoff, N. Andrew, & W. Prinz (Eds.), *The imitative mind: Development, evolution, and brain bases* (pp. 311–330). New York: Cambridge University Press.

Kinsbourne, M. (2005). Imitation as entrainment: Brain mechanisms and social consequences. In S. Hurley & N. Chater (Eds.), *Perspectives on imitation: From neuroscience to social science* (pp. 163–172). Cambridge, MA: MIT Press.

Kinsbourne, M., & Jordan, J. S. (2009). Embodied anticipation: A neurodevelopmental interpretation. *Discourse Processes, 46*, 103–126.

Kirsch, P., Esslinger, C., Chen, Q., Mier, D., Lis, S., Siddhanti, S., . . . Meyer-Lindenberg, A. (2005). Oxytocin modulates neural circuitry for social cognition and fear in humans. *The Journal of Neuroscience, 25*, 11489–11493.

Kleinhans, N. M., Johnson, C., Richards, T., Mahurin, R., Greenson, J. G., Dawson, G., & Aylward, E. (2009). Reduced neural habituation in the amygdala and social impairments in autism spectrum disorders. *American Journal of Psychiatry, 166*, 467–475.

Klin, A., Jones, W., Schultz, R., & Volkmar, F. (2003). The enactive mind, or from actions to cognition: Lessons from autism. *Philosophical Transactions of the Royal Society of London B, 358*, 345–360.

Klin, A., Jones, W., Schultz, R. T., Volkmar, F., & Cohen, D. (2002). Visual fixation patterns during viewing of naturalistic social situations as predictors of social competence in individuals with autism. *Archives of General Psychiatry, 59*, 807–826.

Klin, A., Lin, D. J., Gorrindo, P., Ramsay, G., & Jones, W. (2009). Two-year-olds with autism orient to non-social contingencies rather than biological motion. *Nature, 459*, 257–261.

Kosfeld, M., Heinrichs, M., Zak, P. J., Fischbacher, U., Fehr, E., (2005). Oxytocin increases trust in humans. *Nature, 435*, 673–676.

Kuhl, P. K., Coffey-Corina, S., Padden, D., & Dawson, G. (2005). Links between social and linguistic processing of speech in preschool children with autism: Behavioral and electrophysiological evidence. *Developmental Science, 8*, F1–F12.

Lakin, J. L., Jefferis, V. E., Cheng, C. M., & Chartrand, T. L. (2003). The chameleon effect as social glue: Evidence for the evolutionary significance of nonconscious mimicry. *Journal of Nonverbal Behavior, 27*, 145–162.

Leighton, J., Bird, B., Chaiman, T., & Hayes, C. (2008). Weak imitative performance is not due to a functional "mirroring" deficit in adults with autism spectrum disorders. *Neuropsychologia, 46*, 1041–1049.

Limoges, E., Mottron, L., Bolduc, C., Berthiaume, C., & Godbout, R. (2005). Atypical sleep architecture and the autism phenotype. *Brain, 128*, 1049–1061.

Magnee, M. J. C. M., deGelder, B., van Engeland, H., & Kemner, C. (2007). Facial electromyographic responses to emotional information from faces and voices in individuals with pervasive developmental disorder. *Journal of Child Psychology and Psychiatry, 48*, 1122–1130.

Marsh, K. L., Richardson, M. S., & Schmidt, R. (2009). Social connection through joint action and interpersonal coordination. *Topics in Cognitive Science, 1*, 320–339.

McHugo, G. J., Lanzetta, J. T., Sullvan, D. G., Masters, R. D., & Englis B. G. (1985). Emotional reactions to a political leader's emotional displays. *Journal of Personality and Social Psychology, 49*, 1513–1529.

McIntosh, D. N. (1996). Facial feedback hypotheses: Evidence, implications, and directions. *Motivation and Emotion, 20*, 121–147.

McIntosh, D. N., Reichmann-Decker, A., Winkielman, P., & Wilbarger, J. L. (2006). When the social mirror breaks: Deficits in automatic, but not voluntary mimicry of emotional facial expressions in autism. *Developmental Science, 9*, 295–302.

Macrae, C. N., Duffy, D.K., Miles, L. K., & Lawrence J. (2008). A case of hand waving: Action synchrony and person perception. *Cognition 109*, 152–156.

Meltzoff, A. N. (1995). Understanding the imitations of others: Re-enactment of an intended act by 18-months-olds. *Developmental Psychology, 31*, 838–850.

Meltzoff, A. N., & Moore, M. K. (1977). Imitation of facial and manual gestures by human neonates. *Science, 198*, 75–78.

Meltzoff, A. N. (2002). "Like me": A foundation for social cognition. *Development Science, 10*, 126–134.

Moody, E. J., McIntosh, D. N., Mann, L. J., & Weisser, K.R. (2007). More than mere mimicry? The influence of emotion on rapid facial reactions to faces. *Emotion, 7*, 447–457.

Moore, G. A., & Calkins, S. D. (2004). Infants' vagal regulation in the still-face paradigm is related to dyadic coordination of mother-infant interaction. *Developmental Psychology 40*, 168–1080.

Nacewicz, B. M., Dalton, K. M., Johnstone, T., Long, T. M., McAuleffe, E. M., Oakes, T. R. . . . Davidson, V. J. (2006). Amygdala volume and nonverbal social impairment in adolescent and adult males with autism. *Archives of General Psychiatry, 83*, 1417–1428.

Nadel, J., Prepin, K., & Okanda, M. (2005). Experiencing contingency and agency first step toward self-understanding in making a mind? *Interaction Studies, 3*, 447–462.

Neumann, R, Spezio, M. L., Piven J & Adolphs, R (2006). Looking you in the mouth: Abnormal gaze in autism resulting from impaired top-dawn modulation of visual attention. *Social, Cognitive and Affective Neuroscience 1*, 194–202.

Neumann, R., & Strack, F. (2000). "Mood contagion": The automatic transfer of mood between persons. *Journal of Personality and Social Psychology, 79*, 211–223.

Nicholas, B., Rudrasingham, V., Nash, S., Kirov, G., Owen, M.J., & Wimpory, D.C. (2007). Association of Per1 and Npaas2 with autistic disorder: Support for the clock genes/timing hypothesis. *Molecular Psychiatry, 12*, 691–692.

Niedenthal, P. M., Barsalou, L. W., Ric, F., & Krauth-Gruber, S. (2005). Embodiment in the acquisition and use of emotion knowledge. In L. F. Barrett, P. M. Niedenthal, & P. Winkielman (Eds.), *Emotion and Consciousness* (pp. 21–50). New York: Guilford Press.

Oberman, L. M., Winkielman, P., & Ramachandran, V. S. (2009). Slow echo: Facial EMG evidence for the delay of spontaneous, but not voluntary, emotional mimicry in children with autism spectrum disorders. *Developmental Science, 12*, 510–520.

Oberman, L., Hubbard, E., McCleery, J. P., Altschuler, E., Ramachandran, V., & Pineda, J. A. (2005). EEG evidence for mirror neuron dysfunction in autism spectrum disorders. *Cognitive Brain Research, 24*, 190–198.

Oberman, L., & Ramachandran, V. (2007). The simulating social mind: The role of the mirror neuron system and simulation in the social communicative deficits of autism spectrum disorders. *Psychological Bulletin, 133*, 310–327.

Ohman, A. (2002). Automaticity and the amygdala: Nonconscious responses to emotional faces. *Current Directions in Psychological Science, 11*, 62–66.

Ozonoff, S., Iosif A-M., Baquio F., Cook, I. C., Hill, M. M., Hutman, T., — Young, G. S., Pardo, C. A., Vargas, D. L., & Zimmerman, A. W. (2005). Immunity, neuroglia and neuro-inflammation in autism. *International Review of Psychiatry, 17*, 485–495.

Penman, R., Meares, R., Baker, K., & Milgrom-Friedman, J. (2003). Synchrony in mother-infant interaction: A possible neurophysiological base. *British Journal of Medical Psychology, 56*, 1–7.

Perry, A., & Bentin, S. (2009). Mirror activity in the human brain while observing hand movements: A comparison between EEG desynchronization in the u-range and previous fMRI results. *Brain Research, 1282,* 126–132.

Pfeifer, J. H., Iacoboni, M., Mazziotta, JC., & Dapretto, M. (2008). Mirroring others' emotions relates to empathy and interpersonal competence in children. *Neuroimage, 15,* 2076–2085.

Pierce, K. & Redcay, E. (2008). Fusiform function in children with an autism spectrum disorder is a matter of "who." *Biological Psychiatry, 64,* 552–560.

Pierce, K., Haist, F., Sedaghat, F., & Courchesne, E. (2004). The brain response to personally familiar faces in autism: Findings of fusiform activity and beyond. *Brain, 127,* 2703–2716.

Pineda, J. S. (2008). Sensorimotor cortex as a critical component of an "extended" mirror neuron system: Does it solve the development, correspondence, and control problems in mirroring? *Behavioral and Brain Functions, 4,* 47.

Platek, S. M., Critton, S.R., Myers, T.E., & Gallup, G. G., Jr. (2003). Contagious yawning: The role of self-awareness and mental state attribution. *Cognitive Brain Research, 17,* 223–227.

Polleux, F., & Lauder, J. M. (2004). Toward a developmental neuropsychology of autism. *Mental Retardation and Developmental Disabilities Research Reviews, 10,* 303–317.

Porges, S. W. (2003). The polyvagal theory: Phylogenetic contributions to social behavior. *Physiology & Behavior, 79,* 503–513.

Prinz, W. (1990). A common coding approach to perception and action. In O. Neumann & W. Prinz (Eds.), *Relationships between perception and action: Current approaches* (pp. 167–201). Berlin: Springer.

Provine, R. R. (1989). Faces as releasers of contagious yawning: An approach to face detection using normal human participants. *Bulletin of the Psychonomic Society, 27,* 211–214.

Ramachandran V.S. (2000) Mirror neurons and imitation as the driving force behind the "great leap forward" in human evolution. www.edge.org.

Reiss, A. L., Eckert, M. A., Rose, F. E., Karchemskiy, A., Kesler, S., Chang, M. — Galaburda A . . . (2004). An experiment of nature: Brain anatomy parallels cognition and behavior in Williams syndrome. *The Journal of Neuroscience, 24,* 5009–5015.

Robins, B., Dautenhahn, K., & Dubowski, J. (2006). Does appearance matter in the interaction of children with autism with a humanoid robot? *Interaction Studies, 7,* 509–542.

Rogers, S. B. (2009). What are infant siblings teaching us about autism? *Autism Research, 2,* 125–137.

Rogers, S. J. (2006). Studies of imitation in early infancy. In Rogers, S. & Williams, J. (Eds) *Imitation and the Social Mind: Autism and Typical Development* (pp. 3–26). New York: Guilford Press.

Rubenstein, J.L., & Merzenich, M.M. (2003). Model of autism: Increased ratio of excitation/inhibition in key neural systems. *Genes Brain Behavior, 2,* 255–2_7.

Scambler, D. J., Hepburn, S., L., Rutherford, M.D., Wehner, E.A., Rogers,S.J. (2006). Emotional

responsivity in children with autism, children with other developmental disabilities, and children with typical development. *Journal of Developmental Disorders, 37,* 553–563.

Schultz, R. T., Gauthier, I., Klin, A., Fulbright, R. K., Anderson, A. W., Volkmar, F. . . . Gore, J. C. (2000). Abnormal ventral temporal cortical activity during face discrimination among individuals with autism and Asperger syndrome. *Archives of General Psychiatry, 57,* 331–340.

Sebanz, N., Bekkering, H., & Knoeblich, G. (2005). Joint action: Minds and bodies moving together. *Trends in Cognitive Science, 10,* 70–76.

Senju, A., Maeda, M., Kikuchi, Y., Hasegawa, T., Tojo, Y., & Osanai, H. (2007). Absence of contagious yawning in children with autism spectrum disorder. *Biology Letters, 3,* 706–708.

Shapiro, T., Sherman, M., Calamari, G., & Koch, D. (1987). Attachment in autism and other developmental disorders. *Journal of the American Academy of Child and Adolescent Psychiatry, 26,* 480–484.

Sigman, M., & Ungerer, J. A. (1984). Attachment behaviors in autistic children. *Journal of Autism and Developmental Disorders, 14,* 231–244.

Siller, M., & Sigman, M. (2002). The behaviors of parents of children with autism predict the subsequent development of their children's communication. *Journal of Autism and Developmental Disorders, 32,* 77–89.

Singer, T., Seymour, B., O'Doherty, J., Kaube, H., Dolan, R. J. & Frith, C. D. (2004). Empathy for pain involves the affective but not sensory components of pain. *Science, 303,* 1157–1162.

Simner, M. L. (1971). Newborn's response to the cry of another infant. *Developmental Psychology, 5,* 136–150.

Sonnby-Borgstrom, M. (2002). Automatic mimicry reactions as related to differences in emotional empathy. *Scandinavian Journal of Psychology, 43,* 433–443.

Spezio, M. L., Huang, P. S., Castelli, F. & Adolphs, R. (2007). Amygdala damage impairs eye contact during conversations with real people. *The Journal of Neuroscience, 27,* 3994–3997.

Sprengelmeyer, R., Young, A. W., Schroeder, U., Grossenbacher, P.G., Federlein, J., Buttner, T., & Przuntek, H. (2006). Knowing no fear. *Proceedings of Biological Sciences: The Royal Society B, 266,* 2451–2456.

Stefanatos, G. A. (2008). Regression in autistic spectrum disorder. *Neuropsychology Reviews, 18,* 305–319.

Stefanatos, G. A., Kinsbourne, M., & Wasserstein, J. (2002). Acquired epileptiform aphasia: A dimensional view of Landau-Kleffner syndrome and the relation to regressive autistic spectrum disorder. *Clinical Neuropsychology, 8,* 195–228.

Stel, M., van den Heuvel, C., & Smeets, R.C. (2008). Facial feedback mechanisms in autistic spectrum disorders. *Journal of Autism and Developmental Disorders, 38,* 1250–1258.

Striano, T., Henning, A. & Stahl, D. (2005). Sensitivities to social contingencies between 1 and 3 months of age. *Developmental Science, 8,* 509–518.

Swettenham, J., Baron-Cohen, S., Charman, T., Cox, A., Baird, G., Drew, A. . . . Wheelright, S. (1998). The frequency and distribution of spontaneous attention shifts between social and non-social stimuli in autistic, typically developing and non-autistic developmentally delayed infants. *Journal of Child Psychology and Psychiatry, 39,* 747–754.

Termine, N. & Izard, C. E. (1988). Infants' responses to their mother's expressions of joy and sadness. *Developmental Psychology, 24,* 223–229.

Tkach, D., Reimer, J., & Hatsopoulos, N. G. (2007). Congruent activity during action and action observation in motor cortex. *The Journal of Neuroscience, 27,* 13241–13250.

Tomasello, M. (1996). Do apes ape? In C. Heyes & B. Galef (Eds.) *Social learning in animals: The roots of culture* (pp. 319–346). San Diego, CA: Academic Press.

Tomasello, M., Carpenter, M., Call, T., Behne, T., & Moll, H. (2005). Understanding sharing intentions. *The origins of cultural cognition. Behavior and Brain Sciences, 28,* 675–697.

Trevarthen, C. & Daniel, S. (2005). Disorganized rhythm and synchrony: Early signs of autism and Rett syndrome. *Brain & Development, 27,* S25–S34.

Tronick, E. Als, H. & Brazelton, T. B. (1977). Mutuality in mother-infant interaction. *The Journal of Communication, 27,* 74–79.

Ulhaas, P. J., Pipa, G., Lima, B., Melloni, L., Neuenschwander, S., Nikolic, D., & Singer, W. (2009). Neural synchrony in cortical networks: History, concepts and current status. *Frontiers in Integrative Neuroscience, 3,* 17.

van Baaren, R.B., Holland, R. W., Kawakami, K., & van Knippenberg, A. (2004). Mimicry and prosocial behavior. *Psychological Science, 15,* 71–74.

Varela, F. J., Thompson, E., & Rosch, E. (1992). *The embodied Mind: Cognitive science and human experience.* Cambridge, MA: MIT Press.

Vargas, D. L., Nascimbene, C., Krishnan, C., Zimmerman, A. W., & Pardo, C. A. (2005). Neuroglial activation and neuroinflammation in the brain of patients with autism. *Annals of Neurology, 57,* 67–81.

Vaughan, K., & Lanzetta, J. (1980). The effect of modification of expressive displays on vicarious emotional arousal. *Journal of Experimental Social Psychology, 17,* 16–30.

Verte, S., Roeyers, H., & Buysee A., (2003). Behavioral problems, social competence and self-concept in siblings of children with autism. *Child: Care, health and development, 29,* 193–205.

Wang, A. T., Lee, S. S., Sigman, M., & Dapretto, M. (2007). Reading affect in the face and voice: Neural correlates of interpreting communicative intent in children and adolescents with autism spectrum disorders. *Archives of General Psychiatry, 64,* 698–708.

Warner, R. M. (1992). Sequential analysis of social interaction: Assessing internal versus social

determinants of behavior. *Journal of Personality and Social Psychology, 63,* 51–60.

Watanabe, T., Okubo, M., & Kuroda, T. (1996). Analysis of entrainment in face-to-face interaction using heart rate variability. *Robot and Human Communication, 5th IEEE International Workshop,* Cambridge MA, 141–145.

Waterhouse, L., Fein, D., & Modahl, C. (1996). Neurofunctional mechanisms in autism. *Psychological Review, 103,* 457–489.

Welsh, J. P., Ahn, D. S., & Placantonakis, E. G. (2005). Is autism due to brain desynchronization? *International Journal of Developmental Neuroscience, 23,* 253–263.

Weissberg, D. S., Keil, F. C., Goodstein, J., Rawson, E., & Gray, J. R. (2008). The seductive allure of neuroscience explanations. *Journal of Cognitive Neuroscience, 20,* 470–477.

Wicker, B., Keysers, C., Plailly, J., Royet, J. P., Gallese, V., & Rizzolatti, G. (2003). Both of us Disgusted in my insula: The common neural basis of seeing and feeling disgust. *Neuron, 40,* 655–664.

Wilbarger, J. L., McIntosh, D., M., & Winkielman, P. (2009). Startle modulation in autism: Positive affective stimuli enhance startle response. *Neuropsychologia, 47,* 1323–1331.

Willemsen-Swinkels, S. H. N., Buitelaar, J. K., Dekker, M., & van Engeland, H. (1998). Subtyping stereotypic behavior in children: The association between stereotypic behavior, mood and heart rate. *Journal of Autism and Developmental Disorders, 28,* 547–557.

Williams, J. H. G. (2008). Self-other relations in social development and autism: Multiple roles for mirror neurons and other brain bases. *Autism Research, 1,* 73–90.

Williams, J. H., Whiten, A., Suddendorf, T., & Perrett, D. I. (2001). Imitation, mirror neurons and autism. *Neuroscience and Biobehavioral Reviews, 25,* 287–295.

Wiltermuth, S. S. & Heath, C. (2009). Synchrony and cooperation. *Psychological Science, 20,* 1–5.

Yirmiya, N., Gamliel, I., Pilowsky, T., Feldman, R., Baron-Cohen, S. & Sigman, M. (2006). The development of siblings of children with autism at 4 and 14 months: Social engagement, communication and cognition. *Journal of Child Psychology and Psychiatry, 47,* 511–523.

Zahn-Waxler, C., Radke-Yarrow, M., & King, R. A. (1979). Child rearing and children's prosocial initiations toward victims of distress. *Child Development, 50,* 319–330.

Zajonc, R.B., Adelmann, P.K., Murphy, S.T., & Niedenthal, P.M. (1987). Convergence in the physical appearance of spouses. *Motivation and Emotion, 11,* 335–346.

Zwaigenbaum, L., Bryson, S., Rogers, T., Roberts, W., Brain, J., & Szatmari, P. (2005). Behavioral manifestations of autism in the first year of life. *International Journal of Developmental Neuroscience, 23,* 143–152.

Chapter 19

Repetitive Movements and Arousal

Marcel Kinsbourne

This discussion of neuropsychological aspects of autistic spectrum disorder (ASD) is focused on aberrant behaviors, with respect to their role in the self-regulation of the individual, and on the underlying neurobiology. Where knowledge is incomplete, it suggests in which direction the scientific winds are blowing.

REPETITIVE MOVEMENTS

In contrast to the intense, ongoing attention to the social and cognitive aspects of ASD, there is a dearth of empirical and theoretical interest in the attentional, sensory, and motoric aspects of the disorder. Individuals with autism are notoriously impaired in relating to others. However, the other side of the coin is that they persist unduly in self-involved activities. Not directing themselves toward any discernible outward goal, they turn inward, and address subjective imperatives that others can only guess at. The perplexed observer sees

what appear to be constraints on attention, a rigid application of rules, circumscribed interests, the use of unusual postures, and apparently purposeless routines and actions.

Repetitive behaviors in autism include bursts of coordinated, rhythmically repetitive movements such as spinning, flapping, touching, or self-mutilating. Bauman (1999) characterizes these movement sequences as follows: "rhythmic rocking of the body from foot to foot while standing, rhythmic flapping of the arms and hands, or repetitive flicking of the fingers in front of the eyes. Inanimate objects may be incorporated into this behavior, such as string that is twirled, wheels of toys that are spun, or repetitive tapping of blocks, toys or eating utensils" (p. 602).

Recent reviewers are in agreement that the cause or causes of repetitive movements are not definitively established. However, a definitive experiment is a largely mythical concept in cognitive neuroscience. As in other areas dealing with behavior, the solution is more a matter of pattern perception of convergent findings, than the uncovering of the totally convincing clue. I will present findings from a wide range of sources, no one of them by itself convincing, but together pointing toward the same solution. This discussion considers neuropsychological aspects of this repetitive behavior, with an emphasis on its motoric manifestations. The question is, what kind of a theory should we be looking for?

Any neurological symptom or symptom complex (i.e., syndrome) is of one of three types: *deficit, disinhibition,* or *compensation.* Deficit implies loss, such that the behavioral deviation is *negative*: Due to the lack of a previously functional brain operation, or its deficient development, the patient's behavioral repertoire is being correspondingly depleted or made incomplete. Severe cases of ASD exhibit a failure of development of language, and even of intellect in general. However, there is no known concomitant location of structural damage, and some persons on the spectrum have a command of language and an intellect that is normal, if not above average. There seems to be no unifying neurocognitive deficit that characterizes the essence of being autistic, only characteristic deviations in behavior.

In any case, no structural impairments of the developing brain have been reliably associated with repetitive behaviors. Such abnormalities as have become apparent through postmortem microscopic studies are not clearly related to the movement aspects of ASD. Some in vivo structural MRI studies have pointed to group differences between people with ASD and controls with respect to the volume of brain structures within cortico-basal ganglia circuitry (reviewed by Lewis & Kim, 2009). With respect to repetitive movements, Rojas et al. (2006) found significant positive correlations between the volume of the caudate nucleus and scores in the ADI-R repetitive and stereotyped behavior domain. If this finding turns out to be reliable, what does it imply? More functional substance? More immature substance that has been insufficiently synaptically pruned? Or perhaps swollen by inflammation? It remains unclear what type of pathology the volume abnormality indicates. And most critically, before offering any interpretation, how specific is the volume change to stereotypies in ASD?

Damasio and Maurer (1978) suggested that repetitive movements are dystonias, related to mesolimbic dopaminergic dysfunction. But unlike dystonias, they are not thought to be outside voluntary control, and as we shall see, they serve an adaptive purpose. Ornitz (1983) argued that the movements are products of dysfunction in central vestibular connections. The same objection applies. Turner (1999) described them as analogous to frontal lobe perseverations. She overlooks the basic distinction: perseverations occur when the patient attempts meaningful responses, whereas repetitive movements occur outside the context of attempted goal-directed action.

If disinhibition is the problem, brain damage or dysfunction has released a normally inhibited pattern of behavior to be realized in novel *positive* symptoms. The atypical autistic behaviors are certainly positive symptoms. However, they may only in part be disinhibitory, and in other part manifestations of attempts to compensate (Kinsbourne, 1979).

Bailey, Phillips, and Rutter (1996) noted that current neuropsychological theory in autism is heavily weighted toward cognitive models, and this is still the case. A major weakness of current models is that they cannot account for the third mandatory symptom set in autism, repetitive behaviors (as well as sensory abnormalities and behavioral rigidity). Thus, *deficient Theory of Mind* (Baron-Cohen, Leslie, & Frith, 1985) lacks generality. It does not address the attentional, sensory, and movement abnormalities of autism, and it cannot account for the origins of autistic symptoms as early as the first year of life, when Theory of Mind is still far in the future for any child. *Weak central coherence theory* (Happé & Frith, 2006) gives a useful account of local preference in autism as a cognitive style, but does not address the autistic disorders of social interaction and of movement (South et al. 2005). There is ample evidence for *deficiencies in executive functions* in autism (Ozonoff et al. 2001), but no apparent link to repetitive movements. Furthermore, executive dysfunction is an amalgam of diverse constructs, such as planning, impulse control, working memory, initiation, and monitoring of action, and does not offer a unitary explanation (Banich 2009). Liss et al. (2001) performed executive-function testing on 21 children with high-functioning autism. They found some types of difficulty in these tests, but none likely to result in autistic behaviors or deficits. The prefrontal dysfunction is probably secondary to another cause that is more central to the disorder. Ohnishi et al. (2000) found two distinct factors in their ASD population. Factor one was comprised of sociocognitive problems, and featured prefrontal cortical abnormality in regional blood flow. Factor two, the need for sameness factor, denoting repetitive behaviors, was associated with abnormal right medial temporal blood flow. The authors suggest that need for sameness is not related to executive dysfunction, but rather to a deficit in orienting to novelty. They reference corroborative medical literature. The findings of Ohnishi at al. (2000) relate repetitive movements in autism to abnormalities in the control of arousal state, rather than to cognitive problems.

BEHAVIOR THAT REFLECTS INTERNAL STATES

A closer scrutiny of the nature and determinants of repetitive movements will show how unlike they are to any static manifestation of focal brain damage. In the case of repetitive behaviors, there are many tantalizing clues that point toward the third alternative; bursts of repetitive actions act as partial *compensation* for core deficiencies in the brain organization of people with ASD. To expand on this direction of inquiry, we first consider the range of behaviors that are encompassed by repetitive movements. We then delineate their distribution across autistic and non-autistic syndromes, as well as normal people and even normal animals. Finally, we tentatively apply simplifying generalizations that might illuminate the atypical habitual behavior of people with autism to the diverse expressions of repetitive behavior that appear both across human disease categories and across species. This discussion is focused on the expression of repetitive behaviors in autism in sustained rhythmical movement routines.

DIAGNOSIS

Restricted or repetitive movements are included in a domain of behavior that is required for a diagnosis of autistic spectrum disorder (ASD) as per the *DSM-IV* and *DSM-IV-TR*. These movements distinguish people with ASD from people with other disorders not on the spectrum, not necessarily by qualitative differences, but by their frequency and intensity (e.g. Bodfish, Symonds, Parker, & Lewis, 2000). Behaviors that were characterized by a repetitive movement factor were significantly more prevalent in ASD than in other developmental disorders, or than they are at a younger age during typical development (Richler, Bishop, Kleinke, & Lord, 2006).

Whereas DSM-IV categories A and B for the diagnosis of autistic disorder refer to social interaction and communication respectively, the remaining category C overviews "restricted repetitive and stereotyped patterns of behavior, interests, and activities, as manifested by at least two of the following:

1. Encompassing preoccupation with one or more stereotyped and restricted patterns of interests that is abnormal either in intensity or focus:
2. Apparently inflexible adherence to specific, nonfunctional routines or rituals.
3. Stereotyped and repetitive motor mannerisms (e.g. hand or finger flapping or twisting, or complex whole-body movements).
4. Persistent preoccupation with parts of objects.

The Autism Diagnostic Interview-Revised (ADI-R) is organized into three sections: Language/Communication, Reciprocal Social Interactions and Restricted and Repetitive and Stereotypes Behaviors and Interests. The latter category comprises at least two factors, (Richler, Bishop Kleinke and Lord (2007), a repetitive sensorimotor (RSM) factor and an insistence on sameness (IS) factor.

Lewis and Bodfish (1998) tabulated normed instruments for the assessment of repetitive behaviors. Repetitive behaviors tend to abate with increasing age (Esbensen, Seltzer, Lam, & Bodfish, 2009). South et al. (2005) found high internal consistency between the components of category C, providing evidence for a unitary repetitive behaviors factor. The repetitive behaviors either have no reference to objects in the external world, or deal with objects in ways that are tangential to their known functions and familiar uses (e.g. lining things up rather than using them). McDougle et al. (1995) compared the thoughts and actions of people with ASD to those of people with obsessive-compulsive disorder. They concluded that, "Repetitive ordering; hoarding; telling or asking (trend); touching, tapping, or rubbing; and self-damaging or self-mutilating behavior occurred significantly more frequently in the autistic patients, whereas cleaning, checking, and counting behavior was less common in the autistic group than in the patients with obsessive-compulsive disorder" (p. 772)

Repetitive movements are only a subset of the abnormal postures and movements that appear sporadically in people with autism; for an exhaustive description of the dazzling profusion of aberrant movements in autism, see Ornitz (1973) and Leary and Hill (1996).

Repetitive behaviors are on their face self-involved. Although no one's subjective state is transparent to an observer, the observed activities appear to be reactive to internal states rather than to events and goals in the external environment. Most obviously self-centered is the propensity of autistic people to engage in repetitive movement routines, which, while not unique to their condition, are particularly obtrusive, prolonged, and detached from outside reality. For the duration of the bout of stereotypic behavior, the individual shuts out external events, and excludes any attempt at social interaction. Dwelling on fragmentary sensations, recurrent memories, stereotyped verbalizations, and esoteric preoccupations completes the picture of individuals whose attention is compulsively turned toward their inward reality. However, while people with obsessive-compulsive disorder readily express the anxiety that they attempt to control with ritualistic behavior, people with ASD offer no such explanation of what they do. An exception is the following meditation by the noted veterinary scientist, Temple Grandin, who characterizes her own Asperger perspective and that of others as follows: "the manner in which the person with autism spectrum disorders perceives his world (is that) his mind is one of absolutes, of thinking patterns that are rigid and repetitive, where minute details become focal points of obsessive attention and self-involvement takes precedence over exploration" (Grandin & Barron, 2005, p. 83). At the stereotypic motoric level as well as the subjective, this characterization also seems on point. Dr. Grandin's comment about self-involvement is particularly pertinent to this discussion. Perhaps their action patterns originated so early in life, that most other high-functioning persons on the spectrum cannot remember any different way of functioning and consider their own behavior and mental states to be mundane and unremarkable. Elsewhere, Dr. Grandin remarked that she herself is oversensitive to certain stimuli (touch hurts, sounds are deafening, faces are threatening), to the extent of being impelled to withdraw from them (Grandin, 1996). From the perspective of neuropsychology one would seek to characterize these internal states that so effectively draw attention away from the ordinary traffic of the outside world, and delineate the underlying structural and/or neurochemical deviations in the brain. How exactly might stereotypic movement routines arise from aberrant states of mind or feelings?

REPETITIVE MOVEMENTS

Action sequences can be structured or repetitive. If repetitive, the repetitions may be appropriate to a task (unscrewing a bottle, chopping wood, winding a watch, or applauding, for example). Alternatively, the repetitions may be unrelated to any instrumental action on the outside world. Apparently purposeless, such behavior may be targeted at the person's own state of mind.

Repetitive movements that are out of context are rhythmic, and maintain the same repetition rate throughout their duration. With the exception of body rocking, Ritvo et al. (1968) found the repetition rate to be the same for different movements and among different individuals with autism. They are not restricted to any one category of disorder. Like all manifestations of psychopathology, the aberrant repetitive movements of people with autism are exaggerations of movement routines that are observed in typically developing people, and particularly in typically developing infants and toddlers. No one type of action sequence is unique to individuals with autism. The fact that repetitive movements occur so broadly and vary so greatly in their form has to qualify accounts of the role they presumably play in self-regulation. But repetitive movements in normal development might constitute a microcosm of repetitive movements in autism and related disorders, occurring for similar reasons, although within much narrower boundary conditions.

Typically functioning adults do, on occasion, exhibit bursts of repetitive movements. These include finger-drumming and heel-tapping during states of nervous anticipation, pacing during anxious waiting, habitual self-touching when anxious or self-conscious (such as rearranging hair, adjusting tie, pulling down skirt, picking lint off clothing, scratching scalp, thumb sucking, or nose picking; Grant, 1968). Chewing on inedible objects is common, as chewing is stress reducing (Scholey et al., 2009), and is perceived as such by its practitioners, who include not only autistic individuals, but baseball coaches and players when they are on the sidelines during games.

Repetitive reciprocal kicking of the legs is universal among infants. Thelen (1981) reported that infants behave in rhythmically repetitive fashion much of their waking day, with peak incidence at 2 years of age. As children grow older, the action sequences gain in complexity (Militerni et al., 2002). Infants who are deprived of the expected level of social interaction with caretakers, as in poorly run orphanages, are well-known to be apt to develop social and repetitive autistic behaviors. These behaviors slowly dissipate when normal adult-child interactions are initiated.

Congenitally blind children are notable for their repetitive movements. Repetitive movements are also more frequent than in the general population in numerous other disorders, in some of which other autistic traits are expressed to a variable extent, such as fragile X syndrome, Rett syndrome, and mental retardation. For this reason, many commentators have argued that the repetitive movement phenotype is quite variable, and neither the origins nor the functions of the movements can be assumed to be the same across different disorders. That is undoubtedly correct. However, much of the etiological diversity of relevant disorders may be reduced to a functional convergence at the phenotypic level. At least some of the disorders, such as fragile X and Rett syndromes, often present with autistic-like states (not just isolated repetitive movements). Certainly, many mentally retarded people exhibit repetitive movements. They are particularly common in Down syndrome. The frequency of repetitive movements in mentally retarded children suggests that cortical control of subcortical motor centers failed to develop. Mental states that are conducive to stereotypical activities may occur across a wide range of etiologies and disease entities.

Even if they address comparable mental states, the form of the repetitive movements may differ between different disorders. For example, the stereotypies in Rett syndrome prominently feature hand posturing, which is not among the typical stereotypies in autism. No doubt there is a physiological explanation. But, like the stereotypies in autism, they occur against a background of heightened sympathetic arousal.

Prader-Willi syndrome is a genetic disorder of development that is characterized by multiple cognitive and behavioral abnormalities (Butler et al., 2004). The repetitive behaviors of people with Prader-Willi syndrome are more externalizing than those in fragile X, and include anger, aggression, and repeatedly asking questions to which they know the answer. These stand in opposition to the more internalizing behavior of people with fragile X, such as anxious and

repetitive behaviors, and sometimes motor stereotypies (Woodcock et al., 2009). But in both syndromes, the repetitive behaviors are usually precipitated by changes in routines or expectations. People react in different ways, but the precipitant is much the same: uncertainty, which they experience as aversive. The reactions, whatever form they take, are also much the same in that they are repetitive. Moss et al. (2009) investigated the prevalence and phenomenology of repetitive behavior in the following genetic syndromes: Cornelia de Lange, Cri-du-Chat, Angelman, fragile X, Prader-Willi, Lowe, and Smith-Magenis. The highest prevalence was in fragile X syndrome. Prader-Willi, Cri-du-Chat and Smith-Magenis syndromes exhibited unique profiles of repetitive behavior. Some neurotypical people engage in self-injury (Nock, 2009), a practice that is often classified among repetitive behaviors. Self-injury often is triggered by high aversive arousal, and people who injure themselves display elevated arousal (skin conductance) in response to a laboratory stressor.

TAXONOMY

Turner (1999) subdivided repetitive behaviors into "lower-order" actions that entail the repetition of specific movements, and "higher-order behaviors" that reflect the adherence to a rule, such as compulsions, rituals, and insistence that circumstances remain the same and focus of interest remains the same. Factor analyses have largely endorsed this conceptual subdivision, with repetitive movements constituting one factor, and resistance to change, insistence on sameness, circumscribed interests, or inflexible behavior adhering to some rule, constituting another (e.g., Lam, Bodfish, & Piven, 2008; Szatmari et al., 2006). The first factor comprises behaviors that attempt to compensate for overarousal that is already in place, whereas the second factor comprises behaviors that attempt to avoid arousal or fend it off (Kinsbourne, 1987). Autistic children's preference for working with limited sets, and their aversion to open-ended situations, implies that they are "more comfortable when the range of cues is limited. . . . Gaze avoidance, isolation and need for sameness obviously could be, and have often been, interpreted as being defensive, minimizing the possibility of encountering a novel and therefore arousing input" (p. 117). Anxiety would be the prime candidate for such a state.

Liss et al. (2006) reported the result of a cluster analysis on data derived from parent ratings on two scales that featured various anomalies of perception, attention, and action. The analysis revealed a cluster, which represented a pattern of overfocused attention and overreactivity, comprised of 43% of the sample. The authors discussed this outcome in relation to an overarousal hypothesis. This behavioral cluster applies across the autistic spectrum, ranging from its mildest manifestations in Asperger's disorder, and the even more borderline syndrome of overfocusing (Kinsbourne, 1991), to severe autistic disorder. Overfocused attention thus can coexist with cognitive deficits of various degrees of severity, but can also manifest in their absence or near-absence, as a disorder of cognitive style rather than cognitive impairment. Much milder than Asperger syndrome in terms of the considerable social impairment (see Table 1, page 710 in Szatmari et al., 1989), overfocusing as a freestanding disorder of cognitive style of autistic type can easily be mistaken for a variant of ADHD. It represents a distinct factor in the ASD complex, which could be due, in part if not wholly, to sympathetic overarousal. Overfocusing does feature repetitive movements. They are typically telltale unsustained bursts of rotation or flexion-extension (flapping), symmetrical at the wrists, elicited by uncertainty and anticipation of a positive or negative event.

This description seems as though it should indicate obvious pathology. However, in practice, the manifestations are often so mild that the child is taken to be merely obstinate and insufficiently disciplined. In the classroom, he comes to the teacher's attention because he does not respect transitions, but insists on completing the current project in what some might consider excessive detail. He seems "not to hear" instructions that are contrary to his current goal. Teachers usually consider that the child has an attention deficit with an oppositional trait. The child may be very bright, and thought to be an eccentric, gifted person. Attempts to change overfocusers' behavior by threats or exhortations fail. Referred to pediatricians, these children are diagnosed with ADHD or ADD, and often treated with stimulant drugs, to which they respond partially at best, and only when the dose is small. Overfocusers' behavior is characterized in detail in Kinsbourne (1991). A 25-item rating scale describing the essence of overfocusing is also found in Kinsbourne (1991), and Table 19-1. Based on

currently available norms, the criterial score for the diagnosis of overfocusing is 40. For more information on clinical use of this scale, please contact Kinsbourne (see Table 19-1 for contact information).

Liss et al. (2006) studied their sample of children with ASD on this scale, which was completed by the parents of 144 children with ASD, mean age 8.5 years, 80% male. Ratings were on a 4-point scale (0–3), such that the maximum score would be 75.

Factor analysis revealed three strong factors: sensitivity/perseveration/social withdrawal, fixations, and inattentiveness. The sample yielded four clusters. Cluster 1 (n = 17), who were high-functioning, had a mean score of 61, well above Kinsbourne's cutoff of 40 for overfocusing. A second cluster (N = 50), had a score of 30, which was non-diagnostic of overfocusing. The third cluster (n = 44) comprised low-functioning children, with mean scores of 45. The fourth group (n = 47) was described as mildly overfocused, with a score of 49. Thus, 75% of this ASD sample belonged to clusters that were marked, mildly or strongly, by overfocusing behaviors.

The salient finding of this study for present purposes is that the cluster of overfocused behaviors, which appears in isolation in children diagnosed as overfocusers, characterized children with ASD at all levels of cognitive function. Thus, overfocusers exemplify one factor in the ASD symptom complex. This factor may appear in isolation, or in association with a wide range of other autistic characteristics and along an axis of levels of functioning, from borderline mainstream to very low.

Overfocusing puts into particularly sharp relief a question that pertains to the great range of levels of function in ASD. Is autism a syndrome of deviant behavior, or is it a syndrome of deviant plus or minus delayed (i.e., impaired or underdeveloped) behavior? Should the sometimes very severe mental retardation that attends the autistic behavior of many individuals be considered a comorbid disorder, or should it all be dubbed autism because it is happening in the same child? For this discussion, this question is relevant to the further question: What is the scope of the theoretical understanding for which we strive? Is it to explicate the deviant behaviors termed autistic, or also the mental retardation found in many people with autism? In the present discussion the goal is the former—to cast light on the deviant autistic behavior (and wait for separate explanation of the so-called "delays").

Table 19-1 Kinsbourne Overfocusing Scale

Please rate the child's behavior on each item listed below over the last six months. Please circle only one of the following ratings:
0 = behavior occurs not at all; 1 = it occurs sometimes; 2 = it occurs pretty often; 3 = it occurs very often

Prefers sameness, upset by sudden changes in routine.	0	1	2	3
Socially withdrawn and unskilled, especially with strangers.	0	1	2	3
Works slowly and may be compulsive.	0	1	2	3
Resists being hurried or told to do more than one thing at a time.	0	1	2	3
Organization is difficult (for instance, organizing schoolwork, keeping up with assignments, cleaning up room), especially at the beginning of tasks.	0	1	2	3
Often seems preoccupied with his/her own thoughts.	0	1	2	3
Is bothered by loud noises.	0	1	2	3
Unusually sensitive hearing.	0	1	2	3
Has a narrow scope of interest.	0	1	2	3
Prefers to focus on one thing at a time.	0	1	2	3
Explores topics of own choosing in depth.	0	1	2	3
Resists shifting attention or changing activities on someone else's timetable.	0	1	2	3
Worrier, anxious.	0	1	2	3
Overly sensitive to negative feedback.	0	1	2	3
May interpret a parent's frown as indicating anger or a teacher's scolding as directed specifically at him/her.	0	1	2	3
Has trouble "remembering" (for instance, remembering more than one instruction at a time, classroom assignments, chores).	0	1	2	3
Is quietly oppositional, stubborn.	0	1	2	3
May have explosive outbursts, and takes a considerable time to cool off.	0	1	2	3
Performs better on tasks and in situations after getting used to them (for instance, at the end of school year than at beginning, or after trying a task one or more times).	0	1	2	3
May keep the same posture of facial expression for unusually long periods of time.	0	1	2	3
Is frightened of anticipated new or intense experiences (for instance, meeting new people or undertaking new activities).	0	1	2	3
Becomes preoccupied with impending, anticipated events.	0	1	2	3
Engages in repetitive movements (for instance, tapping, self-touching).	0	1	2	3
Often sits "hunched over" when working.	0	1	2	3
Is shy.	0	1	2	3

Contact: M. Kinsbourne, MD, 80 Fifth Avenue, #704, NY, NY 10011; kinsbouM@newschool.edu

DISPLACEMENT BEHAVIORS IN ANIMALS

Cognitive theories of autism in general have failed to explain, or even address, the repetitive movement component of autism. Perhaps the core of the aberrant behaviors in ASD (if there is a core) is sensory and autonomic, and not cognitive at all. What do repetitive movements have in common across the various situations and conditions under which they occur? We consider repetitive behaviors that are reactive to dysphoric states, in animals and humans, both in neurotypical and in autistic individuals.

Bursts of self-directed repetitive movements, which ethologists have termed *displacement behaviors* (Hinde, 1970), are provoked in animals by response conflict, frustration, thwarting, and novelty, all of which are presumably stressful. Some habitual species-specific behavior cannot be carried out, some goal cannot be attained, some attempt at self-regulation cannot be implemented. Stereotypies are virtually unknown in free-living wild animals, and do not occur in wild-caught adult animals.

They generally arise from the frustration of behaviors that the animals are highly motivated to perform: burrowing, nesting, foraging, hiding, escaping, gnawing, and exploring (Balcombe, 2006). They are high frequency, but non-urgent, behaviors that relate to bodily largely homeostatic needs. In the event of certain stresses, they are "displaced" from their usual role in the behavioral repertoire. (See Kinsbourne, 1980, for a review.) They are stress reducing, and ultimately they usher in sleep (Delius, 1969); in the course of the movement routine, cortisol levels drop, heart rate declines. Troisi (2002) concluded,

"In both nonhuman primates and human subjects, displacement behavior appears in situations characterized by social tension and is likely to reflect increased autonomic arousal. Pharmacological studies of nonhuman primates have shown that anxiogenic compounds increase displacement behavior and anxiolytic drugs decrease it. Ethological studies of healthy persons and psychiatric patients during interviews have found that increased displacement behavior not only correlates with a subjective feeling state of anxiety and negative affect but also gives more veridical information about the subject's emotional state than verbal statements and facial expression."(page 47)

Naturally, displacement behaviors are observed with great frequency in domestic animals, and in wild animals that are confined in cages (as well as in laboratory experiments). When they occur, they may consume many hours of the day.

Displacement routines take on species-specific forms, which are not necessarily similar to those observed in typical and in autistic humans. However, whether they occur in humans or animals, the movements have in common the fact that they are without perceptible purpose in the context in which they occur, though they are well represented within the animal's response repertoire (e.g. pecking by pigeons in the absence of grain, out-of-context grooming by cats). Confinement is a potent trigger for displacement behavior. Wild animals pace repetitively in confined spaces. Floeter and Greenough (1979) reported that monkeys that were reared in isolation rocked and engaged in stereotyped behavior. However, monkeys that were kept in single cages from which they could see and hear other monkeys, and where they could

play for four hours daily with another monkey, exhibited little abnormal behavior. Dogs placed in isolated cages become hyperexcitable (Melzack and Burns, 1965). Korda (1978) kept kittens blindfolded from birth onwards. One third of the kittens developed stereotyped walking by the fourth month of life. In the general human population, analogous behaviors emerge under conditions of state anxiety when goals are in sight, but not necessarily attainable. In these instances, when the individual does not approach the goal, it is not because he is at rest, but because the perceived risks of action outweigh the perceived benefits.

Berkson et al. (1963) reported that chimpanzees exhibit their highest level of displacement behaviors when they are confined in enclosed cubicles, and when they are exposed to fear-inducing stimuli. The authors conclude that displacement behaviors are directly associated with the level of arousal. The lowest level of arousal occurs when the chimpanzees are free to manipulate objects. The level of sympathetic arousal thus rises under two contrasting conditions: When animals are overstimulated, as in fear-provoking circumstances, and when they are thwarted, as in confinement. Both conditions raise sympathetic tone. For instance, Dickens (2009) reported that as wild starlings entered captivity, their heart rate remained elevated for several days, and their sympathetic tone exerted more control than their vagal tone over their heart rate. Bachmann et al. (2003) reported that horses that engaged in crib-biting routines had a higher basal heart rate in response to thwarting than those who did not. Their basal vagal tone was lower and their basal sympathetic tone was higher. The crib-biters were thought to be more sensitive to stress.

Garner et al. (2003) demonstrated that parrots that engage in stereotypic behavior also perseverate on a cognitive task. They assert relevance to humans. "As stereotypies in captive animals develop in response to the captive environment, these results also emphasize the role that the environment may play in eliciting or exacerbating stereotypy in human patients" (p. 125). Displacement behaviors in animals clearly occur in response to various stresses, including confinement. Do autistic people restrict their arena of exploration because they are afraid to enlarge it? Do they cause their own confinement through self-imposed restrictions, deprive themselves of the benefits of human interaction, and then react to that self-imposed confinement with compensatory displacement activity?

DISPLACEMENT BEHAVIORS IN HUMANS

The insistence on sameness is an obvious instance of efforts to minimize potential exposure to environmental stresses, Avoiding face-to-face interactions with eye contact is another (Chapter 18). Circumscribed interests and inflexibly rule-bound behavior are yet others. Indeed, autistic children have a substantially more limited range of exploration than typical controls, and spend less time exploring (Pierce, 2009). In this respect their self-imposed confinement puts autistic children on a par with the socially deprived or blind infant. The amount of exploration and of repetitive movements are both significantly correlated with the extent of cerebellar vermis hypoplasia of lobules VI-VII.

Infants implement their purposes largely indirectly, by summoning the attention and enlisting the help of the caretaker. When neurotypical infants are denied normal social interaction with caretakers, repetitive movements become conspicuous. Infants respond adversely to lack of human interaction, at least in part due to not being hugged and cuddled. Babies reared in institutions fail to thrive unless they are cuddled. Tactile and kinesthetic stimulation has a beneficial effect on premature infants (White & Labara, 1976, Solkoff et al. 1969). Provence and Lipton (1962) found that institutionalized babies started to rock at 5 to 8 months of age. Even earlier, they had become stiff and resistant when they were held. Tactile stimulation had a beneficial effect on these infants, even when it was undertaken much later. Thelen (1981) showed that stereotypies were at their maximum when infants were confined in baby seats and when they were not in direct contact with their caretakers. The movements were at a minimum when the child was rocked, bounced, or carried, in direct contact with a caretaker. A small number of typically developing children exhibit autistic-like stereotypies. However, they are transitory and disappear before the age of 5 years. Typically developing children have been observed to swing their legs rhythmically in the classroom when they are confronted with problems that they find difficult, and their heart rate decreases (Soussignan & Koch, 1985).

Repetitive movements called "blindisms," seen in congenitally blind children, can be similarly conceived of as resulting from the much smaller than usual action space that results from the absence of targets in the visual field (Fazzi et al., 1999). Mentally retarded adults exhibited the most stereotypies when they were confined in unfamiliar spaces, and the least when they were given opportunity for independent action (Berkson & Mason, 1963). Mentally retarded people could be diverted from stereotypic behavior by being offered alternative activities, or by being handed objects. They would not reach for objects spontaneously while engaged in rocking. When mentally retarded people were confined in unfamiliar spaces, they were highly aroused (Davis et al., 1969). A restricted environment can render both people and animals more sensitive to stimuli.

RITUALS

Repetitive movement routines become more complex as the individual matures, and they are more complex in relatively high-functioning individuals. Though they are more complex still, ritualistic stereotypical behaviors are also multiply repeated, and occur in the general population, especially in young children, and with greater frequency in autism and other internalizing psychopathologies, notably obsessive compulsive disorder. In addition to their culturally determined social functions when they are performed in public, rituals are a means for allaying the anxiety that comes with uncertainty. Rituals are motivated by apprehension as to dangers not yet in evidence (Boyer & Lienard, 2006). The tendency to engage in rituals is correlated with anxiety or fearful traits (Zohar & Felz, 2006. Laver (1975) explained, "Ritual turns on how agents objectify the normal by turning uncertainties into manageable risk" (p. 217). Some rituals were accompanied by obsessive behavior (Russell, 2006). While the rituals of people with autism are far simpler and more rigid even than most of the rituals found in the general population, and lack their social implications, they could also be attempts to cope with the stress of uncertainty, by counteracting it with the admittedly fanciful powers of superstitious behavior. Without attributing elaborate states of mind to people with autism, the basic uncertainty counteracting and anxiety reducing function of rituals seems also to apply.

ANXIETY IN AUTISM

Schultz et al. (2000) comment that people with autism are very frequently abnormally fearful and anxious.

A growing literature notes that anxiety is frequently, if not invariably, observed in people with ASD (Bellini, 2004; Muris, Steerneman, Merckelbach, Holdrinet, & Meesters, 1998,). Baron et al. (2006) offer an extended multiauthored discussion of stress and anxiety in ASD, and the consequences for treatment. In a chapter in that volume, Romanczyk and Gillis (2006) highlight the near ubiquity of anxiety in ASD, and explain its psychophysiological concomitants. Though sometimes described as comorbid with autism (Muris et al., 1998), that term is not helpful when the apparently comorbid condition is nearly always present. Instead anxiety seems to be an integral part of autistic symptomatology. Steingard et al. (1997) describe the surge of anxiety that individuals with ASD experience when their need for sameness is infringed upon, and when they are in transition from one arena of functioning to another. Thus these cardinal symptoms of autistic disorders are reactions to anxiety generated by novel events. Steingard et al. (1997) discuss the anxiolytic benefits of sertraline in ASD.

Fear is a negatively valenced arousal state in response to an apparent threat, whereas anxiety is a state of negative arousal to an anticipated threat. Commenting on the amygdala theory of autism, Amaral and Corbett (2003) argued that the amygdala is not essential for social behavior, but does "have a role in detecting threats in the environment" (p. 185). Indeed, the central nucleus of the amygdala is described as the central mechanism of fear (LeDoux Iwata, Cicchetti, & Reiss, 1988). It can impact social behavior by generating anxiety when it is overactive. LeDoux and colleagues state, "anxiety is an extremely common feature of the autism spectrum disorders" (p. 184), and cite studies to that effect. Neuroimaging studies indicate that the amygdala shows heightened activity during anxious states. Removal of the amygdala in non-human primates produced "animals that were less fearful of inanimate objects as well as other monkeys." Overarousal of the amygdala might provide a neurological substrate for excessive fearfulness and anxiety in ASD. Anxiety is also frequent in people with obsessive-compulsive disorder, and they too have high levels of arousal, which their compulsive behaviors serve to reduce (Walton and Mather 1964, Russell, Mataix-Cols, Anson, & Murphy, 2005).

Anxiety-related traits are fundamental, enduring, and continuously distributed dimensions of normal human personality (Lesch et al. 1996). Children within the mainstream who are shy (behaviorally inhibited to the unfamiliar) have been described as maintaining higher tonic sympathetic arousal than children who are not shy, and been credited with greater reactivity of the amygdala to uncertainty (Kagan, Reznick, & Snidman, 1987). This trait is related to a serotonin transporter polymorphism (Arbelle et al., 2003), which had also been related to autism (Brune et al., 2006; Klauck et al., 1997). The anxious reaction to uncertainty of autistic children appears to lie on a continuum with a lesser form of that tendency in shy children, and both groups share associations to the same serotonin genetic variant. In both shy and autistic children, sympathetic nervous system activity and the reactivity of the amygdala are heightened.

OVERAROUSAL IN AUTISM

Animals exhibit displacement behaviors when they are highly aroused. Is this also the case for repetitive behaviors by humans with autism? When the autistic brain is overaroused, because the individual perceives threat or is in an excited state (for instance, while unwrapping a present), she feels dysphoric and anxious. This "defense reaction" leads to restriction of sensory input, turning attention inward such that through sensory rejection, the organism becomes oblivious of external events. The child will avoid potential sources of stimulation, and protect himself against the arousing effects of unexpected motion and change. He will engage in solitary occupations and become engrossed in unusual topics of interest, seek to isolate himself, and minimize eye contact and other human interaction until the brain activation level has subsided. To make this happen, the child engages in stereotypical and manneristic behaviors, which are to be understood as being dearousing maneuvers, analogous to displacement behaviors in animals, though longer lasting (Kinsbourne 1980, 1987). As they continue, stereotypies lower neural excitation levels. Repetitive movements have been described as having a calming effect on children with autism (Willemsen-Swinkels, Buitelaar, Dekker, & van Engeland, 1998). However, while they run their course, they discourage and even block human interaction, further exacerbating the social isolation and imperviousness to learning of the autistic individual.

Hutt, Hutt, Lee, and Ounsted (1965) introduced the overarousal model for autism. They reported that stereotypies increased with increased task complexity and with environmental novelty. Hutt and Hutt (1965) observed autistic children under four conditions of increasing complexity. Stereotyped behavior increased as complexity increased. They also reported desynchronized EEGs indicative of heightened arousal, which became somewhat attenuated after a bout of stereotypies. They resorted to the construct of overarousal to explain major aspects of autistic behavior. Numerous subsequent studies have found support for the view that autistic children are overaroused. Stroh and Buick (1968) found that stereotypies increased when novelty or complexity were introduced into the environment. Cohen and Johnson (1977) concluded, "Some autistic children characteristically may be in a state of sensory rejection associated with generally higher levels of arousal or defense against environmental bombardment" (p. 561).

Kootz et al. (1982) found psychophysiological indications that lower-functioning autistic children behaved in ways that were consistent with

sensory rejection . . . consistent with their need to preserve sameness. Autistic children appear to be more sensitive to the environment and may use behavioral strategies, such as avoiding environmental change and social interaction, as methods of reducing further disorganizing experiences. Disturbances in filtering environmental stimulation and modulating response to novelty may be part of the basic pathology of autism that becomes apparent during the 1st year of life." (p. 185)

Raymaekers et al. (2004) gave adults with high-functioning autism syndrome a go/no-go reaction time task. The adults with autism were as successful as controls in inhibiting false positive go responses at relatively slow rates of stimulus presentation, but under the more arousing conditions of fast presentation they made significantly more false positive errors than controls. The authors concluded that the adults with autism could inhibit responses as long as they were not in a high arousal state, under which condition inhibition becomes problematic.

Zentall and Zentall (1983) attributed to autistic children a heightened tendency to avoid stimulation so as to moderate their own arousal levels. Their extreme withdrawal is the overriding feature of the autism. Zentall and Zentall cited evidence that any repetitive monotonous stimulation will attenuate arousing responses. Thus the behavior either

directly or indirectly blocks or avoids the processing of distal or intense stimulation. Indeed, "time-out," generally considered to be punishing, sometimes has a reinforcing effect on autistic children. If, however, they are subjected to inescapable arousing conditions, they switch their defensive reaction from flight to fight, with outbursts of intractably disruptive behavior. Ming et al. (2005) reported reduced parasympathetic activity in children with autism, resulting in unrestrained sympathetic activity. Low basal parasympathetic tone results in hyperactive heart rate and blood pressure responses. Autistic children often have sluggish pupillary responses, cold and clammy extremities, urinary retention and disturbed sleep, all signs that are suggestive of autonomic dysfunction.

Baron et al. (2006) reviewed evidence for overarousal in autistic spectrum disorder. It was particularly the higher-functioning individual who seemed overaroused. A minority seemed lethargic and underaroused, generally those who were most intellectually handicapped. Liss et al. (2006) arrived at a similar conclusion based on the results of cluster analysis of parents' responses to questionnaires about their children with ASD. The parents were most likely to describe their higher functioning children as overaroused. Goodwin et al. (2006) documented a high basal heart rate in an ASD group, 20 beats per minute higher on average than controls. "The high basal heart rate was interpreted as due to increased general arousal, and the reduced responsivity to the potential stressors was taken to be evidence for autonomic defensiveness or sensory rejection in an attempt to escape threatening stimuli" ((Lacey, 1967, p. 53). It reflects increased sympathetic tone, which results either from sympathetic arousal or relaxation of the vagal brake, or both. Ming et al. (2004, 2005) and Hirstein et al. (2001) reported similar findings.

OVERAROUSAL IN OTHER CONDITIONS

Autism and autistic features are commonly seen in fragile X syndrome (Cornish et al., 2004), and fragile X syndrome is characterized by repetitive movements (Turk & Graham, 1997). According to Hagerman, Rivera, and Hagerman (2008), psychophysiological studies in fragile X have demonstrated hyperarousal of the autonomic system with sensory stimuli, particularly enhancement of the sympathetic response, as measured by the sweat response in electrodermal studies and by decreased vagal tone. This was particularly the case in individuals with fragile X who were also autistic. The sympathetic hyperarousal was coupled with stress and anxiety and the enhanced release of cortisol. Miller et al. (1999) conducted a study of phasic electrodermal responses to sensory stimuli by people with fragile X syndrome. They observed exaggerated enhancement of responses attributable to sympathetic hyperarousal. This finding was consistent with clinical reports and previous research that documented tonic hyperarousal. Investigating the typical gaze avoidance that people with fragile X syndrome display during social interactions, Hall et al. (2009) observed higher than expected heart rates, lower vagal tone, and lower heart rate variability during social interaction in fragile X syndrome. They considered their observations to be consistent with gaze avoidance actuated by anxiety. Roberts et al. (2006) observed low and inconstant vagal tone in boys with fragile X syndrome, associated with hyperarousal. Cohen (2005) related inconstant arousal modulation in people with fragile X syndrome to difficulties in acquiring and utilizing cognitive skills.

Rett syndrome (Cooper & Kerr, 1998) is characterized by its hand-wringing mannerisms and a mix of other stereotypies as well (Temudo et al., 2008). Julu et al. (1997) found an unstable sympathetic predominance in cardiorespiratory control in Rett syndrome. Glaze (2005) reported cortical hyperexcitability in Rett syndrome, as indicated by evoked potential and EEG studies. So both people with Fragile X and with Rett syndrome, who exhibit repetitive movements and other autistic features, such as social withdrawal, but are not classically autistic, also showed evidence of sympathetic overarousal. Repetitive movements, stereotypies, and mannerisms are also frequent in schizophrenia, as is a high basal level of autonomic arousal and vulnerability to stress (Dawson, Nuechterlein, Schell, Gitlin, & Ventura, 1994). People with schizophrenia and those who overdose on amphetamines are known to be susceptible to overarousal. They describe their repetitive movements as having a calming effect (Fox, 1971). People with autism may also derive a calming effect from their repetitive movements. Post-traumatic stress disorder is also characterized by a tonic state of overarousal (Cohen, 2009).

MECHANISM OF OVERAROUSAL

Further evidence for overarousal in autism derives from studies of eye contact. Nichols and Champness (1971) studied GSR responses when typical adults were instructed to make eye contact with another person, or to avert their gaze. Both the frequency and the amplitude of GSR responses were greater during eye contact. Dalton et al. (2005) studied "gaze fixation," or the failure of individuals with autism to make and maintain eye contact, in relation to the level of activation of the amygdala. They found that unlike neurotypical individuals, the autistic individuals exhibited strong activation in the amygdala while they were fixating gaze on other people. "Amygdala hyperactivation in the autistic group . . . is specific to the amount of eye fixation" (p. 524). They conclude: "we suggest that within the autistic group, eye fixation is associated with negatively valenced arousal, mediated by activation in limbic regions such as the amygdala. We propose that diminished gaze fixation within the autistic group may facilitate reduction of overarousal to social stimuli" (p. 524). The argument that people with ASD have no interest in their fellow humans, and therefore fail to engage them in face-to-face eye contact, is not compatible with these findings. Indeed, it is well-known that, while disengaging from confrontation with others, autistic people are apt to keep them in their peripheral field of vision (Hirstein, Iverson, & Ramachandran, 2001), indicating a continuing interpersonal interest, rather than indifference.

Rubenstein and Merzenich (2003) are recent exponents of the overactivation/overarousal model of ASD. They suggest, "These children have noisy and unstable cortical networks. This type of cortex will lead to broad ranging abnormalities in perception, memory and cognition and motor control" (p. 256). Furthermore, "Higher-than normal noise in cortical processes . . . could plausibly account, for example, for the strong aversive reactions to auditory, tactile and visual stimuli that are commonly recorded in autistic individuals" (p. 260). Belmonte et al. (2003) likewise referred to "neural systems prone to noise and cross-talk, resulting in hyperarousal and reduced selectivity" (p. 651).

Describing stereotypic and repetitive movements in children with autism, Baumann (1999) noted, "They appear most often among autistic children that are mentally retarded, and are progressively less apparent with increased IQ. It has been noted, however, that among normally intelligent autistic children stereotypies may be exacerbated during periods of stress on into adulthood" (p. 602). Referring to stereotypies in children in residential care, Baumann (1999) remarked, "These stereotypies appear to be associated with concentration, arousal, frustration, boredom and distraction and seem to stabilize the child's level of arousal in monotonous, frustrating or overwhelming situations. Given these observations, it is possible that stereotypic behavior may be playing a similar role for autistic children" (p. 602). Also consistent with the theory that autism is characterized by a liability to hyperarousal is the finding that children who have recovered from autism nonetheless still are apt to have anxiety disorders (Helt et al., 2008).

Gal et al. (2002) exposed children with autism to stimuli that were neutral, aversive, or attractive. Stereotypic movements increase following the onset of an aversive stimulus, and they decrease after an attractive stimulus. The children also initiated or increased stereotyped movements during periods of neutral stimulation. "Neutral" may not appear so to autistic children. Toichi and Kamio (2003) and Ming (2004) reported that children with ASD find it aversive to be maintained under "neutral" stimulation.

REPETITIVE MOVEMENTS WHILE "AT REST"

Repetitive movements can also arise in contexts that would not normally be regarded as arousing. One possibility is that if these movement routines turn out to be reinforcing in minimizing the subjective concomitants of stress, they could become habitual even in nonstressful neutral conditions. This might particularly occur in mentally handicapped individuals, who have only a limited motor repertoire from which to select their actions. Another frequent interpretation is that the autistic individuals are underaroused, and that the repetitive movements raise the arousal level to within an optimal range. This notion may have arisen from a misunderstanding of what Lovaas et al. (1987) meant by "self-stimulation"; in fact, they meant perceptual reinforcement (see below). Unlike normal children, autistic children may experience overarousal in the resting (i.e., behaviorally inactive) state. Under quieter circumstances, movements often called "stimming" are observed. May stimming reflect inner overarousal in a quiet environment, and be performed for its calming effect?

Toichi and Kamio (2003) reported a paradoxical heightened autonomic response of autistic children when at "rest," rather than only when active. The finding "suggests that some autistic subjects were more stressed under 'resting' conditions than while performing mechanical or repetitive mental tasks" (Abstract, page 417). "Some individuals with autism may not be adequately relaxed under seemingly 'resting' conditions" and "they might obtain relaxation by devoting themselves to a certain activity" (p. 423). The authors refer the reader to several studies that "reported sensory rejection patterns in cardiovascular response to environmental stimuli, which seems consistent with the hyperarousal view of autism" (p. 424). Ming et al. (2004) stated: "It is often inferred that many autistic patients are withdrawn to themselves with little or no interaction with the outside environment around them. The patients are labeled as not interested . . . This simplistic interpretation of autism requires further clinical evaluation" (p. 519). In a single case study of an individual with autism who had been labeled noncompliant, and who appeared to be unresponsive to requests to exert pressure by gripping a handgrip device, Ming et al. (2004) showed that increases in sympathetic tone betrayed the fact that the patient was trying to comply by exerting mental effort. Correspondingly, Ming et al. (2005) reported increased sympathetic tone in autistic children although they were at rest ("baseline").

What can one infer about a person with autism who appears to be at rest? Only that they are not currently interacting with the environment. Despite the alternative interpretations discussed above, two further possibilities remain. One is that a subset of individuals with ASD, perhaps those who are most severely cognitively handicapped, does tend toward pathologically low rather than high arousal, for whatever reason. The other is that sympathetic tone, though typically exaggerated in most people with autism, is also in dyscontrol and liable to extreme fluctuation.

Recent neuroimaging findings have delineated a neural "default network," which consists of structures in the brain that are activated when individuals are not engaged in active, goal-directed interaction with external targets (Buckner, Andrews-Hanna, & Schacter, 2008), and are apparently at rest. This network includes the medial prefrontal cortex, rostral anterior cingulate, posterior cingulate, and precuneus. Normally these structures become deactivated when the individual engages in cognitively demanding tasks. The role of the default network has been variously characterized as subserving spontaneous mental activity without external stimulation, remembering one's autobiographical past or projecting it into the future, inferring others' mental states, self-referential processing, and moral decision making. Given the massive amount of neuronal circuitry in structures that constitute the network, many or all of these attributions may well be correct (Spreng, Mar, & Kim, 2009). They have in common inwardly directed attention. The network deactivates when attention turns outward during task performance. Kennedy et al. (2006) discovered that in the autistic brain, the default network fails to deactivate when the individual engages in cognitive performance. One interpretation would be that autistic people have persistently inwardly directed attention, which continues to be the case even when they are active within their surroundings. Severe anxiety could draw attention inward.

Zaid et al. (2002) reported that the ventromedial prefrontal cortex (VMPFC), a component of the default network, is activated when negative emotion is linked with autonomic responses. They comment,

> The extent to which VMPFC activity changes during overtly stressful situations is closely related to anxiety. Normally the VMPFC rCBF decreases when subjects move from a resting state to a more active attention demanding cognitive state. The extent of this decrease is inversely correlated with the amount of anxiety experienced by subjects in the more active state . . . Those subjects who fail to lower activity in the VMPFC experience the greatest level of transient anxiety when anticipating a potentially aversive stimulus." (p. 2453; see also Nagal et al. 2004)

They also point out that the retrosplenial region, another component of the default network, frequently activates during exposure to negative mood factors both in t,he presence and absence of overtly anxiety evoking stimuli. Therefore, the persistent activation of the default network during task performance in autism indicates the presence of both phasic and tonic negative mood states, notably anxiety. In summary, the failure of the default network to deactivate as expected in autism suggests that the individual is in a continual state of anxiety, both when anxiety-provoking stimuli are present as well as when they are not.

Lombardo et al. (2009) compared the functional effect of mentalizing about oneself with mentalizing about the Queen of England. Unlike in controls, the activity level of VMPFC was the same under both conditions in the autistic subjects. They infer that these autistic subjects have difficulty with self-representation. An alternative notion would be that their "default" inwardly turned attention persists even when the Queen is concerned.

The individual who is "at rest" could be in a state of anguished emotional arousal for all we know, but simply not exhibiting any outward telltale signs of arousal. Children with autism are perhaps more overaroused when "at rest," and doing something repetitively may make them more comfortable than doing nothing. The case studies reviewed above teach us that the initial arousal levels can be high when the individual with autism is in a quiescent state. The repetitive movements may have the function of lowering high arousal levels.

NEUROBIOLOGY OF THE DEAROUSING EFFECT OF REPETITIVE MOVEMENTS

Stress and Dopamine

As classically explained by Cannon (1929), the visceral and hormonal changes that accompany fear and rage reactions are adaptations that prepare an organism to cope with an emergency, and specifically to prepare the individual for the extreme muscular exertion that is called for by the "fight-or-flight" response to a perceived threat, or to overcome stress. This preparatory reflex is mediated by arousal of the sympathetic nervous system. It includes visceral components, notably cardiovascular rearrangements that shift blood flow to structures which are essential for the preservation of the individual. Correspondingly, homeostatic processes are temporarily inhibited (Hilton, 1982).

The stress system has the following components: Corticotropin-releasing hormones (CRH), locus coeruleus–norepinephrine (LC-NE)-autonomic systems and their peripheral effectors, the pituitary-adrenal axis, and the limbs of the autonomic system. Stress activates the brain's monoaminergic systems, increasing serotonin, norepinephrine, and dopamine (DA) neurotransmission. The CNR and LC/Ne systems stimulate arousal and attention, as well as the mesocorticolimbic dopaminergic system (Tsigos & Chrousos, (2002). The dopaminergic projections from the ventral tegmentum to the prefrontal cortex (PFC) (Gao et al. 2001) are particularly sensitive to the activating effect of stress, and the mesoaccumbens and mesostriatal dopamine systems are also activated. The medial PFC, particularly on the right, regulates the neuroendocrine (hypothalamic-pituitary-adrenal) and autonomic (vagal) responses to stress, enabling coping behaviors (Sullivan & Gratton, 1999). Hilz et al. (2006) reported that the right ventromedial PFC tonically inhibits sympathetic arousal. Injury to this area of the PFC releases a heightened sympathetic stress response with anxiety among its consequences. Nagal et al. (2004) summarize the situation as follows: "activity within the VMPFC and OFC reflects a dynamic between exteroceptive and interoceptive deployment of attention" (p. 243).

Arnstein (2009) reviewed evidence that stress inactivates the PFC, such that control of behavior switches to the basal ganglia. This switch from PFC to basal ganglia control facilitates highly overlearned familiar behaviors, at the expense of more complex cognitions, including working memory. If this switch occurs in autistic people as a stress response, the inhibition of PFC would explain why they are so often found to have disproportionate difficulty on tests of executive function. Berridge et al. (1999) remark, "The near-obligatory nature of the PFC DA response in stress has made this response a primary index of stress" (p. 188). Ernst et al. (1997) reported diminished medial prefrontal dopaminergic activity in autistic children. Anxiolytics, such as the benzodiazepines, attenuate the stressor-induced PFC DA response, whereas anxiogenic agents increase the DA response. Stereotypic activities are linked to excessive dopamine activity in the nigrostriatal circuitry. Robbins and Koob (1980) reported that an experimental analogue of displacement behavior in the rat depended upon the integrity of the mesolimbic dopaminergic projection to the nucleus accumbens and olfactory tubercle. Lesions of the mesolimbic dopamine system disrupt displacement behavior.

In summary, the following sequence of events may be involved in the stress response and its attenuation by repetitive movements: Stress causes activation of mesolimbic dopamine circuitry, the projection of which inhibits the functioning of the VMPFC. The VMPFC loses control of the amygdala and sympathetic overarousal results. Concurrently, control of behavior switches to the basal ganglia, which generate simple overlearned behaviors. The repetitive movements moderate the dopamine effect in VMPCF, thus reducing arousal levels.

Serotonin agonists have beneficial effects on human stereotypies, and opiate agonists have effects that are more complex. It appears that, in both cases, the effects are mediated through input to basal ganglia dopaminergic structures (Lewis & Bodfish, 1998).

Stress and Cortisol

Focusing on the striking propensity of people with autism to avoid novel situations, Corbett et al. (2006) tested the functioning of the hypothalamic-pituitary-adrenal axis, a system that is sensitive to stress, in children with ASD and matched controls. The children were subjected to a mild stress, and cortisol levels in salivary samples were repeatedly measured. Corbett et al. (2006) found no difference between the groups in baseline level, but 8 of 12 children with ASD responded to the novel situation with sharp increases in cortisol within 20 minutes, which had not yet dropped back to control levels after one hour.

Stress and Repetitive Behaviors

The general stress response is not detected in experiments in which stressed rats had the opportunity to chew on or gnaw inedible objects. As noted earlier, chewing is known to attenuate a variety of physiological indices of stress, in humans as well as experimental animals. This repetitive activity is considered to be a coping response. Berridge et al. (1999) studied the effect of chewing in rats and mice, measuring the levels of DA and its catabolites as indices of DA turnover. The DA response to aversive novelty was maximal in the right PFC. Concurrent chewing attenuated this response. The authors remark,

> Chewing and other relatively stereotyped behavioral responses have long been noted to occur under behaviorally activating, or stressful conditions. Examples of these behaviors include chewing grooming, fighting and stimulant-induced stereotypy. These so-called displacement activities were originally noted because they appeared to occur out of context, elicited by environmental stimuli not 'normally' associated with that specific behavioral response." (p. 195)

They continue by remarking that chewing and fighting have been shown to attenuate indices of stress/arousal. Thus "some displacement behaviors may not, in fact, be inappropriate. Rather, these behaviors may serve to modify certain physiological responses to stress" (p. 195).

Berridge et al.'s (1999) animal model provides the neurobiology that underlies the dearousing effect of autistic stereotypies (Kinsbourne, 1980). The results also explain the well-documented amphetamine stereotypies that result when experimental animals are overdosed with dopamine agonists such as amphetamine (Randrup & Munkvad, 1967). The rats pass through a stage of increased repetitive locomotion as the drug takes effect, and at peak effect they relentlessly, and with a mechanically precise repetition rate, gnaw the wire netting of the cage. The drug toxicity elicits the defensive reaction and an intense form of displacement behavior in response. Amphetamine stereotypies in rats depend on the integrity of the corpus striatum (Fog, Randrup, & Pakkenberg, 1970).

Ueda et al. (2003) report that the expectancy of unpleasant stimuli produces activation in the right PFC, right amygdala, and left anterior cingulate cortex. (Pleasant stimuli activate structures on the opposite sides.) The amygdala, via direct connections with pontine autonomic nuclei, is further implicated in translating psychological stress into bodily arousal. Other studies, reviewed by Shackman et al. (2009), have indicated that the human right PFC is sensitive to uncertainty and ambiguity, relative to signals generated elsewhere (amygdala, anterior cingulate, etc.). If the individual cannot immediately resolve the cause of the uncertainty, she continues to be vigilant in order to gather the information that would resolve the uncertainty. This sequence of events represents a function of the behavioral inhibition system (BIS) and is in itself a physiological reaction that, as has been remarked, is also found in the general populatio. The BIS is "responsible for generating anxiety and organizing defensive responses to threat and punishment" (Shackman, McMenamin, Maxwell, Greischar, & Davidson, 2009, p. 1500). The consequent tonic activity in the right dorsolateral PFC may be moderated by repetitive activity.

The "fear network" involves activation of the anterior cingulate, amygdala, hippocampus, and periaqueductal gray matter (Mathews, Yiend, & Lawrence, 2004). Santini et al. (2004) offer evidence for the role of medial prefrontal cortex in the mechanism of fear extinction through measurement of local protein synthesis "the mPFC is a critical storage site for extinction memory, rather than simply a pathway for expression of extinction" (p. 5704). Schultz et al. (2000) explain how loss of VMPCF control handicaps the extinction of the fear response when the cause for fear is no longer in evidence.

> The medial prefrontal cortex may be essential to the "turning off" of the amygdala fear systems when they are no longer necessary. When medial prefrontal cortex malfunctions, the uninformed amygdala continues to send out its cry of alarm because it has not received the safety signal from the prefrontal cortex indicating that the situation is no longer fearful . . .If the amygdala is "stuck on" because of inadequate medial prefrontal input, a continuous tonic, anxiety-producing output from the central nucleus of the amygdala directly to autonomic centers of the hypothalamus will result. In this state, although arousal and general anxiety may increase, the individual is unable to mount a normal emotional response to fear and other emotional stimuli because the circuit may be already nearly fully activated. Since the amygdala circuitry is already fully engaged, the affected individual is not able to appreciate and respond to new social-emotional events (pp. 28–29)

Correspondingly, Goodwin et al. (2006) found that children with autism, although they had a tonically elevated heart rate, did not react with heart rate changes to events that would have induced cardiac acceleration in typical children. Heart rate accelerates for internal observation, and decelerates for external observation (Porges & Raskin, 1969, Tursky, Schwartz, & Crider, 1970).

The paraventricular nucleus of the hypothalamus is integral to the generation of a defensive response. It is in dynamic balance with other hypothalamic structures. The neural substrate of fear is turned off by activation of the paraventricular nucleus, which results in the production of oxytocin and leads to profound bradycardia through activation of the parasympathetic system (Darlington, Miyamoto, Keil, & Dallman, 1989). Oxytocin controls autonomic arousal by exciting the central nucleus of the amygdala, thus exerting an inhibitory effect on the basolateral nucleus and so modulating the autonomic expression of fear (Huber, Veinante, & Stoop 2005), enhancing trust and generosity instead, and reducing the disturbed feelings that are evoked by stressful situations (Rodriguez et al. 2009). Oxytocin is anxiolytic (Ring et al., 2006). Administering oxytocin reduced repetitive behaviors in adults with autistic and Asperger's disorders (Hollander et al., 2003), presumably because it activates parasympathetic opposition to sympathetic overarousal.

Differential activation of sympathetic arousal by gender may account for the highly reliable preponderance of males among people with autism, 4 to 1 or greater (Scott, Baron-Cohen, Bolton, & Brayne, 2002). According to Dart et al. (2002), males tend to sympathetic dominance, whereas females tend to parasympathetic dominance. Evans et al. (2001) arrived at the same conclusion, and referred to additional studies that corroborated this gender difference. According to Hinojosa-Laborde et al. (2002) "in females, the regulation of the SNS is altered such that sympatho-adrenal activation is attenuated or sympatho-adrenal inhibition is augmented" (p. 122). Knight et al. (2002) noted that gender differences in aggression appear to be a function of corresponding differences in the ability to regulate arousal. The extent to which males were more aggressive than females increased as contexts became more emotionally arousing. Kimmerly et al. (2009) were able to relate this sex difference to differential activation of control mechanisms at the cerebral level. Thus the 4 to 1 predominance of males in ASD could be due wholly or in part to their greater baseline degree of sympathetic activation or readiness to activate fight-flight responses as compared to females. Knickmeyer et al. (2005) and Auyeung et al. (2009) proposed that people with autism were in fact analogous to "extreme males" (see Chapter 17), and argued for the importance of fetal testosterone in the genesis of ASD, presumably through its effect on fetal neurological development. Knickmeyer and colleagues pointed to evidence that females with autism have enhanced production of androgens. Testosterone has the effect of activating the synthesis of noradrenaline, and reducing its clearance (Dart, Du, & Kingwell, 2002), which elevates sympathetic tone, whereas estrogen has the reverse effect. So testosterone (and estrogen) may be the mechanisms for the greater male propensity to sympathetic arousal, and therefore for the preponderance of males among people with ASD. This greater propensity for sympathetic arousal on the part of males may also be why males with autism, though on average less handicapped cognitively than females with

autism, have a greater incidence of restricted, repetitive, and stereotyped behavior (Hartley & Sikora, 2009).

Behaviors that are analogous to the hypothesized predisposition to fearfulness in autism are observed in a well-developed animal model of autism, in the rat. The dam is treated with an injection of valproic acid (VPA) during her pregnancy. Valproic acid is an antiepileptic agent that is apt to cause autism in the offspring of epileptic women treated with VPA during pregnancy. This animal model features repetitive behavior among other "autistoid" traits (Markram, Rinaldi, La Mendola, Sandi, & Markram, 2008). Fear memories were stronger, more generalized, and more difficult to extinguish in VPA-treated offspring than in control animals. The authors suggested a hyperreactive amygdala as the underlying pathology; when activated, the amygdala unleashes a suite of defensive reactions, including autonomic arousal.

DIRECT MEASUREMENTS OF AROUSAL

Given the significant circumstantial evidence for a self-regulatory role for repetitive movements, one would expect to find such unequivocal direct evidence for hyperarousal among the majority of individuals with autism. Indeed, Dawson and Lewy (1989) stated, "The behavioral and physiological evidence suggests that that autism is associated with aversive responses to novelty and with chronic high levels of autonomic arousal (e.g. high heart rate) . . . If novelty detectors of the cortex are oversensitive to changes in the environment, this may well result in a aversive response or a failure to respond to that stimulus" (p. 163). However, Rogers and Ozonoff (2005), in a careful survey of the literature, listed a range of studies with dependent variables that are relevant to generalized cerebral arousal. Only one study documented hyperarousal (James & Barry, 1980) and two others arrived at the opposite conclusion. Rogers and Ozonoff concluded, "There is little evidence of general baseline overarousal in subjects with autism" (p. XX).

On the other hand, there is consistent evidence for sympathetic overarousal, at least phasic, from work already cited by Baron, Goodwin, Ming and Hirstein, and their respective colleagues. Hirstein et al. (2001) attributed the inconsistent results of research on the arousal levels of people with autism to the failure of investigators to consider the impact of repetitive movements on the child's level of arousal at the time of measurement. "A child may not show chronically hyperactive sympathetic activity . . . because of the tremendous capacity the children have for reducing autonomic activity via repetitive and/or somaesthetic activity . . . (the) child has either hyperactive or hypoactive sympathetic activity depending on what the child is doing" (1886). Indeed, they continue, "The large reduction in sympathetic activity that we observed could explain why autistic children so relentlessly seek out self-stimulatory actions" (p. 1886). They see the limbic-autonomic axis as bestowing markers of significance on experiences. If the system is overactive, significance is promiscuously bestowed, (over-meaningfulness, as discussed by Shapiro, 1973), and if the system fluctuates, the attaching of significance becomes chaotic and unmanageable. In either case, the child may shut the system down, with predictable adverse consequences for learning.

The negative studies that Rogers and Ozonoff (2005) cited in several earlier negative reports, referenced by Kinsbourne (1987), call into question the pervasive presence of sympathetic arousal in ASD. The striking contradictions between studies indicate the need for repeated measures in the same children. Immediately after a bout of repetitive movements, a child's arousal level might temporarily approximate the mainstream level, or drop even lower. Alternatively, overarousal might be phasic, rather than tonic, in some or many of the subjects. Also, as Zentall and Zentall (1983) emphasized, autistic children may have a low and narrow range of optimal stimulation, such that levels of arousal that fall within the normative mainstream may be higher than they can tolerate. Group studies may be clouded by heterogeneity of subjects with respect to their liability to overarousal.

More direct measurement of the state of the cortex may resolve the issue. Moreover, more direct appraisal of the cortical overarousal hypothesis has become technologically possible. Frye and Beauchamp (2009) measured the level of cortical excitation in high-functioning autistic individuals directly by means of magnetoencephalograohy; they reported that the cortex was hyperexcitable. The inconsistency of findings across psychophysiological studies could be due to the fact that the experimental measurement conditions could themselves be perceived as stressful by the participants, to a variable degree.

RECIPROCITY BETWEEN SOCIAL ENGAGEMENT AND DEFENSE/IMMOBILIZATION

What is the role of the sympathetic state (and its remedies) in autism spectrum disorders? Specifically, does the sympatheticotonus have explanatory value for aspects of autism beyond repetitive movements, and other defensive readjustments to avoid sources of overstimulation? According to one theory, the sympathetic predominance has serious consequences for the other side of the autistic coin—namely, the dearth of social interaction. Parasympathetic predominance has the opposite effects—an example of this is the beneficial effect of oxytocin.

Porges (2004) has hypothesized that a fundamental reciprocity exists between social and defensive states, which is intertwined with three distinct states of the autonomic nervous system (Porges refers to this as the "polyvagal theory"). These are: *social engagement*, linked to facial expression, vocalization, and listening; *mobilization*, linked to the fight-or-flight response, and; *immobilization*, linked to behavioral shutdown. The social engagement system depends on the myelinated vagus nerve. This component of the parasympathetic nervous system fosters calm behavior by inhibiting the sympathetic system and the hypothalamic-pituitary axis. The mobilization system depends on the sympathetic nervous system, and the immobilization system depends on the unmyelinated dorsal vagus nerve. Porges suggests that autism, "in which compromised social behavior is a diagnostic feature"... "is associated with neurobiological states that foster defensive and not social behaviors" (p. 7), with defensive states including both mobilization and immobilization.

The brain stem nuclei of the cranial nerves—which control eyelid opening, emotional expression, extracting the human voice from background noise (by tensing the muscles that approximate the ossicles in the middle ear), mastication, prosody, and head turning and tilting (orienting)—foster social engagement. These nuclei, of the 5th, 6th, 7th, 9th, 10th, 11th, and 12th nerves, communicate with an inhibitory neural system that slows heart rate, lowers blood pressure, and reduces arousal to promote calm states. These nuclei, in turn, are controlled by the frontal cortex. According to Porges, difficulty in holding a gaze, extraction of human voice, maintenance of facial expression, and regulation of hand gestures and prosody are common features of individuals with autism. Congenital anomalies of these nuclei have been implicated in the genesis of autism (Rodier, Ingram, Tisdale, Nelson, & Romano, 1996). Interestingly, the cranial nerve nuclei that control the facial maneuvers of social engagement are incapacitated for congenital reasons in Moebius syndrome (Gillberg & Stauffenberg, 1989); about one-third of Moebius patients are autistic.

When social engagement is compromised, the resulting changes in autonomic state support a range of adaptive defensive behaviors, mediated by the sympathetic system and the dorsal vagal system. This makes risk assessment the central priority. Structures that appraise risk include areas of temporal cortex. If the degree of risk is appraised to be high, the periaqueductal grey matter and the central nucleus of the amygdala become activated. In this case, the physiological state limits the range of social behavior.

The relevance of Porges' model to this discussion is that it points to a neurobiological mechanism that could identify the prevalent state in autism as defensive, and has that state compete with, and suppress, a contrasting state of openness to social engagement. The sympathetic hyperarousal would then either result in, or be accounted for by, the social deficiencies of autism. In other words, a primary failure of the emergence of the social engagement system might disinhibit sympathetic hyperarousal, or alternatively, sympathetic hyperarousal might overwhelm the social engagement system. Either way, the person with autism would experience dysphoric arousals, which he could readily identify subjectively as anticipatory fear or dread.

Gergely (2001) presented a novel mechanism to account for many features of autism. He summarized research that showed that neurotypical infants initially have a preference for perfect response-contingent stimulation, but show greater interest in slightly imperfect contingent displays after they are about 3 months old. Autistic children continue to exhibit a preference for perfectly response-contingent displays at an age at which neurotypical infants have long since switched their preference. He infers a "contingency detection module," which typically switches from perfect to imperfect at 3 months of age, but fails to switch in the case of an autistic child. He offers explanations for other components of the autistic symptom complex based on this hypothesized preference for perfect contingency, which in nature is only to be attained when the infant experiences the results of her own movements.

These are provocative findings, but yet another uncorroborated static brain module may not be needed to explain them. The young infant learns to identify her body parts by determining which of the sensations that she experiences are due to self-movement, and which sensations implicate the outside world (Kinsbourne, 2001). Once the infant has successfully determined the range and limits of the body parts, and as the infant's capabilities for exploring the ambient space mature, so attention is more readily also focused on the environment. Inspection of Gergely's (2001) data shows that both autistic and control children in fact spend about the same amount of time on observing imperfectly contingent events. The difference resides in the extent of attention to perfect contingencies. The greater interest of the autistic children in perfect contingencies can be ascribed to the aforementioned proclivity toward directing attention inward. One reason why repetitive movements appear to be calming and reinforcing in autism may be because they result in the familiar, reassuring, and therefore de-arousing sensation of perfect response contingency.

If, as argued above, the autonomic state determines the subjective feeling (Critchley, 2005), the sympathetic arousal would be experienced as free-floating fear. This, in turn, would engender behavioral inhibition, avoidance reactions, and hypervigilance in the search for the nonexistent external source of the experienced threat. The "fear network" involves activation of the anterior cingulate, amygdala, hippocampus, and periaqueductal gray matter (Mathews et al., 2004). Lowenstein et al. (2001) conceptualized risk assessment as "risk as feeling." When emotional reactions to risky situations diverge from cognitive reactions, the cognitive appraisal does not necessarily dispel the feeling that there is risk, and it is the emotion that often drives the behavior. The tuning of the perceptual systems toward inferring threat during uncertainty would recruit the mobilization (sympathetic) system.

MINIMIZING AROUSAL BY ELIMINATING OR ATTENUATING STEREOTYPIES BY BEHAVIORAL MEANS

Repetitive movements are recognized to be *automatically reinforcing*. Lovaas et al. (1987) introduced this term into the autism literature to indicate that the behavior was self–stimulating in the sense of being self–reinforcing. That is to say, flapping and spinning are their own reward; the sensation that the movement itself elicits reinforces the movements. Lovaas et al. (1987) and subsequent behaviorist students of repetitive behaviors have not hazarded a guess as to the precise nature of the reinforcing subjective sensation that the movements engender. The studies reviewed above lead me to surmise that it is the sensation of calming in the face of overarousal that makes repetitive behaviors so persuasively reinforcing and so hard to extinguish. Parenthetically, when behaviorists refer to self- stimulation, or "stimming," they are not referring to an attempt generally to increase arousal levels, but only to the self-generation of a rewarding sensory experience. Lovaas et al. (1987) explained how the fact that the behavior is itself the reinforcement explains accounts for it being so durable and so effective in blocking new learning.

If that experience is of a calming effect, and if the anxiety of hyperarousal is indeed a significant contributor to the genesis of autistic behavior, then eliminating these compensatory movements should engender an observable aggravation of the child's condition. Does it? There is no medical literature that directly addresses this question in a controlled manner. Instead, there are a number of single-case studies that present various means for controlling the tendency to generate repetitive movements (reviewed by Cunningham & Schreibman, 2008). Various means are applied, including positive and negative reinforcement, and offering the child a more attractive alternative occupation. These methods sometimes succeed in eliminating, or at least attenuating, the movement tendency, and the studies typically conclude with an anecdotal statement that the child became better, did not change, or became worse. Meaningful long-term follow-up is lacking. We do not know how long the movements remain controlled, or in many cases even whether they remained controlled outside the test situation. If they do, we are not informed of any beneficial or adverse long-term effects. We do not know whether the anxiety is better, worse, or the same as before, and we have no published report of arousal levels after treatment as compared to before treatment. In the present state of knowledge, the effect of counteracting stereotypies has not been delineated in a manner that could cast light on the hypothesis that they are compensatory dearousing activities.

MINIMIZING AROUSAL WITH DRUGS

The pharmacological treatment of repetitive movements in ASD, which largely centers on serotonin uptake inhibitors and opioid antagonists, is beyond the scope of this discussion (see Rapp & Vollmer, 2005). However, it would be of interest, if it were possible, to assist people with autism in switching away from sympathetic overarousal, instead of seeking to arrest the downstream consequences of the arousal with dopamine antagonists or serotonin agonists. The potential use of oxytocin has been mentioned. More directly, one might use beta-adrenergic blocking agents such as propranolol. These drugs curb aggression (Haspel, 1995), and there is pilot data that suggests "subtler changes in speech and socialization" in adults with autism (Ratey et al., 1987, p. 439). In an "open-label" study, Ratey and colleagues gave propranolol or nadolol, both beta-blockers, to eight autistic adults. They reported dramatic improvement in two of the participants, and all eight manifested better attention spans and fewer impulsive, aggressive, and ritualistic behaviors. Six improved their social skills, and sought more human contact. They improved in communicative speech and seemed more aware of how others felt. Ratey et al. (1987) suggested that people with autism are in chronic hyperarousal, which is ameliorated by the beta-blockers. Beversdorf et al. (2008) reported that propranolol generally impairs verbal problem-solving, but improves it in ASD. Sporadic publications attest to the benefits of alpha-2 adrenergic agonists for people with autism; these drugs show improvements in hyperactivity, impulsiveness, and inattention in several categories of developmental disorder, including pervasive developmental disorders (Scahill, 2009). These agents are thought to reduce arousal by decreasing the rate of firing of neurons in locus coeruleus. They include clonidine, which binds to all three subtypes of alpha-2 receptors, and guanfacine, which binds more selectively to alpha 2-a receptors, and enhances prefrontal function.

Although the above scatter of findings is somewhat suggestive, it does not seem that any anti-anxiety drug treatment has radically ameliorated the autistic pattern of behavior as such. It may be that the sympathetic arousal component, though significant, is only a part of a more general overactivation of the forebrain, as Hutt et al. (1965) originally, and Rubenstein and Merzenich (2003) more recently, have suggested.

CONCLUSION

Taking the totality of the available information into consideration, there is little doubt that autistic repetitive activities serve self-regulation; since they are presumably reinforcing, over time additional motivators for these behaviors may be acquired (Willemsen-Swinkels et al. 1998), to the point that they become functionally autonomous. Their primary function is to moderate the arousal levels of autistic people, who perceive circumstances as being taxing and potentially overwhelming. Evidence for their role in counteracting sympathetic hyperarousal is gathering momentum. The intimate neurochemistry and regional brain activations that are involved are coming into focus on the basis of animal studies.

The fact that repetitive behaviors are compensatory does not necessarily make them optimally adaptive. Indeed, studies of successful behavioral attenuation of these movement patterns have not reported symptom substitution, or any exacerbation of the autistic condition (albeit, these studies are typically narrowly focused, and lacking in follow-up). At the very least, a less disabling alternative form of compensation would be beneficial. Repetitive movement routines obstruct human interaction and isolate the child from learning, as well as socializing influences. A logical target for therapy would be the hyperarousal that occasions the stereotypies, or the environmental circumstances that fuel the arousal. A further benefit would follow if the not-yet-realized remedy extended to thought processes. Presumably the restricted range of interests and need for sameness extends beyond repetitive action to repetitive thought. If so, the freedom to extend the range of ideas might be highly adaptive.

The larger question is whether the lowering of arousal levels has an impact, alone or in interaction with other factors, beyond the individual's autonomic well-being, on other major elements of the autistic syndrome, ranging from need for sameness, restricted interests, and sensory deviances, to disorders of social interaction, language, and communication. It is not difficult to derive any or all of these features (except perhaps delayed language development), from a radical shift to defensive reactions mediated by increased sympathetic tone and related cortical overactivation (Kinsbourne, 1987). On the other hand, trials of anxiolytic agents that downregulated sympathetic arousal have not reported remission in the autistic disorder as such, only benefits for anxiety, self–injury, aggression and the like. However, these studies have not addressed the possible benefits for autism in any systematic manner. To test these predictions, one might begin by examining people with autism when they are overaroused and when they are within normal bounds of arousal. When people with autism are not overaroused, would their performance on perceptual, cognitive and even language tasks improve, and would they exhibit more nearly normal behavior? To what extent is the autistic syndrome itself a consequence of near-constant overarousal? These questions would begin to be addressed, were one to study the same individual both in the overaroused and the less-aroused state, with well-validated test instruments and experimental procedures the address all the chief elements of autism. The less-aroused state might occur due to spontaneous downward fluctuation when state is unstable, after the deployment of stereotypical behaviors by the autistic individual, or through the use of beta-blockers and allied agents which are known to reduce sympathetic arousal.

The preceding discussion has focused on autonomic arousal. However, central arousal in autism, as indicated by desynchronization in the EEG, which was first reported by Hutt, Hutt, Lee and Ounsted (1965), has not been extensively studied. Overarousal may not be limited to increased sympathetic tone, but may also characterize the functioning of other parts of the forebrain, and other arousal systems (Jones, 2003). Glutamatergic neurons in the reticular formation stimulate cortical activity by exciting the projecting neurons of the nonspecific thalamo-cortical projection. Cholinergic, noradrenergic, serotonergic, and histaminergic systems independently enhance cortical activation. Writing about locus coeruleus noradrenergic neurons, Jones (2003) states: "These neurons may accordingly correspond to a central sympathetic system that stimulates and enhances cortical activation and arousal, particularly during periods of stress, but is not necessary for the simple occurrence of these during waking" (p. 441). Samuels and Szabadi (2008) explain how amygdala activation leads to sympathetic arousal, and also leads to locus coeruleus activation, which in turn projects norepinephrine to activate wide areas of cerebral cortex, activating widespread cortical neuronal systems in addition to the sympathetic arousal.

If, as seems possible, the basis of the autism is neuroinflammation (Pardo-Villamizar, 2008), a process that results in the widespread release of excess of the excitatory neurotransmitter glutamate, the brain's excitation/inhibition ratio would shift upward. A wide range of variation in how much of the brain is involved might account for the perplexing association of autistic behavior with cognitive skills that range from the superior to the profoundly impaired, as well as for motor anomalies that are just as diverse and wide-ranging. Referring to the well-established early cerebral overgrowth in at least half of infants with early presenting autism, Courchesne and Pierce (2005) suggested that, on account of neuroinflammatory processes, the developing prefrontal cortex becomes internally overconnected, but externally underconnected, diminishing its influence both horizontally, on posterior areas of the cortex, and vertically, on the amygdala and basal ganglia, among other areas. If these hypothesized processes lead to cognitive and emotional alterations, then one would not expect antidotes to sympathetic overarousal to suffice in correcting autistic constraints in behavior. Repetitive movements may mitigate sympathetic arousal, but not affect overactivation of cognitive central neuronal systems.

Repetitive and restricted behaviors are such a pervasive component of autistic behavior that their presence is mandatory for diagnosing autism. This may be because it is an enduring, even primary, necessity for people with autism to regulate their errant arousal levels, and is something that they find hard to do. Lowering arousal levels by repetitive movements can be a time-consuming endeavor, which leaves little opportunity to turn one's attention outward to one's fellow humans and the world beyond the self. This is, perhaps, an aspect of the dynamics of the autistic experience. But even if overarousal mediates much of the anomalous nature of autistic behavior, the pattern of brain dysfunction that renders everyday situations of human experience so unmanageably overarousing for people with autism remains to be definitively established.

References

Amaral, D. G., & Corbett, B. A. (2003). The amygdala, autism and anxiety. In G. Bock & J. Goode (Eds.), *Autism: Neural basis and treatment possibilities (Novartis Foundation Symposium)* (pp. 177–187). Chichester UK; Wiley.

Arbelle, S., Benjamin, J., Golin, M., Kremer, I., Belmaker, R. H., & Ebstein, R. P. (2003). Relation of shyness in grade school children to the genotype for the long form of the serotonin promoter region polymorphism. *American Journal of Psychiatry, 160,* 671–676.

Arnstein, A. F. T. (2009). Stress signaling pathways that impair prefrontal cortex structure and function. *Nature Reviews Neuroscience, 10,* 410–422.

Auyeung, B., Wheelwright, S., Allison, C., Atkinson, M., Samarawickrema, N., & Baron-Cohen, S. (2009). The children's empathy quotient and systematizing quotient: Sex differences in typical development and in autistic spectrum conditions. *Journal of Autism and Developmental Disorders, 38,* 1230–1240.

Bachmann, I., Bernasconi, P., Herrmann, R., Weishaupt, M. A. & Stauffacher, M. (2003). Behavioral and physiological responses to an acute stressor in crib-biting and control horses. *Applied Animal Behaviour Science, 82,* 297–311.

Bailey, A., Phillips, W., & Rutter, M. (1996). Autism, Towards an integration of clinical, genetic, neuropsychological and neurobiological perspectives. *Journal of Child Psychology and Psychiatry and Allied Disciplines, 37,* 89–126.

Balcombe, J. P. (2006). Laboratory environments and rodents' behavioral needs, A review. *Laboratory Animals, 40,* 217–235.

Banich, M. T. (2009). Executive function, The search for an integrated account. *Current Directions in Psychological Science, 19,* 89–93.

Baron, M. G., Groden, J., Groden, G., & Lipsitt, L. P. (2006). *Stress and coping in autism.* New York: Oxford University Press.

Baron-Cohen, S., Leslie, A. M., & Frith, U. (1985). Does the autistic child have a "theory of mind"? *Cognition, 21,* 37–46.

Bauman, M. L. (1999). Motor dysfunction in autism. In A. B. Joseph & R. R. Young (Eds.), *Movement disorders in neurology and neuropsychiatry* (2nd ed.). (pp. 601–605). Oxford, Blackwell.

Bellini, S. (2004). Social skills deficits and anxiety in high-functioning adolescents with autism spectrum disorders. *Focus on Autism and Other Developmental Disorders, 19,* 78–86.

Belmonte, M. K., & Yurgelun-Todd, D. A. (2003). Functional anatomy of impaired selective attention and compensatory processing in autism. *Cognitive Brain Research, 17,* 651–664.

Berkson, G., & Mason, W. A. (1963). Stereotyped movements of mental defectives, III. Situation effects. *American Journal of Mental Deficiency, 68,* 409–412.

Berridge, C. W., Mitton, E., Clark, W., & Roth, R. H. (1999). Engagement in a non-escape (displacement). behavior elicits a selective and lateralized suppression of frontal cortical dopaminergic utilization in stress. *Synapse, 32,* 187–197.

Beversdorf, D. Q., Carpenter, A. L., Miller, R. F., Cios, J. S., & Hillier, A. (2008). Effect of propranolol on verbal problem solving in autism spectrum disorder. *Neurocase, 14,* 378–383.

Bodfish, J. W., Symons, F. J., Parker, D. E., & Lewis, M. H. (2000). Varieties of repetitive behavior in autism, Comparison to mental retardation. *Journal of Autism and Developmental Disorders, 39,* 237–243.

Boyer, P., & Lienard, P. (2006). Why ritualized behavior? Precaution systems and action parsing in developmental, pathological and cultural rituals. *Behavioral and Brain Sciences, 29,* 596–613.

Brune, C. W., Kim, S-J., Salt, J., Leventhal, B. L., Lord, C., & Cook, E. H. (2006). 5–HTTLPRgenotype-specific phenotype in children and adolescents with autism. *American Journal of Psychiatry, 163,* 2148–2156.

Buckner, R. L., Andrews-Hanna, J. R., & Schacter, D. L. (2008). The brain's default network, Anatomy, function and relevance to disease. *Annals of the New York Academy of Sciences, 1124,* 1–38.

Butler, M. G., Bittel, D. C., Kibiryeva, N., Talebizadeh, Z., & Thompson, T. (2004). Behavioral differences among subjects with Prader-Willi syndrome and type I or type II deletion and maternal disomy. *Pediatrics, 113,* 565–557.

Cannon, W. B. (1929). *Bodily changes in pain, hunger, fear and rage* (2nd ed.). New York: Appleton.

Cohen, H. (2009). Analysis of heart rate variability in posttraumatic stress disorder patients in response to a trauma-related reminder. *Biological Psychiatry, 44,* 1054–1059.

Cohen, D. J., & Johnson, W. T. (1977). Cardiovascular correlates of attention in normal and psychiatrically disturbed children, Blood pressure peripheral blood flow and peripheral vascular resistance. *Archives of General Psychiatry, 34,* 561–567.

Cohen, I. (2005). An analysis of the role of hyperarousal in the learning and behavior of fragile X males. *Mental Retardation and Developmental Disabilities Reviews, 4,* 286–291.

Cooper, R. A., & Kerr, A. M. (1998). Rett syndrome, Critical examination of clinical features, serial EEG and video-monitoring in understanding and management. *European Journal of Paediatric Neurology, 2,* 1127–1135.

Corbett, B. A., Mendoza, S., Abdullah, M., Wegelin, J. A., & Levine, S. (2006). Cortisol circadian rhythms and response to stress in children with autism. *Psychoneuroendocrinology, 31,* 59–68.

Cornish, K. M., Turk, J., Wilding, J., Sudhalyter, V., Muniz, F., Kooy, F., & Hagerman, R. (2004). Annotation: Deconstructing the attention deficit in fragile X syndrome: a developmental neuropsychological approach. *Journal of Child Psychology and Psychiatry, 54,* 1042–1053.

Courchesne, E., & Pierce, K. (2005). Why the frontal cortex in autism might be talking only to itself, local over-connectivity but long-distance disconnection. *Current Opinion in Neurobiology, 15,* 225–230.

Critchley, H. D. (2005). Neural mechanisms of autonomic affective and cognitive integration. *Journal of Comparative Neurology, 493,* 154–166.

Cunningham, A. B., & Schreibman, L. (2008). Stereotypy in autism, The importance of function. *Research in Autism Spectrum Disease, 2,* 469–479.

Dalton, K. M., Nacewicz, B. M., Johnstone, T., Schaefer, H. S., Gernsbacher, M. A., Goldsmith, H. H., Alexander, A. L., & Davidson, R.J. (2005). Gaze fixation and the neural circuitry of face processing in autism. *Nature Neuroscience, 8,* 519–526.

Damasio, A. R., & Maurer, R. G. (1978). A neurological model for childhood autism. *Archives of Neurology, 35,* 777–786.

Darlington, D. N., Miyamoto, M., Keil, L. C., & Dallman, M. F. (1989). Paraventricular stimulation with glutamate elicits bradycardia and pituitary responses. *Integrative and Comparative Physiology, 256,* 112–119.

Dart, A. M., Du, X-J, & Kingwell, B. A. (2002). Gender, sex hormones and autonomic nervous control of the cardiovascular system. *Cardiovascular Research, 53,* 678–687.

Davis, K. V., Sprague, R. L., & Werry, J. S. (1969). Stereotyped behavior and activity level in severe retardates, The effects of drugs. *American Journal of Mental Deficiency, 73,* 721–727.

Dawson, G. & Lewy, A. (1989). Reciprocal cortical-subcortical influences in autism. The role of attentional mechanisms. In G. Dawson (Ed.). *Autism, nature, diagnosis and treatment* (pp. 144–173). New York: Guilford Press.

Dawson, M. E., Nuechterlein, K. H., Schell, A. M., Gitlin, M., & Ventura, J. (1994). Autonomic abnormalities in schizophrenia, trait or state indicators? *Archives of General Psychiatry, 51,* 813–824.

Delius, J. D. (1969). Irrelevant behavior, information processing and arousal homeostasis. *Psychol. Forsch, 33,* 165–185.

Dickens, M. J. (2009). Wild European starlings (Sturnusvulgaris). adjust to captivity with sustained sympathetic nervous system drive and a reduced fight-or-flight response. *Physiological and Biochemical Zoology, 82,* 603–610.

Ernst, M., Zametkin, A. J., Matochik, J. A., Pascualvaca, D., & Cohen, R. M. (1997). Reduced medial prefrontal dopaminergic activity in autistic children. *Lancet, 350,* 638.

Esbensen, A. J., Seltzer, M. M., Lam, K. S. L., & Bodfish, T. W. (2009). Age-related differences in restricted repetitive behaviors in autism spectrum disorders. *Journal of Autism and Developmental Disorders, 39,* 57–66.

Evans, J. M., Ziegler, M. G., Patwardhan, A. R., Ott, J. B., Kim, C. S., Leonelli, F., & Knapp, C. F. (2001). Gender differences in autonomic cardiovascular regulation, spectral, hormonal and hemodynamic indexes. *Journal of Applied Physiology, 98,* 2611–2618.

Fazzi, E., Lanners, J., Danova, S., Ferrari-Ginevra, O., Gheza, C., Luparia, A., Balottin, U., & Lanzi, G. (1999). Stereotyped behaviours in blind children. *Brain and Development, 21,* 522–528.

Floeter, M. K., & Greenough, W. T. (1979). Cerebellar plasticity, Modification of Purkinje cellstructure by differential rearing in monkeys. *Science, 206,* 227–229.

Fog, R., Randrup, A., & Pakkenberg, H. (1970). Lesions in corpus striatum and cortex of rat brains and the effect on pharmacologically induced stereotyped, aggressive and cataleptic behavior. *Psychopharmacology, 18,* 346–356.

Fox, M. W. (1971). Psychopathology in man and lower animals. *Journal of the American Veterinary Association, 159,* 66–77.

Frye, R. E., & Beauchamp, M. S. (2009). Receptive language organization in high-functioning autism. *Journal of Child Neurology, 24,* 231–236.

Gal, E., Dyck, M., & Passmore, A. (2002). Sensory differences and stereotyped movements in children with autism. *Behavior Change, 19,* 207–219.

Garner, J. P., Meehan, C. L., & Mench, J. A. (2003). Stereotypies in caged parrots, schizophrenia and autism, evidence for a common mechanism. *Behavioral Brain Research, 145,* 125–134.

Gergely, G. (2001). The obscure object of desire. "Nearly but clearly not, like me.", Contingency preference in normal children versus children with autism. *Bulletin of the Menninger Clinic, 65,* 411–426.

Gillberg, C., & Steffenburg, S. (1989). Autistic behavior in Moebius syndrome. *Acta Paediatrica, 78,* 314–316.

Glaze, D. G. (2005). Neurophysiology of Rett syndrome. *Journal of Child Neurology, 20,* 740–746.

Goodwin, M. S., Groden, J., Velicer, W. F., Lipsitt, L. P., Baron, M. G., Hofmann, S. G., & Groden, G. (2006). Cardiovascular arousal in individuals with autism. *Focus on Autism and other Developmental Disabilities. 21,* 100–123.

Grandin, T. (1996). *Thinking in pictures.* New York: Vintage.

Grandin, T., & Barron, S. (2005). *The unwritten rules of social relationships.* Arlington, Texas: Future Horizons.

Grant, E. C. (1968). An ethological description of non-verbal behavior during interviews. *British Journal of Medical Psychology, 41,* 177–186.

Hagerman, R. J., Rivera, S. M., & Hagerman, P. J. (2008). The fragile X family of disorders, A model for autism and targeted treatments. *Current Pediatric Reviews, 4,* 40–52.

Hall, S. S., Lightbody, A. A., Huffman, L. C., Lazzeroni, L. C., & Reiss, A. L. (2009). Physiological correlates of social avoidance behavior in children and adolescents with fragile X syndrome. *Journal of the American Academy of Child and Adolescent Psychiatry, 48,* 320–329.

Happé, F., & Frith, U. (2006). The weak coherence account, Detail-focused cognitive style in autism spectrum disorder. *Journal of Autism and Developmental Disorders, 36,* 5–25.

Hartley, S. L., & Sikora, D. M. (2009). Sex differences in autism spectrum disorder: An examination of developmental functioning, autistic symptoms, and coexisting behavior problems in toddlers. *Journal of Autism and Developmental Disorders, 39,* 1715–1722.

Haspel, T. (1995). Beta-blockers and the treatment of aggression. *Harvard Review of Psychiatry, 2,* 274–281.

Helt, M., Kelley, E., Kinsbourne, M., Pandey, J., Boorstein, H., Herbert, M., & Fein, D. (2008). Can children with autism recover? If so, how? *Neuropsychology Review, 18,* 339–366.

Hilton, S. M. (1982). The defence-arousal system and its relevance for circulatory and respiratory control. *Journal of Experimental Biology, 100,* 159–174.

Hilz, M. J., Devinsky, O., Szczepanska, H., Borod, J., Marthol, H., & Tutaj, M. (2006). Right ventromedial prefrontal lesions result in paradoxical cardiovascular activation with emotional stimuli. *Brain, 129,* 3343–3355.

Hinde, R. A. (1970). *Animal behavior: A synthesis of ethology and comparative psychology.* New York: McGraw-Hill.

Hinojosa-Laborde, C., Chapa, I., Lange, D., & Haywood, J. R. (2002). Gender differences in sympathetic nervous system regulation. *Clinical and Experimental Pharmacology and Physiology, 26,* 122–126.

Hirstein, W., Iverson, P., & Ramachandran, V. S. (2001). Autonomic responses of autistic children to people and objects. *Proceeding of the Royal Society, London, Series B, 286,* 1883–1888.

Hollander, E., Novotny, S., Hanratty, M., Yaffe, R., DeCaria, C. M., Aronowitz, B. R., & Mosovich, S. (2003). Oxytocin infusion reduces repetitive behaviors in adults with autistic and Asperger's disorders. *Neuropsychopharmacology, 28,* 193–198.

Huber, D., Veinante, P., & Stoop, R. (2005). Vasopressin and oxytocin excite distinct neuronal populations in the central amygdala. *Science, 308,* 245–248.

Hutt, C., & Hutt, S. J. (1965). Effects of environmental complexity on stereotyped behaviors of children. *Animal Behavior, 13,* 1–4.

Hutt, C., Hutt, S. J., Lee, D., & Ounsted, C. (1965). A behavioral and electroencephalographic study of autistic children. *Journal of Psychiatric Research, 3,* 181–198.

James, A. L., & Barry, R. J. (1980). Respiratory and vascular responses to simple visual stimuli in autistics, retardates and normals. *Psychophysiology, 17,* 541–547.

Jones, B. E. (2003). Arousal systems. *Frontiers in Bioscience, 8,* 438–451.

Julu, P. O., Kerr, A. M., Hansen, S. A., Partopoulos, F., & Jamal, G. A. (1997). Functional evidence of brain stem immaturity in Rett Syndrome. *European Journal of Child and Adolescent Psychiatry, 6, Suppl 1,* 47–54.

Kagan, J., Reznick, J. S., & Snidman, N. (1987). Biological basis of childhood shyness. *Science, 240,* 167–171.

Kennedy, D. P., Redcay, E., & Courchesne, E. (2006). Failing to deactivate: Resting functional abnormalities in autism. *Proceedings of the National Academy of Sciences, 103*, 8275–8280.

Kinsbourne, M. (1979). The neuropsychology of infantile autism. In L. H. Lockman, K. F. Swaiman, J. S. Drage, K. B. Nelson, & K. H. Marsden (Eds.), *Workshop on the neurobiological basis of autism, NINCDS monographs 23*. Bethesda, MD: Dept HEW.

Kinsbourne, M. (1980). Do repetitive movement patterns in children and animals subserve a dearousing function? *Journal of Developmental and Behavioral Pediatrics, 1*, 39–42.

Kinsbourne, M. (1987). Cerebral-brainstem relations in infantile autism. In E. Schopler & G. B. Mesibov (Eds.), *Neurobiological issues in autism* (pp. XX–XX). New York: Plenum.

Kinsbourne, M. (1991). Overfocusing: An apparent subtype of attention deficit-hyperactivity disorder. In N. Amir, I. Rapin, & D. Branski (Eds.), *Pediatric neurology: Behavior and cognition of the child with brain dysfunction* (pp. 18–35). Basel: Karger.

Klauck, S. M., Poustka, F., Benner, A., Lesch, K. P., & Poustka, A. (1997). Serotonin transporter (5-HTT). gene variants associated with autism? *Human Molecular Genetics, 6*, 2233–2238.

Knickmeyer, R., Baron-Cohen, S., Raggatt, P., & Taylor, K. (2005). Foetal testosterone, social relationships and restricted interests in children. *Journal of Child Psychology and Psychiatry, 46*, 198–210.

Knight, G. P., Guthrie, I. K., Page, M. C., & Fabes, R. A. (2002). Emotional arousal and gender differences in aggression, A meta-analysis. *Aggressive Behavior, 28*, 366–393.

Kootz, J. P., Marinelli, B., & Cohen, D. J. (1982). Modulation of response to environmental stimulation in autistic children. *Journal of Autism and Developmental Disorders, 12*, 185–193.

Korda, P. (1978). Locomotor stereotypy in visually-deprived kittens. *Acta Neurobiologica Exp., 38*, 343–351.

Lacey, J. I. (1967). Somatic response patterning and stress: Some revisions of activation theory. In M. H. Appley & R. Trumball, (Eds.), *Psychological stress: Issues in research* (pp. 14–42). New York: Appleton-Century-Crofts.

Lam, K. S., Bodfish, J. W., & Piven, J. (2008). Evidence for three subtypes of repetitive behavior in autism that differ in familiarity and association with other symptoms. *Journal of Child Psychology and Psychiatry, 49*, 1193–1200.

Laver, J. (1975). Communicative function of phatic communion. In A. Kendon, K. M. Harris, & M. Ritchie. (Eds.), *Organization of behavior in face-to-face communion* (pp. 217–238). The Hague: Mouton.

Leary, M. R., & Hill, D. A. (1996). Moving on: Autism and movement disturbance. *Mental Retardation, 14*, 39–53.

LeDoux, J. E., Iwata J., Cicchetti, P., & Reiss, D. J. (1988). Different projections of the central amygdaloid nucleus mediate autonomic and behavioral correlates of conditioned fear. *The Journal of Neuroscience, 8*, 2517–2529.

Lesch, K-P., Bengel, D., Heils, A., Sabol, S. Z., Greenberg, B. D., Petri, S., Benjamin, J., Muller, C. R., Hamer, D. H., & Murphy, D. L. (1996). Association of anxiety-related traits with a polymorphism in the serotonin transporter gene regulatory region. *Science, 274*, 1527–1531.

Lewis, M., & Kim, S-J. (2009). The pathophysiology of restricted repetitive behavior. *Journal of Neurodevelopmental Disorders, 1*, 114–132.

Lewis, M. H., & Bodfish, J. W. (1998). Repetitive behavior disorders in autism. *Mental Retardation and Developmental Disabilities Research Reviews, 4*, 80–89.

Liss, M., Fein, D., Allen, D., Dunn, M., Feinsten, C., Morris, R., Waterhouse, L., & Rapin, I. (2001). Executive functioning in high functioning children with autism. *Journal of Child Psychology and Psychiatry, 42*, 261–270.

Liss, M., Saulnier, C., Fein, D., & Kinsbourne, M. (2006). Sensory and attentional abnormalities in autistic spectrum disorders. *Autism, 10*, 155–172.

Lombardo, M. V., Chakrabati, B., Bullmore, E. T., Sadek, S. A., Pasco, G., Wheelwright, S. J., Suckling, J., MRC AIMS Consortium, & Baron-Cohen, S. (2009). Atypical neural self-representation in autism. *Brain, 1093*, 1–14.

Lovaas, I., Newsom, C., & Hickman, C. (1987). Self-stimulatory behavior and perceptual reinforcement. *Journal of Applied Behavior Analysis, 20*, 45–68.

Lowenstein, G. F., Weber, E. U., Hsee, C. K., & Welch, N. (2001). Risk as feelings. *Psychological Bulletin, 127*, 267–286.

Markram, K., Rinaldi, T., La Mendola, D., Sandi, C., & Markram, H. (2008). Abnormal fear conditioning and amygdala processing in an animal model of autism. *Neuropharmacology, 33*, 901–912.

Mathews, A., Yiend, J., & Lawrence, A. D. (2004). Individual differences in the modulation of fear-related brain activation by attentional control. *Journal of Cognitive Neuroscience, 16*, 1683–1694.

McDougle, C. J., Kresh, L. E., Goodman, W. K., Naylor, S. T., Volkmar, F. R., Cohen, D. J., & Price, L. H. (1995). A case-controlled study of repetitive thought and behavior in adults with autistic disorder and obsessive compulsive disorder. *American Journal of Psychiatry, 152*, 772–777.

Melzack, R., & Burns, S. K. (1965). Neurophysiological effects of early sensory restriction. *Experimental Neurology, 13*, 63–175.

Miller, L. J., McIntosh, D. N., McGrath, J., Shyu, V., Lampe, M., Taylor, A. K., Tassone, F., Neitzel, K., Stackhouse, T., & Hagerman, R. J. (1999). Electrodermal responses to sensory stimuli in individuals with Fragile X syndrome. *American Journal of Medical Genetics, 83*, 268–279.

Ming, X., Julu, P. O. O., Brimacombe, M., Connor, S., & Daniels, M. I. (2005). Reduced cardiac parasympathetic activity in children with autism. *Brain and Development, 27*, 509–516.

Ming, X., Julu, P. O. O., Wark, J, Apartopoulos, F & Hansen S(2004). Discordant mental and physical efforts in an autistic patient. *Brain and Development, 26*, 519–524.

Militerni, R., Bravaccio, C., Falco, C., Fico, C., & Palermo, M. T. (2002). Repetitive behaviors in autistic disorder. *European Child and Adolescent Psychiatry, 11*, 210–218.

Moss, J., Oliver, C., Arron, K., Burbidge, C., & Berg, K. (2009). The prevalence and phenomenology of repetitive behavior in genetic syndromes. *Journal of Autism and Developmental Disorders, 39*, 572–588.

Muris, P., Steerneman, P., Merckelbach, H., Holdrinet, I., & Meesters, C. (1998). Comorbid anxiety symptoms in children with pervasive developmental disorders. *Journal of Anxiety Disorders, 12*, 387–393.

Nagal, Y., Critchley, H. D., Featherstone, E., Trimble, M. R., & Dolan, R. J. (2004). Activity in ventromedial prefrontal cortex covaries with sympathetic skin conductance level, a physiological account of a "default mode" of brain function. *Neuroimage, 22*, 243–251.

Nichols, K. A., & Champness, B. G. (1971). Eye gaze and the GSR. *Journal of Experimental Social Psychology, 7*, 623–626.

Nock, M. K. (2009). Why do people hurt themselves? New insights into the nature and functions of self-injury. *Current Directions in Psychological Science, 18*, 78–83.

Ohnishi, T., Matsuda, H., Hashimoto, T., Kunihiro, K., Nishikawa, M., Uema, T., & Sasaki, M. (2000). Abnormal regional cerebral blood flow inchildhood autism. *Brain, 123*, 1838–1844.

Ornitz, E. M. (1973). Childhood autism–A review of the clinicaland experimental literature (Medical Progress). *California Medicine, 118*, 21–47.

Pardo-Villamizar, C. A. (2008). Can neuroinflammation influence the development of autisms spectrum disorders? In A. Zimmerman (Ed.), *Autism, current theories and Evidence* (pp. 329–346). Totowa, NJ: Humana.

Pierce, K. (2009). Evidence for a cerebellar role in reduced exploration and stereotyped behavior in autism. *Biological Psychiatry, 49*, 655–664.

Porges, S. W. (2004). The role of social engagement in attachment and bonding. In C. S. Carter, A. Lieselotte, K. E. Grossman, S. B. Hrdy, M. E. Lamb, S. W. Porges, & N. Sachser (Eds.), *Attachment and bonding: A new synthesis (Dahlem Workshop Reports)* (pp. (272–306). Cambridge, MA: MIT Press.

Porges, S. W., & Raskin, D. C. (1969). Respiratory and heart rate components of attention. *Journal of Experimental Psychology, 81*, 497–503.

Provence, S., & Lipton, R. C. (1962). *Infants in institutions*. Oxford: International Univ. Press.

Randrup, A., & Munkvad, I. (1967). Stereotyped activities produced by amphetamine in several animal species and man. *Psychopharmacologia, 11*, 300–310.

Rapp, J. T., & Vollmer, T. R. (2005). Stereotypy II: A review of neurobiological interpretations and suggestions for an integration with behavioral methods. *Research in Developmental Disabilities, 26*, 548–564.

Ratey, J. J., Bemporad, J., Sorgi, P., Bock, P., Polakoff, S., O'Driscoll, G., & Mikkelsen, E. (1987). Brief report: Open trial effects of beta-blockers on speech and social behaviors in 8 autistic adults. *Journal of Autism and Developmental Disorders, 17*, 439–446.

Raymaekers, R., van der Meere, J. J., & Roeyers, H. (2004). Event rate manipulation and its effect on arousal modulation and response inhibition in adults with high-functioning autism. *Journal of Clinical and Experimental Neuropsychology, 26*, 74–82.

Ring, R. H., Marberg, J. E., Potestio, L., Ping, J., Boikess, S., Luo, B., Schechter, T. E., Rizzo, S., Rahman, Z., & Rosenzweig-Lipson, S. (2006). Anxiolytic-like action of oxytocin in male mice, behavioral and autonomic evidence, therapeutic implications. *Psychopharmacology, 185*, 218–225.

Ritvo, E. R., Ornitz, E. M., & La Franchi, S. (1968). Frequency of repetitive behaviors in early infantile autism and its variants. *Archives of General Psychiatry, 19*, 341–347.

Roberts, J. E., Boccia, M. L., Hatton, D. D., Skinner, M. L., & Sidetis, J. (2006). Temperament and vagal tone in boys with fragile X syndrome. *Journal of Developmental and Behavioral Pediatrics, 27*, 193–201.

Robbins, T. W., & Koob, G. F. (1980). Selective disruption of displacement behaviour by lesions of the mesolimbic dopamine system. *Nature, 285*, 409–412.

Rochas, D. C., Peterson, E., Winterrowd, E., Reite, M. L., Rodgers, S. S. J., & Tregelles, J. R. 2006). Regional gray matter volumetric changes in autism associated with social and repetitive behavior symptoms. *BMC Psychiatry, 6*, 56–64.

Rodier, P. M., Ingram, J. L., Tisdale, B., Nelson, S., & Romano, J. (1996). Embryological origin for autism, developmental anomalies of the cranial nerve motor nuclei. *Journal of Comparative Neurology, 370*, 247–261.

Rodrigues, S. M., Saslow, L. R., Garcia, N., John, O. P., & Keltner, D. (2009). Oxytocin receptor genetic variation relates to empathy and stress reactivity. *Proceedings of the National Academy of Sciences USA, 106*, 21437–21441.

Rogers, S. J., & Ozonoff, S. (2005). Annotation: What do we know about sensory dysfunction in autism? A critical review of the empirical evidence.

Journal of Child Psychology and Psychiatry, 46, 1255–1268.

Romanczyk, K., & Gillis, J. M. (2006). Autism and the physiology of stress and anxiety. In M. G. Baron, J. Groden, G. Groden, L. P. Lipsitt (Eds.), *Stress and coping in autism* (pp. 183–204). New York: Oxford University Press.

Rubenstein, J. L. R., & Merzenich, M. M. (2003). Model of autism, increased ratio of excitation/inhibition in key neural systems. *Genes, Brain and Behavior, 2,* 255–267.

Russell, A. J., Mataix-Cols, D., Anson, M., & Murphy, D. G. M. (2005). Obsessions and compulsions in Asperger syndrome and high functioning autism. *British Journal of Psychiatry, 186,* 525–552.

Samuels, E. R., & Szabadi, E. (2008). Functional neuroanatomy of the noradrenergic locus coeruleus: Its role in the regulation of arousal and autonomic function. Part I: Principles of functional organization. *Current Neuropharmacology, 6,* 235–253.

Santini, E., Ge, H., Ren, K., de Ortiz, S. P., & Quirk, G. J. (2004). Consolidation of fear extinction requires protein synthesis in the medial prefrontal cortex. *The Journal of Neuroscience, 24,* 5704–5710.

Scahill, L. (2009). Alpha-2 adrenergic agonists in children with inattention, hyperactivity and impulsiveness. *CNS Drugs, 23,* 43–47.

Scholey, A., Haskel, C., Robertson, B., Kennedy, D., Milne, A., & Wetherell, M. (2009). Chewing gum alleviates negative mood and reduces cortisol during acute laboratory psychological stress. *Physiology and Behavior, 97,* 304–312.

Schultz, R. T., Romanski, L. M., & Tsatsanis, K. (2000). Neurofunctional models of autistic disorder and Asperger syndrome. In A. Klin, F. R. Volkmar, & S. S. Sparrow (Eds.), *Asperger syndrome* (pp. 179–209). New York: Guilford.

Scott, F. J., Baron-Cohen, S., Bolton, P., & Brayne, C. (2002). Brief report, prevalence of autism spectrum conditions in children aged 5–11 years in Cambridgeshire, UK. *Autism, 6,* 231–237.

Shackman, A. J., McMenamin, B. W., Maxwell, J. S., Greischar, L. L., & Davidson, R. J. (2009). Right dorsolateral prefrontal cortical activity and behavioral inhibition. *Psychological Science, 20,* 1500–1506.

Shapiro, D. (1973). *Neurotic styles.* New York: Basic Books.

Sokoloff, N., Yaffe, S., Weintraub, D., & Blase, B. (1969). Effects of handling on the subsequent development of premature infants. *Developmental Psychology, 1,* 765–768.

Soussignan, R., & Koch, P. (1985). Rhythmical stereotypies (leg-swinging) associated with reductions in heart-rate in normal school children. *Biological Psychology, 21,* 161–167.

South, M., Ozonoff, S., & McMahon, W. M. (2005). Repetitive behavior profiles in Asperger syndrome and high-functioning autism. *Journal of Autism and Developmental Disorders, 35,* 145–158.

Spreng, R. N., Mar, R. A., & Kim, A. S. N. (2009). The common neural basis of autobiographical memory, prospection, navigation, theory of mind and the default mode: A quantitative meta-analysis. *Journal of Cognitive Neurosciences, 21,* 489–510.

Steingard, R. J., Zimnitsky, B., DeMaso, D. R., Bauman, M. L., & Bucci, J. P. (1997). Sertaline treatment of transition-associated anxiety and agitation in children with autistic disorder. *Journal of Child and Adolescent Psychopharmacology, 7,* 9–15.

Stroh, G., & Buick, D. (1968). The effect of relative sensory isolation on two autistic children. In S. J. Hutt & C. Hutt (Eds.), *Behavior studies in psychiatry* (pp. 161–174). New York: Pergamon.

Sullivan, R., & Gratton, A. (1999). Lateralized effects of medial prefrontal cortex lesions on neuroendocrine and autonomic stress responses in rats. *The Journal of Neuroscience, 19,* 2834–2840.

Szatmari, P., Bartolucci, G., & Bremner, R. (1989). Asperger's disorder and autism: Comparison of early history and outcome. *Developmental Medicine and Child Neurology, 31,* 709–720.

Szatmari, P., Georgiades, S., Bryson, S., Zwaigenbaum, L., Roberts, W., Mahoney, W., Goldberg, J., & Tuff, L. (2006). Investigating the structure of the restricted, repetitive behaviours and interests domain of autism. *Journal of Child Psychology and Psychiatry, 47,* 582–590.

Temudo, T., Ramos, E., Dias, K., Barbot, C., Viera, J. P., Moreira, A.,... Maciel P (2008). Movement disorder in Rett syndrome: An analysis of 60 patients with detected MECP2 mutation and correlation with mutation type. *Movement Disorders, 23,* 10,1384–1390.

Thelen, E. (1981). Kicking, rocking and waving: Contextual analysis of rhythmical stereotypies in normal human infants. *Animal Behaviour, 29,* 3–11.

Toichi, M., & Kamio, Y. (2003). Paradoxical autonomic response to mental tasks in autism. *Journal of Autism and Developmental Disorders, 33,* 417–426.

Troisi, A. (2002). Displacement activities as a behavioral measure of stress in nonhuman primates and human subjects. *International Journal on the Biology of Stress, 5,* 47–54.

Tsigos, C., & Chrousos, G. P. (2002). Hypothalamic-pituitary-adrenal axis, neuroendocrine factors and stress. *Journal of Psychosomatic Research, 53,* 865–871.

Turk, J., & Graham, P. (1997). Fragile X syndrome, autism and autistic features. *Autism, 1,* 175–197.

Turner, M. (1999). Annotation: Repetitive behaviour in autism: A review of psychological research. *Journal of Child Psychology and Psychiatry, 47,* 839–849.

Tursky, B., Schwartz, G. E., & Crider, A. (1970). Differential patterns of heart rate and skin resistance during a digit-transformation task. *Journal of Experimental Psychology*, 83, 451–457.

White, J. L., & Labara, R. C. (1976). The effects of tactile and kinesthetic stimulation on neonatal development in the premature infant. *Developmental Psychobiology*, 9, 569–577.

Willemsen-Swinkels, S. H. N., Buitelaar, J. K., Dekker, M., & van Engeland, H. (1998). *Journal of Autism and Developmental Disorders*, 28, 547–557.

Woodcock, L., Oliver, C., & Humphreys, G. W. (2009). Associations between repetitive questioning, resistance to change, temper outbursts and anxiety in Prader-Willi and fragile X syndromes. *Journal of Intellectual Disability Research*, 53, 265–278.

Zaid, D. H., Mattson, D. L., & Pardo, J. V. (2002). Brain activity in ventromedial prefrontal cortex correlates with individual differences in negative affect. *Proceedings of the National Academy of Sciences*, 99, 2450–2454.

Zentall, S., & Zentall, T. R. (1983). Optimal stimulation: A model of disordered activity and performance in normal and deviant children. *Psychological Bulletin*, 94, 446–471.

Zohar, A. H., & Felz, L. (2006). Ritualistic behavior in young children. *Journal of Abnormal Child Psychology*, 29, 121–128.

Chapter 20

Neural Network Models of Context Utilization

Ananth Narayanan and David Q. Beversdorf

Several psychological theories (described in Chapter 5) have been proposed to explain the features found in autism, including decreased central coherence, Theory of Mind deficits, and bias toward local, as compared to global, processing. Neural network models attempt to illustrate a mechanism by which these psychological principles may manifest in the brain, utilizing varying degrees of input from the underlying pathological features. Connectionist models view higher-level cognition as a product of extensive interaction between multiple layers of simple processing units. They utilize a model using certain physical and biochemical properties of neurons and their activation patterns, without incorporating the general complexity of the structure of the brain. This allows us to view higher-level cognitive deficits as a result of alterations to the basic structure and topology of these connections, thereby enabling us to explore the nature of the relationship between developmental abnormalities and the emergence of characteristic pathological behaviors. This, particularly

when considered in combination with information derived from functional brain mapping and our understanding of other principles of brain organization, yields a potentially powerful technique for determining the inner workings of the brain. The most widely modeled aspects of autism to this point have been issues related to decreased central coherence.

NEURAL NETWORKS

Computational neuroscience can model complex neural and cognitive functioning, and can also be used to solve problems that elude traditional statistical techniques. A traditional neural network consists of more than one layer of processing units. These units are connected with different strengths, depending on the association of an output pattern with an input pattern. Figure 20-1 demonstrates a putative network by which each word selectively activates itself and other words related to it. The nodes on the left

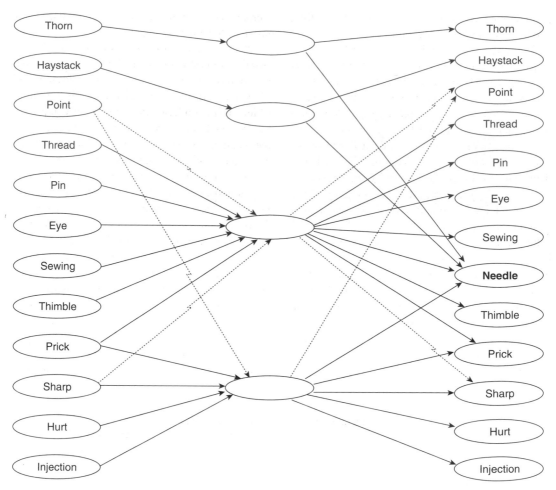

Figure 20-1 This is a typical feed-forward neural network with multiple layers. This is an exemplar of a network model as applied to the "false memory" word list, implying that the activation received by each word also activates overlapping aspects represented by these inputs. One or more input units are interconnected with one or more hidden layers, each one of which is connected to one or more output elements. Whereas in some feed-forward neural networks, the hidden layers can each be connected to all of the input and output units, this is not always the case. As is observed in this example, some of the input units are connected with only one of the units in the hidden layer, which are in turn, connected to only certain specific units in the output layer in this network. The interconnections between different units allows for the distribution of information across the entire network. The connection strengths (not shown in the figure) may also vary to yield strong or weak activations depending on the strength of the individual connections (from Beversdorf et al, 2007).

represent the words entered into the network. The hidden nodes are those in the middle. They are not directly observable in the input or output (hence the term "hidden nodes"), but rather represent intermediary processing within the network as related by meaning. The nodes on the right represent the resulting activation patterns from the network. Neural network models try to integrate the structural and functional features of the brain in patient populations with the emergence of atypical behaviors in these disorders, using the general principles of brain functionality. In other words, they propose to establish a model for a link between brain structure and behavior (Gluck & Myers, 2001). Several investigators have used this concept to explain the neurological basis of behaviors in autism. This chapter gives a brief overview of several proposed neural network models relevant to autism, and thoughts for future directions.

Learning in any simple network model, such as a parallel distributed processing (PDP) network (Rumelhart & McClelland, 1986; McClelland, 2000), occurs by selective modification of the strengths of connections between the processing units. When a new pattern is introduced to the network, learning occurs by building upon the previous state of the neural network. Therefore, learning is state dependent; that is, it engages the knowledge accumulated in all the other patterns stored in the network at that stage, and builds upon it. As a result, similar patterns of input will tend to yield similar behaviors. This pattern overlap creates a shared use of preexisting knowledge present in the neural network prior to training. Learning occurs using the Hebbian process, which states that the strength of connection between two directly connected neurons is directly proportional to the frequency at which one neuron activates the other. Using this general principle, the weights or the connection strengths are modified based on feedback from the previous outputs, so as to optimize the

appropriateness of the network and to statistically minimize the error (see Figure 20-2).

Effective storage of memories in the complicated neural network structure of the brain must address the two contrasting characteristics of generalization and interference. In order to understand this, one must achieve a basic understanding of how any component is represented in a neural network. Storing a memory that incorporates multiple senses such as smell, taste, and sight involves breaking the complex aspects of those senses (olfactory, gustatory, visual, etc.) into simpler forms of their basic components that can be easily represented in the system. For example, a cherry-flavored Popsicle would be represented as "red," "solid," "cold," and "sweet" (along the aspects of color, texture, temperature, and flavor), while the corresponding representation of cocoa would be "brown," "hot," "liquid" and "sweet." In this example, both the Popsicle and the cocoa share the property of being "sweet." This similarity in the properties of different items gives rise to the emergent property of association. In other words, the network associates each of the distinct properties with the appropriate

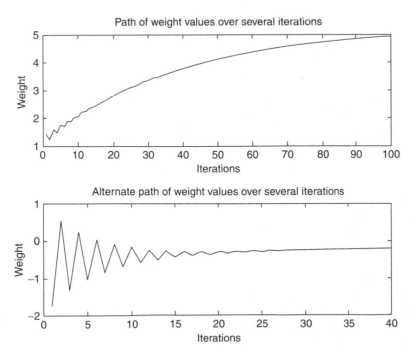

Figure 20-2 Depending on the network parameters and the inputs themselves, the weights may be convergent (in a stable network) or divergent (in an unstable network). This figure shows two of the ways in which a convergent weight would converge on a particular value upon further iteration. The weights in an unstable network (not shown) oscillate infinitely about a value or diverge to infinity.

input. The significance of this will become apparent in later parts of the chapter. Furthermore, using this basic principle, a simple association can be made between, for example, the physical appearance and the taste of a particular food—say, steak—such that the image of a steak is associated with the taste. Therefore, the visual image of a steak elicits a memory of its taste. The entire network is structured in such a way that the same network can be used to process multiple distinct inputs by creating and modifying associations. A similar association can be made using the same network, with a different food, such as a Popsicle. This particular input would evoke very different visual and gustatory responses in the network. However, as the number of food items represented in this network is increased, with varying degrees of overlap (ice cream will overlap with the sweet and cold aspects of the Popsicle, but the richness and intensity of the flavor may align it somewhat with steak), significant levels of cross-talk would lead to the operational essence of these neural networks, which brings us to another main property of such networks: generalization.

When two different inputs overlap to some degree, rather than remaining completely independent, pattern overlap forces shared use of knowledge which has been acquired independently from multiple inputs. Using Hebbian learning, as described above, the strength of the connection between the active units increases. If there are common elements to different input patterns, these common elements are strengthened preferentially (relative to the rest), leading to a representation where the associations of the more frequent component are "learned" preferentially, thereby producing a robust response to any input combination. For example, if the input "dark beer" is seen by the network much more frequently than "root beer," the network will learn to associate "brown," "bubbly," and "liquid" with dark beer more than it will with root beer. On the other hand, the basic components ("brown," "bubbly," and "liquid") will be preferentially strengthened over any other components that might be present in the aforementioned network when both "dark beer" and "root beer" are activated in equal proportions. Interestingly, this also leads to the converse, ensuring the activation of both dark beer and root beer upon encountering the basic components, "brown," "bubbly," and "liquid." If two similar inputs are fed into the neural network, the network will tend to react similarly to those inputs,

with only minor differences. If several similar trial items are fed into the neural network, slight increases are seen in the connection strengths after every run leading to a comprehensive strengthening of common elements according to the Hebbian rule. This yields a robust representational system which can deal with most inputs that contain any combination of the simple components of the inputs that have been used to train the network.

On the other hand, interference stems from the inability of the network to differentiate the nuanced distinctions associated with the complex cognitive processes necessary for the regular functioning of the human brain. In particular, when an input pattern is too similar to other patterns of inputs that have been seen by the network before, the network tends to activate outputs that have been generated by the network previously, even if this is not appropriate, thereby leading to inefficiency. However, a technique called *conjunctive coding* can be used to avoid this problem. In this technique, the combined activation of two or more units is necessary for a higher-level (conjunctive) unit to be activated. In other words, every salient combination of units is assigned to another unit, to ensure that the simultaneous occurrences of two simple components are represented by that one higher-level unit. For example, in Figure 20-3, only the activation of both of the outside units will result in the activation of the higher-level conjunctive unit shown in the bottom. The activation of any other combination of units will not result in the activation of the conjunctive unit. The ability of networks to generate useful conjunctions allows it to more efficiently collapse multiple representations, as well as create distinct representations. This principle was described as it applies to autism by McClelland (2000).

MCCLELLAND'S MODEL

With neural networks, McClelland (2000) explains the hyperspecificity of memory in autistic individuals, utilizing these basic Hebbian principles. Children with autism are known to be highly specific in their representation of information. McClelland (2000) gave an example of a child who was at a birthday party and had to go to the bathroom. However, the child was unable to recognize the bathroom at the home of the host, because it was different that what he was accustomed to at home, and had to be taken home to

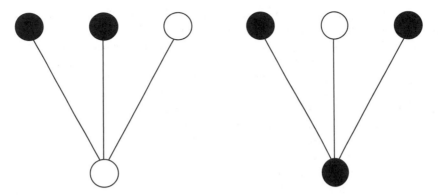

Figure 20-3 In the above figure, the unit in the bottom is a higher-level conjunctive unit that is primed to activate if and only if two preidentified units upstream of it fire simultaneously. The shaded units represent activated units. As can be seen in this figure, only the activation of the both the left and right units simultaneously will result in the activation of the conjunctive unit. In the case that either one of those preidentified units are inactive, the conjunctive unit will remain inactive.

use his own bathroom. This hyperspecific representation of information is related, it has been suggested, to decreased central coherence, or an inability to extract information in context (Happé, 1996). They are also known to have preserved memories in context-independent forms (Beversdorf et al., 2000). McClelland (2000) proposes that the hyperspecificity encountered in children with autism stems from a highly conjunctive representation, as described above, while typically developing children use a representational system that preserves the individual elements. According to this theory, learning in typical individuals is characterized by a tendency to discover appropriate representations that allow effective generalization, thereby progressively creating more subtle and nuanced distinctions to categorize knowledge, whereas individuals with autism may be predisposed to use an excessively conjunctive form of neural encoding, resulting in hyperspecificity.

APPLICATION OF MCCLELLAND'S MODEL TO A MEMORY TASK

One interesting task that reveals a potential consequence of network hyperspecificity and decreased central coherence is the "false memory" task (Roedinger & McDermott, 1995). In our previous work, high-functioning participants with ASD were presented with a list of semantically and associatively related words, and then tested for recognition of an index item, or critical lure, which was closely related to all the words on the list but was not presented. Subjects with ASD were found to be less susceptible than a matched comparison group in reporting that they recognized the critical lure (Beversdorf et al., 2000). This appears to be demonstrated even more robustly for visuospatial items (Hillier et al., 2007).

Using a simple network model, rather than making use of hidden nodes or other complex features, Beversdorf and colleagues (2007) utilized data from the previously described "false memory" task (Beversdorf, 2000) in order to generate an application of the principles of McClelland (2000). Each word in this model was assumed to activate all related words, including the critical lure (which was related to all words on the list). The activation scores, or the strength of activation, of each word on the list, and the corresponding effects for the primacy (occurring first) and recency (occurring last) were estimated for controls and ASD populations using previous research on semantic association (O'Connor, 1967). These cross-activation scores were applied as connection weights to this model, and the overall strength of activation was calculated for each word on the list, including the critical lure, after exposure to each word on the list through the model. With this examplar 2-layer network generated (as opposed to a 3-layer network with hidden nodes in Figure 20-1), the false memory task was assessed, and due to weaker activation of the associated words in autism, the autism exemplar model demonstrated superior performance on discriminating true and false items (critical lures) on "false memory" tasks in recognition testing.

Interestingly, the model may also explain the diverging results of free recall on the "false memory" task. Individuals with autism are known to have impairments in executive function (Russell, 1997), which plays a large role in the use of search strategies. Free recall is dependent on both search strategies and access to networks, and is therefore also impaired in ASD. With a restricted network in the setting of a less efficient search strategy, the search through the network involved in free recall is proposed to yield a lower probability of free recall for individuals with ASD, since inefficient strategy would cause several target words to be missed during the search, with the possible inclusion of extraneous, less-related words, in an effort to generate the expected number of words (Beversdorf, Narayanan, Hillier, & Hughes, 2007). In contrast, better connections strengthened by semantic and associative relations between different nodes would result in cross-activations among recall words, and with a more efficient search strategy, would lead to the higher degree of recall seen in the non-ASD population. Thus, the proposed model also predicts the findings of impaired performance of ASD participants on free recall during the "false memory" task, as has been observed by Bowler et al. (2000).

ATTENTIONAL CONTRIBUTORS, AND GUSTAFSSON AND PAPLINSKI'S SELF-ORGANIZING MAP

Courchesne et al. (1994a; 1994b) proposed an anatomical mechanism as the source of the attentional impairment seen in children with autism. In particular, patients with autism and patients with acquired cerebellar lesions showed similar impairment in a task requiring rapid shifts in attention between multimodal stimuli requiring high levels of accuracy; it was therefore proposed that cerebellar abnormalities may contribute to the observed attention-shift impairments in autism. According to Courchesne (2002), the attention-shift impairments may interfere with encoding certain aspects of the events, leading to fragmented memory formation in autism. They also argue that this might lead to certain characteristics commonly observed in autism, such as obsessive insistence on sameness (Courchesne et al., 1994a).

However, others (Dawson, Meltzoff, Osterling, Rinaldi, & Brown 1998) have suggested that attention-shift impairments are, at least in part, a manifestation of aversion to social stimuli rather than a root cause of autism, since children with autism demonstrated significantly reduced response to social stimuli (hand clapping, name calling) as compared to non-social stimuli (rattling, or a musical jack-in-the-box). Yet other studies have shown that children with autism could form strategies during some strategy-dependent problem-solving tasks, but struggled to shift strategies to fit modified task parameters (Pascualvaca, Fantie, Papageorgiou, & Mirsky 1998), suggesting that additional external feedback was being rejected. In addition, aspects of saccadic eye movements which are controlled by the neocortex are abnormal in autism, but those movements under cerebellar control are normal (Minshew, Luna, & Sweeney 1999). Minshew and colleagues (1999) also proposed that autistic children are averse to novelty itself, and that social stimuli, being associated with novelty more than most other stimuli, will result in children being socially avoidant; the aversion to novelty would also result in attentional impairments, thereby resulting in the characteristics that are often associated with autism.

Gustafsson and Paplinski (2004) tested these various hypotheses regarding attentional impairment in autism using the organization of a simple artificial neural network (ANN) (Haykin, 1999) model to study developmental differences between different types of attention-shifting impairments: first, when they were unconditional and modulated by cerebellar abnormalities (Courchesne et al., 1994a, 1994b), and then when they were attenuated due to familiarity preference (Minshew et al., 1999). In this study, a specific type of ANN, called self-organizing maps (SOMs) (Kohonen, 2001), which are known to produce topographical feature maps that seem to match feature maps in sensory cortices very closely, are used for this purpose. SOMs are a unique category of neural network that simulates the development and the continued refinement of cortical feature maps, such as the changes that occur with experience in the somatosensory cortex (Gustafsson & Paplinski, 2004; Kohonen, 2001).

In contrast to connectionist models described above, in SOMs, information is conceptualized as stored topographically from inputs in a 2-dimensional, 3-dimensional, or higher- dimensional map, mapped onto one or two dimensions. The outputs are generally organized into groups of distinct nodes or regions represented within the map. They are referred to as "self- organizing," because they preserve the topological properties of the data (Principe, Euliano, & Lefebvre, 2000). In other words, data points in the input that are close to each other are also close to each other upon being processed by the network. As mentioned above, the salience of SOMs is supported by their resemblance to what occurs during information processing in the cerebral cortex (Gustafsson & Paplinski, 2004; Kohonen, 2001). These neural networks have the ability to store tremendous amounts of detail, by breaking down the similarities and differences between different memories and storing them in hierarchies of such cortical features. This is most easily demonstrated by mapping items in multiple dimensions across a plane, to generate a self-organizing map of the items based on these features. The topology and architecture of the input-output combinations yields a self-organizing map, as described above. In more complex maps, each stimulus is represented by a set of individual values across a number of features, which is then mapped onto a field of x dimensions where x equals the number of features used in generating the map. Hermelin (1978) showed that autistic children have difficulty recoding sensory information into more abstract forms, which Gustafsson and Paplinski (2004) propose is related to their difficulty with seeing what typical individuals regard as salient features of a situation (Gustafsson & Paplinski, 2004; Happé, 1991). The learning process for an ANN in autism may result in an inadequate feature map, resulting in incorrect classification of stimuli (Gustafsson & Paplinski, 2004).

Gustafsson and Paplinski's SOM simulations show that learning with familiarity preference results in maps with characteristics such that the stimuli of one source will be preferentially learned. If one source has decreased variability, it may dominate the map such that other sources will not be detected. This seems similar to learning tendencies in people with autistic characteristics, where learning occurs in great detail, but only within a narrow field. Learning with attention-shift impairments results in maps that seem normal, though the learning process itself in the model was reported to be highly chaotic, with a slightly better capacity for discrimination than in normal learning, which could relate to curious special abilities more frequently observed in autism, such as perfect pitch.

As attentional impairment is common in autism, it was unclear how attention-shifting impairment, strong familiarity preference, or aversion to novelty each contributed to the features of autism. By comparing these deficits in a SOM simulation, potential links between these deficits and behavior related to autism are detected (Gustafsson & Paplinski, 2004), suggesting by the simulations that familiarity preference could result in detailed learning within a narrow field, and that the attention-shift impairments could result in better discrimination ability than learning ability, both of which can be observed in autism.

HISTOLOGICAL CONTRIBUTORS

Some studies have revealed that individuals with autism have too many or too few neurons in various regions of the brain. Increased neuronal density and smaller neurons were noticed in the hippocampus, enterohinal cortex, the amygdalae, the mammillary body, the medial septal nucleus, and the cingulate cortex (Bauman & Kemper, 1985, 1994). Neuronal loss is also observed in certain areas of the cortex, as well as in the fastigial, globose, and emboliform nuclei. Reduced dendritic branching was observed in CA1 and CA4, and reduced area of the perikaryon was observed in CA4 neurons of the hippocampus (Raymond et al., 1996). There are also reports of increased cell-packing density in the same temporal lobe structures (Bauman & Kemper, 1994). In general, though variable in location, the types of structural deficiencies appear to be consistent (Bauman, 1991)—namely, there are too few neurons in some areas and too many neurons in other areas. Other anatomical considerations, such as minicolumns (Casanova, 2002), will be discussed below.

COHEN'S MODEL

Cohen (1994, 1998) modeled this neuroanatomical pattern of autism using scores on various aspects of behavior derived from the Autistic Behavior Interview (Sparrow, Balla, & Cicchetti 1984), and varying the number of neuronal connections in the intermediate layer and the number of trials in the training period. This study showed a trade-off between learning and generalization, where having too many processing elements in the data set led to good learning but weak generalization, and having too few processing elements led to weak learning and weak generalization. While the generalization was accurate with one of the test data sets, it was relatively poor with the other. In the network with one processing unit (or few units) in the hidden layer, acquisition of information appeared to interfere with generalization. In the network with nine hidden-layer processing elements (or many elements), the nuances had been learned with excessive detail, leading to deterioration of performance in the test set. This weak generalization ability, in combination with overselective features of the network, was similar to the behavioral characteristics of some children with autism.

Converging lines of evidence suggest that people with autism have the ability to recognize and discriminate among complex patterns in all modalities, including visual, spatial, temporal, and auditory (Happé, 1996; Shah & Frith, 1983, 1993). Cohen's (1994) model attempted to provide an explanation of how the anatomic abnormalities in autism translate into the behavioral realm, as exemplified by the attention to context-irrelevant details at the expense of generalization. This might also contribute to the "Theory of Mind" deficits (Baron-Cohen, 1985; Frith & Baron-Cohen, 1987) noticed in autism, through weak generalization of another person's perceptions. This would also explain the results that children with autism, when learning, focus on a characteristic of the stimulus that interferes with generalization of a related stimulus (Lovaas, Schreibman, Koegel, & Rehm 1971; Schreibman & Lovaas, 1973). From these observed results, Cohen predicts that "this overselectivity phenomenon is a direct consequence of the child's neuronal connectivity pattern, is functionally related to the child's experience with stimuli that require discrimination, and will depend on when it is assessed during learning" (p. 16). According to Cohen, children who attend to a restricted range of stimuli and have difficulty acquiring simple discriminations may fall into the category of subjects who have too few neurons or neuronal connections in areas such as the amygdala and hippocampus (Raymond, 1996), which are essential for learning about stimulus-stimulus or stimulus-reinforcer associations; as a result, these children may not learn how to discriminate salient features in order to permit generalization. Other children with superior pattern discrimination ability but difficulty abstracting would have too many neurons in these same brain regions, leading them overlearn the minute associations that would tend to interfere with generalization. It is also proposed that deficiency in upstream processing of multilayered neural networks might result in a deficiency in the proper functioning of downstream modules, in spite of otherwise perfect integrity of the downstream modules. This could explain the inability of the children with autism to perceive more complex abstract relationships among the patterns, such as with semantic comprehension.

LOCAL HYPERCONNECTIVITY/ GLOBAL UNDERCONNECTIVITY

Casanova et al. (2002) report abnormalities in minicolumnar organization in the cerebral cortex in autism, indicating that minicolumns are smaller and their component cells are more dispersed than those observed for control subjects. In a follow-up study, Casanova et al. (2006) reported a 23% higher cell-packing density in autism, but with smaller cells (as indicated by neuronal and nuclear cross sections) compared to controls, suggesting a greater number of minicolumns and shorter connecting fibers, favoring local connectivity over long-distance connectivity. Behavioral studies also demonstrated superior aspects in perceptual function in autism, particularly when the task benefits from greater local and less global processing (Mottron & Burack, 2001). Examples of this aspect of functioning in autism includes their superior performance in tasks that involve attention to focused local information, such as block-design tasks (Shah & Frith, 1993), the embedded figures test (Shah & Frith, 1983), and the resistance to visual illusions (Happé, 1996). This is reinforced by reports (Just, Cherkassky, Keller, & Minshew 2004) of decreased connectivity during sentence comprehension in autism between the distant brain regions involved in this task. However, Belmonte and Yurgelun-Todd (2003) reported that individuals with autism showed a variable modulation of activation in the superior parietal lobe, decreased modulation in the ventral occipital cortex, and an increased modulation in the left intraparietal sulcus in a task involving bilateral visuospatial attention, suggesting local over-connectivity. Therefore, while the global connectivity is significantly decreased in individuals with autism (Just, 2004), there is evidence of an increase in local connectivity in the affected brain regions (Belmonte et al., 2004b; Belmonte & Yurgelun-Todd, 2003; Rubenstein & Merzenich,

2003). Belmonte et al. (2004a) therefore advocate inclusion of these global and local features in future neural network models of autism (see Chapter 21). Lewis et al. (2008) have also proposed, in a network model, that the altered growth trajectory in autism, with larger brain sizes in early childhood, could lead to selective disruption of long-distance connectivity, with the observed behavioral consequences.

FUTURE DIRECTIONS

In the future, other features of autism must also be considered. For example, Beversdorf et al. (1998) compared the effects of central coherence and emotion on memory to determine whether separable contributions could be identified. Whereas this very high-functioning group of subjects did utilize semantic and syntactic context as much as controls in recall—in contrast to previous results in somewhat lower-functioning individuals (Hermelin & O'Connor, 1970; O'Connor & Hermelin, 1967)—emotional context did not increase recall in autism as it did in controls, suggesting that impairments in emotional processing cannot be considered as simply an effect of the lack of central coherence in autism. This was proposed to be related to amygdalar function. As mentioned above, postmortem neuroanatomical studies showed increased cell density in the amygdala in the presence of normal amygdalar volume (Bauman & Kemper, 1994; Rapin & Katzman, 1998). Otherwise healthy subjects with amygdala lesions are also known to have impaired social judgment (Adolphs, Tranel, Damasio, & Damasio, 1994; Young, Hellawell, De Wal, & Johnson, 1996). Furthermore, individuals with autism activate the amygdala to a lesser degree when processing emotional faces, and appear to compensate for the lack of amygdalar activation by placing a greater load on temporal lobe structures, which are specialized for verbal naming of complex visual stimuli and processing of faces and eyes (Baron-Cohen et al., 2000). Therefore, aspects of amygdalar function would be a critical component of future neural network models of autism.

The importance of specific anatomical regions being linked in a specific type of task network must also be considered in future network models. One example is the social network (Baron-Cohen & Belmonte, 2005). Brothers (1990) and Brothers et al. (1990) suggested that "social intelligence" is dependent on three brain regions—namely, the amygdala, the orbitofrontal cortex (OFC), and the superior temporal sulcus and gyrus (STG)—terming these regions the "social brain." Therefore, it is possible that deficits in each of these three structures might lead to autistic tendencies. Results of SPECT activity in the OFC (Baron-Cohen et al., 1994) and fMRI findings (Baron-Cohen et al., 2000) support these conclusions about this network in autism.

Other imaging aspects would also need to be integrated; for example, the increased thalamocortical connectivity observed in autism (Mizuno, Villalobos, Davies, Dahl, & Müller, 2006) would need to be incorporated into future models. Neuropharmacological and genetic aspects would also need to be included, including the finding of common types of mutations such as those of the neurexin and neurligin family (Autism Genome Project Consortium, 2007), and postmortem findings suggestive of altered GABAergic system function (Blatt et al., 2001; Guptill et al., 2007; Yip, Soghomonian, & Blatt, 2008), and their known effects on neuronal communication. Effects of pharmacological interventions also present a future opportunity for utilization of neural network models, such as the effects we have demonstrated for noradrenergic agents (Beversdorf et al., 2008; Narayanan et al., 2010).

References

Adolphs, R., Tranel, D., Damasio, H., & Damasio, A. (1994). Impaired recognition of emotion in facial expressions following bilateral damage to the human amygdala. *Nature*, 372, 669–672.

The Autism Genome Project Consortium. (2007) Mapping autism risk loci using genetic linkage and chromosomal rearrangements. *Nat Genet*, 39, 319–328.

Baron-Cohen, S., & Belmonte, M. K. (2005). Autism: A window onto the development of the social and the analytic brain. *Ann Rev Neurosci*, 28, 109–126.

Baron-Cohen, S., Leslie, A. M., & Frith U. (1985). Does the autistic child have a "theory of mind"? *Cognition*, 21, 37–46.

Baron-Cohen, S., Ring, H. A., Bullmore, E. T., Wheelwright, S., Ashwin, C., & Williams, S. C. (2000). The amygdala theory of autism. *Neurosci Biobehav Rev.*, 24, 355–364.

Baron-Cohen, S., Ring, H., Moriarty, J., Shmitz, P., Costa, D., & Ell, P. (1994). Recognition of mental state terms: A clinical study of autism, and a functional neuroimaging study of normal adults. *Br J Psychiatry*, 165, 640–649.

Bauman, M., & Kemper, T. (1994). *The neurobiology of autism*. Baltimore: Johns Hopkins.

Bauman, M., & Kemper, T. L. (1985). Histoanatomic observations of the brain in early infantile autism. *Neurology, 35*, 866–874.

Bauman, M. L. (1991). Microscopic neuroanatomic abnormalities in autism. *Pediatrics, 87*, 791–796.

Belmonte, M. K., Allen G., Beckel-Mitchener, A., Boulanger, L. M., Carper, R. A., & Webb, S. J. (2004a). Autism and abnormal development of brain connectivity. *J Neurosci, 24*, 9228–9231.

Belmonte, M. K., Cook, E. H., Jr., Anderson, G. M., Rubenstein, J. L., Greenough, W. T., Beckel-Mitchener, A., Courchesne, E., Boulanger, L. M., Powell, S. B., Levitt, P. R., Perry, E. K., Jiang, Y. H., DeLorey, T. M., & Tierney, E. (2004b). Autism as a disorder of neural information processing: Directions for research and targets for therapy. *Mol Psychiatry, 9*, 646–663.

Belmonte, M. K., & Yurgelun-Todd, D. A. (2003). Functional anatomy of impaired selective attention and compensatory processing in autism. *Brain Res Cogn Brain Res., 17*, 651–664.

Beversdorf, D. Q., Anderson, J. M., Manning, S. E., Anderson, S. L., Nordgren, R. E., Felopulos, G. J., Nadeau, S. E., Heilman, K. M., & Bauman, M. L. (1998). The effect of semantic and emotional context on written recall for verbal language in high functioning adults with autism spectrum disorder. *J Neurol Neurosurg Psychiatry, 65*, 685–692.

Beversdorf, D. Q., Carpenter, A. L., Miller, R. F., Cios, J. J., & Hillier, A. (2008). Effect of propranolol on verbal problem solving in autism spectrum disorder. *Neurocase, 14*, 378–383.

Beversdorf, D. Q., Smith, B. W., Crucian, G. P., Anderson, J. M., Keillor, J. M., Barrett, A. M., Hughes, J. D., Felopulos, G. J., Bauman, M. L., Nadeau, S. E., & Heilman, K. M. (2000). Increased discrimination of "'false memories'" in autism spectrum disorder. *Proc Natl Acad Sci U S A, 97*, 8734–8737.

Beversdorf, D. Q., Narayanan, A., Hillier, A., & Hughes, J. D. (2007). Network model of decreased context utilization in autism spectrum disorder. *J Autism Dev Disord, 37*, 1040–1048.

Blatt, G. J., Fitzgerald, C. M., Guptill, J. T., Booker, A. B., Kemper, T. L., & Bauman, M. L. (2001). Density and distribution of hippocampal neurotransmitter receptors in autism: An autoradiographic study. *J Autism Dev Disord, 31*, 537–543.

Bowler, D. M., Gardiner, J. M., Grice, S. J., & Saavalainen, P. (2000). Memory illusions: False recall and recognition in adults with Asperger's disorder. *J Abnorm Psychol, 10*, 663–672.

Brothers, L. (1990). The social brain: A project for integrating primate behaviour and neurophysiology in a new domain. *Concept Neurosci 1990, 1*, 27–51.

Brothers, L., Ring, B., & Kling, A. (1990). Responses of neurons in the macaque amygdala to complex social stimuli. *Behav Brain Res, 41*, 199–213.

Casanova, M. F., Buxhoeveden, D. P., Switala, A. E., & Roy, E. (2002). Asperger's disorder and cortical neuropathology. *J Child Neurol, 17*, 142–145.

Casanova, M. F., van Kooten, I. A., Switala, A. E., van Engeland, H., Heinsen, H., Steinbusch, H. W., Hof, P. R., Trippe, J., Stone, J., & Schmitz, C. (2006). Minicolumnar abnormalities in autism. *Acta Neuropathol, 112*, 287–303.

Cohen, I. (1998).Neural network analysis of learning in autism. In D. Stein & J. Ludick (Eds.), *Neural networks and psychopathology* (pp. 274–315). Cambridge: Cambridge University Press.

Cohen, I. L. (1994). An artificial neural network analogue of learning in autism. *Biol Psychiatry, 36*, 5–20.

Courchesne, E. (2002).Deciphering the puzzle: Unusual patterns of brain development in autism. Paper presented at the Inaugural World Autism Congress, Melbourne, Australia.

Courchesne E, Townsend, J, Akshoomoff, N. A., Saitoh, O, Yeung-Courchesne, R., Lincoln, A. J., James, H. E., Haas, R. H., Schreibman, L., & Lau, L. (1994a). Impairment in shifting attention in autistic and cerebellar patients. *Behav Neurosci, 108*, 848–865.

Courchesne, E., Townsend, J., Akshoomoff, N., Yeung-Courchesne, R., Press, G., Murakami, J., Lincoln, A., James, H., Saitoh, O., Eggas, B., Haas, R., & Schreibman, L. (1994b). A new finding: Impairment in shifting attention in autistic and cerebellar patients. In S. Broman & J Grafman (Eds.), *Atypical cognitive deficits in developmental disorders: Implications for brain function* (pp. 101–137). Hillsdale, NJ: Erlbaum.

Dawson, G., Meltzoff, A. N., Osterling, J., Rinaldi, J., & Brown, E. (1998). Children with autism fail to orient to naturally occurring social stimuli. *J Autism Dev Disord, 28*, 479–485.

Frith, U., & Baron-Cohen, S. (1987). Perception in autistic children. In D. J. Cohen, & A. M. Donnellan (Eds.), Handbook of autism and pervasive developmental disorders (pp. 85–102). New York: Wiley.

Gluck, M. A., & Myers, C. E. (2001).Gateway to memory: An introduction to neural network modeling of the hippocampus and learning. Cambridge, MA: MIT Press.

Guptill, J. T., Booker, A. B., Gibbs, T. T., Kemper, T. L., Bauman, M. L., & Blatt, G. J. (2007).[3H]-flunitrazepam-labeled benzodiazepine binding sites in the hippocampal formation in autism: A multiple concentration autoradiographic study. *J Autism Dev Disord, 27*, 911–920.

Gustafsson, L., & Papliński, A. P. (2004). Self-organization of an artificial neural network subjected to attention shift impairments and familiarity preference, characteristics studied in autism. *J Autism Dev Disord., 34*, 189–198.

Happé, F. (1991). The autobiographical writings of three asperger syndrome adults: Problems of identification and implications for theory. In U. Frith

(Ed.), *Autism and asperger syndrome* (pp. 207–252). Cambridge: Cambridge University Press.

Happé, F. G. E. (1996). Studying weak central coherence at low levels: Children with autism do not succumb to visual illusions. A Research Note. *J Child Psychol Psychiatry, 37,* 873–877.

Haykin, S. (1999). *Neural networks—A comprehensive foundation* (2nd ed.). Upper Saddle River, NJ: Prentice Hall.

Hermelin, B. (1978). Images and language. In M. Rutter & E. Schoppler (Eds.), *Autism: A reappraisal of concept and treatment* (pp. 141–154). New York: Plenum.

Hermelin, B., & O'Connor, N. (1970). Psychological experiments with autistic children. Oxford: Oxford University Press.

Hillier, A., Campbell, H., Keillor, J., Phillips, N., & Beversdorf, D. Q. (2007). Decreased false memory for visually presented shapes and symbols among adults on the autism spectrum. *J Clin Exp Neuropsychol, 29,* 610–616.

Just, M. A., Cherkassky, V. L., Keller, T. A., & Minshew, N. J. (2004). Cortical activation and synchronization during sentence comprehension in high-functioning autism: Evidence of underconnectivity. *Brain, 127,* 1811–1821.

Kohonen, T. (2001). *Self-organising maps* (3rd ed.). Berlin: Springer.

Lewis, J. D., & Elman, J. L. (2008). Growth-related neural reorganization and the autism phenotype: A test of the hypothesis that altered brain growth leads to altered connectivity. *Dev Sci., 11,* 135–155.

Lovaas, O. I., Schreibman, L., Koegel, R., & Rehm, R. (1971). Selective responding by autistic children to multiple sensory input. *J Abnorm Psychol, 77,* 211–222.

McClelland, J. L. (2000). The basis of hyperspecificity in autism: A preliminary suggestion based on properties of neural nets. *J Autism Dev Disord, 30,* 497–502.

Minshew, N. J., Luna, B., & Sweeney, J. A. (1999). Oculomotor evidence for neocortical systems but not cerebellar dysfunction in autism. *Neurology, 52,* 917–922.

Mizuno, A., Villalobos, M. E., Davies, N. M., Dahl, B. C., & Müller, R. A. (2006). Partially enhanced thalamocortical functional connectivity in autism. *Brain Res, 1104,* 160–174.

Mottron, L., & Burack, J. A. (2001). Enhanced perceptual functioning in the development of autism. In J. A. Burack, T. Charman, N. Yirmiya, & P. R. Zelazo (Eds.), *The development of autism: Perspectives from theory and research* (pp. 131–148). Mahwah, NJ: Lawrence Erlbaum Associates.

Narayanan, A., White, C. A., Saklayen, S., Scaduto, M. J., Carpenter, A. L., Abduljalil, A., Schmalbrock, S., & Beversdorf, D. Q. (2010). Effect of propranolol on functional connectivity in autism spectrum disorder – a pilot study. *Brain Imag Behav, 4,* 189–197.

O'Connor, N., & Hermelin, B. (1967). Auditory and visual memory in autistic and normal children. *J Mental Deficiency, 11,* 126–131.

Pascualvaca, D. M., Fantie, B. D., Papageorgiou, M., & Mirsky A. F. (1998). Attentional capacities in children with autism: Is there a general deficit in shifting focus? *J Autism Dev Disord, 28,* 467–478.

Principe, J. C., Euliano, N. R., & Lefebvre, W. C.(2000). *Neural and adaptive systems, competitive and kohonen networks.* Hoboken, NJ: Wiley.

Rapin, I., & Katzman, R. (1998). Neurobiology of autism. *Ann Neurol, 43,* 7–14.

Raymond, G. V., Bauman, M. L., & Kemper, T. L. (1996). Hippocampus in autism: A Golgi analysis. *Acta Neuropathol, 91,* 117–119.

Roediger, H. L., & McDermott, K. B. (1995). Creating false memories: Remembering words not presented in lists. *J Exp Psychol: Learn Mem Cogn, 21,* 803–814.

Rubenstein, J. L., & Merzenich, M. M. (2003). Model of autism: Increased ratio of excitation/inhibition in key neural systems. *Genes Brain Behav, 2,* 255–267.

Rumelhart, D. E., & McClelland, J. L. (1986). *Parallel distributed processing: Explorations in the microstructure of cognition, Vols. 1 and 2.* Cambridge, MA: MIT Press.

Russell, J. (1997). Introduction. In J. Russell (Ed.), *Autism as an executive disorder* (pp. 1–20). New York: Oxford University Press.

Schreibman, L., & Lovaas, O. I. (1973). Overselective responding to social stimuli by autistic children. *J Abnorm Child Psychol, 1,* 152–168.

Shah, A., & Frith, U. (1983). An islet of ability in autistic children: A research note. *J Child Psychol Psychiatry, 24,* 613–620.

Shah, A., & Frith, U. (1993). Why do autistic individuals show superior performance on the block design task? *J Child Psychol Psychiatry, 34,* 1351–1364.

Sparrow, S. S., Balla, D. A., & Cicchetti, D. V. (1984).*Vineland adaptive behavior scales. Interview Edition. Survey from Manual.* Circle Pines, MN: American Guidance.

Yip, J., Soghomonian, J. J., & Blatt, G. J. (2008). Increased GAD67 mRNA expression in cerebellar interneurons in autism: Implications for Purkinje cell dysfunction. *J Neurosci Res, 86,* 525–530.

Young, A., Hellawell, D., De Wal, C., & Johnson, M. (1996). Facial expression processing after amygdalectomy. *Neuropsychologia, 34,* 31–39.

Chapter 21

Structural and Functional Brain Development in ASD: The Impact of Early Brain Overgrowth and Considerations for Treatment

Karen Pierce and Lisa T. Eyler[1]

The biology of the autistic brain has long been a mystery. This is because autism was originally cast as a predominantly psychological, not neurobiological, disorder (Bettelheim, 1967; Kanner, 1943), and this hindered basic scientific research for decades. Today much is known about the disorder, including that it is more heritable than breast cancer or diabetes, and that concordance rates for monozygotic twins, particularly if the broader phenotype is considered, can be as high as 90% (Bailey et al., 1995; Ritvo, Freeman, Mason-Brothers, Mo, & Ritvo, 1985; Steffenburg et al., 1989). At its most macroscopic level, autism is clearly a *neuro*biological disorder; the gamut of symptoms— from social aloofness to repetitive behavior—stem from faulty neural function.

Magnetic resonance imaging (MRI), electroencephalography (EEG), and postmortem techniques are powerful tools which are used to examine the brains of individuals with autism, and studies that utilize these techniques have been accumulating over the past 20 years. A superficial examination of brain research findings, however, illustrates a seemingly complex—and on the surface somewhat conflicting— profile, including: reduced width of cortical mini-columns (Casanova, Buxhoeveden, Switala, & Roy, 2002; Casanova & Trippe, 2009) and increased cell packing density in some brain areas (Bauman & Kemper, 2005), yet a decreased number of neurons in other brain areas (Schumann & Amaral, 2006; van Kooten et al., 2008; Whitney, Kemper, Bauman, Rosene, & Blatt, 2008); hyperplasia in cerebellar hemispheres (Courchesne et al., 1994) and hypoplasia in the cerebellar vermis (Courchesne, Yeung-Courchesne, Press, Hesselink, & Jernigan, 1988; Kaufmann et al., 2003); reduced whole brain gray matter volume (McAlonan, et al. 2005) and enlarged whole-brain gray-matter volumes (see Brambilla et al., 2003; and Chapter 3 for reviews); neurofunctional

1. This work was supported by NIMH grant 1R01MH080134, awarded to Karen Pierce.

hypoactivity (Bird, Catmur, Silani, Frith, & Frith, 2006; Castelli, Frith, Happe, & Frith, 2002; Just, 2004) and neurofunctional hyperactivity (Noonan, Haist, & Muller, 2009); and enhanced amplitude of EEG components as well as a reduction in the same components (see Jeste & Nelson, 2009, for a review).

While there are several different factors that may give rise to the apparent contradictions and complexities in brain research findings to date, we believe that two are particularly important. The first, and most crucial, factor relates to evidence that biological abnormalities in autism begin shortly after birth, or perhaps even prenatally. Developmental age-related changes lead to different neurobiological effects at different ages. Despite this, the majority of brain research on the disorder has been conducted on high-functioning adults with the disorder—20 or 30 years after the onset of symptoms (Courchesne et al., 2007). To the extent that compensatory mechanisms, plasticity, and even the effects of epigenetics may differ among individuals as well as across development, research findings with adults represent only a small part—a relative end state—of development in autism. Thus, while the mature phenotype is essential to study, it illuminates the state of autism after a lifetime of interactions between and among biological and environmental mechanisms. An understanding of the neurobiology of autism might come into clearer focus if the vital period of early development were more closely examined, and research findings were consistently placed in a developmental context.

A second factor that contributes to challenges in interpreting autism research is that there may be multiple, heterogeneous pathologies that all give rise to broadly similar behavioral profiles that are recognized as autism spectrum disorders. For example, some children with autism may have copy-number mutations (Sebat et al., 2007), chromosome-15 abnormalities (Cook et al., 1998; Depienne et al., 2009; Filipek et al., 2003; Hogart, Wu, Lasalle, & Schanen, 2008; Miller et al., 2009; Ouldim, Natiq, Jonveaux, & Sefiani, 2007; Simic & Turk, 2004), or associated conditions such as tuberous sclerosis (Jeste, Sahin, Bolton, Ploubidis, & Humphrey, 2008; Wong, 2006), while others do not, yet they all are diagnosed as autistic. Furthermore, across the spectrum there is considerable heterogeneity in symptom presentation—such as a presence of language abilities in some children, and a lack of speech in others—which may or may not be related to differences in etiologies. Thus, the forces of

both etiological *and* symptom heterogeneity have a significant, but currently poorly understood, impact on brain research in the field of autism. New approaches, such as brain-gene mapping, hold promise as ways to disentangle this heterogeneity.

Evidence now suggests that there are underlying developmental principles that guide the development of the neurobiological phenotype of autism. As such, this chapter will broadly characterize structural and functional brain imaging findings about autism as applying to either the early (birth to 5 years) or late (adolescence through adulthood) time periods. The middle childhood years, while important, have not been extensively researched at the neurobiological level, and will thus be discussed infrequently. A particularly strong emphasis will be placed on the early period, because we believe that careful examination of this stage may hold the key to some of the most pressing autism questions of the day. Fortunately, there have been several pioneering studies and concepts that have started us on our way. First is the discovery that the autistic brain undergoes accelerated rates of brain growth during early development (Courchesne et al., 2001; Courchesne, Carper, & Akshoomoff, 2003). Based on these findings and studies that have followed, we have recently theorized that autism involves three phases of brain growth: early overgrowth during the first years of life, arrest of growth during middle childhood, then a decline during adulthood (Courchesne, 2004; Courchesne et al., 2007; Courchesne & Pierce, 2005a, 2005b). Second is the realization that in vivo sleep MRI and fMRI can be used as powerful tools to safely study the living autistic brain as early as the first days of life (Redcay, Kennedy, & Courchesne, 2007). Third, and finally, is the demonstration that brain-behavior studies during early development are not only essential, but possible to perform (Dawson et al., 2002; Dawson, Webb, Carver, Panagiotides, & McPartland, 2004; Kuhl, Coffey-Corina, Padden, & Dawson, 2005; Pierce & Courchesne, 2001; Redcay & Courchesne, 2008; Redcay et al., 2007).

Within the framework of early/late and functional/structural brain studies of autism, we believe strong consideration should be given to three pivotal ideas about the disorder previously articulated by our laboratory (Courchesne, 2004; Courchesne, et al., 2007; Courchesne & Pierce, 2005a, 2005b). First, autism involves three phases of aberrant brain growth as described above. Second, the result of this overgrowth, which may stem from an excess number of neurons, is an increase in the ratio of local—relative to long-distance—connections. Third, because the frontal lobes have the most protracted development and are undergoing intense refinement during the peak overgrowth period (roughly 9–24 months of age), this brain region may be the most severely affected, both structurally and functionally, in autism. In this chapter we will further refine these hypothesized principles as well as consider a new, fourth, principle regarding brain development in autism. Namely, we introduce what we call the "threshold theory," which posits that resting functional networks are established as faulty during the early brain overgrowth period in autism. These faulty resting networks may explain why functional magnetic resonance imaging studies in autism almost unilaterally report hypoactivity during task conditions in widespread cortical and subcortical areas, including (but not limited to) the fusiform gyrus, amygdala, hippocampus, precuneus, posterior cingulate, anterior cingulate, orbitofrontal cortex, medial frontal cortex, inferior temporal gyrus, middle temporal gyrus, and superior temporal sulcus. Specifically, we hypothesize that in many cases, the stimulus condition—be it a face-processing, executive-functioning, or other task—is unable to modulate the normal balance between resting and task-activated networks. The threshold theory is particularly strongly supported by consideration of specific examples in the literature on face processing. If the threshold theory holds true, then it may not be the case that defects in individual brain regions per se are immediately responsible for the autism phenotype. Rather, defects in coordinated switching between resting and stimulus-evoked networks are more relevant to understanding behavioral deficits in autism.

In light of these ideas, we consider, as others have before us (Dawson, 2008), perhaps the most important question in the field of autism: *Can abnormal brain connectivity patterns in autism be changed?* The chapter then concludes with a discussion of future directions in the study of autism, especially those that will further test the theory of abnormal growth and development of connectivity in the autistic brain.

AUTISM DURING THE EARLY PERIOD: BRAIN STRUCTURE

There is arguably no other period during development that encapsulates such a wide range of dynamic changes as the first three years of life. At the molecular level, processes that started before birth continue to operate in order to strengthen active neural connections, prune out redundant or unused connections, and increase the efficiency of long-distance neural communication through increases in myelination. At the macroscopic level, these processes result in increases in head size, grey matter volume, and white matter volume, as well as changes in the organization and integrity of white matter, as observable by diffusion tensor imaging. The newborn brain begins at only 25% of its adult size, but the dramatic growth in the first two years of life brings it to about 75% of its adult volume, while true adult size is not fully achieved until 12–16 years of age (Courchesne et al., 2000). At the behavioral level, the infant enters the world unable to perform little more than regulatory and reflexive actions. By the time that same infant is 3 years old, she can speak in sentences, use a wide range of complex emotions and gestures to convey meaning, and regulate and control her own behavior to achieve goals (Kochanska, Coy, & Murray, 2001). Given that children with autism either fail to achieve or are delayed in achieving these same skills, it is no surprise that brain structure and function in autism are abnormal. Unfortunately, virtually nothing was known or discovered about the brain in autism during the first years of life for almost 50 years after the disorder was first described. This lack of progress is somewhat ironic, given that in the first description of the disorder in 1943, Leo Kanner made the striking observation that children with autism seemed to have large heads, and thus potentially large brains (Kanner, 1943).

THE DISCOVERY OF EARLY BRAIN OVERGROWTH IN AUTISM

Head Circumference Studies

It was not until 2003 that the first empirical demonstration of abnormal brain size in autism during the infancy period came to light (Courchesne et al., 2003). This study used a simple and inexpensive technology to make inferences about the brain in autism: a tape measure. Although a weak indicator of brain size later in life, head circumference strongly correlates (r = 0.93) with actual brain size, based on MRI, up to 6 years of age (Bartholomeusz, Courchesne, & Karns, 2002). Since the initial discovery, multiple studies have used retrospective head circumference values to document abnormal rates of brain growth and brain size in autism (Dawson et al., 2007; Dementieva et al., 2005; Fukumoto et al., 2008; Hazlett et al., 2005; Mraz, Green, Dumont-Mathieu, Makin, & Fein, 2007; Sacco et al., 2007; Webb et al., 2007).

Collectively, head circumference studies illustrate two essential points regarding the neuroanatomic profile of autism. First, at the time of birth, overall brain size is not enlarged, but instead is similar to, or slightly smaller than, the normal average (Courchesne et al., 2003). For instance, infants later diagnosed with autism in the Courchesne et al. (2003) study had head circumference values slightly below the 50th percentile at birth (see Redcay & Courchesne, 2005, for meta-analysis and review). By 12–14 months, however, values jumped up to above the 95th percentile in many cases, as was also found in other later studies (Dawson et al., 2007; Dissanayake, Bui, Huggins, & Loesch, 2006; Webb et al., 2007). Thus, it is the relative *rate of change* that may most strongly characterize autism. Figure 21-1 shows brain growth patterns based on head circumference in 3 children with an autism spectrum diagnosis. Note that in the first two children with an ASD illustrated in Figure 21-1, head circumference values were *below* the 50th percentile at birth (i.e., a Z score of 0), and jumped one or more standard deviations above the normal mean in the relatively brief period of 6 months. This is in contrast to typically developing children, who may also have large head sizes, but generally do not exhibit rapid changes to the same extreme as is seen in some cases of autism. Overall, rates of brain growth in children with an ASD can usually be characterized as one of three types: those that show persistent enlarged brain sizes and meet criteria for macrencephaly (i.e., > 97th percentile); those that show large changes in brain size, relative to head circumference at birth, but do not meet criteria for macrencephaly; and those that do not exhibit dramatic changes in brain size at all (University of California San Diego Autism Center of Excellence, 2010).

Macrencephaly per se, however, is not specific to autism. Many syndromes—including Sotos, Canavan, Simpson-Golabi-Behmel, neurofibromatosis, Cowden, Macrocephaly-Cutis Marmorata Telangiectatica Congenita (M-CMTC) and Perlman—all display macrencephaly during childhood (see reviews of disorders associated with macrencephaly in Cohen, 2003, and Courchesne & Pierce, 2005a). Although there can be some social withdrawal associated with Sotos syndrome (Rutter & Cole, 1991) and neurofibromatosis (Noll et al., 2007), children with these disorders of enlarged brain volumes generally do not display symptoms of autism. In contrast to autism, children with all of the aforementioned disorders are born with macrencephaly, suggesting that brain growth accelerated prenatally. Thus, the distinguishing feature between autism and these other disorders of brain growth is the very brief and rapid period of brain-size change that generally begins several months after birth.

MRI Studies

Although head circumference studies show that brain growth peaks around the first birthday, MRI studies show that brain enlargement in autism can still be detected at 2–4 years in age, and is about 10% larger relative to typically developing children (Courchesne et al., 2001; Hazlett et al., 2005; Redcay & Courchesne, 2005; Sparks et al., 2002; Stanfield et al., 2008). A meta-analysis of all published MRI brain size data on children, adolescents, and adults through early 2005 showed that the period of greatest brain enlargement in autism is during the toddler years and early childhood (Redcay & Courchesne, 2005).

These striking findings have led researchers to examine more specific structures within the brains of children with autism, in hopes of finding regional abnormalities that would help to explain the unique behavioral features of the disorder. Studies comparing and contrasting multiple brain regions in young children with autism are sparse, but recent work suggests that the frontal and temporal lobes may be particularly affected (Carper & Courchesne, 2005; Carper, Moses, Tigue, & Courchesne, 2002). This is not surprising, given that higher-order executive and social functions, such as the ability to have a meta-representation of other minds (or Theory of Mind), appear most impaired in autism (Baron-Cohen, 2009). It is the frontal lobes that are commonly thought to be integral for most of these functions (Adolphs, 2009).

Some studies have examined the size of the cerebellum and its subregions in young children with autism. In general, increased total cerebellar volume has been observed, which appears to be proportional to total cerebral volume increases (Courchesne et al., 2001; Herbert et al., 2003; Palmen et al., 2005; Sparks et al., 2002). However, subregions within the cerebellum

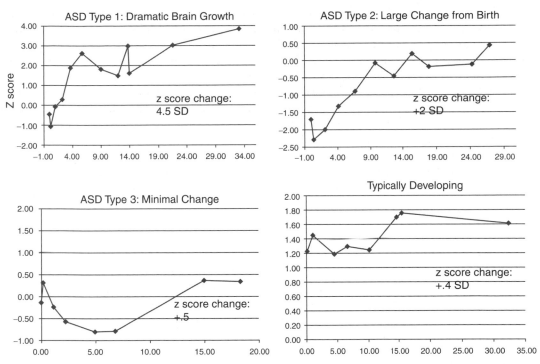

Figure 21-1 Representative examples of types of changes in brain growth as indexed by head circumference in 3 infants with an ASD from the UCSD Autism Center of Excellence, and one typically developing infant. Brain growth characteristics in children with an ASD generally fall into one of 3 types. Type 1 exhibits extreme changes in brain size across the first 24 months of life, usually > 3 SD above the normal mean and meets criteria for macrencephaly. Type 2 exhibits large changes in brain size from birth to about 2 years, but absolute head size is not excessive. Type 3 shows little change across development and never meets criteria for macrencephaly. Finally, it is important to note that many typically developing children also have large head sizes, as is illustrated in the last panel.

appear to vary in whether they are reduced or enlarged in autism. Reduced relative volume of the cerebellar vermis was observed in young children with autism, particularly lobules VI-VII (Carper & Courchesne, 2000; Courchesne et al., 2001; Kates et al., 1998; Kaufmann et al., 2003; Webb et al., 2009). Findings for other subregions, however, have been more mixed (Courchesne et al., 2001; Webb et al., 2009; see Stanfield et al., 2008 for a review).

Other studies have focused on the amygdala because of its role in emotion processing, an area of considerable deficit in autism. Few studies have examined children with autism, but those that have focused on the early period found enlargement of amygdala volume among those with the disorder (Mosconi et al., 2009; Munson et al., 2006; Sparks et al., 2002; Schumann, Carter, Lord & Courchesne, 2009), and this may continue into the early childhood years (Schumann et al., 2004). This contrasts with fairly

consistent findings of amygdala volume reductions in adults with autism spectrum disorders. In two studies, amygdala enlargement in toddlers with autism was found to be associated with social functioning deficits (Munson et al., 2006; Schumann, Carter, Lord & Courchesne, 2009). A longitudinal study examined amygdala growth from 2 to 4 years of age and confirmed enlargement at both time points in the autism spectrum disorder group, and also observed a relationship between volume at age 4 and joint attention ability in the autistic group (Mosconi et al., 2009; see Chapter 3 for a general review of neuroanatomy in autism).

DTI and Autism: Clues To Structural Connectivity?

Diffusion tensor imaging (DTI) allows an in vivo look into the microstructure of white matter in the brain, and is an important complement to volumetric studies of specific structures, such as the amygdala. DTI may be particularly informative in the study of autism, because it has been speculated that white-matter defects may be even more pronounced than gray-matter defects for affected individuals (Herbert, 2005). Furthermore, in contrast to gray matter, white-matter volume continues to increase across childhood and adolescence (Courchesne et al., 2000; Durston et al., 2001; Giedd et al., 1999), thus allowing for analyses of growth curves and changes specific to the microstructure of axons.

Studies that utilize DTI technology generally describe two characteristics of white matter: the overall *quantity* of the diffusion of water molecules (often referred to as mean diffusivity), and the *directionality* of the diffusion of water molecules (often referred to as anisotropy) within a particular voxel. Diffusion imaging takes advantage of the fact that the myelin sheath surrounding an axon restricts the diffusion of water perpendicular to the axon, while allowing relatively free diffusion of water parallel to the axon. This partially restricted motion is referred to as *anisotropic* diffusion, and carries a theoretical maximum value of one. In contrast, completely free diffusion of water, as is found in ventricles, is said to be *isotropic* and theoretical FA values should be near zero. As a concept, fractional anisotropy (FA) is thought to reflect both the size and number of myelinated axons and the coherence of axonal orientation (Neil et al., 1998). Thus, low FA values may suggest decreased fiber density, reduced myelination of fiber tracts, or less directionally coherent organization of fibers within a voxel. White matter injuries, such as a stroke, result in low FA values, and studies have shown a correlation between low FA values and reduced cognitive performance (Skranes et al., 2007). FA values also decrease as a consequence of healthy aging (Kochunov et al., 2007), and can be even more severely reduced in degenerative cases of aging such as Alzheimer's disease (Chua, Wen, Slavin, & Sachdev, 2008). In contrast, high FA values are thought to reflect coherently bundled, myelinated fibers oriented along the axis of greatest diffusion, or a general increase in the size or number of myelinated axons within a particular voxel (for an excellent review of how brain diffusion properties are affected in clinical samples, see Cascio, Gerig, & Piven, 2007).

Given an abnormal brain growth trajectory in autism, what profile of white matter microstructure, as characterized by diffusivity and FA values, would be predicted? During the first phase of brain growth in autism, namely the overgrowth phase, there is no clear prediction. That is, FA values could theoretically be either increased, reflecting greater number of axons and increased myelination, or decreased, reflecting poorly organized fiber tracts within cortex particularly in the frontal lobes. In the only study to use DTI to examine white matter during a time period that coincides with early brain overgrowth, Ben Bashat et al. (2007) examined FA and diffusivity indices (i.e., displacement) in seven toddlers with confirmed autism ranging in age from 1.8 to 3 years. Contrasting DTI values were also obtained from a sample of over 40 typically developing infants and children. Although the autism sample size was small, results were remarkably consistent: 100% of the toddlers with autism had FA values that exceeded the normal mean in some brain regions, such as the forceps minor region (the anterior portion of the corpus callosum that extends into the frontal lobes). Region of interest analyses revealed that the largest FA increases were in the genu of the corpus callosum, posterior limb of the internal capsule and corticospinal tracts. The authors interpret their findings as evidence of accelerated maturation of white matter in autism (see Figure 21-2). Although it is only one study, results from Ben Bashat et al. (2007) suggest that FA values in particular may be increased during the overgrowth phase of brain development in autism.

Advanced visualization of DTI data can be obtained via a method commonly referred to as "tractography" or "DTI fiber tracking." Fiber tracking uses the diffusion tensor of each voxel to follow an axonal tract in three dimensions from voxel to voxel through the human brain. Because DTI provides only microstructural information at relatively low spatial resolution, DTI fiber tracking is often combined with functional or higher resolution anatomic information to delineate specific pathways. Currently there are no published tractography studies in infants and young children with autism. The University of California, San Diego (UCSD) Autism Center of Excellence currently has studies under way to examine white matter structure in infants at risk for autism using both DTI and tractography. As can be seen in Figure 21-2, tractography may be an excellent mechanism to visualize aberrant white matter tract projections in infants at risk for autism. Both infants at risk for autism shown in Figure 21-2 illustrate excess white matter

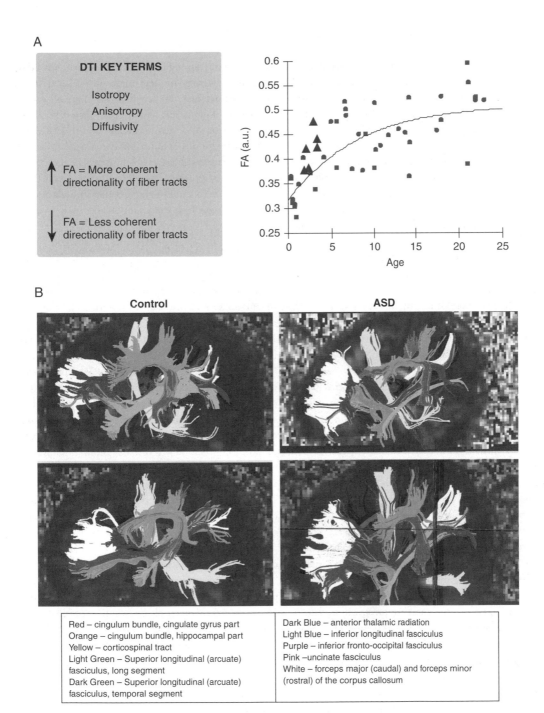

A

DTI KEY TERMS

Isotropy
Anisotropy
Diffusivity

↑ FA = More coherent
directionality of fiber tracts

↓ FA = Less coherent
directionality of fiber tracts

B

Control   ASD

Red – cingulum bundle, cingulate gyrus part
Orange – cingulum bundle, hippocampal part
Yellow – corticospinal tract
Light Green – Superior longitudinal (arcuate)
fasciculus, long segment
Dark Green – Superior longitudinal (arcuate)
fasciculus, temporal segment

Dark Blue – anterior thalamic radiation
Light Blue – inferior longitudinal fasciculus
Purple – inferior fronto-occipital fasciculus
Pink –uncinate fasciculus
White – forceps major (caudal) and forceps minor
(rostral) of the corpus callosum

Figure 21-2 A. Values of fractional anisotropy (FA) in the forceps minor (the anterior portion of the corpus callosum that extends into the frontal lobes) plotted for 7 toddlers with autism (triangles) against typically developing subjects ages 4 months–23 years. Note that FA values were increased for all 7 ASD toddlers relative to the normal mean (from Ben-Bashat, et al., 2007). B. DTI tractography images from 14-month-old (top) and 20-month-old (bottom) ASD and typically developing infants. The inferior longitudinal fasiculus (ILF) is diminished in the infants at risk for an ASD, as is the superior longitudinal arcuate fasiculus (SLAF), a fiber tract involved in language processing. Note that the forceps minor region of the corpus callosum (CC-FMin) that extends into the frontal lobes (shown in white) is enlarged relative to normal. This finding is consistent with Ben Beshat et al. (2007), who reported increased FA in the forceps minor portion of the corpus callosum (Unpublished data from the University of California San Diego Autism Center of Excellence). (See color Figure 21-2.)

tracts in the frontal lobes, likely the result of early brain overgrowth.

Is There a Relationship Between Early Brain Overgrowth and Autism Symptoms?

Although it is plausible to hypothesize that children with the most excessive brain overgrowth are also most affected clinically, whether such a linkage exists is currently unknown. One study designed to address this issue found that those children with the most enlarged brains were more likely to be diagnosed with Autistic disorder than with the symptomatically milder pervasive developmental disorder, not otherwise specified (PDD-NOS), while other studies found no such relationship (Akshoomoff et al., 2004; Mraz et al., 2007). A recent study, however, found a relationship in the opposite direction; namely, children with greater rates of accelerated brain growth during the first year of life had better adaptive functioning and less social impairment during childhood (Dementieva et al., 2005). Finally, a new study found a relationship between head circumference and outcome in a high-risk sample of infant siblings. Specifically, findings indicated that infants with larger HC values at 12 months and greater deceleration of growth between 12 and 24 months were more likely to receive a final diagnosis on the spectrum than those who did not exhibit this profile (Elder, Dawson, Toth, Fein, & Munson, 2008).

It may also be useful to examine the temporal relationship between early brain overgrowth and the onset of observable autism symptoms, a research goal most directly achievable by the use of prospective study designs. Consider that the first prospective study of autism (Zwaigenbaum et al., 2005) utilizing the infant-sibling approach found no difference in a range of social and attention tasks between infants eventually diagnosed as having an ASD and those that were typically developing prior to 12 months of age. At 12 months however, deviations from normal development emerged in a wide range of behaviors from language, to attention, to social functions. Temporally, the period of peak brain overgrowth as identified by a recent meta analysis (12–14 months; Redcay & Courchesne, 2005) overlaps with the rapid decrease in social behavior for the infants in the Zwaigenbaum study, also characterized in detail as single-case studies (Bryson et al., 2007) who eventually were diagnosed with autism (see Figure 21-3). Although direct evidence of a relationship between early brain overgrowth and the onset of autism symptoms has not yet been demonstrated in humans, studies of rodents have shown that genetic mutations leading to brain overgrowth result in abnormal social behavior in some (Kwon et al., 2006; Page, Kuti, Prestia, & Sur, 2009), but not all (Moy et al., 2009) mouse models. In autism, it may be the case that upregulation of key genes relating to brain growth may serve as early warning signs that may actually precede brain overgrowth, as well as observable symptoms.

Genetic, Cellular, and Molecular Basis of Early Brain Overgrowth

It is no surprise that genes regulating brain growth have been studied extensively in autism. Mutations in PTEN, a gene involved in cell-cycle regulation, have been found in a small subset of autistic subjects with macrencephaly (Butler et al., 2005; Goffin, Hoefsloot, Bosgoed, Swillen, & Fryns, 2001; Herman et al., 2007; Varga, Pastore, Prior, Herman, & McBride, 2009). In addition, polymorphisms of genes related to the serotonin system have recently been linked to brain overgrowth in young children with autism (Davis et al., 2008; Wassink et al., 2007). Serotonin plays a role in normal brain development (Sodhi & Sanders-Bush, 2004), and several lines of evidence suggest serotonergic abnormalities in autism (Chugani et al., 1997, 1999; Cook et al., 1997). In one study that examined the relationship of serotonin-linked genes to brain size in children, a functional, variable number, tandem repeat polymorphism in the monoamine oxidase A gene (MAO-A), which regulates serotonin levels, leading to lower MAO-A activity (thus, higher serotonin levels) was found to be associated with larger brain volumes in a sample of 2- and 3-year-old boys with autism (Davis et al., 2008). The same group (Wassink et al., 2007) found that the short allele of the serotonin transporter gene was positively associated with cerebral gray matter volume in a dose-dependent fashion in two samples of young (3- and 4 years old) boys with autism. This finding is not entirely consistent with the MAO-A gene association, since the short allele polymorphism is associated with lower serotonin uptake (Lesch et al., 1996), but the studies collectively support a link between genetic abnormalities in the serotonin system and early brain overgrowth. Examination of genes alone likely will not be sufficient to understand early brain overgrowth and anatomical connectivity deficits in autism, because these processes are dynamic, whereas the genetic code is fixed. Recent studies have begun to look at levels of

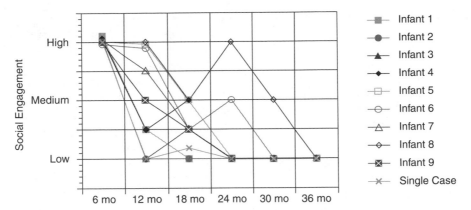

Figure 21-3 Graphic illustration of the levels of social engagement of 9 high-risk infants between the ages of 6 and 36 months eventually diagnosed as having an ASD, as described in previously published case studies. Data from the first 9 cases are adapted from Bryson et al., 2007 and the final case is from Dawson et al., 2005. Note that all 10 high-risk infants showed high levels of social engagement at 6 months. Also note that the decline in social responsiveness was inconsistent between children with some declining rapidly by 12 months and others not until 24 or 30 months. High Social Engagement refers to a consistent interest or pleasure in, and responsiveness to, others. Medium Social Engagement refers to inconsistent interest or pleasure in, and responsiveness to, others. Low Social Engagement refers to little or no interest or pleasure in, and responsiveness to, others. (See color Figure 21-3.)

gene expression, which is likely to reflect the interaction of both genetic and environmental factors across development. Examining gene expression in blood cells is a minimally invasive way to potentially identify biomarkers for autism. Using microarray technology, studies have identified dysregulation of blood-based gene expression in gene families related to cell growth and maintenance, development, metabolism, and signal transduction among children with autism (Enstrom et al., 2009; Gregg et al., 2008). Studies such as this are ongoing in our lab and others, and, in combination with other measures of brain and behavior, may lead to a sensitive and specific marker for autism and provide further evidence regarding the pathophysiology of the disorder.

At the cellular and molecular level, the mechanisms that may underlie early brain overgrowth and altered connectivity patterns, particularly in the frontal lobe, are as yet unknown. One idea we have proposed is that the brain overgrowth reflects an excess of neurons, possibly as a result of failure of normal apoptosis, which normally occurs during typical development (Courchesne et al., 2007; Courchesne & Pierce, 2005a, 2005b). Since pyramidal neurons predominate in the cortex, increases in the number of these neurons would lead to findings (reviewed above) of increases in grey and white matter volume and overall brain size. Interestingly, since pyramidal neurons are excitatory, a selective increase in these types

of neurons might alter the balance of excitatory and inhibitory inputs, and also lead to some of the functional brain response deficits reviewed below. Cortical imbalances in excitation and inhibition has been a longstanding theoretical description of autism, first postulated by Rubenstein and Merzenich in 2003 and later considered by others (Carper & Courchesne, 2005; Courchesne et al., 2007; Courchesne & Pierce, 2005a, 2005b; Persico & Bourgeron, 2006; Rubenstein & Merzenich, 2003; Vaccarino, Grigorenko, Smith, & Stevens, 2009).

The Importance of Frontal Pyramidal Neurons In Early Brain Enlargement

Given that brain overgrowth seems to be greatest in the frontal cortex, the role of frontal pyramidal neurons in autism is of particular interest. Only one stereological study in autism has been published that specifically addresses neuron numbers in frontal cortex. In this study, Kennedy and colleagues (2007) found 58% more spindle neurons, which are large specialized pyramidal cells thought by some to be important elements in social processing circuits, in a 3-year-old autistic case, as compared to an age and hemisphere matched control. Overall, however, there were no group differences in spindle neuron counts between ASD and controls, likely because this study contained a wide age range (3–41 years), and age effects were not specifically analyzed (Kennedy et al., 2007). In other postmortem investigations, abnormalities in minicolumn width defects are widespread across the cortex, with the greatest defects in the frontal lobes, and significant developmental trends suggesting possible early overproduction of neuropil (Buxhoeveden et al., 2006; Casanova, et al., 2006; Casanova, Buxhoeveden, & Brown, 2002;).

Frontal pyramidal neurons may play an especially important role in connectivity defects in autism simply because they stand at the epicenter of cortical circuits—thus constituting the sole output from, and the largest input system to, the cortex, as well as the major target of all inputs to the cortex. Pyramidal neurons of the deepest layers (VI and V) send subcortical projections to the thalamus, and brain stem and spinal cord, respectively, while those of the upper layers (II-IV) exclusively form intracortical connections. Furthermore, pyramidal neurons in prefrontal cortex in particular are unique in that they display larger dendritic trees and up to 20 times as many dendritic spines than those in primary cortices (Elston, 2000; 2003). Research by Herbert and colleagues (see Chapter 3) revealed that it is the outer radiate portion of white matter that may be selectively enlarged in autism, and the enlargement was greatest in the frontal cortex (Herbert et al., 2004). Pyramidal neurons in these upper layers (II-IV) form intra-cortical connections. Increased neurons, and thus increased connections, may result in the abnormal development of resting functional networks, an idea that we will elaborate on later in this chapter.

The timing of overgrowth and first emergence of dysfunctional behaviors associated with autism is coincident with the period of maximal development in the frontal, and also temporal, cortex. If there are too many neurons, and a relative imbalance of excitatory and inhibitory input in these regions, it is easy to see how the development of coordinated neural circuits underlying normal social, emotional, and language function would be impaired. In particular, local increases in neuron number would potentially serve to strengthen local and short-distance communication at the relative expense of long-distance connections, via a process of activity-based competition (Courchesne et al., 2007).

Synapses and Autism

An imbalance of excitation and inhibition can be achieved by means that may or may not be directly related to an excess number of neurons. Neuroligins and neurexins are molecules that are vital to the normal structure of synapses that connect nerve cells sending and receiving signals, and are thought to pay a major role in plasticity (Sudhof, 2008; see Figure 21-4). Recently, several genetic studies have reported defects in genes that code for neuroligins and neurexins in a few cases of autism (Jamain et al., 2003; Laumonnier et al., 2004). Since the initial discovery by Jamain (2003), several other studies have noted mutations in synaptic proteins (Arking et al., 2008; Bakkaloglu et al., 2008; Durand et al., 2007; Kim et al., 2008). In general, synapses can be either excitatory, typically when the neurotransmitter glutamate is released, or inhibitory, typically with the release of the neurotransmitter GABA. The ratio of excitatory or inhibitory synapses on a neuron determines whether or not it will fire in any given situation. While there is an exuberance of synaptic connectivity during the first years of life, not all synaptic connections will be kept. Thus, the first few years of life are critical for brain circuit formation. Neuroligin and neurexin pathways are likely critical to the stabilization phase of synapses, in response to neuronal activity (Bourgeron, 2009). Indeed, synapses not only transmit signals, but also transform and refine them (Sudhof, 2008). In an attempt to explain the mechanism that may cause symptoms of autism, Tabuchi and colleagues (2007) demonstrated in a mouse model that overexpression of neuroligin-1 leads to excitatory transmission at synapses, whereas neuroligin-2 overexpression leads to inhibition. Tabuchi and colleagues (2007) speculated that an alteration in either neuroligin could affect the excitatory-inhibitory balance, subtly changing the number of neurons that are firing during brain development. Such disruptions could eventually produce the symptoms of autism, because synapses change with use, becoming more or less sensitive to stimuli depending on experience. This activity-dependent "synaptic plasticity" is the basis for circuit formation and learning and memory functions, and thus likely plays a major role in the development of language and social behavior as well. Although phenotypic fidelity of a complete mouse model of autism is debatable, such models are powerful tools for studying particular aspects of the disorder. Studies to date have provided provocative evidence of disrupted synaptic function in mouse models of autism: namely, excessive or diminished excitatory synaptic connectivity (Chao, Zoghbi, & Rosenmund, 2007; Hanson & Madison, 2007),

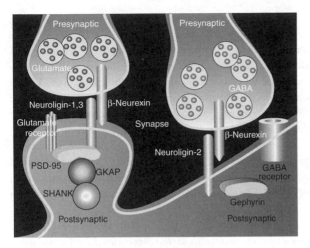

Neuroligins are are molecules that ensure signal transitions between nerve cells. **Neuroligins** are expressed on the surface of the postsynaptic neuron and bind to **nuerexins** which are proteins on the presynaptic neurons. It is thought that **neurologins** and neurexins together play key roles in the forming and functioning of synapses and are often thought of as "glue" that binds pre and postsynaptic neurons together.

There are 5 neuroligins genes in the human genome: **NLGN1, NLGN2, NLGN3, NLGN4** and **NLGN4Y**

Schematic of a chemical synapse between an axon of anc neuron and a dendrite of another. Synapses are specialized minute gaps between neurons. Electrical impulses arriving at the axon terminal trigger the release of packets of chemical messengers (neurontranmitters), which diffuse across the synaptic cleft to receptors on the adjacent dendrite, temporarily affecting the likelihood that an electrical impulse will be triggered in the latter neuron. Once released, the neurotransmitter is rapidly metabolized or is pumped back into a neuron.

Figure 21-4 Neuroligins, neurexins, and the synapse. Adapted from Garber, K. (2007). Autism's cause may reside in abnormalities at the synapse. Figure 2 called "Autism's origin." *Science, 317*(5835), 190–191. (See color Figure 21-4.)

and alterations in the balance of excitation and inhibition (Dani et al., 2005).

Overall, whereas an increase in neuron number or a decrease in cell death could lead to an imbalance in excitation and inhibition in the cortex, so could a defect in neuroligins, neurexins, and other synaptic binding proteins. Whether an excess of neurons or mutations in binding proteins is the cause of synaptic imbalance is unknown. Furthermore, the same mutations can be associated with different phenotypes in different people. For example, a microdeletion in NLGN4 was found to cause severe autism in one brother and Tourette's syndrome in another (Lawson-Yuen, Saldivar, Sommer, & Picker, 2008).

AUTISM DURING THE EARLY PERIOD: BRAIN FUNCTION

If early brain overgrowth is true for at least some children with autism, then what might be the functional consequences of such deviant growth patterns? Direct examinations of early functional brain development using modern techniques such as electroencephalography (EEG), event related potential (ERP), near-infrared spectroscopy (NIRS), magnetoencephalography (MEG) and functional magnetic resonance imaging (fMRI) are virtually non-existent for infants and toddlers at risk for an ASD. This is due in part to the challenges inherent in working with infants and young children whether normal or autistic, particularly the high susceptibility of such subjects to inducible motion artifacts. Additionally, until very recently, autism was not diagnosed until ages 3-4 years, thus largely eliminating the possibility of studying the disorder during the infancy and toddler periods. However, EEG and ERP technology has been used to examine some functions in ASD immediately following diagnosis, namely within the 3 to 4 year old range (Dawson, et al., 2002; Kuhl, et al., 2005). With the tide turning toward earlier diagnoses, at least one new study has used functional imaging techniques to examine children with autism as young as 24 months old (Redcay & Courchesne, 2008).

FUNCTIONAL STUDIES OF EARLY BRAIN DEVELOPMENT

Functional magnetic resonance imaging (fMRI) is arguably one of the most powerful imaging tools available, but it requires the subject to lie still for extended periods of time, a prerequisite that eliminated toddlers and young children from participating in studies of this type in the past. Recently, however, scientists have revealed that fMRI images of the young brain can be successfully obtained during unsedated, natural sleep. Sleep fMRI studies have demonstrated that cognitive processing persists during natural sleep, including processing one's own name as well as responding to environmental sounds such as a phone ringing, non-verbal tones, and language (Redcay, Haist, & Courchesne, 2008). Furthermore, studies using this method with infants and young children suggest that the functional patterns of activity are similar (although reduced in power) to what would be expected in awake children (Dehaene-Lambertz, Dehaene, & Hertz-Pannier, 2002; Wilke, Holland, & Ball, 2003). Functional brain activity during the early periods has been more widely studied using electroencephalography (EEG), particularly with typically developing infants. Although more widely used and potentially easier to implement than sleep fMRI studies, this technology has its own set of methodological issues which, like fMRI, largely relate to measurement error (Gaillard, 1988). Despite the challenges of research with infants and young children, much is known about typical functional brain development during the first years of life. In addition, a large body of developmental literature in animal models also exists, and this can guide hypotheses about functional brain development. Studies in this area highlight several important characteristics of early brain functional development from which we can begin to interpret research, and thus make speculations about brain development in autism.

Putative Developmental Principle #1: The Cortex is initially responsive in a widespread fashion, but becomes more focal over time

Although not universally accepted, there is considerable evidence to suggest that cortical functional activity in response to specific stimuli during infancy is initially widespread, but becomes more focal over time, allegedly as the result of learning and environmental input.

This principle is consistent with Mark Johnson's *interactive specialization* (IS) *theory* (Johnson, et al., 2009), and evidence in support of this theory can be found across a range of functional domains from language to face processing. For example, in language studies of cortical evoked potentials by Mills,

Coffey-Corina, and Neville (1993, 1997), 13- to 20-month-old infants were presented single words. Among the 13- to 20-month-old infants, event-related potential (ERP) differences between known and unknown words were widespread over both cerebral hemispheres. In contrast, 20-month-old infants displayed more focal patterns of responding to comprehended words in the expected left hemisphere. As another example, Johnson and colleagues (2005) showed that a few months after birth, wide areas of the cortex are functionally active in response to faces. By 6 months, however, the adult-expected right side dominance appears (de Haan & Nelson, 1997). Neurofunctional specialization extends well into the childhood years, so that more widespread cortical activation can be expected even during the childhood years, relative to adults. For example, in a study by Wang and colleagues (2006) 7- to 9-year-old children showed greater functional activity in frontal and temporal areas than adults (although note that adults show greater functional activity in some brain regions relative to children; see Figure 21-5). In summary, developmental theories suggest that children are not born with circumscribed "modules" for language- or face-processing, but such specialized cortical responding happens over time as the result of experience and competition in initially widespread areas of the cortex (Johnson et al., 2009; Karmiloff-Smith, 2007).

Whereas many regions of the cortex become more functionally specialized (and in many cases more focally activated) across development, connectivity between brain regions, on the other hand, increases in strength across development. For example, a recent developmental study of coordinated neural activity at rest, as measured by functional magnetic resonance imaging, found significantly greater correlation strength between the medial prefrontal cortex and other brain regions in the default mode network, such as the posterior cingulate, in adults as compared to 7- to 9-year-olds (Fair et al., 2008). These principles are illustrated in Figure 21-5.

Based on Principle #1, tasks that are more difficult or novel recruit more cerebral tissue than tasks that have been mastered already, and this general phenomenon of cortical activity holds true across development, even into the adult years. For example, within the same subjects, normal adults recruited more widespread areas of activity in response to a complex language task than in response to a simple one (Just, Carpenter, Keller, Eddy, & Thulborn, 1996). If the principle

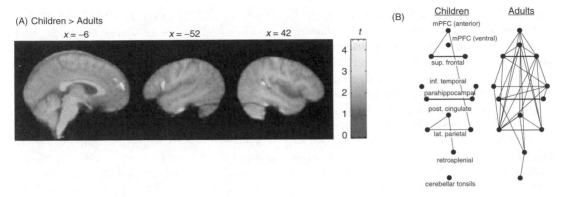

Figure 21-5 Examples of 2 theorized principles of brain development. (A). Example of more widespread activity earlier in development. In a task where children were to perceive irony, children showed significantly greater activity than adults in the MPFC (x = –8, y = 58, z = 20; P < 0.05), the left inferior frontal gyrus (x = –48, y = 16, z = 14; P = 0.05) and the right posterior STS (x = 42, y = –44, z = 16; P < 0.05). (From Wang, Lee, Sigman, & Dapretto, 2006). Johnson, Grossmann, & Cohen Kadosh (2009) cite this example of more widespread activity in children than adults in some brain regions as support of the view that functional activity becomes more focal across development. (B). Example of increased connectivity of networks later in development. Graphic visualization of the brain regions that are significantly correlated based on functional connectivity analyses. Brain regions in the default mode network (e.g., medial prefrontal cortex and posterior cingulate) are only very sparsely connected in children aged 7–9 years. In adults aged 21–31 years, the default regions are highly integrated (strongly functionally connected). (From Fair et al., 2008). (See color Figure 21-5.)

guiding specialization is true, *more* widespread functional activation might be expected in autism, given that most tasks would be more challenging for children with the disorder, and brain development likely has not yet reached a similar level of specialization, in comparison with typically developing children. As will be reviewed later, fMRI findings in adults with autism generally report hypoactivity of many brain regions, including the fusiform face area, amygdala, medial frontal lobes, and parietal lobes (Baron-Cohen et al., 1999; Critchley et al., 2000; Dapretto et al., 2006; Humphreys, Hasson, Avidan, Minshew, & Behrmann, 2008; Kennedy & Courchesne, 2008; Pierce, Haist, Sedaghat, & Courchesne, 2004; Pierce, Muller, Ambrose, Allen, & Courchesne, 2001; Schultz et al., 2000; Soulieres et al., 2009). Considering slightly younger children, results are more mixed. Children with autism ages 6–12, in the study by Pierce et al. (2008), showed strongly bilateral activation in response to familiar faces, whereas the typical children showed the more focal, and expected, right-side-dominance pattern. Finally, in the only fMRI study published on toddlers and young children with autism, Redcay and Courchesne (2008) presented children with autism, ages 25–46 months and mental- and

chronological-age-matched infants, forward and backward speech during natural sleep. The mental-age-matched typical infants (mean age 19 months) recruited widespread frontal and temporal areas while listening to the speech sounds. This is consistent with early (Mills et al., 1993) and recent (Johnson et al., 2009) ERP studies that suggest that the brain recruits widespread neural tissue during the early phases of learning. In contrast to the younger infants, the chronological-age-matched infants (mean age 36 months) showed more focal activity restricted to traditional language areas in the temporal lobe. The children with autism (mean age 36 months) displayed neither the pattern of widespread functional activity of their mental-age-matched peers, nor the focal activity of their chronological-age-matched peers. Instead, they displayed a pattern somewhere in between, consisting of some frontal activity and some temporal activity.

Putative Developmental Principle #2:
Intrinsic and extrinsic factors play a large
role in gene expression across development

At every stage of brain development—from genesis, migration, naturally occurring cell death, axon and dendritic growth, and synaptogenesis, to circuit formation and function—and in every region, it is likely that there are distinctive and pivotal stage- and region-dependent patterns of expression of large networks of genes. Significant perturbations in a stage or region could have the potential to impact patterns that emerge at later developmental stages or in other interconnected neural regions. While much remains to be discovered, a general biological principle is that the functional expressions of many genes are modifiable by either intrinsic (e.g., mutations, spontaneous neural activity, etc.) or extrinsic factors (e.g., behavioral experience) that affect patterns of neural activity *and* that those alterations change subsequent neural growth, function and behavior. For example, in a genetically normal but monocular-deprived animal, light in the *non*-deprived eye causes a host of genes that regulate axonal and dendritic growth and synapse formation to change expression in a way that drives abnormally excessive size and number of neuronal elements (Majdan & Shatz, 2006); see Shatz, 1990 for a review). Collectively, animal model-based research in this area suggests a possible mechanism by which experience and genes can interact to influence brain development which is likely at work in humans as well, and may be influential in developmental deficits in autism.

While most of what we have learned comes from animal models involving developing sensory or motor systems, the general principles are thought to apply as well to higher-order functions in humans. Higher social and language functions involve large-scale, long-distance networks in the frontal, temporal, and parietal cortices; examples include the resting network, the task positive network, and the mirror neuron system. Correlated activity within such networks may spontaneously fluctuate and be anti-correlated with other networks. Although it is unknown what conditions enable their development, it is likely that numerous intrinsic factors are involved, such as a suitable number of neurons, a balance of inhibitory and excitatory neurons at local nodes within a network, and a balance of axonal connections between nodes within a network relative to connections to opposing networks; numerous but poorly understood extrinsic factors such as changing forms of social and language activity and experience are likely also essential. The temporal and spatial orchestration of the development of such networks probably depends on a changing score of stage- and region-dependent dynamic interactions between patterns of expression, neural activity and extrinsic experience.

The interactive specialization theory of how function-specific networks are formed (described above) can therefore be generalized to include the idea of interactive "gene expression-neural activity" specialization; gene-expression patterns can modify neural activity, and neural-activity patterns can modify gene expression. That is, the underlying mechanism for the gradual specialization and stabilization of social and language networks is the modification of gene expression patterns by neural activity, whether intrinsic, including spontaneous, or extrinsic in origin.

This has numerous implications for autism. For example, toddlers with autism have abnormal language network activity (Redcay & Courchesne, 2008). This research finding suggests two simple conclusions: First, in locations of abnormally present or absent activity, gene expression patterns must also be aberrant. Gene expression studies of tissue from such key cortical locations could therefore offer extremely valuable insight into the molecular defects that give rise to the disorder. Further, gene expression-fMRI association studies in living autistic toddlers may reveal key genetic markers and pathways involved in dysregulation of core autism symptoms. Knowledge of such molecular defects, markers, and pathways opens avenues of progress toward discovery of early-warning biomarkers of autism, its prognosis in identified individuals, and perhaps, eventually, molecular interventions that augment current behavioral ones.

Second, such abnormal neural activity in autistic toddlers in social, emotion, and language systems might drive still further gene expression abnormality, which in turn could lead to further changes in neural pathology at an older age. The older the autistic child or adult, the further downstream one is from detecting patterns of neural and gene expression activity that existed at the time of first symptoms. For instance, while Sparks et al. (2002), Mosconi et al. (2009) and our laboratory (Schumann, Carter, Lord & Courchesne, 2009 have each found abnormal enlargement of the amygdala in 2- to 4-year-olds with autism, between the ages of 10 and 44 years, the amygdala is found to be missing its normal number of neurons (Schumann & Amaral, 2006). This outcome state is not the cause of autism, but instead reflects powerful and very abnormal changes in gene expression functions that ultimately turned abnormal early gain into abnormal later loss. Research is needed to test the hypothesis that some form of deviant neural activity—and perhaps excess neuron number—in early development in autism causes changes in gene expression levels that later promote cell death.

It has been hypothesized that the abnormal fMRI activation in social, emotion, and language regions in autistic toddlers may be due to the neural pathology that underlies early brain overgrowth. As described earlier, among the various possibilities for overgrowth in autism are excessive neuron numbers and/or synaptogenesis in frontal and temporal cortices—regions that are pivotal to the development of large-scale, long-distance social, emotion, and language networks. Elsewhere (Courchesne et al., 2007; Courchesne & Pierce, 2005a, 2005b), it has been argued in detail that such excesses will alter local as well as long-distance connections, and could lead to increased diffuse activity, reduced selective responsiveness, reduced temporal coherence in local and long-distance networks, and disorganized spontaneous as well as evoked neural activity in these important higher-order cortical regions. The main point here, however, is that these many and major alterations in neural activity would be predicted to induce significant changes in gene expression, disrupting the normal level of expression of genes that lay the foundation for further specialization and elaboration of social, emotion, and language neural networks. The gene networks that make growth and function possible in these neural networks must be many and dynamic in their expression during the first years of life. Since the background genetics of each autistic infant are different, the effect of the overgrowth perturbation on these dynamic gene networks could well differ across individuals. Observations at older ages could therefore reflect individual differences in the way such gene networks respond to the early pathological perturbation. That is, functional connectivity patterns, as well as gene expression profiles, at older ages might be thought of as the "whisper of the bang" that began maldevelopment.

Putative Developmental Principle #3: Early learning is strongly socially mediated

The third principle is one that takes into consideration how the typical baby learns many functions: that is, socially. Research has shown that language and communication in particular are deeply embedded in social interaction. The most compelling example of this fact is a study wherein 9-month-old English-speaking American infants were exposed to a foreign language, Chinese Mandarin, for 25 minutes across 12 weeks. One group was exposed to the language via a live actor who read books and played with the infant. The other two groups were exposed to the same words and quantity of language across the 25-minute period, but only via television or an audio recording. Following the play sessions, infants exposed to Mandarin via a live actor performed significantly better on a Mandarin phoneme-contrast test than the children in the television or audiotape conditions who performed no better than chance (Kuhl, Tsao, & Liu, 2003). As another example of socially mediated communication learning, babies that were smiled at and touched by their mothers immediately following a verbalization produced more vocalizations than babies who were touched and smiled at an equal amount, but not in a manner contingent upon their own vocalizations (Goldstein, King, & West, 2003). A recent near-infrared spectroscopy study also showed that brain responding is enhanced when infants listen to speech that is more socially animated than when they listened to backward speech or silence. In this study, 6- to 9-month old infants showed more functional brain activity in the left temporal lobe in response to "mothcrese" (speech that contains exaggerated pitch contours yet sounds soothing and melodic), than when they listened to backward speech or silence (Bortfeld, Wruck, & Boas, 2007). Given the importance of social cues and responsiveness to learning and the known deficits in such processing in autism, it is clear that this principle is of great potential relevance to understanding functional brain development in autism, as will be discussed below.

While there are no functional brain imaging studies in autism that speak directly to this phenomenon, studies of language development in young children with autism strongly support the contribution of social deficits to individual differences in language abilities. For example, three longitudinal studies have shown that, independent of other baseline factors such as IQ, mental age, or initial language abilities, a child's early ability to respond to others' bids for joint attention is highly predictive of later language proficiency (Anderson et al., 2007; Sigman et al., 1999; Siller & Sigman, 2008). A recent study found a link between joint attention deficits and amygdala enlargement in 4-year-olds with autism (Mosconi et al., 2009), suggesting a possible brain mechanism for these social deficits which may, in turn, influence development of functional networks responsible for language processing. There have been no functional imaging studies of joint attention in young children with autism, but a study of joint attention in healthy adults identified several activated regions, including areas such as the ventromedial prefrontal cortex, that are also abnormally responsive in adolescent or adult individuals with autism during a variety of emotional and cognitive tasks (Williams, Waiter, Perra, Perrett, & Whiten, 2005). One functional study in young children with autism has been conducted that directly tests the link between brain function abnormalities during language processing and social deficits. Kuhl and colleagues (2005) showed that, as a group, children with autism ages 3–4 years showed abnormal ERP responses to various mismatch phonemes. Strikingly, however, the subset of children with autism who preferred to listen to motherese speech as opposed to a computer-generated voice showed an ERP response similar to that of typically developing children. Although only speculative, children with autism who were more social tended to have more typical brain responses to language. The brain systems involved in understanding irony, a complex communicative task, have also been tested in older children and adolescents (age 7–17) with autism. Medial prefrontal cortex activity was reduced during this task in the autism group, and the degree of medial prefrontal deficit correlated directly with levels of social impairment (Wang, Lee, Sigman, & Dapretto, 2007).

AUTISM DURING THE LATE PERIOD: BRAIN STRUCTURE

Notwithstanding caveats such as the impact of mental retardation on brain size (Freitag et al., 2009), a meta-analysis of cross-sectional studies throughout the life span in autism reveals that whole brain volume actually declines during the adulthood years (Redcay & Courchesne, 2005). A relative reduction in whole brain volume in autism is mirrored by a reduction in discrete brain areas such as the thalamus, after correcting for whole brain volume (Tsatsanis et al., 2003), amygdala (Aylward et al., 1999; Pierce et al., 2001), and planum temporale (Rojas, Bawn, Benkers, Reite, & Rogers, 2002). Some brain regions, such as the caudate and the medial frontal lobes, may remain enlarged during adulthood (Haznedar et al., 2006; Rojas et al., 2006; for thorough reviews of MRI studies with adults

with autism, see Amaral, Schumann, & Nordahl, 2008; Stanfield, et al., 2008). A recent longitudinal study also supported the idea of cortical declines, and showed that these may begin in late childhood. Hardan et al. (2009) studied changes in gray matter volume and cortical thickness over a 30-month period in children with ASD and typically developing children who were 8–12 years of age at baseline. The rate of change in total gray matter volume and regional cortical thickness was steeper in the ASD group, although only occipital thickness differences survived corrections for multiple comparisons. As in studies of children, there has been some interest in linking structural findings to particular genes. In adolescents and adults with ASD, associations between the serotonin transporter gene polymorphism and brain size were not supported (Raznahan et al., 2009). This is perhaps not surprising, given that the role of genes is likely to be age-dependent, and that many environmental or epigenetic influences may intervene across development and lessen the importance of genotype.

Studies that use DTI to examine white matter in adults with autism are strikingly consistent. Barnea-Goraly (2004) reported reductions in FA in high-functioning adolescents and adults (ages 11–18) in brain regions involved in social cognition, such as the ventromedial prefrontal cortex. Alexander (2007) and Keller (2007) both reported reduced FA in the corpus callosum. Overall, at least 10 studies have reported reduced FA values in older children or adults with autism (Alexander et al., 2007; Ke et al., 2009; Keller et al., 2007; J. E. Lee et al., 2007; Pardini et al., 2009; Sundaram et al., 2008; Thakkar,et al., 2008). Reduced FA values in autism during adulthood has been shown to be associated with weaker cognitive abilities (Pardini et al., 2009), greater symptom severity (Cheung et al., 2009), and increased rates of repetitive behavior (Thakkar et al., 2008). This pattern of increased FA early in life (Ben Bashat et al., 2007), as described earlier, followed by reduced FA values in adulthood, is consistent with the idea that the adult phase is one of active degeneration. The DTI findings in adults also are consistent with the functional underconnnectivity results reviewed below. It is not yet known, however, how FA abnormalities might relate to connectivity abnormalities if measured in the same sample of individuals.

The two studies that reported both increases and decreases in FA values in their autism samples (Cheung et al., 2009; Ke et al., 2009) included subjects with ages that fell within both the early and middle periods. For example, Ke and colleagues (2009) studied subjects as young as 6 years old in combination with subjects over 11 years old, and Cheung (2009) studied children ranging in age from 6 to 14 years old. This transition, or "middle" childhood, period is a clear example of the transition between early overgrowth and arrest of growth.

Overall, the adult phase in autism appears to be largely characterized by neuronal decline, although the precise mechanisms leading to this are unclear. Postmortem studies of adults have found evidence for molecular processes, possibly neuroinflammatory, that serve to reduce neuron number (Vargas, Nascimbene, Krishnan, Zimmerman, & Pardo, 2005). Depending on when these mechanisms may begin to have effects, neuroinflammation may well help to explain the arrest of growth and decline that follows early brain overgrowth. Further postmortem work, particularly on the brains of children, will be crucial to examine what kinds of cellular abnormalities predominate, and to link these to expression of genes, particularly those related to cell growth and death.

AUTISM DURING THE LATE PERIOD: BRAIN FUNCTION

Regionally Specific Functional Brain Imaging In Adults With Autism

While the literature on the development of functional brain abnormalities in autism is just beginning to take shape, there is a wealth of knowledge about brain function in adulthood. Although not unilaterally the case (Dichter, Felder, & Bodfish, 2009; Schmitz et al., 2008), overall, reports of functional activity in adults with autism generally report *hypoactivity* in brain regions that would be expected to be recruited by a particular task. For example, there have been ample reports of reduced medial frontal lobe (Kennedy & Courchesne, 2008; Pierce et al. 2004), inferior frontal (Dapretto et al., 2006), and amygdala activity during socioemotional tasks (Baron-Cohen et al., 1999; Critchley et al., 2000), reduced parietal activity during spatial-attention and visual-reasoning tasks (Soulieres et al., 2009), and reduced fusiform face activity during face-processing tasks (Humphreys et al., 2008; Pierce et al., 2001; Schultz et al., 2000). This is consistent with the final phase of brain

growth we have described in autism—namely, decline. The nature of this decline, however, is unclear. While studies reviewed above suggest the possibility of neuron loss, there are no reports of widespread, whole-brain, volume reductions in autism during the adult period. From a neurofunctional perspective, it is important to consider that formerly hypoactive patterns of brain activity can be altered to respond more normally. For example, Pierce and colleagues (2001) showed that adults with autism exhibited a reduction in FFA activity relative to controls during the presentation of stranger faces. Our group (Pierce et al., 2004) showed that, in contrast, when more interesting and personally meaningful faces were used, such as the participant's mother's face, normal FFA activity was found. A similar phenomenon is observed in mu activity in response to tasks thought to engage the mirror neuron system (Oberman, Ramachandran, & Pineda, 2008). Finally, Pierce and colleagues (2008) demonstrated that children with autism showed extremely low levels of functional brain activity in response to stranger adult faces, and that the same children showed normal levels of brain activity in response to familiar faces. Using an event-related design, this within-subject contrast clearly demonstrated that, under certain possibly attention-grabbing conditions, the brain in autism can respond more normally. Cumulatively, the studies by Pierce and colleagues raise the possibility of a very fundamental principle in autism—namely, that resting networks are abnormally engaged in autism, and the degree to which certain tasks may, or may not, evoke normal functional brain activity has more to do with functional networks than neuronal degeneration per se. This "threshold theory," centered on the degree to which stimuli are capable of breaking through abnormally tuned resting networks, may be a unique signature of autism that is particularly strong during the adult years. This new idea needs to be tested in further studies (see Figure 21-6).

Functional Connectivity Studies in Adults With Autism

Recent studies have used functional magnetic resonance imaging (fMRI) or positron emission tomography (PET) not only to identify areas of regional abnormality, but also to examine the correlation between the responses of distributed regions within the brain. Whereas the typical functional-imaging paradigm compares regional brain response between

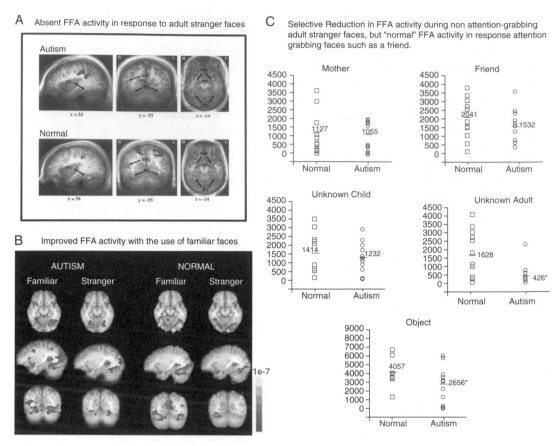

Figure 21-6 Fusiform activity in autism across three separate studies. In panel A (Pierce et al., 2001), adults with autism showed reduced fusiform activity in response to faces of strangers. In panel B (Pierce et al., 2004), adults with autism showed modestly reduced activity in response to faces of strangers, but normal levels on fusiform activity in response to familiar faces. Panel C (Pierce et al., 2008) shows that in 6- to 12-year-olds with autism, the number of voxels that were active in response to faces of strangers were only ½ to ¼ the number seen in response to mothers or friends face. Collectively the studies by Pierce and colleagues demonstrate that the fusiform can be active at normal levels in individuals with autism. The degree to which the fusiform functions normally may have more to do with a stimulus' ability to break through a strong and aberrantly connected resting network (i.e., the "threshold effect") than defects in the fusiform per se. (See color Figure 21-6.)

individuals with autism and those without the disorder either during a resting state or during a cognitive challenge, functional connectivity studies emphasize the degree to which brain response is or is not *coordinated* across regions, and how the patterns of correlation may differ depending on the presence of autism. Such correlation-based analyses can either be conducted on data collected during a stimulation-free period, or during a behavioral challenge. In healthy individuals who are not engaged in a particular cognitive task (at "rest"), it has been established that there are low-frequency oscillations of neurophysiological signals

that temporally correlate between distributed brain regions. These correlations are present during sleep and even during coma, and are thought to reflect low-frequency fluctuations in local field potentials (Leopold, Murayama, & Logothetis, 2003). There are likely multiple such networks of correlated activity at rest, but one network has received particular attention because it resembles the network that is seen to "turn off," or show decreased response in the context of a cognitive task. This network, which includes the medial prefrontal cortex, posterior cingulate/precuneus, and angular gyrus, has been referred to as the Default Mode Network (DMN), or the Task Negative Network, and is thought to reflect the combination of social, emotional, and introspective processing that predominates in healthy individuals when not engaged in a cognitively demanding task. This interpretation of the functional role of the DMN has been supported by evidence showing that these regions respond positively when individuals are explicitly instructed to perform self-reflective, social, or emotional tasks. Given that these are the very behavioral areas of primary concern in autism, it is clear that examination of the DMN in the disorder is of great relevance. An additional reason to study functional connectivity in autism is that studies of regional differences, compared to healthy individuals, using fMRI and PET have not found a particular region of functional deficit that could serve as a smoking gun to explain all behavioral symptoms. Furthermore, many of the functional imaging studies have shown that some areas are under-responsive in autism, while others are over-responsive, suggesting that there is dysregulation between regions. Finally, as reviewed above, there is growing evidence from MRI and postmortem studies that there is likely to be disordered anatomical connectivity in the autistic brain that could have deleterious consequences for the functional coordination between brain regions.

Table 21-1 lists the characteristics and results of 23 studies published to date that have included analyses of interregional correlations in brain response using fMRI and PET. Although EEG and MEG studies have also examined correlations between different brain areas, we did not include them in the review due to the lower spatial resolution of these techniques. We will return later, however, to the idea that combining the powerful temporal information from EEG/MEG with the good spatial resolution of fMRI may prove most useful in understanding connectivity deficits in autism.

As with many of the findings reviewed so far in this chapter, most of the functional connectivity studies in autism have been conducted with samples of high-functioning adults. All but two of the existing studies of functional connectivity in autism have been conducted with samples of adolescents or young adults. As suggested by Just (2004) and Hughes (2007), a pattern emerges from these studies of underconnectivity in adult autism. All but two of the reviewed studies (Noonan et al., 2009; Welchew et al., 2005) found some evidence for smaller correlations between the functional response of brain regions among participants in the ASD group than among healthy individuals. Underconnectivity between cortical regions was observed under a variety of conditions, including during tasks of finger movement (Mostofsky et al., 2009), attention (Bird et al., 2006), Theory of Mind (Castelli et al., 2002; Mason, Williams, Kana, Minshew, & Just, 2008), language (Just 2004; Kana, Keller, Cherkassky, Minshew, & Just, 2006), executive function/working memory (Just, Cherkassky, Keller, Kana, & Minshew, 2007; Koshino et al., 2005, 2008), response inhibition/cognitive control (Kana, Keller, Minshew, & Just, 2007; P. S. Lee et al., 2009; Solomon, et al., 2009), face perception (Kleinhans et al., 2008), and emotion processing (Wicker et al., 2008), and also during periods of non-stimulation (Cherkassky, Kana, Keller, & Just, 2006; Horwitz, Rumsey, Grady, & Rapoport, 1988; Kennedy & Courchesne, 2008; Monk et al., 2009), or after having statistically controlled for task-related effects (Turner, Frost, Linsenbardt, McIlroy, & Muller, 2006; Villalobos, Mizuno, Dahl, Kemmotsu, & Muller, 2005). The methods of determining functional connectivity varied widely across studies, as did the methods for determining which regions to examine for altered correlations. Many studies used information from a traditional task-related analysis to narrow down the regions to examine, thus focusing on the interconnections between nodes in a putative network responsible for task performance. Other studies examined regions of interest that were determined in an a priori fashion based on past anatomical or functional studies to be related either to autism or to task performance or to a particular resting network. Fourteen studies found evidence for underconnectivity between regions of the prefrontal cortex and posterior regions (Cherkassky et al., 2006; Horwitz et al., 1988; Just, 2004; Just et al., 2007; Kana et al., 2006, 2007; Kennedy & Courchesne, 2008; Koshino et al., 2008; Mason et al., 2008; Monk et al., 2009; Mostofsky et al., 2009; Solomon et al., 2009; Villalobos et al., 2005; Wicker et al., 2008), although some studies showed overconnectivity between frontal and other regions, particularly subcortical ones (Koshino et al., 2005; Mizuno, Villalobos, Davies, Dahl, & Muller, 2006; Noonan et al., 2009; Turner et al., 2006). The regions within the prefrontal cortex that have been shown to have abnormal functional connectivity have been varied. The pattern of results, therefore, is generally consistent with the idea of reduced long-distance connectivity between

Table 21-1

Task-related Connectivity Studies:

Paper	Clinical Group	Sample Size (ASD; HC)	Age (ASD: mean [SD] years, range; HC: mean [SD] years, range)	M: F ratio (ASD; HC)	IQ (ASD: mean [SD]; HC: mean [SD])	Imaging Modality (PET or fMRI)	Task or State	Functional Connectivity Analysis Method	Group Difference in Connectivity	Under vs. Over Connectivity
Bird, Catmur, Silani, Frith, & Frith, 2006	ASD (Autism, n=1; Aspergers, n=15)	ASD: 16; HC: 16	ASD: 33.3 (11.5); HC: 35.3 (12.1)	ASD: 14:2; HC: 14:2	ASD: 119 (14); HC: 119 (13.2)	FMRI	Selective attention task (same vs. different judgment for face or house stimuli with two distractor stimuli)	Dynamic causal modeling of left hemisphere time series in three ROIs derived from the task-related analysis and localizer task (face- and house-specific regions and a nonspecific V1 region)	Lack of feedback from face and house-specific regions to V1 region and feedforward modulation from V1 to face-selective region in ASD	Under
Castelli, Frith, Happé, & Frith, 2002	ASD (Autism or Asperger's)	ASD: 10; HC: 10	ASD: 33 (7.6); HC: 25 (4.8)		Verbal ability: ASD: 61st percentile (24); HC: 76th percentile(11)	PET (H215O)	Moving triangles in 3 conditions: Theory of Mind, Goal Directed, Random	Correlation between extrastriate region (more active in Theory of Mind than Random in both groups) and rest of brain	Reduced correlation between extrastriate region and region of superior temporal sulcus in ASD	Under

Citation	Population	Sample	Age	Gender	IQ	Method	Task	Analysis	Findings	
Just, Cherkassky, Keller, & Minshew, 2004	Autism (high-functioning)	ASD: 17; HC: 17	NG (matched between groups)	NG	NG (matched between groups, > 80)	FMRI	Sentence comprehension	Correlation between time course (fixation time points excluded) of activated (greater in sentence comprehension than fixation) voxels within 35 anatomically-determined ROIs	Significantly lower correlations in the autism group in 10 (out of 186) pairwise comparisons (none significantly higher).	Under
Just et al, 2007	Autism (high-functioning)	ASD: 18; HC: 18 (ASD:12 and HC: 9 partici-pated in Just et al, 2004)	ASD: 27.1 (11.9); HC: 24.5 (9.9)	ASD: 17:1; HC: 15:3	ASD: 109.3(17.7); HC: 108.1(13.8)	FMRI	Tower of London task (forced choice response of minimum moves required)	Correlation between time course (fixation time points excluded) of activated (greater in Tower of London than fixation) voxels within 15 ROIs active in the group map for each group	Lower correlations between frontal and parietal regions (intra and interhemispheric) in autism; degree of connectivity related to ADOS scores	Under
Kana, Keller, Cherkassky, Minshew, & Just, 2006	Autism (high-functioning)	ASD: 12; HC: 13	ASD: 22.5 (8.8); HC: 20.3 (4.0)	ASD: 11:1; HC: 12:1	ASD: 110.7 (9.2); HC: 113.2 (9.2)	FMRI	Evaluating sentences as true or false that require low or high imagery to respond correctly	Correlation between time course (fixation time points excluded) of activated (greater in sentence comprehension than fixation) voxels within 21 ROIs active in group map for each group; separate analyses for low and high imagery	Decreased frontal-parietal correlation in autism relative to healthy when compared to all other pair-wise correlations; no interactions with imagery condition	Under

(continued)

Table 21-1 (Continued)

Paper	Clinical Group	Sample Size (ASD; HC)	Age (ASD: mean [SD] years, range; HC: mean [SD] years, range)	M: F ratio (ASD; HC)	IQ (ASD: mean [SD]; HC: mean [SD])	Imaging Modality (PET or fMRI)	Task or State	Functional Connectivity Analysis Method	Group Difference in Connectivity	Under vs. Over Connect-ivity
Kana, Keller, Minshew, & Just, 2007	Autism (high-functioning)	ASD: 12; HC:12	ASD: 26.8 (7.7); HC: 22.5 (3.2)	ASD: 11:1; HC: 11:1	ASD: 110.1 (12.6); HC: 117.0 (8.7)	FMRI	Response inhibition (either to a particular target or to a temporal combination of targets ["1-back"])	Correlation between time course (fixation time points excluded) of activated (greater in response inhibition than fixation) voxels within 21 ROIs active in group map for each group, separately for the two inhibition conditions; factor analysis to create composite indices of networks	In autism group (but not in healthy group), right middle frontal and right intraparietal sulcus did not load with other "inhibitory" regions during 1-back condition; inhibitory factor less correlated with right inferior parietal areas	Under
Kleinhans et al., 2008	ASD (Autism = 8, Asperger's = 9, PDD-NOS = 2)	ASD: 19; HC: 21	ASD: 23.5 (7.8), 18-44; HC: 25.1 (7.6), 18-43	NG	ASD: 106.7 (15.7); HC: 109.1 (14.4)	FMRI	1-back identification of face or house stimuli	Difference between Face and House conditions in correlation between activity in each individual's right fusiform face area (functionally defined in fusiform for Face vs. House) and 6 predefined ROIs (also whole brain)	Lower connectivity in ASD between right FFA and left amygdala, bilateral posterior cingulate, and left cuneus. Right FFA to amygdala connectivity negatively related to social deficit severity	Under

Study	Condition	Sample	Age	Sex ratio	IQ	Modality	Task	Analysis	Results	Under and over
Koshino et al., 2005	Autism (high-functioning)	ASD: 14; HC: 14	ASD: 25.7; HC 29.8	ASD: 13:1; HC: 13:1	ASD: 100.1; HC: 109.1	FMRI	N-back working memory for letters (0-, 1-, and 2-back)	Comparisons and factor analysis of correlations between average timecourse (for 2-back condition) within 24 anatomical ROIs conducted for each group separately	Autism factor structure different: fewer ROIs in "working memory" factor, "posterior" factor in autism group; lower correlations in autism group between left inferior parietal lobe and other ROIs; higher correlation between left DLPFC and right inferior temporal lobe	Under and over
Koshino et al., 2008	Autism (high-functioning)	ASD: 11; HC: 11	ASD: 24.5 (10.2); HC: 28.7 (10.9)	ASD: 11:0; HC: 10:1	ASD: 104.5 (13.1); HC: 108.6 (9.1)	FMRI	N-back working memory for faces (0-, 1-, and 2-back)	Comparison and factor analysis of correlations between the average timecourse of activated voxels within 13 functional ROIs (determined by conjunction of activated clusters for all conditions vs. fixation in both groups)	Lower correlation between left frontal and left and right fusiform in autism vs. HC; more factors in autism than HC; fusiform regions loaded with different frontal regions in the two groups; less frontal-parietal connectivity in the autism group	Under

(continued)

Table 21-1 (Continued)

Paper	Clinical Group	Sample Size (ASD; HC)	Age (ASD: mean [SD] years, range; HC: mean [SD] years, range)	M: F ratio (ASD; HC)	IQ (ASD: mean [SD]; HC: mean [SD])	Imaging Modality (PET or fMRI)	Task or State	Functional Connectivity Analysis Method	Group Difference in Connectivity	Under vs. Over Connectivity
Lee et al., 2009	ASD	ASD: 12; HC: 12	ASD: 10.2 (1.6), 8-12; HC: 11.0 (1.8), 8-12	ASD: 9:3; HC: 8:4	ASD: 113.3 (17.3); HC: 114.9 (10.3)	FMRI	Go/No-Go (press for all letters vs. do not press for X)	Derived 10 ROIs based on No-Go vs. Go activation of all participants (none sig diff betweeen groups): time series of seed regions (left and right inferior frontal gyrus) correlated with time series of other 8 ROIs	No difference in connectivity except when age used as a covariate; age negatively related to degree of correlation between right IFC and bilateral pre-SMA and between right IFC and right caudate among ASD but not HC	Under (but only among the oldest ASD participants)
Mason, Williams, Kana, Minshew, & Just, 2008	Autism (high-functioning)	ASD: 18; HC: 18	ASD: 26.5; HC: 27.4	ASD: 17:1; HC: 16:2	ASD: 101.9; HC: 105.5	FMRI	Theory of Mind: reading sentences that provide context vs. require an inference that involves physical, intentional, or emotional state of the protagonist	Correlation between time course of activated voxels (during the inference condition, separately for each passage type) among 11 functional ROIs (determined based on activity in all three conditions vs. fixation) in both groups	Lower correlations in autism group among ROIs within "Theory of Mind" network (left medial frontal with right temporoparietal junction) and between language and "Theory of Mind" regions	Under

Study	Diagnosis	Sample	Age	Sex	IQ; Scanner	Task	Analysis	Results	Over/Under
Mostofsky et al., 2009	Autism	ASD: 13; HC: 13	ASD: 10.9 (1.5), 8-12; HC: 10.5 (1.4), 8-12	ASD: 11:2; HC: 11:2	ASD: 103 (18); HC: 118 (14); FMRI	Tap each finger to thumb in succession	Bivariate correlation between mean filtered timecourse from active voxels within 7 functionally determined motor network ROIs and two control regions (for entire task, left hand trials only, right hand trials only, and rest only)	Autism group had reduced connectivity between motor regions but not control regions compared to HC (for entire task and left and right hand trials; less different for rest trials)	Under
Solomon et al., 2009	ASD (Autism=10, Asperger's= 12)	ASD: 22; HC: 23	ASD: 15.2(1.7), 12-18; HC: 15.9(2.1), 12-18	ASD: 17:5; HC: 18:5	ASD: 107(14); HC: 113(11); FMRI	Preparing to Overcome Prepotency test: green cue (75% of trials) = congruent button press, red cue (25%) = incongruent response	Pairwise correlation between mean timecourse for correct trials in red and green trials (separately) in 20 ROIs active in red vs green contrast during cue period for either group. Factor analysis of this matrix. Seed analysis based on "beta series" also used	Reduced correlationss in ASD group in several regions during both red and green trials; ASD group had two factor solution (vs. 1 factor for HC); seed analysis revealed underconnectivity with prefrontal regions	Under
Welchew et al., 2005	Asperger's	ASD: 13; HC: 13	ASD: 31.2 (9.1); 25.6 (5.1)	ASD: 13:0; HC: 13:0	ASD: 108.6 (17.1); HC: 117.9 (9.6); FMRI	Facial affect processing: high fear, low fear, neutral, and scrambled	Mean timecourse within 45 anatomical ROIs used to create distance matrices separately for each group as input for multidimensional scaling; permutation analyses to determine reliable differences in configuration between groups	No overall difference in configuration of connectivity, but regionally, right and left para-hippocampal gyrus and left amygdala showed differences in connectivity between groups (higher correlations with rest of brain in ASD vs. HC)	Over (regionally)

(continued)

Table 21-1 (Continued)

Paper	Clinical Group	Sample Size (ASD; HC)	Age (ASD: mean [SD] years, range; HC: mean [SD] years, range)	M: F ratio (ASD; HC)	IQ (ASD: mean [SD]; HC: mean [SD])	Imaging Modality (PET or fMRI)	Task or State	Functional Connectivity Analysis Method	Group Difference in Connectivity	Under vs. Over Connect-ivity
Wicker et al., 2008	ASD (Autism = 8, Asperger's = 4)	ASD: 12; HC: 14	ASD: 27 (11); HC: 23.4 (10)	ASD: 11:1; HC: 14:0	ASD: 81.8; (not matched with HC)	FMRI	Judge emotion vs. age of video stimuli of actor's face showing anger or happiness with either directed or averted gaze	Structural equation modeling to test model with 7 ROIs and connections between them (based on known anatomy); mean time series for the Emotion condition calculated from cluster of activity around the peak voxel in each ROI and path coefficients calculated for each individual; within and between group t-tests of the path coefficients	ASD had reduced connectivity between amygdala and dorsomedial frontal, between dorsomedial and dorsolateral prefrontal, between dorsolateral and ventral prefrontal, and between ventrolateral prefrontal and superior temporal sulcus; ASD had enhanced connectivity between left prefrontal and fusiform gyrus	Under (and over)

Resting or Non-Stimulus Period Connectivity Studies:

Paper	Clinical Group	Sample Size (ASD; HC)	Age (ASD: mean [SD] years, range; HC: mean [SD] years, range)	M: F ratio (ASD; HC)	IQ (ASD: mean [SD]; HC: mean [SD])	Imaging Modality (PET or fMRI)	Task or State	Functional Connectivity Analysis Method	Group Difference in Connectivity	Under vs. Over Connect-ivity
Cherkassky, Kana, Keller, & Just, 2006	Autism (high-functioning)	ASD: 57; HC: 57	ASD: 24 (10.6); HC: 24 (9.0)	ASD: 53:4; HC: 52:5	ASD: 106 (16.2); HC: 113 (11.3)	FMRI	Fixation baseline from 6 separate studies	Pairwise correlation of average time series (during fixation) in 12 ROIs determined to be task-related across all tasks and the combined group	94% of the 66 pair-wise correlations showed lower correlation in the autism group; including lower anterior cingulate to posterior cingulate / precuneus, left parahippocampal gyrus to other ROIs, and within right hemisphere correlations	Under

Horwitz, Rumsey, Grady, & Rapoport, 1988	Autism	ASD: 14; HC: 14	ASD: 27 (6.6), 18-39; HC: 27 (6.6)	ASD: 14:0; HC: 14:0	ASD: 94.4 (19.2); HC: NG	PET (FDG)	Rest (eyes covered, ears plugged)	Correlations between metabolism in 59 ROIs (normalized by global metabolism)	Fewer positive correlations between frontal and parietal regions, especially with left and right inferior prefrontal, and lower correlations between subcortical and frontal/parietal regions in the autism group	Under
Kennedy & Courchesne, 2008	ASD (Autism = 6, Asperger's = 6)	ASD: 12; HC: 12	ASD: 26.5 (12.8), 15.7-52.0; HC: 27.5 (10.9), 15.9-45.4	ASD: 12:0; HC: 12:0	ASD: 101.6 (15.2); HC: 111.5 (8.3)	FMRI	Resting state (stare at fixation; not in context of a task)	Correlation between time course in six seed regions (from "task-positive network"[TPN] or "task-negative network"[TNN]) and rest of brain used to find TPN and TNN clusters at the group level; average timeseries in each node within each network was correlated with all the other nodes' averaged timeseries	TNN network more sparse in ASD and within node correlations reduced compared to HC. Correlation of medial prefrontal and left angular gyrus with all other nodes was reduced in ASD. TPN nodes and connectivity not different between groups.	Under

(continued)

Table 21-1 (Continued)

Paper	Clinical Group	Sample Size (ASD; HC)	Age (ASD: mean [SD] years, range; HC: mean [SD] years, range)	M:F ratio (ASD; HC)	IQ (ASD: mean [SD]; HC: mean [SD])	Imaging Modality (PET or fMRI)	Task or State	Functional Connectivity Analysis Method	Group Difference in Connectivity	Under vs. Over Connectivity
Mizuno, Villalobos, Davies, Dahl, & Muller, 2006	Autism (high-functioning)	ASD: 8; HC: 8	ASD: 28.4, 15–39; HC: 28.1, 21–43	ASD: 8.0; HC: 8.0	ASD: 92.3 (nonverbal)	FMRI	Visuomotor task (visually-guided sequence of button presses vs. single button)	Mean timecourse within bilateral and unilateral thalami calculated and correlated with that of all other voxels (task-related effects statistically controlled)	Higher correlations in autism group between thalamus and bilateral frontal and pericentral regions and left inferior parietal lobe; lower correlations between thalamus and lateral and medial temporal lobes	Over and under
Monk et al., 2009	ASD (Autism = 7, Asperger's = 2, PDDNOS = 3)	ASD: 12; HC: 12	ASD: 26 (5.9); HC: 27 (6.1)	ASD: 11:1; HC: 10:2	Verbal: ASD: 117 (13.7); HC: 110 (18.0)	FMRI	Resting state (stare at fixation cross for 10 minutes; not in context of a task)	Whole brain analysis of correlation beween seed square centered on posterior cingulate voxel in default network and rest of brain; group differences tested in 11 default mode ROIs	Reduced connectivity in ASD with right superior frontal gyrus; greater connectivity with right temporal lobe and right parahippocampal gyrus; Under-connectivity of right superior frontal gyrus related to severity of social deficits; over-connectivity with parahippocampal gyrus related to more severe restricted and repetitive behaviors	Under and over (both related to symptom severity)

Study	Diagnosis	N	Age	Gender	IQ	Modality	Task	Method	Results	Over/Under
Noonan, Haist, & Muller, 2009	ASD (Autism = 6, Asperger's = 4)	ASD: 10; HC: 10	ASD: 23.0 (9.9), 14-43; HC: 25.8 (9.9)	ASD: 10:0; HC: 10:0	ASD: 96.7 (16.1); HC: 110 (15.8)	FMRI	Intentional auditory or visual deep encoding of words; recognition memory for study source (auditory or visual or new)	Whole brain analysis of correlation between seed volume timecourses in three regions active during source recognition memory (one only in HC, one only in ASD, and one active in both) and rest of brain; task-related effects statistically controlled	Greater connectivity with left middle frontal gyrus and left superior parietal lobe seed volumes in ASD than HC, particularly in right hemisphere; fewer areas of overconnectivity in ASD compared to HC with left middle occipital gyrus seed volume	Over
Turner, Frost, Linsenbardt, McIlroy, & Muller, 2006	Autism	ASD: 8; HC: 8	ASD: 28.1 (8.9), 15-39; HC: 28.6, 21-43	ASD: 8:0, HC: 8:0	ASD: 92.3 (nonverbal)	FMRI	Visuomotor task (visually-guided sequence of button presses vs. single button)	Mean timecourse within bilateral and unilateral caudate calculated and correlated with that of all other voxels (task-related effects statistically controlled)	Higher correlations in autism group between caudate and diffuse regions of frontal, parietal, and occipital lobes; lower correlations between caudate and right superior frontal gyrus (and in temporal and occipital regions if right caudate used as seed)	Over and under
Villalobos, Mizuno, Dahl, Kemmotsu, & Muller, 2005	Autism	ASD: 8; HC: 8	ASD: 28.4 (8.9), 15-41; HC: 28.6, 21-43	ASD: 8:0, HC: 8:0	ASD: 92.3 (nonverbal)	FMRI	Visuomotor task (visually-guided sequence of button presses vs. single button)	Mean timecourse within bilateral primary visual cortex (area 17) calculated and correlated with that of all other voxels (task-related effects statistically controlled)	Lower correlation in autism group between primary visual cortex and bilateral inferior frontal cortex, right superior frontal gyrus, and paracentral lobule; and with bilateral thalamus, right basal ganglia, and cerebellar vermis	Under

anterior and posterior cortical regions (Courchesne & Pierce, 2005b). There is less evidence from the functional imaging literature to support the idea of local cortical overconnectivity, but this may be due to difficulties in observing such functional relationships on the temporal and spatial scale that is typical of MRI or PET studies. It may be necessary to combine EEG and MEG studies (like that of Murias et al., (2007)) with functional MRI in order to address the hypothesis of local overconnectivity. It also seems to be the case that overconnectivity is more likely to be observed during periods of non-stimulation (Koshino et al., 2005; Mizuno et al., 2006; Monk et al., 2009; Noonan et al., 2009; Turner et al., 2006), which is consistent with the "threshold theory" introduced above. The functional connectivity studies reviewed above also hint at a pattern of heightened correlations between subcortical and cortical regions. This overconnectivity may be equally detrimental to behavior as underconnectivity (for example, if it reflects more widespread and diffuse functional connections that are not properly specialized; see Muller, 2008). The distinction between cortical-cortical and cortical-subcortical connections deserves further study in order to determine whether the two types of functional connectivity abnormality are driven by the same or different pathological processes.

We have emphasized throughout this chapter that studies of the adult autistic brain represent a relative end state, and may reflect the compensatory actions of the brain, over years, in response to altered neural substrates and sensory inputs. Thus, it is clearly important to contrast the development of functional brain networks in typical and autistic children. Unfortunately, there have been no functional connectivity studies in young children with autism. There have been two studies conducted with children during the middle childhood years (P. S. Lee et al., 2009; Mostofsk, et al., 2009), both of which contrasted functional brain correlations between ASD and healthy individuals who ranged in age from 8–12 years. Mostofsky et al. (2009) examined connectivity during appositional finger movements. They found that children with ASD had reduced correlations between nodes within the motor system compared to typically developing children. Lee et al. (2009) studied functional connectivity during a response inhibition (Go/ No-Go) task. This investigation found no differences in connectivity between the autism group and the typically developing group, until age was introduced as a covariate.

Follow-up analyses showed that correlations between the inferior frontal cortex and both the bilateral pre-supplementary motor area and right caudate lessened with age in the autism group only, so that only the oldest autistic children (11–12 year olds) showed underconnectivity relative to typical children. Recent developmental studies of resting functional connectivity in healthy children, adolescents, and adults have demonstrated a strengthening of long-distance functional associations across age groups, and a decrease in short-range functional correlations (Fair et al., 2008). Further work with young samples of autistic individuals will be needed to demonstrate whether there is a disruption in the developmental trajectory of functional connectivity in autism, as well as the nature of any such disruption.

Can Connectivity Be "Normalized" in Autism?

For the first time, the notion that autism can be cured, or is "reversible," is a question under serious consideration (Dawson, 2008; Helt et al., 2008). A recent review suggests that 3–25% of affected children can expect to achieve age-appropriate functioning in cognitive and language behaviors following a period of intensive early behavioral treatment (Helt et al., 2008). Even more dramatic are findings from the first comprehensive study on this topic by Lovaas in 1987, which reported a 47% "recovery" rate for autistic children between the ages of 3 and 5 years following intensive behavioral therapy (Lovaas, 1987). Because early intervention studies tend to focus on outcome variables such as changes in language and cognition, less clear is the degree to which fully normal social behavior can be achieved. Furthermore, the design of treatment studies does not allow for an interpretation that a small percentage of children may improve regardless of treatment, perhaps due to a set of protective genes or other innate mechanisms. Nonetheless, the undeniable gains in cognitive and language skills experienced by a subset of children with autism following intensive early treatment is remarkable, and stands in contrast to outcomes in the not-so-distant past, which were bleak (DeMyer, et al., 1973), and often included years of institutionalization (Treffert, McAndrew, & Dreifuerst, 1973).

The opportunity for early treatment is the direct product of early identification. In the past, more intensive and focused treatment generally began once a child reached school age, or somewhere around age 5 years (Fenske, Zalenski, Krantz, & McClannahan, 1985; Rogers, 1998). The advent of early identification tools, such as the Modified Checklist for Autism in Toddlers (MCHAT) (Robins, Fein, Barton, & Green, 2001), are facilitating treatments as young as 18 months of age (such as a recently funded study led by Catherine Lord and Amy Wetherby) and in some cases as young as 12 months (Pierce, et al., 2010). This time window shift, from treatment beginning at 5 and older, to treatment beginning at 3 and younger, has the powerful advantage of moving treatment initiation into an epoch characterized by high brain plasticity. Consider, for example, that children and infants between the ages of 1 month to 3 years who undergo a hemispherectomy (due to intractable seizures) achieve virtually normal social, language, and cognitive functioning (Byrne & Gates, 1987). Similarly, infants and young children with focal lesions in Broca's area, located in the inferior frontal gyrus, go on to achieve normal language function as well (Mosch, Max, & Tranel, 2005; Wulfeck, Bates, Krupa-Kwiatkowski, & Saltzman, 2004). The remarkable outcome experienced by such infants and children is largely due to the *timing* of the neural insult—namely, one that occurred very early in development. An essential point is that the insult occurs *prior* to the mastery of complex skills such as language. By contrast, a similar neural insult in older children and adults rarely results in a full recovery (Mosch et al., 2005). Plasticity, then, is very closely linked to critical periods in development. Based on his research with guinea pigs, John Beard described a critical period as a time in which there is sudden anatomic, biochemical, and functional maturation of the brain (Beard, 1896). In humans, there is no single critical period of brain development, because developmental neural events are heterosynchronous; neurogenesis, neuronal migration, axon outgrowth, and dendrite and synapse formation occur during different times throughout pre- and postnatal development. With the exception of the dentate gyrus neurons in the hippocampus (E. Lee & Son, 2009; Suh et al., 2007), and interneurons in the olfactory bulb, neurogenesis is largely concluded by birth. In contrast, synpatogenesis begins during the last trimester of pregnancy and peaks in the infant at around 12 months of age in the prefrontal cortex and at 36 months in Heschel's gyrus and Wernicke's area, two brain regions heavily involved in language development. Synpatogenesis,

at slower rates, continues throughout adolescence. Huttenlocher (2002) stresses that the first two years of life, a time when synpatogenesis is at its peak, may be a particularly important time period for plasticity effects, and writes:

> Environmental factors become more important during the later phases of development, especially those related to synaptogenesis. . . . The development and maintenance of synapses in the cerebral cortex differs from the earlier developmental steps (e.g., neurogenesis, neuronal migration), which are largely under genetic control. In contrast, environmental factors become important in synaptogenesis, especially in the stabilization of the initial synaptic contacts. Some of these early synapses are incorporated into functioning circuits and are stabilized (persist), while others are useless and are reabsorbed. It is here that the environmental input to the cerebral cortex becomes essential for further development." (p. 36)

In a remarkable example of the importance of sensitive periods, Nelson and colleagues (2007) studied the outcomes of institutionalized infants placed in foster care after various periods of time. Results indicated that institutionalized infants placed into foster care by 18 months had a mean developmental quotient (DQ) based on the Mullen Scales of Early Learning of 94 when tested at 42 months in age. In contrast, infants who remained in an institution until at least 2 years but were placed in foster care later, displayed mean IQ scores at least 14 points lower when tested at 42 months (i.e., DQ of <80).

The period following peak synaptogenesis is mirrored by an explosion of skill development in the normal infant. Between the ages of 12 and 24 months, an infant's vocabulary grows from approximately 12 to 300 words; during this age span, the infant learns an average of 3 new words per day (Fenson et al., 1994). Joint attention emerges and is mastered, wherein infants can both respond to and direct the attention of others (Tomasello, Carpenter, Call, Behne, & Moll, 2005); an understanding of objects as permanent (Spelke, Gutheil, & Van de Walle, 1995) and the ability to display clear signs of empathy in response to others in distress (Spinrad & Stifter, 2006; Young, Fox, & Zahn-Waxler, 1999) all emerge.

For the child with autism, the brain undergoes a period of rapid overgrowth that generally peaks around age 1, as discussed earlier in the chapter. Although the etiology of this overgrowth is unknown, one viable hypothesis is that it is the result of an excess number of neurons, which would in effect lead to an excess number of synapses formed. Figure 21-7 shows developmental mean synaptic density plots from Huttenlocher (1997) and illustrates a key point: children with autism experience brain overgrowth during the same time period in development when the brain is already experiencing a spike in synaptogenesis. It also illustrates the protracted course of development in the frontal lobes, which does not peak in synapse numbers until approximately age 40 months. Early intervention, or environmental enrichment, during this time period is essential to strengthen appropriate connections or eliminate those that are non-functional. Left without appropriate environmental input, it is easy to imagine how such a system could go awry.

Brain imaging technology offers the potential to measure changes in functional circuitry as the result of treatment. Changes in connectivity patterns have certainly been achieved following pharmacological intervention, such as increases in frontal lobe activity

and concomitant increases in verbal fluency in healthy controls following administration of the performance-enhancing drug erythropoietin (Miskowiak et al., 2008). Changes in functional connectivity as the result of purely behavioral intervention have been largely studied with stroke patients, a research area that has shown considerable evidence for cortical reorganization and plasticity, even in adults (Rossini et al., 2007). Such pre- and post-treatment imaging studies, however, have yet to be carried out in autism. Although laudable, such endeavors suffer from difficult, if not impossible, problems, such as conducting fMRI with awake toddlers, challenges in controlling for cortical changes that happened naturally during development regardless of environment, differing baseline functioning levels of participants, challenges inherent in ensuring that environmental stimulation (i.e., therapy) is equal across participants, and finally the ethics involved in having a no-treatment, or even a different treatment, control group.

Despite an absence of data and thorny methodological challenges, it is still essential to ask *what brain changes may be occurring in response to treatment in*

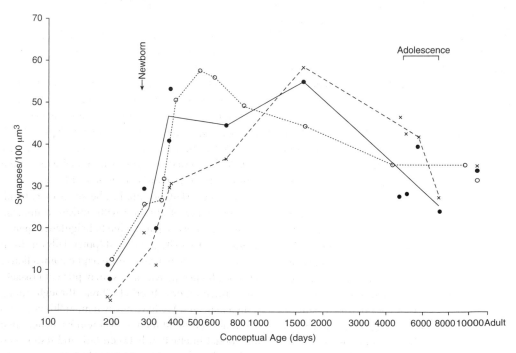

Figure 21-7 Mean synaptic density in synapses/100 μm³ in auditory, calcarine, and prefrontal cortex at various ages. Open circles, visual cortex (area 17); filled circles, auditory cortex; x, prefrontal cortex (middle frontal gyrus). (From Huttenlocher & Dabholkar, 1997).

autism, particularly those with a successful outcome? Do children change by way of compensatory mechanisms or strengthening existing but weak systems? The first possibility, that compensatory mechanisms may come into play as in the infant with a focal lesion, suggests that the child's brain recruits non-damaged tissue to execute functions that were lost. This rests on the idea that a particular brain region or system is particularly compromised in autism, such as the amygdala (Baron-Cohen et al., 2000). Early intervention would, in effect, recruit alternate brain regions and systems to perform functions of regions and systems that are deviant. If this were the case, then one would expect different areas of brain activity to be seen during fMRI studies, for example. Although not a ubiquitous phenomenon, some studies with adults with autism have found evidence of fractionated and unexpected functional maps (e.g., Müller, Pierce, Ambrose, Allen, & Courchesne, 2001; Pierce et al., 2001; Schultz et al., 2000), evidence that non-traditional pathways may be used to perform some cognitive tasks in autism. Furthermore, even after successful training to identify faces, functional activity in the FFA did not increase in adults with autism (Bolte et al., 2006).

As we have outlined in this chapter, however, we propose that autism is the result of early brain overgrowth, and the manifestation of symptoms coincides with this event. Although more pronounced in the frontal and temporal lobes (Carper et al., 2002), early brain overgrowth is likely a general phenomenon in autism, and as such would not result in a defect in a particular brain region or system per se. Such neural overgrowth, and potential concomitant spike in synapses, would result in many inefficient connections, or perhaps even excessive connectivity in some expected areas. Treatment would, in effect, simply strengthen appropriate connections. If this were the case, then the adult neuroimaging literature may reveal situations wherein functional connectivity patterns are normal in autism, or can be modulated to a more normal state. Research by Pierce and Redcay (2004) demonstrated this phenomenon. In that study, the traditional neural system involved in face processing that engaged the fusiform gyrus was hypoactive in response to some face stimuli, but normally active in response to other face stimuli, suggesting that connectivity in autism is generally weak, but not entirely dysfunctional, and may not be the result of compensatory mechanisms. This research was conducted with adults with autism, and the quantity and quality of early

treatment that they may have received is unknown. It stands, however, as an example of normal functional activation patterns in autism and lends support to the idea that it is connectivity per se that is the problem, not one brain system. By default, it is connectivity that would be manipulated during successful treatment.

Another mechanism that might shed light on this issue would be the examination of individuals with autism who have "recovered" in comparison to those that have not, also referred to "optimal outcome" cases (Sutera et al., 2007). Although there is ample evidence to suggest that *symptoms* can dramatically improve following treatment in autism, an understanding of concomitant changes in the brain is nonexistent. Nonetheless, the type of neural abnormality we describe in this chapter—namely early brain overgrowth—combined with some adults with autism showing the possibility of normal circuitry, leads us to strongly consider the possibility that connectivity can indeed be normalized in autism, and may be the precise mechanism resulting from treatment.

CONCLUSIONS AND FUTURE DIRECTIONS

There is ample evidence illustrating autism as a disorder of early brain overgrowth, although our understanding of the mechanisms that contribute to this profile and their functional consequences is far from complete. Despite this, a number of conclusions come out of this review. First, it is unlikely that early brain development in autism adheres to typical developmental principles, such as the tendency for new skills to functionally recruit widespread areas of the cortex early in development, followed by more focal patterns as the skill, or stimulus, becomes more familiar. The failure of children with autism to undergo this normal process may be due to heightened spontaneous neural activity during rest (potentially due to an excess number of neurons and synaptic connections). This heightened activity at rest may prevent task-activated structures or networks to "break through" strong resting networks. We have newly named this phenomenon the "threshold theory," wherein we believe that the normal fluctuation between task and resting networks is altered in autism from the first days or months of life. This may account for findings of hypoactivity observed in the only published fMRI study of children with autism (Redcay & Courchesne, 2008) as well as the failure to show differential Nc and P400 responding between face and object conditions in early ERP studies with 3- and 4-year-old children with the disorder (Dawson et al., 2002). Second, since neural activity modifies gene expression, and gene expression modifies growth of neural circuits, altering this cycle would require that intervention begin prior to the formation of firmly established functional circuits. How can this best be accomplished? We speculate that the most powerful method for changing functional connectivity patterns is based on the developmental principle that learning is strongest when placed within a social context. While this presents a challenge in the field of autism, since the disorder's cardinal feature is a reduction in social interest, it is not a barrier. That is, pockets of social interest exist in children with the disorder that can be gradually expanded by the use of naturalistic early teaching strategies, such as pivotal response training (Pierce & Schreibman, 1995). To the extent that Applied Behavioral Analysis (ABA) treatments also focus attention on social rewards, this may explain the efficacy of these strategies in some groups of children with autism. Thus, we predict that treatment methods that are fundamentally aimed at normalizing attention to the social milieu and utilizing residual social interests would have the best chance of normalizing gene expression and eventually circuit formation, if begun within the first year or two of life. Rote training methods such as Discrete Trial Training, or computer-based training methods, while important for teaching discrete skills particularly later in development, may not hold the key for the formation of normal brain circuitry early in development.

A close examination of brain structure and function during the early period also brings with it direct clinical benefits, not the least of which is the opportunity to discover an early neurobiological signature of autism at or under one year of age. Can a specific set of neural characteristics, such as a reduced hemodynamic response to speech sounds, or increased white matter tracts in frontal lobes, validly signal an infant's risk for manifesting symptoms of autism? Is the quest for early brain markers of autism a realistic goal? If the answer is yes, and we believe that it is, then such discoveries of "early neural signatures" will have a profound impact on the early diagnosis and treatment of autism. The ultimate goal, of course, is to push the age of diagnosis and treatment to a time period that

precedes the onset of full-blown symptoms, allowing for at least the opportunity to prevent the symptoms from manifesting in their totality. As stated above, the reality is, however, that the overall impact of early brain overgrowth must be the abnormal construction of neurofunctional networks early in life which, in turn, impacts gene expression, which impacts behavior. It is an empirical question if and whether early interventions are capable of normalizing functional patterns of brain activity. This is an exciting area of research that awaits future discovery.

In reality, studying the developing human brain presents several challenges for both functional and structural investigations. Using sleep fMRI, for example, brings with it myriad complications such as considering sleep stage and k-complexes as factors in analyses, as well as the logistical challenges inherent in obtaining successful brain images in infants as they sleep. Structural efforts, such as DTI, are also challenging because values for water diffusion parameters vary considerably with age. As a result, much of the knowledge regarding DTI derived from studies of the mature adult human brain is not directly applicable to the developing brain, thus making interpretations of DTI data with infants relatively uncharted waters (Huppi & Dubois, 2006).

While studying the developing brain may yield great leaps forward in the field of autism, studying older children and adults with autism has yielded many significant findings in the field in the past, particularly in the areas of fMRI and genetics. Functional connectivity studies with adults with the disorder raise the intriguing possibility that resting functional networks are abnormal in autism (Kennedy, Redcay, & Courchesne, 2006), and reports of hypoactivity commonly found in the field may be the result of task-related networks having difficulties in "breaking through" resting networks. This threshold theory has been supported by the handful of resting network studies in autism that report hyperconnectivity (Murias et al., 2007). The threshold theory speculates that the interpretation of hypoactivation in various systems as a defect in that particular structure or region may be incorrect. This threshold theory, although provocative while considering research with adults with autism, may also have support in younger children and infants at risk for the disorder as well.

Studying older individuals with the disorder also represents a unique opportunity to discover neurobiological correlates of those with an "optimal

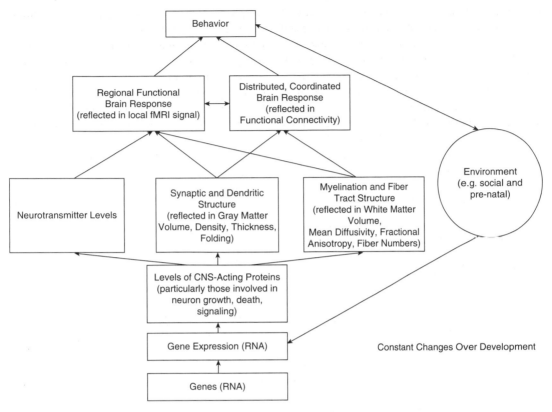

Figure 21-8 Constant Changes Over Development.

outcome—that is, those who successfully participate in society in the context of employment, school placement, and interpersonal relationships. Generating profiles of those with an optimal outcome may aid in treatment decisions, as well as generate a genetic understanding of those individuals with the disorder who may improve in the absence of any treatment at all.

In order to understand autistic behavior and ultimately have a hope of improving functioning, it is also important that research into the neural basis of the disorder encompass an examination of deficits at many different levels of analysis ,from genes to transcription to proteins to brain structure to brain function (see Figure 21-8). Luckily, the arsenal of techniques in each of these areas is growing rapidly. Microarray technology has quickly expanded our ability to examine both genes and gene expression, stereological techniques have improved the reliability and validity of postmortem investigations, and brain imaging modalities have exploded in the past few decades,

allowing more detailed examination of the living brain than has ever before been possible. The growing technology holds promise for a greater understanding of autism that is only beginning to be realized.

References

Adolphs, R. (2009). The social brain: Neural basis of social knowledge. *Annu Rev Psychol*, 60, 693–716.

Akshoomoff, N., Lord, C., Lincoln, A., Courchesne, R. Y., Carper, R. A., Townsend, J., & Courchesne, E. (2004). Outcome classification of preschool children with autism spectrum disorders using MRI brain measures. *J Am Acad Child Adolesc Psychiatry*, 43(3), 349–357.

Alexander, A. L., Lee, J. E., Lazar, M., Boudos, R., DuBray, M. B., Oakes, T. R., . . . Lainhart, J. E. (2007). Diffusion tensor imaging of the corpus callosum in Autism. *Neuroimage*, 34(1), 61–73.

Amaral, D. G., Schumann, C. M., & Nordahl, C. W. (2008). Neuroanatomy of autism. *Trends Neurosci*, 31(3), 137–145.

Anderson, D. K., Lord, C., Risi, S., DiLavore, P. S., Shulman, C., Thurm, A., . . . Pickles, A. (2007).

Patterns of growth in verbal abilities among children with autism spectrum disorder. *J Consult Clin Psychol*, 75(4), 594–604.

Arking, D. E., Cutler, D. J., Brune, C. W., Teslovich, T. M., West, K., Ikeda, M., . . . Chakravarti, A. (2008). A common genetic variant in the neurexin superfamily member CNTNAP2 increases familial risk of autism. *Am J Hum Genet*, 82(1), 160–164.

Aylward, E., Minshew, N., Goldstein, G., Honeycutt, N. A., Augustine, A. M., Yates, K. O., . . . Pearlson, G. D. (1999). MRI volumes in amygdala and hippocapus in non-mentally retarded autistic adolescents and adults. *Neurology*, 53, 2145–2150.

Bailey, A., Le Couteur, A., Gottesman, I., Bolton, P., Simonoff, E., Yuzda, E., & Rutter, M. (1995). Autism as a strongly genetic disorder: Evidence from a British twin study. *Psychological Medicine*, 25(1), 63–77.

Bakkaloglu, B., O'Roak, B. J., Louvi, A., Gupta, A. R., Abelson, J. F., Morgan, T. M., . . . State, M. W. (2008). Molecular cytogenetic analysis and resequencing of contactin associated protein-like 2 in autism spectrum disorders. *Am J Hum Genet*, 82(1), 165–173.

Barnea-Goraly, N., Kwon, H., Menon, V., Eliez, S., Lotspeich, L., & Reiss, A. L. (2004). White matter structure in autism: Preliminary evidence from diffusion tensor imaging. *Biol Psychiatry*, 55(3), 323–326.

Baron-Cohen, S. (2009). Autism: the empathizing-systemizing (E-S) theory. *Ann N Y Acad Sci, 1156*, 68–80.

Baron-Cohen, S., Ring, H., Wheelwright, S., Bullmore, E. T., Brammer, M. J., Simmons, A., & Williams, S. C. R. (1999). Social intelligence in the normal and autistic brain: An fMRI study. *European Journal of Neuroscience, 11*, 1891–1898.

Baron-Cohen, S., Ring, H. A., Bullmore, E. T., Wheelwright, S., Ashwin, C., & Williams, S. C. R. (2000). The amygdala theory of autism. *Neuroscience and Biobehavioral Reviews*, 24(3), 355–364.

Bartholomeusz, H. H., Courchesne, E., & Karns, C. M. (2002). Relationship between head circumference and brain volume in healthy normal toddlers, children, and adults. *Neuropediatrics*, 33(5), 239–241.

Bauman, M. L., & Kemper, T. L. (2005). Neuroanatomic observations of the brain in autism: A review and future directions. *Int J Dev Neurosci*, 23(2-3), 183–187.

Beard, J. (1896). *On certain problems of vertebrate embryology*. Jena: G. Fischer.

Ben Bashat, D., Kronfeld-Duenias, V., Zachor, D. A., Ekstein, P. M., Hendler, T., Tarrasch, R., . . . Ben Sira, L. (2007). Accelerated maturation of white matter in young children with autism: A high b value DWI study. *Neuroimage*, 37(1), 40–47.

Bettelheim, B. (1967). *The empty fortress: Infantile autism and the birth of the self*. New York: Free Press.

Bird, G., Catmur, C., Silani, G., Frith, C., & Frith, U. (2006). Attention does not modulate neural responses to social stimuli in autism spectrum disorders. *Neuroimage*, 31(4), 1614–1624.

Bolte, S., Hubl, D., Feineis-Matthews, S., Prvulovic, D., Dierks, T., & Poustka, F. (2006). Facial affect recognition training in autism: Can we animate the fusiform gyrus? *Behav Neurosci*, 120(1), 211–216.

Bortfeld, H., Wruck, E., & Boas, D. A. (2007). Assessing infants' cortical response to speech using near-infrared spectroscopy. *Neuroimage*, 34(1), 407–415.

Bourgeron, T. (2009). A synaptic trek to autism. *Curr Opin Neurobiol* 19(2), 231–4.

Brambilla, P., Hardan, A., di Nemi, S. U., Perez, J., Soares, J. C., & Barale, F. (2003). Brain anatomy and development in autism: Review of structural MRI studies. *Brain Res Bull*, 61(6), 557–569.

Bryson, S. E., Zwaigenbaum, L., Brian, J., Roberts, W., Szatmari, P., Rombough, V., & McDermott, C. (2007). A prospective case series of high-risk infants who developed autism. *J Autism Dev Disord*, 37(1), 12–24.

Butler, M. G., Dasouki, M. J., Zhou, X. P., Talebizadeh, Z., Brown, M., Takahashi, T. N., . . . Eng, C. (2005). Subset of individuals with autism spectrum disorders and extreme macrocephaly associated with germline PTEN tumour suppressor gene mutations. *J Med Genet*, 42(4), 318–321.

Buxhoeveden, D. P., Semendeferi, K., Buckwalter, J., Schenker, N., Switzer, R., & Courchesne, E. (2006). Reduced minicolumns in the frontal cortex of patients with autism. *Neuropathol Appl Neurobiol*, 32(5), 483–491.

Byrne, J. M., & Gates, R. D. (1987). Single-case study of left cerebral hemispherectomy: Development in the first five years of life. *J Clin Exp Neuropsychol*, 9(4), 423–434.

Carper, R. A., & Courchesne, E. (2000). Inverse correlation between frontal lobe and cerebellum sizes in children with autism. *Brain*, 123, 836–844.

Carper, R. A., & Courchesne, E. (2005). Localized enlargement of the frontal cortex in early autism. *Biological Psychiatry*, 57(2), 126–133.

Carper, R. A., Moses, P., Tigue, Z. D., & Courchesne, E. (2002). Cerebral lobes in autism: Early hyperplasia and abnormal age effects. *Neuroimage*, 16(4), 1038–1051.

Casanova, M. F., Buxhoeveden, D. P., & Brown, C. (2002). Clinical and macroscopic correlates of minicolumnar pathology in autism. *J Child Neurol*, 17(9), 692–695.

Casanova, M. F., Buxhoeveden, D. P., Switala, A. E., & Roy, E. (2002). Minicolumnar pathology in autism. *Neurology*, 58(3), 428–432.

Casanova, M. F., & Trippe, J. (2009). Radial cytoarchitecture and patterns of cortical connectivity in autism. *Philos Trans R Soc Lond B Biol Sci*, 364(1522), 1433–1436.

Casanova, M. F., van Kooten, I. A., Switala, A. E., van Engeland, H., Heinsen, H., Steinbusch, H. W., . . . Schmitz, C. (2006). Minicolumnar abnormalities in autism. *Acta Neuropathol*, 112(3), 287–303.

Cascio, C. J., Gerig, G., & Piven, J. (2007). Diffusion tensor imaging: Application to the study of the developing brain. *J Am Acad Child Adolesc Psychiatry*, 46(2), 213–223.

Castelli, F., Frith, C., Happe, F., & Frith, U. (2002). Autism, Asperger syndrome and brain mechanisms for the attribution of mental states to animated shapes. *Brain*, 125(Pt 8), 1839–1849.

Chao, H. T., Zoghbi, H. Y., & Rosenmund, C. (2007). MeCP2 controls excitatory synaptic strength by regulating glutamatergic synapse number. *Neuron*, 56(1), 58–65.

Cherkassky, V. L., Kana, R. K., Keller, T. A., & Just, M. A. (2006). Functional connectivity in a baseline resting-state network in autism. *Neuroreport*, 17(16), 1687–1690.

Cheung, C., Chua, S. E., Cheung, V., Khong, P. L., Tai, K. S., Wong, T. K., . . . McAlonan, G. M. (2009). White matter fractional anisotrophy differences and correlates of diagnostic symptoms in autism. *J Child Psychol Psychiatry*, 50(9), 1102–1112.

Chua, T. C., Wen, W., Slavin, M. J., & Sachdev, P. S. (2008). Diffusion tensor imaging in mild cognitive impairment and Alzheimer's disease: a review. *Curr Opin Neurol*, 21(1), 83–92.

Chugani, D. C., Muzik, O., Behen, M., Rothermel, R., Janisse, J. J., Lee, J., & Chugani, H. T. (1999). Developmental changes in brain serotonin synthesis capacity in autistic and nonautistic children. *Annals of Neurology*, 45(3), 287–295.

Chugani, D. C., Muzik, O., Rothermel, R., Behen, M., Chakraborty, P., Mangner, T., . . . Chugani, H. T. (1997). Altered serotonin synthesis in the dentatothalamocortical pathway in autistic boys. *Ann Neurol*, 42(4), 666–669.

Cohen, M. M., Jr. (2003). Mental deficiency, alterations in performance, and CNS abnormalities in overgrowth syndromes. *Am J Med Genet C Semin Med Genet*, 117(1), 49–56.

Cook, E. H., Jr., Courchesne, R., Lord, C., Cox, N. J., Yan, S., Lincoln, A., . . . Leventhal, B. L. (1997). Evidence of linkage between the serotonin transporter and autistic disorder. *Molecular Psychiatry*, 2(3), 247–250.

Cook, E. H., Jr., Courchesne, R. Y., Cox, N. J., Lord, C., Gonen, D., Guter, S. J., . . . Courchesne, E. (1998). Linkage-disequilibrium mapping of autistic disorder, with 15q11-13 markers. *Am J Hum Genet*, 62, 1077–1083.

Courchesne, E. (2004). Brain development in autism: Early overgrowth followed by premature arrest of growth. *Mental Retardation and Developmental Disabilities Research Reviews*, 10(2), 106–111.

Courchesne, E., Carper, R., & Akshoomoff, N. (2003). Evidence of brain overgrowth in the first year of life in autism. *Journal of the American Medical Association*, 290(3), 337–344.

Courchesne, E., Chisum, H. J., Townsend, J., Cowles, A., Covington, J., Egaas, B., . . . Press, G. A. (2000). Normal brain development and aging: quantitative analysis at in vivo MR imaging in healthy volunteers. *Radiology*, 216(3), 672–682.

Courchesne, E., Karns, C., Davis, H. R., Ziccardi, R., Carper, R., Tigue, Z., . . . Courchesne, R. Y. (2001). Unusual brain growth patterns in early life in patients with autistic disorder: An MRI study. *Neurology*, 57, 245–254.

Courchesne, E., & Pierce, K. (2005a). Brain overgrowth in autism during a critical time in development: implications for frontal pyramidal neuron and interneuron development and connectivity. *Int J Dev Neurosci*, 23(2-3), 153–170.

Courchesne, E., & Pierce, K. (2005b). Why the frontal cortex in autism might be talking only to itself: local over-connectivity but long-distance disconnection. *Curr Opin Neurobiol*, 15(2), 225–230.

Courchesne, E., Pierce, K., Schumann, C. M., Redcay, E., Buckwalter, J. A., Kennedy, D. P., & Morgan, J. (2007). Mapping early brain development in autism. *Neuron*, 56(2), 399–413.

Courchesne, E., Saitoh, O., Yeung-Courchesne, R., Press, G. A., Lincoln, A. J., Haas, R. H., & Schreibman, L. (1994). Abnormality of cerebellar vermian lobules VI and VII in patients with infantile autism: identification of hypoplastic and hyperplastic subgroups by MR imaging. *American Journal of Roentgenology*, 162, 123–130.

Courchesne, E., Yeung-Courchesne, R., Press, G. A., Hesselink, J. R., & Jernigan, T. L. (1988). Hypoplasia of cerebellar vermal lobules VI and VII in autism. *New England Journal of Medicine*, 318(21), 1349–1354.

Critchley, H. D., Daly, E. M., Bullmore, E. T., Williams, S. C. R., Van Amelsvoort, T., Robertson, D. M., . . . Murphy, D. G. M. (2000). The functional neuroanatomy of social behavior: Changes in cerebral blood flow when people with autistic disorder process facial expressions. *Brain*, 123, 2203–2212.

Dani, V. S., Chang, Q., Maffei, A., Turrigiano, G. G., Jaenisch, R., & Nelson, S. B. (2005). Reduced cortical activity due to a shift in the balance between excitation and inhibition in a mouse model of Rett syndrome. *Proc Natl Acad Sci U S A*, 102(35), 12560–12565.

Dapretto, M., Davies, M. S., Pfeifer, J. H., Scott, A. A., Sigman, M., Bookheimer, S. Y., et al. (2006). Understanding emotions in others: Mirror neuron dysfunction in children with autism spectrum disorders. *Nat Neurosci*, 9(1), 28–30.

Davis, L. K., Hazlett, H. C., Librant, A. L., Nopoulos, P., Sheffield, V. C., Piven, J., & Wassink, T. H. (2008). Cortical enlargement in autism is associated with a functional VNTR in the monoamine oxidase A gene. *Am J Med Genet B Neuropsychiatr Genet*, 147B(7), 1145–1151.

Dawson, G. (2008). Early behavioral intervention, brain plasticity, and the prevention of autism spectrum disorder. *Dev Psychopathol*, 20(3), 775–803.

Dawson, G., Carver, L., Meltzoff, A. N., Panagiotides, H., McPartland, J., & Webb, S. J. (2002). Neural correlates of face and object recognition in young children with autism spectrum disorder, developmental delay, and typical development. *Child Dev*, 73(3), 700–717.

Dawson, G., Munson, J., Webb, S. J., Nalty, T., Abbott, R., & Toth, K. (2007). Rate of head growth decelerates and symptoms worsen in the second year of life in autism. *Biol Psychiatry*, 61(4), 458–464.

Dawson, G., Webb, S. J., Carver, L., Panagiotides, H., & McPartland, J. (2004). Young children with autism show atypical brain responses to fearful versus neutral facial expressions of emotion. *Dev Sci*, 7(3), 340–359.

de Haan, M., & Nelson, C. A. (1997). Recognition of the mother's face by six-month-old infants: A neurobehavioral study. *Child Dev*, 68(2), 187–210.

Dehaene-Lambertz, G., Dehaene, S., & Hertz-Pannier, L. (2002). Functional neuroimaging of speech perception in infants. *Science*, 298(5600), 2013–2015.

Dementieva, Y. A., Vance, D. D., Donnelly, S. L., Elston, L. A., Wolpert, C. M., Ravan, S. A., . . . Cuccaro, M. L.(2005). Accelerated head growth in early development of individuals with autism. *Pediatr Neurol*, 32(2), 102–108.

DeMyer, M. K., Barton, S., DeMyer, W. E., Norton, J.A., Allen, J., & Steele, R. (1973). Prognosis in autism: A follow-up study. *Journal of Autism & Childhood Schizophrenia*, 3(3), 199–246.

Depienne, C., Moreno-De-Luca, D., Heron, D., Bouteiller, D., Gennetier, A., Delorme, R., . . . Betancur, C. (2009). Screening for genomic rearrangements and methylation abnormalities of the 15q11-q13 region in autism spectrum disorders. *Biol Psychiatry*, 66, 349–359.

Dichter, G. S., Felder, J. N., & Bodfish, J. W. (2009). Autism is characterized by dorsal anterior cingulate hyperactivation during social target detection. *Soc Cogn Affect Neurosci*, 4(3), 215–226.

Dissanayake, C., Bui, Q. M., Huggins, R., & Loesch, D. Z. (2006). Growth in stature and head circumference in high-functioning autism and Asperger disorder during the first 3 years of life. *Dev Psychopathol*, 18(2), 381–393.

Durand, C. M., Betancur, C., Boeckers, T. M., Bockmann, J., Chaste, P., Fauchereau, F., . . . Bourgeron, T. (2007). Mutations in the gene encoding the synaptic scaffolding protein SHANK3 are associated with autism spectrum disorders. *Nat Genet*, 39(1), 25–27.

Durston, S., Hulshoff Pol, H. E., Casey, B. J., Giedd, J. N., Buitelaar, J. K., & van Engeland, H. (2001). Anatomical MRI of the developing human brain: What have we learned? *J Am Acad Child Adolesc Psychiatry*, 40(9), 1012–1020.

Elder, L. M., Dawson, G., Toth, K., Fein, D., & Munson, J. (2008). Head circumference as an early predictor of autism symptoms in younger siblings of children with autism spectrum disorder. *J Autism Dev Disord*, 38(6), 1104–1111.

Elston, G. N. (2000). Pyramidal cells of the frontal lobe: all the more spinous to think with. *J Neurosci*, 20(18), RC95.

Elston, G. N. (2003). Cortex, cognition and the cell: New insights into the pyramidal neuron and prefrontal function. *Cereb Cortex*, 13(11), 1124–1138.

Enstrom, A. M., Lit, L., Onore, C. E., Gregg, J. P., Hansen, R. L., Pessah, I. N., . . . Ashwood, P. (2009). Altered gene expression and function of peripheral blood natural killer cells in children with autism. *Brain Behav Immun*, 23(1), 124–133.

Fair, D. A., Cohen, A. L., Dosenbach, N. U., Church, J. A., Miezin, F. M., Barch, D. M., . . . Schlaggar, B. L. (2008). The maturing architecture of the brain's default network. *Proc Natl Acad Sci U S A*, 105(10), 4028–4032.

Fenske, E. C., Zalenski, S., Krantz, P. J., & McClannahan, L. E. (1985). Age at intervention and treatment outcome for autistic children in a comprehensive intervention program. *Analysis Intervention Dev Disabilities*, 5, 49–58.

Fenson, L., Dale, P. S., Reznick, J. S., Bates, E., Thal, D. J., & Pethick, S. J. (1994). Variability in early communicative development. *Monogr Soc Res Child Dev*, 59(5), 1–173; discussion 174-185.

Filipek, P. A., Juranek, J., Smith, M., Mays, L. Z., Ramos, E. R., Bocian, M., . . . Gargus, J. J. (2003). Mitochondrial dysfunction in autistic patients with 15q inverted duplication. *Ann Neurol*, 53(6), 801–804.

Freitag, C. M., Luders, E., Hulst, H. E., Narr, K. L., Thompson, P. M., Toga, A. W., . . . Konrad, C. (2009). Total brain volume and corpus callosum size in medication-naive adolescents and young adults with autism spectrum disorder. *Biol Psychiatry*, 66(4), 316–319.

Fukumoto, A., Hashimoto, T., Ito, H., Nishimura, M., Tsuda, Y., Miyazaki, M., . . . Kagami, S. (2008). Growth of head circumference in autistic infants during the first year of life. *J Autism Dev Disord*, 38(3), 411–418.

Gaillard, A. W. (1988). Problems and paradigms in ERP research. *Biol Psychol*, 26(1-3), 91–109.

Giedd, J. N., Blumenthal, J., Jeffries, N. O., Castellanos, F. X., Liu, H., Zijdenbos, A., . . . Rapoport, J. L. (1999). Brain development during childhood and adolescence: A longitudinal MRI study. *Nat Neurosci*, 2(10), 861–863.

Goffin, A., Hoefsloot, L. H., Bosgoed, E., Swillen, A., & Fryns, J. P. (2001). PTEN mutation in a family with Cowden syndrome and autism. *Am J Med Genet*, 105(6), 521–524.

Goldstein, M. H., King, A. P., & West, M. J. (2003). Social interaction shapes babbling: Testing parallels between birdsong and speech. *Proc Natl Acad Sci U S A*, 100(13), 8030–8035.

Gregg, J. P., Lit, L., Baron, C. A., Hertz-Picciotto, I., Walker, W., Davis, R. A., . . . Sharp, F. R. (2008). Gene expression changes in children with autism. *Genomics*, 91(1), 22–29.

Hanson, J. E., & Madison, D. V. (2007). Presynaptic FMR1 genotype influences the degree of synaptic connectivity in a mosaic mouse model of fragile X syndrome. *J Neurosci*, 27(15), 4014–4018.

Hardan, A. Y., Libove, R. A., Keshavan, M. S., Melhem, N. M., & Minshew, N. J. (2009). A Preliminary Longitudinal Magnetic Resonance Imaging Study of Brain Volume and Cortical Thickness in Autism. *Biol Psychiatry*, 66(4), 313–315.

Hazlett, H. C., Poe, M., Gerig, G., Smith, R. G., Provenzale, J., Ross, A., . . . Piven, J. (2005). Magnetic resonance imaging and head circumference study of brain size in autism: Birth through age 2 years. *Arch Gen Psychiatry*, 62(12), 1366–1376.

Haznedar, M. M., Buchsbaum, M. S., Hazlett, E. A., LiCalzi, E. M., Cartwright, C., & Hollander, E. (2006). Volumetric analysis and three-dimensional glucose metabolic mapping of the striatum and thalamus in patients with autism spectrum disorders. *Am J Psychiatry*, 163(7), 1252–1263.

Helt, M., Kelley, E., Kinsbourne, M., Pandey, J., Boorstein, H., Herbert, M., & Fein, D. (2008). Can children with autism recover? If so, how? *Neuropsychol Rev*, 18(4), 339–366.

Herbert, M. R. (2005). Large brains in autism: The challenge of pervasive abnormality. *Neuroscientist*, 11(5), 417–440.

Herbert, M. R., Ziegler, D. A., Deutsch, C. K., O'Brien, L. M., Lange, N., Bakardjiev, A., . . . Caviness, V. S. (2003). Dissociations of cerebral cortex, subcortical and cerebral white matter volumes in autistic boys. *Brain*, 126(Pt 5), 1182–1192.

Herbert, M. R., Ziegler, D. A., Makris, N., Filipek, P. A., Kemper, T. L., Normandin, J. J., et al. (2004). Localization of white matter volume increase in autism and developmental language disorder. *Ann Neurol*, 55(4), 530–540.

Herman, G. E., Butter, E., Enrile, B., Pastore, M., Prior, T. W., & Sommer, A. (2007). Increasing knowledge of PTEN germline mutations: Two additional patients with autism and macrocephaly. *Am J Med Genet A*, 143(6), 589–593.

Hogart, A., Wu, D., Lasalle, J. M., & Schanen, N. C. (2008). The comorbidity of autism with the genomic disorders of chromosome 15q11.2-q13. *Neurobiol Dis*, 38(2), 181–191.

Horwitz, B., Rumsey, J. M., Grady, C. L., & Rapoport, S. I. (1988). The cerebral metabolic landscape in autism. Intercorrelations of regional glucose utilization. *Archives of Neurology*, 45(7), 749–755.

Hughes, J. R. (2007). Autism: The first firm finding = underconnectivity? *Epilepsy Behav*, 11(1), 20–24.

Humphreys, K., Hasson, U., Avidan, G., Minshew, N., & Behrmann, M. (2008). Cortical patterns of category-selective activation for faces, places and objects in adults with autism. *Autism Res*, 1(1), 52–63.

Huppi, P. S., & Dubois, J. (2006). Diffusion tensor imaging of brain development. *Semin Fetal Neonatal Med*, 11(6), 489–497.

Huttenlocher, P. (2002). *Neural plasticity: The effects of environment on the development of cerebral cortex.* Cambridge, MA: Harvard University Press.

Huttenlocher, P. R., & Dabholkar, A. S. (1997). Regional differences in synaptogenesis in human cerebral cortex. *Journal of Comparative Neurology*, 387(2), 167–178.

Jamain, S., Quach, H., Betancur, C., Rastam, M., Colineaux, C., Gillberg, I. C., . . . Paris Autism Research International Sibpair Study (2003). Mutations of the X-linked genes encoding neuroligins NLGN3 and NLGN4 are associated with autism. *Nat Genet*, 34(1), 27–29.

Jeste, S. S., & Nelson, C. A., III. (2009). Event related potentials in the understanding of autism spectrum disorders: an analytical review. *J Autism Dev Disord*, 39(3), 495–510.

Jeste, S. S., Sahin, M., Bolton, P., Ploubidis, G. B., & Humphrey, A. (2008). Characterization of autism in young children with tuberous sclerosis complex. *J Child Neurol*, 23(5), 520–525.

Johnson, M. H., Griffin, R., Csibra, G., Halit, H., Farroni, T., de Haan, M., . . . Richards, J. (2005). The emergence of the social brain network: Evidence from typical and atypical development. *Dev Psychopathol*, 17(3), 599–619.

Johnson, M. H., Grossmann, T., & Cohen Kadosh, K. (2009). Mapping functional brain development: Building a social brain through interactive specialization. *Dev Psychol*, 45(1), 151–159.

Just, M. A., Carpenter, P. A., Keller, T. A., Eddy, W. F., & Thulborn, K. R. (1996). Brain activation modulated by sentence comprehension. *Science*, 274(5284), 114–116.

Just, M. A., Cherkassky, V. L., Keller, T. A., Kana, R. K., & Minshew, N. J. (2007). Functional and anatomical cortical underconnectivity in autism: evidence from an FMRI study of an executive function task and corpus callosum morphometry. *Cereb Cortex*, 17(4), 951–961.

Just, M. A., Cherkassky, V. L., Keller, T. A., Minshew, N. J. (2004). Cortical activation and synchronization during sentence comprehension in high-functioning autism: Evidence of underconnectivity. *Brain*, 127(Pt 8), 1811–1821.

Kana, R. K., Keller, T. A., Cherkassky, V. L., Minshew, N. J., & Just, M. A. (2006). Sentence comprehension in autism: Thinking in pictures with decreased functional connectivity. *Brain*, 129(Pt 9), 2484–2493.

Kana, R. K., Keller, T. A., Minshew, N. J., & Just, M. A. (2007). Inhibitory control in high-functioning autism:

decreased activation and underconnectivity in inhibition networks. *Biol Psychiatry, 62*(3), 198–206.

Kanner, L. (1943). Autistic disturbances of affective contact. *Nervous Child, 2,* 217–250.

Karmiloff-Smith, A. (2007). Atypical epigenesis. *Dev Sci, 10*(1), 84–88.

Kates, W. R., Mostofsky, S. H., Zimmerman, A. W., Mazzocco, M. M., Landa, R., Warsofsky, I. S., . . . Reiss, A. L. (1998). Neuroanatomical and neurocognitive differences in a pair of monozygous twins discordant for strictly defined autism. *Annals of Neurology, 43*(6), 782–791.

Kaufmann, W. E., Cooper, K. L., Mostofsky, S. H., Capone, G. T., Kates, W. R., Newschaffer, C. J., . . . Lanham, D. C.(2003). Specificity of cerebellar vermian abnormalities in autism: A quantitative magnetic resonance imaging study. *J Child Neurol, 18*(7), 463–470.

Ke, X., Tang, T., Hong, S., Hang, Y., Zou, B., Li, H., . . . Liu, Y. (2009). White matter impairments in autism, evidence from voxel-based morphometry and diffusion tensor imaging. *Brain Res, 1265,* 171–177.

Keller, T. A., Kana, R. K., & Just, M. A. (2007). A developmental study of the structural integrity of white matter in autism. *Neuroreport, 18*(1), 23–27.

Kennedy, D. P., & Courchesne, E. (2008). The intrinsic functional organization of the brain is altered in autism. *Neuroimage, 39*(4), 1877–1885.

Kennedy, D. P., Redcay, E., & Courchesne, E. (2006). Failing to deactivate: Resting functional abnormalities in autism. *Proc Natl Acad Sci U S A, 103*(21), 8275–8280.

Kennedy, D. P., Semendeferi, K., & Courchesne, E. (2007). No reduction of spindle neuron number in frontoinsular cortex in autism. *Brain Cogn, 64*(2), 124–129.

Kim, H. G., Kishikawa, S., Higgins, A. W., Seong, I. S., Donovan, D. J., Shen, Y., . . . Gusella, J. F. (2008). Disruption of neurexin 1 associated with autism spectrum disorder. *Am J Hum Genet, 82*(1), 199–207.

Kleinhans, N. M., Richards, T., Sterling, L., Stegbauer, K. C., Mahurin, R., Johnson, L. C., . . . Aylward, E. (2008). Abnormal functional connectivity in autism spectrum disorders during face processing. *Brain, 131*(Pt 4), 1000–1012.

Kochanska, G., Coy, K. C., & Murray, K. T. (2001). The development of self-regulation in the first four years of life. *Child Dev, 72*(4), 1091–1111.

Kochunov, P., Thompson, P. M., Lancaster, J. L., Bartzokis, G., Smith, S., Coyle, T., . . . Fox, P. T. (2007). Relationship between white matter fractional anisotropy and other indices of cerebral health in normal aging: tract-based spatial statistics study of aging. *Neuroimage, 35*(2), 478–487.

Koshino, H., Carpenter, P. A., Minshew, N. J., Cherkassky, V. L., Keller, T. A., & Just, M. A. (2005). Functional connectivity in an fMRI working memory task in high-functioning autism. *Neuroimage, 24*(3), 810–821.

Koshino, H., Kana, R. K., Keller, T. A., Cherkassky, V. L., Minshew, N. J., & Just, M. A. (2008). fMRI investigation of working memory for faces in autism: Visual coding and underconnectivity with frontal areas. *Cereb Cortex, 18*(2), 289–300.

Kuhl, P. K., Coffey-Corina, S., Padden, D., & Dawson, G. (2005). Links between social and linguistic processing of speech in preschool children with autism: Behavioral and electrophysiological measures. *Dev Sci, 8*(1), F1–F12.

Kuhl, P. K., Tsao, F. M., & Liu, H. M. (2003). Foreign-language experience in infancy: effects of short-term exposure and social interaction on phonetic learning. *Proc Natl Acad Sci U S A, 100*(15), 9096–9101.

Kwon, C. H., Luikart, B. W., Powell, C. M., Zhou, J., Matheny, S. A., Zhang, W., . . . Parada, L. F. (2006). Pten regulates neuronal arborization and social interaction in mice. *Neuron, 50*(3), 377–388.

Laumonnier, F., Bonnet-Brilhault, F., Gomot, M., Blanc, R., David, A., Moizard, M. P., . . . Briault, S. (2004). X-linked mental retardation and autism are associated with a mutation in the NLGN4 gene, a member of the neuroligin family. *Am J Hum Genet, 74*(3), 552–557.

Lawson-Yuen, A., Saldivar, J. S., Sommer, S., & Picker, J. (2008). Familial deletion within NLGN4 associated with autism and Tourette syndrome. *Eur J Hum Genet, 16*(5), 614–618.

Lee, E., & Son, H. (2009). Adult hippocampal neurogenesis and related neurotrophic factors. *BMB Rep, 42*(5), 239–244.

Lee, J. E., Bigler, E. D., Alexander, A. L., Lazar, M., DuBray, M. B., Chung, M. K., . . . Lainhart, J. E. (2007). Diffusion tensor imaging of white matter in the superior temporal gyrus and temporal stem in autism. *Neurosci Lett, 424*(2), 127–132.

Lee, P. S., Yerys, B. E., Della Rosa, A., Foss-Feig, J., Barnes, K. A., James, J. D., . . . Kenworthy, L. E. (2009). Functional connectivity of the inferior frontal cortex changes with age in children with autism spectrum disorders: A fcMRI study of response inhibition. *Cereb Cortex, 19*(8), 1787–1794.

Leopold, D. A., Murayama, Y., & Logothetis, N. K. (2003). Very slow activity fluctuations in monkey visual cortex: implications for functional brain imaging. *Cereb Cortex, 13*(4), 422–433.

Lovaas, O. I. (1987). Behavioral treatment and normal educational and intellectual functioning in young autistic children. *Journal of Consulting and Clinical Psychology, 55*(1), 3–9.

Majdan, M., & Shatz, C. J. (2006). Effects of visual experience on activity—dependent gene regulation in cortex. *Nat Neurosci, 9*(5), 650–659.

Mason, R. A., Williams, D. L., Kana, R. K., Minshew, N., & Just, M. A. (2008). Theory of mind disruption and recruitment of the right hemisphere during narrative comprehension in autism. *Neuropsychologia, 46*(1), 269–280.

McAlonan, G. M., Cheung, V., Cheung, C., Suckling, J., Lam, G. Y., Tai, K. S., . . . Chua, S. E. (2005). Mapping the brain in autism. A voxel-based MRI study of volumetric differences and intercorrelations in autism. *Brain, 128*(Pt 2), 268–276.

Miller, D. T., Shen, Y., Weiss, L. A., Korn, J., Anselm, I., Bridgemohan, C., . . . Wu, B. L. (2009). Microdeletion/duplication at 15q13.2q13.3 among individuals with features of autism and other neuropsychiatric disorders. *J Med Genet, 46*(4), 242–248.

Mills, D. L., Coffey-Corina, S., & Neville, H. J. (1993). Language acquisition and cerebral specialization in 20-month-old infants. *Journal of Cognitive Neuroscience, 5*(3), 317–334.

Mills, D. L., Coffey-Corina, S., & Neville, H. J. (1997). Language comprehension and cerebral specialization from 13 to 20 months. *Dev Neuropsychol, 13*, 397–446.

Miskowiak, K., Inkster, B., O'Sullivan, U., Selvaraj, S., Goodwin, G. M., & Harmer, C. J. (2008). Differential effects of erythropoietin on neural and cognitive measures of executive function 3 and 7 days post-administration. *Exp Brain Res, 184*(3), 313–321.

Mizuno, A., Villalobos, M. E., Davies, M. M., Dahl, B. C., & Muller, R. A. (2006). Partially enhanced thalamo-cortical functional connectivity in autism. *Brain Res, 1104*(1), 160–174.

Monk, C. S., Peltier, S. J., Wiggins, J. L., Weng, S. J., Carrasco, M., Risi, S., & Lord, C. (2009). Abnormalities of intrinsic functional connectivity in autism spectrum disorders. *Neuroimage, 47*(2), 764–772.

Mosch, S. C., Max, J. E., & Tranel, D. (2005). A matched lesion analysis of childhood versus adult-onset brain injury due to unilateral stroke: Another perspective on neural plasticity and recovery of social functioning. *Cogn Behav Neurol, 18*(1), 5–17.

Mosconi, M. W., Cody-Hazlett, H., Poe, M. D., Gerig, G., Gimpel-Smith, R., & Piven, J. (2009). Longitudinal study of amygdala volume and joint attention in 2- to 4-year-old children with autism. *Arch Gen Psychiatry, 66*(5), 509–516.

Mostofsky, S. H., Powell, S. K., Simmonds, D. J., Goldberg, M. C., Caffo, B., & Pekar, J. J. (2009). Decreased connectivity and cerebellar activity in autism during motor task performance. *Brain, 132*(9), 2413–2425.

Moy, S. S., Nadler, J. J., Young, N. B., Nonneman, R. J., Grossman, A. W., Murphy, D. L., . . . Lauder, J. M. (2009). Social approach in genetically engineered mouse lines relevant to autism. *Genes Brain Behav, 8*(2), 129–142.

Mraz, K. D., Green, J., Dumont-Mathieu, T., Makin, S., & Fein, D. (2007). Correlates of head circumference growth in infants later diagnosed with autism spectrum disorders. *J Child Neurol, 22*(6), 700–713.

Muller, R. A. (2008). From loci to networks and back again: Anomalies in the study of autism. *Ann N Y Acad Sci, 1145*, 300–315.

Müller, R. A., Pierce, K., Ambrose, J. B., Allen, G., & Courchesne, E. (2001). Atypical patterns of cerebral motor activation in autism: a functional magnetic resonance study. *Biological Psychiatry, 49*, 665–676.

Munson, J., Dawson, G., Abbott, R., Faja, S., Webb, S. J., Friedman, S. D., . . . Dager, S. R. (2006). Amygdalar volume and behavioral development in autism. *Arch Gen Psychiatry, 63*(6), 686–693.

Murias, M., Webb, S. J., Greenson, J., & Dawson, G. (2007). Resting state cortical connectivity reflected in EEG coherence in individuals with autism. *Biol Psychiatry, 62*(3), 270–273.

Neil, J. J., Shiran, S. I., McKinstry, R. C., Schefft, G. L., Snyder, A. Z., Almli, C. R., . . . Conturo, T. E. (1998). Normal brain in human newborns: Apparent diffusion coefficient and diffusion anisotropy measured by using diffusion tensor MR imaging. *Radiology, 209*(1), 57–66.

Nelson, C. A., 3rd, Zeanah, C. H., Fox, N. A., Marshall, P. J., Smyke, A. T., & Guthrie, D. (2007). Cognitive recovery in socially deprived young children: The Bucharest Early Intervention Project. *Science, 318*(5858), 1937–1940.

Noll, R. B., Reiter-Purtill, J., Moore, B. D., Schorry, E. K., Lovell, A. M., Vannatta, K., & Gerhardt, C. A. (2007). Social, emotional, and behavioral functioning of children with NF1. *Am J Med Genet A, 143A*(19), 2261–2273.

Noonan, S. K., Haist, F., & Muller, R. A. (2009). Aberrant functional connectivity in autism: Evidence from low-frequency BOLD signal fluctuations. *Brain Res, 1262*, 48–63.

Oberman, L. M., Ramachandran, V. S., & Pineda, J. A. (2008). Modulation of mu suppression in children with autism spectrum disorders in response to familiar or unfamiliar stimuli: The mirror neuron hypothesis. *Neuropsychologia, 46*(5), 1558–1565.

Ouldim, K., Natiq, A., Jonveaux, P., & Sefiani, A. (2007). Tetrasomy 15q11-q13 Diagnosed by FISH in a Patient with Autistic Disorder. *J Biomed Biotechnol, 2007*(3), 61538.

Page, D. T., Kuti, O. J., Prestia, C., & Sur, M. (2009). Haploinsufficiency for pten and serotonin transporter cooperatively influences brain size and social behavior. *Proc Natl Acad Sci U S A, 106*(6), 1989–1994.

Palmen, S. J., Hulshoff Pol, H. E., Kemner, C., Schnack, H. G., Durston, S., Lahuis, B. E., . . . Van Engeland, H. (2005). Increased gray-matter volume in medication-naive high-functioning children with autism spectrum disorder. *Psychol Med, 35*(4), 561–570.

Pardini, M., Garaci, F. G., Bonzano, L., Roccatagliata, L., Palmieri, M. G., Pompili, E., . . . Emberti Gialloreti, L.(2009). White matter reduced streamline coherence in young men with autism and mental retardation. *Eur J Neurol, 16*(11), 1185–1190.

Persico, A. M., & Bourgeron, T. (2006). Searching for ways out of the autism maze: genetic, epigenetic and environmental clues. *Trends Neurosci*, 29(7), 349–358.

Pierce, K., Carter, C., Weinfeld, M., Desmond, J., Hazin, R., Bjork, R., & Gallagher, N. (2010). *Catching, studying, and treating autism early: The 1-Year Well-Baby Check-Up Approach*. Manuscript submitted for publication.

Pierce, K., & Courchesne, E. (2001). Evidence for a cerebellar role in reduced exploration and stereotyped behavior in autism. *Biol Psychiatry*, 49(8), 655–664.

Pierce, K., Haist, F., Sedaghat, F., & Courchesne, E. (2004). The brain response to personally familiar faces in autism: findings of fusiform activity and beyond. *Brain*, 127(Pt 12), 2703–2716.

Pierce, K., Muller, R. A., Ambrose, J., Allen, G., & Courchesne, E. (2001). Face processing occurs outside the fusiform "face area" in autism: evidence from functional MRI. *Brain*, 124(Pt 10), 2059–2073.

Pierce, K., & Redcay, E. (2008). Fusiform function in children with an autism spectrum disorder is a matter of "who." *Biol Psychiatry*, 64(7), 552–560.

Pierce, K., & Schreibman, L. (1995). Increasing complex social behaviors in children with autism: Effects of peer-implemented pivotal response training. *J Appl Behav Anal*, 28(3), 285–295.

Raznahan, A., Pugliese, L., Barker, G. J., Daly, E., Powell, J., Bolton, P. F., & Murphy, D. G. (2009). Serotonin transporter genotype and neuroanatomy in autism spectrum disorders. *Psychiatr Genet*, 19(3), 147–150.

Redcay, E., & Courchesne, E. (2005). When is the brain enlarged in autism? A meta-analysis of all brain size reports. *Biol Psychiatry*, 58(1), 1–9.

Redcay, E., & Courchesne, E. (2008). Deviant functional magnetic resonance imaging patterns of brain activity to speech in 2-3-year-old children with autism spectrum disorder. *Biol Psychiatry*, 64(7), 589–598.

Redcay, E., Haist, F., & Courchesne, E. (2008). Functional neuroimaging of speech perception during a pivotal period in language acquisition. *Dev Sci*, 11(2), 237–252.

Redcay, E., Kennedy, D. P., & Courchesne, E. (2007). fMRI during natural sleep as a method to study brain function during early childhood. *Neuroimage*, 38(4), 696–707.

Ritvo, E. R., Freeman, B. J., Mason-Brothers, A., Mo, A., & Ritvo, A. M. (1985). Concordance for the syndrome of autism in 40 pairs of afflicted twins. *American Journal of Psychiatry*, 142(1), 74–77.

Robins, D. L., Fein, D., Barton, M. L., & Green, J. A. (2001). The modified checklist for autism in toddlers: An initial study investigating the early detection of autism and pervasive developmental disorders. *J Autism Dev Disord*, 31(2), 131–144.

Rogers, S. J. (1998). Empirically supported comprehensive treatments for young children with autism. *J Clin Child Psychol*, 27(2), 168–179.

Rojas, D. C., Bawn, S. D., Benkers, T. L., Reite, M. L., & Rogers, S. J. (2002). Smaller left hemisphere planum temporale in adults with autistic disorder. *Neurosci Lett*, 328(3), 237–240.

Rojas, D. C., Peterson, E., Winterrowd, E., Reite, M. L., Rogers, S. J., & Tregellas, J. R. (2006). Regional gray matter volumetric changes in autism associated with social and repetitive behavior symptoms. *BMC Psychiatry*, 6, 56.

Rossini, P. M., Altamura, C., Ferreri, F., Melgari, J. M., Tecchio, F., Tombini, M., . . . Vernieri, F. (2007). Neuroimaging experimental studies on brain plasticity in recovery from stroke. *Eura Medicophys*, 43(2), 241–254.

Rubenstein, J. L., & Merzenich, M. M. (2003). Model of autism: Increased ratio of excitation/inhibition in key neural systems. *Genes Brain Behav*, 2(5), 255–267.

Rutter, S. C., & Cole, T. R. (1991). Psychological characteristics of Sotos syndrome. *Dev Med Child Neurol*, 33(10), 898–902.

Sacco, R., Militerni, R., Frolli, A., Bravaccio, C., Gritti, A., Elia, M., . . . Persico, A. M. (2007). Clinical, morphological, and biochemical correlates of head circumference in autism. *Biol Psychiatry*, 62(9), 1038–1047.

Schmitz, N., Rubia, K., van Amelsvoort, T., Daly, E., Smith, A., & Murphy, D. G. (2008). Neural correlates of reward in autism. *Br J Psychiatry*, 192(1), 19–24.

Schultz, R. T., Gauthier, I., Klin, A., Fulbright, R. K., Anderson, A. W., Volkmar, F., . . . Gore, J. C. (2000). Abnormal ventral temporal cortical activity during face discrimination among individuals with autism and Asperger syndrome [see comments]. *Archives of General Psychiatry*, 57(4), 331–340.

Schumann, C. M., & Amaral, D. G. (2006). Stereological analysis of amygdala neuron number in autism. *J Neurosci*, 26(29), 7674–7679.

Schumann, C. M., Barnes, C. C., Lord, C., & Courchesne, E. (2009). Amygdala enlargement in toddlers with autism related to severity of social and communication impairments. *Biological psychiatry*, 66, 942–949.

Schumann, C. M., Hamstra, J., Goodlin-Jones, B. L., Lotspeich, L. J., Kwon, H., Buonocore, M. H., . . . Reiss, A. L. (2004). The amygdala is enlarged in children but not adolescents with autism; The hippocampus is enlarged at all ages. *Journal of neuroscience*, 24, 6392–6401.

Sebat, J., Lakshmi, B., Malhotra, D., Troge, J., Lese-Martin, C., Walsh, T., . . . Wigler, M. (2007). Strong association of de novo copy number mutations with autism. *Science*, 316(5823), 445–449.

Shatz, C. J. (1990). Impulse activity and the patterning of connections during CNS development. *Neuron*, 5(6), 745–756.

Sigman, M., Ruskin, E., Arbeile, S., Corona, R., Dissanayake, C., Espinosa, M., . . . Zierhut, C. (1999). Continuity and change in the social competence of children with autism, Down syndrome, and developmental delays. *Monogr Soc Res Child Dev*, 64(1), 1–114.

Siller, M., & Sigman, M. (2008). Modeling longitudinal change in the language abilities of children with autism: parent behaviors and child characteristics as predictors of change. *Dev Psychol*, 44(6), 1691–1704.

Simic, M., & Turk, J. (2004). Autistic spectrum disorder associated with partial duplication of chromosome 15: Three case reports. *Eur Child Adolesc Psychiatry*, 13(6), 389–393.

Skranes, J., Vangberg, T. R., Kulseng, S., Indredavik, M. S., Evensen, K. A., Martinussen, M., . . . Brubakk, A. M. (2007). Clinical findings and white matter abnormalities seen on diffusion tensor imaging in adolescents with very low birth weight. *Brain*, 130 (Pt 3), 654–666.

Sodhi, M. S., & Sanders-Bush, E. (2004). Serotonin and brain development. *Int Rev Neurobiol*, 59, 111–174.

Solomon, M., Ozonoff, S. J., Ursu, S., Ravizza, S., Cummings, N., Ly, S., . . . Carter, C. S. (2009). The neural substrates of cognitive control deficits in autism spectrum disorders. *Neuropsychologia*, 47, 2515–2526.

Soulieres, I., Dawson, M., Samson, F., Barbeau, E. B., Sahyoun, C. P., Strangman, G. E., . . . Mottron, L. (2009). Enhanced visual processing contributes to matrix reasoning in autism. *Hum Brain Mapp*, 30(12), 4082–4107.

Sparks, B. F., Friedman, S. D., Shaw, D. W., Aylward, E. H., Echelard, D., Artru, A. A., . . . Dager, S. R. (2002). Brain structural abnormalities in young children with autism spectrum disorder. *Neurology*, 59(2), 184–192.

Spelke, E., Gutheil, G., & Van de Walle, G. (1995). The development of object perception. In S. Kosslyn & D. Osherson (Eds.), *Visual cognition. An invitation to cognitive science* (2nd ed., pp. 297–330). Cambridge, MA: MIT Press.

Spinrad, T. L., & Stifter, C. A. (2006). Toddlers' empathy-related responding to distress: Predictions from negative emotionality and maternal behavior in infancy. *Infancy*, 10(2), 97–121.

Stanfield, A. C., McIntosh, A. M., Spencer, M. D., Philip, R., Gaur, S., & Lawrie, S. M. (2008). Towards a neuroanatomy of autism: a systematic review and meta-analysis of structural magnetic resonance imaging studies. *Eur Psychiatry*, 23(4), 289–299.

Steffenburg, S., Gillberg, C., Hellgren, L., Andersson, L., Gillberg, I. C., Jakobsson, G., & Bohman, M. (1989). A twin study of autism in Denmark, Finland, Iceland, Norway and Sweden. *Journal of Child Psychology and Psychiatry and Allied Disciplines*, 30(3), 405–416.

Sudhof, T. C. (2008). Neuroligins and neurexins link synaptic function to cognitive disease. *Nature*, 455(7215), 903–911.

Suh, H., Consiglio, A., Ray, J., Sawai, T., D'Amour, K. A., & Gage, F. H. (2007). In vivo fate analysis reveals the multipotent and self-renewal capacities of Sox2+ neural stem cells in the adult hippocampus. *Cell Stem Cell*, 1(5), 515–528.

Sundaram, S. K., Kumar, A., Makki, M. I., Behen, M. E., Chugani, H. T., & Chugani, D. C. (2008). Diffusion tensor imaging of frontal lobe in autism spectrum disorder. *Cereb Cortex*, 18(11), 2659–2665.

Sutera, S., Pandey, J., Esser, E. L., Rosenthal, M. A., Wilson, L. B., Barton, M., . . . Fein, D. (2007). Predictors of optimal outcome in toddlers diagnosed with autism spectrum disorders. *J Autism Dev Disord*, 37(1), 98–107.

Tabuchi, K., Blundell, J., Etherton, M. R., Hammer, R. E., Liu, X., Powell, C. M., & Sudhof, T. C. (2007). A neuroligin-3 mutation implicated in autism increases inhibitory synaptic transmission in mice. *Science*, 318(5847), 71–76.

Thakkar, K. N., Polli, F. E., Joseph, R. M., Tuch, D. S., Hadjikhani, N., Barton, J. J., & Monoach, D. S. (2008). Response monitoring, repetitive behaviour and anterior cingulate abnormalities in autism spectrum disorders (ASD). *Brain*, 131(Pt 9), 2464–2478.

Tomasello, M., Carpenter, M., Call, J., Behne, T., & Moll, H. (2005). Understanding and sharing intentions: the origins of cultural cognition. *Behav Brain Sci*, 28(5), 675–691; discussion 691-735.

Treffert, D. A., McAndrew, J. B., & Dreifuerst, P. (1973). An inpatient treatment program and outcome for 57 autistic and schizophrenic children. *Journal of Autism & Childhood Schizophrenia*, 3(3), 138–153.

Tsatsanis, K. D., Rourke, B. P., Klin, A., Volkmar, F. R., Cicchetti, D., & Schultz, R. T. (2003). Reduced thalamic volume in high-functioning individuals with autism. *Biol Psychiatry*, 53(2), 121–129.

Turner, K. C., Frost, L., Linsenbardt, D., McIlroy, J. R., & Muller, R. A. (2006). Atypically diffuse functional connectivity between caudate nuclei and cerebral cortex in autism. *Behav Brain Funct*, 2, 34.

University of California San Diego Autism Center of Excellence (2010). Unpublished raw data.

Vaccarino, F. M., Grigorenko, E. L., Smith, K. M., & Stevens, H. E. (2009). Regulation of cerebral cortical size and neuron number by fibroblast growth factors: Implications for autism. *J Autism Dev Disord*, 39(3), 511–520.

van Kooten, I. A., Palmen, S. J., von Cappeln, P., Steinbusch, H. W., Korr, H., Heinsen, H., . . . Schmitz, C. (2008). Neurons in the fusiform gyrus are fewer and smaller in autism. *Brain*, 131(Pt 4), 987–999.

Varga, E. A., Pastore, M., Prior, T., Herman, G. E., & McBride, K. L. (2009). The prevalence of PTEN mutations in a clinical pediatric cohort with autism spectrum disorders, developmental delay, and macrocephaly. *Genet Med*, *11*(2), 111–117.

Vargas, D. L., Nascimbene, C., Krishnan, C., Zimmerman, A. W., & Pardo, C. A. (2005). Neuroglial activation and neuroinflammation in the brain of patients with autism. *Annals of Neurology*, *57*, 67–81.

Villalobos, M. E., Mizuno, A., Dahl, B. C., Kemmotsu, N., & Muller, R. A. (2005). Reduced functional connectivity between V1 and inferior frontal cortex associated with visuomotor performance in autism. *Neuroimage*, *25*(3), 916–925.

Wang, A. T., Lee, S. S., Sigman, M., & Dapretto, M. (2006). Neural basis of irony comprehension in children with autism: The role of prosody and context. *Brain*, *129*(Pt 4), 932–943.

Wang, A. T., Lee, S. S., Sigman, M., & Dapretto, M. (2007). Reading affect in the face and voice: Neural correlates of interpreting communicative intent in children and adolescents with autism spectrum disorders. *Arch Gen Psychiatry*, *64*(6), 698–708.

Wassink, T. H., Hazlett, H. C., Epping, E. A., Arndt, S., Dager, S. R., Schellenberg, G. D., . . . Piven, J. (2007). Cerebral cortical gray matter overgrowth and functional variation of the serotonin transporter gene in autism. *Arch Gen Psychiatry*, *64*(6), 709–717.

Webb, S. J., Nalty, T., Munson, J., Brock, C., Abbott, R., & Dawson, G. (2007). Rate of head circumference growth as a function of autism diagnosis and history of autistic regression. *J Child Neurol*, *22*(10), 1182–1190.

Webb, S. J., Sparks, B. F., Friedman, S. D., Shaw, D. W., Giedd, J., Dawson, G., & Dager, S. R. (2009). Cerebellar vermal volumes and behavioral correlates in children with autism spectrum disorder. *Psychiatry Res*, *172*(1), 61–67.

Welchew, D. E., Ashwin, C., Berkouk, K., Salvador, R., Suckling, J., Baron-Cohen, S., . . . Bullmore, E. (2005). Functional disconnectivity of the medial temporal lobe in Asperger's syndrome. *Biol Psychiatry*, *57*(9), 991–998.

Whitney, E. R., Kemper, T. L., Bauman, M. L., Rosene, D. L., & Blatt, G. J. (2008). Cerebellar Purkinje cells are reduced in a subpopulation of autistic brains: a stereological experiment using calbindin-D28k. *Cerebellum*, *7*(3), 406–416.

Wicker, B., Fonlupt, P., Hubert, B., Tardif, C., Gepner, B., & Deruelle, C. (2008). Abnormal cerebral effective connectivity during explicit emotional processing in adults with autism spectrum disorder. *Soc Cogn Affect Neurosci*, *3*(2), 135–143.

Wilke, M., Holland, S. K., & Ball, W. S., Jr. (2003). Language processing during natural sleep in a 6-year-old boy, as assessed with functional MR imaging. *AJNR Am J Neuroradiol*, *24*(1), 42–44.

Williams, J. H., Waiter, G. D., Perra, O., Perrett, D. I., & Whiten, A. (2005). An fMRI study of joint attention experience. *Neuroimage*, *25*(1), 133–140.

Wong, V. (2006). Study of the relationship between tuberous sclerosis complex and autistic disorder. *J Child Neurol*, *21*(3), 199–204.

Wulfeck, B., Bates, E., Krupa-Kwiatkowski, M., & Saltzman, D. (2004). Grammaticality sensitivity in children with early focal brain injury and children with specific language impairment. *Brain Lang*, *88*(2), 215–228.

Young, S. K., Fox, N. A., & Zahn-Waxler, C. (1999). The relations between temperament and empathy in 2-year-olds. *Dev Psychol*, *35*(5), 1189–1197.

Zwaigenbaum, L., Bryson, S., Rogers, T., Roberts, W., Brian, J., & Szatmari, P. (2005). Behavioral manifestations of autism in the first year of life. *Int J Dev Neurosci*, *23*(2-3), 143–152.

Chapter 22

Neuropeptide and Steroid Hormones

Suma Jacob, Maria Demosthenous, and C. Sue Carter

INTRODUCTION

Autism spectrum disorders (ASD) are increasingly recognized and diagnosed, but the mechanisms that lead to the development of these disorders are poorly understood. Autism is diagnostically characterized by qualitative impairments in three domains: social interactions, communication, and restrictive/repetitive behaviors and interests (American Psychiatric Association, 2000). Autism spectrum disorders include Autistic disorder, pervasive developmental disorder not otherwise specified (PPD-NOS), and Asperger's disorder. With the emergence of improved diagnostic measures and genetic technology, the field has realized that phenotypic heterogeneity across the autism spectrum is likely due to multiple etiologies and complex inheritance patterns. In addition to the broad variability found under the clinical and diagnostic umbrella of the autism spectrum, there are additional differences observed within sub-domains due to comorbid neuropsychiatric disorders,

including epilepsy, intellectual disabilities, anxiety, and depression.

Epidemiological studies have revealed autism to be the most heritable psychiatric syndrome (Bailey et al., 1995). Research to date has failed to find evidence for a single locus or cause for autism, although a small percentage of autism cases can be ascribed to single-gene disorders and diverse chromosomal abnormalities (Veenstra-VanderWeele & Cook, 2004). ASD may be due to multiple common polymorphisms that confer risk (Folstein & Rosen-Sheidley, 2001) with a complex genetic inheritance pattern (see Chapters 2 and 24). With larger study samples, rare genetic variants are also being found in autism and other neuropsychiatric disorders (Cook & Scherer, 2008). Rare variants may have individually larger effects, but with high-locus heterogeneity.

Models that have examined heritability in monozygotic and dizygotic twins suggest that each domain of behavior used to describe the autism spectrum—including repetitive behaviors, communication, and social behavior—is highly heritable. These domains are not strongly affected by environment and are relatively independent of each other (Ronald et al., 2006). Because several genes confer susceptibility to a disorder with phenotypic heterogeneity, examining males and females or other relevant subgroups separately (e.g. those with different neurochemical profiles) may help us identify different etiological pathways. Focusing on specific behavioral subdomains or symptom clusters may be an alternative way to elucidate the independent contributions of pathophysiological systems or genes. Many biological mechanisms are involved in ASD and contribute to the range of differences observed in behaviors, communication, social abilities, and learning and developmental trajectories.

Several lines of scientific inquiry suggest a connection between neuropeptide or steroid hormones and specific behaviors that are characteristic of ASD. In this chapter, we will explore hormonal mechanisms that influence social interactions, communication, or repetitive behaviors, as well as their potential role in autism. We focus on neuropeptide hormones including oxytocin (OT) and vasopressin (AVP), as well as the steroid hormones, such as testosterone and cortisol, because they have been studied more extensively than other hormones in ASD.

Hormones have been investigated in a range of medical disorders that have higher or lower incidences in males versus females, or influence the timing or susceptibility of the disorder within a particular sex. In autism, the ratio of males to females has been estimated at 4:1, and may be even higher in high-functioning autism or Asperger's disorder (Fombonne, 2003; Volkmar et al., 1993). The male-bias found in autism could be due to range of reasons, including: 1) early risk or protective exposure of hormones that mediate sex differences (e.g. testosterone, estrogen, AVP, OT, etc.); 2) interactions with etiological factors that are modulated by neurohormones; or 3) gene products regulated by sex chromosomes or autosomal chromosomes, with pathway genes differentially expressed in males and females.

Given the high heritability of autism, genes with different expression or function in males versus females are interesting candidates for altered risk and hormone pathway genes. Some risk alleles may contribute risk only in males or only in females, and may be detectable only through subgrouping based upon sex or other stable characteristics. For example, boys in a general population are more vulnerable to

sociocommunicative deficits, and interesting interactions with IQ have been illuminated (Skuse, Morris, & Lawrence, 2008). Statistical interactions suggested that verbal IQ was protective against social communication impairments in girls, but not boys with above-average IQ. Given that some girls do develop ASD, specific subdomains in ASD may be more useful for studying hormonal vulnerabilities associated with developing a disorder than broad diagnostic criteria. As summarized in Figure 22-1, complex interactions exist between developmental and genetic factors, and sex differences may contribute risk or protective factors for ASD.

Hormones have been studied in ASD because they modulate and influence social communication or repetitive behaviors in humans or highly investigated animal models. For example, oxytocin has been shown to influence social memory and modulation of reactivity to social stress, reproductive and parenting behaviors, affiliation and attachment, and response to facial expressions (Carter, Grippo, Pournajafi-Nazarloo, Ruscio, & Porges, 2008; Domes, Heinrichs, Michel, Berger, & Herpetz, 2007). Vasopressin plays a role in vigilance and mobilization, restricted behaviors, reduced fear in the face of challenge, and aggression (Carter et al., 2008; Heinrichs & Domes, 2008). Testosterone variation has been associated with differences in pragmatic language skills, restricted interest, repetitive behaviors, quality of social relationships, and aggression (Knickmeyer et al., 2005). Fetal testosterone in ASD models has received attention because of theoretical suggestions that cognitive strengths and deficits in ASD reflect an extreme pattern observed in men rather than women (Baron-Cohen, Knickmeyer, & Belmonte, 2005; see Chapter 17). In addition, cortisol functioning in ASD has been studied because some research has suggested that some behavioral disturbances are related to basal stress levels, heightened or altered stress responses, and variation in arousal (Lam, Aman, & Arnold, 2006).

Hormones have also been studied in ASD because they are included in neurochemical investigations of living and postmortem samples within this clinical population. In a range of neurobiological disorders, including Parkinson's disease, cerebrospinal or blood chemical studies have generated theories and treatment approaches. Monoamines, neurotransmitters, and other neuropeptides—including opioids, brain-derived neurotrophic factor (BDNF), and melatonin—have been measured in ASD and are reviewed in

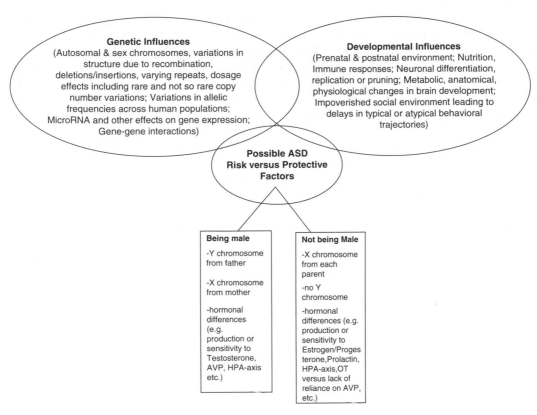

Figure 22-1 Potential Factors Contributing to Sex Differences in ASD (Modified from Jacob et al. 2009).

detail by Posey et al in this volume. Given the heritability of ASD, candidate hormone and receptor genes have also been studied, and will be discussed further in this chapter for oxytocin, vasopressin, and our overview discussions of steroid hormones. In summary, increased male vulnerability for ASD, animal models related to ASD, hormonal modulation of atypical social and repetitive behaviors, differences in neurohormonal measurements in ASD versus controls, and ASD genetic findings related to hormone systems have made this a promising area of research. In this chapter, androgens and cortisol hormone research related to ASD will be summarized and followed by a more detailed review of oxytocin and vasopressin neuropeptide hormone ASD studies.

ANDROGENS AND AUTISM SPECTRUM DISORDERS

Androgens, such as testosterone, have important sensitive periods of development, and have long-term

effects on the brain and behavior as well. Testosterone plays a key role in the development of brain structures, specifically the hypothalamus, limbic structures, and neocortex (Arnold & Gorski, 1984; Breedlove, 1994; MacLusky & Naftolin, 1981). During development, animal studies have shown that fetal testosterone influences neural structure and function by averting programmed cell death, influencing neural connectivity, and altering neurochemical profiles (Knickmeyer, et al., 2005).

Additionally, testosterone impacts behavior by biologically influencing sex differences in social behaviors and affective reactions. Given theories about the role of testosterone in autism and male cognitive patterns, there are ongoing studies investigating the relationship between prenatal fetal testosterone levels and postnatal human social behaviors (Knickmeyer et al., 2005). The longitudinal Cambridge fetal testosterone project has been following up on the relationship between prenatal amniotic fluid testosterone levels and postnatal behavior in approximately 100 children. The Children's Communication Checklist, measured at age 4, shows that high levels of testosterone during development were negatively correlated to social relationship skills, and positively correlated to restricted behaviors (Knickmeyer et al., 2005).

The theory that the presence of high levels of testosterone during early development may create a predisposition to autism spectrum disorders and produce phenotypic cognitive changes is called the "extreme male brain" theory of ASD (Baron-Cohen et al., 2005; Knickmeyer et al. 2005; Lutchmaya et al., 2004; Tordjman, Ferrari, Sulmont, Duyme, & Roubertoux, 1997; see also Chapter 17). It proposes that individuals with ASD are characterized by impairments in empathizing in conjunction with intact, or even superior, systematizing (Knickmeyer et al., 2005). When ASD patterns are compared against the distribution of typical sex differences, the ability to have Theory of Mind and affective reactions are skewed toward, or overlap with, the male pattern. Females with congenital adrenal hyperplasia (CAH) and related high fetal testosterone exposure have been reported to have higher Autism Spectrum Quotient subscale scores related to social skills and imagination than unaffected females (Knickmeyer et al., 2006), suggesting that some but not all subdomains or behaviors may be influenced by fetal testosterone or metabolite levels. Females with CAH did not have higher scores than typical males, nor were their significant differences between typical males and males with CAH.

Genetic variation in the androgen receptor was examined in autism, and no rare variants or mutations were identified in one study (Henningsson et al., 2009). Inconsistent results were also reported, with two of three polymorphisms (CAG repeat and rs6152) studied in exon 1 showing an association with autism in the case-control comparison, in contrast to the third polymorphism (GGN repeat) studied, which showed an association within their family-based study.

Testosterone is only one of the many hormones or brain factors that are associated with sex-specific differences in cognitive-behavioral patterns. Measuring specific fetal neurochemicals and the maternal-fetal exchange during sensitive periods of brain development with longitudinal outcome measures is challenging, especially in humans. The risk or protective role and complex developmental interactions of other gonadal and adrenal steroids, neuropeptides, and amine-derived neurohormones need to be further examined and integrated in studies of ASD.

CORTISOL AND AUTISM SPECTRUM DISORDERS

Cortisol is an essential hormone in the regulation of the limbic-hypothalamic-pituitary-adrenal (LHPA) axis, which in turn affects the management of reactions to stressful experiences. This system is highly regulated, involving multiple brain components, and shows a diurnal rhythm. It has been known for a long time that children with ASD have atypical responses to stress or physiological challenge tests (Hoshino et al., 1984; Maher, Harper, Macleay, & King, 1975). They show some dysregulation in diurnal rhythms, often having significant variability in morning cortisol and higher than normal evening cortisol levels (Corbett, Mendoza, Wegelin, Carmean, & Levine, 2006, 2008). Within the ASD population, there are also significant individual differences in cortisol levels, which demonstrate subgroup variability in stress response or clinical subphenotype (Corbett, Schupp, Levine, & Mendoza, 2009).

Fewer studies of ASD have examined cortisol and its relationship with other hormones and physiological variables in ASD during a challenge or behavioral paradigm. One study involved adults diagnosed with ASD who were asked to perform in a public speaking task. Interestingly, in this study, there was no significant overall difference between ASD adults versus controls during the task in cortisol, norepinephrine, epinephrine, OT, or AVP (Jansen et al., 2006). However, both basal OT levels and heart rate were elevated in the ASD group compared to healthy controls.

Interplay between cortisol and OT may influence stress responses or the effects of social interactions. The factors regulating endogenous OT levels are not well understood. However, OT may reduce LHPA-axis reactivity to social stressors, possibly by reducing uncertainty (Domes et al., 2007) and increasing trust (Baumgartner, Heinrichs, Vonlathen, Fischbacher, & Fehr, 2008). It has also been suggested that AVP may amplify the effects of cortisol in times of social stress. Figure 22-2 demonstrates the interactive and potentially opposite roles OT and AVP have in regulation of stress reactivity. These relationships are important to explore because children with ASD are at greater risk for anxiety problems and related psychiatric comorbidities (Kim, Szatmari, Bryson, Streiner, & Wilson, 2000). The brain and hypothalamic-pituitary-adrenal axis (HPA-axis) may show atypical responses to stressors, but more research is required to ascertain if there are specific

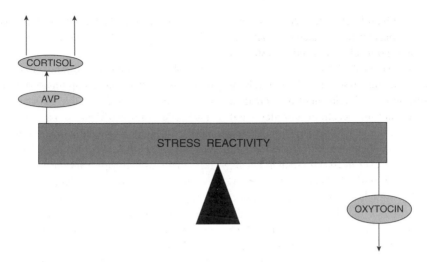

Figure 22-2 Interplay Between Cortisol AVP and OT in Times of Stress.

differences in response for ASD or diagnostic subdomains compared to non-specific, atypical responses found in other or all neurodevelopmental disorders.

NEUROPEPTIDES AND AUTISM SPECTRUM DISORDERS

Two neuropeptides, OT and AVP, have received particular attention in the context of autism (Insel, O'Brien, & Leckman, 1999; Leckman & Herman, 2002; Welch et al., 2005; Young, Nilsen, Waymire, MacGregor, & Insel, 1999, 2002), because animal research has demonstrated that both play an important role in social as well as repetitive behaviors. OT and AVP evolved from a common ancestral gene. Both consist of a six-amino-acid ring, with a three-amino-acid tail. The molecular structures of OT and AVP differ by two of nine amino acids. OT and AVP are synthesized primarily in the hypothalamus and released into the bloodstream from the posterior pituitary. OT and AVP are also released into the central nervous system, diffusing from the site of synthesis to affect receptors in brain regions some distance from the cells of origin (Landgraf & Neumann, 2004).

Neuropeptide hormones and animal models

Oxytocin and AVP hormonal systems have been manipulated in several animal models, creating behavioral deficits that may relate to autism. Studies conducted on prairie voles, mice, rhesus monkeys, and rats examined behavioral changes that occur when these two neuropeptide systems are altered (Carter, 2007). See Table 22-1 for a summary of behavioural changes that have been studied in animals with changes in the OT and AVP systems.

In animal models, OT has been shown to play a critical role in social processing, recognition, and bonding; it also influences stereotyped behaviors, such as exaggerated grooming (Carter, 2003; Van Wimersma Greidanus, Kroodsma, Pot, Stevens, & Maigret, 1990; Winslow & Insel, 2004). OT knockout mice have been shown to maintain olfaction and cognitive performance, but suffer deficits in social recognition; these deficits were recovered by intraventricular OT but not by AVP administration (Ferguson et al., 2000). Compared to wild type, OXTR knockout mice emit fewer ultrasonic vocalizations in response to social isolation, experience deficits in social discrimination, and demonstrate more aggressive behavior (Takayanagi et al., 2005). Additionally, the absence of exposure to OT during development in these mice is associated with abnormalities in the development of emotional behavior and in the management of stressful experiences (Amico et al., 2004; Mantella, Vollmer, Li, & Amico, 2003).

Similarly, AVPR1A knockout mice have been reported to exhibit social memory deficits (Bielsky & Young, 2004), and expression of the receptor gene in the lateral septum enhances social recognition (Bielsky, Hu, Ren, Terwilliger, & Young, 2005). Increases in AVP often are associated with stressful

Table 22-1 Social, Stress and Repetitive Behavior Findings in Animal Studies

Model Species	Nursery Reared (light stressor) Rhesus	OTA PN Day 1 Prairie vole	OTKO Mouse	OXTR KO Mouse	AVP adult Rat	AVP Antagonist Rat	AVPR 1A KO Mouse
Behavior							
Social	↓	↓	↓	↓	↑ (♂)	↓	↓
Repetitive	↑						
Stress/ Anxiety		↑	↑				↓ (♂) nc (♀)
AVP involvement							
AVP peptide	Nc	↓ (♂)		nc	↑ (♂)	↓	
AVPRV1a		↓ (♂) nc (♀)					↓
OT involvement							
OT peptide	↓	↑ (♀)	↓	nc			
OXTR		nc		↓			

Table 1 (modified from Carter, 2007): Unless otherwise indicated studies were done in males (♂) versus females (♀). nc = no change or a nonsignificant difference. PN = postnatal; OT = oxytocin; OXTR = OT receptor; AVP = vasopressin; AVPR1a = AVP receptor; OTA = OT antagonist; KO = knockout or gene deletion.

or defensive circumstances, especially when a strategy of mobilization or reduced fear in the face of challenge is adaptive. In humans, AVP acts to amplify the actions of corticotrophin-releasing factor (CRF) (DeBold et al., 1984). AVP also is capable of increasing certain forms of aggressive behaviors (Ebner, Wotjak, Landgraf, & Engelmann, 2005; Ferris, 2000;Winslow et al., 1993), and may be associated with repetitive and defensive behaviors (Albers, 2002). Both OT and AVP may directly or indirectly influence cellular growth, death or motility, and inflammation or differentiation (Paquin et al., 2002; Theodosis, Trailin, & Poulain, 2006). The potential to remodel the nervous system, especially in early life, offers another process through which disruptions in OT or AVP system could play a role in atypical neurodevelopment.

Vasopressin and sex differences

Sex differences in OT and AVP and their pathways have been consistently found in all vertebrate classes (De Vries & Panzica, 2006). In males, AVP is synthesized in sexually dimorphic areas, including the bed nucleus of the stria terminalis (BNST), the lateral septum, and the medial amygdala (Lonstein et al., 2005). AVP production is androgen-influenced in

these regions and dysregulation of the AVP system during development changes behavior in male, but not female, mice (Lim, Bielsky, & Young, 2005).

Androgens alter the activity of a variety of neuropeptides and other neurochemicals (Pinna, Agis-Balboa, Doueri, Guidotti, & Costa, 2004), which in turn could play a role in ASD. Included among the brain areas in which male humans have higher levels of androgen receptors than females is the paraventricular nucleus of the hypothalamus (PVN; Swaab et al., 2003), a central relay point involved in stress and coping responses, and also a major site for the synthesis of AVP and OT (Hirasawa et al., 2003). AVP synthesis is androgen-dependent in the medial amygdala and BNST, areas with dense projections into the lateral septum. Androgens also may alter the activity of OT or the response to OT. The relationship between testosterone and central AVP could contribute to increased male vulnerability for ASD.

Females have lower central levels of AVP, insensitivity to AVP, or even show directionally different effects when exposed to AVP (Bielsky et al., 2005; Thompson, Gupta, Miller, Mills, & Orr, 2004; Winslow et al., 1993). Several of the functions normally served by AVP in males rely on OT in females. The lack of dependence on AVP reflects a difference in female brains that may be neurodevelopmentally protective. In addition, females may be protected through active mechanisms that rely on OT, estrogen or other neurohormones (see Figure 22-1). AVP-synthesizing neuronal sex differences in the lateral septum may be due to genes on the sex chromosome other than those responsible for testicular differentiation and subsequent sex hormone differences in early development (Gatewood et al., 2006). Differences in expression of AVPR1a receptors occur between some species, and there may be individual differences within species for males (Fink, Excoffier, & Heckel, 2006; Young, Winslow, Nilsen, & Insel, 1997).

In human males, higher mean levels of AVP are detected in the peripheral blood (van Londen et al., 1998), and AVP-synthesizing neurons are reportedly larger in males than in females (Ishunina & Swaab, 1999; Swaab, Purba, & Hofman, 1995). Following intranasal AVP administration, healthy men 1) perceived unfamiliar same-sex faces as less friendly, and 2) responded to those faces with facial motor patterns that occur in situations of threat or conflict (Thompson et al., 2004). In contrast, women perceived unfamiliar same-sex faces as more friendly and responded with more affiliative facial motor patterns following intranasal AVP administration.

Taken together, these studies suggest that sex differences can occur both in the availability of these peptides and in the capacity to respond to these peptides. Because both OT and AVP have the potential to regulate social and emotional systems, such differences could contribute to male vulnerability to ASD. Given that human data shows that AVP has socio-communicative effects in non-clinical populations, studying AVP in relation to this ASD subdomain may be a direction for future hypothesis driven studies in ASD.

Oxytocin levels in Autism Spectrum Disorders

In human studies, OT administration has been shown to increase trust (Kosfeld, Heinrichs, Zak, Fischbacher, & Fehr, 2005) and to reduce amygdala activation (measured by fMRI) compared to placebo in healthy males (Kirsch et al., 2005). Elevated OT has been reported in obsessive-compulsive disorder (Leckman et al., 1994; Swedo et al., 1992) and in Prader-Willi syndrome (Martin et al. 1998). There is one report that children with autism have lower average levels of blood OT (Modahl et al., 1998). Although this was significant for the overall group with autism, a subgroup of children who were rated "aloof" using Wing's topology showed stronger correlations between behavior and OT. This sample of children with autism also showed a higher level of an extended form of OT (OT-X) that typically is expressed at higher levels in early development, and then decreases (Green et al., 2001). Because the OT-X form may be less active than normal OT, elevations in OT-X could be evidence of dysfunction at the level of peptide availability, or in the metabolism of this peptide. In contrast, a study of adults with ASD suggested that OT might be elevated (Jansen et al., 2006) and varies with age.

Oxytocin administration

There are recent reports that treatment with peripheral OT, given as intravenous infusions, reduced repetitive behaviors (Hollander et al., 2003) and increased comprehension of affective speech (Hollander et al., 2006) in adults with autism and Asperger's syndrome. Preliminary treatment results of intranasal OT in autism appear to be promising in improving social function in a small sample of adults (Bartz & Hollander, 2006). If recent investigations appear to show treatment benefits with OT in autism, examining the OT- and AVP-related pathways may help identify genetic risk factors in development, as well as the subset of individuals with autism who may benefit from specific neuropeptide treatment approaches.

Oxytocin and arginine vasopressin receptors

There is one known oxytocin receptor (OXTR), which is present in both neural tissue and in other parts of the body, including the thymus, heart, and reproductive organs (Gimpl & Fahrenholz, 2001). The OXTR is a G protein coupled receptor, and positively coupled to phospholipase C (Wotjak et al., 1996). In contrast, three distinct receptor subtypes have been identified for AVP (Birnbaumer, 2002; Delville, 1994; Ring, 2005). The V1a receptor (AVP1aR) is found in abundance in the brain, and is associated with behavior and cardiovascular functions. AVP, acting at the AVP1aR, plays a central role in social bonding (Winslow et al., 1993), and can facilitate positive social behaviors (Cho, DeVries, Williams, & Carter, 1999).

Embedded in the mechanisms of AVP's actions are the capacity to both upregulate and downregulate reactions to stressors (Kajantie & Phillips, 2006; Ring, 2005). The AVP1b (also known as V3) receptor is expressed in pituitary and the brain (Lolait et al., 1995), and has been associated with ACTH release in the pituitary gland and the regulation of stress responses; blocking the AVP1b receptor was associated with reduced levels of defensive behaviors (Serradeil-Le Gal et al., 2005).

The V2 receptor (V2R) is most abundant in the kidneys, and plays a critical role in water retention, thus accounting for the fact that AVP is also known as the antidiuretic hormone. In general, V2Rs are less abundant in the brain, and less is known regarding the role of V2Rs in the brain or behavior functions (Ring, 2005).

AVP has been associated with social behaviors (Carter et al., 2008; Heinrichs & Domes, 2008), obsessive-compulsive behaviors (Altemus et al., 1992; McDougle, Barr, Goodman, & Price, 1999), and stress responses (Lightman, 2008). The androgen-dependence of AVP, especially in the central axis that includes the amygdala, BNST, and lateral septum, and the possible increased sensitivity of males to AVP, may also be relevant to the etiology of ASD. In the context of ASD, dysfunction in either the synthesis of AVP or the function of the receptors for AVP might contribute to male vulnerability for some neurodevelopmental disorders.

Anatomical distribution of oxytocin and arginine vasopressin receptors

Receptors for both OT and AVP are localized in areas of the nervous system, and especially in brain stem regions that play a role in reproductive, social, and adaptive behaviors (Gimpl & Fahrenholz, 2001; Insel & Young, 2001; Witt, 1997; Young et al., 1999), and in the regulation of the HPA axis and the autonomic nervous system (Huber, Veinante, & Stoop, 2005; Neumann, 2001; Porges, 2001; Sawchenko & Swanson, 1982). Research in animal models suggests that OXTRs are expressed at higher levels in early development (Shapiro & Insel, 1989; Tribollet, Charpak, Schmidt, Dubois-Dauphin, & Dreifuss, 1989), suggesting that the effects of OT are of particular developmental significance. It was recently reported that OT an excitatory-to-inhibitory switch in GABA (gamma-aminobutyric acid) actions in immature neurons and serves a neuroprotective function in fetal rats (Tyzio et al. 2006). In addition, variation in receptors for AVP or OT, especially during early life, may play a role in early brain development as described below.

Molecular variation of arginine vasopressin receptors and animal models

The AVPV1aR exhibits exceptional variance, both across species and within individuals (Phelps & Young, 2003), due at least in part to the presence of variable microsatellites in the promoter region (Hammock & Young, 2005). The pattern of AVPR1a receptor expression in the brain appears to be influenced by variation in the length of a microsatellite in the promoter region of the gene (Hammock & Young, 2005). Male prairie voles with a longer (compared to shorter) version of these microsatellites had higher levels of the AVP1aR in the lateral septum and olfactory bulb, and were more likely to form a partner preference. In addition, increasing the availability of the AVP1aR, added by viral vectors, can facilitate social behaviors (Lim et al., 2004).

Neuropeptide hormones and autism genetics

Oxytocin and AVP pathway genes are of particular interest in autism spectrum disorders, because sex differences in expression of these genes have been reported in animals. Animal studies have detailed the role of OT and AVP in both affiliative behaviors and pair bonding (Insel et al., 1999). These animal studies inspired work that led to the discovery that genetic polymorphisms in the promoter region of the central AVP receptor (AVPR1A) relate not only to social behavior, but also to where the receptors are localized within the brain (Lim & Young, 2006).

The human AVPR1A gene is located at chromosome 12q14-15, and encodes a 418-amino-acid protein with seven transmembrane domains. A number of microsatellite loci with varying lengths of simple, repeat-sequence polymorphisms have been characterized in the human AVPR1A gene (Thibonnier, Coles, Thibonnier, & Shoham, 2002). There is an overall association with one of these microsatellites (RS3) in the 5' flanking region in children and adolescents with autism (Kim et al., 2002). In an independent sample, another microsatellite (RS1) was found to be associated with autism, and more strongly associated

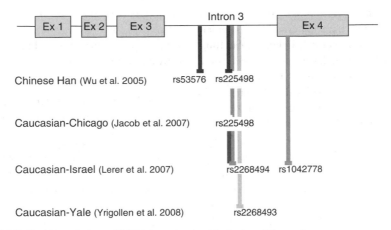

Figure 22-3 OXTR (3p25) and Some SNPS Associated with Autism Diagnosis.

in a subgroup of children who had less severe language impairment (Wassink et al., 2004). A third independent study showed association with autism and another microsatellite (AVR) as well as a highly significant haplotype association, including all three microsatellites (AVR-RS1-RS3), and the overall ADOS score (Yirmiya et al., 2006). These significant associations of microsatellites in AVPR1A and ASD are summarized in Figure 22-4.

Genetic associations of the human OT receptor (*OXTR*) with autism have recently been found. The *OXTR* gene encodes a 389-amino-acid protein and is a seven-transmembrane-domain, G-protein-coupled receptor (Gimpl & Fahrenholz, 2001; Wotjak et al., 1996). *OXTR* is located at chromosome 3p24-26 and has four exons, the latter two encoding the sequence for the receptor (Gimpl & Fahrenholz, 2001).

Combined linkage analysis of two independent samples of 314 Finnish families demonstrated linkage in the 3p24-25 region containing the *OXTR* gene (Ylisaukko-oja et al., 2006). Two SNPs were associated with autism in the Chinese Han population (Wu et al., 2005). Our study (Jacob et al., 2007) genotyped two OXTR SNPs, and observed a significant association with a single SNP with autism in a Caucasian sample. In an Israeli population, a study of 18 tagged SNPs in the OXTR genes was conducted, revealing an association between single SNPs and haplotype in autism, and with IQ and total Vineland scores (Lerer et al., 2008). Another independent autism study examined several genes related to affiliative behaviors and reported a significant SNP for overall autism in a similar region of the OXTR (Yrigollen et al., 2008). In addition, they found a SNP within the oxytocin peptide gene on chromosome 20p13 that was associated with stereotyped behaviors, but not with overall autism. Moreover, a study looking for de novo copy number mutations reported a child with

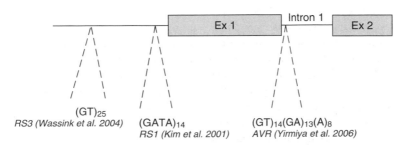

Figure 22-4 AVPR1A (12q14–15) and Microsatellites Associated with Autism Diagnosis.

the diagnosis of Asperger's disorder who had a deletion, involving the 20p13 region, of approximately 27 genes, including the adjacent oxytocin and vasopressin peptide genes (Sebat et al., 2007).

Interactions between oxytocin and arginine vasopressin systems

It is important to examine both OT and AVP together because of their evolutionary history, overlapping functions, and ability to influence each other's pathways or receptors throughout development (Hirasawa et al., 2003; Landgraf & Neumann, 2004; Ragnauth et al., 2004). The fact that OT and AVP peptides differ by only two amino acids may help to explain the interactions between these molecules. Peptide manipulations during development can alter the sensitivity of the adult nervous system toward subsequent hormonal or stress experiences (Csaba, 1987). In rats, neonatal stress can influence hippocampal OXTRs (Noonan et al., 1994), and early exposure to AVP inhibits OXTRs in the paraventricular nucleus (Vaccari et al., 1996). Although more data is needed concerning interactions at an in vivo level, AVP was four times more potent than OT in human uterine tissue, and AVP had effects on both OXTR and AVPR1a, whereas OT's effects were only seen on OXTR (Bossmar et al., 1995). Recently, plasma levels of both OT and AVP hormones examined in social vervets were found to be highly heritable and correlated with each other (Bailey et al., 2006). Experimental studies in prairie voles of immunoreactive central OT and AVP, as well as peripheral measures of these peptides, suggest positive correlations between OT and AVP (Carter, unpublished data), so studying both peptides in the same samples yields valuable information.

SUMMARY AND DIRECTION FOR FUTURE RESEARCH

Autism spectrum disorder is a phenotypically heterogeneous and complex genetic syndrome. It has been suggested that the increased risk of developing ASD symptoms may be related to early developmental brain differences occurring in varying hormonal milieus. As a result, androgen, cortisol, oxytocin, and vasopressin have been studied in both animals and human subjects. In addition, genetic changes affecting hormones, genes, and receptors result in altered social and repetitive behaviors in animal models.

Descriptions of hormonally influenced behaviors overlap with the range of behavioral deficits observed in ASD. Sex-related steroid hormones, particularly fetal testosterone, have been studied in ASD because of their potential contributions to male cognitive patterns and males' increased risk for developing ASD. Cortisol and the HPA stress-response system, including corticotropin-releasing hormone (CRH), may be perturbed in a prominent subset of those with ASD, and contribute to behavioral problems and challenges with learning and development. OT and AVP have been particularly emphasized in ASD research because they are involved in social and repetitive behaviors, as illustrated by studies with both animals and typically developing humans. There have been at least eight human genetic studies that have reported either linkage or association of ASD with polymorphisms in the OXTR and AVPR1A genes. Additionally, both OT and AVP also interact with other hormones, such as cortisol and testosterone, in development, or to regulate stress response and anxiety. These hormone systems are particularly interesting given their influence in social processing in the amygdala, and its reported abnormalities in structure or function in ASD (Skuse et al., 2003).

Data on clinical ASD phenotypes are derived from diagnostic measures that were designed to evaluate whether specific behaviors exceeded a threshold to fulfill a criterion for consensus diagnoses. Therefore, the challenges in understanding the role of hormones in development and in the severity of ASD symptoms rest on broadening our understanding of the range of variable physiological and behavioral expression within ASD. In addition, there is limited data on the normal range of behaviors that reflect hormonal influences on the typically developing brain during early childhood. Autism may be an umbrella for a collection of neurodevelopmental conditions; the way they are currently grouped together results in challenges for finding specific etiologies. Animal research demonstrates that the same pathophysiological mechanisms may present differently, and are influenced by age, sex, learning abilities, environment, and even subtle differences in genetic backgrounds.

Additional research which takes into account the broad range of individual phenotypes in ASD is needed. As previously described, multiple genetic studies have reported associations between autism and the brain receptors of AVP, OT, and more recently, the androgen receptor. Several steps are needed to connect the clinical presentation of autism spectrum disorders with physiological and genetic differences of OT, AVP, and other hormone pathways in humans. We need to establish whether observed associations may correspond to a particular symptom domain or subgroup of patients. It will be important to understand whether physiological differences of hormones or gene expression in individuals with ASDs are associated with specific behaviors or symptoms, or create different risks for males versus females. For example, do children with more frequent repetitive behaviors have higher average AVP levels? Do boys with a particular *AVPR1a* receptor polymorphism have increased repetitive behaviors because of receptor distribution or its interaction with testosterone, while girls do not? Do young children with ASD and low levels of non-verbal social communication have high OT, but do the levels of this subgroup drop when they are adults?

Hormones appear to have both trait and state influences, so the time course of peripheral or central levels may be an important variable to study. Large samples are required to investigate a spectrum disorder with notable individual and subgroup differences. In order to start answering these complex questions, future ASD work needs to: 1) test hypotheses informed by animal research and evolutionary contexts; 2) examine genetic, clinical, behavioral, physiological, and neurochemical measures simultaneously; and 3) investigate these relationships within a developmental framework.

References

Albers H. E., H. K., Meisel RL. (2002). *Hormonal basis of social conflict and communication* (Vol. vol 1). San Deigo: Academic Press.

Alstein, M., Whitnall, M. H., House, S., Key, S., & Gainer, H. (1988). An immunochemical analysis of oxytocin and vasopressin prohormone processing in vivo, *Peptides* (Vol. 9, pp. 87–105.).

Altemus, M., Pigott, T., Kalogeras, K. T., Demitrack, M., Dubbert, B., Murphy, D. L., et al. (1992). Abnormalities in the regulation of vasopressin and corticotropin releasing factor secretion in obsessive-compulsive disorder. *Arch Gen Psychiatry*, 49(1), 9–20.

Albers HE, H. K., Meisel RL. (2002). *Hormonal basis of social conflict and communication* (Vol. 1). San Deigo: Academic Press.

Alstein, M., Whitnall, M. H., House, S., Key, S., & Gainer, H. (1988). An immunochemical analysis of oxytocin and vasopressin prohormone processing in vivo, *Peptides* (Vol. 9, pp. 87–105.).

Altemus, M., Pigott, T., Kalogeras, K. T., Demitrack, M., Dubbert, B., Murphy, D. L., et al. (1992). Abnormalities in the regulation of vasopressin and corticotropin releasing factor secretion in obsessive-compulsive disorder. *Arch Gen Psychiatry*, 49(1), 9–20.

Amico, J. A., Mantella, R. C., Vollmer, R. R., & Li, X. (2004). Anxiety and stress responses in female oxytocin deficient mice. *J Neuroendocrinol*, 16(4), 319–324.

APA. (2000). Diagnostic and statistical manual of mental disorders : DSM-IV-TR.

Arnold, A. P., & Gorski, R. A. (1984). Gonadal steroid induction of structural sex differences in the central nervous system. *Annu Rev Neurosci*, 7, 413–442.

Bailey, A., Le Couteur, A., Gottesman, I., Bolton, P., Simonoff, E., Yuzda, E., et al. (1995). Autism as a strongly genetic disorder: Evidence from a british twin study. *Psychological Medicine*, 25(1), 63–78.

Bailey, J., Bales, K., Jorgensen, M., & Fairbanks, L. (2006). *Plasma oxytocin and vasopressin are highly inheritable in a pedigree of vervet monkeys*. Paper presented at the XIV World Congress on Psychiatric Genetics, Congress Centre Fiera Internazionate della Sardegna, Cagliari, Italy.

Bales, K. L., Plotsky, P. M., Young, L. J., Lim, M. M., Grotte, N., Ferrer, E., et al. (2006). Neonatal oxytocin manipulations have long-lasting, sexually dimorphic effects on vasopressin receptors. *Neuroscience*.

Baron-Cohen, S., & Belmonte, M. K. (2005). Autism: A window onto the development of the social and the analytic brain. *Annu Rev Neurosci*, 28, 109–126.

Baron-Cohen, S., Knickmeyer, R. C., & Belmonte, M. K. (2005). Sex differences in the brain: Implications for explaining autism. *Science*, 310(5749), 819–823.

Bartz, J. A., & Hollander, E. (2006). The neuroscience of affiliation: Forging links between basic and clinical research on neuropeptides and social behavior. *Horm Behav*, 50(4), 518–528. Epub 2006 Aug 2001.

Baumgartner, T., Heinrichs, M., Vonlanthen, A., Fischbacher, U., & Fehr, E. (2008). Oxytocin shapes the neural circuitry of trust and trust adaptation in humans. *Neuron*, 58(4), 639–650.

Bielsky, I. F., Hu, S. B., Ren, X., Terwilliger, E. F., & Young, L. J. (2005a). The V1a vasopressin receptor is necessary and sufficient for normal social recognition: A gene replacement study. *Neuron*, 47(4), 503–513.

Bielsky, I. F., Hu, S. B., & Young, L. J. (2005b). Sexual dimorphism in the vasopressin system: Lack of an altered behavioral phenotype in female V1a receptor knockout mice. *Behav Brain Res, 164*(1), 132–136.

Bielsky, I. F., & Young, L. J. (2004). Oxytocin, vasopressin, and social recognition in mammals. *Peptides, 25*(9), 1565–1574.

Birnbaumer, M. (2002a). *Vasopressin receptor* (Vol. vol III). San Deigo: Academic Press.

Birnbaumer, M. (2002b). *Vasopressin receptors* (Vol. vol III). San Deigo: Academic Press.

Bolton, P., Macdonald, H., Pickles, A., Rios, P., Goode, S., Crowson, M., et al. (1994). A case-control family history study of autism. *J Child Psychol Psychiatry, 35*(5), 877–900.

Born, J., Lange, T., Kern, W., McGregor, G. P., Bickel, U., & Fehm, H. L. (2002). Sniffing neuropeptides: A transnasal approach to the human brain. *Nat Neurosci, 5*(6), 514–516.

Bossmar, T., Akerlund, M., Szamatowicz, J., Laudanski, T., Fantoni, G., & Maggi, M. (1995). Receptor-mediated uterine effects of vasopressin and oxytocin in nonpregnant women. *Br J Obstet Gynaecol, 102*(11), 907–912.

Breedlove, S. M. (1994). Sexual differentiation of the human nervous system. *Annu Rev Psychol, 45,* 389–418.

Brune, C. W., Kim, S.-J., Salt, J., Leventhal, B. L., Lord, C., & Cook, E. H., Jr. 5-HTTLPR genotype-specific phenotype in children and adolescents with autism. *Am J Psychiatry.*

Campbell, C. D., Ogburn, E. L., Lunetta, K. L., Lyon, H. N., Freedman, M. L., Groop, L. C., et al. (2005). Demonstrating stratification in a European American population. *Nat Genet, 37*(8), 868–872.

Carter, C. S. Sex differences in oxytocin and vasopressing: Implications for autism spectrum disorders? *Behavioral Brain Research.*

Carter, C. S. (1998). Neuroendocrine perspectives on social attachment and love. *Psychoneuroendocrinology, 23*(8), 779–818.

Carter, C. S. (2003). Developmental consequences of oxytocin. *Physiol Behav, 79*(3), 383–397.

Carter, C. S. (2007). Sex differences in oxytocin and vasopressin: Implications for autism spectrum disorders? *Behav Brain Res, 176*(1), 170–186.

Carter, C. S., Grippo, A. J., Pournajafi-Nazarloo, H., Ruscio, M. G., & Porges, S. W. (2008). Oxytocin, vasopressin and sociality. *Prog Brain Res, 170,* 331–336.

Chakrabarti, S., & Fombonne, E. (2001). Pervasive developmental disorders in preschool children. *Journal of the American Medical Association, 285*(24), 3093–3099.

Chakrabarti, S., & Fombonne, E. (2005). Pervasive developmental disorders in preschool children: Confirmation of high prevalence. *Am J Psychiatry, 162*(6), 1133–1141.

Cho, M. M., DeVries, A. C., Williams, J. R., & Carter, C. S. (1999). The effects of oxytocin and vasopressin on partner preferences in male and female prairie voles

(microtus ochrogaster). *Behav Neurosci, 113*(5), 1071–1079.

Choleris, E., Kavaliers, M., & Pfaff, D. W. (2004). Functional genomics of social recognition. *J Neuroendocrinol, 16*(4), 383–389.

Cook, E. H., Jr., & Scherer, S. W. (2008). Copy-number variations associated with neuropsychiatric conditions. *Nature, 455*(7215), 919–923.

Corbett, B. A., Mendoza, S., Abdullah, M., Wegelin, J. A., & Levine, S. (2006). Cortisol circadian rhythms and response to stress in children with autism. *Psychoneuroendocrinology, 31*(1), 59–68.

Corbett, B. A., Mendoza, S., Wegelin, J. A., Carmean, V., & Levine, S. (2008). Variable cortisol circadian rhythms in children with autism and anticipatory stress. *J Psychiatry Neurosci, 33*(3), 227–234.

Corbett, B. A., Schupp, C. W., Levine, S., & Mendoza, S. (2009). Comparing cortisol, stress, and sensory sensitivity in children with autism. *Autism Res, 2*(1), 39–49.

Csaba, G. (1987). Receptor ontogeny and hormonal imprinting. *Experientia Suppl, 53,* 79–102.

De Vries, G. J., & Panzica, G. C. (2006). Sexual differentiation of central vasopressin and vasotocin systems in vertebrates: Different mechanisms, similar endpoints. *Neuroscience, 138*(3), 947–955. Epub 2005 Nov 2028.

DeBold, C. R., Sheldon, W. R., DeCherney, G. S., Jackson, R. V., Alexander, A. N., Vale, W., et al. (1984). Arginine vasopressin potentiates adrenocorticotropin release induced by ovine corticotropin-releasing factor. *J Clin Invest, 73*(2), 533–538.

Delville Y, K. E., Ferris CF. (1994). *Sexual differences in magnocellular vasopressinergic system in golden hamsters.*

Dickel, D. E., Veenstra-VanderWeele, J., Cox, N. J., Wu, X., Fischer, D. J., Van Etten-Lee, M., et al. (2006). Association testing of the positional and functional candidate gene slc1a1/eaac1 in early-onset obsessive-compulsive disorder. *Arch Gen Psychiatry, 63*(7), 778–785.

DiLavore, P., Lord, C., & Rutter, M. (1995). Pre-linguistic autism diagnostic observation schedule (pl-ados). *Journal of Autism and Developmental Disorders, 25,* 355–379.

Domes, G., Heinrichs, M., Michel, A., Berger, C., & Herpertz, S. C. (2007). Oxytocin improves "Mind-reading" In humans. *Biol Psychiatry, 61*(6), 731–733.

Dong, W., Seidel, B., Marcinkiewicz, M., Chretien, M., Seidah, N. G., & Day, R. (1997). Cellular localization of the prohormone convertases in the hypothalamic paraventricular and supraoptic nuclei: Selective regulation of pc1 in corticotrophin-releasing hormone parvocellular neurons mediated by glucocorticoids. *J Neurosci, 17*(2), 563–575.

Ebner, K., Wotjak, C. T., Landgraf, R., & Engelmann, M. (2005). Neuroendocrine and behavioral response to social confrontation: Residents versus intruders, active versus passive coping styles. *Horm Behav*, 47(1), 14–21.

Ferguson, J. N., Young, L. J., Hearn, E. F., Matzuk, M. M., Insel, T. R., & Winslow, J. T. (2000). Social amnesia in mice lacking the oxytocin gene. *Nat Genet*, 25(3), 284–288.

Ferris, C. F. (2000). Adolescent stress and neural plasticity in hamsters: A vasopressin-serotonin model of inappropriate aggressive behaviour. *Exp Physiol*, 85 *Spec No*, 85S–90S.

Fink, S., Excoffier, L., & Heckel, G. (2006). Mammalian monogamy is not controlled by a single gene. *Proc Natl Acad Sci U S A*, 103(29), 10956–10960. Epub 12006 Jul 10910.

Folstein, S. E., & Rosen-Sheidley, B. (2001). Genetics of autism: Complex aetiology for a heterogeneous disorder. *Nat Rev Genet*, 2(12), 943–955.

Fombonne, E. (2003). The prevalence of autism. *JAMA*, 289(1), 87–89.

Gatewood, J. D., Wills, A., Shetty, S., Xu, J., Arnold, A. P., Burgoyne, P. S., et al. (2006). Sex chromosome complement and gonadal sex influence aggressive and parental behaviors in mice. *J Neurosci*, 26(8), 2335–2342.

Geier, M. R., & Geier, D. A. (2005). The potential importance of steroids in the treatment of autistic spectrum disorders and other disorders involving mercury toxicity. *Med Hypotheses*, 64(5), 946–954.

Gimpl, G., & Fahrenholz, F. (2001). The oxytocin receptor system: Structure, function, and regulation. *Physiol Rev*, 81(2), 629–683.

Green, L., Fein, D., Modahl, C., Feinstein, C., Waterhouse, L., & Morris, M. (2001). Oxytocin and autistic disorder: Alterations in peptide forms. *Biol Psychiatry*, 50(8), 609–613.

Gunnar, M. R., Bruce, J., & Hickman, S. E. (2001). Salivary cortisol response to stress in children. *Advances in Psychosomatic Medicine*, 22, 52–60.

Hammock, E. A., & Young, L. J. (2005). Microsatellite instability generates diversity in brain and sociobehavioral traits. *Science*, 308(5728), 1630–1634.

Hardiman, A., Friedman, T. C., Grunwald, W. C., Jr., Furuta, M., Zhu, Z., Steiner, D. F., et al. (2005). Endocrinomic profile of neurointermediate lobe pituitary prohormone processing in PC1/3- AND PC2-null mice using SELDI-TOF mass spectrometry. *J Mol Endocrinol*, 34(3), 739–751.

Hashimoto, K., Azuma, C., Koyama, M., Nobunaga, T., Kimura, T., Shimoya, K., et al. (1997). Biparental alleles of HLA-G are co-dominantly expressed in the placenta. *Jpn J Hum Genet*, 42(1), 181–186.

Hedeker, D., & Gibbons, R. D. (2006). *Longitudinal data analysis*. New Jersey: John Wiley & Sons, Inc.

Heinrichs, M., & Domes, G. (2008). Neuropeptides and social behaviour: Effects of oxytocin and vasopressin in humans. *Prog Brain Res*, 170, 337–350.

Henningsson, S., Jonsson, L., Ljunggren, E., Westberg, L., Gillberg, C., Rastam, M., et al. (2009). Possible association between the androgen receptor gene and autism spectrum disorder. *Psychoneuroendocrinology*, 34(5), 752–761.

Hirasawa, M., Mouginot, D., Kozoriz, M. G., Kombian, S. B., & Pittman, Q. J. (2003). Vasopressin differentially modulates non-nmda receptors in vasopressin and oxytocin neurons in the supraoptic nucleus. *J Neurosci*, 23(10), 4270–4277.

Hollander, E., Bartz, J., Chaplin, W., Phillips, A., Sumner, J., Soorya, L., et al. (2006). Oxytocin increases retention of social cognition in autism.

Hollander, E., Chaplin, W., Phillips, A., Sumner, J., Soorya, L., Anagnostou, E., et al. (2005). *Oxytocin increases social cognition in autism*. Paper presented at the American College of Neuropsychiatry 44th Annual Meeting.

Hollander, E., Novotny, S., Hanratty, M., Yaffe, R., DeCaria, C. M., Aronowitz, B. R., et al. (2003). Oxytocin infusion reduces repetitive behaviors in adults with autistic and Asperger's disorders. *Neuropsychopharmacology*, 28(1), 193–198.

Hoshino, Y., Ohno, Y., Murata, S., Yokoyama, F., Kaneko, M., & Kumashiro, H. (1984). Dexamethasone suppression test in autistic children. *Folia Psychiatr Neurol Jpn*, 38(4), 445–449.

Huber, D., Veinante, P., & Stoop, R. (2005). Vasopressin and oxytocin excite distinct neuronal populations in the central amygdala. *Science*, 308(5719), 245–248.

Insel, T. R. (2006). From species differences to individual differences. *Mol Psychiatry*, 11(5), 424.

Insel, T. R., O'Brien, D. J., & Leckman, J. F. (1999). Oxytocin, vasopressin, and autism: Is there a connection? *Biol Psychiatry*, 45(2), 145–157.

Insel, T. R., & Young, L. J. (2001). The neurobiology of attachment. *Nat Rev Neurosci*, 2(2), 129–136.

Ishunina, T. A., & Swaab, D. F. (1999). Vasopressin and oxytocin neurons of the human supraoptic and paraventricular nucleus: Size changes in relation to age and sex. *J Clin Endocrinol Metab*, 84(12), 4637–4644.

Jacob, S., Brune, C., Carter, S., Leventhal, B., Lord, C., & Cook, E. (2007). Association with oxytocin receptor gene (oxtr) in children and adolescents with autism. Neurosci Lett. Apr 24;417(1):6–9.

Jacob S, Landeros-Weisenberger A, Leckman JF. Autism spectrum and obsessive-compulsive disorders: OC behaviors, phenotypes and genetics. Autism Res. 2009 Dec;2(6):293–311.

Jansen, L. M., Gispen-de Wied, C. C., Wiegant, V. M., Westenberg, H. G., Lahuis, B. E., & van Engeland, H. (2006). Autonomic and neuroendocrine responses to a psychosocial stressor in adults with autistic spectrum disorder. *J Autism Dev Disord*, 36(7), 891–899.

Jensen, J. B., Realmuto, G. M., & Garfinkel, B. D. (1985). The dexamethasone suppression test in infantile autism. *J Am Acad Child Psychiatry*, 24(3), 263–265.

Jorde, L., Hasstedt, S., Ritvo, E., Mason-Brothers, A., Freeman, B., Pingree, C., et al. (1991). Complex segregation analysis of autism. *American Journal of Human Genetics*, 49, 932–938.

Kajantie, E., & Phillips, D. I. (2006). The effects of sex and hormonal status on the physiological response to acute psychosocial stress. *Psychoneuroendocrinology, 31*(2), 151–178.

Keenan, K., & Jacob, S. Regulatory processes in the development of child behavior problems: Biological, behavioral, and social-ecological processes context matters: Exploring definitions of a poorly modulated stress response. In S. L. Olson & A. J. Sameroff (Eds.). New York, NY: Cambridge University Press.

Kim, J. A., Szatmari, P., Bryson, S. E., Streiner, D. L., & Wilson, F. J. (2000). The prevalence of anxiety and mood problems among children with autism and asperger syndrome. *Autism, 4*(2), 117–132.

Kim, S.-J., Cox, N., Courchesne, R., Lord, C., Corsello, C., Akshoomoff, N., et al. (2002a). Transmission disequilibrium mapping in the serotonin transporter gene (slc6a4) region in autistic disorder. *Molecular Psychiatry, 7*(3), 278–288.

Kim, S. J., Cox, N., Courchesne, R., Lord, C., Corsello, C., Akshoomoff, N., et al. (2002b). Transmission disequilibrium mapping at the serotonin transporter gene (SLC6A4) region in autistic disorder. *Mol Psychiatry, 7*(3), 278–288.

Kim, S. J., Young, L. J., Gonen, D., Veenstra-VanderWeele, J., Courchesne, R., Courchesne, E., et al. (2002c). Transmission disequilibrium testing of arginine vasopressin receptor 1a (APVR1A) polymorphisms in autism. *Mol Psychiatry, 7*(5), 503–507.

Kimura, T., Saji, F., Nishimori, K., Ogita, K., Nakamura, H., Koyama, M., et al. (2003). Molecular regulation of the oxytocin receptor in peripheral organs. *J Mol Endocrinol, 30*(2), 109–115.

Kirsch, P., Esslinger, C., Chen, Q., Mier, D., Lis, S., Siddhanti, S., et al. (2005). Oxytocin modulates neural circuitry for social cognition and fear in humans. *J Neurosci, 25*(49), 11489–11493.

Knickmeyer, R., Baron-Cohen, S., Fane, B. A., Wheelwright, S., Mathews, G. A., Conway, G. S., et al. (2006). Androgens and autistic traits: A study of individuals with congenital adrenal hyperplasia. *Horm Behav, 50*(1), 148–153.

Knickmeyer, R., Baron-Cohen, S., Raggatt, P., & Taylor, K. (2005). Foetal testosterone, social relationships, and restricted interests in children. *J Child Psychol Psychiatry, 46*(2), 198–210.

Kosfeld, M., Heinrichs, M., Zak, P. J., Fischbacher, U., & Fehr, E. (2005). Oxytocin increases trust in humans. *Nature, 435*(7042), 673–676.

Kozorovitskiy, Y., Hughes, M., Lee, K., & Gould, E. (2006). Fatherhood affects dendritic spines and vasopressin v1a receptors in the primate prefrontal cortex. *Nat Neurosci, 9*(9), 1094–1095. Epub 2006 Aug 1020.

Kramer, K. M., Cushing, B. S., & Carter, C. S. (2003). Developmental effects of oxytocin on stress response: Single versus repeated exposure. *Physiol Behav, 79*(4-5), 775–782.

Kramer, K. M., Cushing, B. S., Carter, C. S., Wu, J., & Ottinger, M. A. (2004). Sex and species differences in plasma oxytocin using an enzyme immunoassay. 82, 1194–1200 JF -. Canadian Journal of Zoology.

Kubota, Y., Kimura, T., Hashimoto, K., Tokugawa, Y., Nobunaga, K., Azuma, C., et al. (1996). Structure and expression of the mouse oxytocin receptor gene. *Mol Cell Endocrinol, 124*(1-2), 25–32.

Lam, K. S., Aman, M. G., & Arnold, L. E. (2006). Neurochemical correlates of autistic disorder: A review of the literature. *Res Dev Disabil, 27*(3), 254–289.

Landgraf, R., & Neumann, I. D. (2004). Vasopressin and oxytocin release within the brain: A dynamic concept of multiple and variable modes of neuropeptide communication. *Front Neuroendocrinol, 25*(3-4), 150–176.

Leckman, J. F., Goodman, W. K., North, W. G., Chappell, P. B., Price, L. H., Pauls, D. L., et al. (1994a). Elevated cerebrospinal fluid levels of oxytocin in obsessive-compulsive disorder. Comparison with Tourette's syndrome and healthy controls. *Arch Gen Psychiatry, 51*(10), 782–792.

Leckman, J. F., Goodman, W. K., North, W. G., Chappell, P. B., Price, L. H., Pauls, D. L., et al. (1994b). Elevated cerebrospinal fluid levels of oxytocin in obsessive-compulsive disorder. Comparison with tourette's syndrome and healthy controls. *Arch Gen Psychiatry, 51*(10), 782–792.

Leckman, J. F., & Herman, A. E. (2002). Maternal behavior and developmental psychopathology. *Biol Psychiatry, 51*(1), 27–43.

Lerer, E., Levi, S., Salomon, S., Darvasi, A., Yirmiya, N., & Ebstein, R. P. (2008). Association between the oxytocin receptor (OXTR) gene and autism: Relationship to vineland adaptive behavior scales and cognition. *Mol Psychiatry, 13*(10), 980–988.

Lightman, S. L. (2008). The neuroendocrinology of stress: A never ending story. *J Neuroendocrinol, 20*(6), 880–884.

Lim, M. M., Bielsky, I. F., & Young, L. J. (2005). Neuropeptides and the social brain: Potential rodent models of autism. *Int J Dev Neurosci, 23*(2-3), 235–243.

Lim, M. M., Wang, Z., Olazabal, D. E., Ren, X., Terwilliger, E. F., & Young, L. J. (2004). Enhanced partner preference in a promiscuous species by manipulating the expression of a single gene. *Nature, 429*(6993), 754–757.

Lim, M. M., & Young, L. J. (2006). Neuropeptidergic regulation of affiliative behavior and social bonding in animals. *Horm Behav, 50*(4), 506–517. Epub 2006 Aug 2004.

Lolait, S. J., O'Carroll, A. M., Mahan, L. C., Felder, C. C., Button, D. C., Young, W. S., 3rd, et al. (1995). Extrapituitary expression of the rat v1b vasopressin receptor gene. *Proc Natl Acad Sci U S A, 92*(15), 6783–6787.

Lonstein, J. S., Rood, B. D., & De Vries, G. J. (2005). Unexpected effects of perinatal gonadal hormone manipulations on sexual differentiation of the extra-hypothalamic arginine-vasopressin system in prairie voles. *Endocrinology*, 146(3), 1559–1567. Epub 2004 Dec 1559.

Lord, C., Risi, S., Lambrecht, L., Cook, E. H., Jr., Leventhal, B. L., DiLavore, P. C., et al. (2000). The autism diagnostic observation schedule-generic: A standard measure of social and communication deficits associated with the spectrum of autism. *Journal of Autism and Developmental Disorders*, 30(3), 205–223.

Lord, C., Rutter, M., & Le Couteur, A. (1994). Autism diagnostic interview - revised: A revised version of a diagnostic interview for caregivers of individuals with possible pervasive developmental disorders. *Journal of Autism and Developmental Disorders*, 24(5), 659–685.

Lutchmaya, S., Baron-Cohen, S., Raggatt, P., Knickmeyer, R., & Manning, J. T. (2004). 2nd to 4th digit ratios, fetal testosterone and estradiol. *Early Hum Dev*, 77(1-2), 23–28.

MacLusky, N. J., & Naftolin, F. (1981). Sexual differentiation of the central nervous system. *Science*, 211(4488), 1294–1302.

Maher, K. R., Harper, J. F., Macleay, A., & King, M. G. (1975). Peculiarities in the endocrine response to insulin stress in early infantile autism. *J Nerv Ment Dis*, 161(3), 180–184.

Mantella, R. C., Vollmer, R. R., Li, X., & Amico, J. A. (2003). Female oxytocin-deficient mice display enhanced anxiety-related behavior. *Endocrinology*, 144(6), 2291–2296.

Martin, A., State, M., Anderson, G. M., Kaye, W. M., Hanchett, J. M., McConaha, C. W., et al. (1998a). Cerebrospinal fluid levels of oxytocin in Prader-Willi syndrome: A preliminary report. *Biol Psychiatry*, 44(12), 1349–1352.

Martin, A., State, M., Koenig, K., Schultz, R., Dykens, E. M., Cassidy, S. B., et al. (1998b). Prader-Willi syndrome. *Am J Psychiatry*, 155(9), 1265–1273.

McDougle, C. J., Barr, L. C., Goodman, W. K., & Price, L. H. (1999). Possible role of neuropeptides in obsessive compulsive disorder. *Psychoneuroendocrinology*, 24(1), 1–24.

Modahl, C., Green, L., Fein, D., Morris, M., Waterhouse, L., Feinstein, C., et al. (1998). Plasma oxytocin levels in autistic children. *Biological Psychiatry*, 43(4), 270–277.

Muhle, R., Trentacoste, S. V., & Rapin, I. (2004). The genetics of autism. *Pediatrics*, 113(5), e472–486.

Mulder, E. J., Anderson, G. M., Kema, I. P., Brugman, A. M., Ketelaars, C. E., de Bildt, A., et al. (2005). Serotonin transporter intron 2 polymorphism associated with rigid-compulsive behaviors in Dutch individuals with pervasive developmental disorder. *Am J Med Genet B Neuropsychiatr Genet*.

Neumann, I. D. (2001). Alterations in behavioral and neuroendocrine stress coping strategies in pregnant, parturient and lactating rats. *Prog Brain Res*, 133, 143–152.

Noonan, L. R., Caldwell, J. D., Li, L., Walker, C. H., Pedersen, C. A., & Mason, G. A. (1994). Neonatal stress transiently alters the development of hippocampal oxytocin receptors. *Brain Res Dev Brain Res*, 80(1-2), 115–120.

Pan, H., Nanno, D., Che, F. Y., Zhu, X., Salton, S. R., Steiner, D. F., et al. (2005). Neuropeptide processing profile in mice lacking prohormone convertase-1. *Biochemistry*, 44(12), 4939–4948.

Paquin, J., Danalache, B. A., Jankowski, M., McCann, S. M., & Gutkowska, J. (2002). Oxytocin induces differentiation of P19 embryonic stem cells to cardiomyocytes. *Proc Natl Acad Sci U S A*, 99(14), 9550–9555.

Phelps, S. M., & Young, L. J. (2003). Extraordinary diversity in vasopressin (v1a) receptor distributions among wild prairie voles (microtus ochrogaster): Patterns of variation and covariation. *J Comp Neurol*, 466(4), 564–576.

Pinna, G., Agis-Balboa, R. C., Doueiri, M. S., Guidotti, A., & Costa, E. (2004). Brain neurosteroids in gender-related aggression induced by social isolation. *Crit Rev Neurobiol*, 16(1-2), 75–82.

Porges, S. W. (2001). The polyvagal theory: Phylogenetic substrates of a social nervous system. *Int J Psychophysiol*, 42(2), 123–146.

Prathikanti, S., & Weinberger, D. R. (2005). Psychiatric genetics-the new era: Genetic research and some clinical implications. *British Medical Bulletin*, 73 and 74, 107–122.

Ragnauth, A. K., Goodwillie, A., Brewer, C., Muglia, L. J., Pfaff, D. W., & Kow, L. M. (2004). Vasopressin stimulates ventromedial hypothalamic neurons via oxytocin receptors in oxytocin gene knockout male and female mice. *Neuroendocrinology*, 80(2), 92–99. Epub 2004 Nov 2002.

Ring, R. H. (2005). The central vasopressinergic system: Examining the opportunities for psychiatric drug development. *Curr Pharm Des*, 11(2), 205–225.

Ronald, A., Happe, F., Price, T. S., Baron-Cohen, S., & Plomin, R. (2006). Phenotypic and genetic overlap between autistic traits at the extremes of the general population. *J Am Acad Child Adolesc Psychiatry*, 45(10), 1206–1214.

Salzberg, A. D., & Swedo, S. E. (1992). Oxytocin and vasopressin in obsessive-compulsive disorder. *Am J Psychiatry*, 149(5), 713–714.

Sawchenko, P. E., & Swanson, L. W. (1982). Immuno-histochemical identification of neurons in the paraventricular nucleus of the hypothalamus that project to the medulla or to the spinal cord in the rat. *J Comp Neurol*, 205(3), 260–272.

Sebat, J., Lakshmi, B., Malhotra, D., Troge, J., Lese-Martin, C., Walsh, T., et al. (2007). Strong association of de novo copy number mutations with autism. *Science, 316*(5823), 445–449.

Serradeil-Le Gal, C., Wagnon, J., 3rd, Tonnerre, B., Roux, R., Garcia, G., Griebel, G., et al. (2005). An overview of SSR149415, a selective nonpeptide vasopressin V(1b) receptor antagonist for the treatment of stress-related disorders. *CNS Drug Rev, 11*(1), 53–68.

Shapiro, L. E., & Insel, T. R. (1989). Ontogeny of oxytocin receptors in rat forebrain: A quantitative study. *Synapse, 4*(3), 259–266.

Skuse, D., Mandy, W., Steer, C., Miller, L., Goodman, R., Lawrence, K., et al. (2008). Social communication competence and functional adaptation in a general population of children: Preliminary evidence for sex-by-verbal iq differential risk. *J Am Acad Child Adolesc Psychiatry.*

Skuse, D., Morris, J., & Lawrence, K. (2003). The amygdala and development of the social brain. *Ann N Y Acad Sci, 1008,* 91–101.

Smalley, S. L., Asarnow, R. F., & Spence, M. A. (1988). Autism and genetics. A decade of research. *Arch Gen Psychiatry, 45*(10), 953–961.

Smeltzer, M. D., Curtis, J. T., Aragona, B. J., & Wang, Z. (2006). Dopamine, oxytocin, and vasopressin receptor binding in the medial prefrontal cortex of monogamous and promiscuous voles. *Neurosci Lett, 394*(2), 146–151. Epub 2005 Nov 2009.

Spielman, R. S., McGinnis, R. E., & Ewens, W. J. (1993). Transmission test for linkage disequilibrium: The insulin gene region and insulin-dependent diabetes mellitus. *American Journal of Human Genetics, 52,* 506–516.

Steffenburg, S., Gillberg, C., Hellgren, L., Andersson, L., Gillberg, I. C., Jakobsson, G., et al. (1989). A twin study of autism in Denmark, Finland, Iceland, Norway and Sweden. *J Child Psychol Psychiatry, 30*(3), 405–416.

Suresh, R., Ambrose, N., Roe, C., Pluzhnikov, A., Wittke-Thompson, J. K., Ng, M. C., et al. (2006). New complexities in the genetics of stuttering: Significant sex-specific linkage signals. *Am J Hum Genet, 78*(4), 554–563. Epub 2006 Feb 2001.

Sutcliffe, J. S., Delahanty, R. J., Prasad, H. C., McCauley, J. L., Han, Q., Jiang, L., et al. (2005). Allelic heterogeneity at the serotonin transporter locus (SLC6A4) confers susceptibility to autism and rigid-compulsive behaviors. *Am J Hum Genet, 77*(2), 265–279. Epub 2005 Jul 2001.

Swaab, D. F., Chung, W. C., Kruijver, F. P., Hofman, M. A., & Hestiantoro, A. (2003). Sex differences in the hypothalamus in the different stages of human life. *Neurobiol Aging, 24 Suppl 1,* S1–16; discussion S17-19.

Swaab, D. F., Purba, J. S., & Hofman, M. A. (1995). Alterations in the hypothalamic paraventricular nucleus and its oxytocin neurons (putative satiety cells) in Prader-Willi syndrome: A study of five cases. *J Clin Endocrinol Metab, 80*(2), 573–579.

Swedo, S. E., Leonard, H. L., Kruesi, M. J., Rettew, D. C., Listwak, S. J., Berretini, W., et al. (1992a). Cerebrospinal fluid neuro-chemistry in children and adolescents with obsessive-compulsive disorder. *Arch Gen Psychiatry, 49,* 29–36.

Swedo, S. E., Leonard, H. L., Kruesi, M. J., Rettew, D. C., Listwak, S. J., Berrettini, W., et al. (1992b). Cerebrospinal fluid neurochemistry in children and adolescents with obsessive-compulsive disorder. *Arch Gen Psychiatry, 49*(1), 29–36.

Takayanagi, Y., Yoshida, M., Bielsky, I. F., Ross, H. E., Kawamata, M., Onaka, T., et al. (2005). Pervasive social deficits, but normal parturition, in oxytocin receptor-deficient mice. *Proc Natl Acad Sci U S A, 102*(44), 16096–16101. Epub 2005 Oct 16025.

Theodosis, D. T., Trailin, A., & Poulain, D. A. (2006). Remodeling of astrocytes, a prerequisite for synapse turnover in the adult brain? Insights from the oxytocin system of the hypothalamus. *Am J Physiol Regul Integr Comp Physiol, 290*(5), R1175–1182.

Thibonnier, M., Coles, P., Thibonnier, A., & Shoham, M. (2002). Molecular pharmacology and modeling of vasopressin receptors. *Prog Brain Res, 139,* 179–196.

Thompson, R., Gupta, S., Miller, K., Mills, S., & Orr, S. (2004). The effects of vasopressin on human facial responses related to social communication. *Psychoneuroendocrinology, 29*(1), 35–48.

Tordjman, S., Ferrari, P., Sulmont, V., Duyme, M., & Roubertoux, P. (1997). Androgenic activity in autism. *Am J Psychiatry, 154*(11), 1626–1627.

Tribollet, E., Charpak, S., Schmidt, A., Dubois-Dauphin, M., & Dreifuss, J. J. (1989). Appearance and transient expression of oxytocin receptors in fetal, infant, and peripubertal rat brain studied by autoradiography and electrophysiology. *J Neurosci, 9*(5), 1764–1773.

Tribollet, E., Goumaz, M., Raggenbass, M., & Dreifuss, J. J. (1991). Appearance and transient expression of vasopressin and oxytocin receptors in the rat brain. *J Recept Res, 11*(1-4), 333–346.

Vaccari, C., Carter, C. S., & Ostrowski, N. L. (1996). *Neonatal exposure to arginine AVP alters adult AVPV1a and OT receptor mRNA expression in rat brain.* Paper presented at the Soc Neurosci Abst.

van Londen, L., Kerkhof, G. A., van den Berg, F., Goekoop, J. G., Zwinderman, K. H., Frankhuijzen-Sierevogel, A. C., et al. (1998). Plasma arginine vasopressin and motor activity in major depression. *Biol Psychiatry, 43*(3), 196–204.

Van Wimersma Greidanus, T. B., Kroodsma, J. M., Pot, M. L., Stevens, M., & Maigret, C. (1990). Neurohypophyseal hormones and excessive grooming behaviour. *Eur J Pharmacol, 187*(1), 1–8.

Veenstra-VanderWeele, J., & Cook, E. H. (2004). Molecular genetics of autism spectrum disorder. *Mol Psychiatry, 9,* 819–832.

Volkmar, F. R., Szatmari, P., & Sparrow, S. S. (1993). Sex differences in pervasive developmental disorders. *J Autism Dev Disord*, 23(4), 579–591.

von Eggelkraut-Gottanka, R., & Beck-Sickinger, A. G. (2004). Biosynthesis of peptide hormones derived from precursor sequences. *Curr Med Chem*, 11(20), 2651–2665.

Wassink, T. H., Piven, J., Vieland, V., Pietila, J., Goedken, R. J., Folstein, S., et al. (2004). Examination of avpr1a as an autism susceptibility gene. *Molecular Psychiatry*, 9(10), 968–972.

Waterhouse, L., Fein, D., & Modahl, C. (1996). Neurofunctional mechanisms in autism. *Psychol Rev*, 103(3), 457–489.

Welch, M. G., Welch-Horan, T. B., Anwar, M., Anwar, N., Ludwig, R. J., & Ruggiero, D. A. (2005). Brain effects of chronic ibd in areas abnormal in autism and treatment by single neuropeptides secretin and oxytocin. *J Mol Neurosci*, 25(3), 259–274.

Windle, R. J., Kershaw, Y. M., Shanks, N., Wood, S. A., Lightman, S. L., & Ingram, C. D. (2004). Oxytocin attenuates stress-induced c-fos mRNA expression in specific forebrain regions associated with modulation of hypothalamo-pituitary-adrenal activity. *Journal of Neuroscience*, 4, 2974–2982.

Winslow, J. T. (2005). Neuropeptides and non-human primate social deficits associated with pathogenic rearing experience. *Int J Dev Neurosci*, 23(2-3), 245–251.

Winslow, J. T., Hastings, N., Carter, C. S., Harbaugh, C. R., & Insel, T. R. (1993). A role for central vasopressin in pair bonding in monogamous prairie voles. *Nature*, 365(6446), 545–548.

Winslow, J. T., Hearn, E. F., Ferguson, J., Young, L. J., Matzuk, M. M., & Insel, T. R. (2000). Infant vocalization, adult aggression, and fear behavior of an oxytocin null mutant mouse. *Horm Behav*, 37(2), 145–155.

Winslow, J. T., & Insel, T. R. (2002). The social deficits of the oxytocin knockout mouse. *Neuropeptides*, 36(2-3), 221–229.

Winslow, J. T., & Insel, T. R. (2004). Neuroendocrine basis of social recognition. *Curr Opin Neurobiol*, 14(2), 248–253.

Winslow, J. T., Noble, P. L., Lyons, C. K., Sterk, S. M., & Insel, T. R. (2003). Rearing effects on cerebrospinal fluid oxytocin concentration and social buffering in rhesus monkeys. *Neuropsychopharmacology*, 28(5), 910–918. Epub 2003 Mar 2026.

Witt, D. M. (1997). Regulatory mechanisms of oxytocin-mediated sociosexual behavior. *Ann N Y Acad Sci*, 807, 287–301.

Wotjak, C. T., Kubota, M., Liebsch, G., Montkowski, A., Holsboer, F., Neumann, I., et al. (1996). Release of vasopressin within the rat paraventricular nucleus in response to emotional stress: A novel mechanism of regulating adrenocorticotropic hormone secretion? *J Neurosci*, 16(23), 7725–7732.

Wotjak, C. T., Naruo, T., Muraoka, S., Simchen, R., Landgraf, R., & Engelmann, M. (2001). Forced swimming stimulates the expression of vasopressin and oxytocin in magnocellular neurons of the rat hypothalamic paraventricular nucleus. *European Journal of Neurosciences*, 13(12), 2273–2281.

Wu, S., Jia, M., Ruan, Y., Liu, J., Guo, Y., Shuang, M., et al. (2005). Positive association of the oxytocin receptor gene (oxtr) with autism in the chinese han population. *Biol Psychiatry*, 58(1), 74–77.

Yirmiya, N., Rosenberg, C., Levi, S., Salomon, S., Shulman, C., Nemanov, L., et al. (2006). Association between the arginine vasopressin 1a receptor (avpr1a) gene and autism in a family–based study: Mediation by socialization skills. *Mol Psychiatry*, 11(5), 488–494.

Ylisaukko-oja, T., Alarcon, M., Cantor, R. M., Auranen, M., Vanhala, R., Kempas, E., et al. (2006). Search for autism loci by combined analysis of autism genetic resource exchange and finnish families. *Ann Neurol*, 59(1), 145–155.

Young, L. J., Nilsen, R., Waymire, K. G., MacGregor, G. R., & Insel, T. R. (1999). Increased affiliative response to vasopressin in mice expressing the V1a receptor from a monogamous vole. *Nature*, 400(6746), 766–768.

Young, L. J., Pitkow, L. J., & Ferguson, J. N. (2002). Neuropeptides and social behavior: Animal models relevant to autism. *Mol Psychiatry*, 7 Suppl 2, S38–39.

Young, L. J., Winslow, J. T., Nilsen, R., & Insel, T. R. (1997). Species differences in V1a receptor gene expression in monogamous and nonmonogamous voles: Behavioral consequences. *Behav Neurosci*, 111(3), 599–605.

Yrigollen, C. M., Han, S. S., Kochetkova, A., Babitz, T., Chang, J. T., Volkmar, F. R., et al. (2008). Genes controlling affiliative behavior as candidate genes for autism. *Biol Psychiatry*, 63(10), 911–916.

Zak, P. J., Kurzban, R., & Matzner, W. T. (2005). Oxytocin is associated with human trustworthiness. *Hormones and Behavior*, 48(522–7).

Chapter 23

Redefining the Concept of Autism as a Unitary Disorder: Multiple Causal Deficits of a Single Kind?

Jill Boucher

INTRODUCTION

From Kanner (1943) onwards, it has been widely assumed that the co-occurrence in a proportion of the human population of the constellation of behavioral anomalies associated with autism, does not occur by chance. If this assumption is correct, there must be some explanation for this non-random co-occurrence, and a great deal of theorizing and research has been devoted to identifying a single first cause or common pathway capable of explaining why these behaviors occur together. Recently, however, the concept of autism as a unitary disorder comparable to, for example, Down's syndrome or phenylketonuria, has weakened to the point of being abandoned.

The issue of the randomness or relatedness of behaviors associated with autism is of critical importance both practically and theoretically. Specifically: understanding of the causes of autistic spectrum disorders (ASDs) has implications for interventions that might be designed to prevent, cure, or alleviate maladaptive autism-related behaviors—or, just as importantly, to ensure that certain notably adaptive capacities associated with high-functioning autism remain in the gene pool and are not jeopardized phenotypically. In this chapter I argue that abandoning the search for causal relationships among autism-typical behaviors would be premature, and that instead there is a need to rethink the issues and to be prepared to redefine what might be meant by "unitary." First, however, the history of single-factor explanations of autism is reviewed.

HISTORICAL BACKGROUND

Single-Factor Theories

Theories positing a common etiology and shared causal pathways thereafter

In the first three decades following Kanner's (1943) report, there was a widespread assumption that autism derives from the same etiological factors in all cases. So, for example, Kanner himself proposed that autism resulted from a "lack of the innate ability to form the usual biologically provided affective contact with people," implying a shared genetic basis and abnormal brain development and function. Similarly Rimland (1964), having noted that many children with autism had been given oxygen postnatally because of respiratory distress, proposed a genetically determined hypersensitivity to oxygen as the initial cause of autism, arguing that this would disrupt the normal development of the reticular activating system, which he identified as the malfunctioning brain system underlying autism-related behaviors.

Other early theorists identified environmental factors as the initial cause of autism in all cases. Psychoanalysts such as Mahler (1952) and Bettelheim (1967), for example, argued that autism resulted from emotionally cold parenting and failure to establish the usual mother-child bond. At a later date, a similar argument was made by Welch (1984), who viewed autism as an attachment disorder. When the psychoanalytic model gave way to a behavioral model as the dominant one for understanding psychological disorders, autism was hypothesized by some to result from maladaptive learning associated with inappropriate reinforcement of behaviors during infancy (e.g., Ferster, 1961).

Theories positing a common brain basis and shared pathways thereafter

Some early theorists proposed that abnormalities affecting specific brain regions were common to all cases of autism, remaining agnostic concerning underlying etiology. For example, Hutt et al. (1964) hypothesized, as did Rimland (1964), that the reticular activating system in the brain stem malfunctions in autism in ways affecting arousal, attention, and responsivity, and hence learning capacities. Ornitz and Ritvo (1968) hypothesized that abnormal function within the vestibular system affecting the ability to integrate sensory and motor processes could explain autism-related behaviors. Left-hemisphere dysfunction resulting in severe language disorder was identified as the critical source of autistic behaviors by McCann (1981), while right-hemisphere dysfunction associated with emotional and social impairments was identified as critical by Fein et al. (1984). Damasio and Maurer (1978) proposed a model of autism as resulting from

basal ganglia and mesial frontal lobe abnormalities. Hetzler and Griffin (1981) proposed bilateral medial temporal lobe abnormalities, noting that these could explain both the social and the cognitive impairments in autism[1].

Theories positing a common psychological deficit manifesting in autism-related behaviors

A further group of early theorists proposed single-factor causal hypotheses at the psychological level, remaining agnostic concerning underlying brain abnormalities as well as underlying etiology. Some of these theories identified one of the diagnostic features of autism-related behavior as primary in the sense of being the immediate cause of other autism-related behaviors. Notable among these were a group of theories proposing that autism was a type of language disorder severe enough to cause autism-related communication and social interaction impairments, as well as repetitive behaviors and resistance to change (e.g., Churchill, 1972; Rutter, 1968). Some theorists identified the language impairment as a form of developmental dysphasia (specific language impairment), not going beyond this in attempting to explain developmental dysphasia itself. Other theorists, however, suggested that a more fundamental psychological deficit, such as impaired symbolizing (Ricks & Wing, 1975) or impaired sequencing (Tanguay, 1984), caused the language impairment (and thereafter the socio-communication impairment and repetitive behaviors), with additional effects on thinking and reasoning such as were manifested in intellectual disability.

It may strike contemporary readers as odd that so much emphasis was placed on language impairment, in the sense that impaired language needed to be explained, let alone in the sense that language impairment might be able to explain other behavioral abnormalities associated with autism. However, until *DSM-III(R)* was published in 1987, structural language

---

1. My own suggestion that the hippocampus might be a site of dysfunction in people with what is now known as autistic disorder has often been interpreted as a single-factor neurobiological explanation of the totality of autism-related behavior. However, it was not intended as such, as is clear from the quote included in the section on Goodman's model.

impairment was a diagnostic criterion for autism, in addition to social interaction impairments, repetitive behaviors, and resistance to change. This illustrates a point made later in the chapter, concerning the fact that definitions of autism, and thereby concepts of "what has to be explained," constitute a moving target of research. In addition, at the time when these language-focused explanations were being proposed, psycholinguistics was an "in" field of study, under the influence of Chomsky's recently published linguistic theories. This illustrates again how the prevailing models within a discipline influence theorizing (and it is worth pondering what models are influencing current theorizing, given the declining influence of cognitivist, computer-based models).

A more recent group of theories pitched at the psychological level of explanation also identified a single primary psychological deficit as leading either directly to each of the diagnostic behaviors, or as leading directly to one (or two) and indirectly to the other(s). Thus, Russell (1997) argued that executive dysfunctions were the immediate cause of all three defining features of behavior—namely social and communication impairments (no longer necessarily including structural language impairment), and restricted and repetitive behaviors. Baron-Cohen (1989) hypothesized that the social and communication impairments could be explained by a defective metarepresentation mechanism resulting in impaired 'theory of mind', with repetitive behaviors occurring secondarily as a result of disorientation and anxiety. Similarly, Frith (1989) initially hypothesized that impaired mentalizing, leading to impaired social interaction and communication, could be explained in terms of a weak drive for central coherence, with repetitive behaviors occurring secondarily. These three well-known single-factor theories, all pitched at the level of psychological explanation, battled unproductively for supremacy through the last 15 years of the twentieth century and beyond, long after their original proponents had retreated from their early claims (see Rajendran & Mitchell, 2007, for a detailed review).

Goodman's model of diversity within a unitary concept of autism

Goodman (1989) proposed a notably different model of the causes of autism in a paper entitled "Infantile autism: A syndrome of multiple primary deficits?" As is evident from the title of his paper, Goodman—like other theorists referred to above—conceived of autism as a syndrome and to this extent a unitary disorder with, by implication, a single causal explanation at some or other level of analysis. However, unlike other theorists up to that time, Goodman argued that behaviors diagnostic of autism as then defined result from pathology within different brain systems. He further argued that the co-occurrence of neuropathology in diverse brain systems results from shared vulnerability to certain genetic or environmental effects mediated by factors such as the physical proximity of the brain systems involved, their shared blood supply, shared sensitivity to an environmental toxin, shared susceptibility to nutrient deficiency, shared neurotransmitters, shared viral receptors, or shared developmental periods of maximum vulnerability. Thus, instead of identifying a single specific etiological, neurobiological, or psychological factor as the sole cause of autism (as other theories reviewed above had done), Goodman identified "shared vulnerability" as critical, and spelled this out in terms of possible *kinds* of shared causes.

Goodman's suggestions resemble some I had made several years earlier concerning common pathways to autism, when I wrote:

> There is no a priori reason to suppose that all the presenting symptoms of autism stem from a single primary impairment of behavior, whether this be abnormal social avoidance or impaired language acquisition: both social abnormalities and cognitive abnormalities associated with language may be primary features of behavior. A neuropsychological approach . . . can provide a framework within which various different aspects of behavior may be seen as related because, for example, they are mediated by a single brain structure that has a variety of functions, or because they are mediated by areas of the brain which are related in some way, such as topographically, functionally, biochemically or in having a common blood supply." (Boucher, 1975, pp. 68–69; see also Boucher, 1976).

I suggest later in this chapter that Goodman's notion of "shared vulnerability" has relevance for understanding how diversity among behaviors associated with ASDs and their brain correlates may nevertheless be understood as causally related, and to this extent, compatible with a unitary concept of autism.

Loosening the Concept of Autism as a
Unitary Disorder as Traditionally Defined

From the 1980s onwards, the concept of autism as a unitary disorder comparable to conditions such as Down's syndrome or phenylketonuria was increasingly called into question. In 1979, Wing and Gould published their epidemiological study demonstrating the dissociability of certain strands of autism-related behaviors; and in 1981 Wing published her case studies and discussion of individuals with Asperger syndrome, bringing Asperger's work to the attention of English-speaking researchers for the first time. As a result of her research and clinical observations, Wing (1988) proposed the notion of a spectrum of overlapping but non-identical disorders characterized by social and communication impairments and lack of imagination, sometimes but not always accompanied by language and learning impairments, and often accompanied by a range of other physical, developmental, and mental health anomalies and problems. Wing's work led to a major shift in the concept of autism, from that of a syndrome with more or less invariant symptomology and a single cause, to that of a dimensional disorder consisting of certain characteristics that tend to occur together but which do not invariably do so, and that have importantly different causal antecedents. This shift was recognized in part by the identification of subtypes of autism-related disorders in *ICD10* (World Health Organization, 1992) and *DSM-IV* (American Psychiatric Association, 1994).

Further evidence of the dissociability of subsets of ASD-related behaviors came from studies of families in which at least one family member was diagnosed with an ASD. These studies showed that isolated facets of ASD-related behavior occur with unusual frequency in family members who do not warrant the diagnosis of an ASD. So, for example, several studies demonstrated higher-than-expected frequencies of ASD-typical social interaction anomalies, or of obsessive tendencies, in each case occurring independently of each other in relatives of probands with autism (see Dawson et al., 2002; Pickles et al., 2000, for reviews). Similarly, Happé, Frith and Briskman (2001) reported that a "piecemeal processing" style occurred in a group of fathers of autism probands, although none of the fathers had a diagnosis of autism themselves. Some studies also reported that structural language impairments were unusually common in non-autistic family members (e.g., Bolton et al., 1994; Folstein et al.,

1999; but see Williams, Botting, & Boucher, 2008, for a critique of these findings). Findings such as the above led to the now widely accepted concept of the broader autism phenotype, or lesser variant autism, in which a single facet of ASD-related behavior occurs in an individual who does not warrant a diagnosis of any subtype of autistic spectrum disorder.

During the 1990s, evidence of autistic behaviors in blind children (Brown et al., 1997), and in children who had been materially and psychologically deprived in their early years (Rutter et al., 1999), suggested that a diagnosis of an ASD might apply in cases where the causal factors involved were not shared at the etiological or neurobiological levels, nor in any clear-cut way at the psychological level (although stimulus deprivation might be said to be involved in both conditions). These observations raised further questions concerning the validity of conceiving of autism, or ASDs, as unitary in any way except as a name for a certain set of behaviors when occurring together. And if blind children and children raised in deprived conditions were agreed to have "autism," as opposed to "pseudo-autism," "quasi-autism," or some differently named autism-like condition (see below), then the scope for identifying common causal pathways would be severely curtailed.

More recently, Happé, Ronald, and Plomin (2006) published a paper entitled "Time to give up on a single explanation for autism?" In this paper, Happé et al. argued that available evidence indicates not only that each member of the triad of diagnostic impairments can occur in isolated form, but also that attempts to explain these behaviors by a single deficit at either the psychological or the neurobiological level have failed; and that recent evidence, including some of their own, indicates that the genes underlying each of the diagnostic impairments are also largely unshared.

Finally, I have pointed out elsewhere that we do not know the incidence of each of the diagnostic impairments in the general (non-autistic) population, and therefore cannot calculate the frequency with which they might co-occur by chance, undermining the usual grounds for seeking single-factor explanations (Boucher, 2006).

It appears, therefore, that the concept of autism as a unitary disorder resulting from a single common cause at some or other level of explanation may be at the point of being abandoned, to give way to a model of the routes to ASD-related behaviors as both multiple and independent. In the following sections I will argue against allowing the pendulum to swing this far, and in favor of reconsideration of the issues, including possibilities for a different kind of understanding of what might make 'ASD' in some sense a unitary condition.

RETHINKING THE CONCEPT OF AUTISM AS A UNITARY DISORDER

I suggest first that there is, in fact, evidence for the non-random co-occurrence of ASD-related behaviors, other than evidence that might be obtained by assessing the incidence of each facet of autism-diagnostic behavior in the general population and multiplying these probabilities. This opens the way for working with a concept of autism as a spectrum of overlapping conditions in which potentially dissociable behavioral (and physical) anomalies tend to occur together more often than would be predicted by chance—a concept that recognizes dimensionality without abandoning the notion of "unitary" in the sense of causally related. I suggest next that the set of "potentially dissociable behavioral and physical anomalies that tend to occur together"—i.e., what has to be explained—needs to be reformulated and expanded in order to allow for an eventual understanding of how these anomalies are all related. I then argue for more explicit recognition of the complexity of causal routes to ASD-related behaviors, with the aim of differentiating the necessary and sufficient causes from the many aggravating causes of these behaviors. Finally, I suggest that ways of conceptualizing the relatedness of causal routes to ASDs are already available within the recent literature.

Evidence for the Non-random Co-occurrence of ASD-Related Anomalies

Autistic traits, and sometimes behaviors warranting a diagnosis of Asperger syndrome or autistic disorder, occur more often than would be predicted by chance in association with certain congenital medical conditions. For example, tuberous sclerosis is known to occur in 0.01% of the general population, but in approximately 2% of all people with ASDs: i.e., 200 times more often, and at even higher rates if those with autistic traits are included (Gutierrez, Smalley, & Tanguay, 1998). Similarly, fragile X syndrome occurs in approximately 0.03% of the general popula-

tion, but in approximately 3% of people diagnosed with an ASD; moreover, the rate of diagnosed ASD in the population of individuals with fragile X syndrome is estimated at between 15 and 25% (Bailey, Phillips, & Rutter, 1996; Dykens & Volkmar, 1997). Various other congenital medical conditions occur more often in the autistic population than the general population, including phenylketonuria, Turner syndrome, Down's syndrome, and Williams syndrome (see Filipek, 2005, for a review).

The fact of higher-than-expected rates of comorbidity of full forms of ASD (Asperger syndrome or autistic disorder) with these conditions provides incontrovertible evidence that ASD-related behaviors do not co-occur by chance. At the same time, the higher-than-expected rates of isolated facets of ASD-related behavior in some of these conditions confirm the dissociability of each of the major features of autistic behavior.

The Need to Clarify What Has to be Explained: Reduction and Expansion

When fragile X syndrome was first identified and studied, it was claimed by some researchers that up to 60% of individuals with fragile X also had autism. This much higher rate of comorbidity than is now accepted was found because some of the behavioral characteristics of people with fragile X resemble behaviors associated with ASDs, although on more detailed analysis this resemblance turns out in most instances to be superficial. This cautionary tale emphasizes the importance of detailed qualitative descriptions of behaviors characteristic of people with ASDs: there is no point in attempting to identify common causes of behaviors that have only superficial resemblance. The large bodies of psychological research into some major facets of ASD-related behavior over recent decades have contributed greatly to the detailed characterization that is needed. In particular, a great deal is now known about the precise patterns of spared and impaired social cognition, emotion processing, pragmatic language impairments, executive functions, sensory-perceptual processing and motor skills characteristic of individuals with ASDs, especially those with AS/HFA. However, structural language impairment as it occurs in individuals with lower-functioning autism remains in need of detailed characterization to avoid falling into the "superficial resemblance" trap (Boucher et al., 2008; Williams et al., 2008).

Detailed qualitative description of ASD-related behavior can help to discriminate between what may be referred to as "prototypical ASDs," as opposed to non-prototypical cases, where behaviors superficially resemble those characteristic of ASDs. Age of onset, course, and response to treatment may also be used to discriminate between prototypical ASDs and non-prototypical cases. So, for example, cases of pervasive developmental disorder not otherwise specified (PDD-NOS) with atypical symptomology, and cases of late-acquired and transient ASD-related behaviors resulting from Herpes encephalitis (Ghaziuddin et al, 1992; Gillberg, 1986), are clearly non-prototypical. If longitudinal studies were to show that the course and outcome of late-onset or regressive autism differ from the course and outcome of early-onset autism, then regressive autism might also be described as non-prototypical (but the evidence for reaching a conclusion on this point is not available). Ongoing study of blind or deprived individuals with autistic-like behaviors should demonstrate not only how closely behaviors resemble those of prototypical ASDs, but also whether or not response to intervention and eventual outcome are prototypical (here again, conclusive evidence is lacking). Tustin (1981; 1991) has long argued for the existence of a condition she calls "psychogenic autism," distinct from what might be termed "organic autism." Regardless of whether or not one accepts Tustin's specific argument, recognition of non-prototypical conditions such as psychogenic autism, late-acquired autism, deprivation autism, and possibly regressive autism may be useful in clarifying what does *not* have to be causally explained. This does not imply that there are no interesting issues concerning possible relationships between these suggested subtypes, but rather that for present purposes these issues can be set aside.

If at some future date it were to be shown that the ASD-related behaviors sometimes associated with known medical conditions, such as tuberous sclerosis or Turner's syndrome, do not closely resemble those in people with ASDs who do not suffer from any such medical condition, or if it were to be shown that the typical course, outcome, or response to treatment differed, then my argument that these conditions provide evidence for the non-random co-occurrence of behaviors diagnostic of ASDs would be undermined. At the same time, the description "prototypical autism" would apply to a correspondingly reduced set of cases. In theory, this process might continue until all cases

of ASD could be assigned to a particular subtype identified by cause in addition to detailed behavioral profile, age of onset, etc. As differentiable subtypes proliferated, the notion of autism as unitary in any meaningful sense would be eroded and might eventually be abandoned. This, I take it, is the situation that Happé et al. (2006) foresee. I would argue that we have not yet reached this situation, but that allowing that some differentiable subtypes, or cases of quasi- or pseudo-autism, exist, and identifying a narrowed concept of "prototypical autism" is helpful when considering whether or not ASDs are in any sense a unitary condition.

Having argued for a reduction in what has to be explained, I will now argue for an expansion. One of the earliest attempts to establish diagnostic criteria for autism was what came to be known as Creak's Nine Points (Creak, 1961). The committee of practitioners chaired by Creak suggested nine diagnostic criteria for a diagnosis of "early infantile autism," based on an interpretation of Kanner's descriptions and their own clinical experience. The nine points were: gross and sustained impairment of emotional relationships; serious retardation with islets of normal or exceptional intellectual function; apparent unawareness of personal identity; pathological preoccupation with particular objects; sustained resistance to change; abnormal response to perceptual stimuli; acute and illogical anxiety; speech absent or underdeveloped; and distorted motility patterns.

A decade or so later, Rutter (1968) in the U.K. and Ritvo and Freeman (1977) in the U.S. had more or less agreed on an abbreviated set of diagnostic criteria, and these were incorporated into *DSM-III* (American Psychiatric Association, 1980), in which an entry for "infantile autism" appeared for the first time. These criteria were: lack of responsiveness to others; impaired language and communication skills; bizarre responses to aspects of the environment; and onset prior to 30 months. In *DSM-III (R)* (American Psychiatric Association, 1987), impaired language was omitted as a criterion, leaving "communication" as the second member of what later became known as the triad of impairments. Differing criteria for the subtypes of Asperger syndrome, autistic disorder, and PDD-NOS were not included until *DSM-IV* (American Psychiatric Association, 1994).

Since the publication of DSM-IV, most attempts to explain ASDs in terms of shared causal factors have focused exclusively on Asperger syndrome (AS) and high-functioning autism (HFA), defined in terms of impaired social interaction, impaired communication, and restricted and repetitive behaviors in the absence of cognitive impairment or current structural language impairment. The rationale for this strategy is that AS and HFA constitute the purest forms of ASD, uncontaminated by intellectual impairment or structural language impairment which, it is implied, sometimes co-occur with "pure" autism by chance (although the frequency of co-occurrence is so high that this could hardly be the case). Popular use of the term "syndrome" in "Asperger syndrome" further implies that this form of ASD may be unitary as generally understood (although, notably, *DSM-IV* uses the term "disorder" rather than "syndrome"). The durability of the *DSM-IV* criteria is rarely if ever questioned by those currently investigating possible common pathways to ASDs. Correspondingly, the *soi-disant* "gold standard" ascertainment methods, though recognized to be in need of some revision to be in perfect accord with *DSM-IV* criteria, are heavily relied on in selecting participant groups in causal investigations. *DSM-V*, when it appears, will make significant changes in terminology and definitions of 'autism spectrum disorders' and, no doubt, these ascertainment instruments will be revised accordingly.

The point being made here is that there is an ongoing and as yet incomplete process of definition and redefinition of what is meant by "autism" or "autistic spectrum disorders," and we remain a long way from knowing for what characterization of ASDs it might be "time to give up on a single explanation". A subsidiary point is that, valuable as "gold-standard" methods are for operationalizing and ensuring shared usage of whatever definition of ASDs is current, they are only as good as the current definition. Moreover, if taken to be the end-point in diagnostic ascertainment for purposes of theoretical research, these instruments run the risk of impeding progress toward improved understanding in that they instantiate circularity; that is, they imply that this is what autism is because this is what we see in people selected using these criteria (a similar point is made by Rajendren & Mitchell, 2007). I have argued elsewhere (Boucher, 2009) that for the purpose of explaining ASDs (and possibly for purposes of clinical diagnosis, but that is a different issue and beyond the scope of the present argument), there is a need to make certain changes and additions to "what has to be explained", and to remain open to the possibility of future changes. A summary of some changes I have argued for (Boucher, 2009) is given below.

In the first place, social interaction impairments and communication impairments—in the sense of impaired use of linguistic or non-linguistic signaling systems—should be recognized as indissolubly linked, and identified as such under the heading "socio-communicative impairment." This suggestion derives from the fact that all social interaction involves communication, and all human communication involves social interaction—you cannot have one without the other, and they do not require substantially different explanations.

I also argue that there is now overwhelming evidence of anomalous emotion-processing at the heart of the interaction impairment, and that for the purposes of explanation this should be recognized by further expansion of a socio-communicative impairments into a set of "socio-emotional-communicative impairments." This is necessary because if we seek to explain only the socio-cognitive aspects of the interaction impairments we will not have explained enough, and we will almost certainly have arrived at an incorrect or incomplete explanation of the behavior in question.

A corollary and linked change in the formulation of "what has to be explained" is that clinically significant structural language impairments (impairments of the language system itself—that is, of linguistic knowledge, as opposed to use of this knowledge) should be separated from the use-of-language communicative impairment and recognized as characteristic of only a proportion of people with an ASD. In addition, recognition of the frequently made point that intellectual disability in people on the autistic spectrum derives primarily from low verbal IQ (e.g., Bailey et al., 1996; Boucher, Mayes, & Bigham, 2008; Lord & Paul, 1997) dictates that the *combination* of structural language impairment and intellectual disability in most cases of autistic disorder (as currently defined) needs to be explained[2].

---

2. Structural language impairment sometimes occurs in individuals with ASD and normal full-scale IQ (Kjelgaard & Tager-Flusberg, 2001). It will be important in future research into the causes of language impairment in ASDs to compare the characteristics of language impairment yoked to intellectual disability with the characteristics of language impairment when it occurs in otherwise high-functioning individuals. My prediction is that the language impairments will be found to be qualitatively different, and that different explanations will apply.

Finally, sensory-perceptual anomalies are almost certainly universal and of a kind specific to people with ASDs, and must be included among behaviors to be explained (and possibly reinstated as a diagnostic criterion, as Mottron & Burack, 2006, have argued).

In sum, and taking it as read that *repetitive behaviors and lack of imagination* need to be explained, to this I would add *socio-emotional-communicative impairments* and *sensory-perceptual anomalies* in all people with full forms of ASD, plus the *combination of structural language impairment and intellectual disability* in low-functioning ASD only. *Spared abilities* across the spectrum must also be taken into account, both because they need to be explained (especially when superior) and because they may be part of the explanation (see, for example, Mottron & Burack's, 2001, enhanced perceptual function theory; see also Chapter 7, where it is argued that exploitation of spared memory capacities can explain certain superior abilities in both high- and low-functioning individuals). Uneven patterns of motor skills are also almost certainly universal in individuals with full forms of ASD, and this will eventually need to be explained. However, motor skills across the spectrum are not well characterized and are possibly heterogenous, therefore they are not included in the suggested list of "what has to be explained."

In the longer term, the physical as well as the behavioral phenomena associated with ASDs must also be explained. For example, certain sensory and neuromuscular disorders are more common in the autistic population than in the general population. These include hearing impairment (Rosenhall, Nordin, Sandstroem, Ahlsen, & Gillberg, 1999) and visual impairment (Dakin & Frith, 2005), and both hyper- and hypotonia (Rapin, 1996) as well as dyspraxia (Dzuik et al., 2007; Page & Boucher, 1998). Epilepsy is known to occur in association with ASD-related behavior with far greater frequency than in the general population (Tuchman & Rapin, 2002). To these must be added the occasional but above chance comorbidity with ASDs of conditions such as Turner's syndrome and Prader-Willi syndrome, as noted above. Autoimmune disorders (Ashwood & Van de Water, 2004) and gastrointestinal disorders (Erickson et al., 2005) may also occur more often in the autistic than in the non-autistic population, although the evidence here is controversial.

Expansion of what has to be explained beyond the dyad of socio-communicative impairments and repetitive, non-productive behaviors should not be seen as making the explanatory task more difficult, but as making it easier. This is because each example of non-random co-occurrence—whether universal or rare—provides clues to the causes of ASDs. For example, the genetic bases of all the medical conditions discussed in the section on "Evidence for non-random co-occurrence" are known in general terms, if not in precise detail. Similarly, the routes from these genetic abnormalities to a characteristic set of physical, developmental, and behavioral features are at least partially understood in all of these conditions. Hypotheses concerning why and how the genetic abnormalities involved in each type of condition also sometimes lead to ASD-related behaviors are under investigation by various groups of researchers. These investigations are likely to be highly informative about both similarities and differences among the numerous causal routes to these behaviors.

The Need to Clarify the Set of Candidates for Critical Causes of ASDs: Reduction and Expansion

Life would be easier for those seeking to understand the causes of ASDs if each of the defining features of behavior had just one clear-cut explanation. Unfortunately this is not the case: for each set of defining behaviors there are numerous contributory causal factors. For example, the socio-emotional-communicative impairments may result mainly from problems of primary intersubjectivity (dyadic relating) as is now commonly suggested (see Boucher, 2009, for a review). However, obsessive interests, abnormalities of attention or perception, and poor language comprehension when present may also contribute. Similarly, key facets of restricted, repetitive behavior and lack of imagination may result mainly from specific executive dysfunctions, as also commonly suggested. However, anxiety, maladaptive learning, or brain abnormality associated with compulsive, obsessive behavior may also contribute.

Practitioners with responsibilities for intervention or care may need to unravel all the causal antecedents of particular behaviors in any one individual. However, theoreticians concerned with identifying causal pathways to prototypical ASDs need only identify the necessary and sufficient cause(s)—what might be referred to as the "critical" causes—of ASD-related behavior. So, for example, anxiety is neither necessary nor sufficient to cause the restricted and repetitive behaviors, and can be eliminated as a critical cause. This is because not all individuals with an ASD have high levels of anxiety, but all do have restricted and repetitive behavior: anxiety is not, therefore, a necessary cause. At the same time, many individuals in the wider population have clinically significant levels of anxiety but do not have ASD-typical restricted and repetitive behaviors: anxiety is not, therefore, a sufficient cause.

Candidates for causes of ASD-related behaviors at the psychological level of explanation are further reduced by the fact that at least three of the major strands of ASD-related behavior (impaired social interaction, behavioral rigidity, and "piecemeal processing") can occur independently of the others, as shown in evidence leading to the concept of the broader autism phenotype. None of these strands can therefore by itself be a sufficient cause of any other strand. Arguments concerning whether or not impaired theory of mind/mindreading/mentalizing might constitute a sufficient explanation of executive function impairments, or vice versa, were therefore always misconceived for at least this reason, as pointed out in the past (e.g., Boucher, 1996). Similarly, piecemeal processing cannot by itself provide a sufficient explanation of either the social impairment or the behavioral rigidity. This argument does not of course rule out the possibility that one or other of the major strands of ASD-related behavior is a *necessary contributory* cause of one or more of the others—nor does it rule out the fact that each type of behavioral anomaly exacerbates the others when all are present.

The above argument does, however, imply that explanations of each major set of ASD-typical behaviors must involve at least one necessary causal factor at the psychological level of explanation that is not shared by other sets (see Bishop, 1989, for an early exposition of this argument). Causal explanations of "pure" autism must therefore identify at least three different critical causal factors at this level. Current candidates are, as indicated above: primary intersubjectivity impairments (as the critical cause of socio-emotional-communication impairments); certain types of executive dysfunction (as the critical cause of restricted and repetitive behaviors); and either weak central coherence (Happé,

& Frith, 2006) or enhanced perceptual processing (Mottron & Burack, 2001) as the critical cause of sensory-perceptual anomalies. The co-occurrence of structural language impairment and intellectual disability in autistic disorder requires identification of at least one further critical factor. Current candidates include comorbid specific language impairment (of unspecified origin) as a cause of language impairment only (Kielgaard & Tager-Flusberg, 2001), and impaired declarative memory as a cause of the combined impairment of language and learning (Boucher et al., 2008; see also Chapter 7, this volume).

At the neurobiological level of explanation, each of these causal factors must be associated with some structural or functional abnormality within the brain. Thus, the socio-emotional-communicative impairments are likely to be associated with abnormalities within the neural circuit that includes the amygdala, fusiform gyrus, superior temporal sulcus, ventromedial prefrontal cortex, and orbitofrontal cortex (Pelphrey, Adolphs, & Morris, 2004; Schultz, 2005), and possibly with abnormality within the mirror neuron system (Oberman & Ramachandran, 2007). It would also be widely agreed that impaired executive functions of various kinds are associated with abnormalities within subregions of the frontal, and especially prefrontal, cortex (Ozonoff et al., 2004). There is less agreement concerning the brain correlates of sensory-perceptual anomalies. Proponents of the weak-central-coherence hypothesis have returned to their original suggestion of impaired global processing, linking this to a lack of top-down, frontally mediated control (Happé & Frith, 2006). Proponents of the enhanced perceptual processing hypothesis, on the other hand, emphasize hyper-efficient processing in regions of sensory cortex (Mottron & Burack, 2001). In either case, however, the cause of the observed bias toward the processing of parts rather than wholes is hypothesized to reflect an imbalance between the contributions of local as opposed to more global neural networks in the processing of sensory-perceptual information (Rippon et al., 2007). The brain correlates of language and learning impairments in autistic disorder are less well researched (but see Chapters 6 and 7).

At the etiological level of explanation there is an even greater proliferation of candidates for possible causes of ASDs. In particular, there is indisputable evidence that genetic factors are involved in most if not all cases, the current consensus being that a number of susceptibility genes may contribute, and that these may vary across individuals (Bespalova, Reichert, & Buxbaum, 2005; Rutter, 2005). However, the precise genes that may contribute have not been conclusively identified. There is also evidence to suggest that certain environmental factors, especially those impinging on the developing fetus, may cause or contribute to the development of an ASD. For example teratogens, such as thalidomide and valproic acid, have been implicated in the past (Arndt, Stodgell, & Rodier, 2005). There are also claims that viral infections in the mother (Libby, Sweeten, McMahon, & Fujinami, 2005), hormones released in response to stress (Beversdorf et al., 2005), maternal alcohol or drug abuse (Harris, MacKay, & Osborn, 1995; Hultman, Sparen, & Cnattingius, 2002), and abnormally high levels of testosterone (Baron-Cohen, 2003; Baron-Cohen, Knickmeyer, & Belmonte, 2005) can lead to, or predispose an individual toward, the development of an ASD. It has not, however, been shown that any of these factors can by themselves cause prototypical forms of ASD, and in the case of one such factor (maternal rubella) longitudinal research demonstrated an atypical course and outcome (Chess, 1977).

Commonalities Among Neurobiological Factors Contributing to ASDs?

Given the multiplicity of causal factors involved at all levels of explanation, plus the dissociability of the behaviors diagnostic of ASDs, it is unsurprising that numerous writers on autism have argued against single-factor explanations of ASDs—at least of the kind that have been suggested in the past (Bishop, 1989; Boucher, 1976, 1996; Coltheart & Langdon, 1998; Goodman, 1989; Happé et al., 2006). In this final section of this chapter I argue that, before concluding that prototypical forms of ASDs represent the effects of multiple independent factors at all levels of explanation, other formulations of the concept of "unitary" should be considered.

There is no question, from my reading of the literature, that the etiological factors capable of causing prototypical forms of ASD are many and cumulative. Moreover, these factors almost certainly vary not only in their specific identifying descriptions (e.g., 'the genes on chromosome 15q11-q13'), but also in kind, being either genetic or environmental (again of various kinds, such as teratogens or viral infections). Similarly, it has been argued above that there are several critical

psychological causes of the various strands of ASD-related behavior and that these vary in kind, relating respectively to primary intersubjectivity, executive functions, and the balance between local and global processing, according to current opinion. As with the different kinds of etiological factor, the specific psychological causes of each strand of ASD-related behavior may vary within any one kind of cause. For example, the capacity for primary intersubjectivity might be impaired because of defective social orienting (e.g., Leekam, 2005), imitation (e.g., Williams et al., 2001), or timing (Wimpory, Nicholas, & Nash, 2002; see also Feldman, 2007), or because of impaired integration of the cognitive and affective components of social experience (e.g., Mundy, 2003).

By contrast, in the literature on the neurobiology of ASDs it is now common to describe the set of overlapping conditions as a disconnection syndrome in which the critical brain abnormalities are of a single kind, in that they are all characterized by a lack of structural or functional connectivity (Belmonte et al., 2004; Courchesne, 2004; Geschwind & Levitt, 2007). Thus the social interaction impairments (in which I would include emotion-processing and communicative use-of-language impairments) are seen as deriving from impaired connectivity within amygdala-prefrontal circuitry; restricted, repetitive behaviors and lack of imagination may be seen as deriving from impaired connectivity between certain frontal regions and distal cortical regions; and sensory-perceptual anomalies may be seen as deriving from impaired connectivity favoring activity within local neural networks as opposed to more global networks. To this I—and many others—would add impaired connectivity within circuitry subserving emotion-related and declarative forms of memory, including the amygdala, hippocampus, and subregions of prefrontal cortex; plus peri- and entorhinal medial temporal cortex in the case of LFA only.

Baron-Cohen's (2003) "extreme male brain" theory is another in which brain abnormalities leading to ASD-related behaviors are seen as all of a kind, and in this respect unified. Similarly, it has been suggested that ASDs result from an imbalance between the development of gray and white matter (Bonilha et al., 2007). According to all these theories, the varied set of behaviors associated with ASDs are explicable in terms of a single kind of brain abnormality, in much the same way as the varied set of behavioral presentations in tuberous sclerosis are explicable in terms of the different sites in the brain in which tuberous growths have formed.

Regardless of how one rates the individual theories in terms of evidence and argument, it is easy to see how, in each case, a single kind of brain abnormality might "fan out" to produce dissociable psychological deficits and diverse behavioral impairments. It will be very much harder to explain how the multiplicity of susceptibility factors underlying ASDs might in their different combinations "fan in" to produce a disconnection syndrome, let alone an extreme form of the male brain (Fisher, 2006)[3]. Even in the case of tuberous sclerosis, where the genetic bases of the condition are relatively well understood, environmental factors in the broadest sense—i.e., considered to include the internal environments in which development takes place from conception onwards—must almost certainly be invoked to explain variations in brain development across individuals (see, for example, explanations for the fact that monozygosity is not invariably associated with concordance for autism: Kates et al., 2004; Le Couteur et al., 1996). However, Goodman's (1989) concept of shared vulnerability, mediated by factors such as shared neurotransmitters or shared developmental periods of maximum vulnerability, offers the right kind of explanation, and the concept of shared vulnerability now figures in most hypotheses concerning links between etiological factors and brain anomalies in people with ASDs (for examples, see Bauman & Kemper, 2005).

Future accounts of any "fan in" processes (assuming that the model of convergence onto a single kind of brain abnormality is upheld) will also have to explain why certain facets of ability are so notably spared, not only in high-functioning individuals but also in some with low-functioning autistic disorder. The common and possibly universal co-occurrence of uneven motor skills, and the less common but nevertheless non-random co-occurrence of numerous other psychological and physical abnormalities, will also have to be explained. This may seem like a counsel of perfection. However, the practical importance of differentiating causal routes to the life-enhancing capacities associated with ASDs from causal routes to those characteristics that limit possibilities for a high quality of life, increases as possibilities for prevention draw closer.

---

3. The phrases "fan in" and "fan out" are taken from Belmonte et al., 2004.

References

American Psychiatric Association. (1980). *Diagnostic and Statistical Manual of Mental Disorders* (3rd ed.). Washington D.C.: Author.

American Psychiatric Association (1987). *Diagnostic and Statistical Manual of Mental Disorders* (3rd ed., revised). Washington D.C.: Author.

American Psychiatric Association (1994). *Diagnostic and Statistical Manual of Mental Disorders* (4th ed.). Washington D.C.: Author.

Arndt, T., Stodgell, C., & Rodier, P. (2005). The teratology of autism. *International Journal of Developmental Neuroscience, 23*, 189–199.

Ashwood, P., & Van de Water, J. (2004). Is autism an autoimmune disease? *Autoimmunity Reviews, 3*, 557–562.

Bailey, A., Phillips, W., & Rutter, M. (1996). Autism: Toward an integration of clinical, genetic, neuropsychological, and neurobiological perspective. *Journal of Child Psychology and Psychiatry, 37*, 89–126.

Baron-Cohen, S. (1989). Do autistic children have obsessions and compulsions? *British Journal of Clinical Psychology, 28*, 193–2000.

Baron-Cohen, S. (2003). *The Essential difference: Male and female brains and the truth about autism.* New York: Basic Books.

Baron-Cohen, S., Knickmeyer, R., & Belmonte, M. (2005). Sex differences in the brain: Implications for explaining autism. *Science, 310.no.5749*, 819–823.

Bauman, M. L., & Kemper, T. L. (2005). *The neurobiology of autism.* Baltimore, MD: Johns Hopkins Press.

Belmonte, M., Cook, E., Anderson, G., Rubenstein, R., Greenough, W., Beckel-Mitchener, A.,Tierney, E. (2004). Autism as a disorder of neural information processing: Directions for research and targets for therapy. *Molecular Psychiatry, 9*, 646–663.

Bespalova, I., Reichert, J., & Buxbaum, J. (2005). Candidate susceptibility genes for autism. In M. Bauman & T. Kemper (Eds.), *The neurobiology of autism* (pp. 217–232). Baltimore: John Hopkins.

Bettelheim, B. (1967). *The empty fortress: Infantile autism and the birth of the self.* New York: The Free Press.

Beversdorf, D., Manning, S., Hillier, A., Anderson, S., Nordgren, R., Walter, S., Nagaraja, H., Cooley, W., Gaelic, S., & Bauman, M. (2005). Timing of prenatal stressors and autism. *Journal of Autism and Developmental Disorders, 35*, 471–478.

Bishop, D. V. M. (1989). Asperger's syndrome and semantic-pragmatic disorder: Where are the boundaries? *British Journal of Disorders of Communication, 24*, 107–121.

Bolton, P., Macdonald, H., Pickles, A., Rios, P., Goode, S., Crowson, M.... Rutter, M. (1994). A case-control family history study of autism. *Journal of Child Psychology and Psychiatry, 35*, 877–900.

Bonilha, L., Cendes, F., Rorden, C., Eckert, M., Dalgalarrondo, P., Min Li, L., & Steiner, C. (2007). Gray and white matter imbalance–Typical structural abnormality underlying classic autism? *Brain and Development, 30,* 396–401.

Boucher, J. (1975). A neuropsychological approach to the study of autism: Two exploratory hypotheses. Unpublished doctoral dissertation, University of Birmingham, UK.

Boucher, J. (1976). Is autism primarily a language disorder? *British Journal of Disorders of Communication, 11,* 135–143.

Boucher, J. (1996). What could possibly explain autism? In P. Carruthers & P. K. Smith (Eds.), *Theories of theory of mind* (pp. 223–241). Oxford: Oxford University Press.

Boucher, J. (2006). Is the search for a unitary explanation of autism justified? *Journal of Autism and Developmental Disorders, 36,* 289.

Boucher, J. (2009). *The autistic spectrum: Characteristics, causes and practical issues.* London: Sage.

Boucher, J., Mayes, A., & Bigham, S. (2008). Memory, language, and intellectual ability in low functioning autism. In J. Boucher & D. M. Bowler (Eds.), *Memory in Autism* (pp. 268–290). Cambridge: Cambridge University Press.

Brown, R., Hobson, R. P., Lee, A., & Stevenson, J. (1997). Are there "autistic-like" features in congenitally blind children? *Journal of Child Psychology and Psychiatry, 38,* 693–703.

Chess, S. (1977). Follow-up report on autism in congenital rubella. *Journal of Autism and Childhood Schizophrenia, 7,* 69–81.

Churchill, D. W. (1972). The relation of infantile autism and early childhood schizophrenia to developmental language disorders of childhood. *Journal of Autism and Childhood Schizophrenia, 2,* 182–197.

Coltheart, M., & Langdon, R. (1998). Autism, modularity and levels of explanation in cognitive science. *Mind and Language, 13,* 138–152.

Courchesne, E. (2004). Brain development in autism: Early overgrowth followed by premature arrest of growth. *Mental Retardation and Developmental Disabilities Research Reviews, 10,* 106–111.

Creak, M. (1961). Schizophrenic syndrome in childhood: Progress report of a working party. *Cerebral Palsy Bulletin, 3,* 501–504.

Dakin, S., & Frith, U. (2005). Vagaries of visual perception in autism. *Neuron, 48,* 497–507.

Damasio, A., & Maurer, R. (1978). A neurological model for childhood autism. *Archives of Neurology, 35,* 777–786.

Dawson, G., Webb, S., Schellenberg, G., Dager, S., Friedman, S. et al. (2002). Defining the broader phenotype of autism: Genetic, brain, and behavioral perspectives. *Development and Psychopathology, 14,* 581–611.

Dykens, E. & Volkmar, F. (1997). Medical conditions associated with autism. In D. Cohen & F. Volkmar (Eds.), *Handbook of autism and pervasive developmental disorders* (2nd ed) (pp. 388–407). New York: John Wiley.

Dziuk, A., Larson, J. G., Apostu, A., Mahone, E., Denkla, M., & Mostofsky, S. (2007). Dyspraxia in autism: Association with motor, social, and communicative deficits. *Developmental Medicine and Child Neurology, 49,* 734–739.

Erickson, C., Stigler, K., Corkins, M., Posey, D., Fitzgerald, J., & McDougle, C. (2005). Gastrointestinal factors in autistic disorder: A critical review. *Journal of Autism and Developmental Disorders, 35,* 713–727.

Fein, D., Humes, M., Kaplan, E., Lucci, D., & Waterhouse, L. (1984). The question of left hemisphere dysfunction in infantile autism. *Psychological Bulletin, 95,* 258–281.

Feldman, R. (2007). Parent-infant synchrony and the construction of shared timing; physiological precursors, developmental outcomes, and risk conditions. *Journal of Child Psychology and Psychiatry, 48,* 329–354.

Ferster, C. B. (1961). Positive reinforcement and behavioral deficits of autistic children. *Child Development, 32,* 437–456.

Filipek, P. (2005). Medical aspects of autism. In F. Volkmar, R. Paul, A. Klin, & D. Cohen (Eds.), *Handbook of autism and pervasive developmental disorders* (3rd ed., pp. 534–578). New York: John Wiley.

Fisher, S. (2006). Tangled webs: Tracing the connections between genes and cognition. *Cognition, 101,* 270–297.

Folstein, S. E., Santangelo, S. L., Gilman, S. E., Piven, J., Landa, R., Lainhart, J....Wzorek, M. (1999). Predictors of cognitive test patterns in autism families. *Journal of Child Psychology and Psychiatry, 40,* 1117–1128.

Frith, U. (1989). *Autism: Explaining the enigma* (1st ed.). Oxford: Blackwell.

Geschwind, D. & Levitt, P. (2007). Autism spectrum disorders: Developmental disconnection syndromes. *Current Opinion in Neurobiology, 17,* 103–111.

Ghaziuddin, M., Tsai, L. Y., Eilers, L., & Ghaziuddin N. (1992). Autism and herpes simplex encephalitis. *Journal of Autism and Developmental Disorders, 22,* 107–114.

Gillberg, C. (1986). Onset at age 14 of a typical autistic syndrome. A case report of a girl with herpes simplex encephalitis. *Journal of Autism and Developmental Disorders, 16,* 369–375.

Goodman, R. (1989). Infantile autism: A syndrome of multiple primary deficits? *Journal of Autism and Developmental Disorders, 19,* 409–424.

Gutierrez, G., Smalley, S., & Tanguay, P. (1998). Autism in tuberous sclerosis complex. *Journal of Autism and Developmental Disorders, 28,* 97–104.

Happé, F. & Frith, U. (2006). The weak coherence account: Detail-focused cognitive style in autism spectrum disorders. *Journal of Autism and Developmental Disorders, 36,* 5–23.

Happé, F., Frith, U., & Briskman, J. (2001). Exploring the cognitive phenotype of autism: Weak "central coherence" in parents and siblings of children with autism: I. Experimental findings. *Journal of Child Psychology and Psychiatry, 42*, 299–307.

Happé, F., Ronald, A., & Plomin, R. (2006). Time to give up on a single explanation for autism. *Nature Neuroscience, 9*, 1218–1220.

Harris, S., MacKay, L., & Osborn, J. (1995). Autistic behaviors in offspring of mothers abusing alcohol and other drugs: A series of case reports. *Alcoholism: Clinical and Experimental Research, 19*, 660–665.

Hetzler, B., & Griffin, J. (1981). Infantile autism and the temporal lobe of the brain. *Journal of Autism and Developmental Disorders, 11*, 317–330.

Hultman, C., Sparen, P., & Cnattingius, S. (2002). Perinatal risk factors for infantile autism. *Epidemiology, 13*, 417–423.

Hutt, S., Hutt, C., Lee, D., & Ounsted, C., (1964). Arousal and childhood autism. *Nature, 204*, 908.

Kanner, L. (1943). Autistic disturbances of affective contact. *Nervous Child, 2*, 217–250.

Kates, W., Burnette, C., Eliez, S., Strunge, L.A., Kaplan, D. , Landa, R.... Pearlson, G. (2004). Neuroanatomic variation in monozygotic twin pairs discordant for the narrow phenotype for autism. *American Journal of Psychiatry, 161*, 539–546.

Kjelgaard, M., & Tager-Flusberg, H. (2001). An investigation of language profiles in autism: Implications for genetic subgroups. *Language and Cognitive Processes, 16*, 287–308.

Le Couteur, A., Bailey, A., Goode, S., Pickles, A., Robertson, S., Gottesman, I., & Rutter, M. (1996). A broader phenotype of autism: The clinical spectrum in twins. *Journal of Child Psychology and Psychiatry, 37*, 785–801.

Leekam, S. (2005). Why do children with autism have a joint attention impairment? In N. Eilan, C. Hoerl, T. McCormack, & J. Roessler (Eds.), *Joint attention: Communication and other minds* (pp. 205–229). Oxford: Oxford University Press.

Libby, J., Sweeten, T., McMahon, W. & Fujinami, R. (2005). Autistic disorder and viral infections. *International Journal of Developmental Science, 23*, 235–243.

Lord, C., & Paul, R. (1997). Language and communication in autism. In D. Cohen & F. Volkmar (Eds.), *Handbook of autism and pervasive developmental disorders* (2nd ed., pp. 195–225). New York: John Wiley.

McCann, R. (1981). Hemispheric asymmetries and early infantile autism. *Journal of Autism and Developmental Disorders, 11*, 401–411.

Mahler, M. (1952). On child psychosis and schizophrenia: Autistic and symbiotic psychosis. *Psychoanalytic Study of the Child, 7*, 286–305.

Mottron, L., & Burack, J. (2001). Enhanced perceptual functioning in the development of autism. In J. Burack, T. Charman, N. Yirmiya, & P. R. Zelazo (Eds.), *The Development of Autism: Perspectives From Theory and Research* (pp. 131–148). Hove: Lawrence Earlbaum Associates.

Mottron, L., & Burack, J. (2006). Editorial preface. *Journal of Autism and Developmental Disorders, 36*, 1–3.

Mundy, P. (2003). The neural basis of social impairments in autism: The role of the dorsal medial-frontal cortex and anterior cingulate system. *Journal of Child Psychology and Psychiatry, 44*, 793–809.

Oberman, L., & Ramachandran, V. (2007). The simulating social mind: The role of the mirror neuron system and simulation in the social and communicative deficits of autism spectrum disorders. *Psychological Bulletin, 133*, 310–327.

Ornitz, E., & Ritvo, E. (1968). Neurophysiologic mechanisms underlying perceptual inconstancy in autistic and schizophrenic children. *Archives of General Psychiatry, 19*, 76–98.

Ozonoff, S., Cook, I., Coon, H., Dawson, G., Joseph, R., Klin, A., McMahon, W., Minshew, N., Munson, J., Pennington, B., Rogers, S., Spence, M., Tager-Flusberg, H., Volkmar, F., & Wrathall, D. (2004). Performance on Cambridge neuropsychological test automated battery subtests sensitive to frontal lobe function in people with autistic disorder. *Journal of Autism and Developmental Disorders, 34*, 139–150.

Page, J., & Boucher, J. (1998). Motor impairments in children with autistic disorder. *Child Language, Teaching, and Therapy, 14*, 233–259.

Pelphrey, K., Adolphs, R., & Morris, J.P. (2004). Neuroanatomical substrates of social cognition dysfunction in autism. *Mental Retardation and Developmental Disabilities Research Reviews, 10*, 259–271.

Pickles, A., Starr, E., Kazak, S., Bolton, P., Papanikolaou, K., Bailey, A.... Rutter, M. (2000). Variable expression of the autism broader phenotype: Findings from extended pedigrees. *Journal of Child Psychology and Psychiatry, 41*, 491–502.

Rajendran, G., & Mitchell, P. (2007). Cognitive theories of autism. *Developmental Review, 27*, 224–260.

Rapin, I. (1996). Neurological issues. In I. Rapin (Ed.), *Preschool children with inadequate communication* (pp. 98–112). Cambridge: Mac Keith Press.

Ricks, D. M. & Wing, L. (1975). Language, communication, and the use of symbols in normal and autistic children. *Journal of Autism and Developmental Disorders, 5*, 191–221.

Rimland, B. (1964). *Infantile autism*. New York: Appleton-Century-Crofts.

Rippon, G., Brock, J., Brown, C., & Boucher, J. (2007). Disordered connectivity in the autistic brain: Challenges for the new psychophysiology. *International Journal of Psychophysiology, 63*, 164–172.

Ritvo, E., & Freeman, B. (1977). National Society for Autistic Children definition of the syndrome of autism. *Journal of Pediatric Psychology, 2*, 146–148.

Rosenhall, U., Nordin, V., Sandstroem, M., Ahlsen, G., & Gillberg, C. (1999). Autism and hearing loss. *Journal of Autism and Developmental Disorders, 29*, 349–357.

Russell, J. (1997). How executive disorders can bring about an inadequate "theory of mind." In J. Russell (Ed.), *Autism as an executive disorder* (pp. 256–299). Oxford: Oxford University Press.

Rutter, M. (1968). Concepts of autism: A review of research. *Journal of Child Psychology and Psychiatry*, 9, 1–25.

Rutter, M. (2005). Aetiology of autism: Findings and questions. *Journal of Intellectual Disability Research*, 49, 231–238.

Rutter, M., Anderson-Wood, L., Beckett, C., Bredenkamp, D., Castle, J., Groothues, C.... O'Connor, T. (1999). Quasi-autistic patterns following severe early global privation. *Journal of Child Psychology and Psychiatry*, 40, 537–550.

Schultz, R. (2005). Developmental deficits in social perception in autism: The role of the amygdala and fusiform gyrus. *International Journal of Developmental Neuroscience*, 23, 125–141.

Tanguay, P. (1984). Toward a new classification of serious psychopathology in children. *Journal of the American Academy of Child Psychiatry*, 23, 378–384.

Tuchman, R., & Rapin, I. (2002). Epilepsy in autism. *Lancet Neurology*, 1, 352–358.

Tustin, F. (1981). *Autism and childhood psychosis.* London: Hogarth Press.

Tustin, F. (1991). Revised understanding of psychogenic autism. *International Journal of Psychoanalysis*, 72, 585–591.

Welch, M. (1984). Retrieval from autism through mother-child holding. In E. Tinbergen & N. Tinbergen (Eds.), *Autistic children–New hope for a cure* (pp. 322–336). London: Allen & Unwin.

Williams, D., Botting, N., & Boucher, J. (2008). Language in autism and specific language impairment: Where are the links? *Psychological Bulletin*, 134, 944–963.

Williams, J., Whiten, A., Suddendorf, T., & Perrett, D. (2001). Imitation, mirror neurons and autism. *Neuroscience and Biobehavioral Reviews*, 25, 287–295.

Wimpory, D., Nicholas, B., & Nash, S. (2002). Social timing, clock genes and autism: A new hypothesis. *Journal of Intellectual Disability Research*, 46, 352–358.

Wing, L. (1981). Asperger's syndrome: A clinical account. *Psychological Medicine*, 11, 115–129.

Wing, L. (1988). The continuum of autistic characteristics. In E. Schopler and G. Mesibov (Eds.), *Diagnosis and assessment in autism* (pp. 91–110). New York: Plenum Press.

Wing, L., & Gould, J. (1979). Severe impairments of social interaction and associated abnormalities in children: Epidemiology and classification. *Journal of Autism and Childhood Schizophrenia*, 9, 11–29.

World Health Organization (1992). *International classification of mental and behavioral disorders: Clinical descriptions and diagnostic guidelines* (10th ed.). Geneva: Author.

Chapter 24

Autism Endophenotypes Are Not Unified by Gene Variants or Chromosome Number Variants

Lynn Waterhouse

INTRODUCTION

Researchers have claimed that it is crucial to study homogeneous autism samples in order to determine the genetic basis of autism (Folstein, 2006; Goos, 2008; Vernes et al., 2008). Forming homogeneous autism samples is difficult, however, because the diagnosis of autism includes immense phenotypic heterogeneity. Goos (2008) asserted that using diagnosis as a phenotype in genetic studies "is a very serious mistake, as heterogeneity is rampant within diagnostic categories, and individuals with the same diagnosis may vary significantly in phenotype and etiology, even in the presence of high heritability" (p. 270). Consequently, autism endophenotypes—brain deficits or behavioral impairments thought to be linked to a single gene mutation or chromosome alteration—may offer a better opportunity to map brain or behavior autism traits onto genetic variants (Duvall Lu, Cantor, Constantino, & Geschwind, 2007; Happé & Ronald, 2008; Lam, Bodfish, & Piven, 2008;

Liu, Paterson, & Szatmari, 2008; Reiss, 2009; Spence et al., 2006).

However, the majority of gene mutations and chromosome copy number variants (CNV) associated with autism are also associated with non-autism phenotypes (Abrahams & Geschwind, 2008; Happé & Ronald, 2008; Joober & Bokva, 2009; Kramer & Bokhov, 2009; Lintas & Persico, 2009; Marshall et al., 2008; Morrow et al., 2008; Schanen, 2006; Veenstra-VanderWeele, Christian & Cook, 2004). This link between autism and non-autism phenotypes is both the result of pleiotrophic effects of single gene mutations on phenotypic traits, and of dosage effects in chromosome duplications and deletions. Consequently, autism endophenotypes also share gene variants and chromosome copy number variants with other syndromes and conditions (Christian et al., 2008; Hoffman & State, 2010; Lintas & Persico, 2009; Marshall et al., 2008; Schanen, 2006). Therefore, as the autism phenotype and individual autism endophenotypes share nearly all their many gene, chromosomal, or epigenetic sources with other disorders, it may be more useful to define multiple subsyndromes by unitary gene system causes, rather than by the general behavioral syndrome of autism. One reason is that future genetic treatments will require the identification of gene system causes (the problem of diagnosis and gene causal factors is discussed in section three below).

This chapter comprises three sections. The first section summarizes current revisions to molecular genetics which are relevant to the increasing complexity facing genetics research in autism. This section argues that new findings for genetic and chromosomal variation and molecular epigenetics will help uncover many more gene-system sources for autism. The second section reviews gene-system sources associated with autism endophenotypes. This section reports that the three diagnostic endophenotypes—social impairment, language impairment, and restricted and repetitive behaviors—and two nondiagnostic endophenotypes—macrocephaly and intellectual disability—are each associated with more than one gene-system source. As these five endophenotypes are not differentiated by gene-system source, they do not serve to form meaningful causal groups. The third section considers the efforts to maintain the syndrome diagnosis of autism, despite the wide range of recent genetic and chromosomal findings. This section argues that because single-gene mutations and chromosome copy number variants associated with autism have pleiotrophic expressions, wherein autism is just one expression of many varied expressions, the coherence of the autism syndrome is increasingly frayed, as more gene-system sources for autism are discovered. The chapter concludes that autism is a portmanteau syndrome (Waterhouse, 2009), the contents of which must be separated out one by one in order to provide a coherent basis for genetic screening, or possible future treatment research.

RECENT REVISIONS TO MOLECULAR GENETICS

Until recently, molecular genetics research was based on a model in which only 1.2% of the human genome contained all 20,000 genes, and wherein each gene generates one protein, and each protein has one function. Gene-based diseases and disorders were thought to be caused either by rare single-gene mutations, or by the accumulation of multiple common chromosomal copy number variants (CNVs). A CNV is a segment of DNA of 1000 base pairs or more containing either multiple duplications or multiple deletions of DNA base pairs. Although these DNA base-pair duplications or deletions usually occur at a single locus, surprisingly, the duplications or deletions may occur at different loci on the chromosome. CNV regions may include hundreds of genes, disease-linked loci, and functional elements (Joober & Bokstra, 2009). Although researchers have identified more than 300 single-gene mutations linked to specific disorders, and more than 1400 CNVs have been discovered, these single-gene mutations and CNVs have only been able to account for less than 5% of the genetic heritability of common diseases, such as diabetes and heart disease. A massive amount of "genetic dark matter" is missing (Maher, 2008). Although twin and family studies suggest a 90% heritability for autism, autism-linked gene mutations and known CNVs identified to date explain perhaps 7–10% of that heritability (Abrahams & Geschwind, 2008; and see Chapter 2).

The missing "genetic dark matter" that might explain the heritability of autism and other disorders, such as diabetes and schizophrenia, may be found in novel mutations in genes and CNVs, and in the myriad of processes involved in the regulation of gene expression. Research has now shown that alternate splicing allows a single gene to generate multiple transcripts, each of which may produce a different protein (Seringhaus & Gerstein, 2008). Moreover, although gene exon regions were previously thought to be the only coding elements of the gene, it is now known that exons can be excluded from the final product, and non-gene sequences can be spliced into the transcript to produce a different protein. Still more surprising, Kapranov, Willingham, and Gingeras (2007) reported that more than 90% of the human genome could be transcribed. Transcription outside the known genes includes "pseudogenes, regions of the genome long considered fossils of past genes" (Seringhaus & Gerstein, 2008, p. 468). Adding further complexity to the system is the fact that many different genome variants overlap and "multifunctional usage of the same genomic space is common" (Kapranov et al., 2007, p. 414).

Greater variation in the genome base pair sequences has also recently been discovered. Khaja et al. (2006) reported finding 1,447 copy number variant (CNV) chromosome regions including approximately 30 million base pairs that span the entire

3 billion base pairs of our genome, and cover more than 2,900 genes, including many of the 285 single genes known to be associated with diseases. These 1,447 copy number variants are likely to co-function with the 2,900 genes they overlap, and perhaps co-function with non-gene regions of the genome as well. Christian et al. (2008) discovered 51 CNVs in 12% of 397 individuals with autism, and Marshall et al. (2008) reported 277 CNVs in 44% of ASD families. Joober and Bokstra (2009) noted that, although humans are resilient to many structural variants that affect hundreds of genes, CNVs are likely to explain a significant subpopulation of autism, because autism appears early in development and usually has a severe clinical expression.

In addition to the expanding DNA-sequence variation, greater epigenetic variation has also been uncovered, and the epigenome code is now seen as a significant force in the production of phenotypic traits. Epigenetics includes both the transitory and the heritable changes in gene function that occur without a change in the DNA sequence. Epigenetic action involves DNA methylation, histone acetylation, and RNA interference. DNA methylation marks the genomic chromatin to regulate gene expression. Even a histone code has been identified: histones control access to regulatory proteins and act in phosphorylation for DNA replication, thus contributing to regulation of gene expression (Happel & Doenecke, 2009).

Kaminsky et al. (2009) found significant variation in monozygotic (MZ) co-twin DNA methylation in the absence of DNA sequence variation. They concluded that an individual's epigenome could account for considerable phenotypic variation. Reid, Gallais, and Metivier (2009) asserted that gene expression depends on which gene transcript is produced and what epigenetic modifications of chromatin have been made. Epigenetic mechanisms include *imprinting*, in which one parent's allele controls gene expression, *X-inactivation* of one of the two copies of the X chromosome, *gene silencing*, wherein histone modification switches off a gene, and many other mechanisms as well. Kaduake and Blobel (2009) proposed that even the physical structure of chromatin is likely to have phenotypic effects. They reported that chromatin loops form to block gene expression through blocking gene "enhancers and promoters from interacting productively perhaps by separating them physically" (p. 22).

In sum, the new data on the epigenome, the histone code, the CNV findings, and genome sequence functional complexity together create a revised model that seriously "challenges the notion that a DNA sequence in a single region is sufficient to describe a gene" (Seringhaus & Gerstein, 2008, p. 469).

This complexity can be seen in the finding that mutations in MECP2, a chromatin-associated protein that binds methylated CpGs to activate or repress transcription, is the cause of Rett syndrome, an autism spectrum disorder (Swanberg, Nagarajan, Peddada, Yasui, & LaSalle, 2009). The researchers found an interactive relationship between MECP2 and the activity-dependent early growth response gene 2 (*EGR2*), which is required for both brain development and mature neuron function. Most importantly, they reported that Rett syndrome and autism postmortem cortex samples showed a significant reduction in EGR2 protein, suggesting that EGR2 affects neuron development in both syndromes, even though MECP2 function in autism without Rett syndrome does not produce typical Rett syndrome phenotypic features.

Schanen (2006) claimed that autism linkage peaks met imprinting zones at 15q11–13, 7q21–31.31, 7q32.3–36.3, 4q21–31, 11p11.2–13, and 13q12.3, and epigenetic imprinting theories of autism have been proposed. Crespi and Badcock (2008) theorized that aberrant DNA methylation in imprinting can yield both psychosis and autism, leaving social cognition underdeveloped in autism, but dysfunctionally overdeveloped in psychosis. Jones, Skinner, Friez, Schwartz, and Stevenson (2007) theorized that autism is caused by hypomethylation or hypermethylation of CpG sites within gene promoters on the X chromosome, which leads to overexpression or partial silencing of one or more brain-expressed genes. Mehler and Purpura (2008) theorized that a dynamic epigenetic remodeling of the locus coeruleus and of the noradrenergic network of pre- and postsynaptic receptors might be the basis for autism.

GENE SYSTEM SOURCES OF AUTISM ENDOPHENOTYPES

Goos (2008) argued, "The use of endophenotypes in the study of complex psychiatric disorders is increasing, and has been shown to facilitate the identification of genetic risk factors" (p. 270). The majority of the few genetic studies that have explored autism endophenotypes have identified endophenotypes as the triad of diagnostic features of autism: impaired social function, impaired communication, and restricted, repetitive, and stereotyped patterns of behavior, interests, and activities.

Gene System Findings for Endophenotypes of Diagnostic Criteria for Autism

Happé and Ronald (2008) reported that each member of the diagnostic triad (impaired social interaction, communication deficits, and rigid or repetitive behaviors) is separately heritable. Vernes et al. (2008) also proposed that the diagnostic triad should be the basis for endophenotypes of autistic spectrum disorders. Happé, Ronald, and Plomin (2006) noted the lack of replication of linkage studies in autism, and they claimed that the triad of autism diagnostic features was only weakly correlated. Happé et al. (2006) and Mandy and Skuse (2008) proposed that studies should be conducted in autism samples that expressed primarily social impairment, or primarily communication impairment, or primarily restricted, repetitive, and stereotyped patterns of behavior, interests, and activities.

Table 24-1 outlines a selected set of recent findings for diagnostic and non-diagnostic autism endophenotypes. These findings for genetic studies of the three diagnostic autism endophenotypes are mixed.

Social impairment

Liu and colleagues (2008) found no genome-wide linkage for reciprocal social interaction in 976 multiplex families from the Autism Genome Project consortium. Duvall and colleagues (2007) also reported that a diagnostic endophenotype measure of social responsiveness was not significantly linked to any chromosomal regions they explored, although they did detect two possible associated regions on chromosome 11 and 17.

Conversely, Yrigollen and colleagues (2008) reported evidence for polymorphisms of the *PRL*, *PRLR*, and *OXTR* genes in 177 individuals diagnosed with ASD. Oxytocin (OT) is a peptide involved in affiliative behavior. Autistic children have been shown to have abnormal levels of plasma OT (Green et al., 2001; Modahl et al., 1998). Prolactin (PRL) is a pituitary hormonal peptide also found to play a key role in affiliative behaviors. The researchers found significant correlations between the presence of PRL receptor

gene (*PRLR*) polymorphisms and an endophenotype of social skill impairment.

Communication impairment

Vernes et al. (2008) found an association between the language endophenotype of nonsense word repetition and polymorphisms in the exon 13–15 region of *CNTNAP2* in children with specific language impairment. Alarcón et al. (2008) reported evidence of a significant link between a language endophenotype (age at first spoken word) and polymorphisms in the exon 13–15 region of *CNTNAP2* in autism. Vernes et al. argued that *CNTNAP2*-caused deficits appear in a pure form in specific language impairment, but *CNTNAP2*-caused deficits are only one contributor to the gene-system basis of autism. A genome-wide association study (GWAS) of individuals with autism by Arking and colleagues (2008) detected a significant linkage signal in the 7q35 region involving the *CNTNAP2* gene. Bakkaloglu and colleagues (2008) reported evidence for an association of autism and rare *CNTNAP2* variants.

Yrigollen et al. (2008) reported a pattern of significant correlations between polymorphisms of the *OXTR* and *OXT* genes and diagnostic endophenotypes for impaired communication skills in a sample of 177 autistic patients. However, Spence and colleagues (2006) found no linkage in a sample of 133 multiplex autism families for any chromosomal loci and either of two language endophenotypes: the delayed production of words, and the delayed production of phrases. Their study, however, did identify loci on chromosomes 1, 2, 4, 6, 7, 8, 9, 10, 12, 15, and 19 that showed somewhat higher linkage signals in the two language endophenotype subgroups.

Restricted or repetitive activities and interests

Lam and colleagues (2008) found familial aggregation associated with subtypes of the diagnostic endophenotype of restricted or repetitive activities and interests. Lam et al. (2008) identified three subgroups within the endophenotype: repetitive motor behaviors, insistence on sameness, and circumscribed interests. Using sibling-pair correlations, the researchers found that insistence on sameness and circumscribed interests were family-linked features. Yrigollen et al. (2008) found significant correlations between the

Table 24-1 Genetic Findings for Diagnostic and Non-Diagnostic Endophenotypes of Autism

Endophenotypes based on diagnostic criteria			
Authors	Sample	Endophenotype	Genetic Association
Duvall et al. (2007)	190 autism probands	social skill	weak linkage chromosome 11, 17
Liu et al. (2008)	976 autism families	social skill	no linkage
Yrigollen et al. (2008) from 151 families	177 ASD probands	social skill	PRLR polymorphisms
Spence et al. (2006)	133 autism families	language delay	no linkage
Alarcón et al. (2008) of autism families	304 parent-child trios	language delay	exon 13–15 region of CNTNAP2
Yrigollen et al. (2008) from 151 families	177 ASD probands	impaired communication	OXTR, OXT polymorphisms
Liu et al. (2008)	976 multiplex families	restricted, repetitive behaviors	no linkage
Yrigollen et al. (2008) from 151 families	177 ASD probands	restricted, repetitive behaviors	OXTR, OXT polymorphisms
Lam et al. (2008)	316 autism probands and 316 sibs	repetitive motor behaviors insistence on sameness circumscribed interests	no familial trait aggregation familial trait aggregation familial trait aggregation
Endophenotypes based on associated non-diagnostic features			
Authors	Sample	Endophenotype	Genetic Association
Butler et al. (2005)	18 autism patients with macrocephaly	macrocephaly	3 males with PTEN mutations
Buxbaum et al. (2007a)	88 autism patients with macrocephaly	macrocephaly	1 individual with PTEN mutation
Buxbaum et al. (2007b)	88 autism patients with macrocephaly	macrocephaly	no link to NSD1 gene mutations
Sacco et al. (2007)	241 patients with autism	macrocephaly	no link to serotonin (5-HT) blood levels
Mefford et al. (2008)	8 individuals duplication of 1q21.1	macrocephaly	4 individuals with autism and
Orrico et al. (2008)	40 patients with neuro-developmental disorders and macrocephaly	macrocephaly	PTEN mutations in 3 patients, 2 with autism
Tsuchiya et al. (2008)	17 males with autism	macrocephaly	inverse correlation of serum levels of PECAM-1 with head size
Brunetti-Pierri et al. (2008)	36 individuals with 1q21.1 deletions or duplications	intellectual disability	3 individuals with autism and intellectual disability
Mefford et al. (2008)	8 individuals with duplication of 1q21.1	intellectual disability	4 individuals with autism and intellectual disability
Cai et al. (2008)	279 autism patients	intellectual disability	4 with duplications in 15q11-q13 2 with duplications in 22q11 2 with duplications TM4SF2 gene

(continued)

Table 24-1 (continued)

	Endophenotypes based on non-diagnostic criteria		
Authors	Sample	Endophenotype	Genetic Association
			16 with ASMT duplications Xp22.32
			1 with ASPA deletion in 17p13
			1 with PAX6 deletion in 11p13
			1 with EXT1 deletion in 8q24
			1 with ARHGEF6 deletion in Xq26
Loat et al. (2008)	219 autism families	intellectual disability	significant link to MECP2 (Rett) site
Weiss et al. (2008)	811 patients with autism or intellectual disability	intellectual disability	8 with duplication in 16p11.2 4 with deletion in 16p11.2
Zingerevich et al. (2009)	48 children with FRX	intellectual disability	60% diagnosed with autism or ASD and intellectual disability

presence of PRL receptor gene (*PRLR*) polymorphisms and an endophenotype of stereotyped behaviors. The researchers also found a pattern of significant correlations between polymorphisms of the *OXTR* and *OXT* genes and diagnostic endophenotypes for stereotyped behaviors.

However, Liu and colleagues (2008) found no genome-wide linkage for restricted, repetitive, and stereotyped patterns of behavior in 976 multiplex families from the Autism Genome Project consortium.

Summary

Taken together, the evidence for gene-system sources for endophenotypes of autism based on diagnostic criteria suggests that not much explanatory ground has been gained by limiting studies to such endophenotypes. For example, although Yrigollen et al. (2008) found significant correlations between autism diagnostic endophenotypes and oxytocin and prolactin gene polymorphisms, the correlations were indiscriminate: i.e., polymorphisms of the *OXTR*, *OXT*, and *PRLR* genes were significantly correlated with *both* the diagnostic endophenotype for impaired communication skills *and* the diagnostic phenotype for stereotyped behaviors.

Gene System Findings for Endophenotypes of Non-Diagnostic Features of Autism

Macrocephaly and intellectual disability (ID) (formerly mental retardation)are two non-diagnostic features commonly found in significant subgroups of individuals diagnosed with autism. The prevalence of atypical increased head size (macrocephaly) or atypical increased brain size (megalencephaly) in autism has been identified variously at 0%, 14%, and 75%, depending on sample size and measurement employed (Redcay & Courchesne, 2005), and the prevalence of intellectual disability in autism is over 60% (Amaral, Schumann, & Nordahl, 2008). While both macrocephaly and ID may be meaningful endophenotypes of autism, neither of them can help to limit associated gene and chromosome variants, because it is already known that in samples of non-autistic patients, both ID and macrocephaly are associated with multiple single-gene mutations and CNVs.

Macrocephaly

Williams, Dagli, and Battaglia (2008) identified 164 conditions associated with macrocephaly. The condition most commonly found in autism with macrocephaly is a *PTEN* gene mutation. The *PTEN* gene generates the phosphatase and tensin homolog protein, in which the phosphatase is involved in preventing cells from growing and dividing too rapidly. As can be seen in Table 24-1, Orrico et al. (2009) reported that in 40 patients with neurodevelopmental disorders and macrocephaly, three novel de novo missense *PTEN* gene mutations were found (p.H118P, p.Y176C, p.N276S) in two severely intellectually disabled patients with autism, and in a subject with neurodevelopmental disorders without autistic features. Butler et al. (2005) studied 18 children with autism spectrum disorder and macrocephaly. Of these 18 boys and girls, each with a head circumference range from 2.5 to 8.0 standard deviations above the mean, the three boys with the largest head circumference were found to carry previously undescribed germline PTEN mutations: H93R (exon 4), D252G (exon 7), and F241S (exon 7). Buxbaum et al. (2007a) found only one boy with PTEN mutations in a sample of 88 individuals with autism who also had macrocephaly.

However, Buxbaum et al. (2007b) screened for the NSD1 gene in a sample of 88 individuals diagnosed with autism who also had macrocephaly; the researchers found no mutations or deletions in the NSD1gene and concluded that the related Sotos syndrome is a rare cause of autism macrocephaly. Moreover, Sacco et al. (2007) studied 241 patients with autism and found no association between macrocephaly and blood levels of serotonin (5-HT).

Other genes and chromosome copy number variants have been associated with macrocephaly in autism. Tsuchiya et al. (2008) reported that serum levels of platelet-endothelial adhesion molecule PECAM-1 and vascular cell adhesion molecule VCAM-1 in subjects with high-functioning autism were lower than those of age-matched controls, and that serum levels of PECAM-1 were negatively correlated with head circumference at birth in autism. Both VCAM-1 and PECAM-1 contribute to the regulation of endothelial cells.

Intellectual disability

The 60% of individuals with autism and intellectual disability have not often been studied as a group, because the presence of intellectual disability has been incorrectly argued to be a separate comorbid syndrome affecting individuals with autism (Waterhouse, 2008). However, the 66 single-gene mutations Wall and colleagues (2009) identified as present in autism families are associated with mild to moderate intellectual disability. Moreover, the chromosome region copy number variants associated with autism (1p, 1q, 2q37, 3q, 4q21–31, 5p, 6q, 7q21–31.31, 7q32.3–36.3, 8q, 11p11.2–13, 13q12.3, 15q11–13, 15q24, 16p11.2, 17q11, 19p, 22q11.2, and Xq 6, 21, 30, 62, 82, 102, 110, 120; Veenstra-VanderWeele et al., 2004) are associated with phenotypic expression of mild to moderate intellectual disability. Joober and Bokva (2009) noted, "low IQ is a quasi-constant manifestation of large chromosomal anomalies" (p. 58).

Kramer and van Bokhoven (2009) stated that 2 to 3% of the world population has some form of intellectual disability: over 300 genes have been identified, and there are already more than a thousand Mendelian disorders associated with intellectual disability.

The current world population prevalence of autism is estimated to be seven-tenths of one percent, of which more than 60% have intellectual disability. As 90% of autism is estimated to have a genetic basis, therefore nearly one half of one percent of the general world population would be expected to have gene-based autism with intellectual disability. This autism with intellectual disability population is likely to express autism and ID as a consequence of gene-system variants that give rise to both autism and ID.

In fact, the pleiotrophic effects of a given individual gene mutation, or the dosage effects of chromosome copy number variant, do not just include autism features co-occurring with intellectual disability: the pleiotrophic variation and dosage range of phenotypic traits can be extremely large. For example, Miller et al. (2008) reported that 10 of 1,441 individuals with autism spectrum disorders (ASD) had segmental alterations at breakpoints four and five (BP4-BP5) of chromosome 15q13.2q13.3. The BP4-BP5 alterations included deletions and duplications spanning CHRNA7, a candidate gene for seizures. However, none of the 10 individuals with the BP4-BP5 alterations had epilepsy or seizures, although one individual had an abnormal EEG. These ten individuals did have significant expressive language deficits, and subsets of the 10 individuals were diagnosed with autism, ADHD, anxiety disorder, and mood disorder. Cognitive impairment varied from moderate intellectual disability to normal IQ with learning disability. This pleiotrophic range illustrated by Miller and colleagues (2008) better explains intellectual disability in autism, than does the claim that intellectual disability in autism is a separate comorbid disorder.

Table 24-1 outlines the association of intellectual disability and autism. Cai and colleagues (2008) found that about 1% of their autistic sample had chromosome and gene duplications and deletions. Duplications included 15q11-q13, 22q11, TM4SF2 gene, ASMT Xp22.32, and deletions occurred in ASPA in 17p13, PAX6 in 11p13, EXT1 in 8q24, and ARHGEF6 in Xq26. These duplications and deletions also produced intellectual disability.

Loat et al. (2008) found MECP2 in association with autism and develop delay. Weiss et al (2008) found intellectual disability and autism in association with deletions and duplications in 16p11.2. Brunetti-Pierri et al. (2008) and Mefford et al. (2008) found intellectual disability and autism in association with deletions or duplications in 1q21.1.

Intellectual disability and macrocephaly

A problem with defining intellectual disability (ID) and macrocephaly as separate endophenotypes of autism is that they can occur together as related features. At least one chromosomal locus linked to autism, 1q21.1, yields both abnormal head size and intellectual disability. Brunetti-Pierri and colleagues (2008) studied a large sample of individuals with microdeletion and microduplication at 1q21.1. The researchers found dosage effects such that head circumference was significantly smaller in 21 of 29 individuals, with a microdeletion at 1q21.1, whereas head circumference was significantly larger in 10 of 24 individuals, with microduplication at 1q21.1. Mefford and colleagues (2008) screened 5218 individuals with idiopathic intellectual disability, autism, or congenital anomalies and found 25 unrelated individuals with overlapping deletions of 1q21.1 and 8 individuals with the reciprocal duplication of 1q21.1. Mefford et al. (2008) also reported significant dosage effects for 1q21.1: deletions were associated with microcephaly, and duplications were associated with macrocephaly. Both deletions and duplications, however, were associated with mild-to-moderate intellectual disability. Seven of the eight individuals who were carriers of the 1q21.1 duplication had intellectual disability, and four of the seven had macrocephaly. The researchers also found that four of the seven had autistic behaviors or autism. In these two studies macrocephaly, autism, and intellectual disability are co-occurring phenotypic features of the 1q21.1 duplication.

As can be seen in the data in Table 24-1, and from Miller et al. (2008), Joober and Bokva (2009), and Wall et al. (2009), and the reviews of Abrahams and Geschwind (2008) and Veenstra-VanderWeele et al. (2004), as well as Chapter 2, intellectual disability *cannot* be an endophenotype of autism. Ramocki and Zoghbi (2008) concluded that chromosome deletion and duplication, the "functional loss or gain of proteins or RNAs involved in diverse processes leads to intellectual disability, autism and other neuropsychiatric symptoms" (p. 217). They also argued that there are likely to be thousands of genes whose alteration results in intellectual disability or autism or both.

Intellectual disability and autism diagnostic features may occur together when they are pleiotropic effects of a single gene mutation, or when they are phenotypic expressions of the same chromosome copy number variant. There are so many CNVs and single-gene mutations that give rise to autism co-occurring with intellectual disability, that creating an ID endophenotype of autism gains no inferential ground.

Summary

As with the diagnostic endophenotypes, explorations of intellectual disability and macrocephaly as endophenotypes of autism have so far done little to increase the homogeneity of gene sources. Instead, new findings have suggested the inherent complexity of single-gene mutation pleiotrophy and chromosome number duplication and deletion dosage effects in creating a wide range of aspects of phenotypic expression, and have highlighted the co-occurrences of autism and intellectual disability, as well as autism and intellectual disability and macrocephaly.

GENE SOURCES UNDERMINE THE AUTISM DIAGNOSTIC PHENOTYPE

Maher (2008) noted that, "Medicine tries hard to lump together a complex collection of symptoms and call it a disease. But if thousands of rare genetic variants contribute to a single disease, and the genetic underpinnings can vary radically for different people, how common is it? Are these, in fact, different diseases?" (p. 7). At present, despite the wide variation in gene-based sources, and despite the syndrome overlaps between autism and other syndromes, autism continues to be diagnosed as a unitary behavioral syndrome, and research is conducted on samples defined by diagnosis. The problems with maintaining autism as a single syndrome are revealed in the effort to isolate syndromic autism from idiopathic autism, in the effort to construct unified gene-based theories of autism, in the lack of coverage of gene and CNV findings to date, and in the emerging case-carrier examinations of individual chromosome copy number variants.

The Effort to Maintain Syndromic Autism versus Idiopathic Autism: Fragile X Syndrome, Rett Syndrome, Cortical Dysplasia-Focal Epilepsy Syndrome and Autism

The problem of "what makes autism a syndrome?" can be seen in the relationship of autism to fragile X syndrome (FRX), Rett syndrome (RTT), and to cortical dysplasia-focal epilepsy syndrome (CDFES). A diagnosis of autism in fragile X syndrome, Rett syndrome, or cortical dysplasia-focal epilepsy syndrome has been defined as "syndromic autism," and has been argued to include only 10% of cases of autism (Lintas & Persico, 2009). The remainder of autism is identified as "idiopathic autism." Although fragile X and Rett syndrome are both now excluded from the diagnosis of autism, shared gene-system sources do link autism to Rett syndrome, fragile X syndrome, and cortical dysplasia-focal epilepsy syndrome.

Rett syndrome and autism

Monteggia and Kavalali (2009) noted that Rett syndrome is defined by mutations in the *MECP2* gene in the 15q11-13 region. They concluded that epigenetic regulation of gene expression for those genes within the 15q11-13 region for all these disorders is critical for development of the neural circuits involved in social behaviors, language, and cognition. Thus, Rett syndrome with autism diagnostic features, Rett syndrome without autism diagnostic features, and autism without Rett syndrome may all arise from mutations in the *MECP2* gene within the CNV in 15q11-13.

Schanen (2006) claimed that duplications of the *MECP2* gene in chromosome 15q11–13 occurred in up to 5% of individuals with ASD, and that parent-of-origin effect on chromosome 15q duplications indicated that imprinted genes in this region contributed to ASD. Hogart, Nagarajan, Patzel, Yasui, and LaSalle (2007) posited that epigenetic dysregulation of the 15q11-13 GABAA receptor cluster results in aberrant expression levels of *GABRB3* in multiple neurodevelopmental disorders, including Rett syndrome and autism. The researchers noted that epigenetic methylation of an intronic sequence of *GABRB3* serves as a binding site for MECP2, and that MECP2 is a positive regulator of *GABRB3* expression. Hogart et al. (2007) found that autism samples with loss of biallelic expression of any one of the 15q11-13 GABAA receptor subunit genes had significantly reduced GABRB3 protein levels. Swanberg and colleagues (2009) reported that EGR2 and MECP2 co-regulate one another in both Rett syndrome and autism.

Should there be an *EGR2-MECP2-GABRB3* gene mutation network Rett syndrome? This would imply an *EGR2-MECP2-GABRB3* gene mutation network autism-without Rett syndrome features, and an *EGR2-MECP2-GABRB3* gene network mutation Rett syndrome without autism features.

How should non-Rett syndrome autism and Rett syndrome with an associated diagnosis of autism be differentiated where both are linked to the presence of a *MECP2* gene mutation and an associated dysfunction in a gene network?

Fragile X syndrome and autism

Zingerevich et al. (2009) reported that 60% of a sample of 48 children with fragile X syndrome met the diagnostic criteria for autism or ASD. Similarly, Bearden et al. (2008) reported that 30% of males with fragile X syndrome could be diagnosed with autism, and that a much greater percentage had some features of autism. Fragile X syndrome, the most common inherited form of intellectual disability in males, results from an expanded repeat mutation of the fragile X mental retardation 1 (*FMR1*) gene on the X chromosome. Affected females have a milder form of the disorder. The associated protein, FMRP, contributes to the organization of neuron structure in development, and reduced FMRP is associated with abnormalities of the cerebellar vermis and enlargement of the caudate, both of which have been found in autism without fragile X syndrome phenotypic features (Redcay & Courchesne, 2005; Stanfield et al. 2008).

As noted above, the convention has been to define an autism diagnosis in fragile X syndrome as fragile X syndrome, and to define the presence of the *FMR1* gene mutation in autism without the physical features of fragile X syndrome as "syndromic autism." However, the behavioral diagnosis of autism should provide a label for *all* individuals whose behaviors meet the criteria for autism.

Cortical dysplasia-focal epilepsy syndrome and autism

Cortical dysplasia-focal epilepsy syndrome is associated with a mutation of the Contactin-associated protein-like 2 (*CNTNAP2*) gene, a member of the neurexin family. On the basis of research reports by Alarcón et al. (2008), Arking et al., (2008) and Bakkaloglu et al. (2008), Stephan (2008) argued that it was "reasonable at this point to define *CNTNAP2* mutation-positive autistic cases as having 'Type 1 autism'" (p. 7). However, *CNTNAP2* mutation-positive individuals already have their own defined syndrome: cortical dysplasia-focal epilepsy syndrome.

More importantly, Bakkaloglu et al. (2008) reported that there was *no* significant increased *CNTNAP2* gene mutation in the individuals with autism, compared to controls. The researchers identified only 27 of 635 individuals with autism as having variants of the *CNTNAP2* gene, and identified 35 of 942 individuals in a control group as having variants of the *CNTNAP2* gene. Although Alarcón et al. (2008) admitted that "large CNVs at the CNTNAP2 locus are not a common cause of autism or a major contributor to the language disorders" (p. 156), the researchers did claim that both rare and common variants of the *CNTNAP2* gene contributed to a behavioral endophenotype of autism. However, the behavioral endophenotype is broadly conceived to include intellectual disability, repetitive motor behaviors, seizures and language delay (Alarcón et al., 2008). Importantly, as was noted in the discussion of the work by Yrigollen et al. (2008) above, an association between the presence of the *CNTNAP2* gene mutation and many behaviors—here, intellectual disability, repetitive motor behaviors, seizures, and language delay—in individuals is not circumscribed by finding a significant correlation between the presence of the *CNTNAP2* gene mutation and language delay.

Summary

The mutation of the CNTNAP2 gene is associated with cortical dysplasia-focal epilepsy syndrome, the FMR1 gene variant is associated with fragile X syndrome, and the MECP2 gene variant is associated with Rett syndrome. All three gene variants are linked to delayed language and cognition problems. Delayed language and cognition problems are symptoms of many neurodevelopmental disorders including autism. If the pleiotrophic phenotypic expression patterns for many different single gene mutations are similar, what should be the defining point for a syndrome? Should there be a CNTNAP2 gene-associated autism, and a CNTNAP2 gene-associated learning disability, and a CNTNAP2 gene-associated language delay, as well as the originally defined CNTNAP2 gene syndrome of cortical dysplasia-focal epilepsy syndrome?

The Effort to Construct Unified Gene-Based Theories of Autism

Researchers are aware of the many single-gene mutations and chromosomal duplications and deletions associated with autism (see Abrahams & Geschwind, 2008; Glessner et al., 2009; Hoffman & State, 2010; Lintas & Persico, 2009; Ma et al., 2009; Marshall et al., 2008; Pinto et al., 2010; van der Zwaag et al., 2009; Veenstra-VanderWeele et al., 2004; Wang et al., 2009; and Chapter 2) . Efforts to unify the gene bases for autism have included the creation of models of gene and CNV relationships and the selection of a limited set of genes or CNVs as crucial to autism.

Models of gene mutation and CNV relationships in autism

Ramocki and Zoghbi (2008) argued that the wide range of single-gene mutations and CNVs could be bound into a unified pattern by considering homeostasis. They claimed that failure of homeostasis is the mechanism common to all such gene mutations, and they argued that any loss or gain of a protein that influences synaptic function might be the source of neurological or psychiatric phenotypes, because changes in synaptic function will eventually exhaust the ability of neural circuits to establish homeostasis. Morrow et al. (2008) theorized that impairment of neural activity-dependent regulation of synapse development might be common to a group of mutations associated with autism, and that loss of proper regulation of gene dosage may be a core genetic deficit in autism.

Zhao et al. (2007) proposed a template pattern of inheritance that needs to be filled in by a variety of spontaneous mutations, as well as specific modifier genes. The researchers argued that most forms of autism are the result of de novo mutations that appear in the parental germ line. These mutations affect males more than females. Resistant females carry the de novo mutation and pass the mutation to their children, who are more likely to display the autism symptoms if they are male. The researchers claimed that the de novo and inherited mutation expressions are likely to account for the majority of cases of autism.

Identifying a limited set of genes or CNVs as crucial to autism

Ma et al. (2009), Wang et al. (2009), and Glessner et al. (2009) reported concurrent GWAS findings for common variants in the region of chromosome 5p14.1 in a combined cross-study sample of over 10,000 individuals. Wang et al. (2009) noted that SNPs with higher association P values identified a linkage disequilibrium block within the intergenic region between CDH10 (cadherin 10) and CDH9 (cadherin 9) genes. Wang and colleagues (2009) further reported that a group of 25 related cadherin genes showed more significant association with ASD than all other genes, and also noted that combining the 25 cadherin genes with eight neurexin family genes (NRXN1 to NRXN3, CNTNAP1 to CNTNAP5) revealed a still more significant association with ASD. Wang et al. (2009) claimed that their data, combined with evidence for brain underconnectivity in ASD, "convergently indicate that ASDs may result from structural and functional disconnection of brain regions that are involved in higher-order associations, suggesting that ASDs may represent a neuronal disconnection syndrome" (p. 5).

However, Wang and colleagues (2009) noted that several other loci contained SNPs with suggestive association signals, including 13q33.3, 14q21.1, LRFN5, Xp22.32, NLGN4X, and a SNP on the Y chromosome located within an ubiquitin gene. Additionally, Glessner and colleagues (2009) also reported evidence that CNVs in their ASD sample were associated with the genes outside the cadherin/ neurexin gene families. They found that genes from the ubiquitin pathway (UBE3A, PARK2, RFWD2 and FBXO40) were another possible ASD susceptibility source.

Van der Zwaag et al. (2009) explored CNVs in 105 ASD patients and 267 healthy individuals and found evidence for an association between ASD and genes RAI1, BRD1, and LARGE. They reported that a group of seven genes functioning in glycobiology that included the LARGE gene was associated with seven CNVs specifically identified in autism patients, where three of the seven CNVs were de novo in the patients. They argued that gains and losses of genes associated with glycobiology are important contributors to the development of ASD.

Wall et al. (2008) proposed that sets of genes that are under differential gene regulation in autism include multiple genes that influence transmission of nerve impulses, nervous system development, synaptic transmission, cell–cell signaling, brain development, generation of neurons, regulation of cell proliferation, cell migration, and homeostasis, cell morphogenesis, ion transport, and cell differentiation. Through an analytic network strategy they discovered nine new candidate genes (SLC16A2, SLC6A8, OPHN1, FXN, AR, L1CAM, FLNA, MYO5A,

PAFAH1B1) that were differentially expressed in "autism sibling disorders," which they defined as Rett, fragile X, Asperger's disorder, intellectual disability, Angelman syndrome, tuberous sclerosis, hypotonia, ataxia, hypoxia, seizure disorders, spasticity, and microcephaly.

Lintas and Persico (2009) argued that the six most important single gene mutation causes of autism would be HOXA1, NLGN3, NLGN4, NRXN1, PTEN, and SHANK3. Abrahams and Geschwind (2008) identified nine genes associated with autism (UBE3A, SHANK3, CNTNAP2, FMR1, DHCR7, MECP2, CNA1C, TSC1, and TSC2), but they claimed that the most promising candidate gene for autism was RELN. In order to boost the possibility of finding inherited factors, Morrow et al. (2008) recruited a sample of individuals with autism spectrum disorders whose parents shared ancestors. The researchers reported deletions in PCDH10 (protocadherin 10), NHE9, and in a researcher-defined potential new gene region DIA1 (deleted in autism1, or c3orf58).

Weiss and colleagues (2008) and Marshall and colleagues (2008) both reported that a chromosome number variant alteration at 16p11.2 was present in 1% of their autism spectrum samples. However, Weiss and colleagues (2008) also reported that 1 of 648 patients with schizophrenia, 1 of 420 patients with bipolar disorder, 1 of 203 patients with ADHD, 1 of 748 patients with dyslexia, and 1 of 3000 patients with panic disorder, anxiety, depression, or addiction had the same CNV at 16p11.2. As noted earlier, Marshall and colleagues (2008) reported finding 277 CNVs in 44% of ASD families, Christian et al. (2008), reported finding 51 CNVs in 12% of their sample of individuals with autism, and Sebat et al. (2007) reported that de novo CNVs occurred in 10% of their sample of individuals with autism.

Summary

Many gene variants and CNVs have been interpreted as the set of genetic sources for autism. Evidence does suggest that Rett and fragile X syndromes arise from gene variants that generate the symptoms of autism, that CNVs at 16p11.2 are likely to represent 1% of ASD (Marshall et al., 2008; Weiss et al., 2008), and that cadherin and neurexin gene variants may be linked to some as-yet-unknown percentage of ASD patients. These sources, though, cannot define autism as its own multi-gene mutation, multi-CNV syndrome for two reasons. First, a majority of these single-gene mutations and chromosome alterations are not unique to ASD. Second, as gene variants and CNVs account for less than 10% of ASD (Lintas & Persico, 2009), at present it is most likely that more complex epigenetic and multi-variant potential sources of ASD have yet to be discovered.

The Lack of Coverage of Gene and CNV Findings to Date

Despite the large number of individual gene and CNV variants discovered to date, as noted above, the coverage for autism is low. Lintas and Persico (2009) claimed that only 10% of autistic cases could be linked to known genetic syndromes (such as fragile X, Rett Syndrome, neurofibromatosis, tuberous sclerosis, or Angelman syndrome) or CNVs (such as duplication of the maternal 15q11-13 region, deletions of chromosome 2q37, 7q31, 22q11, and microdeletions of chromosome 22q11.2). Sebat and colleagues (2007) reported that 10% of individuals diagnosed with autism were carriers of novel CNVs that were quite varied and included mutations of single genes. Abrahams and Geschwind (2008) argued that 1–2% of ASD was linked to 15q11–15q13 duplications, 2–4% of ASD was linked to FXS and Angelman syndrome, and 1–3% of ASD was linked to all other chromosomal abnormalities. Schanen (2006), however, argued that up to 5% of ASD was linked to 15q11–15q13 duplications alone. Weiss and colleagues (2008) and Marshall and colleagues (2008) both reported that CNV alteration at 16p11.2 was present in 1% of their autism spectrum sample.

Summary

The current coverage of gene-system findings is generally thought to cover about 10% of gene-based autism. The missing "genetic dark matter" may include more single-gene mutations and more CNVs. It is also possible that the complex processes in regulating gene expression will be a large component of the missing genetic matter.

Case-Carrier Examinations of Individual Chromosome Copy Number Variants

Abrahams and Geschwind (2008) argued that the autism phenotype can be examined for single-gene

mutations and CNVs based on a search for mutation specific phenotypic signatures. However, this method, as has already been demonstrated by work conducted to date, has yielded, at best, 10% coverage. Moreover, case carrier phenotype studies have begun to reveal the difficulty of attempting to find phenotypic signatures that are isolable to a particular single mutation.

Case carrier phenotype studies

Case carrier phenotype studies are best illustrated by the explorations of Mefford et al. (2008) and Brunetti-Pierri et al. (2008) of the phenotypes found for carriers of 1q21.1 duplications and deletions. As was outlined in Section Two above, these two groups of researchers screened large samples to find small groups of carriers of 1q21.1 duplications and deletions. Exploring these carriers in a case-by-case fashion revealed the massive pleiotrophic effects and dosage effects of the 1q21.1 chromosomal alterations. Both groups found differential microdeletion and microduplication dosage effects influencing head size. Both groups found a wide range of outcomes for the carriers. Duplications of 1q21.1 were associated with macrocephaly, autism, depression, anxiety, speech delay, learning disability, seizure disorder, macrocephaly, dysphagia, Chiari malformation, hydrocephalus, toe-walking, cryptorchidism, right-sided hyperpigmentation, Raynaud's phenomenon, hypospadias, hypotonia, nerve paresis, fifth-finger clinodactyly, scoliosis, and advanced bone age. Deletions of 1q21.1 were associated with microcephaly, autism, schizophrenia, hallucinations, depression, anxiety, antisocial behavior, ADHD, learning problems, speech delay, seizure disorder, Chiari malformation, hydrocephalus, agenesis of the corpus callosum, trigonocephaly, scoliosis, 11 pairs of ribs, short stature, various eye disorders including cataracts, postaxial polydactyly, two- to three-toe syndactyly, precocious puberty, cryptorchidism, multiple sclerosis, hemangioma, and isolated heart defects.

Summary

Although these widely varied phenotypic findings are likely to reflect mutation across multiple genes within the 1q21.1 region, the phenotypic variation is extremely wide. This wide phenotypic variation is a clear example of the significant limitation to the goal of determining mutation-specific phenotypic signatures.

CONCLUSION

The syndrome definition problem considered throughout this chapter is not a trivial one. The study of brain deficits and behavioral impairment in autism research has not produced any reasonable standard causal theory of autism (Happé & Ronald, 2008; Reiss, 2009; Waterhouse, 2008). The myriad of competing neural and behavioral theories of autism, while supported by evidence, are nonetheless unsynthesized, and remain competing visions.

The increased prevalence of autism, and the widening range of social action groups pushing for a "cure" for autism, create a strong social force against admitting that autism is not one disorder. However, heightened public concern and attention increases the need to generate productive and predictive understandings of autism. Although all researchers understand that gene-based autism is a behavioral aggregation of phenotypic traits based on pleiotrophic and dosage and epigenetic effects, nonetheless research continues to focus on the genetics of "autism." Real progress leading to treatment will not happen if genetic researchers continue to treat autism as a unitary syndrome (Stephan, 2008; Wall et al., 2008; Zhao et al., 2007). Researchers should concede a paradigm shift, and acknowledge that gene-system variation in autism cannot be encompassed by a single, overarching model.

Veenstra-VanderWeele et al. (2004) argued that the integration of genetic findings for autism "may not be feasible" (p. 396), or may not happen because "some of those investigating autism . . . are sometimes too rigid and compulsive to make the creative leaps necessary to solve the puzzle of autism most efficiently and rapidly" (p. 396). But "puzzle" may be the wrong metaphor. A better metaphor may be "portmanteau," or "carryall" (Waterhouse, 2009). Given that only 10% of autism is tied to gene-system variants, and that these variants are associated with other phenotypic syndromes, it appears that autism is a portmanteau syndrome, a carryall phenotype encompassing so many gene and non-gene sources (as well as so many neural deficits) that no single solution could possibly provide a unified basis for genetic screening, or possible future genetic treatment research.

According to Volkmar, State, and Klin (2009), "The use of newly developed alternative, dimensional assessments may help disentangle much of the current confusion about ASDs broadly defined and their relationship to more strictly diagnosed autism.

The ability to provide better sample specification, e.g., through additional ratings of levels of communicative or cognitive ability would greatly add to the diagnostic system" (p. 112). The genetic research conducted to date suggests, however, that "more strictly diagnosed autism," will not prove helpful to future genetic research or treatment.

Worse still, Joober and Boksa (2009) cautioned that genome-wide association studies and CNV studies have only been able to examine a tiny portion of the human genome, and study of the entire human genome is needed to completely understand the role of genes in illnesses. Kapranov et al. (2007) concluded that the possibility of thousands of additional coding sites and thousands of additional regulators of gene expression "significantly increase the diversity of both transcripts and proteins" (p. 417). Moreover, Janssens and van Duijn (2008) argued that simply finding all the gene mutations and chromosomal alterations would not be enough. The study of the epigenetic code and gene networks is just beginning, and it may require a complete knowledge of the dynamic mechanisms in gene expression in order to understand the entire causal mechanisms of autism. Janssens and Duijn (2008) proposed that disorders like autism might never be completely understood in individuals, as the unraveling of their complete unique causal pathways may prove impossible.

Gene-based autism is a portmanteau phenotype containing pleiotrophic expressions of many different single-gene variants, of the dosage effects of many chromosome copy number duplications and deletions, and of presently unknown epigenetic effects. Genetic research based on the autism diagnostic phenotype and autism endophenotypes, although productive, continue to reveal increasing gene source heterogeneity. Two studies that explored the range of individual phenotypes for carriers of 1q21.1 duplications and deletions (Brunetti-Pierri et al., 2008; Mefford et al., 2008) offered a detailed description of dosage variation and apparent pleiotropic variation within a dosage level expressed in the phenotypes of these carriers. If this case-carrier analytic approach is applied to all the gene mutations and chromosome copy number variants associated with autism, it might be possible to ultimately generate a description of the majority of gene system variants that result in the autism phenotype. This description, however, will most certainly fail to find any overarching "genome variant story" for autism.

Similar to the case-carrier studies outlined above, Reiss (2009) argued that research in developmental disorders such as fragile X syndrome, Rett syndrome, and autism should consider using gene and chromosomal variants as a means to sort associated behaviors. Reiss also argued that the use of endophenotypes would be valuable. But, as reviewed in this chapter, to date no unifying endophenotypes have emerged. It may be that micro-endophenotypes based on narrow neural deficits will be discovered in future research. However, the evidence at present suggests that research employing diagnostic or non-diagnostic endophenotypes of autism will continue to uncover increasing gene-system heterogeneity within endophenotypes. The portmanteau of autism must be carefully and completely unpacked to allow for the development of genetic testing for those individuals with gene-based autism, and for future possible case-specific treatment interventions.

References

Abrahams, B. S., & Geschwind, D. H. (2008). Advances in autism genetics: On the threshold of a new neurobiology. *Nature Review Genetics, 9*, 341–355.

Alarcón, M., Abrahams, B. S., Stone, J. L., Duvall, J. A., Perederiy, J. V., Bomar, S. M., ... Geschwind, D. H.e (2008). Linkage, association, and gene-expression analyses identify CNTNAP2 as an autism-susceptibility gene. *American Journal of Human Genetics, 82*, 150–159.

Amaral, D. G., Schumann, C. M., & Nordahl, C. W. (2008). Neuroanatomy of autism. *Trends in Neuroscience, 31*, 137–145.

Arking, D. E., Cutler, D. J., Brune, C. W., Teslovich, T. M., West, K., Ikeda, M., ... Chakravarti, A. (2008). A common genetic variant in the neurexin superfamily member CNTNAP2 increases familial risk of autism. *American Journal of Human Genetics, 82*, 160–164.

Bakkaloglu, B., O'Roak, B. J., Louvi, A., Gupta, A. R., Abelson, J. F., Morgan, T. M., ... State, M. W. (2008). Molecular cytogenetic analysis and resequencing of contactin associated proteinlike 2 in autism spectrum disorders. *American Journal of Human Genetics, 82*, 165–173.

Bearden, C. E., Glahn, D. C., Lee, A. D., Chiang, M-C., van Erp, T. G. M., Cannon, T. D., ... Thompson, P. M. (2008). Neural phenotypes of common and rare genetic variants. *Biological Psychology 79*, 43–57.

Brunetti-Pierri, N., Berg, J. S., Scaglia, F., Belmont, J., Bacino, C. A., Sahoo, T., ... Patel, A. (2008). Recurrent reciprocal 1q21.1 deletions and duplications associated with microcephaly or macrocephaly and develop and behavioral abnormalities. *Nature Genetics, 40*, 1466–1471.

Butler, M. G., Dasouki, M. J., Zhou, X. P., Talebizadeh, Z., Brown, T., Takahashi, T. N., ... Eng, C. (2005) Subset of individuals with autism spectrum disorders and extreme macrocephaly associated with germline PTEN tumour suppressor gene mutations. *Journal of Medical Genetics, 42*, 318–321.

Buxbaum, J. D., Cai, G., Chaste, P., Nygren, G., Goldsmith, J., Reichert, J., ... Betancur, C. (2007a). Mutation screening of the PTEN gene in patients with autism spectrum disorders and macrocephaly. *American Journal of Medical Genetics Part B Neuropsychiatric Genetics, 144B*, 484–491.

Buxbaum, J. D., Cai, G., Nygren, G., Chaste, P., Delormes, R., Goldsmith, J., ... Betancur, C. (2007b). Mutation analysis of the NSD1 gene in patients with autism spectrum disorders and macrocephaly. *BMC Medical Genetics, 8*, 68.

Cai, G., Edelmann, L., Goldsmith, J. E., Cohen, N., Nakamine, A., Reichert, J. G., ... Buxbaum, J. D. (2008). Multiplex ligation-dependent probe amplification for genetic screening in autism spectrum disorders: Efficient identification of known microduplications and identification of a novel microduplication in ASMT. *BMC Medical Genomics, 1*, 50.

Christian, S. L., Brune, C. W., Sudi, J., Kumar, R. A., Liu, S., Karamohamed, S., ... Cook, E. H., Jr. (2008). Novel Submicroscopic chromosomal abnormalities detected in autism spectrum disorder. *Biological Psychiatry, 63*, 1111–1117.

Crespi, B., & Badcock, C. (2008). Psychosis and autism as diametrical disorders of the social brain. *Behavioral and Brain Sciences, 31*, 241–320.

Duvall, J. A., Lu, A., Cantor, R. M., Constantino, J. N., & Geschwind, D. H. (2007). A quantitative trait locus analysis of social responsiveness in multiplex autism families. *American Journal of Psychiatry, 164*, 656–662.

Folstein, S. (2006). The clinical spectrum of autism. *Clinical Neuroscience Research, 6*, 113–117.

Glessner, J. T., Wang, K., Cai, G., Korvatska, O., Kim, C.E., Wood, S., ... Hakonarson, H. (2009). Autism genome-wide copy number variation reveals ubiquitin and neuronal genes. *Nature, 459*, 569–573.

Goos, L. M. (2008). Imprinting and psychiatric genetics: Beware the diagnostic phenotype. *Behavioral and Brain Sciences, 31*, 271–272.

Green, L., Fein, D., Modahl. C., Feinstein C., Waterhouse, L., & Morris, M. (2001) Oxytocin and autistic disorder: Alterations in peptide forms. *Biological Psychiatry, 50*, 609–613.

Happé, F., & Ronald, A. (2008). "Fractionable autism triad": A review of evidence from behavioural, genetic, cognitive and neural research. *Neuropsychology Review, 18*, 287–304.

Happé, F., Ronald, A., & Plomin, R. (2006). Time to give up on a single explanation for autism. *Nature Neuroscience, 9(10)*, 1218–1220.

Happel, N. & Doenecke, D. (2009). Histone H1 and its isoforms: Contribution to chromatin structure and function. *Gene, 431(1-2)*, 1–12.

Hoffman, E. J., & State, M. W. J. (2010) Progress in cytogenetics: implications for child psychopathology. *Journal of the Academy of Child and Adolescent Psychiatry, 49*, 736–751.

Hogart, A., Nagarajan, R. P., Patzel, K. A., Yasui, D. H., & Lasalle, J. M. (2007).15q11–13 GABAA receptor genes are normally biallelically expressed in brain yet are subject to epigenetic dysregulation in autism-spectrum disorders. *Human Molecular Genetics, 16*, 691–703.

Janssens, A. C., & van Duijn, C. M. (2008). Genome-based prediction of common diseases: advances and prospects. *Human Molecular Genetics, 17(R2)*, R166–173.

Jones, J. R., Skinner, C., Friez, M. J., Schwartz, C. E., & Stevenson, R. E. (2007). Hypothesis: Dysregulation of methylation of brain-expressed genes on the X chromosome and autism spectrum disorders. *American Journal of Medical Genetics Part A, 146A (17)*, 2213–2220.

Joober, R., & Bokva, P. (2009). A new wave in the genetics of psychiatric disorders: The copy number variant tsunami. *Journal of Psychiatry and Neuroscience, 34*, 55–59.

Kaduake, S., & Blobe, G. A. (2009). Chromatin loops in gene regulation. *Biochimica et Biophysica Acta, 1789*, 17–25.

Kaminsky, Z. A., Tang, T., Wang, S-C., Ptak, C., Oh, G. H., Wong, A. H., . . . Petronis, A. (2009). DNA methylation profiles in monozygotic and dizygotic twins. *Nature Genetics, 41*, 240–245.

Kapranov, P., Willingham, A. T., & Cingeras, T. R. (2007). Genome-wide transcription and the implications for genomic organization. *Nature Review Genetics, 8*, 413–423.

Khaja, R., Zhang, J., MacDonald, J. R., He, Y., Joseph-George, A. M., Wei, J., . . . Feuk, L. (2006). Genome assembly comparison to identify structural variants in the human genome. *Nature Genetics, 38*, 1413–1418.

Kramer, J. M., & van Bokhoven, H. (2009). Genetic and epigenetic defects in intellectual disability. *The International Journal of Biochemistry and Cell Biology, 41*, 96–107.

Lam, K. S. L., Bodfish, J. W., & Piven, J. (2008). Evidence for three subtypes of repetitive behavior in autism that differ in familiality and association with other symptoms. *Journal of Child Psychology and Psychiatry, 49*, 1193–1200.

Lintas, C., & Persico, A. M. (2009). Autistic phenotypes and genetic testing: State-of-the art for the clinical geneticist. *Journal of Medical Genetics, 46*, 1–8.

Liu, X. Q., Paterson, A. D., Szatmari, P., & The Autism Genome Project Consortium. (2008). Genome-wide linkage analyses of quantitative and categorical autism subphenotypes. *Biological Psychiatry, 64*, 561–570.

Loat, C. S., Curran, S., Lewis, C. M., Duvall, J., Geschwind, D., Bolton, P., & Craig, I. W. (2008). Methyl-CpG-binding protein 2 polymorphisms and vulnerability to autism. *Genes, brain, and behavior, 7*, 754–760.

Ma, D., Salyakina, D., Jaworski, J. M., Konidari, I., Whitehead, P. L., Andersen, A. N., . . . Pericak-Vance, M. A. (2009). A genome-wide study of autism reveals a common novel risk locus at 5p14.1. *Annals of Human Genetics, 73, pt. 3*, 263–273.

Maher, B. (2008). The case of the missing heritability. *Nature, 456, 6*, 18–21.

Mandy, W. P., & Skuse, D. H. (2008). Research review: What is the association between the social-communication element of autism and repetitive interests, behaviours, and activities? *Journal of Child Psychology and Psychiatry, 49*, 795–808.

Marshall, C. R., Noor. A.,Vincent, J. B., Lionel, A. C., Feuk, L., Skaug, J., . . . Scherer, S. (2008). Structural variation of chromosomes in autism spectrum disorder. *American Journal of Human Genetics, 82*, 477–488.

Mefford, H., Sharp, A., Baker, C., Itsara, A., Jiang, Z., Buysse, K., . . . Eichler, E. (2008). Recurrent rearrangements of chromosome 1q21.1 and variable pediatric phenotypes. *The New England Journal of Medicine, 359, 16*, 1685–1699.

Mehler, M. F., & Purpura, D. P. (2008). Autism, fever, epigenetics and the locus coeruleus. *Brain Research Reviews, 59*, 388–392.

Miller, D. T., Shen, Y., Weiss, L. A., Korn J, Anselm, I., Bridgemohan, C., . . . Wu, B-L. (2009). Microdeletion/duplication at 15q13.2q13.3 among individuals with features of autism and other neuropsychiatric disorders. *Journal of Medical Genetics, 46*, 242–248.

Modahl, C., Green, L., Fein, D., Morris, M., Waterhouse, L., Feinstein, C., & Levin, H. (1998). Plasma oxytocin levels in autistic children. *Biological Psychiatry, 43*, 270–277.

Monteggia, L. M., & Kavalali, E. T. (2009). Rett syndrome and the impact of MeCP2 associated transcriptional mechanisms on neurotransmission. *Biological Psychiatry, 65*, 204–210.

Morrow, E. M., Yoo, S. Y., Flavell, S. W., Kim, T. K., Lin, Y., Hill, R. S., . . . Walsh, C. A. (2008). Identifying autism loci and genes by tracing recent shared ancestry. *Science, 321(5886)*, 218–223.

Orrico, A., Galli, L., Buoni, S., Orsi, A., Vonella, G., & Sorrentino, V. (2009). Novel PTEN mutations in neurodevelop disorders and macrocephaly. *Clinical Genetics, 75*, 195–198.

Pinto, D., Pagnamenta, A. T., Klei, L., Anney, R., Merico, D., Regan, R., Conroy. J. (2010). Functional impact of global rare copy number variation in autism spectrum disorders. *Nature, Volume: 466*, Pages: 368–372.

Ramocki, M. B., & Zoghbi, H. Y. (2008) Failure of neuronal homeostasis results in common neuropsychiatric phenotypes. *Nature, 455(7215)*, 912–918.

Redcay, E., & Courchesne, E. (2005). When is the brain enlarged in autism? A meta-analysis of all brain size reports. *Biological Psychiatry, 58*, 1–9.

Reid, G., Gallais, R., & Metiviér, T. (2009). Marking time: The dynamic role of chromatin and covalent modification in transcription. *International Journal of Biochemistry and Cell Biology, 41*, 155–163.

Reiss, A. (2009). Childhood develop disorders: An academic and clinical convergence point for psychiatry, neurology, psychology and pediatrics. *Journal of Child Psychology and Psychiatry, 50*, 87–98.

Sacco, R., Militerni, R., Frolli, A., Bravaccio, C., Gritti, A., Elia, M., Curatolo, P. (2007). Clinical, morphological, and biochemical correlates of head circumference in autism. *Biological Psychiatry, 62*, 1038–1047.

Schanen, N. C. (2006). Epigenetics of autism spectrum disorders. *Human Molecular Genetics, 15*, R138–R150.

Sebat, J., Lakshmi, B., Malhotra, D., Troge, J., Lese-Martin, C., Walsh, T., . . . Wigler, M. (2007). Strong association of de novo copy number mutations with autism. *Science, 316* (5823), 445–449.

Seringhaus, M., & Gerstein, M. (2008). Genomics confounds gene classification. *American Scientist, 96*, 466–473.

Spence, S. J., Cantor, R. M., Chung, L., Kim, S., Geschwind, D. H., & Alarcón, M. (2006). Stratification based on language-related endophenotypes in autism: Attempt to replicate reported linkage. *American Journal of Medical Genetics Part B Neuropsychiatric Genetics, 141B*, 591–598.

Stephan, D. A. (2008). Unraveling autism. *The American Journal of Human Genetics, 82*, 7–9.

Stanfield, A. C., McIntosh, A. M., Spencer, M. D., Philip, R., Gaur, S., & Lawrie, S. M. (2008). Towards a neuroanatomy of autism: A systematic review and meta-analysis of structural magnetic resonance imaging studies. *European Psychiatry, 23*, 289–299.

Swanberg, S. E., Nagarajan, R. P., Peddada, S., Yasui, D. H., & LaSalle, J. M. (2009). Reciprocal co-regulation of EGR2 and MECP2 is disrupted in Rett syndrome and autism. *Human Molecular Genetics, 18*(3), 524–534.

Tsuchiya, K. J., Hashimoto, K., Iwata, Y., Tsujii, M., Sekine, Y., Sugihara, G., . . . Mori, N. (2008). Decreased serum levels of platelet-endothelial adhesion molecule (PECAM-1) in subjects with high-functioning autism: a negative correlation with head circumference at birth. *Biological Psychiatry, 62*, 1056–1058.

van der Zwaag, B., Franke, L., Poot, M., Hochstenbach, R., Spierenburg, H. A., Vorstman, J. A., . . . Staal, W. G. (2009). Gene-network analysis identifies susceptibility genes related to glycobiology in autism. *PLoS ONE, 4*(5), e5324.

Veenstra-VanderWeele, J., Christian, S. L., & Cook, Jr., E. H. (2004). Autism as a paradigmatic complex genetic disorder. *Annual Review of Genomics and Human Genetics, 5*, 379–405.

Vernes, S. C., Newbury, D. F., Abrahams, B., Winchester, L., Nicod, J., Groszer, M., . . . Fisher, S. E. (2008). A functional genetic link between distinct develop language disorders. *The New England Journal of Medicine, 359, 22*, 2337–2345.

Volkmar, F. R., State, M., & Klin, A. (2009). Autism and autism spectrum disorders: Diagnostic issues for the coming decade. *Journal of Child Psychology and Psychiatry, 50*, 108–115.

Wall, D. P., Esteban, T. F., DeLuca, M., Huyck, T. Monaghan, N., Velez de Mendizabal, N., . . . Kohane, I. S. (2009). Comparative analysis of neurological disorders focuses genome-wide search for autism genes. *Genomics, 93*, 120–129.

Wang, K., Zhang, H., Ma, D., Bucan, M., Glessner, J. T., Abrahams, B. S., . . . Hakonarson, H. (2009). Common genetic variants on 5p14.1 associate with autism spectrum disorders. *Nature, 459*, 528–533.

Waterhouse, L. (2008). Autism overflows: increasing prevalence and proliferating theories. *Neuropsychology Review, 18*, 273–286.

Waterhouse, L. (2009). Autism is a portmanteau syndrome. *Neuropsychology Review, 19*, 275–276.

Weiss, L. A., Shen, Y., Korn, J. M., Arking, D. E., Miller, D. T., Fossdal, R., . . . Daly, M. J. (2008). Association between microdeletion and microduplication at 16p11.2 and autism. *The New England Journal of Medicine, 358*, 667–675.

Williams, C. A., Dagli, A., & Battaglia, A. (2008). Genetic disorders associated with macrocephaly. *American Journal of Medical Genetics Part, 146A*, 2023–2037.

Yrigollen, C. M., Han, S. S., Kochetkova, A., Babitz, T., Volkmar, F. R., Leckman, J. F., . . . Grigorenko, E. L. (2008). Genes controlling affiliative behavior as candidate genes for autism. *Biological Psychiatry, 63*, 911–916.

Zhao, X., Leotta, A., Kustanovich, V., Lajonchere, C., Geschwind, D. H., Law, K., . . . Wigler, M. (2007). A unified genetic theory for sporadic and inherited autism. *Proceedings of the National Academy of Sciences U S A, 104*, 12831–12836.

Zingerevich, C., Greiss-Hess, L., Lemons-Chitwood, K., Harris, S. W., Hessl, D., Cook, K., & Hagerman, R. (2009). Motor abilities of children diagnosed with fragile X syndrome with and without autism. *Journal of Intellectual Disability Research, 53*, 11–18.

Chapter 25

A Whole-Body Systems Approach to ASD

Martha R. Herbert

INTRODUCTION

Although autism is defined at the level of behavior, it is becoming clear that there is much more than behavior impairments to autism. For a long time, the focus of autism research has been on genetics and neurobiology. The high heritability factor has supported a strong interest in genetics, while the brain basis of behavior, combined with findings documenting brain differences in autism, has supported a neurobiological focus.

In recent years, a growing amount of attention has been devoted to a range of somatic features in autism. Prominent among these are disturbances in gastrointestinal, immune, and metabolic functioning. Understanding the role these features play in autism is complicated by the fact that they do not present in any one uniform fashion, nor are abnormalities in these domains measurable in every autistic individual. While somatic features have often been classified as "secondary" in comparison to the "core" features of autism, this classification is increasingly challenged by advances in peer-reviewed scientific

research, and more generally, in our understanding of gut-brain and immune-brain relationships, and of metabolic influences on brain functioning.

Going forward, it will be important to develop awareness of these whole-body and systems issues in autism, in order both to include them in thorough appreciation and documentation of clinical history, and to more fully appreciate scientific and clinical advances in these autism-relevant domains.

EVIDENCE AND RATIONALE FOR LINKING SOMATIC AND SYSTEMIC FEATURES WITH AUTISM

Evidence for, and considerations relevant to, whole-body and systems features of autism will be organized around the following propositions:

1) Biomedical problems are present in many individuals with ASD.

2) Biomedical problems are often related to each other, and also to neurobehavioral problems in autism.

3) Common underlying mechanisms may be found in various behavioral and biomedical features of ASD.

4) Biomedical problems may begin early in development, and in many cases may even precede the onset of ASD behavioral features.

There is substantial growing support for the first three propositions, but the fourth, while supported by significant anecdotal evidence, has received only limited systematic investigation, which has generally been retrospective and therefore based on medical records and questionnaires, rather than direct and prospective measures. These propositions will be discussed more thoroughly below.

Proposition 1) Biomedical problems are present in many individuals with ASD

Evidence for the common presence of biomedical features in autism can be organized into a set of domains; areas to be highlighted here are gastrointestinal symptoms, disordered sleep, electrophysiological and seizure abnormalities, immune system abnormalities, and metabolic and other laboratory abnormalities.

Gastrointestinal System

Divergent recruitment and ascertainment methodologies employed to assess the prevalence of gastrointestinal problems in ASD have yielded a wide range of prevalence estimates. Several recent publications based on prospective data show that gastrointestinal (GI) problems are more common in autism than in the general population. D'Souza and colleagues (2006) report 80% of their autistic subjects (n=54) had GI complaints, versus 32% of the control group; Valicenti-McDermott and colleagues (2006) report that 70% of their autistic subjects (n=50) had GI complaints, versus 28% of controls. Melmed, Schneider, and Fabes (2000) and Levy et al. (2003) report in the range of 50%—a substantial proportion but somewhat lower than the prior two studies. All of these publications drew their subjects from a general population of autistic subjects, without prior selection for previous complaints of GI problems. These numbers conflict with several retrospective reports which place the

incidence of GI problems in autism at a much lower level, of 9–18% (Black, Kaye, and Jick, 2002; Taylor et al., 2002). These lower numbers were the yield of retrospective reviews of the patients' histories as recorded by psychiatrists and general practitioners, who may not have pursued signs and symptoms of gastrointestinal illness as they may present themselves in nonverbal or communicationally impaired autistic individuals who may also have atypical sensory thresholds and pain processing; therefore, these reports are unlikely to be as reliable as prospectively collected data.

A range of gastrointestinal disturbances has been reported in ASD. Horvath et al. (1999) performed endoscopic evaluations of the upper GI tract of 36 autistic children referred to their clinic because of GI complaints. Evaluations included an EGD (esophagogastroduodenoscopy), measurement of small intestine and pancreatic enzymes, biopsy samples, and bacterial and fungal cultures. Reflux esophagitis was found in 69.4% of patients. Chronic stomach inflammation was found in 42%, and inflammation in the duodenum in 67%. Abnormal carbohydrate digestive enzyme activity was found in 58% of patients. (Horvath & Perman, 2002; Jass, 2005). D'Eufemia et al. (1996), using the lactulose-mannitol test, found abnormal intestinal permeability in 43% of their autistic cohort of 40 patients, versus 0% of controls. Horvath and Perman (2002) found abnormal permeability in 76% of their cohort of autistic children with GI symptoms. Abnormal intestinal microflora colonization has been found in several recent studies, including those by Parracho et al. (2005) and Finegold and colleagues (Finegold et al., 2002; Song, Liu, and Finegold, 2004).

Sleep

Sleep disorders are found in a large majority of children with ASD—up to 80% (Malow, 2004). Atypical sleep architecture is common in ASD, and may include longer sleep latency, more frequent nocturnal awakenings, lower sleep efficiency, increased duration of stage 1 sleep, decreased non-REM sleep and slow-wave sleep, fewer stage 2 EEG sleep spindles, and a lower number of rapid eye movements during REM sleep than in non-autistic individuals (Honomich, Goodlin-Jones, Burnham, Gaylor, and Anders, 2002; Limoges, Mottron, Bolduc, Berthiaume, Godbout, 2005).

Epilepsy

A common accompaniment of autism is epilepsy, developing in approximately one-third of individuals with autism. EEG abnormalities are quite common in ASD, even in individuals who do not have epilepsy, though the proportion of individuals in whom this may be documented has varied widely depending upon study design. Percentages of individuals with autistic disorder or ASD who have epilepsy have ranged from 7.4–46%; part of the variability may be related to the subtype (e.g. presence or absence of additional neurological disorder; Canitano 2007). The potential impact of interictal epileptiform abnormalities is emerging as an area of active research interest. Such non-epileptic EEG abnormalities are more likely to be focal than primarily generalized. Autism may follow infantile spasms, which occur mainly during the first year of life. Continuous spike-wave during slow-wave sleep, which can be associated with language regression, can also be associated with autism, as well as with cognitive decline. Seizures and epilepsy are more common among children with autistic spectrum disorder with language regression, especially those who experience language regression after the age of 2 years, and particularly in autistic children with mental retardation and motor abnormalities (Trevathan, 2004).

Abnormal sensory responsiveness

There is a high prevalence of abnormal sensory processing in autism (see Chapter 11). In one study, out of a sample of 281 children with ASD, 95% exhibited sensory processing dysfunction on the Short Sensory Profile (Tomchek & Dunn 2007). Abnormal sensory responsiveness seems to be pervasive in ASD, affecting all main sensory modalities though not equally in every individual, as well as multimodal sensory processing (Leekam, Nieto, Libby, Wing, Gould, 2007), with severity of sensory processing dysfunction being correlated with autism severity in children, though not in adolescents and adults (Kern et al., 2006).

Autonomic nervous system abnormalities

Autonomic nervous system (ANS) disorders have been documented in autism. Additional autonomic abnormalities that have been reported include abnormal skin conductance, blunted autonomic arousal to social stimuli, and increased tonic electrodermal activity (Zimmerman, Connors, & Pardo, 2006) The frequently encountered sleep disorders, as well as gastrointestinal symptoms such as chronic constipation or diarrhea, may have a major autonomic component. Atypical autonomic response to mental and physical tasks has been reported (Goodwin et al. 2006; Ming et al., 2004, 2005; Toichi & Kamio 2003). Autonomic hyperarousal appears to be a common feature of autism, although hypoarousal has also been seen (Hirstein, Iversen, & Ramachandran, 2001). Abnormal arousal is likely to be a significant exacerbating factor in ASD, with contributors to this problem from both physiological factors (e.g. neurologically based high or low sensitivity to sensory stimuli), and from anxiety responses to ineffective coping with stressors.

Immune system

Reported immune abnormalities have included autoantibodies (particularly to central nervous system proteins; Ashwood & Van de Water, 2004b), and deficits in immune cell subsets, cytokine abnormalities, impaired responses to viral infections, and prolonged and recurrent infections (Ashwood & Van de Water 2004a), activation of the inflammatory response, (Croonenberghs, Bosmans, Deboutte, Kenis, & Maes, 2002), as well as vulnerability factors, including family history of autoimmune disease (Comi, Zimmerman, Frye, Law, Peeden, 1999; Sweeten, Bowyer, Posey, Halberstadt, McDougle, 2003) and genetic variants associated with autoimmunity (Ashwood & Van de Water, 2004b; Torres, Maciulis, & Odell 2001;). Immune activation has been demonstrated in brain tissue and CSF (Li et al. 2009; Vargas, Nascimbene, Krishnan, Zimmerman, Pardo, 2005), and brain-specific antibodies have been identified in the plasma of subjects with ASD (Cabanlit, Wills, Goines, Ashwood, Van de Water, 2007), and associated with parent report of behavioral regression (Braunschweig et al. 2008).

Metabolic abnormalities

Mitochondrial abnormalities

Features of mitochondrial abnormalities have been found in autism, including elevated lactic acid, (Chugani, Sundram, Behen, Lee, Moore, 1999;

Clark-Taylor & Clark-Taylor, 2004; Correia et al., 2006; Filipek et al. 2003; Filipek, Juranek, Nguyen, Cummings, Gargus, 2004; Oliveira et al., 2005) and reduced free and total carnitine (Filipek et al. 2004). Other features of autism, such as oxidative stress, can lead to mitochondrial damage and impair mitochondrial function (Cadenas & Davies, 2000). Children with diagnosed mitochondrial disorders frequently present with features of autism (Marin-Garcia, Ananthakrishnan, Goldenthal, Filiano, Sarnat, 1999). It is becoming appreciated that metabolic perturbations can be acquired and not only inherited (Filiano, Goldenthal, Mamourian, Hall, Marin-Garcia, 2002; Graf et al., 2000; Poling, Frye, Shoffner, Zimmerman 2006; Zecavati & Spence, 2009).

Inborn errors of metabolism

Autism is associated with a variety of inborn errors of metabolism, and moreover modulation of autism severity in some such settings by treatment has been reviewed (Page, 2000) and further documented. Autistic symptoms are reduced in PKU by a low phenylanlanine diet (Gillberg & Coleman 2000); in hyperuricosuric autism by a low-purine diet with or without allopurinol (Coleman,1989; Gillberg & Coleman, 2000; Page & Moseley, 2002); in patients with low CSF biopterin by biopterin supplementation (Fernell et al. 1997); in some hypocalcinuric autistic patients by calcium supplementation (Coleman, 1989); in some patients with lactic acidemia by thiamine and/or ketogenic diet (Coleman, 1989); in cerebral folate deficiency by folinic acid supplementation (Bauman, 2006; Moretti et al. 2005); and in Smith-Lemli-Opitz syndrome by cholesterol treatments (Aneja & Tierney, 2008; Natowicz 2004).

Proposition 2) Biomedical problems are often related to each other and also to neurobehavioral problems in autism

Interrelationships have been discussed, both in the autism literature and in the peer-reviewed scientific literature more broadly, in multiple combinations of the above domains.

Gastrointestinal-immune

Many of the reported gastrointestinal abnormalities are of an immune character, such as altered mucosal immunity (Ashwood et al. 2003; Ashwood, Anthony, Torrente,. Wakefield, 2004; Furlano et al. 2001; Torrente et al. 2002); atypical immune responses to certain dietary components have also been reported (Jyonouchi, Geng, Ruby, Reddy, Zimmerman-Bier, 2005a, 2005b; Jyonouchi, Sun, & Itokazu, 2002; Murch, 2005; Vojdani et al. 2002). The gastrointestinal tract contains gut-associated lympoid tissue (GALT), which constitutes about 70% of the body's immune system tissue.

CNS, GI and immune systems may all interrelate as well; for example, the neurotransmitter serotonin, which has been documented in various ways as abnormal in autism, is prominent in the intestine and may be modulated by immune factors (Ashwood & Van de Water, 2004a; Barkhudaryan & Dunn, 1999); this type of multisystem involvement can be described for other neurotransmitters as well. An animal model of gut-brain interaction showed that inflammatory bowel disease activates areas of the brain implicated in autism (Welch et al. 2005), and in a fashion consistent with an underlying inflammatory pathophysiology, such as has been documented in postmortem brains of individuals with autism (Vargas, Nascimbene, Krishnan, Zimmerman, Pardo, 2005).

CNS immune activation and systemic inflammation

Systemic inflammation may lead to exacerbation of central nervous system inflammation (Perry, Newman, & Cunningham 2003); in one study, induction of TNF-alpha was shown to peak in serum in one hour and return to normal levels in six hours, and to peak in the liver in nine hours, but to persist in the brain for ten months (Qin, et al. 2007). Increased intestinal permeability has been found even in autistic individuals without gastrointestinal symptoms (D'Eufemia et al. 1996); such permeability has been associated with endotoxemia, which may render the blood-brain barrier more permeable (Kowal et al. 2004), and facilitate the impact of systemic immune alterations on the CNS. The proinflammatory cytokine profiles reported in the CSF and the peripheral blood overlapped, in that both showed MCP-1, but much else did not overlap (Vargas et al., 2005); tumor necrosis factor-alpha has been found in cerebrospinal fluid (Chez, Dowling, Patel, Khanna, Kominsky, 2007).

Immune activation, cytokines and epilepsy

There is an extensive literature about the general role of immune activation, inflammation, and cytokines in modulating seizure thresholds (Vezzani & Granata, 2005; Vezzani, Moneta, Richichi, Perego, De Simoni, 2004;). However, literature linking immune findings with electrophysiological findings in autism is just emerging (Connolly et al., 2006).

Immune system, infection and sleep

Immune-brain and brain-immune signaling are well known to mediate and modulate sleep regulation (Lorton et al. 2006), with cytokines and endotoxins playing a significant role in this mediation. Although both immune dysregulation and disordered sleep are common in autism, their relationship has not been studied.

GI and sleep

Gastrointestinal conditions that may occur in ASD can be associated with pain which, in turn, disrupts sleep. The inflammatory component of GI conditions may contribute through immune modulation of sleep. This has received little systematic study.

GI and oxidative stress

Reports of low-antioxidant and anti-inflammatory nutrient levels in autistic children (Audhya, 2005; Jory, 2005; Yorbik, Sayal, Akay, Akbiyik, & Sohmen, 2005) suggest a potential self-amplifying feedback loop between (possibly inflammation-related) intestinal malabsorption, which exacerbates poor nutritional status, and low levels of nutrients, which exacerbate inflammation, oxidative stress, and gut disease. These problems may reduce systemic metabolic resiliency, which could make the manifestation of problems more likely in other organ systems.

Epilepsy and language impairment

Various epileptic encephalopathies, including Landau-Kleffner syndrome, are associated with autism (Tuchman, 2006). However, it does not appear that language problems in typical autism can be attributed to epilepsy or epileptiform changes (Deonna & Roulet, 2006).

GI and problem behaviors

Pain, poor intake, and malabsorption of nutrients such as essential fatty acids can be associated with behavioral dysregulation (Garland et al. 2007). Inflammatory bowel disease has also been associated with neurobehavioral symptomatology (Solmaz, Kavuk, & Sayar, 2003).

Sleep and neurobehavioral problems

As compared with good sleepers with ASD, poor sleepers with ASD also had higher scores related to affective problems on the Child Behavior Checklist, and more problems with reciprocal social interaction on the ADOS (Malow et al., 2006). Disordered or insufficient sleep can affect cognitive functioning, attention, and information consolidation (Femia & Hasselmo, 2002).

Autonomic disturbance, abnormal arousal, and problem behaviors

Literature suggests that many of the behaviors associated with ASD are related to arousal, as stressful events frequently precipitate the maladaptive behavior problems seen in this population, such as aggression, self-injury, tantrums, and destruction of property (Groden, Cautela, Prince, & Berryman, 1991). Stereotypic behaviors including echolalia, twirling, rocking, flicking, and hand-flapping are also found to increase when this population is exposed to events commonly defined as stressors in the typical population (Howlin, 1998; Hutt & Hutt, 1968).

Proposition 3) Common underlying mechanisms may underlie various behavioral and biomedical features of ASD

A growing body of empirical evidence, and a number of models of autism, identify common pathophysiological features which can result from various combinations of genetic and environmental interactions, and which can manifest in multiple organ systems (Chauhan, Chauhan, & Brown, 2009; Herbert, 2009).

Increased excitation/inhibition ratio

The idea that information-processing problems in autism may be related to an increased ratio of excitation to inhibition in the central nervous system has been widely advanced (Levitt, 2005; Rubenstein & Merzenich, 2003). This model links diverse findings in autism, including sensory issues, arousal issues, and seizures. It can also result from many different candidate genes, as well as environmental toxins. Intriguingly, such mechanisms may not be restricted to brain. For example, peripheral GABA receptors are widely distributed in multiple systems, and the peripheral GABAergic system is implicated in cardiovascular disease, lung disease, and intestinal and endocrine disorders (Akinci & Schofield, 1999; Gladkevich, Korf, Hakobyan, & Melkonyan, 2006; Veenman & Gavish, 2006).

Disturbed connectivity

Coordination of brain activation appears to be suboptimal in autism (Just et al., 2004; see Chapter 21). Murias and colleagues (2007) have found robust contrasting patterns of over- and underconnectivity at distinct spatial and temporal scales in adult ASD subjects, in the eyes-closed resting state, when compared to controls. This altered pattern of information processing may underlie multiple seemingly distinct behavioral impairments, related to impairments of central coherence (Happé & Frith, 2006) or complex information processing (Williams, Goldstein, & Minshew, 2006). Systemic metabolic and immune dysregulation is plausibly pertinent to disordered synaptic and network functioning (Anderson, Hooker, & Herbert, 2008; Herbert & Anderson, 2008) and long-distance white-matter connectivity (Herbert, 2005).

Immune dysregulation

Reduction in the regulatory cytokine transforming growth factor beta 1 has been associated with lower adaptive behaviors and worse behavioral symptoms (Ashwood et al., 2008). The intriguing report of transient improvement in core features of autism in the setting of fever (Curran et al., 2007) could be consistent with an immune linkage to behavioral dysregulation.

Methylation

Abnormal levels of metabolites in methionine transmethylation and transsulfuration pathways have been measured in autism (James et al. 2006; Suh, Walsh, McGinnis, Lewis, Ames, 2008). Methylation is criti-

cal for regulation of gene expression, neurotransmitter synthesis, and other vital processes. Methylation abnormalities have been implicated in numerous other neurological disorders as well (Mattson & Shea, 2003; Muntjewerff et al., 2003; Pogribna et al., 2001; Schulz, Lindenau, Seyfried, Dichgans, 2000; Serra et al. 2001).

Oxidative stress

A growing body of literature has documented oxidative stress in autism by a variety of measures (Chauhan & Chauhan, 2006; James et al., 2006). Oxidative stress is found in many other neurological and chronic conditions. Redox abnormalities are a final common pathway of myriad genetic and environmental stressors, e.g. methylmercury (Kaur, Aschner, & Syversen, 2006), tributyltin (Liu et al., 2006), cadmium (Yang et al., 2007), and paraquat (Castello, Drechsel, & Patel, 2007), to name just a few, and the cell does not appear to distinguish sharply between different toxicants in its molecular and cellular responses (Li et al., 2007).

Energy metabolism

Mitochondrial metabolism abnormalities and oxidative stress can contribute to altered energy metabolism in ASD, which has been documented (Chugani et al., 1999; Minshew et al., 1993). Network activity in the brain can be highly sensitive to mitochondrial function (Huchzermeyer et al., 2008)

All of the above metabolic abnormalities are consistent with the idea that the neurological disturbances in autism could be a manifestation of systemic metabolic dysregulation or disruption (Anderson, Hooker, & Herbert 2008; Herbert, 2009; Herbert & Anderson, 2008).

Proposition 4) Biomedical problems may begin early in development, may have developmental trajectories, and in many cases may even precede the onset of ASD behavioral features

This proposition has been investigated through medical record review and other retrospective methods in the some of the at-risk siblings studies performed to date. For example, increased frequency of ear infections, greater use of antibiotics, and more illness-related fevers have been documented (Niehus & Lord,

2006), and there were more gastrointestinal symptoms in children with ASD and regression, than in children with ASD and no regression (Richler et al., 2006). Prospective measures of head circumference have demonstrated that rapid head growth during the first year of life decelerates in the second year, at the same time as symptoms worsen (Dawson et al., 2007), while one neuroimaging study supports an increased rate of head growth starting around 12 months of age (Hazlett et al. 2005).

The idea that the pathophysiological accompaniments of autism may themselves undergo development, and may interact significantly with the emergence of behavioral features, is only beginning to be investigated. Studies aimed at elucidating physiological development only become conceivable as a worthwhile endeavor once epigenetics and gene-environment interactions are more thoroughly considered as possible contributors to autism. Careful documentation of physiological and behavioral development in autistic cases may contribute significantly to generating new insights about development and vulnerability in autism.

OPEN QUESTIONS IN CONSIDERING WHOLE BODY AND SYSTEMS FEATURES IN AUTISM

There are a number of questions that will need to be addressed going forward to make sense of the relationship between core behavioral features and somatic or systemic features in autism (Bolton, 2009). These include: 1) determining whether somatic and systemic features are secondary or intrinsic to the autism; 2) investigating the relationship between somatic and systemic features of brain structure and function changes; 3) looking for covariations in somatic and behavioral phenotypic features; 4) assessing whether interventions in one domain or level have an impact at other levels—e.g., whether treating gastrointestinal disease can reduce aggression, or whether treating immune function can improve sleep, sensory processing, or epilepsy; and 5) developing animal models that embody not only brain and behavior but also somatic features (MacFabe et al. 2007; Shultz et al., 2008a, 2008b). Including somatic features in phenotyping may also contribute to identifying meaningful subgroups.

If active pathophysiological processes, such as immune dysregulation, turn out to be contributors to aspects of the behavioral phenotype in autism, this raises a particularly clinically relevant consideration: Are language, communication, and Theory of Mind impairments intrinsic static deficits, and a manifestations of psychologically based lack of motivation, or do they at least in part derive from a physiologically based inability to mobilize cellular activity that is strong or organized enough to drive these functional systems? Insofar as these behaviors may be influenced by somatic physiological status, this raises the possibility that the core "impairments" we see in autism may be the effects at the behavioral level of a pathophysiology based *obstruction* of a capacity that is potentially still at least partly present, rather than an intrinsic and irretrievable impairment.

To the extent that somatic and systemic features in autism are recognized and considered as worthy of documentation, investigation, and reflection, ongoing research and clinical experience may yield interesting insights into the above questions, and hopefully also an expanded and more comprehensive set of interventions, which will take these whole-body dimensions of autism more systematically into account.

References

Akinci, M. K., & Schofield, P. R. (1999). Widespread expression of GABA (A) receptor subunits in peripheral tissues. *Neurosci Res, 35*(2), 145–153.

Anderson, M. P., Hooker, B. S., & Herbert, M. R. (2008). Bridging from cells to cognition in autism pathophysiology: Biological pathways to defective brain function and plasticity. *American Journal of Biochemistry and Biotechnology, 4*(2), 167–176.

Aneja, A., & Tierney, E. (2008). Cholesterol deficit in autism: Insights from Smith-Lemli-Opitz syndrome. In A. Zimmerman (Ed.), *Autism: Current theories and evidence* (pp. 69–79). Totowa, NJ: Humana Press.

Ashwood, P., Anthony, A. Pellicer, A., Torrente, F., Walker-Smith, J. A., & Wakefield, A. J. (2003). Intestinal lymphocyte populations in children with regressive autism: Evidence for extensive mucosal immunopathology. *J Clin Immunol, 23*(6), 504–517.

Ashwood, P., Anthony, A., Torrente, F., & Wakefield, A. J. (2004). Spontaneous mucosal lymphocyte cytokine profiles in children with autism and gastrointestinal symptoms: Mucosal immune activation and reduced counter regulatory interleukin-10. *J Clin Immunol, 24*(6), 664–673.

Ashwood, P., & Van de Water, J. (2004a) A review of autism and the immune response. *Clin Dev Immunol, 11*(2), 165–174.

Ashwood, P., & Van de Water, J. (2004b) Is autism an autoimmune disease? *Autoimmun Rev, 3*(7–8), 557–562.

Ashwood, P., Enstrom, A. Krakowiak, P., Hertz-Picciotto, I., Hansen, R. L. Croen LA, Ozonoff S, Pessah, I. N, Van de Water J. (2008). Decreased transforming growth factor beta1 in autism: a potential link between immune dysregulation and impairment in clinical behavioral outcomes. *J Neuroimmunol, 204* no (1-2), 149–53.

Audhya, T. (2005) Nutrients, toxins, enzymes and oxidative biomarkers in children with autism. *Oxidative stress in autism symposium, New York State Institute for BasicRresearch in Developmental Disabilities, Staten Island NY*, p 3 (abstract).

Barkhudaryan, N., & Dunn, A. J. (1999). Molecular mechanisms of actions of interleukin-6 on the brain, with special reference to serotonin and the hypothalamo-pituitary-adrenocortical axis. *Neurochem Res, 24*(9), 1169–1180.

Bauman, M. (2006). Beyond behavior—Biomedical diagnoses in autism spectrum disorders. *Autism Advocate, 45*(5), 27–29.

Black, C., Kaye, J. A., & Jick, H. (2002). Relation of childhood gastrointestinal disorders to autism: Nested case-control study using data from the UK General Practice Research Database. *BMJ, 325*(7361), 419–421.

Bolton, P. F. (2009). Medical conditions in autism spectrum disorders. *J Neurodevelop Disord, 1,* 102–113.

Braunschweig, D., Ashwood, P., Krakowiak, P. Hertz-Picciotto, I., Hansen, R., Croen, L. A.,... Van de Water, J. (2008). Autism: Maternally derived antibodies specific for fetal brain proteins. *Neurotoxicology, 29*(2), 226–231.

Cabanlit, M., Wills, S., Goines, P. Ashwood, P., & Van de Water, J. (2007). Brain-specific autoantibodies in the plasma of subjects with autistic spectrum disorder. *Ann N Y Acad Sci, 1107,* 92–103.

Cadenas, E., & Davies, K. J. (2000). Mitochondrial free radical generation, oxidative stress, and aging. *Free Radic Biol Med, 29*(3–4), 222–230.

Canitano, R. (2007). Epilepsy in autism spectrum disorders. *Eur Child Adolesc Psychiatry, 16*(1), 61–66.

Castello, P. R., Drechsel, D. A., & Patel, M. (2007). Mitochondria are a major source of paraquat-induced reactive oxygen species production in the brain. *J Biol Chem, 282*(19), 14186–14193.

Chauhan, A., & Chauhan, V. (2006). Oxidative stress in autism. *Pathophysiology, 13*(3), 171–181.

Chauhan, A., Chauhan, V. & Brown, T. (2009). *Autism: Oxidative stress, inflammation and immune abnormalities.* Boca Raton, FL: Taylor & Francis/CRC Press.

Chez, M. G., Dowling, T., Patel, P. B., Khanna, P., & Kominsky, M. (2007). Elevation of tumor necrosis factor-alpha in cerebrospinal fluid of autistic children. *Pediatr Neurol, 36*(6), 361–365.

Chugani, D. C., Sundram, B. S., Behen, M., Lee, M. L., & Moore, G. J. (1999). Evidence of altered energy metabolism in autistic children. *Prog Neuropsychopharmacol Biol Psychiatry, 23*(4), 635–641.

Clark-Taylor, T., & Clark-Taylor, B. E. (2004). Is autism a disorder of fatty acid metabolism? Possible dysfunction of mitochondrial beta-oxidation by long chain acyl-CoA dehydrogenase. *Med Hypotheses, 62*(6), 970–975.

Coleman, N. (1989). Autism: Nondrug biological treatments. In C. Gillberg (Ed.), *Diagnosis and treatment of autism* (pp. 219–235). New York: Plenum Press.

Comi, A. M., Zimmerman, A. W., Frye, V. H., Law, P. A., & Peeden, J. N. (1999). Familial clustering of autoimmune disorders and evaluation of medical risk factors in autism. *Journal of Child Neurology, 14*(6), 388–394.

Connolly, A. M., Chez, M., Streif, E. M., Keeling, R. M., Golumbek, P. T., Kwon, J. M... . Deuel, R. M. (2006). Brain-derived neurotrophic factor and autoantibodies to neural antigens in sera of children with autistic spectrum disorders, Landau-Kleffner syndrome, and epilepsy. *Biol Psychiatry, 59*(4), 354–363.

Correia, C., Coutinho, A. M. Diogo, L., Grazina, M., Marques, C., Miguel, T... . Vicente, A. M. (2006). Brief report: High frequency of biochemical markers for mitochondrial dysfunction in autism: No association with the mitochondrial aspartate/glutamate carrier SLC25A12 gene. *J Autism Dev Disord, 36*(8), 1137–1140.

Croonenberghs, J., Bosmans, E., Deboutte, D., Kenis, G., & Maes, M. (2002). Activation of the inflammatory response system in autism. *Neuropsychobiology, 45*(1), 1–6.

Curran, L. K., Newschaffer, C. J., Lee, L. C., Crawford, S. O., Johnston, M. V., & Zimmerman, A. W. (2007). Behaviors associated with fever in children with autism spectrum disorders. *Pediatrics, 120*(6), e1386–1392.

D'Eufemia, P., Celli, M., Finocchiaro, R., Pacifico, L. Viozzi, L., Zaccagnini, M., Cardi, E., & Giardini, O. (1996). Abnormal intestinal permeability in children with autism. *Acta Paediatr, 85*(9), 1076–1079.

D'Souza, Y., Fombonne, E., & Ward, B. J. (2006). No evidence of persisting measles virus in peripheral blood mononuclear cells from children with autism spectrum disorder. *Pediatrics, 118*(4), 1664–1675.

Dawson, G., Munson, J., Webb, S. J., Nalty, T., Abbott, R., & Toth, K. (2007). Rate of head growth decelerates and symptoms worsen in the second year of life in autism. *Biol Psychiatry, 61*(4), 458–464.

Deonna, T., & Roulet, E. (2006). Autistic spectrum disorder: Evaluating a possible contributing or causal role of epilepsy. *Epilepsia, 47*(Suppl 2), 79–82.

Femia, L. A., & Hasselmo, M. E. (2002). Is autism partly a consolidation disorder? *Behav Cogn Neurosci Rev, 1*(4), 251–263.

Fernell, E., Watanabe, Y., Adolfsson, I., Tani, Y., Bergstrom, M., Hartvig, P... . Langstrom, B. (1997).

Possible effects of tetrahydrobiopterin treatment in six children with autism—Clinical and positron emission tomography data: A pilot study. *Dev Med Child Neurol, 39*(5), 313–318.

Filiano, J. J., Goldenthal, M. J., Mamourian, A. C., Hall, C. C., & Marin-Garcia, J. (2002). Mitochondrial DNA depletion in Leigh syndrome. *Pediatr Neurol, 26*(3), 239–242.

Filipek, P. A., Juranek, J., Nguyen, M. T., Cummings, C., & Gargus, J. J. (2004). Relative carnitine deficiency in autism. *J Autism Dev Disord, 34*(6), 615–623.

Filipek, P. A., Juranek, J., Smith, M., Mays, L. Z., Ramos, E. R., Bocian, M... . Gargus, J. J.(2003). Mitochondrial dysfunction in autistic patients with 15q inverted duplication. *Ann Neurol, 53*(6), 801–804.

Finegold, S. M., Molitoris, D., Song, Y., Liu, C., Vaisanen, M. L., Bolte, E... . Kaul, A. (2002). Gastrointestinal microflora studies in late-onset autism. *Clin Infect Dis, 35*(Suppl 1), S6–S16.

Furlano, R. I., Anthony, A., Day, R., Brown, A., McGarvey, L., Thomson, M. A... .Murch, S. H. (2001). Colonic CD8 and gamma delta T-cell infiltration with epithelial damage in children with autism. *J Pediatr, 138*(3), 366–372.

Garland, M. R., Hallahan, B., McNamara, M., Carney, P. A., Grimes, H., Hibbeln, J. R... . Conroy, R. M. (2007). Lipids and essential fatty acids in patients presenting with self-harm. *Br J Psychiatry, 190*, 112–117.

Gillberg, C., & Coleman, M. (2000). *The biology of the autistic syndromes (Clinics in developmental medicine)*.Cambridge: Cambridge University Press.

Gladkevich, A., Korf, J., Hakobyan, V. P., & Melkonyan, K. V. (2006). The peripheral GABAergic system as a target in endocrine disorders. *Auton Neurosci, 124*(1–2), 1–8.

Goodwin, M. S., Groden, J., Velicer, W. F., Lipsitt, L. P., Baron, M. G., Hofmann, S. G., & Groden, G. (2006). Cardiovascular arousal in individuals with autism. *Focus on Autism and Other Developmental Disabilities, 21*(2), 100–123.

Graf, W. D., Marin-Garcia, J., Gao, H. G., Pizzo, S., Naviaux, R. K., Markusic, D... . Haas, R. H. (2000). Autism associated with the mitochondrial DNA G8363A transfer RNA (Lys) mutation. *J Child Neurol, 15*(6), 357–361.

Groden, J., Cautela, J., Prince, S., & Berryman, J. (1991). The impact of stress and anxiety on individuals with autism and developmental disabilities. In E. Schopler & G. Mesibov (Eds.), *Behavioral issues in autism* (pp. 178–190). New York: Plenum Press.

Happé, F., & Frith, U. (2006). The weak coherence account, detail-focused cognitive style in autism spectrum disorders. *J Autism Dev Disord, 36*(1), 5–25.

Hazlett, H. C., Poe, M., Gerig, G., Smith, R. G., Provenzale, J., Ross, A... . Piven, J. (2005). Magnetic resonance imaging and head circumference study of brain size in autism: Birth through age 2 years. *Arch Gen Psychiatry, 62*(12), 1366–1376.

Herbert, M. R. (2005). Large brains in autism: The challenge of pervasive abnormality. *Neuroscientist, 11*(5), 417–440.

Herbert, M. R. (2009). Autism: The centrality of active pathophysiology and the shift from static to chronic dynamic encephalopathy. In A. Chauhan, V. Chauhan, & T. Brown (Eds.), *Autism, oxidative stress, inflammation and immune abnormalities* (pp. 343–387). Boca Raton, FL: Taylor & Francis/ CRC Press.

Herbert, M. R., & Anderson, M. P. (2008). An expanding spectrum of autism models: From fixed developmental defects to reversible functional impairments. In A. Zimmerman (Ed.), *Autism: Current theories and evidence* (pp. 429–463). Totowa, NJ: Humana Press.

Hirstein, W., Iversen, P., & Ramachandran, V. S. (2001). Autonomic responses of autistic children to people and objects. *Proc R Soc Lond B Biol Sci, 268*(1479), 1883–1888.

Honomich, R., Goodlin-Jones, B., Burnham, M., Gaylor, E., & Anders, T. (2002). Sleep patterns of children with pervasive developmental disorders. *Journal of Autism and Developmental Disorders, 32*, 553–561.

Horvath, K., Papadimitriou, J. C., Rabsztyn, A., Drachenberg, C., & Tildon, J. T. (1999). Gastrointestinal abnormalities in children with autistic disorder. *J Pediatr, 135*(5), 559–563.

Horvath, K., & Perman, J. A. (2002). Autistic disorder and gastrointestinal disease. *Curr Opin Pediatr, 14*(5), 583–587.

Howlin, P. (1998). *Children with autism and Asperger syndrome: A guide for practitioners and carers.* Chichester, UK: Wiley.

Huchzermeyer, C., Albus, K., Gabriel, H. J., Otahal, J., Taubenberger, N., Heinemann, U... . Kann, O. (2008). Gamma oscillations and spontaneous network activity in the hippocampus are highly sensitive to decreases in pO2 and concomitant changes in mitochondrial redox state. *J Neurosci, 28*(5), 1153–1162.

Hutt, S. J., & Hutt, C. (1968). Stereotypy, arousal and autism. *Hum Dev, 11*(4), 277–286.

James, S. J., Melnyk, S., Jernigan, S., Cleves, M. A., Halsted, C. H., Wong, D. H... . Gaylor, D. W. (2006). Metabolic endophenotype and related genotypes are associated with oxidative stress in children with autism. *Am J Med Genet B Neuropsychiatr Genet, 141*(8), 947–956.

Jass, J. R. (2005). The intestinal lesion of autistic spectrum disorder. *Eur J Gastroenterol Hepatol, 17*(8), 821–822.

Jory, J. (2005). Oxidative stress in autism, A role for zinc. *Oxidative Stress in Autism Symposium, New York State Institute for Basic Research in Developmental Disabilities*, Staten Island NY, p. 2 (abstract).

Just, M. A., Cherkassky, V. L. Keller, T. A., & Minshew, N. J. (2004). Cortical activation and synchronization during sentence comprehension in high-functioning autism: Evidence of underconnectivity. *Brain*, *127*(Pt. 8), 1811–1821.

Jyonouchi, H., Geng, L., Ruby, A., Reddy, C., & Zimmerman-Bier, B. (2005a). Evaluation of an association between gastrointestinal symptoms and cytokine production against common dietary proteins in children with autism spectrum disorders. *J Pediatr*, *146*(5), 605–610.

Jyonouchi, H., Geng, L., Ruby, A., & Zimmerman-Bier, B. (2005b). Dysregulated innate immune responses in young children with autism spectrum disorders, their relationship to gastrointestinal symptoms and dietary intervention. *Neuropsychobiology*, *51*(2), 77–85.

Jyonouchi, H., Sun, S., & Itokazu, N. (2002). Innate immunity associated with inflammatory responses and cytokine production against common dietary proteins in patients with autism spectrum disorder. *Neuropsychobiology*, *46*(2), 76–84.

Kaur, P., Aschner, M., & Syversen, T. (2006). Glutathione modulation influences methyl mercury induced neurotoxicity in primary cell cultures of neurons and astrocytes. *Neurotoxicology*, *27*(4), 492–500.

Kern, J. K., Trivedi, M. H., Garver, C. R., Grannemann, B. D., Andrews, A. A., Savla, J. S.... . Schroeder, J. L. (2006). The pattern of sensory processing abnormalities in autism. *Autism*, *10*(5), 480–494.

Kowal, C., DeGiorgio, L. A., Nakaoka, T., Hetherington, H., Huerta, P. T., Diamond, B., & Volpe, B. T. (2004). Cognition and immunity: Antibody impairs memory. *Immunity*, *21*(2), 179–188.

Leekam, S. R., Nieto, C., Libby, S. J., Wing, L., & Gould, J. (2007). Describing the sensory abnormalities of children and adults with autism. *J Autism Dev Disord*, *37*(5), 894–910.

Levitt, P. (2005). Disruption of interneuron development. *Epilepsia*, *46 Suppl 7*, 22–28.

Levy, S. E., Souders, M. C., Wray, J., Jawad, A. F., Gallagher, P. R., Coplan, J... . Mulberg, A. E. (2003). Children with autistic spectrum disorders. I, comparison of placebo and single dose of human synthetic secretin. *Arch Dis Child*, *88*(8), 731–736.

Li, X., Chauhan, A., Sheikh, A. M., Patil, S., Chauhan, V., Li, X. M... . Malik, M. (2009). Elevated immune response in the brain of autistic patients. *J Neuroimmunol*, *207*, 111–116.

Li, Z., Dong, T., Proschel, C., & Noble, M. (2007). Chemically diverse toxicants converge on Fyn and c-Cbl to disrupt precursor cell function. *PLoS Biol*, *5*(2), e35.

Limoges, E., Mottron, L., Bolduc, C., Berthiaume, C., & Godbout, R. (2005). Atypical sleep architecture and the autism phenotype. *Brain*, *128*(Pt. 5), 1049–1061.

Liu, H. G., Wang, Y., Lian, L., & Xu, L. H. (2006). Tributyltin induces DNA damage as well as oxidative damage in rats. *Environ Toxicol*, *21*(2), 166–171.

Lorton, D., Lubahn, C. L., Estus, C., Millar, B. A., Carter, J. L., Wood, C. A., & . Bellinger, D. L. (2006). Bidirectional communication between the brain and the immune system: Implications for physiological sleep and disorders with disrupted sleep. *Neuroimmunomodulation*, *13*(5–6), 357–374.

MacFabe, D. F., Cain, D. P., Rodriguez-Capote, K., Franklin, A. E., Hoffman, J. E., Boon, F... . Ossenkopp, K. P. (2007). Neurobiological effects of intraventricular propionic acid in rats: Possible role of short chain fatty acids on the pathogenesis and characteristics of autism spectrum disorders. *Behav Brain Res*, *176*(1), 149–169.

Malow, B. A. (2004). Sleep disorders, epilepsy, and autism. *Ment Retard Dev Disabil Res Rev*, *10*(2), 122–125.

Malow, B. A., Marzec, M. L., McGrew, S. G., Wang, L., Henderson, L. M., & Stone, W. L. (2006). Characterizing sleep in children with autism spectrum disorders: A multidimensional approach. *Sleep*, *29*(12), 1563–1571.

Marin-Garcia, J., Ananthakrishnan, R., Goldenthal, M. J., Filiano, J. J., & Sarnat, H. B. (1999). Skeletal muscle mitochondrial defects in nonspecific neurologic disorders. *Pediatr Neurol*, *21*(2), 538–542.

Mattson, M. P., & Shea, T. B. (2003). Folate and homocysteine metabolism in neural plasticity and neurodegenerative disorders. *Trends Neurosci*, *26*(3), 137–146.

Melmed, R. D., Schneider, C. K., & Fabes, R. A. 2000. Metabolic markers and gastrointestinal symptoms in children with autism and related disorders. *J Pediatr Gastroenterol Nutr*, *88*, 731–736.

Ming, X., Julu, P. O., Brimacombe, M., Connor, S., & Daniels, M. L. (2005). Reduced cardiac parasympathetic activity in children with autism. *Brain Dev*, *27*(7), 509–516.

Ming, X., Julu, P. O., Wark, J., Apartopoulos, F., & Hansen, S. (2004). Discordant mental and physical efforts in an autistic patient. *Brain Dev*, *26*(8), 519–524.

Minshew, N. J., Goldstein, G., Dombrowski, S. M., Panchalingam, K., & Pettegrew, J. W. (1993). A preliminary 31P MRS study of autism: Evidence for undersynthesis and increased degradation of brain membranes. *Biological Psychiatry*, *33*, 762–773.

Moretti, P., Sahoo, T., Hyland, K., Bottiglieri, T., Peters, S., del Gaudio, D... . Scaglia, F. (2005). Cerebral folate deficiency with developmental delay, autism, and response to folinic acid. *Neurology*, *64*(6), 1088–1090.

Muntjewerff, J. W., van der Put, N., Eskes, T., Ellenbroek, B., Steegers, E., Blom, H., & Zitman, F. (2003). Homocysteine metabolism and B-vitamins in schizophrenic patients: Low plasma folate as a possible independent risk factor for schizophrenia. *Psychiatry Res*, *121*(1), 1–9.

Murch, S. (2005). Diet, immunity, and autistic spectrum disorders. *J Pediatr, 146*(5), 582–584.

Murias, M., Webb, S. J., Greenson, J., & Dawson, G. (2007). Resting state cortical connectivity reflected in EEG coherence in individuals with autism. *Biol Psychiatry, 62*(2), 270–273.

Natowicz, M. (2004). Personal communication.

Niehus, R., & Lord, C. (2006). Early medical history of children with autism spectrum disorders. *J Dev Behav Pediatr, 27*(2 Suppl), S120–127.

Oliveira, G., Diogo, L., Grazina, M., Garcia, P., Ataide, A., Marques, C., Miguel, T., Borges, L., Vicente, A. M., & Oliveira, C. R. (2005). Mitochondrial dysfunction in autism spectrum disorders: A population-based study. *Dev Med Child Neurol, 47*(3) 185–189.

Page, T. (2000). Metabolic approaches to the treatment of autism spectrum disorders. *J Autism Dev Disord, 30*(5), 463–469.

Page, T., & Moseley, C. (2002). Metabolic treatment of hyperuricosuric autism. *Prog Neuropsychopharmacol Biol Psychiatry, 26*(2), 397–400.

Parracho, H. M., Bingham, M. O., Gibson, G. R., & McCartney, A. L. (2005). Differences between the gut microflora of children with autistic spectrum disorders and that of healthy children. *J Med Microbiol, 54*(Pt 10), 987–991.

Perry, V. H., Newman, T. A., & Cunningham, C. (2003). The impact of systemic infection on the progression of neurodegenerative disease. *Nat Rev Neurosci, 4*(2), 103–112.

Pogribna, M., Melnyk, S., Pogribny, I., Chango, A., Yi, P., & James, S. J. (2001). Homocysteine metabolism in children with Down syndrome, in vitro modulation. *Am J Hum Genet, 69*(1), 88–95.

Poling, J. S., Frye, R. E., Shoffner, J., & Zimmerman, A. W. (2006). Developmental regression and mitochondrial dysfunction in a child with autism. *J Child Neurol, 21*(2), 170–172.

Qin, L., Wu, X., Block, M. L., Liu, Y., Breese, G. R., Hong, J. S... . Crews, F. T. (2007). Systemic LPS causes chronic neuroinflammation and progressive neurodegeneration. *Glia, 55*(5), 453–462.

Richler, J., Luyster, R., Risi, S., Hsu, W. L., Dawson, G., Bernier, R... . Lord, C. (2006). Is there a "regressive phenotype" of autism spectrum disorder associated with the measles-mumps-rubella vaccine? A CPEA study. *J Autism Dev Disord, 36*, 299–316.

Rubenstein, J. L., & Merzenich, M. M. (2003). Model of autism, increased ratio of excitation/inhibition in key neural systems. *Genes Brain Behav, 2*(5), 255–267.

Schulz, J. B., Lindenau, J., Seyfried, J., & Dichgans, J. (2000). Glutathione, oxidative stress and neurodegeneration. *Eur J Biochem, 26*(16), 4904–4911.

Serra, J. A., Dominguez, R. O., de Lustig, E. S., Guareschi, E. M., Famulari, A. L., Bartolome, E. L., & Marschoff, E. R. (2001). Parkinson's disease is associated with oxidative stress: Comparison of peripheral antioxidant profiles in living Parkinson's, Alzheimer's and vascular dementia patients. *J Neural Transm, 108*(10), 1135–1148.

Shultz, S. R., Macfabe, D. F., Martin, S., Jackson, J., Taylor, R., Boon, F... . Cain, D. P. (2008a). Intracerebroventricular injections of the enteric bacterial metabolic product propionic acid impair cognition and sensorimotor ability in the Long-Evans rat: Further development of a rodent model of autism. *Behav Brain Res, 200*, 33–41.

Shultz, S. R., Macfabe, D. F., Ossenkopp, K. P., Scratch, S., Whelan, J., Taylor, R., & Cain, D. P. (2008b). Intracerebroventricular injection of propionic acid, an enteric bacterial metabolic end-product, impairs social behavior in the rat: Implications for an animal model of autism. *Neuropharmacology, 54*(6), 901–911.

Solmaz, M., Kavuk, I., & Sayar, K. (2003). Psychological factors in the irritable bowel syndrome. *Eur J Med Res, 8*(12), 549–556.

Song, Y., Liu, C., & Finegold, S. M. (2004). Real-time PCR quantitation of clostridia in feces of autistic children. *Appl Environ Microbiol, 70*(11), 6459–6465.

Suh, J. H., Walsh, W. J., McGinnis, W. R.,Lewis, A., & Ames, B. N. (2008). Altered sulfur amino acid metabolism in immune cells of children diagnosed with autism. *American Journal of Biotechnology and Biochemistry, 4*(2), 105–13.

Sweeten, T. L., Bowyer, S. L., Posey, D. J., Halberstadt, G. M., & McDougle., C. J. (2003). Increased prevalence of familial autoimmunity in probands with pervasive developmental disorders. *Pediatrics, 112*(5), e420.

Taylor, B., Miller, E., Lingam, R., Andrews, N., Simmons, A., & Stowe, J. (2002). Measles, mumps, and rubella vaccination and bowel problems or developmental regression in children with autism: Population study. *BMJ, 324*(7334), 393–396.

Toichi, M., & Kamio, Y. (2003). Paradoxical autonomic response to mental tasks in autism. *J Autism Dev Disord, 33*(4), 417–426.

Tomchek, S. D., & Dunn, W. (2007). Sensory processing in children with and without autism: A comparative study using the short sensory profile. *Am J Occup Ther, 61*(2), 190–200.

Torrente, F., Ashwood, P., Day, R., Machado, N., Furlano, R. I., Anthony, A... . Murch, S. H. (2002). Small intestinal enteropathy with epithelial IgG and complement deposition in children with regressive autism. *Mol Psychiatry, 7*(4), 375–82, 334.

Torres, A. R., Maciulis, A., & Odell, D. (2001). The association of MHC genes with autism. *Front Biosci, 6*, D936–43.

Trevathan, E. (2004). Seizures and epilepsy among children with language regression and autistic spectrum disorders. *J Child Neurol, 19 Suppl 1*, S49–57.

Tuchman, R. (2006). Autism and epilepsy: What has regression got to do with it? *Epilepsy Curr, 6*(4), 107–11.

Valicenti-McDermott, M., McVicar, K., Rapin, I., Wershil, B. K., Cohen, H., & Shinnar, S. (2006). Frequency of gastrointestinal symptoms in children with autistic spectrum disorders and association with family history of autoimmune disease. *J Dev Behav Pediatr, 27*(2 Suppl), S128–36.

Vargas, D. L., Nascimbene, C., Krishnan, C., Zimmerman, A. W., & Pardo, C. A. (2005). Neuroglial activation and neuroinflammation in the brain of patients with autism. *Ann Neurol, 57*(1), 67–81.

Veenman, L., & Gavish, M. (2006). The peripheral-type benzodiazepine receptor and the cardiovascular system. Implications for drug development. *Pharmacol Ther, 110*(3), 503–24.

Vezzani, A., & Granata, T. (2005). Brain inflammation in epilepsy, experimental and clinical evidence. *Epilepsia, 46*(11), 1724–43.

Vezzani, A., Moneta, D., Richichi, C., Perego, C., & De Simoni, M. G. (2004). Functional role of proinflammatory and anti-inflammatory cytokines in seizures. *Adv Exp Med Biol, 548*, 123–33.

Vojdani, A., Campbell, A. W., Anyanwu, E., Kashanian, A., Bock, K., & Vojdani, E. (2002). Antibodies to neuron-specific antigens in children with autism: Possible cross-reaction with encephalitogenic proteins from milk, Chlamydia pneumoniae and Streptococcus group A. *J Neuroimmunol, 129*(1–2), 168–77.

Welch, M. G., Welch-Horan, T. B., Anwar, M., Anwar, N., Ludwig, R. J., & Ruggiero, D. A. (2005). Brain effects of chronic IBD in areas abnormal in autism and treatment by single neuropeptides secretin and oxytocin. *J Mol Neurosci, 25*(3), 259–274.

Williams, D. L., Goldstein, G., & Minshew, N. J. (2006). Neuropsychologic functioning in children with autism: Further evidence for disordered complex information-processing. *Child Neuropsychol, 12*(4–5), 279–98.

Yang, Z., Yang, S., Qian, S. Y., Hong, J. S., Kadiiska, M. B., Tennant, R. W… . Liu, J. (2007). Cadmium-induced toxicity in rat primary mid-brain neuroglia cultures: Role of oxidative stress from microglia. *Toxicol Sci, 98*(2), 488–94.

Yorbik, O., Sayal, A., Akay, C., Akbiyik, D. I., & Sohmen, T. (2005). Investigation of antioxidant enzymes and trace element levels in children with autistic disorder. *Oxidative Stress in Autism Symposium, New York State Institute for Basic Research in Developmental Disabilities, Staten Island NY*, p. 10 (abstract).

Zecavati, N., & Spence, S. J. (2009). Neurometabolic disorders and dysfunction in autism spectrum disorders. *Curr Neurol Neurosci Rep., 9*(2), 129–36.

Zimmerman, A. W., Connors, S. L., & Pardo, C. A. (2006). Neuroimmunology and neurotransmitters in autism. In R. Tuchman & I. Rapin (Eds.), *Autism: A neurobiological disorder of early brain development* (pp. 141–59). London: Mac Keith Press.

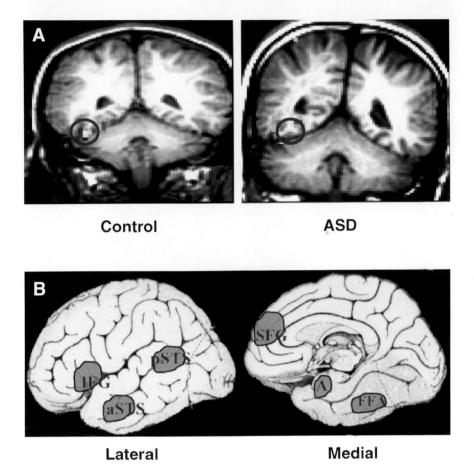

Figure 12-1 Functional MRI abnormalities observed in autism spectrum disorders (ASD). A, these coronal MRI images show the cerebral hemispheres above, the cerebellum below, and a circle over the fusiform gyrus of the temporal lobe. The examples illustrate the frequent finding of hypoactivation of the fusiform gyrus to faces in an adolescent male with ASD (right) compared with an age- and IQ-matched healthy control male (left). The red/yellow signal shows brain areas that are significantly more active during perception of faces; signals in blue show areas more active during perception of nonface objects. Note the lack of face activation in the boy with ASD but average levels of nonface object activation. B, Schematic diagrams of the brain from lateral and medial orientations illustrating the broader array of brain areas found to be hypoactive in ASD during a variety of cognitive and perceptual tasks that are explicitly social in nature. Some evidence suggests that these areas are linked to form a "social brain" network. IFG, Inferior frontal gyrus (hypoactive during facial expression imitation); pSTS, posterior superior temporal sulcus (hypoactive during perception of facial expression and eye gaze tasks); SFG, superior frontal gyrus (hypoactive during theory of mind tasks, i.e., when taking another person's perspective); A, amygdala (hypoactive during a variety of social tasks); FFA, fusiform face area (hypoactive during perception of personal identity). (From DiCocco-Bloom et al., 2006).

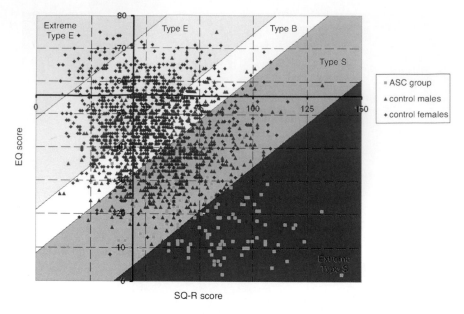

Figure 17-1 SQ and EQ Scores for All Participants with the Boundaries for Each Brain Type.

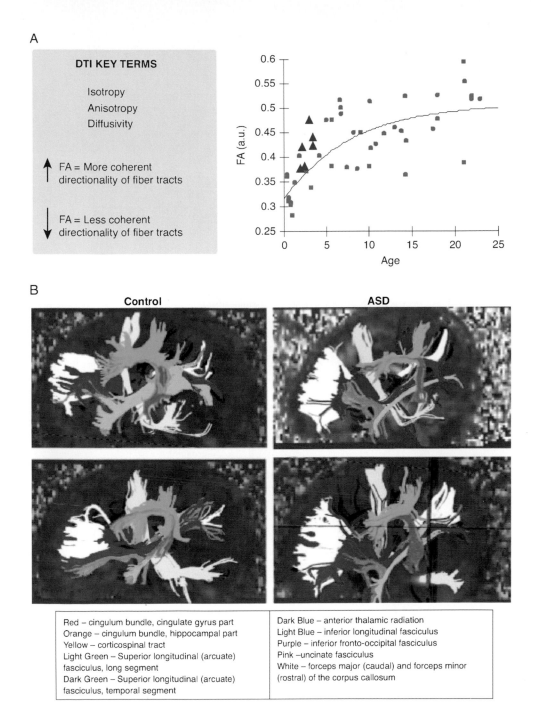

A

DTI KEY TERMS

Isotropy

Anisotropy

Diffusivity

↑ FA = More coherent
directionality of fiber tracts

↓ FA = Less coherent
directionality of fiber tracts

B

| Control | ASD |

Red – cingulum bundle, cingulate gyrus part
Orange – cingulum bundle, hippocampal part
Yellow – corticospinal tract
Light Green – Superior longitudinal (arcuate)
fasciculus, long segment
Dark Green – Superior longitudinal (arcuate)
fasciculus, temporal segment

Dark Blue – anterior thalamic radiation
Light Blue – inferior longitudinal fasciculus
Purple – inferior fronto-occipital fasciculus
Pink –uncinate fasciculus
White – forceps major (caudal) and forceps minor
(rostral) of the corpus callosum

Figure 21-2 A. Values of fractional anisotropy (FA) in the forceps minor (the anterior portion of the corpus callosum that extends into the frontal lobes) plotted for 7 toddlers with autism (triangles) against typically developing subjects ages 4 months–23 years. Note that FA values were increased for all 7 ASD toddlers relative to the normal mean (from Ben-Bashat, et al., 2007). B. DTI tractography images from 14-month-old (top) and 20-month-old (bottom) ASD and typically developing infants. The inferior longitudinal fasiculus (ILF) is diminished in the infants at risk for an ASD, as is the superior longitudinal arcuate fasiculus (SLAF), a fiber tract involved in language processing. Note that the forceps minor region of the corpus callosum (CC-FMin) that extends into the frontal lobes (shown in white) is enlarged relative to normal. This finding is consistent with Ben Beshat et al. (2007), who reported increased FA in the forceps minor portion of the corpus callosum (Unpublished data from the University of California San Diego Autism Center of Excellence).

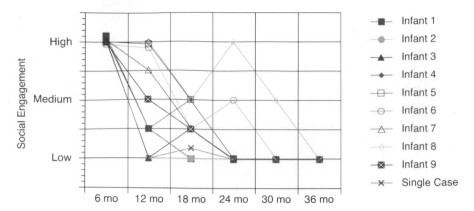

Figure 21-3 Graphic illustration of the levels of social engagement of 9 high-risk infants between the ages of 6 and 36 months eventually diagnosed as having an ASD, as described in previously published case studies. Data from the first 9 cases are adapted from Bryson et al., 2007 and the final case is from Dawson et al., 2005. Note that all 10 high-risk infants showed high levels of social engagement at 6 months. Also note that the decline in social responsiveness was inconsistent between children with some declining rapidly by 12 months and others not until 24 or 30 months. High Social Engagement refers to a consistent interest or pleasure in, and responsiveness to, others. Medium Social Engagement refers to inconsistent interest or pleasure in, and responsiveness to, others. Low Social Engagement refers to little or no interest or pleasure in, and responsiveness to, others.

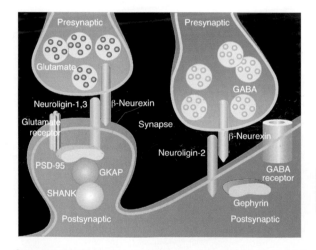

Neuroligins are are molecules that ensure signal transitions between nerve cells. **Neuroligins** are expressed on the surface of the postsynaptic neuron and bind to **nuerexins** which are proteins on the presynaptic neurons. It is thought that **neurologins** and neurexins together play key roles in the forming and functioning of synapses and are often thought of as "glue" that binds pre and postsynaptic neurons together.

There are 5 neuroligins genes in the human genome: **NLGN1, NLGN2, NLGN3, NLGN4** and **NLGN4Y**

Schematic of a chemical synapse between an axon of ane neuron and a dendrite of another. Synapses are specialized minute gaps between neurons. Electrical impulses arriving at the axon terminal trigger the release of packets of chemical messengers (neurontranmitters), which diffuse across the synaptic cleft to receptors on the adjacent dendrite, temporarily affecting the likelihood that an electrical impulse will be triggered in the latter neuron. Once released, the neurotransmitter is rapidly metabolized or is pumped back into a neuron.

Figure 21-4 Neuroligins, neurexins, and the synapse. Adapted from Garber, K. (2007). Autism's cause may reside in abnormalities at the synapse. Figure 2 called "Autism's origin." *Science, 317*(5835), 190–191.

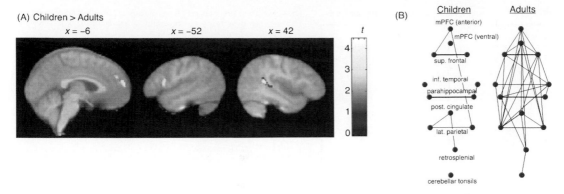

Figure 21-5 Examples of 2 theorized principles of brain development. (A). Example of more widespread activity earlier in development. In a task where children were to perceive irony, children showed significantly greater activity than adults in the MPFC (x = –8, y = 58, z = 20; P < 0.05), the left inferior frontal gyrus (x = –48, y = 16, z = 14; P = 0.05) and the right posterior STS (x = 42, y = –44, z = 16; P < 0.05). (From Wang, Lee, Sigman, & Dapretto, 2006). Johnson, Grossmann, & Cohen Kadosh (2009) cite this example of more widespread activity in children than adults in some brain regions as support of the view that functional activity becomes more focal across development. (B). Example of increased connectivity of networks later in development. Graphic visualization of the brain regions that are significantly correlated based on functional connectivity analyses. Brain regions in the default mode network (e.g., medial prefrontal cortex and posterior cingulate) are only very sparsely connected in children aged 7–9 years. In adults aged 21–31 years, the default regions are highly integrated (strongly functionally connected). (From Fair et al., 2008).

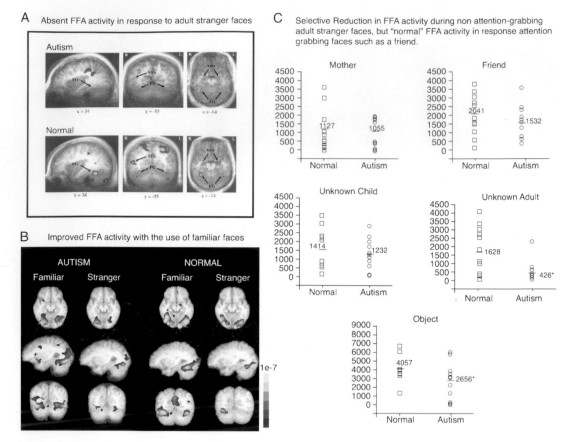

Figure 21-6 Fusiform activity in autism across three separate studies. In panel A (Pierce et al., 2001), adults with autism showed reduced fusiform activity in response to faces of strangers. In panel B (Pierce et al., 2004), adults with autism showed modestly reduced activity in response to faces of strangers, but normal levels on fusiform activity in response to familiar faces. Panel C (Pierce et al., 2008) shows that in 6- to 12-year-olds with autism, the number of voxels that were active in response to faces of strangers were only ½ to ¼ the number seen in response to mothers or friends face. Collectively the studies by Pierce and colleagues demonstrate that the fusiform can be active at normal levels in individuals with autism. The degree to which the fusiform functions normally may have more to do with a stimulus' ability to break through a strong and aberrantly connected resting network (i.e., the "threshold effect") than defects in the fusiform per se.

Chapter 26

Future Directions in ASD Research

Deborah Fein, Katarzyna Chawarska, and Isabelle Rapin

INTRODUCTION

Each expert who contributed to this book was asked to discuss the most up-to-date research on an aspect of autism, and all provided state-of-the-art reviews of one of the complex clinical or research topics related to the disorder. The task of this closing chapter is to provide a bird's-eye view of where the field of autism has arrived after a third of a century of widely disparate efforts, and of what seem like the most promising and pressing areas of research for the immediate future. We emphasize that, in this chapter, when we say "autism" we are referring to the autism spectrum disorders (ASDs) and not specifically.to Autistic Disorder, as diagnosed by *DSM-IV* criteria,

There is incontrovertible evidence that autism is not a "disease," in the sense of a unitary condition with one well-defined biological cause, and a singular underlying pathology and biochemistry. It is at the behavioral level that a unitary core of symptoms makes diagnosis easy in some affected individuals, in others

more difficult. This is not to say that there is universal agreement on the exact delineation of the core symptoms, but there is consensus that autism is a syndrome characterized by profound deficits in sociability, communicative skills, and various aspects of language, as well as a lack of behavioral flexibility, with a strong tendency toward repetitive verbal and behavioral perseveration. Much remains to be understood about this unitary behavioral syndrome: how are its core symptoms interrelated, how are they related to the many other behavioral features that characterize some affected individuals and not others, and to such overall behavioral features as drive, arousal, mood, cognition, memory, and others?. What brain systems, if any, must be dysfunctional in all affected individuals, as opposed to others that may be dysfunctional in only those who manifest specific non-core symptoms?

The fact that, at the biological level, there is no "autism disease" is still not universally appreciated by parents, the public, and, surprisingly, by many scientists, who view autism from the perspective of their narrow but deep knowledge of their field of expertise. The evidence, however, is overwhelming: autism, or at least marked autistic behaviors, can arise as the consequence of a multitude of genetic abnormalities and, occasionally, by a fortuitous environmental cause deleterious to the developing brain, such as infection, stress, birth injury, or social deprivation, among others. The current view is that individual life events and environmental effects and genetics are inextricably linked by the ongoing epigenetic control of gene expression that modulate brain development and function. Therefore, the biologic scientists, like the behavioral scientists, need to consider whether the many correlates they are uncovering at an accelerating pace represent necessary and sufficient explanations for the core features of autism, or explanations for multiple syndromes that may include some autistic features.

In this final chapter, we will attempt to identify the areas of research that seem to be the most promising, or the most necessary in order to advance our understanding of the causes, pathophysiology, prevention, and treatment of autistic spectrum disorders. In many ways, this is an impossible task. While in the middle of a line of research, it is not possible to know for sure whether it be a fruitful path or a dead end. In addition, it is obviously impossible to forecast with any certainty advances in other realms of basic science, such as genetics, that will be applicable to autism. Nevertheless, we have contemplated recent advances in autism research, identifying those that seem most promising in yielding a deeper understanding, as well as areas that seem to be crucial gaps in knowledge that might respond to current methods or those under rapid development. We will discuss each of these areas of research; in many cases, the reader will note that they may depend on each other or have overlapping content.

CLASSIFICATION AND CLINICAL PRESENTATION ISSUES

The ASDs share with other developmental disorders and psychiatric illnesses the fact that all are defined on the basis of descriptive behavioral criteria, even though all are the consequences of atypical development of the brain. This means that the diagnostic criteria for all of them are dimensional, not dichotomous, and therefore none of these disorders has sharp margins.

Major efforts have been expended to devise valid and reliable tools, such as the Autistic Diagnostic Interview-Revised (ADI-R) the Diagnostic Observation Schedule (ADOS), and others appropriate for individuals of different ages and abilities. Such standardized instruments are widely accepted, and essential for uniformity of subject selection for research. Clinical diagnosis by experienced clinicians fulfills many practical needs more efficiently but less reliably than these standardized behavioral tools. In turn, the rigidity of these instruments makes them miss some "pastel classic," (term suggested by Martha Bridge Denckla) mildly affected persons at the borderline of the syndrome, whose symptoms nevertheless deserve explanation and remediation.

Classification based on sharp criteria is essential for epidemiology. Diagnostic criteria for ASDs have broadened markedly. Contributing to this is heightened awareness of professionals, parents, and the general public, as well as the use of standardized instruments which pick up both mildly affected individuals, and severely affected persons with other evidence of brain damage or dysfunction. This change in criteria has had a major impact on epidemiologic estimates of the actual prevalence of ASDs and on the delineation of subtypes, not to mention its influence on the demands it makes on educational systems and their budgets. Continued efforts toward devising more robust and accepted diagnostic criteria are needed for scientific as well as political reasons. The new effort, just beginning at the time of this writing, at devising a classification system for psychiatric entities based on their biology (the "Research Domain Criteria") will no doubt in the long run apply to autism as well. A major problem is the many dozens, and perhaps hundreds, of biologic causes already identified as responsible for or contributors to the autism phenotype. As with other disorders, classification based on genetics and pathophysiology will provide a more rational approach to prevention and treatment, although in cases where biological underpinning can either not be identified or cannot be treated, behavioral treatment based entirely on clinical symptoms will no doubt continue to be helpful.

Even in the area of phenotypic manifestations, the subject of ASD research for 50 years, certain areas have been less thoroughly investigated than others. Motor and sensory deficits in autism, even though prominent and very frequent, have been inadequately studied. To what degree stereotypies are behavioral strategies to decrease anxiety, as suggested by Kinsbourne (see Chapter 19) and others, calls for additional rigorous research. As stereotypies are not universal in autism and may not be associated with ostensibly aversive circumstances, they may represent movement disorders which, like tics and other movement disorders, are modulated by emotion. The detailed circuitry that underlies their production has yet to be defined. Motor control and learning, and the role of networks engaging cortical prefrontal, supplementary motor, and parietal areas with subcortical, especially cerebellar and basal ganglia, activity, can now be investigated behaviorally and with electrophysiological and functional imaging, as indicated in Chapter 10. Deficits in sensory perception and intersensory integration, emphasized by parents, occupational therapists, and many affected persons, is another surprisingly neglected biological research area (see Chapter 11). Better understanding of sensorimotor deficits would significantly improve the design of innovative and better targeted interventions, as well as our understanding of basic biological processes.

Progress has been made in defining the language deficits of children with autism, which vary much more than widely appreciated until recently, as discussed in Chapter 6 (Allen & Rapin, 1992; Rapin, Dunn, Allen, Stevens, & Fein, 2009). Detailed analysis of transcripts will yield rich dividends for understanding which parts of the language networks are dysfunctional in which subtype of language disorder, especially if the same children are also studied with electrophysiologic and functional imaging tools. There is critical need for the referral of toddlers for study at the time they are actively undergoing language/autistic regression. Thus far all that is known is that epilepsy appears not to play the major role in causing the regression, but there are no data on potential inflammatory or other factors, or possible stresses in its causation.

EPIDEMIOLOGIC AND DEMOGRAPHIC ISSUES

This is an area where much further work is needed, but definitive figures will not become available until widely acceptable uniform classification criteria are adopted worldwide, which is not likely to happen any time soon. According to many epidemiologists, the main reasons for the so-called contemporary "autism epidemic" are the broadening of criteria just mentioned, shifting diagnostic criteria, and increased public awareness of the autism diagnosis (Fombonne, 2005), which often brings with it desirable, more intensive interventions than do other developmental disorders. From 1970 to 1980, epidemiologists pegged the prevalence of autism at 4/10,000 (1/2,500), whereas the most recently quoted figure is 1/100, although the latter encompasses the whole autism spectrum. Based on scattered evidence, parents incriminate as potential contributors to this 25-fold increase environmental toxins, an increased number of immunizations, undiagnosed infections of the pregnant mother or the infant, and older ages of both fathers and mothers at conception (King, Fountain, Dakhlallah, & Bearman, 2009).

Epidemiologic evidence has thoroughly discredited the measles vaccine and the preservative thimerosal (ethyl mercury) as significant causes of autism (Offit, 2009). There is no convincing evidence for increased toxic exposure, infection, or immune factors in large numbers of cases, although the latter may play a role in a small fraction of children (Patterson, 2009). It has been suspected for decades that nuclear or mitochondrial gene mutations or copy number variations (CNV) of single stranded DNA provide a likely explanation for atypical individual reactions to medications, toxins, infections, or immune factors, and current progress in genetics and especially epigenetics supports this hypothesis. These atypical responses are the exception, and at present are not well enough understood to alter medical practice.

Another factor, and a difficult one to investigate, is the potential role of stress, either on the infant, or even on the fetus of a mother who experiences stress or an illness while pregnant (Kinney, Munir, Crowley, & Miller, 2008). There is some evidence that the male sex may enhance vulnerability to stress. The 4:1 predominance of autism in boys over girls is incontrovertible, yet sex-related differences in autistic symptomatology and explanations for the differential prevalence have barely been explored (see Chapter 17 for one theory).

Thus, while some careful epidemiological studies have been done throughout the world, different diagnostic criteria, different applications of such criteria, and differences in public and professional awareness make it extremely difficult to draw any conclusions about changes in incidence, or related demographic factors that may eventually be important to understanding etiologies. While no convincing evidence exists as yet for environmental contributions to significant numbers of autism cases, the possible role of the enormous numbers of potential toxins, nutrients, infections, or other environmental factors has only begun, and judgment on their potential role in autism must await careful and large-sample studies.

GENETIC AND EPIGENETIC ISSUES

The search for a single gene responsible for most cases of autism is, unfortunately, no longer a reasonable goal. Geneticists need to look for criteria that fall into three categories (Kumar & Christian, 2009). The first, based on pedigree analysis, is new single Mendelian or mitochondrial mutations with strong effects responsible for well-defined "diseases" like PKU (phenylketonuria) which may or may not be associated with autistic symptomatology. The second is microscopically detectable deletions, duplications, translocations, or other chromosomal rearrangements of whole chromosomes or chromosomal fragments in which a group of contiguous genes are affected together, generally resulting in a recognizable complex phenotype like Down's, Williams, or Turner syndrome. The third are microscopic, single-stranded DNA copy number variations (CNVs) of various sizes detectable by whole genome microarray technology; although linkage to autism may be clear, their probable phenotypic relevance requires work at the molecular, cellular, and brain levels. Chapter 2 points out the spectacular progress made in understanding the genetics of autism, and Chapter 24 analyzes the complexities involved in the cross-level relationships between genetic/epigenetic and phenotypic variation.

What geneticists are finding are numerous new abnormalities in all three categories. Some are causal of rare, biologic syndromes which have autism as one of their manifestations. Many more, especially CNVs, contribute to the core autism phenotype or to one of its behavioral features either as single mutations or, more often, by multiple weak influences. The relationship of such genetic or chromosomal variations to disturbed brain development and function is not generally well understood, although very interesting and promising suggestions have been made, such as the role of specific deletions in synaptic function (Morrow et al., 2008). Since Zoghbi (2003) suggested that synaptic function might be a common factor among autism susceptibility genes, this suggestion has been fruitfully used to narrow down likely target genes in chromosome segments (e.g. Kumar et al, 2008). The reversal of some Rett symptoms in mice by treatment with IGF-1 peptide, which increased spine density, synaptic amplitude, and cortical plasticity, seems to open the door to exploration of potential treatments of syndromes with decreased or abnormal synaptic function (Tropea et al., 2009).

Genome-wide microarray studies are uncovering many CNVs; their function in, and relevance to, the autism phenotype are unknown. Understanding their relevance to autism requires multidisciplinary approaches, such as statistical analysis in well-studied homogeneous populations, multiplex families with more than one affected member, and controls in order to evaluate the probability that detected abnormalities play a pathogenic role. This also means that robust clinical features (endophenotypes) need to be detected and used as a basis for classification, be they behavioral or biologic, such as a subtype of language disorder, the presence or absence of epilepsy, stereotypies, big heads or minor congenital abnormalities, extraordinary talents, or a history of autistic/language regression, as well as other neuropsychological traits, or the response to particular medications or educational approaches. We stress that these genetic studies may be addressing the brain basis of an associated feature of autism, and not its core deficits.

Because behavior arises from the dysfunction of more than a single brain network, few genes can be expected to map directly onto behavioral endophenotypes (see Chapter 24). Genes are responsible for the multitude of complex molecular microcircuitries that orchestrate cellular function, and thus brain development, structure, and function, as well as its responses to environmental inputs. Therefore, from a classification standpoint, it is the mapping of genes to brain cells that requires continued investigation, with the understanding that genes are active in only some subpopulations of neurons and glia, and are turned off in others. Some environmental influences may also be quite selective, as will be their behavioral and physical effects. Genes and environment affect the development, structure, and function of the brain synergistically, and thus together they mold the behavioral phenotype of the individual. Hierarchical levels, from genes to brain circuitry to behavior, must be kept firmly in mind by investigators of all the many biologic and behavioral aspects of the ASDs.

It is, of course, the case that particular mutations often produce recognizable phenotypes like fragile X, with its cognitive impairment, anxiety, and attention deficits, but they do so indirectly, in this case at least in part by the effect of lack of the fragile X protein (FMRP) on neuronal spine genesis, and thus synaptic function. Molecular work is crucial for devising therapies effective for at least selected symptoms of autism. In mice engineered to lack the FMRP, providing an enzyme that inhibits actin, a critical protein for spine genesis, partially corrected the spine deficit morphologically and electrophysiologically in neurons, as well as improved behavior (Hayashi et al., 2007). This molecular information does not fully explain how the lack of FMRP affects the development of neuronal spines, or other biochemical/cellular effects of the fragile X mutation on growth of the face, ears, and testes. Again, multidisciplinary investigation will continue to be required to reap more complete understanding of gene effects in the causation of complex disorders like the ASDs, which may, like fragile X and Rett syndrome, or may not have associated somatic effects.

There is a strong need to understand stark phenotypic differences between individuals who are carriers of the same gene mutation. Polygenetic and epigenetic background effects are likely to explain part of the variability in single-gene phenotypes; in some cases, for example in tuberous sclerosis, phenotypic variability can range from non-penetrance to disparate associated neurologic and somatic manifestations, to infantile spasms, with an autistic phenotype in only a fraction of affected individuals. An exciting and very new area of work in ASD is the study of *epigenetics*, processes that modulate gene function without changing DNA sequence. There is substantial complexity here, with processes including chromatin marking, RNA transcription, post-transcriptional modification, translation, and post-translational modification resulting in cell and tissue-specific functional regulation (Mattick, Amaral, Dinger, Mercer, & Mehler, 2009; Mattick, Taft, & Faulkner, 2010; Rando & Chang, 2009). In some definitions (e.g. Mattick et al., 2009), these processes include only heritable ones, such as imprinting, gene silencing by microRNAs, and X-inactivation, while other, broader, definitions (e.g. Crews, 2008) include environmental effects on gene expression, such as those of toxins.

Understanding of this area is just starting, and has major implications for classification and symptom causation. Epigenetics plays a crucial role in brain (and body) development, and in mediating environmental influences on function. Epigenetics may explain phenotypic differences in identical twins who share all their DNA but experience different environmental exposures (Raynes et al, 1999). Future epigenetic studies may help explain variability among individuals in responses to drugs and stresses. It will need to be determined whether comorbidity of autism with other neuropsychiatric conditions, such as attention-deficit/hyperactivity disorder, bipolar disease, or even schizophrenia (Rapoport, Chavez, Greenstein, Addington, & Gogtay, 2009), is another example of phenotypic variability of a given gene, or is due to the coincidence of inheriting several genes with pathologic consequences.

BRAIN STRUCTURE AND FUNCTION

Understanding the biology of autism will entail understanding of at least four interrelated aspects of neural function: the anatomy of the brain once autism is manifest, the cell biology and biochemistry of the autistic brain, the development of the autistic brain both pre- and postnatally, and specific pathological processes that may influence brain development and function. Because autism is not a "disease" but a behaviorally defined syndrome, it is no surprise that studies of its biology come to different, in some cases conflicting, conclusions. Because the autistic spectrum disorders share distinct core behavioral characteristics, it is reasonable to assume that they must have some commonalities at the brain level, despite highly disparate etiologies. Although a great deal has been learned about the biology of autism, research has not yet reached comprehensive understanding of its pathophysiology.

Chapter 3 reviews what has been learned about the brain anatomy of autism, including especially unusual asymmetries (or lack of asymmetry), ventricular dilatation, increased brain size, differential volumes of grey versus white matter, and regional variations, including the limbic system, cerebellum, and cortical areas—especially the frontal lobes, basal ganglia, and thalamus. Herbert presents a comprehensive review of this large, complex, and conflicting literature, and concludes that the developmental trajectories of different brain circuits and structures differ in timing and trajectory. Interpretation of these detailed anatomic changes, alterations in connectivity among cortical and subcortical brain areas and in blood perfusion is complicated by substantial methologic differences among studies. Yet recent substantial progress in morphologic and functional brain imaging technology bodes well for accelerating anatomic and physiologic understanding of autism.

Studies of brain chemistry in autism, although not as extensive as anatomical studies, are equally complex and contradictory. This literature is reviewed in Chapter 4, including early studies of neurotransmitter metabolite levels, through modern postmortem studies and imaging studies focusing on monoamines, glutamate and GABA, and peptides. In Chapter 4, Posey et al. conclude that evidence for a consistent role of monoamines in autism is weak, except for the early and replicated finding of platelet hyperserotonemia in a sizable minority of affected individuals, serotonergic abnormalities in brain, and the effect of serotonergic drugs on some autistic behaviors. Genetic, MRS, and postmortem studies support a possible role for GABA and glutamate in autism, but most of these studies are relatively new and carried out in small samples; much more needs to be done to replicate these findings and associate them with clinical features. Neuropeptides are less well supported as playing a role in autism (but see Chapter 22 for a discussion of oxytocin).

The study of brain development, of course, overlaps with all of the other topics (anatomy, chemistry, pathological processes), but is an area of study in itself. The well-replicated finding of accelerated head and brain growth during the first two years of life, preceding the emergence of signs of autism in many cases, suggests that the study of brain growth is likely to be revealing, particularly a focus on the specific growth of regional grey and white matter. The first such study has recently appeared, tracking by MRI the regional development of the brain in 41 toddlers showing signs of autism as early as 1.5 years, with diagnosis later confirmed (Schumann et al., 2010). The investigators found that all regions (cerebral gray, cerebral white, frontal gray, temporal gray, cingulate gray, and parietal gray) except occipital gray developed at an abnormal growth rate in the affected children. As the authors point out, abnormal development, as indexed by head circumference, begins younger than 1.5 years, and therefore prospective studies in high-risk children starting at birth will be needed to complete the picture of abnormal regional brain growth (see discussion of prospective baby sibling studies, below). Of course, the understanding of relative growth rates of different CNS areas is just the beginning; what is needed is a deep understanding, ultimately to the molecular level, of how the abnormal growth impacts later processes such as anatomical and functional connectivity (Courchesne & Pierce, 2005), and of the processes influencing such abnormal development, such as overgrowth of white matter versus inflammation versus failure of pruning (Herbert, 2005) and, equally important, how these growth parameters correlate with behavioral development and with treatment effects.

Specific perinatal and neonatal pathological processes, such as inflammation, infection, hypoxic-ischemic injury, prematurity, prenatal drug exposure, overall obstetric suboptimality, and genetically determined growth abnormalities such as failure of neuronal pruning, have been subjects of recent speculation and study, but none has a clearly established role in a large number of autism cases (see review by Newschaffer, Fallin, & Lee, 2002). There is some as yet sparse evidence for abnormal activation of immune responses, including activated astroglia and microglia, and an increase in pro-inflammatory cytokines in brain tissue (see Chapter 25), but the number of brains available for postmortem study is still so small—typically one or two to less than a dozen in individual studies— that the generality of findings is tentative at best, in view of the well-documented multiplicity of potential causes of autism and intervening illnesses. In the aggregate, environmental causes may be more numerous than previously appreciated, as there are reports of associations of autism with premature birth (Limperopoulos et al., 2008), suboptimal birth (Hultman et al., 2002), and pregnancy (Newschaffer et al., 2002), including precipitous, induced, or prolonged labor (Juul-Dam, 2001), neonatal requirement for oxygen administration, hyperbilirubinemia and RH incompatibility (Juul-Dam, 2001), uterine bleeding during gestation (Juul-Dam, 2001), certain maternal gestational infections, notably rubella, CMV, and influenza (Newschaffer et al.,2002), and drug exposure, specifically valproic acid and thalidomide (Williams and Casanova, 2010), but not specifically hypoxic injury (Rennie et al., 2009). Although these factors were elevated in autism samples, they clearly could not independently account for a large number of cases (Newschaffer et al., 2002), and equally clearly, serious and large-scale efforts at replication are crucial.

It is also clear that the timing, nature, and severity of injury influences the nature and region of the resulting insult to the fetal brain, as well as the unfolding of interrelated long-term consequences. Rees and Inder (2005) provide a most useful review of animal models of various forms of pre- and perinatal injury, focusing on hypoxic-ischemic injury, inflammatory/infective insults, and preterm birth. Not only must the direct and interacting effects of such pathological processes be understood, but the cascading post-injury reorganization of undamaged systems must be studied as well. Interacting effects, in particular, will be very difficult and complex to untangle, as will the influence of timing of injury, which can have dramatically different effects in different periods of gestation and postnatally.

As has been illustrated in many chapters in this book, it will not be sufficient to collect a sample of individuals with "autism" and perform imaging or other neural studies, and analyze group data, as has very often been done in the studies reviewed in these chapters. Neural development and pathological findings must be studied in relation to specific behaviors and symptoms and to later brain outcome measures, if they are to be ultimately revealing about the way in which the autistic clinical pictures develop. For example, Rees and Inder (2005) point out that animal models suggest that chronic mild placental insufficiency can result in long-term deficits in neural connectivity. A comprehensive model of autism will encompass etiologies, timing, the cascading neural effects, and the behavioral outcomes, as well as, ultimately, the neural effects of successful behavioral or medical interventions.

THE EARLIEST EMERGENCE OF SYMPTOMS, PROSPECTIVE AND LONGITUDINAL STUDIES

The overt behavioral symptoms of autism typically are discerned in the second year of life, enabling clinicians to diagnose ASD with considerable certainty (Brian et al., 2008; Bryson et al., 2007; Chawarska, Klin, Paul, Macari, & Volkmar, 2007, 2009; Landa & Garrett-Mayer, 2006; Pandey et al., 2008). This is not to say that symptoms may not be present in the first year, as discussed below, but it is mostly in retrospect that their import is appreciated. Due to increasing awareness of early symptoms of autism among parents

(Chawarska et al., 2007; Ozonoff et al., 2009) and professionals (Johnson et al., 2007; Myers et al., 2007; Zwaigenbaum et al., 2009), as well as owing to the development of early screening instruments (Robins, Fein, Barton, & Green, 2001; Stone, McMahon, & Henderson, 2008; Wetherby et al., 2004), the number of toddlers undergoing comprehensive diagnostic evaluations and entering early intervention programs has increased considerably in the past decade (Chawarska, Klin, & Volkmar, 2008; Dawson, 2008; Dawson et al., 2010; Koegel, Koegel, Fredeen, & Gengoux, 2008; Wetherby & Woods, 2008; Zwaigenbaum et al., 2009). Although much more work is needed to ensure that high-quality, early diagnostic and therapeutic resources are available universally regardless of racial, ethnic, and socioeconomic status (Mandell, Ittenbach, Levy, & Pinto-Martin, 2002; 2007), current practice represents major progress in the clinical care of young children affected by this complex disorder.

The key impairments notable in the second year of life either emerge at some point during that year, or have their precursors in the first year of life. These include affective responsivity to social partners, capacity for dyadic reciprocal exchanges, intentional communication, and joint attention, to mention a few. Experimental studies of autism in the second year of life also suggest impairments of early emerging elementary aspects of social cognition, including impairments in attentional bias for faces (Chawarska et al., 2003, 2010), visual recognition and scanning of faces (Chawarska & Shic, 2009; Chawarska & Volkmar, 2007), perception of speech (Paul, Chawarska, Fowler, Cicchetti, & Volkmar, 2007), perception of biological motion (Klin, Lin, Gorrindo, Ramsay, & Jones, in press), as well as social (Jones, Carr, & Klin, 2008) and activity monitoring (Shic, Bradshaw, & Chawarska, submitted). The precursors of most of these skills are also typically present in the first months of life, suggesting that the roots of an array of social and communicative deficits noted in toddlers with autism might already be present in the first year. For many decades, studies of early emergence relied on retrospective parental report, or on review of video diaries. However, discovery of the increased genetic risk for autism among younger siblings of children with the disorder enabled researchers to study the emergence of autism in *status nascendi*. This approach involves following pre- and postnatal development of younger siblings, to capture their unfolding neural and behavioral development using state-of-the-art measures.

According to the current conceptualization of the disorder, social and communicative deficits are both defining and primary in autism. Based on the existing, albeit limited, experimental evidence and theoretical considerations, it is likely that deficits in the social domain are the first to differentiate infants with autism from their developmentally delayed peers, because social reciprocal interaction skills emerge prior to intentional communication in typical infants. However, whether or not early social development in infancy is governed by a specialized and distinct brain subsystem is a matter of ongoing discussion. While some advocate a strong version of the social-infant hypothesis, suggesting that the processing of social and nonsocial information relies on a separate innate learning mechanism and neural systems (e.g., Ellsworth, Muir, & Hains, 1993; Trevarthen & Aitken, 2001), others argue that social and nonsocial cognitive development relies on the same ubiquitous mechanisms (Watson, 1979). Others suggest that specialization of the social cognition system emerges over time as a result of interplay of non-specific innate perceptual biases and learning mechanisms with species-typical social experiences in early ontogenesis (Karmiloff-Smith, 2002). In this view, specialization of the social cognition system would reflect outcome of an experience-dependent process rather than merely an expression of a hard-wired system (see Klin, Jones, Schultz, & Volkmar, 2003 for review).

Thus, it is essential to understand development of infants at high risk for autism along multiple dimensions, including the development of brain structure and connectivity, and brain chemistry and electrophysiology, as well as to investigate complex genetic and environmental influences on the early phenotype. Furthermore, behavioral measures need to target early emerging skills relevant to autism, including perceptual preferences for visual, tactile, and auditory social and nonsocial stimuli. It is also necessary to perform analysis of visual exploratory behaviors in response to a variety of socially and biologically relevant stimuli, vocal development, capacity for social engagement and nonverbal communication involving affective expressions, eye contact, and gestures, and ability to explore the environment and develop early discrimination and categorization skills. Examination of the developmental profiles across domains in conjunction with the biological measures will lead to identification of the primary deficits in autism and their underlying mechanisms, enabling researchers to design targeted treatments that might not only change the developmental trajectories of children with autism, but possibly even prevent emergence of the full-blown syndrome (Dawson, 2008).

There is little direct empirical evidence regarding the exact timing and manner of symptom onset in autism. Based primarily on retrospective data, several patterns of onset have been hypothesized: the "early onset" pattern, where symptoms become apparent shortly after birth (Kanner, 1943/1968); the "plateau" pattern, where after a period of more or less typical development, rate of skill acquisition slows down and the child appears to stagnate (Chawarska et al., 2007; Ozonoff, Heung, Byrd, Hansen, & Hertz-Picciotto, 2008; Siperstein & Volkmar, 2004); and the "set-back" or regression pattern, in which a child loses previously acquired social and communication skills in the second year of life (Eisenberg & Kanner, 1956; Kurita, 1985; (Rapin, 1996); Werner & Dawson, 2005). Still others report the presence of early deficits combined with loss of skills (Ozonoff, Williams, & Landa, 2005; Werner & Dawson, 2005). The empirical validity of the hypothesized patterns remains to be determined, as does their potential link to specific etiological factors and outcome.

The first empirical reports regarding the development of infants who later develop autism have begun to emerge. The extant evidence suggests that most infants appear to have relatively intact eye contact and social smile at 6 months of age (Bryson et al., 2007; Landa & Garrett-Mayer, 2006; Ozonoff et al., 2010; Young, Merin, Rogers, & Ozonoff, 2009; Zwaigenbaum et al., 2005), with the frequency and quality of these social behaviors declining between 6 and 12 months (Ozonoff et al., 2010). (But see new study by Bhat et al, 2010, reporting equal responses to caregivers, but less self-initiated socially directed gaze to caregivers, among 6-month-old infant sibs of children with autism compared to controls.) Such observations of behaviour during the second half of the first year have led to the presentation of a hypothesis that symptoms of autism might not be present at birth or shortly thereafter, but emerge over time through a process marked by decline in social-communicative functions (Ozonoff et al., 2010). Future studies will reveal whether these findings reflect the natural history of autism spectrum disorders, or instead, limited sensitivity of the existing methods for detection of more subtle signs of social disability in the first months of life. There is, however, an emerging consensus across a number of research studies that symptoms of social disability become more apparent, at least on the group level, around 12 months of age (see Rogers, 2009, for a review). Behaviors affected at this age include responsivity to name (Nadig et al., 2007), atypical object exploration and repetitive behaviors (Ozonoff et al., 2008), and language and nonverbal communication (Landa & Garrett-Mayer, 2006; Presmanes, Walden, Stone, & Yoder, 2007; Yoder, Stone, Walden, & Malesa, 2009). However, the specificity of these findings to ASD at this age remains to be clarified because, in most cases, control groups consisted of typically developing children or siblings at risk whose development turned out to be typical. Thus, as the expression of autism in the second year is becoming better understood, the next challenge is to identify the timing and domains in which developmental trajectories of infants who later develop autism begin to diverge from those of typically developing infants. These findings will need to be integrated with neurodevelopmental, biochemical, genetic, and brain imaging data to identify meaningful subtypes within the autism spectrum with regard to etiology, course, and outcome, as well as specific targets for intervention and the optimal timing for initiation of treatment.

MEDICAL CAUSES OF AUTISM: THE MATTER OF CO-MORBIDITY

Because autism is a behavioral diagnosis, the biologic cause of the autism may be irrelevant to its diagnosis. Many would still limit the diagnosis of "autism" to individuals with "primary autism/ASD," in whom the reason for the autism is unknown because they do not carry a diagnosable medical or psychiatric condition or have associated findings on physical/neurologic examination. Such a view would classify those in whom the cause is known as "secondary autism," or "autistic-like," or "having-autistic-traits-but-not-autistic." This position ignores the fact that autism is defined by behavioral criteria, and not by the cause of the brain dysfunction responsible for the behaviors. The DSM is cognizant of this, because it states that there are no exclusionary criteria for making a diagnosis of autism. It also states that if the affected individual fulfills criteria for another behavioral disorder (like intellectual deficiency, attention deficit disorder, or

obsessive/compulsive disorder, for example), the primary diagnosis should be the autism diagnosis, and the other disorders should be considered associated or comorbid symptoms. In fact comorbid diagnoses are frequent in persons with autism, especially those with intellectual limitations and severe language disorders. This brings us back to the issue of the dimensional nature of behavioral diagnoses and their fuzzy margins. These fuzzy margins provide ample opportunities for overlap and reemphasize the non-dichotomous nature of behavioral diagnostic labels.

With regard to medical conditions associated with autism, the DSM classifies them on a different diagnostic axis than behavioral diagnoses. Almost none of these medical conditions are inexorably associated with autism, and each of them accounts for a small proportion of all affected individuals. There is no credible evidence for the autism of tuberous sclerosis or fragile X being pathognomonic of that particular genetic disorder, or differing in kind from "primary autism." Fragile X is particularly likely to be associated with social anxiety (Tsiouris & Brown, 2004), and tuberous sclerosis with infantile spasms (Curatolo, Seri, Verdecchia, & Bombardieri, 2001), but again, these are not unique features of that particular genetic cause of autism. It makes more sense to compare, for example, the prevalence of autism in individuals with tuberous sclerosis with and without epilepsy, or with and without intellectual deficiency, than to contrast autism to tuberous sclerosis (chapter 2 provided a useful review of current genetic principles and listed some of the less rare syndromes or specific molecules now known to be associated with autism in some individuals or families). Correlation, however, does not imply causation. In the future, we hopefully will refine our genetic concepts and add many more associated syndromes or molecules. What is particularly needed is to gain an understanding of the influence of the genetic background of individuals, and of gene-gene interactions that account for the phenotypic diversity of given mutations. Another urgent need is to understand how environmental influences can modulate epigenetically the phenotypic expression of such genes, or can cause autism by their direct effects on the immature brain.

In addition, some specific medical conditions not necessarily directly linked to CNS function, such as gastrointestinal dysfunction or allergies, have been suggested to appear in autism at above-chance levels. Data on these conditions, as well as other, more directly CNS-linked abnormalities such as sleep disorders, abnormal response to painful stimuli, and behavioral improvement with fever (Mehler & Purpura, 2009), are not yet definitive and much more information is needed on their possible links to autism. Similarly, the possibility of immune processes in the etiology of some ASD cases has been raised, and there is some small-sample evidence for this, but the role of immune factors in all but a handful of cases remains in doubt. Chapter 25, on multisystem disease, reviewed some of this literature and offered a possible approach to conceptualizing autism as a set of disorders that affect multiple systems besides the CNS.

CLINICAL ASSESSMENT

Guidelines for clinical assessment and management have been published in practice parameters, papers, and books by panels and practicing clinicians, but very little has been done to empirically investigate the most effective assessment practices. This is true as much for psychological, speech and language, and educational assessments as for medical assessments (such as EEG, metabolic, or imaging tests). Yearly assessment (or more frequent for very young children) of such functions as language, reading, and social skills, as well as continuous data collection on behavioral or social problems, would seem an obious contribution to more effective programming, but data to substantiate this claim are largely lacking. Nor are they likely to be obtained soon, because of the ethical problems inherent in letting some children go without assessments that clinicians believe will provide data to guide therapy. Unfortunately, as financial resources of educational systems are squeezed and insurance companies grow more reluctant to pay for "medically unnecessary" assessments, parents or school systems with good financial means will be the only ones who can provide for their children the detailed assessments necessary, so that the educational systems can fine-tune their programming.

The richness of the genetic data that allows for understanding the pathophysiology of autism at the cellular and brain level—and, eventually, for developing targeted pharmacologic interventions for some of its behavioral symptoms-raises the question of how deeply and universally to test children on the autism spectrum for the underlying biologic causes of their autism. Which children need to be studied

morphologically, electrophysiologically, or genetically? Current guidelines (American Academy of Child and Adolescent Psychiatry, 1998; Filipek et al., 2000; Lintas & Persico, 2009) suggest that the answer depends on the goal of biologic testing and on the resources available. Universal in-depth testing is out of the question, because of the behavioral and biological costs and manpower required, and because of the very low yield outside of specific indications. Further, testing without any hypothesis in mind is likely to generate data, some of it false positives, which call for repeated or expanded testing, all of which further increase costs in both money and parental stress. The clinical goal is to uncover a biologic condition or behavioral symptom complex that demands a specific intervention for the welfare of the affected individual, provides a definitive biologic diagnosis for the proband and family, or, rarely and only in interested families, genetic counseling and prevention of the birth of a severely affected child. Among the guidelines are a positive family history of autism or related developmental or psychiatric disorder, clinical features suggesting a known genetic syndrome, like tuberous sclerosis or Rett syndrome, severe cognitive impairment, certain types of epilepsy, or a history of severe language/autistic regression, especially if persistent or progressive.

Brain imaging is rarely clinically indicated in ASDs; it is not part of practice parameters without specific indications. Functional brain imaging including fMRI, PET, diffusion tensor imaging (DTI) of white-matter tracts, and other techniques are research tools or have very limited and specific clinical indications. As more information about anatomy or functional systems is gathered through research, the application of these methods to standard clinical assessment may expand.

EEG and magnetoenceophalography are critically important for those individuals with ASD who have epilepsy, and of course for research on cognition, attention, and especially on the relation of epilepsy to autistic/language regression. However, they may not be particularly helpful or necessary in children with no such indications. Therefore the practice parameters do not recommend EEG as a routine test, because of its low rate of abnormality in the absence of a suspicion of epilepsy. Even in children with language/autistic regression, its yield is modest (McVicar, Ballaban-Gil, Rapin, Moshé, & Shinnar, 2005). For research, electrophysiology—and especially event-related potentials (ERPs)—yield unique functional data in the millisecond domain to which functional imaging is blind with current technology. The information on sensory processing, motor programming, and cognitive activities discussed in multiple chapters in the second section of this book shows that imaging, ERPs, and behavioral testing provide complementary data. Innovative approaches to their integrative use are being developed (Banaschewski & Brandeis, 2007). No doubt as the genetic, imaging, and EEG and MEG correlates of various forms of autism are better understood, clinical practice parameters will change and expand.

INTERVENTIONS AND OUTCOME

Interventions for ASD fall into two main groups: behavioral and educational interventions—including applied behavior analysis (ABA), other educational strategies, speech therapy, and motor therapies such as occupational therapy (OT) and physical therapy (PT)—and biological interventions. Biological interventions also fall into several categories, including psychiatric and neurological medications, and "biomedical" interventions that include unproved or disproved manipulations such as dietary supplements, chelation, and hyperbaric oxygen, Regarding the latter, although some have been shown to be ineffective and even potentially dangerous, it is essential to conduct one or two well-controlled, blinded studies of treatments adhered to by significant numbers of parents and not conducted in a center that offers one of these unproven therapeutic options (and is financially invested in said option).

There is widespread public misconception that autism is "curable," and such a cure could be brought about, if we only took the right medication, or followed the right diet. It is conceivable that we may learn enough about autism to prevent its occurrence or soften its severity, but being able to replace a missing molecule or altering the genome of an already symptomatic infant does not seem likely at this point. Many psychotropic medications are prescribed to individuals with ASD in the hopes of mitigating one or several of their undesirable behavioral symptoms such as aggression, self-injury, inattention, irritability, mood disorder, or sleep problems. This extensive pharmacology is based mainly on evidence gleaned from the treatment of adult psychiatric disorders and

from anecdotal reports. There is no drug specifically geared toward the treatment of autism. The only drug the FDA has approved for autism is risperidone, a so-called atypical antipsychotic. The FDA's approval rested primarily on evidence from a rigorously conducted double-blind study of its administration for 8 weeks to 101 children with autism (McCracken et al., 2002). The FDA's indications are limited to irritability and aggression, although it is widely touted clinically as having favorable efficacy on many other autistic behaviors. Risperidone has serious potential side effects, the most frequent being weight gain, and at high and prolonged doses apathy, movement disorders (tardive dyskinesia and others), and other rare toxicities. Evidence for efficacy of other widely prescribed medications such as stimulants, antidepressants, anxiolytics and others is mainly anecdotal and unblinded.

Development of novel medications depends almost entirely on the translation of progress in molecular biology research to a clinical application. Mutations exert their effects by altering complex biochemical cascades at the cellular level. As the cellular neurobiology of a behavioral syndrome is worked out in tissue culture and experimental animals, and the effect of biochemical alterations on the behavior of animal models are progressively clarified, it seems likely that this logical approach may lead to the development of new experimental drugs which must be evaluated in the laboratory before their effects and toxicities ever reach human trials. It takes years and requires millions of dollars to develop a novel drug, even one that is a minor modification of an existing drug, and that is not what is needed in autism. This pharmacologic effort needs to continue and will, but to our knowledge, a blockbuster new category of medication for autism is not on the close horizon.

Many behavioural and educational interventions have not been well studied, but have face validity, such as teaching and practicing specific social skills. As noted by Martha Denckla, "what you teach is what you get" (personal communication, 2010). This commonsense dictum is consistent with the research literature, which suggests that teaching such tangential skills as crawling, or swinging the child in a chair when you want to teach him to talk, are inefficient at best, and that direct teaching of deficient skills, whether they are reading in a dyslexic child or social and language skills in an autistic one, are the most efficient paths to take. Many studies have supported the efficacy of direct, step-by-step teaching of specific skills, using the well-established principles of learning theory. Heroic and effective programs have been developed not only to teach skills but also to control aggressive, non-compliant, destructive, and repetitive behaviors (see any issue of the *Journal of Applied Behavior Analysis*, for example). One line of research that certainly needs to be continued is the development of effective teaching and behavior-control programs, as well as the best combinations of medication with behavior therapy to control interfering behaviors (e.g. Aman et al., 2009).

In addition, there is a huge range of outcomes for children receiving intensive, effective, early therapy, from full "recovery" to severe disability. There is little known as yet about what early-childhood characteristics predict what level of outcome, although milder symptoms, especially in the repetitive domain, higher intellectual and language function, and quick response to intervention have some predictive value (reviewed by Helt et al., 2008). The possibility of "recovery" or "optimal outcome" (reviewed by Helt et al., 2008) is at the core of many outstanding and important questions: What percent of children with ASD have the potential for "optimal outcome"? Is behavioral treatment a prerequisite, or can other treatments or maturation alone account for some cases? Are there behavioral or biological markers of this potential (e.g., head circumference does NOT predict the possibility of optimal outcome; see Mraz et al., 2009)? Are there residual vulnerabilities that persist in these children (Helt et al., 2008, suggested that attention problems and anxiety, in particular, tend to persist)? What are the neurological mechanisms that allow "recovery"? A number of studies (Dawson, 2008; Dawson & Zanolli, 2003; Helt et al., 2008) speculate on some possible mechanisms, including normalization of development of neural circuitry if intervention begins early enough, and compensation using other brain systems, but evidence on such mechanisms is virtually nonexistent as yet. Some functional-imaging research to study these mechanisms have just begun. Even for children who do not "recover," specific treatment regimens can greatly improve areas of function such as specific language functions and face-processing skills; functional imaging pre- and post-intervention, along with behavioral measurement, may be extremely illuminating about the mechanisms of successful intervention. Ongoing attention is required to the escalating social demands "recovered" and persistently

symptomatic maturing children have to learn to confront and how adults in their lives can help them with these challenges (Fein and Dunn, 2007).

CONCLUSIONS

It is perhaps a good thing that those of us working in the neuropsychology of autism many years ago could not have foreseen the complexity of the task as it appears today. A conception of autism as one primary psychological problem underlain by one anatomical region or system utilizing one neurotransmitter, causation by one genetic defect, and a behavioral syndrome perhaps soluble with one therapy—that was the vision that lay behind much of the early work. As has been shown in each chapter of this book, it is an understatement to say that each of these assumptions proved incorrect. However, the progress made in the last 40 years in virtually all areas of autism research is truly remarkable, and the pace is accelerating. One challenge for the next period will be to avoid oversimplified thinking, and to try to face, with intellectual courage, the beautiful but daunting complexity of the developing nervous system. Another will be to undertake basic research to better understand the fundamental processes involved, while we try to forge ahead in the pragmatic domains of early detection, timely diagnosis, useful and valid assessments, and new therapies.

References

Allen, D. A., & Rapin, I. (1992). Autistic children are also dysphasic. In H. Naruse & E. Ornitz (Eds.), *Neurobiology ofi Infantile autism* (pp. 73–80). Amsterdam: Excerpta Medica.

Aman, M. G., McDougle, C. J., Scahill, L., Handen, B., Arnold, L. E., Johnson, C... . Wagner, A. (2009). Medication and parent training in children with pervasive developmental disorders and serious behavior problems: Results from a randomized clinical trial. *Journal of the American Academy of Child and Adolescent Psychiatry*, 48(12), 1143–1154.

American Academy of Child and Adolescent Psychiatry (1998). Summary of the practice parameters for the assessment and treatment of children and adolescents with language and learning disorders. *Journal of the American Academy of Child & Adolescent Psychiatry*, 37, 1117–1119.

Banaschewski, T., & Brandeis, D. (2007). Annotation: What electrical brain activity tells us about brain function that other techniques cannot tell us—A child psychiatric perspective. *Journal of Child Psychology and Psychiatry and Allied Disciplines, 48*, 415–435.

Bhat, A.N., Galloway, J.C., and Landa, R.J. (2010) Social and non-social visual attention patterns and associative learning in infants at risk for autism. *Journal of Child Psychology and Psychiatry and Allied Disciplines,*51(9), 989–997.

Brian, J., Bryson, S., Garon, N., Roberts, W., Smith, I., Szatmari, P.... Zwaigenbaum, L. (2008). Clinical assessment of autism in high-risk 18-month-olds. *Autism, 12*(5), 433–456.

Bryson, S. E., Zwaigenbaum, L., Brian, J., Roberts, W., Szatmari, P., Rombough, V., & McDermott, C. (2007). A prospective case series of high-risk infants who developed autism. *Journal of Autism and Developmental Disorders, 37*(1), 12–24.

Chawarska, K., Klin, A., Paul, R., Macari, S., & Volkmar, F. (2009). A prospective study of toddlers with ASD: short-term diagnostic and cognitive outcomes. *Journal of Child Psychology and Psychiatry, 50*(10), 1235–1245.

Chawarska, K., Klin, A., Paul, R., & Volkmar, F. (2007). Autism spectrum disorder in the second year: Stability and change in syndrome expression. *Journal of Child Psychology and Psychiatry, 48*(2), 128–138.

Chawarska, K., Klin, A., & Volkmar, F. (2003). Automatic attention cueing through eye movement in 2-year-old children with autism. *Child Development, 74*(4), 1108–1122.

Chawarska, K., Klin, A., & Volkmar, F. R. (2008). *Autism spectrum disorders in infants and toddlers: Diagnosis, assessment, and treatment.* New York: Guilford Press.

Chawarska, K., Paul, R., Klin, A., Hannigan, S., Dichtel, L. E., & Volkmar, F. (2007). Parental recognition of developmental problems in toddlers with autism spectrum disorders. *Journal of Autism and Developmental Disorders, 37*(1), 62–72.

Chawarska, K., & Shic, F. (2009). Looking but not seeing: Atypical visual scanning and recognition of faces in 2 and 4-year-old children with autism spectrum disorder. *Journal of Autism and Developmental Disorders, 39*(12), 1663–1672.

Chawarska, K., & Volkmar, F. (2007). Impairments in monkey and human face recognition in 2-year-old toddlers with autism spectrum disorder and developmental delay. *Developmental Science, 10*(2), 266–279.

Chawarska, K., Volkmar, F., & Klin, A. (2010). Limited attentional bias for faces in toddlers with autism spectrum disorders. *Archives of General Psychiatry, 67*(2), 178–185.

Courchesne, E., & Pierce, K. (2005). Brain overgrowth in autism during a critical time in development: Implications for frontal pyramidal neuron and interneuron development and connectivity.

International Journal of Developmental Neuroscience, 23(2–3), 153–170.

Crews, D. (2008). Epigenetics and its implications for behavioral neuroendocrinology. *Front Neuroendocrinology, 29*(3), 344–357.

Curatolo, P., Seri, S., Verdecchia, M., & Bombardieri, R. (2001). Infantile spasms in tuberous sclerosis complex. *Brain Development, 23*, 502–507.

Dawson, G. (2008). Early behavioral intervention, brain plasticity, and the prevention of autism spectrum disorder. *Development and Psychopathology, 20*(3), 775–803.

Dawson, G., Rogers, S., Munson, J., Smith, M., Winter, J., Greenson, J.... Varley, J. (2010). Randomized, controlled trial of an intervention for toddlers with autism: the Early Start Denver Model. *Pediatrics, 125*(1), 17–23.

Dawson, G., & Zanolli, K. (2003). Early intervention and brain plasticity in autism. In G. Bock & J. Goode (Eds.), *Autism: Neural bases and treatment possibilities. Novartis Foundation Symposium, 251*, 266–280.

Eisenberg, L., & Kanner, L. (1956). Early infantile autism, 1943–55. *American Journal of Orthopsychiatry, 26*, 556–566.

Ellsworth, C. P., Muir, D. W., & Hains, S. M. (1993). Social competence and person-object differentiation: An analysis of the still-face effect. *Developmental Psychology, 29*(1), 63–73.

Filipek, P. A., Accardo, P. J., Ashwal, S., Baranek, G. T., Cook, E. H., Jr., Dawson, G.... Volkmar, F. R. (2000). Practice parameter: Screening and diagnosis of autism: Report of the Quality Standards Subcommittee of the American Academy of Neurology and the Child Neurology Society. *Neurology, 55*, 468–479.

Fein, D. and Dunn, M. A. *Autism in your classroom: a general educator's guide to students with autism spectrum disorders.* 1, 1-319. 2007. Bethesda MD, Woodbine House.

Fombonne, E. (2005). Epidemiology of autistic disorder and other pervasive developmental disorders. *Journal for Clinical Psychiatry, 66*(10), 3–8.

Hayashi, M. L., Rao, B. S., Seo, J. S., Choi, H. S., Dolan, B. M., Choi, S. Y.... Tonegawa, S. (2007). Inhibition of p21-activated kinase rescues symptoms of fragile X syndrome in mice. *Proceedings of the National Academy of Sciences of the United States of America, 104*, 11489–11494.

Helt, M., Kelley, E., Kinsbourne, M., Pandey, J., Boorstein, H., Herbert, M., and Fein, D. (2008). Can children with autism recover? *If so, how? Neuropsychology Review, 18*, 339–366.

Herbert, M. (2005). Large brains in autism: The challenge of pervasive abnormality. *The Neuroscientist, 11*(5), 417–440.

Hultman, C., Sparen, P., & Cnattingius, S. (2002). Perinatal risk factors for infantile autism. *Epidemiology, 13*, 417–423.

Johnson, C. P., & Myers, S. M. (2007). Identification and evaluation of children with autism spectrum disorders. *Pediatrics*, 120(5), 1183–1215.

Jones, W., Carr, K., & Klin, A. (2008). Absence of preferential looking to the eyes of approaching adults predicts level of social disability in 2-year-old toddlers with autism spectrum disorder. *Archives of General Psychiatry*, 65(8), 946–954.

Juul-Dam, N., Townsend, J., Courchesne, E. (2001). Prenatal, perinatal, and neonatal factors in autism, pervasive developmental disorder-not otherwise specified, and the general population. *Pediatrics*, 107(4), 63.

Kanner, L. (1968). Autistic disturbances of affective contact. *Acta Paedopsychiatrica: International Journal of Child & Adolescent Psychiatry*, 35(4–8), 98–136. (Original work published 1943).

Karmiloff-Smith, A. (2002). Development itself is the key to understanding developmental disorders. In M. H. Johnson, Y. Munakata, & R. O. Gilmore (Eds.), *Brain development and cognition: A reader* (2nd ed., pp. 375–391). Malden, MA: Blackwell Publishers.

King, M. D., Fountain, C., Dakhlallah, D., & Bearman, P. S. (2009). Estimated autism risk and older reproductive age. *Am. J. Public Health*, 99, 1673–1679.

Kinney, D. K., Munir, K. M., Crowley, D. J., & Miller, A. M. (2008). Prenatal stress and risk for autism. *Neuroscience Biobehavior Review*, 32, 1519–1532.

Klin, A., Jones, W., Schultz, R., & Volkmar, F. (2003). The enactive mind, or from actions to cognition: Lessons from autism. *Philosophical Transactions of the Royal Society of London Series B: Biological Sciences*, 358(1430), 345–360.

Klin, A., Lin, D. J., Gorrindo, P., Ramsay, G., & Jones, W. (2009). Two-year-olds with autism orient to non-social contingencies rather than biological motion. *Nature*. 459, 257–261.

Koegel, L. K., Koegel, R. L., Fredeen, R. M., & Gengoux, G. W. (2008). Naturalistic behavioral approaches to treatment. In K. Chawarska, A. Klin, & F. Volkmar (Eds.), *Autism spectrum disorders in infants and toddlers: Diagnosis, assessment, and treatment* (pp. 207–242). New York: The Guilford Press.

Kumar, R. A., & Christian, S. L. (2009). Genetics of autism spectrum disorders. *Curr. Neurol. Neurosci. Rep.*, 9, 188–197.

Kumar, R. A., Mohamed, S. K., Sudi, J., Conrad, D. F., Brune, C., Badner, J. A... . Christian, S. L. (2008). Recurrent 16p11.2 microdeletions in autism. *Human Molecular Genetics* 17(4), 628–638.

Kurita, H. (1985). Infantile autism with speech loss before the age of thirty months. *Journal of the American Academy of Child and Adolescent Psychiatry*, 24, 191–196.

Landa, R., & Garrett-Mayer, E. (2006). Development in infants with autism spectrum disorders: A prospective study. *Journal of Child Psychology and Psychiatry*, 47(6), 629–638.

Lintas, C., & Persico, A. M. (2009). Autistic phenotypes and genetic testing: State-of-the-art for the clinical geneticist. *Journal of Medical Genetics*, 46, 1–8.

Limperopoulos, C., Bassan, H., Sullivan, N., Soul, J., Robertson, R., Moore, M... . Plessis, A., (2008). Positive screening for autism in ex-preterm infants: Prevalence and risk factors. *Pediatrics*, 121(4), 758–765.

Mandell, D. S., Ittenbach, R. F., Levy, S. E., & Pinto-Martin, J. A. (2007). Disparities in diagnoses received prior to a diagnosis of autism spectrum disorder. *Journal of Autism and Developmental Disorders*, 37(9), 1795–1802.

Mandell, D. S., Listerud, J., Levy, S. E., & Pinto-Martin, J. A. (2002). Race differences in the age at diagnosis among Medicaid-eligible children with autism. *Journal of the American Academy of Child & Adolescent Psychiatry*, 41(12), 1447–1453.

Mattick, J. S., Taft, R. J., & Faulkner, G. J. (2010). A global view of genomic information–moving beyond the gene and the master regulator. *Trends in Genetics*, 26, 21–28.

Mattick, J. S., Amaral, P. P., Dinger, M. E., Mercer, T. R., & Mehler, M. F. (2009). RNA regulation of epigenetic processes. *Bioessays*, 31: 51–59.

McCracken, J. T., McGough, J., Shah, B., Cronin, P., Hong, D., Aman, M. G... . McMahon, D. (2002). Risperidone in children with autism and serious behavioral problems. *The New England Journal of Medicine*, 347, 314–321.

McVicar, K. A., Ballaban-Gil, K., Rapin, I., Moshé, S. L., & Shinnar, S. (2005). Epileptiform EEG abnormalities in children with language regression. *Neurology*, 65, 129–131.

Mehler, M. F., & Purpura, D. P. (2009). Autism, fever, epigenetics and the locus coeruleus. *Brain Research Reviews*, 59, 388–392.

Morrow, E., Yoo, S., Flavell, S., Kim, T., Lin, Y., Hill, R... . Walsh, C. (2008). Identifying autism loci and genes by tracing recent shared ancestry. *Science*, 321(5886), 218–223.

Mraz, K. D., Dixon, J., Dumont-Mathieu, T., & Fein, D. (2009). Accelerated head and body growth in infants later diagnosed with autism spectrum disorders: A comparative study of optimal outcome children. *Journal of Child Neurology*, 24, 833–845.

Myers, S. M., & Johnson, C. (2007). Management of children with autism spectrum disorders. *Pediatrics*, 120(5), 1162–1182.

Nadig, A. S., Ozonoff, S., Young, G. S., Rozga, A., Sigman, M., & Rogers, S. J. (2007). A prospective study of response to name in infants at risk for autism.[see comment]. *Archives of Pediatrics & Adolescent Medicine*, 161(4), 378–383.

Newschaffer, C., Fallin, D., & Lee, N. (2002). Heritable and nonheritable risk factors for autism spectrum disorders. *Epidemiologic Reviews*, 24, 137–153.

Offit, P. A. (2009). *Autism's false prophets: Bad science, risky medicine, and the search for a cure.* New York: Columbia University Press.

Ozonoff, S., Heung, K., Byrd, R., Hansen, R., & Hertz-Picciotto, I. (2008). The onset of autism: Patterns of symptom emergence in the first years of life. *Autism Research*, 1(6), 320–328.

Ozonoff, S., Iosif, A., Baguio, F., Cook, I. D., Hill, M. M., Hutman, T... . Young, G. S. (2010). A prospective study of the emergence of early behavioral signs of autism. *Journal of the American Academy of Child & Adolescent Psychiatry*, 49(3), 258–268.

Ozonoff, S., Macari, S., Young, G. S., Goldring, S., Thompson, M., & Rogers, S. J. (2008). Atypical object exploration at 12 months of age is associated with autism in a prospective sample. *Autism*, 12(5), 457–472.

Ozonoff, S., Williams, B. J., & Landa, R. (2005). Parental report of the early development of children with regressive autism: The delays-plus-regression phenotype. *Autism*, 9(5), 461–486.

Ozonoff, S., Young, G. S., Steinfeld, M. B., Hill, M. M., Cook, I., Hutman, T... . Sigman, M. (2009). How early do parent concerns predict later autism diagnosis? *Journal of Developmental and Behavioral Pediatrics*, 30(5): 367–375.

Pandey, J., Verbalis, A., Robins, D. L., Boorstein, H., Klin, A., Babitz, T... . Fein, D. (2008). Screening for autism in older and younger toddlers with the modified checklist for autism in toddlers. *Autism*, 12(5), 513–535.

Patterson, P. H. (2009). Immune involvement in schizophrenia and autism: Etiology, pathology and animal models. *Behavioural Brain Research*, i, 313–321.

Paul, R., Chawarska, K., Fowler, C., Cicchetti, D., & Volkmar, F. (2007). "Listen my children and you shall hear": Auditory preferences in toddlers with autism spectrum disorders. *Journal of Speech, Language, and Hearing Research*, 50(5), 1350–1364.

Presmanes, A. G., Walden, T. A., Stone, W. L., & Yoder, P. J. (2007). Effects of different attentional cues on responding to joint attention in younger siblings of childen with autism spectrum disorders. *Journal of Autism and Developmental Disorders*, 37(1), 133–144.

Rando, O. J., & Chang, H.Y. (2009). Genome-wide views of chromatin structure. *Annual Review of Biochemistry*, 78, 245–271.

Rapin, I. (1996). Historical data. In I. Rapin (Ed.), *Preschool children with inadequate communication: Developmental language disorder, autism, low IQ* (pp. 58–97). London: Mac Keith Press.

Rapin, I., Dunn, M., Allen, D. A., Stevens, M., & Fein, D. (2009). Subtypes of language disorders in schoolage children with autism. *Developmental Neuropsychology*, 34, 1–9.

Rapoport, J., Chavez, A., Greenstein, D., Addington, A., & Gogtay, N. (2009). Autism spectrum disorders and childhood-onset schizophrenia: clinical and biological contributions to a relation revisited. *Journal of the American Academy of Child and Adolescent Psychiatry*, 48, 10–18.

Raynes, H.R., Shanske, A., Burde, R., Rapin, I. (1999): Joubert syndrome: Monozygotic twins with discordant phenotype. *Journal of Child Neurology*, 14, 649–654.

Rees, S., & Inder, T. (2005). Fetal and neonatal origins of altered brain development. *Early Human Development*, 81(9), 753–761.

Rennie, J., Hagmann, C., & Robertson, N. (2009). Outcome after intrapartum hypoxic ischaemia at term. *Seminars in Fetal and Neonatal Medicine*, 12(5), 398–407.

Robins, D. L., Fein, D., Barton, M. L., & Green, J. A. (2001). The Modified Checklist for Autism in Toddlers: An initial study investigating the early detection of autism and pervasive developmental disorders. *Journal of Autism & Developmental Disorders*, 31(2), 131–144.

Rogers, S. J. (2009). What are infant siblings teaching us about autism in infancy? *Autism Research*, 2, 125–137.

Schumann, C., Bloss, C., Barnes, C., Wideman, G., Carper, R., Akshoomoff, N... . Courchesne, E. (2010). Longitudinal magnetic resonance imaging study of cortical development through early childhood in autism. *The Journal of Neuroscience*, 30(12), 4419–4427.

Shic, F., Bradshaw, J., Klin, A., & Chawarska, K. (submitted). *Limited activity monitoring in toddlers with autism spectrum disorder*.

Siperstein, R., & Volkmar, F. (2004). Brief report: Parental reporting of regression in children with pervasive developmental disorders. *Journal of Autism & Developmental Disorders*, 34(6), 731–734.

Stone, W. L., McMahon, C. R., & Henderson, L. M. (2008). Use of the screening tool for autism in two-year-olds (STAT) for children under 24 months: An exploratory study. *Autism*, 12(5), 557–573.

Trevarthen, C., & Aitken, K. J. (2001). Infant intersubjectivity: Research, theory, and clinical applications. *Journal of Child Psychology & Psychiatry & Allied Disciplines*, 42(1), 3–48.

Tropea, D., Giacometti, E., Wilson, N. R., Beard, C., McCurry, C., Fu, D. D... . Sur, M. (2009). Partial reversal of Rett Syndrome-like symptoms in MeCP2 mutant mice. *National Academy of Sciences of the USA*, 106(6), 2029–2034.

Tsiouris, J. A., & Brown, W. T. (2004). Neuropsychiatric symptoms of fragile X syndrome: Pathophysiology and pharmacotherapy. *CNS. Drugs*, 18, 687–703.

Werner, E., & Dawson, G. (2005). Validation of the phenomenon of autistic regression using home videotapes. *Archives of General Psychiatry*, 62(8), 889–895.

Wetherby, A., & Woods, J. (2008). Developmental aproaches to treatment. In K. Chawarska, A. Klin, & F. Volkmar (Eds.), *Autism spectrum disorders in infants and toddlers: Diagnosis, assessment, and treatment* (pp. 170–206). New York: The Guilford Press.

Wetherby, A. M., Woods, J., Allen, L., Cleary, J., Dickinson, H., & Lord, C. (2004). Early indicators of autism spectrum disorders in the second year of life. *Journal of Autism & Developmental Disorders*, 34(5), 473–493.

Williams, E. and Casanova, M. (2010) Potential teratogenic effects of ultrasound on corticogenesis: Implications for autism. *Medical Hypotheses*, 75(1), 53–58.

Yoder, P., Stone, W. L., Walden, T., & Malesa, E. (2009). Predicting social impairment and ASD diagnosis in younger siblings of children with autism spectrum disorder. *Journal of Autism and Developmental Disorders*, 39(10), 1381–1391.

Young, G. S., Merin, N., Rogers, S. J., & Ozonoff, S. (2009). Gaze behavior and affect at 6 months: Predicting clinical outcomes and language development in typically developing infants and infants at risk for autism. *Developmental Science*, 12(5), 1381–1391.

Zoghbi, H. Y. (2003). Postnatal neurodevelopmental disorders: Meeting at the synapse? *Science*, 302, 826–830.

Zwaigenbaum, L., Bryson, S., Lord, C., Rogers, S., Carter, A., Carver, L. Yirmiya, N. (2009). Clinical assessment and management of toddlers with suspected autism spectrum disorder: Insights from studies of high-risk infants. *Pediatrics*, 123(5), 1383–1391.

Zwaigenbaum, L., Bryson, S., Rogers, T., Roberts, W., Brian, J., & Szatmari, P. (2005). Behavioral manifestations of autism in the first year of life. *International Journal of Developmental Neuroscience*, 23(2–3), 143–152.

Index

Note: Page references followed by "*f*" and "*t*" denote figures and tables, respectively.

A

Abnormal arousal, 503
Abnormal sensory responsiveness, 501
Abrahams, B. S., 494
Acetylserotonin methyltransferase (ASMT), 88
AD. *See* Autistic disorder (AD)
Adamo, M., 166
ADC. *See* Apparent diffusion coefficient (ADC)
Adelmann, P. K., 340
ADHD. *See* Attention-deficit/hyperactivity disorder (ADHD)
ADI-R. *See* Autism Diagnostic Interview-Revised (ADI-R)
Adolescence
  ability of individuals with ASs, 20
  behavioral problems with ASD patients, 13
  cognitive improvement in, 13–14
  manifestation of ASD symptoms during, 13
  self-help skills of ASD patients, 13

ADOS. *See* Autism Diagnostic Observation Schedule (ADOS)
AF. *See* Amygdalo-fusiform (AF) pathways
Aggression, 82
Aldred, S., 84
Alexander, A. L., 422
Allelic diversity, 36, 39–40
Allelic heterogeneity, 37
Allen, D. A., 21
Allman, J. M., 344–45
Alpha-amino-3-hydroxy-5-methyl-4-isoxazole propionic acid (AMPA), 84
Alpha-[^{11} C]methyl-L-tryptophan (AMT), 82
Alzheimer's disease, 60
AMPA. *See* Alpha-amino-3-hydroxy-5-methyl-4-isoxazole propionic acid (AMPA)
Amygdala, 61, 103–5, 142
  anxiety in autism and role of, 376
  frontal connections, 232
  mimicry and role of, 355–56

Amygdalo-fusiform (AF) pathways, 108
Androgens, and ASD, 453–54
  genetic variation in, 454
Angelman (15q11-13), 38*t*
Animal models, of autism research, 108–9
ANN. *See* Artificial neural network (ANN)
Anti-saccade task, 189
Anxiety
  in autism, 375–76
  disorders, 110
Apparent diffusion coefficient (ADC), 51
Applied Behavior Analysis, 132
Arachnoid cysts, 54
Architectonic asymmetries, 57
A4 receptor, 63
A7 receptor, 63
Arginine vasopressin receptors
  anatomical distribution of, 458
  interaction with oxytocin, 460
  molecular variation of, 458
  oxytocin and, 457–58

Arnott, S. R., 343
Arnstein, A. F. T., 381
Arousal abnormalities, in autism,
    110, 340
    direct measurements of, 383–84
    eliminating/attenuating
        stereotypies, minimizing by,
        385–86
    minimizing by drugs, 386
    self-injury and, 371
Arrieta, A., 84
Arterial spin labeling (ASL), 52
Artificial neural network
    (ANN), 400
Aseptic meningitis, 17
ASL. See Arterial spin labeling
    (ASL)
ASMT. See Acetylserotonin
    methyltransferase (ASMT)
Asparagine, 84
Asperger, Hans, 35, 210, 340
Asperger's disorder (AS), 16, 20–21,
    37, 42, 81, 84, 124, 131, 188,
    195, 372
Asymmetrical ventricles, 54
Asymmetries, of 5-HT synthesis, 82
Attentional impairments, in autism,
    104–5, 109, 301
    clinical implications, 176–78
Attention-deficit/hyperactivity
    disorder (ADHD), 83–84, 98
Attention deficits, in children with
    ASD, 11
Atypical features, of ASD, 47–48
Atypical social development,
    225–26
Autism brain research, 48
Autism Diagnostic Interview-
    Revised (ADI-R), 16, 81, 369
Autism Diagnostic Observation
    Schedule (ADOS), 16, 81,
    236, 347
Autism Spectrum Quotient
    (AQ), 327
Autism Tissue Program, 53
Autistic disorder (AD), 9
Autobiographical memory, 144
Automatically reinforcing, 385–86
Autonomic arousal, oxytocin for,
    382–83
Autonomic disturbance, 503
Autonomic nervous system
    abnormalities, 501
AVP1aR. See V1a receptor
    (AVP1aR)
AVP1b, 458
AVPR1A gene, 458–59
    significant microsatellites of, 459f
AVPR1A knockout mice, 455

AVR-RS1-RS3, 459
Azmi, S., 151

B
Bachmann, I., 374
Baddeley, A., 172
BADS. See Behavioral Assessment
    of Dysexecutive Syndrome
    (BADS)
Bailey, A., 14, 54, 368
Baird, G., 15
Barnard, L., 98
Barnea-Goraly, N., 422
Baron-Cohen, S., 17, 100, 106, 130,
    195, 348, 471
Basal ganglia, abnormalities, 66
Battaglia, A., 488
Bauman, M. L., 54, 367
Bayley Scales of Infant
    Development, 297
BDNF. See Brain-derived
    neurotrophic factor (BDNF)
Beall, P. M., 347
Beckwith Weidemann (11p15), 38t
Bed nucleus of the stria terminalis
    (BNST), 456
Behavioral abnormalities, 37
Behavioral Assessment of
    Dysexecutive Syndrome
    (BADS), 198
Behavioral inhibition system (BIS),
    382
Behavioral Rating Inventory of
    Executive Functioning
    (BRIEF), 196
Behrmann, M., 354
Bekkering, H., 348
Belmonte, M. K., 166, 357, 402–3
Bennetto, L., 125, 173
Benton Test of Facial Recognition,
    300
Benuzzi, F., 345, 352
Berkson, G., 374
Bernasconi, P., 374
Berridge, C. W., 382
Bettelheim, B., 123, 470
Beversdorf, D. Q., 109, 478
Bigham, S., 152
Bird, B., 354
BIS. See Behavioral inhibition
    system (BIS)
Blair, R. J. R., 142, 350
Blais, C., 356
Blakemore, S.-J., 350
Bleuler, Eugen, 35
Block Span Backward task, 192
Blue M. E., 87
BNST. See Bed nucleus of the stria
    terminalis (BNST)

Bodfish, J. W., 369
Booth, R. D. L., 100
Borjas, L., 84
Bott, L., 141, 149
Boucher, J., 140, 146, 149–52,
    302, 356
Bowler, D. M., 141, 143–46, 148
Brain
    asymmetries, 57–58
    growth, types of changes in, 411
    lesions, 48
    maturation, 48
Brain–behavior correlation,
    modular approach to, 48
Brain-derived neurotrophic factor
    (BDNF), 89
Brain development
    constant changes over, 441f
    cortex function and, 418–19
    fMRI studies, 417–18
    functional studies of early,
        417–22
    intrinsic and extrinsic factors role
        in gene expression, 419–21
    learning and, 421–22
    putative developmental principle,
        418–22
Brain enlargement
    frontal pyramidal neurons and
        early, 415–16
Brain function
    autism and early, 417
    autism and late, 423–39
    future directions, 515–17
Brain–neurofunction relationships,
    stages of, 48
Brain overgrowth, in autism, 108
    autism symptoms and
        early, 414
    diffusion tensor imaging and,
        411–14
    discovery of early, 409–17
    future directions for, 439–41
    genetic, cellular, and molecular
        basis of, 414–17
    head circumference studies,
        409–10
    MRI studies of, 410–11
Brain stem nuclei, of cranial nerves,
    384–85
Brain structure, in autism
    early period, 409
    functional connectivity studies in
        adults, 423–36
    future directions, 515–17
    late period and, 422–23
    normalized connectivity and,
        436–39
    overview, 407–9

regionally specific functional brain imaging in adults, 423–36
Brayne, C. E., 15
BRIEF. *See* Behavioral Rating Inventory of Executive Functioning (BRIEF)
Brixton Test, 188–89
Broader Phenotype of Autism Symptom Scale, 102
Brodeur, D., 164
Brodmann's Area (BA), 88
Broks, P., 356
Brothers, L., 343, 403
Bryson, S. E., 208
Buccino, G., 345, 352
Buitelaar, J. K., 21
Bullmore, E. T., 356
Buttner, T., 355
Buxbaum, J. D., 489
Buxhoeveder, D. P., 356
Byrd, R., 13

C
Caccioppo, J., 341
CACNA1C, 37
CAH. *See* Congenital adrenal hyperplasia (CAH)
Calcitonin gene-related peptide (CGRP), 89
Caldara, R., 356
California Card Sorting Test, 197
California Proverb Test, 197
California Trails, 197
California Word Context Test, 197
Calvo-Merino, B., 345, 352
Cambridge Neuropsychological Testing Automated Battery (CANTAB), 171, 173, 196–97
Canessa, N., 345, 352
Cannon, W. B., 196
CANTAB. *See* Cambridge Neuropsychological Testing Automated Battery (CANTAB)
Caregiver's attention, to egocentric autistic child, 352
Carpenter, M., 130
Carter, C., 169
Casanova, M. F., 60, 356, 402
Casey, B., 167
Caudal anterior/middle cingulate cortex (cACC/MCC), 331
Cavum septum pellucidum, 54
CDD. *See* Childhood disintegrative disorder (CDD)
CELF-4. *See* Clinical Evaluation of Language Fundamentals, Version 4 (CELF-4)

Central-Coherence theory of autism, 99, 130
Cerebellar hypo- and hyperplasia, 98
Cerebellar vermal lobules VI–VII hypoplasia, 64
Cerebellum, neuropathological studies of
gray and white matter changes, 65
vermis area, 64–65
volumetric changes, 65
Cerebral hypoperfusion, 60
Cerebral palsy, 88
Cerebral perfusion abnormalities, 60
Cerebrospinal fluid homovanillic acid (CSF HVA) levels, 83
CGRP. *See* Calcitonin gene-related peptide (CGRP)
Chakrabarti, S., 17
Chartrand, T. L., 342
Chawarska, K., 13
Cheng, C. M., 342
Chewing
of inedible objects in adults, 370
stress and, 381–82
Chiari I malformations, 54
Childhood Autistic Rating Scale-Tokyo Version, 63
Childhood disintegrative disorder (CDD), 18–19, 42
Children's Memory Scales, 300
Children with ASD
attention deficits, 11
clinical presentation, 12–13
daily living skills, 13–14
deficits in daily living skills, 13
diagnostic criteria, 10
early markers, 12
electroencephalography (EEG) recordings, 13
executive functioning abilities, deficits in, 11
initiation of social activities, 10
loss of language, 12
manifestations, 13
peer relationships, 10, 23
personal hygiene needs, 13
predictor of positive outcomes, 14–15
prevalence of, 15
prognosis, 13
regression in, 12–13
regulatory difficulties, 12
repetitive behaviors, 10–11, 13
residual pragmatic language difficulties, 15
restricted interests, 10–11
seizures, 13
symptoms, 11–14

Children with autism
emotional contagion in, 347
Choline-containing compounds (Cho), 82
Chong, T., 353
Chromosome copy number variants (CNV)
case-carrier examinations of individual, 494
DNA-sequence variation, 485
identifying limited set of genes, 492–93
models of gene mutation and, 492
overview, 483–84
recent revisions to molecular genetics, 484–85
Classical conditioning, 149
Classification issues, in ASD, 512–13
Clinical assessment, of autism, 520–21
Clinical Evaluation of Language Fundamentals, Version 4 (CELF-4), 131, 299
Clinical neuroradiological imaging, 53–54
Clinical presentation issues, of ASD, 512–13
CNS immune activation, 502
CNTNAP2 gene. *See* Contactin-associated protein-like 2 (*CNTNAP2*) gene
CNV. *See* Chromosome copy number variants (CNV)
Cognition, multiple distinct disorders of, 42
Cognitive flexibility, 98
Cognitive testing, 298
Cohen, D. J., 347, 369
Cohen's model, 401–2
Common coding, of perception and action, 345–46
Communication impairment, 10
and endophenotypes of autism, 486
Comorbid conditions, in ASDs, 24–25
Complex response inhibition, 189–90
Comprehensive Assessment of Spoken Language, 131, 299
Condon, W. S., 340, 351
Congenital adrenal hyperplasia (CAH), 454
Congenitally blind children, and repetitive movements, 371
Conjunctive coding, 398
Conklin, H. M., 173
Connectivity, in autism, 100, 108

Contactin-associated protein-like 2 (CNTNAP2) gene, 37, 491–92
Contactin 4 (CNTN4), 41
Contagious crying, early mimetic behaviors and, 343
Contagious yawning, mimicry and, 343
Contingency detection mechanism, 110
Continuous Performance Test (CPT), 170, 301
Controlled (or selective) attention, 162
  in individuals with ASD, 168–70
  measuring of, 167
  neural basis, 167–68
  neuroimaging studies, 170–71
  typical development, 168
Cook, E. H., 81, 87
Copy number variation (CNV), 36, 41
Corpus callosum enlargement in autism, 57
Cortical dysplasia focal epilepsy (7q35-36), 38t, 491–92
Corticotropin-releasing factor (CRF), 456
Corticotropin-releasing hormones (CRH), 380
Cortisol
  and ASD, 454–55
  interplay with oxytocin, 454–55
  stress and, 381
Courchesne, E., 55, 98, 166, 340, 345, 400
Cowden/Bannayan Riley-Ruvalcaba syndrome (10q23), 38t
Cowell, P. E., 356
Cox, A., 13
CPT. See Continuous Performance Test (CPT)
Craig, J., 195
Craik, F., 150–52
Cranial nerves, brain stem nuclei of, 384–85
Crawley, J. N., 235
Creak's Nine Points, 474
Creatine plus phosphocreatine, 82
CRF. See Corticotrophin-releasing factor (CRF)
CRH. See Corticotropin-releasing hormones (CRH)
Critchley, H. D., 356
Critton, S. R., 343
Croen, L. A., 89
Crowson, M., 132
Cued recall, 143–44, 151
Cummings, N., 169
Cunnington, R., 353

D
Dagli, A., 488
Daly, E. M., 356
Damasio, A., 368, 470
Daniel, S., 348
Dapretto, M., 346, 349
Dart, A. M., 383
DA-ß-hydroxylase (DßH) gene, 83
Dawson, G., 98–99, 102, 104, 110, 128, 227, 356
DBM. See Deformation-based morphometry (DBM)
Declarative memory, 141
Default Mode Network (DMN), 424–25
Default system, 340
Deformation-based morphometry (DBM), 50
DeGelder, B., 347
Deixis, 126–27
Delayed Alternation, 191
Delayed echolalia, 10
Delayed Non-Match-to-Sample task, 191
Delayed recall, 143
Delay of gratification task, 189
Delis-Kaplan Executive Function System (D-KEFS), 197, 302
Delwiche, L., 16
Dementieva, Y. A., 55
Demographic issues, in ASD, 513–14
Depression, 100
Developmental delay (DD), 82
Developmental language disorder (DLD), 22, 55
Developmentally delayed (non-autistic) children, 127
DeVincent, C., 24
DHCR7, 37
Dhossche, D., 84
Diagnostic and Statistical Manual of Mental Disorders—III (DSM-III), 15, 140, 474
Diagnostic and Statistical Manual of Mental Disorders—IV (DSM-IV), 16
Diagnostic and Statistical Manual of Mental Disorders—IV Text Revision (DSM-IV-TR), 24
  criteria for AD, 21
  criteria for AS, 20
  diagnosis of ASD, 9
  PDD in children, 15
Diagnostic assessment, of ASDs
  attentional difficulties, 297–98, 301
  characteristics of individuals, 297–98

child-specific factors, 297
cognitive ability and adaptive skills, 298
executive functioning deficits, 301–2
higher-functioning individuals, 298
imitation, 299–300
language, 299
memory, 302
motor difficulties, 301
repetitive behaviors, 300–301
sensory impairments, 300
social behavior and social cognition, 300
speed of information processing, 298
tests, 297
Diagnostic criteria
  for ASDs, 9–10, 16
  PDD-NOS, 10
Dickens, M. J., 374
Diffusion tensor imaging (DTI), 51–52, 58–59, 108
  in brain overgrowth, 411–14
  fiber tracking, of brain growth, 412–14
Digit Span Backward task, 192
Dilated Virchow-Robin spaces, 54
Dinstein, I., 354
Discrete trial training, 132
Displacement behavior
  in animals, 373–74
  confinement, 374
  defined, 373
  in humans, 375
Dissanayake, E., 344
Divided attention, 11
DLD. See Developmental language disorder (DLD)
DLPFC. See Dorsolateral prefrontal cortex
DMN. See Default Mode Network (DMN)
DNA-sequence variation, of CNV, 484
Dopamine
  genetics, 83
  and metabolites, 82–83
  neuroimaging, 83
  reward circuit, 102
  stress and, 380–81
Dopamine transporter (DAT1) gene, 83
Dorsal medial cortex, 104
Dorsolateral prefrontal cortex (DLPFC), 146, 175
  delayed response, 99
Dowd, J. M., 344

Down's syndrome, 24, 38*t*, 99
  repetitive movements and, 371
D$_1$ receptor (DRD1) gene, 83
D-serine, 84
DTI. *See* Diffusion tensor imaging
  (DTI)
Du, X-J., 383
Dunn, M., 127
Dyadic entrainment, 340
Dysfunctional features, of ASD, 47
Dysmorphism, 37

E

Early-emerging deficits, in autism,
  103
Early growth response gene 2
  (EGR2), 485
Early markers, of ASDs, 12
Eaves, L. C., 13–14
Echolalia, 10, 13, 352
EFT. *See* Embedded figures task
  (EFT)
Egocentric autistic child, caregiver's
  attention to, 352
EGR2. See Early growth response
  gene 2 (*EGR2*)
EGR2-MECP2-GABRB3 gene
  mutation, 491
Eisenmajer, R., 21
Elder, L. M., 55
Electromyography (EMG)
  facial mimicry, 343
  mimicry for actions and emotions,
    347–48
Embedded figures task (EFT), 166
Embodied simulation, 107
EMG. *See* Electromyography
  (EMG)
Emotional contagion, 321
  behavioral measures of, 346–47
  empathy and, 341
  in human infants, 342
  in preschool-age children with
    ASD, 347
Emotional recognition, 107, 321
Emotional resonance, 321
Empathizing, 319–20
  neural systems, 331–32
  relationship with systemizing,
    327–28
  typically development, 321–22
Empathizing-systemizing (E-S)
  theory, of autism, 106, 317–31
Empathy, 319
  emotion recognition in, 321
  mimicry and, 341
Empathy Quotient (EQ), 323–27
Enactive Mind model, 103
Endophenotypes of autism, 485–90

communication impairment and,
  486
diagnostic criteria for autism,
  486–88
  intellectual disability, 489
  macrocephaly, 488–89
  non-diagnostic features of autism,
    487–90
  restricted or repetitive activities
    and interest, 487–88*t*
  social impairment and, 486
Energy metabolism, 504
Enhanced perceptual functioning
  (EPF) model, 330
Enns, J., 164
Epidemiological studies of
  ASDs, 17
Epidemiologic issues, in ASD,
  513–14
Epigenetic issues, in ASD, 514–15
Epilepsy, 89
  and autism, 500
  cytokines and, 503
  and language impairment, 503
Episodic information, 141
Episodic memory, 140, 146, 148
EQ. *See* Empathy Quotient (EQ)
Ernst, M., 83
Erythropoietin, 438
Even-related potential (ERP), 102,
  227
Executive-dysfunction theory of
  autism, 130, 301–2
Executive function (EF) theory, of
  autism, 97–99, 186–87
  Brixton Test, 188–89
  in broader autism phenotype, 198
  cognitive control, 195–96
  construct validity, 196
  fluency, 194–95
  inhibition, 189–90
  Intradimensional/
    Extradimensional (ID/ED)
    Shift, 188
  planning, 194
  set-shifting, 187
  Wisconsin Card Sort Test
    (WCST) performance,
    187–88
  working memory, 190–94
Executive functioning abilities,
  deficits in children with
  ASD, 11
Exogenous attention, 164
Experience-driven developmental
  processes, 103
Experience-expectant
  neurodevelopmental processes,
  104

F

FA. *See* Fractional anisotropy (FA)
Face processing, 102
Facial electromyography
  (EMG), 107
Facial expression processing, 230
Facial mimicry, 107, 342
False memory task, 399–400
Familiarity, 146
Family studies of autism, 106
Fantie, B. D., 170
Farley, A. H., 205
Farrant, A., 150, 356
FDOPA. *See* [^{18}F]fluorodopa
  (FDOPA)
Federlein, J., 355
Fein, D., 100–101, 372
Feldman, R., 348
Feldstein, S., 348
Fenfluramine, 81
Fernald, R. D., 235
FFA. *See* Fusiform face area
  (FFA)
[^{18}F]fluorodopa (FDOPA), 83
FG. *See* Fusiform gyrus (FG)
Fitzgerald M., 84
Floeter, M. K., 374
FMR1 gene, 37
FMRI. *See* Functional magnetic
  resonance imaging (fMRI)
Forceps minor, values of fractional
  anisotropy in, 413*f*
Form-function distinction, 126
Fractional anisotropy (FA), 51, 108
  for brain growth, 412–13
Fragile X syndrome, 24, 38*t*,
  37, 371
  and autism, 491
  and overarousal, 377–78
  and unitary disorder, 473
Fraiberg, S., 352
Freeman, B., 474
Free recall, 143–44, 151, 153
Free verbal recall, 144
Friedrich, F. J., 162
Frith, C., 350
Frith, U., 149, 151, 471
Frontal pyramidal neurons
  early brain enlargement,
    importance in, 415–16
  role in connectivity defects, 416
Functional magnetic resonance
  imaging (fMRI)
  to study brain development,
    417–18
  to study brain structure, 423–36
Fusiform activity, in autism, 424*f*
Fusiform face area (FFA), 348
Fusiform gyrus (FG), 102

G

GABA receptor subunit ß-3 gene (GABRB3), 87
GABRB3, 491
GAD. *See* Glutamic acid decarboxylase (GAD)
GAD65, 87
GAD67, 87
Gadow, K., 24
Gaigg, S. B., 141
Gait apraxia, 19
Gallup, G. G., Jr., 343
Gamliel, I., 348
Garner, J. P., 374
Garretson, H. B., 170
Gastrointestinal abnormalities, 502
    and oxidative stress, 503
    and problem behaviors, 503
    and sleep, 503
Gastrointestinal system, in autism, 500
Gaze aversion, 340
Gender differences, and prevalence rate of ASD, 17–18
Gene mutation, causes of autism, 493
Gene sources, undermine autism diagnostic phenotype, 490–94
    case-carrier examinations of individual CNV, 494
    effort to construct unified gene-based theories of autism, 492–94
    lack of coverage of gene and CNV findings to date, 494
    syndromic autism vs idiopathic autism, 490–92
Gene system sources, of autism endophenotypes, 485–90
    diagnostic criteria for autism, 486–88
    non-diagnostic features of autism, 488–90
Genetic concepts, basic
    cell-adhesion molecules, involvement, 41
    DNA segments, 36
    genetic models, 42
    genotype–phenotype relationships, 41
    positions of genomes, 36–37
Genetic issues, in ASD, 16–17, 514–15
    evidence, 36
    pragmatic difficulties, 129
    at risk, 36
    role of genomic positions (or loci), 36
Genetic variation, 39–40

in androgens in autism, 454
Genome-wide association studies (GWAS), 39
Geographic distribution, of ASD, 17
Gergely, G., 110, 385
Geschwind, D. H., 494
Gillberg, C., 16, 83
Glaser, D. E., 345, 352
Global developmental delay, 22–23
Global processing deficits, 100
Glutamate decarboxylase 67 isoform (GAD67), 64
Glutamate/GABA, neurochemical studies of
    GABA receptors, 87
    glutamate receptor, 86–87
    glutamic acid decarboxylase (GAD), 87
    measurements, 84–86
    mitochondrial aspartate/ glutamate carrier, 87–88
    selected studies, 85–86t
Glutamate receptor AMPA 1 (GluR1) gene, 87
Glutamate receptor 6 (GluR6) gene, 86
Glutamate receptor ionotropic kainate 2 gene (GRIK2), 86
Glutamate receptors, 84
Glutamate uptake, 60
Glutamic acid decarboxylase (GAD), 84
Glycine, 84
Goldstein, G., 101, 170, 174
Go/No-Go task, 167–71, 301
Goodale, M. A., 343
Goodman, J. R. L., 348
Goodman, R., 479
    model of diversity, unitary disorder, 471
Goodman, W. K., 369
Goodwin, M. S., 382
Goos, L. M., 483, 485
Gordon, B., 141, 149
G protein dysfunction, 64
Grammar, 125–27
Grandin, T., 370
Greenough, W. T., 374
Grèzes, J., 345, 352
Griffith, E., 173, 192
GRIK2. *See* Glutamate receptor ionotropic kainate 2 gene (GRIK2)
Grossenbacher, P. G., 355
Grotemeyer, K. H., 84
Gustafsson, L., 400
Guthrie, D., 205
GWAS. *See* Genome-wide association studies (GWAS)

H

Haarmann, F. Y., 84
Habitual self-cueing strategies, 144
Haggard, P., 345, 352
Haist, F., 166
Hakeem, A. Y., 344–45
Hala, S., 145
Haloperidol, 82
Hamilton, A. C., 354
Hammer, J., 100
Hand flapping, 11
Happé, F., 100, 235
    Stories task, 322
Hardan, A. Y., 422
Hare, D. J., 151
Haswell, C. C., 210
Hatfield, E., 341
Hatsopoulos, N. G., 345
Hauck, M., 150
Hauser, S., 140
Hayes, C., 354
Head circumference (HC), review of, 54–55
    accelerated head growth and behavioral correlates, 55–56
    brain asymmetries, 57–57, 409–11
    corpus callosum size changes, 57
    developmental trajectory, 58
    gray-matter changes, 56
    higher-order associational areas, 58
    right-hemisphere dysfunction, 58
    volumetrics, 56
    white-matter changes, 56–57
Heath, C., 344
Hebbian process, 397
Heeger, D. J., 354
Heller's disintegrative psychosis, 19
Helt, M., 15
Henning, A., 342
Hensley, R., 152
Hepburn, S. L., 347
Herbert, M. R., 58
Heritability, of autism, 452
Hermelin, B., 149–50, 401
Herpes encephalopathy, 61
Herrmann, R., 374
Hertz-Picciotto, I., 16
HF. *See* Hippocampofusiform (HF)
HFA. *See* Highfunctioning autism (HFA)
Higgins, J. P., 15
Higher-order planning, 99
High-functioning autism (HFA), 55, 106, 128–29, 188
    abnormalities of prefrontal regions, 142
    functional anomalies, 142

immediate memory span and
    working memory, 142
impaired fear conditioning, 141
impaired motor skills, 141
implicit category formation, 141
long-term declarative memory,
    142–45
motor abnormalities, 142
nondeclarative memory, 141–42
perceptual priming, 142
procedural memory deficits, 142
verbal working memory, 142
visuospatial working memory, 142
Hill, D. A., 370
Hillier, A., 142–43
Hinojosa-Laborde, C., 383
Hippocampal function and
    connectivity, 146
Hippocampal lesions, 148
Hippocampofusiform (HF), 108
Hirstein, W., 377, 383
Ho, H. H., 13–14
Holden, J. J., 83
Homovanillic acid (HVA), 83
Hood, B., 169
Hooper, C. J., 173
Howard, M. A., 356
Howlin, P., 124
5-HT transporter (5-HTT). *See*
    Serotonin
Hutt, C., 356
Hutt, S. J., 356
Huttenlocher, P., 437–38
Hyperactivity, 82
Hyperplasia, 98
Hyperserotonemia, 37, 78, 81
Hypersystemizers, 332
Hypoempathizers, 332
Hypoperfusion, 60
Hypoplasia, 98
Hypothalamus, paraventricular
    nucleus of, 382
Hypotonia, 37

I
Iacoboni, M., 346
Imaginative play, 22
Imitation
    of actions involving objects, 245
    automatic, 244
    debate on the nature of, 256
    elicited, 245
    encoding process, 247–52
    execution phase, 255–56
    of incomplete acts, 245
    neuropsychological models,
        245–47
    of non-meaningful body gestures
        and oral-facial movements, 244

spontaneous, 245
testing, 299–300
transformation phase, 252–55
Immobilization, 384–85
Immune activation, 503
Immune dysregulation, 504
Immune system, and autism, 501
Impaired emotional processing, in
    autism, 105
Impaired joint attention, 10
Impaired motor skills, 37
Impaired nonverbal behavior, 10
Impaired reciprocity, 10
Impaired recollection/spared
    familiarity hypothesis, 147
Implicit learning abilities, in ASD
    inconsistencies, 275*t*
    neural foundations, 268–69
    and savant skills, 274
    social cues, 273–74
    verbal, 271–73
    visuo-motor learning, 269–71
Inborn errors of metabolism, 502
Individuals with Disabilities
    Education Act (IDEA), 16
Infant mimicry, 321
    development and, 342–43
    mechanisms, 349–52
Inferior temporal gyrus, 102
Information processing theory, of
    autism, 99–101
Inhibitory condition, in ASD,
    189–90
Inhibitory control, 98
Input (or spatial) attention
    exogenous processes, 164
    measuring, 162–63
    neural basis of, 163
    neuroimaging studies, 166
    typical development, 164
    visual orientation, in ASD
        patients, 164–65
Insel, T. R., 235
Insula, 346
Intact memory, 147
Intellectual disability, 489
    and macrocephaly, 490
Interactional synchrony, 340
    in infancy, 344
Interactive specialization (IS)
    theory, 418
*International Classification of
    Diseases, 10th Revision*
    (ICD-10), 15
Interpersonal coordination, 340–41
    in people with autism, 346–49
    in typical individuals, 340–46
Interventions, for ASD, 521–22
Intonation, 13

Intradimensional/Extradimensional
    (ID/ED) Shift, 188
Inverse problem, 35
Ionotropic receptors, 84
IQ measures, in ASD patients
    distribution, 281–82
    etiology, 286–90
    genetic causes, 285–86
    predictability and stability,
        282–84
    relationship to severity, adaptive
        functioning, and outcomes,
        284–85
    sex differences, 282
Isenhower, R. W., 348

J
Jack, R. E., 356
Jarrold, C., 149, 169
Jefferis, V. E., 342
Jeon, O. H., 87
Johnson, C. R., 170
Joint attention behaviors, in autism,
    103–4, 322
Jones, S., 343
Jones, W., 347
Jordan, R., 130

K
Kainate, 84
Kaminsky, Z. A., 485
Kamio, Y., 128, 143
Kana, R. K., 106, 171
Kanner, L., 35, 42, 54, 97, 123,
    339–40, 469
Kanwisher, N., 353
Kehrer, H., 84
Keller, T. A., 422
Kemner, C., 347
Kemper, T. L., 54
Kennedy, D. P., 234, 340, 345, 417
Kern, J. K., 63
Khaja, R., 484
Kiddie Stroop tasks, 189
Kingwell, B. A., 383
Kinsbourne, M., 110, 342, 344, 349,
    356, 372
    overfocusing scale, 373*t*
Kleinhans, N. M., 63
Klin, A., 21, 103, 110, 230, 347
Klinger, L. G., 128
Knickmeyer, R., 383
Knight, G. P., 383
Knockout mice models, 109
Knoeblich, G., 348
Koboyashi, R., 13
Konstantareas, M. M., 348
Korda, P., 374
Kramer, J. M., 489

Kresh, L. E., 369
Kuhl, P. K., 422

L
La Franchi, S., 370
Lagravinese, G., 345, 352
Lainhart, J. E., 55
Lakin, J. L., 342
Landau Kleffner syndrome, 350
Langdell, T., 227
Language abilities, of individuals
    with autism
    articulation, 125
    assessment, 131–32
    echolalia, 126
    embedded sentences and relative
        clauses, 126
    grammar, 125–27
    history and overview, 123–24
    morpheme, 125
    nonverbal communication, 128
    oro-motor dyspraxia, 125
    phonology and prosody, 124–25
    pragmatics, 128–29
    prognosis, 133
    pronoun reversal, 126
    semantic aspects, 127–28
    simple sentence structures, 126
    speech fluency, 125
    syntactic ambiguity, 125
    testing, 299
    treatment, 132
Language delays, 10
Language impairment, 100
    and epilepsy, 503
Lateralized left hemisphere
    dysfunction, 100
Learning
    disability, 98
    with Hebbian process, 397
    and neural networks, 397
Leary, M. R., 370
Lecavalier, L., 24
Lee, D., 356
Lee, E., 436
Lee, J. E., 63
Lee, S. S., 349
Leighton, J., 354
Lewis, M. H., 369
Lewis, V., 150–51
Lewy, A., 110
Lexical fluency, 127
Leyfer, O., 24
LFA. See Low-functioning autism
    (LFA)
LHPA. See Limbic-hypothalamic-
    pituitary-adrenal (LHPA)
Limbic-hypothalamic-pituitary-
    adrenal (LHPA), 454
Limbic systems, abnormalities in

DTI analysis, 63
MRS analysis, 63
neuroimaging, 62
neuropathology, 62
shape measurement
    methodologies, 63
Liss, M., 368, 372, 377
Lord, C., 14, 127–28
Lovaas, I., 385–86
Lovaas method, 132
Low-functioning autism (LFA), 55
    V-LFA groups, 149–50, 152
L-serine, 84
Luciana, M., 173
Lui, F., 345, 352
Luna, B., 98, 175

M
Ma, D., 492
Macciardi, F, 83
Macroanatomical studies, of autism
    brain size, 54
    CT scan, 54
    head circumference (HC), 54–55
    structural MRI, 54–55
Macrocephaly, 488–89
    intellectual disability and, 490
Macrocephaly-Cutis Marmorata
    Telangiectatica Congenita
    (M-CMTC), 410
Macroscopic methods, of assessment
    diffusion tensor imaging findings,
        51–52
    magnetic resonance spectroscopy
        study, 52
    MRI-based morphometric
        methods, 50
    perfusion analysis, 52
    raw brain-size data analysis, 51
    surface-based measures, 51
    volume-based normalizations, 51
Magnee, M. J. C. M., 347
Maher, B., 490
Mahler, M., 470
Maintenance of information, 171
Maladaptive features, of ASD, 47
Manipulation working memory
    tasks, 174
Mann, T., 166
MAOA. See Monoamine oxidase A
    (MAOA)
Marsh, K. L., 343, 348
Mason, R. A., 234
Mason, W. A., 374
Mattingly, J., 353
Maurer, R., 368, 470
Maurice, C., 162
Mazziotta, J. C., 346
McCauley, J. L., 87
McClelland's model, 398–99

application in memory task,
    399–400
McCrory, E., 144
McDougle, C. J., 369
MCHAT. See Modified Checklist
    for Autism in Toddlers
    (MCHAT)
M-chlorophenylpiperazine
    (m-CPP), 81
McIntosh, D. N., 347
M-CMTC. See Macrocephaly-Cutis
    Marmorata Telangiectatica
    Congenita (M-CMTC)
M-DLPFC. See Mid-dorsolateral
    prefrontal cortex (m-DLPFC)
MECP2 gene, 19, 37, 491
Medial temporal lobe epilepsy, 63
Medical causes, of autism,
    519–20
Meehan, C. L., 374
Melke, J., 88
Mellor, C., 151
Meltzoff, A. N., 98–99
Memory, in.ASDs, 302
    high-functioning individuals,
        141–48
    history, 139–40
    low-functioning individuals,
        148–54
    theoretical framework and
        terminology, 140–41
    Tulving's systems approach, 141
Mench, J. A., 374
Mental retardation (MR) without
    autism, 88
Merzenich, M. M., 84
Metabolic abnormalities, 501–5
    CNS immune activation, 502
    gastrointestinal abnormalities,
        502
    inborn errors of metabolism, 502
    mitochondrial abnormalities,
        501–2
    systemic inflammation, 502
3-Methoxy-4-hydroxyphenylglycol
    (MHPG), 84
3-Methoxytyramine (3MT), 83
Methylation, 504
MHPG. See 3-methoxy-4-
    hydroxyphenylglycol (MHPG)
Microexpressions, 321
Microscopic imaging, of brain,
    52–53
Mid-dorsolateral prefrontal cortex
    (m-DLPFC), 172
Mid-gestation respiratory
    infection, 63
Millward, C., 151–52
Milne, E., 165
Mimicry

of actions and emotions, 341–42, 346–48
in adults, 343
and common perceptual and motor coding, 349
contagious crying and, 343
defined, 341
and development, 342–43
echolalia, 352
empathy and, 341
facial, social impact of, 342
lack of social attention and diminished, 351
mechanisms of, 349–52
mirror neuron theory, 353–55
neurobiological mechanisms for disrupting, 352–57
neurochemical and anatomical underpinnings of, 344–45
overarousal theory, 356–57
and reduced social perception, 352
role of amygdala, 355–56
and synchrony of rhythm, 343–44, 348–49
timing deficit theory, 355
voluntary, 321
Mindblindness theory of autism, 105, 320
Minderaa, R. B., 84
Mind Reading DVD, 330
Minicolumnar alterations, 59–61
Minshew, N. J., 98, 100–101, 145–46, 148, 170, 174
Mirror neuron dysfunction, 353–54
Mirror neuron theory
of autism, 107–8, 209
mimicry, 353–55
Mirsky, A. F., 170
Mitochondrial abnormalities, 501–2
Mitochondrial aspartate/glutamate carrier, 87–88
MMR vaccine and ASD, 17
Modahl, C., 101
Modified Checklist for Autism in Toddlers (MCHAT), 437
Moebious syndrome, 24
Molesworth, C., 141
Monoamine oxidase A (MAOA), 82, 414
"low activity" allele (MAOA-L), 82
Monoamines, neurochemical studies of, 78
CSF 5-HIAA levels, 78
dopamine and metabolites, 82–83
dopamine genetics, 83
dopamine neuroimaging, 83
5-hydroxytryptophan (5-HTP), 81
norepinephrine and metabolites, 84
platelet 5-HT levels, 78

selected studies, 79–80t
serotonin and metabolites, 77–81
serotonin genetics, 81–82
serotonin neuroimaging, 82
tryptophan depletion, 81
urinary levels of 5-hydroxyindoleacetic acid (5-HIAA), 78
Moody, E. J., 347
Moore, K. M., 84
Moreno-Fuenmayor, H., 84
Morphemes, 125
Morton-Evans, A., 152
Mostofsky, S., 141
Motor abnormalities, in ASD, 301
learning, 208–9
magnetoencepholgraphy (MEG) findings, 211
measures, 206–8
neuroanatomical motor correlates, 210–11
sensory/social functioning, 209–10
Motor deterioration stage, of RD, 19
Mottron, L., 127
Moy, S. S., 236
Mraz, K. D., 55
Mullen Scales of Early Learning, 437
Mundy, P., 104, 132
Murata, T., 13
Murphy, D. G. M., 356
Murphy, S. T., 340
Myers, T. E., 343
Myo-inositol (mI), 82

N
NAA. See N-acetylaspartate (NAA)
N-acetylaspartate (NAA), 58, 63, 65, 82
creatine ratios, 63
Nadel, J., 349
NALIQ. See Non-autistic low IQ (NALIQ)
Naltrexone, 88
Nativist position, of neurofunctional capabilities, 48
Navon letter task, 161
Naylor, S. T., 369
N4 brainwaves, 127–28
NE + epinephrine (EPI), 83
Neologisms, 127
NEPSY, 197–98
NEPSY-II, 300
Nerve growth factor (NGF), 89
Nervous system function, role in ASD, 47
abnormalities in limbic systems, 61–63

and accelerated head growth, 55–56
anatomical changes, 49
basal ganglia abnormalities, 66
brain asymmetries, 57–58
brain enlargement, 56
brain size measures, 54–56
cerebellum abnormalities, 63–65
clinical neuroradiological imaging, 53–54
computerized tomography (CT) scans, 54
corpus callosum enlargement, 57
diffusion tensor imaging findings, 58–59
frontal lobe volume changes, 67
gray matter and white matter during development, 56
head circumference (HC) measures, 54
1H-MRS studies, 58
magnetic resonance spectroscopy study, 58
minicolumnar alterations, 59–61
MRI, 54–55
nativist framework, 48
neuroanatomical investigations, 49–50
neuroconstructivist framework, 48–49
neuroinflammation, 59–61
neuronal integrity, 58
neuropathology findings, 59–61
occipital lobe changes, 67
parietal lobe involvement, 67
postmortem and microscopic analysis, 52–53
region-oriented neuroanatomical studies, 61
sensitivities and constraints of methods, 49–50
structural neuroanatomy, investigation of, 49
temporal lobe changes, 67
thalamus abnormalities, 65–66
volumetric imaging, 50–52
white matter integrity, study of, 58–59
white-matter parcellation technique, 56–57
Neural network models, of autism research, 109–10, 395–98
learning and, 397
local/global hyperconnectivity, 402–3
typical feed-forward, 396f
Neurexin 1 (NRXN1), 41
Neurexins, 416–17
Neuroanatomy, 48

Neurobehavioral problems, sleep and, 503
Neurobiology of dearousing effect, of repetitive movements, 380–83
Neuroconstructivist position, of neurofunctional capabilities, 48–49
Neurofunctional homunculus, 48
Neuroinflammation, 59–61, 63
Neuroligin 3 gene–a mutation, 235
Neuroligins, 416–17
Neuronal loss, in cortex, 400
Neuropeptides, study of
  analysis from blood samples, 88–89
  and animal models, 455–56
  and ASD, 455–60
  and autism genetics, 458–60
  investigations of CSF ß-endorphin levels, 88
  melatonin, 88
  opioid dysregulaton, evaluation of, 88
  urinary opioid peptides, 88
Neurotransmitter receptor, 49
NGF. See Nerve growth factor (NGF)
Nicotinic abnormalities, 65
Niedenthal, P. M., 340
Nissl staining, 64
NMDA. See N-methyl-D-aspartate (NMDA)
N-methyl-D-aspartate (NMDA), 84
Noens, I. L. J., 130
Non-autistic low IQ (NALIQ), 55
Nonsyndromic autism, 54
Nonverbal learning disabilities, 22–23
Non-word repetition, 192
Norepinephrine and metabolites, 84
NSD1 gene, 489

O
Oberman, L. M., 347
Obsessive-compulsive disorder (OCD), 22–23, 110
Occipital lobe changes, 67
OCD. See Obsessive-compulsive disorder (OCD)
O'Connor, N., 149–50
Oculomotor Delayed Response (ODR) task, 171
ODD. See Oppositional defiant disorder (ODD)
ODR. See Oculomotor Delayed Response (ODR) task
OFC. See Orbitofrontal cortex (OFC)

Okanda, M., 349
Opiate agonists, for human stereotypies, 381
Opioid dysregulation and autism, 88
Oppositional defiant disorder (ODD), 24
Orabona, G., 82
Orbitofrontal cortex (OFC), 403
  and gray matter volume, 67
Ornitz, E. M., 205, 370
Oro-motor dyspraxia, 125
O'Shea, A., 144
Osterling, J., 98–99
OT-X. See Oxytocin-X (OT-X)
Ounsted, C., 356
Overarousal
  in autism, 376–77
  fragile X syndrome and, 377–78
  mechanism of, 378–79
  Rett syndrome and, 378
Overarousal theory, mimicry, 356–57
Overfocused attention, 372
Overfocusing, 372
Oxidative stress, 504
  and gastrointestinal abnormalities, 503
Oxman, J., 348
OXTR gene, 459f
Oxytocin, 88, 235
  anatomical distribution of, 458
  and animal models, 455–56
  and arginine vasopressin receptors, 457–58
  for autonomic arousal, 382–83
  disruption in autism, 102
  interaction with arginine vasopressin systems, 460
  interplay with cortisol, 454–55
  levels in ASD, 457–60
Oxytocin receptor gene in autism, linkage studies, 109
Oxytocin-X (OT-X), 457
Ozonoff, S., 13, 98, 169, 383–84

P
PACAP. See Pituitary adenylate cyclase-activating polypeptide (PACAP)
Palmieri, L., 88
PANDAS. See Pediatric Autoimmune Neuropsychiatric Disorders Associated with Streptotoccus (PANDAS)
Papageorgiou, M., 170
Paplinski, A. P., 400
Parallel distributed processing (PDP) network, 397

Paraventricular nucleus, of hypothalamus, 382
Parent-child synchrony
  in dyads, 348
  overarousal and early, 356
Parent-infant synchrony, 348
Pascualvaca, D. M., 170
Passingham, R. E., 345, 352
Pastteri, I., 345, 352
PDD-NOS. See Pervasive Developmental Disorder, Not Otherwise Specified (PDD-NOS)
16p11 deletion, 38t, 42
3p Deletion/ duplication, 38t
PDP network. See Parallel distributed processing (PDP) network
Peabody Picture Vocabulary Test, 127
  Fourth Edition (PPVT-IV), 299
PECAM-1, 489
PECS. See Picture Exchange Communication System (PECS)
Pediatric Autoimmune Neuropsychiatric Disorders Associated with Streptotoccus (PANDAS), 66
Peer relationships, in children with ASDs, 10, 23
Pennington, B. F., 130, 173
Perceptual memory, 140
Pervasive developmental disorder, not otherwise specified (PDD-NOS), 10, 15, 21–22, 63, 414, 474
Pervasive developmental disorder (PDD), in children, 15, 42, 53
PET. See Positron emission tomography (PET)
Petersen, S., 163
Peterson, E., 368
Pevsner, J., 87
PFC. See Prefrontal cortex (PFC)
Pfeifer, J. H., 346
Phillips, W., 368
Phonological abilities, of individuals with autism, 124–25
Physical Prediction Questionnaire (PPQ), 323, 329
Picture Exchange Communication System (PECS), 132
Pierce, K., 423, 439
Pilowsky, T., 348
Pineda, J. S., 345
Pituitary adenylate cyclase-activating polypeptide (PACAP), 89

PK11195, 60
Plaisted, K., 11
Platek, S. M., 343
Plomin, R., 235
Polyvagal system, deficient, 357
Polyvagal theory, 357
Pomeroy, J., 24
POP. *See* Preparing to Overcome Prepotency (POP) Task
Porges, S. W., 110, 384
Positron emission tomography (PET), 52, 60
Posner, M. I., 162–63
Postmortem studies
    glutamate receptor abnormalities, 87
    nervous system functions, 52–53
Potocki-Lupski Duplication (17p11), 38*t*
Potter, D., 16
PPQ. *See* Physical Prediction Questionnaire (PPQ)
Prader-Willi syndrome, 38*t*, 371
Pragmatics, 128–29
Pre-autistic infants, deficits in mimicry and, 351
Prefrontal cortex (PFC), 146
    stress and, 381
Preparing to Overcome Prepotency (POP) Task, 169–70
Prepin, K., 349
Preschool-age children with ASD, emotional contagion in, 347
Prevalence
    of ASD, 15–17
    Asperger's disorder (AS), 16
Price, L. H., 369
Priming, 149
Prinz, W., 345
Procedural memory, 140
Processing bias, in ASD, 100
Prosody, 124–25
Proto-conversations, 321
Proton magnetic resonance spectroscopy (H1-MRS), 58, 82
Provencal, S., 98
Przuntek, H., 355
Psychological deficit manifesting, in autism, 470–71
PTEN gene mutation, 488–89
Purcell, A. E., 87
Purkinje cells, 64

Q
1q21.1, deletion, 41
7q11.23 deletion, 41
15q13 deletion, 38*t*
22q13 deletion, 38*t*
22q11 deletion (aka VCFS/DiGeorge), 38*t*
22q11 deletion syndrome, 24
1q21 duplication, 38*t*, 41
7q11 duplication, 38*t*
15q duplication (maternal), 38*t*
Quantitative T2 transverse relaxation time, 50

R
Rabionet, R., 88
Rafal, R. D., 162
Ramachandran, V. S., 347, 353
Rapson, R., 341
Raymaekers, R., 169
Reciprocal conversation and interactive play, lack of, 10
Recollection, 146, 148
Redcay, E., 439
Reed, C. L., 347
Rees, L., 11
Refrigerator mother, 123
Regionally specific functional brain imaging, in adults, 423–36
Region-oriented neuroanatomical studies, in autism, 61
Reichmann-Decker, A., 347
Reimer, J., 345
Reite, M. L., 368
"Remember-know" paradigm, 144
Renner, P., 165
Repetitive behaviors, of children with ASDs, 10–11, 98, 300–301
    animal studies, 456
Repetitive Behavior Scales–Revised, 300
Repetitive motor mannerisms, 81
Repetitive movements, 367–71
    arousal and. *See* Arousal
    behavior reflects internal states, 369
    congenitally blind children and, 371
    diagnosis, 369–70
    displacement behavior and, 373–75
    neurobiology of dearousing effect of, 380–83
    neurological symptom, 368
    overarousal and. *See* Overarousal
    phenomenology in genetic syndromes, 371
    repetitive reciprocal kicking of legs in infants, 370–71
    at rest, 379–80
    ritualistic stereotypical behavior and, 375
    stress and, 381–83
    taxonomy, 371–72
Repetitive reciprocal kicking, of legs in infants, 370–71
Rett syndrome, 18–20, 38*t*, 371
    and autism, 491
    and overarousal, 378
Richardson, M. J., 348
Right hemisphere abnormalities, 100
Rimland, B., 140, 470
Rinaldi, J., 98–99
Risperidone, 82
Ritualistic behaviors, of children with ASDs, 10–11
Ritvo, E. R., 370, 474
Rizzolatti, G., 345, 352, 354
6R-L-erythro-5,6,7,8,-tetrahydrobiopterin (R-BH$_4$), 83
Roberts, J. A., 126
Roberts, N., 356
Robertson, D. M., 356
Robinson, P. D., 83
Rogers, S. J., 13, 125, 130, 173, 368, 383–84
Rojas, D. C., 368
Rolf, L. H., 84
Ronald, A., 235
Rourke, B., 23
Roy, E., 356
Rubenstein, J. L. R., 84
Russell, J., 149, 169, 471
Rutter, M., 368, 474

S
Sander, L. W., 340, 351
Saulnier, C., 372
Saunders, K., 17
Schanen, N. C., 485
Scheepers, C., 356
Schizophrenia, 100
Schmidt, R. C., 348
Schmitz, N., 98
Schroeder, U., 355
Schultz, R. T., 103, 347
Schutz, C. K., 83
Schyne, P. G., 356
Sears, L. L., 141
Sebanz, N., 348
Seizures, 13, 37
Selective attention, 11, 109, 162
Self-injurious behavior, 82, 132
Self-ordered pointing, 192
Self-organizing maps (SOM), 400–401
    ANN and, 400
Semantic-clustering strategy, 143–44
Semantic memory, 140, 146
Semantics, 127–28

Semendeferi, K., 345
ß-endorphin, evaluations of, 88
Sensorimotor resonance, 322, 331
Sensory hypersensitivity, 330
Sensory-perceptual anomalies, 476
Sensory-processing abnormalities, in
    ASD, 300
    auditory mismtach paradigm,
        219–20
    auditory processing, 219
    neural substrates, 221
    somatosensory perception,
        220–21
    visual perception, 216–17
    visual processing of non-
        biological motion, 217–18
    visual processing of stationary
        "low-level" visual stimuli,
        218–19
Sensory Profile, 300
Serotonergic dysfunction, 78
Serotonin
    genetics, 81–82
    and metabolites, 77–81
    neuroimaging, 82
Serotonin agonists, for human
    stereotypies, 381
Serotonin neurons, 78
Serotonin transporter, 37
Set-shifting in ASD, 187–89
Sex differences
    in ASD, potential factors
        contributing to, 453f
    IQ measures, in ASD patients,
        282
    vasopressin and, 456–57
Sex discrepancy, within autism, 37
Sham depletion, 81
SHANK3, 41–42
Shared attention, 104–5
Sigman, M., 348–49
Siller, M., 348
Silva, P., 348
Simple response inhibition, 189
Singhal, A., 343
Single nucleotide polymorphisms
    (SNPs), 36, 81, 459f
Single photon emission computed
    tomography (SPECT), 52,
    60, 82
Single-trial learning, 146–47
SLC6A4 gene, 81
SLC25A12 gene, 87–88
    polymorphisms, 88
Sleep, 500
    gastrointestinal abnormalities
        and, 503
    immune system, infection
        and, 503

and neurobehavioral problem,
    503
SLI. See Specific Language
    Impairment (SLI)
SLP. See Speech and language
    pathologist (SLP)
SMA. See Supplementary motor
    area (SMA)
Smeets, R. C., 347
Smith, H., 165
Smith, I. M., 208
Smith-Lemli-Opitz (11q13), 38t
Social attention, 103
Social brain circuitry, in
    infancy, 102
Social cognitive theory, of autism,
    105–6
Social-communicative impairments,
    104
Social deficits, in ASD
    amygdala's role, 231–33
    animal models of social cognition,
        234–35
    eye tracking, 230
    facial identity processing,
        227–30
    functional connectivity for face
        processing, 230–31
    mirror neurons, 233
    neuroimaging studies, 233–34
    primary, 225–27
    repetitive behaviors and impaired
        reciprocal social interaction,
        235–36
    social motivation, 231–32
    testing, 300
    therapeutic interventions, 236
    voice perception, 234
Social engagement, in autism, 101,
    384–85
    levels in high-risk infants, graphic
        illustration, 415
Social findings, in animal studies,
    456
Social impairment, 10
    and endophenotypes of autism,
        486
Social information, processing
    of, 10
Social motivation theory, of autism,
    101–5
Social perception, mimicry and
    reduced, 352
Social Skills Improvement System
    (SSRS), 300
Social stimuli, in autism, 101
Social Stories Questionnaire (SSQ),
    323
Social symptoms, 339–40

Socioeconomic status, and
    prevalence rate of ASD, 18
Socorro-Candanoza, L., 84
Solomon, M., 169
SOM. See Self-organizing maps
    (SOM)
Somatic and systemic, features with
    autism, 499–505
    abnormal sensory responsiveness,
        501
    autonomic nervous system
        abnormalities, 501
    disturbed connectivity and, 504
    energy metabolism, 504
    epilepsy, 500
    excitation/inhibition ratio, 503–4
    gastrointestinal system, 500
    immune dysregulation and, 504
    immune system and, 501
    metabolic abnormalities and,
        501–5
    sleep, 500
Source memory, 152
    tests, 144
South, M., 98
Spatial working memory,
    dysfunction of, 98
Specific Language Impairment
    (SLI), 124, 126
SPECT. See Single photon emission
    computed tomography
    (SPECT)
Speech and language pathologist
    (SLP), 132
SPM. See Statistical parametric map
    (SPM)
Spotlight of attention, in ASD
    patients, 165–66
Sprengelmeyer, R., 355
SQ. See Systemizing Quotient (SQ)
SSQ. See Social Stories
    Questionnaire (SSQ)
SSRS. See Social Skills
    Improvement System (SSRS)
Stahl, D., 342
Stanfield, A. C., 55
Stark, S., 141, 149
Statistical parametric map (SPM),
    50
Stauffacher, M., 374
Stefanatos, G. A., 13
Stel, M., 347
STG. See Superior temporal sulcus
    and gyrus (STG)
Stop Signal task, 167, 169
Strayer, D., 169
Stress
    cortisol and, 381
    dopamine and, 380–81

findings, in animal studies, 456
  repetitive behavior and, 381–83
Striano, T., 342
Stroop task, 167–69
STS. *See* Superior temporal sulcus
  (STS)
Suitala, A. E., 356
Sumatriptan, 81
Summers, J., 150–52
Sundaram, S. K., 58
Sung, Y., 102
Superior temporal gyrus (STG), 403
Superior temporal sulcus (STS),
  102, 403
Supplementary motor area
  (SMA), 211
Sutera, S., 15
Svennerholm, L., 83
Sweeney, J. A., 98
Swettenham, J., 11
Sympathetic arousal
  in animals, 374
  differential activation by gender,
    383
  testosterone in, 383
Sympathetic hyperarousal, 378
Symptomatology, of ASD, 11–14,
  102, 176–77
Symptom clusters, of ASD, 10
Symptoms, of ASD, 9–10
Synapse, 417
  and autism, 416–17
Synaptic density, mean, 438
Synaptogenesis, 437
Synchrony of rhythm, mimicry and,
  343–44, 348–49
Syndromes related, to ASDs, 37–39
Syndromic autism vs idiopathic
  autism, 490–92
Systemic inflammation, 502
Systemizing, 318–19
  in low functioning and high
    functioning individuals, 320t
  neural systems, 331–32
  in people with ASC, 322–23
  relationship with empathizing,
    327–28
  testing of skills, 323–27
Systemizing-Empathizing extension,
  of ToM hypothesis, 106
Systemizing Quotient (SQ), 323,
  327

T
Tabuchi, K., 235
Tactile stimulation, in infants, 375
Tager-Flusberg, H., 126–28, 151
Tang, T., 485
Tantrum-throwing behaviors, 132

Temporal lobe abnormalities, 67
Temporo-parietal junction
  (TPJ), 331
Test for Reception of Grammar,
  Second Edition
  (TROG-2), 131
Test of Language Competence,
  Expanded Edition, 131
Test of Pragmatic Language, Second
  Edition (TOPL2), 131
Testosterone
  sex differences in ASD, 453–54
  in sympathetic arousal, 383
Tetreault, N. A., 344–45
Thalamocortical dysrhythmia, 51
Thelen, E., 370, 375
Theory of Mind (ToM), 100, 102,
  104–6, 130–31, 140, 233,
  320, 331
Thomas, C., 354
Timing deficit theory,
  mimicry, 355
Timothy syndrome (12p13), 38t
Tissue parameter mapping, 50
Titchener, E., 319
Tkach, D., 345
Toichi, M., 143
Tomasello, M., 341
TOPL-2. *See* Test of Pragmatic
  Language, Second Edition
  (TOPL2)
Tordjman, S., 88
Tourette's disorder (TD), 22–24
Tower of Hanoi task, 98
Tower of London task, 98, 194
Townsend, J., 166
TPH1, 82
TPH2, 82
Trail-Making Test, 197
Transmission/disequilibrium test
  (TDT), 81
Treatment considerations
  attention, 307
  cognitive ability and adaptive
    skills, 304
  educational setting, 303
  executive functions, 307–8
  imitation, 304–5
  language skills, 304
  memory, 308
  models, 302–3
  pharmacotherapy, 303
  repetitive behaviors, 306–7
  sensory and motor function, 306
  social cognition, 305–6
Tregellas, J. R., 368
Trevarthen, C., 348
Triad deficits, 41
Trisomy Chr.21, 38t

TROG-2. *See* Test for Reception of
  Grammar, Second Edition
  (TROG-2)
Troisi, A., 374
Tronick, E. Z., 344
Tryptophan depletion, 81
Tryptophan 2,3 dioxygenase
  (TDO2), 82
TS. *See* Tuberous sclerosis (TS)
Tuberous sclerosis (TS), 24, 39t
Tumors, 48
Turner, M., 368, 371
Tustin, F., 474
Twenty Questions, 197
Twin studies, of ASD, 17
Type E brain, 327–28, 332
Type S brain, 327–28, 332

U
Unified gene-based theories of
  autism, 492–94
Unimpaired free recall, 144
Unitary disorder
  fragile X syndrome and, 473
  Goodman's model of
    diversity, 471
  historical background, 469–73
  loosening concept of autism as,
    traditionally defined, 472–73
  non-random co-occurrence of
    ASD-related anomalies,
    evidence for, 473
  overview, 469
  rethinking of concept of autism
    as, 473–79
  single-factor theories, 470–72

V
Vaccination, and prevalence of
  ASD, 17
Valera, V., 84
Valproic acid (VPA)
  during pregnancy, 383
Van Amelsvoort, T., 356
Van Berckelaer-Onnes, I. A., 130
Van Bokhoven, H., 489
Van den Heuvel, C., 347
Van der Gaag, R., 21
Vanderwal, T., 234
Van Engeland, H., 347
Vanillylmandelic acid (VMA), 84
V1a receptor (AVP1aR), 457–58
Vargas, D. L., 59
Vargha-Khadem, F., 147
Variable number tandem repeat
  (VNTR) functional
  polymorphism, 83
Vasoactive intestinal peptide (VIP),
  88–89

Vasopressin
and animal models, 455–56
disruption, in autism, 102
and sex differences, 456–57
and Von Economo neuron,
344–45
VBM. *See* Voxel-based
morphometry (VBM)
VCAM-1, 489
Veenstra-VanderWeele, J., 495
Ventral prefrontal cortex
(VPFC), 172
Ventromedial prefrontal cortex
(VMPFC), 381, 388
Verbal Fluency test, 197
Vermal lobules, 63–64
Verté, S., 142
Vineland Adaptive Behavior Scales,
55, 298
VIP. *See* Vasoactive intestinal
peptide (VIP)
VMA. *See* Vanillylmandelic acid
(VMA)
VMPFC. *See* Ventromedial
prefrontal cortex (VMPFC)
VNTR. *See* Variable number
tandem repeat (VNTR)
functional polymorphism
Volden, J., 127, 129
Volkmar, F. R., 21, 347, 369
Volume-based normalizations, 51
Von Economo neuron, 344–45
Voxel-based morphometry (VBM),
50, 65
VPFC. *See* Ventral prefrontal cortex
(VPFC)
V2 receptor (V2R), 458

W
Walker, J. A., 162
Walker, P., 166
Wall, D. P., 493
Wang, A. T., 349
Wang, K., 492–93
Waring R. H., 84
Warrington, E., 140, 149, 151
Waterhouse, L., 101
Watson, J. S., 110
Watson, K. K., 344–45
WCC. *See* Weak central coherence
(WCC)
WCST. *See* Wisconsin Card Sort
Test (WCST)
Weak central coherence (WCC),
99–101
Webster, C. D., 348
Wechsler intelligence tests, 130
Wehner, E., 173
Weisbrot, D., 24
Weishaupt, M. A., 374
Weiss, L. A., 493
Welch, M., 470
Westerfield, M., 166
White, B. N., 83
White matter differences, 61, 65, 82
hyperintensities, 56–57
Wilbarger, J. L., 347
William, J., 345
Williams, C. A., 488
Williams, D. L., 145–46, 148, 174
Williams, J. H., 233, 354
Williams, J. G., 15
Williams, M., 353
Williams, S. C. R., 356
Williams–Beuren Syndrome, 41

Williams syndrome, 100, 356
Wiltermuth, S. S., 344
Wing, Lorna, 16, 18
Winkielman, P., 107, 347
Winterrowd, E., 368
WISC-IV, 171–72, 174
Wisconsin Card Sort Test (WCST),
98, 187–88
Working memory, 98, 141
complex WM tasks, 192–93
in individuals with ASD, 173–75,
193–94
measuring of, 171–72
neural correlates, 172–73
neuroimaging studies, 175
simple span/STM, 190–92
typical development, 173

X
X-linked or Y-linked syndromes, 37

Y
Yarger, R. S., 173
Yirmiya, N., 348
Yoshinaga, K., 13
Young, A. W., 355
Yurgelun-Todd, D. A., 166,
357, 402

Z
Zajonc, R. B., 340
Zhang, J., 484
Zimmerman, A. W., 87
Zingerevich, C., 491
Zinke, K., 142